"Value-packed, accurate, and comprehensive..."
—*Los Angeles Times*

"Unbeatable..."—*The Washington Post*

LET'S GO:
ISRAEL & EGYPT

is the best book for anyone traveling on a budget. Here's why:

No other guidebook has as many budget listings.

In Luxor, we found 16 hotels or hostels for under $4 a night; in Tel Aviv, we found 9 hotels or hostels for under $9. In the countryside we found hundreds more. We tell you how to get there the cheapest way, whether by bus, plane, or ferry, and where to get an inexpensive and satisfying meal once you've arrived. There are hundreds of money-saving tips for everyone plus lots of information on student discounts.

LET'S GO researcher-writers have to make it on their own.

Our Harvard-Radcliffe researcher-writers travel on budgets as tight as your own—no expense accounts, no free hotel rooms.

LET'S GO is completely revised every year.

We don't just update the prices, we go back to the places. If a charming café has become an overpriced tourist trap, we'll replace the listing with a new and better one.

No other budget guidebook includes all this:

Coverage of both the cities and the countryside; directions, addresses, phone numbers, and hours to get you there and back; in-depth information on culture, history, and the people; listings on transportation between and within regions and cities; tips on work, study, sights, nightlife, and special splurges, city and regional maps; and much, much more.

LET'S GO is for anyone who wants to see Israel and Egypt on a budget.

Books by Let's Go, Inc.

Let's Go: Europe
Let's Go: Britain & Ireland
Let's Go: France
Let's Go: Germany, Austria & Switzerland
Let's Go: Greece & Turkey
Let's Go: Israel & Egypt
Let's Go: Italy
Let's Go: London
Let's Go: Paris
Let's Go: Rome
Let's Go: Spain & Portugal

Let's Go: USA
Let's Go: California & Hawaii
Let's Go: Mexico
Let's Go: New York City
Let's Go: The Pacific Northwest, Western Canada & Alaska
Let's Go: Washington, D.C.

LET'S GO:

The Budget Guide to

ISRAEL & EGYPT

1993

Gary Jonathan Bass
Editor

Richard G. Abramson
Assistant Editor

Written by
Let's Go, Inc.
a wholly owned subsidiary of
Harvard Student Agencies, Inc.

ST. MARTIN'S PRESS
NEW YORK

Helping Let's Go

If you have suggestions or corrections, or just want to share your discoveries, drop us a line. We read every piece of correspondence, whether a 10-page letter, a tacky Elvis postcard, or, as in one case, a collage. All suggestions are passed along to our researcher-writers. Please note that mail received after May 5, 1993 will probably be too late for the 1994 book, but will be retained for the following edition. Address mail to:

> *Let's Go: Israel & Egypt*
> **Let's Go, Inc.**
> **1 Story Street**
> **Cambridge, MA 02138**

In addition to the invaluable travel advice our readers share with us, many are kind enough to offer their services as researchers or editors. Unfortunately, the charter of Let's Go, Inc. and Harvard Student Agencies, Inc. enables us to employ only currently enrolled Harvard students.

Maps by David Lindroth, copyright © 1993, 1992, 1991, 1990, 1989, 1986 by St. Martin's Press, Inc.

Distributed outside the U.S. and Canada by Pan Books Ltd.

ISBN: 0-312-08240-1

First edition
10 9 8 7 6 5 4 3 2 1

Let's Go: Israel & Egypt is written by the Publishing Division of
Let's Go, Inc., 1 Story Street, Cambridge, Mass. 02138.

Let's Go® is a registered trademark of Let's Go, Inc.
Printed in the U.S.A. on recycled paper with biodegradable soy ink.

Editor	Gary Jonathan Bass
Assistant Editor	Richard G. Abramson
Contributing Editor	Muneer I. Ahmad
Managing Editor	Tim Whitmire
Publishing Director	Paul C. Deemer
Production Manager	Mark N. Templeton
Office Coordinator	Bart St. Clair
Office Manager	Anne E. Chisholm

Researcher-Writers

Israeli North Coast, Galilee, *and Golan Heights*	Adina Rachel Astor
Nile Valley, Western Desert Oases, *and Red Sea Coast*	Joshua A. Brown
Jerusalem (New City), Israeli Central and *South Coasts, Negev, and Sinai*	Daniel Jacob Libenson
Jerusalem (Old City and East Jerusalem), *West Bank, and Jordan*	Aseel M. Rabie
Cairo, Mediterranean Coast, Suez, *Alexandria, and Siwa Oasis*	Diana O. Yousef

Sales Group Manager	Tiffany A. Breau
Sales Group Representatives	Frances Marguerite Maximé
	Breean T. Stickgold
	Harry James Wilson
Sales Group Coordinator	Aida Bekele
President	Brian A. Goler
C.E.O.	Michele Ponti

Acknowledgments

It's 4:20am here at 1 Story Street, the night before deadline, and I can't shake this eerie feeling I've forgotten something. Something important. Possibly big and triangular.

In this cluttered office, walls covered with postcards and toys and copy, and floor buried under a small *tel* built out of roughly a third of Harvard's collection of Middle East books, there are two big maps of the Eastern Mediterranean, dotted with five different colors of pins. Each color represents the soul of this book: a researcher-writer who boldly went where no budget traveler had gone before. Generally, each *Let's Go* book has one or two star R-Ws; *I&E* had five this summer.

The independent-minded Adina Astor (blue) showed off her impressive journalistic skills on my old route in north Israel; anything less would have been a crime. She never got her way on format, so here you go: arch*ae*ology. She also went beyond mere budget travel when *Let's Go,* via Adina, scooped the world press on the Israeli election. Thanks for the treasured, if illegal, election memorabilia—if Avoda figures it out, you're in serious trouble. I'll buy you that They Might Be Giants tape when you get back.

Somewhere between heaven and hell, there is Josh Brown (red). Utterly unfazed by the infamous Nile and Oases itinerary, Josh sent scrawled masterpieces that were a treat to read, when they were legible. Last seen going downhill fast in Sohag, Josh was as resilient as he was blasé. He headed out for Kharga leaving only a postcard reading: "Off to the desert, Josh." We were appropriately awed.

My old friend Dan Libenson (white) cruised through south Israel and the Sinai, occasionally cursing Ashdod and Be'ersheva and the editor who sent him there. "You did this to me!!!" he wrote from Sharm. "I'll remember this!" With that phlegmatic attitude, he narrowly avoided arrest for illegal taxi-riding, and then survived a friendly man with a very heavy sledgehammer. I'll remember this, too, Dan—thanks.

In the H.K. of J. and the occupied West Bank, Aseel Rabie (green) was cool and collected. Her copy was prompt (Mumtaz Post is *mumtaz*), obsessively thorough, and a breeze to edit. Her street smarts and sensitivity kept everything well under control, even when I worried more than her mother. And her rambling, semi-coherent letters, ending off with the inevitable smiley-face, made my day.

Diana Yousef (orange), armed with a black-belt in karate, sent us classy, well-organized copy from Cairo and the Egyptian coast. Her work was excellent, overcoming some real hardships. And her insights on the Copts are a valuable addition.

Meanwhile, back in Cambridge. My indefatigable co-worker Rick Abramson is single-handedly responsible for saving me and the book more times than I care to count. For example, I woke up one day to discover we had a GI; another that we had macros; and most every morning to find that yet another copy batch was entered, rendered into English and ready for me to screw up. It was a beautiful thing. I can't think of a better AE, with fine Al Gore rhythms. Thank you, my Chattanoogan friend. You're not really fired.

Muneer Ahmad was invaluable with Arabic, Islam, and with thorny political issues. Thanks to him, CE now means something other than "Christo et Ecclesiae." I respect him as much as I like him, which, by the way, is a lot.

Other friends helped too. Tim Whitmire left no nook (er, cranny) unexplored in his amazingly thorough MEing; I appreciate all his work. Mark Templeton outdid himself with virtuoso genius on the computers, Hebrew, and Arabic—*shukran.* Chris Capozzola, who puts the ME in *mensch*, fought an unmentionable bloated evil entity in New York on my behalf. Thanks also to Lorraine Chao, the 1992 *I&E* editor, for putting up with my questions. René Celaya's language skills were crucial, even though he thinks Aqaba is in Japan. As time got short, Jen Medearis, Liz Stein, Pete Keith, and Rebecca Jeschke did valuable proofing.

Jody Dushay, my editor when I was a R-W on the 1991 *I&E*: thank you for giving me a chance. It was the best of times, it was the worst of times.

vii

You don't "acknowledge" friends; you say hi. I've already mentioned some; this covers the rest of The Office. Carolyn McKee, dear summertime companion, I will miss you next year—politics, potato breaks, neuroses, Pamplona, Connor the *shwarma*, and all that. (Sigh.) Peter Lindberg, fellow resident of the *BIIELon* Tomb, still startles Café of India waiters. My best also to Blythe Grossberg, Steve Mazie, Becca Knowles, Elijah Siegler (who loaned me Muneer), Zach Schrag, and Harry Wilson.

From my pre-*Let's Go* life, thanks to my parents, Arthur and Karen (I'll take a break soon, guys), both sets of grandparents, and the whole family—including Chester. And my love to people who know who they are in Toronto, at Penn, in the spring 1990 transfer class, from *Foreign Policy,* in Israel, at Harvard, Hillel, Lowell House, and *The Crimson*. More specifically (this isn't the whole list; remember, it's late): Josh Kolko, Joel Gerwin, Andrzej Klonecki, Hugh Cleland, Mukhlis Balbale, Glen Schwaber, Julia Fayngold, Ariela Dubler, Jack Levy, Sanjay Wagle, Elie Fishman, Mike Kaplan (*mazel tov*), Mike Dorff (*mazel tov*), Mike Grunwald (don't you dare), Richard Primus, Mark Wiedman, Alison Wakoff, Sarah Cahn, Jon Gross, Rebecca Musher, Harley Guttman, Josef Joffe, and Stanley Hoffmann.

I have no right to dedicate this book to anyone, but I'll dedicate my bits to my genetically redundant brother, Warren Frank Bass, who's been there.

(A final note. King Hussein wrote in *Uneasy Lies the Head,* "I was very much impressed by the atmosphere of Yale, and I remember wishing that I could have attended such a university." I wish he could have too. Goodbye, Harvard.)

—GJB

My only regret about working on this book is not having been able to find a place for the phrase "uglier than the northbound end of a southbound camel." Other than that, *I&E '93* has been a wonderful experience, one that I'm sad to see drawing to an end. Over the last few months, I helped make hummus, I debated political correctness, and I learned to decode secretive editing abbreviations like "MEGO" and "WTF." I even took part in the Hegelian dialectical development of the general introduction. Most of all, I had a really great time, due in large part to the following people.

First of all, to Gary "I'm not all that into hierarchy" Bass, who knows more about the Middle East than anyone in their right mind would ever want to know, thanks for teaching me the merits of the *insha'allah—bukhra—maalish* approach to editing, which I plan to use for my thesis. Just so you know, I envy your writing ability even more than I hate {pb}hummus. Even when it looked like *nahnu mela'un* would be our epigraph (and our epigram), I knew that E.W.D.G.S. was just a façade to fool the rest of the office. Knock 'em dead at *The New Republic* next year, and give me a call the next time you want to sing the *Aleinu* at midnight on a Saturday night.

Next, to Tim Whitmire, thanks for being as devoted to the ITABIIELON staff as you were to our book. M.E.T.C. was definitely *not* a façade. A special thanks goes to Mark Templeton, one of those rare individuals who epitomizes both genius and *mensch*, and to Muneer Ahmad, a veritable fountain of Middle East knowledge and a helluva nice guy to boot.

And now the true authors of this book: Adina Astor, Josh Brown, Dan Libenson, Aseel Rabie, and Diana Yousef. The hard part was completely yours. Congratulations on surviving and on doing an incredible job.

A smooth shout-out also goes to JK, AS, SK, EP, GT, LK, MS, BT, EY, WH, GA, SH, R(T)K, CG, KK, TB, LF, KL, JW, DB, SJJ, AE, AZA, and everyone else who didn't contribute directly to the book but who have all somehow conspired to make life very, very cool. Sadly, JF and CH can never be a part of the *Let's Go* experience, because they both go to a yucky West Coast school where the sun shines entirely too much.

Last but in no way least, thanks to Mom, Dad, and Mike for absolutely everything. Y'all are simply *mahvelous*.

Ever notice how similar the words *salaam* and *shalom* are?...

—RGA

Contents

List of Maps

About Let's Go

A generation ago, Harvard Student Agencies, a three-year-old nonprofit corporation dedicated to providing employment to students, was doing a booming business booking charter flights to Europe. One of the extras offered to passengers on these flights was a 20-page mimeographed pamphlet entitled *1960 European Guide,* a collection of tips on continental travel compiled by the HSA staff. The following year, students traveling to Europe researched the first full-fledged edition of *Let's Go: Europe,* a pocket-sized book with tips on budget accommodations, irreverent write-ups of sights, and a decidedly youthful slant.

Throughout the 60s, the series reflected its era: a section of the 1968 *Let's Go: Europe* was entitled "Street Singing in Europe on No Dollars a Day." During the 70s *Let's Go* gradually became a large-scale operation, adding regional European guides and expanding coverage into North Africa and Asia. Now in its 33rd year, *Let's Go* publishes 17 titles covering more than 40 countries. This year *Let's Go* proudly introduces two new guides: *Let's Go: Paris* and *Let's Go: Rome.*

Each spring 80 Harvard-Radcliffe students are hired as researcher-writers for the summer months. They train intensively during April and May for their summer tour of duty. Each researcher-writer then hits the road on a shoestring budget for seven weeks, researching six days per week, and overcoming countless obstacles in a glorious quest for better bargains.

Back in a basement deep below Harvard Yard, an editorial staff of 32, a management team of six, and countless typists and proofreaders—all students—spend four months poring over more than 75,000 pages of manuscript as they push the copy through a rigorous editing process. High tech has recently landed in the dungeon: some of the guides are now typeset in-house using sleek black desktop workstations.

And even before the books hit the stands, next year's editions are well underway.

A NOTE TO OUR READERS

The information for this book is gathered by Let's Go's researchers during the late spring and summer months. Each listing is derived from the assigned researcher's opinion based upon his or her visit at a particular time. The opinions are expressed in a candid and forthright manner. Other travelers might disagree. Those traveling at a different time may have different experiences since prices, dates, hours, and conditions are subject to change. You are urged to check beforehand to avoid inconvenience and surprises. Travel always involves a certain degree of risk, especially in low-cost areas. When traveling, especially on a budget, you should always take particular care to ensure your safety.

Don't let bad water ruin your trip.

One out of two world travelers will get sick. Drinking contaminated water is the number one cause. PŪR water purifiers make the water safe to drink.

You're planning a great trip—investing lots of time and money. You don't want to miss a thing. But you worry. You've heard stories. Will you get sick? Is any water really safe? Will you be out enjoying the day as planned? Or will you be spending your days with cramps and diarrhea, hoping the medications will work?

Don't let bad drinking water turn your trip-of-a-lifetime into a nightmare. Wherever you travel, before you drink the local water, purify it with PŪR™ water purifiers—The only ones that instantly remove Giardia and eliminate all other microorganisms including bacteria and viruses. PŪR water purifiers are affordable, lightweight, and easy to use.

Don't let bad water ruin your trip. Make sure it's safe. Make sure it's PŪR.

For more information or to order,

Call 1-800-845-PURE

Water Purifiers

"My fellow travelers experienced stomach upset and worse while I was completely fine."
—Ellen R. Benjamin, Ph.D.

LET'S GO: ISRAEL AND EGYPT, Including Jordan and the West Bank

General Introduction

There are very few casual travelers to Israel, Egypt, Jordan, and the West Bank. Just about anyone who ventures to this region, seen in most of the English-speaking world as both impossibly exotic and more than a little dangerous, has a serious reason to go. Some people are searching for their roots, for their own identity, or for their God. Others go for the wonders of civilizations long turned to dust. Some want to take sides in the intractable conflicts of the area, still others want to make peace. People don't just wander over here to play in the sand. This, in other words, isn't Florida.

The Eastern Mediterranean is the cradle of civilization and of three major world religions; it's also the cradle for a number of young states, toddling amidst the wreckage of ancient imperial rubble and rubbish. The region's timeless legacy of blooming civilizations and withering empires is overshadowed by some of the most bitter international turmoil anywhere. This area is never dull—when the rest of the world gets bored, it picks up a newspaper to see what's going on here.

To the kind of tourists who travel 7000 miles in search of a pizza place just like home, who moan that the Pyramids aren't air-conditioned, this place is impossible—the sun is too hot, the food wreaks gastronomic havoc, and the phones don't work.

Let anyone who thinks that go to Florida. You, come with us.

Using Let's Go

Let's Go: Israel & Egypt is written especially for the adventurous budget traveler. In the summer of 1992, our five stalwart researcher-writers set out for the Middle East with the same goals as yours: getting from place to place, filling their stomachs, taking in the sights, absorbing the culture, enjoying the evenings, and getting some sleep, all in the most economical way possible. (We made sure of that—we didn't give them much money.) Our researcher-writers then offered their honest appraisals of budget accommodations and inexpensive restaurants in Israel, Egypt, Jordan, and the West Bank, with candid reviews of everything from hostels to hummus.

Let's Go lists economical places to eat and sleep throughout the region, telling you which places are great bargains and which places are out to rip you off. In addition, *Let's Go* outlines the transportation options to get you to your destination, and we orient you with maps and directions once you get there. We'll point out the sights and entertainment you won't want to miss, and we'll note the location of the nearest post office, emergency center, and laundromat. We'll find the cheapest places to buy souvenirs, and we'll give you hints for bargaining with the locals.

The General Introduction contains information you'll need to know before beginning your journey. Within the General Introduction, the Planning Your Trip section

1

advises you on tourist seasons and climate (see When To Go); lists embassies, consulates, hostel associations, and other important organizations (see Useful Organizations and Publications); explains the details about passports, visas, and other forms of red tape (see Documents and Formalities); discusses currency exchange and traveler's checks (see Money); suggests what to bring along (see Packing); addresses health and safety concerns (see Health, Safety, and Security); lists work and study options (see Alternatives to Tourism); offers recommendations for travelers with special needs (see Additional Concerns); and gives hints on bargaining and travel etiquette (see Other Tips). The Getting There section provides a list of transportation options. Finally, the About the Middle East section provides a brief discussion of the history, architecture, and religions of the Middle East.

Furthermore, Israel, Egypt, Jordan and the West Bank each have their own introductions within this book, including information on accommodations, communication, currency, language, transportation, and lifestyles in each region.

Remember that *Let's Go* is just intended to make your travels easier. They remain, above all, *your* travels. We're glad you brought us along, and we hope we can straighten out some details and entertain you in interminable bus lines. But don't forget to sometimes close your *Let's Go* and explore by yourself.

A Few Gentle Suggestions

You will probably learn the most about new cultures by dissolving discreetly in them. An effort at assimilating goes a long way; obnoxious behavior does too, but in the other direction. Except if you're desperately homesick, eat falafel instead of junk from Pizza Hut. Talk to the people around you, in their own language if possible; even a few phrases of Arabic or Hebrew will be appreciated. (A glossary is included at the back of this book for that purpose.) In this part of the world, politics are unavoidable. The West has not made a very positive impression on the Middle East this century, and a little sensitivity can't hurt. If a Jordanian resents the British government for the Gulf War, or if an Israeli bad-mouths George Bush, don't take it personally. Most people will be interested in your country, too, politics aside. Listen and be respectful.

A monumental statue of Ramses II, whatever its other virtues, is a poor conversationalist; an Egyptian with green sunglasses who speaks Japanese is far more fun and educational. Your fondest memories will be of the kid who fed you free beans in Akko, not of the tourist office there.

Price Warning

This book was researched during the summer of 1992. Inflation, though largely stabilized in recent years, will probably have raised many prices since then. Inflation in Israel was at -0.4% as *Let's Go* went to print, but prices were still climbing.

Planning Your Trip

The more you know about your destination before you get there, the more you'll appreciate your trip. And when every city seems to have 27 museums, 73 archeological sites, and 388 tombs to visit, relax—you don't *have* to cover everything your itinerary lists. Keep your eyes open for new discoveries and vary your travels. When ancient ruins begin to look like heaps of rocks, slow down and do something different. Go to a café and unwind or relax on the banks of the Nile or the beaches of the Mediterranean.

Budget travel is a fine thing, but don't make it an obsession. Many travelers will stay in the most wretched fleabag hostel, eat the least sanitary food, and devote themselves to living cheaply rather than enjoying their trip. You'll know when you're overdoing it, because you'll spend a third of your time bitching. When the blues hit, treat yourself to a decent room or a special meal; a few pounds, shekels or dinars will be put to good use if they soothe you and put you in a frame of mind to get the most out of your travels.

When To Go

Israel and the **West Bank** have two high tourist seasons. Summer is favored by North Americans and students; winter is preferred by Europeans who come to bask in the Middle Eastern warmth. **Egypt** has different high and low seasons depending on the region. In Alexandria and Marsa Matruuh, summer is the high season; in Cairo, in the Sinai, and around the Dead Sea, winter is the high season, when it's bearable to frolic in the sun. **Jordan** has its peak seasons in spring and autumn.

If you can stand the climate, off-season travel means fewer tourist crowds, lower prices, cheap airfares, and greater local hospitality.

Climate

Israel has hot, dry summers and mild, wet winters. The coastal plain is humid in summer and rainy in winter. Because of the sea's moderating influence, winter may bring rain to Jerusalem but more often causes only a cooling frost. The Negev and Jordan Valley have extreme desert climates. Though only pleasantly warm from November to March, summer temperatures often venture uncomfortably far above the 33 C (91 F) mark. Desert nights can be surprisingly cool.

The landlocked and hilly **West Bank** is spared the humidity of Israel's coastal regions, but not the heat. Summer afternoons are scorching; nights are cool. Winters are mild, though it has been known to snow.

Egypt may be the hottest place regularly visited by English-speaking tourists; in the south, temperatures in the summer often reach 49 C (120 F) and sometimes push 54 C (129 F). Fortunately, the climate is extremely dry, and the body's cooling system operates efficiently in the low humidity. Cairo itself is only marginally hotter than Tel Aviv or Amman, but air pollution can make the afternoons uncomfortable. Alexandria is temperate year round, but the humidity is much higher. During the winter the temperature climbs no higher than the low 20s, and nights get much cooler.

Jordan combines warm days and cool nights in spring and autumn. During the winter, when snow falls in the mountain regions, sunny Aqaba becomes popular.

Average Daily Temperatures

	January	July
Alexandria	11-19 C	23-30 C
Amman	4-12 C	18-32 C
Aqaba	10-21 C	30-42 C
Aswan	10-25 C	26-42 C
Cairo	8-19 C	22-36 C
Eilat	10-21 C	30-42 C
Ḥaifa	10-29 C	21-35 C
Jerusalem	6-20 C	19-38 C
Luxor	6-24 C	23-42 C
Nablus	10-28 C	22-37 C
Tel Aviv	11-20 C	23-30 C

Weights, Measures, and Time Zones

1 meter(m)=1.09 yards
1 kilometer(km)=0.62 mile
1 kilogram(kg)=2.20 pounds
1 liter(l)=1.06 quarts
C =5/9(F -32)

Israel, Egypt, Jordan, and the West Bank are seven hours ahead of Eastern Standard Time and two hours ahead of Greenwich Mean Time.

Useful Organizations and Publications

Tourist Offices

Israel, Egypt, and Jordan all take tourism seriously. The agencies and organizations listed below are usually quick to respond to queries, but contact them well in advance of your departure just in case. You can request general information (e.g., what's fun in Jordan), or you can ask specific questions (e.g., how do I go about crossing from the Sinai into Israel).

Egyptian Tourist Authority: USA: 630 Fifth Ave., New York, NY 10111 (tel. (212) 246-6960, fax (212) 956-6439); Wilshire San Vicente Plaza, 83 Wilshire Blvd., #215, Beverly Hills, CA 90211 (tel. (213) 653-8815, fax (213) 653-8961); 645 N. Michigan Ave., Ste. 829, Chicago, IL 60611 (tel. (312) 280-4666, fax (312) 280-4788). **Canada:** Place Bonaventure, Frontenac 40, P.O. Box 304, Montréal, Qué. H5A 1B4 (tel. (514) 861-4420 or 851-4606, fax (514) 861-8071). **U.K.:** 168 Piccadilly, London W1V 9DE (tel. (071) 493 52 82/3, fax (071) 408 02 95).

Israel Government Tourist Office (GTIO): U.S.: 350 Fifth Ave., New York, NY 10118 (tel. (212) 560-0650); 6380 Wilshire Blvd., Los Angeles, CA 90048 (tel. (213) 658-7462); 5 S. Wabash Ave., Chicago, IL 60603 (tel. (312) 782-4306); 420 Lincoln Rd., Miami, FL 33139 (tel. (305) 673-6862). **Canada:** 180 Bloor St., W. Toronto, Ontario M5S 2V6 (tel. (416) 964-3784). **U.K.:** 18 Great Marlborough St., London W1V 1AF (tel. (071) 434 36 51).

Jordan Information Bureau: 2319 Wyoming Ave. NW, Washington, DC 20006 (tel. (202) 265-1606).

Embassies and Consulates

Egyptian Embassies: U.S.: 2310 Decatur Pl. NW, Washington, DC 20008 (tel. (202) 232-5400). **Canada:** 454 Laurier Ave., E. Ottawa, Ont. K1N 6R3 (tel. (613) 234-4931 or (613) 234-4935, fax (613) 234-9347). **U.K.:** 26 South St., London W1Y 6DD (tel. (071) 499 24 01). **Australia:** 125 Manaro Crescent, Red Hill, Canberra ACP 2603 (tel. (06) 95 03 94 or 95 03 95).

Egyptian Consulates: U.S.: 1110 Second Ave., New York, NY 10022 (tel. (212) 759-7120); 3001 Pacific Ave., San Francisco, CA 94115 (tel. (415) 346-9700); 30 South Michigan Ave., 7th flr., Chicago, IL 60603 (tel. (312) 443-1190); 2000 W. Loop South #1750, Houston, TX 77027 (tel. (713) 961-4916); 2310 Decatur Pl. NW, Washington DC 20008 (tel. (202) 234-3903). **Canada:** 3754 Côte-des-Neiges, Montréal, Qué. H3H 1V6 (tel. (514) 937-7781 or 937-7782). **U.K.:** 19 Kensington Palace Garden, London W8 (tel. (01) 229 88 18 or 229 88 19).

Israeli Embassies: U.S.: 3514 International Drive NW, Washington, DC 20008 (tel. (202) 364-5500). **Canada:** 50 O'Connor St., Suite 1005, Ottawa, Ont. K1P 6L2 (tel. (613) 237-6450 or 237-8865). **U.K.:** 2 Palace Green, London W8 4QB (tel. (01) 937 80 50). **Australia:** 6 Turrana St., Yarralumla, Canberra ACT 2600 (tel. (06) 273-1300 or 273-1309). **New Zealand:** 13th Level, Williams City Center, Plimmer Steps, P.O. Box 2171, Wellington (tel. (06) 273-2045).

Israeli Consulates: U.S.: 800 Second Ave., New York, NY 10017 (tel. (212) 351-5200); 6380 Wilshire Blvd. #1700, Los Angeles, CA 90048 (tel. (213) 651-5700); 111 E. Wacker Dr. #1308, Chicago, IL 60601 (tel. (312) 565-3300). Other offices in Atlanta, Boston, Houston, Miami, Montreal, Philadelphia, San Francisco, and Washington, DC. **Canada:** 180 Bloor St. W. #700, Toronto, Ont. M5S 2V6 (tel. (416) 961-1126). **Australia:** 37 York St., Sydney 2000 (tel. (26) 479 33).

Jordanian Embassies: U.S.: 3504 International Dr. NW, Washington, DC 20008 (tel. (202) 966-2664). **Canada:** 100 Bronson Ave. #701, Ottawa, Ont. K1R 6G8 (tel. (613) 238-8090). **U.K.:** 6 Upper Philimore Gardens, London W8 7HB (tel. (4471) 937 36 85). **Australia:** 20 Roebuck St., Red Hill, Sydney 2603 (tel. (06) 95 99 51).

Jordanian Consulates: U.S.: 866 United Nations Plaza, Room 552, New York, NY 10017 (tel. (212) 752-0135); 708 Main St., Suite 930, Houston, TX 77002 (tel. (713) 224-2911).

Budget Travel Services

Council on International Educational Exchange (CIEE), 205 E. 42nd St., New York, NY 10017 (tel. (212) 661-1414). Information on academic, work, voluntary service, and professional opportunities abroad. Administers ISIC, FIYTO, and ITIC cards. Write for *Student Travels* (free, postage US$1), CIEE's biannual travel magazine for college students. Also available are *Work, Study, Travel Abroad: The Whole World Handbook* (US$12.95, postage $1.50); *Going Places: The High School Student's Guide to Study, Travel, and Adventure Abroad* (US$13.95, postage $1.50); and *Volunteer! The Comprehensive Guide to Voluntary Service in the U.S. and Abroad* (US$8.95, postage $1.50).

Always travel with a friend.

Get the International
Student Identity Card,
recognized worldwide.

For information call toll-free **1-800-GET-AN-ID**.
or contact any Council Travel office. (See inside front cover.)

 Council on International Educational Exchange
205 East 42nd Street, New York, NY 10017

Council Travel: A budget subsidiary of CIEE. Offices throughout the U.S., Europe, and Asia, including 205 E. 42nd St., New York, NY 10017 (tel. (212) 661-1450); 729 Boylston St., #201, Boston, MA 02116 (tel. (617) 266-1926); 1093 Broxton Ave., Los Angeles, CA 90024 (tel. (310) 208-3551); 1153 N. Dearborn St., Chicago, IL 60610 (tel. (312) 951-0585); 919 Irving St., San Francisco, CA 94122 (tel. (415) 566-6222); 2000 Guadalupe St., Austin, TX 78705 (tel. (512) 472-4931); 28A Poland St., London, England W1V 3DB. Sells travel gear, discount card memberships.

Federation of International Youth Travel Organizations (FIYTO): 81 Islands Brygge, DK-2300, Copenhagen S., Denmark (tel. (31) 54 60 80, fax (31) 54 88 90). Sponsors an International Youth Card (IYC) for anyone under 26. See Student and Youth Identification under **Documents and Formalities,** below.

International Student Travel Confederation (ISTC): Gothersgade 30, 1123 Copenhagen K, Denmark. Umbrella organization for the following associations: the International Student Identity Card Association, the International Student Insurance Services, the International Association of Education and Work Exchange Programmes, and the Student Air Travel Association. Members of these associations include CIEE/Council Travel Services (U.S.); Travel CUTS (Canada); STA Travel (U.K.); SSA/STA (Australia); Student Travel (New Zealand), and others. Issues the International Student Identity Card (ISIC). See Student and Youth Identification under **Documents and Formalities,** below.

Israel Students Travel Company, Ltd. (ISSTA): 109 Ben-Yehuda St., Tel Aviv 63401 (tel. (03) 527 01 11; fax (03) 527 03 12). Information on tours, student discounts, ID cards, air ticket prices, accommodations, and land arrangements.

Let's Go Travel Services: Harvard Student Agencies, Inc., Thayer Hall-B, Harvard University, Cambridge, MA 02138 (tel. (617) 495-9649 for budget travel info or (800)-5-LETS-GO (553-8746) for credit card purchases and flight reservations). Offers discount flights, ISIC and YIEE cards, International Hostel Membership Cards, travel guides and maps (including the *Let's Go* series—big surprise), and a complete line of budget travel gear. All items available by mail.

London Student Travel, 52 Grosvenor Gardens, London SW1W OAG (tel. (071) 730 3402 European, (071) 730 8111 worldwide). Competitive European rail, coach, and air fares for both students and the independent traveler. Flexible low-cost charter flights, value travel insurance, and most discount cards.

STA Travel: U.S.: 17 E. 45th St., New York, NY 10017 (tel. (800) 777-0112 or (212) 986-9643); 7202 Melrose Ave., Los Angeles, CA 90046 (tel. (213) 934-8722); 166 Geary St., #702, San Francisco, CA 94108 (tel. (415) 391-8407); 273 Newbury St., Boston, MA 02116 (tel. (617) 266-6014). **U.K.:** 74 and 86 Old Brompton Rd., London SW7 3LQ (tel. (071) 937 9921 for European travel, (071) 937 9971 for North American travel, and (071) 937 9962 for everywhere else). **Australia:** 222 Faraday St., Carlton, Melbourne, Victoria 3053 (tel. (03) 347 69 11). **New Zealand:** 10 High St., Auckland (tel. (09) 39 04 58). A worldwide travel company specializing in low-cost international airfares, offering off the beaten track travel arrangements for students and young independent travelers.

Travel CUTS (Canadian Universities Travel Service, Ltd.): Canada: 187 College St., Toronto, Ont. M5T 1P7 (tel. (416) 979-2406). **U.K.:** 295A Regent St., London W1R 7YA (tel. (071) 637 3161). 35 branch offices including offices in Burnaby, Calgary, Edmonton, Halifax, Montreal, Ottawa, Quebec, Saskatoon, Sudbury, Vancouver, Victoria, Waterloo, and Winnipeg. Distributes HI, ISIC, FIYTO, and international youth cards. Discount airfares and charters.

WST Charters: Priory House, 6 Wright's Lane, London W8 6TA (tel (071) 938 4362; Fax (071) 937 7154). Specializing in low-cost flights, accommodations, and tours of Israel and Egypt. Flights to Tel Aviv daily except Fridays. Charters to Egypt available.

Publications

The **U.S. Government Printing Office** offers several publications for travelers including *Key Officers of Foreign Serving Posts,* a quarterly State Department publication that lists all U.S. embassies, consulates general, and missions abroad (US$2.75 for a single issue, $5.00 for a subscription). Other items available include *Your Trip Abroad* ($1.25), *A Safe Trip Abroad* ($1), *Tips for Travelers to the Middle East and North Africa* ($1), and *Health Information for International Travel* ($5). Write to Superintendent of Documents, U.S. Government Printing Office, Washington, DC 20402-9325 (tel. (202) 783-3238). The pamphlets *Foreign Entry Requirements* and *Tips for Travelers* (50¢ each) are available from the **Consumer Information Center,** Dept. 454V, Pueblo, CO 81009 (tel. (719) 948-3334).

The *Handbook for Women Travellers,* by Maggie and Gemma Ross, is available from Piatkus Books, 5 Windmill St., London W1 (tel. (071) 631 0710) for £7.99. The *Jewish Travel Guide*, published by Sepher-Hermon Press, 1265 46th St., Brooklyn, NY 11219 (tel. (718) 972-9010), lists Jewish institutions, synagogues, and kosher restaurants in over 80 countries (US$11.50). Including Israel. See the Additional Concerns section below for listings of books for senior travelers, disabled travelers, and gay and lesbian travelers. Some bookstores will order these books for you.

Hostel Associations

Hostelling International (HI)—previously the International Youth Hostel Federation (IYHF)—is an umbrella organization that coordinates the activities of 60 national hostelling associations and a number of associate agencies around the world. HI membership is required to stay in some of Israel and Egypt's hostels; you can sometimes buy membership on the spot, or sleep there at a higher price. One-year membership cards are readily available from national hostel associations (see below) and from many budget travel agencies (see above). HI publishes an annual *Guide to Budget Accommodation*, which contains up-to-date hostel listings. You may purchase an International Guest Card from local associations or from many larger hostels. Contact your national association for more details.

American Youth Hostels (AYH)/Hostelling International - USA: 733 15th St. NW, #840, Washington, DC 20005 (tel. (202) 783-6161, fax (202) 783-6171).

Australian Youth Hostels Association (AYHA)/Hostelling International - Australia: 10 Mallett St., Level 3, Camperdown, New South Wales 2050 (tel. (02) 565 16 99).

Hostelling International - Canada: 1600 James Naismith Dr., #608, Gloucester, Ont. K1B 5N4 (tel. (613) 748-5638).

Youth Hostels Association of England and Wales (YHA)/Hostelling International - England and Wales: Trevelyan House, 8 St. Stephen's Hill, St. Albans, Herts AL1 2DY (tel. 44 727 55215).

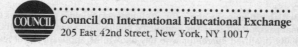

Youth Hostels Association of New Zealand (YHANZ)/Hostelling International - New Zealand: P.O. Box 436, 173 Gloucester St., Christchurch 1 (tel. 64 3 799970).

You can also contact the Egyptian and Israeli hostel associations directly.

Egyptian Youth Hostels Association/Hostelling International - Egypt: 1 El-Ibrahimy St., Garden City, Cairo (tel. 354 05 29, fax 355 03 29). Write for information on their 15 youth hostels. An International Guest Card will cost LE24.

Israel Youth Hostel Association/Hostelling International - Israel: 3 Dorot Rishonim St., P.O. Box 1075, Jerusalem 91009 (tel. (02) 25 27 06, fax (02) 25 06 76). Operates 30 hostels. Write for the pamphlet *Israel on the Youth Hostel Trail*.

Documents and Formalities

This can be a hassle. File all necessary applications early, preferably months—not weeks—before your planned departure. When you have a nonrefundable $1000 ticket, you can't afford to have your visa a little late.

Passports

A valid passport is required to enter Israel, Egypt, and Jordan and to return to your own country. Once you obtain a passport, be sure to record your passport number in a separate place, or even memorize it. If you do lose your passport, notify the local police and your embassy or consulate as soon as possible. Embassies can issue temporary passports immediately in a crunch. Carry a second proof of citizenship (birth certificate or driver's license will do) separately from your passport, as well as a photocopy of the passport.

A **U.S. passport** may be obtained at designated courthouses and post offices or at any of the 13 regional offices of the U.S. Passport Agency. You may also apply by mail if your previous passport was issued after your sixteenth birthday and in the twelve years prior to the date of the new application. Applications require proof of citizenship (e.g., your birth certificate), two identical recent photographs, proof of identity (e.g., a driver's license or student ID), and the correct fee (US$55 for adults and $30 for children, plus a $10 execution fee if this is your first passport). Adult passports (18 and over) are valid for ten years; children's passports are valid for five. Average processing time is 2-3 weeks, but rush processing is available with proof of departure date. Apply between August and December for fastest processing. For a recorded message giving complete information regarding U.S. passports, call (202) 647-0518 anytime. For more detailed information, contact the Washington Passport Agency, Dept. of State, 1425 K St. NW, Washington, DC 20522-1705 (tel. (202) 326-6060).

For information about second passports valid only for travel to Israel, see Travelling to Arab Nations and Israel, below.

Canadian passports may be obtained in person at one of 26 regional passport offices or by mail from the Passport Office, Department of External Affairs, Ottawa, Ont. K1A OG3. Passport requirements include (1) a completed application (available at passport offices, post offices, and most travel agencies in Canada; if outside Canada, available from the nearest Canadian mission); (2) original documentary evidence of Canadian citizenship; and (3) two identical photographs (three if applying outside Canada), both signed by the holder and one certified by a guarantor from an approved list. The guarantor also signs the application form. A list of eligible guarantors and all requirements for obtaining a Canadian passport are outlined on the application form. Children may be included on a parent's passport; they also need proof of Canadian citizenship. The fee is CDN$35, and Canadian passports are valid for five years. Passports normally require five working days at a regional office, while mailed applications require three weeks from the day the application is received. For more information, consult the booklet *Bon Voyage, But...*, available free from the Passport Office.

British citizens can apply for a full passport at main post offices or at one of six regional passport offices. The completed application must be countersigned by a professionally qualified guarantor who has known the applicant for at least two years, and the application must include (1) two recent identical photographs, one countersigned by the guarantor; (2) an original birth certificate and/or marriage certificate (if applicable); and (3) £15 by check or money order. Passports of those 16 and older are valid for 10 years and can be renewed. Children's passports are valid for five years, after which they may be extended for another five years at no extra charge. Passport extensions for travelers already abroad can be obtained at the nearest British High Commission or Consulate. Processing usually takes from four to six weeks; the busy season is between February and August. Rush processing is available.

Irish citizens should pick up an application at a local guard station or request one from one of the two passport offices. If you have never had a passport, you must send your birth certificate, the long application, and two identical pictures to Passport Office, Setanta Centre, Molesworth St., Dublin 2 (tel. (01) 711 633) or Passport Office, 1A South Mall, Cork, County Cork (tel. (021) 272 525). To renew, send your old passport, the short form, and the photos. Passports cost IR£45 and are valid for 10 years. Rush processing is available.

Applicants for an **Australian passport** must apply in person at a passport office, at an Australian diplomatic mission overseas, or at a post office, where an appointment may be necessary. A parent may file for an applicant who is under 18 and unmarried. Applications must include (1) two recent identical photos, countersigned by a guarantor; (2) proof of Australian citizenship (e.g., a birth certificate); (3) proof of identity (e.g., a driver's license); (4) proof of present name; and (5) marriage certificate (if applicable). All documents must be originals. Application fees are adjusted every three months; call the toll free information service for current details (tel. 13 12 32 or (008) 02 60 22). Processing takes about two weeks, though rush service is available. The passport is valid for 10 years. Departure tax stamps can be purchased wherever passport applications are available.

Applicants for a **New Zealand passport** must contact their local Link Centre, travel agent, or New Zealand Representative for an application form, which they must complete and mail to the New Zealand Passport Office. Completed application forms must include evidence of New Zealand citizenship (e.g., original birth certificate); two identical, correctly certified photographs; and the appropriate fee (NZ$56.25 for adults and NZ$25.30 for children under 16 if the application is lodged in New Zealand). Children are required to have separate passports and their names can no longer be endorsed in the passport of their parents or guardians. Children's passports have a maximum validity of five years. Standard processing time is 21 days, but urgent applications will be given priority. For more information, contact the New Zealand Passport Office, Documents of National Identity Division, Department of Internal Affairs, Box 10-526, Wellington (tel. (04) 474 8100).

Visas and Visa Extensions

A **visa** is written permission granted by a government to allow foreigners to enter its country for a specific period of time. Note that while some visas can be obtained abroad, it's both faster and safer to secure them before your trip. The pamphlet *Foreign Visa Requirements* is available for 50¢ from the Consumer Information Center, Department 454V, Pueblo, CO 81009 (tel. (719) 948-3334). Americans can also write to the Bureau of Consular Affairs, Passport Services, Dept. of State #5807, Washington DC 20524 (tel. (202) 647-0518).

Israel does not require that you obtain a visa beforehand if you are not going to study or work; a tourist visa will be issued free of charge to U.S., British, Australian, New Zealand, and Canadian citizens at the port of entry. However, your passport must be valid at least nine months beyond your time of arrival. These tourist visas are valid for three months but are extendable (see below). Study visas can be obtained from an Israeli embassy or consulate prior to departure or from the Office of the Interior once in Israel (in all large cities). You must provide proof of acceptance at an educational institution (such as a letter of sponsorship or acceptance), a medical statement from your doctor, and two photos. If you secure a job in Israel, you should have your employer in Israel contact the Office of the Interior in order to arrange a work visa for you before you leave.

Egyptian visas, which you must obtain prior to entering the country, are available by mail or in person at the nearest consulate. You must present your completed application along with (1) your passport, which must be valid at least six months past the date of your planned entry into Egypt; (2) a passport-sized photo; and (3) the fee, either in cash or a certified check (US$12 for U.S. citizens; more for Australian, British, Canadian, and New Zealand citizens). Include a stamped, self-addressed certified envelope if applying by mail, and allow at the very least 10 days to receive the visa. If you apply in person, the process usually takes two to three days, but keep in mind that the consulate has limited hours, so try to apply early in the day. The visa is valid for six months beginning from the date of issue. Although an Egyptian visa can also be issued at the airport in Cairo or at the port of Alexandria, it is strongly recommended that you obtain one in advance. Visas are available in Tel Aviv but not at the borders of Israel (Rafiah and Taba) or Jordan (Suez). An Egyptian visa does not permit the holder to work.

You must register your passport in Egypt with the police within seven days of your arrival or risk a heavy fine (LE40). It's one form. Ask the tourist office or your hotel manager where to register—frequently the manager will handle the paperwork for you. You may register at a passport office in any regional center (Cairo, Alexandria, Aswan, Luxor, Sharm al-Shaikh, or Marsa Matruuh), or with the less reliable local police in smaller areas. If you are unable to register, don't panic. The U.S. embassy issues a free letter of apology for U.S. citizens, with which you may register late at the Mugama Building at Tahrir Square in Cairo.

Jordanian visas may be obtained in person or by mail at the Jordanian embassy or at any consulate in two days. Visa requirements include (1) a valid passport that does not contain an Israeli seal or stamp (see Travelling to Arab Nations and Israel, below); (2) a completed application form with one photo; (3) a letter explaining the purpose of your visit to Jordan and the approximate date of departure from the U.S.; and (4) a self-addressed stamped envelope. Visas are issued free of charge for U.S. citizens; all others should contact their Jordanian embassy. A group visa can be issued for tour groups of ten persons or more provided all members possess valid American passports.

Visa extensions will normally be granted for six months to one year in Israel, Egypt, and Jordan. Israeli visa extensions are available at any Ministry of the Interior, Egyptian visa extensions in Cairo at the Mugama Building or at any police station, and Jordanian visa extensions at the Ministry of the Interior in Amman. To apply for an Egyptian visa extension, you must submit a photograph with your passport and a LE5-6 fee. Applicants must also be able to prove that they have enough foreign currency to cover the expenses of an extended stay.

Traveling to Both Arab Nations and Israel

> You will *not* be allowed to enter any Arab country except Egypt if you have an Israeli stamp on your passport. Israeli passport officials, however, will give you a detachable visa stamp upon request, allowing you to eliminate evidence of your having been in Israel. However, any other indications of a visit to Israel, such as an Egyptian entry stamp from Rafiah or Taba, will keep you out of Jordan, Syria, and the Sudan. The Egyptians are not as accommodating as the Israelis in providing detachable border stamps.

On April 25, 1992, the U.S. State Department announced that it would no longer issue second passports valid only for travel to Israel. Passports valid only for Israel will be cancelled and replaced free of charge with a two-year passport that has no geographic limitations. The State Department will help Americans obtain travel visas by issuing a limited-duration (2 yrs.) second passport. In order to obtain a second passport, you must include with your application a written statement explaining that you require a second passport in order to facilitate obtaining travel visas for Israel and

Arab countries. For more information, contact the Washington Passport Agency, Dept. of State, 1425 K St. NW, Washington, DC 20522-1705 (tel. (202) 326-6060).

Customs

Your luggage and yourself will be examined as you pass through customs—often with exasperating thoroughness. Certain items may have to be declared upon entry, including jewelry, computers, cameras, portable radios, and sports equipment. Ordinarily, these items can be brought in duty-free as long as you take them with you upon departure. It's a good idea to make a list of the serial numbers of all the expensive items you are taking with you and to have it stamped by the customs office upon departure. See the Entry section of the Israel, Egypt, and Jordan introductions for declaration and duty information specific to each country.

The U.S., Canada, the U.K., Australia, and New Zealand all prohibit or restrict the import of firearms, explosives, ammunition, fireworks, plants, animals, lottery tickets, obscene literature and film, controlled drugs, and bootleg Bart Simpson T-shirts. To avoid problems when carrying prescription drugs, make sure bottles are clearly marked, and have a copy of the prescription ready to show the customs officer. You must declare all items acquired abroad upon returning to your own country.

U.S. citizens may bring back a maximum of US$400 worth of goods duty-free every 30 days; the next $1000 is subject to a 10% tax. Duty-free goods must be for personal or household use (this includes gifts). To reimport expensive foreign-made articles duty-free, register them with any Customs Office or bring proof of domestic purchase. One unsolicited gift worth less than US$50 may be mailed duty-free from abroad per day, as long as it is not liquor, perfume, or tobacco. Spot checks are made on parcels, so write the accurate price and nature of the gift on the outside of the package. If you send back parcels worth more than US$50, the Postal Service will collect the duty plus a handling charge upon delivery. If you mail home personal goods of U.S. origin, mark the package "American Goods Returned" in order to avoid duty charges. Certain items manufactured in Israel, Egypt, and Jordan may be excluded from the U.S. customs tax beyond the normal US$400 limit under the Generalized System of Preferences (GSP), a program designed to build the economies of developing nations through export trade. For more information on all aspects of U.S. customs, including tobacco and alcohol allowances, write for the brochure *Know Before You Go,* available as item 477Y from the Consumer Information Center, Pueblo, CO 81009. You can also directly contact the U.S. Customs Service, Dept. of the Treasury, 1301 Constitution Ave., Washington, DC 20229 (tel. (202) 566-8195). Foreign nationals living in the U.S. are subject to different regulations; ask for the leaflet *Customs Hints for Visitors (Nonresidents).*

Before departure, **Canadian citizens** should identify all valuables with serial numbers on a Y-38 form at a Customs Office or at their point of departure; these goods may then be reimported duty-free. Once every calendar year after a minimum seven-day absence, citizens may bring in goods duty-free up to a value of CDN$300. You may send gifts valued up to CDN$40 duty-free. For more information, including tobacco and alcohol allowances, write for the pamphlet *I Declare/Je Declare,* available from the External Affairs, Ottawa, Ont. K1A OG2 (tel. (613) 993-6435). You can also directly contact the Revenue Canada Customs and Excise Department, Communications Branch, Mackenzie Ave., Ottawa, Ont. K1A OL5 (tel. (613) 957-0275).

British citizens may bring back a maximum of £32 duty-free. For tobacco and alcohol allowances or for more information, write Her Majesty's Customs and Excise Office, Custom House, Nettleton Rd., Heathrow Airport North, Hounslow, Middlesex TW6 2LA (tel. (01) 081 750) for more information.

Irish citizens may import a maximum of IR£34 per adult traveler duty-free (IR£17 per traveler under the age of 15). You may import as much currency into Ireland as you wish. For tobacco and alcohol allowances or for more information, write Division 1, Office of the Revenue Commissioners, Dublin Castle, Dublin 1 (tel. 679 27 27).

Australian citizens age 18 and over may bring back a maximum of AUS$400 duty-free (AUS$200 for travelers under 18). You may mail back personal property as long as you purchased it over 12 months previously, and you may mail back unsolicited gifts duty-free as long as they legitimately look like gifts. These and other restrictions, including alcohol and tobacco allowances, may be found in the brochure Customs Information for all Travelers, available from local customs offices or from Australian consulates.

Citizens of New Zealand may bring in NZ$700 worth of duty-free goods as long as the goods are intended for personal use or as unsolicited gifts. Tobacco and alcohol allowances as well as other information can be found in the New Zealand Customs Guide for Travelers and If You're Not Sure About It, DECLARE IT are both available from any customs office. For more information, contact New Zealand Customs, P.O. Box 29, Auckland (tel. (9) 773 520).

Student and Youth Identification

The **International Student Identity Card (ISIC)** is the most widely accepted form of student identification, providing discounts at museums, archeological sites, retail stores, flights, trains, buses, and accommodations. The US$15 16-month card also provides medical insurance up to US$3000, plus US$100 a day up to 60 days of in-hospital illness. Wave your card everywhere for discounts. Applications must include (1) current, dated proof of full-time student status (e.g., a transcript); (2) a 1.5-inch by 2-inch photo with your name printed on the back; (3) proof of age (12 or over); (4) proof of nationality; (5) name and address of beneficiary (for insurance purposes); and (6) a certified check or money order for US$15. The card is valid for 16 months, from Sept. 1 until December of the following year.

You may obtain an ISIC from CIEE/Council Travel, Let's Go Travel Services, Travel CUTS, STA Travel, Student Travel, or any other agency sponsored by the International Student Travel Confederation (see Budget Travel Services under **Useful Organizations and Publications** above). In addition, over 450 campus offices distribute the ISIC at universities around the United States. The annual International Student Travel Guide, available wherever you apply for the card, lists some of the discounts available with the ISIC. With an increase in the use of counterfeit ISICs, many airlines and other establishments may request double proof of student status. Student travelers may want to bring along a school ID or a signed statement from their registrar.

The **International Youth Card (IYC)** is available to students and nonstudents under the age of 26. The IYC gives access to discounts on international transportation, accommodations, restaurants, cultural activities, and tours. In the Middle East, the card gives discounts on Dan Tours in Israel and on ferry travel connecting Israel, Egypt, Greece, and Italy. The IYC is available from CIEE, Council Travel, Let's Go Travel, and other agencies; applications must include proof of age, a passport-sized photo, and the appropriate fee (US$10 without insurance, US$15 with insurance). For more information, contact the Federation of International Youth Travel Organization (see Budget Travel Services under Useful Organizations and Publications).

International Driver's License

An **International Driving Permit** is required for driving in Egypt and Jordan and is highly recommended for driving in Israel. The permit is available from any office of the **American Automobile Association (AAA)**. You will need (1) a completed application, (2) two recent passport-size photographs, (3) a valid U.S. driver's license, and (4) US$10. Applicants must be at least 18 years old, and the permit is processed and issued while you wait. If you hold a Canadian driver's license, an IDP can be obtained through any office of the **Canadian Automobile Association (CAA)** for CDN$10. Address specific questions about IDPs to AAA Travel Agency Services, 1000 AAA Drive (mail stop 100), Heathrow, FL 32746-5063 (tel. (407) 444-7883). Your domestic driver's license must accompany the International Driver's Permit, so don't forget to take your original driver's license with you.

An **International Insurance Certificate** or "green card" is required to drive in Israel, Egypt, Jordan, and the West Bank. Most rental agencies include this coverage in their prices. Otherwise, obtain this certificate from the dealer from whom you are leasing or buying.

Money

Currency and Exchange

The exchange rates valid at press time (Sept. 1992) are listed at the beginning of each country's section; however, rates fluctuate—often dramatically—so check them in the financial pages of a national newspaper when planning your trip. Before leaving home, buy about $50 in the currency of the first country you will visit. This will save you hours at the airport.

Since commissions can vary greatly, be sure to compare rates when exchanging money. Train stations, luxury hotels, and restaurants generally offer the worst rates. Try not to purchase more of a currency than you'll need in a particular country, for every time you re-convert money you incur a loss. If the dollar is falling, however, you will save money if you exchange as much money as is practical at the beginning of your trip. Divide your money among pockets, bags, and a moneybelt.

Traveler's Checks

Traveler's checks, recognized for cash or exchange at almost every bank in the Middle East, are the safest way to carry money. If lost or stolen, traveler's checks can be replaced. Checks are available in various currencies; the smallest denomination is usually US$20 or equivalent. Get a few of these so that if you have to exchange money at a poor rate you won't lose too much. The US$50 checks are the most convenient denomination and will save you money if a fee is charged for each exchange transaction.

Traveler's check companies offer a variety of additional services besides refunding lost or stolen checks, such as medical and legal referrals, emergency message relay, interpretation help, guaranteed hospital entry, and lost document assistance. Some companies will also provide insurance coverage for trip delays, lost luggage, and accident or sickness.

Banks and agencies worldwide sell traveler's checks. Sometimes you will be charged a commission of about 1-2%, sometimes a set fee, and sometimes, particularly if you are a customer of that bank, nothing at all. Listed below are some major traveler's check companies; to find the closest vendor of a particular brand, consult your local telephone book or bank, or call a number listed below.

American Express: World Financial Center, American Express Tower, 200 Vesey St., New York, NY 10285 (tel. (800) 221-7282 in the U.S. and Canada, request the "Ask the President" unit for questions regarding international travel; (0800) 52 13 13 in the U.K.; (02) 886 06 89 in Australia; elsewhere call U.S. collect at (801) 964-6665 for referral to offices in individual countries). Checks available in 7 currencies. 3 offices in Israel (look for their affiliated company Meditrad), 16 in Egypt, and 2 in Jordan (look for International Traders). Holders of AmEx traveler's checks or credit cards can use most AmEx offices as a mailing address free of charge. For refunds, call collect (03) 546 92 92 in Israel, (44) 273 57 16 00 in Egypt, and (973) 256 834 in Jordan. Call a travel service office to get the helpful *Traveler's Companion*. The **American Automobile Association (AAA)** sells AmEx traveler's checks commission-free to AAA members.

Bank of America Traveler's Office: P.O. Box 37010, San Francisco, CA 94137 (tel. (800) 227-3460 from within the U.S.; from Canada and elsewhere, call California collect (415) 574-7111). Checks available in U.S. dollars only. Commission 1% for non-Bank of America customers.

Barclays Bank: tel. (800) 221-2426 from within the U.S. and Canada; (202) 67 12 12 in the U.K.; from elsewhere, call New York collect (212) 858-8500. Checks available in 4 currencies. Commission 1%.

Citicorp: tel. (800) 645-6556 from within the U.S. and Canada; from elsewhere, call U.S. collect (813) 623-1709. Checks available in 4 currencies. Commission 1-1.5%.

MasterCard International/Thomas Cook: tel. (800) 223-7373 or (800) 223-9920 from within the U.S.; from elsewhere call New York collect (212) 974-5696. Checks available in 11 currencies; Thomas Cook charges a 1% commission, and since their checks must be purchased through an affiliated bank, the seller may levy an additional fee.

Visa: tel. (800) 227-6811 from within the U.S. and Canada; (071) 937 8091 in the U.K.; from elsewhere call New York collect (212) 858-8500. Checks available in 13 currencies. Visa charges no commission, but your bank probably will, about 1%.

American Express, Barclays, and Visa are the best bets for obtaining refunds for in Israel, Egypt, and Jordan. Even in the best of circumstances, the refund process involves a fair amount of red tape and delay. To expedite a refund, separate your check receipts and keep them in a safe place. It is vital that you record check numbers as you cash them so that you can identify exactly which checks are missing. As an additional precaution, leave a list of check numbers with someone at home. Most importantly, keep a separate supply of cash and/or traveler's checks for financial emergencies.

Credit Cards and Cash Cards

Credit cards are of limited day-to-day value to the budget traveler because most small, inexpensive establishments will not honor them. Credit cards are invaluable, however, in a financial emergency. With major credit cards, you can receive an instant cash advance as large as your remaining credit line from banks that issue the card. Both **Visa** (tel. (800) 223-9920) and **MasterCard** (tel. (800) 223-9920) can give cash advances at any of their affiliated banks; just look for the Visa or MasterCard logo on the door.

American Express (tel. (800) 528-4800) will cash personal checks for greencard-holders overseas up to US$1000 every 21 days (up to US$200 in cash; the rest will be disbursed in traveler's checks) in many, but not all, of their offices. Goldcard-holders can cash a personal check abroad for up to US$5000 every 21 days, the first US$500 of which can be in cash. This quick transfusion of cash may be your only source of money, since many traveler's check vendors will not cash a personal check and transatlantic cables for money take at least 24 hours. American Express is affiliated in Israel with Meditrad, Ltd. and in Jordan with International Traders. American Express will allow you to use its offices as mailing addresses free of charge with its card or its checks, but check in the *Traveler's Companion* first, since not all offices offer this service. The *Traveler's Companion,* which lists all American Express offices throughout the world, is available from their travel service offices. (Also see Traveler's Checks, above.)

Cash cards are slowly but steadily making their way into the Middle East. There are now 170 Cirrus **automated teller machines (ATMs)** in Israel (at Bank HaPoalim branches), and 90 for Visa cardholders, but none in Jordan or in Egypt.

Sending Money

Do your best to avoid it. Carry a credit card or a separate stash of traveler's checks.

Money can be sent from your home bank to a branch abroad with a **cable transfer** (in either U.S. or foreign currency) within 24 hours to a major city, a bit longer to a less central location. You pay cabling costs plus the commission charged by your bank (approximately US$25 per $1000). Before you leave home, visit your bank to obtain a list of its corresponding banks in Israel, Egypt, and Jordan. You can also arrange in advance for your bank to send money from your account to foreign banks on specific dates. Remember that you will always need ID to pick up money that has been sent to you.

Western Union offers a convenient though expensive service for cabling money to Israel from the U.S. Using MasterCard or Visa, a sender can cable up to US$2000 by calling Western Union's toll-free numbers, (800) 325-4176 or (800) 325-6000. Without a card, a sender must go in person to a Western Union office with cash or a cashier's check (no money orders accepted) but is not restricted to the $2000 limit. The commission charged by Western Union varies depending on how much money you send. Expect a charge of US$75 per $1000, plus the inevitable bank fee. The money will arrive at the central telegram office or main post office of the city the sender designates and may be picked up by showing photo ID. Money will generally arrive within two to five business days. The recipient will not be notified by the receiving office when the money arrives, so the sender will have to notify the traveler where and when

Don't forget to write.

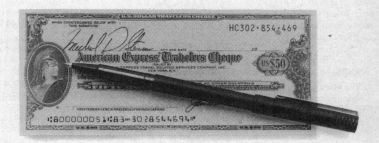

Now that you've said, "Let's go," it's time to say, "Let's get American Express® Travelers Cheques." Because when you want your travel money to go a long way, it's a good idea to protect it. So before you leave, be sure and write.

the money can be expected. Unfortunately, Western Union does not cover Egypt or Jordan.

Bank of America (tel. (800) 237-8052) will send money to any of their affiliated banks throughout the world. Allow three to five working days and expect a US$45 charge per $1000 (US$30 for Bank of America customers). Sender can bring cash, credit card or cashier's check.

Money cabled through **American Express** offices (tel. (800) 543-4080) is guaranteed to arrive within 72 hours. Money will be dispersed in U.S. dollar traveler's checks. The cost to send US$1000 to Cairo is $70. American Express does not transfer money to Israel or to Jordan.

The **Bureau of Consular Affairs' Citizens Emergency Center** (tel. (202) 647-5225) will deliver money to you if you're an American abroad and very, very desperate. The State Department defines emergencies as cases of destitution, hospitalization, or death. The Department will assist by contacting your family or friends in the U.S. and arranging for them to send you money. They prefer to transmit sums not greater than a few hundred dollars. For more information and a complete list of services, write Citizens Emergency Center, Dept. of State, 2201 C St. NW, #4811, Washington, DC 20520.

Packing

It's just too darn hot in the Middle East to worry about fashion. Pack lightly. A tried and true method is to set out everything you think you'll need for your trip, eliminate half of it, and take more money. A heavy bag will create extra transportation problems and make you *really unhappy* whenever you move; your life should fit on your back.

Decide first whether a backpack, light suitcase, or shoulder bag is most suitable for your travels. If you're planning on covering miles of ground by foot, a sturdy **backpack,** preferably with several compartments, is hard to beat. With the weight on your back, your hands will be free to handle maps, tickets, and *Let's Go*. Internal frames are less cumbersome and sturdier, but external frames lift the pack off your body so your back is less likely to become a sweaty swamp in the heat. Backpacks that convert into soft-sided shoulder bags are another good option. Their versatility enables you to move from urban hotel to desert camping with ease, and they allow you to fool hotel managers prejudiced against backpackers.

Regardless of what kind of luggage you choose, a small **daypack** is indispensable for plane flights, sightseeing, and holding your valuables. On short trips, daypacks are useful for carrying your lunch, camera, canteen, and notebook. To avoid theft, guard your money, passport, and other important articles in a neck pouch or moneybelt. For added security, get a few combination luggage locks for your bags (though remember that these aren't invulnerable). Label everything everywhere.

Natural fibers or cotton blends beat synthetics hands down in the heat. Be sure to take clothes that can be washed in a sink. While dark-colored clothes will hide dirt better, light ones are more comfortable in hot weather. Better yet, do as the locals have done for centuries—wear long, pale, gauzy shirts or skirts. You can buy such items once there; light cotton clothing is available everywhere. Skip clothes like cut-offs and tank tops (and of course tube tops) that may be culturally offensive and will brand you as the typical out-of-towner. In Egypt, Jordan, the West Bank, and any holy site, both men and women should keep their knees and shoulders covered to avoid offending local rules of modesty. Breaking accepted standards will only draw unwelcome attention. (See Travel Etiquette under Other Tips, below.) When packing, remember that the temperature drops considerably at night.

Appropriate **footwear** is crucial. Tennis or well-cushioned running shoes are adequate for walking. Buy suitable boots if you plan to do extensive hiking and break them in *before* you go. Talcum powder sprinkled inside your shoes and on your feet can prevent sores, and moleskin is great for blisters. Israel's famous high quality leather sandals (*sandalim*) are good for short walks or evening idling, but they will hurt unaccustomed feet.

Laundromats are often hard to find, so bring along a supply of mild laundry soap. Dr. Bronner's castile soap (available in camping stores) claims to serve as everything from dish detergent to shampoo to toothpaste.

Electric current in Israel, Egypt, and Jordan is 220 volts. Travelers with appliances designed for 110 volts should bring a converter. A few machines are already equipped with a switch-operated converter, but since outlets are designed to receive round prongs, you'll still need an adapter to change the shape of the plug. Converters and adapters are available in department, hardware, and electrical equipment stores. Pay attention to the difference between a converter and an adapter lest you inadvertently ruin your appliances.

Film is generally more expensive abroad. Some foreign airport X-ray machines are film-safe and some are not—better to play it safe and protect your film with a special lead-lined bag available from any photo shop. (You can also ask security to check the film by hand.) Prepare your photo equipment for the dusty Middle East climate with lens paper, which is not widely available there.

Camping Equipment

Prepare ahead of time if you intend to camp. It's better to spend the money on good-quality camping gear than to cope with broken equipment in the field. The basic camping ingredients are a sleeping bag, foam pad, and tent (although often just a sleeping bag will do). Synthetic-filled sleeping bags are adequate for the mild Middle East, and they're cheaper and more durable than down. Mummy bags (very appropriate in Egypt) are lighter and more compact than regular bags. Buy your sleeping bag with the worst imaginable weather in mind. Synthetic bags usually cost at least US$45, while down bags for below-freezing temperatures begin at about US$135. Simple foam sleeping pads cost about US$10; the best air mattress or a sophisticated hybrid such as the Therm-A-Rest costs more than US$50.

Modern tents are remarkably clever. The best tents are easy to set up, self-supporting (with their own frame and suspension systems), and often don't require staking. When purchasing a tent, make certain it has a rain fly and bug netting. It should weigh no more than 3.5kg. Pay attention to the material as well—synthetic canvas is less expensive, lighter, and more water resistant than cotton canvas, but is also less "breathable." Backpackers and cyclists may wish to pay a bit more for a sophisticated, lightweight tent; some two-person tents weigh only 1kg. Expect to pay at least US$95 for a simple two-person tent and over US$120 for a serviceable four-person. Sometimes you can find the previous year's version at half-price, but check it out carefully and be sure you can return it in case of problems.

Other camping basics include a battery-operated lantern (never gas) and a simple plastic groundcloth to protect the tent floor. If you plan on roughing it in extremely isolated areas, water sacks and a solar shower can be very helpful amenities. A small campstove (from US$40) that runs on butane or white gas is also quite useful; the Middle East is not filled with firewood. Always bring waterproof matches. **Wilderness Press,** 2440 Bancroft Way, Berkeley, CA 94704-1676 (tel. (800) 443-7227 or (510) 843-8080), publishes useful books such as *Backpacking Basics* and the *Backpacker's Sourcebook* (both US$7.95 ppd). Call or write for a free catalog.

Some reputable mail-order camping stores in the U.S. include **Campmor,** 810 Rte. 17N, P.O. Box 997-LG92, Paramus, NJ 07653-0997 (tel. (800) 526-4784); **L.L. Bean,** 1 Casco St., Freeport ME 04033 (tel. (800) 221-4221); and **Recreational Equipment Co. (REI),** Sumner, WA 98352 (tel. (800) 426-4840). All will mail orders overseas. Their prices are generally lower, but local dealers will have more advice close at hand.

Health, Safety, and Security

Common sense and a few precautions should carry you safely through your travels. Large cities demand extra caution. Even if the city is familiar, avoid bus and train stations and public parks after dark. Stick to busy, well-lit streets and at all times beware of pickpockets. Hotel or hostel managers are often valuable sources of advice on specific areas. You may also feel safer staying in places with a curfew or a night-attendant. If you're in a dormitory-style room or have no lock on your door, sleep with all valuables on your person or under your pillow; laying your pack alongside the bed won't do. A money belt or neck pouch worn under a shirt are the most theft-resistant. Thieves who prey on backpackers are exceedingly clever, and crowded youth hostels and overnight trains are favorite hangouts for petty criminals.

Politics can intrude on travel, although this is rare. Keep apprised of events through a reliable newspaper. U.S. citizens can check on the latest government travel advisories by calling or writing the State Department's 24-hour Citizens Emergency Center, Rm. 4800, U.S. Department of State, Washington, DC 20520 (tel. (202) 647-5225).

While traveling, steer clear of empty train compartments, particularly at night. Don't check your luggage on trains, especially if you are switching en route; luggage is often lost this way. If you plan to sleep outside or simply don't want to carry everything with you, try to store your gear in a locker at a train or bus station. However, bomb scares and terrorism have greatly curtailed the availability of these lockers.

This will probably be useless advice, but it can't hurt: In case of tear gas, do *not* splash water on your face—the chemical reaction will make your entire face burn, not just your eyes.

> **Hitchhiking is dangerous. Don't try it. A particular warning—women traveling alone, or even in groups, should *never* hitchhike.**

Insurance

For further security, the following firms offer insurance against theft, loss of luggage, and injury, as do some travel agents. Check whether your homeowner's insurance (or your family's coverage) covers theft during travel. University term-time medical plans often include insurance for summer travel. Homeowner's insurance will generally cover the loss of travel documents such as passports, plane tickets, rail passes, etc., up to US$500. Canadians may be covered by their home province's health insurance plan up to 90 days after leaving the country. Also note that AmEx cardholders are often covered. The ISIC comes with a certain amount of insurance (see Student and Youth Identification under Documents and Formalities). In addition, those under 23 should check whether their parents have taken out any coverage on their behalf.

Insurance companies generally require a copy of the police report filed at the time of the theft before they will honor your claim, which can only be filed upon your return home. Similarly, with medical expenses you must submit evidence that you did indeed pay the charges for which you are requesting reimbursement. Check the time limit on filing claims to ensure that you will be home in time to secure reimbursement. Remember to keep all documents which could potentially be useful. The companies listed below can arrange on-the-spot payment of these bills for you.

Council on International Educational Exchange (CIEE): 205 E. 42nd St., New York, NY 10017 (tel. (212) 661-1414). "Trip-Safe" covers medical treatment and hospitalization, accidents, baggage, and flights missed due to illness.

Edmund A. Cocco Agency/GlobalCare Travel Insurance: 220 Broadway, #201, Lynnfield, MA 01940 (tel. (800) 821-2488 or (617) 595-0262). Accident, sickness, medical evacuation, and cancellation/interruption coverage. Payment of medical expenses on-the-spot worldwide. Group rates available.

Travel Assistance International/Europe Assistance Worldwide Services: 1133 15th St. NW, #400, Washington, DC (tel. (800) 821-2828 or (202) 331-1609). Probably the most extensive coverage available. Round-the-world assistance programs available round-the-clock in the event of financial and medical emergencies. Short-term plans available.

The Travelers Insurance Co.: 1 Tower Sq., Hartford, CT 06183 (tel. (800) 243-3174; in CT, HI, and AK call (203) 277-2138). Insurance for accidents, sickness, trip cancellation, and emergency medical evacuation. Also offers baggage-only policies, but at steeper rates.

Alcohol and Drugs

Despite vocal complaints from observant Muslims, alcohol is legal for all ages in Egypt and Jordan. Israel's drinking age is 18.

Never buy, possess, or use drugs in any country. Israeli, Egyptian, and Jordanian authorities all regard drug possession as an extremely serious offense. If you're lucky, you'll only be kicked out of the country. Don't expect much consolation from your consulate either. Consular officers can visit the prisoner, provide a list of attorneys, and inform family and friends. They cannot obtain any more lenient treatment than that dictated by the laws of the country.

Likewise, *never* bring drugs across borders. You and your belongings may be searched thoroughly whether you enter a country by land, sea, or air. Make certain to avoid unintentional involvement—refuse to carry or deliver packages for strangers, no matter how convincing or persuasive their stories. For more information on international drug restrictions and what the American consulate can and cannot do, send a self-addressed, stamped envelope for the brochure *Travel Warning on Drugs Abroad,* Bureau of Consular Affairs, Dept. of Public Affairs #5807, U.S. Dept. of State, Washington, DC (tel. (202) 647-1488).

Health Concerns

The hot temperatures and exotic foods of the Middle East can make even the most careful traveler ill. Drink *lots* of water, try to eat nutritious foods, and avoid overextending yourself physically. The intensity of prolonged travel can be very stressful; keeping your daily mileage down will help reduce anxiety. Avoid excessive caffeine and alcohol, both of which cause dehydration. Steer away from dirty restaurants and from street vendors, or your uninitiated stomach may protest vehemently.

Drink plenty of fluids, even when you don't feel thirsty. The sun can dehydrate you quickly and imperceptibly—as much as 10 liters of water per day may be necessary to stay healthy. If you're drinking enough water, your urine will be close to clear; a deep yellow hue can indicate dehydration. Be sure to wear a hat while in the sun and a shirt while snorkeling or swimming lest you find yourself with a blistering sunburn that could keep you in the shade for weeks. It's a good idea to carry a high sun protection factor (SPF) sun block. Remember that ultraviolet rays penetrate clouds, so even on overcast days you're not safe from sunburn. The desert is not the place to work on a tan—even the dark-skinned or already tan are not immune.

If you're traveling by car in the desert, carry plenty of extra water for the radiator as well as for drinking. Don't attempt to walk for help in the event of a breakdown; stay put and wait for a passing motorist. Distance and incline can be deceiving, and walking in the heat can fry you. If the car begins to overheat, put the engine in neutral and gun it periodically.

Note that **heatstroke** can occur without direct exposure to the sun. If ignored, heatstroke can lead to serious medical problems and even death. Symptoms include cessation of sweating, increased body temperature, flushed skin, and intense headache. If you suspect you have heatstroke, get out of the heat and sun immediately, cover yourself with wet towels, and drink water or fruit juice. Seek medical help as soon as possible.

Relying on bottled mineral water is a sensible precaution, especially in Egypt and Jordan. To save money you may want to use water-purification tablets instead of bottled water. In some places locals may tell you that the water is safe, but often they have developed antibodies that tourists have not. Also, heavy chlorination may disturb some stomachs. Anywhere you've been warned not to drink the water, pass up ice cubes, green salad, and unpeeled fruit. Sprinkling lime juice on salad may remove some of the bacteria, but don't rely on this tactic. Always carry a canteen filled with bottled water if you plan to spend time outside the cities. Perspiration carries away salt that also must be replaced. Lightly salting your food occasionally should suffice.

But, alas, sooner or later, no matter how careful you are, you probably will get traveler's diarrhea—affectionately known among its victims as "Pharaoh's Revenge." (Israelis call it *shil-shoul*, onomatopoeically.) The Revenge typically strikes 10-12 days after arrival and lasts from two to four days if you rest up. The diarrhea is usually accompanied by fever and fatigue. When you get sick, drink plenty of liquids to keep well-hydrated. Two tried and sometimes true domestic remedies are fresh yogurt, and lemon or lime juice into which a small quantity of salt has been dissolved. Commonly recommended American medications for diarrhea are Bactrim, Lomotil, Immodium, and Pepto-Bismol. Pharmacists can provide a number of locally produced medicines as well.

If you feel ill for a substantial amount of time, seek medical attention. Before you leave, consider writing to the **International Association for Medical Assistance to Travellers (IAMAT)** for their pamphlets *How to Avoid Traveler's Diarrhea* and *How to Adjust to the Heat* (417 Center St., Lewiston, NY 14092 (tel. (716) 754-4883); in Canada, 40 Regal Rd., Guelph, Ont. N1K 1B5 (tel. (519) 836-0102)). IAMAT can provide a directory of English-speaking physicians whose services are available at fixed and generally reasonable rates. This way you can ensure that the doctor understands that your tooth hurts, not your appendix. Membership is free, but donations are encouraged. Alternatively, the American, Australian, British, and Canadian embassies and consulates, as well as American Express and Thomas Cook offices, can identify English-speaking doctors. The first-aid centers listed for major cities can also provide assistance.

Take extra precaution against **infection** in Egypt and the rural areas of the Jordan Valley. Cuts and bruises must be properly dressed. If you contract an eye infection, see a physician immediately. Take care not to walk barefoot in the mud or on lawns that are wet with Nile River water. Thread-thin worms await to wriggle betwixt your toes and burrow their way to your intestines for a good meal. Don't swim in the Nile, and never drink from it, unless you want a terminal case of Pharaoh's Revenge.

Travelers with a medical condition requiring medication on a regular basis should consult a physician before leaving. Persons with diabetes, for example, may need advice on changing insulin levels for flights across multiple time zones. **The American Diabetes Association,** 1660 Duke St., Alexandria, VA 22314 (tel. (800) 232-3472) may have further information. Those with medical conditions that cannot be easily recognized (e.g., allergies to antibiotics, diabetes, epilepsy, heart problems) should obtain a **Medic Alert** identification tag, which can communicate vital information in an emergency. The tag also provides the number of Medic Alert's 24-hr. hotline, through which attending physicians can obtain information about the member's medical history. Lifetime membership is included in the price of the ID tag: US$35 for steel, US$40 for silver, and US$50 for gold-plated. Contact the **Medic Alert Foundation International,** P.O. Box 1009, Turlock, CA 95381-1009 (tel. (800) ID-ALERT (432-5378)).

Although no special **immunizations** are required to travel to Israel, Egypt, or Jordan, a shot of gamma globulin to protect against hepatitis as well as boosters against typhoid, tetanus, and diptheria are all wise precautions. Check with your doctor about incidence of malaria in the areas you intend to visit and take appropriate medication. Egypt and Jordan require cholera and yellow fever certificates from travelers arriving from countries where these diseases exist. If you don't have the necessary inoculations, you will be put in quarantine for several days, which is as ugly as it sounds. For more information on U.S. public health recommendations, write the Superintendent of Documents, U.S. Government Printing Office, Washington, DC 20402-9325 (tel. (202) 783-3238) for their book *Health Information for International Travel* (US$5).

A good compact traveler's medical kit should include a mildly antiseptic soap, vitamins, bandages, a thermometer in a sturdy case, mosquito repellent, motion sickness medicine (such as Dramamine), a small pocket knife with tweezers, calamine lotion for sunburn and insect bites, and an antihistamine (the centuries of dust in some places can trigger allergic reactions you never knew you had).

Bring a high SPF sunscreen and a lip balm. Bring an extra pair of glasses or contact lenses along with plenty of solution. Contraceptives are not always available or safe in the Middle East. All travelers on prescription drugs should carry a generous supply with them, preferably in carry-on items in case luggage goes astray. Those who use syringes, narcotic drugs, or other potentially illegal items should carry a legible copy of the prescription from their doctor to avoid problems at border crossings and customs.

An excellent book which addresses all these concerns, including a special section on AIDS, is *How to Stay Healthy Abroad* (US$8.95) by Richard Dawood, published by Viking-Penguin, Inc. This book has recently gone out of print, but you may still be able to get a hold of a copy at a local bookstore. You may also want the *Family Medical Encyclopedia* (US$5.95), ISBN 0671-741-918, published by Simon & Schuster, Order Dept., Old Tappan, NJ 07675 (tel. (800) 223-2348).

Women Travelers

Women may find traveling in Israel, Egypt, Jordan, and the West Bank uncomfortable at times. Israeli standards of dress are more Westernized, and women will experience less verbal harassment there than in Arab countries. In all these areas, however, women should be especially sensitive to different cultural traditions. Jordan is even more conservative than Egypt, the West Bank, and Arab parts of Israel.

Men may not understand that you are irritated or angered by their pursuit. Some may confuse the relative freedom of Western women with sexual willingness. In most cases, the best answer to come-ons is none at all. It may help to wear headphones, as men will be less likely to direct aggressive comments toward you if they think you can't hear them. On the other hand, passivity may be taken as tacit acceptance of the situation. The tricky task of firmly signaling that you've had enough without being hostile is necessary when the proverbial cold shoulder doesn't work. Asking an older man for assistance may also shame the offending parties into backing down. If a situation becomes genuinely threatening, enter tirade mode. Scream and yell in any language—it works, really. *Let's Go* lists emergency, police, and consulate phone numbers in most cities.

Common sense and cultural sensitivity are the best means of avoiding threatening situations in all Middle Eastern countries. In major cities and in tourist sites, locals are more accustomed to Western codes of dress. Away from the metropolitan areas of Egypt and Jordan and in the West Bank and both the Orthodox Jewish and Arab sections of Israel, however, it's advisable to emulate the dress and behavior of local women as much as possible. A shawl and a *djellaba* (a long garment with sleeves and a hood) may not make you blend in if your backpack, features, and height give you away first, but the covering allows you to travel more comfortably as a guest in another culture. If you choose to take public transportation, remember to cover up when going from urban areas to tourist sights (such as Saqqara or Dendera in Egypt or Petra in Jordan), because en route you will be off the most widely used thoroughfares. Once you arrive, you can peel off some portion of your coverings for relief from the heat. Only on or very near the beaches of large tourist resorts are locals used to seeing women in bathing suits. Don't smoke in public in Arab areas, and avoid sitting alone in cafés.

You improve your chances of avoiding harassment if you look as though you know where you're going—an air of confidence and composure works wonders. A good rule of thumb is to dress more a bit more modestly than you think is appropriate; it's hard to go wrong that way. Avoiding eye contact will also reduce the chances of an uncomfortable situation. Forego cheaper accommodations in remote areas of town in favor of youth hostels or more centrally located hotels. Stay away from empty train compartments, especially at night. If you take a *felucca* cruise, it's best to bring along a male companion. Avoid walking in unpopulated alleys and dark streets. If you think you are being followed, walk quickly and confidently to the nearest public area. Be aware that hostel proprietors have keys to your rooms and often segregate the sexes, so you run risks even if traveling with a man. *Never* hitchhike—it's especially dangerous in Israel—and beware of cars that may be following you. When riding in cabs keep your luggage handy and the door next to you unlocked. Be cautious in crowds or situations in which you find yourself confined with males, such as in an elevator. Strolling arm in arm with another woman, a common Middle Eastern practice, may be helpful. Wearing a wedding ring (or in Israel a gold watch, a common engagement gift) is a smart tactic, especially if you're traveling with a man, since out-of-wedlock intimacy between the sexes may be perceived as immoral. The *Handbook for Woman Travellers* (see Publications, above) provides additional information for women traveling alone.

Terrorism

The *Jerusalem Post* runs a filler advertisement that reads, "Suspicion saves! Beware of suspicious objects." A suspicious object—in Hebrew, *ḥefetz ḥashoud*—is reason enough for the authorities to evacuate the area; if you see an orderly and somewhat annoyed mob going one way and muttering about a *ḥefetz ḥashoud,* join it. Whether in Israel, Egypt, Jordan, or the West Bank, if you see an unattended package or bag, contact the police or army immediately: it could be a bomb. Terrorists often use extremely sophisticated bombs, so that even a wallet, roll of bills, or loaf of bread may be an explosive device. Call the police or inform anyone in military dress. If the police start clearing the area, follow their instructions. Though there has been a perceptible increase in terrorism against Israel associated with the turmoil in the occupied territories, attacks against Westerners remain rare. Random acts of violence, however, place everyone in danger. Keep your eyes open.

Alternatives to Tourism

Work and Study

American Zionist Youth Foundation, University Student Department/Israel Action Center: 110 E. 59th St., 3rd flr., New York, NY 10022 (tel. (800) 27-ISRAEL or (212) 339-6941). Clearinghouse for all programs to Israel, offering short-term tours and long-term university study or work/volunteer/internship/archeological dig programs. University programs offer classes in English and Hebrew. Fully accredited programs in Jerusalem, Tel Aviv, Ḥaifa, and Be'ersheva.

Archeological Institute of America 627 Commonwealth Ave., Boston, MA 02216 (tel. (617) 353-9361). Publishes the *Archeological Fieldwork Opportunities Bulletin* (1993 edition will be available Jan. 1, 1993). Lists field projects in the Middle East and throughout the world.

Council on International Educational Exchange (CIEE): 205 E. 42nd St., New York, NY 10017 (tel. (212) 661-1414). CIEE offers several publications on work and study abroad, including *Work, Study, Travel Abroad: The Whole World Handbook* (US$12.95, postage $1.50), *Volunteer! The Comprehensive Guide to Voluntary Service in the U.S. and Abroad* (US$8.95, postage $1.50), *Going Places: The High School Student's Guide to Study, Travel, and Adventure Abroad* (US$13.95, postage $1.50), and their biannual *Student Travels* magazine (postage US$1).

Institute of International Education (IIE): 809 UN Plaza, New York, NY 10017-3580 (tel. (212) 883-8200). Information on study and teaching opportunities abroad. Write for a list of their publications, which includes *Academic Year Abroad* (US$39.95, $3 postage), *Vacation Study Abroad* (US$31.95, $3 postage), and *Financial Resources for International Study* (US$36.95, $5.75 postage).

International Association for the Exchange of Students for Technical Experience (IAESTE): 10 Corporate Center #250, Columbia, MD 21044 (tel. (410) 997-2200). IAESTE operates 8 to 12-week trainee/intern programs in Israel, Egypt, and Jordan, and over 50 other countries for university-level students who have completed at least two years of study in a technical field.

Office of Overseas Schools: Rm. 245 SA-29, Dept. of State, Washington, DC 20522-2902 (tel. (703) 875-7800). Maintains a list of agencies that arrange teaching positions for Americans in elementary and secondary schools abroad.

Volunteers for Peace: 43 Tiffany Rd., Belmont, VT 05730 (tel. (802) 259-2759). Publishes the International Workcamp Directory (US$10) and a free newsletter. Arranges placement in 34 countries.

Additional Concerns

Senior Travelers

The following organizations can provide discount information and assistance for senior travelers. The International Youth Hostel Federation (HI) sells membership cards to persons over 55 for only US$15.

American Association of Retired Person (AARP), 601 E St., Washington, DC 20049 (tel. (202) 434-3680). U.S. residents over 50 and their spouses receive benefits which include travel programs and discounts for groups and individuals, as well as discounts on lodging, car rental, air arrangements, and sightseeing. US$8 annual membership fee.

Bureau of Consular Affairs: Bureau of Consular Affairs, Superintendent of Documents, U.S. Government Printing Office, Washington, DC 20402 (tel. (202) 783-3238). Write for a copy of *Travel Tips for Senior Citizens,* which provides information on passports, visas, health, and currency for older Americans planning trips abroad.

Elderhostel: 75 Federal St., 3rd flr., Boston, MA 02110 (tel. (617) 426-7788). Offers short-term residential educational programs at over 1500 locations internationally, including Egypt and Israel. Must be 60 or older, though companions may be 50 or over. No membership dues or formal education needed. Programs generally include room, board, tuition, and airfare. Scholarships available. Wide variety of subjects.

National Council on Senior Citizens: 1331 F St. NW, Washington, DC 20004 (tel. (202) 347-8800). Information on discounts and travel abroad. Membership fees are US$12 per year, $150 lifetime. Supplemental Medicare insurance offered to those over 65.

Pilot Books: 103 Cooper St., Babylon, NY 11702 (tel. (516) 422-2225). Publishes the *Senior Citizens' Guide to Budget Travel* (US$5.95 plus $1 postage) and *The International Health Guide for Senior Citizens* (US$4.95 plus $1 postage).

Travelers With Disabilities

Israel, Egypt, and Jordan have in recent years developed facilities to respond to the needs of travelers with disabilities. Double-check information from tourist offices to ensure that facilities are appropriately equipped. *Access to the World: A Travel Guide for the Handicapped* provides information on tours and organizations and is available from Facts on File, Inc., 460 Park Ave. S., New York, NY 10016 (tel. (800) 322-8755) for US$16.95 plus tax. The following organizations can also provide information.

ETAMS Tours, 13 Kasr al-Nil St., 3rd Flr. #8, Cairo (tel. 75 47 21 or 75 24 62; fax 574 14 91). Dr. Samy Bishara organizes both individual and group tours to Cairo and Luxor.

Evergreen Travel Service, Inc.: 4114 198th St. SW, Ste. 13, Lynnwood, WA 98036-6742 (tel. (800) 435-2288 or (206) 776-1184). Runs Wings on Wheels Tours for travelers with disabilities to Israel and Egypt. Other services include White Cane Tours for blind or deaf travelers and tours for "slow walkers."

Flying Wheels Travel: 143 West Bridge St., Owatonna, MN 55060 (tel. (800) 535-6790). Operates independent and group travel for travelers with disabilities to Israel and Egypt.

Mobility International USA (MIUSA): U.S.: P.O. Box 3551, Eugene, OR 97403 (tel. (503) 343-1284); **U.K.:** 228 Borough High St., London SE1 1JX (tel. (01) 403 56 88). Provides information on travel programs, international work programs, accommodations, access guides, and organized tours all over the world. Publishes *World of Options for the 1990s: A Guide to International Educational Exchange, Community Service, and Travel for Persons with Disabilities* (US$14 for members, $16 for nonmembers, postage included).

Pauline Hephaistos Survey Projects: 39 Bradley Gardens, West Ealing, London W13 8HE, England. Publishes *Access in Israel*.

Twin Peaks Press: P.O. Box 129, Vancouver, WA 98666 (tel. (800) 637-2256 or (206) 694-2462). Publishes *Directory of Travel Agencies for the Disabled* (US$19.95), *Travel Guide for the Disabled* (US$19.95), and *Wheelchair Vagabond* (US$14.59). Postage US$2 for first book, $1 for each additional book.

The Yad Sarah Organization: 43 HaNevi'im St., P.O. Box 6992, Jerusalem 91609 (tel. (02) 24 42 42). Free loan of medical and rehabilitative equipment in Israel. Also offers transport services, laundry services, and workshop facilities for individuals who are disabled or elderly.

Gay and Lesbian Travelers

Tel Aviv and Alexandria are the most tolerant cities in the region, but an openly gay lifestyle is generally taboo throughout the Middle East. Authorities in Israel, Egypt, and Jordan are usually unsympathetic, if not outright hostile, to homosexual concerns. Although Israel does have support organizations, gay and lesbian assistance in Egypt and Jordan is nonexistent.

The primary organization for gay and lesbian concerns in Israel is the **Society for the Protection of Personal Rights,** P.O. Box 37604, Tel Aviv 61375 (tel. (03) 29 36 81). Community center, library, and coffee shop is located at 28 Naḥmani St., Tel Aviv. The society also operates a gay and lesbian switchboard, the **White Line**, (HaKav HaLavan), tel. (03) 62 56 29, which operates Sun., Tues., and Thurs. 7:30-11:30pm.

There are a variety of publications available for gay and lesbian travelers. **Giovanni's Room,** 345 S. 12th St., Philadelphia, PA 19107 (tel. (215) 923-2960), an international bookstore with mail-order service, is the best source for gay travel books. **INLAND Book Company,** P.O. Box 120261, E. Haven, CT 06512 (tel. (203) 467-4257) publishes a new book called *Women Going Places*, a women's travel/resource guide "for lesbians and all women" emphasizing female-owned and female-operated enterprises. **The Spartacus Guide for Gay Men** provides an extensive list of gay bars, discos, beaches, hotels, campgrounds, restaurants, cafés, stores, and bookshops in over 150 countries. It's available from Giovanni's Room (see above); from Renaissance House, P.O. Box 292, Village Station, New York, NY 10014 (tel. (212) 674-0120); from 100 E. Biddle St., Baltimore, MD 21202 (tel. (301) 727-5677); and from P.O. Box 30 13 45, D-1000, Berlin 30, Germany (tel. 49 30 254 98 200).

Vegetarians

The Middle East is a vegetarian's delight. Many of the cheapest foods are vegetables, grains, and fruit. Street food is mostly vegetarian as well. Check under the **Food** listings for each country for more comprehensive gastronomic information of all kinds. More information may be available from the **North American Vegetarian Society,** P.O. Box 72, Dodgeville, NY 13329 (tel. (518) 568-7970), or from the **Vegetarian Society of the U.K.,** Parkdale, Dunham Rd., Altrincham, Cheshire WA14 4QG (tel. (061) 928 07 03).

Other Tips

Bargaining

Bargaining is a skill that many Westerners have not fully developed. Prices are negotiable in the markets, street stands, small stores, and even the taxis, but not in the large department stores or better quality shops.

One method is to ask the price of the article in a somewhat blasé, offhand fashion. Offer about half the asking price, act firm, and be ready to begin the bidding game. Don't be intimidated into paying more than you wish. At the same time, though, be prepared to pay any price you utter. If you give a price and the seller says yes, the article is yours. Even after you leave the store, the seller may follow you into the street, where the haggling continues.

Another approach is less obnoxious: generously praise the fine store and its honest proprietor, note how much you'd like to shop there, but that as a wretched backpacker you have limited means. It's honest, and it just might work.

Travel Etiquette

Standards of dress and behavior are much more conservative in the Middle East than they are in the West. Israel tends to be the most Westernized, while Jordan tends to be the most traditional. Consult the introductions to individual countries and cities for more specific information about proper etiquette.

In holy places, shorts or sleeveless shirts should never be worn. Do not visit sanctuaries during services unless you are worshipping, in which case you are always welcome. Remove your shoes before entering a mosque. Men should cover their heads when visiting a synagogue.

You should try to arrange your travel itinerary with an awareness of religious holidays. In Israel, many businesses close Friday afternoons in preparation for *shabbat,* the Jewish sabbath, and do not reopen until Saturday after sundown. In Muslim countries, many businesses are closed on Friday, the day of the weekly juma prayer. Businesses are closed on the major Jewish holidays in Israel and during Muslim observances in Egypt, Jordan, and the West Bank. Visitors may find it particularly difficult to travel in Egypt, Jordan, and the West Bank during Ramadan, the yearly month-long fast during which Muslims abstain from food and drink from sunrise to sunset. (In 1993, Ramadan will be approximately February 22-March 24.)

Photography is often forbidden in holy places, archeological sites, and museums. If you are unsure, ask. Photography is absolutely forbidden at all military installations, including border crossings, railroad stations, bridges, ports, and airfields. If you decide to play secret agent and take pictures here, your film will be confiscated and you may be held for questioning.

Getting There

By Plane

Off-season travelers will enjoy lower fares and a greater availability of inexpensive seats. Peak season rates begin about May and run until about September. Actual dates differ depending on your airline and destination—peak seasons in Israel, for instance, correspond to religious holidays as well as to summer high season. If you arrange your travel dates carefully, you can travel in summer and still save with shoulder- or low-season fares. When planning your trip, try to keep your schedule and itinerary flexible—an indirect flight via Brussels or Athens could cost considerably less than a direct flight to Tel Aviv or Cairo. The budget flight plans outlined below differ from one another in economy and flexibility.

Find a good travel agent, ideally one who specializes in Middle East travel. Commissions are smaller on budget flights, so some agents may not have incentive to search for the cheapest fare. The Sunday *New York Times* lists bargain fares, and CIEE or other student travel organizations might offer special student deals.

Charter flights offer consistently economical airfares. Charters may be booked until the last minute, though most summer flights fill up several months in advance. Later in the season companies often have many empty seats and either offer special prices or cancel flights. Charters are more of a bargain in high season, because APEX fares (see below) on commercial carriers are competitively priced during the winter. Fares advertised in the newspapers are usually the lowest possible, but never overlook the fine print. Charter flights allow you to stay abroad up to one year, and often let you "mix-and-match" arrivals and departures from different cities. Once you have made your plans, however, the flexibility wanes. You must choose your departure and return dates when you book your flight, and if you cancel your ticket within 14 or 21 days of departure, you will lose some or all of your money. Travel insurance usually does not cover cancellations for reasons other than serious unforeseen illness, natural disaster, or death (in which case you wouldn't want to go anyway).

Although charter flights are cheaper, figure in the cost of being crowded and spending your vacation waiting in the majestic airports of the world. Ask a travel agent about the charter company's reliability. Charter companies reserve the right to cancel flights up to 48 hours before departure. Though charters will do their best to find you another flight, the delay could be days, not just hours. The companies also reserve the right to add fuel surcharges even after you have made final payment. To be sure you're on your flight, pick up your ticket well before the departure date and arrive at the airport several hours early. Charter companies often have messy reservation systems.

Charter coverage of Israel, Egypt, and Jordan varies from year to year, so consult a travel agent for companies offering flights. Let's Go Travel, CIEE, and Travel CUTS usually offer flights to the Middle East (see Useful Organizations under Planning Your Trip). If you don't mind leaving home without a return ticket in your pocket, you can try to secure an inexpensive charter flight out of Israel to Europe and North America. **Israel Student Travel Association (ISSTA)** (see Useful Organizations) has flights from Tel Aviv to London, Paris, and many other European cities.

If you choose to fly with a commercial airline, you'll be paying for greater reliability and flexibility. You can't fly standby to Israel, Egypt, and Jordan. **Advanced Purchase Excursion Fares (APEX)** provide confirmed reservations and permit you to arrive at and depart from different cities. Reservations usually must be made 21 days in advance with 7- to 14-day minimum and 60- to 90-day maximum stay limitations. Beware of hefty penalties for cancellations and altering reservations.

El Al is the national airline of Israel (tel. (800) 223-6700); **EgyptAir** is Egypt's (tel. (800) 334-6787); and **Alia** is the Jordanian national airline (tel. (800) 223-0470). As of summer 1992, a peak-season round-trip restricted APEX fare from New York to Tel Aviv on El Al was US$1354 plus $33 tax, New York to Cairo on EgyptAir was US$1431 plus $33 tax, and New York to Amman on Alia was US$1499 plus $18 tax. El Al, EgyptAir, and Alia all offer youth and student discounts. Other airlines may be cheaper; you might want to look into Lufthansa to Cairo or Amman.

Airline ticket consolidators sell unbooked commercial and charter airline tickets. Most charge a yearly membership fee of about US$40 which allows you to book flights with them, but the fares can be extremely low. Ask about cancellation penalties and advance purchase requirements and, in general, be wary. The details of flight delays and cancellations are beyond the control of these companies, so the traveler is at the mercy of the particular carrier. A few consolidators are Dollarwise Travel (tel. (305) 592-3343), specializing in flights to the Middle East, and Tourlite International (tel. (800) 272-7600), specializing in budget flights to Greece, with extensions to Egypt and tours to Egypt and Israel.

Travel by **courier** is another option. **Now Voyager,** 74 Varick St., #307, New York, NY 10013 (tel. (212) 431-1616), matches companies that need freelance couriers to fly to different countries, including those in the Middle East, with eager travelers. Most flights originate in New York. Couriers are limited to carry-on luggage only. You can also contact **Halbert Express** at (718) 656-8189 or **World Courier** at (800) 221-

6600. Since air courier services spring up like mushrooms you should check your local yellow pages under "Air Courier Service" for the latest crop.

By Bus and Train

Buses and **trains** can bring you from Northern Europe to ports along the Mediterranean where you can board a ferry to Israel or Egypt. **Magic Bus,** 20 Filellinon, Syntagma, Athens, Greece (tel. (01) 32 37 471/4) has cheap rail, bus, and boat tickets to and from Europe, North America, Africa, and the East. If you're under 26, **BIJ tickets** can provide discounts of up to 50% on regular second-class rail fares on international train runs. Always inquire about other student discounts.

By Boat

Several **ferry lines** sail from Europe to Israel. Fares vary considerably, depending mainly on your tolerance for discomfort. Outdoor deck seats may cost as little as US$50-60 for a three-day trip, but beware that clean bathrooms are hard to come by. More comfortable are the three- or four-berth inside cabins that many companies offer at reduced student and youth fares. The following companies service Europe to Ḥaifa:

Afroessa Lines: Israel: Mano Seaways Ltd., 60 Ben-Yehuda St., Tel Aviv (tel. 528 21/2/3). **Greece:** 1 Charilaou Trikoupi St., Piraeus (tel. 41 83 777). Boats between Ḥaifa and Piraeus leave Tuesdays at 8pm. Deck chair 1-way US$90 including port tax. June 12-Sept. 17 $US97. Double berth with bathroom and shower US$207 high season, US$188 low season (per person).

Arkadia Lines: Israel: Mano Seaways Ltd., 60 Ben-Yehuda St., Tel Aviv (tel. 528 21 21/2/3). **Greece:** 34 Amalias Ave., Athens (tel. 3248 158). Boats between Ḥaifa and Piraeus leave Sunday at 8pm. Deck chair one-way US$121 including port tax if under 26 years old or with ISIC; others US$147. June 4-Sept. 17 under 27/student US$145, others US$177. Double berth with bathroom and shower US$352 per person high season, US$292 low.

Stability Line: Israel: Kaspi Ltd., 76 Ha'Atzma'ut Rd., P.O. Box 27, Ḥaifa (tel. (04) 67 44 44); 4 Yanai St., Jerusalem (tel. (02) 24 73 15 or 24 42 66); 1 Ben-Yehuda St., Tel Aviv (tel. (03) 51 06 834). **Greece:** 11 Sachtouri St., Piraeus (tel. 413 23 92). Operates the *Vergina* between Piraeus and Ḥaifa once per week April 2-Oct. 30, stopping in Iraklion, Rhodes, and Limassol. Deck seats 1-way during high season (June 25-Sept. 16) US$80, in low season US$62.

Ferries also shuttle from Europe to Egypt (for example, the Piraeus-Alexandria run is made by the **Adriatica** line, c/o Menatours, Sa'ad Zaghloul Sq., Alexandria, tel. 80 69 09), but they are usually much more expensive than to Israel. It's cheaper to take a ferry from Greece to Ḥaifa and then take buses to Cairo.

Border Crossings

Border crossing policies in the Middle East fluctuate with political tides, so be sure to check with travel agents, tourist offices, and your nation's government for the most up-to-date information.

> All Arab nations except Egypt refuse to admit travelers with evidence of a visit to Israel in their passports.

If you plan to visit Israel first and then want to travel to an Arab country, tell the Israeli passport officials when you enter. They will usually put your visa stamp on a removable slip of paper rather than directly in your passport (see Travelling to Both Arab Nations and Israel, under Documents and Formalities).

Since the Camp David Accords in 1977, foreigners have been allowed to travel freely between Israel and Egypt. But if you intend to travel to another Arab country, you should obtain an Egyptian visa outside Israel. Note also that an Egyptian entry or exit stamp from the Israeli border at Taba or Rafiah is a clear indication that you've been in Israel and thus prevents you from entering other Arab nations.

Between Israel and Egypt

Tour buses are the best budget option for travel between Israel and Egypt. Several companies operate out of Tel Aviv, Jerusalem, and Cairo, offering bus transport, three days in a shared room at a tourist-class hotel in Cairo, and an open-ended return ticket.

Egged Tours: 15 Frischman St., Tel Aviv (tel. (03) 527 12 12). Offers over 60 tours.

Galilee Tours: 142 HaYarkon St., Tel Aviv (tel. (03) 29 13 10 or 29 08 28); Center 1, 43 Yermiyahu St., Jerusalem (tel. (02) 38 34 60); and 10 HaYarden St., P.O. Box 250, Tiberias (tel. (06) 72 26 60 or 72 05 50).

Mazada Tours: 141 Ibn Gvirol St., Tel Aviv (tel. (03) 546 30 75), 24 Ben Sira St., Jerusalem (tel. (02) 25 54 53), and Paulus VI St., Nazareth (tel. (06) 56 59 37). Round-trip from Tel Aviv to Cairo for US$35, one way US$20 (more from Jerusalem and Nazareth). New midnight express service to Cairo via Taba Border. In Egypt contact them at the Cairo Sheraton Hotel (tel. 34 88 700). Youth and student discounts.

Neot HaKikar Touring Co.: 78 Ben-Yehuda St., Tel Aviv (tel. (03) 22 81 61/2/3); 36 Keren HaYesod St., Jerusalem 92149 (tel. (02) 63 64 94/65 03); HaTmarim Blvd., Eilat (tel. (07) 37 69 08). Much cheaper than its firmly established rivals, Galilee Tours and Egged Tours. Sinai tours from Eilat, Egypt tours from Tel Aviv or Jerusalem.

United Tours: 113 HaYarkon St., Tel Aviv (tel. (03) 754 34 10 or 527 10 10); 4 Bograshov St., Tel Aviv (tel. (03) 75 43 412/3/4); the King David Hotel, Jerusalem (tel. (02) 25 21 87); branch in Eilat (tel. (07) 37 17 20).

Local buses also travel to the border, and from there another relatively inexpensive bus or taxi will take you across (for example, via bus from Eilat to Taba). **Flights** between Israel and Egypt are offered by Israel's El Al and Egypt's Air Sinai. Air Sinai, a sidekick of EgyptAir, was created especially for service to Israel and the Sinai so that EgyptAir would not be denied access to other Arab countries. You must pay an exit tax each time you leave Israel. If you don't already have an Egyptian visa, you can get one at a diplomatic mission; processing takes just a few hours but the lines can get uncomfortably long, especially during Ramadan (see Tel Aviv Practical Information, Eilat, and Sinai). You can't get anything other than a Sinai-only visa at the border.

Between Jordan and the West Bank

Conflict over national claims complicates travel between Jordan and the Israeli-occupied West Bank. Jordan does not recognize Israel as a sovereign nation. In order to enter Jordan, you must bear a passport free of any evidence that you've ever set foot in Israel.

Travel between the two regions is not impossible, just tricky. As far as the Jordanian authorities are concerned, when you cross the King Hussein/Allenby Bridge from the West Bank, you are coming from occupied Palestine, since Israel does not exist and thus cannot have a border. Therefore, Jordanian authorities will probably allow you to enter, as long as your passport does not have an Israeli stamp. Other incriminating evidence includes any visa issued in Israel (including one for Egypt) or an Egyptian entry or exit stamp from either Taba or Rafiah on the Egypt-Israel border. Unlike in Israel, Egyptian authorities do not offer the convenience of giving you an entry stamp on a separate piece of paper.

Crossing from the West Bank to Jordan

Proceed approximately as follows. First, purchase a pocketful of Jordanian dinars ahead of time, as the border exchange facilities are unreliable. Then travel to Jericho, 11km west of the King Hussein/Allenby Bridge, by taking an Arab bus from Damascus Gate, an Egged bus from the central bus station, or a shared taxi from the stand near Damascus Gate. Get off the bus in Jericho when you see the large mosque in the city center. Take a right at the mosque to the square where the *service* taxis wait. The only taxis licensed to go all the way to the bridge (past the first security checkpoint) are those lined up under the big blue "Jericho Municipality" sign. Others will drop you off at an earlier checkpoint where you'll have to wait for the rare shared taxi with an empty seat.

The **King Hussein/Allenby Bridge** across the Jordan River is open only in the morning; arrive as early as possible to ensure that you get through. The bridge is occasionally closed for political or religious events; consular officers, taxi drivers, and bus drivers all keep abreast of the latest political developments. For most foreigners (with the possible exception of Arabs and Jews from any country), the searches are mild, the officers respectful, and the waiting rooms air-conditioned. The U.S. Department of State warns that "American citizens with Arab surnames may encounter delays or obstacles" in bringing items from electronics to toothpaste across the bridge. At the bridge checkpoint, you must pay a departure tax. After your luggage has been inspected, you'll have to wait for one of the approved buses. You cannot drive a vehicle across the bridge.

Once on the East Bank, you'll be issued a permit (in Arabic) saying that you came over the bridge and are prohibited from returning to the West Bank. Though you shouldn't lose the evidence that you entered the country legally, don't keep it in an obvious place either, since it announces that you were on the West Bank. This souvenir could prevent you from being issued a West Bank permit later. Note that the Jordanians do not recognize the bridge as an international border, so you will not receive an entry or exit stamp in your passport. If you are merely returning over the bridge after a Jordan-based visit, only your West Bank permit will be stamped. Once on the Jordanian side, you may catch a shared taxi to Amman.

Crossing from Jordan to the West Bank

This is comparatively hassle-free if you came into Jordan from Egypt, Syria, or elsewhere, but highly problematic if you entered Jordan from the West Bank. Regardless, you'll need a West Bank permit issued by the Ministry of the Interior in Amman (closed on Fri.; see Amman Practical Information for details). The process takes three working days and two revenue stamps, available at post offices or sometimes from a kiosk near the ministry. Preferred religions on the application are Christianity and Islam, but the most difficult application blank will be "port of entry to Jordan." Applicants listing Queen Alia International Airport, Aqaba, or Ramtha (on the Syrian border) have experienced the least problems.

If you came from the West Bank and indicate the King Hussein/Allenby Bridge as point of entry, however, you are implying that you consider the West Bank to be Israeli territory and will be summarily denied a permit. Write Jerusalem or try leaving the question blank and explaining that you never entered Jordan since the bridge is not an international border. Those trying a West Bank-Jordan-West Bank itinerary may be denied a permit solely because of an officer's crotchety mood; try again if you are denied the first time.

With West Bank permit in hand, you're free to leave Jordan via the King Hussein/ Allenby Bridge. To reach the bridge from Amman, catch a shared taxi from Abdali Station or reserve a seat on the daily JETT bus. (See Amman Practical Information for more information on transportation.) A JETT bus will take you all the way to the Israeli checkpoint. A taxi will take you only as far as the terminal for foreigners; from there, you'll have to take a shuttle bus to the Israeli side. Israeli officials will occasionally ask young travelers for evidence of financial security, and they will always search your luggage—and person—thoroughly.

From the border, shared taxis in the West Bank run to many destinations. The Shaheen Bus Company provides air-conditioned transport roughly on the hour between 11am and 3 or 4pm. You may pay for transportation on the West Bank with Jordanian dinars.

Between Egypt and Jordan

Traveling between Egypt and Jordan should pose few problems. You can obtain visas in the respective capital cities; Jordan requires a letter of introduction from your embassy or consulate. (See Cairo and Amman Practical Information for embassy listings.) Instead of flying between the two countries (an expensive option), consider taking a ferry from Nuweiba in Egypt's Sinai to Aqaba, Jordan (see Nuweiba and Aqaba sections for details).

Life in Israel, Egypt, Jordan, and the West Bank

Note: Because the region covered here encompasses three different religions, the dates in this book are given using BCE (Before Common Era) and CE (Common Era), which are numerically equivalent to BC (Before Christ) and AD (Anno Domini).

History

Archeological findings in present day Israel, Jordan, and Egypt indicate that human settlement in the region began during the Paleolithic Age (1 million-70,000 BCE). Excavations at Ein Mallaha and Jericho in the 1920s established a cultural link between the first inhabitants of ancient Palestine and the Neanderthal tribes of Southern Europe. The Natufians, who first appeared along the banks of the Sea of Galilee during the early Mesolithic period (14,000-7500 BCE), left behind flint sickles and grain grinding equipment, which chronicles the first rudimentary attempts at agriculture in the area.

In ancient Egypt, Paleolithic hunter-gatherers migrated in small groups toward the Nile Valley, as climactic changes caused the expansion of the Sahara Desert and the dessication of most of the rest of Northeast Africa. Around 6000 BCE, settlers along the southwest edge of the Delta began growing cereal crops. By 5000 BCE, settlers had established a primitive but productive fishing industry in the ancient lakes of the Fayyum. As walled settlements sprang up throughout the Jordan River Valley and Mediterranean coastal plain, political power emanated for the first time from emerging city-states and rival petty kingdoms.

Ancient Egypt

Conquering Lower Egypt and then uniting it with Upper Egypt, King Menes, the semi-mythical first pharaoh, founded one of the most powerful and lasting civilizations of the ancient world. From the capital of Memphis, supposedly built by Menes around 2900 BCE, successive pharaohs oversaw the construction of complicated irrigation systems and grandiose monuments. Less than 100 years after the first step pyramid was built at Saqqara, the pharaohs of the Old Kingdom (approx. 2665-2180 BCE) were organizing skilled builders and hundreds of thousands of laborers to build the classic, smooth-sided pyramids. At a time when even China had scarcely emerged from the Stone Age, Egyptians had invented writing and papyrus, recorded the regnal years of pharaohs, and were crafting extraordinarily creative ivory and metal art. Many view this era as the apex of ancient Egyptian civilization.

The authority of the pharaoh, previously absolute and godlike, began to wane and the Old Kingdom drew to an end as petty kings and provincial administrators gained power. A cycle of unification and disintegration persisted until the demise of pharaonic rule. After a century of rule by a succession of intermittently feuding petty kings, Mentuhotep II allied with the princes of Thebes to establish the Middle Kingdom (approx. 2050-1786 BCE).

During the Middle Kingdom, Egypt's culture flourished and spread as contact with the southern kingdoms of Nubia and Kush spawned subsidiary pharaonic cultures. Internal political rivalries, however, weakened the Egyptian-Theban dynasty until the Hyksos invaded and conquered Egypt. Upon the expulsion of the Hyksos almost a century later, Egypt was resuscitated in the form of the New Kingdom (approx. 1555-1075 BCE). During this phase, Egypt invaded Africa, Palestine, and Syria. Although the Israelites may have helped build the many monuments left by Ramses II, his successor left behind the victory inscription, "Israel is desolated and has no seed."

The New Kingdom, too, crumbled over time. After a last-ditch attempt by the conservative Kushites (Ethiopians in Sudan) to help Egypt re-establish centralized authority, the Assyrians, soon followed by the Persians, pounced "like wolves on the fold."

The Persian dynasty was Egypt's first completely foreign rule and was loathed deeply. For the next 200 years the Egyptians struggled to overthrow the Persians, periodically succeeding only to be subjugated again. When Alexander the Great arrived in 322 BCE, he was received as a liberator. After ousting the Persians, Alexander set off for the oracle of Amon in the distant Siwa Oasis. There, he was promptly declared the Son of Amon and the legitimate pharaoh of Egypt. But after dutifully founding another Alexandria, the new pharaoh went on his way and never returned. When Alexander's empire was divided upon his death, Ptolemy, son of Lagus, took control of Egypt and became the pharaoh Ptolemy, Son of God. Alexandria swelled and became a cosmopolitan center of trade and learning; its 750,000 volume library contained most of the Greeks' knowledge under one roof.

The Greek and Egyptian religions mingled, and the Ptolemies encouraged the cult of Sarapis, an Egyptian god syncretized with Zeus. The Ptolemies, furthermore, revived the New Kingdom custom of sibling marriage. As the royal family tree became more complex, Rome emerged as an anxious and competent rival.

In 48 BCE, more than a century after Rome made its first, tentative overtures to the ever-feuding Ptolemies, Julius Caesar came to Egypt in pursuit of his rival Pompey and fell captive to the allure of Cleopatra VII, Queen of Egypt. Cleopatra, facing challenges from other claimants to the throne, accepted an alliance with Caesar which left her secure until his assassination four years later. Sensing danger as well as opportunity, Cleopatra conspired with Mark Antony, one of three successors vying for Caesar's empire. Although these events sparked one of history's most celebrated love affairs, political celebration was left to Octavian, who grabbed the empire for himself, ruthlessly crushing the affair and the Ptolemy dynasty in 30 BCE.

Political stability and an increasingly entrenched bureaucracy characterized the subsequent Egypt, that of Imperial Rome and then Byzantium. In 451 CE, not quite two centuries after the Byzantine heirs of the Roman Empire adopted and promoted Christianity, the Coptic Church split from the church of Constantinople due to heretical doctrines (these doctrines influenced subsequent European heretical movements such as the Manichaeans).

Islam and Empires

After the death of the Prophet Muhammad in Medina in 622 CE, Bedouin armies, inspired by Islam and the prospect of substantial spoils, ventured outside their traditional strongholds in Central Arabia and, in a series of protracted battles between 639 and 642, conquered Egypt. Weary of the rigidity of the Greek Orthodox Church, many Egyptians resented Byzantine rule and appreciated, if not the Islamic religion itself, the arriving armies' relative tolerance.

The death of Muhammad gave rise to political confusion, as no successor to the Prophet had been previously designated. Amid vigorous debate as to whether the successor had to be a blood relative, Abu Bakr, confidante of Muhammad and father of his wife A'isha, was chosen as the first successor (*khalifa*, or caliph). Ruling from 523-24, he was followed by Umar (634-44), Uthman (644-56), and finally Ali (656-61). The election of Ali, the Prophet's nephew and son-in-law, to the caliphate incited a civil war and produced a lasting schism in Islam between the Sunni (the "orthodox," who opposed a blood-relative caliphate), and the Shi'i (the "party," who supported Ali's claim). This division notwithstanding, the first four caliphs are known to most Muslims as the Rashidun (the Rightly Guided Caliphs). With the advent of the Ummayad Dynasty, founded by the Caliph Mu'awiya in Damascus in 661, Shi'i opposition was muted, a Sunni hereditary monarchy was installed (unrelated to the Prophet), and the lands between the Nile and Oxus Rivers pacified. By 750, when the Abassids overthrew the Umayyads, the majority of the peasantry had converted to Islam. A mammoth bureaucracy composed of everything from tax officials to scribes to Islamic jurists (*ulama*) assisted in the daily administration of the empire.

Successive Abassid caliphs, usually ensconced in Baghdad, were never without challenges; in addition to the standard unpredictability of palace politics, the rival Umayyad family had managed to establish a potentially troublesome dynasty in Spain and various Shi'i dynasties flourished on the borders of the Abassid empire. The Shi'i Fatamids, attacking northwards from their domain in the fertile Nile Valley, expelled the Abassids from Egypt in 969. They established Cairo as their new capital to replace the old center, Fustat. The Fatamids captured most of Palestine, controlled Jerusalem, and prospered through trade with Spain. This success failed to daunt Salah al-Din (a Kurd, also known as Saladin), founder of the short-lived Ayyubid Dynasty (1171-1250), who dethroned the Fatamids in 1192 with the forces of a vast army of Turkish slaves.

Although Salah al-Din's military victories over the onslaughts of crusading Crusaders earned him a place in history, and in Bocaccio's *Decameron* as well, the finely disciplined slave (*mamluk*) armies upon which he relied became a scourge for his successors. Purchased as young boys, then trained and equipped by the palace, Mamluks were technically property of the Sultan. The actual power structure, however, in no way reflected their official status as peons; as a clique whose members shared a common militaristic upbringing, the Mamluks threatened the Sultan's authority, which was often tenuous at best. In 1250, a Mamluk of the Bahri clan resolved to dispense with formality as well as the Ayyubids so as to rule the sultanate directly. An era of chronic instability and infighting followed. Lifestyles for those at the top were still lavish; life expectancies, however, decreased dramatically.

When the Ottoman Empire, expanding out from Anatolia, gained formal sovereignty over Egypt and Palestine in the early part of the 16th century, Mamluks still retained most of their political power. But through the use of elaborate schemes, official appointments, bribery, and assassination, the Ottoman sultans maintained real and effective control. Manipulating their local "representatives" and playing them against one another, the Ottoman rulers enjoyed their seemingly indelible authority. To learn more about Egyptian and Arabic history, read Albert Hourani's masterpiece *A History of the Arab Peoples.* If you've a long flight, an interest in detail, and a backpack the size of Rhode Island, Marshall Hodgson's three volume *Venture of Islam* might be of interest.

Ancient Palestine

The Bible begins the recorded history of the area with the story of Abraham, the first of the Patriarchs. The semi-nomadic Aramaean tribes' migration to Palestine almost four thousand years ago has been linked by archeologists with the biblical tradition of Abraham's (Avraham in Hebrew, Ibrahim in Arabic) journey from Chaldea. In the 13th or 14th century BCE, however, famine forced some of the Semitic groups in Palestine to flee to Egypt where, according to the Bible, the Pharaoh bound them into servitude. Meticulous Egyptian records (today a vexing rarity) attest to the existence of a foreign group called the Habiri (or Khapiru), a name thought possibly to be the ancestor of the word "Hebrew." But, as told by the Torah, the combination of Moses' (Moshe in Hebrew, Musa in Arabic) initiative and several plagues ultimately convinced an Egyptian pharaoh (quite possibly Ramses II) to allow the Hebrews to leave Egypt. After an arduous journey across the Sinai Peninsula, the Hebrews returned to Canaan, much of which was controlled by a group called the Philistines. After Moses' death, Joshua led the newly constituted twelve tribes of Israel across the Jordan River and conquered Jericho. The battle against the Philistines continued after Joshua's death.

At the end of the 11th century BCE, the Israelite tribes united under King Saul. The kingdom reached its peak of power during the reign of Saul's successor, David, and that of his son, Solomon. The construction of the Temple of Jerusalem is considered perhaps Solomon's most formidable feat, yet the cost of the Temple and other civil projects proved a heavy burden for his subjects. After Solomon's death in 922, unrest spread and the empire split into the Kingdom of Israel in the north and the smaller Kingdom of Judah (Judea) in the south.

The Assyrians conquered Israel in 724 BCE and made Judah a vassal state of the Assyrian empire. Over 100 years later, the Babylonians destroyed Ninevah and crushed Assyria. The Babylonian King Nebuchadnezzar razed the Temple, burned Jerusalem, and deported many Jews to Mesopotamia in the Babylonian Captivity or Exile in 587 BCE. When the Persians defeated Nebuchadnezzer's successor some 50 years later, Jews were permitted to return to Jerusalem and to build a Second Temple. Nevertheless, Palestine again fell prey to foreign invaders. Alexander the Great conquered the region in 333 BCE, and his heirs, the Ptolemies, followed the leader in 323.

The Seleucids displaced the Ptolemies in 198 BCE and attempted to forcibly Hellenize the Jews. Judas Maccabeus (Judah the Hammer), responding to the persecutions of Antiochus IV, led the Jewish revolt against this "abomination of desolation." Victorious, the Maccabees resanctified the Temple in 164 and founded the Hasmonian Dynasty. In spite of potent internal conflict, the Hasmonian Dynasty ruled Palestine independently for over a century.

In 63 BCE, the Romans swept in and took over the area. All Jewish rebellions were invariably crushed; nonetheless, in 70 CE the Roman military governor, peeved by the Jews' persistence, ordered the destruction of the Second Temple and the whole of Jerusalem. Josephus records that of a probable three million Jews, more than a million died during the siege of Jerusalem alone. Three years later, upon capturing the last Jewish stronghold at Masada, the Romans took no prisoners—the defenders, rather than surrendering, took their own lives. Rome gave the land a new name: Palestine.

Byzantine replaced Roman rule in Palestine in 330 CE. Although little changed administratively, the adoption of Christianity by the Emperor Constantine in 331 created an increased interest in what, to many, was the "Holy Land." Pilgrims and devout financiers built churches and endowed monasteries and schools. Newly-found political stability, disrupted only during the Samaritans' revolt in 529 and the brief Persian invasion a few decades later, fostered a new sense of prosperity in the region.

The Muslims arrived in the 7th century, continuing their inveterate drive to push Byzantine armies all the way back to Constantinople. Jerusalem, site of Muhammad's "night journey" to heaven, capitulated in 638. For four and a half centuries thereafter, Palestine was ruled from abroad by the Umayyads, the Abassids, the Fatamids (see above), and, eventually, Turkish Selçuks. Rumors of dubious Selçuk policies regarding the treatment of Christian pilgrims prompted the Europeans to launch a series of crusades aimed at the recapture of the Holy Land. Impelled by a surfeit of inspiration and by more worldly concerns about fame, fortune, and Pope Urban II's offer of indulgences, Crusaders wrought havoc. After massacring both Muslim and Jewish inhabitants of Jerusalem in 1099, the Crusaders established a feudal fiefdom in Akko under Baldwin I.

It didn't last. The second and third Crusades were choked at the hands of Salah al-Din. The following century's subsequent five crusades all floundered, as Mamluks controlled the outpost at Akko and other key fortresses (for instance, Shobak and Montfort) by the close of 1291. After two more centuries of instability, the Ottomans defeated the Mamluk chieftains in 1517, and thus Palestine became merely one of the many administrative units of the empire.

The Collapse of the Ottoman Empire and the Rise of Modern Nationalism

When the gates of Vienna closed on Ottoman armies in 1683, Turkey began worrying about the fate of its increasingly decrepit empire. Napoléon Bonaparte's 1798 invasion of Egypt, however, shocked even the grumpiest pessimist. While Europe had grown more and more powerful economically and militarily, the Ottoman Empire had languished. At one time, the animated ports of Aleppo, Palestine, and Egypt had provided the sole access to the East; now, they were relegated to insignificance as Portuguese sailors finagled their way around the Horn of Africa. Egypt's economy—for two centuries buttressed by trading Arabian and Yemeni coffee—collapsed when European investors cultivated their own, cheaper coffee in the Java islands and, turning the tables, sold it to Cairene merchants. Similarly, the European discovery of alternative silk sources hurt Palestine's economy. Spanish silver from the New World was simultaneously inundating the world, paralyzing agrarian economy. The once-formidable Ottoman Empire came to be known as "the sick man of Europe."

The French occupation of Egypt, a failure despite Napoléon's attempts to be more Muslim than the Muslims, marked the first intrusion of modern European colonialism into the Middle East. Upon the withdrawal of the French army in 1801, resurgent Mamluks scuttled about to regain former prerogatives. A Circassian slave named Muhammad ibn Ali fortified the inchoate power structure, crushing his rivals in a bloody, invitation-only dinner party at the Citadel in Cairo. Muhammad Ali built upon the administrative apparatus left by the French, modernized the civil service, created a regular tax system, and attempted to introduce land reform aimed at the vast feudal estates of his enemies. To stock his army, in lieu of buying more potentially rebellious slaves, Muhammad Ali conscripted peasants. Those peasants who managed to avoid the army labored under watch to build the new and massive irrigation network indispensable to the modernization of Egyptian agriculture.

Naturally, the recrudescent Egypt led by a nominally faithful "servant" perturbed the Ottoman sultan. Evading a direct confrontation, the sultan ordered Muhammad Ali to send Egypt's armies to face the Wahhabi revolt and, shortly thereafter, the Greek revolt. The dramatic Greek victory, though, enraged Muhammad Ali far more effectively than it weakened him. By the late 1830s, Muhammad Ali's violent forays into Palestine, Syria, Lebanon, and Arabia left him with more of the Ottoman Empire than the sultan himself controlled. But when Muhammad Ali threatened to march on stanbul—his armies actually entered Anatolia—France and Britain came to the sultan's aid and unambiguously threatened intervention if that was what it took to maintain the European balance of power. Muhammad Ali was forced to withdraw to Egypt. By the time the Ottoman sultan granted the Europeans unrestricted access to Egypt's markets, Muhammad Ali could scarcely more than whimper.

Muhammad Ali's successors certainly felt the effects of the dearth of improvement. Although the Ottoman Empire initiated a series of reforms known as the *tanzimat*, economic and political crises went unabated. Continuing attempts to modernize the economy (and to finance the Egyptian rulers' trips to foreign spas) heavily indebted Egypt to British and French bankers. At the same time, the developing strategic interest in the newly completed Suez Canal became the subject of many a chess game between British, French, and German foreign ministers.

The Egyptian government's declaration of bankruptcy and a series of stirrings in the Egyptian army prompted the British to send an expeditionary force, which captured Egypt in 1882 after only a few short skirmishes. Although the Egyptian Khedive remained on the throne, all decisions were the charge of British Consul General Lord Cromer (alias Evelyn Baring, alias "Lord Over-Baring") who dominated Egypt for almost three decades. Lord Cromer monitored Egyptian finances with a tight fist, salaried the Khedive and the royal family, and made it his task to ensure full payment to British bondholders who had invested in Egypt.

Meanwhile, European Jews had begun to ponder Palestine. By the late 19th century, Jews began to doubt the rumored improvements in their status as promised by the Enlightenment. In Czarist Russia, Jews crammed into the notorious "Pale of Settlement" were victims of increasingly violent government-sponsored pogroms. In Germany and Austria, anti-Semites had banded into powerful political parties. In the wake of the Dreyfus affair (where anti-Semitic mobs cried "*A mort les juifs*" in the streets of Paris), even France, the role model for liberal revolutions, seemed an unwelcoming option.

The growing Zionist movement gained momentum with the 1896 publication of a small pamphlet entitled *The Jewish State*. The work of Theodor Herzl, a journalist who personally covered the degradation of Captain Alfred Dreyfus for Vienna's leading newspaper, this pamphlet trumpeted the establishment of a Jewish homeland as the only effective answer to Jewish persecution. Although this idea had been proposed earlier in works such as Leo Pinsker's *Auto-Emancipation*, never before had a secular, pro-Enlightenment Jew like Herzl so unequivocally despaired of the possibility of Jews ever being accepted as equals or even tolerated by other Europeans. Herzl, like many others, believed that Jews needed a new state rather than the lands of Palestine. However, as the options (such as Uganda and South America) for settlement plans for Jews were broached, it became apparent that only Palestine had the emotional lure to prompt Jews to immigrate by the hundreds of thousands.

Unlike the small numbers of Jews who had returned to Palestine over the centuries, the late 19th and early 20th century immigrants thoroughly transformed the Jewish community in Palestine (the "Old Yishuv") and profoundly affected the political status of the region. Agricultural settlements, the fruits of the toil of members of the first *aliya* (1882), grew ripe for development into cooperative agricultural settlements, or *kibbutzim,* by the members of the second *aliya* (1904-1914). Far from a mere klatch of disaffected East European youth, the leadership of the second *aliya* shared the socialist principles, sense of urgency, and nationalist sentiment needed to keep the Zionist ideals alive. Two distinct strands of Zionism evolved in the Yishuv: the mainstream Labor movement under David Ben-Gurion, and the more militant, nationalistic and anti-British Revisionist movement under Ze'ev Jabotinsky and Menaḥem Begin.

During World War I, the British government, at war with pro-German Turkey, conducted secret and separate negotiations with both the Arabs and the Zionists to enlist their help in the war. In order to obtain Arab support, Britain pledged in the 1915-16 Hussein-McMahon correspondence (between Sharif Hussein of Mecca and British High Commissioner in Egypt Sir Henry McMahon) to back "the independence of the Arabs" in exchange for an Arab declaration of war against Turkey. The Arab revolt started in June 1916. At the same time, Britain hoped to gain political support from Jews worldwide by offering sympathy to the growing Zionist movement. The November 1917 Balfour Declaration stated that Britain viewed "with favour the establishment in Palestine of a national home for the Jewish people, it being clearly understood that nothing shall be done which may prejudice the civil and religious rights of existing non-Jewish communities in Palestine." Many Arabs were outraged, and Sharif Hussein's suspicions of his British allies grew. The vague wording in the Balfour Declaration and the ambiguity of the boundaries agreed upon in the McMahon-Hussein correspondence did nothing to simplify the situation.

On top of their double game of overtures to both Arabs and Zionists, the British and French had reached a distinctly separate agreement amongst themselves. The 1916 Sykes-Picot Agreement divided the region into zones of permanent British and French influence, rather than giving control of the Middle East to local Arab or Jewish inhabitants. After the war it became apparent that British promises to the Arabs and Jews were largely worthless. France, for its part, drove Sharif Hussein's son Faisal out of Syria, where he had attempted to seize control. In 1921, Britain made good on one part of its promises to the Arabs, or at least to the Hashemites: Faisal's wily younger brother Abdallah was established as *emir* (prince) of Palestine east of the Jordan, dubbed the Emirate of Transjordan. In 1946, Britain granted Transjordan independence. At the San Remo Conference in 1923, the victors of World War I implemented Sykes-Picot with only minor changes. Britain received a mandate to administer Iraq and Palestine, while France was given control over Syria and Lebanon; the crushed Ottoman Empire retired to the dustbin of history.

Throughout the inter-war years, British and French colonial rule was constantly contested from below by a rising tide of Arab and Jewish nationalism. In Egypt, Sa'ad Zaghloul founded the Wafd party, which forcefully criticized English rule and the corrupt Egyptian monarchy. After a relatively minor skirmish between British soldiers and Egyptian peasants, Britain granted King Fuad nominal independence, taking care to sign treaties that protected British military bases, economic interests, and the Suez Canal.

In Palestine, however, conflict between Palestinian Arabs and Jews intensified. British attempts at maintaining order proved insufficient as Jewish and Arab "self-help" groups rose to battle each other in the streets. Britain, to no avail, published the Passfield White Paper in 1930, an attempt to clarify the Balfour Declaration by distinguishing between a Jewish "national home" and a full-fledged "sovereign state." With the anti-British and anti-Zionist Palestinian Arab Revolt in 1936-39, Britain became fearful that the Arabs would revolt on the side of Nazi Germany if the foreshadowed war broke out. Thus, in the White Paper of 1939, Britain severely curtailed Jewish immigration to Palestine as Jewish refugees fled the impending Holocaust. As Hitler's genocide began, Zionists were desperate to establish their own state as a safe haven from the ultimate expression of anti-Semitism. Palestinian Arabs, meanwhile, resented that a "European" problem be solved at their own expense.

The War of Israeli Independence

Several British and United Nations commissions suggested partitioning Palestine as Britain, frustrated by the intercommunal strife there, gave up on its mandate. On November 29, 1947, the United Nations voted to partition the Palestine Mandate into an Arab state and a Jewish state, and to set aside Jerusalem as an international city. The Jews accepted the partition plan; the Arabs rejected it. A bloody civil war broke out between Jews and Palestinian Arabs. The British, although attacked sporadically by both Arab and Jewish groups, remained for the most part on the sidelines.

On May 14, 1948, the British mandate over Palestine ended and David Ben-Gurion declared the independence of the State of Israel. The next day, a poorly-coordinated Liberation Army of Syrian, Iraqi, Lebanese, Saudi, Egyptian, and Jordanian troops marched into Israel from the north, west, and south. Few observers gave the new state much chance for success, but by the signing of the armistices in the spring of 1949, the results of Israel's War of Independence were clear. From the land that was supposed to be a Palestinian Arab state, Egypt had managed to secure the Gaza Strip, and Jordan the West Bank and half of Jerusalem; Israel controlled its allotted territory and some other land. Thousands of Palestinian refugees, displaced in the fighting, crowded into hastily constructed camps in the West Bank, Gaza, and the bordering Arab states—a defeat bitterly remembered by Palestinians as *an-Nakba*, the catastrophe.

Abdallah annexed the West Bank in 1950 and declared the unified Hashemite Kingdom of Jordan. This move, however, met an icy reception by Palestinians and other Arab governments. Sentiment that Jordan was becoming too accommodating of Israeli interests spread, and in 1951, Abdallah, praying in al-Aqsa Mosque in Jerusalem, was assassinated by a Palestinian youth. The crown passed to Abdallah's oldest son Talal, but he voluntarily resigned six months later due to schizophrenia. King Hussein smoothly assumed control after a one-year regency. Not quite 18 when he assumed the throne—which he holds to this day—Hussein embarked on a bold agenda aimed at raising Jordan's status in the Arab world.

The Suez War

Egypt, weakened by persistent struggles between Wafdist nationalists and the monarchy, was in a shambles after its 1948 loss to Israel. In 1952, subsequent to a bloody confrontation between British soldiers and Egyptian police officers, a group of young army officers led by the charismatic Col. Gamal Abd al-Nasser bloodlessly seized power from the late King Fuad's corrupt son, Farouk. Calling themselves the "Free Officers," Nasser's cabinet instituted major economic reforms and foreign policy changes, siding with the Non-Aligned Movement in the Cold War. Drawing from the writings of countless Arab nationalists, Nasser espoused a highly emotive brand of pan-Arabism based on the hope of unifying the Arabic-speaking masses under one huge state powerful enough to resist imperial encroachments and to reconquer Palestine. When Nasser forced Britain to withdraw in 1954, many of the conservative Arab leaders dependent on foreign assistance to maintain their rule became alarmed by Nasser's growing popularity.

The United States and other foreign powers, who had undertaken extensive development of the oil fields of Arabia, feared that arrangements they had cultivated with local, conservative monarchs would collapse if Nasserism spread. Nasser, alarmed by a British-led alignment of conservative Mideast states called the Baghdad Pact, had begun buying Soviet arms via Czechoslovakia in defiance of a 1950 Western-sponsored arms control deal. In 1956, the United States clumsily attempted to end Nasser's adventurism by withdrawing an offer to finance the Aswan High Dam. Rather than yield, though, Nasser stood up to the snub and nationalized the Suez Canal in order to use its revenues to pay for the dam.

Israel, angry that Nasser had recently blockaded Israeli shipping in and out of the Gulf of Aqaba, annoyed by Egyptian sponsorship of *fedayeen* raids, and fearful of Nasser's growing military power, joined Britain and France in a scheme to retake the canal and reopen shipping lanes. Israel was to attack Egypt with the logistical support of the French, an invasion to be followed by a French-English "peace-keeping" force. Initially, the conspiratorial plan worked well: Israel successfully conquered the Sinai and dealt Nasser's military a major setback. An Anglo-French force subsequently entered Egypt and commenced the seizure of the canal under the dubious pretext of separating Egyptian and Israeli combatants. But Britain, France and Israel had failed to take into account world reaction to their adventure. The United States and the Soviet Union, both furious, together applied intense diplomatic pressure. When Israel, Britain, and France withdrew their troops to placate an enraged President Dwight Eisenhower, Nasser was heralded as the savior of the Arab world although he had never won a single military battle.

Syria, racked with internal feuding, joined with Egypt in 1958 to form the United Arab Republic (UAR). Although Nasser trumpeted the creation of the UAR as a triumph of pan-Arabism, the UAR's unwieldy government consistently irritated the Syrians by giving Egypt the upper hand. But after the 1961 secession of Syria from the UAR, Nasser remained at the forefront of Arab politics. In 1964, he hosted two Arab summits and created the Egypt-based Palestine Liberation Organization (PLO), keeping the Palestinian movement under Cairo's suspicious eye. A more radical group, al-Fatah, led by a fiery young Palestinian nationalist named Yasir Arafat, operated under Syrian tutelage.

The Six-Day War/The June War

From bases in Jordan, Syria, and Lebanon, al-Fatah and the PLO initiated terrorist raids into Israel. Though these raids were largely ineffectual, Israel retaliated with airstrikes. The cycle of Palestinian raids and Israeli reprisals created tension on Israel's northern border, including a spectacular Israel-Syria air battle in April 1967. When Syria's hard-line government turned up the rhetoric, Nasser finally stepped in. First, Egypt concentrated its army in the Sinai, and then demanded the withdrawal of the UN buffer-zone troops stationed since 1957, who meekly bowed out just when a buffer was most needed. Israeli Prime Minister Levi Eshkol nervously warned that a blockade of the Strait of Tiran would be taken as an act of war. But Nasser, caught up in his bluff and escalation, initiated the blockade on May 22, 1967.

When Jordan, Iraq, and Syria began deploying troops directly along Israel's borders, the latter was hard-pressed to counter. On June 5, 1967, skeptical of its capacity to sustain an adequate defense indefinitely and fearing imminent attack, Israel launched a preemptive strike on the force of some 250,000 Arab troops splayed against it. Eshkol warned Jordan not to get involved, but King Hussein attacked anyway. One stunning Israeli blow eliminated the Egyptian Air Force and after six days, the Arab states were forced to accept a humiliating ceasefire. From Egypt, Israel had taken all of the Sinai and the Gaza Strip, from Syria the strategic Golan Heights, and from Jordan the West Bank and Arab East Jerusalem—which was promptly annexed. Nasser publicly resigned in disgrace, but a swell of public sympathy prompted him to reclaim his post.

Staggered by the defeat of the Arab states, Palestinian radicals looked to themselves to carry on the struggle. Arafat's al-Fatah took over the PLO from its humiliated pro-Nasserist leadership, and pursued the liberation of Palestine through fighting its own battles, engaging in terrorism.

With the USSR behind the pro-Nasser Arab states and the U.S. behind Israel, a local conflict now raised the threat of superpower confrontation. UN Security Council Resolution 242, passed in November 1967 and eventually accepted by all parties to the conflict, attempted to reach peace by stipulating "withdrawal of Israeli armed forces from territories occupied in the recent conflict" and "acknowledgment of the sovereignty, territorial integrity, and political independence of every State in the area." Bickering over the deliberate ambiguity in the document began almost immediately and continues to the present day. The uneasy peace which followed the war soon degenerated into an almost constant border skirmish known as the War of Attrition.

Civil War in Jordan

King Hussein's government was possibly the weakest of all after Israel's victory in 1967. Besides the massive problem of 400,000 additional Palestinian refugees to care for, Jordan had lost the West Bank to Israel. Complicating the situation was the continuation of agitation by the PLO, strong enough now as to resemble a state-within-a-state, to pursue the "liberation of Palestine." Finally, after a hard-line and anti-Hashemite PLO faction tried to force the King's hand by hijacking a number of commercial airliners in September 1970, Hussein declared war on the PLO. Martial law was imposed and fighting between Jordanian and PLO troops began, the death toll rising into the thousands. When Syrian tanks rolled into Jordan to assist the out-gunned PLO, Israeli forces mobilized in the Golan, and Syria backed down. This, coupled with the decision by the Commander of the Syrian Air Force, Hafez al-Asad, to deny the PLO air cover, devastated the PLO. After Arab League mediation and President Nasser's personal intervention, an agreement was forged in late September and the PLO reluctantly moved its headquarters to Lebanon.

The Yom Kippur War/The October War

The exhausted Nasser died suddenly of a heart attack that month and Vice President Anwar al-Sadat assumed control. Sadat catalyzed the dismantling of Nasser's legacy. Whereas Nasser, for over two decades, had promoted state socialism and massive government involvement, Sadat announced the *infitah,* or economic opening, in order to promote foreign investment and revive Egypt's sickly economy. Furthermore, anxious about the security of his own position, Sadat began exposing Nasser's extensive secret police network and released political prisoners, including members of the religious opposition whom Nasser had ruthlessly suppressed.

Meanwhile, the War of Attrition along the Suez Canal was becoming an increasingly heavy burden for Egypt to bear. In order to alleviate the financial crisis, Sadat sought to reopen the lucrative canal and reclaim the desperately needed Sinai oil fields. Although Soviet advisors were assisting the Egyptian military, Sadat viewed their role as merely keeping him from fighting. Seeing little hope in negotiations, Sadat began making preparations to attack Israel.

On October 6, 1973, a day when virtually all Israelis were in synagogues observing Yom Kippur (the Jewish Day of Atonement), Egypt launched its surprise assault. In the war's first three days, Egypt overwhelmed Israeli defenses in the Sinai, and Syrian forces thrust deep into the Golan and threatened Galilee. Because Egypt's preparatory moves had been perceived by the Israeli government to be simple bluffs, Israel's reserves had not been activated and it appeared that Israel was on the verge of defeat. "The fate of the Third Temple is at stake," Defense Minister Moshe Dayan warned. Sadat, who had originally planned only to cross the Sinai and hold the position, decided to press the battle further. But after U.S. assistance arrived, Israel was able to regain its position and, over a number of weeks, push the Egyptians and Syrians back. A tactical mistake left the Egyptian Third Army caught between the Suez Canal and the Israeli army, which promptly laid siege.

All the parties finally agreed to disengage their forces on January 18, 1974, in an agreement negotiated by U.S. Secretary of State Henry Kissinger. The Sinai I and II agreements returned some of the Sinai to Egypt. Both sides, though, had suffered tremendous losses. Israeli public uproar over the government's unpreparedness prompted Prime Minster Golda Meir to resign in April, and left deep scars on the nation. Israel had won, but the aura of invincibility which it had earned over the years had been shattered.

In September 1974, Egypt and Syria attempted to punish Jordan for not assisting in the Yom Kippur War by declaring that the PLO, not Jordan, was "the sole legitimate representative of the Palestinian people." This incensed King Hussein, but after 20 Arab states assented to PLO representation at the Rabat Arab League summit, he had no option but to agree. In November 1974, the United Nations General Assembly voted to give the PLO observer status.

Throughout the 1970s, increasing numbers of Israelis began to settle in the occupied territories. In 1976, the UN Security Council condemned this West Bank policy and demanded that Israel follow the Geneva Convention's rules regarding occupied territory. Although Prime Minister Yitzhak Rabin (of the traditionally dominant left-leaning Labor party) discouraged permanent West Bank settlement, the next government, under Prime Minister Menahem Begin (of the newly ascendant right-wing Likud bloc) drove vigorously in the other direction after its 1977 victory.

The Camp David Accords and Israel-Egypt Peace

In October 1977, Sadat announced that he would travel to the ends of the earth, even Jerusalem, in order to make peace. With a stunning public visit to Jerusalem the next month, Sadat convinced Israelis of his sincere interest in coexistence.

By September 1978, Begin and Sadat had forged a two-part agreement with the help of U.S. President Jimmy Carter at Camp David. The first part of the Camp David Accords stipulated that Palestinians living in the West Bank and Gaza would receive autonomy within five years. Under the second part, Israel agreed to relinquish the Sinai in exchange for peace and full diplomatic relations with Egypt. Although the treaty's second provision has held, the guarantee for autonomy persists as a source of intense controversy. The relationship between Egypt and Israel has never been warm, but a cold peace is far better than a hot war.

After the Camp David Accords, early hopes that other Arab states would negotiate with Israel evaporated. The Arab rejectionist states and the PLO bitterly denounced Sadat as a traitor to Palestine; Syria and Jordan were adamant about guarantees for the Palestinians; other countries, such as Saudi Arabia and Jordan, disapproved too. Egypt was left isolated, and found itself needing to turn to the United States for financial support. Islamists, whom Sadat had courted in his battles against the Nasserist left, increasingly doubted the wisdom of such an open alliance with the West. When Sadat attempted to crack down, he was assassinated. The Egyptian government acted swiftly to crush an Islamist riot in Assyut and Hosni Mubarak, Sadat's Vice President, was sworn in. Although reaction in the West to Sadat's assassination was widespread and open, Egyptian streets were empty. The hundreds of thousands who had mourned at Nasser's funeral were nowhere to be seen.

The Israeli Invasion of Lebanon

It soon became apparent that the June 1982 Israeli invasion of Lebanon, called Operation Peace for Galilee by its architect, renegade Defense Minister Ariel Sharon, had objectives of crushing the PLO that went beyond its originally stated goal of creating a protective buffer zone against PLO shelling of the Galilee. Begin and Sharon had embarked on the first Israeli war that was not waged out of what Israelis call *ein breira* (no choice), and the first that faced widespread domestic opposition. When the Israeli army, after surrounding the PLO in Beirut, began shelling the city at an enormous civilian cost, Israeli citizens joined in the world-wide chorus of condemnation. With the massacre of civilians at Sabra and Shatila by Lebanese Christian Phalangists operating in Israeli-controlled territory, Israel's political position eroded even further. Under an agreement negotiated by the United States, most fighting ended in 1983. But Israel, worried about a continued Syrian presence and Shi'i harassment, did not fully withdraw until 1985 and today continues to maintain a narrow strip of Lebanese territory along its northern border as a security zone.

Since 1985, King Hussein has endeavored to engineer several peace proposals to resolve the Israeli-Palestinian situation. Unfortunately, hard-liners on both sides have refused to accept the other side's preconditions. The situation deteriorated even more in the wake of a burst of terrorist attacks on Israeli civilians. Other incidents as well, such as the murder by a PLO faction of a Jewish-American on the hijacked *Achille Lauro* ship, have complicated prospects for resolution.

The Intifada

In December 1987, as a result of mounting frustration with the political stalemate and the continuing occupation, a relatively minor traffic accident sparked a series of demonstrations which have continued, in some form, to this day. After 20 years of passivity, the Palestinian uprising was a tremendous shock to everyone, the PLO included. At first, Israeli authorities viewed this *intifada* (shuddering, in Arabic) as a short-lived affair which would peter out much like the earlier agitations did. But after Palestinians in the territories began establishing networks to coordinate their hitherto sporadic civil disobedience and strikes, the *intifada* came alive, and gained a shadowy leadership all its own (though in contact with the PLO).

The constant appearance of Israeli soldiers violently suppressing rioters on TV screens throughout the world inspired increased criticism. In 1988, U.S. Secretary of State George Shultz proposed a plan which would involve an international peace conference to be attended by the permanent members of the UN Security Council. The U.S. and Israel, however, refused to allow the PLO to attend until the organization renounced terrorism and accepted—unequivocally—Israel's right to exist.

In the summer of 1988, King Hussein suddenly dropped his claims to the West Bank and ceased assisting in the administration of the territories, which Jordan had been doing since 1967. Hussein's move left Israel and the United States without an adequate negotiating partner; Arafat seized the opportunity to secure the PLO's participation in negotiations by renouncing terrorism, recognizing Israel, and proposing an independent Palestinian state. Israeli Prime Minister Yitzhak Shamir (Likud), still unwilling to work with the PLO, drew up a proposal of his own. Shamir's proposed election plan insisted that the PLO or PLO-sponsored candidates not take part. The PLO, local Palestinians, and Egypt remained at loggerheads with Israel over Jerusalem's status and the role of Palestinians living around the world.

Many factions in the PLO became convinced, by late 1989, that Arafat had given away the organization's two trump cards—recognition of Israel and renunciation of terrorism. Subsequently, one PLO faction launched an armed speed-boat attack against hotels along the Tel Aviv coast. Although the raid was foiled by the Israeli army, Israel, backed by the United States, unsuccessfully pressured Arafat to denounce the incident. Mutually dissatisfied and having achieved little, the United States broke off its discussions with the PLO in the summer.

The Gulf War

Along with the rest of the Middle East, the Eastern Mediterranean was plunged into crisis with the August 2, 1990 Iraqi invasion of Kuwait. Before the invasion, Iraqi President Saddam Hussein personally assured Mubarak that he would do no such thing. As U.S.-led forces built up in Saudi Arabia, Mubarak and King Hussein's attempts at an "Arab solution" to the crisis came to nothing.

Early in the crisis, Saddam Hussein had, with the support of Jordan and the PLO, suggested "linkage" as a way of solving the Gulf crisis; that is, he would withdraw from Kuwait when Israel withdrew from the West Bank, Gaza, and Golan, and Syria from Lebanon. This gesture and promises to liberate Palestine won Saddam the support of desperate Palestinians. Tensions were further inflamed when, on October 7, 1990, Israeli police killed 17 Palestinians and wounded almost 150 in a riot on the Temple Mount—the worst single day of violence in Israel since the 1967 war. Egypt challenged Saddam's bid to lead the Arab world, with Mubarak joining the U.S.-led coalition along with such Arab states as Saudi Arabia, the Gulf states, and Syria. O n January 18, 1991, immediately after the outbreak of war in the Gulf, the first of 39 Iraqi Scud missiles fell on Tel Aviv and Haifa. 47 Israelis were hurt in the attacks, and the country, fearing chemical strikes, donned gas masks. But Shamir, fearing the possibility of an Arab-Israeli conflagration and of chaos in Jordan, did not retaliate, preferring to let the coalition take on Iraq. Israel accepted the token protection of U.S.-manned Patriot anti-Scud missile batteries.

The Peace Process

The war left King Hussein shaken, as Jordan struggled to absorb approximately 300,000 Palestinians and Jordanians no longer welcome or even tolerated in the Gulf countries. Across the river, Israel's demographics were also in flux, as the country took in 400,000 Jews fleeing the former Soviet Union and Ethiopia.

The U.S. had promised that the defeat of Iraq would open a window of opportunity for Arab-Israeli peace, and began vigorous diplomacy after the war. On October 30, 1991, Shamir sat down at the Madrid peace conference with the foreign ministers of Syria, Lebanon, Egypt, and a joint Jordanian-Palestinian delegation. This unprecedented gathering—the first time Syria and Jordan had officially negotiated with Israel, and the first such official Israeli-Palestinian talks—quickly bogged down in discussions of UN Resolution 242, Palestinian autonomy and rights, Jerusalem, settlements, and the PLO's role. Subsequent sessions, including a historic discussion of regional issues in Moscow attended by many Arab states and Israel, got no further. But on June 23, 1992, an Israeli election ousted Shamir's Likud, whose West Bank settlements had attracted U.S. ire, and brought in a pragmatic Labor-led government under Yitzhak Rabin. Rabin promptly curtailed settlement and promised Palestinian autonomy. Although Syria remains particularly obstinate, the prospects for peace among the peoples covered in this book appear, if not bright, at least not altogether gloomy.

Religion

Islam

Bismillah ar-Rahmani ar-Rahim. In the Name of God, the merciful and the compassionate. Pious Muslims begin every undertaking in their lives with this invocation. The Arabic word *islam* means in its general sense "submission," and Islam the religion is the faithful submission to God's will.

Islam has its roots in the revelations received from 610 to 622 CE by **Muhammad,** who was informed by the Angel Gabriel of his prophetic calling. These revelations, received in Arabic, form the core of Islam, the **Qur'an** (recitation). Muslims believe the Arabic text to be perfect, immutable, and untranslatable—the words of God embodied in human language. Consequently, the Qur'an appears throughout the Muslim world—the majority of which is non-Arabic speaking—in Arabic. Muhammad is seen as the "seal of the prophets," the last of a chain of God's messengers which included Jewish and Christian figures such as Abraham, Moses, and Jesus, and the Qur'an incorporates many of the Biblical traditions associated with these prophets.

Muhammad slowly gathered followers to his evolving faith. Staunchly monotheistic, Islam was met with ample opposition in polytheist Arabia, leading to persecution in Muhammad's native city of **Mecca** in Arabia. In 622, he and his followers fled to the nearby city of **Medina,** where he was welcomed as mediator of a long-standing blood feud. This **Hijrah** (flight, or emigration) marks the beginning of the Muslim community and indicates the beginning of the Muslim calendar. For the next eight years, Muhammad and his community at first defended themselves against raids and later battled the Meccans and neighboring nomadic tribes, until in 630 Mecca surrendered to the Muslims, making Muhammad the most powerful man in Arabia. After the surrender, numerous Meccans converted to the new faith voluntarily. This established the pattern for *jihad* (struggle), a term often grossly misunderstood by non-Muslims. *Jihad* refers, first and foremost, to the spiritual struggle against one's own desires which are in conflict with the precepts of Islam. Another facet of *jihad* is the struggle to make one's own Muslim community as righteous as possible. A third sense of *jihad* is that of the struggle against outsiders who wish to harm one's Muslim community. It is this last idea of *jihad* which is most familiar to the West. War was intended to be waged only against non-Muslims in order to ensure that cities were ruled in accordance with Islam. A city was approached and given three choices: conversion to Islam, payment of the *jizya* (a special tax imposed on non-Muslims), or war. Individual conversions often followed because of the appeal of the Muslim message.

Islam continued to grow after the Prophet's death, flourishing in the "Age of Conquest." The four Rightly Guided Caliphs who succeeded Muhammad led wars against apostate nomadic tribes, and by the year 640 the Muslims had defeated the Byzantine and Persian empires. The fourth Caliph, Muhammad's nephew and son-in-law Ali, was the catalyst for the major split in the Muslim world; for the first time Muslims fought against Muslims. Ali slowly lost power, and was murdered in 661. The *Shi'at Ali* (Partisans of Ali or Shi'is) believe Ali as a blood relative of the Prophet to be the only legitimate successor to Muhammad, thus separating themselves from **Sunni** (orthodox) Islam. Contrary to popular Western perception, **Shi'ism** is not a creed of fanaticism or fundamentalism, but is Islam with a sharp focus on divinely chosen leaders (or *Imams*) who are blood descendants of the Prophet through Ali and his wife, the Prophet's daughter Fatima.

Pillars of Islam

"Allahu akhbar. La ilaha il'Allah Muhammadun rasul Allah. God is great. There is no god but God. And Muhammad is His prophet." This beginning of the call to worship (the *adhan*) punctuates daily life in Muslim areas, sounding five times each day from the mosques. It expresses some of Islam's most important beliefs. The first line glorifies God, using the word for God in Arabic, *Allah*. Praise of God and the Prophet is a pious and meritorious action. These words are whispered into the ears of newborn babies, and are the last words uttered by dying Muslims. The next lines of the call form the *shahadah,* the testimony of faith. The *shahadah* is the first of the five pillars of Islam. It reflects the unity of God *(tawḥid)*, which is Islam's strongest belief, and the special place of Muhammad as God's final Messenger.

Testifying to God's unity through the *shahadah* is the only one of the **five pillars** of Islam to be an article of belief. The second pillar is prayer *(salat)*, recited five times per day in imitation of the practice of Muhammad. Prayers, preceded by ablutions, begin with a declaration of intent and consist of a set cycle of prostrations. No designated person is necessary to lead prayers—they are often done wherever the Muslim happens to be at the time of prayer. On Fridays, congregational prayer is encouraged; this is the only distinguishing feature of the Muslim "sabbath."

The third pillar is **charity** *(zakat,* or purification). Although giving to worthy causes individually often substitutes, *zakat* is technically an assessed tax on property given to a carefully regulated communal fund. However, in Pakistan and Saudi Arabia the government levies a *zakat* tax on all citizens.

It is believed that Muhammad received the Qur'an during the month of **Ramadan.** Fasting during this holy month is the fourth pillar. Not simply a month without eating, Ramadan is a time of daylight fasting and meditation; nights are filled with feasting and revelry. During Ramadan (February 22-March 24 in 1993), offices and businesses not catering to tourists may be closed or keep shorter hours.

The last pillar, which is required only once in a lifetime, is **pilgrimage** (the *hajj*). Every Muslim who can afford it and is physically able should journey to Mecca during the last month of the Muslim calendar.

In this aspect of Islam, as in many others, the Muslim is imitating the Prophet's actions. Muhammad is not believed to be divine; he is the human channel of God's word. His actions, however, are believed to be sanctified because God chose him to be the recipient of revelation, and several verses of the Qur'an demand obedience to the Prophet. The traditions about the Prophet's practices, passed on as *sunnah,* are the revered norms of society, and the derivation of the name for the majority **Sunni Muslims.** The primary source for *sunnah* is the **Hadith,** a written collection of Muhammad's sayings which guide Muslim life. Agreement and social harmony are essential in Islam. Muhammad once said, "My people will not agree on an error," and when *ijma* (consensus) is reached, Sunnis see it as correct. In the 10th century, under the weight of tradition and consensus, Muslim scholars (*ulama*) proclaimed "the gates of *ijtihad* (individual judgment)" closed; new concepts and interpretations could no longer stand on their own but had to be legitimized by tradition. This proscription notwithstanding, *ijtihad* continues today, though not on the scale of the first centuries of Islam.

The **Sufis** are a mystical movement within Islam, stressing the goal of unity with God. They are organized in orders, with a clear hierarchy from master to disciple. Sufi *shayks* (masters) are reputed to perform miracles, and their tombs are popular pilgrimage destinations.

Mosques

Any place where Muslims pray is a *masjid,* a mosque. The word is best translated as "place of prostration." Beautiful buildings glorify God, and an Islamic ban on images, inspired by Islam's vehement opposition to idolatry of any kind, has lead to an incredible ingenuity in geometric and calligraphic decoration. The direction facing Mecca, in which all prayer is spoken, is called the *qibla.* It is marked by a niche, the *mihrab.* The *imam* (leader of prayer, not to be confused with the Shi'i leaders) gives a sermon (*khutba*) on Friday from the *minbar* (pulpit). There are two basic designs for mosques: the Arab style, based on Muhammad's house, has a pillared cloister around a courtyard (hypostyle); and the Persian style has a vaulted arch (an *iwan*) on each side. There are no religious restrictions on non-Muslims entering mosques, but other restrictions may have been adopted for practical reasons in areas with mobs of tourists. Prayer is not a spectator sport, and visitors should stay away during times of worship and always wear modest dress.

For more thorough introductions to Islam, try *An Introduction to Islam* by Frederick Denny, *Islam: The Straight Path* by John Esposito, or *Ideals and Realities of Islam* by Seyyed H. Nasr. A sampling of Islamic texts can be found in Kenneth Cragg and Marston Speight's *Islam from Within.* If you feel inspired enough to study the Qur'an, read Muhammad Marmaduke Pickthall's *Meaning of the Glorious Koran.*

Judaism

Foundations of Judaism

"In the beginning," the Bible relates, "God created the heavens and the earth." Nineteen generations and a flood later, Judaism began with a man called Avram. According to Genesis 17, God appeared to Avram when he was 99 years old, telling him "thou shalt be the father of a multitude of nations" and dubbing him **Avraham** (Abraham), from *Ab,* "father," and *raham,* Arabic for "multitude." The covenant between God and Avraham was sealed with Avraham's circumcision, and the covenant between God and the Jewish people is symbolically reaffirmed with the ritual circumcision (*brit mila*) of Jewish males when they are eight days old.

Avraham's descendants eventually migrated to Egypt to escape famine, but they were bound into servitude (Exodus 1). After the **exodus** from Egypt, the Hebrews spent forty years wandering in the desert, during which time God gave the Torah to **Moshe** (Moses) at Mt. Sinai. In approximately 1200 BCE, the Hebrews settled in the land of Canaan.

As detailed in the Bible, Judaism suffered but managed to continue in roughly the same form throughout the rule of the judges and the kings, the Babylonian Exile, and several invasions by foreign cultures. (See History of Ancient Palestine, above.) However, when the Romans destroyed the Second Temple in 70 CE and the Jews entered the Diaspora, Judaism underwent a major upheaval, with Temple worship and sacrifice being replaced by Torah study (*midrash*) and prayer (*tefila*).

The **Torah** is the central, fundamental text of Judaism. Although it was received over three thousand years ago, the Torah has been continuously interpreted and re-interpreted throughout the centuries in an effort to maintain its vitality and applicability. The Written Torah, which consists of the first five books of the Bible, formed the template for the Oral Torah, a series of interpretations and teachings eventually codified in final form around 200 CE as the *Mishnah*. The Mishnah became the starting point for the Babylonian and Jerusalem Talmuds, finalized sometime in the fifth century CE. Likewise, the Talmud was the springboard for a whole new series of interpretations and teachings that continued to build upon each other throughout the Middle Ages and on into modern times. "Torah," which has come to refer to the entirety of Jewish thought and teachings, has been at the core of Jewish life throughout most of history.

. Prayer in the Diaspora was modeled at first on Temple worship and gradually evolved during the Middle Ages, incorporating new elements of praise and supplication. The liturgy reached its final form about a century ago but has had the same general outline for over a millennium. The main themes are thanks to God for His blessings; praise for God's greatness, power, mercy, and forgiveness; supplication for peace, health, wisdom, etc.; and prayer for the coming of the Messiah (or the Messianic Age). The *Sh'ma,* recited daily, represents Judaism's ultimate proclamation of God's unity and divinity: *Hear, O Israel: The Lord is our God, the Lord is One* (Deuteronomy 6:4).

Jewish Life

Although Judaism stresses faith in God, it places greater emphasis on observing God's commandments. There are 613 *mitzvot* (commandments) in the Torah, including directives for ritual observances and instructions concerning moral behavior. **Halakha** refers to the set of laws and established customs that dictate how one is to lead one's life; by remaining consistent with the *halakha*, traditional Jews affirm Jewish values and ideals, secure their bond with the larger Jewish community, and demonstrate their devotion to God.

Observant Jews pray three times daily: in the morning (the *shaḥarit* service), in the afternoon (the *minḥa* service), and in the evening (the *ma'ariv* service). During the morning service, observant Jews will put on *tefillin*, or phylacteries, in observance of Deuteronomy 6:8. The *talit*, or prayer shawl, contains *tzitzit*, or fringes, in observance of Numbers 15:37-41. Observant Jews keep their heads covered, often with *kipot* (skullcaps), as a sign of reverence for God. The laws of *kashrut* dictate which foods are kosher and which are not (see Leviticus 11 and Deuteronomy 14:3-20).

The seventh day of the week is **shabbat**, the Sabbath, a holy day of rest. Other important Jewish holidays include **Rosh HaShana,** the Jewish New Year; **Yom Kippur,** the solemn day of atonement; **Sukkot,** a festival of thanksgiving that recalls the ancient Hebrews' period of wandering in the wilderness; **Simḥat Torah,** a celebration of the Torah; **Ḥanukah,** which commemorates the resanctification of the Temple of Jerusalem in 164 BCE; **Purim,** which celebrates the Jews' deliverance from threatened persecution as detailed in the book of Esther; **Pesaḥ** (Passover), which recalls the Exodus from Egypt; **Shavuot,** which commemorates the revelation of the Torah at Mt. Sinai; **Tisha B'Av,** which memorializes the destruction of the First and Second Temples; and **Tu B'Shevat,** an ancient Arbor Day celebration. Of more recent and secular vintage, **Yom Ha'Atzma'ut** is the Israeli Independence Day, and **Yom HaShoa** recalls the tragedy of the Holocaust.

Much of modern Jewish life revolves around the **synagogue** (*beit knesset* in Hebrew, *shul* in Yiddish), traditionally a place for worship, study, and communal assembly. In the synagogue, the *aron hakodesh* (the ark) houses the Torah scrolls, which are brought out to be read on Mondays, Thursdays, *shabbat,* and many holidays. According to *halakha*, a *minyan* (prayer quorum) is constituted by at least ten Jews who have reached their 13th birthday; when one turns 13, one becomes a *Bar/Bat Mitzvah,* literally a "son/daughter of the commandments," a Jewish adult and thus legally responsible to fulfill the *mitzvot.*

Most Jews consider themselves to be affiliated with one of four major movements within Judaism: Orthodox, Conservative, Reform, and Reconstructionist. These groups emerged over the past 200 years as different approaches towards adapting the *halakha* to life in the modern world. Each of the four movements incorporate the *halakha* in different degrees, with some elements of the *halakha* being rejected as outdated. While the movements disagree over the interpretation of legal matters such as *kashrut* regulations and *shabbat* prohibitions, the similarities between the movements outweigh the differences. With few exceptions, each movement within Judaism retains a firm commitment to the same ethical values, each manifests the same distinctly Jewish identity, and each associates itself with other Jews around the world.

Judaism, by Michael Fishbane, provides an excellent, concise introduction to the religion. Other good sources include Bernard Bamberger's *The Story of Judaism*, Isadore Epstein's *Judaism*, and Milton Steinberg's *Basic Judaism*.

Christianity

Christianity began in Palestine with the followers of one man: Jesus. The Jesus of history and critical interpretation of the Gospels differs from the Jesus Christ of faith and literal interpretation.

The Life of Jesus

The most significant sources on the life of Jesus are the **Gospels.** Scholars agree that the "synoptic gospels" of Mark, Matthew, and Luke were written in that order after 70 CE, drawing on a "saying source" which recorded the words of Jesus; they were followed by the Gospel of John (after 100 CE, but having older roots). John deviates from the synoptic gospels, and the three also represent often-conflicting traditions. The sources provide a history informed by belief in Jesus Christ, rather than a purely objective history.

Various datings of historical events put the birth of Jesus, the man regarded by millions as their savior, between 4 BCE and 6 CE. In Matthew, Bethlehem is the birthplace of Jesus, and Mary and Joseph move to Nazareth to protect him; in Luke, Jesus' parents are only temporarily in Bethlehem; and in Mark and John, the birth is not even mentioned. The Bible states Jesus was conceived and brought forth by Mary, a virgin, making him a product of God's creative power and free from humanity's original sin. Catholics believe additionally in the Immaculate Conception, which holds that Mary conceived without sin.

Jesus was baptized (ritually washed) in the Jordan River as a young man by John the Baptist, a religious leader later hailed as the herald of the Messiah. Afterwards, Jesus began preaching in the Galilee at places such as Capernaum. He spoke passionately for the poor and the righteous, most notably in the **Sermon on the Mount,** and called twelve **disciples** during this period.

After a year of preaching, Jesus went to Jerusalem, where the **Passion,** the story of his death, was enacted. The Gospels give slightly differing accounts, but key events in the story are Jesus throwing the money-changers out of the Temple, eating the Last Supper, being betrayed by Judas, being arrested in the Garden of Gethsemane, and being condemned to death by crucifixion by Pontius Pilate and the Romans at the urging of the Pharisees. On Good Friday, he carried his cross down the Via Dolorosa, stopping at what became known as the Stations of the Cross, until he reached Golgotha (or Calvary; now marked by the Church of the Holy Sepulchre). There he was crucified, a common Roman method of execution.

History of Christianity

Three days after Jesus' crucifixion, on what is now Easter, three women returned to his tomb to anoint his body and discovered the tomb empty. An angel announced that Jesus had been resurrected. Jesus subsequently appeared to the Disciples and performed miracles. Later, on **Pentecost,** the Disciples were given "tongues of fire," and were directed to spread the Gospel (Greek for "good news"). At first, Christianity was a sect of Judaism, accepting the Hebrew Bible. Gradually, it diverged further and further, as it proclaimed that Jesus was the Christ (a translation of Messiah) and began to accept uncircumcised members into the faith. The **Book of Acts** documents these early Christians, and the **Letters of Paul,** which comprise most of the rest of the New Testament, gave advice to the early Christian communities.

In 325 CE, the Roman Emperor **Constantine** ended the persecution and martyrdom of Christians, and made Christianity the official religion of the ailing Roman Empire.

He convened the Council of Nicea, which came up with an explicit creed. The Church Fathers declared that Jesus Christ was of the same essence as the Father, and that there were three equal parts to God. This crucial doctrine of the **trinity** maintains that the Father, Son, and Holy Spirit are distinct persons yet all one God.

The Church was called "the body of Christ" and believed to be integral and indivisible. Nonetheless, the Christian community has suffered numerous schisms. The **Egyptian (Coptic) Church** broke off in the 3rd century (see below). In 1054, the Great Schism split Christendom into the western **Roman Catholic Church** and the eastern **Greek Orthodox Church.** In 1512, Martin Luther started the Reformation, which began **Protestantism.** Protestantism is itself composed of hundreds of sects, which generally believe in salvation through faith rather than actions. It is only in the 20th century that the ecumenical movement has put these diverse churches on speaking terms.

Most Christians adhere to a common set of beliefs that revolve around Jesus Christ as the savior of humanity. According to this belief, individuals are fatally flawed because they are descendants of Adam and Eve, who disobeyed God. Jesus's death and the rite of Baptism, however, absolve humankind of this "original sin." Christianity places high value on a morally disciplined life that avoids sins such as promiscuity, adultery, and greed. The religion differentiates between the base desires of the flesh, which trace from original sin, and the higher needs of the spirit. Christianity involves a call to virtuous actions, such as charity, and places an emphasis on striving to love others and God in the same unconditional manner in which God loves His creation, expecting nothing material in return.

A good introductory book on Christianity is Steven Reynolds's *Christian Religious Tradition.* Other sources include the works of Denise and John Carmody. Reading the New Testament will expose you to the core from which Christian belief is derived.

The Coptic Church

"Copt" derives from the Greek word for Egyptian, *Aiguptious,* shortened in Egyptian pronunciation to *qibt,* the Arabic word for Copt. Usually, a tattoo of either a domed cathedral or a tiny cross on one's wrist indicates this religious affiliation. Of 56 million Egyptians, 7-8 million are Copts; it's estimated that some 4 million Copts live in Cairo alone. Today, portions of the liturgy are still conducted in Coptic, though most of the service is in Arabic. The Copts recognize a separate pope from John Paul II—their spiritual authority resides in Cairo and serves both Copts and Greek Orthodox followers.

According to Coptic tradition, St. Mark introduced Christianity to Egypt in 62 CE, founding what was to become the Coptic Church. Although mass conversions transformed Alexandria into a Christian spiritual center, Roman persecutions increased accordingly, reaching a bloody height under Diocletian. Diocletian murdered so many Christians that the Copts date their **Martyr's Calendar** from 284 CE, the beginning of his reign.

In 451, the Alexandrian branch of the Church declared theological and political independence from Constantinople, forming the **Coptic Orthodox Church.** The split derived from a doctrinal dispute regarding the interpretation of the Trinity. While the Ecumenical Council at Chalcedon defended the definition of Christ's nature as diphysite, i.e., one in which the human and the divine aspects are clearly differentiated, the doctrine of the new Coptic Orthodox Church centered around **monophysitism,** which holds that Christ's nature is of such unity that the human and divine elements are fused and indivisible.

Ascending to the throne in the wake of these developments, the Roman Emperor Justinian sought to restore unity by exiling Coptic clergy to isolated desert monasteries. Rebellious Copts thus welcomed the Persians as liberators when they captured Egypt in 619. Since the 7th century, the Egyptian Christian community has lived as a religious minority in an Islamic state. The relationship between the Copts and the Muslims has vacillated throughout history, as the Islamic government has used Qur'anic verses and extracts from the Hadith to justify either lenient or oppressive treatment of the Copts. Recently, the Coptic community has felt besieged by Egypt's increasingly vocal Islamists, and acts of sectarian violence have been reported.

Both culturally and intellectually, Coptic Christianity served as a link between the pharaonic and Islamic eras, leaving its own mark on modern Egypt. Coptic art incorporates the influences of the Pharaonic and Hellenistic cultures. The Coptic cross refers back to the *ankh,* the hieroglyphic sign for "life," as well as to the crucifix on Golgotha. Embroidered tapestries and curtains displaying nymphs and centaurs owe their heritage to Greco-Roman mythology. Islamic art often borrows from the Coptic style; many of Cairo's mosques were engineered by Coptic architects. In fact, a number of mosques are converted Coptic churches. Unlike the monumental art of the pharaohs, the art of the Copts tends to be a more popular folk medium

Coptic churches usually have one of three shapes: cross-shaped, circular (to represent the globe, the spread of Christianity, and the eternal nature of the Word), or ark-shaped (the Ark of the Covenant and Noah's Ark are symbols of salvation). The churches are divided into three chambers. The eastward **sanctuary** (*haikal*) containing the alter lies behind a curtain or *iconostasis,* a wooden screen of icons. The next chamber, the **choir,** is the section reserved for Copts. Behind the choir is the **nave,** which consists of two parts, the first of which is reserved for the *catechumens* (those who are preparing to convert). The back of the nave is for the so-called weepers, or sinners. These Christians, having willfully transgressed, were formerly made to stand at the very back of the church. Above every Coptic alter hang ostrich eggs, which symbolize the Resurrection (life coming out of what seems lifeless); the ostrich egg was chosen because the mother ostrich cares for her eggs for a fairly long time, an echo of God's eternal love and care for the Church.

Sources on Coptic Christianity include Jill Kamil's *Coptic Egypt: History and Guide,* Barbara Watterson's *Coptic Egypt,* and Iris H. Elmasry's *Introduction to the Coptic Church.*

Other Sects

The Druze

The faith of the Druze, a staunchly independent sect of Shi'i Muslims, centers around a hierarchy of individuals who are the sole custodians of a religious doctrine hidden from the rest of the world. Many Druzes consider themselves a separate ethnicity as well as a religious group, while others consider themselves Arab. The Druze believe that the word of God is revealed only to a divinely chosen few, and these blessed few must be followed to the ends of the earth. Wherever the Druze settle, however, they generally remain loyal to their host country. Israel's 85,000 Druzes are among its best soldiers, while 500,000 Syrian and 300,000 Lebanese Druzes serve with equal fervor in the armies of Israel's enemies.

The Druze religion was founded in 1017 by an Egyptian chieftain named ad-Darazi who drew upon various beliefs in the Muslim world at the time, especially Shi'ism. The religion differs from both Sunni and Shi'i Islam, however, on key tenets. The Druze believe that God was incarnated in human forms, the final incarnation being al-Hakim. The religion emphasizes moral principles over ceremony. The Druze have suffered a history of persecution and repression for their beliefs, which may partially explain the group's refusal to discuss its religion. The Druze prospered in the late 1600s and under Emir Fakhir ad-Din, the Druze kingdom extended from Lebanon to Gaza to the Golan Heights. Sixteen villages were built from the Mediterranean Sea to the Jezreel Valley in order to guard the two major roads on which goods and armies were transported. In 1830, a Druze revolt against the Egyptian pasha was crushed, along with all but two of the 14 Druze villages in the Carmel. In the 1860s, Ottoman rulers encouraged Druzes to return to the Carmel.

Because the Druze will not discuss their religion, most of what Westerners know about them comes from British "explorers" who fought their way into villages and stole holy books. The religion is not known even to some Druzes. Insofar as anyone knows, Jethro, father-in-law of Moses, is their most revered prophet. The most important holiday falls in late April, when Druzes throughout Israel gather in the holy village of Ḥittim, near Tiberias. Devout Druzes are forbidden to smoke, drink alcohol, or eat pork, but many young Druzes do not adhere strictly to these prohibitions. Gabriel Ben-Dor's *The Druze in Israel: A Political Study* details the ideology, lifestyle, and political situation of the Druze.

The Baha'i

The Baha'i movement began in Tehran in 1817 with the birth of Mirza Hussein Ali. At the age of 46, this son of Persian nobility renamed himself Baha'u'llah, which means "Glory of God," and began preaching non-violence and the unity of all religions. Baha'u'llah's arrival had been foretold in 1844 by the Persian Siyyid Ali Muhammad (also known as El Bab, or "Gateway to God"), the first prophet of the Baha'i religion, who had heralded the coming of a new religious teacher and divine messenger. Baha'u'llah was imprisoned and then exiled to Palestine, where he continued his teachings in the city of Akko. Baha'u'llah is buried near Akko, and El Bab is buried in Ḥaifa, which is currently home to a large Baha'i population.

Baha'u'llah's teachings fill over 100 volumes. In keeping with his message, the Baha'i religion incorporates elements of major Western and Eastern religions. Baha'is believe in a Supreme Being, accepting Jesus, Buddha, Muhammad, and Baha'u'llah as divine prophets. Baha'i Scripture includes the Bible, the Qur'an, and the Bhagavad-Gita. A central doctrine of the faith regards the Baha'i vision of the future. As opposed to both Western and Eastern religions that warn of a final Judgement Day or an end of the world as we know it, Baha'u'llah prophesied a "flowering of humanity," an era of peace and enlightenment to come. Before this new age can arrive, however, the world must undergo dreadful events to give civilization the impetus to reform itself. The Baha'is espouse racial unity, sexual equality, global disarmament, and the creation of a world community. The rapidly-growing Baha'i faith currently boasts about five million adherents, with 1.5 million converts world-wide in the last six years.

Architecture

The Middle East's architectural remains testify to its history of conquest. As ruling dynasties tumbled after each other, new architectural modes syncretized with local forms. The result is a patchwork of Roman ruins, Crusader fortifications, and native styles overlaid with Muslim monumentality.

The **Egyptians** are justly known as the builders of antiquity. Massive blocks of limestone, granite, and sandstone were employed for tombs and temples, and the Nile allowed easy transport of building materials. Architectural remains today are mainly temples and tombs, since most other buildings, including the royal palaces, were built from biodegradable materials which have dissolved back into mud. The Egyptians believed that their life in the afterworld depended upon the preservation of their earthly bodies. The earliest tombs were pits covered with bricks or Nile mud to prevent sands from scattering in the wind. Dignitaries of the Old Kingdom were buried in *mastabas,* rectangular structures surmounting underground burial chambers and abutted by a small court for mourners. The royal *mastabas* were later enlarged and surrounded with series of outer casings to produce step pyramids, forerunners of the true pyramids.

The Roman historian Pliny disparaged the pyramids, an "idle and foolish exhibition of royal wealth." They took fantastically immense amounts of labor: the Great Pyramids of Giza were constructed of huge stone blocks weighing up to 7.5 tons each, pulled for miles on wooden rollers by hundreds of thousands of workers. The royal pyramids were surrounded by throngs of *mastaba* tombs of dignitaries hoping to enter the afterlife with the pharaoh.

The **Israelites** did not build on a similar scale. Nothing remains of King Solomon's Temple. Effort was expended on walls and waterworks; defense and drink came before glory. King Hezekiah dug a tunnel, which still remains, to channel the only nearby spring into the walls of Jerusalem.

Architecture flourished during the several centuries that the **Roman Empire** controlled the Middle East, especially under King Herod. Most of these structures have since been destroyed or plundered, leaving little but skeletons of aqueducts and amphitheaters to tell the tale of Roman might. The most impressive remains of this period are the ruins of Caesarea and the Western Wall in Jerusalem, a retaining wall of the Second Temple. In Jordan, the Romans spent a large part of their four-hundred-year domination building the stone cities of the Decapolis. Significant remains litter Pella, Gedara (Um Qeis), Gerasa (Gerash), and Philadelphia (Amman).

The extant architecture from the **Crusaders,** notably the prison-fortress at Akko, is characterized by its bulk. These structures were built primarily for protection—the Crusader hold over the land was tenuous and required ceaseless defense. Castles and fortresses were built European-style and not modified to suit the climate of the Middle East—the walls are thick, the windows are small, and the atmosphere is that of a Finnish sauna. From the **Romanesque** period, only the Church of the Holy Sepulchre and the Church of St. Anne are still in use.

Coptic architecture in Egypt consists mainly of tombs, monasteries, and churches. These structures were constructed of limestone and timber. Granite columns contain detailed reliefs and carvings of crosses, flowers, and other patterns. Two sites at which tombs can be viewed today are the catacombs of Alexandria and the cemetery of el-Bahnasa, at which the form of the small funerary basilica was perfected. The Dayr el-Abyad Monastery, with its decorated niches and frescoes which once covered the whole surface of the walls, is a fine example of early Christian architecture. The churches of Old Cairo have been influenced by both Arab mosques and Western churches.

Muslim architecture varies regionally, as Muslims adapted prevailing styles to their own needs as they conquered each new area. The minaret, however, is distinctly Islamic, and, along with multiple arches, became a characteristic of the mosque. Many mosques also have domes, which usually rise from square brick bases. What distinguishes Egyptian Islamic architecture is its spareness; there are no glimmering, dazzling faience tiles as in Safavid Iran, and the buildings are massive and plain. The geometrical logic in Islamic buildings recalls the pyramids of the past. The mosques are decorated with Qur'anic inscriptions glorifying Allah and Muhammad, since Sunni Muslims believe that depictions of nature are a blasphemous usurpation of God's prerogative. The Dome of the Rock in Jerusalem (built 692) is an unusual structure. Instead of the standard "borrowing" of Roman pillars to form their own archways, the Muslim conquerors copied the Roman and Byzantine rotunda, or circular building plan, in place of their customary square courtyard. The Mosque of Ibn Tulun brought a new style to Egypt, noted for pointed brick arches and arcades. This mosque now lies in ruins, but it remains one of the great landmarks of Muslim architecture.

The **Mamluk** period is distinguished by an increased richness and variety of crafts and ornamentation. Mamluk architecture is characterized by flat façades with few, if any, projections and sunken panels containing rows of arched windows. Mamluk mosques include ornate *mihrabs* (prayer niches) on the wall, pointing worshipers toward Mecca. **Ottoman** architecture is perhaps best represented by the wall around Jerusalem built under the rule of Suleiman. For more information on architecture read John D. Hoag's *Islamic Architecture.*

Tel Aviv and **Jerusalem** reflect two city-wide experiments in modern architecture. Ariyeh Sharon, an Israeli architect of the Bauhaus school, brought functionalism to Tel Aviv in an attempt to give some coherence to a city erected hastily to house a flood of new immigrants to Israel. He talked the municipal authorities into allowing him to put most new buildings two and half meters off the ground on stilts, or pilotis. The result is nonsense on stilts. Jerusalem has undergone a different kind of experiment, started by Governor Sir Ronald Storrs during British rule. Storrs put a Jerusalem city law into effect stipulating that all buildings must be faced with square, dressed stone; the law is still observed throughout the city. It's hard to make something ugly out of Jerusalem stone, much to the benefit of Jerusalem.

ISRAEL (YISRAEL) יִשְׂרָאֵל

US $1 = 2.39 shekels (NIS)	NIS 1 US $0.42
CDN $1 = NIS 2.02	NIS 1 CDN $0.50
UK £1 = NIS 4.61	NIS 1 = UK £0.22
IR £1 = NIS 4.33	NIS 1 = IR £0.23
AUS $1 = NIS 1.75	NIS 1 = AUS $0.57
NZ $1 = NIS 1.30	NIS 1 = NZ $0.77

> For information on Documents and Formalities, Money, Safety and Security, Climate Concerns, Transportation Options, Border Crossings, History, Religion, and Travel Etiquette, see the General Introduction to this book.

At age 45, a fractious Israel still doesn't know what it wants to be when it grows up. The world's only Jewish state is variously "a light unto the nations," a pariah among its neighbors, and a country like all the others. From persecution culminating in the Holocaust, Israelis have come together to build a new country in the midst of imperial ruins, mingling diverse cultures and backgrounds to make a brand new kind of state and to remake themselves in the process. With the country's identity at stake, all Israelis have their own vision of what Israel should be. To give one eloquent example, Amos Oz, Israel's leading novelist, sees his fellow Israelis not as "the 'Maccabeans reborn' that Herzl talked of, but a warm-hearted, hot-tempered Mediterranean people that is gradually learning, through great suffering and in a tumult of sound and fury, to find release both from the bloodcurdling nightmares of the past and from delusions of grandeur, both ancient and modern." Of course, many Israelis see Oz as a snob and a kvetch, and will tell you at length how *they* see their country (as the saying goes, if you have two Israelis in a room, you have three opinions). Finally, this intense self-analysis is going on in the midst of the intractable brawl of the Arab-Israeli conflict, known here simply as *HaMatzav* (The Situation). Talk with Israelis about their whirling, bewildering, endearing country's situation for long enough, and they will finally smile or shrug and say, "*Yihiyeh b'seder*" (It'll be OK).

Planning Your Trip

Work

Unemployment in Israel is high (currently about 11.6%), and this greatly limits legal employment opportunities for foreigners in Israel. Foreigners looking for work in Israel will have to compete with the wave of *olim ḥadashim* (new immigrants) from the Soviet Union who are struggling to secure their place in Israel's erratic economy. American or European companies with branches in Israel are a possible source of legal employment. If you obtain paid work, your employer must secure a work visa for you through the Ministry of the Interior. Another option is volunteer work in exchange for room and board.

Apprenticeships

Israel belongs to the **International Association for the Exchange of Students for Technical Experience (IAESTE).** This organization operates exchange programs lasting between two and 18 months for undergraduate and graduate students. (See Useful Organizations in the General Introduction.) The **Jewish Agency** also offers a six-month internship for young people with experience or education in a specific field.

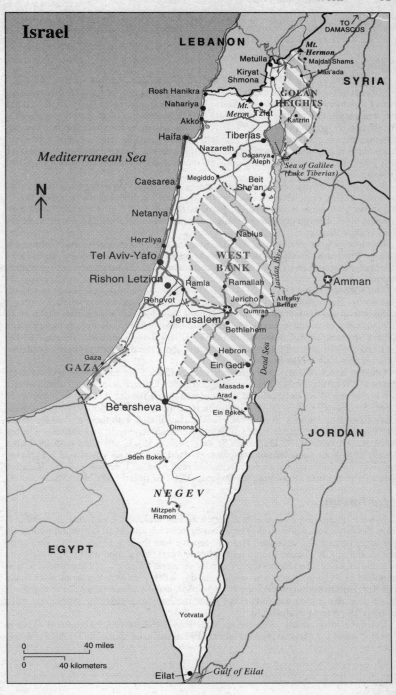

Israel

TO DAMASCUS

LEBANON

SYRIA

Mt. Hermon
Metulla
Majdal Shams
Kiryat Shmona
Mas'ada
Rosh Hanikra
GOLAN HEIGHTS
Nahariya
Mt. Meron
Zfat
Akko
Katzrin
Haifa
Tiberias
Nazareth
Mediterranean Sea
Deganya Aleph
Sea of Galilee (Lake Tiberias)
N
Caesarea
Megiddo
Beit She'an
Netanya
Herzliya
Nablus
Tel Aviv-Yafo
WEST BANK
Rishon Letzion
Ramla
Ramallah
Jordan River
Amman
Rehovot
Jericho
Allenby Bridge
Jerusalem
Qumran
Bethlehem
Hebron
Gaza
Ein Gedi
GAZA
Dead Sea
Masada
Arad
Be'ersheva
Ein Bokek
Dimona
JORDAN
Sdeh Boker
NEGEV
Mitzpeh Ramon
EGYPT

0   40 miles
0   40 kilometers

Yotvata

Eilat   *Gulf of Eilat*

Write to the Center for Ulpanim and Counseling for Young Adults (UCYA), 12 Kaplan St., Tel Aviv (tel. (03) 25 83 11).

Kibbutzim

Israel's 250 kibbutzim—communal settlements whose members divide work and profits equally—are always eager for volunteers. Kibbutzim vary greatly in size, number of volunteers, and ideological basis. Volunteers generally work six six-hour days per week with several days off per month, and may receive a small monthly allowance in addition to various other benefits. If you're already in Israel, visit a kibbutz and talk to volunteers before you commit yourself. Otherwise try to get a written promise of placement on a specific kibbutz before arriving in Israel. Kibbutz life can be seductive in its routine, and many volunteers find themselves staying longer than they had planned.

Jobs for volunteers can be fun, monotonous, or weird. Don't be surprised to find yourself tossing chickies into boxes or chasing renegade ponies across eggplant fields. You may also work in orchards or gardens or end up washing laundry or dishes. Though work assignments theoretically rotate, the needs of the kibbutz will come before your preferences.

If you wish to combine work with study, a suitable option may be the **Kibbutz Ulpanim Program,** available on more than 60 kibbutzim. This program provides 24 hours of classroom instruction per week in exchange for 27 hours of work (see Study below).

The **Kibbutz Aliya Desk,** 110 E. 59th St., 4th flr., New York, NY 10022 (tel. (212) 318-6130), has representatives throughout the U.S. and Canada who will help arrange volunteer work. **Project 67,** 10 Hatton Garden, London EC1N 8AH (tel. (01) 831 76 26), also places volunteers on kibbutzim, and moshavim for one to four months. The **Israel Student Travel Association (ISSTA),** 109 Ben-Yehuda St., Tel Aviv 63401 (tel. (03) 544 01 11), will provide information about the different packages available. Write to them six weeks in advance.

Once in Israel you may apply directly to the office of the appropriate kibbutz association in Tel Aviv. Each kibbutz is affiliated with a kibbutz association, which in turn are organized along political and ideological lines. **Kibbutz Artzi,** 13 Leonardo da Vinci St. (tel. (03) 25 39 05 or 43 52 62), is affiliated with the left-wing party; **Kibbutz HaDati,** 7 Dubnov St. (tel. 695 72 31), is affiliated with the National Religious Party (only Jews accepted, some religious observance required); and **Takam—United Kibbutz Movement,** 82 HaYarkon St. (tel. 545 25 55), is affiliated with the Labor Party. Bring your passport and two passport-sized photos with you if you're applying for work on a kibbutz. For more information read *Kibbutz Volunteer* (£4.95), Vacation Work Publications, 9 Park End St., Oxford, OX1 1HJ (tel. (0865) 24 19 78).

Moshavim

Moshavim provide a somewhat different agricultural work experience from kibbutzim. Moshavim are agricultural communities in which almost all farms and homes are privately owned and operated. You will receive free lodging either with a family on the moshav or in a house shared with other workers. Your appointed family will also provide meals or a food allowance. Laundry services, toiletries, and aerograms will be supplied as well. In return, you work a six-day week with a minimum of eight hours per day. Unlike kibbutz work, workers are paid, usually about US$250 per month. A labor shortage at most moshavim has made moshav work plentiful. Applicants must be ages 18-35 and physically fit.

For more information, write the organizations listed above for kibbutzim. Once in Israel, contact the **Moshavim Movement,** 19 Leonardo da Vinci St., Tel Aviv (tel. 695 84 73).

Archeological Digs

Working on an archeological dig is yet another earthy way to earn your keep. The work consists largely of digging pits, shoveling shards, and hauling baskets of dirt for eight to 10 hours per day in searing heat; work begins at 5am. Don't let dreams of discovering ancient treasures prevent a realistic assessment of your physical stamina and seriousness of interest. In many cases a dig can be a rewarding educational experience and an excellent way to meet people who share your interests.

Every February the **Israel Antiquities Authority,** P.O. Box 586, Jerusalem 91911 (tel. (02) 29 26 07), compiles a list of excavations that are open to volunteers in the summer (must be at least 17 and in excellent shape). Every January the **Archeological Institute of America,** 627 Commonwealth Ave., Boston, MA 02216 (tel. (617) 353-9361) publishes a thorough listing of digs in its *Fieldwork Opportunities Bulletin* (US$8); it sells out quickly. Another good source is the *Biblical Archeology Review,* 3000 Connecticut Ave. NW, #300, Washington, DC 20008; tel. (202) 387-8888.

Apply directly to the dig leader. Volunteers usually must be able to work a minimum of two weeks. Be sure to indicate any previous experience or knowledge of archeology, geology, or anthropology in your application, although none is typically required. Many excavations also charge an application fee. Volunteers are usually responsible for their own travel arrangements to and from Israel, and most excavations charge for food and accommodations. Accommodations range from camping at the site to a nearby hostel, hotel, or kibbutz. The Department of Antiquities recommends that volunteers come fully insured, as most excavations provide only minimal insurance.

Another excavation program is provided through the **Israel Student Travel Association (ISSTA),** 109 Ben-Yehuda St., Tel Aviv 63401 (tel. (03) 544 01 11), which has arrangements with Tel Aviv University for students interested in working on digs. Again, the work is long and arduous, and intended only for archeology fiends.

The "Dig for a Day" program is designed more for the curious tourist. The program includes a three-hour excavation, seminars on methodology, tools, and history, and a tour of the entire site. The cost for students is about US$13. For more information contact **Archeological Seminars, Inc.,** 34 Ḥabad St., Jewish Quarter or P.O. Box 14002, Jaffa Gate, Jerusalem 91140 (tel. (02) 28 22 21 or 27 35 15), from July through August.

Volunteers for Israel

The Volunteers for Israel program places participants in non-combat support jobs in the Israeli military. Volunteers began in 1982 during the Lebanon War to give reserve soldiers with businesses and families a chance to return to their domestic affairs. The 23-day program involves menial work, such as washing dishes, polishing boots, or packing equipment. Unless your home is encircled with barbed wire and rifle-toting guards, an army base will be a new, perhaps startling environment. You will wear army fatigues, army boots, and sleep in army barracks, but don't expect to carry an Uzi or keep the uniform afterwards. The program offers reduced airfare on El Al or Tower Air, providing you fulfill your commitment. The round-trip ticket is good for 180 days and can be extended once you have finished the program for US$50 per 180 days. If you wish to leave early, the airline will charge an additional US$50 for your return ticket. There is sometimes a special fare for students under 26 with a letter from your university registrar proving enrollment. Write to **Volunteers for Israel,** 330 W. 42nd St., #1818, New York, NY 10036-6902 (tel. (212) 643-4848). Application must include a US$50 registration fee.

Living Experiences

A blend of work, study, and life in general, **Otzma** incorporates kibbutz and moshav life, youth villages, and Hebrew study (tel. (212) 475-5000). In the **Isaac Mayer Wise-Inside Israel Program,** you live with an Israeli family as well as on a kibbutz, and learn Hebrew to boot. Contact Paul Reichenback, Union of American Hebrew

Congregations, 838 Fifth Ave., New York, NY 10021 (tel. (212) 249-0100 ext. 546). **Livnot U'Lehibanot: To Build and Be Built,** is a three-month intensive program of study and restoration in the old city of Tzfat (110 E. 59th St., 3rd Flr., New York, NY 10022 (tel. (212) 752-2390). Other programs that may be of interest are the Peace Corps-style **Sherut La'Am** (tel. (212) 339-6002), and the **NAAM Internships** (tel. (212) 339-6060), both affiliated with the American Zionist Youth Foundation.

Study

Ulpanim

An *ulpan* is a short-term study program for foreign students that provides intensive Hebrew and Jewish culture instruction. There are about 100 *ulpanim* throughout Israel. **Kibbutz Ulpanim** offer 24 hours of classroom instruction per week in return for work (see Work above). Studies emphasize conversation and simple reading in Hebrew, and include seminars on current events. Kibbutz Ulpanim run for 3 to 6-months. Participants must be between 17 and 35, single or a couple without children, and in good physical shape. Many American universities recognize Kibbutz Ulpanim for foreign language and elective credits. For more information contact the **Kibbutz Aliya Desk.** (See address above under Kibbutzim.)

The **Ulpan Akiva Netanya** runs a series of three- to 20-week study programs in Hebrew and Arabic. The programs include 4 or 5 Hebrew study hours per day and cultural activities in the evening, and are open to both Jews and non-Jews from ages 18-80. Costs vary according to duration of program. Write to Ulpan Akiva Netanya, P.O. Box 6086, Netanya 42160 (tel. (535) 23 12 13). Other programs are sponsored by **Beit Ha'Noar Ha'Ivri,** HaRav Herzog 105, Jerusalem 92622 (tel. (02) 78 94 41), **Beit Ha'Am,** Rehov Bazelel 11, Jerusalem (tel. (02) 25 41 56), and **Mo'adon Ha'Oleh,** Rehov Alkalai 9, Jerusalem (tel. (02) 63 37 18). Contact the **World Zionist Organization,** 515 Park Ave., New York, NY 10022 (tel. (212) 339-6000) for more information.

The Jerusalem municipality also runs inexpensive *ulpanim* (about US$130 per month). For information contact the Municipality of Jerusalem, Department of Culture, *Hanhalat HaLashon* unit in Beit Ha'Am, 11 Bezalel St., Jerusalem 94591 (tel. (02) 22 41 56).

Universities

Israel has six institutions of higher learning, with universities in Tel Aviv, Jerusalem, Haifa, and Be'ersheva, and technical and scientific institutes in Haifa and Rehovot. Programs for foreign students range in length from one summer to four years. **Year-abroad** programs usually begin with a 4 to 9-week *ulpan* to learn Hebrew before the semester begins in October, after the Jewish holidays. The courses for these programs are usually in English; if you know Hebrew, you have the option of taking regular university courses. Israeli universities also offer full-time **degree programs** on both the undergraduate and graduate levels, usually preceded by a *mekhina* (see Mekhinot below). Admission to undergraduate bachelor programs ordinarily requires proficiency in Hebrew and at least one year of college.

Several universities currently operate overseas student programs. You must apply directly to the university through its New York office. Some scholarships are available. Ask at your university career office or write to the **Institute of International Education (IIE),** 809 United Nations Plaza, New York, NY 10017 (tel. (212) 888-8200), for their free pamphlet *Basic Facts on Foreign Study* or other helpful publications. The various Friends Committees also offer scholarship assistance. American Guaranteed Student Loans (GSL) may be applied to study in Israel.

Tel Aviv University offers both single-semester and full-year programs for overseas students; the application deadline is May 1 for fall semester or year programs, November 1 for the spring semester, and April 15 for summer. The fall and full-year program is preceded by an *ulpan*. For more information write to the Office of Academic Affairs, American Friends of Tel Aviv University, 360 Lexington Ave., 3rd flr., New York, NY 10017 (tel. (212) 687-5651).

The **Hebrew University of Jerusalem** offers summer and full-year programs primarily in Judaic, Middle Eastern, and Israeli studies. Courses are also offered in modern and biblical Hebrew, Yiddish, and literary and spoken Arabic. Month-long programs during the summer cost between US$400 and 500, and tuition for full-year programs is US$3900. The university also has programs for graduate study. Courses are often taught in English. For information and application forms write to the Office of Academic Affairs, Hebrew University, 11 E. 69th St., New York, NY 10021 (tel. (212) 472-2288); Friends of Hebrew University, 3 St. John's Wood Rd., London NW8 8RB (tel. (071) 286 11 76); Canadian Friends of Hebrew University, 3080 Yonge St., Ste. 5024, Toronto, Ont. M4N 3P4 (tel. (416) 485-8000, outside Toronto (800) 668-3956). In Israel write Hebrew University, Goldsmith Building, Mount Scopus, Jerusalem (tel. (02) 88 26 02).

For information on the various programs offered by other universities write to these addresses: **Bar Ilan University,** 91 Fifth Ave., #200, New York, NY 10003 (tel. (212) 337-1270/86); **Ben-Gurion University of the Negev,** Overseas Study Program, 342 Madison Ave., #1924, New York, NY 10173 (tel. (212) 687-7721); American Friends of Haifa University, 41 E. 42nd St., #828, New York, NY 10017 (tel. (212) 818-9050). For **Technion-Israel Institute of Technology,** contact Registration and Admission Center, Technion City, Haifa (fax (4) 32 45 30).

For information about all programs contact the **Israel Student Authority,** 15 Hillel St., Jerusalem (tel. (02) 24 11 21). Additional information on study opportunities is available at the Institute of International Exchange and at the New York consulate's Office of Academic Affairs, or call the University Student Department of the Israel Action Center in the U.S. at (800) 27-ISRAEL (274-7723).

Mekhinot

Students who do not have the required proficiency in Hebrew but wish to enter a full undergraduate degree program usually first enroll in *mekhina* programs. The *mekhina* provides a year of intensive Hebrew instruction and a chance to develop study plans as well. *Mekhinot* are offered by the universities and other schools of post-secondary education. Note, *mekhina* participation does not guarantee acceptance to a university; students must still take entrance examinations. At Hebrew University, Technion, and Practical Engineering Colleges, the *mekhina* opens in September or October. The program for Practical Engineers in Be'ersheva begins in August and February. *Mekhinot* begin in August at all other schools.

Once There

Entry

Security upon your arrival into Israel is seemingly relaxed, especially when compared to the scrutiny your luggage will receive at Ben-Gurion Airport upon your departure. For the most part, you can take the "Green Channel" to exit the airport. Most items can be brought in duty-free as long as you intend to carry them out when you depart. Take the "Red Channel" if you need to declare articles. Duty must be paid on large quantities of perfume, alcohol, and cigarettes.

For the nervous or clueless, there is an Israeli **Government Tourist Information Office (GTIO)** in the arrival hall at Ben-Gurion. Very soothing. Egged **buses** run regularly to major cities (#475 to Tel Aviv), and United Tours bus #222 chugs to Tel Aviv (NIS5). *Sherut* **(shared) taxis** run regularly from the airport to Jerusalem (NIS24).

Useful Organizations

Embassies and Consulates

U.S.: Embassy, 71 HaYarkon St., Tel Aviv (tel. (03) 65 43 38). **Consulates,** in Tel Aviv, at embassy; in East Jerusalem, 27 Nablus Rd. (tel. 23 42 71); in New City, 18 Agron Rd. (tel. 28 22 31/2); in Ḥaifa, 12 Jerusalem St. (tel. 67 06 15).

Canada: Embassy, 220 HaYarkon St., Tel Aviv (tel. (03) 22 81 22). **Consulate,** 7 Ḥavakuk St. (tel. (03) 546 58 10).

Britain: Embassy, 192 HaYarkon St., Tel Aviv 63405 (tel. (03) 24 91 71). **Consulate** at embassy; in East Jerusalem on Rajib St. near Sheikh Jarrah (tel. (02) 28 24 81/2).

Australia: 37 King Saul St., 4th floor, Tel Aviv 64928 (tel. (03) 25 04 51).

Tourist and Travel Services

Israel Ministry of Tourism: Jerusalem, 24 King George St. 94262 (tel. (02) 23 73 11); **Tel Aviv,** 7 Mendele St. (tel. (03) 22 32 66/7); **Ḥaifa,** 18 Herzl St. (tel. 66 65 21) and 14 other cities. Maps, train schedules, and information on current events. The **Voluntary Tourist Service (VTS)** arranges for tourists to spend an evening with Israeli families (ask about the *Meet the Israelis* program).

Israel Youth Hostel Association: 3 Dorot Rishonim St., P.O. Box 1075, Jerusalem 91009 (tel. (02) 25 27 06). Operates 30 hostels. Organizes tours for groups and individuals to Israel, Sinai, Jordan, and Egypt.

National Parks Authority: 4 Rav Aluf M. Makleff St., P.O. Box 7028, Tel Aviv 61070 (tel. (03) 25 22 81). Material on parks and historical sites. Also sells a 14-day ticket (US$12) covering admission to all sites. Ticket available in Tel Aviv only.

Society for the Protection of Nature in Israel (HaḤevra LeHaganat HaTeva, SPNI): Jerusalem, 13 Heleni HaMalka St. (tel. (02) 22 23 57); **Tel Aviv,** 4 HaShfela St. 66183, near the central bus station (tel. (03) 38 25 01); **Ḥaifa,** 8 HeMenahem St. (tel. (04) 66 41 35); **Be'ersheva,** Sderot Utvia (tel. (057) 321 56). In the **U.S.,** contact ASPNI, 475 Fifth Ave., 23rd floor, New York, NY 10117 (tel. (212) 685-3380). In the **U.K.,** UKSPNI, 25 Lyndale Ave., London NW2 2QB (tel. (01) 435 68 03). Organizes hikes and camping trips. Dues US$36 per year, US$30 for students.

Israel Camping Union: P.O. Box 53, Nahariya 22100 (tel. (04) 92 53 92). Write for information about organized camping tours and a full list of campsites.

Israel Student Travel Association (ISSTA): Jerusalem, 5 Eliashar St. (tel. (02) 22 72 57); **Tel Aviv,** 109 Ben-Yehuda St. 63401 (tel. (03) 544 01 11); **Ḥaifa,** 29 Nordau St. 33124 (tel. (04) 66 91 39). Information about tours, student discounts, and ID cards.

Safety and Emergency Information

Emergency assistance is available throughout Israel, and most doctors speak English. **Magen David Adom,** the Israeli Red Star of David (Red "Cross") provides first-aid and other emergency help. Emergency hospitals and pharmacies are open 24 hours, *shabbat,* and on holidays.

Communication

Mail

Post offices are usually open 8am-12:30pm and 3:30-6pm except Wednesday (8am-2pm) and Friday (8am-1pm), and are closed Saturday and holidays. In the larger cities some offices may keep longer hours. Mail from North America to Israel can take up to two weeks; mail sent from Israel to North America is considerably faster. Be sure to write "Air Mail" on the envelope, lest it be sent across the ocean in a bottle. On the street, red mailboxes are for all mail, while yellow mailboxes are for mail within the same city. If you need to mail something to North America within 72 hours, the central post offices in Jerusalem, Tel Aviv, and Ḥaifa offer reasonably reliable International Express Mail service (hours vary, but are generally Sun.-Thurs. 7:45am-12:30pm and 4-6pm, Fri. morning only).

Travelers have three means of receiving mail: Poste Restante (*doar shamur* in Hebrew), American Express, and ISSTA. Poste Restante functions in Israel, though you must ask repeatedly to receive all your letters (address them: Name, Poste Restante, Main Post Office, name of city, Israel). Have tellers check under both first and last names, and, if possible, check yourself. Always bring your passport or other proper identification. Lines at American Express are short, and employees often let you check the letter pile. Lines at ISSTA are another story.

Telephone

Public telephones are everywhere, and generally work. Older telephones insatiably munch *asimonim* (tokens) for local calls, which are available at post offices, hotel reception desks, and newsstands for about NIS0.50. Avoid calling long distance direct from an old pay phone—making a connection may take hours and handfuls of *asimonim*.

Beige-colored public telephones, a new breed, do not eat *asimonim*; instead, they scan Telecards (the moral equivalent of *asimonim*). These credit cards can be bought at post offices and bus stations (10 units of calling time NIS4.80, 20 units NIS9). Telecards are good for local, long distance, and international calls. Bezek, Israel's phone company, has metered phones for international calls in some cities.

English telephone directories are available at hotels and the main post offices, or dial 144 for assistance. You can dial direct overseas from central post offices in major cities, which will save both time and money. Dial 00, then the country code (U.S. and Canada code: 1, Great Britain: 44, Australia: 61, New Zealand: 64), area code, and telephone number. For collect and credit card calls, dial 188 for the overseas operator. The Tel Aviv operator (tel. (03) 62 28 81/2/3) may make your connection more quickly.

The **international phone code** for calling to Israel is 972.

Telegram

You can send a telegram by dialing 171. Post offices and hotels will also send telegrams for you. **Telex** service is available in Tel Aviv at the Mikveh Israel post office (see practical information in Tel Aviv) and in Jerusalem at the central post office.

Currency and Exchange

The primary unit of currency in Israel is the **new Israeli shekel (NIS).** Notes come in denominations of NIS100, NIS50, NIS20, and NIS10; coins come in NIS5, NIS1, NIS.50, 10 agorot, and 5 agorot. The triple-digit hyperinflation of the early 1980s has now been almost completely curtailed as a result of the wage and price freeze instituted during the summer of 1985 (see Economy). That September the new shekel was introduced, equivalent to 1000 existing shekels and divided into 100 agorot.

Money can be exchanged at any bank or authorized hotel; always bring your passport. Hotel rates of exchange are usually slightly worse than those in banks. **Bank Leumi** will exchange foreign currency for shekels with no commission for a minimum US$100 conversion. Shekels can be freely reconverted to a maximum of US$100. To change more than US$100 show a receipt which verifies your original conversion into shekels. (Banks usually open Sun., Tues., and Thurs. 8:30am-12:30pm and 4-5:30pm, Mon. and Wed. 8:30am-12:30pm, Fri. and holidays 8:30am-noon. The **First International Bank** and many hotels have additional hours.)

Use of Foreign Currency

Many services and shops accept U.S., Canadian, and Australian dollars as well as Pounds Sterling, but are under no obligation to accept foreign currency. If you do pay in foreign currency (traveler's checks and credit cards included), expect your change to be in shekels. When you use foreign currency, you are exempt from the domestic **Value Added Tax (VAT)** on goods and services (18%). Many shops include VAT in listed prices, so you may have to insist on a discount. VAT refunds can also be obtained by presenting all receipts of purchases made with foreign currency at any export bank upon your departure. The refund will be in the currency you used; if the bank cannot make the refund, it will be mailed to your home address. A new policy allows Eurocheques to be written in shekels and counted as foreign currency for discounts.

You may bring an unlimited amount of currency, foreign or shekels, into the country in any form. Upon departure you are permitted to take up to US$100 cash. Anything over this must be accompanied by receipts to prove that it was brought into the country. Unless you want to frame them or wallpaper your kitchen, exchange all your shekels before you leave Israel. Few foreign banks are willing to buy them.

Tipping

Do not feel obligated to tip except in Western-style restaurants, hotels, or other touristy establishments; often a service charge is already included in the bill. If the bill says "service not included," tipping is customary. Taxi drivers will cheerfully accept tips but they are not expected. Israelis usually tip only a barber or hairdresser.

Black Market

Avoid exchanging your money in unofficial, black market booths. They are illegal and hurt Israel's economy. Furthermore, the improving health of the economy has made the premium offered on the black market less significant.

Business Hours

Business hours in Israel are difficult to pinpoint—generally, they're when everyone goes home. Because of the variety of religions, different shops close on different days. Most Jewish shops, offices, and places of entertainment are closed for *shabbat* from early Friday afternoon until after sundown on Saturday. State-run public transportation, including Egged bus lines, also shuts down throughout the country except in Haifa, where the local ruling coalition does not include the religious party. Don't expect to catch a bus after 2pm on Friday. Arab buses continue to run, primarily to the West Bank. Arab-owned establishments close on Fridays and, in some cases, for strikes; Christian businesses close on Sundays. Typical shopping hours are Monday-Thursday 8am-1pm and 4-7pm, Friday 8am-2pm. Due to the *intifada,* many Palestinian businesses are on strike and open in the mornings only.

On the major Jewish holidays (Rosh HaShana, Yom Kippur, Simhat Torah, Pesah, Yom Ha'Atzma'ut, and Shavuot) businesses are closed, and have Friday hours the day before. During Sukkot and Pesah, each of which lasts seven days, shops close entirely for the first and last days and are open until early afternoon during intermediate days. "Lesser" holidays are marked by early closing only. In Israel's predominantly Arab areas, some restaurants close for the entire month of Ramadan; many others close during the day. (See Festivals and Holidays.)

Accommodations

Hostels

Although often crowded in summer, Israel's **Hostelling International (HI)** youth hostels are usually clean and close to historic sites and scenic areas. You can obtain a list of hostels from the **Israel Youth Hostel Association.** (See Useful Organizations.) Hostel locations are also listed on the back of the Government Tourist Office's survey map. Most HI hostels accept reservations. They have no age limit, but a few have a maximum stay of three nights. The HI hostels are generally more expensive than the unofficial hostels. Individuals 18 and under may receive a discount. Hostels usually offer lunch and supper for an additional fee. In addition, many hostels follow a strict schedule: they are open from 5-9pm for check-in, from 7-9am for check-out, and are closed the rest of the day (check the specific listing). There are many excellent unofficial hostels and pensions in Israel. Regardless of whether they are affiliated, hostels are not known for safety. Guard your valuables with your life.

The Israel Youth Hostel Association also offers package tours for individuals and groups. Write to them for information on the "Israel on the Youth Hostel Trail" deals.

Hotels

Hotel accommodations are usually too costly for the budget traveler. The Ministry of Tourism rates hotels on a five-star basis, with five stars signifying the highest quality and most expensive hotels. There are some reasonably priced one- and two-star hotels in the larger cities; a few have singles for approximately NIS40 and doubles for NIS60. Prices can often be bargained down substantially when business is slow. Ask at tourist offices for the booklets *Israel: A Youth and Student Adventure* and *Israel Tourist Hotels.*

Camping

Israel's campsites provide electricity, sanitary facilities, public telephones, first-aid, a restaurant and/or store, and a night guard. Swimming areas are either on the site or nearby. During July and August most camping places charge NIS10-15 per night for adults. For more information write to the **Israel Camping Union.** (See Useful Organizations.)

Think twice before unrolling your sleeping bag in areas not officially designated for camping. Certain stretches of beach are off-limits for security reasons (for example, the Mediterranean coast north of Nahariya), and others have a high incidence of robbery (near Haifa, Tel Aviv, and Eilat). **Women should not camp alone.** Finally, **heed mine field warning signs** unless you fancy yourself triple-jointed and edible.

Alternative Accommodations

If you plan to sleep in Bethlehem, Nazareth, or Jerusalem, the three major Christian sites in Israel, consider staying in one of the many **Christian hospices.** There are also hospices on Mount Tabor, in Tiberias, and in Tel Aviv. Most hospices are old monasteries or Franciscan settlements. They are officially designed to provide reasonably priced room and board for Christians on pilgrimages to the Holy Land, but all the hospices listed in this book welcome both tourists and pilgrims.

The 40 hospices in Israel are run by organizations representing various Christian denominations and a host of nations. Bed and breakfast costs US$12-16 per person at most places. Dorm beds can be as cheap as US$3. Though austere, the hospices are usually quiet, clean, and comfortable. In addition, most serve cheap, filling meals, and are conveniently located in important religious centers. But the number of rooms is limited, and they can be difficult to obtain in the tourist season. For a list of these hospices write to the **Ministry of Tourism,** Pilgrimage Promotion, Youth and Students Division, P.O. Box 1018, Jerusalem 91009 (tel. (02) 24 05 53 or 23 73 11).

In some cities (such as Tzfat and Eilat), the cheapest alternative to camping or a youth hostel is a **private home.** The Government Tourist Office and some private travel agencies can arrange accommodations. The Patra Travel Agency, 63 Nahalat Binyamin St. or P.O. Box 1074, Tel Aviv 61009 (tel. (03) 62 34 11) rents rooms in Tel Aviv starting at US$18 for singles and US$23 for doubles, with a 10% discount for students. A less expensive alternative is to find a place on your own. Prices should be no more than what you would pay at a local hostel. Exercise caution, as always.

Some kibbutzim also offer accommodations at **Kibbutz Hotels.** Most are rated three-star by the Ministry of Tourism, and prices run as high as US$35 for singles and US$45 for doubles. For more information contact them at 90 Ben-Yehuda St., Tel Aviv 61031, (tel. (03) 24 61 61 or 544 80 86). Finally, try **ISSTA** (see Travel Services) for cheap package deals on accommodations.

Transportation

Bus

Buses are the most popular and convenient means of traveling around Israel. Except for the **Dan Company** in Tel Aviv and the **Arab buses** serving the West Bank and Gaza, the **Egged Bus Cooperative** (something of an oxymoron) has a monopoly on buses, serving nearly every settlement and city in Israel. Several express and local buses travel between the major cities each day. Buses are generally modern, air conditioned, and quite inexpensive. Students with ISIC and passport receive a 10% discount on all fares; just be sure to show your ID a number of times—first to the ticket seller, then to the driver, then to the ticket inspector, then to interested passengers.

Buses are sometimes crowded, especially on Saturday nights after *shabbat.* Don't be afraid to push your way in and out of the bus door; just preface each push with the word *sliha* (excuse me), as do Israelis.

Egged sells *hofshi hodshi* monthly bus passes, good for unlimited travel in Jerusalem and Haifa. Dan sells the same for Tel Aviv routes. These are well worth the price if you will be staying in one area for a longish time. Otherwise, you can buy a *kartisiya* from any bus driver (NIS20); this useful item gives you 11 rides at a NIS2 savings, but it's no good for the ubiquitous *sherut* taxis (see below). In general, all intra-city routes in Israel cost NIS2 (except in Eilat, where lack of VAT brings the price down to NIS1.50).

Most bus stations have printed schedules—sometimes in English. A better strategy is to call **Egged's toll-free information** at 177 022 55 55 for all the facts on every place you can think of visiting (open Sun.-Thurs. 6:30am-9pm, Fri. 6:30am-3pm, Sat. 4-10pm). For express buses get in line at the platform (they're always marked) and pay on board. Signs directing you to buy tickets at the ticket window can be safely ignored except for highly traveled, long distance routes (such as Jerusalem-Eilat) for which advance reservations are recommended. When planning your itinerary, remember that only Arab buses run during *shabbat.* Buses between cities usually leave from the central bus station *(tahana merkazit).* You can usually buy a round-trip ticket *(halokh v'hazor)* at a 10% discount. Some popular routes—especially to and from Eilat— take reservations and give assigned seating; if you know when you're going, these guaranteed seats can take a load off your mind.

Many tourists prefer to travel on **Egged tour buses.** Egged offers over 100 excursions to various regions in Israel; their tours into the Sinai Desert and along the Red Sea are particularly popular. They're cheaper than the tours run by the Society for the Protection of Nature, though not nearly as good. For more information check with the Egged tour office in the U.S. by calling (800) 682-3333; you can also write to their head office at 15 Frischmann St., Tel Aviv (tel. (03) 24 22 71).

As *Let's Go* was going to press, Egged raised its prices by 12% from the ones listed in this guide. We're as annoyed as the rest of Israel.

Taxi

Israeli companies offer both private and less expensive *sherut* (shared) taxis. All city taxis have meters whose use is mandatory, though the drivers often need to be reminded to turn them on. Bargain if you know how much the ride should cost. Any offers of "special rates" (translation: no meter and an exorbitant charge) should be adamantly refused. Taxis can be called or hailed on the street.

Sherut taxis hold up to seven people. Certain taxi companies operate *sherut* taxis seven days per week from stations or taxi stands in each city. Inter-city *sherut* taxis operate on loose schedules (ask at stations) except on Saturdays, when they simply whiz along the streets in search of passengers. Intra-city *sherut* taxis never follow a schedule, but cruise the streets daily. The price should not be much more than the bus fare for the same route, and always fix the price before starting out. Be particularly insistent about this on Saturdays and late at night when buses don't run and *sherut* drivers may try to rip you off. Most routes, intra-city included, have set fares. Check with Israelis or at the nearest tourist office.

Car

The leading cause of death in Israel is not war, but automobile accidents. A popular bumper sticker during the Gulf War read, "I'm not a Scud and you're not a Patriot, so back off." Extensive public transportation makes a car generally unnecessary but may allow you to reach out-of-the-way places. The brazen can drive in Israel with a valid international driver's license (see the General Introduction); you must be 21. Roads are paved and well marked, and maps are available at all tourist offices. Israelis drive on the right side of the road. The cheapest rentals run about US$18 per day, plus 25¢ per kilometer, or US$32 per day with unlimited mileage. Watch for special deals; Eldan, among others, occasionally offers cut-rate prices. Invest in appropriate insurance and update your will. It is often cheaper to reserve cars from outside Israel; if you know you'll want a car, call ahead. See the Practical Information of each city for agency addresses.

Avis: U.S., (tel. (800) 331-1212); **Canada,** (tel. (800) 268-2319); **U.K.,** dial 100 and ask for Freephone Avis.

Budget: U.S., (tel. (800) 742-3325); **Canada,** (tel. (800) 268-8900); **U.K.,** (tel. 0800 18 11 81). Must be 21.

Eldan: U.S., (tel. (800) 533-8778 or (212) 629-6090); **U.K.,** in London (tel. 951 57 27). Must be 24.

Hertz: U.S., (tel. (800) 654-3001); **Canada,** (tel. (800) 263-0600). Must be 21.

Train

Rail service in Israel, though rather limited, is an excellent alternative for travel between major cities. **Israel Railways** runs a line from Nahariya through Ḥaifa, Tel Aviv, and major towns along the north coast. The Tel Aviv-Jerusalem line is circuitous and slower than travel on the highway but considerably more scenic and relaxing.

Like buses, trains screech to a halt during *shabbat*. Avoid traveling on Friday afternoons when the trains are most crowded. Train fares are slightly cheaper than bus fares. Students with an ISIC receive a 50% discount.

Hitchhiking

Let's Go does *not* recommend hitchhiking. "Tremping" is not what it used to be in Israel. **Women are strongly advised not to hitchhike alone.**

The incidence of sexual harassment and assault has increased dramatically in recent years—so much so that female members of the armed forces are forbidden to hitchhike. The *intifada* has also made hitchhiking a dangerous proposition for everyone.

Male soldiers still hitch, and they have priority at the marked spots for hitchhikers on main roads and near bus stops. License plates carry meaning here; yellow is Israeli, black with a ‫צ‬ is army, and blue is occupied territories. Hitchhiking in the Negev or Golan (where the only option is sometimes military vehicles) runs the risk of getting a ride that doesn't go all the way to your destination, leaving you stranded and fried. One final danger: Sticking your thumb out *Let's Go* style when hitchhiking is equivalent to the American raised middle finger; veteran hikers instead point to the side of the road with the index finger.

Hiking and Biking

Israel's most splendid scenery is often accessible only by foot. **Neot HaKikar** and the **Society for the Protection of Nature in Israel (SPNI)** can provide a wealth of hiking suggestions (see the General Introduction). In general, remember that high altitudes coupled with strong rays may make midday hiking unsafe; consult the SPNI for advice. Cyclists should be aware that two-wheelers are an unfamiliar sight on Israeli roads, and some drivers merely see them as desirable fresh targets.

Life in Israel

Government and Politics

> *This isn't a central government, it's a circus.*
> —*Yitzhak Shamir*

Israel's government is a parliamentary democracy, the only one in the Middle East. Though there is no written constitution, a series of Acts of Parliament (1958) serves as the framework for legislation. Israelis do not vote for a candidate in the general election; instead they vote for a list of candidates from one of more than 20 political parties. The percentage of the popular vote received by a given party is then converted into a proportion of the 120 seats of the Knesset, the Israeli parliament. The party with the majority of representatives selects the prime minister.

But it's not that simple. Never in Israeli history has a party achieved a majority in a general election, which means that the parties must then scramble to form a coalition. They usually squabble and scream, cajole and concede for several weeks until agreements are reached with smaller parties. Once enough parties have banded together to form a majority, the game ends and a prime minister is selected. Under this election system the smallest parties have disproportionate clout in the balance of power. These parties exact concessions, as the largest party may need the two or three seats a minor party can provide to achieve the necessary coalition majority.

The two major parties are **Labor** (in Hebrew *Avoda*, sometimes still referred to by its old name *Ma'arakh*, the Alignment) and **Likud.** Labor's roots are in old-style Labor Zionism, and the Likud is still strongly influenced by Revisionist Zionism. Likud (until recently led by Yitzhak Shamir, who resigned in 1992) is thus the more right-wing of the two, pursuing a hard-line approach to the West Bank problem. Labor (led by Yitzhak Rabin, chief of staff in the Six-Day War and a former prime minister) tends to be left-of-center and is willing to make territorial concessions for peace. The 1984 and 1988 elections ended in ties, with the two big parties forming National Unity Governments, which were largely paralyzed by internal dissent. In 1990, Shamir formed a Likud-led government supported by king-making religious and far-right parties. But a general election in June 1992 decisively ousted Shamir and replaced him with a dovish, pragmatic Labor-led government under Prime Minister Rabin. Labor won 44 Knesset seats to Likud's 32, out of 120 total. Rabin's government includes

Foreign Minister Shimon Peres, secular Education Minister Shulamit Aloni of Meretz, scandal-ridden Interior Minister Ariyeh Deri of Shas, and the brilliant Amnon Rubenstein at Energy and Science, with Rabin serving as his own defense minister and personally looking after the peace process.

After the big two, Israeli parties run the political gamut. Arguing for territorial concessions in the peace process, religious pluralism, electoral reform, and equal rights for women is **Meretz** (12 seats), a new movement made up of three smaller parties, Ratz, Shinui, and Mapam. Meretz is Labor's main partner in the government. Orthodox Jews in Israel are represented by the **National Religious Party** (which, for the first time in Israeli history is not in the current government), **Shas** (a Sephardi party, in the government), and **United Torah Judaism.** The NRP and Shas hold six seats each, and United Torah Judaism four. On the Likud's right, popular former IDF chief of staff Rafael (Raful) Eitan's **Tzomet** quadrupled its size to take eight seats; Tzomet combines a tough stance on the territories with a Meretz-like platform on social policy. Further right, the tiny ultra-right wing **Moledet** (Homeland), led by Rehavam Ze'evi (facetiously nicknamed Gandhi) advocates "transfer" (expulsion) of Palestinians from the territories; Moledet has three seats. The 1992 elections also saw the demise of the right-wing Tehiya party. On the far left, the **Arab Democratic Party** took two seats, and **Hadash,** the Communist party, another two. One group is as yet not organized into a major party—the new immigrants (*olim*), 400,000 strong, from the late USSR and Ethiopia. A few of Israel's more unusual parties did not get enough votes for even one seat in the Knesset: **On Wheels** promised to work for better conditions for taxi drivers, and **The Law of Nature Party** argued that all of Israel's problems would be solved if everyone would do transcendental meditation.

Economy

Israel's economy has suffered a long history of instability and inflation. In the past 10 years the currency has been changed from lirot to shekelim to new shekelim (NIS) in attempts to control the devaluation of Israeli currency. The new shekel is worth one-tenth of an old one, and an old one was worth one-thousandth of a lira.

The government's support of the shekel at an artificially high value, an effort to lower inflation, collapsed in 1983. What followed was a series of devaluations in the shekel, reductions in government spending, and cutbacks in food subsidies. Israelis rushed to buy stable American dollars, and it was even suggested that U.S. dollars be used as legal tender. A new finance minister stopped government support of the shekel, and inflation consequently skyrocketed to more than 400%. Inflation hit a high of 24.3% in October 1984—an annual rate of 1260%. That same month the government implemented an austerity program. Unemployment jumped but inflation dropped to 3.7% in December as a result of a price, wage, tax, and profit freeze. When the program was diluted the following year inflation boomed back to 300%.

Social discontent grew as the standard of living waned. In June a series of strikes was held. Wages, prices, and currency exchange rates were frozen until October, and later extended through July 1986. This time the inflation-reduction methods worked. Israel recorded its first surplus on its balance-of-payments current account in 1985. This "economic miracle," however, went the way of Dukakis's, and today Israel is once again plagued by economic turmoil. The *intifada,* with its boycotts and strikes, has cut off Israel's largest export market after the U.S.—the Palestinians bought US$1 billion worth of goods every year. The *intifada* itself is costly; an estimated US$150 million has been spent in the effort to squash it. Tourism, one of Israel's leading industries and sources of foreign currency, has also been affected by the *intifada* even though most tourist areas remain completely safe. The result is increasing inflation and unemployment and vastly unpopular subsidy cuts. One consistent bonus for the economy is US$3 billion in American aid each year.

The influx of 400,000 new immigrants since 1989 has added to Israel's economic woes; consider that the current population is only five million, with 11.6% unemployment. 40% of these highly skilled *olim* are unemployed. In another complication, Arab citizens complain that they face grimmer statistics than Jewish citizens; of Israel's 915,000 Arabs, 50% live below the poverty line, and 20% are unemployed. Abroad, the United States, annoyed at Shamir's vigorous settlement policy in the occupied territories, initially rebuffed Israel's request for $10 billion in loan guarantees to house the *olim,* compounding Israel's economic problems. But Rabin's promise to curtail construction of new West Bank settlements changed President George Bush's stance, who agreed to the loan guarantees in August 1992.

Kibbutzim and Moshavim

Three percent of the Israeli population lives on kibbutzim, somewhat socialist societies where production is controlled by members. Kibbutzim are responsible for a disproportionate amount of Israel's agricultural, production, and political leadership. The kibbutzim of today hardly resemble the fiercely ideological pioneer settlements that began 70 years ago. Now most have diversified and use state-of-the-art agricultural technology; the Israelis are world leaders in desert irrigation. In addition, the passion for austerity is subsiding; kibbutzniks are now demanding the same luxuries enjoyed by other Israelis (larger living quarters, TVs, VCRs, Bart Simpson rhinestone jackets). Many kibbutz children now live with their parents, whereas just a decade or two ago nearly all lived in separate dormitories.

Today kibbutzim, like the family farm, face mounting problems. Labor shortages increase as two-thirds of younger members leave the settlements to test their skills elsewhere. In addition, debt is becoming a daunting threat; kibbutzim owe a collective US$4 billion, about US$31,000 for each kibbutznik.

Similar to kibbutzim are moshavim, which provide roughly 40% of Israel's food. Members of a moshav typically operate their own piece of land, though the marketing is often done as a collective. Some moshavim also have a crop that all members help cultivate. Moshavim do not have communal dining rooms like kibbutzim. Recently moshavim have begun to industrialize as agricultural profits decline.

The Army

Israel is proud of its army, known as Tzahal (the Hebrew acronym for Tz'va Hagana LeYisrael, Israel Defense Forces; that's IDF in English). All 18-year olds are drafted, with certain exceptions—most notably non-Druze Arabs (who may enlist if they choose but are not conscripted) and *yeshiva* students. The result is an informal and highly-motivated citizens' army, the country in khaki. Tzahal is a fact of Israeli life from 18, when youths hope to enroll in prestigious units like the paratroopers or Givatis, till age 55, when regular reserve duty (*miluim*) call-ups cease. In addition to its obvious military rationale, Tzahal serves as a melting pot to bring Israelis from disparate backgrounds together, helps to forge a sense of national identity, and even offers certain social services and benefits for soldiers.

Religion

Freedom of religion has been safeguarded by the state; in 1967, the Law for the Protection of Holy Places was passed along with the annexation of Jerusalem's sacred sites. **Jews** make up 82% of the population, **Muslims** 13.8%, **Christians** 2.5%, and **Druze** and others 1.7%. Each community operates its own religious courts, funded by the Ministry of Religion, and controls its own holy sites. All religions' days of rest are guaranteed by law.

In an electoral system where Jewish religious parties have often wielded disproportionate power, it's no surprise that there is a religious bureaucracy. But Israeli Judaism is not monolithic. The head of Jewish religious authority is the Chief Rabbinate, composed of Sephardi and Ashkenazi Chief Rabbis and the Supreme Rabbinical Courts.

Sephardic Jews are those who emigrated from North Africa, the Middle East, or the Balkans; **Ashkenazic** Jews came from Europe. Ethnic and social conflicts fester between them. **Orthodox** Jews themselves are also not a solid bloc. The vast majority of Israeli Jews are secular. Two denominations that are small but growing are the **Reform** (*mitkademet,* or Progressive) and **Conservative** (*masorati*) Jews. There are 4,175,000 Jews in Israel.

After Mecca and Medina, the most important Muslim holy sites are in Jerusalem—the Dome of the Rock and the al-Aqsa Mosque. The Qur'an tells of Muhammad's journey from Mecca to al-Aqsa (The Farthest) and up through the Seven Heavens to meet with God. There are 7000 Muslims in Israel proper.

Many Christian sects are represented in Israel, including Armenian Orthodox, Abyssinian, Anglican, Coptic (Egyptian), Greek Orthodox, Roman Catholic, and Syrian Orthodox. The nearly 130,000 Christians in Israel are mostly Christian Arabs, plus some immigrants.

Currently about 85,000 Druze reside in Israel. The friendly relations between Jews and Druze have deteriorated somewhat after the Israeli annexation of the Golan Heights. Unlike Muslims, all Druze serve in the army. The Druze have their own communal institutions and usually hold one or two Knesset seats. There is also a large **Baha'i** population in Israel. Baha'i holy sites are the Tomb of El Bab in Ḥaifa and the Tomb of Baha'u'llah near Akko.

See the General Introduction for a more detailed discussion of Religion.

Festivals and Holidays

All Jewish holidays, including *shabbat,* are officially observed. Each holiday begins at sundown on the evening preceding its calendar date and ends at sundown the next day. The holidays fall on different days each year with respect to the secular calendar because their dates are fixed according to the Jewish lunar calendar. On most holidays and the afternoon before, stores, museums, banks, and government-run offices and services close in Jewish areas.

In 1993, **Rosh HaShana,** the Jewish New Year, will be celebrated September 28-29. Soon after is **Yom Kippur** (Oct. 7), the holiest day of the year. On Yom Kippur, observant Jews fast in atonement for their sins, and Israel shuts down entirely. The mood changes to celebration later in the week with **Sukkot** (Oct. 12-19), the festival of the harvest. Open-roofed booths called *sukkot* are built and decorated with fruits and vegetables, symbolizing both the autumn harvest and the huts of the Israelites during the exodus from Egypt. October 12 and 19 are holidays in Israel. Seven days after the beginning of Sukkot falls **Simḥat Torah** (Celebration of the Law; Oct. 19), when the final chapters of Deuteronomy in the Torah are publicly read and the process immediately commences again with Genesis. Both Jerusalem and Tel Aviv host street festivals.

Ḥanuka (Dec. 20-27), the Festival of Lights, marks the victory of Jews under Yehuda HaMaccabee and the subsequent rededication of the Temple in 164 BCE. Only the first and last days are major holidays. **Purim** (March 7, March 8 in Jerusalem), rich in pageantry and skits, celebrates the Jews' salvation from the Persians in the 5th century by Queen Esther. The eight-day holiday of **Passover (Pesaḥ,** April 6-12) marks the flight of the Jews from slavery in Egypt. During the eight days of Passover Jews eat *matza* (unleavened bread) to commemorate the Israelites' hurried escape when they did not have enough time to let their bread dough rise. April 6 and 12 are holidays. Products made with regular flour and leavening agents may be hard to come by during this week in Israel's Jewish areas. **Yom HaZikaron** and **Yom Ha'Atzma'ut** (April 25 and 26, respectively) are secular holidays. The first commemorates Israeli soldiers who died in war, the second is Independence Day. **Yom Yerushalayim** (Jerusalem Day) is May 19. **Shavuot** (May 26) celebrates the giving of the Torah. The fast day of **Tisha B'Av** (July 27) commemorates the destruction of the First and Second Temples.

The most notable holiday observed in predominantly Arab areas is **Ramadan** (begins approx. February 22 in 1993), a month when the devout fast from dawn to dusk. Some restaurants close for the entire month and many close during the day. The end of Ramadan is celebrated as **Eid al-Fitr** (approx. March 24). Beginning May 31 is the four-day **Eid al-Adha,** the commemoration of Abraham's cancelled sacrifice of his son Ishmael. Muhammad's birthday **(Mawlid an-Nabi)** is another occasion for festive celebration. In the Christian quarters of Israeli cities, major holidays such as the New Year, Easter, and Christmas are celebrated on different days, according to either the Gregorian calendar (observed by Protestants and Catholics) or the Julian calendar (followed by the Greek Orthodox and Armenian churches).

Language

The contemporary Hebrew language was created from biblical Hebrew by **Eliezer Ben-Yehuda,** who compiled the first modern dictionary in the 1920s. Modern Hebrew contains elements of many other European languages; many words for which no equivalent biblical concept exists, such as *psykologia* (psychology), or *cassetta* (cassette), have been lifted almost intact from English. Most Israelis speak some English, and signs are usually written in English and Russian as well as Hebrew and Arabic, the official languages of Israel. You may want to learn a few Hebrew phrases so you won't be directed to the *otoboos* (bus) when you want the *sherutim* (restroom). Or so that you can urbanely comment that the *otoboos* smells uncannily like the *sherutim*. The best phrasebooks are the Dover publication *Say It in Hebrew* and *Berlitz Hebrew for Travelers* (both about US$5).

The appendix of this book contains a guide to the Hebrew alphabet and a list of useful Hebrew words and phrases.

Food

Some Israelis' diets are affected by the Jewish dietary laws called *kashrut*, a Hebrew word meaning proper or properly prepared. *Kashrut* (the noun; *kosher* is the adjective) forbids meat or chicken to be eaten with dairy products and prohibits the consumption of animals that don't have split hooves and chew their cud, and fish that don't have both scales and fins. Consequently, most restaurants serve either meat products or dairy. *Kashrut* also requires animals to be ritually killed according to strict guidelines (severing the jugular vein). Other Israelis, of Muslim faith, keep *halal*.

The variety of ethnic cuisines in Israel far exceeds that available in the West; restaurants run the gamut from Chinese to French, Moroccan to American, with a little Yemenite thrown in for spice. Because of the poor quality and high cost of meat, Israelis rely largely on dairy and vegetable products, especially salads and yogurts (try the sweetened fruit yogurts *Prily* or *Yogli*).

Israel's national food is undeniably falafel—pita bread stuffed with salad and deep-fried ground chickpea balls, topped with *tahina* sauce. Pizza is a close second. Hummus (mashed chickpeas, garlic, and lemon dip served with pita) is a creamy alternative, and *shwarma* (chunks of roast turkey, sometimes posing as lamb, and salad wrapped in pita) is a staple among Arabs and Sephardic Jews. *Melawah,* thin fried dough usually dipped in a watery tomato sauce, is a Yemenite specialty. The typical Israeli eats a large breakfast, returns home for a big mid-day dinner, and has a light, late supper.

Preparing your own food is quite cheap, especially during the summer months when fresh fruits and vegetables are available from kibbutz harvests in every outdoor *shuk* (market). You can buy groceries inexpensively at local *shuks,* at the neighborhood *makolet* (small grocery store), or at the Western-style supermarkets in large cities. On hot summer days street vendors sell what look like hand grenades. Not to worry—these are *sabras* (a prickly cactus fruit), and the inside is edible, although the seeds cause some people indigestion. *Sabra* is also a term for native-born Israelis; both the fruit and the people are said to be thorny on the outside, sweet on the inside.

You may want to carry a canteen filled with water lest you wind up singlehandedly subsidizing the Israeli soda industry. *Mitz tapuzim* (orange juice) and *eshkoliot* (grapefruit juice), cheaper than soda and safer than water, are sold everywhere. The two most common beers are *Maccabee,* a lager, and *Goldstar,* which is slightly stronger and cheaper. *Nesher* is a sickly sweet, non-alcoholic malt beer. If you ask for coffee with no specifications, you'll get a small cup of strong, murky Arabic coffee; if you want something resembling American coffee, ask for *nes,* or *nes kafeh,* and you'll get instant coffee. If you want it with milk, ask for it *im ḥalav.* The secret to getting brewed coffee is asking for *caffe filter.*

The Arts

Literature

The compilation of the biblical narrative was followed by the age of the Mishnah (100 BCE-700 CE) during which time *halakha* (law derived from the Bible) and *agada* (elaboration on non-legal biblical aspects) were compiled. This age also saw the growth of the *piyyut* (liturgical poem). Jewish poetry proliferated in the Middle Ages in such *oeuvres* as *Megillat Antioḥus* and *Megillat Ḥanuka.* Narrative prose of the Middle Ages focused on demonological legends.

The increasing revival of Hebrew as a secular language in the 18th century brought a drastic shift in Hebrew literature. Josef Perl and Isaac Erter parodied Ḥasidic works in their writings. In Tsarist Russia, Abraham Mapu, the first Hebrew novelist, wrote *The Hypocrite,* the first novel to portray modern Jewish social life in a fictional context. Following generations moved toward realism, often employing the more versatile language of Yiddish.

At about the turn of the 20th century, Hebrew was revived for literature by Joseph Brenner, whose hallmark was the tragic, uprooted settler. His works are remarkable not only for their continuing influence on subsequent generations of Israeli writers, but also for their searching and pessimistic depictions of social interaction between Jews and Arabs. In the 1920s and 1930s Nobel Laureate Shmuel Yosef (Shai) Agnon confronted the breakdown of cultural cohesion among modern Jews in his writings. His works include *A Guest for the Night, The Bridal Canopy,* and *Twenty-One Stories.* Leah Goldberg infused the harsh realities of life into her poetry—for example, "Tel Aviv 1935."

Just prior to the creation of the State of Israel, a new group of native Hebrew authors arose with a fresh style characterized by a concern for the landscape and the moment, exemplified by S. Yizhar's *Efrayim Returns to Alfalfa.* Beginning in the late 1950s, writers such as Amos Oz and A.B. Yehoshua began to experiment with psychological realism, allegory, and symbolism. In the 1960s new skepticism surfaced in Israeli literature. Yehoshua, for example, wrote about tensions between generations, Arabs and Jews, and Sephardim and Ashkenazim in his "Facing the Forests" and his collection of short stories *Three Days and a Child.* David Shahar has been called the Proust of Hebrew literature for his *The Palace of Shattered Vessels* set in Jerusalem in the 1930s and '40s. Ya'akov Shabtai's *Past Continuous,* about Tel Aviv in the 1970s, was perhaps the best Israeli novel of the decade.

More recently, a number of people have written fascinating accounts of their experiences in Israel. Oz's *In the Land of Israel* is a series of interviews with native Israelis and West Bank residents that documents the wide range of political sentiments; his *A Perfect Peace* is a semi-allegorical account of kibbutz life just before the Six-Day War. The poet Yehuda Amiḥai offers insight into the soul of the modern Israeli in his *Selected Poems.* Both books, as with most major Israeli works, have been translated to English. Other personal observations of Israel include Saul Bellow's *To Jerusalem and Back* and journalist Lawrence Meyer's *Israel Now.* David Grossman's *Yellow*

Wind tells of one Israeli Jew's journey to the West Bank just prior to the uprising. *The West Bank Story* by Rafik Halabi, an Israeli Druze television reporter, is an informative account. Fawaz Turki's *The Disinherited* offers a thoughtful autobiography of a Palestinian Arab, and Ze'ev Chafetz's *Heroes and Hustlers, Hard Hats and Holy Men* is a hilarious look at Israeli society and politics.

For a look backward from the modern day into the past of Jewish experience, read Nobel Laureate Elie Wiesel's *Night, Dawn,* or *Souls on Fire.* Aharon Appelfeld offers a survivor's account of the Holocaust in *The Age of Wonders* and *Badenheim 1939. Voices Within the Ark,* by Howard Schwartz and Anthony Rudolph is an anthology of 20th-century Jewish poetry, much of which derives from the Israeli experience. David Grossman's *See Under: Love* is a complicated account of coming to terms with the Holocaust.

Israel's short but tumultuous history has inspired a number of historical novels. Consider reading Ḥayim Potok's *Wanderings,* James Michener's *The Source,* and Leon Uris's *Exodus.* For a more sober textbook history of the land read Barbara Tuchman's *Bible and Sword,* which chronicles Palestine from the Bronze Age to the Balfour Declaration of 1917. The works of Solomon Grayzel are also authoritative and elegant for historical background. An account of Israeli-Arabs can be found in the dense but provocative *The Arabs in Israel* by Sabri Jiryis. Serious academic types should pick up Nadav Safran's hefty *Israel: The Embattled Ally* or Conor Cruise O'Brien's lighter *The Siege.*

The Israeli press is far livelier than the Western norm; politics is taken seriously here, and opinions are expressed vociferously. The liberal *Ha'Aretz* is the most respected daily; *Yediot Aḥronot* is more tabloid-style and the most widely-read. *The Jerusalem Post,* the only English-language daily, is generally right-wing and can be a bit spotty in its reporting, while the biweekly English-language *Jerusalem Report* offers high-quality reporting and analysis from more dovish editors. The *Post* reprints *The New York Times* "Week in Review" section each Monday.

Music

Music became an organized facet of Israeli culture after World War I, when enthusiastic amateur and professional musicians assembled chamber groups, a symphony orchestra, an opera company, and a choral society. During the 1930s with the rise of Nazism in Europe, hundreds of Jewish music teachers, students, composers, instrumentalists and singers, and thousands of music lovers, streamed into the country. This influx spurred the formation of music schools, the Palestine Symphony in 1936 (today the internationally acclaimed Israel Philharmonic Orchestra), and the formation of a radio orchestra (currently the Jerusalem Symphony Orchestra of the Israel Broadcasting Service).

These professional organizations have been joined by the Ḥaifa Symphony Orchestra, the Israel Chamber Orchestra (Tel Aviv), and, in the early 1970s, by the Israel Sinfonietta (Be'ersheva) and the Netanya Orchestra. Major choral groups include the Tel Aviv Choir (est. 1941) and the Rinat Choir (1955). Seasonal music activities from October into July include the subscription series of the major orchestras, as well as many concerts and recitals by small ensembles and individual performers. Concerts are held in such varied settings as the historic Knight's Hall in the Crusader Castle at Akko to the modern, 3000-seat Mann Auditorium in Tel Aviv.

A peculiar and singular style has been adopted by some Israeli composers as an attempt to break new classical ground. The "Mediterranean" style is informed by traditional Eastern and Western melodies, by the cantillation of ancient prayer, and by the dissonant legacy of Schönberg.

Israeli rock, at times drawing on folk, synth, Middle Eastern and European rhythms and at other times simply kicking butt, has been outstanding ever since Danny Sanderson and Kaveret invented the genre. Yehudit Ravitz, Etti Ankri, Matti Caspi, Etnix (that's אתניקס), Ḥava Albershtein, Gidi Gov, No'ar Shulayim (Juvenile Delinquents), and Mashina are favorites; Arik Einshtein and Miki Gabrielov's *On the Verge of Light* is the lyrical and witty Israeli answer to the Beatles' *White Album*. Israeli rock themes range from love to Lebanon, and lyrics are often very sophisticated. For example, Yehuda Poliker's "Hurts But Less" is about being the son of Holocaust survivors; Shlomo Artzi's "New Land" sparked controversy for its dovish take on the Arab-Israeli conflict; and Shalom Ḥanokh's "Messiah's Not Coming" expresses his despair in the face of Israel's great expectations. American, British, and Israeli groups often perform in HaYarkon Park in Tel Aviv and Sultan's Pool in Jerusalem. You've never lived till you've done air guitar to Etnix's "To the Light."

Jerusalem (Yerushalayim, al-Quds)
القدس ירושלים

Pray for the peace of Jerusalem
They shall deserve quietness that love thee
Peace be within thy walls
Calm within thy palaces

—Psalm 122: 6-7

When the sun sets over the Judean hills, the white dressed stone of Jerusalem really does turn gold, and peace seems to be within the high walls too. Sometimes it is. But don't stop praying for the peace of Jerusalem too soon; around you, three religions and two warring peoples stake claims to a single acre of land. The blinding white Jerusalem stone, by law the construction material of every building in the city, has seen more than its fair share of blood, all in the name of love for the city.

At its worst, Jerusalem is vicious. "Jerusalem," reflected Muhammad ibn Ahmad al-Muqaddasi in the 10th century, "is a golden basin filled with scorpions." At its best, it is more magnificently spiritual than perhaps any place on earth. In a weird way, this can be difficult, too; the Israeli poet Yehuda Amiḥai sighed that the "air over Jerusalem is saturated with prayers and dreams, like the air over industrial cities. It's hard to breathe."

The spiritual, religious, and nationalistic charms of Jerusalem attract all kinds of people. Ultra-Orthodox *ḥaredi* Jews, Christian pilgrims, Armenians, Palestinians, secular Israelis, Mormon missionaries, annoying American tourists, fanatics, saints, mystics, and raving lunatics exist side by side. (Figuring out which is which is a good trick.) Mayor Teddy Kollek, with his One Jerusalem Party, struggles tirelessly to hold the city together—it is his municipal government that puts up signs that say, of course, "Pray for the peace of Jerusalem."

And what will bring that peace? Prayer, to be sure; this is Jerusalem, after all. But maybe something else, too. Sitting by Jaffa Gate, Amiḥai once heard a guide telling some tourists, "You see that man with the baskets? Just right of his head there is an arch from the Roman period. Just right of his head." Amiḥai, a sensitive sort, thought to himself: "Redemption will come only if their guide tells them: 'You see that arch from the Roman period? It's not important, but next to it, left and down a bit, there sits a man who's bought fruit and vegetables for his family.'"

History

During Jerusalem's 3000 years, 18 conquerors have presided over the city. Archeological findings indicate that Jerusalem was a Canaanite city for 2000-3000 years before King David's conquest around 1400 BCE. David established Jerusalem as the capital of the Israelite kingdom, then Solomon, his son, extended the city's boundaries northward to include the present-day Temple Mount. There Solomon built the First Temple, wherein sacrificial observances were to be centralized and the Ark of the Covenant kept.

The Israelite kingdom split shortly after Solomon's death in 933 BCE. The tribes of the northern Kingdom of Israel created their own capital, while those of the south retained Jerusalem as the center of the Kingdom of Judah. Internal disunity and strife left the land of Judah vulnerable to ruinous invasions. The Babylonian army led by King Nebuchadnezzar succeeded in besieging the city and forcing its capitulation in 596 BCE. The Babylonians, like most other empires bent on world conquest, were extremely concerned with keeping Jerusalem and all of Judah disarmed and powerless. When Zedekiah instigated a rebellion ten years later, a wrathful King Nebuchadnezzar took even more drastic measures; he ordered the burning of Jerusalem's finest buildings, including the Temple, and the exile of the Jews to Babylon. In 539 BCE, though, the Babylonians succumbed to Cyrus of Persia who permitted the Jews to return from exile. Reconstruction commenced soon thereafter, and in 515 BCE the Second Temple was rededicated. But the restoration of Jerusalem was not consummated until Nehemiah, the prophet who moonlighted as Governor of Judah, rebuilt the city walls in 445 BCE.

Jerusalem enjoyed more than a century of undisturbed revival until Alexander the Great swept through in 332 BCE. The subsequent wave of Hellenization soon swamped much of the population. After a century and a half of Hellenic rule and a brief spell of Egyptian Ptolemaic control, the Seleucid Empire took Jerusalem in 198 BCE. King Antiochus IV forbade all Jewish practices, including *shabbat* observance, circumcision, and any reading of the Torah. When he installed the cult of Zeus in the temple, the "abomination of desolation," the non-Hellenized Jews revolted. The rebels, led by Yehuda HaMaccabee (derived from the ancient word for hammer) nailed the Seleucids, resanctifying the temple in 164 BCE and giving the priestly hierarchy secular power over the city. Thus began the Hasmonian dynasty, which ruled an independent Jewish nation for the next century.

The Roman general Pompey seized control of Jerusalem in 64 BCE, ushering in several centuries of Roman rule. The Romans installed Herod the Great, son of a Jewish father and Samaritan mother, to reign over what they called the Kingdom of Judea. While occupying the throne (37-4 BCE), Herod commanded the reconstruction of the temple and the creation of the well-known and partially extant Western Wall to better support the enlarged Temple Mount. In 6 CE the Romans bequeathed the governance of the province to a series of procurators, the most famous of whom was Pontius Pilate. After another sixty years, though, the Jews revolted against Rome. The Roman commander Titus crushed the revolt four years later, destroyed the temple, razed the city, and cast many Jews into slavery or exile; life in the Diaspora was thus began. After the Bar Kokhba Revolt, a second Jewish revolt named for its leader, ended in 135, the city was again destroyed by Emperor Hadrian and Jerusalem again declared off limits to the Jews.

That very year Hadrian built a new city, Aelia Capitolina, on Jerusalem's site to serve as a Roman colony. The pattern of the present-day Old City still corresponds to the plan of Hadrian's city which was to be divided into quarters by two major roads and orientated north to south. When in 331 Roman Emperor Constantine accepted and legalized Christianity, his mother Helena visited the Holy Land in order to identify and consecrate Christian sites. Subsequent Byzantine rulers devoted their energies to the construction of basilicas and churches for the glorification and celebration of the city's Christian heritage.

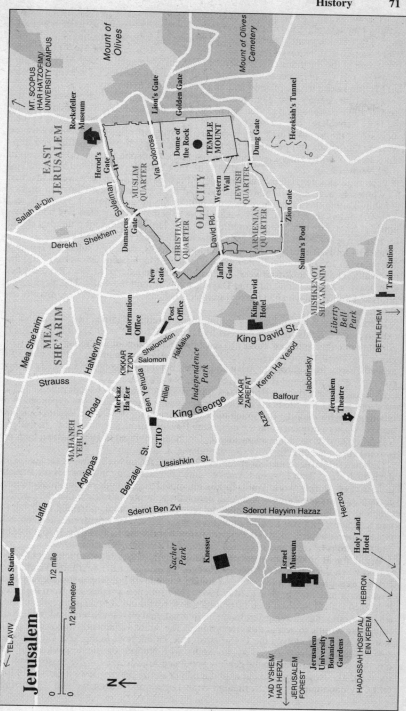

Jerusalem

← TEL AVIV

0
0
1/2 mile
1/2 kilometer

N ←

Bus Station

Mea She'arim

MEA
SHE'ARIM

Strauss

HaNevi'im

Road

Merkaz
Ha'Eer

MAHANEH
YEHUDA

Agrippas

Jaffa

Betzalel   St.

Ussishkin   St.

GTIO

Ben Yehuda

Hillel

King George

Sderot Ben Zvi

Sacher
Park

Knesset

Jerusalem
UNIVERSITY
BOTANICAL
Gardens

YAD V'SHEM/
HAR HERZL

JERUSALEM
FOREST

KIKKAR
TZION

Information
Office

Shelomzion

Salomon

HaMalka

Post
Office

Independence
Park

KIKKAR
ZAREFAT

Keren Ha Yesod

Azza

Balfour

Jabotinsky

Jerusalem
Theatre

Sderot Hayyim Hazaz

Israel
Museum

HADASSAH HOSPITAL/
EIN KEREM

Herzog

Holy Land
Hotel

HEBRON

MT. SCOPUS
(HAR HATZOFIM)/
UNIVERSITY CAMPUS

Mount of
Olives

Mount of Olives
Cemetery

Rockefeller
Museum

EAST
JERUSALEM

Salah al-Din

Derekh   Shekhem

Suleiman

Herod's
Gate

Damascus
Gate

New Gate

MUSLIM
QUARTER

CHRISTIAN
QUARTER

Via Dolorosa

Lion's Gate   Golden Gate

Dome of
the Rock   TEMPLE
MOUNT

Western
Wall

JEWISH
QUARTER

OLD CITY

ARMENIAN
QUARTER

David Rd.

Jaffa
Gate

Dung Gate

Zion Gate

Hezekiah's Tunnel

Sultan's Pool

King David
Hotel

King David St.

MISHKENOT
SHA'ANANIM

Liberty
Bell
Park

Train Station

BETHLEHEM

Following a brief period of Persian rule in the early 7th century, Jerusalem was taken in 638 CE, six years after the death of Muhammad, by the Muslim caliph Umar, who cleansed and hallowed the Temple Mount anew as a center of Muslim worship. Umar, one of the Rashidun (Rightly Guided Caliphs), personally accepted Aelia's surrender. In 691 CE his successors completed the Dome of the Rock. Under more tolerant Muslim rule, a trickle of Jews was allowed to return to the city.

In the 10th century Jerusalem fell into Egyptian hands. The Fatamid despots destroyed all synagogues and churches (around 1010, the "mad caliph" al-Hakim sacked the Holy Sephulcre), and passed on their policy of persecuting non-Muslims to their successors, the Seljuk Turks. Their rumored closing of pilgrimage routes enraged Western Christians and prompted the Crusades, a series of bloody battles and ferocious feuds over the Holy Land, culminating in the Christian capture of Jerusalem in 1099. With cries of *"Deus vult"* (God wills it), the Crusaders slaughtered Muslims and Jews as they took Jerusalem. The Crusader Kingdom lasted almost 90 years, marked by wholesale massacres of non-Christians and desecration of non-Christian sites of worship. During this time, churches were built or rebuilt and hospices, hospitals, and monastic orders founded. In 1187 Salah al-Din expelled the Crusaders and both Muslims and Jews once again began resettling the city. Jerusalem became a thriving center for Muslim scholarship from the 13th-15th centuries under the Mamluks.

In 1516 Jerusalem capitulated to the Ottoman Turks, the city's rulers for the next 400 years. In 1537 Ottoman Emperor Sulayman the Magnificent set out to rebuild the city walls. The task took four years and still the planners deviated from the older design, leaving Mount Zion and King David's tomb beyond the walls. This negligence infuriated Sulayman who had the two architects beheaded; their graves are directly inside Jaffa Gate.

In attempts to limit Turkish expansion, many foreign countries began demanding extra-territorial rights for their citizens living under Turkish rule. The world political climate forced the sultan of Turkey to issue the 1856 "Edict of Toleration" for all religions. The small, deeply religious Jewish and Christian communities in Jerusalem still needed charity from abroad to make ends meet, but the trickle of Jews and Christians coming from Europe and Russia increased to a steady flow.

Sir Moses Montefiore, a British Jew, undertook several trips to Palestine in 1854, sponsoring Jewish settlements outside the city walls. These areas soon expanded into bustling neighborhoods, the foundation of Jerusalem's New City. Resulting from heavier Western influence and the increasing flow of European immigrants, Jerusalem was designated as an independent *sanjak* (Ottoman province) in 1889, its own ruler or *(pasha)* appointed directly from Constantinople.

Ottoman rule over Jerusalem ended in 1917 when the city fell without resistance to the British army. Both Jews and Arabs resented the increasing influence of the British in Jerusalem. During World War I, Britain attempted to gain kudos by making separate declarations to both Zionists and Arab nationalists, implying to each that they would eventually gain sole sovereignty over the city. In the end, though, Britain kept Palestine for themselves as a League of Nations Mandate. Under British rule, tension between the Jewish and Arab communities heightened, bursting into violent confrontations in 1929 and 1933, and virtual civil war between 1936-1939.

World War II brought an uneasy truce between Arabs and Jews, which quickly dissolved when the war ended. Violence ravaged Palestine for the next three years. The British announced that they were no longer capable of governing the country and would terminate the Mandate in May 1948. They solicited a settlement from the newly formed United Nations; their resolution was to partition Palestine into separate Jewish and Arab states, leaving Jerusalem an international city. Jews, who had nothing to lose, were willing to accept this compromise. The Arabs vehemently rejected it.

In the war that followed the 1948 British evacuation, Jews in the New City and the Jewish Quarter were besieged by the Arabs, who blocked the single road out of the city that linked Jerusalem to the densely populated Jewish areas on the coastal plain to the west. The New City held out until the first ceasefire, but the Jewish Quarter of the Old City capitulated to the Jordanian Arab Legion after extensive and exhausting house-to-house fighting. Jordan demolished the ancient Jewish Quarter of the city and dynamited synagogues. The remaining two sectors of the city were separated by a buffer zone.

This division lasted nearly two decades. When the 1967 war broke out, Israel requested that Jordan not get involved; King Hussein attacked Jewish Jerusalem nonetheless. In the Six-Day War, Israel captured East Jerusalem from the Jordanians and regained control of the sacred Temple Mount. On the 29th of June that year Israel declared the newly unified Jerusalem its eternal capital. The Mandelbaum Gate and the walls separating the Israeli and Arab sectors were torn down. The decrepit homes in the Jewish quarter of the Old City were torn down. Following excavations, the section was extensively cleaned and rebuilt, incorporating many of the ancient architectural features. New shops were opened along the ancient Cardo market left over from Roman times. In contrast to the other sections of the Old City, the Jewish Quarter has a breezy shopping-center style polish.

The two decades following the Six-Day War also saw large scale construction outside the Old City. Neighborhoods for young Israeli-born couples as well as for new *olim* (immigrants) were built north and south of the city. The old campus of the Hebrew University on Mount Scopus, deserted since the Jordanian occupation of East Jerusalem, was also rebuilt. Intensive gardening projects blossomed throughout the city, and verdant parks encircled the old city.

The recent and constant waves of *olim,* mostly from the Soviet Union and Ethiopia, have contributed to the skyrocketing of housing prices and burgeoning homeless problem in Jerusalem and throughout Israel.

Since the beginning of the *intifada* in December 1987, East Jerusalem and the Arab sections of the Old City have on occasion been virtually shut down. Shopowners willingly or unwillingly participating in strikes work only morning hours, usually 9am-1pm, although certain events may prompt establishments to close for the entire day. Visitors should not stray too far into the City of David, nor should they wander in Arab sections at night: rock-throwing and other sporadic acts of violence are not uncommon. Jerusalem's long-time and popular mayor, **Teddy Kollek,** nonetheless envisions and works tirelessly to keep peace among the diverse communities in the fractious holy city.

Orientation

The city is known as Yerushalayim in Hebrew, and al-Quds (the Holy) in Arabic.

The old Green Line marking the pre-1967 ceasefire runs straight through Jerusalem, separating the Old City and East Jerusalem from the New City. But that fact, while of intense concern to diplomats, is an abstraction to tourists; Jerusalem is an open city today, and there is nothing to impede moving around.

The presence of the *intifada* renders East Jerusalem and parts of the Old City unsafe at times. If a demonstration erupts near you, *get away*—this is not a spectator event. The army will tear-gas tourists and protestors alike, and cameras are often impounded.

The **New City,** seat of the national government, is also the administrative and commercial center of Jerusalem. Most of the city's restaurants and services are located here, as well as virtually all of its nightlife. The New City's main street is **Jaffa Road** (Reḥov Yafo), which runs from the central bus station to the Old City's Jaffa Gate (Sha'ar Yafo). At the midway point between the two, Jerusalem's triangular downtown area (Merkaz Ha'Ir) prospers. With Jaffa Rd. as one of the sides, **King George Street** (Reḥov HaMelekh George) and **Ben-Yehuda Street** enclose the area. The corner of Ben-Yehuda and Jaffa is the site of **Zion Square** (Kikar Tzion), and on Ben-Yehuda between Jaffa and King George is a popular *midreḥov* (pedestrian mall). In the direction of the bus station between Jaffa Rd. and **Agrippas Street** you'll find the New City's chaotic open-air market, **Maḥaneh Yehuda.**

Jerusalem's most important historical and religious sites are concentrated within the walls of the **Old City,** which is still divided into the four quadrants originally laid out by the Romans in 135 CE. To get from downtown to the Old City, continue on Jaffa Rd. past the post office all the way to **Jaffa Gate.** Here you can follow the promenade along the ancient walls to the seven other gates. The main road in the Old City is **David Street,** an extension of which, **Bab as-Silsileh** (Gate of the Chain) runs to the Western Wall. The **Armenian Quarter** is to the right as you enter through Jaffa Gate and is directly accessible from Zion Gate. Left of Jaffa Gate is the **Christian Quarter,** which can also be reached straight through New Gate. Damascus Gate provides direct entry into the heavily populated **Muslim Quarter.** To get there from Jaffa Gate, turn left onto **Khan az-Zeit** from David Rd. and it will be on the right. In the wake of the *intifada,* the *souk* is not the place to proclaim support for Israel or dazzle shopkeepers with your Hebrew. A right turn off David Rd. onto **HaYehudim** leads to the **Jewish Quarter** which is directly accessible via Dung Gate.

In contrast to the Old and New Cities, **East Jerusalem** is almost wholly Palestinian. **Suleiman Street,** in front of **Damascus Gate,** and **Salah al-Din St.** which runs out from Herod's Gate are East Jerusalem's main roads. The latter is a haven for many professional offices and stores. Two Arab bus stations serve the area, the larger of which is located on Suleiman St. between **Nablus Road** (Derekh Shkhem) and Salah al-Din. The other station, located on Nablus Road., serves routes northward. **HaNevi'im Street** (Musrada in Arabic) which, with Nablus Rd., converges at Damascus Gate, has many dry goods stores and hostels. Unlike the Old City's *souk,* which is lined with small and incongruous shops, East Jerusalem is the financial and cultural center for local Arab communities.

You can reach any section of the city by bus from the **central bus station** on Jaffa Rd (NIS2). Egged buses stop along the road outside the station entrance, and in front of Binyenei Ha'Ouma (across the street through the underpass). Only Arab buses run during *shabbat*; Egged service stops about 3:30pm on Fridays and resumes after sunset Saturday night.

#1 (Platform D): To Mea She'arim, Jaffa Gate, Mt. Zion and the Old City's Jewish Quarter.

#5, 6, 13, 18, 20, 21 (Platform A): To the New City center. Get off at the intersection of Jaffa Rd. and King George St. All but #13, 18, and 20 go to the train station.

#9 (Platform A): To the Knesset and the Israel Museum, Mt. Scopus, New City center, and Hebrew University at Givat Ram.

#13, 20, 23 (Platform A): Down Jaffa Rd., to Jaffa Gate by the Old City.

#27 (Platform A): To the New City center, Damascus Gate, and East Jerusalem. Note the broken windows.

#99, the Jerusalem Circular Line (from Jaffa Gate): 34 major tourist sights. Oy gevalt. Sun.-Thurs. at 10am, noon, 2pm, 4pm, Fri. at 10am, noon, 2pm. One loop costs NIS5. For information, tel. 24 81 44 or 24 77 83.

The tourist office usually distributes two different maps of the city: the brown Ministry of Tourism map and the pink Gabrieli map. The Gabrieli map is much more detailed, but is only occasionally available at the King George St. office. Aharon Bier's excellent map of the Old City, superimposed over an aerial photograph, gives an extremely helpful three-dimensional perspective and shows every courtyard and alley within the city walls; the map is available at the tourist office inside Jaffa Gate and at the SPNI Bookstore. For maps deluged with detail, try the Department of Surveys (1 Heshin St., around the corner from the MTIO). An excellent and detailed English bus route map is available free from the Egged Public Relations office, in the Beit Egged office building, 208 Jaffa Rd., Rm. 305 (3rd floor). (Open Sun.-Thurs. 7:30am-noon and 1-3:30pm.)

Practical Information

Government Tourist Information Office (GTIO): Main Office: 24 King George St. (tel. 75 49 10/2 or 75 48 63/4), corner of Schatz St. in the New City, in the old Knesset building. The new

Teletext TV screen provides a wealth of information for your viewing pleasure, as does the newer Golden Screen computer. **Branch office** inside Jaffa Gate in the Old City (tel. 28 22 95). Sets up short visits or meals with Israeli families. Both offices have maps, brochures, bus schedules, and a calendar of local events. Both open Sun.-Thurs. 8:30am-6pm, Fri. 8:30am-2pm (in winter, Sun.-Thurs. 8:30am-5pm, Fri. 8:30am-1pm).

Tourist Police: inside Jaffa Gate, to the right (tel. 27 32 22, ext. 33 or 34). Office open 6:30am-10pm. When closed, call police station at the Russian Compound (tel. 39 11 11). For emergencies dial 100.

Municipal Tourist Information Office (MTIO): 17 Jaffa Rd. (tel. 25 88 44) at Tzahal Sq. Although most of their literature is in Hebrew, the staff is helpful and the office uncrowded. Free Saturday walking tours (2pm). Open Sun.-Thurs. 8:30am-4:30pm, Fri. 8:30am-1pm.

Christian Information Center: Inside Jaffa Gate and to the right, just past the Citadel (tel. 27 26 92; mailing address P.O. Box 14308). Provides meticulously detailed lists of Christian services, hospices, and sites in Jerusalem. Sells books on religion and archeology (US$3). Call or write to reserve tickets to midnight Mass in Bethlehem. Open Mon.-Fri. 8:30am-12:30pm and 3-6pm, Sat. 8:30am-12:30pm; in winter Mon.-Fri. 8:30am-12:30pm and 3-5:30pm, Sat. 8:30am-12:30pm.

Franciscan Pilgrims Office: Same building as Christian Information Center (tel. 27 26 97; mailing address P.O. Box 186). Makes reservations for Mass at all Franciscan sanctuaries. Pilgrimage certificates available (US$3). Open Mon.-Fri. 8:30am-noon and 3:30-5:45pm, Sat. 8:30am-noon; in winter Mon.-Sat. 8:30am-noon and 3:30-5:30pm.

Heritage House Jewish Information Office: 5 Tiferet Yisrael St., Jewish Quarter (tel. 28 00 61, evenings 27 22 24), off the main square. Meir Schuster's staff is eager to place Jewish travelers in the Heritage House Hostel (see Accommodations) and provide information about short and long term study programs, Jewish museums, art, and culture. Offers a free tour of the Jewish Quarter (Sun.-Thurs. at 11:55am). The office makes dinner arrangements for *shabbat*. Open Sun.-Thurs. 10am-4pm, Fri. 10am-2pm.

Jewish Student Information Center: 5 Beit El, Jewish Quarter (tel. 28 83 38 or the omnipresent Jeff Seidel's 24-hr. answering service, 53 21 31 ext. 1792), across from the Ḥurva Arch. A myriad of free services for Jewish travelers, including light refreshments, accommodations, *shabbat* dinner arrangements, a library, and tours Sun.-Tues. and Thurs. at 3pm, and Sat. to be announced in the near future. Nightly movies and seminars. Can be persistent. Open Sun.-Thurs. 9am-midnight, Fri. 9am until 2 hrs. before *shabbat;* in winter, Sun.-Thurs. 9am-7pm, Fri. 9am until 2 hrs. before *shabbat.*

Torah Outreach Program, Jewish Information Office: 54 Ḥabad St., Jewish Quarter (tel. 28 89 68). An extensive collection of videos (in English) on Zionist issues and a library, both free. Introductory Torah lessons Tuesdays at 10am. Call for information on current Torah classes. Open Sun.-Thurs. 9am-6:30pm, Fri. 9am-3pm.

Neot HaKikar, 36 Keren HaYesod St. (tel. 63 65 03), across from King Solomon Hotel. The first stop for information on hiking or touring in Israel and Sinai. Usually the best prices of any major company. Great guides; excellent reputation at home and abroad. Open Sun.-Thurs. 9am-6pm, Fri. 9am-12:30pm.

Society for the Protection of Nature (SPNI): 13 Helena HaMalka St. (tel. 25 23 57 or 24 46 05), the 3rd left off of Jaffa Rd. when walking towards the Old City. "Off-the-Beaten-Track" tours in Jerusalem and throughout the country (US$32-275). Guides speak excellent English; investigate their field seminars on botany and wildlife. The store sells guidebooks (including *Quartertour*), maps, and camping equipment. Open Sun.-Thurs. 9am-3:45pm, Fri. 9am-12:30pm.

Budget Travel: ISSTA, 5 Eliashar St. (tel. 22 72 57). From Jaffa Rd., turn left on Eliashar St. at the bright yellow sign 1 block from Zion Sq. toward the Old City. ISIC costs NIS25; bring proof of student status and a photo from the shop around the corner on Jaffa Rd. Services include student discounts on flights to Europe, buses and flights to Cairo, car rentals, and Eurail Passes. Lines can be long. Not always the best deal in town. Open Sun.-Thurs. 9am-1:30pm and 3-6pm, Fri. 9am-1:30pm. Also on Mt. Scopus next to the Rothberg School in the Goldsmith Building, Hebrew U. (tel. 82 61 18). Open Sun. and Tues. 9am-5:30pm, Mon., Wed.-Fri. 9am-3:30pm.

Consulates: U.S., 18 Agron St. in New City (tel. 25 32 88) and 27 Nablus Rd. in East Jerusalem. Open Mon.-Fri. 8:30-4pm, closed Israeli and U.S. holidays. Visas (open Mon.-Fri. 8:30am-noon) and passports (open Mon.-Thurs. 8:30am-noon and 1:30-3pm, Fri. 8:30am-noon) should be obtained in the office on 27 Nablus Rd. **U.K.,** 19 Nashashibi St. (tel. 82 82 81), near Shaikh Jarrah in East Jerusalem. Open Mon.-Fri. 8am-noon. No **New Zealand** embassy in Israel.

Banks: Bank Leumi, main office on 21 Jaffa Rd. (tel. 25 74 71), next to the post office. Open Sun., Tues., and Thurs. 8:30am-12:30pm and 4-5:30pm, Mon. 8:30am-1:30pm, Wed. 8:30am-

12:30pm, and Fri. 8:30am-noon. **Bank HaPoalim** (tel. 20 70 70), 1 Kikar Tzion. Open Sun., Tues., and Thurs. 8:30am-12:30pm and 4-6pm, Mon. and Wed. 8:30am-12:30pm, Fri. 8:30am-noon. **First International** (tel. 75 68 88), 10 Hillel St. Open Sun., Tues. and Thurs. 8:30am-2pm, Mon.-Wed. 8:30am-2pm and 4-7pm, Fri. 8:30am-2pm.

American Express: Meditrad, Ltd., 27 King George St. (tel. 25 22 11), near Ben-Yehuda St. Mail held and personal checks approved for cardholders. Sells, replaces, refunds traveler's checks. AmEx card replacement. Open Sun.-Thurs. 9am-5pm.

Post Office: 23 Jaffa Rd. (tel. 29 08 98). Open Sun.-Thurs., 7am-7pm, Fri. 7am-noon. **Poste Restante** here. Express mail goes out every day at 5pm. **Telegrams** in the main building or dial 171. First 7 words NIS17.30, NIS0.85 each additional word. **Fax** service also available here (open 24 hrs). **Parcel Service** (tel. 29 09 15), around the building to the right. Open Sun., Tues., and Thurs. 8am-12:30pm and 3:30-6pm, Mon. and Wed. 8am-1:30pm, Fri. 8am-noon. Special rates for books. Keep boxes open to be searched; bring along tape to seal them. **Branch post offices** throughout the city (ask for the DO-ar).

International Telephones: Bezek, 1 Koresh St. (tel. 188), in back of the post office. Open Sun.-Thurs. 8am-9pm, Fri. 8am-2pm. Payment in shekels only. For collect calls from a pay phone dial 188. **Telephone code:** 02.

Flight information: tel. (03) 971 24 84. For daily arrival information call 38 11 11 in Jerusalem. **El Al** has an advance check-in procedure in Jerusalem: bags for morning flights can be checked in and inspected the night before at Center 1, 49 Yirmiyahu St. (tel. 24 67 25), corner of Jaffa Rd. (open Sun.-Thurs. 1-10pm, Sat. one hour after sunset until 10pm). For El Al information, reservations, and flight confirmation, call tel. 24 67 25 (7:30am-11:30pm) or stop by the office at 12 Hillel St. (open Sun.-Thurs. 8:30am-4:45pm). Buses to **Ben-Gurion Airport** leave from the central bus station, but for early morning flights you may want to pay extra for a *sherut*. (See below).

Train Station: Remez Sq. (tel. 73 37 64), just southwest of the Old City at the southern end of King David St. From downtown, take bus #5, 6, or 8. Two trains per day to Tel Aviv (8am and 4pm) NIS6.50, students NIS5. Slower than buses but a bit cheaper and gorgeous scenery.

Egged Central Bus Station: Jaffa Rd. (tel. 30 47 04), west of the city center. General information, posted lists of destinations and fares, and ticket windows to the right as you enter. Staff speaks limited English. 10% discount with ISIC and passport. To: Tel Aviv (every 10 min., 5:50am-midnight, Fri. 5:50am until 2hr. before *shabbat*, Sat. after *shabbat* until midnight; NIS9); Ḥaifa (roughly every 20min. until 8pm, Fri. 7:30am-3.5hr. before *shabbat*, Sat. after *shabbat* until 10:30am; NIS16.50); Ben-Gurion Airport (every 30min. 6am-8pm, Fri. 6am-3.5 hours before *shabbat*, Sat. 8:40pm, 9pm, 9:30pm, 10:30pm; NIS9); Eilat (Sun.-Thurs. at 7am, 10:30am, 2pm, 5pm, and 12:30am; Fri. at 7am, 10am, and 1pm; NIS28, round trip NIS50; book in advance); and Be'ersheva (every 30min. 6am-8:30pm, NIS14). **Baggage check** across the street, NIS4 per item per day. Open Sun.-Thurs. 7am-5pm, Fri. 7am-3pm.

Arab Bus Stations: Suleiman St. Station, in East Jerusalem between Herod's and Damascus Gates, serves routes south. Bus #23 to Hebron (every 10min. until 8pm, NIS1.50), #22 to Bethlehem (every 15min. until 7pm, NIS1.50), #28 to Jericho (every 20min., NIS1.80), and #36 to Bethany (every 30min., NIS1). **Nablus Rd. Station** serves points north. Bus #18 to Ramallah (NIS1), #23 to Nablus (NIS2.50). On Sat., Arab buses go up Nablus Rd. to Mt. Scopus, and down Hebron and Bethlehem Rd. to the train station, Talpiyot, and Ramat Raḥel.

Taxis within Jerusalem: Jerusalem Taxi, 6 Histadrut St. (tel. 25 52 33), near the junction of King George and Ben-Yehuda St.; **David Citadel Taxi,** Jaffa Gate (tel. 28 43 34); **Ben-Yehuda Taxi,** Herbert Samuel St. (tel. 25 55 55); **HaBira,** 1 HaRav Kook St. (tel. 38 99 99), corner of Jaffa Rd.; **Kesher-Aviv,** 12 Shammai St. (tel. 22 73 66), off of Yoel Salomon St. To hail a taxi hold your arm out horizontally and point to the street. Insist upon a *moneh* (meter).

Intercity *Sherut* Taxis: Intercity rates are fixed. 2 pieces of luggage are included in the fare. **Nesher,** 21 King George St. (tel. 95 72 27 or 23 12 31) goes to Ben-Gurion Airport. Must reserve in advance and confirm the night before. Picks you up at your door (NIS24). **Parcel delivery** also available.

English Bookstores: Sefer V'Sefel, 2 Ya'Avetz St. (tel. 24 82 37), near corner of 49 Jaffa Rd.; 3rd door on the right and up the stairs. New and used books and magazines. Browse on the patio while sampling their homemade ice cream and brownies. Open Sun.-Thurs. 8am-8pm (in summer, sometimes stays open until 10pm), Fri. 8am-2:30pm, and Sat. nights 8:30-11:30pm. **Yalkut Books—New and Used,** 8 Aliash St. (tel. 25 70 58), in Kikar Raduan, upstairs from the Lev Yerushalayim Hotel. Open Sun.-Thurs. 8am-7pm, Fri. 8am-1:30pm. **Steimatzky's,** 7 Ben-Yehuda St. (tel. 25 54 87), on the *midreḥov*. New books and magazines. Open Sun.-Thurs. 8:30am-11pm, Fri. 8:30am-2:30pm, Sat. sundown-11pm.

Ticket Agencies: Ben Naim, 38 Jaffa Rd. (tel. 25 40 08); **Bimot,** 8 Shammai St. (tel. 23 40 61); and **Kla'im,** 16 Shammai St. (tel. 25 68 69). All three open Sun.-Thurs. 9am-1pm and 4-7pm, Fri. 9am-1pm.

Laundromats: Baka Washmatic, 35 Emek Refa'im St. (tel. 63 18 78). Take bus #4, 14, 18, or 24 from the city center, get off at the Emek Refa'im post office, and cross the street; it's half a block farther down. Open Sun.-Thurs. 7am-7pm, Fri. 7am-2pm. Wash, dry, and fold with large machine NIS34; with small machine NIS27.50. Last self-service loads Sun.-Thurs. 5:30pm, Fri. 12:30pm. **HaMerkaz Laundry,** 11 KK"L St. (tel. 66 42 46), just off of Ussishkin St. Open Sun.-Thurs. 8am-1pm and 3-7pm, Fri. 8am-1pm. Up to 5kg wash and dry NIS20. **Superclean Laundromat,** 16 Palmah St. (tel. 66 03 67), bus #15. Open Sun.-Thurs. 7am-7pm, Fri. 7am-2pm. Wash, dry, and fold NIS22-30.

Swimming Pools: Beit Taylor, Zangwill St. (tel. 41 43 62), in Kiryat Yovel, open daily 9am-2pm for both sexes, 2:30-7pm for women only (bus #18 or 24; NIS15). **Jerusalem Swimming Pool,** Emek Refa'im St. (tel. 63 20 92) open daily 7:30am-6pm (buses #4 or 18; NIS23). Buy tickets for *shabbat* in advance.

Film Developing: Photo Yehezkil, 47 Jaffa Rd. (tel. 25 55 90), in the alleyway opposite the Lotto booth. NIS7.30 per roll, then NIS.55 for each picture. One free enlargement with every roll. Open Sun.-Thurs. 8:30am-7pm, Fri. 8:30am-2pm. **Photo HaBira,** 91 Jaffa Rd. (tel. 23 19 15). Developing NIS8, each picture NIS.55. Open Sun.-Thurs. 8am-1pm and 4-7pm, Fri. 8am-2pm.

Help Lines: Rape Crisis Center, tel. 51 44 55. 24 hrs. English spoken. They will accompany you to the police and explain procedures. **Mental Health Hotline,** tel. 22 71 71. Called Eran-Emotional First Aid. English spoken. Assists tourists. Open 8am-11pm. When closed, Hebrew recording gives you alternate number to call. **Alcoholics Anonymous,** tel. 63 05 24 or 35 13 03.

Services for the Disabled: Yad Sarah Organization, 43 Nevi'im St. (tel. 24 42 42). Loans medical equipment to the disabled. Free, but deposit of full value required. Extraordinarily helpful. Equipment can be borrowed for one month with an option to extend for up to three months. Look for a big blue former train. Open Sun.-Thurs. 9am-5pm, Fri. 9am-noon.

Pharmacy: Super-Pharm, 5 Burla St. (tel. 63 93 21), near Hebrew U., Givat Ram campus, bus #17. Open 9am-9pm and Sat. night. Also at 3 HaHistadrut (tel. 24 62 44/5), between Ben-Yehuda and King George streets. Open Sun.-Thurs. 8:30am-10pm, Fri. 8:30am-3pm, Sat. sundown-11pm. **Alba Pharmacy,** 7 Ben-Yehuda St. (tel. 25 77 85). Open Sun.-Thurs. 8am-7pm, Fri. 8am-2pm. There are many pharmacies in the City Center area.

Medical Emergency: Tel. 101. Look for **Magen David Adom** (Israeli Red Cross) next to the central bus station or inside Dung Gate in the Old City (tel. 52 31 33). Newspapers list 24-hr. hospitals and pharmacies on duty for emergencies. Blue Cross-Blue Shield members are eligible for prepaid hospitalization at Hadassah Ein Kerem and Mt. Scopus hospitals (tel. 44 60 40 for information).

First Aid for Tourists: Bikur Holim Hospital, 74 Nevi'im St. (tel. 70 11 11), at the corner of Strauss St., the continuation of King George St. past Jaffa Rd. Open 24 hrs.

Police: For emergencies dial 100. Located in the Russian Compound (tel. 39 11 11), off Jaffa Rd. in the New City and inside Jaffa Gate to your right in the Old City (tel. 27 32 22). Information (tel. 24 61 96).

Books and Tours

Jerusalem's legends and history are best absorbed through advance reading or an extensive guided tour. The most interesting, unusual, and easy-to-follow guidebook is *Footloose in Jerusalem* (NIS31) by Sarah Fox Kaminker. For a more humorous look at the City of Gold, buy *Marty's Walking Tours of Biblical Jerusalem* (NIS8). Marty Isaacs outlines itineraries on the Mount of Olives and through the City of David. *Discovering Jerusalem* (NIS90), by Nahman Avigad, is a fascinating description of the most recent digs around the Old City; it's available in hardback only. Nitza Rosovsky's *Jerusalemwalks* (NIS40) is by far the most thoughtful guide to the city's lesser known avenues and well worth the price. David Benvenisti's *Tours in Jerusalem* (NIS23) is cheaper and has good directions. *Quartertour Walking Tour of the Jewish Quarter* (NIS5) is cheaper, more interesting, and more comprehensive than many of the books that describe guided walking tours. *Guide to the Holy Land* (US$11 at Christian Information Center), written by a Franciscan monk, describes sites of Christian significance in exhaustive detail. Architecture buffs will appreciate *The Holyland* (NIS66) by Jerome Murphy O'Connor. Finally, athletes should pick up *Carta's Jogger's Guide to Jerusalem* (NIS25). The book details runs (or long walks) amidst historic areas and sights. Most of these books are available at Steimatzky's and other bookstores throughout the city. **Hebrew Union College,** 13 King David St. (tel. 20 33 33 or 25 14 78), has an air-conditioned library with an extensive collection of books about Jerusalem. Seek in the Bible and ye shall find endless references to Jerusalem (particularly II Samuel 5, I Kings 3 and 6, II Kings 24-25, Psalms 122 and 137, and the Gospels).

Every Saturday at 10am the Jerusalem municipal government sponsors an excellent free **Shabbat Walking Tour** (for information call 22 88 44). Meet at 32 Jaffa Rd. at the entrance to the Russian Compound, near Kikar Tzion. *This Week in Jerusalem* lists the itineraries, which are also posted at the municipal information office at 17 Jaffa Rd. Tours last about three hours and can be very large. The **Society for the Protection of Nature in Israel** (see Practical Information) offers tours daily; SPNI tours usually cost US$36 for a full day of hiking in the West Bank Judean hills or NIS20 for two to three hour walks along unusual routes within the city. Some *shabbat* tours are free. Guided walking tours of Jerusalem are available through the Hostel Jasmine for NIS30. Leaving from Kikar Tzion Wed. and Sat. at 9am, the tours take about nine hours. King George "The Arc" Youth Hostel also arranges US$5 tours (for both, see Accommodations).

New City

Striking and varied in its own right, the New City of Jerusalem includes elegant, thickly gardened neighborhoods such as the German Colony and Talbieh as well as the candy-coated American-dominated Ben-Yehuda *midreḥov,* packed with tourist shops and eateries. During the day one finds most services, museums, parks, cafés and shopping to be in the New City; at night *all* of the action is here. Many places close for *shabbat* from Friday afternoon until sundown on Saturday evening, but an increasing number are opening their doors both Friday and Saturday nights until the wee hours of the morning.

Accommodations and Camping

To fully appreciate and explore Jerusalem's efflorescent nightlife you should register at a hostel with no curfew. (New dance clubs in Jerusalem's southern neighborhood of Talpiot rock until 4-5am on weekends.) Most hostels operate year-round, and, though prices do not automatically drop in the off-season, you can bargain more successfully then. Accommodations in private houses are another option. Locals may approach you at the bus station, but be aware that their places may not be licensed and thus not subject to government inspection. Women should exercise caution. As always, you save the 18% VAT if you pay in dollars.

If you'll be living in Jerusalem for over two months, consider renting an **apartment,** especially during July and August when many Israeli students are on vacation. A single room in a shared flat will cost at least US$200 per month. The best source of information is the classified section of *Kol Ha'Ir*—find someone to translate, and submit an ad of your own requesting a flat. Classified ads are free. A thorough but more expensive option is the **She'al Service,** 21 King George St. (tel. 25 69 19). This agency grants one month's access to its voluminous listings in English for NIS49 (open Sun.-Thurs. 8:30am-1pm and 4-7pm, Fri. 8:30am-noon). The bulletin boards at Hebrew University and upstairs at the Israel Center on the corner of Strauss and HaNevi'im St. may also be helpful. Not least, the "Bed and Breakfast" listings at the GTIO are a thorough and reliable source for monthly rentals.

Bernstein Youth Hostel (HI), 1 Keren HaYesod St. (tel. 22 82 86), at the corner of Agron St., near the Plaza Hotel. A 10-min. walk from downtown on King George St. from the center of town, or take bus #7, 8, 9, or 14 from the central bus station. Closed to the public for summer camp from late June until mid-August. Reading room, coffeehouse, courtyards, and an air-conditioned dining room that serves large meals. Office open 7-9am and 3pm-midnight. No check-out Sat. Curfew midnight with 20-min. grace period. No kitchen facilities, but can store small items in the hostel refrigerator. Dorm beds (4-7 per room; heating in winter) US$12-14. Breakfast included. Always call ahead.

Beit Shmuel Guest House (HI), 6 Shama St. (tel. 20 34 56/9 until 4pm). An expensive architectural jewel tucked behind Hebrew Union College on King David St. Unobstructed view of the Old City across the street. Designed by Israeli architect and Harvard Professor of Design Moshe Safdie, this relatively new hostel is remarkably hotel-like. Lounges, courtyard, member's kitchen, coffee shop, dining hall, and cafeteria, plus full use of the connected Hebrew Union College facilities: classrooms, synagogue, library, museum, and various cultural events. Wheelchair-accessible. Elevator. A/C. Reception 7am-11pm. Dorm beds US$18 (members US$15.50). Singles US$37 (members US$26.50). Doubles US$62 (members US$37). Prices drop during low season. Breakfast included.

Jerusalem Inn Youth Hostel, 6 HaHistadrut St. (tel. 25 12 94, fax 25 12 97), between King George and Ben-Yehuda St. Buses #14, 17, 31, and 32 from the central station. Ideal location and reasonable prices. Immaculate. Four-story stairway looks onto central courtyard with garden. Comfy crayon-decorated reception area has TV and drinks (NIS1.50-2.50). Use of hostel refrigerator. Wash and dry US$5. Free use of safe and luggage storage on front balcony. Outside door always locked, but can ring bell until midnight. All must be quiet in hostel after midnight, but NIS10 deposit or document gets you a key so you can come and go (quietly) as you please. Strict no-visitors rule. 24-hour heating in winter. Sun deck on roof. Exclusive deal with Underground Club gets hostel guests free admission to disco and 20% off drinks. Dorm beds US$9 (US$10 if you're only staying for one day). Singles US$24. Doubles US$28. Triples US$42. Prices lower in winter. Breakfast NIS6. Affiliated with Jerusalem Inn Guest House; get cheap eats there.

King George "The Arc" Youth Hostel, 15 King George St. (tel. 25 34 98). Take bus #14, 17, 31, or 32 to first stop on King George St. Prime location with lively atmosphere, but lacking in some of the extra amenities: bathrooms tidy but ancient and bathtubs have a grey hue. Noah and his beasties parade out of the ark and across the barroom's mural. Lounge with color TV, kitchen facilities, free luggage storage, and lockers for NIS4. Curfew 2am. Dorm beds (6-8 per room) NIS19. Private rooms (for 1 or 2) NIS78. Free tea and coffee. Sells US$5 tickets for walking tour of Jerusalem, leaving Jaffa Gate daily at 9am and 2pm (Sat. 2pm only).

Hotel Noga, 4 Bezalel St. (tel. 25 45 90 until 1pm, 66 18 88 after; ask for Kristal). Near corner of Shmuel HaNagid St. Like having a private apartment. Managers leave at night and give you a key to the front door. Bright white sheets and walls. Great location and facilities. Four airy rooms and a porch and two more rooms on ground floor; cute European furniture. Very homey. Singles (not available in July and Aug.) US$20. Doubles US$25. If you get the porch couch (bathroom attached), it's US$10 per night (less in winter). All rooms heated in winter. Definitely call ahead and make reservations.

Hotel Eretz Yisrael, 51 King George St. (tel. 24 50 71). Head away from town on King George St. and look for the big yellow sign just before the Sheraton Plaza Hotel. No meals served, no kitchen facilities, and not cheap. Run by the Barmatzes, an older couple who will not let an unmarried couple sleep together "even for a million dollars." Main attraction: immaculate, quiet old stone house in a garden of stones and cypress trees just a few blocks from the center of town. Rooms feature normal, American-style mattresses, sink, and chest of drawers. Clean bathrooms in hallway. Free tea and coffee, use of refrigerator, and luggage storage. No new guests accepted during *shabbat*. Singles US$20. Doubles US$30.

Jasmine Bed and Breakfast, 3 Even Sapir St. (tel. 25 30 32, mornings) at the corner of Bezalel St. Bus #17 from central bus station. A few blocks from the center of town in a quiet neighborhood. A bit rough around the edges, but good traveler's atmosphere. Hostel usually fills up by around 4pm in summer. Front door always locked, but everyone gets a key. Lounge has comfy chairs, books, and games; you can also sit on couches in the courtyard. Wash NIS8. Arranges tours to Masada-Dead Sea area leaving Mon., Wed., Fri. at 3am; departure from Kikar Tzion (US$31; 11-13 hours). Also offers 9-hour walking tours of Jerusalem Wed. and Sat. at 9am from Kikar Tzion. Dorm beds NIS14. One private double with toilet and shower NIS50. Breakfast served 8-10:30am (NIS5).

Hotel Merkaz Habira, 4 HaHavatzelet St. (tel. 25 40 75 or 25 57 54) 2nd floor. Across from Kikar Tzion. Large, professional hotel with tidy rooms. Lounge, TV, radio, and refrigerator. Free tea, coffee, luggage storage and use of safe. 24-hr. reception. Rooms are carpeted and have sink, mirror, and closets. Some rooms have strange built-in shower separated from the room by half-height walls only. Dorm beds (available only in July and August) US$15, singles US$22, doubles US$28 (with shower US$34). 10% off for stays over one week.

Kaplan Hotel, 1 HaHavatzelet St. (tel. 25 45 91), across from Kikar Tzion. Kitchen facilities and free tea and coffee. Also free luggage storage and use of washing machine. No curfew. Recently renovated, small rooms with wood panelling. Sparkling clean private bathrooms with showers (many of which were formerly balconies and hence have nice views if you open the windows). Singles US$35. Doubles US$45.

Ritz Hostel, 37 Jaffa Rd., same building as the Arizona disco. If all else fails, crash here. Extremely cheap, but rustic living. Dark and somewhat rickety beds; prime location for Jerusalem night living. Dorm beds NIS12, mattress on roof NIS10.

Suburbs of West Jerusalem

For a quieter, more scenic refuge, try the HI hostels in the hills surrounding Jerusalem. Lodgings listed here are 15-30 minutes by bus from the center of town.

Louis Waterman Wise Hostel (HI), 8 Pisga Rd., Bayit V'Gan (tel. 42 33 66 or 42 09 90). Take bus #18 or 20 to Mt. Herzl. A large, clean hostel with a good reputation in a safe neighborhood. Kitchen for groups only; bring your own utensils. Reception open 7-9am and 5-9pm. No curfew. Dorm beds US$15.50, nonmembers US$14. Singles US$25. Doubles US$34. Breakfast included.

Ein Kerem Youth Hostel (HI), off Ma'ayan St. (P.O. Box 17013; tel. 41 62 82). Take bus #17 to Ein Kerem, walk to the Church of St. John (the tall clock tower nearby), walk down Ma'ayan St. from the church's gate, and hike up the path past Mary's Fountain. Beautiful location and sights. (See Ein Kerem in Near Jerusalem.) Has been used as an immigrant absorption center (*merkaz klita*) and is in a bit worse shape than most HI hostels, but renovations are scheduled for 1993. Stone building in a small forest has a great view of the surrounding hills. Has a small stove, and each room has a small refrigerator. No curfew, but buses stop running around 11:45pm. Dorm beds US$9, nonmembers US$10. Breakfast US$3.50. Dinner US$6. Reservations recommended in summer.

Camping

Several well-equipped campsites around Jerusalem are convenient to the city center. They're also expensive: two-to-four person bungalows rent for NIS25-35. All have telephones and hot showers. None of the campgrounds have kitchens but all will let you use a camp stove without charge. For more details on camping throughout Israel, pick up the pamphlet "Israel Chalets and Camping" at the GTIO.

Ramat Raḥel Camping (tel. 70 25 55), 2km from central Jerusalem (bus #7; get off at the last stop). Owned by Kibbutz Ramat Raḥel. Open 7am-midnight. NIS21 (children NIS11) for tent pitch; bungalows for 2 US$38. Breakfast included. Use of kibbutz swimming pool NIS18.

Beit Zayit Camping, Har Nof (tel. 34 62 17; mailing address: M.P. Harei Yehuda), 6km west of Jerusalem. Take bus #151 (10 per day) from the central bus station to Beit Zayit, the last stop. Tell driver you want the pool. To avoid a long wait take bus #11 or 15-*alef* which leave every 15min. from in front of *Binyenei Ha'Ouma*, across from the central bus station. Ask the driver to tell you when the bus enters Har Nof and get off at the playground. Follow the signs (10-min. walk). At night avoid the trail and take bus #151. Helpful management and free use of refrigerator. Swimming pool NIS20 (children NIS15), Fri. and Sat. NIS25 (children NIS20). Camping: tent space NIS10 per person (children NIS8), Fri. and Sat. NIS20 (children NIS15). Bungalows NIS24 per person (children NIS18), Fri. and Sat. NIS30 (children NIS25).

Food

The spices, aromas, and flavors of Jerusalem's complex edibles come from the Middle East, Eastern Europe, India, China, Ethiopia, Morocco, Yemen, and Russia. For Israelis, dining out is a luxury deserving of time and money. Most eateries close Friday afternoon and reopen Saturday night after sundown, so stock up at the markets on Thursday and Friday mornings. Pick up the *Jerusalem Post* "Good Food Guide" and *Jerusalem Menus* magazine from the tourist office and ask about dinners hosted by Israeli families.

The cheapest food is sold in **Maḥaneh Yehuda,** the raucous open-air market between Jaffa Rd. and Agrippas St., to the west of the city center. Fruit and vegetable stands, pita bakeries, and sumptuous displays of pastries line the alleys, and there's a small grocery store *(makolet)* with rock-bottom prices at almost every corner. You can find pita here at 10 for NIS1.50 or less, and tomatoes at NIS1.50 per kilo. The Yemenite section (follow the alleys leading east from Maḥaneh Yehuda St.) is the cheapest for produce, and the stands along Etz HaHayim St. sell the best *halva* at NIS5 per half kilo. You can find *shishlik* vendors around the outskirts of the market, but the two cheapest and best stands are located off the intersection of Mahaneh Yehuda and Agrippas St. The most popular, **Tzion HaKatan** (47 Mahaneh Yehuda St. tel. 24 44 26) sells *shishlik* in pita with a choice of salads and chips for NIS8 (open Sun.-Thurs. 8:30am-8:30pm, Fri. 8:30am-3pm).

Visit the market at closing time (Sat.-Thurs. 7-8pm, Fri. 1-2 hrs. before sundown) when merchants lower their prices shekel by shekel to sell off the day's goods. Thursdays and Friday afternoons are wildest in Mahaneh Yehuda as thousands elbow and scramble to obtain the food they need for *shabbat*. If you don't want to spend any money, just amble through the meat market in the alleys to the west of Mahaneh Yehuda St.—a stroll among the skinned and dangling beasts may keep you fasting for days. The **supermarkets** (in the basement of HaMashbir department store at the intersection of King George and Ben-Yehuda St. (tel. 25 78 30) and on the corner of Agron and Keren HaYesod St., among others) have moderate prices on packaged foods (loaf of bread NIS1.40, hummus and salads NIS11.80 per half kilo; open Sun.-Thurs. 8am-7:30pm, Friday 8am-2:30pm).

The best quick stops are the self-service falafel stands where you can stuff your pita silly with salad. Most of these places are on King George St. between Jaffa Rd. and Ben-Yehuda, or in Mahaneh Yehuda. If you're looking for really cheap falafel, **Melekh HaFalafel V'HaShwarma** (Falafel and *Shwarma* King), on the corner of King George and Agrippas St. (tel. 35 65 23), is the place for you. A falafel costs a mere NIS2, a huge *esh-tanur* (sort of a double falafel) is NIS3, and a *shwarma* goes for NIS3.50. How does the King do it? Volume, volume, volume. (Open Sun.-Thurs. 8am-midnight, Fri. 8am-4pm.) Falafel connoisseurs should also stop by the tiny **Merkaz HaFalafel HaTeymani** at 48 Nevi'im St. (tel. 24 23 46), the first right off King George St. before it becomes Nathan Strauss if you're coming from Jaffa Rd. (falafel or hummus and salad NIS4; open Sun.-Thurs. 8am-10pm, Fri. 8am-3pm). **Moushiko's** on the *midrehov* also puts together a serious falafel. The best hummus hole is **Ta'ami,** 3 Shammai St. (tel. 25 36 44), where a serving costs only NIS5. (Open Sun.-Thurs. 8am-8:30pm, Fri. 8am-2pm.) Around the corner on Ben-Yehuda, an expensive hummus restaurant, **Shemesh** (tel. 25 24 18), also serves its tasty fare cheaply at an adjacent window called the **Shemesh Quick Bar.** Hummus in pita with salads is NIS3.50 (open Sun.-Thurs. 10am-10pm and Friday 10am-3pm).

The number-one place in Jerusalem for pizza is **Apple Pizza,** 13 Dorot Rishonim St. (tel. 25 04 67), off Ben-Yehuda. The owners are from the "Big Apple," and this is one of the only places in Israel where the pizza (regular slice NIS4) lives up to its namesake. (Open Sun.-Thurs. 8am-midnight, Fri. 8am-4pm, Sat. 8:30pm-midnight.)

For *glida* (ice cream), visit the transplanted **Ben and Jerry's** at 5 Hillel St. (tel. 24 27 67), just off King George St., not far from the tourist office. A small cone scoops NIS4.50 out of your wallet, a large cone NIS8.60. Or try **Carvel** at 16 King George St. (tel. 25 44 10), near the HaMashbir department store. A small cone here is NIS4.

Another imported delicacy is the eponymous product of **Cheese Cake,** 23 Yoel Salomon St., in a large garden café on the second floor of an old house (tel. 24 50 82). NIS9 per slice. This charming establishment features sundaes (NIS16.50), an "obscene Brownie" with ice cream, whipped cream, and chocolate sauce (NIS14.50), and the stupendous "Monster" Sundae (NIS38) with eight scoops of ice cream plus assorted toppings. Extensive sandwich and salad menu NIS10.50-28. (Open Sun.-Thurs. 7:30am-midnight, Fri. 7:30am-before *shabbat,* Sat. sundown-midnight. Kosher.) The **Magic Fruit House,** 26 Ben-Yehuda St., has an unfortunate name but concocts fantastic fresh juices on the spot. Choose from mango, fig, peach, watermelon, and many others. Fig? Regular size NIS2-3.

Some of Jerusalem's best restaurants are located on a new *midrehov* just east of Ben-Yehuda, off Jaffa Rd. **Yoel Salomon** and **Yosef Rivlin Street** comprise the area known as **Nahalat Shiv'a,** a magnificent renovation of one of the oldest neighborhoods in the New City.

The Yemenite Step, 12 Yoel Salomon St. (tel. 24 04 77). Grand stone building with high ceilings. Absolutely outstanding atmosphere and food. Try the scrumptious and very filling *melawaḥ* specialty (NIS6-8.50). Soup NIS10.50-12.50, entrees NIS10-17, "business lunch" (12-4pm) NIS14.50-20.50. Open Sun.-Thurs. noon-1am, Fri. noon-3pm, Sat. sundown-1am. Kosher.

Off the Square, 6 Yoel Salomon St. (tel. 24 25 49), off Kikar Tzion. Popular garden restaurant with huge menu. Try the pizzas (NIS19) and crepes (NIS20). Italian food and "veggie meat" cost NIS17-23. Open Sun.-Thurs. 11am-11pm, Fri. 11am-2pm, Sat. sundown-midnight. A connected deli by the same name and management offers meat entrees for NIS20-40 and a full "business lunch" (11am-4pm) for NIS25. Open Sun.-Thurs. 9:30am-11:30pm, Fri. 9:30am-3:30pm, Sat. sundown-midnight. Kosher.

Tavlin, 16 Yoel Salomon St. (tel. 24 38 47). Dairy and vegetarian fare with excellent blintzes (NIS17) and crepes (NIS21). Dine to classical music in a wood and stucco interior. Open Sun.-Thurs. 8am-12:30am, Fri. 8am-4pm, Sat. sundown-1:30am. Kosher.

Wooden Horse, 3 Yosef Rivlin St. (tel. 25 48 31) off Kikar Tzion. Low-key, boho atmosphere and fantastic food. Steaks NIS28-35, chicken NIS25, pies NIS8. Open daily 5pm-2am.

Primus, 3 Ya'avetz St. (tel. 23 49 17), off Jaffa Rd. and across from Sefer V'Sefel. Yemenite dairy restaurant-bar in a century-old stone building. 12 kinds of delicious *malawaḥ* for NIS6.5-14, 10 types of crêpes NIS13.5-17.5. Open Sun.-Thurs. noon-midnight, Fri. noon-3pm, Sat. sundown-1am. Glatt kosher.

Aluma, 8 Ya'avetz St. (tel. 25 50 14) off 49 Jaffa Rd., between Jaffa Rd. and King George St. Quiet, spacious stone veranda and botanical interior. Everything made from scratch in this crunchy natural food restaurant. Specializes in self-ground, yeastless, whole wheat sourdough bread. Try the grain of the day. Main dishes NIS14-22, all served with sourdough bread and raw vegetables. Open Sun.-Thurs. 10am-11pm, Fri. 10am-2pm, Sat. after *shabbat*-11pm. Glatt kosher.

Tikho House, off 7 HaRav Kook St. (tel. 24 41 86). Dairy and veggie restaurant set on the peaceful grounds of artist Anna Tikho's house and gallery (formerly her husband's eye clinic). Sit inside or under a yellow umbrella on the patio looking onto the splendid park below. Delicious large salads (NIS14-18), cream cheese and raisin crepes (NIS20), stuffed mushrooms, eggplants and artichokes with cheese, nuts, and rice (NIS18), and cakes (NIS8.50). Open Sun.-Thurs. 10am-11:45pm, Fri. 10am-3pm, Sat. sundown-11:45pm. Kosher. The Tikho Museum (free) is open Sun., Mon., Wed., and Thurs. 10am-5pm, Tues. 10am-10pm, Fri. 10am-2pm.

Sergey, Heleni HaMalka St. at the corner of Mounbaz St., next to Glasnost. Intellectual twenty-something and over crowd; beyond chic—they don't even wear black. Italian food. Main courses NIS12-19. Come for late-night coffee and dessert. Open 8pm-3am.

Nargila, 3 Horkenus St. (tel. 23 44 69), corner of Heleni HaMalka St. Fast-paced, crowded, but good Yemenite food whenever you crave it. Soups NIS6, kebabs NIS11-13, *malawaḥ* NIS8.50-12. Breakfast (eggs, salad, pita and butter, date honey) NIS8.90. Open 24 hrs.

Mama Mia's, 38 King George St. (tel. 24 80 80), in the former Mo'adon Tzafta. A change of pace from budget Middle Eastern eating. Occasional owner-performed serenades. Delicious fettucini NIS23, pizza NIS22-24, and great homemade ravioli NIS23-25. Open Sun.-Thurs. noon-midnight, Fri. noon-4pm, Sat. sundown-midnight. Kosher.

Kamin, 4 Rabbi Akiva St. (tel. 25 64 28), near the Jerusalem Towers hotel. A bit upscale, but you can find tuna or cold cut sandwiches for NIS12, large salads for NIS16, and soups for NIS10. More expensive are spaghetti (NIS21-22), fish (NIS27-34), and steak (NIS28). Open Sun.-Thurs. 10am-midnight, Fri. and Sat. noon-1am.

Family Restaurant-Garden, 3 HaMa'alot St. (tel. 23 42 35) on the corner of King George St., a few blocks from city center. White-pebbled garden café and air-conditioned interior. Great prices for delicious food: large selection of salads, *schnitzel*, meat-stuffed artichokes (NIS6), and peppers stuffed with rice (NIS4). Open Sun.-Thurs. 8am-10:30pm, Fri. 8am-4pm. Kosher.

Restaurant-Ḥen Jerusalem, 30 Jaffa Rd. (tel. 22 73 17), in the middle of the block (the whole block is #30). No English sign. Serves *shishlik*, kebab, and Kurdish-style steak—all delicious and quite reasonable (around NIS17). Salads (ḥummus, *taḥina,* and mixed vegetables) NIS4, with meat NIS10. Open Sun.-Thurs. 8am-6pm, Fri. 8am until one hour before *shabbat*.

B'Sograim, 45 Ussishkin St. (tel. 24 53 53), a few blocks from corner of Bazalel St. Somewhat expensive vegetarian restaurant set in an old stone mansion in a pleasant neighborhood. Enjoy dessert in the garden for only NIS7-9. Main dishes include spaghetti (NIS18), omelettes (NIS17-18), and fish (NIS30-32). Open Sun.-Thurs. 9am-12:30am, Fri. 9am-3pm, Sat. 8:30pm-12:30am.

The Promenade Café and Restaurant (tel. 73 12 86 or 73 25 13). Part of the Talpiyot promenade overlooking the Old City; take bus #8 from Jaffa Rd. Watch a riveting sunset from this place and you'll love Jerusalem for life. Café: watermelon NIS5, avocado salad NIS8. Restaurant: meat meals NIS18-28. A la carte service for dinner. Open daily 8am-midnight.

Singha Thai Restaurant, 3 Rivlin St. (tel. 23 14 55). A bit expensive, but you can say you ate Thai food in Israel. Comfortable interior with beautiful table-settings and Thai waiters. Meat meals (NIS22-23), and veggie entrees (NIS16-20). Open daily noon-midnight.

Sights

Since the first Jewish pioneers dared to move outside the protective walls of the Old City in the 1860s, the communities they established in West Jerusalem have thrived. A decree requiring that all buildings be at least faced with Jerusalem stone (dolomite limestone that is white by day, gold by night) affords the New City a certain harmony. As you explore West Jerusalem you'll discover not only impressive museums but also diverse neighborhoods—the cool, shady streets of Reḥavia, the working-class Kata-monim, the winding alleys of Naḥla'ot, and the graceful Arab mansions of Baka, the German Colony, and Talbieh.

One of the most attractive indoor sights in the New City is the **Israel Museum** (tel. 70 88 11/73). From the ticket building, walk along the shrub-lined walkway and up the steps to the main building. (A free shuttle bus makes the trip every ten minutes for disabled or elderly visitors and their escorts; the bus runs all day except 1-1:30pm.) Rock and rust enthusiasts should go straight to the **archeology** section—30,000 years of human habitation in the Fertile Crescent are recorded with an extensive collection of tools and weapons. Guided tours of the archeological galleries are given in English every Monday and Thursday at 3pm and Wednesday at 1:30pm. Straight ahead from the bottom of the steps is the ethnography exhibit, which traces Jewish Life Cycle. Guided tours of the Judaica and ethnography galleries are given Sunday and Wednes-day at 3pm and Monday at 1:30pm. Adjacent is a fascinating display of Semitic cos-tumes and an exhibit of traditional Eastern European household and kitchen paraphernalia.

The Israel Museum is also the place to be for art lovers. The museum features a sec-tion on Israeli art showing older paintings as well as the latest products of the Israeli avant-garde. Visitors will also be surprised by a fairly large collection of Impressionist and Post-Impressionist paintings as well as an entire room transplanted from the Roth-schild house in France. The new **Weisbord Pavilion** directly across from the ticket building houses a small permanent collection of Rodin sculptures and early Modern paintings. Outside, the **Billy Rose Sculpture Garden** contains the works of such mas-ters as Henry Moore and Picasso. Pick up a schedule of evening outdoor concerts at the museum, and try to visit on a Tuesday night when the garden is illuminated.

One of the museum's attractions is the **Shrine of the Book,** which displays the Dead Sea Scrolls. The shape of the building resembles, among other things, the covers of the pots in which the scrolls lay hidden for 2,000 years in the Caves of Qumran near the Dead Sea. Dating from the 2nd century BCE to 70 CE and belonging to an apoca-lyptic, monastic sect called the Essenes, some of the scrolls contain versions of the Hebrew Bible almost identical to the books that passed through the hands of countless Jewish scribes. On the bottom level of the museum is a collection of letters and relics that predate the destruction of the Second Temple and have been crucial to scholars studying that period. Guided tours of the building, shaped like a Hershey's Kiss, are offered in English on Sunday and Thursday at 1:30pm and on Tuesday at 3pm.

Take bus #9, 17, or 24 to the Israel Museum. Open Sun., Mon., Wed., and Thurs. 10am-5pm, Tues. 4pm-10pm (the Shrine opens at 10am as usual), Fri. and Sat. 10am-2pm. Guided tours in English Sun., Mon., and Wed.-Fri. at 11am, Tues. at 4:30pm. Admission to museum and Shrine NIS15, students NIS7. Student annual membership costs NIS23 and allows unlimited entrance to the Israel, Rockefeller, Tel Aviv, and Ḥaifa Museums, as well as discounts on museum programs. In the entrance lobby is a very helpful information booth with museum maps and schedules of current exhibits, special events, lectures, and tours. Specific guide pamphlets are available for NIS1 each.

If you haven't had enough, across the street from the Israel Museum is the brand new **Bible Lands Museum** (tel. 61 10 66), housing the private collection of Dr. Elie Borowski, an avid antiquities collector from Canada. It's no Israel Museum. (Open Sun. and Wed. 9:30am-9:30pm, Mon., Tues., and Thurs. 9:30am-5:30pm, Fri. 9:30am-2pm, and Sat. 11am-3pm. Buy tickets in advance. Admission NIS8, students and children NIS5.)

The **Knesset,** Israel's Parliament, is located on Eliezer Kaplan St. It is directly across the street from the Israel Museum, but you have to walk around the block (around 5 minutes) to the entrance. You must have your passport to visit this seat of Israeli government, and you may be subjected to a body search. It is worth it to see a Knesset session in progress, as the Likud and its opposition partners yell at members of Yitzhak Rabin's Labor-led coalition. The decibel level on the floor can get quite high, with blows narrowly averted. To experience Knesset *mishegahs,* come on Monday or Tuesday from 4-7pm or Wednesday from 11am-7pm. The debates are in Hebrew or Arabic. On Sunday and Thursday from 8:30am-2:30pm you can take a free tour of the building, which includes an explanation of the structure of the Israeli government and a look at the Chagall tapestry and mosaics that adorn the building. Take bus #9 or 24 (tel. 75 33 33 for information).

Yad V'Shem, meaning "a memorial and a name" (tel. 75 16 11), is the most moving of Israel's Holocaust museums. It's actually a complex of buildings. Start at the **historical museum,** which uses photographs, documents, and relics to paint a frightening and tragic picture of the events leading up to the Holocaust and of the Holocaust itself. The exhibit ends with a simple, powerful memorial: symbolic tombs upon which are written the number of Jews who were killed in each country, and finally a tiny shoe that belonged to one of the Holocaust's youngest victims. **The Hall of Names** (open Sun.-Thurs. 10am-2pm, Fri. 10am-2:30pm) contains an agonizingly long list of all known Holocaust victims. Visitors may fill out a Page of Testimony, recording the name and circumstances of death of family members killed by the Nazis. Another building houses a *ner tamid* (eternal fire) to memorialize the Holocaust's victims, with the name of each concentration camp engraved into the floor. The **art museum** nearby houses drawings and paintings made in the ghettos and in the concentration camps by Jewish prisoners; in the museum and on its grounds are a number of evocative works by sculptor Elsa Pollock. By far the most powerful part of Yad V'Shem is the stirring **Children's Memorial,** where mirrors are used to create a spark of light for every youth who perished; a recorded voice recites the name and age of each young victim. An enormous labyrinthine memorial dedicated to the **Destroyed Communities** is located in the valley below. A free guided tour is given in English Sun.-Fri. at 11am. (Open Sun.-Thurs. 9am-4:45pm, Fri. 9am-1:45pm. Free.) To get to Yad V'Shem, take buses #13, 17, 18, 20, 23, 24, or 27 and get off at the huge orange arch sculpture just past Mt. Herzl. Turn around and take a left on Ein Kerem St., then follow the signs down HaZikaron St. (about 8min. to the museum).

You'll also see signs near the bus stop for **Mount Herzl** (Har Herzl), the burial place of the founder of modern political Zionism. The **Herzl Museum** (tel. 51 11 08) encapsulates the energy of a man who made the most prominent modern articulation of Zionism, worked as a newspaper correspondent, and lobbied for the creation of a Jewish state until his death in 1904. (Open Sun.-Thurs. 9am-5pm, Fri. 9am-1pm. Free.) Ze'ev Jabotinsky is also buried here, and the tombs of Levi Eshkol, Golda Meir, and other national leaders are a short walk away in the **Israeli Military Cemetery,** resting place of soldiers. The Military Cemetery is two stops before Mount Herzl, but go to the Herzl Museum first to get a walking map.

The synagogue at the Hadassah Medical Center near Ein Kerem (tel. 77 62 71; not to be confused with Hadassah Hospital on Mt. Scopus) houses the **Chagall Windows,** which depict the 12 tribes of Israel in enchanting abstract stained-glass designs based on Genesis 49 and Deuteronomy 33. Chagall gave the windows to the hospital in 1962. When four of the windows were damaged in the 1967 war, Chagall was sent an urgent cable. He replied, "You worry about the war, I'll worry about my windows." Two years later he installed four replacements. Three of the windows contain bullet holes from the Six-Day War. Take bus #19 or 27. (Free English tours Sun.-Thurs. 8:30-2:30 on the half hour, no tour 1:30pm; Fri. every hour 9:30-11:30am. Synagogue open Sun.-Thurs. 8am-1:30pm and 2-3:45pm, Fri. 8am-12:45pm. Admission NIS4, students NIS2.)

Stained-glass window enthusiasts should not miss the fabulous **Ardon Window** in the Jewish National and University Library in Givat Ram. This is one of the two largest stained glass windows in the world; it depicts *kabbalistic* (Jewish mystical) symbols in rich, dark colors. (Open Sun.-Thurs. 9am-7pm, Fri. 9am-1pm. Library and window free.)

Colored glass and lead also decorate the almost-great **Jerusalem Great Synagogue** on King George St. (tel. 24 71 12), across from the Sheraton Plaza Hotel. The building is ornate, but it's nothing more than a very big synagogue. Dress modestly to visit (open Sun.-Fri. 9am-1pm) and stop at the **Wolfson Museum** next door, on the fourth floor of the Hekhal Shlomo building. The museum contains a large exhibit of Jewish religious and ceremonial objects and a room with dioramas of various scenes from Jewish history. (Museum open Sun.-Thurs. 9am-1pm, Fri. 9am-noon. Admission NIS2.) Services on *shabbat* (Fri. 20 min. after candle-lighting, Sat. 8am) feature a cantor and a choir.

If you take bus #2 from the city center and get off at HaSanhedrin St. (off Yam Suf St.), you'll find a park carpeted with pebbles and pine needles and the **Tombs of the Sanhedrin.** Composed of esteemed male sages and leaders, the Sanhedrin was the high court of ancient times; it ruled on grave legal matters and even reviewed the case of Jesus. Separate burial areas were designated for the corpses of the members. (Open Sun.-Fri. 9am-sunset. Free.)

The **Holyland Hotel** (tel. 43 77 77) has a scholarly and dramatic model of Jerusalem in 66 CE, the time of the Second Temple. Scaled to about one-fiftieth of the city's size, the knee-high model was reconstructed according to historical documents and contains authentic building materials. A step up from the grandeur of Graceland, the model is well done and offers a giant's eye view of a Jerusalem mostly vanished. Take bus #21 from downtown. (Open Sun.-Thurs. 8am-9pm, Fri. and Sat. 8am-5pm. Admission NIS15, students NIS10.)

Tikho House, 7 HaRav Kook St. (tel. 24 50 68), near Kikar Tzion about 2 blocks up the hill, houses numerous scenes of Jerusalem, still life paintings, landscapes, and portraits painted in watercolors or drawn in charcoal by Anna Tikho. The building that houses the late Mrs. Tikho's paintings was once her private home, as well as the renowned eye clinic of her husband Dr. Avraham Tikho. Dr. Tikho once said that he healed people's eyes so that they could see the beauty of his wife's paintings. The building also shows Dr. Tikho's large collection of menorahs, as well as a small collection of documents including his medical license and letters he received while recuperating from an Arab stabbing attack. A small library (open Sun.-Thurs. 10am-4pm, Fri. 10am-noon) has a large collection of art books. Affiliated with the Israel Museum, the building, restaurant (see Food), and spectacular gardens are well groomed and make a relaxing setting for a mid-city respite. (Open Sun., Mon., Wed., and Thurs. 10am-5pm, Tues. 10am-10pm, Fri. 10am-2pm. Free.) The **Mayer Institute for Islamic Art** (tel. 66 12 91), 2 HaPalmah St. near the Jerusalem Theater and the President's residence, displays a significant collection of miniatures, paintings, and artifacts from the Islamic world. Take bus #15 from the center of town. (Open Sun.-Thurs. 10am-5pm, Sat. 10am-1pm. Admission NIS6, students NIS4.50, under 18 NIS2.50. Buy tickets for Saturday in advance.)

Three sights in the New City document Israel's 20th-century struggles. The **Hall of Heroism** inside the Russian Compound on Jaffa Rd. (tel. 25 40 00) commemorates the work of Israel's underground movement in the pre-1948 struggle against British domination. Originally erected by Russian pilgrims, the hall was converted by the British into Jerusalem's main prison. Enter through Heshin St., just off Jaffa Rd. where it splits with Shlomzion HaMalka St. Follow the green signs that say "Museum." (Open Sun.-Thurs. 9am-3pm, Fri. 10am-1pm. Admission NIS4, students NIS3.)

The **Tourjeman Post** (tel. 28 12 78) recounts Jerusalem's history from its division in 1948 to its dramatic reunification in 1967. The building withstood severe shelling during the War of Independence and became an Israeli command post when the Jordanian border was just across the street between 1948 and 1967. Take bus #1, 11, or 27. To reach the building follow Shivtei Yisrael St. away from the Old City and turn right onto Hel Handassa St. (the continuation of Shmuel HaNavi St.). The museum will be on your right. (Open Sun.-Thurs. 9am-4pm, Fri. 9am-1pm; must arrive at least one hour before closing. Admission NIS4, students NIS3.)

Before the Six-Day War, **Ammunition Hill** (Givat HaTahmoshet; tel. 82 84 42) was Jordan's most fortified strategic position in the city, commanding much of northern Jerusalem. Taken by Israeli troops in a bloody battle, the hill now serves as a memorial to the soldiers who died in the 1967 conflict. The somber, architecturally striking museum is housed in a reconstructed bunker and gives an account of the 1967 battle. Buses #4, 9, 25, and 28 let you off at the foot of the hill. (Open Sun.-Thurs. 9am-5pm, Fri. 9am-1pm. Admission NIS4, children NIS3. Disabled access. Call in advance to arrange a guided tour in English.)

Mea She'arim ("Hundredfold," an invocation of plenty) is the world's only remaining example of the Jewish *shtetl* communities that flourished in Eastern Europe before the Holocaust. About 1000 religious Jews live here as their ancestors did, preserving with painstaking diligence traditional habits, dress, customs, and beliefs.

Although few in number, Mea She'arim's extremists are vocal and receive a good deal of publicity. The Neturei Karta, the most extreme sect of the Satmar Hasidim, oppose the Israeli state, arguing that Jewish law prohibits the legitimate existence of a Jewish country until the coming of the Messiah. One famous and recurring piece of graffiti states, "Judaism and Zionism are diametrically opposed." These views do not prevent the believers from living in Israel and accepting money and protection from the state. Their minority support has been intensely courted by the two largest parties—Labor and Likud—because the electoral system often allows the smaller religious parties to tip the political scales. The Labor government elected in 1992 is the first in many years to be able to function without their support.

Signs throughout the neighborhood read, "Daughters of Israel! The Torah requires you to dress modestly," and then proceed to explain exactly what this means. Whether or not you're Jewish, take this warning seriously; otherwise, you'll deeply offend those around you. Women should be covered to the elbow and knee and men should wear long pants. Don't fondle your loved one in this part of town, and always ask before you take photographs. Residents have been known to spit on people who don't conform strictly to their ideas of modesty.

Mea She'arim is probably the cheapest place in the world to buy Jewish books and religious items. Bargaining is the rule for religious objects; try the stores on the easternmost stretch of Mea She'arim St. The neighborhood also has some of the best bakeries in the city. Most remain open all night on Thursdays, baking *hallah* and cake for the Sabbath. The bakery at 15 Rabbenu Gershom St. (off Yehezkil St.) bakes your bubbe's *borekas* and chocolate rolls.

The neighborhoods of **Nahla'ot** and **Zikhronot,** just south of the Mahaneh Yehuda market, are also crowded and predominantly religious. Residents are mostly Sephardic Jews from Yemen, Iran, Turkey, and Morocco, and, increasingly, artists and students in search of cheap housing. The narrow, winding alleys and tiny courtyards are festooned with laundry and lined with barber shops, blacksmiths, and sandal-makers.

On the western edge of the city, the **Jerusalem Forest** is a picnicker's paradise; take bus #5, 6, 18, or 21 and get off at the Sonol gas station on Herzl Blvd. Walk in the direction the bus was traveling, and take the first right onto Yefeh Nof St. The second left, Pirhei Hen St., leads into the forest. The Jewish National Fund runs a **Plant a Tree with Your Own Hands** program among the groves. To leave a verdant token of your visit, take bus #19 or 27 to the last stop; go into the main entrance of Hadassah

Ein Kerem hospital and ask for the Tannenbaum Center where a JNF representative waits to take people to the grove in his car. A tree costs NIS24, and the representative is present Sun.-Thurs. 8:30am-3pm, Fri. 8:30am-noon; if he's not there, wait a few minutes, as he is probably out in the forest with a fellow environmentalist. You can contact the JNF at 1 Keren Kayemet St., P.O. Box 283, Jerusalem 91002. Tel. 70 74 32. Follow Pirḥei Ḥen St. to the Youth Center in the middle of the forest, then proceed along a shady path to the birthplace of John the Baptist in the village of **Ein Kerem** (see Near Jerusalem).

A walk through **Liberty Bell Park (Gan HaPa'amon)**, which contains a replica of the Liberty Bell and runs alongside Keren HaYesod St. (bus #5, 6, or 14), will take you to the restored neighborhood of **Yemin Moshe.** It was here that the English Jew, Sir Moshe Montefiore, first managed to convince a handful of residents from the Old City's overcrowded Jewish Quarter to spend occasional nights outside the city walls, thus founding the New City. To strengthen the settlers' confidence, Montefiore built **Mishkenot Sha'ananim** (Tranquil Settlement), a small compound with crenelated walls resembling those of the Old City. He also put up his famous stone windmill, inside of which is a small museum dedicated to Montefiore. (Open Sun.-Thurs. 9am-4pm, Fri. 9am-1pm. Free.)

Yemin Moshe is one of the most exclusive neighborhoods in the city and has become an artists' hub, with a number of interesting galleries. In the valley below is Sultan's Pool and the Old City is on the valley's opposite bank. Walking back through the Liberty Bell Park and up Jabotinsky St. (1 block past the La Romme Hotel), the neighborhood to the left with monumental Arab houses and abundant gardens is **Talbieh.** (Martin Buber's house is the last one on the right on Ḥovevei Tzion St., 1 block in).

The **Hebrew University of Jerusalem** has two main campuses: **Mount Scopus** and **Givat Ram.** The newer campus, at Mt. Scopus (Har HaTzofim), lies north of the Mount of Olives and is the home of both the Hebrew University and the Hadassah Hospital. Free guided tours of the campus in English depart from the Bronfman Visitors center in the Administration Building Sunday-Thursday at 11am. It's worth coming up here just to see the spectacular new **Hecht Synagogue** overlooking the Old City from the Humanities building; enter via the Sherman Building. (Call 88 38 86 for information about *davening*.) Between 1948 and 1967, Mt. Scopus was a garrisoned Israeli enclave in Jordanian territory. Its summit offers fabulous views of Jerusalem, while the university's gorgeous **amphitheater** looks east to Jordan. Once there, take advantage of the subsidized cafeterias, especially the **Frank Sinatra**—located in the **Nancy Reagan Plaza**—where you can have "lunch." (Full meals NIS7.50-9. Open Sun.-Thurs. 11:15am-4pm.) To get to Mount Scopus, take bus #4-*alef,* 9, 23, 26, or 28. Hebrew University's science campus and the **National Library** are located in **Givat Ram,** near the Knesset. A new **science museum** is scheduled to open here in 1993. Tours of the Givat Ram campus leave Sunday-Thursday at 10am from the Visitors Center in the Sherman Building. For further information call 88 28 19. Last but not least, Jerusalem's southern industrial neighborhood, **Talpiot,** offers a burgeoning selection of dance clubs which rock into the wee hours of the morning from Thursday-Saturday.

Entertainment

A popular Tel Aviv T-shirt features the banner "Jerusalem Night Life" on a plain black shirt. That's not quite fair, although for dancing you're better off in the other big city. For pubs and cafés, though, stay here. In the last few years Jerusalem's nightlife has grown dramatically. The best listings of concerts, exhibits, nightlife, and cultural activities are in *Kol Ha'Ir,* a free weekly newspaper in Hebrew. You might also read the entertainment supplement to Friday's *Jerusalem Post,* the various booklets supplied by the GTIO, and the posters lining the city streets.

The most popular night spot for Jerusalemites is the **Jerusalem Cinematheque** on Hebron Rd. in the Hinom Valley (tel 72 41 31), southwest of the Old City walls (bus #5 or 21), which screens two repertory films per day (Sat., Mon., Tues., and Thurs.

nights and Fri. afternoons). Its main attraction, though, is the avant-garde café with an uninterrupted view of the Old City—spectacular at night when spotlights illuminate the walls. The annual **Israeli Film Festival** brings a selection of fresh international films to Jerusalem and introduces local film students' pieces throughout July. Pick up the free book of listings at the Cinematheque or the Friday supplement of the *Jerusalem Post* and buy your tickets there well in advance. (Tickets about NIS14. Bring your student ID.) Jerusalem's "ordinary" **movie theaters** provide a chance to catch dated flicks that are close to becoming classics. Most are in English (or have subtitles) and star Olivia Newton John. The largest theater is the **Orion Cinema,** 13 Hillel St. (tel. 25 29 14).

Dancing

The city center's dancing scene has been whittled down to only two clubs. **The Underground,** 8 Yoel Salomon St. (tel. 25 19 18), is the more popular, featuring a bar and a Batcave-like disco area downstairs. The disco is musty with funky fluorescent graffiti on the walls, but you won't notice because of all the sweaty, semi-trashed dancers crammed in. **The Arizona,** 27 Jaffa Rd., is a drop smaller but features a cute Western-theme bar, with a buy-one-get-one-free happy hour (7:30-9pm). The Arizona's disco is a twin of the Underground's; in fact, they are only separated by one (all too thin) wall. Neither club has a cover charge, but both require purchase of one drink to get into the disco area. Both open 7:30pm-4am (depending on crowds).

The largest dancing establishments are located in Jerusalem's southern industrial neighborhood, **Talpiot,** down Hebron Rd., and on Yad Ḥarutzim St., parallel to Hebron Rd. There you'll find **HaHungar,** which can satiate literally thousands of dance-craving bodies, **Pythagoras, Ambatya, Exposé, Carlos and Charlies,** and a few smaller hideouts. Cover charges range from NIS15-25 for Friday and Saturday nights; open from about 9pm-5am. **Baraton,** a club at the top of Hebrew University's Mt. Scopus campus, has **folk dancing** on most Saturday and Wednesday nights at 7:30pm (tel. 88 26 70; bus #9 or 28); the **International Cultural Center for Youth** (ICCY), 12a Emek Refa'im St. (tel. 66 41 44), offers folk dancing Sundays and Mondays at 7:30pm (NIS8; bus #4, 14 or 18); the **House for Hebrew Youth** (Beit HaNo'ar), 105 HaRav Herzog St. (tel. 78 86 42), conducts classes on Thursdays at 8pm (bus #19); and outdoor dancing takes place in the **Liberty Bell Gardens** a bit after *shabbat* ends. Each week instructors teach new dances to Astaires of all ages—from traditional folk dances to modern jazz.

Pubs

Glasnost, 15 Heleni HaMalka St. (tel. 25 69 54), off Kikar Tzion, toward the Russian Compound. Plays jazz and funk, with occasional live bands. Sit inside large interior or outside on patio under swooping palm trees. Very, very cool. Great minds have met here. Beer NIS6-8, hard liquor NIS10-20. Also serves food: spaghetti, grilled cheese concoctions, burgers, cakes NIS12-22. Open 7pm-whenever.

Lynch Pub, 17 Jaffa Rd. (tel. 22 54 22), features live jazz, blues, TV theme music, and Brazilian music. Maccabee NIS4. Happy hour 7-9pm. Open 7pm-2am.

The Tavern Pub, 16 Rivlin St. (tel. 24 59 22), off Jaffa Rd. Jerusalem's oldest pub features videos and occasional live music. Open daily 2pm-3am or later.

Champs Pub, 5 Yoel Salomon St., right off Jaffa Rd at Kikar Tzion. Loud, crowded, and MTV-infested. Blue flourescent lights. Open daily noon-2am or later.

The Rock, 11 Yoel Salomon (tel.25 91 70), features good music and a mellow, almost romantic, candle-lit, blue flourescent lighted atmosphere. Happy hour 5-9pm. Open Sun.-Thurs. 5pm-2am, Fri. 10am-4pm, Sat. 10am-2am.

The Good Vintage Pub, 12 Yoel Salomon, attracts a crunchy crowd of Israelis and tourists. Two large-screen TVs show videos by popular request. Fri. and Sat. crowd usually starts prancing. Open Sun.-Thurs. 7pm-2am, Fri. 9:30pm-late, Sat. 8:30pm-late.

HaMirpeset (The Balcony), 59 HaNevi'im St. (tel. 25 13 69), about 1 block from King George St. Occasional live piano music and late-night jam sessions in funky wooden-floored pub. Beer

NIS5-7, hard liquor NIS12 and up. Light food also available, including "hostel platters" (fish, omelettes, and burgers) for NIS7-9, kebabs NIS5-9, and meat dishes NIS14-28. Open Sun.-Fri. 9am-2am, Sat. sundown-2am.

Cafés

Café Atara, 7 Ben-Yehuda St. (tel. 25 01 41). The original meeting place of the Hagana and Jewish writers for the *Jerusalem Post* when it was still the *Palestine Post*. Today, vintage Jerusalem intelligentsia and politicians as well as young journalists linger over coffee here during the day. Disappointing at night: just another face in the crowd of *midrehov* cafés. Try the award-winning French onion soup. Sandwiches NIS7.50-12.50. Open daily 6:30am-midnight. Kosher.

Café Ta'amon, 27 King George St. (tel. 25 49 77), corner of Hillel St. Another legendary hole in the wall; older Israeli writers and intellectuals also frequent this establishment. Owner Mordekhai Kop's book of lengthy IOUs is a veritable list of who's who is Israel. All coffee, tea, "choco," cookies, and sandwiches NIS3. Beer, brandy, and pastries NIS4.50. Open Sun.-Thurs. 6:30am-11pm, Fri. 6:30am-4pm.

Cafe Akrai, A.M. Luntz St. (tel. 25 40 01), between Jaffa Rd. and Ben-Yehuda St. It's the first café on the left coming from Jaffa Rd.; the sign is difficult to spot. Caters to young, chic Israelis. Also popular with gay men and women. Meatless menu; all food homemade. Pasta NIS15-21, sandwiches NIS13-15. Live jazz Thurs. and Fri. afternoons. Desserts NIS11-18. Danish pastries NIS5. Open daily 7:30am-2am.

The Mad Hatter Jazz Club, 6 Yosef Rivlin St. Plays mellow jazz every night. Specializes in goulash soup (NIS11). Food menu includes bacon and ham (NIS11-18). Beer NIS7-10. Open Sun.-Thurs. 8pm-3am, Fri. 9:30pm-4am, Sat. 8:30pm-4am.

HaMizraka Tea House, 12 Yoel Salomon St. (tel. 25 52 22). Serves 24 different kinds of tea (NIS6 per pot) as well as assorted snacks in a candle-lit, cushion-clad cave. Open Sun.-Thurs. 7pm-1am, Fri. and Sat. 9pm-1am.

Jan's, below the Jerusalem Theater. Light fare is delicious but somewhat expensive (NIS10 minimum). Eclectic clientele and opium den-like aura make it well worth the price. Kosher.

Jerusalem Cinematheque, Hebron Rd., directly across from the southeast walls of the Old City. Excellent pasta dishes NIS18. Open daily 11:30am-1am. (See above under Entertainment.)

Cultural Activities

The **Jerusalem Symphony** performs frequently at the plush Jerusalem Theater on David Marcus and Chopin St. (tel. 61 71 67). The theater also hosts numerous plays, dances, lectures, and concerts. Similar events are held at the Israel Museum (tel. 63 62 31), at Binyenei Ha'Ouma (tel. 25 24 81) across from the central bus station, and occasionally at both Hebrew University campuses. The Gerard Bakhar Center at 11 Bezalel St. (tel. 24 21 57), hosts a variety of concerts, including occasional Israeli folk music and jazz. **Asaf's Cave,** in the Mount Zion Cultural Center (tel. 71 68 41), near David's Tomb, stars the Diaspora Yeshiva Band; wish *shabbat* goodbye each week at 9pm (in winter 8:30pm) with Ḥasidic dancing and English, Hebrew, and Yiddish music—a unique Jerusalem experience (cover NIS20, students NIS10; call to make sure there is a performance).

Built by Ottoman Turks in the 1880s as a caravan stop, the **Ḥan** (tel. 71 82 83 or 72 17 82), across from the railway station in Remez Sq., contains an intimate theater, café, art gallery, and Jerusalem's first nightclub (open until 2am). It's rarely frequented by tourists, but its concerts and plays, some only in Hebrew, are critically acclaimed. (Egged buses #6, 7, 8, and 30 or Arab buses #21 and 22 pass by the railway station.) Seize any opportunity to attend a rock, jazz, or classical performance at **Sultan's Pool** (Brekhat HaSultan), a grassy outdoor amphitheater named for Sultan Sulayman the Magnificent, the Ottoman ruler who repaired the ancient aqueduct in 1536. The theater is open in the summer only. Tickets for American or British rock stars cost about NIS40.

Look for schedules of cultural events in the Friday *Jerusalem Post* or in *This Week in Jerusalem* or *Events in Jerusalem*, available in hotels and in the tourist offices.

Old City

Accommodations

Jerusalem's cheapest and some of its most comfortable hostels—from quiet sanctuaries to wild tourist hang-outs—are located within the Arab sector of the Old City. The views from the rooftops and balconies, not to mention the proximity to major sights, make up for the wake-up call provided by *muezzins* at the crack of dawn and by the morning hustle and bustle of the market. Lodgings cluster near Jaffa and Damascus Gates. Accommodations in the Jaffa Gate area are more accessible from the New City: Walk down Jaffa Rd. or Agron St. to the end or take bus #1, 3, 13, 19, 20, or 80. The hotels and hostels in the Damascus Gate area, in the middle of the Arab *souk*, are cheaper and livelier. If business seems slow you can bargain for a lower price. You can reach Damascus Gate by walking to the end of HaNevi'im St. or by taking bus #27. Women should exercise great care if they wander deep into the *souk*. Avoid walking alone through the Damascus Gate area after dark, and don't leave valuables and luggage unattended in Old City hotel rooms if you can avoid it. Only the busiest streets in the Old City are lit at night; learn the way back to your hostel during the day.

Near Jaffa Gate

Old City Youth Hostel (HI), 2 Bikur Holim (tel. 28 86 11). Walk down David St. into the market and follow the signs right onto St. Mark's Rd., right again across from the Lutheran Hostel, and up the narrow street with half-arches. Clean, airy, and located in a renovated hospital. Louse-free lounge and refrigerator, but the kitchen is reserved for the staff. No smoking, TV or radio on *shabbat.* Usually crowded with school groups and soldiers. Closed 9am-5pm. 11pm curfew. US$10, nonmembers US$11. Breakfast US$7.50.

Lutheran Youth Hostel, St. Mark's Rd. (tel. 28 21 20 or 89 47 35). Enter Jaffa Gate, cross the square, turn right onto al-Khattab, left onto Maronite Convent Rd., and right again at St. Mark's Rd. Spacious and spotless. Lush garden. Free lockers. Closed 9am-noon. 10:30pm curfew. Dorm beds NIS15. Doubles in guest house NIS40 per person. Breakfast included in guest house only.

Citadel Youth Hostel, 20 St. Mark's Rd. (tel. 28 62 73). Before the Lutheran Hostel on the right of the winding path. Clean bedrooms. Kitchen and TV room. The interesting (and low) architecture becomes less interesting each time you bump your head. Open 7am-midnight. Dorm beds NIS12. Doubles NIS40.

Lark Hotel, 8 Latin Patriarchate Rd. (tel. 28 36 20). Take the first left from Jaffa Gate. Compact but clean family establishment. Armenian restaurant on the first floor is run by the same family. Singles, doubles, and triples about US$15 per person; prices very flexible. Continental breakfast included.

Alice's Rush Inn Hostel, 42 St. Mark's Rd. (tel. 28 00 74), on the way to the Lutheran Hostel. Beds in crowded bedrooms with equally cramped bathrooms. Rush in for Alice's maternal demeanor. 10:30pm curfew. Dorm beds NIS10.

Jaffa Gate Youth Hostel, on an alley off al-Khattab St. at the entrance to the market; look for the sign. Cavernous, musty rooms are crowded with cots. Kitchen, fridge, TV, and showers. New bathrooms being built upstairs. Open all day. Noon checkout, midnight curfew. Dorm beds NIS12. Doubles NIS35.

New Swedish Hostel, 29 David St., straight into the *souk* from Jaffa Gate. Tidy and newly painted, if a bit cramped. Madonna poster on the door of the women's room. Stay a week and 7th night is free. Dorm beds NIS10.

Petra Hostel, (tel. 28 23 56) on your left on David St., just before you enter the *souk*. If all other beds in town are taken, this place may have room. Dorm beds NIS12. Doubles NIS30.

Near Damascus Gate

Austrian Hospice, 37 Via Dolorosa, P.O. Box 19600 (tel. 89 43 32). Just to the left of al-Wad Rd. Embassy-like. Spacious, walled grounds and spotless rooms. Wheelchair accessible. German library and excellent *aussicht* from the roof. Dorm bed and breakfast US$9. Singles US$35, doubles US$50, and triples US$69 with breakfast.

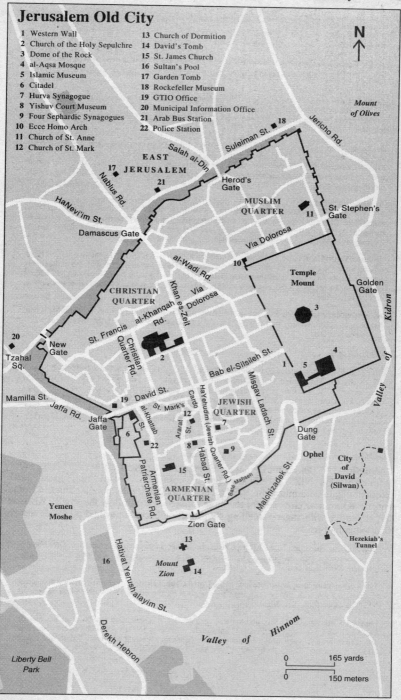

Jerusalem Old City

1 Western Wall
2 Church of the Holy Sepulchre
3 Dome of the Rock
4 al-Aqsa Mosque
5 Islamic Museum
6 Citadel
7 Hurva Synagogue
8 Yishuv Court Museum
9 Four Sephardic Synagogues
10 Ecce Homo Arch
11 Church of St. Anne
12 Church of St. Mark
13 Church of Dormition
14 David's Tomb
15 St. James Church
16 Sultan's Pool
17 Garden Tomb
18 Rockefeller Museum
19 GTIO Office
20 Municipal Information Office
21 Arab Bus Station
22 Police Station

N

Mount of Olives

EAST JERUSALEM

Salah al-Din

Suleiman St.

Jericho Rd.

Herod's Gate

MUSLIM QUARTER

St. Stephen's Gate

Nablus Rd.

HaNevi'im St.

Damascus Gate

Via Dolorosa

al-Wadi Rd.

Temple Mount

Golden Gate

CHRISTIAN QUARTER

Via Dolorosa

Khan es-Zeit

al-Khanqah Rd.

St. Francis

Christian Quarter Rd.

Valley of Kidron

Bab el-Silsileh St.

Misgav Ladach St.

New Gate

Tzahal Sq.

Mamilla St.

Jaffa Rd.

David St.

Jaffa Gate

St. Mark's St.

al-Khattab St.

Cardo

Ararat

HaYehudim (Jewish Quarter Rd.)

Habad St.

JEWISH QUARTER

Bate Mahsen

Dung Gate

Ophel

City of David (Silwan)

Armenian Patriarchate Rd.

ARMENIAN QUARTER

Malchizadek St.

Hezekiah's Tunnel

Yemen Moshe

Zion Gate

Mount Zion

Hativat Yerushalayim St.

Derekh Hebron

Valley of Hinnom

Liberty Bell Park

0   165 yards
0   150 meters

Ecce Homo Convent, Eastern Via Dolorosa, P.O. Box 19056 (tel. 28 24 45). Turn left onto Via Dolorosa from al-Wad Rd.; the small "Notre Dame de Sion" sign is down the road on the door on the left. Beds in cubicles with wooden partitions and curtains. Immaculately conceived. Study area stocked with newspapers and books. Passageway to rooms overlooks the Second Station of the Cross. Kitchen. Cleaning 10am-noon; you're encouraged to step out then. Strict 11pm curfew. Dorm beds (for women only) US$5. Small singles and doubles for men or women (but not both) US$18 per person.

Al-Ahram Hostel, al-Wad Rd. (tel. 28 09 26). Enter Damascus Gate and bear left onto al-Wad at the fork; opposite the third station of Via Dolorosa. Hot showers. Heated rooms in winter for a small fee. Midnight curfew. Roof beds NIS8. Dorm beds NIS12. Doubles with private bathroom NIS45.

Al-Arab, Khan az-Zeit Market Rd. (tel. 28 35 37). From Damascus Gate, bear right onto Khan az-Zeit; it's on the left. TV, kitchen, ping-pong. Lively debates on love, sex, politics, and war. Friendly, relaxed atmosphere compensates for peeling plaster; just don't sleep with your mouth open. Manager Abu Hassan can arrange trips to the refugee camps. 1am curfew. Roof beds NIS8. Dorm beds NIS10.

Armenian Catholic Patriarchate, al-Wad Rd. (tel. 28 42 62). Enter under the "Patriarcat Armenian Catholique" sign just after Via Dolorosa on your left, about 200m down al-Wad from Damascus Gate. Clean and appears safe: no frills. Feels like a monastery. Unmarried couples will be turned away. From 1-3pm is rest time—you may step out but cannot enter. Strict 10pm curfew. Dorm beds US$7. Double without shower US$20, with shower US$25.

Tabasco Youth Hostel and Tea Room, 8 Aqabat at-Takiyeh (tel. 28 34 61), the first left off Khan az-Zeit after Via Dolorosa as you enter from Damascus Gate. Clean, though with the outlandishly patterned floor you might think otherwise. Midnight curfew. Laundry NIS6, breakfast NIS4. Roof beds NIS6. Dorm beds NIS10, students NIS8. Singles NIS30, students NIS25. Free tea, coffee, and tabasco sauce.

Al-Hashimi, Khan az-Zeit Rd., just past al-Arab. Check-in 9-10am, 2-4pm, 7-11pm. Must read list of rules before signing in. Midnight curfew. Breakfast NIS4, dinner NIS6. Roof beds NIS8. Dorm beds NIS10.

Jewish Quarter

Heritage House, for men at 10 HaShoarim St. (tel. 27 22 24), for women at 7 HaMelekh St. (tel. 28 18 20). Kitchen, lounge, and packed bedrooms are yours free during the week and for US$7 Fri.-sundown Sat., but only if you're Jewish. *Shabbat* program includes classes and a stay with a family. For "Jews looking for the Jewish experience." Will try to accommodate groups including non-Jews, but not unaccompanied non-Jews. Expect films. Sun.-Thurs. closed 9am-5pm, midnight curfew (11pm in winter). Fri. closed 9am-3:30pm (2:30pm in winter) and 6-9pm, 11pm curfew. Sat. closed 10am-2:30pm, 11pm curfew.

Food

Abu Shukri (200m from Damascus Gate on al-Wad Rd.) still serves his legendary hummus platters (NIS5). **Linda's,** around the corner on Via Dolorosa, serves equally excellent meals (hummus plate NIS4). The daring can try the popular chicken restaurants on **Khan az-Zeit** (look for the huge rotisseries and follow the smell). Khan az-Zeit also drips with sugary-smelling shops selling honey-drenched Arab pastries for NIS3-5 per half-kg.

Abu Saif and Sons (tel. 28 68 12), just inside Jaffa Gate, beyond the tourist office. Don't be put off by the tourist-infested location. Great chicken and a wide range of spicy Middle Eastern dishes (NIS15). Open 8am-8pm.

The Coffee Shop, near Jaffa Gate next to the Christ Church Hospice. The most pristine restaurant in the Old City, with lovely Jerusalem tiles decorating the tables and walls. Salad and bread NIS9.50. Open Mon.-Sat. 10am-6pm.

Quarter Café (tel. 28 77 70), above the corner of Tiferet Yisrael and HaSho'arim St., Jewish Quarter (look for the sign overhead). Thanks to the miracle of self-service, you can eat *moussaka* and take in an epic view of the Mount of Olives without spending a fortune. Salads and cakes NIS4-7. Open Sun.-Thurs. 8am-6:30pm, Fri. 8am-3:15pm. Kosher.

Sights

Several groups offer complete tours of the Old City. **David's City of David** (tel. 52 25 68) has daily tours of the four quarters leaving at 9am and 2pm from the Citadel courtyard outside Jaffa Gate, as well as other, more specific tours. **Walking Tours, Ltd.** also offers daily tours of the Old City, leaving at the same times and from the same location as City of David tours (3-3.5hrs.; US$7, students US$5). For the same price, **Zion Walking Tours** leave at 9am, 11am, and 2pm from their Jaffa Gate office and include the ramparts walk. **Archeological Seminars Ltd.** offers a variety of tours, all preceded by short seminars, for US$13. Meet at 34 Ḥabad St., above the Cardo. GTIO has schedules for the various tour groups, as well as the monthly schedule for the free walking tours sponsored by the Jerusalem Municipality.

The Walls and the Citadel

The present walls of the Old City were built by Sulayman the Magnificent in 1542 CE. The city had been without walls since 1219, when al-Muazzan tore them down to prevent the Crusaders from seizing a fortified city. There are eight gates. The **Golden Gate** has been sealed since 1530, blocked by Muslim graves. It is thought to lie over the Closed Gate of the First Temple, the entrance through which the Messiah will purportedly pass (Ezekiel 44:1-3). The seven other gates open onto different parts of the city. **Jaffa Gate** is the most convenient entrance from the New City and is the traditional entrance for pilgrims, as there has been a gate here since 135 CE. **Damascus Gate** serves East Jerusalem, and **St. Stephen's Gate,** also called the Lion's Gate, is the beginning of the Via Dolorosa. The **Dung Gate,** first mentioned in 445 BCE by the prophet Neḥemiah, opens near the Western Wall and was given its name in medieval times because dumping dung here was considered an especially worthy act. The **Zion Gate** connects the Armenian Quarter with Mt. Zion. **Herod's Gate** stands to the east of Damascus Gate, and the **New Gate,** opened in 1889 to facilitate access to the Christian Quarter, lies to the west.

You can walk atop all parts of the wall except those surrounding the Temple Mount. In addition to the unsurpassed view of the Old City, this walk will give you an idea of the wall's military importance throughout the centuries. Clearly labelled near Jaffa Gate are slits for pouring boiling oil on attackers. You can ascend the **ramparts** (as the walkway is called) after purchasing tickets at Damascus or Jaffa Gates (tel. 23 12 21). (By the way, some people don't give Jaffa Gate the respect it deserves. Gustave Flaubert, famed author of *Madame Bovary,* recalled: "We enter through Jaffa Gate and I let a fart escape as I cross the threshold very involuntarily. I was even annoyed at bottom by this Voltaireanism of my anus." You would be too.) Each ticket is valid for unlimited admission within two days of the time stamped on your stub (three days if you buy your ticket on Friday). Once you have a ticket in hand, you don't owe a shekel to the self-appointed "guards" who might approach you along the way. Women should *never* walk alone on the walls, even during the day; cases of sexual assault have been reported—even if you can run, you can't hide. (Walls open Sat.-Thurs. 9am-4pm, Fri. 9am-2pm. Admission NIS3.50, students NIS1.70.)

To ascend the ramparts from Damascus Gate, you must go down the steps to the right before you enter the gate, walk under it, and continue through the ancient carriageway to the left of the plaza. The level of the carriageways on either side corresponds to the middle Roman period in the 2nd century CE. At the rampart entrance you can visit the **Roman Square Museum,** which is set among the excavations from Aelia Capitolina. The museum displays a copy of the 6th-century **Madaba map** from Madaba, Jordan; the map is the earliest extant blueprint of the city's layout. The huge centipede that seems to crawl from Damascus Gate at the northern tip to Dung Gate at the southern end is actually a two-dimensional rendition of the **Cardo,** the main thoroughfare; its "feet" are the Roman columns lining the street. The map has aided archeologists in concluding that the Cardo recently unearthed in the Jewish Quarter is not part of the Roman original, but a Byzantine addition. Scholars have also discovered a plaza at the gate's entrance with a statue of Hadrian mounted on a huge column. This image reveals the early origins of the Arabic name for Damascus Gate, *Bab al-Amud,* which means "Gate of the Column." The plaza has been partially uncovered, but the black marble column is missing, so you'll have to settle for the hologram on display. The stones on the floor still show the scars left by Roman chariots. (Museum open Sat.-Thurs. 9am-4pm, Fri. 9am-2pm. Admission NIS1.50, students NIS.70.)

Another place to learn about the history of the Old City is the **Citadel** complex, sometimes called **Migdal David** (the Tower of David), just inside Jaffa Gate and to the right. The citadel resembles a Lego caricature of overlapping Hasmonean, Herodian, Roman, Byzantine, Muslim, Mamluk, and Ottoman ruins—everything but ruins from David's time. The Tower of David is the highest point in the citadel and provides a superb vantage point for surveying the Holy City. The citadel hosts several exhibits, an audio-visual presentation of the city's history and cultural composition, and outdoor concerts in summer. The **Museum of the History of Jerusalem** inside the Citadel offers a high-tech and only slightly biased history of the city through a series of exhibition rooms. (Citadel open Sun.-Thurs. 10am-5pm, Fri. and Sat. 10am-2pm. Admission NIS15, students NIS12. Price includes guided tour in English Sun.-Fri. 11am.) A 45-minute **sound and light show** on the history of Israel is presented in English from April through October, Mon., Wed., and Sat. at 9:30pm. (Tel. 28 60 79; admission NIS12, students NIS10. Combined tickets NIS22, students NIS20.)

Markets

From Jaffa Gate, the quickest way to enter the Old City's markets is to descend David St. Shopkeepers peddling everything from bottled water to jewelry will badger you for a shekel. Haggle a little if you wish to buy, or continue down the slippery stone steps. It's impossible to determine whether the *souk* (*shuk* in Hebrew) smells of mint leaves, hashish, your breakfast, or the greasy cart in front of you. Nonetheless, it is an unforgettable experience.

Although all of the Old City is riddled with shops, there are several concentrated commercial thoroughfares. **David Street** (Souk al-Bazaar Rd.), and its continuation, **HaShalshelet Street** (Bab as-Silsileh St.), run from Jaffa Gate to the Temple Mount. Halfway down David St. on the left are two cavernous rooms that house a **fruit and vegetable market** called *Souk Aftimos*. Extending north from David St. to Damascus Gate is **Khan az-Zeit** and the three-laned **Armenian market.** Built atop the Roman Cardo Maximus, Khan az-Zeit also covers the Cardo's Byzantine addition, and today houses fashionable shops in the Jewish Quarter.

Al-Wad Road connects the Western Wall area to Damascus Gate. A right off al-Wad onto **Via Dolorosa** will lead to an array of small ceramics shops. **Jerusalem Pottery,** a company run by an Armenian family, supplies many shops with their wares (small ceramic tiles from NIS6). Their own shop in the market has a larger, more attractive selection of pieces that sport the company logo on the underside—when buying elsewhere, check for the logo to avoid inferior impostors. Shops also populate the tiny streets between **Christian Quarter Road** and the Church of the Holy Sepulchre.

As you wind your way through the market, look up from time to time. Much of the decorative masonry—stone set within stone over entries and passageways—is characteristic of Mamluk architecture. Paintings of the Dome of the Rock and the Ka'ba, Islam's most sacred shrine, adorn doorways. A painting of the latter signifies that a member of the family has made *hajj,* the pilgrimage to Mecca, and has been to the holy cities of Medina and Jerusalem as well. Walk down David St. from Jaffa Gate, turn right on **Souk al-Hussor,** and climb the metal staircase to your left to reach the market roofs. Although less notoriously dangerous than the Ramparts Walk, women alone should not venture much farther than the top of the staircase.

Ask around to get an idea of starting prices before shopping in the market, and *always* bargain. Merchants ordinarily start by giving you a price often several times the true value. As soon as you hear a price, knit your brow, and proclaim your own figure. Remember that you will not be able to go any lower than your first price. When the seller tells you to forget it, walk out of the store. If you are not called back, either the seller has spotted someone else or your bluff has backfired—hardly a problem since a dozen other shops are bound to sell exactly the same item. Pay in exact change to avoid last minute equivocating. Never buy drugs; dealers and informers are often one and the same. Women should avoid being coaxed into back rooms to look at a "better selection." Modestly dressed women will experience considerably less verbal harassment.

The markets also offer a uniquely Middle Eastern trinket—the elaborate water pipes (*narghila* in Arabic) shared at public coffee houses. Smoking a *narghila* (NIS1-2) is traditionally a masculine pursuit; foreign women are welcome, but should expect curious stares from the local clientele. It is customary to drink thick Arabic coffee while smoking the strong tobacco; if you don't let the coffee grinds sink to the bottom first, however, you'll get a mouthful of soot. Dilettante non-smokers will definitely get a headache. Be like Bill Clinton: try not to inhale the smoke.

The markets, especially around Damascus Gate, have often been scenes of Palestinian-Israeli tension in the past few years. The Israeli army has fired tear gas and rubber bullets into Arab markets on numerous occasions. The rubber bullets, more like lead ball bearings covered with enamel than racquet balls, are nothing to scoff at. Such incidents are also dangerous since masses of panicked people flood the small alleyways trampling over each other in an effort to flee. While such incidents have become rare, they have not disappeared. Be alert—if you sense any increased tension, leave the area immediately. Politics aside, women should be cautious in the markets.

Temple Mount (al-Haram ash-Sharif) and Western Wall (HaKotel HaMa'aravi)

In the southeastern corner of the Old City, the **Temple Mount** (al-Haram ash-Sharif in Arabic, Har Bayit in Hebrew), about the size of the Muslim Quarter, is holy to Christians, Jews, and Muslims alike. The hill is traditionally identified with the biblical Mt. Moriah, on which God asked Abraham to sacrifice his son Isaac (Genesis 22:2). The First Temple was built here by King Solomon in the middle of the 10th century BCE, and destroyed by Nebuchadnezzer in 587 BCE when the Jews were led into captivity in Babylon (I Kings 5-8, II Chronicles 2-7, II Kings 24-25). The Second Temple was built in 516 BCE, after the Jews' return from exile (Ezra 3-7). In 20 BCE, King Herod rebuilt the temple and enlarged the Mount, reinforcing it with four retaining walls. Parts of the southern, eastern, and western retaining walls still stand. Religious scholars believe that the Holy Ark was located closest to the **Western Wall,** making this wall the holiest site in Judaism.

The Second Temple is remembered by Christians as the backdrop to the Passion of Christ. Like the First Temple, it lasted only a few hundred years. In the fourth year of the Jewish Revolt (70 CE) Roman legions sacked Jerusalem and razed the Temple. Attempts to rebuild it during the Bar Kokhba revolt and during the reign of Julian the Apostate failed. Justinian built a church here, but the Temple Mount was barren until the arrival of the Muslims in the 7th century. At that time, the Umayyad Caliphs built the two Arab shrines that still dominate the Temple Mount: the holy, silver-domed **al-Aqsa Mosque** (built in 715 CE and rebuilt several times after earthquakes); and the magnificent **Dome of the Rock** (built in 691 CE). A feast for mind and eye, the complex is the third holiest Muslim site, after the Ka'ba in Mecca and the Mosque of the Prophet in Medina. According to Muslim tradition, the Dome of the Rock is the point from which God took Muhammad on his mystical Night Journey (*miraj*) into heaven (17:17). The Qur'an identifies this spot as al-Aqsa (the Farthest); the nearby mosque commemorates Muhammad's journey. The Dome of the Rock surrounds what Muslims believe was Abraham's makeshift altar where he almost sacrificed Ishmael, his son by his concubine Hagar, and not Isaac as Christians and Jews believe.

Although the dome was once solid gold, it was eventually melted down to pay the caliphs' debts. The domes of the mosques and shrines were plated with lusterless lead until the structures received aluminum caps during the restoration work done from 1958 to 1964. The golden hue on the Dome of the Rock is currently achieved with an aluminum-bronze alloy. Workers are, however, regilding the crescent at the top of the dome with 24kt. gold, and bids have been taken to extend the restoration to the entire dome. Many of the tiles covering the walls of the Dome of the Rock were affixed during the reign of Suleiman the Magnificent, who had the city walls built in the 16th century. Scrutiny will distinguish these from the tiles later pasted on by King Hussein of Jordan.

Next to the Dome of the Rock is the much smaller **Dome of the Chain,** where, according to Muslim legend, a chain hung down from heaven which could be grasped only by the righteous. Presently under renovation, the Dome of the Chain is an exact miniature of the Dome of the Rock, except for the pate, and marks the exact center of al-Haram ash-Sharif. Between the two mosques flows a *sabil* (fountain) called **al-Kas,** where Muslims must perform ablutions before prayer. Built in 709 CE, the fountain is connected to underground cisterns capable of holding 10 million gallons. The arches on the Temple Mount, according to Muslim legend, will be used to hang scales to judge the righteous. On the right as you enter the Temple Mount from the ramp is the **Islamic Museum,** filled with fantastic relics such as the huge cauldrons used for cooking food for the poor, taken from the mosques when the holy sites were restored. (Temple Mount and the museum open Sat.-Thurs. 8am-noon and 1:30-3pm. All hours subject to change during Ramadan, other Islamic holidays, and periods of unrest. Tickets to the mosques and museum available at the booth between al-Aqsa and the museum. Admission NIS13, students NIS8. Ticket booth closes at 3pm.) The Mount is also periodically closed without notice, and you might inexplicably be denied entrance. The Mount, run by the Muslim *Waqf* (religious endowment), is supervised by Arab police who speak neither English nor Hebrew, and Druze Israeli soldiers may also be posted at the entrance as an extra security measure. Dress modestly, and restrain any visible attraction to members of the opposite sex. Long gowns are provided for those who need them. Also be aware that many sections considered off-limits by the police are not marked as such. These include the walls around al-Aqsa, the area through the door to the south between al-Aqsa and the museum, and the Muslim cemetery. Once inside al-Aqsa, stay away from areas where Muslims are praying.

The 18m tall **Western Wall** (HaKotel HaMa'aravi in Hebrew) is part of the retaining wall of the Temple Mount built about 20 BCE, and was the largest section of the Temple area that remained standing after its destruction in 70 CE. It has also been tastelessly referred to as the Wailing Wall because Jews, believing that the divine presence lingers here, have visited the wall for centuries to mourn the destruction of the First and Second Temples and to tuck written prayers into its crannies. Tourists have developed the astonishingly offensive habit of taking out other people's notes and reading them; treat such heathens with contempt. The Wall can be reached by foot from Dung Gate, the Jewish Quarter, HaShalshelet St., or al-Wad Rd. (during the day). About 3m off the ground, a gray line indicates what was the surface level until 1967. About 20m of Herodian wall still lies underground. You can identify the Herodian stones by their carved frames or "dressing"; the stones that lie above were added by Byzantines, Arabs, and Turks.

Pre-1948 photos show Orthodox Jews praying at the wall in a crowded alley; after the Six-Day War, the present plaza was built as a national gathering place. Israeli paratroopers are sworn in at the Western Wall to recall its capture by the unit in 1967. Although the Western Wall is not formally a synagogue, the Ministry of Religion has decreed that all rules applying to Orthodox synagogues also apply to the Wall.

The prayer areas for men and women are separated by a screen (*meḥitza*) with the Torah scrolls kept on the men's side of recently excavated sections of the Wall. **Wilson's Arch** (named for the English archeologist who discovered it), located inside a large, arched room, was once part of a bridge that spanned Cheesemakers' Valley, allowing Jewish priests to cross from their Upper City homes to the Temple. (Women cannot enter.) A peek down the two illuminated shafts in the floor of this room gives a sense of the wall's original height. The wall continues from here through closed tunnels for over half a kilometer. Women and groups can enter the passageways through an archway to the south, near the telephones.

Bar mitzvahs—often five or six at once—occur at the Wall on Monday and Thursday mornings and involve tremendous celebration. On Friday, dancing is organized by Yeshivat HaKotel to usher in *shabbat*. Do not take photographs.

Try to visit at least once at night, when the Wall is brightly lit, the air cool, and the area quiet. The plaza has guards posted 24 hours. Underneath the Western Wall is an underground passage where Jewish radicals hid explosives in the early 1980s in a plot to destroy the Dome of the Rock. Although this tunnel is closed to the public, City of David, Archeological Seminars Ltd., Tower of David Walking Tours, and Zion Walking Tours all offer tours which include the area and other passages in Jerusalem. Check with GTIO for schedules and exact routes.

The excavations at the southern wall of the Temple Mount are known as the **Ophel** region, though "Ophel" technically refers to the hill just outside the southern wall where the City of David is located. The ongoing excavations comprise one of the most important archeological digs in the world. (Open Sun.-Thurs. 9am-5pm, Fri. 9am-3pm. Admission NIS3.50, students NIS1.70.) Scholars have uncovered 22 layers from 12 periods in the city's development. Of particular interest here are the well-preserved remains of a Byzantine home and its mosaic floor. A tunnel brings you outside the city walls to the foot of the reconstructed steps that lead to the Temple Mount. Full appreciation of the Ophel complex requires a guide. Archeological Seminars Ltd. includes the Ophel area in one of its tours. (Sun., Tues., Wed., and Fri., 9:30am; 3.5hrs.)

Jewish Quarter

The Jewish Quarter is in the southeast quadrant of the Old City, the site of the posh Upper City during the Second Temple era. The quarter extends from HaShalshelet St. (Bab as-Silsileh) in the north to the city's southern wall, and from Ararat St. in the west to the Western Wall in the east. You can reach the quarter either by climbing the stairs diagonally across from the Western Wall or by heading down David St. and turning right at the sign for the Cardo Maximus. Jews first settled in this area in the 15th century. The Jewish community grew from 2000 in 1800 to 11,000 in 1865, when Jews started to settle outside the walls. Today, about 650 families live in the Jewish Quarter.

Since the annexation of the Old City in 1967, the Jewish Quarter has been completely and impressively rebuilt, repairing the destruction from the house-to-house fighting in 1948 and deterioration during the Jordanian occupation. Archeological discoveries at every turn of the shovel slowed the rebuilding and remodeling, though city planners have worked hard to gracefully integrate the ancient remains into the stunning new neighborhood.

The **Cardo,** Jerusalem's main drag during Roman and Byzantine times, has been excavated and restored. The uncovered section is built over a Byzantine extension of Emperor Hadrian's Cardo Maximus, which ran from Damascus Gate about as far south as David St. Archeologists suspect that Justinian constructed the addition so that the Cardo would extend to the **Nea Church** (beneath Yeshivat HaKotel). Sheltered by the Cardo's vaulted roof are expensive gift shops and art galleries described on a sign as "a continuation of the existing bazaars." (Hardly.) Near the entrance to the Cardo, you can climb down to an excavated section of the Hasmonean city walls and remains of buildings from the First Temple period. Farther along the Cardo is an enlarged mosaic reproduction of the Madaba Map, the 6th-century plan of Jerusalem discovered on the floor of a Byzantine church in Jordan. After sunset the Cardo is open and illuminated until 11pm.

The **Yishuv Court Museum,** 6 Or HaHayim St. (tel. 28 46 36), exhibits glimpses of life in the Jewish Quarter before its destruction in 1948. To get here, walk up the steps at the southern end of the Cardo, cross over the Cardo on the steps to your left, and look left for the brown and tan sign pointing the way. Or turn left onto St. James St. from Armenian Patriarchate Rd. and follow the signs. (Open Sun.-Thurs. 9am-2pm. Admission NIS5, students NIS4.)

Across Jewish Quarter Rd. and on the left from the southern end of the Cardo, a single white stone arch soars above the ruins of the Hurva Synagogue. Built in 1700 by the followers of Rabbi Yehuda the Hasid, the synagogue was destroyed by Muslims 20 years later. In 1856, it was rebuilt as the National Ashkenazic Synagogue, only to be blown up by Jordan during the fighting of 1948. The **Ramban Synagogue** next door was named for Rabbi Moshe ben Naḥman ("Ramban" is an acronym for his name; he is also known as Naḥmanides). Over the years the building has served as a store, butter factory, and mosque. Displayed inside is a letter written by the rabbi describing the state of Jerusalem's Jewish community in 1267, the year he arrived from Spain. (Open for morning and evening prayers.)

The **Four Sephardic Synagogues** (the synagogue of Rabbi Yoḥanan Ben-Zakkai, that of Elijah the Prophet, the Central Synagogue, and the Istanbuli Synagogue) were built by Mediterranean Jews starting in the 16th century in accordance with a Muslim law that prohibited the construction of synagogues taller than the surrounding houses. To attain an aura of loftiness, these synagogues were paradoxically built in large chambers deep underground. The current structure, though renovated, dates from 1835. The synagogues remain the spiritual center of Jerusalem's Sephardic community, with religious services held here every morning and evening. To reach the Sephardic Synagogues, walk south on Jewish Quarter Rd. almost to the parking lot, turn left onto HaTuppim St., then left again, and walk down the stone staircase. (Open Sun., Mon., Wed., and Thurs. 9:30am-4pm, Tues. and Fri. 9:30am-12:30pm. Free.)

The ruins of the **Tiferet Yisrael Synagogue,** built by Ḥasidic Jews during the 19th century, also merit a visit. The synagogue was captured and destroyed by Jordan in 1948. Its upper portions have been covered with cement, making it look like a massive gray amoeba. The synagogue is on Tiferet Yisrael Rd., which begins at the northeastern corner of the courtyard behind the Ḥurva Synagogue, and is a favorite stop for tour guides wishing to evoke contempt for Jordan.

Farther east on Tiferet Yisrael Rd. smolders the **Burnt House** (tel. 28 72 11), the remains of the dwelling of a wealthy priest's family from the Second Temple era. In 70 CE, the fourth year of the Jewish Revolt, the Romans destroyed the Second Temple and, one month later, broke into Jerusalem's Upper City, burning its buildings and killing its inhabitants. The excavation of the Burnt House provided some of the first direct evidence of the destruction of the Upper City: its charred walls had collapsed, crushing jugs and furniture beneath them, and near a stairwell the grisly bones of a severed arm reached for a carbonized spear. Sound and light shows are set inside the Burnt House, recreating the events of its destruction. (Open Sun.-Thurs. 9am-5pm, Fri. 9am-1pm. Programs in English at 9:30am, 11:30am, 1:30pm, and 3:30pm. Admission NIS3.50, students NIS3. No smoking.) Off of the Jewish Quarter's main square, the Wohl Museum around the side of the Yeshivat HaKotel houses the recently opened **Herodian Quarter** (tel. 28 34 48), which features three mansions built for the Second Temple's high priests (*kohanim*). The houses contain mosaics, several ritual baths (*mikvaot*), and stone and pottery dishes unearthed during excavations. (Open Sun.-Thurs. 9am-5pm, Fri. 9am-1pm. Admission NIS6.50, students NIS6. Combined ticket to Burnt House and Herodian Quarter NIS8, students NIS7.50.)

Following Plugat HaKotel Rd. from the Ḥurva Synagogue Sq. brings you past the **Wide Wall,** remains of the Israelite wall that encircled the City of David, the Temple Mount, and the Upper City. The wall was built by King Hezekiah along with his tunnel (see City of David section for details) to defend the city and ensure water provision during attacks and sieges by Assyrian King Sennacherib in the 8th century BCE.

You can visit some of the small synagogues and *yeshivot* (singular *yeshiva*), tucked away in alleys and courtyards throughout the Jewish Quarter. Young men and, in a few places, young women live in these academic institutions for years as they pursue Judaic learning. Several *yeshivot* have begun wooing Jews with little or no religious background to come for short—or sometimes interminable—stays. Stop in at **Aish HaTorah**—students here are mostly American and welcome visitors, even for only one class (though you may have a tough time leaving). To reach Aish HaTorah from the Western Wall, walk up the stairs to the Jewish Quarter and take your first left onto the street before the covered arcade (Beit HaSho'eva Rd.). Women should apply to the *yeshiva's* administrative office off Shvut Rd. in the Jewish Quarter.

Christian Quarter and Via Dolorosa

In the northwest quadrant of the Old City, the Christian Quarter surrounds the Church of the Holy Sepulchre, the site traditionally believed to be the place of Jesus' crucifixion, burial, and resurrection. Many small chapels and churches of various Christian denominations lie near the Church of the Holy Sepulchre.

The **Via Dolorosa** (Path of Sorrow) is the route Jesus followed from the site of his condemnation to his crucifixion site and grave—from the Praetorium to Calvary. Each stop along the route marks an event, one of the "Stations of the Cross" on Jesus' final journey. The present route along Via Dolorosa was established during the Crusader period, but modern New Testament scholars have suggested alternate routes based on more recent archeological and historical reconstructions.

One spat involves establishing exactly where Jesus began his walk. Everyone agrees that Jesus was brought before Pontius Pilate, the Roman procurator, for judgment. A Roman governor ordinarily resided and fulfilled his duties in the palace of Herod the Great, south of Jaffa Gate and the Citadel area. This evidence places the starting point on the opposite end of the city from the traditional beginning on Via Dolorosa. On feast days when the temple area was hectic, however, the governor and his soldiers presumably based themselves temporarily at Antonia's fortress (also built by Herod) to be closer to the Temple Mount. As Jesus was condemned on a feast day (Passover), the **Tower of Antonia**, near St. Stephen's (Lion's) Gate, remains the traditional First Station, although you may see small groups, notably the Catholic Dominican Order, setting out from Jaffa Gate. The placement of the last five stations inside the Church of the Holy Sepulchre is also contested by those who believe that from where Via Dolorosa ends, the route was likely to have continued north toward the skull-shaped Garden Tomb, since the crucifixion took place on a hill called Golgotha, meaning "place of the skull." On Fridays at 3pm (July-Aug. at 4pm), Franciscan monks lead a procession of pilgrims (which you may join) from al-Omariyeh College.

Along the Via Dolorosa from St. Stephen's Gate, you'll first see the **Church of St. Anne** on your right. Commemorating the birthplace of Jesus' mother Mary, the church is one of the best preserved examples of Crusader architecture in Israel. The church survived intact throughout the Islamic period because Salah al-Din used it as a Muslim theological school, hence the Arabic inscription on the *tympanum* above the church doors. Tradition runs deep here: the simple, solemn, citadel-like structure stands over the ruins of a 5th-century basilica that, in turn, is believed to cover a 2nd- or 3rd-century chapel. The church is tilted to one side, symbolizing the crucifixion.

Within the grounds is the **Pool of Bethesda,** which served as the water source for the temple. Crowds of the infirm used to wait beside the pool for an angel to disturb its waters, which explained the pool's periodic gushing; the first person in after the angel would supposedly be cured. Jesus is believed to have healed a paralytic here as well. The pool is divided into a southern and a northern section, but comprehension of the site is confounded by the remains of a Byzantine cistern and the facade of a Crusader chapel. (Church and grounds open Mon.-Sat. 8am-noon and 2-6pm; in winter 8am-noon and 2-5pm. Free.)

Two hundred meters west of St. Stephen's Gate, a ramp leads to the courtyard of the **al-Omariyeh College,** one site identified as the **first station,** where Jesus was condemned (closed 1-3pm). Opposite the school from the Via Dolorosa, enter the Franciscan monastery; to your left is the **Condemnation Chapel,** the **second station,** where Jesus was sentenced to crucifixion. On the right is the **Chapel of Flagellation** where he was first flogged by Roman soldiers. A crown of thorns adorns the dome and mobs clamor at the windows of the chapel. (Open daily 8am-noon and 2-6pm; in winter, 8am-noon and 1-5pm.)

Continuing along the Via Dolorosa, you pass beneath the **Ecce Homo Arch,** where Pilate looked down upon a scourged Jesus and cried "Behold the Man." The arch is actually a part of the triumphal arch that commemorates Emperor Hadrian's suppression of the Bar Kokhba revolt in the 2nd century. (Open Mon.-Sat. 8:30am-12:30pm and 2-4pm.) Adjacent lies the **Convent of the Sisters of Zion,** beneath which excavations have cleared a large chamber thought by some to be the judgment hall, which would make *it* the first station. The convent is closed to the public; the excavations are not. To get to the excavations, walk down the Via Dolorosa from the second station and turn right on Aqabat ar-Rahbat St. Knock on the brown door on your left. (Open Mon.-Sat. 8:30am-12:30pm and 2-4:30pm. Admission NIS2.50.)

Even though the following stations—the destinations of millions of pilgrims—are all marked, they are nonetheless difficult to spot. At the **third station,** to the left on al-Wad Rd., Jesus fell to his knees for the first time. A small Polish chapel marks the spot; a relief above the entrance depicts Jesus kneeling beneath the cross. At the **fourth station,** a few meters farther on the left, just beyond the Armenian Orthodox Patriarchate, a small chapel commemorates the spot where Jesus met his mother. Turn right on Via Dolorosa to reach the **fifth station,** where Simon the Cyrene volunteered to carry Jesus' cross. Fifty meters farther, the remains of a small column mark the **sixth station,** where Veronica wiped Jesus' face with her handkerchief. The imprint of his face was left on the cloth, which is now on display at the Greek Orthodox Patriarchate on the street of the same name. The **seventh station** marks Jesus' second fall—note the sudden steepness of the road here. In the first century, a gate to the countryside opened here, and tradition holds that notices of Jesus' condemnation were posted on it. Crossing Khan az-Zeit, ascend Aqabat al-Khanqa and look beyond the Greek Orthodox Convent for the clothes hanger directing you to the stone and Latin cross that mark the **eighth station.** Here Jesus turned to the women who mourned him, saying "Daughters of Jerusalem, do not weep for me, weep rather for yourselves and for your children" (Luke 23:28). Backtrack to Khan az-Zeit, ascend the wide stone stairway on the right, and continue through a winding passageway to the Coptic church. The remains of a column in its door mark the **ninth station,** where Jesus fell a third time. Again retrace your steps to the main street and work your way through the market to the entrance of the Church of the Holy Sepulchre, where the Via Dolorosa ends.

The **Church of the Holy Sepulchre** marks Golgotha, also called Calvary, where Jesus was crucified. The location was first determined by Helena, mother of the Emperor Constantine, during a pilgrimage in 326 CE. Helena thought that Hadrian had erected a pagan temple to Venus and Jupiter on the site in order to divert Christians from their faith. She sponsored excavations which soon uncovered the tomb of Joseph of Arimathea and three crosses, which she surmised had been hastily left there after the crucifixion as the Sabbath approached. Constantine built a winsome church over the site in 335, which was later destroyed by the Persians in 614, rebuilt, and again destroyed (this time by the Turks) in 1009. Part of Constantine's church's original foundations buttress the present Crusader structure, which dates from 1048. When the present building was erected, its architects decided to unite all the oratories, chapels, and other sanctuaries that had cropped up around the site under one monumental cross. By 1852, tremendous religious conflicts had developed within the Holy Sepulchre over such seemingly silly issues as who had the right to clean the doorstep. The uninterested Ottoman rulers divided the church among the Franciscan order and the Greek and Armenian Orthodox, Coptic, Syrian, and Ethiopian churches. The first three are the major shareholders, entitled to hold Masses and processions and to burn incense in their shrines and chapels.

One of the most venerated buildings on earth, the church is also somewhat decrepit. The bickering among the various denominations lends the structure some of its fascination and color but also has kept the building in shambles, marred by perpetual construction. The effects of major fires in 1808 and 1949 and an earthquake in 1927 demanded a level of cooperation and a pooling of resources that could not be mustered. Restoration work in any part of the basilica implies ownership, making each sect hesitant to assist and eager to hinder the others. The result is that little, if anything, is ever accomplished. In 1935 the church was in such a precarious state that Britain desperately propped it up with girders and wooden reinforcement. Since 1960, partial cooperation has allowed the supportive scaffolding to be gradually removed, but to this day the question of who gets to change a given lightbulb can turn into a controversy that rages for months.

The sites in the church today bear little resemblance to those described in the Gospels, but discrepancies can be explained. The Gospels place Calvary outside the city walls in ancient times; the site is located on the second floor of the church, within today's Ottoman city walls. At the time of Jesus, according to believers, the basilica's Calvary site was indeed located outside the city walls—the extant walls were built centuries after Jesus' crucifixion and encompass a larger area than the original walls. (Church open daily 5am-8pm; in winter 4am-7pm.) The guards are sticklers about modest dress. The first shop outside the eastern entrance to the courtyard rents skirts for NIS1.50; look for the Kodak sign. Ask for Ibrahim, the church's official photographer, if you have any further problems.

The church's entrance faces the slab on which Jesus was supposedly annointed before he was buried. To continue along the stations, go up the stairs to the right just after you enter. The chapel at the top is divided into two naves: the right one belongs to the Franciscans, the left to the Greek Orthodox. At the entrance to the Franciscan Chapel is the **tenth station,** where Jesus was stripped of his clothes, and at the far end is the **eleventh,** where he was nailed to the cross. The **twelfth station,** to the left in the Greek chapel, is the unmistakable site of the Crucifixion: a life-size Jesus, clad in a metal loincloth, hangs among oil lamps, flowers, and enormous candles. Between the eleventh and twelfth stations is the **thirteenth,** where Mary received Jesus' body. The thirteenth station is marked by a statue of Mary, adorned with jewels, with a silver dagger stuck into her breast.

Jesus' tomb on the ground floor is the **fourteenth (final) station.** The **Holy Sepulchre,** in the center of the rotunda, is a large marble structure flanked by huge candles. The first chamber in the tomb, the Chapel of the Angel, is named after the angel who announced Jesus' resurrection to Mary Magdalene. A tiny entrance leads from the chapel into the sepulchre itself, an equally tiny chamber lit by scores of candles and guarded by priests. The walls of the tomb have been covered, but the priest in charge will show you a small section of the original wall hidden behind a picture of the Virgin Mary. The raised marble slab in the sepulchre covers the rock on which Jesus' body was laid. Nudging the back of the Holy Sepulchre is the tiny Coptic Chapel, in which a priest will invite you to kiss the wall of the tomb. To the right of the Sepulchre, the **Chapel of Mary Magdalene** recalls the place where Jesus appeared to her after his resurrection.

The rest of the church is a dark labyrinth of small chapels, through which priests, pilgrims, and chatty tourists wander. Because a denomination's ability to hang anything on the church's walls also indicates possession, the building houses only religious paintings and spindly oil lamps. Near the eastern end, steps lead down to two cavernous chapels commemorating the discovery of the true cross. In a small chapel on the ground floor just below Calvary, a fissure runs through the rock, supposedly caused by the earthquake following Jesus' death. According to legend, Adam (of Adam and Eve fame) was buried beneath Calvary, allowing Jesus' blood to drip through this cleft and anoint him.

St. Alexander's Church, one block east of the Church of the Holy Sepulchre on Via Dolorosa, houses the Russian mission-in-exile. Prayers for Czar Alexander III are held every Thursday at 7am (the only time the church is open). (Open Mon.-Sat. 9am-1pm and 3-5pm. Admission NIS1.50; ring bell.) Across the street is the **Lutheran Church of the Redeemer** (tel. 28 25 43), entrance on Muristan St. Head up the narrow spiral staircase to its bell tower for a special vertigo experience. (Open Mon.-Sat. 9am-1pm and 1:30-5pm. English service Sun. 9am. Admission NIS1, students NIS.60.) The **Greek Orthodox Patriarchate Museum** (tel. 28 40 06), on the street of the same name, is a more recent addition to the Christian Quarter. Under the present Patriarch, Benedictos Papadopoulos, the scattered liturgical riches, gifts of pilgrims, and early printings of the Patriarchate's 19th-century press have been arranged in a spacious, reconstructed Crusader building. (Open Tues.-Fri. 9am-3pm, Sat. 9am-1pm. Admission NIS1.)

Take a left from the Russian mission, another onto Khan az-Zeit St., and walk up the stairs to the left to reach the **Ethiopian Monastery,** located over part of the Church of the Holy Sepulchre and open all day. The Ethiopians possess no part of the church it-self, so they have become squatters on the roof. The modest compound is comprised of white buildings with green doors. Walk around and follow the "Please Watch Up Your Head" signs to the small but amazing church.

Armenian Quarter

Lying beside Mt. Zion in the southwestern part of the Old City, the Armenian Quar-ter maintains a strong cultural identity despite modernization. Aramaic, the ancient language of the Talmud, is spoken both during services and in casual conversation at the **Syrian Orthodox Convent** on Ararat St. The Syrian Church believes this spot is the site of St. Mark's house and the Last Supper, while most other Christians recog-nize the Cenacle on Mt. Zion as the hallowed place. To reach the convent, enter Jaffa Gate and walk along the Citadel onto Armenian Patriarchate Rd. Take a left onto St. James Rd. and another onto Ararat St. A vivid mosaic marks the door to the convent. You can visit during the afternoon; if the door is closed, ring the bell. The **Armenian Compound,** down Armenian Patriarchate Rd. past St. James Rd., is a city within a city, home to about 1000 Armenians and a slew of buildings closed to tourists.

Farther down Armenian Patriarchate Rd. on the left is the entrance to the **Mardi-gian Museum,** which chronicles the history of Armenia from the beginnings of its Christianization in 46 CE to the Turkish genocide of one and a half million Armenians in 1915. Follow the signs for the Armenian Museum. (Open Mon.-Sat. 10am-4:30pm. Admission NIS3, students NIS2.)

St. James Cathedral is open for services for 30 minutes each day. The original structure was built during the 5th century CE, Armenia's golden age, to honor two St. Jameses. The first martyred Apostle, St. James the Greater, was beheaded in 44 CE by Herod Agrippas. St. James the Lesser served as the first bishop of Jerusalem, but was run out of town by Jews who disliked his version of Judaism. Under the gilded altar rests the head of St. James the Greater, which was supposedly delivered to Mary on the wings of angels. St. James the Lesser is entombed in a northern chapel. Persians destroyed the cathedral in the 7th century, Armenians rebuilt it in the 11th century, and Crusaders enlarged it in the 12th. The entire church is decorated with lovely ceramic tiles—the Armenians make the tiled street signs for the entire Old City—and scores of chandeliers, hanging lamps, and censers. Pilgrims have left the votive crosses in the courtyard before the entrance; the oldest cross dates from the 12th century. Enter the cathedral from Armenian Patriarchate Rd., just past St. James St. (Cathedral open for services daily 3-3:30pm.)

Muslim Quarter

The Muslim Quarter is worth exploring mostly for its architecture, notably that from the Mamluk period (1250-1517). Do not wander through the Muslim Quarter during periods of unrest, however, and do not flaunt your Hebrew here. Several of the tour groups include the Muslim Quarter in their routes. Check at the GTIO for specif-ics.

The stretch of Bab as-Silsileh St. extending to the Temple Mount sports many Bent-leys of the architectural world. Just past Misgav Ladakh Rd. on the right is the **Tasta-muriya Building,** housing the tomb of its namesake (d. 1384) and formerly a *madrasa* (Islamic college).

Continuing down Bab as-Silsileh to its intersection with Western Wall St. (HaKo-tel), you'll arrive at the **Kilaniya Mausoleum,** with its characteristic Mamluk stalac-tite half-dome; the **Turba Turkan Khatun** (Tomb of Lady Turkan) is at #149. At the end of Bab as-Silsileh, on your right and often surrounded by tour guides in training, is the **Tankiziya Building.** This venerated structure, on the site of the original seat of the Sanhedrin, is currently occupied by Israelis due to its proximity to the Western Wall and Temple Mount.

Mount Zion and City of David

Mount Zion (Har Tzion) stands outside the city walls opposite Zion Gate and the Armenian Quarter. At various times since the Second Temple era, however, Mt. Zion has been enclosed by the walls. The mount has long been considered the site of the Tomb of David (though recent archeological evidence suggests otherwise), the Last Supper, and the descent of the Holy Spirit at Pentecost. The name Zion, which is also applied to Israel as a whole, is thought to be derived from the Jebusite fortress called Zion, which was first seized by King David when he conquered the territory to the east. During the siege of the Jewish Quarter in 1948, the area around **Zion Gate** (Sha'ar Tzion) was the scene of some of the fiercest fighting in Jerusalem, as the Hagana tried to break in and end the attack. Vestiges of fighting include the bomb-shell-pocked gate. Egged buses #1 and 38 run between Mt. Zion and Jaffa Gate (#1 goes through Mea She'arim to the central bus station; #38 goes to the center of town). To reach the sights on the Mount, leave the Old City through Zion Gate or approach Zion Gate from either Jaffa or Dung Gates. Turn left coming out of Zion Gate and fol-low the wall around, forking right at the convent. At the next fork, take a left.

A stairway through the green door on your left leads to the bare **Coenaculum,** iden-tified by most as the site of the Last Supper. One of the reasons for its no-frills appear-ance is that Britain, in an effort to avoid sectarian disputes, passed a law during the Mandate forbidding any changes, including decorations, to be made in the church. During the 15th century, the building was used as a mosque and the *mihrab* (prayer niche) is still visible in the southern wall. Beware the little old lady warning you about Armageddon. (Open daily 8:30am-4pm.) Below the Coenaculum is the *beit midrash* (study room) of the **Diaspora Yeshiva,** where many American students learn Torah. Every Saturday night between September and May, visitors are welcome to come sway to live Ḥasidic rock music. (8:30pm; for information, phone 71 68 41.)

To enter **David's Tomb,** go out the green door and turn left. Above the blue velvet-draped tomb in the small cave, the silver crowns, not always displayed, represent the number of years since Israel gained independence. Archeologists refute the authentic-ity of the site because Mt. Zion was never encompassed by David's walls, and it is written that kings and only kings were buried within the city. (Tomb open daily 8am-5pm. Free.)

The **Chamber of the Holocaust** (tel. 71 68 41), through the courtyard and across the street from David's Tomb, commemorates the Jewish communities destroyed dur-ing World War II and displays poignant and grisly artifacts such as rescued Torah scrolls, ashes, and soap made from human tissue. (Open Sun.-Thurs. 8am-5pm, Fri. 8am-1pm. Admission NIS2.) Next door, the affiliated **Museum of King David** at-tempts to convey the spirit and life of David through modern art. (Open irregular hours.) The **Palombo Museum,** across the street and to the left, displays works of the famous sculptor who crafted the entry gate to the Knesset and contributed works to Yad V'Shem. (Open irregular hours, usually in the morning; call 71 09 17. Free.)

The huge, fortress-like **Basilica of the Dormition Abbey** (tel. 71 99 27) lies off the right fork of the road leading to the Coenaculum. The site has harbored many memo-rials; the present edifice, commemorating the death of the Virgin Mary, was built at the turn of the century and completed in 1910. Damaged during battles in 1948 and 1967, parts of the precariously situated basilica have never been repaired. Descend into the crypt to view a figurine of the Virgin. The floor of the ground level is inlaid with symbols of the zodiac from the prophetic tradition. (Open daily 8am-noon and 2-6pm. Free.)

If you have even a fleeting interest in the biblical history of Jerusalem, the **City of David** is a logical place to begin, since this is where the city did. The quest for the or-igins of biblical Jerusalem has been going on since 1850 and only recently have the pieces of the puzzle begun to fit together. Archeologists confirm that the ridge of Ophel—south of the Temple Mount and outside the city walls—is the site of the Canaanite city captured by King David.

Excavations of the earliest Canaanite walls indicate that the Jebusites were confined to an area of about eight acres. The size and location of the city above the Qidron Valley were precisely chosen so that the inhabitants would have access to the nearby water source (the Gihon Spring) and at the same time remain high enough on the Ophel's ridge to ensure adequate defense. In times of peace, townspeople passed through a "water gate" in order to bring water into the city. To allow for continued supply during a siege, the Jebusites dug a shaft from which they could draw water without leaving the walls. David succeeded in capturing the city only after his soldier, Joab, corked the shaft one night. In 1867, Warren confirmed this biblical account when he discovered the long, sleek shaft that now bears his name. In the 1960s, Kathleen Kenyon located the Jebusite city walls dating from 1800 BCE which lie just above the Gihon Spring.

Later King Hezekiah devised a system to prevent David's feat from being turned against the Jews: he built a tunnel to bring the Gihon waters into the city walls and store them in a pool, hiding the entrance of the spring and keeping invaders such as the Assyrians from finding water as they camped outside the wall. According to the biblical account, laborers in Jerusalem dug from opposite ends of the tunnel in order to save time as the Assyrian army approached. Minutes before the enemy's arrival, the laborers heard the picks and voices of their companions on the other side just a few meters off the mark (II Chronicles 32). In 1880, a few years after the tunnel was excavated, a local boy discovered an inscription carved by Hezekiah's engineers. The Siloa inscription describes the tense but jubilant moment when the construction crews completed the tunnel. (The original inscription is in stanbul, but a copy is on display at the Israel Museum.)

You can slosh through **Hezekiah's Tunnel** with a flashlight or a candle, though it is not advisable to do so alone. The water is about 1m high, and wading the 0.5km takes about 30 minutes. Bathing suits or shorts and sneakers for afterwards are useful. Start at the Gihon Spring source on Shiloah Way, which branches to the right from Jericho Rd. as you approach the Qidron Valley from the bottom of the Mount of Olives. Steps from the City of David excavations also lead down to the Gihon Spring. The tunnel ends at the Pool of Shiloah (Silwan in Arabic, Siloam in Hebrew). You can then walk back to the road to your left and catch an Arab bus up the valley. (Open all day. Free, although several little boys will try to convince you otherwise.)

About 100m down from the entrance to the City of David there's a small museum with photos of the most recent excavations. A spiral staircase leads down to **Warren's Shaft.** If you bring a flashlight, you'll be able to see the entire length of the walls that Joab scaled. (Open Sun.-Thurs. 8am-4pm, Fri. 8am-2pm. Admission NIS2.50.)

To witness excavations in progress, walk out of Dung Gate, turn left and walk downhill to the City of David entrance, on your right just past the UNRWA office. The excavations in this particular area of the Ophel, called **Section G,** were halted in 1981 when a group of Orthodox Jews protested that the area might once have been the Jewish cemetery mentioned in the diaries of several medieval pilgrims. After considerable political and sometimes violent ballyhoo, the Supreme Court of Israel ruled that the site should be closed. As a compromise the Israeli government ordered that digging could continue under rabbinic supervision, but no bones have been found. Though numbered and labeled, the ruins adjacent to the route are discombobulated. Several organizations offer tours; check at the tourist office for schedules. If you decide to wander around the area alone, bring a copy of *Marty's Walking Tours.* The site is spectacularly illuminated at night.

Four edifying tombs are located down Shiloah way, in the Kidron Valley. The first, **Absalom's Pillar,** is named by legend as the tomb of David's favored but rebellious son (II Samuel 15-18). Behind it and to the left is the **Tomb of Jehosaphat.** A dirt path on the left leads to the impressive rock-hewn **Tomb of B'nei Hezir** and the **Tomb of Zekhariah.**

East Jerusalem

Annexed by Israel in the aftermath of the 1967 war, East Jerusalem retains a distinctly Arab flavor. Less than 20% of its Palestinian residents accepted Israeli citizenship when it was offered 25 years ago; the majority retained Jordanian passports and were issued East Jerusalem ID cards. Palestinian residents of East Jerusalem share the yellow license plates of Jewish West Jerusalem, and most East Jerusalem schools have remained open during the *intifada*. Nevertheless, the Palestinian residents of East Jerusalem have made it clear that they identify far more with the West Bank than with Israel.

Accommodations

East Jerusalem has often been a hotbed of Israeli-Palestinian tension, but it is ideal for adventurous souls who want a taste of life in an Arab country without leaving Israel. Visibly Jewish travelers (particularly men in *kippot*) should exercise caution and expect at least hostile stares. East Jerusalem's history may not rival that of the Old City, nor its conveniences those of the New City, but you'll find excellent values in accommodations here. Women should be careful walking alone at night in East Jerusalem, but most residents are more than friendly if you make an effort to be sociable. Four hostels cluster on HaNevi'im St., which intersects with Suleiman St. and Nablus Rd. across from Damascus Gate.

Faisal Youth Hostel, 4 HaNevi'im St. (tel. 27 24 92). Clean. Gorgeous view of Damascus Gate from balcony. Kitchen, tea, coffee, and storage available. Midnight curfew. Dorm beds NIS12. Doubles NIS30. Camping on roof NIS8.

Jerusalem Hotel, 4 Antara Ben Shadad St. (tel. 27 13 56 or 28 32 82). Follow Nablus Rd. from Damascus Gate; it's just north of the Arab bus station. Quite comfortable. Courtyard, modern rooms, and exceptionally outgoing management. TV lounge, jazz musician in the winter. Popular with young professionals working in the West Bank. No curfew. Singles US$25. Doubles US$35 with breakfast.

Palm Hostel, 6 HaNevi'im St. (tel. 28 21 89). Clean and green. "Run by tourists for tourists." Beware of Jack's overpriced tours. Dorm beds NIS22. Doubles NIS58.

Ramsis Youth Hostel, 20 HaNevi'im St. (tel. 28 48 18). Huge windows and high ceilings. Some rooms have balconies. Lounge with TVs. Free storage, fridge, hot pot, and dishes. 11:30pm curfew. Dorm beds NIS10. Singles NIS16. Doubles NIS30.

New Raghadan Hostel, 10 HaNevi'im St. Easygoing atmosphere littered with kitschy art. Cluttered but clean. Balcony, dining and sitting room, and kitchen. Filled with Russian-Israeli immigrants working in Israel. Curfew 11pm, but keys available. Dorm beds NIS10. Singles NIS25. Doubles NIS25.

Food

Although East Jerusalem may not look like a paragon of cleanliness, excellent and usually safe falafel and spicy kebabs can be purchased from street vendors for less than NIS2. **Nasser Eddin Bros.** on Suleiman St., across from Damascus Gate and to the right, just past the bus station, stocks almost everything but fresh produce. (Open daily 8am-3pm.) **Salah al-Din Street** buzzes with restaurants open on Saturday. The following restaurants are open on Fridays and during Ramadan:

Abuzeid Oriental Sweets, Suleiman St. (tel. 27 50 52). A bakery with primarily Arab clientele. *Baklava* NIS20 per kilo. Tasty *knaffeh* NIS2 or NIS4 a plate. Open daily 8am-3pm, sometimes later.

Petra Restaurant, 11 Rashid St. (tel 28 36 55). Fancy dining room interior. Salads NIS2. Entrees NIS20-30. Complete meal US$15. Open daily noon-11:30pm.

Café Europe, 11 az-Zahra St. (tel. 28 43 13). *The* place if you have the craving. Delicious milkshakes, hamburger, and chips. Try the "Last Tango of Mangoes" with rum and vanilla ice cream. Open daily from around 11am until late.

Philadelphia, 9 az-Zahra St., off Salah al-Din. Philip Habib and Jimmy Carter's favorite pit-stop. Expensive, but the availability of a Valentine's Day atmosphere in July makes it worth the price. Complete meal costs approximately NIS40. Open daily noon-midnight or 1am.

Sights

Midway between Damascus and Herod's Gates, **Solomon's Quarries** plunge to the city's bowels, providing a welcome refuge from the midday heat. Many believe that it was in these cool caves, which extend about 250m beneath the Old City, that workers quarried limestone for the building of ancient Jerusalem during the First Temple period. To separate blocks of stone from the cave walls, wooden planks were set in crevices and soaked with water; as the planks expanded they wedged the stone apart. Tradition has it that Zedekiah, Judah's last king, fled the city through a passage to Solomon's quarries when King Nebuchadnezzer of Babylonia invaded in 587 BCE. The sign for the quarries reads "Zedekiah's Cave." Although closed to the public during the summer of 1992, the quarries may have reopened by 1993.

Farther east on Suleiman St., opposite the northeastern corner of the city walls, a driveway leads to the **Rockefeller Archeological Museum** (tel. 28 22 51), one of the country's best showcases. Its benefactor, John D. Rockefeller, once asked to be reminded "whether it was one or two million dollars I donated towards the museum." Needless to say, budget travel was not a concern of his. The museum's collection records the region's history, beginning with the remains of 100,000-year-old Mt. Carmel Man, and illustrates the cultural impact of various conquering civilizations. The layout of the museum can be confusing—try to visit on a Sunday or Friday morning for the free guided tours at 11am. (Open Sun.-Thurs. 10am-5pm, Fri.-Sat. 10am-2pm. Admission NIS6, students NIS5. Take Egged bus #27 or 23.)

A short distance up Nablus Rd., on Schick St., a sign points toward the **Garden Tomb,** noticed first by Otto Thenius in 1860 and popularized by the British General Gordon. The garden is possibly Golgotha, the site of Christ's crucifixion. The hill does indeed resemble a skull, and some claim that a nearby tomb is that of Joseph of Arimathea, who placed Jesus' body in his own tomb after the crucifixion. (Open Mon.-Sat. 8am-12:15pm and 2:30-5:15pm. English service Sun. at 9am.) As you continue along Nablus Rd., stop at **St. George's Cathedral,** one of the least visited yet loveliest structures in Jerusalem. The cathedral houses modest collections of Palestinian embroidery and Dothan pottery.

Following Salah al-Din St. up to where it intersects with Nablus Rd., look for the Tombeau des Rois sign on your right just before the intersection. The sign indicates the gate of the **Tomb of the Kings.** Judean kings were originally thought to be buried here, but recent evidence shows that the tomb was in fact built in 45 CE by the Mesopotamian Queen Helena for her family. Bring along a candle or flashlight. (Open Mon.-Sat. 8am-12:30pm and 2-5pm. Admission NIS10, students NIS5.)

The bone-dry slopes of the **Mount of Olives** (Har HaZitim in Hebrew), to the east of the Old City, are dotted with churches marking the sites of Jesus' triumphant entry into Jerusalem, his teaching, his agony and betrayal in Gethsemane, and his ascension to heaven. That the Mount of Olives has three gardens of Gethsemane and two points of Ascension may cast doubt on the accuracy of the locations, but nothing can detract from the splendor. In Jewish tradition, the Mount of Olives holds importance for the future as well: the thousands buried in the cemetery here will be the first to greet the Messiah on Judgment Day.

A walk down the hill, with pauses at the numerous churches, tombs, and gardens, is most enjoyable in the morning when the sun shines at your back, permitting clear views and photographs of the Old City. Since most churches are closed on Sundays and afternoons from about noon-3pm, mornings are also the most practical time to come. Arab bus #75 runs from the station across from Damascus Gate to the Mount of Olives.

Northeast of the Intercontinental Hotel (behind it and to the right), the domineering **Bell Tower** of the Russian convent marks the highest point in Jerusalem. Unfortunately, the compound is closed to the public. South of the hotel along the main road, the **Church of Eleona** and the **Church of the Paternoster** are tucked behind one gate.

Both churches were founded by Queen Helena in the 4th century. The Church of the Eleona marks the spot where Jesus revealed to his disciples the "inscrutable mysteries"—his foretelling of the destruction of Jerusalem and his Second Coming. The Church of the Paternoster (Latin for "Our Father") commemorates the first recital of the Lord's Prayer. Linguists can read the prayer in 77 languages (including Esperanto) on the tiled walls. In the midst of the translations is the grotto of the Princesse de la Tour d'Auvaigne, the woman who financed and worked for 17 years (1857-74) on excavations and renovations here. (Open Mon.-Sat. 8:30-11:45am and 3-4:45pm.) Its credibility contested only by the nearby Russian bell tower, the **Chapel of Christ's Ascension** is farther north along the same road. Inside there is a sacred footprint. (Ring the bell if closed. Admission NIS1.50.)

Down from the Mount of Olives and the Intercontinental Hotel, a gate on the left leads to two tunnels, traditionally identified as the **Tombs of the Prophets** Malahi, Haggai, and Zekhariah. Archeological evidence, however, suggests that the graves are far too recent—probably dating from the 4th century CE. (Open daily 8am-3pm.) The orange sign with black Hebrew lettering marks the **Common Grave** of those who died defending the Jewish Quarter in 1948. Next to the Common Grave lies the **National Cemetery,** and farther down the path sprawls the immense **Jewish Graveyard,** the largest Jewish cemetery in the world.

Farther down the path and to the right, the **Sanctuary of Dominus Flevit** ("the Lord wept") was erected in 1955 to mark the spot where Jesus wept for Jerusalem. During the construction, supervised by the renowned Italian architect Antonio Barluzzi, several unrelated ruins were unearthed. (Open daily 8am-noon and 2:30-5pm; April-Oct. 8am-noon and 2:30-6pm.) Continuing down the road, on the right stands the **Russian Church of Mary Magdalene.** Its seven golden cupolas not only resemble the Kremlin, but also mark the Mount of Olives in the same way that the Dome of the Rock distinguishes the Temple Mount. Czar Alexander III built the church in 1885 in the lavish 17th-century Muscovite style and dedicated it to his mother, the Empress Maria Alexandrovna. The crypt houses the body of a Russian grand duchess, smuggled to Jerusalem via Beijing after her death in the Russian Revolution. Now a convent, the church basks in the aura of the sacred shrines that surround it, and even claims a part of the Garden of Gethsemane. (Ordinarily open Tues. and Thurs. 10-11:30am. Call 28 28 97 to be sure. Free.)

At the bottom of the path, deep in the valley, the **Church of All Nations** (Basilica of the Agony) faces west toward the Old City. Enter through the gate to the Garden of Gethsemane, just below the Church of Mary Magdalene. The garden is another place where Jesus purportedly spent his last night in prayer and was betrayed by Judas (Mark 14:32-42). Although the site has been venerated since the 4th century, the present building, also designed by Barluzzi, was built after World War I with international support. Inside, mosaics depict the last days of Jesus' life while outside, the mosaic on the façade portrays Jesus bringing peace to all nations. (Open 8:30am-noon and 2:30-6pm; Nov.-March 2:30-5pm.) The Grotto further downhill is open until 5pm.

Entertainment

Whereas there has been little to laugh about in East Jerusalem since the beginning of the *intifada,* visitors are not entirely without opportunities for Palestinian cultural activity. The **Palestinian National Theater** (Al-Hakawati), on Nuzah St. (tel. 28 09 57) near the American Colony Hotel, stages plays that are unabashedly political and quite interesting; English synopses are provided. Walk up Nablus Rd. and take the first right after the intersection with Salah al-Din St. Walk 100m and the theater will be on your right, at the end of a short driveway. Locals greet visitors cordially, making this an excellent opportunity to experience Palestinian hospitality. The IDF occasionally shuts down the theater, but otherwise, the show goes on. Performances daily at 3, 4, and 5pm; admission NIS5.

Near Jerusalem

Ein Kerem עין כרם

Formerly an Arab village, tiny Ein Kerem (fountain of vines) is the traditionally professed birthplace of John the Baptist. His mother certainly chose the spot well; rivals to the beauty of this village are scarce. Come here for an afternoon, bring a picnic lunch, and wander through the village's charming alleys and tranquil streets. You'll see plenty of painters attempting to commit the scenery to canvas.

The **Church of St. John** (tel. 41 36 39), with its soaring clock tower, marks the exact spot where John was born. Inside are several noteworthy paintings, including the *Decapitation of Saint John.* (Open Mon.-Sat. 8:30am-noon and 2:30-6pm, Sun. 9am-noon and 2:30-5pm; Oct.-Feb. Mon.-Sat. 8am-noon and 2:30-5pm, Sun. 9am-noon and 2:30-5pm. Mass celebrated at 7:15am, Sun. 8:15am. Dress modestly. Free.) In the **Grotto of the Nativity** below the church there is a lovely Byzantine mosaic of pheasants—the symbol of the Eucharist. Ask the guardian for a key.

Across the valley, down Ma'ayan St. from St. John's gate, the **Church of the Visitation** (tel. 41 72 91) recalls Mary's visit to Elizabeth and contains a rock the infant St. John supposedly hid behind when the Romans came looking for babies to kill. The newer Upper Chapel depicts the glorification of Mary. (Open daily 8-11:45am and 2:30-6pm; Oct.-Feb. daily 8-11:45am and 2:30-5pm.) **Mary's Well,** an ancient spring, is a small stone trough below the **Youth Hostel** (see Accommodations, Suburbs) off Ma'ayan St. The pink tower above the hostel belongs to the **Russian Monastery** (tel. 25 25 65 or 41 28 87), which you can visit only by appointment. The handful of cafés in Ein Kerem are expensive for meals (entrees NIS15-20) but worth a quick stop for coffee and snacks.

To reach Ein Kerem take city bus #17, which runs every 20-30 minutes from the central bus station and the center of town. Ein Kerem is also a 15-minute walk along a footpath to or from the Hadassah Medical Center and the stop for bus #19.

Abu Ghosh אבו גוש

Thirteen kilometers west of Jerusalem lies the Arab village of Abu Ghosh, whose inhabitants aided the Jews in the 1948 war. In the 18th century Sheikh Abu Ghosh required pilgrims to pay a toll here as they traveled to Jerusalem; the town was the last of a series of caravan stops en route to the Holy City. Christians and Jews alike revere Abu Ghosh as the original site of the Ark of the Covenant, which was moved by King David to Jerusalem. The **Notre Dame de l'Arche d'Alliance** (Our Lady of the Ark of the Covenant) was built on the site of the ark. (Open daily 8:30-11:30am and 2:30-6pm.)

Below the sacred hill stands the magnificently preserved, turreted **Crusader Church of the Resurrection,** built in 1142 and acquired by the French government in 1873. Excavations beneath the church have uncovered remains dating back to Neolithic times. The church lies below the main road; head for the minaret of the attached mosque. (Open Mon.-Wed. and Fri.-Sat. 8:30-11am and 2:30-5:30pm. Free.)

A **War Memorial** stands at **Kibbutz Kiryat Anavim** near Abu Ghosh in memory of the Palmah soldiers who fell fighting on the road to Jerusalem during the 1948 war. Three kilometers down the road toward Jerusalem is a **campground** (tel. 53 77 17) run by the moshav at Beit Zayit.

To reach Abu Ghosh, take Egged bus #185 or 186 (NIS3.70), leaving hourly from the central bus station. *Sherut* taxis traveling between Jerusalem and Tel Aviv will stop at the exit, 2km from Abu Ghosh.

Latrun לטרון

Located on Jerusalem's main artery, halfway to Tel Aviv, Latrun was the site of fierce fighting during the 1948 war. From Latrun, Arab forces closed the only road by which food and supplies could have been brought to the besieged inhabitants of Jerusalem. The Arab Legion held this strategic junction against numerous Hagana attacks. Eventually the Jews secretly constructed a new passage, called the Burma Road, outside the range of the Arab guns in order to bring food to the starving residents of West Jerusalem. The rusting red vehicles you see on the road testify to those who never made it up the hill. Latrun remained in Arab hands until the 1967 Six-Day War. The coveted fort that guards the junction of the Jerusalem-Tel Aviv road with the Ashkelon-Ramallah road is now an Israeli army base.

Across the road from the fort is the **Monastery of Latrun,** built in 1927 by the French Trappist Order on the ruins of a 12th-century Crusader fortress. This is said to be the site of the home of one of the thieves crucified at the side of Jesus; the name Latrun comes from the Latin *latro*, "thief." (Open daily 7:30-11:30am and 2:30-5pm. Free.)

Canada Park, one of many spots in Israel forested with the help of the Jewish National Fund, is on the edge of the West Bank just north of Emmaus. Virtually all the trees you see here were planted during the last 50 years. When you wander through the grounds, look carefully—the place is peppered with archeological remains.

Farther north along the edge of the West Bank, **Modi'in,** a mesmerizing archeological site, features the **Tombs of the Maccabees.** Every year on the first night of Hanuka a team of runners carries a torch, lit near the tombs, to Jerusalem where it is used for the ceremonial lighting of the Hanuka candles.

Latrun can be reached by bus #402, 403, 404, or 433 passing between Jerusalem and Tel Aviv every 30 minutes (NIS3).

Sorek Cave in the Avshalom Reserve מערת שורק

The stalagmite *and* stalactite cave of Avshalom contains amazing speliological splendors. Even the ridiculously large numbers of tour groups that converge on this place won't overshadow the majesty of the caverns. Obey the rule about not taking pictures; repeated exposure to flashes damages the mineral formations. Admission (NIS9, children NIS4.50) includes a slide show and guided tour (tel. 91 11 17). The cave lies 19km southwest of Jerusalem next to the village of Nes Harim. Due to the lack of direct public transportation and the 7km distance between Nes Harim and the cave, Sorek is all but inaccessible unless you join an organized tour (try Egged Tours). Stalwart hikers can take bus #184 or 413 (NIS5) to Nes Harim and walk to the cave. (Open Sat.-Thurs. 8:30am-3:30pm, Fri. 8:30am-12:30pm.)

Tel Aviv and the Central Coast

Roughly two-thirds of Israel's population lives between Haifa and Tel Aviv along 70 miles of muggy coastal plain. The moisture that hangs in the air soaks out orthodoxy: in Haifa, buses run on *shabbat,* and in Tel Aviv most establishments stay open Friday night. Well-irrigated kibbutzim along this part of the coast subscribe to an equally secular work ethic. This region includes the country's wealthiest, most commercial city as well as state-of-the-art agricultural centers—all in all, the no-nonsense, secular heart of Israel, the way it behaves when there are no tourists around.

Tel Aviv תל אביב

The introduction to *This Week in Tel Aviv* welcomes you to the city "where life is lived to the fullest, 24 hours a day." That doesn't leave too much room for a late train, but if there's a city in Israel that can legitimately lay claim to that description, it is Westernized and lively Tel Aviv. Israel's foremost Mediterranean city is vibrant, modern, and progressive. In 1990, a Tel Aviv belly dancer, challenged by the Rabbinate, successfully defended her right to perform in hotels. The country's most outspoken gay writer, Yotam Reuveni, makes his home here.

It's only a 50-minute ride from Jerusalem to Tel Aviv, but in that short time, the stone and conservatism of the former cracks, and the concrete and liberalism of the latter sets in. Amos Oz, Israel's preeminent novelist, chuckles over the Tel Aviv-Jerusalem differences: If Tel Avivians see the Holy City "as a fanatical loony bin," Jerusalemites see their Mediterranean neighbor as "a shallow steam bath, hurried and noisy, a little like a shtetl, petit-bourgeois, somewhat bohemian in a vulgar way, somewhat working-class with pseudo-proletarian pretensions. In short, a hick town, shrill, ugly, and very, very plebeian." Nonsense, of course, but the world's first modern Jewish city invariably inspires emotion among travelers—some fall in love, and some catch the first bus to Jerusalem.

In his turn-of-the-century utopian novel *Altneuland* (Old-New-Land), Theodor Herzl pictured a city in a Jewish homeland established entirely by contemporary Jews; the Hebrew translation of the city's name was Tel Aviv (hill of spring). The development of Israel's largest city began with Jewish settlement in Yafo (anglicized as Jaffa) in 1820. Yafo at that time served as Palestine's major port and the arrival destination for immigrants. Shortly thereafter, enough Jews had settled in Yafo to create the first two exclusively Jewish neighborhoods just to the north, **Neveh Tzedek** in 1887 and **Neveh Shalom** in 1891. As the Jewish population in Yafo continued to increase, settlers founded a suburb in this area to the north. On April 11, 1909, they parceled out their newly acquired land north of Yafo, naming the area, with sober Labor Zionist practicality, **Aḥuzat Bayit** (Housing Property). One year later, the suburb's name was changed to **Tel Aviv.** Its first main streets included Herzl St., Aḥad Ha'Am St., and Rothschild St.; all are still busy thoroughfares.

Immigration and settlement continued under British rule. In 1949, Yafo and Tel Aviv were merged into one city, and residents quickly transformed sandy stretches into a steel and concrete landscape. As the only entirely Jewish city of its time, Tel Aviv became the center of Jewish art and culture. Though scorned as a modern Gomorrah by some Jerusalemites, Tel Aviv is the base for the Israel Philharmonic, the HaBima and HaKameri Theaters, ballet companies, galleries, and museums. The Suzanne Dellale Center houses several renovated theaters for dance and drama, and at Kassit an older generation of artists and intellectuals still thrives.

In 1983, the municipality of Tel Aviv banned the conversion of new office space in the city in an attempt to curb the tremendous flow of Tel Aviv residents outward to the suburbs. Various regions of the city, such as Neveh Tzedek, are being gentrified while ethnic neighborhoods like Kerem HaTemanim (the Yemenite Quarter) maintain their traditional appeal.

Although Israel was not in the 1991 Gulf War, Tel Aviv nonetheless became a target for Iraqi Scud missile attacks. Two years later, the damage has been patched up, and life is back to its usual bustle. In Tel Aviv, you will find plenty of opportunities to live secular modern Israeli life to the fullest, 24 hours a day.

Orientation

Located in the center of Israel's Mediterranean coastline, Tel Aviv is 63km (a 50-min. bus ride) west of Jerusalem, and 95km (a 2.5-hr. bus ride) south of Ḥaifa.

The two main points of entry into Tel Aviv are Ben-Gurion Airport (at Lod) and the central bus station. Buses stop running from the airport at noon, but due to the raging hostel-war in Tel Aviv, several establishments send vans to pick up and pester potential clients.

As early Tel Aviv's leading architect Ariyeh Sharon put it, the city "just growed." The best solution to the haphazard street layout is a bus map (NIS2.50) available at the **Dan Bus Company** headquarters on the corner of HaGalil St. and HaSharon St. at the central bus station. House numbers generally increase from the sea eastward and from

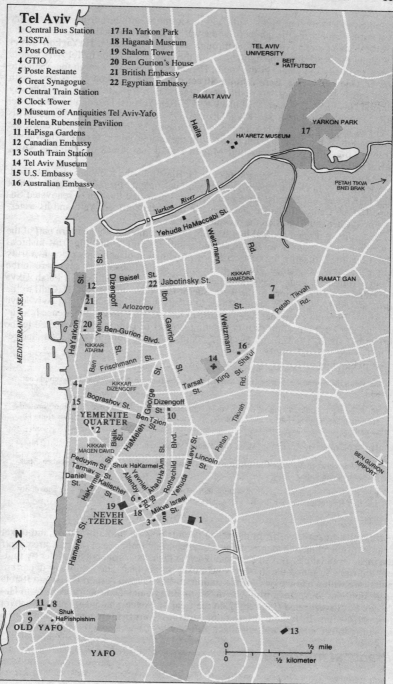

Tel Aviv

1 Central Bus Station
2 ISSTA
3 Post Office
4 GTIO
5 Poste Restante
6 Great Synagogue
7 Central Train Station
8 Clock Tower
9 Museum of Antiquities Tel Aviv-Yafo
10 Helena Rubenstein Pavilion
11 HaPisga Gardens
12 Canadian Embassy
13 South Train Station
14 Tel Aviv Museum
15 U.S. Embassy
16 Australian Embassy
17 Ha Yarkon Park
18 Haganah Museum
19 Shalom Tower
20 Ben Gurion's House
21 British Embassy
22 Egyptian Embassy

the more modest southern part of the city up to the wealthier north. Almost every street corner announces the numbers on the wall of the nearest building.

Several major streets run parallel through the downtown area. **HaYarkon Street** runs along the beach from the northern tip of the city, and is home to Tel Aviv's more expensive hotels and cafés. In the south, HaYarkon leads you through the Yemenite Quarter. One block east, **Ben-Yehuda Street** parallels HaYarkon and is lined with travel agencies and more affordable restaurants. Ben-Yehuda turns into **Allenby Road,** at November 2 Square. One block east of Ben-Yehuda, Dizengoff runs parallel until the popular Dizengoff Sq. (Kikar Dizengoff) where it branches further east. (This street and meeting place honor the city's first mayor, Meir Dizengoff.) Allenby, the continuation of Ben-Yehuda, intersects with the anachronistic **HaMelekh George Street** (King George St.) at Kikar Magen David just south of which is **Shuk HaKarmel** (Karmel Market).

The *midrehov* (pedestrian streets) of Nahalat Binyamin and Rambam also run south from Kikar Magen David. Neveh Tzedek, with its student clientele, lies just south of Shuk HaKarmel and Nahalat Binyamin. You can also find the newly renovated Suzanne Dellale Center for dance and drama in this neighborhood. Yafo and its waterfront lie further south, outside the downtown area.

The confusing **Egged central bus station,** in the crumbling southeastern part of the downtown area, spans several blocks and winds through a bustling fruit-fashion-falafel market. Arguably the best earthly approximation of hell, this place is a truly unique Tel Aviv experience. On the up side, you can get absolutely anywhere in the country from here. Four streets flank the station's main islands: Derekh Petah Tikva (the entrance to the station) to the west, Sderot Har Tzion to the east, HaGalil to the north, and Shomeron to the south. Buses to points inside and outside Tel Aviv leave from here. Become a nuisance, keep a sense of humor, remember that patience is a virtue, and just keep repeating your destination; sooner or later you'll be steered to the correct bus stand. The last city bus is 12:30am. Buses do not run on *shabbat* and resume service at 5pm Saturday evening.

Six **urban bus** routes are important to visitors:

#4: From the central bus station, runs parallel to the coastline up Allenby and Ben-Yehuda and back.

#5: From the central bus station, runs north along Rothschild Blvd. and Dizengoff, turns around at Nordau and Yehuda HaMaccabee (2 blocks from the Back Pack Hostel), and returns along Dizengoff.

#10: Runs from city hall to Yafo along Ben-Yehuda St. and returns via HaYarkon.

#25: Runs between Tel Aviv University and Bat-Yam via Haifa Rd., Yehuda HaMaccabee, Shuk HaKarmel, and Yafo.

#27: From the central bus station, runs along Petah Tikva Rd. and Haifa Rd. to Tel Aviv University and Beit HaTfutzot, through Tel Barukh and back.

#46: From the central bus station, runs along Petah Tikva Rd., to Yafo and back.

Intercity buses leave from the seven islands outside the information and ticket counter. If traveling to a major city on a bus departing from one of the side streets (off the main terminal plaza), you can usually avoid the chaos around the counter by finding the right stop and purchasing your ticket on the bus. The following departure points are within a few blocks of the station: to Ben-Gurion Airport (Lod) and Ramla from Finn St.; to Netanya from Hagra St.; to Hadera and Zikhron Ya'akov from HaNegev St.; to Azor and Bat Yam from the field of Neveh Sha'anan; and to Rehovot from HaGedud Ha'Ivri St. Intercity bus travel is surprisingly cheap: NIS16 for a roundtrip ticket between Jerusalem and Tel Aviv.

Practical Information

Government Tourist Information Office (GTIO): 5 Shalom Aleichem (tel. 66 02 59/61), near the beach between HaYarkon St. and Ben-Yehuda St. Maps of Tel Aviv and other cities. Schedules of cultural events. An excellent new computer system puts all the information you need on accommodations, food, shopping, and tours at your fingertips. Limited number of tickets to the Israeli Philharmonic. With 48 hr. notice, will arrange a visit to meet Israelis in their homes. Open Sun.-Thurs. 8:30am-5pm, Fri. 8:30am-2pm.

Budget Travel: ISSTA, 109 Ben-Yehuda St. (tel. 52 70 11), at Ben-Gurion St. Cheap plane and ferry fares, tours, and information. For an ISIC, bring a photo, proof of student status, and NIS25. Open Sun.-Thurs. 8:30am-1pm and 3-6pm, Fri. 8:30am-1pm. **GSTS International:** 57 Ben-Yehuda St. (tel. 22 22 61), next to the GTIO. Cheap fares on scheduled airlines, charters, train and boat tickets, car rental, and hotel bookings. Open Sun.-Thurs. 8:30am-1pm and 3:30-6pm, Fri. 8:30am-1pm.

Embassies: U.S.: 71 HaYarkon St. (tel. 517 43 38). Open Mon.-Fri. 8-11am. Library open 10am-4pm, Fri. 10am-1pm. Closed Israeli holidays. For emergencies when closed call 65 43 47. **Canada:** 220 HaYarkon St. (tel. 527 29 29). Open Mon.-Thurs. 8am-4:30pm, Fri. 8am-1:30pm. Consular, passport, and visa services, 7 Havakuk St. (tel. 546 58 10), 1 block north of embassy. Open Mon.-Fri. 8am-noon. **Australia:** 37 King Shaul St., 4th floor (tel. 695 04 51). Open Mon.-Thurs. 8-11am. **U.K.:** 192 HaYarkon St. (tel. 510 01 66). Consular section open Mon.-Fri. 8am-1pm. Applications for visas and letters of consent, Mon.-Fri. 8-11:30am. Travelers from **New Zealand** should contact the British embassy. **Egypt:** 54 Basel St. (tel. 546 41 51/2, fax 544 16 15), just off Ibn Gevirol St. Visa section open Sun.-Thurs. 9-11am. Bring your passport, a photo, and NIS40 (NIS30 for Americans). Get there early. Pick up your passport with visa at 1:30pm.

Banks: Most open Sun., Tues., and Thurs. 8:30am-12:30pm and 4-5:30pm, Mon., Wed., and Fri. 8:30am-noon. Main bank offices: **Bank Hapoalim,** 104 HaYarkon St. (tel. 524 33 11); **Israel Discount,** 16 Mapu St. (tel. 524 72 76); **Bank Leumi,** 130 Ben-Yehuda St. (tel. 522 92 31). **First International,** 9 Aḥad Ha'Am St. (tel. 519 61 11). Branches throughout the city and suburbs. Some banks in hotels stay open later. **Israel Discount** has a branch in the Hilton Hotel, Independence Park (tel. 524 54 29), open Sun.-Thurs. 8am-noon and 2:30-7:30pm, Fri. 8-11:30am, and another branch in the Dan Hotel, 59 HaYarkon St. (tel. 523 32 83).

American Express: Meditrad Ltd., 16 Ben-Yehuda St. (tel. 29 46 54). Mail held. Cardholders can buy traveler's checks with personal checks (with a passport and 1.25% charge) for up to $1000 every 21 days. Travel agency offers discounts for cardholders. Open Sun.-Thurs. 9am-5pm.

Post Office: 132 Allenby Rd. (tel. 62 15 09). Open Sun.-Thurs. 9am-5pm. **Poste Restante** is two blocks east at 7 Mikveh Yisrael St. (tel. 564 36 53/51 or toll free 177 022 21 21). Open Sun.-Thurs. 8am-10pm, Fri. 8am-noon. Tel Aviv has several branch offices that are usually open Sun.-Thurs. 8am-12:30pm and 3:30-6pm, Fri. 8am-1 or 2pm. Ask for the nearest *doar.* **Telegrams** can be sent from any post office or hotel, or by dialing 171.

Telephones: Bezek, 13 Frischmann St. is most convenient for international calls. Open Sun.-Thurs. 9am-11pm, Fri. 8am-2:30pm, Sat. 8:30pm-midnight. To make international calls from outside the phone office, dial 188; for collect calls, dial 177 100 27 27 (AT&T), 177 150 27 27 (MCI), or 177 102 27 27 (Sprint). Learn Arabic, Hebrew, and Russian as the recording drones on. For **directory information** dial 144.

Telephone code: 03.

Airport: Ben-Gurion Airport, 22km southeast of Tel Aviv in Lod. For recorded information about flights on all airlines, call 971 10 70 or 971 10 79 (recording is in Hebrew). Egged bus #475 to the airport leaves from Finn St. near the central bus station every 20min., Sun.-Thurs. 5:10am-4pm. United Tours bus #222 leaves from the central train station hourly and goes down HaYarkon St. to the airport (Sun.-Fri. 3:45am-midnight, Sat. 11:45am-midnight; 30min.; NIS5).

Trains: Information tel. 542 15 15 (open 6am-8pm). Several trains to Ḥaifa, Netanya, and Nahariya leave from the central train station (Arlozorov St. across Ḥaifa Rd.) approx. every hour on the hour Sun. 6am-8pm, Mon.-Thurs. 7am-8pm, and Fri. 6am-3pm. One train to Jerusalem leaves Sun.-Fri. at 8:15am from B'nei Brak near Ramat Gan Stadium, returning at 4pm. 20% student discount. Slower, but more pleasant and slightly cheaper than bus travel. Compare a 50-min. bus ride from Tel Aviv to Jerusalem at NIS8 to a more scenic and relaxing 2.5hr. train ride at NIS6.5. Purchase tickets onboard. Take bus #62 or 64 from Ben-Yehuda to the station. The Hebrew word for train is *rakevet.*

Buses: For Egged intercity information, call 177 022 55 55 (toll free from anywhere), or for tours, 527 12 12. For Dan information in Tel Aviv, call 561 44 44 or 754 33 33; for tours, 29 10 28. Sun.-Thurs. 6:30am-9pm., Fri. and holidays 6:30am-3pm. (See Orientation above for more information.)

Ferries: Mano Passenger Lines Ltd., 60 Ben-Yehuda St. (tel. 528 21 21/2/3). Books tickets on ships to Greece. Boats leave Sun. and Tues. 8pm. Deck chair one way US$73 (June 12-Sept. 17 US$80). Port tax additional US$17. Additional US$25 to Marmais, Turkey. Open Sun.-Thurs. 9am-6pm, Fri. 9am-1pm. (See Budget Travel above.)

Taxis: Salomon St., opposite the central bus station, for cars to the suburbs, Ḥaifa, and Jerusalem. Allenby Rd. and HaMoshavot Sq. to most other major cities. Cost about the same as buses. *Sherut* **taxis** run Fri. evenings and Sat., with a 20% *shabbat* surcharge. *Special taxis* operate with meters. It is illegal for a special taxi to carry you without a meter. Finally, *sherut moniyot* operate only between Ben-Gurion Airport and Jerusalem. They are shared, and take you to your door (NIS40).

Car Rental: Avis (tel. 38 42 42): US$67 (in summer US$90) per day with insurance. **Budget** (tel. 562 12 92): US$75 per day with insurance. **Eldan** (tel. 537 22 66/7/8): US$34 per day with insurance. **Hertz** (tel. 562 21 21): US$58 per day with insurance. Prices in shekels are considerably higher. Legal driving age is 17, but most agencies will only rent to persons 24 or older. Most major car rental agencies honor an American license. Others should procure an international driving license.

Shopping hours: In general, 8:30am-1pm and 4-7pm.

Information: Tel. 144.

English Bookstores: Pollak's Used Books, 36 HaMelekh George St. (tel. 528 86 13), has a 100-year tradition of buying and selling used books. Open Sun.-Fri. 9am-1:30pm, Tues. 4-7pm as well. **Book Boutique,** 170 Ben-Yehuda St. Best used bookstore in town. Over 13,000 titles, including out-of-print books and best-sellers. Good conversation as well. Open Sun.-Thurs. 10am-7pm, Fri. 10am-3pm. **Steimatzky's,** 109 Dizengoff St. (tel. 22 15 13). Open Sun.-Thurs. 8:30am-9:50pm, Fri. 8:40am-2:50pm, Sat. 8pm-10pm.

Tours: Society for the Protection of Nature in Israel (SPNI): 4 HaShfela St. (tel. 38 25 01), near the central bus station. English-guided hiking trips to all parts of the country, year-round. Most tours venture far off the tourist track, and last from a day (US$35) to 7 days (up to US$295).

Neot HaKikar (Oases of the Desert), 78 Ben-Yehuda St. (tel. 22 81 61/2/3). Good for guided hiking and camping tours in Israel and Egypt by foot, jeep, camel, or your own combination. Well-informed and reasonably priced. 1-day Sinai Desert Safari to Santa Katarina US$53. 4 days in 3-star hotels in Egypt US$160, and 6 days of camel trekking in Sinai US$350. Special budget 4 day and 3 night Egypt trip US$95.

Camping Supplies: LaMetayel, Dizengoff Center, Gate 3 or 5 (tel. 528 68 94), near the Lev Cinema. The largest and cheapest camping store in Israel. Books, maps, guides, information, and a full range of equipment. Open Sun.-Thurs. 9:30am-7:30pm and Fri. 9:30am-2pm. **HaYeḥida,** 25 Tchernihovsky St. (tel. 65 02 60), off of Bialik. Open Sun.-Thurs. 9am-7pm, Fri. 9am-3pm, Sat. from end of *shabbat* until 10pm.

Kibbutz and Moshav Offices: Takam (United Kibbutz Movement), 82 HaYarkon St. (tel. 545 25 55). **HaKibbutz Ha'Artzi,** 13 Leonardo da Vinci St. (tel. 43 52 22). Takam and Ha'Artzi offices open Sun.-Thurs. 8am-2pm. **HaKibbutz HaDati,** 7 Dubnov St. (tel. 695 72 31), accepts only religious Jews. **Moshav Movement,** 19 da Vinci St. (tel. 695 84 73), open Sun.-Thurs. 9am-noon. **Moshav Volunteer Office,** 5 Tiomkin St. (tel. 560 08 06 or 560 53 16), off Yehuda HaLevi St., open Sun.-Thurs. 9am-3pm. **Meira's Volunteers for Moshav,** 103 Ben-Yehuda St. (tel. 523 73 69 or 523 80 73). To apply for work bring 2 passport photographs and your passport. You must be 18-32 years old and agree to work for at least 2 months.

Laundromats: 51 Ben-Yehuda St. (tel. 22 29 54). Coin-operated washers and dryers. Wash NIS7, soap NIS1, 30min. drying NIS6. For NIS2 more, they'll do it for you. Open Sun.-Thurs. 8am-6pm, Fri. 8am-2pm. **Buot,** 49 Sheinkin (tel. 528 83 94). For NIS18 they will pick up and clean up to 6kg of laundry and drop it off on your doorstep. Ironing is NIS3 per item.

Help Lines: Crisis Intervention: tel. 25 33 11. **Rape Crisis:** tel. 523 48 19, 24 hrs. **Drug Counseling:** tel. 546 35 87. **Gay and Lesbian Hotline: White Line** (HaKav HaLavan), tel. 62 56 29. Sun., Tues., and Thurs., 7:30-11:30pm.

Pharmacy: HaGalil Pharmacy, 80 Ben-Yehuda St. (tel. 22 33 58). English spoken. Open Sun.-Thurs. 8:30am-7pm, Fri. 8:30am-3:30pm. There are no 24-hr. pharmacies in Tel Aviv. Two are open until 11pm every night on a rotating schedule. Schedules available at any pharmacy.

Fire: Tel. 102.

First Aid: Tel. 101.

Police: Tel. 100.

Accommodations

Most of Tel Aviv's cheap hostels are located on or around Ben-Yehuda and Dizengoff St. You can also find a few hostels and cheaper hotels near the beach on and just off of Allenby Rd. and HaYarkon St. The traffic of the main roads can keep you up nights; check the noise level before you take any room, because what you hear at midday will continue through most of the night. Hostels in Tel Aviv fill up quickly, especially during the summer. Prices drop by about 10% in the off season. Paying in foreign currency will save you the 18% VAT. Sleeping on the beach is illegal and you should be aware that there have been many cases of theft and sexual assault; single women in particular should *not* sleep on beaches. If you must, go as far north as possible (staying south of the port) and sleep on your wallet.

Tel Aviv Youth Hostel, 36 B'nei Dan St. (tel. 544 17 48 or 546 07 19, fax 544 10 30), in north Tel Aviv, a bit far from the city center; buses #5, 24, 25, 27 have stops nearby. Well-furnished, airy rooms all have attached bathroom with toilet and shower. Lobby with snack bar and candy machines. Large dining hall serves dinner (US$6, open 7-8pm). Lockers available for NIS3 per day. Two handicapped-accessible rooms. A few blocks south of World Union of Progressive Judaism center. No curfew. Open 24 hours. Guest house (4 per room) US$15; hostel (5-6 per room) US$13. Nonmembers add US$1.50. Breakfast included.

No. 1 Hostel 84 Ben-Yehuda St., 4th floor (tel. 523 78 07). Formerly the "Top Hostel." Yes, *4th floor,* but No.1 offers the unrivaled hostel luxury of a quietly efficient elevator. Each dorm room (of 4, 6, or 8 beds) has private shower. The bird's eye view from the bar and cable TV room faces *east,* but long balconies on three sides, a sunny, hospital-clean interior, and laundry facilities for NIS8 make this a particularly comfortable environment. Fine views even from the kitchen and laundry, and a tasty limited menu with occasional barbeques NIS3.50-6. Kitchen closes at 11pm. Lockout 11am-2:30pm. No curfew. Lockers for NIS3 per day; free use of safe. Dorm beds NIS19-22, private single NIS60. In summer, mattresses on roof for NIS19. Breakfast included.

Old Yafo Hostel, 8 Olei Zion St. (tel. 82 23 70, fax 82 23 16), right in the middle of the Shuk HaPishpishim in the center of Yafo. This clean, friendly place has been recently restored and is one of Tel Aviv's best hostels. Just a short bus ride from the middle of Tel Aviv. If you let them know exactly when you are coming, they'll send a free van to pick you up at the airport. Israeli breakfast (NIS5), all-you-can-eat vegetarian dinner (NIS6), beer (NIS3.50), and other goodies can be purchased on credit for up to one week. Free use of kitchen and safe. Laundry machine (NIS8). Check-in 8am-midnight. No curfew. No lockout. Dorm beds (8 per room) NIS15, mattress on roof NIS12, rooftop "bungalow" NIS15, singles NIS50.

The Greenhouse, 201 Dizengoff St. (tel. 523 59 94). Take bus #5 all the way up Dizengoff. Extremely clean, airy rooms, no bunk beds, kitchen facilities, spotless showers, great location, telephone, and no curfew. Coffee, beer, and soda sold in a homey TV room. Rooftop bar open until 1-2am (only in summer). Beach campers can use shower and kitchen facilities for NIS7. Dorm beds NIS22 (in summer NIS25). Doubles NIS56. Apartments for 2, NIS91; for 3, NIS108.

Momo's Hostel, 28 Ben-Yehuda St. (tel. 528 74 71). Another centrally located hostel. It's not pristine or even renovated, but cleanliness is a high priority. As Momo insists, "I clean the toilets twice a day with Lysol." Rooftop sunning a pleasant bonus. Bar downstairs has pleasantly gritty, relaxed atmosphere. Mix ethnic cuisines at the well-stocked, inexpensive snack bar. Free use of safe. Laundry service. TV and VCR in bar. Kitchen facilities. Separate sex and mixed rooms. No curfew. Check out at 11am. Dorm beds (4, 6, or 8 per room) NIS15; add NIS3 for breakfast.

Hotel Yosef, 15 Bograshov St. (tel. 528 09 55), off Ben-Yehuda St. Specifically for students and "young travelers." Clean. Bar closes 1am (happy hour 9-11pm). Use of kitchen facilities 1-11pm. Information and arranging of cheap flights, kibbutz and moshav volunteering, and available jobs. Lockers for NIS4 per day, free luggage storage and use of safe. Lockout 11am-2pm. Curfew 1:30am but flexible, especially in summer. Dorm beds NIS17.50; beds or mattresses on roof NIS16. Breakfast NIS5, NIS6 if ordered in advance.

Traveler's Hostel, 40 Ben-Yehuda St. (tel. 525 09 99). Small but clean, with cable TV and bar in garden below. Kitchen facilities. Curfew 3am. Dorm beds NIS15, singles NIS60, includes breakfast (served 8-10am). Will arrange visas to Egypt, cheap flights, jobs.

Gordon Hostel, 2 Gordon St. (tel. 22 98 70), corner of HaYarkon St. Great location near top hotels, with several rooms looking onto the Med. Same ownership as the No. 1 Hostel. Kitchen, hot showers, and free coffee and tea in reception/TV room. Arranges cheap flights and tours. Rooftop bar open 4pm-midnight. Lockers NIS3; free use of safe for documents. Hot meals for NIS6-8. Arrive early in the day. No curfew. Dorm beds (6 per room) NIS17.

Riviera Hostel, 52 HaYarkon St. (tel. 65 68 70). Near the beach, but separated from the sand by a block of long-term construction. Interior includes stained glass windows over stairway, wrought iron railing, and panelled walls. Cramped but reasonably clean rooms. Pub with music and video bar open 6pm-3am (happy hour 6-10pm). No curfew. Dorm bed NIS13, with breakfast NIS17. Singles NIS55, with shower NIS65. Doubles NIS65, with shower NIS75.

The Home, 6 Frischmann St., corner of HaYarkon, #16 (tel. 22 26 95). The name fits the place. Newly renovated rooms are spotless, cozy, and fully furnished with carpeting, small refrigerators, hot plates, and private bathrooms. New balconies overlook the sea. TV available for small fee, and telephones supplied with US$100 deposit. A/C. Singles US$250 per week. Some doubles and triples available. 10% discount for students with ISIC. Reception open daily 9am-2pm.

Hotel Nes Tziona, 10 Ness Tziona St. (tel. 510 34 04), just off Ben-Yehuda St. Superb location and service. Of its 22 rooms, 16 have showers, 8 have bathrooms, and 11 have sinks. Free fans on request. Singles NIS50-60. Doubles NIS70-80. Triples NIS90-95. One small room on ground floor NIS40.

The Hostel, 60 Ben-Yehuda St., 4th floor (tel. 528 70 88 or 528 15 00). Convenient, if lofty, location. Inexpensive but somewhat dark and more regimented than other hostels. Lights and TV off at midnight, checkout by 9:30am, and closed for cleaning until 1pm. 2am curfew. Dorm bed (3-4 per room) NIS18-20, 8 per room NIS15. Double NIS45.

Hotel Tamar, 8 Gnessin St. (tel 528 69 97), near Cinema Hod. Follow Mendele St. east (away from the sea) from Ben-Yehuda; at the end of Mendele make first right. Quiet and tidy rooms, with telephone and bathroom. Singles NIS40, with private shower NIS60. Doubles NIS50, with private shower NIS70.

Immanuel House Christian Hospice, 12 Be'er Hoffmann St. (tel. 82 14 59 or 82 47 21), in Yafo, at the corner of Auerbach. Take bus #44 or 46 and get off after the Paz gas station on Eilat St. A neat, friendly, relaxing place outside the city center. Built by Peter Ustinov's father. Professional chef cooks lunch (NIS18) or supper (NIS10) on request. 11pm curfew. Dorm beds NIS24. Doubles with bath NIS120.

Allenby Street has a row of hotels located near the beach at the corner of HaYarkon. The bright white complex, including arcade with gargling fountain, offers a welcome respite from Tel Aviv's largely poverty-stricken south. Coffee shops and ice cream stores alternate with fairly inexpensive accommodations.

Hotel Galim, 9 Allenby St. (tel. 65 57 03). Dirt-free, airy rooms, each with a private shower and two beds. Kitchen facilities. Dorm beds NIS15 (4-5 in room). Singles NIS50. Doubles NIS60.

Miami Hotel, 8 Allenby St. (tel. 510 38 68). Small but comfortable and clean rooms with plenty of light, phone, and bathrooms with shower. Singles US$30. Doubles US$40.

Food

Follow the locals to one of the many neighborhoods that specialize in street food. Head for the self-service eateries on Ben-Yehuda St. or the innumerable falafel stands; those around Shuk HaKarmel and along Bezalel St. off Allenby and HaMelekh George stay open the latest. Mix either (but not both) *ḥarif,* the red-hot sauce, or the yellow mustard sauce with lots of *taḥina.* One portion (a *mana*) costs about NIS3.

The **Kerem HaTemanim,** between Shuk HaKarmel and the beach, houses many inexpensive Yemenite and Middle Eastern restaurants between its small red-roofed houses and narrow streets. **Maganda,** 26 Rabbi Meir St. (tel. 65 99 90 or 66 18 95), **Shaul's Inn,** 11 Eliashiv St. (follow the signs) (tel. 65 76 19), and **Zion Restaurant,** 28 Peduyim St. (tel. 65 87 14) all serve such delicacies as brains and lungs, but the prices take guts (entrees NIS14-30). You can always get fall back on the old reliable: a ḥummus platter for NIS5.

For NIS3 you can eat at an *al ha'esh* ("on the fire") stand along Kanfe Nesharim St., which runs north-south in the Neveh Tzedek area. Ask around for someone selling homemade *marak basar* (a delicious Yemenite meat soup) or *malawaḥ* (fried, salted dough dipped in *srug, khelbe,* or another sharp sauce). A family's tureens are usually empty by noon or 1pm, so try to eat early.

Dizengoff Street's restaurants run the gamut of intercontinental cuisine: from Russian to Argentinian, and everything in between. Dizengoff also has the most restaurants open on *shabbat.* On the northeast side of Dizengoff Sq., there are several sub shops where you can stuff your own buns with cheese, salads, vegetables, or meat. Skip the mildly sinister **McDavid's** and **Burger Ranch,** unless you're a junk-food junkie. A number of new American chains such as **Philadelphia Hoagy, Wendy's,** and **Pizza Hut** have opened recently in the area as part of their ongoing campaign of cultural imperialism.

For a treat, head north towards **Yirmeyahu Street,** which runs between Dizengoff and Ben-Yehuda just before they intersect. This area is quieter and more elegant than downtown. Several of its restaurants and cafés are superb, and you're less likely to choke on bus fumes while dining *al fresco.*

Another alternative is to visit the factories where *begaleh* are made using 1950s equipment. Only the missing centers of these large sesame rings resemble American bagels. Sprinkle each bite with the spices displayed in the paper twists on the counter. There are a handful of *begaleh* bakeries near the central bus station. In the event of a sneak midnight bagel-craving, visit the **all-night bagel factory** at 11 Pines St. The two bagel barns in Yafo just beyond the Old Clock Tower (on the right if you bear left onto Beit Eshel) are a bit more tourist-ridden.

Minimalist spenders should shop at the large, outdoor **Shuk HaKarmel** (Karmel Market). The best deals are on produce and underwear, both of which you can get for bare-ass prices. Most of the produce stands are at the southwestern end of the market, west of HaKarmel St. between Tarmav and Kalisher. To catch prices at their lowest, shop an hour or two before the beginning of *shabbat.* A block south of the *shuk,* **Naḥalat Binyamin Street** and intersecting Rambam St. form a long, wide *midreḥov.* Spend an evening under soft gas lights, listening to street musicians and participating in lazy circle dances in the street. Just north of Naḥalat Binyamin is Sheinkin St., Israel's answer to Greenwich Village, full of art galleries and trendy cafés.

Keep hydrated while about-towning, but be sure to watch prices: a Kinley mango on Dizengoff costs NIS3-4, whereas the same cash at a Ben-Yehuda supermarket nets you a 1.5-liter bottle of mineral water or cola.

Rosemarine, 190 Dizengoff (tel. 524 68 94). Health food from Kibbutz Yotveta, Israel's second largest dairy kibbutz. Fresh salads with a delightful yogurt dressing and sandwiches served indoors or out (NIS14). Freshly squeezed juices (NIS4-5) and homemade cakes and pies (NIS6.50). Add 10% to all prices for takeout. Open Sun.-Thurs. 8:30am-1am, Fri 8:30am-2pm, Sat. 10pm-1am. Kosher.

Eternity, 60 Ben-Yehuda St. (tel. 20 31 51). Run by members of the Black Hebrew community, a group originally from the midwestern United States who have settled in Israel. Their dietary laws prohibit both milk and meat, so you'll find interesting (and neologistic) alternatives, from tofulafel to vegetable burgers and *parve* natural ice cream (made of soybeans). The vegetable *shwarma* and barbecue twist are even better than the real thing. Entrees NIS4-15.30. Open Sun.-Thurs. 8am-11pm, Fri. 8am-3pm (in winter 8am-2pm), Sat. after sundown. Kosher.

Café B'Nordau, 230 Ben-Yehuda St. (tel. 544 17 35), on the corner of Nordau. Botanical life from the plant shop next door spills over into this cozy restaurant. Largely, though not exclusively, gay clientele. Tasty light meals (NIS7-22), and delicious cakes and pies (NIS7-9). Open Sun.-Fri. 8am-2am, Sat. 10am-2am.

Hungarian Blintzes, 94 Dizengoff St. (tel. 23 05 18). Blintzes filled with combinations of cream, chocolate, cinnamon, apples, cheese, nuts, raisins, jam, spinach, and an assortment of other goodies. Two superb blintzes NIS15. Open Sun.-Thurs. 11am-1am, Fri. 11am-3pm.

Cherry's, 116 Dizengoff (tel. 523 46 87) at Ben-Gurion St. Sidewalk tables and air-conditioned interior. Voluminous menu. Gargantuan salads and light meals (NIS10-20), as well as a wide range of desserts. Open daily 8am-2am, Fri. 8am-4am.

Nargila, 10 Frischmann St. (tel. 23 41 54). Traditional Yemenite *malawaḥ* (a thin flour-based pancake) served whole with a choice of 13 toppings (NIS4.50-12) or cut into pieces and mixed with 7 choices of ingredients to make "sweet fatoot" (a dessert; NIS4.50-8). Other Yemenite specialties such as lung, stomach, and tail prepared as soup or entree (NIS5.50-10). Great food, location (one block from the beach), and hours (open around the clock). Inexplicably, cut-outs of nude women adorn all the menus here.

Zion Restaurant, 28 Peduyim St. Follow HaKarmel, the main street of the *shuk,* to Rambam, turn right, and look for narrow Peduyim St. Yemenite dishes served in a traditional Middle Eastern atmosphere. Brave souls can grab gourmet ox testicles. (Remember this place when your Aunt Sonia tells you to have a ball in Tel Aviv.) Prudish eaters can order a ḥummus platter and drink for NIS7.50-9. Entrees NIS14-30. Open daily 10am-1am.

Dalas [sic] Restaurant, 68 Etzel St. (tel. 37 43 49), in Tel Aviv's Hatikva section. They would have been better off calling it Dali's Restaurant—the combination of wall-paintings of Southfork Ranch (of the popular but deceased TV series "Dallas") with outstanding Yemenite food is positively surreal. In one of Tel Aviv's poorer sections, accessible by buses #7a, 15, 16, and 41 and well worth the trip. Plentiful ḥummus salads (NIS4.50), delicious Iraqi pita (NIS1.50), and kebabs (NIS6-11 per skewer) attract many locals. Open Sun-Thurs. 11am-2am, Fri. 11am until 1.5hrs. before *shabbat*.

New York Deli, 164 Dizengoff (tel. 22 59 66). The only restaurant in Israel that makes its own corned beef. Other house specialties include pastrami, beef brisket, and smoked turkey with garlic. Sandwiches NIS20. Open Sun.-Thurs. 9am-1am, Fri. 9am-*shabbat*, Sat. after *shabbat*-1am. Kosher.

Acapulco, the corner of Dizengoff and Frischmann St. (tel. 523 75 52). Great for a cheap kebab dinner. Main dishes NIS7.50-19. Mouthwatering assortment of desserts: the huge "Blintz Acapulco" is an epicurean orgy (NIS15). Open daily 11am-midnight. The meat is kosher, but the *shabbat* hours are not.

Domino's, in the Dizengoff Center mall. Go in gate 3, bear left at HaMashbir, go the end of the hall. Excellent pizza (NIS4-5.50 per slice) and sit-down Italian meals (NIS12-14). Breakfast served (NIS10). Open Sun.-Thurs. 9am-11:30pm, Fri. 9am-1pm, Sat. after *shabbat*-11:30pm. Kosher.

Café Kazze, 19 Sheinkin St. (tel. 29 37 56). Israeli stars can sometimes be seen eating at this trendy café. Small tables in airy rooms or garden patio in back. Try the spaghetti (NIS16.50, comes with salad) or the croissants (NIS4.50-6). Open Sun.-Thurs. 8am-12:30am, Fri. 8am-3:30pm. Kosher.

Chin Chin, 42 Frischmann St. (tel. 524 58 02), off Dizengoff. Tasty, greasy approximations of Chinese food. Good service amidst the flurry of butterfly-dragon wallpaper. Soups NIS4, entrees NIS13.50-15.50.

Sights

The chaos (*balagan* in Hebrew) of **Shuk HaKarmel** (Karmel Market) will entertain even the most jaded of tourists. Near the northern entrance to the market, shopkeepers stand behind piles of clothing and footwear, selling "fashions" which even the Russian *olim* (emigrés) choose to admire from afar. Waving polyester undergarments and red plastic sandals, vendors bellow their products' virtues. Farther south, near the parking lot, you can buy fresh fruit and vegetables at the lowest prices in the city. Huge mounds of chickens plucked bare make the west side of the market look like the morning after a foul barnyard orgy. The entrance to the *shuk* is at **Kikar Magen David** at the intersection of Allenby and HaMelekh George St. The community in **Kerem HaTemanim** (the Yemenite Quarter), northwest along Allenby, retains its traditional character despite the encroachment of stores hawking Simpsons T-shirts. For a more sedate shopping experience, on Tuesdays and Fridays the *midreḥov* of **Naḥalat Binyamin St.**—one block south of Shuk HaKarmel—becomes a street fair. From 10am-4pm (weather permitting) local artists sell jewelry, pottery, paintings, Judaica, and even some bizarre candelabras; the street is also full of magicians, mimes, and musicians. Mmm. Take bus #4 from the central bus station and ask the driver to let you off at the *shuk*.

Just north of the *shuk*, off Allenby, lies Bialik St., named after Ḥayim Naḥman Bialik, one of Israel's greatest poets. His home, now the **Beit Bialik Museum,** 22 Bialik St. (tel. 517 15 30) is maintained exactly as it was when he died. Bialik's manuscripts, paintings, photographs, articles, letters, and 94 books (with translations in 28 languages) are all on display. An English brochure is available, but lack of English translations on the display cases makes this museum difficult for non-Hebrew speakers. (Open Sun.-Thurs. 9am-4:45pm, Sat. 10am-1:45pm. Admission free, but might charge a few shekels by 1993.) Nearby stands the **Museum of the History of Tel Aviv-Yafo,** 27 Bialik St. (tel. 517 30 52), which traces the city's history through photographs, documents, models, dioramas, and a slide presentation. (Open Sun.-Thurs.

9am-2pm. Admission free. Currently under renovation, but library open Sun., Tues, and Thurs. 9:30am-1pm.) At 38 HaMelekh George St. is the brand new **Museum of the Irgun Tzvai Leumi** (tel. 525 13 87 or 528 40 01), which traces the pre-Independence history of Menaḥem Begin's rightist resistance movement. The museum boasts information on all the *Etzel's* battles, models, maps, and a Mount Rushmore-style bust of Ze'ev Jabotinsky, the father of the right-wing philosophy of Revisionist Zionism. (The bust looks remarkably like Yitzḥak Shamir.) Avid Likudniks won't want to miss this one. (Open Sun.-Thurs. 8:30am-4pm, Fri. 8:30am-noon. Admission NIS5, students NIS2, free on Independence Day.) The **Jabotinsky Institute** houses a collection of works written by and about Jabotinsky. 1993 will spotlight an exhibition on Menaḥem Begin as well. (Open Sun., Tues.-Thurs. 8am-2pm, Mon. 8am-5pm, Fri. 8am-noon. Free.)

The **Shalom Tower** stands at the other end of the *shuk* at 1 Herzl St. Soaring a whole forty stories, this is the tallest structure in the Middle East. The Rooftop Observatory (tel. 64 29 45) offers a spectacular view of Tel Aviv and environs. (Open Sun.-Thurs. 9am-7pm, Fri. 9am-2pm. Elevator ride NIS5, children NIS4). Next to the elevator of the observatory is the **Israeli Wax Museum** (tel. 64 29 45 or 65 73 04). Recently updated, the museum shows historical scenes from the Jewish expulsion from Spain to the Madrid peace conference. The wax is a bit unbelievable (the hilarious figure of John F. Kennedy is itself worth the price of admission), but it's a lot of fun. (Open Sun.-Thurs. 9am-5pm, Fri. 10am-2pm. Observatory and museum admission NIS12, children NIS9. Museum admission NIS9, children NIS7.) The tower occupies the site of the **Herzliya Gymnasium,** the first Hebrew school in Israel.

Neveh Tzedek, west of the Shalom Tower, is quickly becoming an artists' quarter. The recently renovated buildings that comprise the new **Suzanne Dellale Center** (tel. 510 56 56), are packed until the wee hours of the morning. Several dance and theater groups, including the Bat Sheva Dance Company and the Inbal Folklore Theater, perform in the center as well as outside in front of the new eateries. Here you can also explore the studios of Israel's avant-garde. Out-of-control art lovers should call 45 12 22 for guided tours of Tel Aviv's galleries and museums.

One of Tel Aviv's most important historical monuments is the **Great Synagogue** just east of the Shalom Tower at 110 Allenby St. (tel. 560 49 05). Completed in 1926 and renovated in 1970, the domed synagogue is ancient only by Tel Aviv standards. On Friday at sunset, observant Jews make their way toward the synagogue, bringing all traffic to a halt.

One block south of the synagogue, at 23 Rothschild Blvd., is the home of Eliyahu Golomb, one of the founders and leaders of the Hagana. The house was one of the first buildings erected in Tel Aviv and is now the **Hagana Museum** (tel. 62 36 24). It contains exhibits tracing the development of the IDF (Israel Defense Force) from its beginnings as an underground movement called the Hagana during the British Mandate through the present. Movies dramatize the Yom Kippur War and the Hagana's efforts to break the British blockade of ships carrying World War II refugees to Palestine. (Open Sun.-Thurs. 9am-4pm and Fri. 9am-12:30pm. Admission NIS5, students and children NIS2.)

Uptown, the **Tel Aviv Museum of Art,** 27 Shaul HaMelekh Blvd. (tel. 696 12 97), has split-level galleries and a sizable collection of Israeli and international modern art. The museum is large, so if your time is limited, head to pavilion #2. The first part contains an impressive collection of Impressionist art, including canvases by Corot, Renoir, Pissaro, Monet, and Dufy, with some works by Utrillo and a Degas sculpture. The second part features post-Impressionist masters such as Picasso, Juan Gris, Kokoschka, Roualt, and Matisse. Call ahead or pick up a copy of the Friday *Jerusalem Post,* which has a supplementary section listing the museum's exhibits and events. Take bus #18, 19, or 70. (Open Sun.-Thurs. 10am-9:30pm, Fri. 10am-2pm, Sat. 10am-2pm and 7-10pm. Admission NIS10, students NIS5.) The ticket for museum admission also entitles you to enter the **Helena Rubinstein Pavilion of Contemporary Art,** (tel. 528 71 96) down the street at 6 Tarsat Blvd., which houses rotating exhibits of modern Israeli art. Take bus #5, 11, or 62.

As you head farther north and toward the shore, visit the **David Ben-Gurion House,** 17 Ben-Gurion Ave. (tel. 22 10 10), to see the exhibition of books, pictures, and mementos of Israel's first prime minister and greatest leader. Included in the exhibition are letters from Ben-Gurion to John F. Kennedy, Winston Churchill, Charles de Gaulle (who all but worshiped Ben-Gurion), and other world leaders, as well as an elephant tusk given to Ben-Gurion by the president of Liberia. In the **Hillel Cohen Lecture Hall** next door you'll find even more Old Man trivia, such as copies of all his passports and even a copy of a 1928 salary slip. Avid Laborites won't want to miss this one. (Open Sun. and Tues.-Thurs. 8am-2pm, Mon. 8am-5pm, Fri. 8am-noon. Free.)

There are several points of interest in Ramat Aviv, the northernmost part of the city. The **Eretz Yisrael Museum** (Land of Israel) on Ha'Universita St. (tel. 641 52 44/8) includes eight pavilions built around an archeological site. For one price (NIS10, seniors and students NIS7) you can visit all eight museums *and* use the Eretz Yisrael Library, containing over 30,000 books and periodicals about the land of Israel.

The most famous attraction in the complex is the **Glass Museum,** offering one of the finest collections of glassware in the world. Exhibits trace the history of glassmaking from the earliest examples of the craft in the 15th century BCE through the Middle Ages. Across the patio, the **Kadman Numismatic Museum** traces the history of Israel through ancient coins. The **Ceramics Pavilion** has an extensive collection of pottery, especially the Gaza and Akko styles of Ibriq pottery. The **Nechustan Pavilion** houses the discoveries of the excavations of the ancient copper industries at Timna, better known as King Solomon's Mines. Walk across the entrance area past the grassy amphitheater to the **Man [sic] and His Work Center,** an exhibition of folk crafts and techniques used in Israel.

To the southeast, still in the museum complex, are the **Tel Qasila Excavations,** which have revealed a 12th-century BCE Philistine port city and ruins dating back to the time of Kings David and Solomon. The temple area at the top of the hill contains the remains of three separate Philistine temples built one on top of another. Down the hill to the south are scattered remains of the residential and industrial quarter of the Philistine town. A useful free guide to the *tel* (multi-level site) is available in the small **Tel Qasila Pavilion** (open Sun.-Thurs. 9am-12:30pm) to the east, which also contains artifacts found at the site.

Past the Philistine town is the **Folklore Pavilion,** with Jewish religious art, ceremonial objects, and ethnic clothing. The room at the rear of the pavilion contains a Florentine synagogue's benches, pulpit, and ornately decorated *aron*. The Eretz Yisrael complex also houses the **Alphabet Museum,** the **Lasky Planetarium** (shows in Hebrew only), and the **Museum of Science and Technology.** Take bus #25 from Yafo or Shuk HaKarmel; #27 from the central bus station. (Complex open Sun.-Fri. 9am-2pm, Tues. 9am-5pm, Sat. 10am-2pm. Library open Sun.-Thurs. 9am-5pm.)

At the Tel Aviv University campus, Gate 2, **Beit HaTfutzot** (Museum of the Diaspora, tel. 646 20 20) documents the Jewish experience in exile through movies, slides, maps, dioramas, and artifacts. One of the most powerful exhibits is "Scrolls of Fire," a collection of documents that give first-person perspectives on massacres from Roman times to the Nazi concentration camps. Mini-cinemas throughout the museum screen short documentaries, as well as recordings of dramatized discussions between historical figures. For NIS3, museum computers will trace the history of Jewish family names. Take bus #25 from Yafo, Karmel Market, or the HI youth hostel; or #27 from the central bus station. Get off at Gate 2 of the university. (Open Sun.-Tues. and Thurs. 10am-5pm, Wed. 10am-7pm, Fri. 9am-2pm. Admission NIS13, students NIS10.) *Chronosphere,* a multi-screen audio-visual display, costs an additional NIS6.

Animal lovers have a wide range of possible activities in Israel. Near HaYarkon Park is the new **Zapari** bird park (tel. 524 73 73). While admission is expensive (NIS18, students NIS12), the park is very relaxing and peaceful with its outdoor aviaries, swans, and cockatoos. An unforgettable bird show featuring Ilan, a bicycle-riding parrot; Alex, a telepathic cockatoo; and Tuvia, introduced as a "real Israeli parrot," who flies into the audience and takes NIS100 from an audience-member is presented every 10 minutes starting at 11am. (Open 9am-6pm daily.)

Another new—and far more reasonable—attraction is the **World of Silence Aquarium** at 1 Kaufman St. (tel. 510 66 70), near the Carmelit bus terminal in south Tel Aviv, on the corner of Herbert Samuel St. For only NIS7 (NIS5 for children) you can see hundreds of fish from the Mediterranean, the Red Sea, and around the world. Another room houses a frightening array of snakes, scorpions, reptiles, and tarantulas. (Open 10am-7:30pm daily. In July and August open 10am-10pm.)

For something completely different, get off the beach and go see a baby rhinoceros at the **Zoological Center** in Ramat Gan (tel. 631 21 81). This combination drive-through safari park and zoo features 250 acres of African game in a natural habitat. You can walk within one meter of African tigers, or stare over a *wadi* at Syrian bears and painfully intelligent-looking gorillas. Bring a picnic, or have lunch at the moderately priced restaurant (excellent view of the long-tailed monkey island). If you don't have a car, call ahead to see if tours are being offered for the pedestrians. Take bus #30, 35, or 43 to Ramat Gan. (Open Sun.-Thurs. 9am-4pm, Fri. 9am-1pm. July and Aug. Sun.-Thurs. 9am-7pm, but no entry after 5pm; Fri. 9am-1pm. Admission NIS20, children NIS15.) Continue your beast watch across the street at the massive **Ramat Gan National Park** (open dawn-dusk; free).

The Jewish National Fund (Keren Kayemet LeYisrael) organizes a tour of the **Modi'in Forest**, where you can plant a tree with your own paws. The tour leaves from the Keren Kayemet Building, 96 HaYarkon St. Reservations are required. For more information call 523 44 49.

Entertainment

A copy of *Tel Aviv Region Events,* issued at the GTIO, lists enough cultural activities to fill an entire vacation; however, most travelers seem to prefer to grease up and fry themselves on the beach. Better learn it now: the Hebrew word for beach is *hof,* as in **Ḥof Ma'ariv**--the southern beach where hundreds gather on Thursday nights for dinner, drinks, and, oddly enough, Brazilian music. Familiarize yourself with the flag language of the beach: black means swimming forbidden, red means swimming is dangerous, white means swim at will. Israelis with cars head north for a less crowded and slightly more pristine waterfront; most of the popular beaches within the city also tend to be in the north, near the Sheraton, Hilton, and Gordon Hotels. The southern coastline, with fewer amenities and no luxury hotels, tends to be quieter during the day. All of Tel Aviv's beaches are rife with theft; if possible, lock your valuables away before you hit the sands. Avoid the grossly overpriced refreshment stands in the northern Atarim Sq. (also known as Namir Sq.); Ben-Yehuda St., with cheap food and drink, is never more than a two-minute walk from the beach. Near Atarim Sq., a marina rents sailboats, surfboards, and windsurfers. Surfers ride the waves between the Carlton and Hilton Hotels. The marina also has an outdoor roller-rink, gym, and municipal pool (tel. 29 85 55; open daily 4:30am-6pm; admission NIS12, children NIS8, NIS2 extra on Sat.).

The Mediterranean art of crowd-gazing can be perfected in Tel Aviv's outdoor eateries, especially in the hours between dinner and dancing. The best places from which to watch are the tables on **Dizengoff** and **Yirmeyahu St.** in the north end. **Dizengoff Square** (Kikar Dizengoff) in the south has been spruced up in recent years with a futuristic pedestrian overpass and a singing fountain designed by the Israeli artist Agam. On the hour, except at 2 and 3pm, the fountain's colorful, three-tiered circular structure rotates and water flashes in synchrony with music ranging from Ravel's *Bolero* to Israeli folk songs. It's like a traffic accident—you don't want to look, but morbid fascination wins out.

The latest Israeli craze is bowling. The **Bowling Center** under the Shalom Tower (tel. 510 07 44) offers 16 lanes, arcade games, a snack bar, and live music on Friday nights after 11pm. Games cost NIS6, after 5pm NIS8, Fri. and Sat. after 8pm NIS10. Shoes NIS1.5. (Open 10am-3 or 4am daily.)

Tel Aviv rocks like no other Israeli city after dark. Club charges, however, range from NIS10 to 20 and pubs charge NIS4-6.50 for a Maccabee beer (mixed drinks run NIS5-20). The legal drinking age in Israel is 18.

Most of Tel Aviv's discos open at 10pm, but few truly hop before midnight. The **Colosseum,** at Atarim Sq. (tel. 528 71 21), attracts the largest crowd with its laser and video show. The cover is NIS15-20 for men, women get in free. Drinks are fairly inexpensive, and the first three are free. On Fridays, men pay NIS30 to enter this revolving inferno—and women still get in free. Get the picture? The place for new wave is **Liquid,** 117 Sh'alma St. (tel. 537 68 14), not far from Herzl St. The comparatively cheap cover charge (weeknights NIS10, weekends NIS20) compensates for expensive beer. (Maccabee NIS5. Open Tues., and Fri.-Sat. 11pm-5am. Live music every few Wednesdays.) **Penguin,** 43 Yehuda HaLevi St. (tel. 61 16 91), just west of Allenby, also spins funk and new wave. (Admission NIS10-15.)

For deafening reggae and rap, vogue over to **Soweto,** 6 Frischmann St. (tel. 524 08 25), corner of HaYarkon. Admission NIS10 and drinks are inexpensive. (Open nightly 10pm until everyone leaves.) To party with Israeli college students, look for **Focus** (tel. 42 30 04) at Tel Aviv University. There are movies at 8 and 10pm every night except Wednesdays (NIS7.50, students NIS6).

The **Metro,** 58 Allenby St. (tel. 65 96 10), next to the Sivan movie theater, is one of the only gay nightspots in Tel Aviv, featuring cheap drinks and disco tunes. (Acid House some Tuesdays. Open Mon.-Sat. 11pm-3 or 4am.)

Tel Aviv also has an array of pubs.

M.A.S.H. (More Alcohol Served Here), 275 Dizengoff (tel. 45 10 07). Most popular with tourists. Music from the '60s, '70s, and '80s. Down-and-dirty drinking. Open Mon. and Fri. 10am-1am, Sat. and Sun. 9am-1am.

Long John Silver's, in an alley just off Dizengoff next to the Ester Cinema (tel. 528 60 84). The best of the 3 pubs in the alley. Relaxed atmosphere, cheap drinks, cheap Clarence Thomas jokes, and classic rock music. Open 8:30pm-2:30am, Fri. 8:30pm-4am.

The Whitehouse, 108 HaYarkon (tel. 523 05 77), near Frischmann St. Cheap beer and predominantly Israeli clientele. Happy hours 5-9pm. Open until 2am.

The Happy Casserole, 344 Dizengoff St. (tel. 44 23 60). A wilder, more expensive Israeli hangout decorated with oldies memorabilia but no noodles. Live music every night, often Israeli folk tunes. When the place gets warmed up, don't be surprised if people start dancing on chairs and singing along. The crowd remains until the musicians collapse.

HaShoftim, at the corner of Ibn Gevirol and HaShoftim St. (tel. 25 17 53). Attracts an almost exclusively Israeli crowd. Lively ambience and mellow prices (Maccabee NIS7). No English menus. Open 11pm-5am.

The Bell, 281 Dizengoff St. (tel. 546 29 48 or 544 38 03), at the junction of Ben-Yehuda and Dizengoff. A healthy balance of Israelis and tourists. Comparatively costly (Maccabee NIS5.50) but a good place to meet people. Upstairs intimate continental restaurant, downstairs pub/café. In winter, open log fire and pianist upstairs. Open 3pm-3am upstairs, 6pm-4 or 5am downstairs.

Beit Lessin, 34 Weizmann St. (tel. 695 62 22). A jazz oasis, this theater/café attracts Israel's best jazz musicians every Sun. starting at 10pm. Open Sun.-Thurs. 10:30am-1:30pm and 5pm-midnight, Fri. 10:30am-1:30pm and 7pm-midnight, Sat. 6pm-midnight.

Gordon's Pub, 17 Gordon St. (tel. 22 21 28). A quiet pub on Tel Aviv's chic gallery-lined lane. One block from the beach. Bizarre entertainment features old cartoons on a 100-in. color video screen—no sound. Maccabees NIS5. Open daily 6pm-2am (sometimes until 4 or 5am).

To temper the hedonism, Tel Aviv offers nightly opera, ballet, jazz and classical concerts, and dance performances. **The Y Studio,** 1 Tveriya St. (tel. 22 36 15), off Bograshov St., is a theater workshop that teaches and trains actors and directors for the professional stage. Performances are given in English every Monday at 8:30pm. **Bikurei Ha'Etim Cellar,** 6 Helftman St. (tel. 697 95 10), offers Israeli folk dancing for all levels, including instruction every Monday, Tuesday, and Thursday at 7 and 9pm and Friday at 9pm. Call ahead: sometimes classes are geared for experienced dancers. The **outdoor theater** in Neveh Tzedek, 6 Yehieli St., often has concerts and dance performances. For schedules, call 517 37 11. (See also the Suzanne Dellale

Center above.) The amphitheater at **HaYarkon Park** features rock and pop performers. For tickets and schedules inquire at Hadran ticket agency, 90 Ibn Gevirol St., north of Malkhei Yisrael Sq. (tel. 524 87 87).

The ticket office for concerts, plays, and other performances is at 93 Dizengoff St. (tel. 524 88 24; open Sun.-Thurs. 9am-1pm and 5-7pm, Friday 9am-1pm.) For the most detailed information on performance schedules and other activities in the Tel Aviv area see *Tel Aviv Today, Hello Israel,* and *This Week in Israel,* all free at the GTIO and major hotels.

Yafo (Jaffa) יפו

The port of Old Yafo is one of the oldest functioning harbors in the world. The main port through which the first waves of Jewish immigrants broke into Palestine, Yafo has been relegated by the modern ports of Haifa and Ashkelon to harboring mainly small fishing boats. Several years ago, Israel undertook a massive renovation project, restoring and cleaning many of Yafo's convents, mosques, and crusader walls. The lively city center and art galleries make for a delightful, easy day trip (if you want more time here, stay at the Old Yafo Hostel in the Accommodations section under Tel Aviv, above). The view of Tel Aviv and the Mediterranean from Yafo's landscaped parks is unsurpassed.

Yafo ("beautiful" in Hebrew), is known in Arabic as Yafa, and in the Bible as Joppa. According to the Bible, the recalcitrant prophet Jonah shirked his divine calling by fleeing to Joppa to catch a boat to Tarshish. When a great tempest threatened to destroy the ship, Jonah asked crewmates to hurl him overboard, for he knew the Lord had created the storm. The sea calmed, but an enormous fish surfaced and swallowed the prophet. After three days and nights, Jonah repented and the fish delivered him safely to dry land. (See Ashdod.)

According to the New Testament, the Apostle Peter brought the disciple Tabitha back to life in Joppa. The latter then dwelt in the seaside house of the town tanner and received divine instructions to preach to non-Jews. To this day, you can still visit the house of Simon the Tanner.

The earliest archeological finds in Yafo date from the 18th century BCE. In 1468 BCE, the Egyptians conquered Yafo by hiding soldiers in life-size clay jars that were brought into the city market. King David conquered the city in about 1000 BCE, and under Solomon it became the main port of Jerusalem, a position it maintained until the development of Caesarea under King Herod. During the 12th century, Yafo was captured by the Crusaders, Salah al-Din, Richard the Lion-Hearted, the Muslims, and finally the Crusaders again, who then built magnificent walls and towers, parts of which are extant still. In 1267 the Mamluks overpowered the city, and Yafo remained an important Arab stronghold until 1948.

Relations between the Arabs in Yafo and the Jews in Tel Aviv were never harmonious. In 1929, 1936, and 1939, Yafo was the scene of anti-Zionist riots. When the Irgun captured the Arab section of Yafo in 1948, shortly before the creation of the State of Israel, most of Yafo's Arab population—some 70,000 strong—fled the city. With the huge influx of Jews, Yafo was officially incorporated into the Tel Aviv municipality in 1949. Today Yafo is one of the few truly mixed neighborhoods in Israel. As the locals say, "Here it's Arab-Jew, Arab-Jew."

Food

The area around the Yafo clock tower is full of food. In this area you can find small fish restaurants, *al ha'esh* stands, and falafel; nearby, *mamtekim* sellers hawk their Middle Eastern sweets every few meters. These cakes and pastries, swimming in warm, sticky honey, are especially popular during the nights of Ramadan. Between the clock tower and the flea market stands **Abu-Lafiah** (open all night), which sells scrumptious homemade pizzas and *borekas* (dough folded over meat, eggs, cheese, or mushrooms), as well as large, soft *begalehs* dipped in *za'atar,* a sage-like spice. For a full seafood meal, try **Fisherman's Restaurant** (Misadat Dagim) on Ha'Aliya HaShniya St., southwest of the clock tower. A dinner on the wharf or inside among the stuffed sharks costs NIS18-34.

For dessert, try an ice cream at **Dr. Lek** just up from the clock tower on 3488 St. (not a typo). Reputedly Israel's best ice cream, you can get a Dr. Lek cone for NIS4.40.

Sights

The **Clock Tower of Yafo,** built in 1906, marks the entrance to the city. A free tour of Old Yafo given by the Association for Tourism of Tel Aviv-Yafo begins here each Wed. at 9:30am (line up at 9am). Next to the clock tower is the minaret of the **al-Mahmudia Mosque,** an enormous structure erected in 1812. Entrance is forbidden for non-Muslims. Down Mifratz Shlomo St. from the mosque, the **Museum of Antiquities of Tel Aviv-Yafo** (tel. 82 53 75) contains artifacts from nearby sites in Old Yafo. The columns and capitals scattered about the museum's courtyard date from the first century BCE and were brought here from Caesarea during the 1800s. (Open Sun.-Wed. 9am-2pm, Tues. 9am-7pm. Admission NIS5, students NIS3.)

Behind the museum lie the grassy **HaPisga Gardens,** which contain a small, modern amphitheater as well as an archeological site with excavations of an 18th-century BCE Hyksos town and a later Egyptian city. A white, ladder-like sculpture dominates one hill in the gardens; its three sections depict the fall of Jericho, the sacrifice of Isaac, and Jacob's dream. Russian musicians play violin music as you stroll through the park.

From the park, a small wooden footbridge leads to **Kikar Kedumim,** Yafo's commercial, historical, and tourist center. In 1740, the first Jewish hostel was established on this site. It included two *mikvaot* (ceremonial baths) and a synagogue. Libyan Jews reopened the synagogue, which is still in use today. After the War of Independence, the striking, abandoned Arab stone buildings in this area became home to a large artists' colony. In the late 1950s the government renovated the neighborhood, and today studios, galleries, and restaurants stand artfully arranged among the reconstructed buildings.

Several interesting sights are located in Kikar Kedumim, including a small, well-preserved archeological site, the colorful Greek Orthodox **Church of St. Michael,** the Roman Catholic **Monastery of St. Peter,** and the **House of Simon the Tanner. Andromeda's Rock,** site of the Greek princess's mythological rescue by Perseus, is visible from the lighthouse a few blocks to the south.

Yafo's large **Shuk HaPishpishim** (Flea Market) is one of the most exciting markets in Israel, with a covered row of overflowing stalls offering endless delights of the traditional Middle Eastern variety, as well as modern Israeli hand-dyed clothing and other crafts. Choose among Persian carpets, leather goods, used clothes, and brassware. A vast selection of enormous *narghilas,* elaborate Middle Eastern waterpipes, is available. Bargaining is a way of life here, and you should begin by offering no more than half the asking price. To reach the flea market from the clock tower, continue 1 block south down Yefet St. and turn left. The market is squeezed between Tzion and MeRagusa St. and is closed on *shabbat.*

Entertainment

Yafo buzzes with nocturnal activity. The discos are wild, crowded, and usually expensive (cover charges NIS15-20), and they are open 10am-4 or 5am. One of the best pubs in Yafo is **Aladin,** 5 Mifratz Shlomo St. (tel. 82 67 66). Take a gander at the gorgeous Mediterranean and Tel Aviv skyline. Open 11:30pm-2am. Rock with raucous Israeli youth at **Steps,** 1 Rabbi Pinhas St. (tel. 24 99 22 or 45 51 66), or **November,** 15 Yeffet St. (tel. 82 12 43), both of which spin disco and new wave. For a more relaxed atmosphere, try **Omar Khayam** (tel. 82 58 65), 5 Netiv HaMasalot St. in Old Yafo at Kikar Kedumim, featuring live entertainment every night 9pm-2am. **The Cave,** 14 Kikar Kedumim (tel. 82 90 18) is an exciting, if expensive, Israeli folklore night club.

Near Tel Aviv

Most of Tel Aviv's suburbs are modern, clean, attractive, and dull. **Petaḥ Tikva** was the site of a heated conflict in 1984 between Orthodox residents of the town and a movie theater owner who wanted to show films on Friday night. The furor has since subsided; Petaḥ Tikva, like Ḥolon, has regained its suburban composure. **Ramat Gan** houses the Tel Aviv Stadium (where every four years Jewish athletes from all over the world compete in the Maccabia Games, patterned after the Olympic Games), and the Elite chocolate factory, every Israeli kid's dream. Ramat Gan earned dubious international renown during the Gulf War as the favorite suburban target of Iraqi Scuds. **Bat Yam** is a seaside resort with alluring beaches and painfully expensive hotels. **B'nei Brak,** re-established in 1924 by Ḥasidic Jews from Warsaw, is a religious neighborhood and a center of Talmudic scholarship. In the 2nd century CE, B'nei Brak was the home of Rabbi Akiva's famous yeshiva.

Herzliya Pituah הרצליה פיתוח

An affluent area of Herzliya, Herzliya Pituaḥ is home to many foreign ambassadors who live and tan themselves there, alongside the luxury hotels that line the town's beautiful beaches.

Budget travel is not impossible here, however, thanks to the **Mittelmann Guesthouse,** 13 Basel St. (tel. (052) 57 65 44). It has cozy rooms with refrigerators, private showers, air conditioning, and access to kitchen facilities; best to ring the bell before entering the courtyard so friendly manager Effie can call off his two dogs. (Singles US$28. Doubles US$38.) From Deshalit Sq., where the bus from Tel Aviv lets you off, follow Basel St. for about 10 min.

Another option is to do as the locals do and camp on the beautiful—and free—**Nof Yam Beach**. Although not an official campground, cookouts and overnight stays are common here. The beach lies 1km north of Herzliya Pituaḥ's hotel-lined main beach, just beyond the dilapidated **Sydne Ali** mosque.

Herzliya Pituaḥ offers a few sights worth seeing in addition to the beach and Sydne Ali mosque. Perched on a ledge one hundred meters north of the entrance to Nof Yam Beach is an inhabited sandcastle known as the **Hermit's House.** Part of it looks like a boat over which a peacock has spread its fan, part like a gargoyle, and the rest like nothing else you've ever seen. The hermit in question, Nissim Kaḥalon, has been building this fantastic structure for the past 19 years with packed sand, tires, bottles, broken plates, and other debris that washes ashore. Peevish Israeli authorities have so far been unable to oust him. Look for his latest creation, the "sand bar" snack stand, featuring cold drinks and watermelon served on a covered veranda. If you can find him, he might be persuaded to give you a tour of his outlandish abode and the surrounding caves. He may even introduce you to his pet peacock. Rumor has it he plans to open a school to teach people "how to survive."

On the cliffs above the beach, a few hundred meters farther north, are the barely discernible ruins of **Apollonia,** a Roman port fortified by medieval Crusaders. Huge chunks of the Crusaders' walls fell from the cliffs when the city was destroyed, and more fell in the winter of 1991-92 due to the exceptionally heavy rains. The pieces lie half-submerged along the beach. To reach Apollonia, take the road east from the beach entrance and turn almost immediately onto a dirt road. Don't venture too close to the nearby ammunition factory, which is surrounded by barbed wire. To reach the beach entrance from Deshalit Sq., walk north along Galei Tekhelet St., bear left at Golda Meir St. and take the immediate left onto the dirt road. Follow Keren HaYesod St. to the end, turn right onto Galei Tekhelet St. If in doubt, ask for directions to the mosque.

Surprisingly, there are a number of reasonably-priced restaurants in Herzliya Pituaḥ. Most notable is **Nargila** (tel. (052) 55 41 03), a 7-minute walk up HaGalim St. from the beach, which features homemade Yemenite specialties and nude women on the menu. Try the *ziva*, thin dough wrapped around melted cheese with tomato sauce (NIS5.50). For the more daring diner, try the fish and grilled dishes at **Ahmad et Salim Restaurant**, attached to the Paz gas station about a 20-minute walk south along the highway from the Keren HaYesod St. bus stop. If you're lucky, you'll have a view of the old buses and cars that sometimes occupy the field behind the restaurant.

United Bus #90 runs from Tel Aviv to Herzliya from 5am to 12:30am every half hour. In Tel Aviv, board outside the Dan Panorama Hotel on Prof. Y. Kaufman St., or on Arlozorov St. near King Solomon St. In Herzliya, #90 runs from the Sharon Hotel, off Deshalit Sq. The ride takes about 30 min. and costs NIS3.60; it also runs on *shabbat*. Egged #601 also makes the trip every 20 minutes from Tel Aviv's central bus station, Sun.-Thurs. 5:30am-10:30pm; Fri. 5:30am-4pm; Sat. 5-10:30pm. Get off at Keren HaYesod St., one stop away from Herzliya Junction.

Rehovot and Rishon L'Tzion רחובות, ראשון לציון

> *The Institute is the fulfillment of a vision and the*
> *translation of a dream into reality.*
> —*Hayim Weizmann*

Rehovot, a quiet and somewhat secluded town, is known primarily for its world-famous **Weizmann Institute of Science.** The institute is named for Israel's first president, Dr. Hayim Weizmann, who was also a research chemist. During World War I, Weizmann discovered an innovative way to produce acetone, which proved essential to the British military effort (as well as to nail polish removal). Weizmann's discovery, combined with his formidable character and arguments, helped persuade Lord Balfour to issue the famous 1917 Balfour Declaration favoring the establishment of a Jewish national homeland.

The institute grounds, once a barren stretch of scrubland, extend over 250 acres of manicured subtropical gardens and lawns. The grounds are so photogenic that newlyweds from all over the country flock here for their wedding pictures. In the southeast corner of the institute, the most verdant part of the grounds, stands the **Weizmann House** (tel. (08) 34 32 30 or 34 33 28), Israel's first presidential residence. Dr. Weizmann is buried adjacent to the house. (Tours every half-hr. Sun.-Thurs. 10am-3:30pm, NIS4.50.) Near the main entrance to the institute are the **Weizmann Archives,** holding Dr. Weizmann's letters and papers.

The institute's scientific staff conducts pioneering research in all of the natural sciences. Projects include research on cancer, immunology, aging, the computer revolution, and the environment. Pick up maps and brochures at the **Visitors Section** (tel. (08) 34 35 97; #504 in the Stone Administration Building, first building on the left as you enter the main gate). There is a free video at the Wix Auditorium, the second building on the left as you enter the main gate (shown Sun.-Thurs. 11am and 2:45pm, Fri. 11am). The main gate to the Weizmann Institute is at the north end of Herzl St., a 20-minute walk from Bilou St., Manchester Sq., and the central bus station. Also on Bilou St., you'll find Rehovot's central fruit and vegetable market. The city's main avenue, Herzl St., is lined with falafel shops and self-service restaurants (falafel NIS3-4). For authentic, spicy Yemenite dishes, head south along Herzl St. several blocks from the bus station, where you'll find a cluster of restaurants. Rehovot has no cheap accommodations. Buses #200 (express) and #201 make the 20km trip from Tel Aviv every 20 minutes (NIS4.20), stopping 30m beyond the institute's large white stone gate.

Between the Weizmann Institute and downtown Rehovot (about a 30-min. walk from the central bus station) and hidden at the end of a group of winding side streets and paths is a small but captivating museum at the site of **Givat HaKibbutzim** (Kibbutz Hill). The museum recalls the double existence led by those who ran a clandestine bullet factory—code-named the Ayalon Institute—for the Hagana during the British Mandate. Ostensibly an orientation center for groups of soon-to-be kibbutzniks (hence the name), the building contained moveable washing machines and bakery ovens hiding the entrances to the underground factory. A short English film explains the Hebrew-labelled exhibits. (Tel. (08) 46 65 52. Open Sun.-Thurs. 8:30am-

4pm, Sat. 9am-4pm; March-Sept., Mon. 8:30am-6pm. Admission NIS5, children/seniors NIS4.) To reach Givat HaKibbutzim from Reḥovot, head north on Herzl St. for about 1km and then turn right at the traffic lights on Meir Weisgal Rd. Continue through the Kiryat Weizmann Science Park to the end (it becomes Pinḥas Sapir St.) and make a right on the unnamed street. Proceed for about 5-7 more minutes up the hill until you see an orange Hebrew sign for the Ayalon Institute. Beware goat herds crossing the road on the way.

On the way to Reḥovot, you'll pass through the small town of **Rishon L'Tzion** (First to Zion), the site of the first Jewish settlement in Palestine. As might be expected, the town contains many Israeli "famous firsts." It was here that the tune to the Israeli national anthem was composed, the world's first national Hebrew school opened, and the Jewish National Fund was created. The **Rishon L'Tzion Museum,** 2-4 Aḥad Ha'Am St. (tel. (03) 94 16 21), traces the history of the town from the early pioneers to the present. For NIS7 you can get a tour of the museum and a sound and light show. (Museum open Sun. and Tues.-Thurs. 9am-2pm, Mon. 9am-1pm and 4-8pm, Fri. 9am-1pm, Sat. 6-9pm. Free tours and admission 10am-2pm on the first Sat. of every month.) At no charge, you can take your own tour of the "Pioneer's Way," a path painted along Rishon's pavement, directing you to 18 of the town's historic sites, each with a plaque to explain its significance. Pick up Israel's version of the "Freedom Trail" at Rothschild St. (Walk south on Herzl St. 2 blocks, turn left onto Rothschild, a pedestrian street, and walk uphill until the pedestrian mall ends.) The yellow line leads down HaCarmel St., where you will pass the **Winery,** 25 HaCarmel St. (tel. (03) 96 42 021), built by Baron Edmond de Rothschild in 1887 and still used today to produce Carmel Mizraḥi wine. One-hr. tours of the winery end with a winetasting session and a souvenir bottle dredged from the grapes of Rothschild. (Open Sun.-Thurs. 8:30am-4pm. Admission NIS9, seniors/students NIS6.) Across the street from the winery, you can buy booze at wholesale prices at **Sokolik** (tel. (03) 96 41 343; open Sun.-Wed. 6am-2:30pm, Thurs. 6am-5pm, Fri. 6am-3pm).

For reasons unknown to locals, Rishon L'Tzion is blessed with its very own **Ben and Jerry's** ice cream, 75 Herzl St., conveniently located 1 block south of the central bus station (two measly scoops NIS6.90. Open Sun.-Sat. 10am-midnight.) Try a less expensive meal at **Kiosk Madar** (sign in Hebrew, but hard to miss the line), a local hole-in-the-wall favorite at the corner of Rothschild St. and Mohliever St., where the street begins after the pedestrian mall. (Falafel NIS3.50.)

Bus #200 runs from Tel Aviv to Reḥovot, stopping in Rishon en route. The 15-20 minute ride from Tel Aviv costs NIS3.30 (NIS3 from Reḥovot). The Rishon L'Tzion **bus station** is on Herzl St.

Ramla רמלע

Ramla ("sand" in Arabic) is the only city in Israel to have been founded and originally developed by Arabs. Built by the Sunni caliph Sulayman in the 8th century, Ramla lay on the strategically important road connecting Damascus and Baghdad with Egypt. For 300 years, Ramla was the center of the Muslim community in Palestine, but during the 11th century, earthquakes and Bedouin looting devastated the city. By the time the Crusaders captured it in 1099, Ramla languished in ruins. In 1267, the Mamluks captured the city, and it prospered until a Turkish conquest in the 17th century. Ramla deteriorated under Turkish rule, but was gradually revived by Jews fleeing persecution in Jerusalem and by Christians serving in the monastery of St. Nicodemus. Ramla became a rest stop for pilgrims on their way to Jerusalem, and Napoléon stayed in the monastery before making his ill-fated attack on Akko.

By the beginning of the 20th century, Ramla was again inhabited mostly by Arabs, and anti-Zionist riots caused the Jewish population to flee in 1936. When the Israelis attacked Ramla in 1948, the town surrendered immediately and almost all the Arab inhabitants of Ramla, together with those from nearby Lod, were deported by the Israeli army. Today, Ramla's population is mostly Jewish and includes 3000 Karaites, members of a literalist religious sect that recognizes only the authority of the Bible. Ramla is also home to scores of immigrants from Russia, Ethiopia, and Vietnam.

The citizens of Ramla often joke that the best thing about Ramla is the road to Tel Aviv. But don't overlook Ramla; there are sights here worth visiting. Three can be found by chasing steeples. Just west of the bus station stands the remarkably well-preserved **Al-Omri Mosque** (tel. (08) 22 50 81), with its slender white minaret. The mosque was originally a Crusader church built in the 12th century. The Muslims made only a few changes in the structure, notably in the outer courtyard and the *mihrab*, the niche in the direction of Mecca. The mosque has remained in constant use. (Open Sun.-Thurs. 8am-1pm. Modest dress required.)

Farther north on Herzl Blvd. is the tower of the **Church of St. Nicodemus and St. Joseph Arimathea** (tel. (08) 22 12 17), which commemorates the saints who took Jesus off the cross. Though parts of the church were built in the 16th century, most was completed in 1902. From Herzl Blvd., turn left on Bialik St., and the entrance is through the first gate on your left. Ring the bell—a jovial Franciscan monk (one of the five living in the monastery's new addition next to the church) will show you the main sanctuary. Ask to see Napoléon's room and you'll be taken upstairs, through the corridors of the old monastery to the chambers where Napoléon had his staff headquarters when he unsuccessfully attempted to seize Palestine from the Turks in 1799. (Open for mass and for visitors Mon.-Fri. 9-11:30am.)

The stubby, square **Tower of the Forty Martyrs** stands alone at the end of Danny Mass St., which branches west off Herzl Blvd., just north of the church. A guard might admit you in the morning. Once inside, you can climb up the tower's musty stairs, which seem to be inhabited primarily by winged beasties. The inscription over the tower's entrance says it was built by Muhammad Abu Kalaon in 1318. In the surrounding fields, farther in from the road, you can see the ruins of the **Jamia al-Abiad Mosque,** the White Mosque, built in 716 CE, for which the tower originally served as a minaret.

The only major sight in Ramla with no religious affiliation and no steeple is the **Pool of St. Helena,** a rain reservoir built in the 8th century for Haroun al-Rashid, a familiar figure from the *Arabian Nights.* Christians later renamed the pool after Emperor Constantine's mother. It is known as the Pool of al-Anazia in Arabic, and Brekhat HaKeshatot (Pool of the Arches) in Hebrew. Walk north on Herzl Blvd. from Danny Mass St. and turn right on HaHagana St. The pool is on the right side of the street, opposite the Hagana Gardens, identified by a Hebrew sign. The small building on the left, next to the blue and white murals, has an entrance leading down to the waters. The pools are neither particularly wide nor particularly deep, and there may be no one to admit you. But other than that, they're a blast. If you get in, you can rent a rowboat. (Open Sun.-Fri. 9am-1pm. Admission NIS1.)

Ramla makes a good daytrip from Tel Aviv. Buses #451 and #455 make the 25-minute run from Tel Aviv to Ramla every 15 minutes, 5am-10:40pm (NIS3.70). Express buses leave Ramla for Jerusalem (NIS8.50) every half hour, 5:50am-8:20pm. The **bus station** is on Herzl Blvd., the town's main street.

Netanya נתניה

Known as the Israeli "Riviera," Netanya has grown into Israel's largest Mediterranean resort. Although the city was founded in the 1920s as an agricultural center, affluent vacationers now enjoy the beautiful beaches and excellent weather. Walking down the quiet streets and the wooden path near the waterfront, you would never guess that this city is also one of Israel's major industrial centers. The diamond-cutting and steel factories hover discreetly at the city's outskirts.

Most of Netanya's hotels and restaurants cater to wealthy Europeans. There are virtually none of the hostels and self-service restaurants which attract budget travelers. The town's cultural offerings also cater to an older, wealthier clientele: an orchestra, a bridge club, and even a series of meetings for single tourists overshadow a handful of cinemas, bars, and discos.

Orientation and Practical Information

From the bus station on Binyamin Blvd. (which turns into Weizmann Blvd. farther north), walk a block north to **Herzl Street,** the town's main shopping avenue. Turn left on Herzl, and after 4 blocks you'll arrive at **Ha'Atzma'ut Square** (Independence Sq.), an attractive park with a fountain. Opposite the bus station, Sha'ar HaGai St. cuts diagonally from Binyamin Blvd. to Herzl St. Sha'ar HaGai St. has less ostentatious shops, cafés, and bakeries, and a large fruit stand.

Government Tourist Information Office (GTIO): small, strangely-shaped, red brick building in the southwest corner of Ha'Atzma'ut Sq. (tel. 82 72 86). City maps, train schedules, and lists of upcoming events. Will arrange a visit to meet Israelis in their homes on three days notice. Open Sun.-Thurs. 9am-7pm, Fri. 9am-noon; July-Aug., Sun.-Thurs. 9am-10pm, Fri. 9am-noon.)

Banks: Central offices: **Israel Discount Bank,** 6 Smilansky St. (tel. 33 47 46) and **Bank Leumi,** 5 Herzl St. (tel. 60 45 11). Open Sun., Tues., and Thurs. 8:30am-12:30pm and 4-6pm, Mon. and Wed. 8:30am-12:30pm, Fri. 8:30am-noon. **First International,** 25 Zion Sq. (tel. 33 04 44). Open Sun., Tues, and Thurs. 8:30am-2pm, Mon. and Wed. 8:30am-2pm and 4-7pm, Fri. 8:30am-noon. **Bank HaPoalim,** 11 Ha'Atzma'ut Sq. (tel. 62 00 11). Open Sun., Tues., and Thurs. 8:30am-12:30pm, Mon. and Wed. 8:30am-12:30pm and 3:45-6pm, Fri. 8:30am-noon.

Post Office: 59 Herzl St. (tel. 411 09). **Poste Restante** here. Branches also at 15 Herzl St. (tel. 422 09) and 8 Ha'Atzma'ut Sq. (tel. 421 05). Open Sun.-Tues. and Thurs. 8am-12:30pm and 3:30-6pm, Wed. 8am-1:30pm, Fri. 8am-noon.

Central Bus Station: 3 Binyamin Blvd. (tel. 33 70 52). Buses to Tel Aviv about every 10 min. (NIS5). Schedule posted on the wall to the left of the information window. **Luggage check,** at the far corner of the station away from the information window, is open Sun.-Thurs. 6:30am-4pm, Fri. 6:30am-noon. NIS3 per day.

Train Station: HaRakevet Rd. (tel. 82 34 70), on the outskirts of town. Follow Herzl St. to the Ḥaifa-Netanya Junction, go right, and it's on your left. From Pinsker St. near the bus station, take bus #5 (runs every half-hr., Sun.-Thurs. 6:10am-8:10pm, Fri. 6:10am-3:05pm). To Tel Aviv (15 trains daily 6:25am-8:30pm, NIS3.50), Ḥaifa (12 trains daily 6:30am-8:45pm, NIS6), and other smaller towns. GTIO has schedules.

Taxis: Hashaḥar, 1 HaMeyasdim St. (tel. 82 46 45), corner of Herzl St. **Sharon,** 2 Smilansky St. (tel. 82 25 25), corner of Herzl St. **Netanya,** 8 Raziel St. (tel. 344 43).

Car Rental: Avis, 1 Ussishkin St. (tel. 33 16 19). **Hertz,** 8 Ha'Atzma'ut Sq. (tel. 82 88 90). **El-dan,** Ha'Atzma'ut Sq. (tel. 61 69 82). Expensive and you must be 23 years old.

English Bookstores: Steimatzky's, 4 Herzl St. (tel. 61 71 54). Best selection. Open Sun.-Mon. and Wed.-Thurs. 8:30am-1pm and 4-7pm, Tues. 8:30am-1pm, Fri. 8:30am-2pm. **The Reader's Corner,** 12 Stampfer St. (tel. 34 57 67). Cheapest new and used books and magazines. They buy and sell. Open Sun., Mon., Wed., and Thurs. 8:30am-1pm and 4-6pm, Tues. 8:30am-1pm, Fri. 8:30am-2pm.

Laundry: Kabes-Na, 27 Dizengoff (tel. 33 39 29), corner of Herzl St. Wash and dry NIS18. Open Sun.-Thurs. 7:30am-8pm, Fri. 7:30am-3pm. **Express Laundry,** 28 Smilansky St., near the corner of Remez St. Wash and dry NIS5 per 7kg load. Your clothes will be washed, dried and folded in one-and-a-half hr., guaranteed. Open Sun.-Mon. and Wed.-Thurs. 7:30am-1pm and 4-6pm, Tues. 7:30am-1pm, Fri. 7:30-noon.

Swimming Pool: Elizur Sports Center (tel. 389 20) on Radak St. Open May-Sept. Sun.-Thurs. 6am-6pm.

Pharmacies: Trufa, 2 Herzl St. (tel. 82 86 56). Open Sun.-Mon. and Wed.-Thurs. 8am-1pm and 4-7pm, Tues. 8am-1pm, Fri. 8am-1:45pm. Others on Herzl St., Weizmann Blvd., and Sha'ar HaGai St. At least one is always open for emergencies; the roster is posted on each door.

Psychological Aid: Tel. 33 53 16

First Aid: Tel. 101 or 233 33.

Police: Tel. 100 or 214 44.

Accommodations and Food

There are no hostels in Netanya and almost all of the hotels are expensive. Many places lower their prices by 10-15% from November to February, but you should bargain at any time of the year. Make it clear that you're on a tight budget, and remind obstinate managers that there are many other hotels in town. Paying in foreign currency spares you the 18% VAT. Camping on the beach is always an alternative but unsafe for single women and unguarded valuables. The most popular areas are near the 24-hr. coffee shops which line the shores.

Orit Pension, 21 Hen Ave. (tel. 61 68 18), off Jabotinsky St., south of Ha'Atzma'ut Sq. Homey, scrupulously clean rooms, and a common room with *The Jerusalem Post* make this the best budget bed in town. Caters to—for some reason—a predominantly Swedish clientele, who get preference for reservations. Call in advance, especially April-Nov. Curfew 11pm. No smoking. Singles US$23, NIS34.80. Doubles US$40. Breakfast included (Sun.-Fri. 8am, Sat. 9am).

Hotel Galei Ruth, 11 David HaMelekh St. (tel. 82 26 47), 2 blocks north of Ha'Atzma'ut Sq. Small, comfortable and clean rooms with private bathroom and shower. Tiny balcony with aging futon and refrigerator in every room. Singles US$30. Doubles US$40. Prices lower Nov.-Feb. Breakfast US$4 at the Park Hotel next door.

Hotel Gal-Yam, 46 Dizengoff St. (tel. 62 50 33), 2 blocks from Herzl St. Clean, cramped rooms with private bathroom and shower. Manager Aharon Zung may be the coolest person between the Jordan and the Mediterranean. Singles US$29. Doubles US$52. Breakfast included.

Motel Landa, 3 Jabotinsky St. (tel. 82 26 34), close to Ha'Atzma'ut Sq. Reasonably large, sunny rooms for 1-5 people with tiny bathrooms and private shower. Several rooms equipped with small kitchens. Large living room with TV and use of motel's common kitchen, located in the front courtyard under a large roof. Singles US$28, NIS70. Doubles US$32, NIS80. Each additional person pays half the double rate, minus US$1. Open 8am-9pm. Prices lower Nov.-Feb.

The mini-markets at Ha'Atzma'ut Sq. and on Herzl St. are overpriced; more affordable alternatives include the **supermarket** on HaRav Kook St. (tel. 496 77; open Sun.-Tues. 7am-1:30pm and 4-7pm, Wed.-Thurs. 7am-1:30pm and 4-8pm, Fri. 7am-2pm). There are larger and slightly more expensive supermarkets at 13 Smilansky St. and 14 Stampfer St. For fresh fruits and vegetables shop at the **open market** on Zangwill St., 2 blocks east of Weizmann Blvd., near the center of town. (Open Sun., Mon., Wed., and Thurs. 7am-8pm, Tues. and Fri. 7am-3:30pm.) Prices are cheapest in the afternoon, especially right before *shabbat,* when merchants desperately vie for the last customers' shekels.

Sha'ar HaGai St. is lined with falafel stands and self-service restaurants, which will stuff just about anything legal into a pita (falafel NIS3, *shwarma* NIS5, chicken *schnitzel* NIS5). If you've hit falafel bloat, try pizza in Ha'Atzma'ut Sq. (NIS4 per slice) or *malawaḥ* (thin fried dough with a watery tomato sauce, NIS5).

A number of restaurants line the cliffs overlooking the beach. For a meal with a view, try the **Mini Golf Restaurant and Pub,** 21 Nice Blvd. (tel. 61 77 35), perched on the edge of a cliff overlooking the sea. From Ha'Atzma'ut Sq. take King David St. past the Hotel Dan Netanya to Nitza Blvd. Their grilled and Italian dishes are excellent (NIS8-32) and the atmosphere is relaxing and romantic. (Open daily noon-2am.) Don't expect to play any golf. A cheaper option is **Pizza Hut,** David HaMelekh St., a half-block from Ha'Atzma'ut Sq., a recent import from the U.S. The Israeli version, however, is set in a beautifully landscaped park. Pizza patrons can watch the sunset over the water through the floor-to-ceiling windows. (Small pizza NIS11.) Farther north down Nitza Blvd. (bus #29 or cab), you will eventually hit **Blue Bay Beach,** where you'll find **Hofeya** (tel. 62 31 41), on the left hand side of the road. At high tide, the waves of the Mediterranean crash up against the windows of this delightful restaurant/pub. The main dishes are a bit expensive (NIS8-32), but you can enjoy the spectacular scenery for the price of a salad (NIS2-9) or *malawaḥ* (NIS5). Live singers perform every Friday night. (Open 24 hours; Sept.-May daily noon-2am.) **Patisserie Antverpia** at 6 Eliyahu Krause St. (tel. 33 53 90), 1 block south of Herzl St. off Smilansky St., serves fresh *challah* and luscious cream pastries at slightly lower prices than its tourist-district counterparts. (Open Sun.-Thurs. 7:30am-9pm, Fri. 7:30am-3pm.)

Vegetarian alternatives include the **Dana Dairy Restaurant,** 2 Eliyahu Krause (tel. 61 90 08) and **Bagel Nash,** 12 Ha'Atzma'ut Sq. (tel. 61 69 20). Dana Dairy is open

Sun-Thurs. 9am-9pm, Fri. 9am-2pm. Bagel Nash is open Sun.-Thurs. 8am-midnight, Fri. 8am-4pm.

Sights and Entertainment

Sand and sun addicts, as well as numerous other crawling critters, converge on Netanya's waterfront. The steps leading to the main **beach** are at the western end of Ha'Atzma'ut Sq. All of Netanya's beaches are free; those to the north, under the small cliffs, are the least crowded.

The Netanya municipality organizes various forms of free entertainment almost every night during the summer, and fairly frequently during the winter. From May through October folk dancing occurs several nights each week at the Netanya Cultural Center, 4 Raziel St. (tel. 60 33 92) and Saturday and Sunday nights in Ha'Atzma'ut Sq. The GTIO has complete listings of concerts, movies, and a host of other activities. During the summer, you can watch the sun set over the Mediterranean while listening to classical muzak in the amphitheater, next to the steps to beach, Sun.-Thurs. 5-7pm.

With its rows of cafés and pubs (some of which are actually frequented by Israelis—always a positive sign), the pedestrian mall on Herzl St. by Ha'Atzma'ut Sq. is a people-watching paradise. Another prime place is the **Kanion HaSharon Mall,** at the junction of Herzl St. and Petaḥ Tikva St. Netanya's three **cinemas** are the **Gil**, at the Kanion (tel. 62 84 52), the **Rav Ḥen**, at the Kanion (tel. 61 85 70), and the **Studio**, 29 Herzl St. (tel. 33 86 76). For tickets to local concerts and plays, call the **Signal Ticket Agency,** Zion Sq. (tel. 82 31 98) or **Mofa,** 20 Herzl St. (tel. 33 03 35). A list of upcoming shows is available at the GTIO.

Sports-enthusiasts can flex racket and muscle at the **tennis courts** in the Maccabee Stadium (tel. 82 46 27) and the Elizur Sport Club on Radak St. (tel. 33 89 20; open Mon.-Thurs. 8:30am-3pm.) For **horseback riding,** trot to the Cliff Ranch (tel. 66 35 25), near the Blue Bay Hotel.

Don't miss a tour of the **Netanya Diamond Center,** 90 Herzl St. (tel. 62 47 70; open Sun.-Thurs. 8am-7pm, Fri. 8am-3pm). If you're in a sour mood, visit the city's **citrus packing plants,** located in the industrial area, Kiryat Eliezer. (Open Sun.-Thurs. 8am-4pm, Fri. 8am-1pm. Dec.-March only.)

Near Netanya

The beautiful **Poleg Nature Preserve,** about 8km south of Netanya, begins where the Poleg River meets the sea. The walk upstream leads past flowering plants and eucalyptus trees planted during the last century to dry up the swamps that once covered the Plain of Sharon. A few kilometers south, near **Kibbutz Ga'ash,** seaside cliffs reach almost 61m. During the summer, you may see hang-gliding here. Egged bus #601 runs every half-hr., 5:30am-10:30pm. Just ask the driver to let you off at Naḥal Poleg.

Less than 5km north of Netanya, in Aviḥa'il, stands the **Jewish Legion Museum** (tel. 82 22 12), dedicated to the Jewish units of the British Army in World War I. Led by the dashing Yosef Trumpeldor, the Zion Mule Corps distinguished themselves in battle at Gallipoli in 1915 against the Ottomans. (Open Sun.-Thurs. 9am-3pm, Fri. 8am-noon.)

Kfar Vitkin, one of the largest *moshavim* in Israel, lies 8km north of Netanya, a short walk from gorgeous, free beaches. The adjoining **Emek Ḥefer Youth Hostel (HI)** (tel. (053) 66 60 32) has sports facilities and impressively clean rooms. Buses #702, 857, 852 from Tel Aviv, #29, 706, 922 from Netanya, and #901, 921 from Ḥaifa travel here. Ask to get off at Tzomet Beit Yanai then look for the hostel sign on the eastern side of the highway. The site is used as a summer camp for children and occasionally as a training camp for soldiers. (NIS35, US$13; nonmembers NIS38, US$14.50). Breakfast included; lunch and dinner available. Reservations recommended July-Sept.) Nearby is the **Ḥanout Shohar Supermarket,** which sells everything from food to artwork (open Sun.-Thurs. 8am-8pm, Fri. 8am-3pm, Sat. 9am-8pm), the

Miss Lucy Pancake House (tel. (053) 66 31 45; open Sun.-Thurs. 7:30am-9pm, Fri. 7:30am-3pm, Sat. 9am-9pm), and a quiet, free beach.

Caesarea קסריה

On the site of a small anchorage named Strato's Tower, Herod the Great built this city (pronounced Kay-SAHR-ya) for his emperor in Rome at the end of the first century BCE. The extensive remains include a Roman theater, Byzantine mosaics, aqueducts, a Crusader city, and a 2000-year old harbor with sophisticated engineering rivaling that of any modern Israeli port. Caesarea deserves a visit despite its inaccessibility; the ruins of the ancient city constitute one of Israel's finest archeological sites. Though the ruins are not yet ruined, a dozen tacky cafés and gift shops, a beach club, a diving center, and even a disco have already been built among them, under the supervision of the ominously named Caesarea Development Corporation.

Phoenician travelers of the 4th century BCE first established a small settlement and harbor called Strato's Tower on the main trading route between Phoenicia and Egypt. The settlement, along with the rest of the coastal strip, eventually fell into the hands of Caesar Augustus, who granted it to Herod the Great, governor of Judea. Because of its choice location and access to the harbor, Herod turned Strato's Tower into one of the great cities of the eastern Roman Empire. Construction began in 22 BCE, and only 12 years later Strato's Tower was a splendid Roman city boasting a theater, a hippodrome, a rhinodome, aqueducts carrying fresh water from the north, and a harbor capable of accommodating 300 ships. Herod named the new city in honor of Caesar Augustus, and in 6 CE. Caesarea (also known as Caesarea Maritima) became the capital of the Roman province of Judea. It remained the seat of Roman power in the area until the downfall of the empire. It was the Roman prefect of Caesarea from 26 to 36 CE, Pontius Pilate, who ordered the crucifixion of Jesus. The first evidence of Pilate's existence outside the accounts of the Gospels and the historian Josephus was found here in 1961.

In 66 CE, a riot between Jews and Romans in Caesarea sparked the six-year Jewish Rebellion, which ended in the destruction of the Second Temple in Jerusalem. When the Romans finally squelched the rebellion in 70 CE (except for the holdouts at Masada), they celebrated by sacrificing thousands of Jews in Caesarea's amphitheater. Sixty years later, a second Jewish uprising, the Bar Kokhba Revolt, was also brought to a bitter end. This time the Romans were more selective—10 Jewish sages, among them the famous Rabbi Akiva, were tortured to death in the arena. Ironically, Caesarea later became a center of Jewish and Christian learning. During the Crusades, Caesarea changed hands four times before its capture in 1251 by King Louis IX of France. Louis strengthened and expanded the city's fortifications, adding most of the massive ramparts and battlements and the impressive moat, all of which are still in excellent condition. Despite these efforts, Caesarea was captured in 1265 by the Mamluk Sultan Baybars, who destroyed it. The city remained uninhabited until 1878 when the Muslim Boshnaqs resettled it. The 1948 war drove out the Arab population, emptying Caesarea once again.

Caesarea's ruins span many historical periods, although very little is left of the Roman city, largely because its magnificent buildings were constantly pillaged by other towns.

Most of the site is well marked. Relics from the Roman period include the main road and several statues; the granaries and residences are Arab remains, while the walls and churches date from the Crusader period. Don't be surprised to find pieces of a marble column used as street pavement—Crusade-era contractors frequently re-used Roman remains when erecting a city. The harbor and beaches of Caesarea are of major archeological significance as well. The engineering of Herod's now-submerged port rivals that of its modern counterparts, and the breakwater he built was the first in the country. Both the dry ground and underwater areas of Caesarea are currently bring excavated by a team of American and Israeli archeologists and volunteers.

Although most of the ruins are within the Crusader walls, the most interesting Roman remnants all lie outside the site proper. Behind the café across from the entrance to the Crusader city are an excavated **Byzantine street,** and Caesarea's most famous finds: colossal Roman statues from the 2nd century CE, one of red porphyry, the other of white marble. The two headless figures were discovered accidentally by kibbutzniks ploughing their fields. A 1km walk north along either the beach or the road that runs along the Crusader walls leads to Caesarea's town beach and the excellently preserved **Roman aqueduct.**

About 1km east, off a dirt road that begins at the aqueduct, are some splendid Byzantine mosaics. Stroll a half-km south of the Crusader city along either the road or the waterfront, and you will reach the enormous and extensively restored **Roman Theater.** Reopened in 1961, it has recently hosted Eric Clapton, the Bolshoi Ballet, and the Alvin Ailey Dance Theater. Ask at the ticket office for concert information. Consult GTIO offices in Tel Aviv or Ḥaifa for more comprehensive listings. Tourists are occasionally inspired by the amphitheater to do impromptu Clapton-style air guitar concerts.

About 1km along the main road running east from the theater stands an archway leading to the ruins of the **Roman hippodrome,** now overgrown with banana and orange groves cultivated by the nearby kibbutz of Sdot Yam. In its heyday, the racetrack could hold 20,000 spectators; it measures 352 by 68 meters. If you get to the Crusader city very early in the morning, you can get in for free—the local fisherfolk leave the gates open. (Site open April-Sept.: Sun.-Thurs. 8am-5pm, Fri. 8am-4pm; Oct.-March: Sun.-Thurs. 8am-4pm, Fri. 8am-3pm. Admission NIS8 for adults and NIS for students to the Crusader city and theater. Other sites free.)

The two hotels on the beach are expensive; head south for cheaper accommodations. Just south of the Roman theater, kibbutz Sdot Yam maintains a number of **guest apartments**, all ideal for families or for groups of 3-4 adults. The apartments are located in the center of the kibbutz and have 2 spacious, clean rooms with private bathroom and shower, small refrigerator, and electric kettle. Guests are entitled to use of the kibbutz sailing center and private beach, cultural and sports facilities, and archeological museum. US$28 per person. Includes only breakfast in kibbutz dining room, but full board available for an additional US$12 per person (tel. (06) 36 44 70, fax (06) 36 22 11). Call in advance. To get to the office, enter the kibbutz through its main gate near the Roman theater. Pass the tile factory and the bus stop, and look for the small white building slightly to the right. If in doubt, ask someone to direct you to the "kef-yam" office. On the other side of the kibbutz is the **Caesarea Sports Center,** which maintains several buildings of rooms and a dining hall adjacent to the diving and boating center. The center frequently hosts various Israeli sports teams and youth groups, as well as the Caesarea excavation team, but rents rooms to individuals if space permits. Rooms in the newer "Beit Gil" building are spotless, air-conditioned, and have private bathroom and shower. Open Sun.-Thurs., NIS109 per person; Fri.-Sat., NIS127 per person. Full board included. The other building is older, has communal bathroom and shower, and has no air-conditioning. Open Sun.-Thurs., NIS72 per person; Fri.-Sat., NIS85. Full board included. Free Israeli folk dancing at the sports center each week. Call in advance (tel. (06) 36 43 94 in Caesarea or (03) 56 12 858 for main office in Tel Aviv). The southernmost (and cheapest) option is the Ḥofshonit beach resort, just south of the Sports Center. Though many visitors to Caesarea simply unroll their sleeping bags on the beach, devotees of organized **camping** can pitch a tent here for NIS20. The resort also rents decrepit, dingy, 3-person bungalows for NIS50. Separate bathroom facilities. No showers. Ḥofshonit is a safer option than the unsupervised beach, but keep a vigilant eye on your valuables in both places. Local archeologists have uncovered not only ancient monuments, but also piles of stolen purses, wallets, and passports.

The easiest way to get to Caesarea is through Ḥadera, the nearest city. A number of intercity Egged buses go through here, including #852, #872 from Tel Aviv, #706 from Netanya, and #922 from Ḥaifa. Bus #76 runs from Ḥadera directly to the entrance of the Crusader City and then down the street to the Roman Theater, ending at Sdot Yam.

Be sure to ask the driver to stop at the ruins (*ha'attikot*), not the affluent housing development named Caesarea, 1km closer. The #76 bus leaves Ḥadera 9 times a day, Sun.-Thurs. 6am-8:30pm, Fri. last bus at 4pm, and returns from Kibbutz Sdot Yam via the ruins Sun.-Thurs. 6:30am-9pm, Fri. last bus at 4:30pm. The trip takes 30 minutes and costs NIS3.50. Buses to Ḥadera from Tel Aviv and Ḥaifa cost NIS6.30. The cost is NIS14 from Jerusalem and NIS4.20 from Netanya. Many intercity buses will stop at the Caesarea exit on the main road. The ruins are a 3km walk east.

Near Caesarea

Just outside Moshav Beit Ḥananya on the old coastal road between Caesarea and Ma'agan Mikha'el arch two well-preserved **Roman aqueducts,** believed to have carried water from the Shuni springs northeast of Binyamina down to the ancient city of Caesarea. North of the moshav, excavations are in progress at **Tel Mevoraḥ,** where several important Roman artifacts have been unearthed. Two of the marble sarcophagi discovered in the ruins of a Roman mausoleum are on display in the Rockefeller Museum in Jerusalem.

Kibbutz Ma'agan Miḥa'el is one of the largest and loveliest kibbutzim in Israel. The huge industrial plant at the entrance belies the cultivated fields and acres of neat, rectangular fish ponds set between the coastal road and the sea. Part of the kibbutz serves as a wildlife preserve with an aviary, and a small museum displays archeological finds from the fields. The preserve runs along the banks of Na{pb}hal HaTaninim (Crocodile River), purportedly the only unpolluted river on the Israeli coast.

The gorgeous beach at **Dor** is protected by four small, rocky islands, each a bird sanctuary, explorable at low tide. The **Tel Dor** archeological site is on the hill at the far northern end of the beach; you'll need shoes to traverse the rusty-wire-and-sand road. Though the site was probably founded in the 15th century BCE and was part of both King David's and King Solomon's empires, most of the important remains at Dor date from the Greek and Roman periods. The site includes temples dedicated to Zeus and the goddess Astarte, and the ruins of a Byzantine church.

Near the southern end of the beach Moshav Dor lies a **campsite** (tel. (06) 39 90 121) built on the ruins of the Arab village of **Tantura.** (NIS7 per person, 3-person bungalows NIS45. Tent sites open May-Oct. Call ahead.) The caves and ruins make beach camping at Tantura more interesting than crashing on your average strip of sand. To reach Dor and Tantura beaches, get off the highway at the sign for Kibbutz Naḥsholim and walk toward the sea, or hike 5km north along the beach from Ma'agan Miḥa'el.

About 5km east of Dor, on a hill overlooking the fertile coastal plain, is **Zikhron Ya'akov,** founded in 1882 by Romanian Jews. The early settlers fought unsuccessfully against malarial swamps until Baron Edmond de Rothschild came to their aid with generous donations, establishing an economy based on vineyards. The town was thus named "Ya'akov's Memorial"; it commemorates the baron's father, James. Since its early start in wine production, Zikhron Ya'akov has come to be known for its **Carmel-Mizraḥi Winery** (tel. (06) 39 67 09), founded 100 years ago by the French Jewish baron. The winery now produces most of Israel's domestic wine, as well as a large stock for export. You can sample the finished product at the end of the tour, and buy some at their store. Walk three blocks north from the central bus station along HaMeyasdim St. and turn right on HaNadiv St. The winery is the huge building at the bottom of the hill. (Open Sun.-Thurs. 8:30am-3:30pm., Fri. 8:30am-1pm. Admission NIS9. Call ahead for tours in English.) The decrepit structure off the shore is a glass factory built by the baron and managed by Meir Dizengoff, the first mayor of Tel Aviv. The factory transformed the white sand on the coast into bottles for the baron's winery. The **Rothschild Family Tomb and Gardens** (tel. (06) 39 78 21) is nearby. (Open Sun.-Thurs. and Sat. 8am-4pm, Fri. 8am-2pm.) The **Aharonson House** (tel. (06) 39 01 20), commemorating NILI, an early Zionist paramilitary intelligence unit originally based in Zikhron Ya'akov, is on HaMeyasdim St. just north of the bus station. The entrance to the museum is on the small street on the right just before the museum. (Open Sun.-Thurs. 8:30am-1pm, Fri. 10am-noon. Admission NIS5.) An added bonus is the Sarah Aharonson "Meteorology Station" outside the museum, consisting of a piece of paper tacked to a board listing the day's wind speed and direction, temperature, and barometric pressure.

Buses #872 from Tel Aviv and #202 from Ḥaifa make the trip to Zikhron Ya'akov.

Haifa and the Northern Coast

Theodor Herzl dubbed modern Ḥaifa "the city of the future," despite the fact that the surrounding area contains pre-historic caves as well as ancient and medieval ruins. Israel's northern coast is a blend of the historical memories and the vastly different cultures that co-exist in the region. Two Druze villages on the slopes of Mount Carmel, for example, tread the fine line between tradition and tourism. Rosh HaNikra, at the Lebanese border, attracts visitors bedecked with state-of-the art cameras, eager to photograph the area's age-old sea caves. The ancient cemetery at Beit She'arim, the imposing Crusader city of Akko, and the seaside resort of Nahariya all beckon the 20th-century traveler to the northern coast.

Haifa חיפה

The wind that gusts from Ḥaifa Bay up the face of Mt. Carmel has lifted the pall of ancient dust from this steeply terraced city. A prosperous city, Ḥaifa boasts ever-expanding urban conveniences, two universities, and open areas that will make even the most jaded squinting eyes open wide. Despite these features, Ḥaifa has often been overshadowed by Israel's other two big cities. Like the poor middle child, Ḥaifa is persistently dogged by comparisons along the hackneyed lines of "less gaudy than Tel Aviv, more fun than Jerusalem, less frenetic than Tel Aviv, more tolerant than Jerusalem," ad infinitum. Try to enjoy the place on its own tidy and egalitarian merits.

Ḥaifa has had a tradition of harboring political and religious minorities since the Hebrew prophet Elijah first fled there from the wrath of King Ahab. Crusaders built the first of several monasteries above Elijah's cave; these temporarily housed many sects before finally giving shelter to the wandering Carmelite Order. Among the other religious minorities who have found refuge in Ḥaifa are German Templars, Druze, and Baha'is. The massive Aliya Bet, the desperate 1930s boat journeys that sought refuge from Nazism in Europe and then braved a British blockade on Palestine, brought so many Jews to Ḥaifa that they became the majority in a formerly Arab-dominated city. The city was the first territory secured after the Israeli Declaration of Independence in 1948. With its port and refineries, Ḥaifa became the early industrial center of the young Israel, a status that earned it the nickname "Red Ḥaifa"—the workers' city. The locals will tell you that "in Jerusalem, *lomdim* (they study), in Tel Aviv, *rokdim* (they dance), but in Ḥaifa, *ovdim!* (we work!)"

While a religiously observant Jewish community does exist in Ḥaifa, the prevailing tenor of the city is secular. In a country fraught with sectarian squabbles, the comparatively harmonious coexistence of secular and Orthodox Jews, Baha'is, Christians, Muslims, and Druze, makes Ḥaifa Israel's most egalitarian city. You won't find a traditional Middle Eastern atmosphere in Ḥaifa; the well-groomed streets and stately residential neighborhoods present a more modern Israeli face.

Orientation

Ḥaifa, Israel's principal port and the departure and destination point of all passenger ferries, is situated on the Mediterranean coast about 100km south of the Lebanese border and due west of the Sea of Galilee. Rising from the sea, Ḥaifa ascends in three tiers of increasing elegance and affluence. The bustling **downtown** around the **port** is a working-class area of outdoor stands and small stores. To the west of the port on the same level is the central **bus station**, and behind it, connected by a tunnel, the **train station**. The newly reopened subway, the **Carmelit**, runs from the port up the Carmel. The middle tier of Ḥaifa is the **Hadar** district, home to many businesses, cafés, bakeries, and moderately priced hotels. Atop the mountain is **Carmel**, characterized by posh homes, five-star hotels, observation points, restaurants, and discos.

The Ḥaifa bus station can be confusing. Like the city, the station has three tiers. Arriving out-of-town buses generally drop off passengers on the third level. Local buses depart from the front of the second level, with Egged Information located in the center. Out-of-town buses depart from the lowest level, where the restrooms, luggage storage, and municipal information booth are located.

Practical Information

Government Tourist Information Office (GTIO): 18 Herzl St. (tel. 66 65 21/2 or 64 36 16) in Hadar. Take bus #10 or 12 from the port area or #21 or 28 from the central bus station. Useful maps, train schedules, and information on current events. Open Sun.-Thurs. 8:30am-5pm, Fri. 8:30am-2pm. Second office in **Passenger Hall** of the Port; open when ships arrive.

Municipal Information Office: Egged Central Bus Station (tel. 51 22 08), conveniently located on lowest level of station. Maps, schedules, and lists of clubs, pubs, museums, and accommodations. Open Sun.-Thurs. 9:30am-5pm, Fri. 9:30am-2pm. Other offices at **City Hall** (tel. 66 65 21) in Hadar, 14 Hassan Shukin St. (open Sun.-Fri. 8am-1pm), and at 106 HaNassi Blvd. (tel. 37 40 10) in Carmel (open Sun.-Thurs. 8am-6pm in winter, 8am-7pm in summer; Fri. 8am-1pm).

Budget Travel (ISSTA): 29 Nordau St. (tel. 66 91 39). Cheap fares and tours. Open Sun.-Thurs. 8:30am-1pm and 4-7pm, Fri. 8:30am-1pm.

U.S. Consulate: 12 Yerushalayim St., in Hadar (tel. 67 06 15). Only for commercial matters; in case of lost passport, the GTIO will telephone the Embassy in Tel Aviv for you. Open Sun.-Tues. and Thurs. 8:30am-12:30pm and 3-4:30pm, Wed. and Fri. 8:30am-12:30pm.

Banks: Barclays Discount, 65 Ha'Atzma'ut St. (tel. 52 22 91); **HaPoalim,** 1 HaPalyam Blvd. (tel. 68 14 11); **Israel Discount,** 47 Ha'Atzma'ut St. (tel. 54 61 11); **Leumi,** in the new HaMeginim Tower at 21 Yafo St. (tel. 54 71 11). Branches located throughout city. General hours 8:30am-12:30pm and 4-5pm (sometimes a little later). All banks closed on Mon. and Wed. afternoons. A Bank HaPoalim is open in the central bus station and in the Passenger Hall for ships. Be wary of random people offering to exchange money.

American Express: Meditrad Ltd., 2 Khayat Sq. (tel. 64 22 66). Entrance in alleyway next to Steimatzky's off Ha'Atzma'ut St., opposite Sha'ar Palmer St. Open Sun.-Thurs. 8:30am-4pm, Fri. 8:30am-1pm.

Post Office: At Shabtai Levi and HaNevi'im St. (tel. 64 09 17), in Hadar. Take bus #41 from station. Also at central bus station, 152 Yafo St., Sha'ar Palmer St.; at 19 HaPalyam Blvd., in port area; at 63 Herzl St., Hadar; and at 7 Wedgewood Blvd. in Carmel. **Poste Restante** services at HaPalyam branch only. HaPalyam office open Sun.-Thurs. 7am-4pm, Fri. 7am-2pm. Hadar office open Sun.-Thurs. 8am-7pm, Fri. 8am-1pm; in winter Sun.-Thurs. 8am-8pm, Fri. 8am-2pm.

International Telephones: At HaPalyam, HaNevi'im, Yafo, Sha'ar Palmer, and Wedgewood post office branches. **Telephone code:** 04.

Train Station: Bat Galim (tel. 542 14 14 or 56 45 64), adjacent and connected by tunnels to central bus station. Trains to Netanya, Akko, Nahariya, and Jerusalem. 20% discount for students with ISIC. GTIO has schedules.

Central Bus Station, Yafo St. (tel. 54 95 49), at beginning of main road to Tel Aviv. **Baggage check** on lower level behind Bank HaPoalim, open Sun.-Thurs. 8am-5pm, Fri. 8am-1pm, with a noon-12:30pm lunch intermission. NIS4 per item. Lost and Found operates from here as well. **Routes:** Buses heading south leave from here; buses to the north and southeast usually stop in Hadar as well. Last trip on Fri. 3-5pm. To Akko and Nahariya: #251 and 271 (via Hadar), Daniel St. off HaNevi'im St. every 15-20min. 5:10am-11:30pm, Sat. every 10-25min. 9am-midnight. To Tel Aviv: #900 and 901, every 10-20min. 5:30am-11pm, on Sat. 2:35-11pm; NIS10. To Jerusalem: #940 and 966, 6:30am-8pm, on Sat. after 5:30pm; NIS16.50. Also to Tzfat and Nazareth. **Bank HaPoalim** branch office here.

Haifa

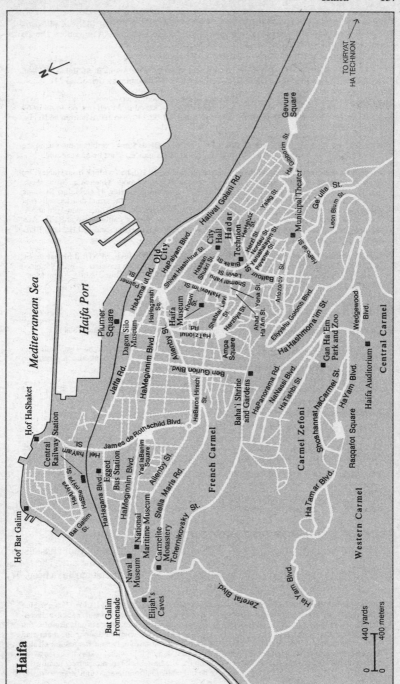

Mediterranean Sea

Haifa Port

Hof HaShaket

Hof Bat Galim

Bat Galim Promenade

TO KIRYAT
HA TECHNION

Gevura
Square

Ge'ulia St.

Municipal Theater

Leon Blum St.

Ha Giborim St.

Hatiyat Golani Rd.

Hadar

Yaliag St.

Hehalutz St.

Herzl St.

Korolau St.

Technion

Shivat Hashimur St.

HaPalyam Blvd.

City
Hall

Shmaryahu
Levin St.

Balfour St.

Yerushalaim St.

Pevsner St.

Artozorov St.

Old
City

Bialik St.

HaNevi'im St.

Arlozorov St.

Hassan
Shukri St.

Dagon Silo
Museum

Plumer
Square

HaAzma'ut Rd.

Palmer St.

Allenby St.

HaMeginnim Blvd.

Jaffa Rd.

HaHaganah
Sq.

Haifa
Museum

Khouri
St.

Ahad / Yona St.

Herzliya St.

HaTz'iyoni
Rd.

Shabtai Levi
St.

Ampa
Square

Eliyyahu Golomb Blvd.

HaHashmona'im St.

Gan Ha'Em
Park and Zoo

Ben Gurion Blvd.

HaBaron Hirsch
St.

Baha'i Shrine
and Gardens

HaPanorama Rd.

Central Carmel

Wedgewood
Blvd.

HaNassi Blvd.

HaTishbi St.

Carmel Zefoni

Haifa
Auditorium

HaYam Blvd.

James de Rothschild Blvd.

Hel haYam St.

Central Railway Station

French Carmel

Shoshannat haCarmel St.

Raqqafot Square

Western Carmel

HaTam'ar Blvd.

Egged
Bus Station

HaHagana Blvd.

HaMeginnim Blvd.

Yad laBanim
Square

Allenby St.

Stella Maris Rd.

Tchernikovsky St.

HaShe St.

HaYuta St.

HaShe St.

Bat Galim
St.

National
Maritime Museum

Naval
Museum

Carmelite
Monastery

Elijah's
Caves

Zefelat Blvd.

Ha Yam Blvd.

Central Post Office

0   440 yards
0   400 meters

Carmelit (subway): from Paris Sq. in the port up to Gan Ha'Em in Carmel. Six years of repairs have paid off; it now takes a mere six minutes to travel the distance. No A/C in stations. Orange and turquoise tiles. NIS2.

Ferries: Terminal at the port, next to the train station. Departures for Cyprus, Crete, and mainland Greece, Sun. and Thurs. 8pm. Buy tickets at **Kaspi Travel,** 76 Ha'Atzma'ut St. (tel. 67 44 44), **Multitour,** 55 HaNamal St. (tel. 66 35 70), and **Mano,** 39 HaMeginim St. (tel. 52 26 24).

Sherut **Taxis: Aviv** (tel. 66 63 33) to Jerusalem (leaves at noon; reservations required), Tel Aviv (hourly), and Tiberias from 5 Yona St. in Hadar behind the Mashbir. **Aryeh** (tel. 66 44 44 or 67 36 66) to Tel Aviv from 9 Be'erwald St. in Hadar. **Amal** (tel. 52 28 28) to Tel Aviv from #6 HeḤalutz in Hadar.

Rental Cars: Budget, 186 Yafo Rd.; **Eldan,** 117 HaNassi Blvd. Same exorbitant rates as in the rest of the country. (Approx. US$315 per week including insurance.) Must be 23 years old.

English Bookstores: Beverly's Books, 18 Herzl St. (tel. 66 48 10), half a block from HaNevi'im St on the second floor. Buys and exchanges used books "if they're good." Open Sun., Mon., Wed., and Thurs. 9am-1pm and 4-6pm, Tues. and Fri. 9am-1pm. **Book Center,** 31 HeḤalutz St. Look for bookshelves in front. **Studio 5,** 5 Derekh HaYam St., in Merkaz HaCarmel district, sells (but doesn't buy) used English language books. Open Sun., Mon., Wed., and Thurs. 9am-1pm and 4-7pm, Tues. and Fri. 9am-1pm. **Steimatzky's,** two in the central bus station. Also at 82 Ha'Atzma'ut St. (tel. 66 53 01) downtown, 16 Herzl St. (tel. 66 50 42) in Hadar, and 130 HaNassi Blvd. (tel. 38 87 65) in Carmel.

Society for the Protection of Nature (HaḤevra LeHaganat HaTeva, SPNI): 8 Menahem St. (tel. 66 41 35), near Nordau St. Informed staff eager to advise rookie travelers. This is the place to ask about hiking trips into the Carmel Mountains. Open Sun. and Thurs. 9am-5:30pm, Mon.-Wed. 9am-3:45pm, Fri. 9am-12:30pm.

Ticket Offices: Ḥaifa, 11 Be'erwald St. (tel. 66 22 44); **Garber,** 129 HaNassi Blvd. (tel. 38 47 77); and **Nova,** 15 Nordau St. (tel. 66 52 72).

Laundromat: 30 Geiela St. (tel. 67 82 38) and 2 Liberia St. (tel. 25 27 64). Take bus #24.

Swimming Pools: Maccabee Pool, Bikurim St., in central Carmel (tel. 38 83 41). Outdoor in summer, heated and covered in winter. Admission NIS8. Closes early Fri. afternoon. **Technion** pool NIS9. **Dan Panorama Hotel** (tel. 35 22 22) NIS15.

Information for Gay and Lesbian Travelers: Ḥaifa Hotline (tel. 25 73 19), P.O. Box 45417, Ḥaifa 31453.

Rape Crisis Center: (tel. 66 01 11), 24 hrs.

Emotional First Aid: (tel. 67 22 22), 24 hrs.

Pharmacies: Shomron, 44 Yafo St. (tel. 52 41 71), downtown. **HeḤalutz,** 12 HeḤalutz St. (tel. 66 29 62) in Hadar. **Merkaz,** 130 HaNassi Blvd. (tel. 38 19 79) in Carmel.

First Aid: 6 Yitzḥak Sadeh St. (tel. 101).

Fire: Tel. 102

Police: 28 Yafo Rd. (tel. 100).

Accommodations and Camping

Two words: slim pickings. Ḥaifa is short on budget hotels, and its youth hostels and campsites, while close to the sea, are not easily accessible from the city. The Hadar district is your best bet if you want to stay in town, but it's still not terribly cheap. Try to stay with Uncle Bernie and Aunt Betty.

Carmel Youth Hostel (HI), 4km south of the city at Ḥof HaCarmel (tel. 53 19 44). Closest of the 3 HI hostels, but still inconvenient. Last stop of bus #43; last bus leaves Hadar at 6:15pm and central bus station at 6:30pm (Fri. 4pm). Bus #30-alef goes past the hostel, which is only useful if you can persuade the Egged driver to stop. If you take bus #45 or 47, which runs along the main road by the water (until about 11:15pm), ask to be dropped off at the Sports and Recreation Center. Cross the street toward the gas station, turn left just past it, then follow the road as it curves to the right. The path is unlit and can be dangerous at night. The hostel is large, near a free, uncrowded beach and has a splendid view. This hostel will be full with *olim* (immigrants) until approximately

March 1993, but, until then, 6-person bungalows with separate showers and bathrooms may be available to tourists for NIS20 per person.

Talpiyot, 61 Herzl St. (tel. 67 37 54). Very clean and convenient, but request a room away from the noisy street and with a private bathroom. Fans. Congenial manager. Singles US$23. Doubles US$33. Buffet breakfast included.

Bethel Tourist Hostel, 40 HaGeffen St. (tel. 52 11 10), west of Ben-Gurion St. Take bus #22 from central bus station to Ben-Gurion St. close to HaGeffen; or walk 15-20min. up James de Rothschild Blvd., following the curve to the left onto HaBaron Hirsch, which becomes HaGeffen. The pamphlets lining the walls hint where the place is coming from (e.g., *My Heart, Christ's Home; Becoming a Christian;* and *Knowing God Personally*), but they're not terribly intrusive about it. Registration Sat.-Thurs. 5-10pm, Fri. 4-9pm, hostel closed 9am-5pm daily. New arrivals can leave bags in locked storage and return to register. Strict 11pm curfew, 7am wake-up. Inexpensive à la carte breakfast available in snack bar. Free soup and dessert in guest lounge on Fridays. Dorm beds US$8.

Nesher Hotel, 53 Herzl St. (tel. 64 06 44), at Ḥayim St. (look for the orange sign). Fairly ordinary. Good breakfast buffet. A/C and fans. 24-hr. check-in. Some rooms have private bathrooms. Singles US$27. Doubles US$40. Breakfast included.

Young Judea Youth Hostel (HI), 18km east of Ḥaifa adjacent to kibbutz Ramat Yoḥanan (tel. 44 29 76). Bus #66 runs twice per day directly to the kibbutz, and buses #62 and 63 run every 20-45min. to Kiryat (until 8pm). Once in Kiryat Ata, you'll have to walk 4km to the hostel or get a ride with a kibbutznik. Primarily for youth groups, which often completely fill it June-Sept.; be sure to call ahead. NIS25, nonmembers NIS27. Family rooms with bath NIS27 per person.

Camping: Kibbutz Neveh Yam (tel. 84 22 40), 18km south of Ḥaifa. Take bus #122 from central bus station. (Buses run from Ḥaifa 6am-7:30pm. Last bus Fri. 4:20pm.) Just off the beach, near the ruins of the Crusader fortress of Atlit (now a military installation closed to tourists). Excellent amenities, including a small store and restaurant. Cooking facilities available. Camping with tent: NIS12, children NIS7. Bungalows for 4 with toilet, shower, and refridgerator NIS80. Open in summer only.

Food

There's lots of it, tasty and cheap. In **Hadar,** both HaNevi'im and HeḤalutz St. are lined with falafel and sandwich stands, some open on Saturday. On HaNevi'im St., vendors hawk *tiras* (corn on the cob), and restaurants offer an eclectic assortment of cuisines, including Moroccan, Italian, and Romanian. The main road of the **Merkaz HaCarmel** district, **HaNassi Boulevard,** is dotted with cafés. Many establishments in the Carmel are open on Friday nights, but there is no public transportation.

Hadar

Nimer, King of Shwarma 136 Yafo St. (tel. 53 87 27), 200m from the central bus station. Made fresh daily from veal and lamb. Probably the best *shwarma* in town (NIS5.50). Try the hot, spicy pickles, served with a blistering yellow sauce called *amba* (which is also terrific and a little daring on *shwarma*). Unlike the stuff hawked on the street, the *shwarma* here hasn't been soaking up car exhaust indefinitely, and is prepared under scrupulously clean conditions—even non-Israeli stomachs can handle a meal here. Open Sun.-Thurs. noon-11pm, Fri. 10am-midnight, Sat. 5pm-midnight.

Avraham, King of Falafel, 36 Allenby St. at HaTzionut St. Sign in Hebrew only, but look for the jokers smiling at you. The locals' favorite falafel stand (NIS4). Across the street is their main competitor, **Ya'akov, King of the King of Falafel.** Ya'akov is obviously dreaming—in an astounding display of the power of the free market, crowds flock to Avraham, and Avraham alone. Open daily 10am-11pm.

At Benny's, 23 HeḤalutz St. (tel. 66 47 51), near the intersection with Herzl St. Typical Middle Eastern restaurant. Ṣalads (NIS4) and *shishlik* (NIS12). Open daily 8am-10pm.

Tzimḥonit Ḥayim, 30 Herzl St. (tel. 67 46 67). Old-style Jewish dairy restaurant, catering to an elderly clientele. Salad from NIS4, fish from NIS5. Open Sun.-Thurs. 9am-8pm, Fri. 9am-1pm.

Beit HaPri, 12 Herzl St. (tel. 67 71 88), attached to the pizzeria. Shakes made from virtually any combination of fruits and vegetables. Try to keep in mind the distinction between adventurous and truly disgusting when choosing. Hebrew sign only, but look for the green awning.

Hamber, 61 Herzl St. (tel. 66 67 39), at the corner of Arlozorov St. Kosher meat meal with salads NIS11. Try the grilled dishes. Open Sun.-Thurs. 8am-10pm, Fri. 8am-2:30pm.

Nir Etzion, 40 Herzl St. near Ḥayim St. (tel. 64 59 76). *Schnitzel* or beef meal with side order NIS10. Soups and salad NIS3 each. Kosher. Comfortable and clean dining area; self-service. Hebrew sign only, but look for the strangely-dressed figure beckoning you from above. Open Sun.-Thurs. 10am-6pm, Fri. 10am-2:30pm.

Merkaz HaCarmel

Ristorante Italiano, 121 HaNassi St. (tel. 38 13 36). A homey place, run by the same family for 30 years. Serves homemade Italian and Middle Eastern food. Spaghetti NIS14.60, homemade minestrone NIS7.90. A favorite among Knesset members and other celebrities—just ask to see the guest book. Look for the brown chairs outside. Open Sun.-Thurs. and Sat. noon-10pm.

Danny's Inn (tel. 37 55 08), 99 Yefeh Nof Rd., at the corner of Sha'ar HaLevanon. Laid-back café with a breathtaking view of the city. Light meals from NIS3, main dishes NIS12. Open daily 9:30am-midnight.

Narghila, 125 HaNassi Blvd. (tel. 37 59 59). The ubiquitous Yemenite restaurant. Open 24 hrs. daily.

Elsewhere

Sinn-Sinn Chinese Restaurant, 28 Yafo Rd., downtown (tel. 64 22 23). Like most Chinese restaurants in Israel, it's run by a Vietnamese family. Soup, eggroll, salad, main course, and rice NIS16.50. Open Mon.-Thurs. noon-10pm, Fri. and Sun. noon-3:30pm.

There is an inexpensive **fruit and vegetable market** just west of the Paris Sq. station between Naḥum and Nathan St. Walking east on Nathanson, the shop at #777 sells Arab delicacies. Although cow spleen is out of the budget range at NIS11, you'll go nuts over the ox testicles at a mere NIS4. Another *shuk* can be found one block down from HeḤalutz in Hadar on Sirkin and Luntz streets.

Sights

The **Ḥaifa Municipal Tourist Office,** 106 HaNassi Blvd. (tel. 37 40 10), offers an excellent free walking tour of Ḥaifa's major attractions every Saturday from 10am to 12:30pm. The tour leaves from the corner of Yefeh Nof (Panorama) St. and Sha'ar HaLevanon; dress modestly for the stops at Baha'i holy places. A few city buses start running about 9:30am, so you can probably catch one to the starting point if you are not staying in the Carmel.

Many of Ḥaifa's most interesting museums are in the Carmel district, an area adorned by fancy homes and luxury hotels. Inexplicably, the Carmel district is called *ha'merkaz* or "the center" of the city, though by not even the farthest stretch of the imagination is it the geographic, business, or political center of Ḥaifa. The 300m ridge affords views of the white cliffs of Rosh HaNikra to the north as well as the ancient fortress of Atlit to the south. Buses #21, 22, 23, 27, and 37 run to Gan Ha'Em, the public park in "Merkaz HaCarmel," the Carmel shopping area.

Gan Ha'Em (Mother's Park) (tel. 37 70 19 or 37 28 86) has a delightful municipal zoo. It's not exactly an African game reserve, but even a work-wearied zoologist may be surprised at some of the beasts indigenous to this small country. (Open Sun.-Thurs. 8am-4pm, Fri. 8am-1pm, Sat. 9am-4pm; June-Sept. Sun.-Thurs. 8am-6pm, Fri. 8am-1pm, Sat. 9am-6pm. Admission NIS15, students NIS12.) Across the park at 124 HaTishbi St. are three museums that offer another perspective on the flora and fauna of northern Israel: the **M. Stekelis Museum of Prehistory,** the **Natural History Museum,** and the **Biological Museum.** (All open Sun.-Thurs. 8am-3pm, Fri. 8am-1pm, Sat. 10am-2pm. Admission to zoo includes museums.)

For a brush with nature in the middle of the city, take the SPNI nature trail that begins in Gan Ha'Em to the right of the shell-shaped stage. Follow the blue signs into the brush; the path will lead you around the zoo and through tangled greenery into a wadi. The trail is 2km long (about 1hr. walking) and ends in the lower Carmel. (Take bus #3 or 5 to get back uptown).

The **Mané Katz Art Museum,** 89 Yefeh Nof Rd. (tel. 38 34 82), just behind Panorama Center, displays sculptures and canvases by Mané Katz, a member of the Paris group of Jewish Expressionists that included Modigliani, Chagall, and Cremegne. (Open Sun.-Thurs. 10am-4pm, Fri. and Sat. 10am-1pm. Free.) Near the intersection of HaPanorama and HaTzionut, opposite 135 HaTzionut, a **sculpture garden** contains striking bronzes by Ursula Malkin. The **Panorama Center,** inside the large twin towers, houses a movie theater, a bookstore, and various boutiques. Exhibits and fashion shows occasionally grace the walkways. Take buses #21, 22, 23, 31, and 37 to all of these sights.

Haifa's two major academic complexes overlook the slopes at the opposite end of the Carmel ridge. To reach **Haifa University,** take bus #24 or 37 from Herzl St. or the central bus station and ask to be let off at the next to last stop. The university's landmark, designed by the renowned architect Niemeier, is the large 30-story **Eshkol Tower,** also known as the "White Elephant." The building is the focus of student activities and always displays art exhibits. From the tower's observatory, Israel itself becomes a work of art. Free guided tours of the campus are conducted by students every hour from 9am to 2pm (until noon on Fri.), starting from the main building. (For more information, call 24 00 03 or 24 00 07.) The **Reuben and Edith Hecht Museum,** (tel. 25 77 73 or 24 05 77) houses a permanent exhibit on "The People of Israel in the Land of Israel," a respectable collection of impressionist and Jewish paintings, including a few temporary exhibits. Tours available if you call ahead. (Open Sun.-Thurs. 10am-4pm, Fri. 10am-1pm, Sat. 10am-2pm. Free.)

The **Technion,** Israel's internationally acclaimed scientific academy, is worth visiting primarily for its campus life. The Technion is divided into two campuses: the older one, on Balfour and Herzl St. in Hadar, houses the school of architecture, while the newer Kiryat HaTechnion (Technion City, which sounds like something out of an Arnold Schwarzenegger movie), on Mt. Carmel, includes the other departments. Take bus #17 from downtown, #31 from Central Carmel, or #19 from the central bus station or Herzl St. to reach Kiryat HaTechnion. (Call 32 06 64 for information on occasional guided tours of the new campus.)

Beneath the slopes of Mt. Carmel in the Hadar district stands the **Haifa Museum,** at 26 Shabtai Levi St. (tel. 52 32 55). The museum contains three separate exhibits: Israeli modern art, ancient art, and Jewish ethnology. The ancient art exhibit on the top floor includes spectacular mosaic floors from Shihmona, where ancient Haifa was probably located, and an extensive collection of sculptures and figurines from the Canaanite era (18th century BCE) through Greek and Roman times. The ethnology exhibit consists of folk costumes, utensils, and musical instruments from Jewish communities around the world. (Open Sun., Mon., Wed., Fri. 10am-1pm; Tues., Thurs. 10am-1pm and 5-8pm; Sat. 10am-3pm and 5-8pm. Admission NIS7, students NIS5; includes coffee. The ticket is also good for the Prehistory and National Maritime Museums.) Buses #10, 12, 22, and 28 travel to the Haifa Museum.

A few blocks east, the **Technoda** (National Museum of Science, Planning, and Technology) contains a collection of functioning models and demonstrations of the principles of physics (tel. 67 13 72). Children and *Let's Go* staff will enjoy the hands-on exhibits. Take bus #12, 21, 28, or 37. Walk uphill on Balfour St. (from the intersection of Balfour and Herzl St.) to the red-and-white sign on the left pointing to the museum. (Open Mon., Wed., and Thurs. 9am-5pm, Tues. 9am-7pm, Fri. 9am-1pm, Sat. 10am-2pm. Admission NIS7, students NIS5.)

Halfway up Mt. Carmel is the golden-domed **Baha'i Temple,** the shrine of a comparatively new religion. Rows of cypress trees surround the temple, while palm and eucalyptus flourish in the gardens. Its architecture is a cross between Baroque Christian (the dome) and Moorish (the archways). The temple commands a film-frying view of the sprawling municipality below.

The Baha'i shrine (tel. 52 17 61), located on HaTzionut Ave., commemorates the Persian Siyyid Ali Muhammad, the first prophet of the rapidly growing Baha'i religion. (See the General Introduction.) The prophet's bones, brought to Haifa in 1909, now lie in the Persian gardens next to the temple. Modest dress required. Take bus #22 from the central bus station or bus #23, 25, 26, or 32 from HaNevi'im and Herzl St. to the shrine. (Open 9am-noon, gardens open until 5pm. Free.)

From the Baha'i shrine, buses #25 and 26 climb Mt. Carmel to the holy places of the Carmelite Order, whose **monastery** stands on a promontory over Haifa Bay. A Latin monk named Berthold founded the order in 1150. Persecution, which most recently took the form of Napoléon's siege and loss of Akko in 1799, forced the Discalced (or "barefoot") Carmelite Order to move to the site of the cloister. The monks currently live in a relatively new church and monastery complex called **Stella Maris** (Star of the Sea), built in 1836 on the ruins of an ancient Byzantine chapel and a medieval Greek church. The church's dome is crowned by paintings depicting biblical prophets including Elijah flying in his chariot of fire, King David plucking his harp, and scenes of the Holy Family. An exquisite statuette of the Virgin Mary (with whom the order is associated) cradling the baby Jesus stands inside. No bare knees or shoulders permitted. (Tel. 52 34 60. Open daily 6am-1:30pm and 3-6pm.) Next to the Carmelite monastery is a small museum containing ruins of former Mt. Carmel cloisters dating from Byzantine and Crusader times. (Open daily 8:30am-1:30pm and 3-6pm. Free.) Take bus #25, 26, or 31.

Given the Carmelites' affinity for Elijah, or Saint Elias, the Feast of St. Elias is a terrific celebration. Christian Arabs set up booths for food and games, and a communal party begins, culminating with special masses on the morning of the Feast of St. Elias.

Across the street from the monastery is the upper station of the **cable car** *(rakhbal),* which runs down the northwestern slope of the Carmel. While the view from the car is striking, the trip is short, and the prerecorded explanation of the view below (your choice of English or Hebrew) is rushed and uninformative. You can board the cars from either station. By foot, walk west on HaHagana Blvd. from the central bus station for five minutes. There is a small walkway going underneath the elevated train tracks on the right. From the tracks, walk one block down Rahaf St. and turn left onto Ha'Aliya HaShniya St. The cable car station is several blocks down. Another approach is to take bus #42. The cable car station is the last stop. (Tel. 33 59 70 or 33 00 09. Open Sat.-Thurs. 10am-6pm, Fri. 9:30am-2pm. Round-trip NIS9, NIS6 one way.)

Opposite the lower cable car station—across the street and tracks—is the **Clandestine Immigration and Naval Museum,** 204 Allenby Rd. (tel. 53 62 49). The museum explains the exciting exploits behind *Ha'apala,* the desperate smuggling of immigrants into Israel during the British Mandate. Take bus #43 or 44: look for the *Af-Al-Pi* (In spite of), an old immigrant ship now perched atop the museum. (The ship's gangway is lowered Sun. and Tues 8:30am-4pm; Mon., Wed., and Thurs. 8:30am-3pm; Fri. 8:30am-1pm. Admission NIS3, students or under 18 NIS2.)

Up the street at 198 Allenby, the **National Maritime Museum** (tel. 53 66 22) contains models of seafaring vessels from ancient times to the present, as well as other nautical exhibits. The prize exhibit is the bronze bowpiece from a 4th-century CE battleship discovered near Atlit in 1980. (Open Sun.-Thurs. 10am-4pm, Sat. 10am-1pm. Admission NIS5, students NIS4. Free on Sat.)

The stairs leading to the entrance of **Elijah's Cave,** 230 Allenby St. (tel. 52 74 30), are just across the street from the naval museum. Like so much of the Holy Land, all three of the country's major faiths revere the spot. In the biblical history of the Israelites, the caves at the base of the mountain sheltered Elijah from the rage of King Ahab and Queen Jezebel after the prophet killed 450 priests of Ba'al at nearby Mukhraqa in the 9th century BCE (I Kings 17-19). Muslims also revere Elijah as Al-Khadar, "the green prophet" of the same-colored mountains. Christians believe the caves safeguarded the Holy Family upon their return from Egypt. Believers of each faith now pray quietly in the dim light. Bus #45 runs to Edmund Fleg St. near the Carmelite Monastery above the caves. As you approach from the monastery, a difficult path leads down the mountainside beginning near the elbow in the road, across the street from the monastery entrance. Modest dress required. (Cave open Sun.-Thurs. 8am-5pm, Fri. 8am-1pm; in winter Sun.-Thurs. 8am-6pm, Fri. 8am-1pm. Free.)

On Ha'Atzma'ut St. near Plumer Sq. stands the **Dagon Silo Grain Museum** (tel. 66 42 21), one of the most extraordinary granaries ever constructed. This curious edifice, the asymmetrical towers of which dominate Ḥaifa's waterfront, looks something like a modern Crusader fortress. The silo is Israel's only grain-receiving depot, storing 90% of the country's grain. A small archeological exhibit stands in the lobby of the silo's tourist center, just east of the main building on Ha'Atzma'ut St. Take bus #10, 12, or 22. The exhibit and models of the silo's facilities can be seen only when free tours are given (Sun.-Fri. at 10:30am or you can avoid the crowds and make an appointment).

Farther down Ha'Atzma'ut St., near Faisal Square, is the **Railway Museum** (tel. 56 42 93). The old Ḥaifa railroad station now houses a collection of train memorabilia and restored locomotives. (Open Sun., Tues., Thurs. 9am-noon.) East of the railway museum, the Shemen Oil Factory is home to the **Edible Oil Museum,** 2 Tuvin St. (tel. 67 04 91), containing artifacts relating to the oil industry in Israel. (Open Sun.-Thurs. 8:30am-2:30pm.) Buses #17, 42, and 193 go to the Railway Museum; bus #2 goes to the Oil Museum. Ask the museum staff for wry Israeli jokes about how their country got the wrong kind of oil.

Entertainment

A number of **beaches** along the north coast past the Dagon Silo provide a welcome escape from the industrial pulse of the city. Ḥof HaShaket, the most convenient, costs NIS3.50; take bus #41 from the Hadar district or the central bus station. Ḥof Bat Galim, also near the central bus station, is small and frequently crowded. On Saturdays, when the beaches to the north of Ḥaifa are packed, it's worth traveling to the south where you can still see the sand between the bathers. Take bus #44 or 45 to Ḥof HaCarmel, a free beach. Ḥof Dror (tel. 51 48 09), a small white building next to the lower cable car station, rents windsurf boards and diving equipment.

When asked about the city's sparse entertainment, Ḥaifa's first mayor pointed to the city's factories and said, "There is our nightlife." Although still an unusually quiet metropolis, Ḥaifa does not lack nocturnal attractions. The GTIO and Municipal Office can both supply information on nightlife. Pick up the free monthly *Events in Ḥaifa and the Northern Region* for a complete listing of daily concerts and special events.

A relaxing evening activity is a walk along **Yefeh Nof St.** (HaPanorama). Catch a bus to Merkaz HaCarmel for a view of twinkling city lights—and not just Ḥaifa's: on a clear night, you can see Lebanon. Nearby **Gan Ha'Em** is always lively and occasionally has free summer concerts. On Mondays, listen for rock concerts at 5:30pm; tickets cost NIS1-20.

The **Ḥaifa Cinematique,** 142 HaNassi Blvd. (tel. 38 34 24 or 38 62 46), a few blocks from Gan Ha'Em, screens three or four English movies every night except Friday (NIS9). Next door is the **Ḥaifa Auditorium,** where the Israel Philharmonic and distinguished musicians perform regularly. The expensive tickets are usually available the day of performances; inquire at the tourist office in the morning for information. On the **Bat Galim Promenade,** along the shore behind the central bus station, you can soothe road-weary nerves with a few waves (i.e., the sea or a liberal libation of Maccabee). On the Promenade, the **Panas Boded Pub** screens your favorite rock videos on strategically placed televisions and serves up Maccabee (NIS6) till dawn. (Open daily from 7pm "until the last person leaves.") Several doors down, **Pub Hayu-Haya** offers similar fare, though only here can you see King Kong surprise an unsuspecting surfer. Closer to the port, the **London Pride Pub,** 85 Ha'Atzma'ut St. at Khayat Sq. (tel. 66 38 39), is a raucous pick-up joint frequented by sailors. The cover charge is NIS6 on weekdays, NIS8 Fridays and Saturdays, first drink included (opens at 8:30pm). In Hadar, three local pubs are **Ha'Olam Hazeh** and **Salamandra** at the Nordau *midreḥov* and **Rodeo** (tel. 67 43 63), 23 Balfour St.

Fun-seekers head to the Carmel about 10:30pm. Popular discos include **Biblos,** 1 Liberia St. (tel. 25 54 81), and **Hitchcock,** 115 Yefeh Nof St. (tel. 37 15 62). The emphasis is more on drinking than dancing at the **Aḥuza Club,** 25 Tcherniḥovsky (tel. 33

88 37), the **Bear Pub,** 135 HaNassi Blvd. (tel. 38 17 03), and **Little Ḥaifa,** 4 Sha'ar HaLevanon St (tel. 38 09 29).

Dances, coffeehouses, and movies at the **Technion** and at **Ḥaifa University** offer excellent opportunities to meet young Israelis, particularly during the school year. Foreign students are welcome at the Technion's nightly dances in July and August. For more information, call 32 06 64; you may have to bring your student ID and passport.

On Sunday evenings during the summer, Dado Beach, on the south western edge of the city, is still stayin' alive with free **disco dancing** outdoors from 8pm until midnight. Take local bus #43, 44, or 45, or regular buses heading south to Jerusalem or Tel Aviv, and get off at the first gas station. On Thursday evenings, on Hassan Shukri St. near Gan HaZikaron, street performers clown around by the flower market. Call the "What's On In Ḥaifa" hotline (tel. 37 42 53) for current entertainment information.

Near Haifa

A common denominator among the eclectic settlements near Ḥaifa is grapes (the name Carmel is a creative linguistic child of Kerem El, "Vineyard of God"). Miles of fine grapevines line the inland foothills (Ein Hod, Daliyat al-Karmel, Isfiya), the plain of Sharon (Atlit, Neveh Yam, Dor, Zikhron Ya'akov, Ma'agan Miḥa'el), the Jezreel Valley (Kiryat Tivon, Beit She'arim), and Zevulun Valley (Kfar HaMaccabbi, Akko, Nahariya, the Akhzivs). Many of these can easily be visited as daytrips from Ḥaifa. Ein Hod, to the south, is a tiny and intriguing artists' village. The ruins and burial catacombs of Beit She'arim offer fascinating insight into the era of Roman rule over Judea. The villages of Isfiya and Daliyat al-Karmel are home to Druze, members of a secretive sect of Shi'i Islam, whose followers maintain a strong religious identity separate from Sunni and other Shi'i Muslims.

Beit She'arim בית שארים

Beneath the fertile soil of Carmel, 19km south of Ḥaifa, the remains of the members of the arcane Hebrew judicial council, the Sanhedrin, rested peacefully for nearly 2000 years. Twenty years ago, excavations at Beit She'arim disturbed their graves when archeologists found an ancient synagogue and astonishing system of catacombs. Beit She'arim was the gathering place of the Sanhedrin, recognized by the Roman Empire in the 2nd century CE as the Supreme Rabbinical Council, the judicial authority over all of world Jewry. Two hundred years later, it had become a sacred (and secret) burial ground for Jews, victims of the Diaspora, who were barred from Jerusalem. Archeologists have uncovered a labyrinth of some 20 caves whose walls are lined with dozens of intricately adorned sarcophagi, including one of Rabbi Yehuda HaNassi, first president of the Sanhedrin and compiler of the Mishnah. According to inscriptions found on the sarcophagi, many of the buried were brought from as far away as Sidon and Tyre, Babylon, and southern Arabia. (Open Sat.-Thurs. 8am-5pm, Fri. 8am-4pm. Admission NIS5.50, students NIS4.10.)

The **archeological site** and a **museum** (tel. 83 16 43) are located in a park near the town of **Kiryat Tivon.** To get to Beit She'arim, take bus #74, 75, 301, 338, or 431 (or #331 to Nazareth) from the central bus station or Herzl St. to Kiryat Tivon (NIS4.20). Buses leave every 20 minutes and the trip takes 40 minutes (last bus leaves Ḥaifa at 11pm, Fri. 3pm). From the bus stop, walk downhill on Alexander Zaid St. to the T-junction at Katzenelson St. (look for a supermarket on your right). Turn left onto Katzenelson, then right onto Sharet Rd. before the school. Follow Sharet until the green metal fence on your right ends at a park. Take the dirt path on the right that starts where the fence ends and make a left at the T-junction. Follow the path down to a second T-junction. The site will be straight ahead through the trees. If the walk takes more than 20 minutes, you have done something wrong and are now lost. Ignore the signs attempting to direct you to the site. The paved road in front of the entrance to the site leads to an ancient olive press and synagogue. The steps next to the canteen take you to the modern Alexander Zaid statue. Zaid was the guardian of these hills during the 1930s until his death in the 1936 uprisings. Because of the esteem in which he was held by local Arabs, he served as the mediator among the Arab *hamulas* (extended families) of the area. His descendants still fill this role today.

Ein Hod עין הוד

Ein Hod (Hebrew for "Spring of Grandeur") was originally Ein Houd (Arabic for "Spring of Garden Rows"), an Arab village of 670 people, located on a hill on the western slopes of Mt. Carmel. The town also served as a resort for Crusaders based at the nearby Atlit fortress. In 1948 the Arab inhabitants fled from the Israeli forces to the south and the deserted village was transformed into a *moshav,* and later an artists' colony. Today it is home to an olio of studios, where artists create everything from traditional needle crafts to abstract paintings. Bronze sculptures grace backyards, mobiles swing between trees, and stone figures recline against fences. Most of the Arab homes are still intact, and the view of the Mediterranean undoubtedly inspires the muse. Although studios are closed to casual visitors, the large **Ein Hod Gallery** (tel. 84 25 48), run by two gregarious women who may proffer their services as tour guides, exhibits works by residents. (Open Sun.-Thurs. and Sat. 9:30am-5pm, Fri. until 4pm. Admission NIS1.) Across from the gallery is the attractive, though somewhat expensive **Artists' Inn Café,** and nearby is Ein Hod's **Janco-Dada Museum** (tel. 84 23 50 or 84 31 52). Stop in to admire the works of Marcel Janco, one of the founders of Dadaism and of Ein Hod. (Open Sun.-Thurs. and Sat. 9:30am-5pm, Fri. 9:30am-4pm. Admission NIS5, students NIS3.)

Ein Hod is 14km south of Ḥaifa. To get there, take **bus** #202 or 921 heading south along the old Ḥaifa-Ḥadera road (NIS3.70). From the Ein Hod junction where the bus lets you off, the town is a 2km walk uphill. To get to the center of Ein Hod, turn right when you reach the playground at the entrance to the village.

Isfiya and Daliyat al-Karmel
עוספיה, דלית אל–כרמל

Isfiya (pronounced "Usfiya" in Arabic, "Usefiya" in Hebrew) and Daliyat al-Karmel villages are the center of Druze life along the northern Israeli coast. An unsuccessful rebellion against the Egyptian pasha in 1830 led to the destruction of 14 of the Druze villages in the Carmel; Daliyat and Isfiya are the only two remaining. In the 1860s, when the Turks were anxious to have the Druze as a buffer against the Bedouin and Christians who were seeking converts, they welcomed the Druze back to these Carmel villages.

Some 17,000 Druze live on Mt. Carmel in the colorful villages of **Isfiya** and **Daliyat al-Karmel.** Druze elders are recognizable by their thick mustaches and flowing white *kaffiyehs* (headdresses), and Druze women are distinctive in their black robes and white shawls. The Druze are known for being extraordinarily congenial, even while hawking their wares.

In **Daliyat al-Karmel,** the bazaar is liveliest on Saturdays, but come on a weekday if you want lower prices and a better opportunity to converse with locals, come on a weekday. You can try to bargain, though vendors generally are determined to extract large sums from tourists. A few words of Arabic or Hebrew can lower prices considerably. Be aware that most of the clothes and jewelry are imported from India, while the furniture comes from Gaza. Wheat stalk baskets, embroidery, and tapestry work are mainly local goods.

The Zionist and Christian mystic, Sir Lawrence Oliphant, was one of few outsiders close to the sect. In the late 19th century, he and his wife lived in Daliyat for five years, helping the Druze build their homes. Since 1980, the Israeli Defense Ministry has been paying for the restoration of Oliphant's house on the outskirts of town. It is now a memorial to the scores of Druze soldiers killed in Israel's wars. Although street names are not used, anyone can direct you to **Beit Oliphant.** Sir Lawrence sheltered Arab and Jewish insurgents against the British in the cave between the sculpture garden in the rear and the main house. Oliphant's secretary, the Hebrew poet Naftali Hertz Imber, later wrote "HaTikva" (The Hope), Israel's national anthem, at this site.

Four kilometers from Daliyat al-Karmel, away from Isfiya, is the site where Elijah massacred 450 priests of Ba'al. **Muhraqa,** the Arabic name, refers to the sacrifice (or "burning") that Elijah offered God from an altar here. It was also from this Mount that Elijah's servant sighted the rain cloud that relieved the land's drought. The Carmelites saw the clouds as a symbol of the Virgin Mary, to whom they are devoted. In 1886 they built a small **monastery** here; from the roof on a clear day you can see snow-capped Mt. Hermon on the horizon. Modest dress advisable. (Monastery open daily 8am-5pm. Admission to the rooftop viewing area NIS1.) There is no bus service to the monastery; you'll have to hire a taxi. If hiking (not advisable), bear left at the only fork along the way or you'll head toward al-Yakim. The **Stella Carmel Hospice** in Is-fiya organizes occasional walking tours to the site for pilgrims. The most eventful day at Muhraqa is the Feast of St. Elias (Elijah), when Christian Arab families party in the park surrounding the monastery.

Isfiya is 4km closer to Haifa than Daliyat al-Karmel. Isfiya's alleys wind between sun-drenched stone houses, and overflow with romping children in the summer. The view from the nearby peaks of Mt. Carmel is magnificent: ridges and forests spread dramatically into the Zevulun valley. Have a picnic.

Isfiya has a Christian population of about 1000 Roman Catholics, in addition to its 4000 Druze. At the lovely Catholic church on the main road, members of the congregation boast that their ancestors were Crusaders from Italy. Isfiya also houses the excellent **Stella Carmel Hospice** (tel. 39 16 92; P.O. Box 7045, Haifa 31070), run by the Anglican Church and open to all. A converted Arab villa, the hospice has a charming lounge filled with antique Persian rugs. The hospice is to the right of the main road from Haifa, at the entrance to the village. Look for the narrow paved road lined with trees. Take bus #192 or a *sherut* taxi from Haifa University (4 buses per day 1pm-4:30pm, last bus on Fri. 2:25pm, last return bus 3pm; in both cases ask the driver for Stella Carmel). Bed and breakfast in the main house is US$18, half-board US$27, full board US$34; bed and breakfast for an outside dorm room US$10, half-board US$19, full board US$26. Unmarried couples will get separate rooms.

The Druze villages make an excellent daytrip from Haifa. **Bus** #192 leaves infrequently from the central bus station and the Hadar district, stopping in both villages on weekdays. The senseless bus schedule, however, makes it impossible to take a bus both to and from the villages. Flag down a *sherut* taxi on the main road next to Haifa University to get to the villages and wait by an Egged bus stop to catch one back. Prices for this route during the day are the same as bus fares. The last bus leaves Daliyat and Isfiya at 3pm, but *sherut* continue to run and stores remain open until about 8pm.

Akko (Acre) עכו

Just across the mouth of Haifa Bay, Akko is centuries apart from its urban neighbor. Akko (historically written "Acre" in English) is not made up of two cities, as many people believe, but rather three. Inside a bastion of crumbling walls, the 200-year-old Arab town is a labyrinth of alleys and stairwells leading up to ancient Turkish fortifications, only to disappear into the chaos of the streets below. Just outside Arab Akko, a rapidly encroaching new city is laying siege to the embattled ancient walls—a familiar struggle throughout Israel. Undisturbed by this contest stands the vast, subterranean Crusader City, still only partially excavated, directly underneath old Akko and predating it by 600 years. The enormous rooms of this basement city and the network of tunnels lacing through them were fortuitously preserved by the Turks, who found the constructions too solid to raze.

The tumultuous history of Akko reflects the ebb and flow of the contending armies that have washed over it, leaving behind their tell-tale architectural jetsam. The Crusaders came to the city in 1140 on their vainglorious campaign to recapture the Holy Land for Christianity. Failing to take Jerusalem initially, they retreated to peaceful

Akko, transforming it into the greatest port of their empire and a worldwide showpiece of culture and architecture. The Mamluks ended Crusader rule in 1290, and almost 500 years later a Bedouin sheikh rebuilt the city. The city that survives today was built by an Albanian adventurer, Ahmad, who ousted the Bedouin and became the Turkish pasha Al-Jazzar ("The Butcher"). Napoléon later claimed, with his typical modesty, that had Akko fallen to him, "the world would have been mine." In the city's most recent clash, Jewish resistance fighters disguised themselves as British soldiers to lead the 1947 Irgun prison break, a prelude to the War of Independence the following year.

Akko was designed for the pedestrian, so allow ample time to amble and explore. During school vacations, you may find yourself awarded an informative, if somewhat tiresome, self-appointed guide in the Arab town. The young men who so boldly approach you are often only interested in practicing their English and impressing their friends, so offering a tip may be taken as an insult. On the other hand, many local men consider picking up foreign women a full-time sport, and what begins as a pleasant chat can turn menacing. Women travelling alone especially should avoid these encounters. Steer clear of any drugs offered on the streets; the police keep a close watch on dealers and usually confine foreign offenders to the local prison for several nightmarish days before expelling them from the country. It's best not to prowl the alleys of the Old City after dark.

Orientation

To reach Akko from Haifa or Nahariya, take bus #252 or 272 (express), which depart every 15 minutes (NIS4.20). New and old Akko are connected by **Hayim Weizmann Street.** From the central bus station, Herzl Street runs to Weizmann. **HaHagana Street** hugs the sea to the west from the new city to the lighthouse. On **Al-Jazzar Street** are the mosque, Crusader City, information office, and Old City bus stops. The central supermarket, central post office, Wolfson Auditorium, and City Hall are on **Ha'Atzma'ut,** the major street of the new city. The Old City, located on a peninsula, is riddled with poorly marked passages. The market winds its way through the middle of the peninsula. The **Southern Promenade,** at the end of HaHagana St., has been developed as a tourist area, with several restaurants and sitting areas built into the old Pisan Harbor walls and towers.

Practical Information

Municipal Information Office: Tourist Center, Al-Jazzar St. (tel. 91 17 64 or 91 02 51), across from the mosque. Information about sites and special events in Akko and a great map of the new and old cities (NIS2.50). Get the map before you attempt the old city. Open Sun.-Thurs. 8am-4pm. On *shabbat* and when the MIO is deserted, check with the Crusader City for information.

Central Post Office: 11 Ha'Atzma'ut St., next to the municipality building. Open July-Aug. Sun.-Thurs. 8am-2:30pm, Fri. 8am-noon; Sept.-June Sun., Tues., and Thurs. 8am-12:30pm and 3:30-6pm, Mon. and Wed. 8am-2pm, Fri. 8am-1pm. Smaller office inside entrance to Crusader City. **International telephones** and **Poste Restante** are available at Ha'Atzma'ut St. **Telephone code:** 04.

Banks: in the Old City, **Barclay's Discount,** corner of Al-Jazzar and Weizmann St., and the **Arab-Israeli Bank,** around the corner on Weizmann St. Open Sun., Tues., and Thurs., 8:30am-1pm and 4-5:30pm, Mon. and Wed. 8:30am-1pm, Fri. 8:30am-noon. In the new city, several banks are located on and near Ben Ami St.

Train Station: David Remez St. (tel. 91 23 50), across from the central bus station. Haifa-Nahariya and Nahariya-Tel Aviv trains stop here.

Central Bus Station: Ha'Arba'a Rd. in the new city (tel. 91 63 33 for information). Buses #251 and 271 to Haifa (NIS4.20) and Nahariya (NIS3.00) are *me'asef,* which means they make a lot of annoying stops. Buses #252 or 272 are express. Buses from platform 3, near the Egged restaurant, will take weary travelers the short distance to the Old City. **Baggage check** open Sun.-Thurs. 7:30am-3pm (NIS4), or stash your stuff at the Knight's Parking Lot on Weizmann in the Old City (just north of Al-Jazzar), open daily 8am-6pm (NIS5). Knights have parking lots?

Taxi: **Akko Tzafon,** tel. 91 66 66; **Ariyeh,** tel. 91 33 69.

Pharmacies: **Akko,** 35 Ben Ami St. (tel. 91 20 21); **Merkaz,** 27 Ben Ami St. (tel. 91 05 27).

Fire: Tel. 91 02 33.

First Aid (**Magen David Adam**): Tel. 101.

Police: 2 Ben Ami St. (tel. 100).

Accommodations and Food

The **Akko Youth Hostel (HI)** (tel. 91 19 82), just across from the old lighthouse, has commodious, comfortable rooms. Emulate royalty for a night in the 200-year-old building: it was once the palace of the Ottoman governor. Located in the Crusader City and rarely full, this is one of the finest (and most expensive) urban hostels in Israel. The airy lounge and several of the rooms have a fabulous view of the sea over the ramparts. To reach the hostel from the bus station, take any bus from platform #16 to the Old City, then make your way through the market, following sparse signs, or walk just north of the old city from the bus, making a left onto Napoléon "Blown-apart" Bonaparte St. and another left onto HaHagana St. when you reach the water. Follow HaHagana to the lighthouse; the hostel is 30m to the left. (10:30pm curfew. NIS25 or US$11, nonmembers NIS28 or US$12. Breakfast included. Dinner NIS12.50.) Alternatively, try **Paul's Hostel and Souvenir Shop,** just opposite the lighthouse at the southern end of HaHagana St., under a white awning with blue metal poles. Ask anyone in the shop for Paul Elias, who will take you to his 10-bed hostel located in his family's building just behind the shop. Hostel guests live in a large, Crusader-domed room with adjacent bathroom with shower and kitchen. Each guest gets a key to the hostel rooms. NIS15. Shop open daily 8am-10pm. No obligation to buy. There are additional unofficial and unregulated hostels or rooms for rent in the Old City, but get the tourist office's opinion of the place before you make a decision you might regret. The port area can be dangerous at night, especially for women alone. Beach camping is forbidden.

The **Lighthouse Restaurant** (tel. 91 76 40), under its namesake near the hostel, has tables overlooking the water and invites evening idling. Hostel patrons receive a 10% discount. Up the street away from the hostel is the more expensive **Abu Christo** restaurant (tel. 91 00 65). Daredevils occasionally take a dive off the three-story store wall into the water near the restaurant. Around the corner from the hostel, heading away from the lighthouse, is the **Pita Bakery,** where hot pita bread is peddled for a pittance in the pre-noon period. A number of inexpensive falafel stands huddle near the corner of Weizmann and Ben Ami St. **Abu Elias,** across from the tourist information office, serves creamy hummus with salad for NIS7. Next door, **The Orient** sells "Foul" for NIS7 (you know, *fowl*). **Café Tuscana,** in the Pisan Harbor en route to the hostel, has the standard Middle Eastern munchies at slightly inflated prices (pita and chips NIS4). It's well worth it, though, for the jaw-dropping view of the sea and Old Akko. You can buy food at the outdoor market next to the central bus station and at the *shuk* in the Old City. Farther from the hostel are the food stands and small supermarkets on Yehoshafat St. off Ben Ami St.

Sights and Entertainment

No itinerary can do justice to the aura of history and conflict that emanates from the ruins and fortifications of old Akko. To reach the **Old City** from the bus station by foot, walk down Ben Ami St. to Weizmann St. and turn left. The entrance to the Old City is just past Eli Cohen Park on the left. As you pass the Al-Jazzar wall, look for the moat beneath the Burj al-Kommander to the left. The entrance to the **Mosque of Al-Jazzar** is to your right on Al-Jazzar St. The third largest mosque in Israel and the most important one outside Jerusalem, it dominates this city of monuments with its green dome and sleek minaret. Ahmed Al-Jazzar ordered its construction in 1781 on what is believed to have been the site of San Croce, the original Christian cathedral of Akko.

Inside is an attractive courtyard with Roman columns taken from Caesarea. The western end of the courtyard rests upon the cellar of a Crusader fortress. The surrounding structures are lodgings for students of the Qur'an and the personnel of the mosque. The small building in front of the mosque houses the sarcophagi of Ahmed Al-Jazzar and his adopted son, Sulayman Pasha. The tower was destroyed by an earthquake in 1927, but promptly restored; the rest of the complex is in magnificent condition.

In front of the mosque sits an octagonal *sabil* (fountain) where the faithful perform *wudhu*, the ritual washing of their heads, hands, and feet before entering the sanctuary. Inside, in the green cage on the balcony to the right, is a shrine containing a hair from the beard of the prophet Muhammad. As in all mosques, prayers are conducted five times per day, and you will be asked to wait or return in 20 minutes if you arrive during a prayer session. To the right of the mosque is a small building containing the sarcophagi of Al-Jazzar and son; you can peek through the barred windows at the marble boxes, now covered with soil and green plants. Al-Jazzar turned the buried Crusader cathedral into an underground water reservoir, filled by rainfall and pipelines. You can enter the recently renovated reservoir through a small door and underground stairway to the left of the mosque. Look for the small green sign and red arrows. Modest dress required; large scarves available for those not already covered. The guides who offer NIS2-4 tours vary in quality. Some are very knowledgeable, while others are merely literate in Arabic and will read you a few inscriptions. (Open daily 8:30am-7pm. Closes one hour earlier in winter. Admission NIS1.50, students NIS1.)

A restored white stone gate, the entrance to the subterranean **Crusader City,** stands across from the mosque on Al-Jazzar St. When first discovered, the rooms were thought to have been built underground, but archeologists have since determined that Al-Jazzar found it easier to simply build his own city above them. Because excavations were halted for fear that the Arab town above might collapse, most of the Crusader City remains buried; only the area originally known as the "Hospitaller's Quarter" is open. In the entrance halls, three enormous pillars stand amidst a variety of architectural styles. Almost anything in these halls decorated with pictorial representations such as flowers or human forms is the work of the Crusaders, while the more abstract embellishments and the Arabic calligraphy are Ottoman additions. The flowers engraved in several of the columns are among the earliest examples of the *fleur-de-lis,* the French imperial insignia. The neighboring halls date from the original 12th-century Crusader City and were probably part of a hospital complex in which the Hospitaller Order gave medical attention to pilgrims. The arches project directly from the floor, indicating that the current foundation is some 4m above the bases on the original level. The barrels and girders throughout the complex were placed there recently to support the original walls.

Proceed from the entrance halls to the courtyard to see some of the fortifications built by Daher al-Omar. Turn left and enter the Hospitaller's fort through the imposing Turkish gate, directly beneath which stands the original Crusader gate. Turning right from here will bring you to the center of the original Crusader complex. These halls are now used for concerts during July by the Haifa Symphony Orchestra, as well as the annual **Israel Fringe Theater Festival.** The week-long extravaganza occurs during the Jewish festival of Sukkot (usually in mid-October), and attracts small theater groups from all over Israel. Only a few of the performances are in English. The **Vocalisa Festival,** also called "Voice from the Wall," brings singing groups to these halls from around the world for Passover (usually in April).

Closed since 1990, the passageway from this part of the Crusader City to the **Refectory** or **Crypt of St. John** is impassable. To reach the crypt, leave the Crusader City the way you came in, turn right, and follow the signs to the crypt entrance. Look for the spooky black-and-white sign on a metal door. The most magnificent and famous of the buried rooms, the crypt once housed Crusader feasts.

Next to the third column in the crypt is a staircase connected to the long underground passageway that leads to six adjacent rooms opening onto a central courtyard. The passageway may have been dug by the Crusaders as a hiding place in case of attack, or possibly as an elaborate sewage system. It was later restored by Al-Jazzar to serve as a means of escape if Napoléon gained entrance to the city walls. The rooms also served as a hospital for wounded knights, and the Turks used it as a post office. The adjacent **Municipal Museum** (accessible either through the metal door opposite the crypt entrance or through the metal door opposite the main entrance around the corner) is essentially a Turkish steam bath that operated until 1947. Random relics are strewn throughout the baths with little explanation. (Crusader City open Sat.-Thurs. 8:30am-4:45pm, Fri. 8:30am-1:45pm. Admission NIS5, students NIS4. Useful pamphlet and map NIS1.) If you're in a group of at least 20, try to see the film *5000 Years: The History of Akko*.

From the Municipal Museum, take a right down the alley and continue to the *souk*, a tumultuous avenue of butchers, grocers, bakers, and copper, brass, and leather vendors. Small eateries throughout the *souk* offer shish kebab, falafel, and sandwiches. (Market open 7am-7pm.) Near the market crouch several caravanserais (*khan* in Arabic), quadrangular inns with large inner courts where travelers and their caravans once lodged. The most impressive among them is **Khan al-Umdan** (Inn of Pillars), just past the Isnan Pasha mosque and the fishing port. Al-Jazzar built this *khan* for Turkish merchants toward the end of the 18th century. The lower stories of the courts served as stalls for horses, camels, and tree sloths, while the upper galleries served as boarding rooms. The *khan* is marked by a slender, square clock tower with the Turkish halfmoon and star. The tower was erected in 1906 to celebrate the jubilee of the Turkish Sultan Abd al-Hamid, who ruled from 1876 to 1918.

Near the Khan al-Umdan is the **Akko Marina.** You can rent diving equipment from **Ramy's Diving Center** (tel. 91 89 90), located inside the Khan al-Umdan on the left. Look for the Ahab's Camel Wash sign. An introductory dive with instructor and equipment will set you back US$40. During July and August, the Arab fisherfolk will take tourists out in boats for views of the sea walls. Set a price before you go (no more than NIS2-3 in a boat with other tourists). Refuse offers for "special" private cruises costing up to NIS20; you can bargain the price down considerably. Women should be on guard against harassment, and no one should expect much from a tour, for many of the fisherfolk do not speak English. You can rent a pedal boat for a hefty NIS25 per hour or a motor boat for NIS45 per hour, on Saturdays only, between 9am-8pm. (Look for the "Boats for Rent" sign on the small orange dock.)

In the northern part of the Old City, the commanding **Citadel** adjoins the Crusader City on HaHagana St., opposite the sea wall. (Navigating the maze of streets in this part of Old City is tricky, especially without one of the GTIO's glossy maps.) This stronghold, used by the British as their central prison, now houses the **Museum of Heroism** (tel. 91 39 00), a monument to Jewish pre-state resistance organizations. The citadel was built in the late 1700s on Crusader foundations of the 13th century, and was used as a prison by the Turks. The most famous inmate during Turkish rule was Baha'u'llah, founder of the Baha'i faith, who was imprisoned here on the second floor in 1868. During the British Mandate, the prison housed about 560 inmates under the guard of about half as many British soldiers. Members of the Palmah, Hagana, and Irgun, including Ze'ev Jabotinsky, were imprisoned here for anti-British activities. Jabotinsky was a key organizer of Menahem Begin's Irgun (later to evolve into the Likud bloc), which lost eight members to the citadel's gallows between 1938 and 1947. The Irgun retaliated by hanging a British officer. **The Gallows Room,** now the museum's most sobering exhibit, displays the noose in place, along with photographs of the eight victims. On May 4, 1947, the Irgun outwitted its British captors by staging a spectacular prison break that freed 11 of its members and 255 other inmates. To reach the museum, follow the stone stairs down to the lower garden, then up the metal stairs and around the side of the prison. (Prison and museum open Sun.-Thurs. 9:30am-5:30pm, Fri. 9am-12:30pm, Sat. 9:30am-5:30pm. Admission NIS6, students NIS4.)

Across the street from the Museum of Heroism looms the **Burj al-Kuraim** (Fortress of the Vineyards), commonly referred to as the British Fortress, despite its Crusader and Turkish builders. Renowned through history as the most secure port in the East, Akko remains a city of battlements and bastions. Akko's defense in recent centuries has relied upon the **Al-Jazzar Wall,** which extends along the northern and eastern sides of the city and is surrounded by a moat of sea water. The best place from which to view the wall is the **Burj al-Kommander** (Commander's Fortress), an enormous Crusader bastion at the northern corner. To enter the watchtower, climb the steps that begin where Weizmann St. crosses the wall.

The city walls originally encompassed the entire harbor, but all that remains is the ruined **Tower of the Flies,** the site of the original lighthouse, solemnly brooding in the middle of the bay. The original fortifications were toppled by a devastating earthquake in 1837. At the eastern corner near the shoreline yawns the so-called **Land Gate,** once the only entrance to the city.

The only part of Akko's new town of interest to tourists is Ḥof **Argaman** (Purple Beach; tel. 91 03 57), which isn't actually purple (the reference is to a type of snail found here). (Open June-Oct. 8am-4pm. Admission NIS5, students NIS4. Weight room and sauna NIS20.) To get to Ḥof Argaman, follow Yonatan HaHashmonai St. from the Land Gate south along the coast for about 10 minutes, taking the detour around the naval school. The only hotels in the new town, the Argaman and the Palm Beach, dominate the beach. Past the Palm Beach Hotel is a free beach just as fine as Ḥof Argaman, but without lifeguards. Just outside the Land Gate, at the less attractive Ḥof HaKhomet (open 7am-6pm, admission NIS5), sailboards are available for NIS10 per hour. None of the several hundred swimmers seem to notice the "bathing prohibited" signs (posted in three languages). There's a changing room through the low door opposite the beach entrance.

Near Akko

Loḥamei HaGeta'ot ("Fighters of the Ghettos"), a kibbutz founded by concentration camp and Warsaw Ghetto survivors, lies outside Akko toward Nahariya. The **Ghetto Fighters' House** (tel. 92 04 12) is dedicated to the memory of World War II resistance fighters and ghetto rebels. The heroic Warsaw Ghetto uprising is examined extensively, as are Nazi atrocities in other countries. Much of the museum displays the rich and vital Jewish cultural life of the Warsaw Ghetto (in particular the poetry of Yitzḥak Katzenelson), as well as paintings, drawings, lithographs, sculptures, and prints by prisoners and survivors. To reach the kibbutz and museum, take bus #271 toward Nahariya (make sure that the bus is *me'asef,* not express, or you'll end up in Nahariya, feeling rather silly). (Museum open Sun.-Thurs. 9am-4pm, Fri. 9am-1pm, Sat. 10am-5pm. Small donation requested.)

The **Roman aqueduct,** just outside the museum to the south, is remarkably well preserved, largely because it's not Roman. Al-Jazzar had it built in 1780 to carry water the 15km from the Kabri springs to their stronghold in Akko. Take bus #271, which runs on Saturday.

Two kilometers south of the kibbutz bloom the **Baha'i Gardens** (tel. 81 27 63), arranged in a riveting combination of Occidental and Oriental styles. The gardens hold the villa and shrine of Baha'u'llah (Glory of God), the prophet and founder of the Baha'i faith. The gardens were planted from 1952-56 to beautify the site. (Shrine open Fri.-Mon. 9am-noon, gardens open daily until 9-5pm. Free.) The gate on the main road is for Baha'is; all other tourists should get off the bus just north of the gate at the sign for Shomrat. Walk east about 0.5km, past **Kibbutz Shomrat,** and enter the gate on the right just past the military camp, marked by a small sign. The gardens are on the main Akko-Nahariya road, accessible by bus #271 (about 10min.). For a more arduous daytrip, consider the 1km hike through **Naḥal Shagur** (also called **Naḥal Beit Hakerem**), a tributary of the Ḥilazon River that extends east of Akko and is part of the valley dividing the Upper and Lower Galilee.

Nahariya נהריה

In a country where the Bible can moonlight as a travel guide, the most remarkable thing about tiny Nahariya is that it is very recently developed and little of particular importance has happened here. Founded by German Jews in 1934 as a farming village, Nahariya was the site of seven illegal immigrant boat landings between 1939 and early 1948. The town has quietly expanded into a pleasant resort, distinguished by a lingering touch of European charm and easy access to first-rate beaches. The Ga'aton River, a sliver of water around which the town initially developed, runs along the middle of the town's main boulevard. (*Nahar* means "river," hence *Nahariya*.) In the heat of the summer, the river dwindles to a pathetic trickle.

Orientation and Practical Information

10km north of Akko and the same distance south of Rosh HaNikra's sea caverns, Nahariya is the northernmost town on Israel's coast. The roads from cities further to the south run to the beaches and parks of Akhziv (3km north, a 40-min. walk). Nahariya itself is miniscule; nearly every service you'll need is located on HaGa'aton Blvd. To reach the beaches, walk a few blocks west on HaGa'aton and stop when you get wet.

Municipal Tourist Information Office (MTIO): HaGa'aton Blvd. (tel. 92 98 00), ground floor, Municipality Building, HaGa'aton Blvd. From the bus station, walk west on HaGa'aton until you reach the plaza on your left just after Herzl St.; the MTIO is the large white building at the end of the plaza. Downright avuncular staff. Open Sun.-Thurs. 8am-1pm and 4-7pm, Fri. 8am-1pm.

Banks: Barclay's Discount (tel. 92 46 11), **Israel Discount** (tel. 92 88 81), and **Leumi** (tel. 92 56 31) are all on HaGa'aton Blvd. Most open Sun., Tues., and Thurs. 8:30am-12:30pm and 4-6pm, Mon. and Wed. 8:30am-12:30pm, Fri. 8:30am-noon.

Post Office: 40 HaGa'aton Blvd. (tel. 92 01 80). Open Sun., Mon., Wed., and Thurs. 7:45am-12:30pm and 3:30-6pm, Tues. 7:45am-2pm, Fri. 7:45am-1pm. **International calls** and **Poste Restante** service available. **Telephone code:** 04.

Train Station: 1 HaGa'aton Blvd., 1 block east (away from the sea) from the bus station. Trains only for Akko, Ḥaifa, Netanya, and Tel Aviv.

Bus Station: 3 HaGa'aton Blvd. (tel. 92 34 44). Buses #272 (express) and 271 depart for Nahariya from both Ḥaifa (45min., NIS5.50) and Akko (20min., NIS3). Buses #20 and 22 to Rosh HaNikra; #22, 24, 25, 26 run regularly to Akhziv 5am-9pm; #44 to Peki'in.

Bookstore: Doron Books, 32 HaGa'aton Blvd. (tel. 92 91 63). Open Sun., Mon., Wed., Thurs. 8am-1pm and 4-7pm, Tues. 8am-1pm, and Fri. 8am-2pm.

Pharmacy: Szabo, 3 HaGa'aton Blvd. (tel. 92 04 54), in front of the bus station. Open Sun.-Thurs. 8am-1pm and 4-7pm.

First Aid: Tel. 82 33 33.

Hospital: Tel. 85 05 05, Ben-Tzvi Ave.

Police: HaGa'aton Blvd. (tel. 92 03 44), just east of the Ḥaifa-Nahariya highway.

Accommodations and Food

During the summer, many rooms and bungalows are available in private homes. "Rooms to Rent" signs are common on Jabotinsky St.; head west on HaGa'aton to the post office and take a right onto Jabotinsky (NIS45 or more, but polite bargaining may help). The MTIO also keeps a list of rooms for rent, but this list doesn't include prices.

Kalman Hotel (HI), 27 Jabotinsky St. (tel. 92 03 55), across from UNIFIL building. Both 3-star hotel rating *and* HI affiliation. Speckless and spacious, with A/C and private bathrooms. Owner Miron Teichner will give you coupons for the beach and restaurants, and you can make collect overseas calls without fee. He'll also show off the signatures of big-shots who've stayed here, including Benny Begin, Ezer Weizman, Pinḥas Sapir, Yigal Allon, Shimon Peres—and Sophia Loren. 1 block from the beach. Fabulous for families. For *Let's Go* holders, singles US$22, doubles US$35. If you're low on cash, ask Miron for room 26, a room that's US$17.50 as a single, US$28 as a double year-round. Don't ask why. If one is available, Miron will give *Let's Go* users a television with no charge. Includes excellent buffet breakfast.

Sirtash House, 22 Jabotinsky St. (tel. 92 25 86). Clean, cozy rooms and private bathrooms. Some rooms have small kitchens. Singles NIS40, doubles NIS70-80.

Motel Arieli, 1 Jabotinsky St. (tel. 92 10 76). Neat rooms with fans in small bungalows and main building. Next to HaGa'aton and the beach. 2-person bungalows NIS50. Doubles in the main building NIS80-100.

Beit Erna, 29 Jabotinsky St. (tel. 92 01 70 or 92 28 32), 1 block from the waterfront. Looks like an American motel thanks to the miracle of renovation. Clean, comfortable, and spacious. A favorite among vacationing UN soldiers. Singles US$35. Doubles US$50. In summer, singles US$45, doubles US$65. Includes breakfast.

Beit Gabiazda, 12 Jabotinsky St. (tel. 92 10 49). Get a suite with a balcony. Doubles NIS80, but try to bargain.

All of the restaurant-cafés and falafel stands lining HaGa'aton Blvd. peddle the same food at outrageous prices. Nahariya's beaches and gardens make delightful picnic grounds; shop at the **Co-op Tzafon supermarket** (tel. 92 72 10) on the corner of HaGa'aton and Herzl St. Fruit and vegetable stores punctuate Herzl between HaGa'aton and HaMeyasdim. A Russian bakery across from the Hod theater on Herzl sells several dozen varieties of cookies for NIS5-6 per kilo.

Sights and Entertainment

The remains of a 4000-year-old **Canaanite Temple** dedicated to Asherah, the goddess of fertility, were accidentally discovered in 1947 on the hill next to the town's shore. To reach the ruins, walk south along the beach for about 20 minutes. While the site itself is unimpressive, a gentle amble along the shore soothes the soul.

The 20th-century Municipality Building near the bus terminal contains a **modern art museum** (5th floor) with very little modern art, a few archeological finds from the area, a malacological section of seashells (6th floor), and an exhibit on the history of Nahariya and the German Jews (7th floor). (Open Sun. and Wed. 10am-noon and 4-6pm, Mon., Tues., Thurs., and Fri. 10am-noon. Free.) An ornate mosaic floor is all that remains of a 4th-century **Byzantine church** (tel. 92 21 21), on Bielefeld St. near the Katzenelson School. (Open daily 9-11am. Free.)

Nahariya's *raison d'être* remains, predictably, tanning and swimming. The main beach is the crowded **Galei Galil,** featuring a lifeguard and a breakwater. Walk down HaGa'aton Blvd. and turn right at the end (open 8am-5pm, admission NIS10). Fee covers admission to the heated indoor pool (open year-round), the Olympic-size outdoor pool, and the kiddy pools. The pools and beach are clean, the bathrooms not as clean. All facilities are jammed on Saturdays. South of Galei Galil is a free beach without a breakwater. Local kids surf here with the same lunatic exuberance that makes driving in Israel so much fun. Thank God surfboards don't have horns. Farther south is a free municipal beach with lifeguards and dressing rooms and a sculpture dedicated to the *ma'apilim,* Jewish refugees who defied the British Mandate to enter Palestine under the cover of darkness. The remains of a ship have been incorporated into the piece.

Horse-drawn **carriage rides** start from the post office and the eastern end of HaGa'aton; follow your nose and the tell-tale signs horses have a way of leaving behind (30min., 8-10 people, NIS20). The **Hod Cinema** (tel. 92 05 02), on the corner of Herzl and HaGa'aton, often shows movies in English, as does the **Hekhal HaTarbout** (tel. 92 79 35) on Ha'Atzma'ut Rd.

What nightlife Nahariya has starts fairly late on Friday and Saturday nights, with options for every budget. A local favorite is **My Pub,** across from the bus station on HaGa'aton (follow the music). **Tropigan** offers live music in botanical environs on a second-floor balcony on HaGa'aton. And for big spenders, or those who can make friends with locals (they all seem to get in free), there's dancing at the **Carlton Hotel disco,** also on HaGa'aton. (Admission normally NIS25.)

Near Nahariya

Rosh HaNikra ראש הניקרה

Although Lebanon, one of the world's most tragically war-torn nations, hovers too close for comfort, Rosh HaNikra's spectacular white cliffs and caves remain open to tourists. When you descend into the serene beauty of the grottos, it's easy to forget the presence of the Israeli border station and patrols overhead. Rosh HaNikra's cool caves have been sculpted out of white soft chalk cliffs by centuries of lashing waves. These natural grottos were enlarged when a tunnel, originally designed as a train route between Haifa and Beirut, was dug through the cliffs by the British during World War II.

The nearby kibbutz, seeing the potential for tourism, blasted additional tunnels through the rock to improve access to the sea caves and topped the cliffs with an observation point and cafeteria. The highway from Nahariya ends at the observation point, making the cable car the only way down to the caves. (Tel. 85 71 08; operates Sun.-Thurs. 8:30am-6pm, Fri. 8:30am-4pm; admission to the caves NIS15, students NIS13. If you can convince the ticket salesman that you're in a group with 14 strangers who took the same bus, everyone gets in for NIS11.) Buses #20 and 22 make the trip from Nahariya to Rosh HaNikra, departing at 9:15am, 11:30am, and 2:30pm. The buses return to Nahariya at 9:30am, 11:50am, and 2:50pm. (Translation: you either have too much time or too little.)

Arrive early, since coach tours and youth groups often spelunk in the afternoon. The worse the weather, the better the show at Rosh HaNikra—waves pound against the natural caverns, forming powerful cross-currents and whirlpools, and echoing thunderously through the subterranean tunnels. If you decide to take an illegal dip and risk joining the legions of ghostly swimmers on the sea floor, take care not to venture out into the waters to the north; the Lebanese border guards have no sympathy for even the most accidental tourists.

Akhziv אכזיב

Akhziv beach, which begins about 4km north of Nahariya, is popular (and populated), proffering showers, shade, changing rooms, and kiosk (admission NIS3). Two roads lead to the beach: the paved road along the coast which ends here, and the unpaved, noncoastal road on which buses stop.

The historical heart of the area is the **Akhziv National Park** (tel. 82 32 63), with its sprawling lawns and sheltered beach (complete with showers and changing rooms), on the remains of an 8th-century Phoenician port town. (Park open daily 8am-5pm, Fri. 8am-4pm; in winter daily 8am-4pm. Closed Dec.-Feb. Admission NIS9.50.) Bordering the park on its northern side is **Akhzivland,** a self-proclaimed independent state founded in 1952 by the wonderfully eccentric Eli Avivi, who leased the land from an unamused Israeli government. An eye-catching figure in his flowing robes, Avivi is unforgettable—particularly when kvetchy customs officials try to figure out the "Akhzivland" stamp on your passport. **Eli's Museum** (tel. 82 32 50), housed in a deteriorated but striking Arab mansion, exhibits the benevolent dictator's extensive and esoteric collection of implements, statue fragments, and maps, mostly from the Phoenician period. (Open daily 8am-5pm; Oct.-March 8am-4pm. Admission NIS5.) Sleeping inside the dilapidated camping area costs NIS20, in one of Eli's newly constructed guest rooms NIS30. Parking and beach admission included.

Across the road is the **Akhziv Diving Center** (tel. 82 36 71), where you can rent a mask, snorkel, and fins for NIS15. Diving classes begin on Sunday and run through Saturday, but they'll wreck your budget at a hefty NIS800. An introductory dive hurts less at NIS90. Call ahead.

Just north is **Gesher HaZiv,** one of 11 bridges blown up on the evening of June 16, 1946 ("the night of the bridges"), to protest the British government's closure of Palestine's ports to Jewish refugees. The **Yad LeYad Memorial,** located near the bridge, honors 14 young men, members of the Hagana, who were killed in an attempt to blow up a bridge. In accordance with Jewish custom, visitors place pebbles on the gravestones.

Much more attractive than Akhzivland are the campsite and hostel, both a short distance up the road. The enormous **Akhziv Campground** (tel. 82 36 02) has 250 tent sites at NIS15 per adult. Two- and four-person bungalows cost NIS35 per adult. Mobile homes for four cost NIS200. Prices are about 15% lower in the off-season. On site are a kitchen and minimarket. Locked refrigerator boxes rent for NIS8. Campers can also rent mattresses for NIS8, and electric light cables can be connected to your tent for NIS8. (Reception open 7am-7pm.)

Yad LeYad Youth Hostel (HI) (tel. 82 33 45), a half-km farther north along the main road, is huge and rarely full, despite its excellent beachside location. You can buy meals at the bar next door or cook them in the hostel kitchen. (Reception open 8am-noon and 5-8pm. Doubles NIS90. Breakfast included.) About 200m north, on the opposite side of the street, the **Society for the Protection of Nature in Israel** (tel. 82 37 62) leads walks in the area (open 8am-4:30pm). The field school rents excellent private rooms for up to six people for NIS130, although it is frequently filled by groups. You can reach the nature field school, hostel, beach, and campground near Akhziv by buses #22, 24, 25, and 26 which depart from Nahariya twice per hour. *Sherut* taxis also run frequently between Akhziv and Nahariya.

Montfort מונפורט

The Crusader castle of Montfort features resplendent ruins and scenery after a challenging hike. Wind-swept and solitary, the fortification juts dramatically over a deep valley of the western Galilee. The main structure, located near the Lebanese border, was built by the Knights Templar early in the 12th century and partially destroyed by Salah al-Din in 1187. Enlarged and strengthened by the Hospitaler Knights in 1230, the fortress was named Starkenburg ("strong castle" in German), as well as Montfort ("strong mountain" in French). You can still see the impressive 18m tower and 20m main hall, along with the remains of the fortress complex.

Buses #40 to #45 leave Nahariya for Mi'ilya throughout the day. From the bus stop at Mi'ilya, follow the road that ascends from the highway for 2.5km, bearing left at every fork until it bends sharply to the right and you see the wooden sign for Montfort. Follow the red-and-white-striped blazes along the path another 1.5km; the path to the castle abruptly turns to the right, up the rocks. You will exert yourself.

Traveling north from the castle, follow the uphill path that forks left at the junction near the ruins of the auxiliary building on the floor of the valley. At the top of the hill is a picnic area. From here, it's a 2km walk to the entrance of the **Keziv Park.** The park lies between the settlements of Goren and Elon on the main road leading west to Rosh HaNikra. You can also continue to follow the red-and-white-striped blazes back, along a slightly different route, to Mi'ilya. Bus #25 from Nahariya runs to and from Goren several times per day.

Both Montfort and **Gadin Castle** (tel. 92 48 09) at Yeḥiam, 8km to the west by the southern road, were built to protect Akko, the Crusader capital. Though destroyed by the Mamluk Sultan Baybars in 1265, the ruins remain impressive and offer yet another view of the western Galilee highlands. (Castle open Sun.-Thurs. 8am-5pm, Fri. and holidays 8am-4pm. Admission NIS3.50, students NIS1.50.) Buses #39 and 42 run several times per day to Yeḥiam.

Peki'in (Bke'ah) פקיעין

Peki'in (Bke'ah in Arabic) is known as the spot where Rabbi Shimon Bar-Yoḥai and his son, Eliezer, fled from a Roman decree prohibiting the study of Torah. For 13 years, the erudite duo hid in a small cave in the hillside, sustained by a nearby spring and fertile carob tree. During this time, some Jews believe they composed the Zohar, the single most important text of Kabbalah (Jewish mysticism). To visit the holy cave, take the winding road leading up from the bus stop to the top of the village. When you reach a marking stone and a blue-and-white sign on your right, take the dirt path down to the stairway. Walk downstairs until a large bush is in front of you, and turn right between two large rocks. The tiny cave is on your right. Continue down the stairway to the bottom. Turn right onto the narrow street and follow it until you reach Kikar

HaMa'ayan ("Spring Square"). You'll see an odd-shaped pool of water fed by the underground spring for which the square is named. From the square, take the small street with the round red-and-white sign. Turn left at the first intersection and follow this curving road down to the white synagogue gate at your right. The synagogue on this site, which stood in the days of Shimon Bar-Yoḥai and his son, is now a small museum. If the synagogue gate is closed, knock on the white metal door with a blue star opposite the gate and go upstairs. Although the museum is theoretically free, you should leave a small donation in the box on the table with the prayer books. (Synagogue open Sun.-Thurs. 8:30am-noon and 2-6pm, Fri. 8:30am-2pm.)

Peki'in itself is an Arab village with a mixed Druze and Christian community. Near the bus stop, two families have opened small cafés, both of which serve fragrant Arabic coffee and sandwiches made from thin *rkak* bread brushed with olive oil, *za'atar* (a tangy ground herb), and *labaneh* (yogurt cheese).

Although part of the Galilee, Peki'in is most accessible from Nahariya. Bus #44 from Nahariya makes the round trip to Peki'in six or seven times per day; be sure to get off at Peki'in Atika (Old Peki'in), not Peki'in Ḥadasha (New Peki'in) one stop earlier. The last stop on the bus is the small Druze village of **Beit Jan,** which is much less commercialized than Daliyat al-Karmel.

Galilee (HaGalil) הגליל

Several millennia of historic sites are squeezed between the Sea of Galilee and the West Bank. Jesus wandered, preached, and fashioned miracles, and Jewish mystics wrote the classics of the *Kabbalah* in these forested hills. The Lower Galilee, which includes Nazareth and Megiddo, is marvelous touring country.

Two facts stand out in the Galilee's recent history. First, what today is Israel's agricultural heartland was once a lifeless swamp. The majestic scenery reflects an intense and painstaking Israeli effort. Second, Israel's northern neighbors have been notably less enthusiastic about this Zionist success story, a sentiment that until recently was expressed with *katyusha* rockets and terrorist raids. In the worst days, Syrian shelling rattled Kiryat Shmona's buildings, and kibbutzniks watched acts of arson consume their crops. Notwithstanding occasional sparks from the *intifada,* the Arabs of the Galilee live quite comfortably beside the Jews; coexistence is never easy in this part of the world, but both sides have made impressive progress here. Today a hard-won quiet prevails, creating the drowsy mood you would expect in such an astoundingly beautiful region.

Nazareth (Natzrat) נצרת

A vibrant center of Arab life in the Galilee, Nazareth is vastly different from the Biblical images of pastoral churches and convents. Sentimental sketches on Christmas cards belie the true nature of Nazareth, an engrossingly gritty town. For a sense of Nazareth's overwhelming importance to Christians, head for the winding back alleys and dim church interiors. Your shaky faith will quickly be cured, however, when a reckless driver misses you by inches on Paul VI St. or when you fight the clamoring crowds in the main business district.

Orientation and Practical Information

Nazareth lies in the Lower Galilee between Ḥaifa (40km northwest) and Tiberias (30km northeast), on a slight elevation north of the Jezreel Valley. The inhabitants of the old **Arab Town,** where the Christian sites are located, resent the encroaching development of the newer **Natzrat Illit** (Upper Nazareth), where more recent Jewish arrivals have built a thriving community. The *intifada* has strengthened many Nazarene Arabs' sense of Palestinian identity, but the city remains relatively free of tension.

Nazareth utterly lacks street signs. When you get lost in the market, just keep walking downhill and you'll eventually come to **Paul VI Street.** This thoroughfare winds uphill from the bus station to Mary's Well and intersects **Casa Nova Street.**

Nazareth's Christian community rolls up the sidewalks on Sundays, but many establishments are open on *shabbat.*

Government Tourist Information Office (GTIO): Casa Nova St. (tel. 57 30 03 or 57 05 55), near intersection with Paul VI St. Try to obtain the city map at another office before braving Nazarene navigation. Open Mon.-Fri. 8:30am-5pm, Sat. 8:30am-2pm.

Banks: HaPoalim, Paul VI St. (tel. 57 09 23), to the right of the Mashbir department store. Open Mon., Tues., and Thurs. 8:30am-1pm and 3:30-6pm, Wed. and Sat. 8:30am-12:30pm, Fri. 8:30am-noon. **Leumi,** on Paul VI, just north of Casa Nova. Open Mon., Tues., and Thurs. 8:30am-12:30pm and 4-5:40pm, Sun. and Wed. 8:30am-12:30pm, Fri. 8:30am-noon.

Central Post Office: north on Paul VI St. (tel. 55 40 19 or 55 51 88), to your left at Mary's Well. **Poste Restante** at far right window. **International calls** available. Open Mon. and Wed. 8am-2pm, Tues., Thurs., and Fri. 8am-12:30pm and 3:30-6pm, Sat. 8am-1pm. **Telephone code:** 06.

Buses: Intercity buses stop along a stretch of Paul VI St. across from HaMashbir department store (tel. 56 25 55). Egged information office on Paul VI St. (open daily from about 6am-6:30pm). Bus #431 comes from Ḥaifa and continues to Tiberias. Buses #823 and 824 run frequently to Afula, bus hub of the Galilee, and Tel Aviv. **Baggage storage** is next door, NIS2 per piece per day. Open Sun.-Thurs. 8am-1pm, Fri. 8am-2pm. Or try the baggage storage operated by a taxi stand north of the GTIO, near the Muzzawi souvenir stand. Open Sun.-Thurs. 8:30am-6pm, Fri. 8:30am-2pm. NIS2 per piece.

Taxis: Ma'ayan, on Paul VI St. (tel. 55 51 05 or 57 09 07), **Abu Elassel** (tel. 55 47 45), **Galil** (tel. 55 55 36), **Diana** (tel. 55 55 54). *Sherut* taxis can be found at the blue signs with the red circle all along Paul VI St. Regular service to Tiberias and Ḥaifa.

Car Rental: Europcar (tel. 57 53 13), **Budget** (tel. 57 63 67). Must be 21 years old. Must also be a Forbes scion: US$100 per day.

Pharmacy: Ferah Pharmacy (tel. 55 40 18), next to Egged information. Open Mon., Tues., Thurs., and Fri. 8:30am-1pm and 3:30-6pm, Wed. 8am-1pm, Sat. 8:30am-1:30pm.

Hospital: Nazareth Hospital (tel. 57 15 01/2), **Holy Family Hospital** (tel. 74 53 56/7).

First Aid: Magen David Adom, tel. 101.

Police: Tel. 100 or 57 44 44.

Accommodations and Food

Inexpensive beds are offered by several Christian hospices. Unfortunately, because sisters from all over the world are frequently here on retreat, you may need to scramble for a bed. A pristine dormitory with superb facilities is run by the **Sisters of Nazareth** (tel. 55 43 04, P.O. Box 274), near the basilica. Walk up Casa Nova St. and take a left after the Casa Nova Hospice; it will be on the right at #306, just past the pink archway. (Check-in 4pm, but you can leave your pack if you arrive earlier. Dorm beds NIS15, private rooms US$12 per person. Includes kitchen, dining room, and living room.) If you arrive when the sisters are on retreat, call the **Frères de Betharram** (tel. 57 00 46) in the Eilout neighborhood, where dormitory beds cost US$20, doubles NIS48, and you can *parlez* the night away. The German-speaking **Sisters of Charles Barrameus** also run a hospice (tel. 55 44 35) behind the Carmelite Convent, with beds for NIS15 per night. The **Casa Nova Hospice** (tel. 71 32 67), on Casa Nova St., is the deluxe option and almost always booked months in advance. (Bed and breakfast US$18.) The **Galilee Hotel,** 6 Paul VI St. (tel. 57 13 11), about a 10-minute walk south of the bus station, has private rooms with showers. (Singles US$35. Doubles US$55. Breakfast included. Call ahead.)

Falafel stands freckle Paul VI St., and numerous cafés specializing in sweet Middle Eastern desserts are scattered throughout the city. Try **Mahroum's Bakery,** on Casa Nova St., for fresh pastries sold by weight (NIS1-3 per piece). There are plenty of small grocery stores and produce markets on Paul VI St. flanking both sides of the central bus station. The **al-Amal Restaurant,** near the corner of Casa Nova and Paul VI St. with a green-and-white sign and white arch doors, serves Middle Eastern fare at prices lower than more glitzy competitors (ḥummus NIS6, chicken dishes NIS15). Open daily 8:30-9pm. Smirchlessness and air conditioning distinguish the **Alje-neenah Restaurant** (tel. 55 40 22), just down the street from St. Gabriel Church and the post office (salads NIS8, meat dishes NIS25; open daily 6am-midnight.) In the market just past the white mosque in Mosque Sq. and next to a large mural is **al-Han-na,** an inexpensive Middle Eastern restaurant where a full meal of salad, ḥummus, a plate of meat, and a drink costs NIS17. (Open Mon.-Sat. 7am-4pm.)

Sights

Nazareth is synonymous with churches. The **Basilica of the Annunciation,** which dominates Nazareth's downtown, is actually two churches built in 1966 over the remains of older structures which date back to 356 CE. The basilica's huge bronze doors depict the life of Jesus. The entry level is built on the site believed to be Mary's house, where the archangel Gabriel appeared to Mary to herald the birth of Jesus. The church's second level contains an intriguing series of international artistic interpretations of the Annunciation, as well as ceramic reliefs of the stations of the cross molded by Christian Arabs. The excavations of the ancient town of Nazareth lie in a garden underneath the plaza, accessible from the upper floor of the church. Ask one of the Franciscan monks to show you around. Modest dress required. To get to the Basilica, walk north from the GTIO; it's the enormous building on your right. (Open Mon.-Fri. 8:30-11:45am and 2-5:45pm, Sun. and feasts 2-5:45pm; in winter, Mon.-Fri. 9-11:45am and 2-4:45pm, Sun. and feasts 2-4:45pm.)

Across the plaza stands **St. Joseph's Church,** where you can look down on the cave thought to be Joseph's house. The present structure, built in 1914, incorporates remnants of an older Byzantine church. Inside, stairs descend to caves that once stored grain and oil. Although this is usually referred to as Joseph's workshop, evidence exists suggesting that these caves have been used since the late Stone Age. The **Greek-Catholic Synagogue Church** in the center of the Arab market is the site of the synagogue where Jesus is believed to have preached as a young man. To get there, enter the *souk* from Casa Nova St., bear left at the first fork, then take the first right; the entrance will be on your right, at the yellow gate. Climb the stairs on your right for a view of Nazareth's rooftops. Following Paul VI St. uphill from the bus station, you come to **Mary's Well,** reputedly still functioning. Many believe that the well's water miraculously heals. Veering left and continuing uphill from the well, you come to the **Orthodox Church of the Archangel Gabriel** which stands over the town's original water source. The original church was erected in 356 CE over the spring where Mary drew water and where the Greek Orthodox believe Gabriel appeared to Mary. The present church, built in 1750, has elaborate Byzantine-style paintings and decorations. Ancient tiles adorn the entrance in the well area. (Ask the caretaker to open it.) To reach the **Maronite Church,** dating from 1770, follow the road past the Greek-Catholic Synagogue Church, take the first left, and follow the signs. The **Mensa Christi Church,** next door on Al-Batris Sq., marks the place where Jesus shared a meal with his disciples after the Resurrection. The building surrounds a 10 ft. by 12 ft. piece of soft limestone (*mensa*). Although the church is unmarked, the colorful mural on the surrounding walls facilitate identification.

For a terrific view over the Galilean hilltops, hike up to the **Salesian Church** at the top of the natural amphitheater. (All churches in Nazareth claim to be open 8:30-11:45am and 2-5:45pm; in winter 9-11:45am and 2-4:45pm. Many churches, however, close in the afternoon. Sunday mornings are reserved for services. Modest dress required at all times.)

Nazareth's lively **market** (open Mon., Tues., Thurs., and Fri. 8:30am-1:30pm, Wed. and Sat. 8:30am-2pm), best reached via Casa Nova St., is the place to go for olive wood camels and Bart Simpson underwear.

Near Nazareth

Kfar Kanna, a village to the north of Nazareth, is said to be the site of Jesus' miraculous transformation of water into wine at the wedding feast (John 2:1-11). A Franciscan church was built here in 1881 to commemorate the event. (Open Mon.-Fri. 8:30-11:45am and 2-5:45pm, Sun. and feasts 2-5:45pm.) Buses leave for Kfar Kanna every 45 minutes from near Mary's Well in Nazareth, or you can take bus #431 to Tiberias and ask to be let off at Kfar Kanna. Bus #431 leaves every 40 minutes from the central bus station. **Mount Tabor,** Har Tavor in Hebrew, (588m) is located 33km from Nazareth. Shared by Franciscan and Greek Orthodox monks, inside Mount Tabor's fortifications are a number of sights. The **Basilica of the Transfiguration,** built in 1924, sits atop a 6th century CE Byzantine church marking the spot where Jesus spoke with Elijah and Moses and was transfigured in the presence of apostles Peter, James, and John (Luke 9:28-36). Nearby, the **Church of Elijah** is built atop the **Cave of Melchizedek,** which can be entered from the outside through a small, iron door. The limestone fortifications, once an Arab fortress called **al-Adil,** date from 1211. Mount Tabor was also the site where the prophetess Deborah led the Israelites into a victory over Sisera's army (Judges 4-5). No shorts are allowed at the site. From the base of the mountain, hike the 3km down the long and winding road. (Site open 8am-noon and 3pm-sunset.)

Megiddo (Armageddon) מגידו

The settlements at Tel Megiddo have been destroyed so many times that the town has truly earned its Latin cognate: "Armageddon." The New Testament forewarns that at the end of the world demons will go out to all the nations, assembling first at Armageddon (Revelations 16:16). Megiddo's used to being a meeting place—in ancient times the fortress town bordered the crucial route between Egypt and Mesopotamia that became the Roman Via Maris.

The *tel* (layered hill) at Megiddo was once thought to date only to King Solomon (c. 950 BCE). Excavations in the 1960s, however, uncovered remains dating back to the Neolithic Age (c. 3500 BCE) with 20 layers of ruins. The ruins are mostly unreconstructed except for the grain silo and water tunnel. The site is nonetheless impressive simply for its sheer size (about 900 ft. by 650 ft.). The silo was built on the top of the hill during the reign of King Jeroboam II (787-747 BCE) to protect its contents from moisture. Because it's difficult to keep all the different sections of the *tel* straight, it's worthwhile to pick up the guide to the site at the ticket window for NIS.50. Major finds include the Temple of Astarte (1900 BCE), ancient stables for some 480 horses, an underground tunnel, the Gate of Solomon (1600 BCE), and a 70 by 75 ft. palace dating from the second half of the 12th century CE. A small **museum** near the entrance contains exhibits explaining the various layers of excavations and a model of Solomon's chariot town. There's also a list of the many biblical references to Megiddo as well.

From the observation point at the site, you can look out over the **Valley of Jezreel** (*Emek Yizre'el*) which was mostly swamp until 1920, when Jewish immigrants drained the land and made it arable. The mountain in the distance is Mt. Tabor.

One of the site's most intriguing features is the tunnel built to conceal the city's water source from invaders and to make the water accessible from inside the city walls. The tunnel terminates with a turnstile into the parking lot, so make sure it's your last stop at the site. When you exit, turn right and walk 0.5km back to the main road. (Site open Sun.-Thurs. 8am-5pm, Fri. 8am-4pm; closes one hour earlier in winter. Admission NIS5.50, students NIS3.) Bus #823 leaves Nazareth for Megiddo every hour during the morning, and every 30 minutes from noon to 7:30pm. Bus #183 runs from Ḥaifa. From Megiddo, buses to Afula, the transportation hub of the Lower Galilee, stop on the south side of the road, while buses to the coast and Tel Aviv stop on the north side, both about every 20 minutes. You can also walk 1km downhill to *tzomet* Megiddo to transfer buses.

Other Sites Near Nazareth

Along the road from Beit She'an to Afula you'll find a several sites of both natural and historical interest. **Beit She'an** is a largely Sephardi development town. Its most famous son is former foreign minister David Levy (or, as he put it, "minister of the out"), the most prominent Sephardi pol in Israel. (Corny David Levy jokes are an Israeli national pastime, to the annoyance of some Sephardim. Stop us if you've heard this one. David Levy gets into a taxi, and the cab driver says, "Hey, have you heard the latest David Levy joke?" David Levy snaps, "Look, I'll have you know, I *am* David Levy." "That's OK," replies the taxi driver, "I'll tell it slowly.") Of more interest to gawking tourists is one of the finest archeological sites in the country, best known for its **Roman amphitheater,** one of the largest extant Roman constructions in Israel. Built in 200 CE by the Emperor Septimius Severus, the ampitheater accommodated 8000 spectators. Other sites in the area include the remains of four Egyptian temple complexes: the **Temple of Amenophis III** dating from 1400 BCE; the **Seth Temple** built around 1300 BCE; a temple built by Ramses I from 1292-1225 BCE, and the **Ashtaroth Temple** built by Ramses III. North of the major excavation mound, **Tel al-Husn,** is the **Monastery of the Noble Lady Maria** which was abandoned after the Persian invasion in 614 CE. From the Beit She'an bus stop, walk straight through the shopping complex, turn left at the end, then right after Bank Leumi. Follow the paved road down to the site. Adjacent to the site is **Gan HaBanim,** a park with a freeze-your-arse pool (NIS6) and a small but shady playground. Beit She'an was bombarded by Syria as recently as 1975. (Open Sun.-Thurs. 8am-5pm, Fri. 8am-4pm. Closes one hour earlier in winter. Admission to the site NIS8, under 18 NIS4.) Buses #415 and 412 leave Afula, transportation hub of the lower Galilee, for Beit She'an every 20 minutes. From Tiberias, take #961, 963, or 964.

Take an afternoon excursion to the lovely park of **Gan HaShlosha,** also known as the **Sahne,** which lies 5km northwest of Beit She'an and 1km southeast of Beit Alpha on the road to Afula. This park made a splash even in Roman times with its waterfalls and crystal-clear swimming holes. Buses #415 and 412 from either Afula or Beit She'an run to the Sahne. (Open Sun.-Thurs., Sat. 7:30am-6pm, Fri. 7:30am-5pm. Admission NIS13, under 18 NIS6.50.) A 10-minute walk along the road behind the park leads to the **Nir David Museum of Mediterranean Archeology** (tel. 58 62 19), an extensive collection of Hellenistic and Islamic art and pottery. Remains gathered locally from a Canaanite temple, an Israelite community, and a Roman weavers' colony trace the peoples who have lived here. (Open Sun.-Fri. 8am-1pm, Sat. 10:30am-1pm. You have to pay for the park to see the museum.)

One kilometer northwest of the Sahne on the road to Afula, within Kibbutz Hepzi-ba, shines the 6th-century CE synagogue of **Beit Alpha** (tel. 53 14 00), including a magnificently preserved mosaic of a zodiac wheel surrounding the sun god, Helios. To reach Hepziba take bus #415 or 412 from either Beit She'an or Afula. (Open Sat.-Thurs. 8am-5pm, Fri. 8am-2pm. Admission NIS4, students NIS3.40.) Do not be misled by the sign for Kibbutz Beit Alpha (1km closer to Beit She'an), which is named after the ancient site.

A few kilometers closer to Afula, the transportation hub of the Lower Galilee, on the eastern side of the road is **Kibbutz Ein Harod** with the **Beit Sturman Museum of Natural History** (tel. 54 89 74). The museum is devoted to studies of the region, and has an archeological garden with pillars and a sarcophagus. (Open Sun.-Thurs. 9am-1pm, Fri. 9am-noon, Sat. 10am-12:30pm. Admission NIS7, students NIS6.50.)

Three kilometers down the road to Afula is the **Ma'ayan Harod Youth Hostel (HI)** (tel. 53 16 60) and **campground** (tel. 53 16 04), both of which lie 1km off the Afula-Beit She'an road. Bus #35 from Afula, leaving at 6am, noon, and 6pm, will take you directly to the hostel. Buses #412, 402 and 405 (not express) bring you to the road leading to the site; from there the walk is about 1km and the route is marked with gorgeous orange signs. The hostel facilities are adequate, the well-stocked kiosk has long hours, and it's also the place where Gideon, guided and inspired by the prophetess Deborah, defeated the Midianites (Judges 7). Sleep inspired. The small cave in the garden contains the grave of one of the Midianite leaders. (Dorm beds or beds in bungalows NIS18, nonmembers 20. Call ahead in July and Aug.)

The Tiberias-Beit She'an bus will let you off at the turn-off to **Belvoir** (tel. 58 70 00), a 12th-century Crusader fort which affords marvelous views over the entire Jezre'el Valley and, on a clear day, the Kinneret. The castle (Kokhav HaYarden, or Star of the Jordan) presides 1800 ft. above the River Jordan, overlooking the medieval trade route from Egypt to Damascus. The area was the scene of several skirmishes between the Crusaders and Muslims until, after the Battle of Hattin in 1187, the Muslims besieged the castle. After 18 months, the knights finally surrendered, and in acknowledgment of their bravery were permitted to depart unharmed. During the early 13th century, the castle was partially destroyed by the sultan of Damascus to preempt a Crusader reoccupation of the stronghold. The interior, constructed with massive 10 ft. thick blocks of black stone and surrounded by a deep moat, is still breath-taking. Unfortunately, no bus runs directly to the castle, and it's a very steep 6km uphill walk to the site from the junction where the bus lets you off. A clear hat-and-water hike. (Open Sat.-Thurs. 8am-5pm, Fri. 8am-2pm. Closes one hour earlier in winter. Admission NIS6.50, students NIS4.85.)

Tiberias (Tveriya) טבריה

Since the Israeli troops took the Golan Heights in 1967, ending the constant shelling of the region, the area around the Kinneret (Sea of Galilee) has become a popular alternative to a Mediterranean holiday. Although tourism has raised prices, it has also brought an abundance of lodgings and a lively weekend nightlife to northern Israel. Tiberias is the only major city on the Kinneret and an ideal touring base for the area, though during July and August the city can be soggily humid due to its location 200m below sea level.

For a resort, Tiberias has a surprisingly noble history. Built in 18 CE by Herod Antipas, King of Judea and tetrarch of Galilee, the city was named for the Roman emperor Tiberius. According to first-century Jewish historian Josephus, the city also took on its namesake's most salient trait—hedonism. Although the Romans attempted to bring in settlers, most Jews, including Jesus, refused to enter the town because it was built upon the site of older Jewish graves. But after the Rabbi Shimon Bar-Yohai declared the town ritually pure, Tiberias became a major center of Jewish scholarship. When the Romans destroyed Jerusalem in response to the Bar Kokhba revolt, Tiberias became perhaps the most serious center of Jewish life and scholarship in the Holy Land. It was here that the *Mishnah* (a collection of Jewish law forming part of the *Talmud*) was codified, the *Talmud* edited, and vowels added to the Hebrew alphabet and sacred texts. The Sanhedrin, the great court of scholars and rabbis, also met here. Along with Jerusalem, Hebron, and Tzfat, Tiberias was deemed one of Israel's holy cities.

Under the Byzantines, Jews from Persia and Babylonia came on pilgrimages to Tiberias, following the legend that the redemption of Israel would begin here. Throughout the Byzantine and Islamic periods Tiberias served as both a significant civic center and a health resort as well. In 1837 Tiberias was devastated by an earthquake that rocked all of northern Palestine. At the turn of the century, Jewish immigrants began to resettle the area until they made up half of the 12,000 inhabitants at the time of the founding of the State of Israel in 1948. The city's population has since doubled and is now almost entirely Jewish.

Practical Information and Orientation

Tiberias has three tiers: the **old city** is by the water, the **new city** (Kiryat Shmuel) up the hill (take bus #1 or 5 from the bus station), and the **uptown** at the top of the hill (bus #7, 8, or 9 from the station). Though the ruins in the old city don't rival ancient counterparts in Akko or Jerusalem, there is still little reason to venture out of this region of the city except to see a movie. **HaGalil Street,** running parallel to the water, is the main thoroughfare in Tiberias.

Government Tourist Information Office (GTIO): on the *midreḥov* (tel. 72 09 92 or 72 20 89). From the corner of HaBanim St. and HaYarkon St. walk towards the Kinneret; GTIO is on the 2nd floor of shops on your left, up the flight of stairs to the right of the Big Ben Pub. Open Sun.-Thurs. 8:30am-5pm, Fri. 8:30am-2pm.

Central Post Office: HaYarden St. (tel. 72 24 32). Take a right as you exit the bus station onto HaYarden St. and walk away from the mountains; the office is on the left just before Alhadef St. Open Sun.-Tues. and Thurs. 8am-12:30pm and 3:30-6pm, Wed. 8am-1:30pm, Fri. 8am-noon. Branch office in Kiryat Shmuel on corner of Bialik St. and Aḥad Ha'am St.

International phone calls: Bezek, above the GTIO on the *midreḥov*. Open Sun.-Thurs. 9am-11pm, Fri. 8am-2pm. **Telephone code:** 06.

Central Bus Station: HaYarden St. (tel. 79 10 80). #961, 963, and 964 to Jerusalem (every 30-45min. 6am-6pm, NIS18); #830, 832, 836, 840, and 841 to Tel Aviv (every hr., 5:30am-8:30pm, NIS14); #430 and 431 to Ḥaifa (every 20-45min. 5:40am-8:30pm, NIS9.50).

Taxis: *Sherut* and private taxis congregate in front of the bus station on the stretch of HaYarden St. running from the bus station to the Kinneret. Regular inter-city service to Ḥaifa only (last car on Fri. 3:30pm). Call the night before, tel. 72 00 98.

Bicycles: Hostel Aviv is best (NIS20 for regular, NIS30 for 18-speed mountain bike per day). Also at Naḥum Hostel, Schwitzer Hostel, and Lake Castle Hostel (all NIS20). See Accommodations below for addresses.

Laundry: Panorama (tel. 72 43 24), south of HaKishon St. 7kg wash, dry, and fold NIS15. Self-service as well. Open Sun.-Thurs. 8am-6pm, Fri. 8am-2pm.

Pharmacy: Center Pharm (tel. 79 06 13), at the corner of Bibass St. and HaGalil St. Open Sun.-Fri. 8am-9pm. **Schwartz Pharmacy** (tel. 72 09 94), on HaGalil St. opposite the park.

English Bookstores: Steimatsky's, 3 HaGalil St. (tel. 79 12 88). Open Sun.-Thurs. 8am-1pm and 4:30-7:30pm, Tues. 8am-1pm, Fri. 8am-2pm. Also in the Lev Ha'Ir shopping mall, corner of Bibass and HaShiloaḥ streets (tel. 72 37 16).

First Aid: Magen David Adom (tel. 79 01 11), corner of HaBanim and HaKishon St. Open 24 hrs.

Police: Tel. 79 24 44.

Accommodations and Camping

For a town this size, Tiberias offers an astonishing number of lodging options. Competition is fierce; you'll probably be bombarded by hostel employees when you arrive at the bus station. See the room before you commit. Prices rise dramatically during the high season, July-Sept. The area is also particularly mobbed during Pesaḥ, Rosh HaShana and Sukkot. Most hostels will arrange Golan tours if you ask.

Meyouhas Hostel (HI), HaYarden St. (tel. 72 17 75 or 79 03 50), at the corner of HaGalil and HaYarden. Centrally located hostel, 2.5 blocks from the bus station. Brightly painted, clean and comfortable, with TV room and balcony. April-Sept., 1am curfew; Oct.-March, midnight curfew. Reception open 7-9am and 4pm-midnight. US$6.50, under 18 US$6, nonmembers add US$1.50. A/C US$.50. Make reservations. HI members have priority.

Naḥum Hostel, Tavor St. (tel. 72 15 05). From HaYarden St. turn south on HaGalil, then turn right on Tavor St. about 100m. About a 5-min. walk from bus station. A lively place with clean rooms, all with A/C and private showers. Rooms on the lower level also have kitchens and private toilets. The rooftop bar features nightly values, a throat-parching view of the Kinneret, and the antics of Ya'akov and Emil. No curfew. Dorm beds US$7 (high season US$9), private rooms US$25 (high season US$30). Israeli breakfast NIS3.

Hostel Aviv, HaGalil St. (tel. 72 00 31), 1.5 blocks south of HaYarden, past the park. Centrally located and popular. Wide halls, TV lounge, bar, and kitchen facilities. Most rooms have A/C and private shower and toilet. No curfew. Dorm beds NIS15 (high season NIS20). Doubles in hostel NIS40 (high season NIS50), in hotel NIS60 (high season NIS80).

Lake Castle Hostel (tel. 72 11 75), next to the Moriah Plaza Hotel. Great location on the promenade with a view of the sea from the terrace. Rooms are clean, and many have A/C, private showers, and kitchen facilities. Several overlook the water. No curfew. Dorm beds NIS15 (high season NIS20). Doubles NIS60. Call ahead during May and June.

Maman Hostel, Atzmon St. (tel. 79 29 86). From HaYarden St., turn south on HaGalil, then bear right on Tavor St.—a sign at the corner of Tavor and Atzmon directs you to the hostel. Easygoing atmosphere, clean toilets and showers. All rooms have A/C. The hostel has a small, unheated pool in back and a popular new restaurant and bar in front. Kitchen facilities and meals available. Dorm beds NIS15 (high season NIS20). Private rooms with kitchen and bathroom NIS60 (high season NIS80).

Schwitzer Hostel, HaShiloah St. (tel. 72 19 91), at the corner of Bibass St., 200m south of the bus station. Unimpressive bathrooms. Kitchen facilities and unlimited free tea or coffee. Some rooms have private shower. Dorm beds NIS15. Two-person private bungalows NIS30. Private rooms NIS50 (NIS60 in high season).

Adina's Hostel, 15 HaShiloah St. Head south along the street from the bus station (tel. 72 25 07). Run by Adina and her family. Pleasant and clean, with kitchen facilities and impressive private bathrooms. Adina is especially friendly if you speak Hebrew or if your name is Adina. Dorm beds NIS20. Doubles NIS50. Private rooms for up to 4 people NIS80.

Church of Scotland Hospice, P.O. Box 104 (tel. 72 11 65). A gray stone building at the corner of HaYarden St. and Gedud Barak Rd., next to the HI hostel. Many of the hotel rooms are spectacular. Dorm rooms are currently under renovation. Reception open 8-10am, 10:30am-12:30pm, 1:30-3:30pm, and 4-6pm. Hotel rooms US$26. Includes breakfast. Make reservations.

Toledo Hotel, HaPrahim St. (tel. 72 16 49). From the bus station, walk one block south on HaShiloah and turn right onto HaPrahim. The hotel is one block down on the right. Rooms are clean and sunny, with A/C, full bathroom, telephone, and radio. Lobby lounge with TV. Singles US$30 (high season US$35). Doubles US$40 (high season US$50). Includes breakfast.

Camping is the best way to escape the city heat. Though camping in the summer will bring you closer to the maddening crowds, official campsites are often cheaper than hostels. Start by getting information at the stand run by the Ministry of Tourism and the Society for the Protection of Nature (tel. 75 20 56) at Tzemah. (Open in summer 8am-5pm; take bus #18, 21, 22, or 24.) Their map details the locations of the 25 campsites on the lake. These sites, identifiable on the map by a tree and picnic bench, cost NIS10-15 per car, regardless of the number of passengers. Ask the SPNI or GTIO about **Ein Gev** (tel. 75 11 77), **Ha'On** (tel. 75 75 55/6), and **Karne Hittim** (tel. 79 59 21) campsites.

Interspersed among the private beaches are stretches of shoreline which allow **free-lance camping.** You provide the food, water, and insect repellent, and the government kicks-in jiffy johns and trash bins at a few of these points. Take the Ein Gev bus from Tiberias and get off wherever you see a site, or walk south along the coast past the Tiberias hot springs. Be wary of theft.

Food

The city *shuk,* occupying a square block starting at Bibass St. and going south, sells cheap, high-quality produce every day except *shabbat.* You can also pick up a light lunch or dinner at one of Tiberias's innumerable falafel spreads on HaYarden St., which runs from HaBanim St. toward the bus station. Most of the grill restaurants near the *midrehov* serve *shishlik* by the skewer (NIS4 each). The seafood restaurants along the waterfront offer idyllic candlelit settings; a tasty dinner of St. Peter's fish, unique to the Sea of Galilee, costs about NIS30. (The fish served at most restaurants, however, are imposters from fish ponds at kibbutzim in the Golan. The large St. Peter's fish are difficult to net in summertime and many restaurants are reluctant to serve the smaller specimens actually caught in the Kinneret. Most establishments instead prepare larger fish. And no, there is no Santa Claus either.) The eateries on HaGalil and HaBanim St. and the squares in between offer cheaper fare. There is a **Co-op Tzafon supermarket** in the Great Mosque Plaza across from Meyouhas Hostel, open 7am-7:45pm most days (closed Sat.).

Avi's Restaurant, HaKishon St. (tel. 79 17 97) between HaGalil and HaBanim St., opposite the Jordan River Hotel. Local atmosphere and tasty food. Pizza NIS12-15, canneloni NIS18. *Tahina* NIS5. Open daily noon-2am.

Maman Restaurant, HaGalil St. (tel. 72 11 26), at the corner of Bibass St. Crammed with Israelis. Middle Eastern fare at reasonable prices. A/C. ḥummus or taḥina NIS5, schnitzel NIS15, chicken hearts NIS17. Open Sun.-Fri. 8am-midnight. Kosher.

Guy Restaurant, Ha Galil St. (tel. 72 19 73), near HaKishon. Moroccan kitchen, but can throw together a serious chopped liver. Closed on *shabbat*. Kosher.

Karamba Vegetarian Restaurant, on Promenade (tel. 79 15 46). Take the alley leading to the waterfront from the Meyouhas hostel. Exotic ambience on the waterfront. Pizza marguereta NIS14, artichoke house-style NIS14.

Dolphin Grill, at the corner of HaBanim St. and the *midreḥov. Shishlik*, kebab, or *schnitzel* with 5 salads and "cheeps" costs NIS15, ḥummus NIS6. The grill's outdoor tables are prime for people-watching.

Eat As Much As You Can (tel. 72 38 99), HaBanim St. across from the *midreḥov*, between HaYarden and HaYarkon. Not the most elegant place in town, but the best way for the budget traveler to get a nice piece of authentic St. Peter's fish. Unlimited amount of small, delicious fresh fish from the Kinneret NIS15. Salad, chips, or ḥummus NIS5 each.

Sesame (tel. 72 00 38), in the thick of the *midreḥov*. Even non-vegetarians appreciate the home-made food and mellow music here. Interesting menu: whole grain pizza NIS14, gazpacho NIS7. Open daily 1pm-2am.

Sights

The **old city,** shaken by earthquakes and conquerors, has vanished but for a few fragments of the walls littering the modern town. To get a sense of its former glory, join a free walking tour offered by the Moriah Plaza Hotel Saturdays at 10am (tours leave from the hotel lobby). Alternatively, an archeologist from the Society for the Protection of Nature in Israel gives a two-hour tour of Tiberias's more obscure attractions.

The meticulously tended **Tomb of Moses Maimonides** on Y. Ben Zakkai St., commemorates the controversial and famous rabbi and physician who attempted a synthesis of Aristotelian and Arabic philosophy with the study of Judaism. According to legend, an unguided camel carried his coffin to Tiberias. To reach the tomb, take HaYarden St. east (toward the water) and turn left on Y. Ben-Zakkai St. The tomb is about two blocks up on the right. The area has a red fence and black pillars; the white half-cylinder with Hebrew writing is the actual tomb. If you need further directions, ask for the tomb of "Rambam," the rabbi's Hebrew acronym (Rabbi Moshe ben Maimon) or get in good with an unguided camel. While you're at it, visit the **Tomb of Rabbi Akiva,** on the hillside above the Kinneret (take bus #4 and ask for directions), and that of **Rabbi Meir Ba'al HaNes,** student of Rabbi Akiva (on the hillside above the hot springs). Tombs open daily 8am-5pm. Modest dress required.

Back on the waterfront promenade, the **Franciscan Terra Sancta Church** (tel. 72 05 16), stands next to the Caesar Hotel. The church was built in the 12th century to commemorate St. Peter's role in the growth of Christianity, and is thus known as St. Peter's. The apse behind the altar is arched like the bow of a boat, in honor of his first career as a fisherman. In the courtyard is a statue to the Virgin built by Polish troops who were quartered in the church from 1942 to 1945. (Open daily 8-11:45am and 2-5pm.)

Farther south stands a blue and red marina, now home to several shops on the bottom and the **Galilee Experience** (tel. 72 36 20) complex on top. The complex includes a bookstore and a plush theater, and is run by group of Christians and Messianic Jews who overrode the protests of the local Orthodox community and overhauled the old marina building. The main attraction here is a 36-minute film that provides an overview of the past 4,000 years in the Galilee, emphasizing the life of Jesus as well as the birth of the modern Israeli state. Attached to the theater is a **bookstore** that sells Jewish ritual objects, Communion grape juice, and both Easter and bar mitzvah cards. A small **café** with a view of the coastline is at the rear of the bookstore. The film is shown daily 8am-10pm (closed Fri. night and Sat. during the day) and costs US$6. Many of the screenings are in English.

Tiberias is the site of one of the world's earliest known **hot mineral springs.** One legend maintains that the springs were formed in the great biblical flood when the earth's insides boiled. Another legend holds that the water was heated by demons under the orders of King Solomon, who then made the demons deaf so that they would never hear of his death and desert their duties. Apparently, they still haven't heard; visitors come to the warm flowing waters for therapy. You can lie in the slimy but incredibly relaxing pools, cleansing body and wallet for NIS24 (Sat. NIS27). A massage is NIS29 (Sat. NIS33), while a mineral bath is NIS25 (Sat. NIS29). The springs are 3km south of town on the coastal road. Either walk or catch bus #2 or 5 from the front of the central bus station or from HaGalil St. The older building, **Tiberias Hot Springs,** serves those with serious ailments. (Open Sun.-Thurs. 6:30am-4pm, Fri. 6:30am-1pm.) The newer building, **Tiberias Hot Springs Spa** (tel. 79 19 67), serves those seeking modest rejuvenation. (Open Sun.-Thurs. 8am-8pm, Fri. 8am-2:30pm, Sat. 8:30am-8pm.)

Across the street are ruins of the **Ḥammat Synagogues,** six ancient buildings constructed one on top of another. The jewel of the excavations is a mosaic floor that was part of three separate synagogues. The four upper synagogues were used in the 6th-8th centuries CE. The small **Lehmann museum** displays other remains. Enter the museum and walk out the back door to reach the ancient synagogues. (Site open Sun.-Thurs. 8am-5pm, Fri. 8am-2pm. Admission NIS3, students NIS2.)

Entertainment

Unlike the shores of the Med, those of this misnamed lake (circumference 58km) have entrance fees, and many lack sand. The shoreline in the city and to the immediate north and south is owned by hotels, which charge a hefty admission but possess changing and shower facilities, boat rentals, and kiosks. The beaches to the north of the city are located along Gedud Barak Rd., off HaYarden.

The **Lido Kinneret,** just off HaYarden St., charges NIS10. NIS50 buys you 30 minutes of waterskiing. (Open daily 8am-6pm.) Just north is the somewhat dilapidated **Nelson Beach,** where kayaks rent for NIS30 per hour, though student discounts are available (admission NIS10; open 7:30am-9pm). As part of its effort to woo a young crowd, the Nelson hosts rock concerts in the summer. You can sleep on Nelson beach for NIS10. Just north are the meticulously tended **Quiet Beach** (NIS10) and **Blue Beach** (NIS12). With some searching, you may find an entrepreneur who will undercut the expensive waterskiing establishments. To the south of Tiberias, about a 15-minute walk or a short ride on bus #2 or 5, the **Municipal Beach** charges only NIS5. Next to it is the beach of **Gannei Hamat** (NIS6). Many beaches also have kiddie pools. Tiberias also maintains a free **separate-sex beach,** open to women on Sun., Tues., and Thurs., to men on Mon., Wed., and Fri.

Nightlife in Tiberias centers on the *midreḥov* and promenade area. In summer, popcorn and cotton-candy vendors and street musicians proliferate. Young Israelis dance on the tables to live rock at **La Pirate Pub,** at the corner of the *midreḥov* and the promenade. The pub's large outdoor section fills to capacity and music begins at 10 or 11pm nightly. (1 liter of beer NIS11. Open daily 8am-4am.) The **Petra Pub,** under the Lake Castle Hostel at the southern end of the promenade, is also popular for late-night drinking and dancing, although mostly with tourists. One of the cavern-like rooms becomes a disco after midnight (Maccabee NIS4). Open daily till the wee hours. The bars at the Maman, Naḥum, and Schwitzer hostels are hip hangouts for backpackers; they all usually serve reasonably priced drinks (Goldstar NIS3) and show videos.

Back on the water, **Blue Beach** on Gedud Barak Rd. opens its disco at 8:30pm during the summer—Israeli folkdancing alternates with top-40 hits (admission NIS12). Wear your bathing suit under (or as) your attire so you can take a dip between sets. You can also try to crash the nightclub shows in the hotels. Lido Kinneret Beach and Kinneret Sailing offer nightly **disco cruises** leaving at 9pm (NIS12). Overindulgence has its consequences—spinning rooms and lolling boats can do interesting things to the inner ear.

Slightly south of Tiberias (1km) is **Luna Beach,** featuring yippee-skip waterslides. (Open 8am-5pm; admission NIS20.) The adjacent **Sironit Beach** has only a few slides but is open 7pm-midnight and charges NIS10. Walk or take bus #2 or 5 from the central bus station or HaGalil St. The best waterpark on the Kinneret, however, is on its eastern shore—**Luna Gal** (tel. 73 17 50), operated by Moshav Ramot. The park has bumper boats, thrilling slides and pools, waterfalls, an inner tube ride, and an excellent beach. (Open daily 9am-9pm; admission NIS35.)

Moshav Ramot, along with several other moshavim and kibbutzim, also operates **jeep trips** (tel. 94 10 91), guided half-day and quarter-day jeep tours of the Upper Galilee and Golan. Two-hour trips cost NIS40 per person; four-hour trips cost NIS60.

If you're sick of sun and water, try bowling—at Tiberias's new ultra-modern 10-pin bowling lanes atop the Lev Ha'Ir shopping mall (corner of HaShiloaḥ and Bibass Streets). The **Tiberias Bowling Club** (tel. 72 45 10) features 12 lanes with computer score-keeping, a snack bar, and a majestic view of the Kinneret. (Open Sun.-Thurs. 10am-1am, Fri.-Sat. 10am-2am; one game costs NIS6-11 per person; shoe rentals cost NIS2.)

For the less uncouth, the **Sea of Galilee Festival,** featuring international folkdancing and singing troupes, usually takes place in Tiberias during the second week of July. Check at the GTIO for details on special events and for information on Ein Gev's **Passover Music Festival.**

Near Tiberias

New Testament Sites

Four of the most significant stories in Christian history are set in the steep hills surrounding the Kinneret's northern coast. The adventurous can tour the holy sights by bicycle to save the hassle of long walks and waiting for buses. A total circuit takes about four hours, plus time to actually visit the sights. Get a mountain bike if possible (Hostel Aviv is your best bet); the knobby tires will supplement your motocross prowess when insane Israeli drivers force you into a roadside ditch. A Kinneret Sailing boat schedule, available from the GTIO, is handy in case you want to take the easy way back from Capernaum.

According to the New Testament, when Jesus walked on water, he walked on the Kinneret. (Today, you can only waterski.) On the **Mount of Beatitudes,** overlooking sea, field, and town, Jesus gave his Sermon on the Mount (Matthew 5). A church, built by Mussolini, of all people, now stands on the Mount. Its octagonal shape recalls Jesus' eight beatitudes. Shorts and bare shoulders are not permitted. To reach the Mount, take bus #841 or 459 from Tiberias; get off at the second stop after the bus turns uphill away from the lake. From here, a sign points the way to the church, 1km along a side road. (Church open daily 8am-noon and 2:30-5pm. Free.)

If you take the path down from the Mount to the coastal road, or get off the bus before it turns up the Mount and hike 3km, you'll find the ancient town of **Capernaum** (Kfar Naḥum) about 1km to the east, where Jesus healed Simon's mother-in-law and the Roman Centurion's servant (Luke 4:31-37 and 7:1-10). This is also the birthplace of Peter; the ruins of a 5th century octagonal church cover the site, believed to be that of Peter's house. Today, a modern church arches over the ruins. Nearby, the ruins of a synagogue, perched between the old town and the Sea of Galilee, contain Corinthian columns and friezes dating from the 2nd century CE. Since Capernaum did not participate in the Jewish revolts, the city was left alone by the Romans as they systematically destroyed other similar towns in the region in retribution. Modest dress required. (Open daily 8:30am-4:15pm. Admission NIS2.) Buses #841, 459, 541, and 963 pass the Capernaum junction about once an hour en route to Kiryat Shmona, Tzfat, and Tiberias.

Two kilometers southwest of Capernaum along the coastal road, in **Tabgha,** stands the **Church of the Primacy,** marking the spot where Jesus made Peter "Shepherd of his People." *Tabgha* (Tabḥa in Hebrew) is an Arabic distortion of the original Greek name for the site, *Heptapegon,* meaning seven springs. According to the Book of

John, after the Resurrection Peter led the apostles on a fishing expedition 100m off-shore from Tabgha. A man on shore called to them to throw their nets over the star-board side and assured them of a catch. When the nets hit the water, a swarm of fish swam in. Jumping off the boat and swimming to shore, Peter found the man, whom he now realized was Jesus, preparing a meal for the Twelve. When the others sailed in, Jesus charged Peter, "Feed my lambs.... Tend my sheep.... Feed my sheep" (John 21: 15-19)—this episode is widely regarded as the basis for the primacy of St. Peter. The Church of the Primacy is built around a rock said to be the table of this feast; the building itself dates only to the 1930s. On the seaward side of the church are the steps from which Jesus called out his instructions, and on the shoreline is a series of six double or heart-shaped column bases built by early Christians and called the "thrones of the Apostles" (tel. 72 10 61; open 8am-4pm).

Just west of the Church of the Primacy along the northern coast of the sea lies the **Church of the Multiplication of the Loaves and Fishes.** A mosaic inside relates how Jesus fed 5000 pilgrims with five loaves and two small fish (Matthew 15:29-30). A section of the mosaic has been removed so you can see the original 4th-century foundations. (Church open Mon.-Sat. 8:30am-5pm, Sun. 9:45am-5pm. Modest dress required.) Around the right side of the church past the "private" sign and up the stairs is a small **hospice** (tel. 72 10 61), primarily for Christian pilgrims but open to anyone if there's room. There is a kitchen and a small food store for guests only.

Migdal, the birthplace of Mary Magdalene ("Magdalene" is a corruption of Migdal), halfway between Tiberias and the Capernaum junction, was a flourishing metropolis during the Second Temple period. Only a tiny, white-domed shrine marks where the city once stood. To reach the shrine, take bus #55 or 54 from Tiberias.

Shores of Yam Kinneret ים כנרת

Horseback is an excellent, albeit expensive, way to explore the northern coast of the lake. The bus stop after the one for the Hospice of the Beatitudes (bus #459 or 841) leaves you at the road to Korazim, in front of the guest farm **Vered HaGalil.** A half-day ride through the Galilean hills down to the sea and then up to the Mount of Beati-tudes costs NIS90 per person. If you call ahead, the owner, Yehuda Avni, will let you camp free and use shower and toilet facilities the night before your ride. Bring your sleeping bag. There's also a bunkhouse where bed and American breakfast cost NIS80 for one, NIS130 for two. The restaurant here may eat up your funds. The stables offer many different kinds of rides, and previous experience isn't necessary. An hour-long rental is NIS18, a horse for a day NIS80. (For reservations, write to Vered HaGalil, Korazim or call 93 57 85.) A number of kibbutzim and moshavim also offer horseback riding. Check at GTIO for details.

The low water level of the Kinneret in 1985-86 had one serendipitous benefit—the discovery of an **ancient boat** off the beach of Kibbutz Ginnosar. The boat was found buried under a segment of newly exposed lakebed. The boat's wooden frame, which had turned to mush after centuries of marinating in mud, was encased in a fiberglass frame and hauled to shore. The boat has been restored to near-pristine condition, and has been dated at 100 BCE-100 CE. It rests in a glass tank filled with water, where it will undergo nine years of cosmetic repair. Noting its age, some Christians have dubbed it "the Jesus boat." While it *is* a fishing boat, even of the sort the apostles might have used, archeologists claim it has no further connection to Jesus. Archeolo-gists suspect it was sunk by the Romans in a great sea battle against the Jews de-scribed by Josephus. Next door is **Ginnosar Beach** (open 8am-6pm; NIS8, children or group members NIS6). The area is green and shady and great for pterodactyls. Paddle boat rentals are NIS25 an hour; NIS15 for kayaks. To reach Ginnosar, take bus #841, 459, or 963 from Tiberias to the new Yigal Allon Center where the boat is soaking (tel. 72 14 95; open Sat.-Thurs. 9am-4pm, Fri. 9am-noon; admission NIS3, students NIS1).

Karne Hittim (the Horns of Hittim) is where Salah al-Din gave the Crusaders their comeuppance in 1187 CE. From this mountain peak, you can see Jordan to the east, the Mediterranean to the west, and Tzfat to the north. Take bus #42 and ask the driver where to get off. The walk to the top of the hill is about 50 minutes, but the view will leave you more breathless than the climb. Open 8am-5pm.

A modern miracle is commemorated near the spot where the Jordan River flows out of the Sea of Galilee, about 8km from Tiberias. Founded in 1910, **Deganya Alef** is Israel's oldest kibbutz, the first Jewish settlement in the Jordan Valley and the birthplace of Moshe Dayan. On May 19, 1948, a few days after the State of Israel was declared, Syria took the nearby town of Tzemah and, armed with tanks, tried to overrun Deganya. The kibbutzniks, with only small-caliber rifles and Molotov cocktails, held them off until one tank pierced the perimeter. The interloper was stopped by a Deganya settler with a homemade grenade, and the other tanks retreated, never to return. The gutted chassis of the Syrian tank rests at an angle on the lawn of the kibbutz, commemorating Deganya's victory. Deganya's diamond tool factory has since made it a wealthy, industrial community. The kibbutz also has two small museums at **Beit Gordon** (tel. 75 00 40), one devoted to the archeology of the Kinneret area, the other to its natural history, replete with exhibits of taxidermal treasures.

Deganya's size and uniformity is conducive to easy misdirection. Take a right after the tennis courts and ambulances and ask directions immediately. Next to Beit Gordon is an ebullient **Society for the Protection of Nature in Israel** office. (Museums open Sun.-Thurs. 9am-4pm, Fri. 9am-1pm, Sat. 9:30am-noon. Admission NIS4, students NIS3.) Deganya can be reached by bus #24 to Hammat Gader or bus #23, 26, 27, 28, or 29 headed for Beit She'an and the Jordan River Valley.

Eight kilometers southeast of Deganya, about 30 minutes from Tiberias, the hot baths of **Hammat Gader** lie on the Jordanian and Syrian borders. Once the site of a large Roman bath complex, the hot sulphur springs have been mostly diverted to a modern pond with a house of ablutions. The Roman ruins are partially reconstructed, with several large bathing areas and a smaller pool that was reserved for lepers. At the southwest corner of the complex is the hottest spring in the area at 51 C. It was named *Ma'ayan HaGehinom* in Hebrew, meaning "Hell's Pool," and *Ain Makleh,* the "Frying Pool," by the Arabs who controlled the baths from 1922 until 1967. The modern hot pool is crowded with families on outings. The leper pool is not. There is also an area with the black mud that purportedly cures skin ailments. In addition, Hammat Gader is the site of an alligator park, where you can observe hundreds of large, somnolent alligators sunning themselves on the banks of their swimming area or slogging though the murky water. Having imported the first generation from Florida, the preserve now raises the young inside a hothouse at the entrance to the ponds. New additions include two waterslides and trampolines as well as a health club with cosmetic treatments, massages, and Izod shirts.

The park also contains the **ruins** of a 5th-century synagogue, just west of the Roman baths and past the picnic area. The synagogue is at the site of a modern border lookout station; to the northwest, spanning the Yarmoukh River, is a bridge dating from the Ottoman railroad. Admission to the entire Hammat Gader complex is NIS8, students and children NIS6. Bus #24 leaves from Tiberias twice in the morning beginning at 8:40am and 10:30am; the last bus back is at 3pm.

Tzfat (Safed) צפת

You needn't be religious or Jewish to be enraptured by the mystical city of Tzfat; anyone who's ever had a semi-profound thought, or faked one, will love it. Set on hazy Mt. Canaan, overlooking the Galilean hills and the Kinneret, Tzfat is a city of mesmerizing beauty. Orthodox Jews believe the Messiah will travel from Mt. Meron to Tzfat before going to Jerusalem; some here even sport buttons that read "We want the Messiah now!" or display "In God We Trust" bumper stickers.

Along with Jerusalem, Hebron, and Tiberias, Tzfat is a Jewish holy city. Sages say each city represents an element: Jerusalem is fire because of the burnt offerings in the Temple; Hebron earth for the land Abraham bought there; Tiberias water for Yam Kinneret; and Tzfat, a walled city perched in the cool Upper Galilee hills, is air. Of course, it's possible to get too much of Tzfat's atmosphere: in 1777, a rabbi who had trekked all the way to Tzfat from Europe ultimately packed up and left for Tiberias, complaining that the angels here kept him up at night.

For all its contemporary serenity, the city's history is messy. Tzfat was originally built by Canaanites and settled by Jews during the time of the First Temple and later by Arabs in the 7th century CE. Plundered first by the Romans and later by the Crusaders led by Tancred, it was ultimately conquered by the Mamluk ruler Beybers in 1266. Having slaughtered the Crusaders, he built Tzfat into a major administrative center for the surrounding region, including Galilee and Lebanon. A thriving Jewish community reemerged in the Middle Ages, when refugees from the Inquisition began to build the synagogues of today's Spanish Quarter. Mystical and scholarly sects settled in Tzfat as well, among them that of Rabbi Isaac Luria Ashkenazi, known to his followers as Ha'Ari, "the Lion." Many of the synagogues of these leaders as well as countless legends about their great works survive. Some of the Ḥasidic Jews who live here today claim to be heirs of the mystical Kabbalists who lived in Tzfat during the 16th century.

During World War I, famine and cholera devastated the Jewish Quarter and the town became predominantly Arab. Jews and Arabs coexisted amicably until 1929, when Tzfat's Arabs participated in bloody anti-Jewish riots sparked by Hajj Amin al-Husseini. In the 1948 War of Independence, Tzfat was fiercely contested because of its strategic position at the heart of northern Galilee. All 12,000 Arab residents fled as the Israeli forces took over the city in May. In recent years, Tzfat's picturesque surroundings, serendipitous alleys, and temperate climate have attracted artists and vacationers from all over the world.

Orientation and Practical Information

Tzfat, transliterated as Zefat, Safed, Safad, and even Cfat, is arranged in circular terraces of streets descending from the castle ruins at the town center. **Jerusalem (Yerushalayim) Street,** the main street, behind the central bus station, makes a complete circle around **Gan HaMetzuda** (Park of the Citadel). **HaPalmaḥ Street** begins off Jerusalem St. near the central bus station and crosses the main street via an arched stone bridge. Think of Tzfat as divided into three semi-distinct districts: the **Park Area,** at the top of the mountain (ringed by Jerusalem St.); the **Artists' Quarter,** southwest and down the hill; and the **Synagogue Quarter** (Old City), immediately to the north of the Artists' Quarter on the other side of Ma'alot Oleh HaGardom. If you arrive by car, you'll need parking permits from the GTIO, NIS1.20 per hour from 8am until 1pm.

Government Tourist Information Office (GTIO): ground floor of the Municipality Building, 50 Jerusalem St. (tel. 93 06 33 or 92 06 66), a 7-min. uphill walk to the right as you leave the central bus station. It's worth buying the new, detailed map for NIS5 if you plan to spend more than a few hours in the city. Open Sun.-Thurs. 8am-6pm, Fri. 8am-1pm.

Banks: Leumi, 33 Jerusalem St.; **HaPoalim,** 72 Jerusalem St.; and **Discount,** 83 Jerusalem St. All open Sun., Tues., and Thurs., 8:30am-noon and 4-6pm, Mon. and Wed. 8:30am-12:30pm, Fri. 8:30am-noon. **First International,** 40 Jerusalem St. open Sun., Tues., and Thurs. 8:30am-2pm, Mon. and Wed. 8:30am-2pm and 4-7pm, Fri. 8:30am-noon.

Central Post Office: HaPalmaḥ St. (tel. 92 04 05), next to a radar dish visible from the corner of HaPalmaḥ St. at Aliya Bet. **Poste Restante** services available. Open Sun.-Tues. and Thurs. 8am-12:30 and 3:30-6pm; Wed. 8am-1:30pm, Fri. 8am-noon. The more convenient branch on Jerusalem St., near GTIO, has similar hours. **Telephone code:** 06.

Central Bus Station: Ha'Atzma'ut Sq. (tel. 92 11 22). Bus #459 travels between Tiberias and Tzfat every 1-2hrs. All buses to Kiryat Shmona from Jerusalem and Tel Aviv stop at Rosh Pina, where you can transfer for a bus to Tzfat, 10km east. There is a direct bus to Jerusalem daily at 7:30am (#964) via the West Bank. Buses #361 and 362 travel to and from Ḥaifa through Akko every 20min. Last bus Sun.-Thurs. 9pm, Fri. 4:45pm. First bus on Sat. at 5pm. **Baggage storage** open Sun.-Thurs. 7am-2:30pm, NIS3 per piece per day. Also at Ascent Institute (tel. 97 14 07) on Ha'Ari St.; take your first right as you ascend Jerusalem St. NIS1 per piece per day, open 7am-10pm.

Taxis: Tel. 97 07 07. Near the central bus station. No *sherut* or intercity service.

First Aid: Magen David Adom (tel. 92 03 33), next to the central bus station.

Police: Tel. 100 in emergencies, otherwise call 92 04 44 or 97 24 44.

Accommodations and Food

Tzfat's youth hostel is well equipped and only a short ride from the bus station. Another option is to sleep in the inexpensive **guest rooms** and separate flats provided by town residents, open primarily in high (summer) season. Most of the rentals are comfortable, with hot showers, living rooms, and separate kitchens for guests. The best way to find one of these places is to let them find you: if you walk around the central bus station forlornly holding your luggage, it shouldn't be long before you are approached. Don't pay until you see the quarters. It's wise to ask the GTIO about any place you're considering renting. You may also want to walk up Jerusalem St. and choose one of the places with a "rooms to let" sign (often in Hebrew only). Ask at the tourist office for the phone numbers listed for rooms to rent. Official prices are NIS50 for a double, but you can bargain, especially during low season. It is wise to check all accommodations for heating or blankets; because of the city's altitude, nights in Tzfat can be chilly.

Beit Binyamin (HI), near the Amal Trade School in South Tzfat (tel. 92 10 86). A 20-min. walk from the bus station, or take bus #6 or 7. From the bus station, follow Jerusalem St. south (left, downhill) and take your first left onto Aliya Bet, which will merge with Hehalutz. Just past the Allon Center, take a right off of Hehalutz onto HaNassi. After HaNassi turns into HaMem-Gimel, head left on Lohamei HaGeta'ot, the second turn-off. Now put your hands on your head. The hostel will be on your right. Commodious, with many amenities, including new kitchen and dining room. US$13, nonmembers US$14.50. Breakfast included, other meals served upon request. Reception open 7-9am and 4-7pm. Call ahead.

Ascent Institute of Tzfat, 2 Ha'Ari St. (tel. 92 13 64). Take the first right off Jerusalem St. heading right up the hill from the bus station. For Jewish travelers. Nightly classes and programs on Tzfat and *Kaballah*; placement with families on *shabbat;* 3-day hikes to Golan or Galilee; shorter hikes in Tzfat area; and walking tours of the city. Refrigerator available. Call ahead, especially for *shabbat* placement and 3-day hikes. Will house non-Jews in a group with Jews, but non-Jews with no Jews will be set up in a rented room for same price as Ascent. Reception open Sun.-Thurs. 7am-10pm, Fri. noon-1:30pm and 3:30-6:30pm but you can always leave your bags. Dorm beds NIS30, less NIS5 rebate for each of two optional classes you attend while there. Friday nights, dorm beds NIS20. Breakfast included.

Hadar Hotel, Ridbaz St. (tel. 92 00 68). Take a right from the bus station and head up Jerusalem St. Ridbaz is an alley off Jerusalem. Look for the yellow sign with an arrow. Cozy atmosphere unquestionably enriches the Tzfat experience, if you have the cash. Rooms include bath. No smoking on *shabbat.* Doubles US$44, July-Aug. US$50.

Beit Natan, on Jerusalem St. (tel. 92 01 21) south of GTIO, by the Davidka monument. Rooms to let in July-Aug. Doubles US$50.

Bear in mind that everything in Tzfat shuts down on *shabbat;* if you don't shop before Friday afternoon, you'll starve. The stretch of Jerusalem St. north of the bridge (to #48) is lined with good, cheap falafel stands and expensive sit-down restaurants. Despite its dubious name, **California Falafel,** 92 Jerusalem St., next to the HaPalmah St. bridge, fries up some of the best falafel (NIS4) in town. (Open weekdays until 10pm, Fri. until 2pm. Kosher.) **HaMifgash Restaurant** (tel. 92 05 10 or 97 47 34), 75 Jerusalem St., just opposite the small observation point and park, serves stupendous food in a homey stone cavern. *Shishlik,* kebab, or hamburgers are an excellent splurge at NIS18-25. (Open Sun.-Fri. 9am-11pm. Kosher.) The **Steakia HaSela** (no English sign), a tiny grill two doors west of the bridge, has some of the best *shwarma* in the country, served in pita with monogrammed salads (NIS6). The most popular place in the Old City is **Big Mo's Dairy Experience,** at HaMeginim Sq. Follow the signs from Jerusalem St. (Mo is short for Mordekhai.) Catch up on international sports scores from Mo and listen to the black hats joke around ("Sure, he *looks* frum...."). Take home their delicious baked goods for *shabbat.* (Pizza NIS3, fish NIS5.50, French onion soup NIS5, soyburger NIS4. Open Sun.-Thurs. 8:30am-11:30pm, Fri. 8:30am-

4:30pm, Sat. 9:30pm-1:30am. Kosher.) A fruit and vegetable **market** is held Tuesdays and Wednesdays 6am-2pm, next to the bus station. There are **supermarkets** in the new shopping complex on the Jerusalem St. *midreẖov,* above the bus station and in the Artists' Colony on the way to the Rimon Inn (open Sun.-Thurs. 8am-7pm, Fri. 8am-2pm).

Sights and Entertainment

As with all the older cities of Israel, the tangled pedestrian streets of Tzfat are sparingly labelled. You're here to wander happily around, anyway. The meager ruins of a 12th-century Crusader fortress that once controlled the main route to Damascus grace **Gan HaMetzuda,** a cool, wooded park and an ideal spot for a picnic. At the summit stands a monument commemorating the Israelis who died here during the 1948 war. The entrance near GTIO is across from the Davidka Monument, memorializing a makeshift weapon used in the War of Independence, effective simply due to a frightening noise it made.

The **Israel Bible Museum** (tel. 97 34 72), just north of the park up the steep stone stairway, displays the work of Phillip Ratner, a modern American artist whose work is in permanent collections at the Statue of Liberty, the White House, and the U.S. Supreme Court. Sculptures, lithographs, graphics, and paintings vividly depict biblical scenes and personalities. Pick up a list of works from the front desk. (March-Sept. open Sun.-Thurs. 10am-6pm, Sat. 10am-2pm; Oct.-Nov. Sat.-Thurs. 10am-2pm; In Dec. and Feb. Sun.-Thurs. 10am-2pm. Closed Jan. Free.) The **Shem V'Ever Cave,** one of several sacred caves in the region, is believed to be the place where Noah's son and grandson, Shem and Ever respectively, studied the Torah and were later buried. If the cave is locked, knock on the door of the nearby small, domed synagogue, and ask the caretaker to open it. The cave is near the top of the bridge off HaPalmaẖ St. At the intersection of Jerusalem and Arlozorov St., a forest of English signs will direct you down the hill to the **General Exhibition** which is housed in the town's former mosque, abandoned in 1948. On the way, detour off Arlozorov into the Artists' Quarter and wander through the alleys and galleries just south of the Jerusalem-Arlozorov intersection. The quality of the art varies, and though the colony has seen better days there is still some decent stuff; the Ora Gallery, the Bible Museum, Victor Havani, Mike Leif, and Reuven and Naomi Spiers merit a browse. Hours vary, as many of the galleries are run by the artists themselves (most are open 10am-1pm and 4-7pm).

Navigating in the gnarled streets of the **Synagogue Quarter** (*Kiryat Batei HaKnesset*), also called the Old City (*Ir Ha'Atika*), is a matter of luck; note landmarks carefully, but when you get lost—and you will get lost—enjoy the experience: there are few nicer places to lose your bearings. The Old City's tiny, ornate synagogues—all of which are still in use—are its most interesting features. Because Tzfat lies to the north of Jerusalem, their holy arks are placed on the southern rather than the eastern wall. Each synagogue has its story. The **Chernobyl Synagogue** was founded by Jews from that luckless Ukrainian town. They claim that the reactor was built over Jewish graves, and that it melted down on the *yartzheit* (anniversary of the death) of the chief rabbi buried beneath it. The **Chertkoff Synagogue's** chief rabbi predicted in 1840 that the messianic redemption (*ge'ula*) would begin when there were 600,000 Jews in the Land of Israel—a population reached with independence in 1948, but with no results so far. The **Caro Synagogue** and **Ha'Ari (Ashkenazi) Synagogue** are the most famous synagogues. To reach the Caro Synagogue, take Ma'alot Oleh HaGardom St. off Jerusalem St. and make a right onto Beit Yosef St. Ask to see the remarkable set of old *sefarim* (books) and Torah scrolls. It was here that Yosef Caro, chief rabbi of Tzfat and author of the vast *Shulẖan Arukh* ("The Set Table," an extensive and standard guide for daily life according to Jewish law), studied and taught in the 16th century. In the basement is the angel with whom he used to confer (Rabbi Alkabetz purportedly witnessed their talks). These days, the angel prefers not to be disturbed. To reach Ha'Ari Synagogue, follow Beit Yosef until it becomes Alkabetz St., make a right up a stairway with stained glass Stars of David above, and continue straight under the stone arch. The synagogue will be to your right on Najara St. Rabbi Isaac Luria, nicknamed the Ari (lion), was the great Kabbalist who introduced the *Kabbalat Shabbat,* an arrangement of prayers in preparation for the Sabbath; Alkabetz, his student, wrote the famous liturgical hymn *Lekha Dodi.* The four pillars that buttress the podium in the middle of the room symbolize the four elements of the world (air, fire, water, and earth) and the four holy cities (Tzfat, Jerusalem, Tiberias, and Hebron). The small hole in the *bima* (pulpit), directly opposite the door, is a scar from an May 1948 Arab shell. Although the synagogue was full at the time, no one was hurt—a miracle attributed to protection by the ghost of the Rabbi Luria. A Sephardic synagogue lies farther down the hill near the cemetery. Just downhill from the Caro Synagogue, off Abuhav St. in the Spanish Quarter, stand the **Abuhav** and **Alsheih Synagogues.** Take a left off Beit Yosef St. onto Alsheih St. and then make a sharp right; both buildings will be to your right. The blue color of the walls symbolizes *malkhut* (God's reign) and the green, also common, symbolizes *tzmihat hage'ula* (the growth of redemption). Dress modestly when you visit synagogues. No cameras on *shabbat* (Fri. night and Sat.). When visiting a synagogue, remember to make a donation, however small, for the synagogue's upkeep.

Three adjoining **cemeteries** sprawl on the western outskirts of the Old City, off Ha'Ari St. Follow the path all the way down, past the complex of new stone buildings on the left. The small building on the left where the path turns right down the hill into the cemetery is Ha'Ari synagogue's men's *mikveh,* or ritual bath (women should not enter). The oldest of the cemeteries contains the 17th century graves of the most famous Tzfat Kabbalists, as well as a domed tomb built by the Karaites of Damascus (a medieval group of Jewish biblical literalists) to mark the grave of the biblical prophet Hosea. On the wall inside the tomb, you'll see an article posted about an eighth-generation Tzfat resident named Mordekhai Shebabo. Shebabo left his position as a fine pedicurist, and single-handedly undertook the restoration of the graves. Any visible grave on the site is the result of this man's manicuring prowess. Shebabo or one of his sons may ask you for a small donation for the upkeep of the cemetery. Legend has it that hidden under this same hill lie Hannah and her seven sons, whose martyrdom at the hands of the Syrians is recorded in the Book of Maccabees. Supposedly you'll know you're walking over their graves because you'll be overcome by a sudden feeling of fatigue. Also buried near here are the children of Tzfat who were killed in May 1974 on a trip to Ma'alot, when PLO terrorists took over the school in which the children were sleeping. A large memorial service is held for them each year.

At the bottom of the Oleh HaGardom steps, **Beit Hameiri** (tel. 97 13 07) contains a museum of old tools and furniture as well as an institute for the study of the history of the Jewish settlement in Tzfat. Bright orange signs with a mango tinge point the way here from anywhere in town. (Open Sun.-Fri. 9am-2pm. Admission NIS3.50.)

The legends of Tzfat, modern and ancient, are best told by locals. **Shlomo Bar-Ayal** (tel. 97 45 97) gives daily tours of the Old City in such vivid detail that he seems to have lived in Tzfat for centuries. When *The New York Times Magazine* wanted a typical Israeli to quote, they went to Shlomo. You judge how typical he is. Tours leave from the GTIO Sun.-Thurs. at 9:30am and 2pm, and Fri. at 9:30am. Several nights per week he leads an evening tour starting from the Rimon Inn; check with the GTIO. Dress modestly. (2hr. US$8, students US$6.)

The Yigal Allon Cultural Center on Hehalutz St. occasionally shows recently released English **movies;** check with the GTIO. In July, the town hosts a wild **klezmer festival** (Eastern European Jewish soul music) that has to be seen to be believed. *Shabbat* in Tzfat brings heightened tranquility and introspection; if you'd rather reflect in the water and not your mind, though, head over to the **swimming pool and leisure center** (tel. 92 02 17) just off Ha'Atzma'ut Rd., behind the central bus station. Walk down from the station, turn left, and the turn-off for the swimming pool will be 100m on the left. (Open in summer only, beginning July daily 9am-5pm. Admission NIS10, children NIS6.) Another pool (tel. 97 42 94), in the industrial district of south Tzfat (take bus #6 or 7) is heated and open year-round. (Sun.-Thurs. 11am-9pm, Fri. 11am-5pm, Sat. 10am-6pm. Admission NIS10, under 18 NIS7. Sauna NIS5.)

Near Tzfat: Meron מירון

Each year on the holiday of Lag Ba'Omer (May 9, 1993), thousands converge on the tiny village of Meron, 4km west of Tzfat, at the tomb of Rabbi Shimon Bar Yohai, the great 2nd-century Talmudic scholar. Some believe he composed the *Zohar* (the central work of Jewish mysticism) while hiding in a cave in Peki'in. According to the Kabbalists, Bar Yohai once vowed to God that the Jews would never forget the importance of the Torah. Mindful of this vow, the Tzfat Hasidim dance and sing their way to his tomb in a joyous procession, accompanied by an ancient Torah scroll from the Bana'a Synagogue in the Spanish Quarter. Contact the GTIO in Tzfat for details.

Near the tomb are the ruins of an outwardly unimpressive but historically noteworthy synagogue dating from the 3rd century CE, when Meron was a center in the booming olive oil trade. From Bar Yohai's grave, walk to your right, past the yeshiva, and follow the uphill path to your left. Virtually all that's left of the synagogue is a lintel. Legend has it that this lintel's fall will herald the coming of the Messiah. The Israeli Department of Antiquities has nervously buttressed the artifact with reinforced concrete, but every year, pious Jews from Tzfat enthusiastically dance and stomp in efforts to accelerate its fall.

Just west of the town is **Mount Meron** (Har Meron), the highest mountain in the Galilee (1208m). A superb trail affords tremendous vistas of Tzfat and the surrounding countryside, and on clear days you can see Lebanon and Syria to the north, the Mediterranean to the west, and the Kinneret to the southeast. It is possible to ascend the mountain from the town of Meron, but a more convenient option is to take bus #43 from Tzfat to Kibbutz Sasa, northwest of the mountain. Buses depart at 7am, 12:30pm, and 5pm, and return about 8am, 1:45pm, and 6:15pm. Catch the early bus to avoid the midday heat. From the kibbutz, where the bus turns around, continue 1km to the turn-off on the left for the Beit Sefer Sadeh (Field School). The field school is 200m up the road and has an information office (tel. 98 00 23). Call ahead to arrange for a guided hike. To reach the trail, walk straight down the road from the Field School turnoff until you pass an army base on the right and a small parking lot on the left. The trail begins from the back of the lot and is indicated by stone markers and black-and-white striped blazes. A one-hour walk brings you to the summit, where the trail is marked with red-and-white blazes. Stay on the trail, which skirts the green-and-white summit, since the very top of the mountain is the site of a crimson-and-white army radar installation. Twenty minutes farther along the path, you'll approach a brown-and-white picnic site with an orange-and-white asphalt traffic circle on a road; don't cross the road, but follow it for 20m to the left to where the trail begins again. A long, easy descent, again marked with the black-and-white-and-red-all-over blazes, ends on a dirt road just above the village of Meron. Return to Tzfat either by retracing your steps to Sasa or by catching one of the frequent buses from Meron.

Kiryat Shmona קרית שמונה

Tel Hai, 3km from Kiryat Shmona, has the dubious distinction of being the site of the first armed conflict between Jews and Arabs within the current borders of the State of Israel. In 1920, a sizable group of Arabs gathered around the settlements of Tel Hai, Kfar Giladi, and Metulla (then part of French-administered Syria and Lebanon) and accused the Jewish settlers of protecting French soldiers charged with encroachment on Arab lands. In an attempt to prove his neutrality, Yosef Trumpeldor, the leader of Tel Hai, allowed four Arabs inside the settlement to search for the French agents. Once inside the complex, the Arabs attacked, killing Trumpeldor and seven others. The six men and two women were buried in Kfar Giladi, where the lion in the Cemetery of the Shomrim (Guardians) now stands. Trumpeldor's last words, "No matter, it is good to die for our country," have passed into legend. (In the classic Israeli coming-of-age movie *Late Summer Blues,* set during the War of Attrition, his words are scorned.) In 1949, in honor of the eight victims, the town that was situated on the ruins of the old Arab village al-Khalsa was dubbed Kiryat Shmona, "town of the eight."

By virtue of its location in the Ḥula plain of Upper Galilee near the Lebanese border, Kiryat Shmona was the target of numerous PLO *katyusha* bombings and terrorist attacks until Israel invaded in 1982, and it has been subject to Hizballah shelling as recently as February 1992. Given the grim nickname Kiryat Katyusha, many of its buildings bear the scars of these assaults on their acned façades. And walking the thin line between humor and horror, three brightly painted tanks sit in a small park near the southern entrance to the town.

Today Kiryat Shmona is the quiet administrative and transportation center of the Upper Galilee, although the city is little more than a pit-stop for most tourists. Buses for the Upper Galilee, the Golan, and Tzfat leave from the **central bus station** (tel. 94 07 40/1), on Tel Ḥai Blvd. The only accommodations in the area are youth hostels in **Tel Ḥai** or **Rosh Pina.** Falafel and *shwarma* stands cluster around the intersection of Tel Ḥai and Tchernihovsky St. Cafés and small restaurants stretch one block north and south of the central bus station. There is a **Co-op Tzafon supermarket** and **HaMashbir department store** in the shopping complex just south of the bus station. On Thursday mornings until noon there's an open air *shuk* on Tel Ḥai St., just north of the bus station. The **post office** is south of the bus station and has **international telephone** and **Poste Restante** services. (Open Sun., Mon., Tues., Thurs. 8am-12:30pm, Wed. 8am-1:30pm, Fri. 8am-noon.) For **first aid (Magen David Adom),** dial 94 43 34; for **police,** dial 94 94 44. The **telephone code** for the Kiryat Shmona area is 06.

Near Kiryat Shmona

Tel Hai תל חי

Three kilometers north of Kiryat Shmona, Tel Ḥai poses on a promontory with an eye-overflowing view of the valley below. First established in 1918 as a military outpost after the withdrawal of British forces from the Upper Galilee, the town has become a symbol of Israel's early pioneer movement and the struggle for the Ḥula Valley region, known until the 1967 conquest of the adjacent Golan Heights as "the Finger of the Galilee." A monument to Yosef Trumpeldor stands on the town's outskirts. The original watchtower and stockade settlement, destroyed by Arabs in 1920, has been reconstructed as a small **museum** (tel. 95 13 33), displaying simple farming tools. (Open Sun.-Thurs. 8am-1pm and 2-5pm; Sept. 2-May 31 Sun.-Thurs. 8am-4pm, Fri. 8am-1pm, Sat. 8:30am-2pm. Admission NIS6, students NIS5.) An excellent slide show in English will be screened for small groups upon request, and an informative brochure is available in English for NIS1.50. Tel Ḥai is also the home of Israel's northernmost **youth hostel** (tel. 94 00 43). Just off the main Metulla-Kiryat Shmona road, the hostel is served by bus #20 and 23 from Kiryat Shmona—ask to go to the youth hostel, not the archeological site. (Reception open daily 8am-12:30pm and 5-7pm. Dorm beds NIS40. Breakfast included.)

Up the road from the hostel is the **military cemetery** containing the graves of the eight of Tel Ḥai, with a statue of a roaring lion facing the mountains to the east. Fifty meters up the road, inside the gates of Kibbutz Kfar Giladi, is **Beit HaShomer** (House of the Guardian, tel. 94 15 65), the IDF museum documenting the history of the early defense organizations in the Upper Galilee and the exploits of the Jewish regiments in the British Army during World War I. (Open Sun.-Thurs. 8am-noon and 2-4pm, Fri. 8am-noon, Sat. 9am-noon. Admission NIS5.)

Nature Reserves

The transformation of the Ḥula Valley in the 1920s by Israel's first Jewish pioneers remains a remarkable achievement. Just south of Kiryat Shmona, the **Ḥula Nature Reserve** (tel. 93 70 69) blossoms where a few decades ago a vast swamp festered. The 775-acre reserve encompasses dense cypress groves and open fields; exotic wildlife such as razorbacks and mongeese dwell within the underbrush. The entrance booth rents binoculars for NIS7, which are helpful for those interested in identifying the infinitude of birds that wings its way over the papyrus thickets, swamps, and reeds. Try to arrive early: the park becomes progressively less serene as families with vocally inquisitive children get there. Buses #840, 841, 511, 541, and 963, leaving frequently from Kiryat Shmona (twice per hour or more), will take you to a junction 2.5km from the entrance to the reserve, and from there you can walk, skip, or crawl. (Open daily 8am-4pm. Admission NIS9, under 18 NIS4.50. English brochure NIS1. Ticket for Hula, Banyas, Gamla, Dan, and Ayun Reserves, available at all 5 sites, NIS19.) The observation area has little shade. There's a kiosk and picnic area for snacks, and a **visitors center** offers exhibits on flora and fauna, and screens a 15-minute film. (Open Sat.-Thurs. 8am-3pm, Fri. 8am-2pm. Admission NIS4.)

Huge oak trees, some nearly 2000 years old, stand in the **Horshat Tal Nature Reserve** (tel. 94 23 60). According to a Muslim legend, the trees, which survive nowhere else in Israel, have been preserved thanks to the 10 messengers of Muhammad who once rested here. Finding a dearth of trees for shade and not a single hitching post for their camels, they pounded sticks into the earth to fasten their mounts. Overnight the sticks sprouted, and the holy men found themselves in a thick forest. The trees now tower over a grassy park which is crammed on Saturdays with picnicking families. Especially enticing is the large, ice-cold **swimming pool**—actually the River Dan ingeniously diverted. (Admission NIS10, children NIS5.) Buses #26, 27, and 36 from Kiryat Shmona all travel the 9km east through Horshat Tal every hour or so. About 100m farther along the road is the **Horshat Tal Camping Ground** (tel. 94 23 60), on the banks of the Dan River. The campground is a convenient base for the rest of the Galilee; however, there's an 11pm curfew and campers must clear out by 1pm. (Tent sites NIS15. 4-person bungalows NIS90.)

One kilometer down the road, **Kibbutz She'ar Yishuv** hosts the SPNI's field school **Beit Sefer Sadeh Hermon** (tel. 94 10 91). Buses #26, 36, and 55 leave from Kiryat Shmona will take you to the kibbutz. The next kibbutz to the northeast, **Kibbutz Dan,** is in the midst of the Hula Valley's thickest **nature reserve** (tel. 95 15 79). The waters come from the Fountain of Dan at the foot of the large Tel Dan, still under excavation. The many springs nourish a dense grove of trees and bushes that grow to record heights. The paths in this small (under 100 acres) but pastoral reserve offer welcome opportunities to cool hot paws in the trickling streams (no swimming allowed). Excavations have revealed the ruins of the ancient Hyksos and Canaanite city of Lakhish, which became the capital city of the tribe of Dan, one of the 12 tribes of Israel. A pre-1948 Arab flour mill has also been restored by the park authorities. To reach the reserve take bus #27 or 36 from Kiryat Shmona to Kibbutz Dan, continue up the main road, and turn left at the sign to the reserve. A 3km walk will bring you to the entrance. (Open daily 8am-5pm, Fri. until 2pm; in winter 8am-4pm. Admission NIS6. The guidebook available at the ticket window is worth the NIS.50.)

Metulla מטולה

Defying its location, Israel's largest village on the Lebanese border stubbornly maintains its sleepy, small-town atmosphere. Metulla, 9km north of Kiryat Shmona, is perfect for those in need of a retreat from the hectic pace of Israeli cities. Only the rumble of transport trucks, the tufts of barbed wire around the town's perimeter, and the brightly painted bomb shelters serve as reminders of its precarious location. Bus #20 runs eight times per day from Kiryat Shmona to Metulla.

Metulla's main spectacle is **Gader HaTova** (The Good Fence) just north of town, an opening in the border barrier between Lebanon and Israel where Lebanese Christians and Druze are allowed to pass through to obtain free medical services, visit relatives, and work in Israel. Israel began passing aid and supplies across the border to Lebanese Christians in 1971, and in 1976 the Good Fence was officially opened. The checkpoint remained open even during the war in Lebanon. From the observation point to the right of the snack bars you can see several Lebanese Maronite Christian villages; on the farthest hill to the right (northeast) stands the Crusader fortress of Beaufort, which was fortified by the PLO and used as a base for shelling Israeli border villages. On the hill farthest to the northwest, look for the Israeli kibbutz Misgav Am, located where the border heads farther north, behind a Lebanese hill. Avoid the cornball "Better a close neighbor than a distant enemy" T-shirts, and get a more intriguing souvenir, sold quietly at the snack bar on the far left: Lebanese money.

Jaded Israelis head to Metulla's new **Canada Centre** (tel. 95 03 70), one of the top sports facilities in Israel and home of its only ice-skating rink. The hefty admission fee of NIS25 entitles you to use the rink, an enormous indoor pool with slides, basketball court, jacuzzi, sauna, and, for an extra NIS3, squash and tennis courts. The complex is located just down the hill from the Yafa Pension. (Open daily 10am-10pm.)

There are two reasonably priced pensions in Metulla, both along the town's main road. The **Yafa Pension** (tel. 94 06 17), at the second bus stop in town and recognizable by its bizarre rock garden and Hebrew sign, has doubles for NIS130 (try to bargain). **Arazim Pension** (tel. 94 41 44), a three-star hotel at the end of the same road, has doubles for US$78 (in summer US$90), including breakfast. The airy restaurant across from the HaMavri Hotel, marked with a prominent English sign reading, logically enough, "Restaurant," serves decent food at low prices. If you continue straight on the main road instead of turning left to the Good Fence, you'll come to the small **Naḥal Ayun Nature Reserve** (tel. 95 15 19) with a picnic area. Through the gate and down the stone steps is a path to the one of the reserve's waterfalls. To reach the Ayun Stream, continue walking south past the brown sign in the picnic area, through the apple groves; the path will lead you to the riverbed beyond which lies Grandmother's house. Unfortunately, in the summer the falls and river run completely dry, except for a few stagnant pools. (Reserve open Sat.-Thurs. 8am-5pm (8am-4pm in winter), Fri. 8am-2pm. Admission NIS6.)

South of Metulla, set back from the road, the cool mountain air is moistened with mist from the **Tanur Waterfall.** With the 18m drop, the density of mist creates the illusion of billowing smoke: *tanur* means "oven." The fall slows to a trickle after June. The Ayun Stream, fed by the pools, later joins the Jordan as it flows south. Local bus #20 from Kiryat Shmona will drop you at the turn-off to the waterfall if you ask; from there it's a three-minute walk to the park.

Kfar Blum כפר בלום

This kibbutz, southeast of Kiryat Shmona, has two unrelated attractions: classical music and kayaking. The **Upper Galilee Chamber Music Days** feature a week-long series of concerts in July by Israel's famous instrumentalists and vocalists as well as lesser-known performers. Tickets are somewhat expensive (NIS17-22 per concert), but rehearsals during the day are free. On a different note, a thrilling 6km kayaking trip (tel. 94 87 55) on the Jordan River costs NIS45 for two people. Bus #29 runs from Kiryat Shmona; schedules are inconvenient.

Golan Heights (HaGolan)
הגולן

The armies of many civilizations have battled over the strategic peaks above the fertile Jordan Valley; the tradition of military conflict here dates back to the Roman siege of Gamla. In more recent times, Israel fought a successful uphill battle in the 1967 Six-Day War to capture the Golan from entrenched Syrian troops. Syria's surprise attack in the 1973 Yom Kippur War pushed Israel back, but the IDF recovered and was successful in its counter-attack. As part of the 1974 disengagement accord outlined in U.S. Secretary of State Henry Kissinger's shuttle diplomacy, Israel returned both this newly conquered territory and part of the land captured in 1967. In 1981, convinced that Syrian possession of the strategically superior Golan could tempt Damascus to attack, Israeli Prime Minister Menaḥem Begin annexed the Heights. This act aroused international protest and considerably upset the Golan's sizeable Druze population, who were now required to carry Israeli identification cards and serve in the Israeli army. Israeli settlements are now scattered amid ruins, rusting tanks, and remote Druze villages. Today, all that remains of the Syrian presence are stone trenches with a commanding view of Israeli communities in the Galilee, and small plastic anti-personnel mines. The eucalyptus trees shading the trenches were planted at the suggestion of Eli Cohen, an Israeli spy in the Damascus government, who in 1967 told Israeli pilots to aim for the distinctive vegetation.

Controversy still simmers over the Heights. Syria claims that the land was seized by an illegal act of aggression and insists on the return of the territory. Israel, for its part, blames the 1967 war on Arab aggression, and counters that Syria's possession of the Golan Heights would pose an intolerable threat to northern Israeli towns.

It is possible to tour most of the Golan by **Egged bus,** but infrequent service along infrequently traveled roads makes careful planning a necessity. Double-check all schedules. In deciding to use buses, you are almost definitely writing off Gamla and Brekhat HaMeshushim; anticipate a fair amount of walking as well, which means you'll need a hat and buckets of water. In general, buses to sites east of and near the Kinneret leave from Tiberias. The Upper Galilee, Ḥula Valley, and northern Golan are served by buses from Kiryat Shmona and occasionally from Tzfat. The bus from Tzfat crosses the **B'not Ya'akov Bridge** over the Jordan River some 10km from Katzrin. According to legend, this is where Jacob and his family were when his daughters predicted the siblings would sell their brother into slavery in Egypt. The name B'not Ya'akov (Daughters of Jacob), however, comes from a Crusader order of nuns by the same name.

Relatively few cars traverse the Golan, and some are driven by people with whom you wouldn't want to spend too much time. There have been reports of attacks in recent years, making hitching a *phenomenally* bad idea. If, despite all this, you are foolhardy enough to set out on your own, be sure to take a good map, a sizable water bottle, and at least a day's worth of food. **Stay on the paved roads, away from leftover Syrian land mines hidden in barren fields. Any fenced-off area should be avoided whether or not there are warning signs.** Despite seasonal minesweeping, the Golan is still littered with the toe- and leg-chomping critters. Hike on marked trails only and avoid fields, fenced areas, or anything that looks suspicious. Heed the warning signs, which are yellow with a red triangle and read "Danger" above Hebrew writing. The Ministry of Tourism *strongly* suggests that visitors to the Golan start from the field school in Katzrin to get maps and information. Many hapless tourists have been known to stray into mine-laden fields, only to be picked up by unamused army personnel.

Organized **tours** of the area are faster, more convenient, and sometimes less expensive in the long run; however, they can be rushed and usually do not allow any time for hiking or swimming. Egged (tel. (06) 79 10 80 or 72 04 74) offers full-day tours of the region from Tiberias on Tuesdays, Thursdays, and Saturdays, and provides an excellent overview of the Upper Galilee and Golan Heights region (US$24, 10% discount with ISIC). There is also a day tour from Tel Aviv (tel. (03) 24 22 71, Thurs. and Sat., US$45). Day tours from Ḥaifa are also available from April to Oct. for US$39. Several private guides, usually based in Tiberias, make similar tours of the Golan and Upper Galilee. From Tiberias, **Moshe Lohen** (tel. 72 16 08) makes the rounds in his taxi for NIS63. Also in Tiberias, **Max Ballhorn** (tel. 79 35 88) gives an Egged-style tour; he is the only licensed operator listed here. In Tzfat, the personable **Shlomo Bar-Ayal** (tel. 97 45 97 or 92 09 61) gives occasional Golan tours at roughly the same price. The best tours are the two- to four-day camping trips organized by the SPNI. Though expensive, the trips visit otherwise inaccessible spots and often include unforgettable funfests like inner-tubing down the Jordan River. For more information ask for the pamphlet entitled *Off the Beaten Track* at any GTIO.

The only other option for fully exploring the Golan is to **rent a car.** While you need a car full of fellow clowns to make it economical, this is an excellent way to tour the area. Eldan, an Israeli company, often undersells Avis, Budget, and Hertz; all four have branches in most cities.

Katzrin קצרין

The young town of Katzrin is the administrative and municipal center of the Golan and an ideal base from which to explore the area. Katzrin enjoys a high standard of living for a young settlement; the town is attractive, but almost numbingly homogeneous with its rows of nearly identical apartment buildings. Ask the bus driver to let you off in front of the **Beit Sefer Sadeh Golan** on Daliyat St. (Golan Field School, tel. 96 12 34), an invaluable source of information on the area; the school even gives lifts in their tour buses when there's room. Their accommodations are often full, but they run an excellent **campground** (tel. 96 12 34), 500m east along the road in front of the school. Registration is ordinarily open 8am-7pm, but if no one is there you can find the manager in the field school. Pleasant bungalows for two cost NIS40, tent sites NIS9 per person.

The **Golan Archeological Museum** (tel. 96 13 50) is in the north end of town, at the opposite end of Daliyat St. from the field school. Despite its tiny size, the museum is one of the most informative of its kind in the country, with thorough explanations in Hebrew and English accompanying most exhibits. The Golan excavations, consisting largely of engraved artifacts of ancient synagogues and houses, testify to agricultural communities dating back to the New Stone Age. (Open Sun.-Thurs. 9am-4pm, Fri. 9am-1pm, Sat. 10am-4pm. Admission NIS7, students NIS4.) Many of the museum's artifacts come from a site south of the city which displays a large synagogue and other public buildings from the Talmudic era. The museum screens an excellent movie in English on the ancient site of Gamla. Ask at the museum for directions to the ruins of the original Katzrin. Next door to the museum there is a **public pool** (open daily 9am-5pm; admission NIS7), a **supermarket,** and the town's few restaurants.

Bus #55 makes two trips per day from Kiryat Shmona, approaching Katzrin from the north and going past the towns at the base of Mt. Ḥermon. Alternatively, bus #841 leaves Kiryat Shmona for Rosh Pina, where you can catch bus #55 or 56 and approach Katzrin from the opposite direction. From Tiberias, bus #19 travels to Katzrin.

A few kilometers north of Katzrin, the road ends in a T heading west to the B'not Ya'akov Bridge or east toward Quneitra. To reach the **Gilabon** (jee-la-boon) and **Dvora waterfalls** in the **Gilabon Nature Reserve,** head 1km east and turn left just before the military base. The approach to the reserve begins about 2km down this road. The reserve contains a well-marked, circular path leading to both waterfalls. Hiking the entire challenging trail takes four to five hours, but if you want a shorter route you can hike down to the Gilabon and back without completing the full circle (2-3 hrs.).

Banyas בניס

The name Banyas comes from the Greek *Paneas* (Pan's Place); the spring here was the site of an ancient sanctuary dedicated to Pan, god of nature and shepherds. Classical Arabic, with no *P* sound, renders "Paneas" *banyas*. These rocks gush with religious and strategic significance: the prophet Elijah (al-Khadar to Muslims) had a shrine by the Banyas. Jesus chose his first disciple here, and prior to 1967, Syria staged attacks into the Ḥula Valley from this spectacularly beautiful site.

The Banyas is in the Golan Heights, but lies only a few minutes down the road from Dan and Ḥorshat Tal in the Upper Galilee. Although the Banyas is the most popular site in the Upper Galilee-Golan area, public transportation to the site is woefully inadequate. Bus #55 travels from Kiryat Shmona through the Golan by way of the Banyas twice per day, but the last bus back to Kiryat Shmona is at noon. If you want to spend the afternoon at the park, you can walk 5km west to Kibbutz Dan; the last bus (#25, 26, or 36) leaves at 7:35pm from the kibbutz. (Park open 8am-5pm, Fri. 8am-4pm. Admission NIS9. Combination ticket to Banyas, Gamla, Dan, Ayun, and Ḥula Valley Reserves NIS19.)

More stunning than the park is the Banyas waterfall (*mapal banyas*), the largest falls in the region. Just across the stream running through the park is a wooden sign marking the beginning of a path to the waterfall. All subsequent signs are in Hebrew, but there is only one fork (just past the pita bakery)—go right. Farther along the path is a clearing that leads to a clean swimming pool fed by the icy waters of the spring; just past the pool three paths intersect; the middle and right-hand paths lead to the waterfall. Local daredevils leap the 15m from the ledge into the foaming pool below. From there the road runs 1km out to the main road, emerging 1km west of the entrance to the park.

Nimrod's Fortress (*Kal'at Nimrod*) stands 1.5km northeast of the Banyas, on a knobby hill visible through the trees. According to the biblical table of Noah's descendants, Nimrod was "the first on earth to be a mighty man" (Genesis 10:8). Legend holds that, as well as fashioning sandals and building the Tower of Babel, he erected this humongous fortress high enough to shoot his arrows up to God. A plaque above one of the many gates reads in Arabic: "God gave him the power to build this castle with his own strength." The strength of his slaves must have been phenomenal as well, judging from the size of the stones they schlepped up the steep cliffs. Historians spoil all the fun and claim that the fortress was actually built by the Muslims, and originally named Qalat Subayba. The view from the top of the fortress is unrivaled anywhere in the Upper Galilee or Golan. You can see Mt. Hermon to the north and the Hula Valley to the southeast. The approach to the castle, from which there is a clear view into the tiny Druze village of Ein Qinya, is just off bus route #55 between Kiryat Shmona and Katzrin; the gate to the road leading to the castle is directly across from the bus stop. The castle is also accessible by a footpath from the Banyas, beginning directly above the springs. The walk takes about 90 minutes each way and has no shade. (Site open 8am-4pm. Admission NIS4.)

Brekhat HaMeshushim בריכת המשושים

A few kilometers southeast of Katzrin, not served by public transportation, is the **Ya'ar Yehudiya Nature Reserve** and the source of the Zavitan River. From just off the road, you can hike down the river through some of Israel's richest greenery. To reach the hiking path head about 2km southeast along the main highway from Katzrin. Watch for a small, weather-beaten orange sign in Hebrew on the right, marking the beginning of the trail. Starting here, you can follow the stream for about two hours through rocky pools swiggling with fish and freshwater crabs during the summer. The trail is clearly marked with red-and-white striped blazes. Before the stream joins the Meshushim stream to the west, the path leads up the steep side of the ravine, across the plateau, and down to Brekhat HaMeshushim (Hexagon Ponds). The formation of hexagonal columns of rocks at the water's edge inspired the name. To leave this area, walk up to the parking lot and follow the 5km access road to the main highway. From here it's 17km to Katzrin; there are no buses. The ponds can also be reached by climbing upriver from the Bet Tzayda Valley (ask for *Tzomet Bet Tzayda*) along the Kinneret or by walking down the path from the deserted village of Jaraba, about 13km south of B'not Ya'akov Bridge off the left side of the road. The river basin is occasionally closed to through traffic due to military maneuvers in the area. More often, temporary roadblocks are set up while mines are detonated a few kilometers ahead.

Gamla גמלא

For years all that was known about the lost city of Gamla was its legend as told by the first-century historian Josephus. Somewhere in the Golan existed the remains of an ancient town whose defenders heroically resisted the Roman army during the Great Rebellion, then chose martyrdom (*The Jewish War*, Book IV, ch. 1). After the Six-Day War, archeologists had the opportunity to scour the area for a spot corresponding to ancient descriptions of the city. Eventually, Shmaryahu Gutman, who claims to have worked with a copy of *The Jewish War* in hand, found the site: 15km southeast of modern Katzrin, on the high escarpments encircling a ridge crowned by the ruins of

Gamla, lay a battlefield missing only the Roman legions. The only access to its walls is via a narrow strip of land connecting it with the higher surrounding ridges. The peak, when viewed from a certain angle, resembles a camel's hump—hence *gamla,* a corruption of the Hebrew *gamal* (camel).

At this site some 2000 years ago, the Romans laid siege to the religious city of Gamla, which was packed with 9000 Jews seeking refuge. After a siege lasting many months, Romans on the nearby hills led the attack down the corridor of land leading to the city. When the legion managed to penetrate Gamla's walls, hordes of Jews were found fleeing up the ridge. The Romans followed, and on the steep trails beyond the confines of the town, the Jews suddenly turned and massacred the legionnaires. Weeks later, a second attack proved too much for the Jews to withstand. Rather than become Roman slaves, these Jews, like those at Masada, chose death, hurling themselves over the steep rock face of the ridge. Only two women survived. Don't miss the outstanding film at the Golan Archeological Museum about Gamla.

Getting to Gamla is tricky without a car. If you catch a ride with a group from the field school you'll also benefit from the guided tour. Otherwise, try to get a ride from Katzrin and walk 1km to the ridge overlooking the ruins. The descent to the ruins along the Roman route takes about 15 minutes, but give yourself time to clamber about the town. The archeologists' camp is at the entrance to the ruins; politely ask someone to show you around. (Site open 8am-4pm.) If you continue on the path past the ruins, you'll reach a lookout point over **Mapal Gamla,** Israel's highest waterfall. The falls are more impressive than the ruins. The path continues above the falls, terminating at the ruins (3hrs.).

Mas'ada and Majdal Shams משעדה, מג׳דל שמס

The Druze of these villages are separated from their Syrian brothers and sisters only by the looming Mt. Hermon. Unlike those on Mt. Carmel, some of these Druze are loyal to Syria. In 1982, they tore up their Israeli citizenship documents in a rebellion backed by PLO-supplied weapons. The Israeli army quickly quashed the revolt, but not the Syrian allegiance. Outwardly, however, the villages are tranquil.

Mas'ada and Majdal Shams are far less primed for tourists than their counterparts in Carmel, with the emphasis here more on tradition than on commercialism. Women walk around swathed in black and men wear the traditional black *shirvelas* (low-hanging baggy pants), which date from Ottoman times. The Qur'an describes Muhammad's reemergence in the world as coming through the "bowels of a man"; devout Turkish Muslims are prepared.

Mas'ada is located at the foot of Mt. Hermon, at the intersection of the roads leading south to Katzrin and west to Kiryat Shmona. Mas'ada's farmers cultivate the valley and terrace the low-lying ridges around the mountain. The numerous Israeli flags and pro-Israel murals are the government's rebuke to the town's demonstrators. Down the road 2km is the famous lake, **Birkat Ram** (in Hebrew, Brekhat Ram). The perfectly round body of water is something of a geological peculiarity, formed not, as it appears, in a volcano-crater, but by underground water-bearing strata. You'll know you've reached the lake when you see the parking lot of the two-story Birkat Ram Restaurant. The restaurant is packed and completely surrounded by fences separating it from the lake. The only decent view is from the porch, and the Druze owners are polite about it although not terribly enthusiastic about gazers. You can rent a paddleboat for NIS10 per hour, or a sailboard for NIS16 for a half hour, but either way you still have to pay NIS1 just to walk down to the dock. Out of the parking lot and to the right you'll see a postcard-worthy view of a striking Druze mosque beneath seasonally snowy Mt. Hermon.

From Mas'ada to **Majdal Shams** ("tower of the rising sun" in Arabic), the largest town in the Golan (pop. 8000), the road runs 5km along a beautiful valley. Two kilometers past Majdal Shams is **Moshav Neveh Ativ,** founded after the mountain was captured in the Six-Day War. The moshav has developed a resort village to take advantage of the ski slopes on the southern face of **Mount Hermon** 10km away; call the ski office at 98 13 37. In summer, bantam two-person bungalows can be rented for NIS48 per night, and lodges for 10-12 people for NIS112 per night. The Alimi family of the moshav rents the guest houses from house #19 (tel. 98 13 33). Bus #55, leaving Kiryat Shmona twice per day, travels to the villages. It's also possible to take a *sherut* taxi from Mas'ada to Kiryat Shmona in the late afternoon for the same price as the bus. The road from Mas'ada to Kiryat Shmona is particularly scenic, running west along a deep gorge and past the hilltop village of Ein Qinya and the silhouette of Nimrod's Fortress.

Continuing toward Syria, still higher levels of the Golan can be reached. About 5km before the border are two kibbutzim, **Merom Golan** and **Ein Zivan.** Merom Golan (Golan Heights) was the first Israeli settlement in the Golan, founded a few months after the Six Day War. Nearby, Mt. Bental is visible; the peak closer to Ein Zivan, blessed with the radio antennae, is Mt. Avital. From the observation point here you can see the destroyed Syrian city of Quneitra. In 1967, Israel captured the town after fierce fighting, only to return it to Syria in the 1974 disengagement agreement. Once a city of 30,000 and headquarters of the Syrian army, Old Quneitra is now a ghost town in the buffer zone of a tense border. Only an occasional UN vehicle breaks its strained silence.

Negev Desert and the Southern Coast הנגב

> We shall bloom the desert land and convert the spacious Negev into a land of strength and power, a blessing to the State of Israel.
>
> —David Ben-Gurion

Ben-Gurion's dream of a transformed Negev has come partially true; in between stretches of land visited only by buses and Bedouin, witness solar-powered highway lights, roadside payphones, and improbable stretches of green culled out of the desert by innovative kibbutz agriculture. In the past year, the Negev has seen blooming of a different sort: its plentiful open land has made it the perfect place for the Israeli government to build housing for the vast numbers of Russian and Ethiopian Jewish immigrants. Especially around Be'ersheva, housing complexes sprout more regularly than any kibbutz's tomatoes.

Come to the Negev to see ancient remains and austere beauty, not to party in its haphazard cities (Eilat perhaps excepted). **Field schools** (Beit Sefer Sadeh) in Sdeh Boker, Mitzpeh Ramon, Ein Gedi, and Eilat should be your first stop for hiking information, guided tours, and hostel accommodations. An inexpensive way to reach most of the Negev's natural sights is to join a **Society for the Protection of Nature in Israel** tour (see Useful Organizations in the Israel Introduction). Alternatively, a bus ride from Be'ersheva through Mitzpeh Ramon—if you watch the scenery and not the soldiers or music videos—can provide an overview of the rugged terrain.

Despite water from the Kinneret piped in to irrigate some of the artificial oases, most of the Negev remains wild and desolate. What success Israel has had in "making the desert bloom," however, symbolizes for Israelis their country's triumph as a whole. Arab farmers, who only very rarely can secure permission to dig needed wells, are resentful. The **Negev Mountains,** in the southwestern part of the desert bordering the Sinai, glory in the most dramatic scenery. At the western edge of the Negev is Israel's south coast, which offers several historical sites and excellent beaches.

To the south of Ashkelon lie the city of **Gaza** (Ghaza in Arabic, Azza in Hebrew) and the **Gaza Strip,** a small stretch of coastline that was captured by the advancing

Egyptian army in 1948 and occupied by the Israeli military in 1967. The Camp David Accords did not return Gaza to Egypt; instead they vaguely promised negotiated autonomy. In December 1987, Gaza was the site where the Palestinian uprising (*intifada*) was sparked. With a population of 775,000 Palestinians crammed into a mere 46km, and 29,000 of them living in refugee camps, conditions are appalling. Gaza, and particularly the refugee camps, have often been the site of the uprising's most violent demonstrations, the harshest Israeli crackdowns, and, more recently, intra-Palestinian clashes. With the exception of the 4000 die-hard Jewish settlers living in the Strip, few Israelis have much desire to continue to rule Gaza. **Visiting here is dangerous and not recommended.** If you do wish to go, though, make sure to do so under the auspices of an appropriate humanitarian agency. Your embassy or consulate might be able to direct you to such an agency; in any case, be sure to check in with your embassy or consulate before going.

Summer visitors to the south coast should be aware that the Dead Sea and surrounding areas, in stark contrast to the arid climate just a few miles inland, are among the most horrendously humid parts of Israel. When in the desert or the heat of the south coast, drink at least a gallon of liquid daily, wear a hat, get an early start, and try to avoid physical exertion between noon and 3pm (see Health in the General Introduction). Wintertime visitors should bring rugged clothing in preparation for harsh winds and rains.

Partly because of the climate, but mostly because of the political tensions near the Gaza Strip, hitchhiking is *not an option;* incidents in recent years have made "tremping" dangerous for both men and women. Knifings of both Arabs and Jews, sadly, are no longer a surprise. Sleeping on the beach, except within the cities of Ashkelon and Ashdod, is definitely out; military patrols comb the beach at night and, especially in the south, often rake the full length of the beach and later check the sand for footprints, looking for infiltrators.

Buses to the Negev, particularly to Be'ersheva, Ashkelon, and Eilat, leave frequently from Tel Aviv and Jerusalem. Buses to Taba (the Sinai) and Rafiah (Cairo) borders leave from Jerusalem, Tel Aviv, Ashkelon, and Eilat.

Be'ersheva באר שבע

Tell any traveler you meet in Israel that you're going to Be'ersheva, and you'll immediately be asked: "Why?" Unless you're a Russian immigration buff or volunteer, or you want to see pioneering first hand, Be'ersheva's only major attraction is the Thursday morning Bedouin market. Consider a Thursday morning trip.

Be'ersheva means both "well of the oath" and "well of seven" in Hebrew, and the Bible (Genesis 21:25-31) offers both etymologies. The story goes that Abimelekh's servants seized a well that Abraham claimed to have dug. The dispute ended with a covenant in which Abraham offered seven ewes to Abimelekh in exchange for recognition as the well's rightful owner. The seven ewes were testimony to Abraham's oath that it was indeed he who dug the well.

When Israel recaptured it from Egypt in 1948, Be'ersheva was a village of under 2000 people. Its growth since then reflects that of Israel; the city is now home to immigrants from Morocco, Syria, Central Europe, Russia, Argentina and Ethiopia, as well as the largest Albanian Jewish community in the world. Today, Be'ersheva is the focal point for Russian immigrant absorption. In what one city official called "the largest home-building enterprise the world has ever seen," Be'ersheva has absorbed over 20,000 immigrants since 1990, building 30,000 housing units. Its population is expected to double by 1994.

Orientation and Practical Information

Be'ersheva is located in the middle of the northern Negev, 40km from both the Mediterranean and Dead Seas, and is approximately 80km southwest of Jerusalem. Begin your Be'ershevian tour by purchasing the indispensable *Big Map*. The relatively useless GTIO is almost always closed. If it is, get your map at the **town hall.** To reach the Old Town—renowned as the Thursday *axis mundi* of Bedouin marketing—walk through the main exit of the bus station (next to the information desk), and turn to the left. Take any bus (signs are in English); most pass the *shuk* (the building with the metal arches) and continue to the Old Town. On foot, cross the parking lot and make a left onto Ben Tzvi St. Make another left onto HaNesi'im Blvd., which turns into Herzl St.; it's a 10-minute trip.

Town Hall: From the central bus station, go left on Ben Tzvi St. and walk one block to HaNesi'im. Turn right and go three blocks up. For NIS8, the *Big Map* will make navigating the lackluster Old Town and hyper-modern New City entirely feasible. A talking computer service says "If you need more information, go ahead, make my day" with an Israeli accent. The advisor to the mayor Yitzhak Yellin (tel. 46 38 79 or 46 37 90/1), a former Bostonian, is eager to assist any *Let's Go*ons. Open 24 hrs.

Government Tourist Information Office (GTIO): (tel. 23 60 01/2/3), across the street from the main entrance to the bus station. Sparse information about accommodations and events. Open Sun.-Thurs. 8:30am-5pm.

Banks: Bank Leumi, to the left of the central bus station (tel. 392 22). Open Sun., Tues., Thurs. 8:30am-12:30pm and 4-5:30pm, Mon. 8:30am-1:30pm, Wed. 8:30am-12:30pm, Fri. 8:30am-noon. Emergency number after hours: 514 94 00. **Bank HaPoalim,** 40 Ha'Atzma'ut St. (tel. 66 26 61), corner of HeHalutz St. Open Mon. and Wed. 8:30am-12:30pm, Sun., Tues., Thurs. 8:30am-12:30pm and 4-6pm, Fri. 8:30am-noon.

Post Office: (tel. 321 75), on the northwest corner of HaNesi'im Blvd. and Ben Tzvi St., across from the bus station. Open Sun.-Tues. and Thurs. 8am-7pm, Wed. 8am-1:30pm, Fri. 8am-noon. **International telephones** and **Poste Restante** here; no phones during renovations. There are smaller branch offices on 51 Hadassah St. and in the bus station. All open Sun.-Tues. and Thurs. 8am-12:30pm and 3:30-6pm, Wed. 8am-1:30pm, Fri. 8am-noon.

Telephone code: 057. Will soon change to 07. 5-digit numbers are being phased out; if it starts with a 3 or a 7, try adding a 2 first. Or call information, 144.

Central Bus Station: (tel. 43 05 85 or 743 43), near the municipal market on the northeastern edge of the Old Town. Buses #443, 445, and 446 run approximately every 30min. to Jerusalem (6:15am-7pm, NIS14). Avoid #440; it also runs to Jerusalem, but it goes through the West Bank with a change of buses in Hebron. Buses #394 (express) and 393 run hourly to Eilat until 5pm (NIS24); #370 runs every 10-15min. to Tel Aviv until 8pm (NIS11), and #369 until 9:45pm. **Luggage storage** open Sun.-Thurs. 8am-4:30pm, Fri. 8am-1pm. NIS4 per piece per day.

Taxis: Yael-Daroma, 195 Keren Kayemet LeYisrael St. (tel. 28 11 44/5). From central bus station make a left on HaNesi'im Blvd., continue for about 10min. and make a right on Keren Kayemet LeYisrael St. *Sherut* taxis to Jerusalem (NIS14.30), Eilat (NIS29), and Tel Aviv (NIS12); cheaper than buses. **HaTzvi Taxi** (tel. 393 32), outside the central bus station, travels within the city and surrounding area. **HeHalutz Taxi** (tel. 33 33 32), corner of Ha'Atzma'ut and HeHalutz.

Car Rental: Rumor has it that car rental agencies charge according to clients' estimated naiveté: Insist on seeing the printed rate sheet. **Eldan** has the cheapest prices of all the major agencies, but you'll have to take a taxi (approx. NIS6.50) to the Desert Inn (Neot HaMidbar) to get to their office (tel. 43 03 44); US$40 per day for 100km and 24¢ per km thereafter. **Hertz** is across from the bus station at 6a Ben Tzvi St. (tel. 738 78); US$47 per day for 200km, and 27¢ per km thereafter.

English Bookstores: Used books at **Mini Book,** 67 HaHistadrut St. (tel. 43 33 96), in the passage way between Hadassah and Histadrut St., opposite Israel Discount Bank. Open Sun.-Wed. 9:30am-1pm and 4-7pm, Thurs.-Fri. 9:30am-1pm. **Steimatzky's,** in the Kanion near the bus station (tel. 303 01). Open Sun.-Thurs. 9am-9pm, Fri. 9am-2pm, Sat. 8-10pm.

Pharmacies: Yerushalayim, 34 Herzl St. (tel. 770 34). Open Sun.-Thurs. 8am-7:30pm, Fri. 8am-2pm. **HaNegev,** 94 Keren Kayemet LeYisrael St. (tel. 277 016). Open Sun.-Thurs. 8am-2pm, 4-7:30pm, Fri. 8am-2pm. **Super Pharm,** in the Kanion (tel. 28 13 71 or 28 07 35/6), enter through door opposite bus station. Open Sun.-Thurs. 9am-midnight, Fri. 9am-3pm.

Hospital: Soroka Hospital, HaNesi'im Blvd. (tel. 66 01 11). Bus #4 or 7, and tell the driver to let you off at the new emergency room.

First Aid: Magen David Adom, 40 Bialik St. (tel. 101 for emergencies, otherwise 783 33).

Police: On Herzl St. at the corner of Keren Kayemet LeYisrael St. (tel. 100 for emergencies, otherwise 46 27 44).

Accommodations

If you can avoid sleeping in Be'ersheva, do so. Your choices here include the expensive four-star Neot Hamidbar, an international youth barracks, and a collection of dimly-lit '50s throwbacks with mix-and-match Eastern European decor. It's wiser to arrive early Thursday morning for the Bedouin market, visit a few museums and maybe the university in the afternoon, and then head to the attractive and reasonably priced hostels at Sdeh Boker and Mitzpeh Ramon. If, however, you insist:

Beit Yatziv Youth Hostel (HI), 79 Ha'Atzma'ut St. (tel. 27 74 44), a few blocks from the Old Town. Bus #13 will take you directly to the hostel from the bus station every 45min., or you can take any bus to the town center and walk past the Negev Museum on Ha'Atzma'ut St. Clean, large complex, but spartan, stuffy rooms (the small windows open only halfway, and without cross-ventilation the fans don't provide much relief). Rooms contain 4 or 8 beds, a desk, and 2 small closets. Only 1 key per room. This 270 bed hostel is almost always full due to special arrangements with conventioneers and military overflow and it is likely that you will be forced to take the smaller, more expensive 4-person room. Reception open until 9pm. No curfew. Lobby features avocado vinyl and brown plastic chairs, postage and coffee machines, pay phone, and snackbar open until 9pm. Private rooms in the guest house just as stifling, but with carpeting and sheets. No kitchen facilities. NIS35 (8-person room), NIS41 (4-person room), nonmembers add NIS3. Private singles in guest house NIS69, doubles NIS104. Large breakfast included.

Aviv Hotel, 40 Mordei HaGeta'ot St. (tel. 278 059), off Keren Kayemet LeYisrael St. Bulgarian owners Berta and Shlomo Ḥalyu run a tidy, pleasant establishment. Side and front rooms have balconies overlooking the center of town, ancient (but functioning) private baths, TVs, phones, and closets. A challenge: try to guess which plants are plastic and which are real. Check-in until 7:30pm. Singles NIS54. Doubles NIS77. Breakfast included.

Arava Hotel, 37 HaHistadrut St. (tel. 278 792), just off Keren Kayemet LeYisrael St. Rooms are plain and a bit cramped, but almost all have A/C and clean private baths. Small TV lounge. Admire longingly the framed camel prints over your 1960s style bed. Kitchen facilities available at manager's discretion. Local calls possible from front desk (NIS1). Many *olim* from Russia and Argentina make permanent homes here. Singles NIS55. Doubles NIS85-97. Breakfast included.

Food

Old Town Be'ersheva's Keren Kayemet LeYisrael St. is lined with numerous excellent falafel, *shwarma*, pizza, and sandwich stands (NIS 2.50-9). For a more serious meal, try **Restaurant Hungarian** at 55 HaHistadrut St. (tel. 35262), just off the *midreḥov* (full meals NIS15-20). **Bis LeḤol Kis**, 98 Mordei HaGeta'ot St., (tel. 277 178) offers large meat- or fish-based homestyle meals (NIS11-15; Open Sun.-Fri. 11:30am-4pm). An excellent bakery on the corner of Smilensky St. and Trumpeldor St. has *borekas*, rolls, and other baked goodies for only NIS1.50-2.50 (open 24 hours).

If you need an American food fix, head to the Kanion HaNegev mall across from the bus station. A food court is on the lower floor. A womba double Bomba burger at **Burger Ranch** costs NIS6.90, and pizza costs NIS4-5. The food court also offers full Chinese meals at **China Town** for NIS 13.50-15. Most restaurants in the Kanion are open Sun.-Thurs. 9am-midnight, Fri. 9am-1am, Sat. 10am-10pm. The mall features a number of boutiques, a department store, a movie theater, and a **Hypershuk supermarket**. (Most stores open Sun.-Thurs. 9am-9pm, Fri. 9am-3pm, Sat. 8-10pm.) T h e cheapest place to buy drinks and fresh produce is the *shuk*, located just south of the central bus station and easily identifiable by its arched metal rooftops. The Thursday Bedouin market also has cheap prices for foodstuffs. Shop for *shabbat* at either **Supermarket Co-op**, 2 Keren Kayemet LeYisrael St., at the corner of Herzl St. and the *midreḥov* (open Sun.-Thurs. 9am-8:30pm, Fri. 9am-2pm) or **Supermarket Aḥim Greenberg**, on the corner of Ha'Atzma'ut St. and Beit Eshel St. (open Sun.-Thurs. 7am-8pm, Fri. 7am-3:30pm). If you forget to buy food in advance, you can eat at the **Jade Palace**, 79 HaHistadrut St. (tel. 753 75 or 711 70), which serves the best Chinese food and is the nicest restaurant in town. Soups NIS6.50, main dishes NIS15-35. (Open daily noon-11:45pm.) For desert dessert, nothing beats **Ice Cream Be'ersheva**, 50 Hadassah St. (tel. 277 072), where a waffle cone with 5 scoops is NIS6. (Open daily 9am-1am.)

Sights

Be'ersheva's chief attraction is its Thursday **Bedouin Market,** located just south of the municipal market and bus station. Trading begins around 6am and concludes by noon. These Bedouin speak relatively intelligible English and may compliment your beautiful eyes while charging six times the going rate. Don't be embarrassed to offer a fraction of the asking price—a small fraction. The best haggling strategy is to offer what *you* want to pay even before inquiring about their prices. Always be polite and friendly. If vendors decline your bid, but call or chase after you, you stand a good chance of getting the item close to or at your original offer. Alternatively, if your Arabic or Hebrew is good, eavesdrop on prices quoted to natives.

Hundreds of Bedouin, both the semi-settled from around Be'ersheva and the nomads from deep in the desert, gather in the area around Hebron St. to sell sheep, goats, clothes, cloth, jewelry, ceramics, spices, and even digital watches. Animals are generally traded and sold on the city's southernmost limits, with camels strictly prohibited from the market. (Security concerns make the commotion of large livestock an unnecessary risk.) The northern part of the market features tremendous quantities of schlocky clothing, amazingly all selling for NIS10. "More fashionable" items may be marked as high as NIS20-30. As you head further south, the quantity of rusty cans, scraps of paper and dust increases, the smell of goat dung becomes stronger, and you can buy yourself live rabbits, chickens, doves, or even parakeets, fruits, vegetables, and nuts, or plastic garbage and trinkets. The southernmost part of the market features the real gems: beaten copperware, Bedouin robes, fabrics, rugs, and ceramic items—all at bargain basement prices.

Be'ersheva's main attraction after the Bedouin market is the **Negev Museum** at 18 Ha'Atzma'ut St. (tel. 391 05; take bus #5, 12, or 13 to the last stop). Set in a Turkish mosque built in 1915, the museum chronicles five millenia of the history of Be'ersheva and the surrounding region—from the Chalcolithic period to the present. The museum focuses on ancient Be'ersheva (Tel Sheva); the models of the site make the museum a wise first stop before visiting the actual *tel*. The museum's prize possession is the **animal mosaic,** a delicate 6th-century CE church floor depicting animals woven together in an intricate geometric design. Because the museum is located across the street from an army base, its minaret is closed to visitors. (The museum is under renovation, and it is unclear exactly when it will reopen. Call ahead.) The adjacent **art gallery** is tiny and houses rotating exhibits of contemporary art. (Open Sun.-Thurs. 10am-6:30pm, Fri. and Sat. 10am-1pm. Admission NIS2.50, children NIS2, Sat. free. One ticket admits you to both the museum and the gallery.)

Five kilometers northeast of the city are the impressive ruins at **Tel Be'ersheva** (tel. 460 103), which have recently been renovated and made a national park. After exalting in remains of a Roman fortress dating from 200 CE, frolic through houses from the 8th century BCE or toss a coin in a dry, 12th century BCE well. Organized tours are most enlightening. Bus #55 runs to the site Sun.-Thurs. at 2:10, 3:15, and 5:45pm (last return bus 6pm), on Friday at 11:15am and 3pm (last return bus 3:15pm; NIS1.80). Next to the ruins is a visitors center with a cafeteria, a nice-but-expensive restaurant, and a small-but-interesting **museum** devoted to the life of the Bedouins. The center is open daily 9am-11pm; the museum is open Sun.-Thurs. 10am-5pm and Fri.-Sat. 10am-1pm (admission NIS2, students NIS1.50); the archeological site is always open and free. Solo women should not accept offers of personal tours of the site.

Nearby is contemporary Tel Sheva, a village of Bedouin where residents wear traditional clothing and retain native customs. To reach the village take bus #55. (Travelers wishing to visit the archeological site will also end up at the village if they don't make their destination absolutely clear to the bus driver.)

Back in town, another historical attraction, **Abraham's well,** is upstaged by the touristy restaurant The Well, which sits over its namesake at the busy intersection of Ha'Atzma'ut and Hebron St. at the southeastern edge of town. This is thought to be the disputed site where Abraham offered Abimelekh seven ewes in exchange for recognition of Abraham's ownership of the well. (Open daily 8am-7pm. Free.) To get to the well, walk down Ha'Atzma'ut St. through the Old Town. Basically, the well consists of 2 holes in the ground covered by ornate black grates, with rotting soda cans on the bottom. None too exciting, but you may be able to get a map of Be'ersheva from the visitor's center attendant. The dearth of maps in the city might make the trip to the well worthwhile for that reason alone.

The large, white, sandcastle-style building next door to the town hall is Yad La-Banim (tel. 377 04), literally, "Memorial to the Sons" (of Be'ersheva fallen in war). The four volumes at the end of the tour provide a poignant look at the personal price paid for Israel's survival—each page offers a photograph and brief biography of a fallen Be'ersheva veteran. (Open Sun.-Thurs. 9am-1pm, 5-8pm, Fri. 8am-12:30pm, Sat. 10am-1pm. Free.) The modern campus of **Ben-Gurion University,** founded in 1969, lies in the northeastern corner of the city. For visits, contact Guest Relations, tel. 46 11 11 or 46 12 79. At Merkaz Ta'obel (tel. 305 20 or 49 22 88), near the university dorms, 40 Ethiopians sell their folk art on Tuesday and Wednesday mornings.

Perhaps the most unusual sight in Be'ersheva is the **Memorial of the Negev Palmaḥ Brigade,** located on the northeastern outskirts of the city and dedicated to the soldiers who fell in the 1948 campaign to capture the desert. Many of the Hebrew inscriptions give day-by-day accounts of the battles; the rest explain the significance of the sculptures. Some of the sculptures with more obvious meanings include a watchtower and aqueduct, a lacerated snake representing the defeated enemy forces, and the perforated and split Memorial Dome (free). It's a long, sweltering walk to the memorial; there is no direct public transportation. Bus #55 passes the spur road (from there it's a 1km walk), or you can take a taxi for under NIS15.

Entertainment

Be'ersheva is a surprisingly lively at night, especially around Trumpeldor St. Most of the pubs open at 8 or 9pm, but remain quiet until about 11pm, when an almost exclusively Israeli crowd starts pouring in. (Maccabee NIS5-6.) **Trombone,** on 18 Ha'Avot St. (tel. 277 670), at the corner of Trumpeldor, is another informal restaurant/pub with a more intimate atmosphere. Beer NIS6 and main dishes from the kitchen NIS7-15. (Open nightly 8:30pm-4am.) The wildest place in Be'ersheva is **HaSimta** (The Alley), 16 Trumpeldor St. Prepare for a deafening mixture of Israeli, American, and European music, and a crowd that sings along. Must be 18. (Open nightly 8pm-3am.)

If you're too sober for the pub scene, head for one of Be'ersheva's several movie theaters. **Hekhal HaTarbut** on HaNesi'im St. (tel. 710 65 or 46 30 71), near the municipality building, **Gilat** (tel. 41 42 19), and the four cinemas in the Kanion mall are the only ones open on Friday night. On Saturday, dive into the **swimming pool** at the Beit Yatziv Youth Hostel, 79 Ha'Atzma'ut St. (Open Sun.-Fri. 8:30am-5pm, Sat. 8:30am-4pm. Admission NIS10, *shabbat* NIS12. NIS3 discount for hostel guests.) More mellow still is an annual international **harmonica and accordion** festival with street performers and classical, pop, blues, and soul concerts. The festival is in early July; ask at the GTIO for details.

Near Be'ersheva

Arad ערד

Located on the border between the Negev and the Judean deserts, the dry climate and unpolluted, pollen-free air of the appropriately named Arad attract asthma sufferers from all over the world. Founded as a small residential settlement in 1960 for laborers from the Dead Sea Works, Arad has grown rapidly (population now 15,000 including writer Amos Oz, an illustrious recent arrival.) The discovery of a nearby natural gas field has made Arad an important industrial area as well.

Arad's **central bus station** is on Yehuda St. across from the town's commercial center. Bus #389 speeds to Tel Aviv (NIS15.50); bus #388 chugs to Be'ersheva

(NIS7.50). There are no direct buses to Jerusalem from Arad; you'll have to change in Be'ersheva. Buses #384 and #385 run to Ein Bokek (NIS7), Masada (NIS9.50), and Ein Gedi (NIS10). Many buses, including some to the Dead Sea, leave from the station up the hill on Yerushalayim St. Special routes apply during the music festival (see below).

Across from the bus station is the town's **commercial center/mall,** containing most of Arad's important institutions. The **tourist office** (tel. 95 81 44) is located on the opposite side of the center from the bus station (open Sun.-Thurs. 9am-noon and 5-7pm, Fri. 9am-noon). Even better is the **Arad Visitor's Center** (tel. 95 44 09), located just across Ben Yair St. from the tourist office. (Office and museum open Sat.-Thurs. 9am-5pm and Fri. 9am-2pm.)

The **post office** (tel. 95 70 88) next door to the tourist office has Poste Restante and **international telephone** services. (Open Sun.-Tues. and Thurs. 8am-12:30pm and 3:30-6pm, Wed. 8am-1:30pm, Fri. 8am-noon.) The commercial center also includes a **pharmacy** (tel. 95 74 39; open Sun.-Thurs. 8:30am-7:30pm, Fri. 8:30am-1:30pm), a **Co-op Supermarket** across the street from the bus station (open Sun.-Tues. 7:30am-1:30pm and 4-7pm, Wed. and Thurs. 7:30am-1:30pm and 4-8pm, Fri. 7am-2pm), and four **banks** (most open Sun., Tues., and Thurs. 8:30am-12:30pm and 4-5:45pm, Mon. and Wed. 8:30am-12:30pm, Fri. 8:30am-noon).

Stay at the quaint **Blau-Weiss Youth Hostel (HI)** on Arad St. (tel. (057) 95 71 50). Walk east on Yehuda St., take a right on Palmaḥ St. past the **police** (tel. 100 or 95 70 44) and **first-aid** (tel. 101 or 95 72 22) stations and follow the signs. The hostel is closed 1:30-4:30pm; you can check in between 4:30pm and 8pm. The rooms are spotless and there is a kitchen and TV room, but no A/C. Make reservations in advance, especially during festival season. (Dorm beds NIS40. Singles NIS69. Doubles NIS104. Nonmembers add NIS3. Breakfast included.)

At ancient Arad (**Tel Arad**), about 10km west of the modern town, two archeological sites have been discovered and partly reconstructed: a 5000-year-old Canaanite city and an Israelite fortress dating from King Solomon's era, with a sanctuary resembling the Temple in Jerusalem. Although the area has been inhabited constantly through the ages, this incarnation of Arad was essentially destroyed in 701 BCE by Sanherib the Assur. (Open Sun.-Thurs. 8am-5pm, Fri. 8am-3pm, Oct.-March Sun. Thurs. 8am-4pm, Fri. 8am-2pm. Admission NIS4.50, students NIS2.50. No public transportation; get information on tours from Visitors Center.)

The best time to visit Arad (or to avoid it if you hate crowds or kids or crowds of kids) is in mid-July during the annual rock festival. Israelis talk about Festival Arad as the local annual Woodstock. Virtually every Israeli rock star (see Music in the Israel introduction) performs during this unique week; therefore, every Israeli kid with any self-respect shows up in Arad this week as well, and hundreds of thousands line the streets, crowding free public campgrounds and public telephone booths (you can forget about making phone calls during the festival). The area around the commercial center fills with milling mobs of merry musicians, mimes, and moshavnikim. Rock and roll is still alive and will probably never die. The rock concerts (tickets cost NIS30) and other cultural events take place in and around Arad, with some also at Masada (special buses run for ticket holders only at the proper times). Bring a sleeping bag with you and join the throngs sleeping in the campgrounds and elsewhere. Food sellers also abound, and restaurants often offer special prices.

Sdeh Boker and Ein Avdat שדה בוקר, עין עבדת

Lost amidst endless Negev desert, verdant Sdeh Boker is named for the mountain behind it. Arabs named this mountain "Jabal Baqara" (Mt. Cow), which Israelis later changed to the closest Hebrew cognate, "Har Boker" (Rancher Mt.). The kibbutz, established in 1952 on a plain, adopted the name Sdeh Boker (Rancher's Field). This aviary/oasis produces olives, apricots, kiwis, and other fruit for domestic and international markets, as well as wheat, corn, and livestock.

David Ben-Gurion, Israel's founding father and first prime minister—and a Sdeh Boker member—considered settlements in the Negev a top priority. When experts advised that developing the Negev was a waste of money and time, Ben-Gurion insisted on searching for unconventional methods of taming the desert. Referring to water preservation techniques employed by an ancient people of the region, he asked, "If the Nabateans can do it, why can't we?" He was so taken with the young pioneers building fledgling Sdeh Boker in a 1953 visit that he decided, at the age of 67, to resign from office and settle in the middle of the Negev desert. Ben-Gurion fans hoping to follow in the Old Man's footsteps by visiting Sdeh Boker would do well to shell out the cash (socialism be damned) and rent a car for the day. With infrequent bus service and rather long distances between areas of interest, travelers not sleeping over may find their idealism evaporating along with all their bodily fluids. It is possible to get around by bus and by foot, but be prepared for interminable waits and aching feet.

Ben-Gurion's home, **Tzreef Ben-Gurion** (tel. (057) 56 03 20 or 55 84 44), only slightly larger than the residences of his neighbors, has been left unaltered except for the installation of glass doors separating visitors from the living room and library. Visitors can see how this brilliant and idealistic man decided to set a personal example for young Israelis to follow. Pictures and documents are on display, giving the visitor some tangible connection to the legendary leader. Only one picture hangs in Ben-Gurion's bedroom: at his own request, Mahatma Gandhi.

Books written by Ben-Gurion are on sale for NIS5.50-46. (Open Sun.-Thurs. 8:30am-3:30pm, Fri. 8:30am-2pm, Sat. and holidays 9am-2:30pm. Free.) Take bus #60, which runs from Be'ersheva (NIS8.40). The stop for the house is one stop after the kibbutz. (Ask for Tzreef Ben-Gurion.)

Next door is the **Sdeh Boker Inn** (tel. 56 03 79), a snack shop where you can get full meals for NIS15 and stock up on liquids. (Open Sun.-Thurs. 8am-4pm, Fri. 8am-3pm, Sat 8:30am-3pm; the management will cook meals for you until 9pm if you call ahead.)

If you take the bus to the road just after Tzreef Ben-Gurion (two stops past the kibbutz and head for the distant complex of buildings, you'll discover a fascinating natural and futuristic world well worth visiting for a day or two.

The **Ben-Gurion Institute for Desert Research** (affiliated with Ben-Gurion University of the Negev) located here is famous for its research into desert food production, reforestation, and solar energy. The *madrasha* (institute) staff conducts studies ranging from applied geobotanics to low-water desert architecture and hydroponics. You must call ahead. As you walk through the large gate near the bus stop continue along the road past the **Ben-Gurion Research Institute and Archives,** where famous scholars including Harvard's Glen Schwaber have been constrained. On your left you will see a shopping center with a **post office** (open Sun.-Thurs. 9-11am and 1-2pm, Fri. 9-11;30am), gift shop, supermarket and ice cream shop.

Also in the shopping center is the office of the **Bet Sefer Sadeh** (best translated as the "School in and of Nature" but usually called the field school). The school sponsors a light and sound show about Ben-Gurion's life and activities at the kibbutz. Individuals should call (tel. 56 57 17 or 56 58 28) to find out about a given day's screenings. (Shows in Hebrew, English or Russian; Admission NIS5, students/children NIS3.) Be sure to take advantage of the field school's superb hiking expeditions in and around Sdeh Boker: trek to the icy spring and waterfall at Ein Avdat, to Ein Akev, or to the nearby **tombs of David and Paula Ben-Gurion.** At NIS150 for four hours of a guide's time, this may be only accessible for groups. Or sleep in the **hostel** on the canyon's edge and spend the evening hobnobbing with students of desert living and Israeli nature guides-to-be. (tel. 56 50 16 or 56 58 28.) Dorm rooms are separated into two areas of three beds each, with spotless, modern, private baths, and incredible views of the Avdat canyon. Kitchen facilities are available. The palm-shaded, sand-colored exterior affords maximum interior coolness and surrounds a lovely courtyard. (Dorm beds NIS19.10. Doubles NIS90.)

Arrangements at the roomier **Sdeh Boker Guest House** should be made at least one day in advance. (Contact Shosh at her home at 56 59 33, or in her office at 56 50 79,

8am-4pm.) Every conceivable amenity. Cavernous common room offers a dizzying view of the canyon. The feature attraction, though, is free use of the swimming pool. Singles US$35, Doubles US$40.

If you want to explore on your own, the tombs of David and Paula Ben-Gurion are 3km from the *tzreef* on a cliff, with a jaw-breaking view of the Canyon of Tzin. Take bus #60 to Ben-Gurion University and follow the signs. The tomb area is immaculately kept. In 1992, ex-USSR ex-president Mikhail Gorbachev lay a wreath at Ben-Gurion's grave and praised the success of Ben-Gurion's style of socialism.

Avdat עבדת

The magnificently preserved ruins of a 3rd-century BCE Nabatean city are perched high upon a hill, 5km south of Sdeh Boker in Avdat. (The sizable oasis just below the ruins grows out of Israeli experimentation with ancient water techniques borrowed from the Nabateans.) At the intersection of the caravan routes from Petra and Eilat, Avdat once thrived as a stopping point for travelers, and as a strategic base for the Nabateans' notorious raids: from Avdat they could see caravans as far away as Mitzpeh Ramon or Sdeh Boker. Romans captured the city in 106 CE and exploited the agricultural expertise of the region's former rulers. The city flourished again during the Byzantine period, and most of the visible ruins date from this time. 7th-century Islamic marauders protected the Roman baths, but not much else. The most important Nabatean remains are a handsome esplanade on top of the hill, a winding staircase which led to a Nabatean temple, and a potter's workshop; all date back to the first century CE. The best of the Byzantine remains include a 20-ft. high wall, a street, a monastery, two churches, and a baptistry, all from the 6th century CE. The park is open daily 6am-7pm (admission NIS5, students NIS4). Drinking water is available near the bathrooms. Bus #60, which also runs to Sdeh Boker, makes the one-hour trip from Be'ersheva 12 times daily Sunday-Thursday and six times on Friday. Make it clear to the driver that you want to go to the archeological site and not Ein Avdat, the mid-desert oasis. Bring water for the 15-minute hike to the ruins since the summit is completely dry.

Mitzpeh Ramon מצפה רמון

In the 1920s and '30s, **Makhtesh Ramon** (the Ramon Crater) did not appear on any British map. After the founding of the State of Israel, the new government came upon the crater during its systematic exploration of the Negev. Until a more direct route to Eilat was built from the Dead Sea about 13 years ago, what came to be known as "Mitzpeh Ramon" (Ramon Observation Point) was the central stop-off en route southward. A camp for highway construction workers developed into a town by 1954, and later evolved into a support unit for the military observatory that crowns a hill to the west. Since the return of the Sinai to Egypt, Mitzpeh Ramon's importance as a southern tourist and military outpost has grown. Unfortunately, in recent years Mitzpeh Ramon has been in the news for another reason: it has Israel's highest unemployment rate.

Mitzpeh Ramon is set 900m above Makhtesh Ramon, the most gargantuan of the Negev's four craters. A half-kilometer deep, 7km wide, and 40km long, it is the largest single natural crater in the world. Its rock formations are millions of years old, its vegetation comes from four different climatic zones, and evidence of human life in the area predates written history. The gaping hole in the ground looks like the imprint of a giant asteroid, but it's actually a natural pit with steep walls, drained by a single wadi. For obvious reasons, the area has been declared a nature reserve, preserving its archeo-geo-ecological extravaganzabonanza.

The large rock and glass sphere that teeters on the edge of the crater houses the new **visitors' center** (tel. (057) 58 86 20 or 58 86 91). Inside, a circular exhibit displays reconstructions of the rock beds and provides information on the flora and fauna of the surrounding area. (Open Sun.-Thurs. and Sat. 9am-4:30pm, Fri. 9am-2pm; admission

NIS9, children NIS4.50.) If you agree to skip the silly 15-minute audio-visual show, they might let you in for free. Free maps.

By far the most amazing attractions are the numerous routes which one can follow along the crater's base, viewing volcanic remains and other geological oddities at close range. If you're not traveling by car, tours by foot, jeep, or desert beast are available. **Desert Shade's** tours of Makhtesh Ramon includes a round of Arabic coffee and a fire next to a Bedouin tent. A 2.5-hour jeep tour costs US$18 per person, and a night of tent living and Bedouin food costs NIS50-55. Call their agent Avi Ḥaklai (tel. 588205 or 586166, fax 588248) for updated information—as far in advance as possible as spaces fill *very* quickly. On holidays, the visitors' center will arrange guides if you supply the tent.

Across from the Makhtesh Ramon visitors' center is the **Mitzpeh Ramon Youth Hostel (HI)** (tel. 58 84 43 or 58 80 74), one of Israel's best hostels. The rooms are spacious and immaculate, all with toilets and showers. There are classrooms, a TV room, and, of course, a disco in the bomb shelter. Reception officially open 5-9pm, but someone is always there. No kitchen facilities and no curfew. Checkout 9am. Dorm beds with six per room NIS37, three per room NIS47 and for two NIS52. Nonmembers add NIS3 per night. Large breakfast included. Kosher lunch and dinner are available for NIS20 (Fri. NIS22) in the roomy, comfortable dining room. Groups of 4 or more may want to consider a flat.

The cheapest accommodations in the area are the flats rented out by **The Art Colony,** 6 Ma'aleh Dekalim St. (tel. 588950 or 588933). From the visitors' center walk down the street to you right, make a right at the swimming pool; the third left is Ma'aleh Dekalim St. and the guest house is the sixth building on the right. The rooms are furnished with modern paintings and carpeting and all come with kitchens and bathrooms. (2-bedroom flat for 4, NIS150.) Another relatively inexpensive place to stay is the hostel in the **field school** run by the Society for the Protection of Nature (tel. 58 86 15/6), which has clean rooms and a kitchen, although the long walk from town makes it a bit more inconvenient. The hostel is often filled with school groups so call ahead to find out if there's space. Office hours are 8am-5:30pm. (Singles or doubles NIS60. Triples NIS90. Breakfast NIS11, meat meal NIS17, and Fri. dinner NIS24. Kosher.) The field school itself is 3km outside the town by road, or a worthwhile 0.5km hike. Nature enthusiasts might be able to find work here in the winter; you work four days, take tours of the crater for three days, and get paid for all seven if you stay in the hostel a minimum of three months.

Hiking in the crater is the primary activity at Mitzpeh Ramon. Do not trailblaze without contacting the extraordinarily helpful field school (see above). Most of their self-guided tour maps are in Hebrew (Negev maps cost NIS28) but they will go out of their way to translate and offer suggestions. A one-day tour by foot is less rewarding than the three-or four-day excursions possible with a car or jeep. The field school runs half-day jeep trips for $130, 2.5-hour camel trips for NIS30, as well as multi-day jeep-based excursions. Otherwise, rent a mountain bike from Ben Meshi, 4 Ramon Rd. (tel. 58 81 40), for NIS35 per day. Hiring English-speaking guides from the field school costs NIS300 per day for groups of any size. Try to tag along with an already formed group. Always bring plenty of water while hiking and cover your head against the deadly desert sun. If you go without a guide, be sure to stay out of the army's firing area, just northwest of the crater. Try not to hike at high noon during the summer; begin at dawn so you can return by noon. In March and April, the desert literally blooms with flowers, making this the most popular time to hike.

Perhaps the most memorable sight in the area is the **llama and alpaca farm** (tel. 588 047), about 2km west of town. (Approximately 0.5km north of the field school, off the main road west out of town. Follow the llama-shaped signs. Open Sun.-Thurs. 9am-4pm, Fri. 9am-2pm.) These surreal-looking South American imports (the alpacas resemble creatures from a *Star Wars* film) live off of Negev scrub, hay, and water and are raised for their wool. Admission NIS5, children NIS3.80.

Back in town, meander through the **statue museum,** a garden filled with modern Israeli sculpture. Turn right after the gas station on the road below the visitors' center and continue until you reach the garden at the edge of the cliff. (Stop there.) Negev critters reside in their natural habitat (more or less) at the **Zoological Garden** (tel. 58 86 91), located directly across from the visitors' center. (Nominal entrance fee.) The **music and cultural center** on 73 Ben-Gurion St. (tel. 58 84 42, 58 88 65, or 58 83 46) hosts Israeli folk dancing every Sun. at 8pm and movies every Sat. and Mon. at 8:30pm (in winter, 8pm).

If you walk "into town," along the road to your right as you walk down the steps of the visitor's center, you'll stumble upon **Ramon's Restaurant** (tel. 58 81 58) where sandwiches go for NIS5-6 and full meals with meat, rice, fries and fruit for NIS17-20. Much better than you'd expect from a restaurant connected to a gas station, Ramon's offers a snack bar, comfortable indoor eating, and a large, covered outside eating area. It's usually either packed with soldiers or totally deserted. (Open Sun.-Thurs. 5am-8pm, Fri. 5am-4:30pm.) Across the street is a shopping center, which includes **Bank HaPoalim** (open Sun., Tues., and Thurs., 8:30am-noon and 4-6pm, Mon. 8:30am-12:30pm; Wed. and Fri. 8:30am-noon) as well as **Pub Ḥaveet,** Mitzpeh Ramon's only night spot. (Attracts soldiers, backpackers and local youth from this small city. Must be 18 or older. Beer NIS5. Open nightly 7pm-1 or 2am.) Next door are two **falafel cafés.** From 7am-11 or 12pm, you can take your shwarma or falafel outside on the mini-mall veranda and listen to rock, reggae, Israeli folk, and even Lucinda Williams blaring from Pub Harvest. In the same complex you'll also find the essential **post office** (open Sun.-Tues. and Thurs. 8am-12:30pm and 3:30-6pm, Wed. 8am-1:30pm, Fri. 8am-noon), **supermarket** (open Sun.-Thurs. 9am-1pm and 4-7pm, Fri. 8:30am-1pm), and a fabulous **indoor pool** with a large waterslide (open daily 10am-6pm; admission NIS12, children NIS5). Bus #60 runs from Be'ersheva to Mitzpeh Ramon (1.5hr., NIS13. Bus #392 continues to Eilat, and #391 to Tel Aviv.

Dimona and Mamshit דימונה, ממשית

Some people will tell you that Dimona is Israel's best kept secret. Others will tell you to ignore the glowing reports you hear and not to believe every Tom, Dick and Mordekhai you talk to. The city boasts a fusion of ethnicities; Indians, Ethiopians, Russians and even a few *sabras* can be seen walking the streets. You can practise your French on the mushrooming North African population. Bus #56 makes the 35-minute trip from Be'ersheva every 20-30 minutes (NIS5.80).

In any event, Dimona is not really a tourist town and has no accommodations for travelers. The **central bus station** (tel. (057)55 24 21) is on Herzl St. From there make a right on Ben-Gurion St. where you'll see the **police station**. Ben-Gurion St. becomes Mem Gimel Hama'apilim St. and you will see the **post office** (open Sun.-Tues. and Thurs. 8am-12:30pm and 3:30-6pm, Wed. 8am-1:30pm, Fri. 8am-noon; at all other times, gone fission). Past the post office is the **commercial center** and a **Co-op supermarket** (open Sun., Mon., Wed., Thurs. 8am-1pm and 4:30-7:30pm, Tues. and Fri. 8am-2pm). **Patisserie Atzma'ut** serves inexpensive sweets. In the same area you will also find a **pharmacy** (open Sun.-Thurs. 8:30am-1pm and 4-7:30pm, Fri. 8:30am-2:30pm), a **bakery** and a *borekas* stand. A bit farther down Mem Gimel HaMa'apilim St., you'll find three **banks**, as well as Dimona's one and only pub, **Pizza Rimini** (Maccabee NIS5, pizza slices NIS4; open daily 8am-1am).

Dimona is famed for only two things, really. The first seems to be officially named the "Nuclear power plant? What nuclear power plant? Who, us?" This is no time to play spy or meditate on the French non-nonproliferation policy of the 1950s. The only real reason to visit Dimona is to see the **Hebrew Israelite Community**. Better known as the Black Hebrews, the members of this curious sect of English-speaking emigrés from the midwestern United States believe that the historical roots of their ancestors can be traced to Israel. The community claims to have evidence that the ancestors of black slaves in antebellum America lived in Israel until they were forced to migrate to Western Africa after the onslaught of the Romans in 70 CE. The group's first vanguard returned to the Holy Land in 1969, under the leadership of their spiritual guide Ben Ammi. When the Israeli government refused to grant them citizenship unless they converted to Judaism, the Black Hebrews insisted that they could not convert because they were already Jews. Community leaders are currently negotiating with the Israeli government to try to improve their legal status in Israel.

To visit the **Hebrew Village** (tel. 55 54 00), continue walking from the central bus station along Herzl St. for about 10 minutes and enter on your left. The community leaders prefer that you call ahead so that they will be able to arrange a tour for you, take you to their restaurant (strict dietary restrictions prohibit the community's members from eating any meat or dairy products, fish, foul, eggs, white sugar or white flour; open Sun.-Thurs. 9am-11pm; sandwiches cost NIS3-4) or to their boutique (open Sun.-Thurs. 10am-1:30pm and 4-9pm) where they sell handcrafts as well as books and tapes about their beliefs. Off the beaten track, and that's what budget travel is all about.

Six kilometers southeast of Dimona is **Mamshit,** a Nabatean city with Roman ruins, Byzantine churches and a name somewhat difficult to pronounce without snickering. (Those with major giggles might well wish to use the Arabic name "Qurnub.") In the nearby Mamshit stream, three large Nabatean dams were discovered along with the underwater reservoirs they supplied. The only really worthwhile attractions in Mamshit besides the rubble of a few Nabatean houses are the two craters just outside the city's limits, **Makhtesh HaGadol** and the more distant **Makhtesh HaKatan** (literally—and ingeniously—"the big and small craters"). Although less geologically diverse than Makhtesh Ramon, Makhtesh HaKatan particularly lends itself to a pleasant day of hiking. Due to its general inaccessibility, however, it is recommended only for the most stalwart of hikers.

Kibbutz Lahav קיבוץ להב

Uncomfortably close to Jordanian troops until 1967, Kibbutz Lahav still marks the northern limit of Bedouin desert tents and the southern edge of the *fellaheen* (Arab farmers) villages. In addition to creating one of the largest wheat farms in Israel, members of Lahav built the **Col. Joe Alon Center** (tel. (057) 91 85 97, fax (057) 91 98 89) which specializes in regional and folkloric studies. Much more intriguing is the **Museum of Bedouin Culture,** the largest such museum in the world. Bedouin tribespeople, scattered throughout the Negev and Sinai, are undergoing a rapid process of modernization and settlement. Traditional dress, household utensils, jewelry, and tools are fast disappearing, and the museum succeeds poignantly in its attempt to preserve artifacts of Bedouin culture. Many Bedouin from the Sinai, the Negev, and even Saudi Arabia have visited and donated family possessions to the museum. The reconstruction of a Bedouin tent is so surprisingly realistic that Bedouin visitors have fallen asleep in it. Sallem, a Bedouin from the neighboring village of Rahat, often sits just outside the museum in another such traditional tent. As he roasts, grinds, and cooks Bedouin coffee for visitors to sample, Sallem explains the extensive customs that govern Bedouin life. He speaks Hebrew, Arabic, and a little bit of English, but someone is usually there to translate. On Saturdays, a Bedouin woman bakes pita in the tent.

An audiovisual presentation of the museum's holdings is offered in English, German, French, Spanish, and Arabic at no extra cost. If you call in advance (tel. 91 32 02), you may be able to arrange for a guided tour of the museum, kibbutz, and surrounding archeological curiosities such as a *fellah's* restored summer cave. You may eat lunch with the kibbutzniks in the Lahav dining hall or use the picnic facilities located in the nearby forest. The museum center's newly built **observatory** offers a splendid view of the northern Negev, the lowlands of Judah, and the southern portion of the Hebron hills in the West Bank. (Complex open Sun.-Thurs. and Sat. 9am-4pm, Fri. 9am-2pm.)

Getting to the kibbutz can be difficult. Bus #369 runs from Be'ersheva to the Lahav-Devir intersection, 10km from the kibbutz. Bus #42 runs directly to the kibbutz, leaving Be'ersheva at 11:50am and 6:50pm Sunday-Thursday (NIS7). The bus stops at Devir first, so make sure you are getting off at the right settlement. If you contact the museum staff, they will try to find you a ride back to Be'ersheva or the main road with the guides who leave the museum at 3pm. In the high season (April-May), the museum often runs a car shuttle service to and from the bus stop at the Lahav-Devir intersection; call in advance to see if it's available. As always, an easier though much costlier option is to rent a car.

Eilat אילת

Yes, Eilat rhymes with hot. Israel's number-one vacation spot, the city is always soaked with the sweat of rowdy Israelis, international backpackers, and European tourists. Some people swear by Eilat, enjoying the sun, the coral, and the night life. Others see Eilat as a cross between Sodom and Gomorrah, a huge tourist trap attached to a nice beach. Travelers should be aware that, unlike some tourist-oriented areas, in Eilat tourists are often not treated as treasures, but taken for granted by some local business-people; if one tourist leaves, another one is sure to come. The obnoxiousness quotient of this city is rather high. Finding a good hostel can do a lot to help you keep your sanity.

In the off season (June-August) temperatures soar to an infernal 42-48 C, at which point most sopping visitors take to the ocean. Eilat's red granite mountains, veined with copper, appear harsh and unlivable but actually shelter a number of camel ranches in their parched folds. The hot, hotter, hottest attraction in Eilat, however, is 20 C cooler and several feet under. Plunge your mask and snorkel under the uniform blue and in order to see the silent, vibrant kaleidoscope of rainbow coral and flourescent sea critters. While above the water line lies a sun-drenched desert, below it's a neon traffic jam as hundreds of scantily clad bathers clog the waterway.

When the Israeli army captured the oasis and revived its biblical name in 1948, Eilat was nothing more than a few Turkish shacks. King David had built his southernmost defense outpost here about 3000 years earlier, but little remained. Most of what is left of ancient and medieval Eilat is located along the beaches of Aqaba, across the border in Jordan. Although under King Solomon Eilat became famous as a center for the gold trade, the town's fortune waned after it was captured by Salah al-Din in 1167. Under Muslim control, Eilat dwindled to a minor military post. It was not until the Israeli capture of the Sinai that the city became the country's major resort and home to 22,000 inhabitants. In the past two decades, dozens of luxury hotels, restaurants, and tourist shops have become familiar (and lucrative) fixtures along a beach that offers year-round swimming. With the return of the Sinai to Egypt in 1982, Eilat is once again Israel's southernmost port and the logical starting point for excursions into the Sinai.

Eilat is a free trade zone and the value added tax (VAT) has been abolished, reducing prices for most goods and services by an average of 18%. All entry and exit taxes at the airport have also been eliminated.

The busiest times here are Passover (April 6-13 in 1993) and Sukkot (Oct. 12-19 in 1993), when nearly 100,000 Israelis descend upon the city and fill all the accommodations. Eilat is a popular place to earn a little extra money. Proprietors at resorts, hostels, cafés, discos, the Lunar Mini Park, and the Zubrensky political circus are often looking for newcomers because of the high turnover. Jobs with hotels and hostels often include lodging, and should offer a pittance as well. Unfortunately, most of the jobs are illegal, the work often long and arduous, and the wages (paid under the table) low (usually about US$400 per month).

Orientation and Practical Information

Located at the southernmost tip of the Negev desert, Eilat is a 5km strip of coastline at the precarious intersection of four Middle Eastern powers: Israel, Jordan, Egypt, and Saudi Arabia; at night you can see the lights of all these countries. The city is divided into three major sections: the town itself, on the hills above the sea; the hotel area and Lagoon Beach to the east; and the port to the south. Farther south lie Coral Beach and Taba, the Egyptian border since 1989.

Just outside the main entrance to the central bus station, **HaTmarim Boulevard** runs southeast (left) toward the megahotels and Lagoon Beach, passing several commercial centers. Opposite the bus station at HaTmarim, the **Commercial Center** houses the post office, international phones, and major banks. Continuing toward the water on HaTmarim, **Rekhtar Center** is next on the right with the Municipal Tourist Office, pharmacies, small markets, and cafés. The last center on the right, **Etzion Center,** frames the Etzion Hotel with eateries and camping supply stores.

On the left side of HaTmarim Blvd. toward the lagoon are two new open-air, multistory shopping and eating complexes. The first one, **Red Canyon Center,** resembles a giant, futuristic Bedouin tent. The second, **Shalom Center,** resembles a square white spaceship on a tiered landing pad. HaTmarim Blvd., ends here, perpendicular to **Ha'Arava Road** and adjacent to the Eilat Airport.

Yotam Street runs parallel to HaTmarim Blvd. (about 3 blocks from the bus station). The **New Tourist Center** (which has *no* tourist information) is just off the intersection of Yotam St. and HaArava Rd. A right on HaArava Rd. takes you out past the HI and port, to Coral Beach and Taba.

Since you'll need only a shirt, shorts, bathing suit, face mask, snorkel, and canteen, consider leaving your pack in the parcel storage at the bus station (terminal open Sun.-Thurs. 6am-6pm, Fri. 6am-3pm; NIS3.50 per day). Most hostels also have lockers, which are more convenient and cost NIS2 every time you open and lock them. Because Eilat is notorious for petty theft, locking up your bags is necessary, especially if you foolishly opt to sleep on the beach.

Before you hit the beach or head south, obtain a hat and at least one large canteen or water bottle. The dry heat here can dehydrate you quickly *sans* sweat; you should drink at least four or five liters of water per day. Eilat's police, with conceivably nothing better to do, can be strangely ruthless when it comes to jaywalkers. Many travelers have been slapped with NIS30 fines. When crossing, be polite and move single file in the pedestrian crossings marked with blue triangles.

Information Center, Durban St. (tel. 37 47 41 or 37 59 44), just across Ha'Arava Road from the New Tourist Center. Look for a booth with lots of video screens and posters all around. Best information service in Eilat. You tell them your budget and they'll help you plan your stay in Eilat—or anywhere in Israel. Helpful staff has information on all Eilat attractions, many discount coupons for sights and nightclubs, and discount slips for changing money at local banks (an invaluable service). Will also help with complaints and refund requests. This free service is the best first stop you can make. Open 24 hours.

Government Tourist Information Office (GTIO): Khan Center (tel. 37 43 53), Ofira Park, P.O. Box 86. Across from the Caesar Hotel (just over the Marina bridge). Offers maps, brochures, transportation schedules, and border information. Will help find accommodations—an invaluable service in the high season. Computer information system available. Open Sun.-Thurs. 8am-6pm, Fri. 8am-1pm. (Take bus #15 from the bus station.)

Municipal Tourist Information: Rekhtar Center (tel. 37 42 33). Good for maps and emergencies. Open Sun.-Thurs. 8am-6pm, Fri. 8am-1pm.

Consulates: Egypt, 68 Ha'Efroni St. (tel. 37 68 82). From the bus station, walk right on HaTmarim Blvd., away from the beach. Make a left on Eilot St., go right at the Moore Center onto Anafa St., take the third left onto Ha'Efroni and look for the flag at the end of the street. You may have to enter through the rear. Visa section open Sun.-Thurs. 9am-noon, Fri. 9am-11am. Visas issued on day of application (NIS30 for citizens of USA, USSR, Germany, Cyprus, Denmark, Yugoslavia, Norway, Finland, Sweden; NIS40 all others). **U.K.,** (tel. 37 23 44) off Yotam St., above the New Tourist Center (next to the Adi Hotel). Call ahead.

Banks: Bank Leumi, HaTmarim Blvd. (tel. 37 41 91), across from the central bus station. Open Mon., Wed., Fri. 8:30am-noon; Sun., Tues., Thurs. 8:30am-noon and 5-6:30pm. The **First International Bank** in the Tourist Center (tel. 37 61 17/8) is the only bank open on Mon. and Wed. afternoons. Open Sun., Tues., Thurs. 8:30am-2pm; Mon. and Wed. 8:30am-2pm and 4-7pm; Fri. 8:30am-noon. **Bank Hapoalim,** Hativat Hanegev St. (tel. 37 51 84), across from the central bus station. Open Sun., Tues., Thurs. 8:30-noon, 4:30-6pm, Mon., Wed., Fri. 8:30am-noon.

Post Office: Red Canyon Center (tel. 37 23 02) next to the airport. Open Sun.-Tues. and Thurs. 8am-12:30pm and 4-6:30pm, Wed. 8am-1:30pm, Fri. 8am-noon. **International telephones** and **Poste Restante** here.

Bezek International Telecommunications: HaTmarim Blvd. (tel. 37 23 23), in the Commercial Center next to the post office. Sun.-Thurs. 7am-1pm and 4-10pm, Fri. and holidays 7am-1pm. Direct and collect phone services available. Cheapest rates on Sun. Unshaded pay phones outside post office.

Telephone code: 07.

Airport: At the intersection of HaTmarim Blvd. and HaArava Rd. **Arkia Airlines** (tel. 37 61 02) service to and from Tel Aviv every hour; Sun. and Thurs. every half hour (NIS167). To Jerusalem 2 or 3 times daily (NIS167), and to Ḥaifa 2 or 3 times daily (NIS195). It's cheapest to pay in shekels.

Central Bus Station: HaTmarim Blvd. (tel. 33 51 61), in the center of town. Reserve all tickets at least 2 days in advance, 4 days in high season. Jerusalem via Dead Sea (5 daily, NIS28). If no seats are available, take a bus to Be'ersheva and transfer; Tel Aviv via Be'ersheva or direct (7 daily, NIS29).

City Buses: #15 runs down HaTmarim Blvd. and HaArava Rd., making a circuit through the hotel area and continuing past the HI and Coral Beach to Taba—basically, everywhere you need to go. #1 and 2 shuttle between the town and hotel area. All buses run every 20-30min., Sun.-Thurs. 7am-9pm. No service Fri. 5pm-Sat. 9am.

In-city taxis: Arava (tel. 37 41 41). **Taba** (tel. 37 22 12). **King Solomon** (tel. 37 31 31). About NIS15-20 to the Taba border. (Israeli taxis cannot enter Taba.)

Car Rental: Hertz, HaTmarim Blvd. (tel. 37 66 82), in the Red Canyon Center; **Budget** (tel. 37 10 63), under the Etzion Hotel on HaTmarim Blvd.; **Europcar** (tel. 37 40 14), and **Eldan** (tel. 37 40 27) both in the Shalom Center. Hertz and Budget have a minimum age requirement of 21, Europcar 23, and Eldan 24. Payment by credit card or US$ only, except at Budget. Prices start at US$26 a day plus 26¢ per km or US$40 a day for 100km and 24¢ per km thereafter (minimum of 3 days). Insurance costs about US$10.50 per day. You cannot bring a hired car into Egypt.

Bike Rental: Red Sea Sports Club (tel. 37 96 85), near King Solomon Hotel, NIS35 per day. Open 8:30am-5pm.

Nature Reserves Authority: Coral Beach (tel. 37 68 29). Information about maps, hiking, and coral reefs.

Laundromat: Mickey Mouse Laundromat, 99/1 Almogim St. (tel. 37 34 95), opposite the Peace Café. Open Sun.-Fri. 8am-8pm.

Pharmacy: Eilat Pharmacy, 25 Eilot St. (tel. 37 46 65), Sun.-Thurs. 8:15am-1:30pm and 4:45-8pm, Fri. 8:15am-2pm. **Michlin Pharmacy** (tel. 37 25 85), in Rekhtar Center. Open Sun.-Thurs. 8:30am-1:30pm and 4:30-8pm, Fri. 8am-2pm.

First Aid: HaTmarim Blvd. (tel. 101 for emergencies, 37 23 33 to chat). Magen David Adom (Israeli Red "Cross"—actually Red Star of David) first aid stations are located on some beaches.

Hospital: Yoseftal Hospital, Yotam Rd. (tel. 35 80 11).

Fire: Tel. 102 for emergencies; 37 22 22 to chat.

Police: Avdat Blvd. at the eastern end of Ḥativat HaNegev (tel. 100 for emergencies; 33 24 44 to chat). Operates a "lost and found" for packs stolen from the beach.

To reach the **Egyptian border,** take bus #15 from a stop across from the central bus station or from stops along HaTmarim Blvd. and HaArava Rd. (except 5pm Fri.-9am Sat.). Taxis to the border cost NIS15-20—insist on a *moneh* (meter). You'll get off at the Israeli checkpoint since no Israeli buses or taxis are allowed into Egypt (look for the Israeli flags marking the station; open 24 hrs.).

For jaunts to **Taba Beach** (where you'll find a Hilton, a more secluded beach, and great snorkeling), you must present your passport at the border. The passport will not be stamped, but it is the only acceptable form of identification. As always at Egyptian borders, declare all cash and valuables so that they will not be confiscated upon your return.

Travel into the **Sinai** can be either a painless endeavor or a bureaucratic nightmare, depending upon your nationality and the duration of your desert stay. See Sinai Bureaucracy in the Sinai section for details. The Israeli station also issues a one-month visa for travelers coming into Israel from Egypt (free).

If you are not American and plan to visit the Sinai and return to Israel, find out ahead of time if you'll be charged a re-entry fee. (For example, Yugoslavs returning to Israel after a 1-day jaunt are slapped with a NIS135 fee.) Call the Israeli passport control at tel. 37 21 04 (mornings only) to check the ever-changing regulations and find out if you'll need to secure a multiple-entry visa to prevent annoying fines. (Don't listen to anyone else's sage advice about re-entry fines.)

Egypt will issue a 2-week Sinai-only visa on the spot at the Israeli border at Taba, but for longer visits to the Sinai or for journeys to Cairo and points west, you'll need to procure an **Egyptian visa** at the Egyptian consulate in Eilat or Tel Aviv. (See Egyptian Consulate.) Buses into the Sinai and points west leave four times per day from Taba, at 10am and 1, 2, and 3pm. The 10am and 2pm buses travel to St. Catherine's with a stop in Nuweiba; the 1pm bus takes the new road directly to Cairo, and the 3pm bus travels along the Eastern Sinai coastline, to Nuweiba, Dahab, and Sharm al-Sheikh, returning to Taba in the morning. A bus from St. Catherine's returns to the border at 1pm. (Due to the length of the trip, visitors to St. Catherine's should plan on staying the night. See St. Catherine's, below.) Egyptian bus schedules are notoriously inaccurate; call the checkpoint or arrive early (by 9am) with your mineral water and something to read (other than this).

Taxis also serve the Sinai, with fares slightly higher than the bus, but fewer hassles. (For taxis to Cairo, you must get your Egyptian visa in advance.) A final word of caution: Don't schlep much baggage to Sinai. It's rough-going and hot, and everyone else looks like a castaway. Leave all but bare essentials at the baggage check in Eilat.

Accommodations and Camping

Finding a cheap room in Eilat is easy. Finding a safe, comfortable, and convenient cheap room is another story. As soon as you arrive at the bus station you'll be harassed by apartment hawkers. Ignore them, yell "*Lo*" ("No" in Hebrew), give them the look of death, walk away. These people will tell you they just want to show you a room and if you don't like it they'll take you back. Don't get into a cab, and don't make any commitments before you see the room and its distance from the center. Accommodations are next to impossible to obtain during Sukkot (Oct. 12-19 in 1993) and Passover (April 6-13 in 1993); many hostel owners double their prices at these times and/or smugly close their doors to dusty backpackers. If you cannot find a room go to the tourist office, a travel agency, or a real estate office and they should be able to find you a place. All hostel prices listed below increase markedly in July and August. Some prices double. As far as hostels go, some of the bigger ones have been known to put out backpackers in favor of large groups of Israelis. The atmosphere of a smaller hostel can add a tremendous amount to your enjoyment of Eilat.

Max and Merran's Hostel, 116/1 Ofarim St. (tel. 37 23 71). Friendliest hostel in Eilat, and cheapest rooms by far in the high season. Previously "Fawlty Towers." Extremely clean large dorm rooms and two doubles available—all at same price, all with A/C. Two large, clean bathrooms make showering a pleasure. Common room decorated with Welsh and Australian memorabilia, latest videos at 2pm and 8pm every day, many dogs and cats. Warm managers Pamela and Chriss make the hostel a highlight of your Eilat stay. Kitchen facilities available until 11pm. Free tea, coffee and ice water bottles to take to the beach; free safe and luggage storage; management helps find cheap medical services for guests who drank the water in Egypt. No curfew, no alcohol allowed, no visitors, no showers 9am-1pm for cleaning. All beds in all seasons for NIS18.

Youth Hostel (HI), Ha'Arava Rd. (tel. 37 23 58 or 37 00 88), on a hill across from the Red Rock Hotel. Take bus #15 or it's a 10-min. walk from the central bus station. Safe, clean, and you pay for both. All rooms have 8 beds, private bathrooms, and A/C. Lockers for guests. Office open 7-11am and 2-10pm. Midnight curfew. Beds NIS38. Breakfast included. Lunch and dinner NIS19 each, Fri. dinner NIS25. Luggage storage NIS3 per day. Work sometimes available: 4 hrs. in exchange for bed and breakfast, 6 hrs. for bed and 3 meals.

Eilat Field School, Ha'Arava Rd. (tel. 37 11 27 or 37 20 21), just across from the Coral Beach Reserve; take bus #15. Best location for snorkeling and frying in Eilat. A spotless complex made up of small stucco buildings surrounded by well-trimmed courtyards. Each room has 4 beds (2 bunks), A/C, and a private toilet and shower. Guides at the field school can give directions and help plan trips into the Red Mountains. Maps and guidebooks (Hebrew only) NIS30 and NIS2.50

respectively. Kitchen facilities and food storage in the school's refrigerator. Safe storage for valuables. Camping also available; see below. No curfew. Office open Sat.-Thurs. 8am-3pm, Fri. 8am-1pm. Single or double NIS132.

Beit Ha'Arava, 106 Almogim St. (tel. 37 10 52 or 37 46 87). From the bus station, take a right at the bus entrance onto Ḥativat HaNegev St. and walk 2 blocks to the end; it's a half block to the left from there. More like a motel than a hostel. Each room locks. Large front room with newspapers and foosball provides view. Veranda, kitchen, A/C. Wash NIS8-10. Lockers NIS3. No curfew. Dorm beds (4 & 6 to a room, some with private shower and bath) NIS20-25. Doubles, with private shower and bath NIS70-80. Breakfast NIS8-10.

The Home, 108/2 Almogim St. (tel. 37 10 01), gate is on Ofarim St. right before HaTmarim. A converted house, the place offers clean, slightly crowded rooms with A/C. Kitchen facilities with free tea, coffee, bread, and jam. Videos every night at 8pm. Free luggage storage. Wash NIS5. Welcomes backpackers in high season. Dorm beds NIS17. New annex, a bit more open to the elements, has beds for NIS15. Breakfast included.

Ofarim Rooms, 116/2 Ofarim St. (tel. 37 62 89). Very clean rooms (4, 6, or 8 beds) all have attached bathrooms with shower, and A/C. More like a rooming house than a hostel. Kitchen facilities till midnight, wash (up to 5 kilos) NIS10, safe NIS5 per day. No curfew. Dorm beds NIS20. Singles NIS40. Doubles NIS60.

Aviv Hostel, 126 Ofarim St. (tel. 37 46 60), at the intersection of Agmonim and Ofarim, 1 block from the Peace Café. Immaculate and modern. Each dorm room has private shower and bath. Separate building in back has full kitchen facilities and refrigerator. Large color TV with cable and video on front veranda. Lockers NIS5 every time you close them. Cold drinks NIS3. Free tea and coffee 24 hrs. and free use of safe. Dorm beds US$6 (July and Aug. up to US$10).

Shalom Hostel, Ḥativat HaNegev St. (tel. 37 65 44), across the street from the bus entrance to the station: look for their red and white sign. Plain rooms with A/C; one key per room. Video games, TV, institutional bathrooms and cheap meals (NIS5-7) in basement. Lockers NIS2 every time you open them. Dorm beds (8 per room) NIS20. Singles NIS60. Doubles NIS100. Add NIS20 for private bath. Prices double in July and Aug. Management holds your passport until you return unstained bed linens.

Taba Youth Hostel, Ḥativat HaNegev St. (tel. 37 59 82, 37 58 15, or 37 34 05), across the street and to the left of the bus entrance to the station. Main building has 2 large unconnected rooms (16 and 22 beds each). New annex has smaller dorm rooms. Clean and neat, with A/C. Kitchen facilities. Management supervises safety and "decorum." Large front lawn has chairs and picnic tables for viewing big screen TV. No curfew. Dorm beds NIS15, Singles NIS25, Doubles NIS50.

Nathan's White House Hostel, 131/1 Retamim St. (tel. 37 65 72), the first right after crossing Ḥativat HaNegev St. from the bus station and go all the way down to the corner. Unadorned converted house. Simple, clean rooms with bath. Kitchen, billiards, TV, and video. No curfew. Friendly staff sells drinks and sandwiches. Dorm beds (6 per room) NIS20, doubles NIS70-80. Breakfast included.

Corinne Room, 127/1 Retamim St. (tel. 37 14 72), corner of HaTmarim St. Small, but clean. Annex on Eilot St. has 2 doubles with private bathrooms and showers. All rooms with A/C. Free coffee, tea, use of refrigerator. Quality of rooms varies; check before committing. Dorm beds NIS15, doubles NIS60. Prices double in July and August.

Igal's House (Housetel), 16 Almogim St. (tel. 37 22 85), opposite the Peace Café, you have to look for the sign. Pretty big hostel, a bit more rustic than most, but clean rooms and bathrooms, all rooms with A/C. Free use of safe and kitchen (minimarket next door), TV with video outside. No curfew. Dorm beds (bathroom nearby) NIS15, Single or Double (bathroom attached) NIS60.

There are two **camping** options in Eilat: official and expensive or unofficial and free. The latter is far more popular but also more dangerous. During July and August, hundreds of people happen not to see the "No Camping" signs and sleep on the public beach. And year after year, many of these morons are victims of theft. Possessions should never be left unguarded and **women should not camp alone.** Another nuisance at these camps are the rats, attracted by the garbage areas on Lagoon Beach, who will enjoy biting your ears and other appendages. To avoid these hassles, go east (toward the Jordanian border), or south of the Red Rock Hotel (toward Coral Beach).

Sleeping and tent-pitching on these beaches is legal, and there are toilets near most of them.

> **Carolina's Camping,** at the municipal campground opposite Coral Beach (tel. 37 19 11 or 37 50 63). Take bus #15. Clean institutional bathrooms and showers and a compact cafeteria. Miniscule bungalows NIS50 for 1 or 2 people, with A/C, lights, and electrical outlets. If you bring your own tent it's NIS9, NIS7 per child. (Lack of shade makes tents unbearable in July and August.) Refrigerators NIS5. Will supply you with bedsheets and pillowcases. All toilets outside. Office open 24 hrs.

> **Eilat Field School,** (tel. 37 20 21 or 37 11 27), across from the Coral Beach Reserve. Hostel is often full, but camping is NIS10 per person (children NIS8). Toilets and showers included. Office open Sat.-Thurs. 8am-3pm, Fri. 8am-1pm.

Food

You'll have to scrounge for inexpensive stomach degrumbling. By far the cheapest places to get a large, cheap meal that is not falafel are at Eilat's many pubs. For example, the popular *faux* **Rock Café** on 179 Eilot St. (tel. 37 13 21), has quality food at cheap prices: *schnitzel* or fish and chips with bread costs NIS7.50, beer NIS2.50. Flags of many nations adorn the walls and ceiling and the restaurant is frequented by travelers from all over the world. (Open daily 5pm-midnight.) If you're famished, try the **Fisherman House** (tel. 37 98 30) adjacent to Coral Beach, where all the grease you can eat costs only NIS16. (Salad bar alone NIS10. A/C and a great view of the sea. Open daily noon-midnight.) **Pancake Eilat** in the Shalom Center (tel. 33 36 92) across from the airport serves excellent steaks (with chips and salads) for NIS15-30. A filling meal of pancakes costs NIS6.50-9.50; choose from a full page of pancake recipes. Many hostels have 15% off coupons. Open 8am-midnight. The **Maman Red Sea Fish Restaurant** (tel. 37 19 58), behind the Moriah Hotel and literally *on* Northern Beach, serves full-meal deals for NIS14-19. Open 8am-3pm.

Since many accommodations in Eilat provide cooking facilities, you can eat well and inexpensively by purchasing food at the **supermarket** at Eilot St. and HaTmarim Blvd., three blocks inland from the bus station (look for the blue and white squares on the building). (Open Sun.-Thurs. 7:30am-7:30pm, Fri. 7:30am-2pm.) Closer to the center of town is **SuperKolbo Supermarket** in the Rekhtar Commercial Center across the street from the central bus station. (Open Sat.-Thurs. 7am-11pm, Fri. 7am-9pm.)

Sights

Spend your Eilat afternoons underwater, in a cerebellum-addling world of coral, butterfly fish, emperor fish, blubberfish, lionfish, and arrays of other brilliantly colored species.

The best places to rent scuba and snorkeling equipment are near **Coral Beach** (tel. 37 68 29), an underwater nature reserve south of Eilat. To reach the Coral Beach Reserve, take bus #15 from the central bus station toward the sea (open 8am-6pm). The beach is run by the Nature Reserves Authority, and the NIS9 (ages 5-18 NIS4.50) entrance fee helps to preserve the area. Once inside you can rent snorkeling equipment (batmask and cape NIS4, snorkel NIS3, and fins NIS5) and follow one of the five "water trails," marked by buoys, through the reef. A "bridge" allows you to get in the water without stepping on corals. This is the cheapest way to get close to Eilat's marine life; come and go as you like all day for the price of one admission. You can also buy a card for five visits for the price of three. Lockers (NIS3 every time you close them), showers, and well-stocked snack bar on site. Brochures, maps, and books on the coral reef are available at the entrance, or at the **Field School** (tel. 37 11 27 or 37 20 21) across the street. The Coral Beach Reserve now operates a "Snuba" program (tel. 37 27 22) for people who have never dived before; the air tank is on a raft to which the Snuba diver is tethered (NIS65 for 1.5 hours of diving and instruction. Sales office open 8am-5pm.)

Novice and advanced scuba divers should look into **Aqua Sport** (tel. 37 44 04), next to Coral Beach (mask US$3, fins US$2, snorkel US$2, complete diving equipment US$40, introductory dive US$40). They also rent **windsurfing equipment** for NIS22 per hour. A six-day international diving course (equipment included) costs US$220 and 10 qualification dives for two-star certification (equipment included) cost US$230 (summer $295). **Sinai Camping and Diving Safaris,** run by Aqua Sport, leave every Thursday at 6:30am for one, three, five or more days of fun down under. (One day US$75, US$65 if just snorkeling; 3 days US$270, including cruise, US$230 for snorkelers; and 5 days US$420, including two cruises, US$390 for snorkelers.) All prices include driver, guide, camping supplies, and meals. Diving prices include tanks, weight belts, and tank refills. **Underwater scooters,** also available from Aqua Sport, are ideal for underwater dives amidst the coral. Operate the battery-run scooter yourself or ride with a trained driver (US$25 per drive, lasts a few hours). If you definitely plan to windsurf or dive, Aqua Sport will accommodate you in their well-kept, sunny hostel (with access to their private beach) for US$10 per person, breakfast included. Classes should be arranged in advance. Call or write Aqua Sport International Ltd., P.O. Box 300, Eilat 88102.

Red Sea Sports Club (tel. 37 65 69) across the street from Aqua Sport offers rentals at similar prices, as well as night dives for NIS36-110, depending on the amount of gear needed. Their office on North Beach near the lagoon rents windsurfing boards for US$12 per hour and sailboats, and also offers waterskiing and parasailing. Upstairs from Red Sea Sports Club, the Red Sea Sport Club Hotel's **Photo Shop** (tel. 37 31 45, ext. 272, fax 37 40 83) rents underwater cameras for NIS50-100 and video cameras for NIS350 per day. Coral Beach is the most trafficked reef territory on the Red Sea— for more privacy with the fishies, head south into Sinai.

Before snorkeling, a judicious stop is the **Coral World Underwater Observatory and Aquarium** (tel. 37 66 66). The circular glass-walled underwater observatory lets you examine the coral reefs and fish at close range without getting your feet wet. Much more impressive than the observatory are the indoor tanks, which feature flourescent fish, an amazing array of multi-colored fish from the Red Sea, huge turtles, frightening sharks, and bizarre bird-like rays. Well-labeled tanks make a guidebook (NIS12) unnecessary. The area also holds a snack bar, a same-day photo shop, a gift shop, and a cafeteria. A full day of fishy fun will cost you, though (NIS24, children NIS14.50; open Sun.-Thurs. 8:30am-5pm, but once you're in you can stay until 6pm; Fri. 8:30am-3pm, once in stay until 4:30pm.)

Even more expensive, but much cooler is the **Yellow Submarine** (tel. 37 63 37) located inside the observatory grounds. This sub makes 4-5 50-minute dives every day between 9am and 4pm. Walking down the ladder, you step into what looks like a space ship with large portholes. As you dive to a depth of 60 meters, you can watch the sub descend on video monitors set up on either side of the cabin. A stewardess describes what you are seeing as elevator music plays through earphones and you gaze at the stunning wall of coral towering above you. Hundreds of varieties of fish swim by the porthole; don't even bother using the fish cards above your head to ID them. As you surface, the long-awaited Beatles tune plays in your headphones and the stewardess gives everyone a dive certificate. (Admission NIS107, includes admission to Coral World.)

One of Eilat's newest attractions is **Dolphin Reef** (tel. 37 18 46 or 37 34 17, fax 37 59 21), just past the port on the #15 bus. The beautiful beach features dolphin and sea lion shows every hour between 10am and 4pm, as well as non-stop nature films, a pub and a cafeteria. For NIS50, you can swim with the dolphins yourself. (Open daily 9am-5pm. Admission NIS18.)

Eilat is perfectly located for bird watching, as migratory groups flapping north from Africa stop at the salt ponds north of the lagoon and in the northern fields of Kibbutz Eilot from mid-February through May. More than one million birds of 30 different species have been counted in the area. Their migratory patterns and nesting habits, however, are seriously threatened by the vaguely sinister Voice of America Towers to be erected nearby. The **International Birdwatching Center** (tel. 37 42 76) in the

Commercial Center coordinates local tours (US$5 for a walking tour, US$50 for a jeep tour) and educational programs from the GTIO in the Khan Center (across from the Caesar Hotel). A birdwatchers' festival, usually held in late March, features daily excursions, extended trips, lectures, and films. Write to the International Birdwatching Center-Eilat (IBCE) at P.O. Box 774, 88106 Eilat for additional information on the festival. (Open Sun.-Thurs. 9am-1pm and 5-7pm, Fri. 9am-1pm.)

Entertainment

Eilat's inspired nightlife rivals its underwater circus. Most pubs and nightclubs open at 10:30-11pm, start rambuncting at midnight or so, and don't close until 5-6am. The discos are expensive (covers around NIS20); most are located in the lagoon area. Although most of the hotels have discos, they are sometimes open only to guests. Don't be put off by imposing lobbies; many hotel discos have side entrances. The dress codes tend to be stricter at hotel clubs: as a rule, shorts and sandals are a bad idea.

Pubs

Yacht Pub (tel. 33 41 11), on the marina by King Solomon's Wharf. Prime location. Live entertainment at 1:30am changes every few nights. Popular Israeli folk singers in the summer, rock for the European winter clientele. Maccabees NIS6.60. Open 9pm-3am.

Tropicana, in the Shalom Center (tel. 37 46 16). Astonishingly hip. Features a movie every day at 3pm and bingo every night at 10pm (winner gets a bottle of champagne). Videos, cartoons, and Charlie Chaplin films shown throughout the day. Cheap beer (half-liter NIS3, small pint NIS1.50 during happy hour). Free beer from 9-9:10pm, free cocktail for "ladies" 8:30-9pm. Open daily 4:30pm-2am.

The Underground (tel. 37 02 39), in the New Tourist Center. Eilat's up-and-coming bar has great deals on meals. After 5pm, the first 50 customers get the meal of the day and a beer for NIS3.50. Meals normally cost NIS4-5 and include spaghetti, chili, and even bacon. Video-bar, live bands, and managerial vision have made this a very popular bar for travelers. Open 24 hrs.

Hard Rock Café, 179 Eilot Street (tel. 37 13 21), steps lead downstairs. Extremely popular among travelers for its cheap food, good atmosphere and lack of fights. Maccabee draft NIS2.50; burgers, *schnitzel*, grill NIS7.50. Happy hour 4-6pm. Open daily 5pm-midnight.

Hard Luck Café, 15 Almogim St., next door to the Peace Cafe. Movie posters cover the walls. Music plays loudly and the TV shows soccer games (pray that England wins). Fish and chips, chicken, spaghetti, burgers, *schnitzel*, all NIS7. Maccabee draft NIS3, NIS2 if you're eating too. Drinks NIS8-12. Open noon-1 or 2am.

Yatush Barosh, Migdal Yam Soof (tel. 37 42 23) in the Marina, underneath spiral. Features the longest bar in Eilat—over 12m of elbow room. The crowd is a mix of Israelis and tourists. If you're lucky, or sufficiently pestilential, they'll take your picture and add it to the hall of shame posted over the bar. Drinks slightly expensive, but the atmosphere is classier than most. Open 8pm-3am.

Peace Café, 13 Almogim St. (tel. 37 16 29). The cheapest and most international place to hang out. Music videos by day, movies by night. Travelers come from all over to swap messages on the "Peace Board" and compare tattoos and bad hygiene. Attracts a slightly rough crowd. Maccabees NIS3. Open 9am-1:30am. Luggage storage (NIS5 per night) and job placement available.

Kermit's Pub, 1 Hativat Golani St. (tel. 37 26 42) above the Fisherman's Boat Restaurant. Froggy midnight performances of jazz, blues, rock, reggae, and more. Maccabee NIS3.50. Open 10pm-2am.

Teddy's Pub, Ofira Park (tel. 37 39 49), opposite Shulamit Gardens Hotel. A staid plaid English pub in the middle of the desert: Tudor exterior to boot. Live music on weekends: jazz and blues on Fri., Israeli soul music and rock on Sat. Open 7pm until Mr. Kollek leaves.

Clubs

Spiral (tel. 37 66 40), in the Red Sea Tower at the Eilat Marina just over the bridge. Pronounced "SPEE-ral." Unquestionably the best disco in Eilat. Overlooking the water, this 2-story nightclub has an enormous video screen, unparalleled lighting, and an excellent sound system that blasts disco, funk, and acid. Must be 18 to get in (17 in summer). Admission NIS20, Fri. NIS25, includes 1 beer or soft drink. Maccabees NIS7; light fare upstairs for under NIS8. Open 10:30pm-about 5am, depending on crowd size.

Sheba's, at the King Solomon Hotel (tel. 37 41 11). Ultra-modern, maximum-reflection atmosphere with a laser sound and light show. The music is a mix of disco, pop, and new wave. High-energy performing bartenders and strong drinks. Admission NIS30, includes first drink. Maccabees NIS8. Open Mon.-Sat. 11pm until people leave.

Sinbad's, at the Sport Hotel (tel. 37 33 33). Designed as the interior of a galleon ship, resembles nothing of the sort. Generally a younger crowd bopping to classic 60s rock, disco, and new wave. Admission NIS12, includes 1 soft drink. Maccabees NIS6. Open 10:30pm-3am.

The tourist office has information about evening shows and concerts at the **Phillip Murray Cultural Center** (tel. 33 22 57) on HaTmarim Blvd. near the bus station. Many of these jazz, classical, rock, and theater performances are worth the price of admission. The center also has a television, reading room, and rotating art exhibits. (Open daily 5-11pm.) Movie buffs can see last year's flicks (NIS13.50) at **Cinema Eilat** in the Red Canyon Center. The Shulamit Gardens Hotel also screens free films every day at 2pm and midnight in the video room.

For juveniles, there is the **Luna Park** (tel. 37 60 95) in front of the Queen of Sheba Hotel. Each ride costs NIS5; kiddie thrills are NIS4. Rides include Bumper Cars and a "Super-X Simulator." What's an X? (Open Mon.-Sat. 6pm-around midnight.) For a four-hour camel trek into the desert, there's the new **Camel Ranch,** next to the Texas Ranch (tel. 37 66 63, after 7pm 37 86 38). Two tours per day: 9am-1pm and 5-9pm (NIS70). The tour includes free tea or coffee and a Bedouin meal prepared by the guide.

Seasonal events in Eilat include the week-long **Hebrew Rock Music Festival** in early August on Eilat Beach and the mid-August **Red Sea Jazz festival,** featuring 10 performances on four stages every day in the port area; local and international performers and workshops. Ask at the GTIO for more information.

Near Eilat

The sheer pulchritude of the red granite mountains that tower over Eilat matches that of the coral reefs, but the mountains are less wet and less accessible in the summer heat. Many tours are organized for hiking and exploring but few are available for English-speaking tourists. The field school has maps of paths in Hebrew (NIS8), and will help translate. Many of the sites around Eilat are accessible by taking northbound buses, such as #393, 394 or 397. Especially in the high season or on Sundays and Fridays, your trip will require advance planning, as these buses fill up with travelers and Israelis on longer trips. Without reservations, you may be stuck at the bus station. Even worse, you may not be able to get back to Eilat when you want to if the southbound bus is full.

Stunning, rugged desert scenery awaits you to the north of Eilat at **Red Canyon Gorge.** From Red Canyon, continue to the lookout above **Moon Valley,** a pocked, moonscape canyon now controlled by Egypt, and to the unusual **Amram's Pillars.** A half-day tour is US$19 (winter only) with Egged Tours (depart from the central bus station; tel. 37 31 48 or 37 31 49). A Jeep trip is also available for US$30 per half-day through **Johnny Desert Tours** in the Shalom Center (tel. 37 26 08 or 37 67 77).

Timna Valley (tel. 35 62 15), a national park that attests to the region's Bronze Age history, lies 30km north of Eilat. The 6000-year-old Timna copper mines, still flawlessly preserved in the southeast corner of the park, were in mint condition during the Egyptian period. One currently out-of-fashion theory of biblical history puts the exodus of the Israelites on the old path from Egypt to Timna Valley, as Israelite slaves would have known the way to the mines. Today you can find remains of workers' camps and cisterns dating from the 11th century BCE scattered about amid the whir of modern mining (mining of the still-rich ore deposits resumed in 1955). The sandstone **King Solomon's Pillars** dominate the desert at a height of 50m near the 14th-century BCE Egyptian Temple of Hathor. There are interesting exhibits of ore and the production process of the copper mines located at the entrance. The park's **lake** offers camping facilities, a restaurant, toilets, and showers on its artificially created shores. United Tours, in the Shalom Center (tel. 37 17 29), runs tours to Timna Valley for about

NIS50 per half day. Otherwise you can take most buses that go to Tel Aviv or Jerusalem and ask to get off at the sign for Alipaz (not at the Timna Mines signpost). Walk or hitch to the entrance 2km away. (Park open 7:30am-6:45pm, admission NIS9, students NIS7, children (5-18) NIS4.50.) Bring water. There are bathrooms just inside the entrance to the park.

Most northbound buses will also take you to the **Hai Bar Biblical Nature Reserve,** a wildlife park designed to repatriate animals indigenous in biblical times, many of which are now rare in the region. (Ask to get off at Yotvata.) The reserve is home to roaming gazelles, donkeys, ostriches, and 11 species of predators mentioned in the Bible, including leopards, wolves, **rabbits**, and striped hyenas. (Open 9am-1:30pm; animal feeding 8-11am. Admission NIS16, children over 5 NIS10, includes Hai Bar Coach tour.) Only closed vehicles are allowed to enter, lest hapless visitors become lunch for endangered predators. Either come on foot (early) and wait for a vehicle with space, or take one of the daily guided tours in **Hai-Bar Coaches** at 9 and 10:30am, noon, and 1:30pm.

The entrance to the park is 1.5km from **Kibbutz Yotvata,** where **Ye'elim Desert Holiday Village** (tel. 37 43 62) has tent space for NIS20 year-round. (Caravan singles NIS78; doubles NIS111. In July and August singles NIS132, doubles NIS189. Check-in open at 2pm.) Swimming pool free for guests, NIS10 for visitors. The **visitor center** (tel. 37 60 18) opposite the kibbutz provides exhilerating information about the area and shows a film about Negev ecology. (Open 8am-3pm. NIS5 for the film, free with ticket to Hai-Bar.) The **cafeteria** serves Yotvata's nationally famous dairy products.

All of the above sights are worth seeing, but probably not worth the price of Eilat-based tours offered by Egged (tel. 37 31 48/9; 10% student discount), **Dan United** (tel. 37 17 29), and **Neot HaKikar** (tel. 37 13 29). The simplest and cheapest way to go is to take bus #394 to Tel Aviv (leaves the Eilat bus station every hour on the half hour; NIS7.50) and get off at Yotvata. Return to Eilat from the same stop on incoming buses.

Ashkelon אשקלון

> And in the houses of Ashkelon
> They shall lie down at evening
> For the Lord their God will be mindful of them.
> —Zephaniah 2:7

If God is mindful of you, you'll crash on Ashkelon's 10km of Mediterranean beaches or lie down at evening in its national park amid archeological ruins. First settled in the 3rd millenium BCE, Ashkelon is one of the oldest inhabited cities in the world. In Biblical times, Ashkelon was one of the five great cities of the Philistines, and the Bible records almost continuous conflicts with the Hebrews: Samson, as a young man, "went down to Ashkelon, and slew thirty men of them" (Judges 14:19). When King Saul was killed, David cried, "Publish it not in the streets of Ashkelon, lest the daughters of the Philistines rejoice" (Samuel 1:20).

Ashkelon, now a city of 63,000, was captured in 1948. The remains of the Biblical Ashkelon can be found solely in the campground area. What is now the Migdal neighborhood was the Arabic town of Mazhdar before 1948. The first Jewish settlers had hoped to establish a moshav at Migdal, but soon abandoned the site. In 1952, however, South African Jews began to inhabit and expand today's plush Afridar district, initiating construction of the modern town of Ashkelon. The city remains one of the fastest-growing in Israel.

Whereas ancient Ashkelon was beset by external strife, today the city suffers from internal rumblings. There are three isolated neighborhoods. The Migdal-Afridar border divides not only geographic ares but also groups of Israelis from different backgrounds. The Ashkenazi (of Western descent)-Sephardi (of Eastern descent) division, apparent throughout the country, has shaped Ashkelon's modern history. Ashkelon is also the site of one of the most important absorption centers in Israel. Jews from all over the world are brought together here and provided with special apartments and orientation classes for their first three months of residency. American, Canadian, Russian, Ethiopian, and European *olim ḥadashim* (new emigrés) populate the *merkaz klita* (absorption center) area—a living example of the coexistence of Israeli unity and tension.

Orientation and Practical Information

Fifty-five kilometers south of Tel Aviv, Ashkelon is made up of several rigidly demarcated districts set in the coastal fertile plain. Each neighborhood has its own character, from the old Arab town of **Migdal** to the swish commercial center of **Afridar,** to the nearby residential suburbs of **Barnea, Zion Hills, Shimshon,** and **Ramat Eshkol.**

Although the bus station may be centrally located, the town's attractions are not. The public bus system, however, makes it possible to get around without a car. Bus #13 runs from the central bus station to the beach, but only in July and August; buses #3 and 9 pass within walking distance of the park behind the beach (ask to get off on Shapiro Rd.) and buses #4 and 5 (and #7 circuitously) let you off at **Zephaniah Sq.** (*Merkaz Afridar*) in the heart of Afridar. Buses #3, 4a, and 9 also serve Migdal. Bus #5 continues to Barnea. If you decide to walk, get the city map at the GTIO in Afridar Center. All transportation comes to a screeching halt on *shabbat*.

Government Tourist Information Office (GTIO): Afridar Center (tel. 324 12). From the central bus station, take bus #4, 5, or 7. Excellent city maps and information on the national park, buses, hotels, and cultural events. Will arrange visits with members of the Ashkelon English-speaking community. Open Sun., Mon., Wed., and Thurs. 8:30am-1pm, Tues. 8:30am-12:30pm.

Banks: Israel Discount Bank Ben-Gurion Blvd., 2 blocks west of the central bus station. **Bank HaPoalim,** 48 Herzl St. (tel. 291 21), in Migdal and also a branch in Civic Center (tel. 384 31) and Afridar Center (tel. 351 31). Open Sun.-Thurs. 8:30am-12:30pm and 4-6pm.

Central Post Office: 18 Herzl St. (tel. 225 02), in Migdal. Open Sun.-Tues. and Thurs. 8am-12:30pm and 3:30-7pm, Wed. and Fri. 8am-noon. **International telephones** and **Poste Restante** here. (Phones close at 6pm, or at the station manager's discretion.) Branch offices in Afridar Center, Shimshon, and Civic Center (near bus station). **Telephone code:** 051.

Central Bus Station: (tel. 75 02 21). Information booth provides bus schedules with destinations in English. To: Jerusalem (bus #437, about every hour until 6:30pm, 2:30pm on Fri., 90min., NIS11); Tel Aviv (bus #300 or 311, every 15min. until 9:30pm, 4:30pm on Fri., NIS8); Be'ersheva (bus #363 or 364 hourly until 9:15pm, 2:30pm on Fri., NIS8.50). **Baggage check** open daily 7:30am-3pm, NIS6 per day.

Taxis: Yael Daroma on Tzahal St. in Migdal (tel. 75 03 34 or 75 01 34/5), runs *sherut* taxis to Tel Aviv (NIS7). You may have to purchase a seat for your pack. Only private taxis operate within Ashkelon and charge up to NIS6 to cross town. Stations are at Keren Kayemet St. in Shimshon (tel. 222 66/7), Beit HaMishpat St. in Barnea (tel. 255 55 or 222 82), and opposite the central bus station (tel. 330 77).

Car Rental: Amadu, 97 HaNassi (tel. 357 77 or 358 20). Also try **Eldan,** on Ben-Gurion Blvd. (tel. 227 24).

Laundry: Orion, 15 Herzl St., Migdal (tel. 75 04 31). Open Sun., Mon., Wed., and Thurs. 7am-1pm and 4-7pm, Tues. and Fri. 7am-1pm.

Pharmacies: Pharmacy Ashkelon, (tel. 342 34), across from the GTIO in Afridar. Open Sun.-Thurs. 8:30am-1pm and 4:30-7pm, Fri. 8:30am-1pm. **Migdal Pharmacy,** Golumb Sq. (tel. 75 03 32), in the old city. Open Sun.-Thurs. 9am-1pm and 4-7pm, Fri. 9am-1pm. **R&N Pharmacy,** 97 HaNassi St. (tel. 355 42). A list of all-night pharmacies is posted at each one.

Fire: Tel. 102.

First Aid: Emergency tel. 101. Information tel. 233 33.

Police: Emergency tel. 100. Information tel. 714 44. Located at the corner of HaNassi and Eli Cohen St.

Accommodations, Camping, and Food

Laskovicz Guest House, 9 Bareket St. (tel. 324 83), in Barnea. The most charming budget option in town. Take bus #5 to Gideon Ben-Yoash St., or call Alan and Adrienne Laskovicz from the central bus station; if someone is home, you've got a ride. Your hosts will do their darnedest to conjure up a friendly atmosphere. They often rent movies at night and play board games with the guests. The rooms are quiet, comfortable, and clean with private shower and toilet. A kitchen and refrigerator are available, and it's only a hop over the fence, past their swimming pool, to the beach. Mind the hibiscus. (Singles US$25. Doubles US$45.)

Samson Gardens, 38 HaTamar St. (tel. 346 66) in Afridar. Go through the municipal gardens, turn right onto Drom Africa Blvd., and make another right on HaTamar St. The rooms all have telephones, radios, A/C, and private bathrooms and showers. (Singles NIS47. Doubles NIS80. Breakfast included.)

Dagon Hotel, 2 Moshe Dorot St. (tel. 972 51 or 361 11/2), on Afridar Beach. Take bus #6 to the old age home on HaTayassim St. and backtrack 1.5 blocks. The rooms smack of the early '70s, but they're spacious and incorrigibly clean. Large dining hall offers moderately priced to expensive meals. 2min. walk to the beach. Large swimming pool in the central courtyard, lit and enlivened by music until at least midnight. Singles US$32, doubles US$64. Breakfast included.

The GTIO arranges rentals of **private rooms** in homes near the Afridar section of town. The price is usually NIS25-30, without meals, and quality varies widely. People also solicit boarders at the bus station and campground. They may begin by asking as much as NIS30 per night, but if you mention camping, prices will quickly plummet to NIS20. These unregulated rooms are often in Migdal, but are usually unmarked and difficult to find.

Ashkelon has one of the best **campgrounds** in Israel. To reach the campground (tel. 367 77, 340 27 or 308 80), take bus #3 or 9, ask the driver to let you off at Shapiro Rd. Or take bus #13 (in July and August), get off at Shapiro Rd., and walk about five minutes south to the entrance of the park; the campground is a 15-minute walk from the entrance. This route is longer, and you have to pay the park's admission fee of NIS9.50, students NIS4.80. The campground welcomes you with a variety of lodgings and services. There are beaches, archeological sites, snack bars, restaurants, and plenty of picnic facilities on the premises. Sagacious campers bring their own superfood from the **Hypercoop Supermarket,** 4 Ben-Gurion Blvd. (tel. 33 30 45), just south of the central bus station (open Sun.-Thurs. 9am-8pm and Fri. 8am-2pm). Look for the large concrete building behind the mini-mall which is next to the bus station.

Camping facilities are under the management of the Israel Camping Union, which standardizes all prices. If you bring your own tent, it costs NIS15 per person, NIS8 for children under 13. Beds in a bungalow are NIS60 for two people and NIS80 for four people. (Translated, a bungalow is a stuffy but quaint wooden octagon with fiberglass roof and mosquito netting. Simple beds and lamp inside suffice for sleeping, but you won't want to linger inside during the swelterfest.) A caravan with four beds is NIS110, NIS125 for six beds. (A caravan is a more recognizably civilized structure akin to a pre-fab home but immovable and without private bath.) Gas costs NIS8 for one day, NIS2 for each additional day. Lamps and refrigerators can be rented for NIS8 per day each. Chalets have been constructed, each including a living room, kitchen, full bath, and bedrooms that can sleep up to six. NIS200 minimum per night for up to four people. Five to six people, NIS240. The campground provides a massive tent that houses its marble-floored and surprisingly pleasant disco (open 9am-whenever).

The campground is often full, especially on Saturdays, so call ahead. Some folks get away with camping in the park for free, since it's large and crowded. Women are advised not to camp alone anywhere.

Camping on the beach adjacent to the city is dangerous and not recommended; those who do sleep in a large group with one person on guard at all times. The northern beaches might be a tad safer, but be extremely wary of thieves on the entire stretch. Respect the *dati* beach in Barnea during July and August where men and women swim separately.

The most popular inexpensive restaurants and stands are all located in Migdal, although the new *midreḥov* has caused price hikes. Take bus #4, 5, or 7 and get off at

Migdal Station. Air-conditioned **Nitzaḥon** 30 Herzl St. (tel. 274 09), near the post office, has the town's best selection of steaks, *me'orav* (mixed grill), kebab, and stuffed cabbage for NIS10-12 per plate. The restaurant at 70 Herzl St. serves meat sandwiches with hot dogs, schnitzel, or kebab for NIS5-6.50. **Mashehu Mashehu,** at 43 Herzl, has similar fare plus *me'orav* (NIS4). For fresh produce, head for the outdoor *shuk* on Remez St. in Migdal (open Mon., Wed., and Thurs. approx. 5am-6pm). A Tunisian Jew named Amos sells authentic Tunisian sandwiches at **Casse Croute Tunisien,** 31 Herzl, on the *midreḥov*. For NIS4, you'll get a baguette stuffed with tuna, capers, cooked and uncooked vegetable salads, potatoes, hot peppers, spicy *harisa,* lemon, and olives.

Sights and Entertainment

Ashkelon's seaside **National Park** (tel. 364 44) is one of the most popular and impressive in Israel. The park was built on the site of 1000-year-old Canaanite remains buried under the ruins of Philistine, Greek, Roman, Byzantine, Crusader, and Muslim cities. The ruins offer extensive evidence supporting Ashkelon's reputation as the oldest city in the world—competition for this title rages throughout the Middle East. You can pick up a free map of the park, which includes most of the archeological ruins, at the main entrance.

Herod the Great, the Hellenized Jewish king who ruled just before the Romans, was born in Ashkelon. He enlarged and beautified his birthplace, but the most extensive ruins date from the Roman era. The most compact portion of the site, situated in the center of the park, features an imposing Roman colonnade and a haphazard collection of Hellenistic and Roman columns, capitals, and statues, including two magnificent Roman statues of Nike, the winged goddess of victory and distant relative of Bo Jackson. If you came through the main entrance, the first section of antiquities you will see is the **Bouleuterion,** which was the Council House Square of Ashkelon when it was an autonomous city-state under Severius in the 3rd century CE. The sunken area with descending steps on the right, which resembles a courtyard, is actually the inside of a Herodian assembly hall. There is also a statue of the goddess Isis with her god-child Horus. These figures, made of marble imported from Italy, were sculpted some time between 200 BCE and 100 CE. Behind the Bouleuterion lies a spectacular **amphitheater,** well worth the five-minute walk.

Along the southern edge of the park are segments of wall from the 12th-century **Crusader city.** The most peculiar feature of the site is the assembly of Roman columns sticking out of the ancient Byzantine sea wall on the beach. Originally these columns were used to support the walls, which were destroyed in 1191 by Salah al-Din. Richard the Lion-Hearted partly restored them in 1192, as did Richard Cornwall in 1240, only to have them finally demolished by the Sultan Baybars in 1270.

Outside the park on the northern end of the beach is the well-preserved **Roman tomb,** believed to have been built for a wealthy Greek family during the 3rd century CE. The frescoes adorning its interior depict scenes from classical mythology and remain in remarkably good condition. You will have to unbolt a waist-high red iron door to get in. Close it on your way out: sand from the beach corrodes the paintings. (Tomb open Sun.-Fri. 9am-1pm, Sat. 10am-2pm. Free.)

Each of Ashkelon's **beaches** has unique charm. **Shimshon Beach,** in the National Park at the southernmost edge of the city possesses a lawn as well as impressive ruins. **Delila Beach,** about 2km further north, features three artificial islands within wading and swimming distance. Another kilometer farther north lies **Bar Kokhba Beach,** followed by **Barnea Beach,** where residents of Ashkelon's wealthier neighborhoods ablute. **Dati Beach** is a religious beach where men and women swim separately. (Feel free to join them, just honor the gender separation.) **Ḥofit Beach,** at the city's edge, is a popular spot for fishing and boating, but there are no lifeguards here.

For fun in the water—*sans* sand—there's the **Ashkeluna** water park near Delila Beach (tel. (051) 399 70). It's the biggest water park in the Middle East and Ashkelon's newest and cheesiest attraction. NIS27 covers a full day of splashy fun. Open daily 9am-5pm.

The most important ruins in the Afridar section of town are two writhing Roman sarcophagi, enclosed in the **Antiquities Courtyard** (tel. 340 19), along with other Roman sculptures. Both date from the 3rd century CE. The first depicts the abduction of Persephone to Hades, and the second depicts armor-clad, helmeted Greeks triumphing over naked barbarians (a true test of might). To the left of the first sarcophagus is the basket of flowers Persephone had been picking before her kidnapping—now slightly wilted. The sarcophagi are across the street from the GTIO (make a right at the post office) next to the commercial center. (Open Sun.-Fri. 7am-2pm. Free.) On your way out of the GTIO you can gawk at, and clamber over, Yigal Tumarkin's sculptures of ancient sundials in the Municipal Gardens.

Barnea, Ashkelon's rapidly expanding northern sector, contains the ruins of a 6th-century **Byzantine church,** and, nearby, a 5th-century **mosaic floor.** Neither is worth going out of your way to see—after the ruins in the national park, the knee-high pillars and ruined walls seem like pebbles and the design on the floor has been weathered to an almost uniform pallor.

The colorful town of **Migdal** has its own interesting history. After Sultan Baybars destroyed Ashkelon in 1270 CE, the site was desolate for several centuries until, in the 19th century, Lady Stanhope claimed knowledge of a treasure buried in nearby Mazhdar. The ruling Turkish *pashas* of Akko and Yafo brought Arab slaves to dig for the riches. Although the treasure was never discovered, the Arabs settled the area. The huge stones they excavated were shipped to Akko and Yafo for use in construction. When Israeli forces captured the town in 1948, almost all of the Arab population fled to Gaza and the new settlers translated the old name into its Hebrew equivalent: "migdal" (tower). Today, a handful of Arab families remain in Migdal, while many Arab workers commute here from Gaza for daywork. Gazans cannot, however, stay overnight without a permit.

With stone houses huddled together, and an occasional minaret and domed roof, Migdal contrasts conspicuously with the modern, spacious layout of Ashkelon's beachside districts. Nonetheless, the Israeli infatuation with the *midrehov* has made its way to this tiny old neighborhood; the pedestrian mall is on Herzl St. and serves as the main shopping district of town, ripening into a fruit and vegetable *shuk* on Mondays and Wednesdays, and evolving into a lively produce, clothing, and jewelry market on Thursdays. In addition to inexpensive perishables, you'll find sandwiches and snack bars—falafel often costs as little as NIS1. Walk north on Herzl St. just past Tzahal St., and you'll see the market in the narrow passageway to your left. Bus #4, 5, or 7 will take you to Migdal. The walk down Eli Cohen St. takes 25 minutes and passes through open fields.

Migdal is also the site of the new **Ashkelon Museum** (tel. 324 12), built in an old caravanserai and located at the corner of Eli Cohen and Herzl St. next to the Khan mosque. The museum traces the history of Ashkelon from Roman times to the present. (Open Sun.-Thurs. 9am-1pm and 4-6pm, Fri. 9am-1pm, Sat. 10am-1pm. Free.)

Pubs, movies, crowds, beaches, and the wonders of nature all contribute to the wild world of the Ashkelon nightlife. There are two pubs located near Afridar Center. **Style** (tel. 343 25) is the most popular local haunt. Its stocked bar and policy of "anything but Middle Eastern music" appeal to Israeli soldiers on break from Gaza, American engineers from the local power plant, Ashdod residents, and kibbutzniks. At **Bayit HaKafri** (the Village House, tel. 310 54), just across the green from Style, drinks are affordable and bands perform every Tuesday and Thursday evening. Attracts a slightly younger crowd.

The **Rahel Cinema** (tel. 314 29) at Zephania Sq. screens a scramble of (sometimes exceedingly unique) foreign films every night at 7:30 and 9:30pm while the **Esther Cinema** (tel. 226 59) in the Zion Hills district runs more recent films in English. Consult the tourist office for a list of monthly **winter concerts.** (Often, there are sound and light shows near the sarcophagi in Afridar, and the nearby Municipal Gardens hosts outdoor plays and concerts.) **Delila Beach** sizzles every night about 6pm with steak, beer, and pizza. The **Wosk Youth and Cultural Center,** 4 Yohannesberg St. (tel. 381 70), in Afridar, offers folk dancing Monday and Thursday nights at 8:30pm. (From the clock tower walk down Herzl St. until it becomes Drom Africa Rd. Make a left into the park and the Youth Center will be on your right). **Bustan HaZeytim** (tel. 364 44), in the national park, features dancing, folksinging, or magicians every Saturday night, and offers food and drink. Most evenings, the fancy hotels, notably the King Shaul and the Shulamit Gardens, sponsor discos or other activities.

Near Ashkelon

Ashdod אשדוד

"And what is, at best, is the city of Ashdod," wrote Amos Oz as the conclusion to *In the Land of Israel* (1983), his sketch of his own country. "A pretty city and to my mind a good one, this Ashdod. And she is all we have that is our own. All those who secretly long for the charms of Paris or Vienna, for the Jewish *shtetl*, or for heavenly Jerusalem: do not cut loose from those longings—for what are we without our longings?—but let's remember that Ashdod is what there is. And she is not quite the grandiose fulfillment of the vision of the Prophets and of the dream of generations; not quite a world premiere, but simply a city on a human scale. If only we try to look at her with a calm eye, we will surely not be shamed or disappointed.

"Ashdod is a city on a human scale on the Mediterranean coast. And from her we shall see what will flower when peace and a little repose finally come."

That's one way of looking at it. And thinking about the city as a metaphor for the Zionist experiment will keep you entertained. But, just to give you fair warning before you rush off to Ashdod with a copy of *The Jewish State* in hand, there's not much here in terms of standard budget-travel. You can come to Ashdod to practice your French, or to see industry relentlessly gulp down land and resources, or, if you're so inclined, perhaps to view the spot where the whale spat out Jonah. You'll be disappointed, though, if you come to Ashdod for blissful rest and relaxation.

The eco-troops rallying against Israel's ancient deforestation are losing the battle here. As you enter the city through its main boulevard, **Jerusalem Street,** you'll be overwhelmed—and disheartened—by kilometers of concrete high rises built on bare dunes. An equally drab, tangled jungle of metal antennaes and solar water heaters extends from every roof. If you stay long enough to visit Lido Beach, you'll find a short stretch of popular bars and cafés right on the water. But even here, bathers enjoying an otherwise beautiful Mediterranean swim are stalked by enormous cargo ships and spindly cranes from Ashkelon's giant port. The fact is that Ashdod exists for industry and not the other way around.

In Biblical times, Ashdod was one of the five cities of giants, the source of the giant grapes in the Ministry of Tourism's emblem. Although Joshua received accurate information from his spies, he did not stoop to conquer Ashdod, and it was here that the Philistines brought the captured Holy Ark. This former city of Gullivers is now home to 80,000 residents and the largest port in Israel, having surpassed Ḥaifa. Its expanding industries include everything from cosmetics and textiles to power plants that produce roughly half the nation's electricity.

Ashdod is on Israel's agenda for tourist development—but you'd never know it. Dubbed "The Big City" for lack of any other distinguishing features, it remains unabashedly ill-equipped to host visitors. The sole accommodations, the Orly and MiAmi hotels, are way out of the budget range. Nevertheless, Ashdodos are exceptionally outgoing and helpful, and their golden sand beaches, Lido and MiAmi, are clean; sleeping here is tolerated, but as always, sleep on your wallet and avoid "beachcamping" alone. There are showers, and it's easy to find shade.

After you get off the bus, head next door to the **Bureau of Public Relations** on the 5th floor—that's the *cinquième étage* if you want to get anywhere around here—of the Municipal Building (tel. (055) 523 01). The guard on duty will speak Hebrew and French, but most likely not a word of English. Do what you must to get their excellent, poster-sized city map (although you should resign yourself to screaming tourist status thereafter). Like Ashkelon, Ashdod has orchards of banks. Near the bus station, in the area known as Rova Daled, there's **Bank Leumi,** 2 Shapiro St. (tel. 55 29 92; open Sun., Tues., Thurs. 8:30am-12:30pm and 4-6pm, Mon. and Wed. 8:30am-12:30pm, Fri. 8:30am-noon) and **Israeli Discount,** 1 Shapiro St. (tel. 55 66 11; open same hours). At 25 Rogozim St., down Shapiro St. from the Municipal Building, is a **supermarket** (open Sun.-Thurs. 7am-7:30pm, Fri. 7am-2pm), and falafel stands and kiosks abound along Rogozim. At the end of the street is the main **post office.** (Open Sun.-Tues. and Thurs. 7:45am-12:30pm and 3:30-8pm, Wed. 7:45am-1:30pm, Fri. 7:45am-noon.) There is **poste restante** here, and public phones next door. The **police** are on Yitzhak HaNassi St., about a 20-minute walk from Rogozim St. (Dial 100 or 54 77 44 for emergencies.) At the end of Rogozim, turn left onto Nordau, and you'll come to the beach. For **taxis,** call **Ron,** 1 Rogozim St. (tel. 52 21 27 or 52 17 41). For **car rental,** there is **Eldan** (tel. 53 41 77). The **telephone code** is 08.

On the southern outskirts of Ashdod lie the remains of a Fatamid fortress (10th century CE) known in Arabic as **Qal'at al-Mine,** in Hebrew as **Metzudat Ashdod Yam,** and in English as **Fortress of the Port.** Until excavations unearthed bits of ceramic pottery, the site was believed to be more recent. An early Arabic document recounts that Byzantine ships used to bring in Muslim prisoners to sell back to their families. As boats appeared off the coast of Ashdod, the Fatamid fortress would send up smoke signals alerting the townspeople to come at once with their offerings. Thousands brought what riches they had, hoping to earn the return of their loved ones. Qa'lat al-Mine, once part of a chain of coastal fortifications, seems to have served as a focal point for these emotional exchanges. Portions of four towers remain. To visit the site, take bus #5 south, and ask to get off at the fortress (at the end of a row of private homes).

The site of the Biblical city of **Tel Ashdod,** southeast of the modern city, comprises 23 levels of virtually unidentifiable ruins. Nothing much remains, although excavations continue. The **Nahal Lakhish Park,** stretching 3km along the river, separates Ashdod's residential town from the industrial areas and the port, offering a super spot for a picnic.

For a striking view of the city and its environs, climb **Givat Yona,** adjacent to the lighthouse at the end of Ya'ir St. in the northern part of the city. According to Muslim tradition, the ruins mark the spot where the whale coughed up Jonah. If you visit Ashdod on a Wednesday, don't miss the **flea market** at Hof Lido (Lido Beach) from 6am until nightfall. Every Saturday, literally thousands of people grit these sands even finer with their happy, dancing feet (roughly 5-8pm in summer and 11am-2pm in winter). Afterward the crowds pour into the beachfront bars.

The most popular Ashdod night spot is **Bulldog** (tel. 56 13 80), a club that plays American rock for no-nonsense dancers. (Admission NIS10, open 10pm-morning.) Take bus #8 and ask the driver to let you off at the nearest stop. **Umbaba** (tel. 55 38 09), with its six illuminated billiard tables (the bar is otherwise completely dark), is a serious, almost vocational, entertainment establishment—the bar is *always* open, though the management admits that there are very few customers from 4-9am. (Beer NIS3-4, hummus NIS5.) No Middle Eastern music, and preference given to loud, uncut versions of African-American tunes. No cover. Another popular pub on Lido Beach is **Briza** (tel. 54 01 69), where you can imbibe a strange mix of reggae, rock, and Middle Eastern music and beverage. This place also has a battalion of billiard tables inside, and an eating area outside on the beach. No cover charge; "never closes."

In August Ashdod hosts an annual **Mediterranean Festival** including song, dance, sculpture, and musical instruments. The festival lasts five days; ask at the Bureau of Public Relations for 1993 dates and more details.

Bus #15 leaves Ashkelon about every hour for Ashdod (NIS3.80). Buses #312 and 314 from Tel Aviv run to Ashdod every 10-20 minutes until 8pm, and continue less frequently until 9:50pm.

Yad Mordekhai יד מורדכי

There's a story here. From May 19th to 24th, 1948, during Israel's War of Independence, the 165 members of Kibbutz Yad Mordekhai withstood an attack by an Egyptian battalion of 2500. Although the kibbutz members eventually had to retreat to nearby Gvar'am, 300 Egyptians were killed, and this delay gave the Hagana time to regroup and save Tel Aviv. To commemorate this deed, the kibbutz has built a model of the battle on the original site, complete with soldiers, tanks, and weapons. A recorded explanation in several languages recounts the battle and various parts of the colossal reconstruction. The kibbutz is named after Mordekhai Anielewicz, leader of the Warsaw Ghetto uprising. A **museum** (tel. (051) 205 28/9) illustrates the story of the Jewish resistance movement, concluding with exhibits about the establishment of the State of Israel and the battle for Yad Mordekhai. (Museum and battlefield open daily 8am-4pm. Admission NIS3.50, students NIS3.)

Bus #19 runs from Ashkelon to Yad Mordekhai Sunday through Thursday at noon, 2:45pm, and 6pm, and Friday at noon and 4:15pm (NIS2.10). Since the last bus returns at 3:10pm (12:40pm Fri.), you'll have to take the noon bus if you don't intend to stay. If you get stuck in the late afternoon, go back to the bus stop on the highway anyway: buses from Rafiah pass by, and you may get a ride.

Other Towns Near Ashkelon

About 22km east of Ashkelon, **Kiryat Gat** is easily accessible from Tel Aviv, Jerusalem, and Ashkelon (bus #25 runs from Ashkelon Sun.-Thurs. every 30min. until 8:30pm, Fri. until 2:15pm; 30-35 min.; NIS3.10). From Ashdod, take bus #212 to *tzomet* Ashdod, then catch a bus heading to Be'ersheva. This small, industrial town is the capital of the Lakhish region—a network of 30 villages established in 1954—and the jumping-off point for exploring several important sites. Tel Gat, the hill to the northeast, was formerly believed to be Gath, one of the five major Philistine cities and the birthplace of Goliath. Excavations, however, have failed to unearth any evidence of an ancient capital.

Beit Guvrin, a modern kibbutz, was built in 1949 on the ruins of the deserted Arab village of Bit Jibrin. The surrounding region is characterized by huge outcroppings of cacti and fig trees, which hide some 3000 caves. Some of the caves were carved naturally as water eroded the soft limestone. Phoenicians carved the others as they scooped limestone out of gigantic holes in the earth for use in the construction of their great port at Ashkelon. As a result, many of the caves have vast bell-shaped rooms with sun roofs. The caves later became natural sanctuaries for hermits and monks of the Byzantine period. St. John and others came here seeking solitude, and often carved crosses and altars into the walls. Modern carving, mutilation, and havoc were wrought here during the filming of the postmodern epic *Rambo III*.

At nearby **Tel Sandahanna** (Arabic for St. John), excavations uncovered vivid, beautifully preserved, Byzantine mosaics of birds and flowers. These served as floors in 5th- and 6th-century churches and can be seen near the top of the *tel*, protected by small sheds. More recently excavations have uncovered a Roman mosaic floor in even better condition. Two of the caves were used for burials and have niches for the appropriate urns. Since the sites are unmarked and the *tel* is large, you should ask for the assistance of one of the kibbutzniks from Beit Guvrin, a 20-minute walk down the hill. Most of the kibbutzniks get off work about 12:30-1:30pm and are willing to show interested travelers around. Ask to see the house of King Abdallah, King Hussein's grandfather, located amidst the Beit Guvrin caves.

Getting to and from Beit Guvrin requires advance planning. Bus #11 from Kiryat Gat goes directly to the kibbutz. (Sun.-Thurs. 6am, 8am, 5:10pm, Fri. 6am, 8am, 2:15pm. You'll have to catch one of the morning buses if you don't want to spend the night.) Some of the Kiryat Gat-Hebron buses pass by Beit Guvrin as well; ask the driver to let you off here since there is no regular stop. Taxis run from the central bus station to Beit Guvrin, Tel Maresha, and Tel Lakhish. To reach the caves, walk to the paved road opposite the kibbutz. The first fork bears left to the resoundmost of the Beit Guvrin bell caves.

The right fork leads to **Tel Maresha,** about 3km southeast of Beit Guvrin. The unbelievable view makes it worth the trip, even if you're crumbling at the sight of ruins. On a clear day, you can see Tel Aviv and the Mediterranean to the west, and the Jordanian hills and the Dead Sea to the east. The ruins include several Phoenician bell caves, one of which has a stone *calumbarium* with thousands of niches, two decorated graves, and a Crusader basilica nearby. The 60 caves around the ruins contain colorful wildlife drawings.

Tel Lakhish lies just north of the moshav of the same name, 2km south of the Beit Guvrin-Hebron road. Although archeologically more important, Tel Lakhish is not as interesting as Tel Maresha. Because of its strategic location at the intersection of the road to Egypt and the approach to Jerusalem, it was often a scene of conflict in ancient times. It is mentioned in the Bible (Joshua 10:31-32) as one of the Canaanite cities destroyed by the Israelites. Excavations have revealed nine levels of settlements dating as far back as the 3rd millenium BCE. There are still remains of Canaanite graves and one of their holy sites, but most of the artifacts have been removed to museums in Jerusalem and Britain. In addition, it's virtually inaccessible without a car, although bus #11 runs to the moshav. Because of this area's isolation, climate, and proximity to the West Bank, moshavniks strongly discourage camping in these hills.

Sdeh Yoav, a small, unofficial stop on the Kiryat Gat route (bus #25), is quickly turning into a malodorous tourist attraction. The reputedly therapeutic sulphur pools and Dead Sea mud are part of Kibbutz Sdeh Yoav's accidental financial jackpot. While digging a pool for irrigation, kibbutzniks chanced upon a hot sulphur spring. They began pumping it for irrigation of sulphur-friendly crops, and gradually found themselves wading in hot, smelly water as they filled the reservoir. When locals started hopping the fence to partake of the sulfur bath's purported healing properties, the Sdeh Yoav kibbutz decided to go commercial; all profits are diverted into developing the site for tourists. Now you'll find a row of Egged tour buses and gaggles of geriatrics easing their aches and pains in the pools. Four mega pools and 14 subdivisions allow almost 100 people to loll hippopotamus-style in the spring water; eight spigots by the larger pool massage those problem areas. Buy your Dead Sea mud, also thought to be therapeutic, in painfully small containers for NIS3. The snack bar sells soft drinks and candy; bring a picnic for a more salubrious swallowings. (Open Sun. and Thurs. 8am-6pm, Mon., Tues., and Wed. 8am-8pm, Fri. 8am-5pm. NIS10, children NIS7.)

Dead Sea (Yam HaMelah)
ים המלח

This is as low as you can stoop—more than 394m below sea level, the Dead Sea is the lowest point on earth. The shiny, happy name was coined by Christian pilgrims astonished by the apparent absence of any form of life in its waters (kill-joy scientists have recently discovered micro-organisms in the lake's water, but that doesn't count). Its Hebrew name, Yam HaMelaḥ (Salt Sea) makes the point: the lake has a salt concentration eight times that of ocean water. Although there is no outlet for the lake's water, the intense sun bearing down on the valley used to evaporate enough water to keep the water level constant. But since Israel now pumps water from the Sea of Galilee for agricultural purposes, the source of water to the Dead Sea has been cut off and the sea is drying up. Israel considered digging a canal from the Mediterranean to refill the Dead Sea, but the Med-Dead canal idea was too pricey.

Swimming in, or rather floating on, the Dead Sea is like nothing else in the world. You just bob up and down like a human cork, suspended on salts and minerals trapped by centuries of evaporation. Bring a newspaper in and annoy everyone around you.

In ancient times, the Dead Sea was a refuge for those in search of religious freedom (the Qumran sect), political freedom (David, who hid at Ein Gedi), or both (the Jewish

LET'S GO® Travel
1992 CATALOG

When it comes to budget travel we know every trick in the book Discount Air Fares, Eurailpasses, Travel Gear, IDs, and more...

LET'S PACK IT UP

Let's Go Supreme

Innovative hideaway suspension with parallel stay internal frame turns backpack into carry-on suitcase. Includes lumbar support pad, torso and waist adjustment, leather trim, and detachable daypack. Waterproof Cordura nylon, lifetime guarantee, 4400 cu. in Navy, Green or Black.

A $165

Let's Go Backpack/Suitcase

Hideaway suspension with internal frame turns backpack into carry-on suitcase. Detachable daypack makes it 3 bags in 1. Waterproof Cordura nylon, lifetime guarantee, 3750 cu. in. Navy, Green or Black.

B $119

Undercover NeckPouch

Ripstop nylon with soft Cambrelle back. 3 pockets. 6 1/2 x 5". Lifetime guarantee. Black or Tan.

C $9.95

Undercover WaistPouch

Ripstop nylon with soft Cambrelle back. 2 pockets. 12 x 5" with 30 x 13cm waistband. Lifetime guarantee. Black or Tan.

D $9.95

Let's Go Backcountry

Full size, slim profile expedition pack designed for the serious trekker. Parallel stay suspension system, deluxe shoulder harness, Velcro height adjustment, side compression straps. Detachable hood converts into a fanny pack. Waterproof Cordura nylon, lifetime guarantee, main compartment and hood 6350 cu. in. extends to 7130 cu.

E $195

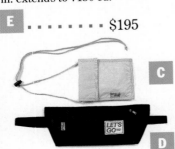

LET'S SEE SOME I.D.

1993 International ID Cards

Provides discounts on accomodations, cultural events, airfares and accident/medical insurance. Valid 9-1-92 to 12-31-93

F1	Teacher (ITIC) • • • • •	$16.00
F2	Student (ISIC) • • • • • •	$15.00
F3	Youth (IYC) • • • • • • •	$15.00

FREE "International Student Travel Guide."

LET'S GO HOSTELING

1993-94 Youth Hostel Card

Required by most international hostels. Must be a U.S. resident.

G1	Adult (ages 18-55) • • • • • •	$25
G2	Youth (under 18) • • • • • • •	$10

Sleepsack

Required at all hostels. Washable durable poly/cotton. 18" pillow pocket. Folds into pouch size.

H	• • • • • • • • • •	$13.95

1992-93 Youth Hostel Guide (IYHG)

Essential information about 3900 hostels in Europe and the Mediterranean.

I	• • • • • • • • • •	$10.95

Let's Go Travel Guides

Europe; USA; Britain/Ireland; France; Italy; Israel/Egypt; Mexico; California/Hawaii; Spain/Portugal; Pacific Northwest/Alaska; Greece/Turkey; Germany/Austria/Swizerland; NYC; London; Washington D.C.; Rome; Paris.

J1	USA or Europe • • • • • •	$16.95
J2	Country Guide (specify) • • •	$15.95
J3	City Guide (specify) • • • •	$10.95

LET'S GO BY TRAIN

Eurail Passes

Convenient way to travel Europe. Save up to 70% over cost of individual tickets. Call for national passes.

First Class

K1	15 days • • • • • • • •	$460
K2	21 days • • • • • • • •	$598
K3	1 month • • • • • • •	$728
K4	2 months • • • • • •	$998
K5	3 months • • • • • •	$1260

First Class Flexipass

L1	5 days in 15 • • • • •	$298
L2	9 days in 21 • • • • •	$496
L3	14 days in 30 • • • • •	$676

Youth Pass (under 20)

M1	1 month • • • • • •	$508
M2	2 months • • • • • •	$698
M3	5 days in 2 months • •	$220
M4	10 days in 2 months • •	$348
M5	15 days in 2 months • •	$474

LET'S GET STARTED

Please print or type. Incomplete applications will be returned

International Student/Teacher Identity Card (ISIC/ITIC) (ages 12 & up) enclose:

1 Letter from registrar or administration, transcript, or proof of tuition payment. FULL-TIME only.
2 One picture (1 1/2" x 2") signed on the reverse side.

International Youth Card (IYC) (ages 12-25) enclose:

1 Proof of birthdate (copy of passport or birth certificate).
2 One picture (1 1/2" x 2") signed on the reverse side.
3 Passport number   **4** Sex: M☐ F

Last Name	First Name	Date of Birth

Street   *We do not ship to P.O. Boxes. U.S. addresses only.*

City	State	Zip Code

Phone	Citizenship

School/College   Date Trip Begins

Item Code	Description, Size & Color	Quantity	Unit Price	Total Price

Shipping & Handling

If order totals: . . . . . . Add
Up to $30.00. . . . . . . $4.00
30.01-100.00. . . . . . . $6.00
Over 100.00 . . . . $7.00

Total Merchandise Price	
Shipping & Handling (See box at left)	
For Rush Handling Add $8 for continental U.S., $10 for AK & HI	
MA Residents (Add 5% sales tax on gear & books)	
Total	

Enclose check or money order payable to: Harvard Student Agencies, Inc.

Allow 2-3 weeks for delivery. Rus orders delivered within one week our receipt.

LET'S G☺ Travel

Harvard Student Agencies, Inc., Harvard University, Thayer B, Cambridge, MA 02138

(617) 495-9649   1-800-5LET'S GO (Credit Card Orders Only)

Prices subject to change

rebels at Masada). The Dead Sea can also name Jesus, King Herod, and John the Baptist among its illustrious, but temporary, residents.

The waters themselves are the subject of controversy—some swear by their curative properties, others say they're useless, and the rest of the world asks if they would mind terribly keeping their voices down. According to a few scientists and all resort owners, concentrations of bromine, magnesium, and iodine 10-20 times higher than in the ocean, reduce skin allergies, stimulate certain glandular functions, and have a soothing effect on the central nervous system. If bromine calms you down, you should take more vacations. The sulphur springs at resorts along the coast seem to alleviate the pains of rheumatism and arthritis, but occasionally have an adverse effect on blood pressure and olfactory functions.

If any of the water gets into your eyes, you're in for several minutes of painful blindness. Rinse your eyes out immediately in the fresh-water showers found on all beaches. Don't shave immediately before swimming here; the water will sear minor scrapes you didn't even know you had. Since you will want to wash off as soon as you get out of the water, you may want to stick to the resorts (Ein Feshka, Ein Gedi, Ein Bokek, and Neveh Zohar), where showers are available.

The Dead Sea does not have an ordinary desert climate—rather than harsh and dry it's harsh and humid. The sticky air, especially in the summer, makes high temperatures barely tolerable. Athletes may enjoy the clean air and a 10% increase in oxygen concentration, but exertion is sane only in the early morning.

Currently the Dead Sea is 65km long, up to 18km wide, and up to 400m deep. The haze that obscures what would otherwise be an otherworldly view of the basin is actually evaporation. The rift in the Earth's crust which created this place is evident in the jagged wall of cliffs, less than 3km apart, which rise on both the Israeli and Jordanian coasts.

From the central bus station in Jerusalem, several **buses** make frequent trips along the bank of the Dead Sea. Buses #421, 486, and 966 stop at Qumran (NIS9.50), Ein Feshka, Ein Gedi, Masada, and Neveh Zohar. Bus #487, also from Jerusalem, runs only to Qumran, Ein Feshka, and Ein Gedi. In addition, bus #385 makes about four trips per day (Sun.-Fri.) between Ein Gedi and Be'ersheva.

If you're planning to stay in the Dead Sea area for a while, stock up on food. The only grocery store is at Neveh Zohar, to the south. The same rules apply as in the desert: Bring a water bottle wherever you go, and keep your head covered with something fashionable or amusing.

Take an organized tour if you want to trek into the desert. The **Metzokei Dragot Desert Tour Village** takes you through rugged desert terrain to major sights. The one-day tour includes refreshments and costs NIS100. Tours of the Dead Sea area leave from the Jerusalem Gate Hotel near the central bus station every Tuesday at 9am. For information and reservations call their offices in Kibbutz Mitzpeh Shalem (tel. (02) 96 45 01/2/3). Or try **Egged** or **SPNI tours.**

Ein Gedi עין גדי

On the approach to the Ein Gedi ("Fountain of the Kid," as in goatling) Nature Reserve, strips of greenery cling to the barren landscape. Ein Gedi's springs bubble in the heights and cascade into refreshing pools and streams. If you hike to the springs via the hot, dry hills, walk back along (or in) the shallow streams.

Practical Information

Buses run to Eilat; Be'ersheva via Arad, Masada, and Ein Bokek; Tel Aviv via Jerusalem; and others. Local buses run to Masada, Ein Bokek, and Neveh Zohar 10 times daily. Reservations for seats on the Eilat bus cannot be made at Ein Gedi or Masada. Your chances of getting an unreserved seat are good at the height of the tourist season, since Egged often runs two buses at a time to accommodate the crowds. If you want to be on the safe side, buy a seat on a bus to Eilat before you leave Jerusalem. When you get off the bus, follow the signs for **Naḥal David,** not for Ein Gedi (this refers to the Ein Gedi kibbutz). Continue 500m south along the main road and you'll pass a roadway on your right that leads to the **Arugot Reserve;** 400m farther down from the nature reserve on your left are the **public campgrounds.** Ein Gedi Kibbutz is 1km farther south; a bus runs to and from the site every 30 minutes. There is a **first-aid station** at the campground.

Accommodations

Along the road to the reserve, a giant leap to the right leads to the hostel and a field school. The prime choice for accommodations in the Dead Sea area is the **Beit Sara Hostel (HI)** (tel. (057) 58 41 65). Despite its 206 beds, this youth hostel is still usually crowded and the management tends to be impersonal. Don't drink any of the tap water from the showers or bathroom; use the drinking fountain instead. The hostel is open from 7am to 9pm; if you come early (before 4pm), management will look after your bags. (Dorm beds NIS35, nonmembers add NIS3. Breakfast included, other meals available.)

Ein Gedi Camping (tel. (057) 58 43 42) is a barren, shadeless beach less than 1km south of the hostel and nature reserve (15-20 min. walk). Since nights at Ein Gedi are almost as hot as days, you should think twice about sleeping without air conditioning. If you decide to camp, the reception office (open 24 hrs.) will store your valuables in a safe. If you bring your own tent, the price is NIS18 (children NIS9). The nearby caravans, which accommodate four to six people, offer A/C and bathrooms. (NIS144 per night for a couple, NIS30 each additional person.) The army discourages free-lance camping.

Sights

David fled to this oasis to escape the wrath of King Saul (I Samuel 23:29). Ein Gedi is also mentioned in the Song of Songs. During the second Jewish revolt, Simon Bar-Kokhba sought refuge here—his hiding place, the Letter Cave, can be visited about 6 km southwest of the main settlement.

But the **Ein Gedi nature reserve** (tel. (057) 58 42 85 or 58 45 17) is the main reason to visit this area. The climbs are not especially difficult, and there are well-placed bars to hold onto in the occasional steep areas. Lighten your load with the lockers at the gift shop (NIS2). Dead Sea temperatures, however, can make even inhaling strenuous, so *only* hike very early in the morning or late in the afternoon. *Always* bring at least two bottles of water (you can fill up at the faucets just outside the gate). If you're short on time, at least hike the 15 minutes up to **Naḥal David** (David's Stream), a slender pillar of water dropping the full length of the cliffside into a shallow pool. Abundant pools nourish the area; investigate the paths that branch off the main trail and disappear into the thicket of giant reeds. (You can drink from the drinking taps scattered throughout the reserve, but *not* from the pools.) Twenty meters below the waterfall on the southern bank of the brook, another trail climbs up the cliffside to **Shulamit Spring.** From the spring you have two options: continuing up the cliff will bring you to **Dodim (Lovers')** Cave, a splendidly cool, mossy niche at the top of the fall (30-min. walk). Don't even think about it. Continuing to the left, you'll see signs to the fenced in **Calcolithic Temple** (20min. from Dodim), built 5000 years ago by the first of an almost unbroken chain of settlers in the region. Beware of the reserve's many leopards; 12 have been tagged so far, and one might try to tag you.

From the Calcolithic Temple, either return as you came or make the steeper descent along a path to **Ein Gedi Spring** (25min.). Despite its pretensions, it is in fact only a water source for the oasis. From Ein Gedi Spring a roundabout path runs to Shulamit Spring, whence you can return to the base of the waterfall at Naḥal David. The map in the brochure available at the entrance to the reserve is not helpful for gauging the ascents and difficulty of the various hikes, but does provide general orientation. The SPNI workers at the field school or at the reserve will help you plan more off-the-beaten-track hikes from the Hebrew-only maps of the area. To allow the leopards time to hunt before dark, the reserve is open 8am-3pm, but you can exit until 4pm (in summer open 8am-4pm, last exit 5pm); you may not start the hike to Dodim Cave and beyond after 1:30pm (in summer 2:30pm). Admission NIS7, children NIS3.50. A food kiosk is open during park hours near the entrance to the reserve.

A fairly difficult climb along **Naḥal Arugot,** which begins in the parking lot of the Naḥal Arugot Rd. about 2km in from Rte. 90, leads to a charming "hidden waterfall." It's a good 90-minute walk from the road (look for the sign), but if you follow the course of the stream you won't get lost. (Open 8am-2pm, last exit 4pm. In summer open 8am-3:30pm, last exit 5:30pm.) The pool at the end, considerably deeper than the others, rewards the exertion. According to Josephus, the Roman statesman and rhetorician G. Levi Primus died here.

Masada (Metzada) מצדה

"Masada shall not fall again," swear the members of the armored division of the Israel Defense Forces each year at this site. The Jewish Zealots' tenacious defense of this formidable rock, though forgotten for centuries, has been fashioned into a vivid symbol for modern Israel, with some controversy about the implications of that metaphor.

The huge fortress (Metzada means fortress) was built as a refuge against marauding Greeks and Syrians by the Jewish High Priest Jonathan Maccabeus around 150 BCE. The 2000 by 750 ft. fortress was expanded a few decades later by Johann Hyrkanus I. In 40 CE, King Herod fled to Masada in order to avoid being massacred by rival Hasmoneans backed by the Parthians. Although Herod was ultimately successful in putting down the revolts, Masada was used once again, in 66 CE, when the Judeans rebelled against Roman occupation; a small band of the rebels, the original Zealots, captured the outpost. The Romans gradually crushed the revolt—taking Jerusalem in 70 CE and destroying the Second Temple—and soon Masada alone was the last holdout. With years' worth of food, water, and military supplies stashed behind its two defensive walls, Masada was ideally suited for resistance. The 967 defenders—men, women, and children—held off thousands of Roman legionnaires through a three-year siege. The Romans, frustrated at first, soon called in their best engineers and constructed a wall and camps in a ring around the mount. With patience and ingenuity, they ultimately built a stone and gravel ramp up the side of the cliff.

When the defenders realized that the Romans would break through the wall the next morning, each family burned its possessions and joined in the plan for a communal suicide. The Jews placed stores of wheat and water in the citadel's courtyard to prove to the Romans that they did not perish from hunger. Ten men were chosen by lot to execute the others and check each house to make sure everyone was dead. Lots were drawn again, and one person was selected to take the lives of the other nine, and finally his own. The following morning, when the Romans burst in, they encountered a deathly silence. The only survivors, two women and five children, told the story of the martyrs of Masada. The story was recorded by Josephus Flavius, a Jewish general in the revolt who had defected to the Romans and become a chronicler.

Practical Information

Masada lies 20km south of Ein Gedi, a few kilometers inland on the road to Arad and Be'ersheva. Buses go to Eilat, Be'ersheva via Arad, Jerusalem, and Ein Gedi. Take the schedules with a grain of Dead Sea salt.

There are three ways to reach the ruins—by cable car or by either of two foot paths. Watch out for Zonker's friend Mr. Sun; a hat is vital. The easier of the two trails, the **Roman Ramp,** starts on the west side of the mountain, on Arad Rd., and takes about 30 minutes to ascend. This trail is not accessible by public transportation, and the walk around the base to the Roman Ramp is extremely arduous and time-consuming. More popular, more scenic, and a bit more difficult is the original **Serpentine Path,** named for its tortuous bends. The path has barely been repaired since the Zealots used it. The hike takes just under an hour, and if you start early enough (gates open at 4:30am), you'll see the sun slowly rising over the Dead Sea 450m below. It is important to start hiking *well* before the afternoon, both to avoid the heat and to leave enough time to tour the extensive ruins. Drinking water is available only at the summit.

The hiking-averse may prefer a **cable car** which stops near the top of Serpentine Path. It starts running at 8am and leaves every few minutes for the three-minute ascent; the last cable car up is at 4pm (summer 5pm), on Friday at 2pm (summer 3pm). (One way fare including admission NIS19.50, youth NIS11, students NIS13.50.) A compromise is to hike up the mountain early and take the cable car down when it starts to get hot. (Site officially open 6:30am-3:30pm. Admission NIS10, youth NIS5, students NIS7.50.) The site officially closes at 3:30pm but the gates are often left open and you can get in free after hours. Guards don't usually ask people to leave until 8pm.

Accommodations and Food

The first thing you'll see when you leave the bus is the **Taylor Youth Hostel (HI)** (tel. (057) 58 43 49). The 150-bed hostel has clean rooms and air conditioning, but is often crowded. Check-in is 4-7pm, but, if you can, try to drop your bags off between 8:30am and 1pm. Lockers NIS3. All rooms are scheduled to have private toilets and showers by 1993. When you check in you can order a bag breakfast to be picked up at 7:30pm. (Dorm beds NIS35, nonmembers NIS38. Breakfast included. Dinner NIS19.) A concrete pavilion in front of the hostel accommodates campers for free. Lockers NIS3; buy locker tokens when you check in. The hostel will allow you to use their showers for NIS2, but they strictly prohibit use of other facilities.

The only other accommodations within reasonable distance are the **campground** at Neveh Zohar to the south, the **youth hostel** in Arad, and the facilities north at Ein Gedi (see the Near Masada and Arad sections for details). Someone rolled off Masada while sleeping on the top several years ago, so you can no longer camp up there.

Next to the hostel at the base of the mountain is an assortment of absurdly priced refreshment stands, a souvenir shop (open 9am-3:30pm), and air-conditioned restaurants (open 11:30am-3pm). The budget exception is the **snack bar,** with large meat or cheese sandwiches for NIS5. The shops all feature overpriced copies of archeologist Yigael Yadin's popular book on Masada, which you can buy for much less at a Steimatzsky's near you. Drinking water is available from a number of faucets and hoses; don't take a sip unless it's marked as drinking water *(mayim leshtiya).*

Sights

The ruins at Masada, as well as some Zealot skeletons, were unearthed in 1963 by a team of archeologists headed by Yigael Yadin. Begin your exploration at the entrance to a huge water cistern—one of seven—located to your right near the last flight of wooden stairs to the summit. It is estimated that the defenders were able to store enough water in the cisterns to last eight years. As you enter the site proper, the enormous store-houses stand to your right. About one-third of the ruins is actually restoration work—a black line runs along the walls to distinguish the original from the reconstructed sections. The main attraction of the palace is the Roman-style **bathhouse,** complete with vomitorium. Traces of all eight Roman camps, appearing as brownish rectangular enclosures, are clearly distinguishable from the mountain summit, and you can make out the outline of a wall that connected them.

At the edge of the northern cliff, with its semicircular patio, lies what archeologists believe was **Herod's private palace.** In the bathhouse of the lowest section, the skeletons of a man, woman, and child were found along with a *tallit* (ceremonial prayer shawl).

Climb back up the steps from Herod's palace and turn right as you reach the summit to find the Zealots' **synagogue,** the oldest known synagogue in Israel. Scrolls were found here containing texts from several books of the Torah. Most are now on display in the Shrine of the Book at the Israel Museum in Jerusalem. Discoveries such as a *mikveh* (ritual bath) and remnants of Torah scrolls indicate that the community followed *halakha* despite mountain isolation and siege. Continuing still farther along the edge you will come to the **Western Palace,** which houses splendid Herodian mosaics, also the oldest in Israel. Masada was occupied for a short time in the 5th century CE by Christian monks who built the **Byzantine Chapel** next to the Western Palace.

A sound and light show runs every Tuesday and Thursday at 9pm (Sept. and Oct. 7pm) in the amphitheater near the bottom of the Roman ramp (not accessible by public transportation). Most viewers come by car from Arad; trekking from the youth hostel is not feasible. The best option is to climb Masada as the sun sets (6pm) and descend at 8pm down the Roman ramp. You still run the risk of not being able to find a ride back to the other side, so this option is only advisable if you can secure a ride while still on Masada. (For more information call Yoel Tours at (057) 58 44 32. Tickets NIS44. No shows Nov.-March.)

Near Masada

The fantastic beach at **Ein Bokek** has made the town one of the most popular resorts on the Dead Sea. Located on the southern half of the sea, 15km south of Masada, Ein Bokek makes a great swim stop on the way to Arad and Be'ersheva if you're going in that direction anyway. Near the hotel area, where the bus lets you off, is an air-conditioned mini-mall featuring a **cafeteria** with meals for NIS16 and a **mini-market** (open 9am-10pm) and a **gift shop.** The most interesting sights around are the salt formations in the southern regions of the Dead Sea, which seem to float like crystalline icebergs but are actually rooted to the sea floor.

Stretching south from Neveh Zohar, the road drops into searing **Sodom,** where Lot's wife was turned into a pillar of salt. The Bible describes Sodom and Gomorrah as the New Yorks of their day, upon which God rained fire and brimstone. Only the family of Lot was spared, on the condition that they not look back to witness their neighbors' plight. Out of sympathy or curiosity, Lot's wife snuck a fateful glance and was transformed into a pile of Morton's (Genesis 18-19).

In modern Sodom the visitor magnet is the column of salt that tour guides introduce as Mrs. Lot. Sodom is also the home of the **Dead Sea Works,** which extract potash and other minerals from the Dead Sea for export. Tours can be arranged through the museum in Neveh Zohar, or in the rear of the main office in Arad. Most of the workers live in nearby Arad and Dimona because Sodom's heat is unbearable—indisputable evidence, it would seem, that it once rained fire and brimstone here. **Buses** #421, 486, and 966 (from Jerusalem) travel as far south as Ein Bokek, Neveh Zohar, and Sodom.

WEST BANK
الضفة الغربية

> Travel in the Israeli-occupied West Bank can be dangerous during times of heightened Israeli-Palestinian tension. The U.S. and U.K. governments officially advise against traveling here. Inform your consulate of your plans if you decide to visit anyway.

The small, rugged towns of the West Bank provide a physical immediacy to the events and characters of the Qur'an and the Bible. Since 1987, the West Bank has made international headlines as the site of the Palestinian uprising, the *intifada*. Today, the relative calm that has returned to parts of the area, as well as the general hospitality of the Palestinian people, makes a visit to the West Bank's historic sites possible.

Still, the precarious political situation makes caution and wise planning an absolute. Use common sense in order to avoid offending or arousing the suspicions of the Palestinians, who categorically do not take kindly to Israelis, or *'amil* (suspected Israeli collaborators): do not speak Hebrew, and avoid socializing with Israeli soldiers. Do everything you can to stress your tourist status: carry a backpack and maps, travel in groups, even wear Hard Rock Café T-shirts. Refer to your surroundings as Palestine (*Filastin*). Refer to Jerusalem by the Arabic *al-Quds* (the Holy), or better yet, say nothing at all. You might also want to pick up a copy of Berlitz's linguistically useless *Arabic for Travellers* and display it prominently. Men should always wear long pants and a shirt; women should wear a long skirt and a long-sleeved shirt.

At the same time, Israeli soldiers are suspicious of tourists who demonstrate knowledge of the Arabic language or local customs. **Travelers who appear to be of Arab descent should be especially cautious and expect attention or sometimes harassment from Israeli troops.**

The most dangerous potential situation for West Bank travelers is getting caught in the crossfire between the plastic bullets and tear gas of Israeli soldiers and the rocks of Palestinians. With proper planning and precautions, though, foreigners can both enjoy the sites and learn a great deal about one of the world's most volatile political conflicts.

Getting There

The sanest way to tour the region is to take daytrips from Jerusalem. Before you leave Jerusalem, consult all available sources, including your consulate, the GTIO (see Jerusalem Practical Information), the Office of Visitor Information of the Civil Administration (212 Jaffa Rd., Jerusalem), friends and neighbors and neighbors' friends. Read a newspaper to stay abreast of current happenings in the towns and be flexible: Don't visit the West Bank if you hear that a general strike has been declared—not only will the transportation system be shut down and the area paralyzed, but violence is a possibility.

The preferred modes of transportation to the West Bank are Arab *service* (shared taxis), private taxis, or Arab buses. Egged buses are a last resort; they cost more, and often only take you to the outskirts of Palestinian towns. Take them only to Jewish settlements. A taxi can drive you right to the sights, often away from the center of town, and wait for you. If you must use a vehicle with yellow (Israeli and East Jerusalem) license plates, make sure "UN" or the name of a Christian service agency is plastered all over the car. Unannounced curfews and roadblocks can materialize in the West

216

Bank at any time. These apply to tourists as well. Unless you plan to stay with close friends, be out of the West Bank by nightfall.

Several organizations aid in planning excursions to the West Bank. The **Palestine Human Rights Information Center** (tel. 28 70 77; open Sat.-Thurs. 8am-2pm), can provide useful information on the current political situation. Director Jan Abu-Shakra gives free lectures on the *intifada* to small groups. Call ahead. (The office is in East Jerusalem, off Salah al-Din St. Turn onto al-Zahra St., and take the first right after the National Palace Hotel. The building is across the street from the Rome-Paris beauty salon and has an "ECRC" sign above the door.) **Al-Haq,** the West Bank affiliate of the International Commission of Jurists, is a Palestinian human rights organization based in Ramallah that publishes informative booklets and reports (tel. 95 64 21). **UNRWA,** the United Nations Relief and Works Agency, may be able to arrange trips to refugee camps (tel. 82 84 51).

Political History

When Jordan conquered the territory in 1948, King Abdallah angered most Palestinians by annexing the region instead of creating a separate state as the UN partition resolution stipulated. Occupied by Israel since the 1967 Six-Day War, the West Bank today is neither autonomous nor officially annexed by Israel, but under Israeli military administration. Israeli civilian law does not apply to non-Israeli citizens.

In December 1987, the Palestinians of the occupied territories began the *intifada.* A minor traffic accident in the Gaza Strip provided the spark, and two decades of occupation and economic stagnation erupted in a deluge of stones and Molotov cocktails. A new generation of Palestinians—those who have known nothing but the reality of Israeli occupation—abruptly upstaged their elders with a widespread resistance movement. While mention of the *intifada* may conjure up images of masked, stone-throwing Palestinians, non-violent resistance has been prevalent as well. The nonpayment of taxes, general strikes, and resignations from government service, constitute much of the latter movement, and Palestinians have formed a loose network of underground "popular committees" to coordinate their efforts for maximum effect. After years of continued struggle since 1987, many Palestinians are frustrated with a diplomatic chess game that has offered few tangible benefits. Palestinian-on-Palestinian violence between members of different and often competing underground movements has become widespread, and Hamas, the Islamist resistance group, has gained in popularity for its uncompromising rejection of negotiations. Moderate West Bank leaders such as Faisal al-Husseini and Hanan Mikhail-Ashrawi have become prominent in the Arab-Israeli peace talks.

The *intifada* has led to several major changes in the nature of the Palestinian-Israeli conflict. The popular nature of the uprising managed to draw far more international attention and sympathy than decades of PLO tactics. American Jewish groups and Israeli liberals have expressed dismay at the sometimes brutal tactics of the Israeli army. Prior to the Gulf War, the focus of the Arab-Israeli dispute appeared to have shifted from Israel's confrontation with the Arab states to the problems of the Palestinians. During the war, Palestinian satisfaction with Saddam Hussein's missile attacks on Israel temporarily squandered some support for Palestinian humanitarian claims, but the post-war Middle East peace process has brought those issues back to center-stage.

Many Israelis today feel that to turn the West Bank over to the Palestinians would be tantamount to guiding a knife to Israelis' own throats, exposing the narrow (9.5 miles at one point) coastal strip that contains three-fourths of Israel's population to hostile neighbors. Eager to create a buffer against Arabs and to cement their own nationalist claim to an area they see as the heart of *Eretz Yisrael* (the land of Israel), right-wing Likud governments have overseen Israeli settlement in the occupied territories—known to rightist Israelis as Judea and Samaria—in direct violation of the Camp David Accords. As both Palestinians and settlers see it, the 110,000 Jews in West Bank settlements are proof that Israel intends to hold onto the area permanently. But Israel's current prime minister, Labor's pragmatic Yitzhak Rabin, opposes Likud's settlements policy and has promised to freeze new settlement activity while simultaneously pursuing peace talks.

From the standpoint of some Israelis, the *intifada* has made clear that incorporating the occupied territories into Israel proper would likely create an internal security threat far more dangerous than the external threat of an autonomous Palestinian enclave. Although many argue that Israel must hold on to specific territory for military and strategic reasons, there are also those who argue that Israel's broader strategic situation might be improved by a territorial compromise that won real peace with Israel's neighbors. It is on such questions that discussions of UN Resolutions 242 and 338 turn. Hammered out in the aftermath of the 1967 war, UN 242's "land-for-peace" formula is still the only settlement acceptable to all parties—as they interpret it.

The *intifada* has exacted a heavy price from the Palestinian community, most painfully in lives lost and rights denied. Israel's economy may have been temporarily stunned when Palestinians first refused to work and boycotted Israeli products; however, like the Arab Revolt of 1936, Palestinian boycotts have severely damaged their own economy. Having feared that a substantial Palestinian involvement in the economy would undermine the nation's Jewish character, many Israelis were amenable to the Palestinians' boycotts. A post-Gulf War influx of Palestinians expelled from the Gulf states has further complicated the situation.

The Jewish holidays and *shabbat* are only observed in West Bank Jewish settlements. The holy month of Ramadan, with its daily fasting and nightly feasting, is observed in Muslim West Bank towns.

Study

At times during the *intifada*, all schools in the West Bank (primary through university) were closed by military authorities. All four West Bank universities, Birzeit, Bethlehem, Hebron, and an-Najah were declared security threats as they were often the venues for demonstrations and violence. Many universities and schools ran underground classes in private homes.

Today, most West Bank schools have resumed classes. If political events have not prompted the reclosing of the schools at the time of your visit, check the programs for foreign students at **Birzeit University** north of Ramallah. The six-week international summer program offers courses in Arabic, Palestinian society, and the Arab-Israeli conflict. (US$300 for language course, US$200 for each of the others. Housing US$200.) Contact the program through the Continuing Education Department, Birzeit University, P.O. Box 14, Birzeit, West Bank, via Israel (tel. 95 62 29 or 95 67 69). Birzeit also sponsors two-week international work camps with Palestinian students during August and September (US$70); contact the Office of the Community Work Program at the above address.

Government and Politics

There are presently several authorities vying for power in the West Bank: the Israeli Military Administration, named the Civil Administration for Judea and Samaria, and the underground Palestinian resistance organizations, including PLO factions and Hamas. The former carries guns, the latter political weight. The PLO's main faction is Yasir Arafat's al-Fatah; more radical is the Popular Front for the Liberation of Palestine (PFLP).

The military administration was established after the 1967 war to govern the Palestinian population, who were not granted Israeli citizenship. Israel maintains control through a rigid system of permits—any Palestinian resident of the West Bank who wishes to construct a building, plant a crop, start a business, or dig a well must first painstakingly obtain permission from the military authorities.

The court system of the West Bank is divided into local and military courts, the former hearing civil cases, the latter cases of Israeli security. But because almost everything that occurs in the West Bank can be considered a security matter, military courts have by far the greater authority. Moreover, all hearings are closed to the public and evidence is commonly kept secret from defendants and their attorneys.

In recent years, Israel has come under international criticism for its failure to observe international human rights standards in the occupied territories. Human rights groups have recorded cases of deportation, shooting of stone-throwers, arrest without charge, collective punishment, and building demolition. The current Israeli government insists that it cannot afford to compromise on matters of security and the safety of civilians.

Israeli settlers have added another dimension to the imbroglio. Viewing the West Bank as part of *Eretz Yisrael* (the land of Israel), the settlers on the West Bank have had little patience with rock-hurling Palestinians and the Israeli government's inability to permanently quell the uprising. Settlers and Palestinians have harassed and killed each other.

Literature

Much of Palestinian literature is concerned with the agony of foreign occupation and exile. Ghassan Kanafani, perhaps the greatest contemporary Palestinian writer, recreates the desperation and aimlessness of the refugee experience in his novel *All That Remains: Palestine's Children.* A book of short stories by the same author looks at Palestine through the eyes of her embattled and sometimes embittered children, while *Men in the Sun and Other Palestinian Stories* portrays the struggle through adult eyes. The longing for a Palestinian homeland is expressed through the poems of Fouzi al-Asmar, collected in *The Wind-Driven Reed and Other Poems.* For a broader anthology of resistance poetry, look for *The Palestinian Wedding,* edited by Abd al-Elmessiri. Other well-known Palestinian writers include Mahmoud Darwish, Samih al-Qassem, and Fawaz Turki. Works on the *intifada* are listed in the General Introduction under the Life in the Middle East section.

Economy

The economy of the West Bank, much to the displeasure of the native Palestinian population, has been dependent on the economy of Israel. The **new Israeli shekel (NIS)** is prevalent, although **Jordanian dinars (JD)** and **U.S. dollars (US$)** are also in use. Because Palestinians are the first to be laid off from their jobs in times of duress, crises in Israel's economy are felt even more sharply in the West Bank.

The economy of the West Bank has been a major battleground of the *intifada.* Palestinians boycott Israeli products in an attempt to rid themselves of economic dependence on Israel, and the Israeli government imposes economic sanctions on the Palestinian community in an attempt to preserve Israeli control over the area.

The uprising has brought economic tensions to a peak. Most merchants have heeded the call of the Unified Command to open shops from 9am-3pm only. Hotels, bakeries, produce stands, street vendors, and pharmacies are exempted from the strike, but on occasional full-strike days even these establishments close. General strikes are held the 6th and the 9th of every month, plus other dates. (The two days commemorate the beginning of the *intifada* in December 1987, but Hamas and al-Fatah can't agree on the date.)

Bethany (Al-Ayzariya) العيزرية

A relatively prosperous Palestinian village, Bethany (al-Ayzariya) was the home of Lazarus and his sisters Mary and Martha. A **Franciscan Church** (tel. 27 17 06) built in 1954 marks the spot where Jesus supposedly slept. The church features several impressive mosaics, including one of the resurrection of Lazarus and another of the Last Supper. Three earlier shrines, the earliest built in the 4th century CE, have been excavated nearby. South of the church lie the remains of a vast abbey built in 1143 CE by Queen Melisende. (Open daily 7-11:45am and 2-5:30pm; in winter, 7-11:45am and 2-5pm. Free.)

Bethany is home to the first-century **Tomb of Lazarus,** which was enshrined in the 4th century. When the Crusaders arrived, they built a church over Lazarus's tomb, a monastery over Mary and Martha's house, and a tower over Simon the Leper's abode (Simon was another resident of Bethany cured by Jesus). In the 16th century the Muslims erected a mosque over the grotto, and in the following century Christians dug another entrance to the tomb so they too could worship there. Head for the silver domes of the **Greek Orthodox Church** above the tomb (the Franciscan Church will be just downhill). As you approach the tomb, a woman will come from across the street to show you the light switch (on the right as you enter) and ask for a donation (NIS2 is appropriate; tomb open daily 8am-6pm). Ten minutes further along the main road, the **Greek Orthodox Convent** shelters the boulder upon which Jesus sat while awaiting Martha from Jericho (ring the bell to see the rock).

To reach Bethany from Jerusalem (4km), take Egged bus #43 or the more frequent Arab bus #36 (NIS2) from Damascus Gate and get off in the town (look for the silver-domed church on your left). There are two #36 buses, so ask for al-Ayzariya before embarking. Women should dress modestly and travel in groups.

Bethlehem (Beit Lahm) بيت لحم

The little town of Bethlehem (Beit Lahm in Arabic, Beit Leḥem in Hebrew) is the biblical setting for Rachel's death, the love of Ruth and Boaz, and the discovery of the lyrical shepherd David, future king of Israel. But what really put Bethlehem on the pilgrimage map was the pastoral birth of Jesus Christ.

Bethlehem has been neither still nor silent since the outbreak of the *intifada*. More than 32 Bethlehem residents have been killed, often by the Israeli army, and the first Israeli casualty of the *intifada* was stabbed here. Since the city relies heavily upon tourism, Bethlehem has been hardest hit by commercial strikes; tourists (and any of their financial benevolence) are welcome here. Churches still hold Christmas and Easter services, and events sponsored by the Bethlehem municipality, including the annual parade from Jerusalem to Bethlehem, continue to take place.

Practical Information

Bethlehem lies 8km east of Jerusalem. Most of what you'll need in Bethlehem is located on or near **Manger Square,** across from the Basilica of the Nativity. The area enclosed by **Najajreh** and **Star Streets,** both of which begin at Manger Sq., contains most of the town's shopping district, including the open-air **market.** This part of town has several **pharmacies,** which take turns staying open in the afternoon during the strikes.

Government Tourist Information Office (GTIO): Manger Sq. (tel. 74 15 81), directly across the Square from the Basilica. Excellent free map of the town (sometimes available at the Jerusalem tourist office), details about special events during Christmas and Easter, and transportation information. They can provide a list of accommodations. Open daily 8am-5pm.

Banks: Leumi (tel. 74 33 30 and 74 29 29), **Barclay's Discount** (tel. 74 25 95), and **Cairo Amman Bank** (tel. 74 49 71), next to GTIO, all in Manger Sq. Open Sun.-Thurs. 8:30am-1pm, Fri. 8:30am-noon.

Post Office: Manger Sq. (tel. 74 26 68), beside the tourist office. Open Mon.-Wed., Fri., and Sat. 8am-3pm, Thurs. 8am-1pm. **Poste Restante** available. International calls possible. **Telephone code:** 02.

Bus Station: Manger St., 50m northwest of Manger Sq., down the hill toward Jerusalem. Arab buses from Damascus or Jaffa Gate in Jerusalem: #22 and 23 (continues to Hebron), 47 (continues east to Beit Sahur), and 60 (continues to Obediya). To Jerusalem (30min., NIS1) last bus back at about 5-6pm. Note that the Hebron bus stops only at Rachel's Tomb and at the intersection with Paul VI St., 3km west of Manger Sq.

Minibuses: Deheisheh (#1) from Manger St. behind the police station, heads north to Rachel's Tomb then south to the Deheisheh refugee camp via the road to Hebron (daily 6am-6pm, every 15-20min., NIS1). To Beit Sahur from same location (NIS1).

Service Taxis: From Jaffa or Damascus Gate in Jerusalem to Manger Sq. until about 7pm (NIS1.50).

Police Station: Manger Sq. (tel. 74 82 22).

Accommodations, Camping, and Food

Although today the town of Bethlehem offers more than mangers, rates and political tension are much higher than in ancient times. Bethlehem doesn't really cater to the budget traveler. Unless you are here during Christmas or Easter, stay in Jerusalem and make Bethlehem a daytrip.

St. Joseph's Home, Manger St. (tel. 74 24 97), 0.5km north of Manger Sq., up Manger St. just past Hamburger House. The sign over the door promises "love and peace." Singles US$12, breakfast included. Half board US$18. Full board US$22.

Al-Andalus Hotel (tel. 74 13 48), in Manger Sq. upstairs next to the Leumi. If door's locked, just knock. Green, green rooms with green, yellow bedspreads. Singles with bath US$20. Doubles with bath US$30. Breakfast included. Bargain down winter price hikes.

Casa Nova, off Manger Sq. (tel. 74 39 80), to the left of the entrance to the Basilica of the Nativity. Marble floor and stained glass windows in lobby might remind you of the set of the 700 Club. Modern rooms and plenty of hot water. Bed and breakfast US$18. Half board US$20. Full board US$24. US$9 extra to convert your double room into a single.

Palace Hotel, Manger St. (tel. 74 27 98 or 74 41 00), to the left as you face the Basilica door. Trees, garden, and clean rooms. Newly renovated. A good deal, better with bargaining. Safe provided. Singles US$18. Doubles US$36. Breakfast buffet included.

Franciscan Convent Pension, Milk Grotto St. (tel. 74 24 41), on your left past the Milk Grotto. Charming rooms overlook a barren valley. *Il faut que vous parlez français.* Curfew 9pm. Bed and breakfast US$18. Dorm beds US$15. Possibility of floor space at holiday time.

For falafel fans and transportation fiends, the stands in Manger Sq. and on Manger St. offer the cheapest stomach stuffers and the most accurate information on bus departures. The **al-Atlal Restaurant,** one block from Manger Sq. on Milk Grotto St., contains neo-Crusader arches and a few crusty farm implements. hummus with meat is NIS12, and a hamburger or omelette with salad and potatoes is NIS5. Another option is **St. George's Restaurant** (tel. 74 18 33), on the same side of Manger Sq. as the GTIO. A meal of kebabs and salad costs US$10. Or try their **Quick, Lunch, Sandwiches** shop right next door (sandwiches NIS6). The only food available later at night is at the **Palace Hotel Coffee Shop** (open 9am-midnight. Salad bar NIS6.)

Sights

A church masquerading as a fortress, the massive **Basilica of the Nativity** on Manger Sq. is the oldest continuously used church in the world. Under the supervision of his mother Helena, Constantine the Great erected the first basilica in 326 over the site of Jesus' birth. During the Persian invasion in 614 virtually every Christian shrine in the Holy Land was demolished with the exception of this basilica, reputedly spared because it contained a potent mosaic of the three wise men which had special anti-artillery powers. The Crusaders extensively renovated the church but it fell into disrepair after their defeat by the Muslims. By the 15th century it had become undeniably decrepit, but the basilica's importance as a holy shrine never waned. Thus during the ensuing centuries, struggle for its control among Catholic, Greek, and Armenian Christians repeatedly led to bloodshed. Not until the 1840s was the church restored to its former dignity, but squabbles between the various sects over the division of the edifice continue. In recent years an elaborate system of worship schedules has harmonized the competing claims of the different groups, but the confusion and tension resulting from the Greek Orthodox Church's rejection of summer daylight savings time demonstrates the teetering balance of this arrangement.

Despite an impressive history, the Basilica of the Nativity is not particularly attractive. The main entrance and windows were blocked up as a safety precaution during medieval times, rendering the façade markedly awkward. To enter you must assume the position and step through the narrow Door of Humility—a remnant of the days when Christians wanted to prevent Muslims from entering the holy place on horseback.

Fragments of beautiful mosaic floors are all that remain of Constantine's original church. View them beneath the huge wooden trap doors in the center of the marble Crusader floor. The four rows of reddish limestone Corinthian columns and the mosaic atoms along the walls date from Justinian's reconstruction. The oak ceiling was a gift from England's King Edward IV, while the handsome icons adorning the altar were bequeathed in 1764 by the Russian imperial family.

The **Grotto of the Nativity** is in an underground sanctuary beneath the church. As you enter the womblike grotto, notice the crosses etched into the columns on both sides of the doorway. This religious graffiti is the work of pilgrims who have visited here over the centuries. A star bearing the Latin inscription: *Hic De Virgine Maria Jesus Christus Natus Est* ("Here, of the Virgin Mary, Jesus Christ was born") marks the spot. The star, added by the Catholics in 1717, was removed by the Greeks in 1847 and restored by the Turkish government in 1853. Silly quarrels over the star supposedly contributed to the outbreak of the Crimean War. (Basilica complex open daily 5:30am-8pm; in winter 7am-6pm. Free, although you are encouraged to make a small donation. Modest dress required. For further information call 74 24 40).

Simple and airy, the adjoining **St. Catherine's Church** (tel. 74 24 25), built by the Franciscans in 1881, is a welcome contrast to the grim interior of the basilica. Use the separate entrance to the north of the basilica, or face the altar in the basilica and pass through one of the doorways in the wall on your left. St. Catherine's broadcasts a Midnight Mass to a worldwide audience every Christmas Eve. Superbly detailed wood carvings of the 14 stations of the Cross line the walls. The first room, the **Chapel of St. Joseph,** commemorates the humble carpenter's vision of an angel who advised him to flee with his family to Egypt to avoid Herod's wrath. The burial cave of children slaughtered by King Herod (Matthew 2:6) lies beneath the altar and through the grille in the **Chapel of the Innocents.** Beyond the altar, a narrow passageway leads to the Grotto of the Nativity. The way is blocked by a thick wooden door pierced by a peephole. During earlier times of hostility between Christian sects, this glimpse was as close as Catholics could get to the Greek Orthodox-controlled shrine. To the right of the altar a series of rooms contain the tombs of St. Jerome, St. Paula, and St. Paula's daughter Eustochia. These lead to the spartan cell where St. Jerome produced the Vulgate, the 4th-century translation of the Hebrew Bible into Latin.

A solemn procession to the basilica and underground chapels is conducted by the Franciscan Fathers on a daily basis. To join in the 20 minutes of Gregorian cantellations and Latin prayer, arrive at St. Catherine's by noon. St. Catherine's (and the tomb of St. Jerome) is open daily 5:30am-noon and 2-8pm.

A five-minute walk from the Basilica of the Nativity down Milk Grotto St. heads to the **Milk Grotto Church** (tel. 74 38 67). The cellar here is thought to be the cave where the Holy Family hid while fleeing from Herod into Egypt. The cave and church take their names from the original milky white color of the rocks, long since blackened by candle smoke. According to legend, some of Mary's milk fell while she was nursing the infant Jesus, whitewashing the rocks forever. Male visitors may be slightly discomfited amid the women who come here to pray for fertility. (Open daily 8am-11:30am and 2pm-5pm.) Ring the bell and wait for a monk to admit you.

About 0.5km north of Manger Sq. along Star St., the three unremarkable restored cisterns of the **Well of David** (tel. 74 24 77; open daily 7am-noon and 2-5pm) squat in the parking lot of the King David Cinema. When a thirsty David, while battling the Philistines, was brought water from the enemy's well, he in turn offered it as a sacrifice to God (II Samuel 23:13-17). From Star St., turn right onto King David St.

The **Tomb of Rachel** (Raḥel) is a sacred site for Jews, a spot where synagogues have been built and destroyed throughout history. On one side are fervently praying Ḥasidic men, and on the other weeping Yemenite women. Rachel died in Bethlehem while giving birth to Benjamin (Genesis 35:19-20), and she became a timeless symbol of maternal devotion and suffering. Despite Rachel's misfortune, the tomb is revered as the place to pray for a child or a safe delivery. Men should be sure to don at least a paper *kippah* (head covering) available at the entrance. The tomb is on the northern edge of town on the road to Jerusalem, at the intersection of Manger St. and Hebron Rd. (Open Sun.-Thurs. 8am-5pm, Fri. 8am-1pm.) All buses between Jerusalem and Bethlehem or Hebron pass the tomb; minibus #1 also swings by. It's only a 20-minute walk from the Basilica.

Bethlehem means "House of Bread" in Hebrew *(Beit Leḥem)* and "House of Meat" in Arabic *(Beit Lahm)*. The yawning **market,** which clings to the town's steep streets, lives up to both names. The market is located up the stairs from Paul VI St. across from the Syrian Church about 2 blocks west of Manger Sq. A few blocks down Paul VI from the market and toward the basilica is the **Bethlehem Museum** (tel. 74 25 89) which exhibits Palestinian crafts, traditional costumes, and a 19th-century Palestinian home. Small fee. (Open daily 10am-noon and 2:30-5pm.)

Near Bethlehem

Herodian

Rising from the plains of the Judean desert 10km southeast of Bethlehem near the village of Asakirah are the ruins of **Herodian,** a winsome fortified palace perched atop a conical peak. King Herod, haunted by fears of assassination, ordered the construction of this hideout in the first century BCE. Enclosed within the massive circular double walls and guarded by four watch towers were all the comforts of Rome: palace, garden and bathhouse. Fifteen meters below the floor, two giant cisterns were filled with water hauled in by donkeys. Though engineered to protect the Roman-sponsored ruler from discontented Jews, the palace actually became a rebel stronghold during the Jewish revolts of the first and second centuries CE. From the top you can see Jerusalem to the north, Bethlehem to the west, the Dead Sea to the east, and the desolate Judean Desert to the south. (Open daily 8am-5pm. Admission NIS8, student NIS6.) To reach Herodian, share a taxi from Bethlehem for NIS30-40 round-trip or hike past Shepherd's Field on the road from Beit Sahur; it's 7km from the marked turn-off.

Shepherd's Field

Beyond the Arab village of Beit Sahur on the eastern edge of Bethlehem is the **Field of Ruth,** believed to be the setting for the biblical *Book of Ruth.* The name of the village in Hebrew is "House of the Shepherds," and Christian tradition holds that this is **Shepherd's Field,** where those tending their flocks were greeted by the angel who pronounced the birth of Jesus (Luke 2:9-11). Take bus #47 (NIS1) from the stop behind the police station in Manger Sq., get off at Beit Sahur, and walk 20 minutes to the site. Otherwise, you can walk the 4km from Bethlehem; follow the signs. (Open daily 8am-12:30pm and 2-5pm.)

The Greek Patriarchate oversees the site where shepherds were told of Jesus' birth. Located 1.5km east of Bethlehem off al-Ruaa St., the site includes a 6th century Byzantine basilica (tel. 74 31 35), monastery, the Holy Cave (350 CE) featuring mosaic crosses in the floor, as well as a small cave filled with human bones. (Open daily 8am-12:30pm and 2-5pm). The Franciscans run a competing shepherd's field 0.5km further down the road. Their site includes a small monastery (400 CE) and a number of ancient cooking pots and coins left by shepherds on the site. (Open daily 8-11:30am and 2-5pm).

Mar Saba Monastery

More remarkable and isolated than Herodian is the **Mar Saba Monastery.** Carved into the walls of a remote canyon, the extensive monastery complex stands precariously above the sewer-esque Kidron River. The monastery was built opposite the cave, marked by a cross, where St. Saba began his ascetic life in 478 CE. The attractive bones of St. Saba are on display in the main church. Women are strictly forbidden to enter and must view the chapels and buildings from a tower near the monastery. Men must wear long pants and long sleeves to be admitted. To enter the monastery, pull the chain on the large blue door. Once inside, you'll be given a five-minute tour in English by one of the monks. The monks occasionally ignore the doorbell on Sundays and late in the afternoon; try to arrive early on a weekday. There is no entrance fee, but it is customary to make a contribution. (Open daily 7am-11am and 1:30pm-5pm).

To reach the monastery, take Arab bus #60, which leaves every couple of hours from the Bethlehem station and travel to the Arab village of Obediya; the last bus returns to Bethlehem at 4pm. Bus #60 originates in Jerusalem.

Jericho (Ariha) أريحا

Descending from Jerusalem into the scorched Jordan River Valley, centuries peel away as you approach the refreshing oasis of Jericho (Ariha in Arabic, Yeriho in Hebrew), one of the oldest continually inhabited sites in the world. A largely abandoned refugee camp stands solemnly on the edge of town—a reminder of the city's 20th-century struggles.

Jericho is best known for the Biblical account of its walls, which came crashing down when Joshua sounded his trumpets after seven days of siege. According to the Bible, two spies sent into town by Joshua were sheltered in the house of the harlot, Rahab. In exchange for the deed, her family was to be spared if she marked her house with a scarlet thread. When the tribes of Israel attacked, the entire city was destroyed save the single house with a scarlet cord dangling from its window (Joshua 2-6).

Practical Information, Accommodations, and Food

40km east of Jerusalem, Jericho lies on the road to Amman at the junction of the highway to the Galilee. The **King Hussein/Allenby Bridge,** located 10km east of Jericho, has served as the only route across the Jordan River since the King Abdallah Bridge to the south was destroyed in the 1967 war. See the General Introduction for information on border crossings.

Arab bus #28 (NIS2) from the Damascus Gate station runs to the bus stop on Ein al-Sultan St., one block north of the central traffic circle. **Egged buses** #961 and 963 (1hr., NIS8.50) and buses to the Galilee leaving from Jerusalem's central bus station will drop you near the ancient city. Arab buses stop running at 4:30pm but you can catch Egged buses for Jerusalem until about 7pm from the stop on the corner of Ein al-Sultan and Jaffa St. in Jericho. After that you may still be able to catch a *sherut* **taxi** from the taxi stand on the square in front of the municipality building. These shared taxis run frequently between Jericho's main square and the Damascus Gate taxi stand in Jerusalem (NIS4-5).

Today's town of 7000 Palestinians is actually a few kilometers south of the ancient city. The main square, really a traffic circle, is the hub of town life and transportation services. Most of Jericho's other services are also located here, including the **police station** (tel. 92 25 21). Since hiking is arduous, the best way to see the sights in Jericho is with an endearingly rickety but functional bicycle. A **bicycle shop,** just off the central square and east of the municipality building, rents balloon-tire bombers for NIS1.50 per hour. The owner may also ask for advance payment—two hours should be enough. Be aware that locals bike on the left side of the road. A **taxi** will take you on a loop of the sights for about NIS60.

Virtually no visitors stay overnight in Jericho during the summer months. The only lodging option, **Hisham's Palace Hotel,** King Hussein's former gambling grounds, is next to the bus stop on Ein al-Sultan St. (tel. 4414), one block north of the main square. (Singles NIS10. Doubles NIS20, NIS30 with shower. Bargain.) Much farther down Ein al-Sultan St. in a residential area is the **Maxim Restaurant.** This all-you-can-eat establishment offers an appetizing selection of salads (NIS6.50) and meats (NIS12). Along the road to ancient Jericho are numerous under-touristed tourist restaurants; falafel stands cluster around the main square.

Sights

Jericho's most popular sights, Hisham's Palace and ancient Jericho, lie on the outskirts of town. Since a cluster of restaurants and a cooling spring near the ancient city provide a pleasant rest stop, visit Hisham's Palace first.

To reach the ruins of **Hisham's Palace,** (tel. 92 25 22) follow the signs along Qasr Hisham St., which heads north from the eastern side of Jericho's main square. The palace is 3km north on paved roads. Coming from ancient Jericho, head north on the main road leading through the **Ein al-Sultan refugee camp.** After 1.5km, turn right on the road back to Jericho town; the turn-off to Hisham's Palace will be almost immediately to your left.

The extensive ruins of Hisham's Palace offer a jaw-dropping example of early Islamic architecture. Known as Khirbet al-Mafjar in Arabic, the palace was designed for the Umayyad Caliph Hisham as a winter retreat from Damascus. The palace was begun in 724 CE and completed in 743, only to be leveled four years later by an earthquake. The window in the courtyard is in the shape of the six-pointed Umayyad star and is the site's most renowned feature. (Open daily, 8am-5pm. Admission NIS6.50, students NIS5.)

To travel the 2km from Hisham's Palace to ancient Jericho, turn right onto the road that runs past Hisham's Palace and then take a left at the end of the road. Follow the "Tel Jericho" signs; about 1.5 km past the synagogue, the Ein as-Sultan spring is on your left. Follow the street around the corner to the right to the entrance. If all else fails, use a map.

Ancient Jericho, thought by some to be the oldest city in the world, is now a heap of ruined walls. Called Tel as-Sultan, the mound contains layer upon layer of garbage from ancient (and modern) cities. The oldest fortifications, 12m down, are 7000 years old. Some of the finds date from the early Neolithic period, leading archeologists to suspect that Jericho was inhabited as early as the eighth millennium BCE. A limited amount of excavation has exposed many levels of ancient walls, some of them 3.5m thick and 5.5m high. Your imagination will have to substitute for visible splendor at this distinctly unphotogenic site. (Tel. 92 29 09; open daily, 8am-5pm. Admission NIS6.50, students NIS4.90.)

An imposing Greek Orthodox **monastery** stands on the edge of a cliff among the mountains west of Jericho; the peak is believed to be the New Testament's Mount of Temptation. The complex of buildings stands before a grotto, said to be the spot where Jesus fasted for 40 days and 40 nights after his baptism in the Jordan River (Matthew 4:1-11). Six wizened Greek monks now live in the monastery, which was built in 1895. Ask one to point out the rock where Jesus was tempted by the devil and served by angels. The road to the monastery heads past the shops near ancient Jericho.

The summit of the mountain, named **Qarantal** after the Latin word for "forty," also serves as a pedestal for the Maccabbean **Castle of Dok,** beside which lie the remains of a 4th-century Christian chapel. (Monastery open daily 7am-3pm and 4-5pm, in winter 7am-2pm and 3-4pm. Modest dress required.)

Near Jericho

The road from Jerusalem to Jericho slices through the harsh desert landscape of the Judean wilderness. About 8km before Jericho the **Mosque of Nabi Musa** stands on a hill in the sea of sand, a short distance from the road. This spot is revered throughout the Muslim world as the grave of the prophet Moses, and many Muslims yearn to be buried by his side after they die. Islamic tradition holds that God carried the bones of the prophet here for the faithful to come and pay their respects. The 13th-century Mamluk mosque containing the prophet's tomb is open daily from 8am-5pm. During Ramadan only Muslims are admitted. Women should bring their own scarf to cover their hair.

About 10km east of Jericho is **al-Maghtes,** the spot on the Jordan River where John the Baptist is believed to have baptized Jesus. A 19th-century Greek Orthodox monastery marks the spot where Christians still come to immerse themselves. The site remains under military supervision, so you need a special permit to get anywhere near it. Permits are available at the military administration center just outside of Jericho, on your left past the Abaqat Refugee Camp as you approach town.

Wadi Qelt وادى قلط

Hiking through **Wadi Qelt** (Naḥal Perat in Hebrew), where the arid Judean desert cracks open and reveals an oasis, is like burrowing through the pantry right after Mother Nature restocks the shelves. Three fresh water springs nourish lush greenery and wildlife, threading 28km between imperious limestone cliffs and undulating ridges of bone-white chalk. Descending 395m below sea level, the wadi is a reasonably safe adventure that offers more drama than the resort oasis at Ein Gedi.

The most interesting and accessible section of the wadi extends from the spring of **Ein Qelt,** past the 6th-century **Monastery of St. George,** and down into Jericho, 10km east. The trek takes about four hours, adventures in dawdledom excluded. The best place to start is at the turn-off from the Jerusalem-Jericho highway about 9km west of Jericho, marked by the orange sign for "St. George's Monastery." Take **Egged bus** #73 (NIS8.50) to the turn-off from the bus stop across from the central bus station; buses depart at 6:15am and 2:30pm. For late risers, **Arab bus** #28 to Jericho (leaving every hour) passes the same turn-off. The trip from Jerusalem takes about an hour. If you're driving it's possible to skip the hike and drive most of the way to St. George's by following signs.

St. George's Monastery dates from the 5th or 6th centuries CE. It was built near the cave of Horeb where the prophet Elijah is said to have hidden to escape the wrath of Jezebel, queen of Samaria (1 Kings 18-19). The floor of St. George's Church is decorated with Byzantine mosaics. Look for the likeness of a two-headed eagle, the Byzantine symbol of power. The neighboring St. John's Church houses a spooky collection of skulls and bones of monks who were slaughtered when the Persians swept through the valley in 614 CE. The Greek Orthodox monks who maintain the monastery can refill your canteen for the rest of the journey into Jericho. (Open daily 8am-1pm and 3-5pm. Leave a donation. Modest dress required.)

On the way to Jericho from St. George's, stop at the ruins of **Tel Abu Alayia** on your right. The palaces with their decorated walls, the bath houses, and the water pools at the site were used by the Hasmoneans and later by King Herod. (Free.)

For those interested in exploring other sections along the wadi and around Jericho, the **Society for the Protection of Nature in Israel** office in Jerusalem sells an excellent detailed Hebrew topographical map of the Judean Desert (NIS12). The staff can also provide information about different routes, though they will probably try to dissuade you from setting off on your own. They offer group tours led by English-speaking guides who are well informed about the wadi's natural and artificial phenomena. Because of the number (up to 20 people) and diversity of participants, however, the pace may be slower than you'd like.

Qumran قمـران

In 1947, a young Bedouin shepherd looking for a wayward sheep wandered into a remote cliffside cave and happened upon a collection of earthenware jars containing parchment manuscripts 2000 years old. These Dead Sea Scrolls have become one of the most important sources on the development of the Bible. The largest, now displayed in the Shrine of the Book at the Israel Museum in Jerusalem, was a 7m long ancient Hebrew text of the Book of Isaiah. Encouraged by the initial discovery, archeologists searched the surrounding caves and undertook excavations at the foot of the cliffs. In 1949, they uncovered the village of the sect that wrote the Dead Sea Scrolls.

Archeological evidence suggests that the site was settled as long ago as the 8th century BCE, reinhabited in the 2nd century BCE, temporarily abandoned during the reign of Herod following an earthquake, and completely deserted after the Roman defeat of the Jewish uprisings in 70 CE. Historians believe that the authors of the scrolls were the Essenes, a Jewish sect whose members were disillusioned by the corruption and Hellenization of their fellow Jerusalemites and therefore sought refuge in the sands. The strict and devout Essenes believed that a great struggle was soon to ensue between the Sons of Light (themselves and the angels) and the Sons of Darkness (everyone else). Excavations at Masada suggest that the members of the Qumran sect joined with the Jews at Masada in their struggle against the Romans.

The main archeological site is compact. Look for the cisterns and channels that were essential for the efficient storage and passage of water in the arid climate. Climb first to the **watchtower** for a panorama of the site. Proceed to the **scriptorium,** the chamber in which the scrolls were probably written. The ruins are clearly marked by Hebrew and English signs and a map of the site is posted just past the entrance. A short rock climb brings you to the caves themselves. It may not seem very far, but bring two or three small bottles of water and wear a hat to avoid dehydrating. If you have a backpack, the staff at the reception booth will usually stare at it for you at no charge.

The site of Qumran lies 43km southeast of Jerusalem; unrest probably won't be a concern. The archeological site is served by Egged buses #486, 421, and 966 from Jerusalem, which let you off at the turn-off to the site (100m from the coastal highway), and by Egged buses from Eilat and Ein Bokek to Jerusalem. Watch for the sign. The national park (tel. (02) 92 25 05) is open in summer Sat.-Thurs. 8am-6pm, Fri. 8am-5pm; in winter daily 8am-4pm. (Admission NIS8.)

Once you've worked up a muddle of moisture beadlets qlambering around Qumran, take advantage of the salt and fresh-water bathing at **Ein Feshka** (tel. (02) 94 23 55), 3km south of the ruins. If you have water but no pack, consider walking from Qumran (south). Unlike other desert respites where mountain streams trickle from the foot of the Judean Hills and collect in channels along the Dead Sea's flat coast, these springs tumble into small pools and wind through the wadi's tangled reeds. Herds of ibex graze in this extraordinarily fertile desert oasis.

The small beach is fairly quiet, except on weekends. From the shore, a dirt road leads inland to the **nature reserve,** where you can wade in femur-deep pools formed by natural springs. Ein Feshka is the only Dead Sea resort with fresh-water ponds adjacent to the swimming area. As the sea level drops, the groundwater level declines as well, bringing plant life eastward in the direction of the receding shoreline. Thus the oasis always maintains its position relative to the sea. Rivulets lace the area and vacationers lounge about, caked head to toe with Dead Sea mud. There are showers, changing rooms, bathrooms, and drinking water. A lifeguard hut separates the beach from the wallow. (Admission NIS10, students NIS8. Open Sun.-Fri. 8am-4:30pm, Sat. 8am-5pm.)

Hebron (al-Khalil) الخليل

Al-Khalil ar-Raḥman (the full Arabic name) means "friend of the compassionate," and the Hebrew name, *Ḥevron,* comes from *ḥaver* (friend). The friend in question is Abraham (Ibrahim/Avraham), traditionally the common ancestor of both peoples. Friendly, however, is hardly the word to describe the Israeli-Palestinian relationship here. The predominantly Palestinian residents of Hebron harbor fierce resentment over the two decades of Israeli occupation, and the combination of Hebron's Palestinians' fearlessness and a large Israeli military presence by the old bus station has been the source of many serious clashes during the intifada. It was in Hebron's Park Hotel that the first Jewish settlement on the West Bank was established, in April 1968. The proximity of Kiryat Arba, a major Jewish settlement, paired with efforts to reestablish a Jewish quarter within the town (550 Jews amidst 65,000 Palestinians), has only exacerbated tensions here.

In Biblical times, Hebron was known as Kiryat Arba (District of the Four). One legend maintains that the "four" referred to four giants who fell from heaven after rebelling against God. In the Book of Numbers, when Moses sent spies to Canaan to bring back a report on the conditions there, the scouts returned with gawkful reports of Hebron's giants. As proof, they brought bunches of grapes so large that a single cluster had to be carried by two people; this image is the symbol of Israel's Ministry of Tourism.

Hebron's Jewish population remained small until the 19th century when many Ḥasidic and Russian Jews emigrated here. In 1925, an entire *yeshiva* moved from Russia to Hebron and a Hadassah medical clinic opened. Local Arabs took offense, and virtually the entire Jewish community perished in the 1929 riots that swept Palestine. The British administrators took the survivors to Jerusalem, and Hebron had no Jewish inhabitants until its capture in 1967. Since then, a significant number of Jews have returned to the area, settling outside the town in the modern Kiryat Arba. Nearby Kfar Etzion, destroyed in 1948, has also been resettled.

Practical Information

Palestinians here carefully distinguish between Israelis and tourists. You can help them and further guarantee your safety by avoiding all things Israeli or Hebrew. If you consult with Israeli soldiers, make it obvious that you are doing so because you are lost. Visitors should make an effort to be respectful of Muslim traditions; Hebron is a very conservative town. Stay in central areas such as King David St. and the area around the Cave of Makhpela. If you do get lost, look it—many young Palestinians in Hebron love to practice their English by giving long-winded directions.

Leave Hebron well before sunset. Don't even think about investigating the nightlife. Before you come, check the security situation in the newspapers, at your consulate, the GTIO, and the Office of Visitor Information (212 Jaffa Rd., Jerusalem). You cannot be too careful. If you encounter stone-hurling youths, try your best not to run; running away frantically only justifies to them their original suspicions.

Located 35km south of Jerusalem on the road to Be'ersheva, Hebron is the only urban center on the West Bank south of Bethlehem. **Egged buses** #34, 440, and 443 (NIS8) come from the Jerusalem central bus station and stop in the main square in front of the Cave of Makhpela after stopping in the Kiryat Arba settlement. Buses run until dark. **Arab bus** #23 (NIS1.50), which runs frequently from Damascus Gate, will drop you in the city center, where King Faisal, King David, and Khalil ar-Raḥman St. converge. From here, a 1km walk along King David Street brings you to the tombs; follow the signs east to the Cave of Makhpela. *Service* **taxis** shuttle between Jerusalem's Jaffa and Damascus Gates and Hebron's King David St., near the cave and the old market. Taxis cost three times as much (NIS4.50) but are faster and run later in the evening. The last Arab bus for Jerusalem departs at about 5:45pm from King Faisal St., just outside the city center.

Most of the town's services, including the **Bank Leumi, post office** (open Sat.-Wed. 8am-3pm, Fri. 8am-1pm), **hospital** (tel. 96 21 26/7), and **police station** (tel. 96 14 44) are also located on King Faisal.

You will be able to purchase food at the **markets;** in the summer season, be sure to try the variety of locally grown grapes (*'anab*). **As-Sayyid Restaurant and Sweets** sells wonderful honey-drenched pastries (NIS1-2) just around the corner from the main square. For the gastronomically adventurous, catch a shared taxi (NIS1) to **Al-Wafa** on Ras al-Jura, by the glass factories. Try the fresh-off-the-carcass lamb baked in a traditional clay oven (US$8, but try to bargain with Jamal). Another Jimmy Carter stop, and a favorite among locals.

The Cave of Makhpela

Abraham chose Hebron, the highest of the four Jewish holy cities (at an altitude of 1030m), as the site of his family cemetery. Beginning with his wife, Sarah (Genesis 23:17-19), all the subsequent matriarchs and patriarchs but one were buried in the Cave of Makhpela. (The exception is Jacob's second wife, Rachel, who died on the way to Bethlehem.) *Makhpela* means a double cave, or cave over a cave. Some claim that Abraham chose the cave because he knew it to be the burial place of Adam and Eve. Consequently, many rabbis explain that Kiryat Arba refers not to four giants, but to the four married couples who are purportedly interred here: Abraham and Sarah, Isaac and Rebecca, Jacob and Leah, and Adam and Eve. The patch of land above the tombs has been fiercely contested throughout history by Crusaders, Muslims, and Jews.

The colossal edifice that now stands over the Cave of Makhpela more resembles a fortress than a house of worship. Both Jewish and Muslim traditions attribute the original stonework of the building to King Solomon's reign. The king is said to have enlisted the help of demons to cut and paste the large blocks. The oldest surviving sections, forming the base of the 3m thick walls, date from King Herod's time. The building fell into disrepair in subsequent centuries, though a small synagogue inside the ruins was continually maintained. In 372 CE the Byzantines built a roof and used the refurbished structure as a church. In 686 CE Muslims took over and added a mosque. In 1103 the Crusaders conquered Hebron and promptly transformed the mosque into a church. As the pattern continued, the Crusaders were driven out and the Mamluks added the current mosque and two square minarets. Until 1929, Jews were allowed to stand and pray, but were permitted to ascend only as far as the seventh step, the level of the holy grotto. The Israelis have now dug the steps away, thereby removing the symbol of their former second-class status. Today, despite political tensions, both Jews and Muslims pray under the same roof.

In the small synagogue large cenotaphs commemorate Jacob and Leah. Across the courtyard, in a second synagogue, two huge boxes covered with elaborate calligraphy stand above the tombs of Abraham and Sarah. The actual remains lie 18m below, within the Cave of Makhpela. A locked trap-door in the mosque leads down to the cave itself. Oil is lowered in to keep the candles burning in the cave. To find the final duo, pass through the synagogue in the **Great Mosque,** where the cenotaphs of Isaac and Rebecca each occupy a small hut. In the small adjoining women's mosque (on your left as you leave the courtyard) is a window containing a stone with an undistinguished imprint. Supposedly, this is Adam's footprint, made when he came here after expulsion from Eden.

Upon entering, male visitors should don a paper *kippah,* available at the top of the staircase. Women may be asked to cover their hair with the furnished scarves. Modest dress is required for both sexes. (Open all day. Mosques closed to non-Muslims during the five prayer times, Muslim holidays, and Fri. Passage through the surrounding hallways and synagogues is permitted when the mosques are closed.)

Other Sights

Hebron's **market** is one of the largest, most interesting, and potentially most dangerous in the West Bank. The vaulted ceilings and booths indicate that the structure is medieval Crusader, but the artifacts sold are distinctly Middle Eastern. Blown glassware made in Hebron's famous factories is the market's specialty. You'll also find skinned camels and various animal heads. Stay close to your companions at all times, and remember the route out.

A five-minute walk west of the town center, down the street from the Arab bus station, stands the **Oak of Abraham** (Balloota in Arabic), the site of the biblical Mamre, where Abraham pitched his tent to welcome tired travelers and entertained three angels who told him of the impending birth of Isaac (Genesis 18). The oak belongs to the Russian Orthodox Church, which built a monastery around it in 1871. According to Christian tradition, the Holy Family rested here on their way back from Egypt. Unfortunately for the tree, travelers since the Middle Ages have removed splinters from it for good luck, and now nails, baling wire, and rusty steel braces have replaced much of the original pith. Despite its convincing decrepitude, some challenge the tree's authenticity and argue that this oak is a mere 600-year-old sapling—they say the oak is referred to in Genesis actually stood at **Alonei-Mamre** north of Hebron on Keizun al-Rama St. If the front gate is locked you can enter from the other side of the monastery's grounds (Gatekeeper Anwar Zablah will let you in most any time; small fee required).

Kiryat Arba, less than 1km northeast of the Cave of Makhpela, is unusual among West Bank settlements for its proximity to a large Palestinian population center. Jewish settlers founded Kiryat Arba in 1972. Tall buildings, wide streets, and green parks contrast sharply with the comparative poverty outside the settlement's barbed wire perimeter. Nevertheless, many of the 5000 residents would eagerly trade their suburbia for an opportunity to reestablish the Jewish Quarter in Hebron, a move that the government has persisted in opposing. English is widely spoken, and in the parks or *yeshiva* (to the left as you enter) you will undoubtedly meet people willing to explain the ideology that has drawn them here.

It is unsafe to walk to Kiryat Arba. Take **Egged bus** #34, 440, or 443, all of which stop within the settlement en route between Jerusalem and Hebron.

Ramallah رام الله

If you are interested in unfiltered West Bank politics, Ramallah is the best place to hear the Palestinian perspective. The Palestinians in Ramallah are friendly to tourists, although less willing to discuss politics than before the *intifada*. In the interest of politeness, respect, and safety, don't argue—just listen.

There are few noteworthy tourist sites in Ramallah, but the town is still equipped to amuse and entertain. Visit the ebullient market next to the bus station or walk around the houses away from the city center. The **Silvana Chocolate Company,** 1.5km down Jaffa Blvd. from Manara Sq., opens its doors to tourists, offering countless free samples. (Open Mon.-Sat. 7:30am-4pm. Call 95 64 58 to arrange a tour).

Ramallah lost its Arab tourist clientele following the 1967 occupation; the uprising has scared away everyone else. There is no longer a tourist office. If the political situation improves, the **Pension Miami** (tel. 95 28 08) on Jaffa Rd. may reopen. **Angelo's Restaurant** (tel. 95 64 08) is rumored to sell the best chicken sandwich in the Middle East (NIS6). Otherwise, good *shwarma* and falafel can be had throughout the town.

To reach Ramallah, take a ***service*** **taxi** (20min., NIS2) from just outside Damascus Gate in Jerusalem. **Arab bus** #18 from the station on Nablus Rd. just north of Damascus Gate (40min., NIS1) stops to pick up every man, woman and child en route. Buses to Jerusalem leave from Jaffa Rd. in Ramallah, just off Manara Sq., the main traffic circle. The last bus leaves around 6pm, the last *service* taxi at about 9pm.

Near Ramallah: Beit-El

The peaceful village of **Beit-El,** 5km northeast of Ramallah on the road to Nablus, is noted on pilgrims' maps as the spot where Jacob lay down to sleep and dreamed of a ladder ascending to heaven with angels going down and up. Upon awakening, Jacob built an altar and named the spot Beit-El, "House of God" (Genesis 28:12-19).

Today, Beit-El is the headquarters of the Israeli civilian administration that governs the West Bank. Although the administration delegates a modicum of authority to Arab mayors and other Palestinian leaders, power remains in the hands of the Israeli officials. The administration center itself is of no interest to tourists, but a visit to the nearby Jewish settlement of Beit-El is worthwhile. Surrounded by tall fences and barbed wire and guarded by army patrols, the settlement provides a glimpse of life in one of the besieged settlements. Most of the working population commutes to Jerusalem, but there are also a few cottage industries, including a workshop that manufactures *tefillin* (religious articles worn by male Jews on the head and arm during prayer).

Beit-El is accessible by **Egged bus** #70 from Jerusalem or El-Bireh. From Ramallah you can walk, take a taxi, or take the bus to Nablus as far as the administrative center.

Birzeit بيرزيت

Twelve kilometers northwest of Ramallah is the largest and most important university on the West Bank. **Birzeit University**'s 2200 students have a history of vocal and sometimes violent opposition to the Israeli occupation; whenever political turmoil forces the Israeli army to tighten security in the West Bank, Birzeit is shut down. In the first years of the *intifada*, Israeli authorities closed down the university altogether. By 1992 it was slowly being reopened. Ask around in Ramallah to make sure it's open before you make the trip. Specify that you want to visit the university *(jam'a)* and not the town. The old campus is next to the last bus stop; the palatial new campus lies 2km out of town on the road back to Ramallah. **Bus** #19 leaves for Birzeit from Radio Blvd. in Ramallah, just off Manara Sq. **Taxis** leave from the same street.

Nablus نابلس

Young Palestinians look upon Nablus (known in the Bible and to many Israelis as Shkhem) as a candidate for the intellectual and administrative capital of their unborn nation. The largest city on the West Bank, it is home to an-Najah University, the territory's second most important university. When you walk off the bus you will be confronted by the bustling business district set in the valley. If you wander around you'll be asked by Palestinians about what you're doing and where you're going. If you walk by Israeli army patrols, their heads will turn in unison, but you shouldn't stop to talk.

After introductions, it is not uncommon for Palestinians to invite you to their homes and possibly offer to show you the *intifada*. Here demonstrations become a matter of tremendous pride, and no story is complete without a detailed account of months (or years) spent in prison. Perhaps the most rewarding way to spend your time here is to accept the residents' hospitality and learn something of the life of West Bank Palestinians.

Practical Information

Nablus lies 63km north of Jerusalem and 46km north of Ramallah—an easy day trip from Jerusalem. Take one of the hourly Tamini Co. **buses** from Nablus Rd. in Jerusalem (1.5-2hrs., NIS6). The last bus to Jerusalem from Nablus leaves at 3pm. *Service* **taxis** cost NIS9, and you may have to change cars in Ramallah.

Sights

After arriving in the center of Nablus, wander south into the crowded streets and passageways of the **market,** overflowing with Nablus merchants, Palestinian customers, and tea-sipping onlookers. Try a piece of the famous, extraordinarily rich *knaffeh nablusia*. Nablus churns out countless trayfuls of this cheese concoction, which is topped with sweet orange flakes and honey (0.25kg NIS2). For the duration of the *intifada,* the market is open 9am-noon. Although you'll feel much more comfortable if you have a guide, stopping to chat and swap stories can often dissipate any awkwardness.

Throughout the market and everywhere in Nablus you'll continue to see the smiling image of Dafer Masri, Nablus's Palestinian mayor. A wreathed monument next to the municipality building marks the spot where he was slain in the winter of 1986. More than likely, his assassins were Palestinians who resented his alleged chumminess with Israeli leadership; the killing is remembered with great bitterness here.

To the east, 3km from the town center, lie two famous though unspectacular pilgrimage sights. **Jacob's Well** (tel. (05) 37 51 23) is now enclosed within a subterranean Greek Orthodox shrine. The well is believed to date from the time when Jacob bought the surrounding land to pitch his tents (Genesis 33:18-19). (Open daily 8am-noon and 2-5pm.) A few hundred meters north of the well lies the **Tomb of Joseph.** According to the Book of Joshua, the bones of Joseph were carried out of Egypt and buried in Shkhem (Joshua 24:32). The tomb was a Muslim shrine until three years ago, when it was taken over by Jewish authorities. Israeli soldiers now guard the unimpressive velvet-shrouded cenotaph and the adjacent *yeshiva.* (Open daily 8am-5pm; no shorts or bare shoulders permitted.) Shared taxis (NIS.70) run to both sites regularly from the center of town.

Mount Gerizim, the tree-covered slope southeast of Nablus, features a terrific view of the Shomron Valley. Since the 4th century BCE, it has been the holy mountain of the Samaritans, who revere it as the spot where Abraham prepared to sacrifice his son Isaac. The Samaritans, an Israelite sect who were excommunicated in biblical times, are distinguished by their literal interpretation of certain scriptures. The highlight of the Samaritan observance of Passover is the sacrifice of sheep atop Mount Gerizim. Tourist buses from Jerusalem and Tel Aviv bring visitors to witness the bloody rite. The hike up the mountain is arduous, but taxis can be hired for about NIS25.

Near Nablus

A resplendent array of Israelite, Hellenistic, and Roman ruins can be found in the multi-colored Shomron Hills, 11km northwest of Nablus. The strategic peak on which the ruins lie was first settled by Omri, King of Israel in the 9th century BCE. Under Herod, the city was made the showpiece of the Holy Land to win the favor of the Roman Emperor. The ruins are just above the present-day Arab town of **Sabastiya.** The beautifully preserved **Roman theater** farther on is more impressive than its famous counterpart at Caesarea. At the top of the hill lie the remnants of Israelite and Hellenistic acropolis walls, and a Roman acropolis, dominated by the enormous column bases of the **Temple of Augustus.** (Site open Sat.-Thurs. 8am-4pm, but the gatekeeper sometimes locks up at 2pm. Admission NIS6, students NIS4.50.) Buses and taxis to Jenin and Tulkarem can drop you off at the turn-off to Sabastiya; walk uphill and take your first right.

EGYPT (MISR) مصر

US $1 = 3.31 Egyptian pounds (LE)	LE1 = US $0.30
CDN $1 = LE 2.94	LE 1 = CDN $0.34
UK £1 = LE 5.56	LE 1 = UK £0.18
IR £1 = LE 5.99	LE 1 = IR £0.17
AUS $1 = LE 2.67	LE 1 = AUS $0.37
NZ $1 = LE 1.80	LE 1 = NZ $0.56

> For important additional information on Climate, Useful Organizations and Publications, Documents and Formalities, Money, Packing, Safety and Security, Alternatives to Tourism, Transportation Options, Border Crossings, Travel Etiquette, and Life in the Middle East, see the General Introduction to this book.

The Arab Republic of Egypt (al-Gumhuriya Misr al-Arabiya) is the child of the Nile Valley, a freak product of northeastern African geography and climate that created the most fertile strip in the world smack in the middle of a desert. The Pharaoh's control of the annual floodwaters was the basis of his power and claim to divinity; modern technology claims that role now. The Aswan High Dam, near the southern border, remains the most profound demarcation of ancient and modern Egypt. Completed in 1970, the dam put an end to the annual flooding of the Nile; Egypt now relies upon irrigation pumps, hydroelectric power, and new technology. Should the dam ever burst, Egypt would be washed into the sea like so much Pharaonic flotsam.

Egypt is a budget traveler's paradise. The sights are stunning, the people and culture fascinating, and you'll almost never get caught in the rain. On the downside, independent travel in Egypt can be difficult; it requires plenty of time, stamina, and an attitude that mixes a dollop of patience with a dash of humor.

Egypt has four regions. The first is the **Mediterranean Coast** bounded by Alexandria, Egypt's summer capital; Marsa Matruuh, home to inviting beaches; and the delightful Siwa Oasis, a pilgrimage to the west.

The second region, the **Nile Valley,** is the most popular and, in terms of distance and sights, the most tremendous. The contrasts are fascinating—one side of the Nile Valley railroad is marked by lush groves of date palms, fig, banana, and mango trees, the other only by vast stretches of sand. Along the Nile, Egypt is divided into two regions: Upper Egypt in the South and Lower Egypt in the North—these names are so designated with respect to the direction of the flowing of the Nile River (upstream and downstream). Lower Egypt includes the Delta and Cairo vicinity, while Upper Egypt includes Luxor and Aswan and extends all the way to Abu Simbel.

The third region is the eastern **Red Sea Coast,** the Arabian Desert, and the Sinai Peninsula, returned to Egypt as part of the Camp David Accords. Snorkeling, hiking, windsurfing, and spectacular scenery at Hurghada and the Aqaba Coast are welcome diversions for museum-mutilated minds.

The last region is the least explored. A trip into the **Western Desert Oases** can include visits to the paradisiac waterholes of Bahariya, Farafra, Dakhla, Kharga, and Baris.

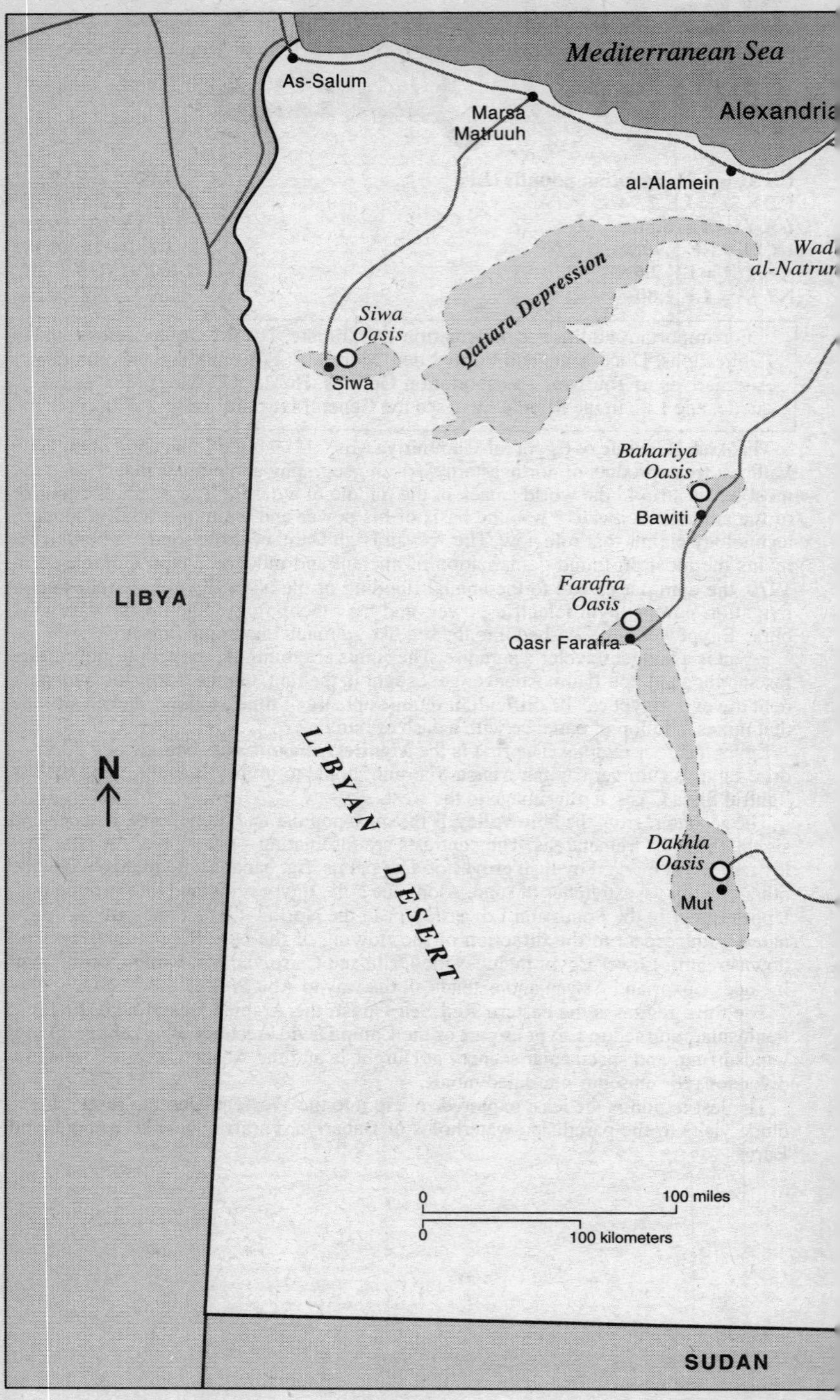
Mediterranean Sea
As-Salum
Marsa Matruuh
Alexandria
al-Alamein
Wadi al-Natrun
Qattara Depression
Siwa Oasis
Siwa
Bahariya Oasis
Bawiti
LIBYA
Farafra Oasis
Qasr Farafra
N
LIBYAN DESERT
Dakhla Oasis
Mut
0
100 miles
0
100 kilometers
SUDAN

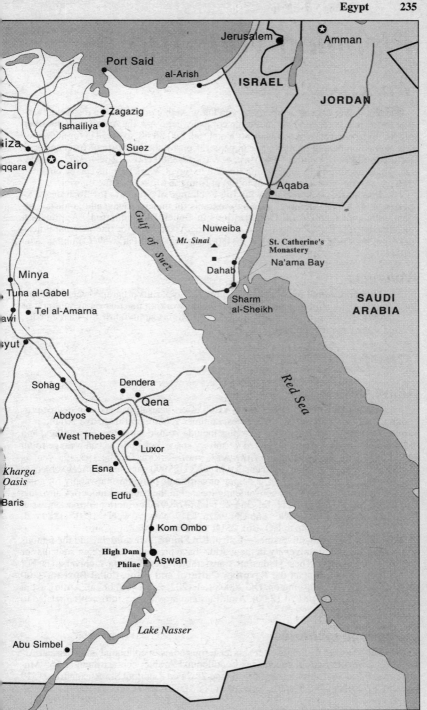

Jerusalem

Amman

Port Said

al-Arish

ISRAEL

JORDAN

Zagazig

Ismailiya

Suez

iza

Aqaba

qqara

Cairo

Nuweiba

Gulf of Suez

Mt. Sinai

St. Catherine's Monastery

Dahab

Na'ama Bay

Minya

Tuna al-Gabel

Sharm al-Sheikh

SAUDI ARABIA

awi

Tel al-Amarna

syut

Red Sea

Sohag

Dendera

Qena

Abdyos

West Thebes

Luxor

Kharga Oasis

Esna

Baris

Edfu

Kom Ombo

High Dam

Philae

Aswan

Lake Nasser

Abu Simbel

Planning Your Trip

Work

Check a university career library. If you know Arabic you'll have a distinct advantage trying to secure work with a foreign company here. Ask the **American Chamber of Commerce** in Cairo at the Marriott Hotel (tel. 340 88 88, ext. 1541) for addresses and phone numbers of its member companies. Consult the **Institute of International Education,** 809 UN Plaza, New York, NY 10017-3580 (fax 212-984-5452), for details about opportunities for teaching English in Egypt. Work permits can be obtained through any Egyptian consulate, or in Egypt from the Ministry of the Interior.

The **International Association for the Exchange of Students for Technical Experience (IAESTE)** sponsors training programs for undergraduate and graduate students in Egypt (see Useful Organizations in General Introduction). Application deadline is Dec. 10. For information, contact the Association for International Practical Training, Parkview Bldg., #320, 10480 Little Papuxent Parkway, Columbia, MD 21044.

Volunteer

The **Higher Council for Youth and Sport** in Egypt runs programs where students of different nationalities spend two to four weeks working together on agricultural or sociological projects. Contact the Council at 10 Modiryiat al-Tahrir St., Garden City, Cairo, or the Egyptian Embassy.

Study

University

The **American University in Cairo (AUC)** offers year-abroad and non-degree programs, bachelor's and master's degrees, summer school, and intensive Arabic programs for foreign students. Course topics include Arabic language, Egyptology, and Middle East studies. There is limited dormitory space, but students can arrange room and board with the assistance of the AUC staff. Tuition for the 1992-93 year is US$3430 per semester; the summer session costs US$900 per course (prices subject to adjustment). U.S. citizens in AUC degree or certificate programs may apply for guaranteed student loans. AUC is conveniently located in the center of modern Cairo, just off Tahrir Sq. (P.O. Box 2511, tel. 354 29 64/5/6/7/8/9). For more information, write to Office of Admissions, AUC, 866 UN Plaza, #517, New York, NY 10017-1889 (tel. (212) 421-6320), or write to P.O. Box 2511, 113 Kasr al-Aini St., Cairo.

Four other Egyptian universities—**Cairo, Ein Shams, Alexandria,** and the famous **Al-Azhar,** the oldest university in the world—have programs for foreign students for one or two semesters. These studies are transferable for credit at most universities. For more information, contact the **Egyptian Cultural and Educational Bureau,** 2200 Kalorama Rd. NW, Washington, DC 20008 (tel. (202) 265-6400) or call **AmidEast** in Cairo (tel. 355 31 70 or 354 13 00). AmidEast can provide any information related to educational concerns.

Language Institutes

Several language institutes offer shorter-term studies in colloquial and classical Arabic. The **Berlitz School** specializes in colloquial Arabic; contact them at 165 Muhammad Farid St., Cairo (tel. 391 50 96) and 28 Sa'ad Zaghloul St., Alexandria 21519 (tel. 80 82 26), or at 40 51st St., New York, NY 10020 (tel. (212) 765-1000). For classical Arabic instruction go to the **Egyptian Center for International Cultural Co-operation,** 11 Shagaret ad-Door St., Zamalek, Cairo (tel. 347 80 05).

Once There

Entry

A **visa** is required to enter Egypt (see Visas in General Introduction). Generally, all personal items brought into the country to be taken out upon departure are exempt from taxes. Unless you are bringing at least US$5000 into the country, there is no formal declaration for personal items. Be sure to save your currency declaration, or your money can be confiscated when you leave Egypt.

Most travelers to Egypt arrive via chaotic, wonderful, befuddling Cairo. To minimize confusion, try to plan your route of escape from the airport, train, or bus terminal before you actually arrive.

Upon arrival at **Cairo International Airport,** purchase a visa stamp if you have not done so already. Visas cost US$2 or LE6.60 for U.S. citizens; the price varies for other nationalities. These rates may rise unexpectedly. Don't panic if an official disappears with your passport; it will be returned, stamped and unharmed.

As (and sometimes even before) you exit customs, you will likely be approached by individuals who claim to be "tourist agents" or employees of the Ministry of Tourism. They wait for unescorted travelers and, pretending to help you, set you up in their employers' hotels, which are usually not a credit to the industry. Do not let anyone direct you to a hotel or even a cab; take cabs from the official stand only, which is monitored 24 hours a day by a Tourist Police officer. All cabs in Cairo are black and white, so it's useless to try to distinguish the Tourist Police cabs by color; look for the officer wearing a black beret and a "Tourist Police" arm band. If you arrive late at night, the safest and easiest move is to get a room at one of the reputable hotels at the airport. Most of these hotels are four- and five-star establishments, so be prepared to splurge the first night of your stay. The least expensive are **Novotel** (singles with bath US$66, doubles with bath US$82; P.O. Box 8, Cairo Airport, Heliopolis, tel. 291 85 77, fax 291 47 94) and **Cairo Airport Hotel** (singles US$29.62, with bath US$37.03; doubles US$37.03, with bath US$44.44; tel. 66 60 74).

To reach the center of town, take red and white **bus** #400 from the rear of the parking lot directly in front of the old airport terminal to **Tahrir Square.** The bus runs 24 hours, twice per hour during the day and every hour late at night and early in the morning (1hr., 10 pt). Roughly. **Minibus** #27 runs between the old airport and the Mugama building in Tahrir Sq. (24 hrs., infrequent at night, 45min., 50pt). There's a free airport shuttle between the old and new airport terminals. Travel by **limousine** is expensive (prices are fixed and posted); bargain with **taxis.**

All trains into Cairo stop at **Ramses Station.** There is absolutely no reason to linger in this chaotic pit. Bus #95 runs from the station to Tahrir Sq. Black and white taxis to Tahrir Sq. cost about LE2. To walk, climb the pedestrian overpass in front of the station and walk south on Ramses St., away from the statue of Ramses II. It's about a 30-minute trek from the station to Tahrir Sq.

Buses from the Sinai, Israel, and Jordan usually drop you off at **Abbassiya Station** in the northern suburb of Abbassiya. To reach Tahrir Sq., hop into a southbound black and white cab (LE2.50-3.50) or walk left down Ramses St. as you leave the station, beyond the overpass, and to the first bus stop on the right. From here most buses pass Ramses Station and many continue to Tahrir Sq.

Useful Organizations

Embassies and Consulates

U.S.: Embassy, 5 Latin America St., Garden City, Cairo (tel. 355 73 71). **Consulate,** in Cairo (tel. 357 22 00), or 110 al-Hurriya Rd., Alexandria (tel. 482 19 11). Use the Cairo embassy for urgent matters. Open Sun.-Thurs. 8am-1pm, closed on Islamic holidays.

Canada: Embassy, 6 Muhammad Fahmi al-Sayid St., Garden City, Cairo (tel. 354 31 10).

U.K.: Embassy, 7 Ahmed Ragheb St., south of the U.S. Embassy, Cairo (tel. 354 08 50/3). **Consulate,** 3 Mena Kafr Abdu St., Roushdy, Alexandria (tel. 84 71 66). In Suez contact the HS Supply Co., 9 Al-Galaa St., (tel. 22 01 45 or 22 53 82) or the Hilton Compound Complex, Rm. 623, Port Said (tel. 23 11 55). Handles affairs for **New Zealand** as well.

Australia: Embassy, Cairo Plaza, 5th floor, 1097 Corniche al-Nil, Bulaq (tel. 77 79 00/94), 4 blocks south of Shepheard's Hotel.

Tourist Services

The **Egyptian General Authority for the Promotion of Tourism (EGAPT)** has offices everywhere. The Egyptian tourist authorities also run a program called the **Tourist Friends Association** (tel. 392 20 36), which matches travelers with Egyptians. For more information, write them at P.O. Box 161 Muhammad Farid, 33 Kasr al-Nil Street, 9th floor, Cairo. The **Tourist Police,** despite the quasi-fascist name, are actually meant to assist visitors with any problems. Go to them in case of theft, or loss of life or limb; most speak some English. The officers are recognizable by their uniforms (black in winter, white in summer) with the words "Tourist Police" on arm bands. Another source of titillating information is the **Egyptian Ministry of Tourism,** 110 Kasr al-Aini St., Bab al-Luq Sq., Cairo (tel. 354 62 95 or 355 55 68).

Medical Emergencies

The major hotels have resident doctors who can prescribe medicine or, in serious cases, arrange for specialists and hospitals. Telephone directories list doctors according to specialization. Ask your embassy for a list of physicians and pharmacists best able to assist foreigners. Several major hospitals provide 24-hour service, including the **Coptic Hospital** (175 Ramses St., Dokki; tel. 90 40 11), the **Anglo-American Hospital** (3 Zohria Garden St., Zamalek; tel. 61 62/3/4/5), and the **al-Salam International Hospital** (Maadi Corniche, Maadi; tel. 363 21 95).

Pharmacies carry most U.S. and European drugs; Egypt is more relaxed about prescriptions than the U.S. Pharmacists are considered doctors in Egypt, and thus are authorized to perform injections. Pharmacies are open 9am-1pm and 4-8pm (often 10pm in summer). Dial 123 for emergencies. (See Health in the General Introduction and Practical Information in the city sections for more information.)

Communication

Mail

An airmail letter from Egypt to the U.S. or Europe costs LE1, postcards the same. The most reliable place to mail letters is, according to local legend, the mailbox near the reception desk at the Nile Hilton. Postcards will more likely reach their destinations if sent from a major hotel rather than a post office. Most hotels sell stamps, although a 5pt surcharge may be added. The most dependable place to receive mail is the main American Express office in Cairo, although Poste Restante functions in most major cities. Confusion over first and last names can be avoided by using an initial and your last name or printing the last name in capitals. Mail can also be addressed to the

American Consulate. As a general rule, mail to Egypt is faster than mail from Egypt. In either case, don't hold your breath—two or three weeks' delivery time is normal.

The process for sending a package is Byzantine. First you must obtain an export license from Cairo International Airport (also available at major hotels and tourist shops). Most souvenir shops will do the dirty work necessary to mail your pyramid paperweights back home, for a fee. In theory, all mail leaving Egypt is opened and inspected. If you must get something to Europe or North America within 72 hrs., go to the main post office at Ataba Square, northeast of Tahrir Sq. The **International Express Mail** office at the side entrance is efficient, albeit expensive. (Open Sat.-Thurs. 7am-7pm.) Also, most hotels can direct you to the nearest **DHL International Courier** office; DHL will deliver anything door-to-door anywhere in the world within 24 hours. The main office is located at 20 Gamal ad-Din Abu al-Mahasin St., Garden City (tel. 355 73 01 or 355 71 18; fax 356 26 01).

Telephone

The Egyptian telephone system promises to be time-consuming and infuriating; you may never say another bad word about Ma Bell and her kids. **Long-distance** or **international calls** are best made from large hotels. **Credit card calls** to the U.S. and Japan can be made from the USCEirect or JapanDirect phones in the lobbies of several five-star hotels. **Collect calls** to Egypt are impossible. The other option is to call from a government telephone office, known fondly as the "Centrale," where maddeningly long waits are usual. If you must make an international call from these offices, go either very early in the morning or very late at night when you stand a better chance of making a connection before you've finished reading your *Let's Go* from cover to cover. At public telephone offices you pay in advance for a specific number of minutes. You'll be cut off abruptly the second your allotted time is up, so err on the generous side. One final headache: if you don't speak Arabic, you may have difficulty communicating your wishes, especially at smaller offices. The **international phone code** for calling to Egypt is 20.

Local calls can be dialed direct to most of Egypt's larger cities and towns. Public pay phones are not common in Egypt, but local calls can be made from many hotels, restaurants, and cigarette kiosks. Be wary of using a phone in a private hotel room; proprietors sometimes levy exorbitant fees. To maximize your probability of success, perform the following ritual: (1) Pick up the receiver, insert your coin, and listen for a continuous ringing noise. (2) Dial slowly. (3) Pray. If you're unlucky on the first try, don't give up—even if you dial faultlessly, you will not necessarily get the correct party. Don't assume that an unanswered ring means no one is home. You are now having fun.

Telegraph

The larger telephone offices and hotels usually provide telex and cable services. In Cairo, go to the Ataba Square telegraph office, opposite the main post office. Dial 124 to send a telegram by phone. It is not always possible to send an international telegram from offices outside of Cairo, but usually at least one major hotel in a town will provide this service. Allow at least two days for the message to reach its destination.

Currency and Exchange

Egypt's array of coins and banknotes is gradually becoming simplified as the old bills and coins pass out of circulation and into the hands of numismatists. The *guinea* (GEE-nay), or **Egyptian pound (LE),** is divided into 100 *airsh,* or **piasters (pt).** Technically, piasters are divided into 100 *millims* (mil-LEEMS), but the only vestige of this minuscule denomination is an extra zero to the right of the decimal point on some posted prices. **Banknotes** are color coded, printed with Arabic on one side and English on the other; the notes come in the following denominations: LE20 (green),

LE10 (red), LE5 (blue), LE1 (brown), 50pt (red and brown), 25pt (blue), 10pt (black), and 5pt (brown). All bills are roughly the same size except for the 10pt and 5pt notes, which are less than half the size of the larger bills. Older banknotes are size-graded throughout. LE50 and LE100 notes are also issued in the new system, but they're rare. In fact, it's best to break your large bills into denominations of LE1 and below because most taxi and bus drivers as well as street vendors cannot or will not make change.

Coins are almost extinct. If you encounter any at all, they'll probably be 10pt and 5pt coins, which are usually silver-colored with ridged edges. For maximum confusion, the copper-colored 1pt and 0.5pt coins are marked with the Arabic numerals 10 and 5, representing millims.

The **currency exchange system** has been completely revised, to the great advantage of the tourist. Beginning in the winter of 1986, the government decided to destroy the black market by co-opting its business—the new **tourist rate** actually beats the previous black-market rate. Be sure to save all exchange receipts. Note that the New Zealand Dollar is not convertible in Egypt (the exchange rate listed in the beginning of the Egypt section was converted from US$).

To buy a plane or boat ticket out of Egypt, find out the price in pounds, exchange exactly that amount at the official rate, and then present your receipt as you purchase the ticket. You are not allowed to carry more than LE20 into or out of Egypt, nor would you want to, so don't exchange more than you think you'll use.

Prices

A brief lesson in Arabic: After *min fadlak* (please) and *shukran* (thank you), the most important word to know is *khoaga* (kho-AH-ga), because you are one. *Khoaga* means "tourist," but is understood locally as "clueless rich one from far away." No matter how destitute you consider yourself, you are probably wealthy by Egyptian standards. Other than those in hotels and restaurants, most prices are not posted, which means *khoagas* are charged more than Egyptians. Avoid salesfolk and shops near tourist hubs, and look upon any unsolicited offer of goods or services with grave suspicion—even if told there is no charge. Always agree upon a price before you accept anything, and do not pay until you receive that for which you bargained. Try to ascertain beforehand how much something is really worth, and pay in exact change. Most importantly, always insist on getting full value, no matter what excuses are offered. Never feel you owe more than the agreed amount no matter how much anyone squawks, and never be afraid to walk away at any time, or to firmly refuse an invitation, however seemingly kind, if you feel you'll have to pay later.

Student discounts of up to 50%, with proper student identification, apply at almost all official sites. The people who work at ticket kiosks will charge you the correct fee, but the guides who solicit your business at sites and museums should be ignored; often they will recite a few memorized phrases in English—"mask of Tuthankamen, solid gold, mummy of Tuthankamen, solid gold"—and then expect outlandish remuneration.

Shopping in Egypt is an adventure that requires patience and discretion. For the basics, simply go where the Egyptians go and pay what the Egyptians pay; rare is the department store clerk or pharmacy that thrives by ripping off *khoagas*. For souvenirs and native sundries, become a cynic. Rare and valuable craftwork is out there—along with pyramid paperweights and fake antiques. Avoid all souvenir shops and kiosks flanking tourist attractions. The bazaars in the cities are chaotic but they are the best places to find authentic woodwork, glassware, textiles and other crafts. The password is: Bargain. (See Other Tips in General Introduction.)

If there is ever a problem with hustlers or rip-off artists, report it to the Tourist Police stationed at every tourist site, transportation centers, and most hotels.

Tipping and Baksheesh

Another crucial Arabic word for *khoagas* to know is *baksheesh,* the art of tipping. It is an ancient tradition in Islamic societies and was going on long before *khoagas* trampled onto the scene. Although *baksheesh* is different from straightforward charity, it stems from the belief that those who have should give to those who have not, particularly in return for a favor or service. There are three kinds of *baksheesh*. The most common is similar to **tipping**—a small reward for a small service. Tipping waiters and cab drivers is routine, as well as maids and cooks after long stays in hotels. Don't feel obligated to give anything more if a "service charge" is added to your bill, as is becoming increasingly common. Do not let yourself be railroaded into forking over huge sums—if a smiling worker demands LE5, say *anna mish khoaga* ("I'm not a dumb tourist") and give 25-50pt. *Baksheesh* becomes most useful when used to procure special favors. Almost any minor rule can be broken for *baksheesh*. If a custodian gives you a private tour of a mosque long after hours, a pound or two is in order. Never expect recipients of *baksheesh* to make change—one more reason to carry small bills. Always ignore the demands for more if you feel you've been fair. Women travellers who feel certain caretakers at monuments and other sites to be harassing or overly friendly should refuse to give *baksheesh* or make some excuse (you don't have your wallet).

The second kind of baksheesh is the giving of **alms.** Everywhere in Egypt you will encounter beggars who are willing to bestow rhetorical blessings upon you in return for a little charity. Deal with them charitably, but be careful of those who try to impose some unwanted service or favor, like opening a door before you can get to it and then demanding *baksheesh*. Refuse all such "favors" loudly and firmly, and if they insist on going ahead with it, thank them and walk away.

The final form of *baksheesh* is simply a bribe. Don't try it.

Women Travelers

Foreign women, especially those traveling alone, should expect to be harassed by Egyptian men. Harassment can take many forms, from a mildly sinister "hello," to the more annoying and frequent *pssst,* to frightening and potentially harmful physical contact. Your stay in Egypt might be a bit more enjoyable if you make it a point to visit crowded areas in lengthier clothing and less crowded sites (tombs, desert areas) with at least one other person. Via Western music, movies, television, and hearsay, some Egyptians have developed the idea that Americans and Europeans are excessively "free" in their dealings and in their behavior. Women are advised to avoid the crowded public buses and most nightclubs ("nightclubs" in the West are equivalent to "discos" in the Middle East; Middle Eastern nightclubs are something completely different, so don't get confused). The best way to deal with harassment is probably to ignore it; repeated advances and extensive verbal harassment, however, are best quelled with a loud, indignant response in front of many people. For more information, see Safety and Women Travelers in the General Introduction. If you feel unduly intimidated or harassed in any way, do not hesitate to alert the police.

Business Hours

On Friday, the Muslim day of communal prayer, most government offices, banks, and post offices are closed (banks are closed on Saturdays as well). Other establishments, such as restaurants, remain open seven days a week. Store hours are ordinarily Saturday-Thursday 9am-2pm and 5pm-8pm (9pm in the summer), with many stores also open Friday. Government office hours are usually 9am-2pm. Do your government business in the morning, as workers often leave before official closing times. Bank hours are ordinarily Sunday-Thursday 8:30am-noon, with money exchange available daily 8:30am-noon and 4-8pm. Foreign banks keep longer business hours, usually Sunday-Thursday 8am-3pm. Archeological sites and other points of interest are typically open 7am-6pm, though in summer the most important ones in the Nile Valley open at 6am and close in the early afternoon.

During the month-long holiday of **Ramadan** (approx. Feb. 22-March 24 in 1993), some restaurants close entirely, while some others open only after sundown when the fast is broken. The streets empty at dusk as everyone sits down to "breakfast," after which business resumes. Shops close at 3:30pm during Ramadan and reopen from 8-11pm. In the middle of the night, about 2-3am, Egyptians sit down for the second daily meal of Ramadan (called *sahur*) before going to sleep. Although traveling during Ramadan can be inconvenient, the excitement of nighttime celebrations offsets daytime hassles.

Accommodations

Hostels

Egypt has 15 youth hostels that vary in quality. Most are bearable, though grungy and crowded, and the unbeatable price (LE3-10 per night) will probably compensate for the less-than-luxurious atmosphere. Keep a careful eye on your valuables and take your passport, visa, and money to bed with you. Advance reservations are usually unnecessary, but arrive early just to be safe. A valid **Hostelling International (HI)** card may not be required, but at most hostels it will save you a pound or two. If you decide to purchase an HI card while you're in Egypt you can get an International Guest Card from all hostels for LE24.

The larger hostels are located in Cairo, Alexandria, Luxor, Port Said, and Sharm al-Shaikh; smaller hostels are in Aswan, Assyut, Damanhour, Marsa Matruuh, Fayyum, Hurghada, Ismailiya, Tanta, Sohag, and Suez. Most hostels have kitchen facilities. For more information write to the **Egyptian Youth Hostel Association,** 1 El-Ibrahimy St., Garden City, Cairo (tel. 354 05 29, fax 355 03 29). The Youth Travel Department can also answer questions, help plan tours, and often provide maps. Write for information on their 15 hostels. Here too, an International Guest Card will cost LE24.

Hotels

Egypt's hotels run the gamut from glistening new resort complexes to spartan, dusty dives in dingy alleys; somewhere in between, clean, comfortable, inexpensive hotels do exist. Most towns and cities have lower-range hotels with rooms for LE10-18, as well as a number of middle-range hotels where you'll pay LE22-28. More comfortable hotels run into the LE30-45 range. Always ask to see the room before you pay. There is a hotel tax which varies by location, from 19% in Cairo to 10-12% in most other places. Unless otherwise noted, the tax should be included.

Prices vary considerably between high and low season. The high season in Alexandria is June-August, in the Nile Valley October-April. If you visit in the high season, expect hotel rates for the Nile Valley (particularly Luxor and Aswan) to be anywhere from *10 to 50% higher* than listed here. In Cairo the high season is also in winter, but the differential between seasonal prices (if it exists) tends to be less.

Not least, realize that hot water and private baths are luxuries in Egypt, and are never free. Don't expect air conditioning, private telephones, or other amenities, including toilet paper; guess what that little squirting pipe in the toilet bowl is for. Go to Egypt's well-stocked pharmacies and street vendors to buy toilet paper.

Transportation

Travel Restrictions

Foreigners are officially required to secure **permits** to travel in the following areas: secondary roads in the Delta; along the Suez Canal between (but not including) Ismailiya and Suez; the coastal road to Libya beyond Marsa Matruuh; any area surrounding (but not including) the Siwa Oasis; the Red Sea coast between (but not including) Suez and Hurghada; and all areas in the Sinai off the main roads and outside the Federation-Klingon Neutral Zone. The Western Desert Oases no longer require a permit. In restricted zones police are allowed to confiscate your passport and hold you for questioning. If you find yourself in such a pickle, sincere apologies and confessions of ignorance may put the matter to rest.

Almost all places of interest to tourists are unrestricted so the above restrictions should seldom interfere with your plans. To undertake unusual expeditions in a restricted area, you must seek permission from the Travel Permits Department of the Ministry of the Interior. Bring two photos, your passport, and patience. In Cairo the office is located at the corner of Sheikh Ridan and Nuban St.; in Alexandria on Ferrana St. off al-Huriyya St. Keep your passport with you at all times.

The law also forbids Egyptians from traveling with foreigners without special permission. A travel agent's license, marriage or birth certificate, and kindergarten report card are required for permission to be granted. To prevent nasty questioning sessions en route, your Egyptian friends may want to check with the local police before accompanying you.

Train

The Egyptian railway system serves almost all major towns and points of interest in the country. First- and second-class trains are relatively comfortable and surprisingly inexpensive. They are also one of the most popular means of transport, with the concomitant long lines and crowded cars. Trains are probably the best option for long-distance travel. For shorter distances, other forms of transportation—particularly *service* taxis—are much faster and more reliable.

The government has hesitated to advertise its train system to tourists because there's barely enough room for Egyptians. Schedules and signs in the anarchic train stations are never in English. The Roman numerals on the trains indicate their class, and fellow passengers are generally helpful in directing you to the correct ticket windows and platforms. Ask at any major station for the invaluable 40-page English version of the *Egyptian Railways Timetable* (LE1).

Student discounts on most major routes can be almost 50%. Riding on the unreserved non-air-conditioned second- and third-class trains may be an adventure, but it's definitely not recommended for long treks. It's better to book seats on **air-conditioned second-class** cars from Cairo; air-conditioned first-class is also available, but the elbow-room is probably not worth the extra cost. **Second-class sleeper cars,** available on regular trains, are an excellent deal for travel to Luxor or Aswan, but are nearly impossible to book. Unmarried couples may not be permitted to share a cabin. Student discounts on sleepers are less than on regular seats; you might not get a discount on the luxurious **wagon-lits.** You can reserve space on a sleeper at the wagon-lit offices in Cairo, Luxor, Aswan, and Alexandria. Other types of train passage can be reserved only at the station of departure, or through a travel agent (for a fee). Reserve seats between Cairo and Upper Egypt several days in advance.

Since round-trip reservations cannot be arranged at the point of origin, always take care of return reservations as soon as you reach your destination, particularly if you intend to take a sleeper. During the last week of Ramadan and the first week after, as well as before Eid al-Adha, reserved seats on all Egyptian trains, especially those to Luxor and Aswan, are completely booked. If you plan to travel during this period book your tickets at least one week in advance.

If your train is full and you're in a hurry, don't worry—simply board the train without buying a ticket. The conductor will sell you one on board for a small fine (about LE1.50 between Cairo and Luxor and Aswan). Your larger problem will be finding a seat or an empty space on the floor. If you are traveling from Cairo to Alexandria or the Delta, you may in fact want to avoid the hassle of waiting in the ticket lines for reserved seating—the trip is short, you may find a seat anyway, and the fine for not having a ticket is nominal.

If you miss your train, immediately return to the back of the ticket windows and find the door to the ticket office. Barge in, ask to see the director, flail your arms, show your tickets, and explain you've just missed your train and that you're a poor student.

You may be amazed—the same lethargic bureaucracy that made you wait for hours to buy the ticket can act with lightning speed under such circumstances. If you're extremely lucky, you may be issued a ticket on the next train out—even if there are officially no seats available for at least a week. Never try to bribe a train station official.

If your antics are unsuccessful, don't throw your money away in despair. It's often possible to return and exchange tickets for a nominal fee. If you want to return reserved tickets, go to the stationmaster's office before the scheduled departure and your money will be refunded minus a small fee.

Finally, women traveling alone should never ride third class; if you have to go this way, try to sit with a group of Egyptian women. Even second-class trains can be an alarming experience for women. Traveling first class to avoid harassment is worth the price.

Bus

Intercity buses are an inexpensive but usually uncomfortable way to travel in Egypt. But despite overcrowding, buses are valuable for short trips, when trains are a hassle. Buses also provide transportation to areas without rail service, such as Hurghada, the Sinai, the Oases, and Abu Simbel. Most routes also offer a slightly more expensive air-conditioned bus, usually early in the morning. Private companies serve routes frequented by wealthier Egyptians (such as Cairo to Alexandria) with special air-conditioned, comfortable, no-standing buses. Bus service in the Sinai, though irregular, is generally comfortable and air conditioned. Note that when you book a ticket for an Egyptian bus you are often assigned a particular seat. Buses traveling between major cities leave frequently throughout the day, although buses to and from the Sinai and the oases often depart only early in the morning. Try to go to the station the day before to confirm departure times.

Numbers and destinations on Egyptian buses are ordinarily written only in Arabic. The conductors who sit at the small kiosks at Tahrir, Ramses, and the other main terminals are usually quite helpful with directions.

Taxi

Taxis are a cheap, convenient option for traveling around Cairo (taxis are black and white) and Alexandria (black and orange). Using the taxis, however, requires some practice. (For tips on how to best flag them down and determine correct payment for your destination, see Cairo Transportation.)

Private taxis (called *taxi spécial*) are much more expensive than the collective variety; use them only for late-night or out-of-the-way travel. The taxi drivers are notorious for exacting inflated fares from naive tourists. To decrease your chances of being ripped off, try to hail a private taxi on the street instead of finding one that is parked, particularly one parked near a popular tourist sight or large hotel. If a cabbie approaches you first, refuse.

Inter-city *service* taxis (*taxi ugra*) link Cairo to other locations. These large, monochrome Peugeot or Mercedes cars seat seven or eight passengers, but sometimes pack in more. *Service* taxis leave from established places in Cairo for a variety of destinations. The cost of a trip, usually fixed (except in Sinai), is split among the passengers. There is no advance purchase of tickets, and cars leave as soon as they are filled. Usually you won't have to wait more than 15 minutes. The major advantage of *service* taxis is their flexibility. You're also less likely to be cheated because all passengers pay the same amount. *Service* taxis can be hired by a group for several hours or for a full day of sightseeing. Tourist offices have the official rates, typically LE20-25 per taxi for a half-day (depending upon the distances involved). One disadvantage of *service* taxis is that they can be dangerous. Although most drivers are responsible, their competence behind the wheel, their addiction to recklessness, and even their sobriety, vary widely.

Service **taxi stands** in large towns are usually well organized. In villages stands may be nothing more than a designated stretch of road. When in doubt, go to the bus station; the taxi stand is usually nearby.

Hitchhiking

Let's Go does *not* recommend hitchhiking. The routes listed elsewhere in this book are not intended to recommend hitchhiking as a means of transport.

Hitchhiking is not common in Egypt, but even within cities Egyptians are usually friendly about picking up foreign hitchers. Rides are reportedly easy to obtain in isolated areas, such as along the Great Desert Road or in remote parts of the Nile Valley, where public transportation is difficult to find. Often, however, drivers who pick up hitchhikers will expect a fare comparable to taxi or bus fare, regardless of whether their passenger is Egyptian or foreign. **Women, whether in a group or alone, should not hitchhike.**

Car Rental

Renting a car may be economical if several people travel in a single vehicle. A car will enable you to visit remote regions such as the Oases or the Red Sea coast. Remember to obtain the necessary permits before cruising on back roads in the Delta or out to Siwa. Bear in mind that there are few places where you can drop off rental cars. An **International Driver's Permit** (see Identification Cards in General Introduction) is required to drive in Egypt. Any insurance you have will not cover you here, so plan to invest in proper coverage. (See Insurance in General Introduction.) Age requirements are not always strictly enforced by rental agencies. The cheapest rentals run about US$70 per day with unlimited mileage. To rent a car once in Egypt, see the Practical Information sections of individual cities. It is often cheaper and easier to make reservations before you leave. Your biggest headache on the road will be the traffic; driving in Egypt demands nerves of steel.

Avis Rent-A-Car: U.S., (tel. (800) 331-1212); **Canada,** (tel. (800) 268-2310); **U.K.,** dial 100 and ask for Freephone Avis; **Egypt,** (tel. (3) 54 70 81 or 54 86 98). Must be 25.

Budget Rent-A-Car: U.S., (tel. (800) 472-3325); **Canada,** (tel. (800) 268-8900); **U.K.,** (tel. 0800 18 11 81). Must be 23.

Hertz Rent-A-Car: U.S., (tel. (800) 654-3001); **Canada,** (tel. (800) 263-0600). Must be 21.

Plane

EgyptAir, the official airline for all domestic flights, serves all major cities out of Cairo International Airport. All prices listed are one-way, economy class. The airline has frequent flights from Cairo to Luxor (1hr., US$85); Aswan (2hr., US$117); Alexandria (30min., US$50 with discounts on round-trip fares); Abu Simbel (US$166); and Hurghada (US$92). EgyptAir's main office in the U.S. is at 720 Fifth Ave., New York, NY 10019 (tel. (212) 581-5600). There are no student discounts or youth fares on domestic flights.

EgyptAir has several offices in Cairo, some more crowded than others. The following offices have staff members who speak English: 16 Adli St., across from the tourist office (tel. 92 09 99), and Nile Hilton, by Tahrir Sq. (tel. 75 98 06). You can reach their central reservations and information service at tel. 75 06 00.

Air Sinai, in the courtyard of the Nile Hilton, is a subsidiary of EgyptAir created to serve the Sinai and Israel so that the Arab states wouldn't blacklist EgyptAir. Foreigners may have to pay in U.S. dollars. Below are one-way fares; the round-trip is probably undiscounted. Air Sinai flies two or three times per week from Cairo to St. Catherine's (US$75), and Sharm al-Shaikh (US$95). Convenient flights also travel from Hurghada to Sharm al-Shaikh (US$65), and St. Catherine's (US$89). Air Sinai's most popular flight connects Cairo and Tel Aviv. For more information, contact the main office at 12 Kasr al-Nil St., Cairo (tel. 75 06 00 or 75 07 29, fax 77 49 66) or any branch office.

Life in Egypt

The burgeoning population of Egypt, 58 million strong, is composed of a broad swath of cultures and classes, including descendants of the Pharaohs, Coptic Christians, and Bedouin, all of whom consider themselves wholly Egyptian. The majority of the population, however, is of Arab ancestry. The upper classes have adopted Western commodity fetishism, while members of the educated middle class do what they can to emulate them on civil-service salaries. The great majority of the lower class lives in appalling poverty, some relying on family and relatives abroad (usually in the Gulf) for support. The cheapest commodity in resource-poor Egypt is labor. Along the banks of the Nile *fellaheen* farm the rich land as their ancestors did 5000 years ago, but Egypt must supplement that with imported food.

In Egypt, the greater honor lies with the host; you won't be there long before you are invited to tea, a meal, or an all-night wedding. Directions and advice are freely offered, but remember that some Egyptians are so eager to help and practice their English they will give incorrect directions rather than fail to offer assistance. Violent crime is not common in Egypt, and it is usually safe to wander in large cities.

Egypt is a conservative, patriarchal society with a strong Islamic tradition. Western mores do not apply, especially in matters of family and sex. For most of this society the role of women is severely limited. The most vocal Egyptian men believe that Western women are free from moral strictures—and will expect (or at least hope) that they will behave accordingly. If foreign women can fend off annoying verbal harassment they'll enjoy the benefits of traveling in a stable and safe society.

From the Western tourist's point of view, a disconcerting feature seems to unite the Egyptian population: the unequivocal lack of concern for time. In Egypt you must simply accept the fact that the economical use of time is not a concern. Just slow down, be excellent to each other, and mellow out.

Your temper is most likely to howl in encounters with Egypt's mind-occluding bureaucracy. You may well feel that you spend more time buying train tickets than exploring ancient temples. Bring every book ever written by Naguib Mahfouz (or better yet, *Let's Go*) to read as you wait in line, and try not to notice that the bureaucrat disappears to chat with friends just as you approach the window.

Government and Politics

According to its 1971 constitution, Egypt is a "democratic, socialist state," but in effect it's neither democratic nor overly socialist. It is more of an election-legitimated authoritarian regime. The president serves a six-year term and can be reelected for additional terms. He appoints the vice president and ministers. Since the 1952 revolution, successions to the presidency have happened only when Gamal Abd an-Nasser died in 1970, and then when his successor Anwar al-Sadat was assassinated in 1981. The legislative branch consists of the 392-member People's Assembly, half of whom must be workers or peasants, and 30 of whom must be women. This assembly ratifies all laws and the national budget. All males over 18 and those women on the register of voters may participate in the election. Despite the regime's ultimate authority, Egypt is among the most liberal Arab countries.

Like that of his predecessor, President Hosni Mubarak's government has been challenged repeatedly by Islamists. Mubarak's inauguration followed the assassination of Sadat by militants whose aim was to overthrow the Egyptian government and establish an Islamic republic in its place.

Islamists gained parliamentary strength in the May 1984 elections for the People's Assembly. The fundamentalist group, the Muslim Brotherhood, joined with the Wafd Party, and the alliance achieved the necessary 8% minimum for parliamentary representation. Meanwhile, Islamists were elected to university student councils, often gaining majorities and faculty support. To try to quell the Islamic militants, the government acquiesced to several fundamentalist demands. Alcohol was banned on EgyptAir flights, and the television program *Dallas* was taken off TV (much to the chagrin of many Egyptians). Furthermore, an aspect of a divorce law enacted by Sadat was declared unconstitutional by the Supreme Court.

Mubarak has employed various strategies to counter the fundamentalist threat to his government. Early in his administration Mubarak appeased Islamic moderates in order to isolate militants, even initiating an Islamic newspaper, *Al-Liwa'al-Islami.* Three years later Mubarak again utilized the government press, this time to mock Islamic militants, employing intellectuals such as Tawfik al-Hakim and Yusuf Idris. (See Literature.)

Meanwhile, though he has stuck to the terms of the 1979 peace treaty, Mubarak has tried to distance Egypt from Israel, keeping the diplomatic air cool. In 1984, as Mubarak reached out to other countries, Egypt restored relations with the Soviet Union and was readmitted to the Islamic Conference. By 1988, the Arab League had invited Egypt to rejoin and dropped demands that Egypt sever ties with Israel. In 1991, having led part of the Arab world against Iraq in the Gulf War, Egypt was invited to head the Arab League, marking the country's re-emergence at the helm of the Arab world. Egypt is also beginning to recapture its former position of power within the world arena; in 1992, Boutros Boutros-Ghali, a respected diplomat involved in the Camp David negotiations, became the new UN Secretary-General.

Economy

At the beginning of this century, Egypt was the richest of the Arab nations. However, Egypt's mushrooming population and shortage of arable land have greatly inhibited its economic development. All but four percent of Egypt is desert, and the little arable land is overcrowded, though extremely fertile. Nonetheless, Nasser's land reform greatly altered the economy's complexion; in 1952 three percent of the population owned more than half of the land, while now no one may own more than 50 acres.

About half of the Egyptian labor force works in the agricultural sector, growing primarily cotton, corn, rice, and grain. Despite the large number of farmers, Egypt, formerly the breadbasket of the world, cannot currently supply enough food for its own population. A growing proportion of workers are involved in manufacturing, which now accounts for as much income as agriculture. The government employs almost all the rest of the work force in its colossal bureaucracy. As the population grows at nearly three percent per year, more and more educated Egyptians leave to find work in wealthy, neighboring oil states. Illiteracy remains high, poverty is widespread, and the typical diet is inadequate.

Seeking to alleviate these problems, Egypt solicits and accepts vast sums of foreign aid. Through the 1970s Saudi Arabia, Qatar, Kuwait, and the United Arab Emirates supplied Egypt with tens of billions in aid, and in 1977 formed the Gulf Organization for the Development of Egypt (GODE). But after the Camp David Accords in 1979, angry Arab states cut off financial support (not GODE). Under the Carter Plan, the U.S., Western Europe, and Japan agreed to provide Egypt with US$12.25 billion over five years. In 1984, Jordan and Iraq restored financial ties with Egypt, though Syria and Libya continue the boycott. The U.S. provides more than US$2 billion in aid to Egypt annually, an incentive first offered to Cairo for making peace with Israel. For its support in the Gulf War, Egypt received further assistance from the West (including the forgiving of US$6.7 billion of military debt to the U.S.) and renewed aid from the Gulf states.

President Hosni Mubarak has tried to diversify the Egyptian economy, encouraging development in the private sector. Foreign investment has grown steadily in recent years, and Arab capital has more than doubled since 1982. In 1987 foreign projects represented 35% of the total investment. Revenue from the Suez Canal has consistently been about US$1 billion per year during the last decade. Most of Egypt's profits are used to purchase foreign grain.

Religion

Ancient Religion

The people of predynastic Egypt were ruled by a bewildering array of local gods representing the cosmos, the natural elements, animals, and the life-cycle. As Egypt was united, these local gods were combined and unified into one syncretic pantheon in which the gods' powers and functions frequently overlapped and/or contradicted one another. The importance of gods often waxed and waned with the fortunes of their home provinces. The basic framework of religious belief, however, remained stable through the three millenia of pharaonic rule.

The central myth of Egyptian religion was the **Osiris cycle.** Seth murdered his brother Osiris, a king from time immemorial, and scattered the pieces of his body throughout Egypt. Subsequently, Osiris's wife and sister Isis conceived and gave birth to Horus, who became Osiris's son and heir. Young Horus avenged Osiris and took back the crown from his usurping uncle. The pharaohs saw Horus as the ideal of the rightful and strong ruler, and identified themselves with Horus while on earth. Upon death they were identified with Osiris, now the king of the dead. The pharaoh was thus literally a god and worshiped as such, and the religious fervor he engendered united the country. Some scholars believe that the Pyramids were built by hundreds of thousands of devout Egyptians out of piety towards their god-king, not by slaves or reluctant non-union labor.

In the Old Kingdom only the pharaoh was believed to be able to enter the afterworld, but gradually the admission standards were loosened until such time as they were comparable to Yale's. Minor royalty took to grouping their tombs around the king's, hoping that the proximity could draw them, too, into the netherworld.

By the time of the Middle Kingdom, the afterlife was open to all of the righteous, and Egyptians' central concern became life after death. Earthly existence was but a short interlude to be endured until the afterlife brought eternal happiness and reward. The divine and secular worlds, however, were not strongly demarcated; the preservation of the earthly body through mummification was considered essential for the afterlife of the *ka,* or soul, and the tomb, the house of the dead, had to be supplied with all the comforts of home (furniture, servants, food, and wine).

The **Pyramid Texts** were spells inscribed on the walls of the royal pyramids to ensure the success of the king or queen's journey to their afterlife. As the underworld *perestroika* took hold, these texts were adopted by more plebeian folk and inscribed on the sides of their coffins. The New Kingdom's *Book of the Dead,* a collection of spells written on papyrus and put in sarcophagi, described not only how to get to the afterworld but also how to enjoy oneself once there; spells detailed how to get a sucker to do one's post-mortem menial labor. The *Book of the Dead* also described the ancient Egyptian version of final judgment—Osiris weighed the heart of a corpse against a feather (truth), and a heavy heart condemned the dead to complete and utter extermination. Few suffered this fate since each corpse had a stone scarab which prevented the heart from providing incriminating testimony.

The Macedonian **Ptolemies,** who ruled Egypt in the wake of Alexander, sought to become pharaonic god-kings to their subjects. By merging Greek and Egyptian elements in the Serapis cult, and building temples to the ancient gods, they achieved what Assyrian and Persian invaders before them never could—they became spiritual successors of the pharaohs. Many of the great temples of Upper Egypt date to Ptolemaic times, including those dedicated to Hathor, the cow-goddess wife of Horus, Sobek, the crocodile god, and Isis, the mother goddess. The conquerors, however, may have been more influenced than influencing; the mystery cults of Osiris, Isis, and Horus spread throughout the Hellenistic world and later throughout the Roman Empire, while Egyptian religion continued fundamentally unchanged.

For more on Egypt's ancient religion and culture consult Nagel's *Encyclopedia-Guide to Egypt.* The *Blue Guide* to Egypt offers detailed descriptions and illustrations of pharaonic sites as well.

Modern Religion

The most common religion in Egypt is Islam; about 85% of the population is Sunni Muslim. Most other Egyptians are Christian Orthodox of the Coptic, or Egyptian, Church. Smaller religious minorities include Shi'i Muslims, Protestants, Roman Catholics, and Jews. (See Religion in the General Introduction.)

Festivals and Holidays

Of the several **mawlid** (birthdays) celebrated throughout the country, the most important is **Mawlid an-Nabi,** the birthday of the prophet Muhammad. Smaller, local *mawlids* take place in mosques or at the shrines of particular religious figures. Check with tourist offices for details. Also festive are the two Sufi rituals of **Zikr** and **Zahr.** In the former, a rhythmic group dance builds in fervor, and the group members become whirling dervishes, mesmerized into a communal trance. The latter is a group dance performed by women, primarily as an exorcism rite. Both rituals are practiced on Fridays in many populous areas.

During the month of **Ramadan** (begins approx. February 22 in 1993), devout Muslims do not eat or drink anything during daylight hours. Ramadan culminates in the three-day festival of **Eid al-Fitr** (approx. March 24). Muslims also celebrate **Eid al-Adha** (May 31), a remembrance of Abraham's intended sacrifice of his son Ishmael which coincides with the *hajj* to Mecca, and **Isra wel Mi'raj** (Jan. 19), which celebrates Muhammad's Night Journey. Government offices and banks close during the festivals, but tourist facilities remain open.

Sham an-Nissim falls on the first Monday after Coptic Easter. Though its origins are a hodgepodge of Coptic and pharaonic influences, it has developed into a secular holiday. Egyptians traditionally spend the day on a picnic eating *fasikh,* a dried, salted fish difficult for most Western palates to appreciate. The Coptic celebrations of Easter and Christmas are tranquil affairs marked by special church services.

The major national holidays, observed officially by banks and government offices but without public celebration are **Sinai Day** (April 25), **Labor Day** (May 1), **Revolution Day** (July 23), and **Victory Day** (Dec. 23).

Language

One of the earliest forms of writing was Egyptian **hieroglyphics** (sacred carvings). This script was used for 3000 years in all formal and decorative writing. Alongside this cumbersome pictorial system developed the **hieratic,** an abbreviated cursive script, which retained only the vital characteristics of the pictures. After the 22nd dynasty, scribes changed the hieratic writing to a form known as **Enchorial** or **Demotic,** used primarily in secular contexts. The *Book of the Dead* was translated into this script. Well before the end of the Roman reign in Egypt, hieroglyphics had been fully replaced by Demotic, Greek, and Latin. Egyptian no longer served as the state language. **Coptic** is a derivation of ancient Egyptian that uses Greek letters and six letters of the Demotic hieroglyphics. Today it is used only in liturgy.

In 1799 Napoléon's Egyptian expedition discovered the **Rosetta Stone,** which provided the necessary clues for interpreting ancient Egyptian. The slab contained a decree written in hieroglyphics, Demotic, and Greek. Jean Champollion used the stone to decipher the Egyptian alphabet and hieroglyphics. The Rosetta Stone is now in the British Museum.

Since the Muslim conquest, the primary language of Egypt has been Arabic. Modern **Egyptian Arabic** differs from classical Arabic, and the Egyptian dialect varies from that used in Jordan and other Arab nations. **Classical Arabic (Fu{pb}sha)** is the 7th-century language of the Qur'an. Its sanctity has preserved it as a living language of liturgy and learned and public discourse. Evening news broadcasts, political speeches in the Assembly, and religious sermons are all given in classical Arabic. Modern written Arabic is classical in form and can be understood by speakers of vastly different dialects even though very few are competent enough grammarians to use it normally. Colloquial Arabic is spoken by everyone in daily life. Even within Egypt the vernacular varies; Cairo, Lower Egypt, and Upper Egypt each have their own dialects. Arabic-language numerals are read from left to right while the language is read from right to left.

The appendix of this book contains a list of useful Arabic words and phrases and a pronunciation guide.

The most comprehensive English-to-Arabic dictionary of Egypt's spoken dialect is the *Pocket Dictionary of the Spoken Arabic of Cairo*, compiled by Virginia Stevens and Maurice Salid, available at the American University of Cairo Bookstore for LE7. The *Cairo Practical Guide* includes a useful list of words; *Berlitz Arabic for Travelers* is helpful if you can master their cryptic transliteration system.

Because of Egypt's 150-year colonial history and its tourist trade, more English is written and spoken here than in other Arab countries. Most educated Egyptians speak at least a bit of English, and some are fluent. French is commonly spoken among the Egyptian upper classes, especially in Alexandria.

Literature

Most of the writings of the **ancient Egyptians** deal with magic and religion in such works as the *Book of the Dead*. Poetic love songs, however, were written as well. The *Song of the Harper* advises immediate gratification in the face of transitory life. Folklore was not as often preserved in stone but *The Tale of the Eloquent Peasant* has survived to tell of a slippery peasant and his travails.

Modern literature offers insights into the nation's culture and curiosities. In 1988, Cairene novelist Naguib Mahfouz became the first Arab to win the Nobel Prize for literature. His *Midaq Alley* describes the life of a stifled young girl along the streets of Islamic Cairo in the 1960s, and his classic allegory *Children of Gebelawi*, banned in Egypt, retells the stories of the Qu'ran in a modern Cairo setting. *Miramar* (about life in an Alexandrian hotel), *Fountain and Tomb, Palace Walk,* and others are also readily available in translation. Yusuf Idris, a leading short-story writer, offers a witty account of modern Egyptian middle-class life in his *Cheapest Nights*. Sunallah Ibrahin's *The Smell of It,* a semi-autobiographical account of his difficulties after his release from prison, was censored in all Egyptian editions, but you may be able to get an unabridged copy in the West. For a range of Egyptian fiction, read *Arabic Short Stories,* edited by Mahmoud Manzalaoui. The Egyptian theater of the absurd is mostly composed of Tawfik al-Hakim's *Fate of the Cockroach and Other Plays*.

Most English translations of modern Egyptian literature are published by **Heinemann Press, Three Continents Press,** or the **American University in Cairo Press.** In the U.S. most of these books are distributed by Three Continents Press, 1901 Pennsylvania Ave. NW, #407, Washington, DC 20006 (tel. (202) 223-2554). Paperback editions cost US$7.50-10 (20% discount on all orders of two or more books) and will be sent promptly by UPS. These books can also be found in Cairo at Madbuli's bookstore in Tala'at Harb Sq.

Several **non-Egyptians** have written accounts of their travels and experiences within the country. In *The Innocents Abroad,* Mark Twain describes his misadventures in

Egypt and other countries. *Flaubert in Egypt* (edited by Francis Steegmuller) also tells tales of strangers-in-a-strange-land variety. In *Maalesh: A Theatrical Tour of the Middle East,* French playwright Jean Cocteau makes insightful and humorous observations about Egypt. For an eye-opening account of early Western explorers exploring the Nile, read Alan Moorehead's *The White Nile.* The companion volume, *The Blue Nile,* includes hair-raising chapters on the French invasion of Egypt and the rise of Muhammad Ali. Another toe-tickling classic for travelers here is Olivia Manning's *Levant Trilogy,* about the wartime marriage of two British citizens who meet in Cairo during the 1940s.

Plenty of **histories** of Egypt have been written, as have cultural, theological, and archeological studies. For an exhaustive eye-witness account of 1850s Egypt and Arabia, dig into Sir Richard Francis Burton's *Narrative of a Pilgrimage to Mecca and Medina.* In *The Riddle of the Pyramids,* the English physicist Kurt Mendelssohn proposes intriguing solutions to archeological puzzles. John Wilson's *Culture of Ancient Egypt* provides an excellent overview for pharaonic-era enthusiasts. E.M. Forster's *Alexandria: A History and a Guide* is a comprehensive guide to the city (for greater amusement read Forster's *Pharos and Pharillon*). E.W. Lane's *An Account of Manners and Customs of the Modern Egyptians,* first published in 1836, is a great companion for touring Islamic Cairo. A superb source of inspiration for adventures in Islamic Cairo is Richard Parker and Robin Sabin's *A Practical Guide to Islamic Monuments in Cairo.* Anwar al-Sadat's autobiography *In Search of Identity* is also engrossing, as is his wife Jehan's book, *A Woman of Egypt.*

Music

Egyptian music falls into the larger category of Arabic music that, between the 7th and 10th centuries, was so highly esteemed by Mideasterners that they took hyperprotective measures against the infiltration of musical trends from the West. Traditional Arabic music therefore has retained its distinct and mesmerizing quality. While Western classical music is characterized by mellifluous harmonies, Arabic music favors simple, extended melodic lines. Usually a single instrument speaks the melody while in the background percussion instruments chant.

In earlier centuries, musicians of the Arab world shunned any Western influence, but they now try to integrate sounds of the West into their works almost indiscriminately. It's Western, therefore it's good, think those Egyptian songwriters as yet blissfully unaware of the existence of Milli Vanilli. While Western musical trends are more and more becoming a part of current Egyptian music, though, the latter still has its foundation in traditional Arabic music. This peculiar combination may surprise the unaccustomed ear, but it has an alluring, mysterious quality to it. You will likely hear Umm Kolthum, the Frank Sinatra of not just Egypt but the entire Arab world for over 50 years, smoking the airwaves.

Food

The influence of Greek, Persian, and Turkish cuisine flavors much of Egyptian fare. Since Egyptian food often wreaks havoc with unhabituated digestive systems, it is mistakenly reputed to be strongly spiced. Actually, it can be rather bland. Plentiful helpings of Egyptian food are available for LE2 or less, but avoid the cheapest street vendors; uninitiated stomachs are bound to protest vehemently within a few hours.

Egyptians generally prefer large, hot meals, which are eaten with flat loaves of bread. *Kebab,* for example, consists of meat roasted on a skewer with salad, dip, and pita bread. *Kufte* is a spiced ground meat wrapped around a skewer and roasted. Chicken is much cheaper and more widely eaten than beef or mutton. But because meat of any sort is a luxury most Egyptians cannot afford regularly, the most common food is *fuul* (brown or black beans served mashed or whole with oil, salt, lemon juice, and sometimes an egg or small pieces of meat; pronounced "FOOL") and *kushari* (a mixture of macaroni, rice, lentils, and tomato sauce). For an exclusively Egyptian dish, try *molokhaya,* a thick, spicy, green stew made from a flat leaf (Jew's Mallow) cooked either by itself or with pieces of chicken, lamb, or rabbit. Like chicken, *samak* (fish) is an inexpensive alternative to red meat. Catfish from Lake Nasser is especially delicious. *Hammam* (pigeon) is also tasty, although you may starve unless you eat two or three. *Fuul mudamas* and *taamiya* (small fried patties or balls of mashed beans and vegetable paste, known as falafel), both served either by themselves or in a sandwich, are the main fare of street stands and small restaurants. *Tahina,* a dip made of sesame-seed paste, and *baba ghanoush,* a mixture of *tahina* and roasted, mashed eggplant, are also popular in these establishments.

Shopping in the *souk* (market) is the cheapest alternative, but you must select your food carefully. Bread, subsidized by the government, is available in three types: *aish baladi* (round unleavened loaves made with coarse flour), *aish shami* (similar to *baladi* but made with refined white flour), and *aish* (leavened "French" style loaves). Street salesfolk offer the flat or pita types, while the leavened loaves must be bought directly from bakeries. Cheese comes in two locally produced varieties: *gibna bay{-pb}da* (white feta cheese) and *gibna rumi* (a hard, yellow cheese with a sharp flavor). You can also purchase imported cheeses at reasonable prices. *Zabadi* (yogurt) comes unflavored and makes a filling addition to any meal, as does *amar ad-din* (apricot jello), which is served frequently during Ramadan.

Egyptian bakers produce a wide range of delicious pastries, including heavenly *baklava* (filo dough, honey or sugar syrup, and nuts), more commonly known as *bu'-LAW-wa,* and *fatir* (pancakes or flake pastry filled with anything from eggs to apricot preserves). Get psyched for the resulting frenzy and indulge. Although a luxury for natives, fruit and fruit juices are some of the best values in Egypt for tourists. Small juice stands litter Egyptian towns, serving fresh fruit drinks in season as well as perennial favorites such as *asab* (sugar cane juice), *tamar hindi* (tamarind), *subiya* (a drink made from rice and sugar quite unlike saki), *farawla* (strawberry juice), and *er-a'a-soose* (karob juice).

Egyptians are coffee and tea fiends. Egyptian tea, similar to the Western variety, is normally taken without milk and with enough sugar to make it syrupy. Though you may get Western-style coffee, Egyptians prefer *ahwa* (Arabic coffee), which comes in three degrees of sweetness: *ahwa sada* (no sugar), *ahwa mazbut* (medium sugar), and *ahwa ziyaada* (with a full year's harvest of sugar cane). Especially when you are in Upper Egypt, try *kirkaday,* a refreshing red drink made by brewing the flower of the fuchsia plant, served hot or cold. Egyptian beer, sold under the brand-name Stella, has a lower alcohol content than European beer and costs between LE1.75 and LE2.50 in restaurants and bars. Egypt produces a selection of justifiably obscure red and white wines, sold for LE2-5 per bottle.

Cairo (al-Qahira) القاهرة

> *I arrived at length at Cairo, mother of cities and seat of Pharoah the tyrant, boundless in multitude of buildings, peerless in beauty and splendor, the meeting-place of comer and goer, the halting-place of feeble and mighty, whose throngs surge as waves of the sea.*
>
> —Ibn Battuta

When greeted at the airport by the "Tourist Official" who assures you that his third cousin's hotel is the cheapest and cleanest in town, or when offered—by a man with impeccable English and a brother in Chattanooga—a vial of worthless priceless per-

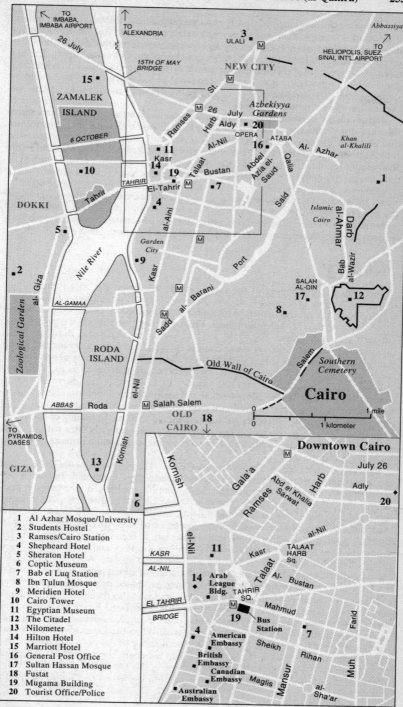

TO IMBABA,
IMBABA AIRPORT

TO ALEXANDRIA

Abbassiya

3
ULALI

TO HELIOPOLIS, SUEZ,
SINAI, INT'L. AIRPORT

26 July

15TH OF MAY BRIDGE

NEW CITY

15

ZAMALEK ISLAND

St.

Ramses

26 July Harb

Azbekiyya Gardens

Khan al-Khalili

6 OCTOBER

Aldy

20

11

Al-Nil

OPERA

16

ATABA

Al- Azhar

Kasr

14

Talaat

Abdel

Qalla

DOKKI

10

TAHRIR

19

El-Tahrir

Bustan

7

Azia el-Saud

Said

Islamic Cairo

1

Darb al-Ahmar

Tahrir

4

al-Aini

Islamic Cairo

Bab al-Wazir

5

Nile River

Garden City

9

Kasr

SALAH AL-DIN

2

al- Giza

AL-GAMAA

Sadd

al- Barani

Port

17

8

12

Zoological Garden

RODA ISLAND

Old Wall of Cairo

Salem

Southern Cemetery

el-Nil

Cairo

ABBAS

Roda

Salah Salem

TO PYRAMIDS, OASES

OLD CAIRO

18

0   1 mile
0   1 kilometer

GIZA

13

6

Downtown Cairo

July 26

Adly

20

Legend

1 Al Azhar Mosque/University
2 Students Hostel
3 Ramses/Cairo Station
4 Shepheard Hotel
5 Sheraton Hotel
6 Coptic Museum
7 Bab el Luq Station
8 Ibn Tulun Mosque
9 Meridien Hotel
10 Cairo Tower
11 Egyptian Museum
12 The Citadel
13 Nilometer
14 Hilton Hotel
15 Marriott Hotel
16 General Post Office
17 Sultan Hassan Mosque
18 Fustat
19 Mugama Building
20 Tourist Office/Police

KASR
AL-NIL
EL TAHRIR
BRIDGE

Kornish

el-Nil

Gala'a

Ramses

Abd el Khalia
Sarwat

Harb

al-Nil

11

Kasr

TALAAT HARB Sq.

14

Arab League Bldg.

TAHRIR SQ.

Al- Bustan

Mahmud

19

Bus Station

Talaat

4

American Embassy

Sheikh

7

British Embassy

Canadian Embassy

Rihan

Mansur

Farid

Muh

Maglis

al-Sha'ar

Australian Embassy

fume, you might conclude that Ibn Battuta was one of the feeble, guileless fellows who escaped Cairo with no more than the sandals on his feet. But Ibn Battuta was a dauntless traveler with 14th-century savvy who saw through Cairo's chaos and Egypt's relentless bureaucratic balderdash to perceive the city's real beauty. The key to enjoying yourself in this absurd and exotic city lies in bringing an inexhaustible sense of humor and learning to interpret the range of Cairene smiles. They can mean anything from "I would like to help you and I expect nothing in return" to "Let me unburden you of your traveler's checks."

A jaunt on the streets of Cairo is an exploration of a vast archeological site where the remnants of different eras overlap in creative disorder. Grand 19th-century colonial buildings encircle ancient statues of Ramses, and pulsing neon stretches across ornate arabesques. Each of Cairo's conquerors from the Romans to the Muslims to the British have left their mark on *al-Qahira* (the Victorious). But don't expect Cairo to be museum gallery of the past. The capital of Egypt and the largest city in Africa, Cairo's concern is with the survival of some 15 million inhabitants, not with antiquity. The noise, the grime, the crowds, and the poverty still shock even the widest-traveled and the most-prepared. The city groans under the weight of its population. Learn to live with the city's rich squalor, its unforgiving sun and its constant cacophony, and you too may find Cairo peerless in excitement, boundless in appeal.

History

The strategic significance of the sandy plateau just below the Nile Delta did not elude the Pharaohs of the Old Kingdom. In the vicinity of contemporary Cairo on the western bank, the ancient capital of Memphis flourished as one of the world's earliest urban settlements. On the eastern bank, Pharaonic remains suggest the presence of similarly important cities—Heliopolis and Khery-Aha, later known as Babylon. These cities, along with the funerary complexes at Saqqara and Giza, were located at the juncture of the newly joined upper and lower lands, at the throat of the new body politic. With this joining of the kingdoms, Memphis became the logical locus of the capital and reached its zenith in the 30th century BCE. Even though the royal capital eventually moved to Thebes and elsewhere, Memphis and Heliopolis remained important political and religious centers until the Ptolemaic period, when Heliopolis faded along with its sun cult. Memphis' eminence endured until the beginning of the Christian era, when massive population shifts left the western bank only Giza with its small settlement and the eastern bank Babylon, an economic base for the Romans, protected by its Byzantine fort.

The early decades of the seventh century CE found Egypt, and the Nile Delta region especially, in the throes of power struggles between the Persian and Byzantine empires. Both the senescent Memphis and the regnant Alexandria changed hands continuously; the excess of warring near Babylon drove many urban dwellers to the villages, leaving the city bereft and deserted at the time of the Arab conquest in 641. General Amr Ibn al-As, head of the invading Arab forces, came to Egypt with specific instructions from the Caliph Omar to center the new state at Babylon, not Alexandria. The former had the appeal of its strategically superior location, and the latter the desert people distrusted because of its swarthy Mediterranean culture. Amr instead founded the outpost of Fustat (the Latin and Byzantine roots of which mean "entrenchment"), the seed of modern Cairo, on part of the plain due east of the ruins of Babylon. Further political expansion and upheavals caused the settlement to expand to the north and northeast. In 868 the Abassid governor Ibn Tulun declared Egypt an independent state. He built a palatial new city around his Grand Mosque, modeling it after the elaborate cities of Iraq, where he had been educated. When the Fatamids swept in from Tunisia in 969 CE, they took the empty northern sector of the plain and there built a magnificent walled city for the new caliph and his court; they dubbed it al-Qahira, "The Victorious." Cairo is the Western corruption of this name. But meanwhile, Fustat continued to swell in size and grandeur, becoming known by the Semitic name for

Egypt, Misr. This was the Golden Age in Cairo when, along with Damascus and Baghdad, it was a center of the most advanced culture west of China.

During the 11th century, the twin cities of al-Qahira and Fustat enjoyed a symbiotic relationship and both thrived. Yet these two metropoli would stand triumphant for not even a century. Fustat suffered from plague, famine, religio-political unrest, and assorted conflagrati, and when Salah al-Din overthrew the Fatamids in 1171 the spoils were few. He opened the walled enclosure of al-Qahira to the populace and built another fortress, the Citadel, on the hills to the south above the rubble of Fustat. During the short reign of the Ayyubites (they, along with the Overbites and the Underbites, blew all their money on expensive orthodontia) and the longer but more violent period of the Mamluk Sultans, the city continued to expand and remained far greater in population and area than any city in Europe throughout the Middle Ages. Almost every sultan or prominent *amir* graced the place with a mosque, school, or hospital, usually raiding the Pharaonic ruins for building materials. The casing stones of the Giza Pyramids and Memphis are now strewn throughout Islamic Cairo.

The Ottoman conquest of 1516 reduced Cairo to a provincial center. The city declined and stagnated until the 19th century, when Napoléon's invasion started tremors that resulted in the ascendancy of the Ottoman Muhammad Ali as ruler. The extravagant royal family built with little respect for Egyptian history, erecting Turkish-style mosques and palaces including the enormous Mosque of Muhammad Ali, a lavish imitation of the grand mosques of Istanbul. These *khedives,* with their European mentors, designed the relatively broad and straight avenues of the New City, built in the lands emptied as the Nile shifted westward. This geological process also spawned Gezira Island.

The early 20th century witnessed the creation of a new Heliopolis, planned by the aristocrat extraordinaire Baron Empain as a haven for Europeans. Population pressure has necessitated the continuous construction of new suburbs ever since. The latest, Madinat Nasr, lies on the edges of the Eastern Desert in an attempt to preserve the precious arable land in the Nile Valley itself. Recent construction has also created satellite cities which hover in the flaming, swelling desert near Cairo.

Orientation

Metropolitan Cairo

Metropolitan Cairo consists of two distinct administrative governates: **Cairo,** on the eastern bank of the Nile, and **Giza,** on the western bank. **Tahrir Square** (*Midan at-Tahrir,* Liberation Square) is the center of the Downtown Cairo area. Among the streets that radiate out from this center, the three most important are **Kasr al-Aini Street, Ramses Street,** and **Tala'at Harb Street.** Kasr al-Aini St. runs south from Tahrir Sq. and ends at **Old Cairo.** Squalid and ungainly, Old Cairo is the most impoverished area of the city. It is known also as Coptic Cairo as it is the historical and spiritual center of the Copts (Egyptian Eastern Orthodox Christians). Sandwiched between Kasr al-Aini St. and the Nile is the serene **Garden City** residential area. Foreign embassies and banks cluster in this neighborhood, where you will also many of the city's best-preserved 19th-century colonial mansions. The American University and various government buildings (Parliament, Ministry of Social Affairs and Ministry of the Interior, among others) line the opposite side of Kasr al-Aini St. Running all the way to the airport, Ramses St. heads northeast away from the Nile. It passes through **Ramses Square,** next to which is the Cairo train station, also called (bingo!) **Ramses Station.** Further out on Ramses St. is **Heliopolis,** the fashionable suburb where you will find colonial architectural extravagances that include the residence of President Mubarak.

The main bridge crossing the Nile from the Downtown area is **Tahrir Bridge,** which, more specifically, connects Tahrir Sq. and the southern tip of **Gezira Island.** Comprising this more verdant end of the island are a large public garden and two private sporting clubs. The northern half is Cairo's ritziest residential area, known as **Za-malek;** this is the name which the entire island often goes by. South of Zamalek is its fellow Nile isle, **Roda Island,** the site of Manial Palace, and the Nilometer.

Past Tahrir Bridge on the western bank of the Nile the Cairo Sheraton Hotel presides over the residential neighborhood of **Dokki,** where a handful of important embassies are located. North of Dokki lies **Mohandiseen** (Engineer's City), designed in the late 1950s by President Nasser as a neighborhood for engineers and journalists. It is now a middle-class residential area. Farther north you'll find **Imbaba,** where a camel-selling extravaganza takes place weekly. South of Dokki past the Zoological Gardens across the Giza Bridge is **Giza Square.** Pyramids Road, whose overpriced bars are the venue for nightly sleazefests, begins at the square and travels to the Pyramids of Giza.

You are as likely to find street signs and posted street numbers, in English or Arabic, as you are to be arrested for jaywalking. To find out which streets you need to jaywalk to get where, acquire a comprehensible, comprehensive street map. The best bet is the large map of Cairo published by Lehnert and Landrock, which includes a brief city history, an index of all the streets and squares, the addresses of banks, travel agencies, embassies, and museums, and a small map of Giza and Saqqara (available at the Nile Hilton for LE7). The *Blue Guide to Egypt* (LE7) and the *AUC Practical Guide* (LE20) also have decent maps and information for travelers planning longer stays. *Cairo A-Z* includes 150 pages of detailed maps of each district of Cairo and its suburbs, along with lists of and directions to sights of interest and a mini-telephone directory. These guides are available at the AUC bookstore (see Practical Information, below).

Downtown Cairo

The New City, now the transportation and commercial hub of Cairo, was conceived in the 19th century. Under the auspices of the benevolent British and French colonialists, the *khedives* then ruling planned the city around a system of *midan* (squares) from which radiate straight avenues; these are named for national heroes and revolutionary activists. Buses leave from two stations on the northern and southern sides of **Tahrir Square** to every metropolitan destination. At the north end of Tahrir facing the square is the sandstone **Egyptian Museum;** adjacent to it on the west side is the blue-and-white Nile Hilton, useful as an air-conditioned mailbox. At the southern end of the square is the concave Mugama Building, the headquarters of Egyptian bureaucracy. Register your passport here within seven days of arrival (for more details, see Practical Information below). The **American University in Cairo (AUC),** directly to the east of the Mugama Building across Kasr al-Aini St., has gardens filled with English-speaking Egyptians and Arabic-speaking Americans, as well as an excellent bookstore offering a variety of guidebooks and maps. Several metropolitan buses depart from a stop in front of the old Arab League Building, to the west of Mugama along Tahrir St., adjacent to the bridge over the Nile.

Tala'at Harb Street runs from the northeast side of Tahrir through Tala'at Harb Sq. Ramses Sq. to the north and Ataba Sq. to the east (both major transportation hubs) form a rough triangle with Tala'at Harb enclosing the main business and shopping district, which is crammed with travel agents, banks, restaurants, juice stands, clothing stores, language schools, and budget hotels. Opera Sq., on the east side of the triangle near Ataba Sq., was the site of two great imperialist monuments, now destroyed: the Opera House and the old Shepherd's Hotel. Only the Azbekiya Gardens, encircled by bookstalls, remain.

Transportation

For information on getting into Cairo from the principal transportation centers, see the Once There section in the Egypt introduction.

Getting around Cairo is cheap, and there are many options. Remember, a little aggravation is good for the soul.

Bus

The red-and-white and blue-and-white public buses in Cairo run often and everywhere, and they're the cheapest available means of transportation. But you get what you pay for—buses have a high breakdown potential and are shabby, stifling, and uncomfortable. Numbers and all destinations are usually written in Arabic, so you'll need to familiarize yourself with the characters. Most buses run 5:30am-12:30am, and during Ramadan from about 6:30am-2am with a break from about 6:30-7:30pm. Two of Cairo's central bus depots are located in Tahrir Sq. The station directly in front of the Mugama serves Giza, points south, and southern portions of Islamic Cairo; the one in front of the Nile Hilton serves points north and the rest of Islamic Cairo. Once you reach the right station, ask someone to point out the correct bus. Most rides cost 10pt, although a few cost 25pt. Outside the main stations, catching a bus is often a matter of running it down and properly timing your leap, as they seldom come to a full stop. The entrance is always through the rear doors (except at a terminus), which have been torn off most buses to facilitate this practice. To disembark, pick a moment when the bus is not moving too rapidly and face the front as you jump off. If you want the bus to come to a full halt at an official bus stop, you must exit through the front door. The front of a bus is generally less crowded than the rear, so it's worth the effort to push your way forward. An *emphatic warning:* when traveling by bus, keep wallets and valuables securely buried on your person. Although violent crime is rare in Cairo, a *khoaga* on a crowded bus is an irresistible opportunity for the occasional pickpocket. Few foreigners actually brave the bus system; women who are so inclined, however, should pass up ridiculously overcrowded vehicles so as to avoid unabashed stares and wandering hands.

From the Mugama Station

#8: Tahrir—Kasr al-Aini—Manial—Giza—Pyramids—Mena House Hotel.

#82, 182: Mausoleum of Imam ash-Shafi'i—Southern Cemetery—Citadel.

#173, 194, 609: Tahrir—Citadel.

#174: Sayyida Zeinab—Ibn Tulun—Sultan Hasan—Citadel.

#900: Tahrir—Kasr al-Aini—Manial—Cairo University—Giza—Pyramids—Holiday Inn Hotel (very crowded except early in the morning).

#913: directly to Sphinx.

#923: Giza Sq.

From the Nile Hilton Station

#50: Abbassiya.

#63, 66: Al-Azhar—Khan al-Khalili.

#72: Sayyida Zeinab—Citadel—Mausoleum of Imam ash-Shafi'i.

#73: Imbaba (camel market).

#75: Islamic Museum—Bab Zuwayla.

#173, 403: Citadel—Sultan Hasan.

#400: Old Cairo Airport via Heliopolis (Midan Roxy).

#422: New Cairo Airport.

#500: Cairo Sheraton.

#510: Heliopolis.

Buses from Tahrir Sq. to Islamic Cairo are usually unbearably crowded. To get to **Ramses Station,** take any bus from the platform farthest to the east.

From the Arab League Building (in between Mugama and the Nile Hilton)

#13: Zamalek.

#110, 102, 203, 19, 166: Dokki.

Inter-city Buses

Unfortunately, Cairo has no single bus depot, which means you'll have to search for the various points of departure. All reservations must be made in person.

Tahrir Square: These buses actually leave from a station behind the Egyptian Museum, under the October 6th Bridge. Reserve seats for Alexandria (LE18) and Marsa Matruuh (LE28) 24 hrs. in advance. (Prices include A/C and TV.) Buses also leave this station for Port Said and Ismailia. See Alexandria and Marsa Matruuh chapters for details.

Ahmed Hilmi Square (ma-HAA-tat Ahmed Hilmi): Behind Ramses Station, accessible by the underground walkway behind the information desk. The station is to the right of the service taxi lot. The **Wagh Ibli Company** (tel. 74 66 58) serves Upper Egypt, with frequent buses to Fayyum (6:30am-6pm, LE2.50), and 2-4 buses per day to Minya (LE10), Mallawi (LE9), Assyut (LE15), Qena (LE17), Luxor (LE25), and Aswan (LE34). Same company also runs to Hurghada (LE21). All prices include A/C and TV.

Abbassiya Station: Usually called Sinai Station. In Abbassiya District, 5km northeast of Ramses Station at the end of Ramses St. From Tahrir or Ramses Sq., you can catch local buses (#54, 710, 728) or minibuses (#24, 32). The **Delta Company** (tel. 76 22 93) and the **South Sinai Company** (tel. 82 47 53) run frequent buses to Sinai destinations as well as to Hurghada, Sharm al-Shaikh, and Dahab; see those chapters for more information.

Kolali Square (Midan Kolali): A 5min. walk from Ramses Sq. across from the train station. Follow the narrow street to the right of the Egyptian State Railway Building. Buses for Port Said (LE10) and Ismailiya (LE5) run hourly 7am-7pm; see respective chapters.

Giza Station: On Nile St. in Giza. Service taxis and buses depart from here to Fayyum and Nile Valley cities.

Buses traveling between major cities leave frequently throughout the day. Buses to and from the Sinai and the Oases often depart only early in the morning. If possible, go to the station the day before to confirm departure times.

Numbers and destinations on Egyptian buses are normally written only in Arabic. If you're in doubt about which bus to take, ask directions. The conductors who sit at the kiosks at Tahrir, Ramses, and the other main terminals can be helpful. A bus service connects Cairo to **Tel Aviv** and **Jerusalem**. Buses leave from either Abbassiya Sq. or from the American Express office in the Cairo Sheraton. Prices range from LE65 to LE84. Call the Sinai terminal (tel. 82 47 53) or the Sheraton's American Express office (tel. 74 04 44) for more information.

Minibus

The Cairo municipal government has introduced red-and-white minibuses along many of the same routes served by the larger, older buses. These vehicles should not be confused with the older, multi-colored taxi-vans that are privately operated. Although more expensive than the regular buses (20-50pt—prohibitively expensive to most Cairenes), the minibuses are far more comfortable. Finding the right bus will inevitably be confusing, but most Egyptians should be glad to help. The following are important minibus routes:

From the Mugama Station

#24: Abbassiya, Roxy.

#27: Masr al-Gadida, Airport.

#30: Nasr City, Abbassiya, Ramses Sq.

#35: Abbassiya, Ismailiya Sq. (Masr al-Gadida), Abbassiya, Ramses Sq., Nasr City, Roxy.

#39, 32: Hada'iq al-Quba, al-Maza, Midan al-Hagaz (Heliopolis).

#49: Tahrir, Zamalek.

#50: Atabah Sq., Citadel.

#52, 56: Maadi, Old Cairo.

#54: Tahrir, Rifi'a Mosque, Ibn Tulun Mosque, Citadel.

#55: Maadi via Dar as-Salaam.

#58: Ramses Sq., Manial (no stop at Tahrir).

#59: Ramses Sq., Tahrir Sq.

#82: Giza, al-Gama'ah, Kasr al-Aini, Faisal Rd.

#83: Dokki, Giza, Midan at-Ta'awon (al-Ahram St., Pyramids Rd.).

From the Arab League Building

#26: Roxy, Tahrir (face the museum), Dokki, Giza (face the Mugama).

#54: Citadel, Cemetery, Bab al-Luuq, Sayyida Zaynab.

#76: Ataba, Zamalek (face the museum), Tahrir, Bulaq ad-Dakrour (face Mugama).

#77: Bulaq ad-Dakrour (face Mugama to catch the bus), Khan al-Khalili (face the Egyptian Museum).

#84: Ataba, Tahrir, Dokki, Giza.

Metro

The Cairo Metro system, completed in 1987, is a world apart from the rest of Cairo public transport. Cool, clean, and efficient, the trains run along a single route linking the southern industrial district of Helwan to the workers' homes north of the city, with a number of stops downtown. Trains run every few minutes 6am-1am (15-50pt). Keep track of your ticket; you'll need it to exit. The downtown stations (look for the enormous red "M" signs) are Mubarak (Ramses Sq.), Orabi (Orabi St. and Ramses St.), Nasser (July 26 St. and Ramses St.), Sadat (Tahrir Sq.), Sa'ad Zaghloul (Mansur St. and Ismail Abaza St.), Sayyida Zeinab (Mansur St. and Ali Ibrahim St.), al-Malik as-Saleh (Salah Salem Road), and Mar Girgis (Old Cairo). Trains are often packed during rush hour; try to avoid Metro travel before 9am and between 5-7pm.

Taxi

Never take the large, unmetered, colorful Peugeot taxis within the city—they charge LE2-3 for a ride around the corner. Instead, lavish your attention lovingly on the metered **black-and-white taxis** that often carry passengers collectively.

To hail a taxi, pick a major thoroughfare headed in the general direction you wish to travel, stand on the side of the street, stretch out your arm as a taxi approaches, and scream out your destination as it goes by. If the drivers are interested in your business, they'll stop and wait for you to run over to their cars. Jump in, and repeat your destination. Don't be alarmed if the taxi seems to be going in the wrong direction; drivers sometimes take circuitous routes to avoid traffic-clogged main arteries, to deposit other passengers, or simply to drive by and say *salaam* to a friend. (Who's in a hurry?)

Meters have been installed in all Cairo taxis, but drivers rarely use them, since passengers jump in and out—haggling only implies that you don't know what you owe. Cairenes simply hail a cab, hop in, and pay what they think is adequate upon arrival. Usually, the most comfortable way to handle the situation is to open the door as you are paying the folded bills and leave the taxi without looking to the driver for approval.

There is a hidden logic of fares. For journeys of 1km or less, 50pt-LE1 is usually sufficient. Add 25pt per kilometer thereafter and about 25% on the entire fare for each additional passenger. You are also expected to pay extra for suitcases and waiting. The fare from Tahrir Sq. to the Northern Cemetery or the Pyramids should be about LE3, to Khan al-Khalili about LE1. Avoid the taxis that park in front of major hotels—the drivers are experts at exploiting tourists and often extort as much as limousines.

Do not expect a taxi driver to speak English, or to know the location of every address or street. Try to identify a major landmark or thoroughfare near your destination and learn to pronounce it in Arabic. Alternatively, have someone write out the address and directions in Arabic. They'll do this for you at the tourist office. Communication is generally neither traumatic nor problematic at most downtown and tourist destinations.

Luggage racks are the only advantage of the expensive, unmetered **Peugeot taxis.** If you're interested in hiring a car for the day, Cairo has a limousine service that rents vehicles with drivers for a daily rate much lower than the cost of a private taxi by the hour. Contact **Limousine Misr** (tel. 91 53 48/9).

Inter-city *service* taxis are best for short trips. Catch them to Alexandria and the Suez Canal next to the Egyptian State Railway Building in Ramses Sq.; south to Fayyum and Minya in Giza Sq. by the train station; to the Delta and Port Said in Ahmed Himli Sq. You'll have to hunt for taxis to the Sinai.

You will also see multi-colored **taxi-vans,** called *arrabeya bil nafar,* all around town. These have the word "taxi" written on the side and carry 12-15 passengers. They function more like buses than taxis, running along fixed routes and often stopping only at certain place (25-50pt). To catch a taxi-van, go to a taxi-van stop (sometimes marked by a wooden shelter) and yell your destination as the van passes. From Ataba Sq. taxi-vans go to Ramses, Tahrir, Northern Cemetery, Zamalek, Islamic Cairo, and Heliopolis. In Tahrir Sq. taxi-vans leave from behind both bus stations and go to Heliopolis, Giza Sq., Dokki, Mohandiseen, and the Pyramids. At the stations, drivers will stand outside their buses and bellow their destinations until the bus is full. Taxi-vans provide the most comfortable means of inexpensive transportation between Cairo and some of the outlying areas, such as Giza.

The only major drawback to ground transportation in Cairo is the harrowing experience of being driven by a sometimes smoking, often newspaper-reading Cairene. Drivers career as if playing a video game, with human life but a lost piaster. **River taxis** provide a more relaxing means of transportation to Old Cairo. Boats run every 30-40 minutes to the Nile barrages and Old Cairo (via Giza) for 50pt. The departure point is on the Corniche in front of the television building, about 1km north of Tahrir Sq.

Train

Ticket windows at Ramses Station are open 8am-10pm. If you have time, first go to the tourist office on Adly St. and have them write out the desired destination and other details in Arabic to avoid confusion. Which line you stand in depends upon whether you are reserving a seat in advance or trying to buy a ticket for the same day (often impossible). Women (and men traveling with women) can take advantage of the special women's line that may form at crowded times, which is much shorter and faster than the corresponding men's line. In addition, women are permitted (possibly expected) to push to the front of the line, head held high. If you give up one day and come back the next, don't assume that you want the same ticket window. If you are willing to travel third class (solo women shouldn't), you can buy tickets from the conductor on the train. Students can get 50% discounts on fares—show an ISIC or student ID.

The trains enter their berths at least half an hour before departure time. None of the train numbers or destinations are in English, but fellow travelers and the tourist police will lend a hand. Nonetheless, be prepared for yet another infusion of confusion. For information at Ramses Station, call tel. 75 35 55. An information desk is directly ahead as you enter the station. Cairo's tourist police office also doubles as a train information office. For more information on trains, see Transportation in the Egypt Introduction.

Walking

One positive aspect of Cairo's absurdly packed layout is that almost everything in the city is within easy walking distance of Tahrir Sq. Though it may take more time, you can see all the sights of Islamic Cairo, the downtown areas, and Roda and Zamalek Islands without once using mechanized transport (an attractive proposition considering Cairo traffic and driving habits). Biking is not a viable option in Cairo—it would be like trying to unicycle blindfolded backwards around a rotary with your feet tied together. Many argue that walking is the only way to see the city; on foot, you will indubitably catch many fascinating glimpses of Cairo life which would go unseen from a bus or car. You will also get your shoes mucked up; many city streets are strewn with garbage and random piles of sawdust.

Traffic is almost always abundant: the only times the streets are empty are during Ramadan and important football (i.e., soccer) matches. Friday, the Islamic day of prayer, is the least crowded day of the week. Cars reign in Cairo; drivers expect pedestrians to look after themselves. Since pedestrians must often take to the streets, it is wise to face oncoming traffic and heed the horns of oncoming cars. A long, uninterrupted honk usually indicates that the driver is either unwilling or unable to swerve. Do not be alarmed if you are lightly pushed or tugged by Egyptians attempting to stay alive. Ignore traffic lights; everyone else does. Cairenes warn against being too careful when you cross a street because if you stop short or break into a run you'll upset the rhythm of the drivers speeding towards you, and they just might hit you.

Practical Information

The most comprehensive compendium of useful information on Cairo is *Cairo: A Practical Guide,* which includes a set of city maps (published by American University in Cairo Press, available at most bookstores for LE25). The most reliable telephone directory for goods and services is the *Cairo Telephone List,* published by the Maadi Women's Guild and available for LE16 at the American Chamber of Commerce, Marriott Hotel, Zemalek (tel. 340 88 88, ext. 1541).

Tourist Office: Main Office, 5 Adly St. (tel. 391 34 54). About a 20-min. walk from Tahrir Sq.: follow Tala'at Harb St. past Tala'at Harb Sq. and turn right on Adly St. The office is 3 blocks down on the left, marked "Tourist Police." Free map. While the staff is short on actual facts, they can usually steer you in more or less the right direction for more information, and will readily write out questions in Arabic (useful for buying train tickets). Open Sat.-Thurs. 9am-2pm. Other offices at the **New Cairo International Airport** (tel. 245 44 00) and **Giza** at the Pyramids (tel. 385 02 59).

Tourist Police: Tel. 126 or 391 33 70 or 75 35 54.

Passport Office: Mugama Bldg., southern end of Tahrir Sq. Passports must be registered within 7 days of arrival. Find "Information" window on 2nd flr. Registration open summer daily 8:30am-2pm and 6-9pm; winter daily 8:30am-2pm and 5-7pm; Ramadan daily 10am-2pm. Evening hours are least crowded. Ask at your hotel; they may register for you. Also come here for **visa extensions**—be sure to bring bank receipts showing that you have exchanged at least US$180 (or the equivalent) into LE. Exchange your money at a bank; receipts from even the most reputable of hotels may not do the job.

Ministry of Tourism, 110 Kasr al-Aini St., Bab al-Luuq (tel. 355 35 66 or 355 55 68). Contact with concerns or with questions about how to acquire a travel permit for the Ghara Oasis. Open Sat.-Thurs. 9am-2pm.

American Embassy: 5 Latin America St. (tel. 355 73 71), 2 blocks south of Tahrir Sq. Lost or stolen passports replaced overnight for LE96; limited passports for travel to Israel issued upon request. Passport photographs at the Nile Hilton. Booklet with advice for American visitors. Passport office open Sun.-Thurs. 9am-12pm; embassy open Sun.-Thurs. 9am-2pm.

British Embassy: 7 Ahmed Ragheb St. (tel. 354 08 50), south of U.S. Embassy. Open Mon.-Fri. 8am-2pm. **New Zealand** has no embassy; the Brits handle their affairs.

Canadian Embassy: 6 Muhammad Fahmi as-Sayid St., Garden City (tel. 354 31 10/9). Open Sun.-Thurs. 7:30am-3pm.

Australian Embassy: Cairo Plaza south, 5th Floor, 1097 Corniche al-Nil, Boulac (tel. 77 79 00/ 94), 4 blocks south of Shepherd's Hotel. Open Sun.-Thurs. 8am-3:45pm. Visa inquiries 9am-12:30pm.

Israeli Embassy: 6 Ibn al-Malek St., Dokki (tel. 361 05 28/45). Cross over to Dokki from Roda Island on University Bridge. The street to the right of and parallel to the bridge is Ibn al-Malek. Look up at the top floors for the Israeli flag or for the security guards by the entrance who will ask to see your passport. Ah, peace. Open Sun.-Thurs. 9am-noon.

Sudanese Embassy: 3 al-Ibrahimi St., Garden City (tel. 354 50 43). US$25, 5 photos, and a letter of recommendation from your embassy are required for a visa. Open Sun.-Thurs. 8:30am-3pm, visas until noon.

Jordanian Embassy: 6 Gohaina, Dokki (tel. 348 55 66), 2 blocks west of the Cairo Sheraton. Visas require a photograph and a letter of introduction, and are free for U.S. and Australian passport holders; LE28 for New Zealand passport holders, LE77 for Britons and Canadians. Open Sat.-Thurs. 9:30am-1:30pm.

Banks: Bank of America, 106 Kasr al-Aini St., Garden City (tel. 354 77 88), and on Sheikh Rihan St. This is the easiest place to obtain advances in LE with a MasterCard or Visa, but it still may take an hour for telex confirmation. Money can be wired to Egypt through **Citibank,** 4 Ahmed Pasha St., Garden City (tel. 355 18 73). **Cairo Barclays International Bank,** 12 Sheikh Yusef Sq., Garden City (tel. 354 21 95), 3 blocks south of Tahrir Sq. along Kasr al-Aini St., accepts traveler's checks and has worldwide money transfer services. All banks offer foreign exchange facilities. Open Sun.-Thurs. 8:30am-2pm; during Ramadan, 10am-1pm. Foreign banks are closed on Fri. and Sat., but most Egyptian banks are open Sat. **Bank Misr** at the Nile Hilton is open 24 hrs. Banking services in other major hotels are open until 8pm.

American Express: 15 Kasr al-Nil (tel. 75 04 55 or 75 01 33), just off Tala'at Harb Sq. toward Ramses St. Best place to have money and mail sent (you must have their traveler's checks or credit card). Also offers USCEirect telephone service. Open daily 8am-5pm. Letter service closed Fri. Other locations: Ramses Hilton (tel. 574 48 99), Nile Hilton (tel. 76 58 10), Marriott Hotel (tel. 341 01 36), Meridien Hotel (tel. 290 91 57), Pullman Maadi (tel. 350 60 93), and Sheraton Giza Hotel (tel. 348 89 37). All Cairo offices provide dollars or LE for traveler's checks, but you need an AmEx card to purchase traveler's checks. Hotel offices provide faster service, but sometimes run out of cash.

Main Post Office: 55 Sarwat St., Ataba Sq. (tel. 91 00 11). Often extremely crowded. Packages require an export license from Cairo International Airport; major hotels and tourist shops also provide this service. **Poste Restante** located around the corner on Bidek St. (open Sat.-Thurs. 8am-6pm). **Express Mail** open Sat.-Thurs. 8am-7pm, also on Bidek St., across from Poste Restante. Main post office open Sat.-Thurs. 9am-4pm. Other post offices open Sat.-Thurs. 8:30am-3pm; during Ramadan 9am-3pm.

Telephone Office: Main Office, Ramses St., 1 block north of July 26 St. Other offices on Tahrir Sq. (76 51 18), Adly St. (390 91 72), and Alfy St. (93 42 09), under the Windsor Hotel. All open 24 hrs. Collect and credit-card calls to Japan and the U.S. available at the USADirect and Japan-Direct phones in the lobbies of the Marriott, Ramses Hilton, and SemiRamis hotels. If you're willing to pay the 25% surcharge, you can make international calls much more easily at the business service offices of the Meridien, Sheraton, and Nile Hilton hotels (24 hrs.). The Nile Hilton has several local pay phones in the lobby. **Telephone Code:** 2.

Telegraph and Telex Office: Ataba Sq., opposite the main post office. Open 24 hrs. Other offices at Tahrir Sq., 26 Ramses St., and Adly St.

Travel Agency for the Disabled: Dr. Sami Bishara organizes individual and group tours to Cairo and Luxor for the disabled. For brochures and advice, contact him at ETAMS, 99 Ramses St., Cairo (tel. 75 24 62; telex: 22 775 ETAMS).

Buses, Trains, Metro, Taxis: See respective sections above in Transportation.

Car Rental: For maniacs willing to risk life and limb to achieve relative freedom of mobility: **Avis** (tel. 76 64 32/3), **Europcar** (tel. 340 11 52), **Hertz** (tel. 347 41 72), and **Budget** (tel. 341 37 90). Rates vary, but a Fiat 128 costs about US$40 per day plus US$0.17 per km over 100km. Age restrictions vary: 21 and older for Hertz, 25 for Europcar and Avis, and 27 for Budget. See Egypt Introduction for more details. You might also want to see Hospitals below.

Lockers: For luggage and valuables storage. Located on the ground floor of Ramses Station, Ramses Sq. 30pt per day for a maximum of 14 days. Walk into the station and ask anyone in uniform, *"Feen al-khazaa'in?"* (Where are the lockers?) Open 24 hrs.

English Bookstores: Shorouk Bookshop, Tala'at Harb Sq., has the best selection and atmosphere. Open daily 9am-8pm. **AUC Bookstore,** Hill House, American University in Cairo, 113 Kasr al-Aini St. (tel. 357 53 77), has a wide range of English literature, guidebooks, and maps. Open Sun.-Thurs. 8:30am-4pm, Sat. 10am-3pm. **Anglo-Egyptian,** 165 Muhammad Farid St. (tel. 391 43 37), has new and used English literature at reasonable prices. Open Mon.-Sat. 9am-1:30pm and 4:30-7:30pm. **Lehnert and Landrock,** 44 Sharif St. (tel. 392 76 06) also has a wide selection. Open Mon.-Sat. 9:30am-1:30pm and 3:30-7:30pm. **Madbuli,** in Tala'at Harb Sq., and the bookstores in the Nile Hilton and other major hotels offer a selection of books on Egypt. Open daily 9:30am-10:30pm. For an astounding collection of rare books and manuscripts go to **L'Orientaliste,** 15 Kasr al-Nil (tel. 75 34 18). Open Mon.-Sat. 10am-7:30pm.

Foreign Newspapers and Magazines: Largest collection is at the kiosks along Tala'at Harb Sq., near AUC, or at the intersection of July 26 and Hassan Sabri St., Zamalek. They stock *Time, Newsweek,* and *The New York Times,* among other titles.

American Cultural Center: 4 Ahmed Ragheb St., Garden City (tel. 354 96 01), across from the British Embassy. If you'll be in Egypt for at least 3 months you are eligible to join. To do so, take along your passport (any nationality) and 2 photos. Members can take out books and cassettes from the library. Occasional free films and lectures. Open Sun.-Fri. 10am-4pm; in winter Mon. and Wed. 10am-8pm, Tues., Thurs. and Fri. 10am-4pm.

British Council: 192 al-Nil St., Agouza (tel. 345 32 81), 1 block south of July 26 St. There is a large library (membership LE20 for 1 year; students LE10) with everything from books to computer software. Also sponsors performances by visiting British cultural groups. Open Mon.-Sat. 9am-2pm and 3-8pm.

Photography and Film Developing: Film and processing is less expensive outside of the major hotels. **Actina,** 4 Tala'at Harb St. (tel. 75 72 36). Open Mon.-Fri. 9am-8pm, Sat. 9am-12:30pm. **Kodak,** 20 Adly St. (tel. 74 93 99), or 159 July 26 St., Zamalek (tel. 740 36) has 1-hr. processing (LE1.50 extra). Open Mon.-Sat. 9am-9pm. **Antar Photo,** 180 Tahrir St. (tel. 354 07 86), right in Bab al-Luq Sq., is known for high-quality processing. Open Mon.-Sat. 9am-10pm.

Swimming Pools: You can pay over LE50 per day to stay at a fancy hotel and swim in an azure, Olympic-size pool. Or you can pay LE5 and swim in the not-quite-Olympic-size, teal-tiled pool on the 7th floor patio of the **Fontana Hotel,** Ramses Sq. (tel. 92 21 45).

Pharmacy: First-Aid Pharmacy, corner of July 26 St. and Ramses St. (tel. 74 33 69), northwest side of intersection. Open 24 hrs. Head pharmacist Dr. Muhammad speaks fairly good English, and is recommended by foreigners. **Ajaz Khanat Sayfa,** 76 Kasr al-Aini St., Garden City (tel. 354 26 78), several blocks south of Tahrir Sq. **Zamalek Pharmacy,** 3 Shagarat ad-Dorr St., Zamalek (tel. 340 24 06), is open 24 hrs.

Hospitals: Anglo-American Hospital, Botanical Garden St., Gezira-Zamalek (tel. 340 61 62/3) next to the Cairo Tower. **As-Salam International Hospital,** Corniche al-Nil, Maadi (tel. 363 21 95). **Cairo Medical Center,** Roxy Sq., Heliopolis (tel. 258 05 25). As-Salam International is the best-equipped.

Private Doctors: Your embassy can provide lists of doctors accessible to foreigners.

Emergency: Ambulance (tel. 123 or 77 01 23); **Fire** (tel. 125 or 91 466).

Police: Tel. 122 or 93 09 00.

Accommodations

You can find any of Cairo's many luxury hotels by looking for the nearest thirty-story pink tower; finding a decent budget hotel is more of a challenge. Full service hotels can be found for as little as LE25 per night, but most of Cairo's mega-cheap hotels are inconspicuous, occupying upper floors of downtown office and apartment buildings along **Tala'at Harb St.** between Tahrir Sq. and July 26 St. In summer, the least expensive hotels fill up quickly. The quality varies; many are dilapidated and some filthy. Be prepared to bargain, especially if you are in a group of two or more. Sometimes it helps to plead your status: student, frugal adventurer, victim of expensive airline fares.

Don't shy away from hotels perched on upper floors. Cairo's streets are noisy throughout much of the night and the increased altitude will aid sleep. Be aware, however, that the uppermost floors of downtown buildings often lack both functioning elevators and running water. Verify that the elevators and taps work before committing.

Even when the daytime is insufferably miserable, nights in Cairo are cool enough that air-conditioning isn't necessary; you can close the windows and muffle the racket coming from the streets below, provided your windows actually function. Many hotels offer rooms facing an inner "courtyard." The windows in these rooms are sometimes locked or broken, and the resulting infernal temperatures can render your stay unbearable. Most places rent fans at reasonable rates and serve tea, coffee, and soft drinks in their lobbies.

Youth Hostel (HI), 135 Malaak Abd al-Aziz al-Saud St., Roda Island (tel. 84 07 29, fax 98 41 07). Take metro to Sayyida Zeinab and cross the Sayala Bridge. Continue along the road, keeping the Manial Palace gardens to your left, until you come to the hostel, across from the Salah ad-Din Mosque. Wall-to-wall bunks in spartan but clean rooms. Centrally located and very crowded from November to May; call ahead. Lockers in every room; padlocks available around the corner for LE2. Bring toilet paper and HI card. Lockout 10am-2pm. 11pm curfew. LE6.50, nonmembers LE8. Breakfast included.

Downtown and Tala'at Harb Street

Fontana Hotel, Ramses Sq. (tel. 92 21 45 or 92 23 21), on your left as you leave Ramses station. Amenities of a first-class hotel: private baths, international phones, A/C, color TV (LE5), psychedelic Arabian disco, and a gift-shop in the lobby. There is also a restaurant, a small but beautiful pool, and a lovely, expensive coffee shop on the roof. Singles with bath LE50.25. Doubles with bath LE72. Breakfast included.

Windsor Hotel, 19 Alfy Bey St. (tel. 91 58 10 or 91 52 77, fax (02) 92 16 21). Beautiful and very clean, with an atmosphere of faded grandeur. Roof garden and restaurant with an opulent bar popular among U.S. and British expatriates. Good place to rendezvous with a Balliol chap and reminisce about that weekend with Lord MacFarquhar. Excellent service. Singles with shower (no toilet) US$18.18, with complete bath, A/C and TV $29.05. Doubles with shower (no toilet) US$24.05, with complete bath, A/C and TV $37.20. Breakfast included. Make reservations.

Grand Hotel, 17 July 26 St. (tel. 75 77 00 or 75 75 09), at the intersection of July 26 St. and Suleiman Basha St. One of the few places in Cairo with truly professional service. Balconies more pleasant than most. The rooms are dressed in oriental rugs and stained glass lamps with lovely tiled bathrooms. In addition to elegant salons and a coffee shop, the "Valley of the Kings" restaurant serves Egyptian and Italian food and boasts a fountain and a large-screen TV (meals LE17). All this makes it worth putting up with the slowest elevator in Cairo. Single with bath A/C, TV, and stereo $32. Doubles with bath, A/C, TV, and stereo $44. Breakfast included. Make reservations 1 week in advance. Visa.

Pensione Roma, 169 Muhammad Farid St. (tel. 391 10 88 or 391 13 40), 2 blocks south of July 26 St. and east of Tala'at Harb St., above the "Gattegno" department store. Clean, airy, tastefully decorated rooms. Decent bathrooms, but the dining room and the salons are truly grand. Singles with bath LE15. Doubles with bath LE29. Breakfast included. This place is no secret; call ahead.

Lotus Hotel, 12 Tala'at Harb St. (tel. 75 06 27 or 75 09 66, fax 92 16 21), 1 block from Tahrir Sq. Professional service, large rooms, hardwood floors, big beds, and clean bathrooms greet the frazzled sojourner. Restaurant, bar, and, coming soon, a solarium. Singles LE22, with shower and A/C LE26. Doubles LE29.50, with shower and A/C LE34.50. Breakfast included. Reserve a day in advance.

Montana Hotel, 25 Sharif St., 7th flr. (tel. 392 86 08 or 392 62 64, international 393 60 25), 2 blocks south of Adly St. Attentive and organized employees keep spotless halls, clean bathrooms, and sharp rooms equipped with internal phones. Singles LE20.50, with bath and A/C LE24.50. Doubles LE31, with bath and A/C LE37. Breakfast included. Montana? Why Montana?

New Hotel, 21 Adly St. (tel. 392 71 76 or 392 70 33), 2 blocks from Tala'at Harb St. The business-minded Al-Houssiny family (including the serious young son) run this place as an escape from Cairo's madness. Though the halls are a bit dingy, the bathrooms and the rooms are large and very clean. Singles LE27.60, with bath LE30.30. Doubles LE43, with bath LE46.35. Breakfast included.

Hotel Tee, 13 Adly St. (tel 391 10 02 or 391 87 10), 3 blocks north of Tala'at Harb Square on Tala'at Harb St. and 2 blocks over on Adly St. This mini-hotel (12 rooms in total) offers spacious rooms and hot water 24 hours a day. Very clean. The entrance of the hotel is always locked. No A/C, but an abundance of fans. Singles LE20, with bath LE25. Breakfast included.

Cleopatra Palace Hotel, 1 Bustan St. (tel. 75 99 00 or 75 99 45), across from the Nile Hilton bus station, above the TWA office. No chocolates on the pillows, or toilet paper, but this large, fully air-conditioned hotel provides clean (though a tad shabby) accommodations. For directions, ask for the "Kilobutra" Hotel. Singles with bath $45. Doubles with bath $58. Breakfast included. Make reservations 3 days in advance.

Anglo-Swiss Hotel, 14 Champollion St., 7th flr. (tel. 75 14 97), 2 blocks west of Tala'at Harb Sq. Quiet, secluded, and clean, this is the place to calm your shattered nerves after a day of sightseeing. Cool stone floors and conservative decor do in fact create a European ambiance. Bathrooms are clean. Singles LE17. Doubles LE32. Breakfast included.

Ismailia House Hotel, 1 & 3 Tahrir Sq. (tel 356 31 22), on the east side of Tahrir Sq. across from AUC. Simple and neat rooms. Hot showers 24 hours a day. Many students stay here and appear to be having a good time; however, privacy seems to be lacking. Singles LE20. Doubles LE40. Breakfast included.

Hotel Oxford, 32 Tala'at Harb St. (tel 75 81 73), 1 block north of Tala'at Harb Sq. A great place to meet foreign students, who are apparently attracted by the dormitory atmosphere. Useable bathrooms, lobby/TV room, and a reputed kitchen. Management is flexible about the number of people in a room. Singles LE12. Doubles LE15.

Hotel des Roses, 33 Tala'at Harb St. (tel. 393 80 22), 2 blocks north of Tala'at Harb Sq. Small, grimy hotel with reasonably clean rooms. Schedule hot showers for sometime between 9am and 2pm. Singles LE12.65, with bath LE16.40. Doubles LE17.65, with bath LE22.85. Fans LE3. Breakfast included.

Crown Hotel, 9 Imad ad-Din St. (tel. 91 83 74). Slow ceiling fans and a 7-ft. galleon adorn the lobby. Dormitory-sized rooms are clean and monastic. Singles LE12. Doubles LE20. LE2 discount for *Let's Go* users. Reserve rooms a day in advance; be sure to ask for a room with a ceiling fan.

Tulip Hotel, 3 Tala'at Harb Sq. (tel. 393 94 33). A clean, cheap hotel beckoning with mint-green walls and lounge with TV. Singles LE11, with shower and phone LE17. Doubles LE26. Breakfast included.

Amin Hotel, 38 Falaky Sq. (tel. 393 38 13), next to the fork of Bustan St. and Tahrir St. Located in bustling Bab al-Louk Sq., this hotel offers only double rooms. The halls are dank and the bathrooms old, but the rooms are surprisingly decent. No A/C, but all the rooms have fans. Doubles LE20.19, with bath LE23. Reserve a day in advance.

Pension Select Hotel, 19 Adly St. (tel. 393 37 07). Clean and quiet. Acceptable rooms with balconies. 3 people of the same gender per room (not a problem if you don't mind living with strangers). A marriage certificate is necessary for man-woman couples. Ask for Ramadan (the man, not the holiday). Dorm beds LE9.

Hotel Beau Site, 27 Tala'at Harb St. (tel 392 99 16 or 392 98 77), 2 blocks north of Tala'at Harb Sq. This quiet hotel is adorned with imitations of ancient Egyptian reliefs. In one corner of the lobby stands a table of books—a "library." The rooms are clean, but the dining hall is a bit shabby and the bathrooms would scare even Ram-beau. [Oog. Our apologies. Diana's joke, not ours. - *Eds.*] Doubles LE16, with fan LE20. Breakfast included. Reserve rooms a day in advance.

Garden City

Garden City House, 23 Kamal ad-Din Salah St. (tel. 354 81 26 or 354 84 00), across from the SemiRamis Hotel. Balconies spill out onto a view of the Nile or of Tahrir Sq. (light sleepers opt for the latter). Although there is no A/C and the furniture is somewhat ragged, the rooms are large and the proprietors feed their patrons well. Singles LE28.50, with bath LE36. Doubles LE48, with bath LE55. (Prices expected to go up in 1993.) Breakfast, one other meal, and all taxes included. Reserve rooms one week in advance Mon.-Sat. from 8am to 12pm.

Zamalek

The Mayfair Hotel, 9 Aziz Osman St. (tel. 340 73 15), on the corner of Ibn Zinky St. across from the French consulate. Relief from the frenzy of Tala'at Harb. Tidy rooms, but dilapidated and dorm-like. Be sure to request a room with a toilet seat, not a hole in the ground. Singles LE14. Doubles LE24. LE2 discount for *Let's Go* users.

Al-Nil Zamalek Hotel, 21 Maahad al-Swissry St. (tel. 340 18 46, international 340 02 20), next to the intersection of Maahad Al-Swissry Street and Muhammad Muzar Street. Quiet and secluded. Rooms are spacious, bright, bemarbled, and modern. All have bath, TV, A/C, fridge, and telephone; many also have extremely nice bathrooms and a balcony overlooking the Nile. Coffee shop, bar, and restaurant with dance floor and live band. Singles with bath LE39. Doubles with bath LE50. Breakfast included.

Khan al-Khalili

El Hussein Hotel, al-Hussein Sq. (tel. 91 80 89 or 91 86 64), next to al-Azhar Sq. on Muski St. Name scrawled in big letters on side of building. Right in the center of Khan al-Khalili, this hotel provides clean rooms with A/C and big balconies, many of which offer splendid views of al-Azhar Mosque. Restaurant and cafeteria. Ask for a room with bath (trust us). Singles with bath LE32. Doubles with bath LE42. Breakfast included.

New Rich Hotel, 47 Abd al-Aziz St. (tel. 390 63 90 or 390 53 80), off Ataba Sq. Delightful rooms and a perfect location for forays into Islamic Cairo. Singles LE30.31, with bath LE39.30. Doubles LE42.83, with bath LE54.38. A/C and breakfast included.

Food

If you're not a stickler for taste and sanitation, you'll need but 25pt to fill your stomach in Cairo on *fuul* and *taamaya*. Pizza-style *fatir,* with vegetables and meats piled on top and stuffed inside, is far tastier than the imitations of Italian pizza in town and, at LE2-3, usually much cheaper. At gastrocenters that do not have servers, you pay first, obtain a ticket, and then exchange your ticket for food. There is a 5% tax on everything and a 10-12% service charge in sit-down restaurants.

Downtown

Felfela, 15 Hoda Sharawy St. (tel. 392 27 51 or 392 28 33), off Tala'at Harb St., 1 block south of Tala'at Harb Sq. Excellent Egyptian food and reasonable prices make this one of the best restaurants in Cairo; every native and every tourist knows it. Busting out all over with bamboo, aquariums, and mosaics. Try their spiced *fuul* (85pt-LE2.80) and *taamaya* dishes (55pt-LE1.25). A full meal can range from *wara'ainab* (stuffed grape leaves, LE5.75) to various meat kebabs (LE9.75-12.65). Also delicious is *om ali,* a pastry baked with milk, honey, and raisins (LE2). Another entrance on Tala'at Harb St. allows access to a self-service take-out counter with cold drinks and a wide selection of Egyptian sandwiches for 40-80pt. Open daily 8am-midnight.

El Tahrir, 169 Tahrir St. (tel. 355 84 18), 3 blocks east of Tahrir Sq. Clean and crowded with Egyptians, featuring tasty *kushari* and *mahellabiah* (milk and rice pudding). Sit down and they'll bring you a huge bowl for LE1.50. Beware: that's hot sauce in the wine bottles. Open daily 6:30am-11pm.

Fatitry Pizza at-Tahrir, 165 Tahrir St. (tel. 355 35 96), 2 blocks east of Tahrir Sq. A small scrumptious *fatir* (with various meats or egg, LE4) or a sumptuous pizza *fatir* topped with meat or seafood, cheese, sauce, and olives (LE6-10) makes a filling meal. Obscenely sweet dessert (with apple jam and powdered sugar) is worth the sin (LE4-6). Open 24 hrs.

Al-Guesh, 32 Falaki Sq., (tel. 354 54 38 or 354 04 72) at the corner of Tahrir and Falaki St., 4 blocks east of Tahrir Sq. Quiet, clean, air-conditioned, and frequented by Egyptians, this spot serves delicious shish kebab (LE7) and grill dishes (*escalope,* kidney, steak, liver, LE6-12). Drinks are 80pt. Open daily 9am-midnight.

Zeina, 32 Tala'at Harb St. (tel. 574 57 58). A midtown bakery and eatery with meals for LE4-10. Outgoing waiter can make his bowtie jump up and down. *Shwarma* (75pt), large selection of fruit juices (70pt), cold drinks, and pastries. Try the *konafa* (80pt) or some *bessboussa* (80pt). Open daily 7am-midnight.

New Kursaal, 5 Imad ad-Din St. (tel. 91 85 78), at the intersection with Alfy Bey St. Professional service and good food. The adventurer can explore the various *taagens* (a mix of potatoes, carrots, onions, and various meats backed in a clay pot) or *kobeba* (ko-BAY-ba, beef with crushed wheat in it). Meals cost from LE3 to LE10. Drinks (LE2), alcoholic beverages (LE5-7.50), and desserts (LE1-2). Open daily 8am-1:30am.

New Hotel Restaurant, 21 Adly St. (tel. 392 71 76), ground floor of the New Hotel. The caricature *garçon,* towel draped over arm, will meet you at the door of this quaint, cool restaurant. Enjoy a nice *repas* of French and Egyptian cuisine: caviar, *fuul, mahshi* (means "stuffed," usually refers to eggplant or cabbage leaves or grape leaves stuffed with meat and/or rice), and hummus range in price from LE3 to LE14. A bit more extravagance (pigeon, brain) costs LE8-18. Open 24 hrs.

Ali Hassan al-Hati, 3 Halim St. (tel. 91 60 55), on the corner between Alfy St. and July 26 St., 1 block south of the Windsor Hotel. Vaulted ceilings and forlorn waiters. Flavorful kebab (LE15) and fish (LE11). The *fattahs* (mixtures of meat, rice, bread, and garlic, LE3.50-10) also do nicely. Open daily noon-11pm.

Alfi Bey Restaurant, 3 Alfi St. (tel. 77 18 88), 1 block north of July 26 St. The oldest restaurant in Egypt (est. 1936) serves up traditional fare: kebab (LE7.80), *escalope* (breaded meat, a favorite among locals, LE13), and a sinful liver-stuffed pigeon (LE6). Open daily noon-1am.

Excelsior, 35 Tala'at Harb St. (tel. 392 50 02), at the corner of Tala'at Harb St. and Adly St. This bright, airy restaurant features Italo-Egyptian specialties: canneloni (LE 4.50), lasagna (LE3.25), *shwarma* (LE8), and *taagen* (LE8). Old-fashioned ice cream bar in the corner. Minimum charge of LE2 per person. Open daily 7am-1am.

Bambo, 39 Tala'at Harb St. (tel. 392 51 79), 1 block from the intersection of Asly St. and Tala'at Harb St. Take away and sit-down restaurant spewing Italian food, Egyptian food, and some American food. For between LE4 and LE7, enjoy a fairly generous meal of pasta, *kufte*, *shwarma*, or hamburgers. "Pizza" is an exaggeration. Open daily 8am-midnight.

Doumyati, on the north side of Falaki Sq. (tel 392 22 93), near the pedestrian overpass, about 4 blocks east of Tahrir Sq. One of the most popular (and cheapest) *fuul* restaurants in Cairo. No menu in English, but it's real simple: *fuul* (50pt), *fuul* with oil (75pt), *taamaya* (20pt), *fuul* sandwich or *taamaya* sandwich (25pt), potato[e] sandwich (30pt), *a'atz* (lentil soup, LE1.10), salad (30pt), and drinks (35pt). Open Sat.-Thurs. 5am-midnight. Closed on Islamic holidays.

Garden City

Take-Away, Latin America St. (tel. 355 43 41), 1 block south of U.S. embassy. Diner cuisine in a diner atmosphere, with a large picture of J.R. on the wall. Full meals LE6-9. The "Mama Burger" is a bargain at LE1.40. Order two. Open daily 8am-midnight.

Khan al-Khalili

Coffee Shop Naguib Mahfouz, 5 al-Badistante Lane (tel. 90 37 88 or 93 22 62), 2 blocks west of al-Hussein mosque in Khan al-Khalili. Expensive but convenient new restaurant in the heart of the Khan. Far from the maddening crowds; a hangout of Nobel laureate and author Naguib Mahfouz. Every night, live music accompanies a Lebanese-style meal: *ema* (dumplings, LE5.75), *shwarma* (LE21.85), kebab or *kufte* (LE20.70), stuffed grape leaves (LE 6.90), *tabouli* or *baba ghanoush* or *tahina* salads (LE3.45). Also various exotic fruit drinks (LE5). Minimum charge LE3.50 per person (plus LE1.10 for music). Open daily 8am-2am, during Ramadan 8am-4am.

El-Dahhan Chicken Home, 82 Gohar al-Qa'it St. (tel. 93 92 78), 1 block down al-Muski St. from ad-Dahhan. Great grilled chicken (LE5) and kebab (LE5-7). Takeout or sit down. Open daily 8am-midnight.

Egyptian Pancakes, 7 al-Azhar Sq. (tel. 90 86 23), 1 block from the intersection of al-Azhar St. and Gohar al-Qa'it St. Meat *fatir* (LE5-9) and sweet *fatir* (LE6-10). Open 24 hrs.

Khan al-Khalili Restaurant, 22 Hussein Sq. (tel. 92 94 69), a few doors down from Hotel El Hussein. Kebab or *kufte* (0.25kg LE10.90). Open Sat-Thurs. 1pm-2am.

El-Dahhan, Hussein Sq. (tel. 93 93 25), 20m from the end of al-Muski. This dark, smoky hole-in-the-wall serves fantastic kebab (LE6 for 0.25kg) and fairly good *mahshi* (LE7). Usually packed with Egyptian families and local traders. Open 24 hrs., 6pm-4am during Ramadan.

Mohandiseen

Tandoori Restaurant and Take-Away, 11 Shehab St. (tel. 348 63 01). Take bus #815 from Tahrir (Nile Hilton station). Incredibly tranquil, with stunning white marble interior. Air-conditioned and spotless. Excellent service and amazing Indian cuisine for LE8-14. Open daily 12:30pm-midnight.

Prestige Pizza, 43 Geziret al-Arab (tel. 347 03 83), just east of Wady al-Nil St. Take bus #888 or #30 from Ramses Sq. The pizza place of choice in Cairo. Pizza (LE6.50-10). Classy atmosphere. Open daily noon-2am.

El Maestro, 26 Syria St., Mohandiseen (tel. 349 06 61/2), inside the Cairo Inn. Take bus #167 from Alaba Sq. The only things Spanish about this place is the music. *Moussaka* (eggplant salad, LE11) or *molokhaya* (a soup of green leaves, pronounced mul-o-KHAY-a, LE15). The restaurant-bar look like something out of *Casablanca* or *Star Wars* (low ceilings, lighted countertops) with live music at night (piano and *mesmar*). Minimum charge (from 5am-3pm LE4, from 3-11pm LE7, from 11pm-5am LE12). Open 24 hrs. US$ accepted.

Al-Omda, 6 al-Gazaer St., a few doors down from the Atlas hotel. Air-conditioned and clean. Kushari (LE4). Open daily 11am-2am.

Zamalek

Restaurant 5 Bells, 13 Ismail Muhammad St. (tel. 340 89 80 or 340 86 35), on the corner of al-Adel Abu Bakr St. Drink in an enchanting Renaissance garden or take refuge from the sun inside a cool, Italian den setting. Backpackers with shorts, Gore-Tex, and velcro might feel out of place—best to pull out the white linen suit, Panama hat, and round wire-rimmed glasses or just a tasteful chemise. Entrees are expensive (LE8-20), but a few of the *mezah* (appetizers, LE1.75-8) make a meal. Open daily noon-2am.

Il Capo, 22 Taha Hussein St. (tel. 341 38 70), half a block from the Chinese embassy. Excellent Italian food in an elegant, air-conditioned dining room. Great pasta (LE9-15). Come here for dinner, then head to **B's Corner** (next door) for music and drinks, and a little dancing . Open daily 1pm-1am.

La Piazza, 4 Hasan Sabri St. (tel. 340 75 10), near the Gezira Club in the Four Corners Complex, a 10min. walk from July 26 St. An elegant Italian restaurant as swank as any in Europe or the U.S., decorated with white marble, potted palms, and fresh roses. Standard pasta cuisine with freshly grated cheese LE12.50. Minimum charge of LE4. Open daily noon-midnight.

Balmoral Chinese Restaurant, (tel. 340 67 61), by the corner of Maahad as-Swissry and July 26 St. Take bus #13 from Tahrir Square to Hassan Sabri Station. Tastefully decorated and overlooking the malnourished gardens of the Center of Arts, this restaurant serves Korean food despite the name (LE14-18). Beware: some dishes are lethally spicy. Open daily 11am-11pm; closed the first Mon. of every month. US$ accepted.

Hana Korean Restaurant, 21 Maahad al-Swissry St. (tel. 340 18 46), next to the El-Nil Zamalek Hotel. This small, charming restaurant serves a variety of Asian dishes, average price LE14. The *sukiyaki* (a do-it-yourself, stir-fry soup) and the *gimshi* (a cabbage concoction, LE15) are delicious. Open daily noon-11pm, closed the last Sun. of every month.

Zamalek Restaurant, 118 July 26 St. (tel. 342 10 98). The cheapest sit-down and takeout restaurant in Zamalek. AUC hangout. Sandwiches: *taamaya* or *fuul* (25pt), liver, *kufte* or sausage (90pt). Open daily 6-2am; open during Ramadan.

Roy Rogers (tel. 784 93), in the Marriott Hotel by the July 26 Bridge. Large salad bar (LE9.50) and omelettes (LE8.75), but the main attractions here are the discomfited Egyptian waiters in cowboy boots, blue jeans, and ten-gallon hats. Poor blokes. Open daily noon-midnight.

Dokki

Swissair Restaurant (Le Chalet), Nile St. (tel. 348 53 21), 4 blocks north of al-Gama'a Bridge. Come here when you're longing for a taste of home, or airline food (even if you're not Swiss). Quiche (LE12.50) and veal escaloppé (LE20.50), as well as French pastries and a *Herald-Trib* to read while you eat. Open daily 10am-11:30.

El Moardi, in the Cairo Sheraton. Café serving delicious *tamaaya* (LE1.25) and *shwarma* in a fly-free environment. Patrons have the option to imbibe a garden: strawberry juice, watermelon juice, canteloupe juice, *mosa bil lebban* (banana juice with milk), *er-a'asoose* (karob juice), *kirkaday* (cold fuchsia-petal tea, pronounced CAIR-ka-day), or *tamrahindi* (hot herbal tea), all for about LE5. After 6pm, there is a minimum charge of LE9 per person. Open daily 8pm-1am.

Teahouses, Pastry Shops, and Cafés

Cairenes' favorite pastime is passing time, catching up with friends and politics and gossip over a cup of tea or a pastry. In headier days, revolutionaries used to plot around café tables. Businessfolk and peddlers share tables in cafés *(ahwa)*, playing backgammon and smoking waterpipes *(sheesha)* for hours at a time. You can find an *ahwa* on almost any street corner east of the Nile, and foreigners are usually welcomed. Egyptian women are never found here, however, and any woman alone will be harassed. Even in the more Western-style establishments, foreign women sitting alone will invariably be approached. In any of the Egyptian pastry shops scattered through downtown, you select your pleasure, pay for it, and take a seat.

Fishawi's Khan al-Khalili (tel. 90 67 55), 4 doors down from El Hussein Hotel, in the same alley. The home of the most famous coffee in Egypt, est. 1752. This traditional tea-house in the heart of the old bazaar is nicknamed Café des Miroirs. Furnished in 19th-century European style with dainty, hammered brass tables. Enjoy the atmosphere with a pot of mint tea (75pt). Let the aroma of the *sheesha* (regular or water-flavored) lull you into a tobacco trance (LE1.50). Open 24 hrs.

Groppi, in Tala'at Harb Sq. (tel. 574 32 44), on the corner of Mahmoud Basuni St. and Kasr al-Nil St. Famous during the days of the Occupation. The ice cream and pastries live up to their reputation; skip the overpriced restaurant. Other locations at 4 Adly St. (near Opera Sq.) with a lush garden, and on Al-Ahram St. in Heliopolis. All 3 open daily 9am-10pm.

La Pergola, Meridien Hotel (tel. 84 54 44), on the corniche. The most romantic view of the Nile at sunset anyone could wish for. Sorbet (LE8.25), exotic fruit juices (LE8.50), gourmet pizza (LE14.50-16.50), and delicious *hawawshi* (meat cooked in pita bread, LE14.50). LE20 minimum charge. Open March-Nov., 11am-2am daily.

La Poire, 18 Latin America St. (tel. 355 15 09), next to TakeAway Restaurant in Garden City. Oozing eclairs and honeysuckle baklava titillate the tongue. All pastries made on the premises (LE1). One of the largest selections of ice cream flavors in Cairo. Open daily 7am-11:30pm.

El Andalusia, 15 July 26 St. (tel. 75 52 05), in front of the entrance of the Grand Hotel. A pleasant outdoor café complete with fountain and backgammon-playing *sheesha* lovers. Try the *sahlab* (hot or cold milk drink with raisins, coconut, and nuts, 50pt) or the *biliari helbah* (a drink made by boiling seeds, 40pt). Open daily 24 hrs.

Tea Island, in Cairo Zoo, Giza (tel. 98 90 89), at the University Bridge. Open-air cafeteria. Features light fare (LE1.50-3.50) and regular meals (LE3-6). Toss your crumbs to the fowl while the flies and mosquitos nibble at your limbs. Open daily 9:30am-4pm.

Simmonds Coffee Shop, July 26 St., Zamalek (tel 340 94 36), just east of the intersection with Hasan Sabri St. Terrific cappuccino, espresso, and hot chocolate (70pt), or lemonade (65pt). Ideal for breakfast and chocolate binges. Open daily 7:30am-9pm.

Ibis Café, Nile Hilton (tel. 76 56 66), on the ground floor. Ideal for breakfast or brunch. Rich tourists in bermudas and Hawaiian shirts, foreign correspondent types with J. Press ties, women with purple hair—could this be you? Club sandwich LE11-20, unlimited salad bar LE7.90. Open 24 hrs.

Abu Ali Café, outside the Nile Hilton hotel. Refreshments in the shade. Prime location. Fresh juice LE4, *kushari* LE3.50. Open daily 11am-11pm.

Khan al-Khalili Coffee Shop, at the Mena House Oberoi Hotel (tel. 383 34 44) at the end of Pyramid St. Funky atmosphere. Arabic coffee (LE2.50), glass of mint tea (LE2). Open 24 hrs.

Rigoletto, 3 Taha Hussein, in the Yamama Center, Zamalek, across from the store Sportic and next to Pour Vous Clothing. A small good-ol' American apple pie (just like Mom used to bake) is LE3.75. A wide selection of ice cream flavors (LE1). LE3 minimum charge. Open daily 8am-midnight.

Brazilian Coffee Shop, 38 Tala'at Harb St. (tel. 75 57 22) at the intersection of Tala'at Harb St, and Adly St. Clean white marble counter. Excellent *café au lait* (LE1.20), cappuccino (LE1.20), and iced coffee (1.30) from Brazilian coffee beans. A magnet for caffeine-crazed students. Open daily 6am-midnight.

In the evenings you can join the swarm of middle-class Egyptian couples at one of the many cafés, called **casinos,** lining the Nile on Gezira Island. Some of these are boats, permanently anchored at the edge of the water with no intention of moving. The **Casino al-Nil,** on the west side of Tahrir Bridge, is one of the best immobile cafés; **Casino A-Z** on Zamalek below July 26 St. serves wonderful coffee, but take your pick from dozens of others, ranging from swank to simple. Most are jammed on Thursday nights, partially because of post-nuptial *haflahs* (parties); Thursday is a popular day to get married in Egypt. Wednesdays during the winter are fairly quiet; everyone is at home avidly watching *Falcon Crest.*

Sights

New City

The sidewalks of the New City teem with thousands of people who seem to be going nowhere, intently. Vendors wander about bellowing the virtues of their plastic baubles while far above the streets laundry flutters from baroque remnants of colonial architecture. In the evening, the latest kung-fu cinematic gem lets out every two hours and hundreds of film connoisseurs flood the streets and pastry shops. Despite the morning heat during the summer and the yearlong bustle, women will find it most comfortable to explore Cairo by day. For groups, the evening is the ideal time to meander through the city.

The best place to acquaint yourself with Cairo's daily life is the market. Each market may be known for a different sort of ware, or in a large market, like the one south of Sayyida Zaynab, each alley may offer a different item. Bus #174 runs from Mugama Station in Tahrir Sq. to Sayyida Zaynab. Other major markets are located northeast of Ataba Sq. and in Bulaq (from Tahrir, walk east along Tahrir St. for Ataba Sq.; take bus #46 for Bulaq). **Bab al-Luq Market,** east and south of Tahrir, is renowned for its cheap produce. While you're in the neighborhood, notice the towering **Statue of Ramses II** in front of the train station. The statue was excavated in 1888 near the remains of the ancient city of Memphis.

Cairo's two main islands merit short visits. Dominating **Zamalek** (also called Gezira or "the island") is the 187m **Cairo Tower.** Early or late in the day, the view from the top of the tower is film-frying—you can see the Pyramids, the medieval citadel, and the Delta. For LE6 you can take the elevator to the observation deck (open daily 9am-midnight). The one-block stretch around and along Hasan Sabri St. north of July 26 St. is lively; colorful, shops, cafés, and grocery stores specializing in imported foods predominate. To the north stretches a serene area with streets, embassies, and diplomatic residences.

On the southern tip of **Roda Island** stands one of central Cairo's most noteworthy ancient monuments. The famous **Nilometer** was designed to measure the height of the river and thereby predict the yield of the annual harvest. The structure dates from the 8th century BCE, though it was restored and the conical dome added under Muhammad Ali's reign. The steps descend into a paved pit well below the level of the Nile, culminating at the graduated column that marks the height of the river. The entrance to the Nilometer is often locked, but if you express interest, one of the local children will pester the custodian who lives nearby (admission LE3). Since the Nilometer lies quite far south, visit it when you tour Old Cairo.

Walking west across the island from the palace and over the Giza Bridge, you'll reach a lush section of the neighborhood of **Giza.** Straight ahead, at the end of the broad boulevard, lies the handsome campus of **Cairo University.** Along the boulevard to the north stretches **al-Urman Garden** (Botanical Gardens), the best place in town to toss a frisbee or vegetate under a shady tree. (Open daily 8:30am-5pm in summer, 8am-4pm in winter; admission 50pt, camera privileges 50pt.) Along the full length of the boulevard to the south and facing the botanical gardens is the **Cairo Zoo.** (Open daily 6am-5pm; crowded on Fri. Admission 50pt.)

Heliopolis was one of the most ambitious urban projects undertaken during the British colonial period of the late 19th and early 20th centuries. The architecture in this district is a strange agglutination of styles; in places an Islamic façade will hide a Western structure. Among the best examples of this are the Palace of Prince Hussayn, the Palace of Prince Ibrahim, the Palace of the Sultana, and the arcades on Abbas Boulevard. The most outrageous example of imported architecture is the **Palace of Empain.** Known locally as "Le Baron" and closed to the public because it has a funny tendency to fall apart, the palace is a replica of a Hindu temple complete with an electrically controlled rotating tower that allowed Empain to follow the sun through the day. To reach Heliopolis from Tahrir Sq., take bus #400 or 500. A taxi will cost about LE6.

A traditional attraction in the New City is the weekly **camel market** at Imbaba. The largest of its kind in the country, the market is held everyday from 5am to 3pm but is reputedly the most fun on Fridays from 7 to 9am. A few of the camels come from the Western Desert, but most of the pitifully lean beasts have trekked all the way from Sudan—a 30-day march to Aswan followed by a 24-hr. truck ride to Cairo. If you're lucky, you'll witness violent arguing, escaping merchandise running precariously on three legs (the fourth is bound so as to prevent just this occurrence), and an occasional goat slaughter. For about LE2200-2500 you can ride off on one of the happy hostages—a small price to pay to surprise the loved ones back home. To reach the market, take bus #172 or 175 from Ataba Sq. or bus #99 from the Nile Hilton to Imbaba (which requires a 10-min. walk upon arrival). You can also catch a cab to Imbaba Airport (from there, cross the railroad tracks and turn right). When the market winds down, traffic along the boulevards of Mohandiseen comes to a standstill as livestock are herded along. (Admission LE1.50).

Islamic Cairo

Cairo's medieval Islamic district is home to resplendent mosques and monuments which are touted as among the finest Islamic architecture in the world. Unlike Damascus and Baghdad, the two other Middle Eastern capitals of the medieval Islamic world, Cairo was spared the devastation of Mongol invasions. But the monuments are only one aspect of life here—once the unrivaled cultural and intellectual center of the Arab world, Islamic Cairo is now a crowded, poverty-plagued neighborhood whose narrow streets will simultaneously dazzle and offend your senses. Don't be too put off by the dirt and sewage; beneath the Muslim city's dingy exterior lies a wealth of ornate friezes, arabesque stucco, finely carved wooden grillwork, and vaulted and domed interiors. Countless minarets serve as observation decks, affording a view of Cairo's splendor.

Allow several hours to thoroughly explore each section of Islamic Cairo on foot. The best time to attempt this is before 9am and the afternoon, although some small palaces and museums close up at 2pm. A practical guide to the Islamic monuments in Cairo is Parker and Sabin's *A Practical Guide to Islamic Monuments in Cairo,* which includes superb maps (LE12). Also worthwhile is *The Beauty of Cairo,* by G. Freeman-Grenville, a shorter and more concise guide (LE12). A set of two detailed maps of Islamic Cairo is published by SPARE (Society for the Preservation of Architectural Resources in Egypt) for LE2.50 each. By far the best maps to have with you are those of the Islamic Monuments on pages 27-32 of *Cairo A-Z* (LE10.80 at the AUC bookstore).

Many of the important monuments charge admission (50% student discount with proper student ID). Caretakers will often serve as tour guides; for ordinary assistance, offer *baksheesh* of about 50pt. If a door is unlocked for you, or if you're shown around in detail, LE1 is appropriate. When visiting smaller monuments or when trying to see the interiors of tombs, don't be bashful about hunting down the custodian. Loudly declare your interest to whomever is about and usually the caretaker will magically swish into being. If you confine your tour of Islamic Cairo to unlocked doors, you'll miss many of the city's treasures.

Visitors must dress modestly in Islamic Cairo; revealing clothing will attract a great deal of unsolicited and unfriendly attention and will prevent admission to many mosques. In some cases head coverings are required (these can usually be rented for a few piastres). In some mosques (such as Muhammad Ali) an entire toga is provided for 50pt (modish, modest, and mint-colored). Sensible shoes are also a must, since most sites are in a state of perpetual renovation. Usually you will be asked to remove your shoes altogether; socks might be a good idea.

Most mosques are open all day, but visitors are not welcome during prayer times. Wait a few minutes after the congregation has finished before entering. Avoid visiting mosques on Friday afternoons when the Muslim community gathers for afternoon prayer. Certain highly venerated mosques—Sayyidna Hussayn, Sayyida Zaynab, and

Sayyida Nafisa—are believed to contain the remains of descendants of Muhammad and are permanently closed to the non-Muslim public. An exception is al-Azhar.

Several architectural feats deserve special attention in Islamic Cairo. Most prominent are the towering minarets from which the solemn chants of the *muezzin* summon the faithful to prayer five times daily. Mosques are generally rectangular with cool arcaded porches *(riwaqs)* surrounding a central open courtyard *(sahn)*. These usually contain a central covered fountain *(sabil)* for ablutions before prayer. The focus of each mosque is the wall *(qibla)*, which holds the prayer niche *(mihrab)* and indicates the direction of Mecca. Particularly in Mamluk mosques, the *mihrab* and *qibla* are elaborately decorated with marble inlay and Kufic inscriptions. Because Muslims consider representations of nature (animals, people) to be blasphemous imitations of God, abstract artwork dominates the mosques' decorations. In the Fatamid period, interlaced foliate patterns in carved stucco and plaster were popular ornamentation. Geometric patterns and elegant calligraphy appeared later in Mamluk times. Particularly beautiful examples of work from this period are found on the pulpits *(minbars)* that usually stand beside the prayer niche. Under the seat of the *minbar*, on the side, there is an archway allowing you to cross through to the other side as you make a wish; this is called a "wishing door."

A wise way to start your tour is to walk to the mammoth south gate of Bab Zuwayla at the intersection of ad-Darb al-Ahmer St. and as-Surugiyya St. Enter the Mosque of al-Muayyad (the large portal inside on the left) and ask to be taken up to one of the two superstratic minarets atop Bab Zuwayla. From there, try to match your two-dimensional map with the three-dimensional array by picking out the minarets and domes of the major monuments. If you wish to plunge straight into the fray, take bus #922 from Tahrir Sq. Alternatively, walk east from Opera Sq. (or Ataba Sq.) on al-Azhar St. Although Islamic Cairo begins at Port Said St., continue on al-Azhar St. about 0.25 mi. to al-Muizz ad-Din Allah, which runs north-south through the medieval city, connecting its northern and southern gates and providing an excellent place to begin your tour of the district. If you stand on the corner of al-Muizz ad-Din Allah and al-Azhar, Bab al-Futuh will be to the north, Bab Zuwayla to the south, and al-Azhar Mosque one block east.

Northern al-Muizz Street

Between al-Azhar Mosque and Bab al-Futuh, al-Muizz St. is lined with Fatamid and early Mamluk architectural attractions. This area is dubbed **Bayn al-Qasrayn**, Arabic for "between the two palaces," after the two Fatamid palaces on al-Muizz St. that once housed 20,000 citizens. Al-Gamaliya St. runs roughly parallel to al-Muizz St., from Bab an-Nasr past the Mosque of al-Hussayn to the square in front of al-Azhar. Walk from al-Azhar up al-Muizz St., through both Bab al-Futuh and Bab an-Nasr, and then return by way of al-Gamaliya St. to minimize mileage. Proceed north on al-Muizz St. from the intersection with Gohar al-Qa'id St., passing four little side streets on the right. You will see the **Tomb and Madrasa of Malik as-Salih Ayyub**, with its nearly square minaret. The *madrasa* has ornate keel-arched windows and the minaret crowns a passageway. Al-Malik as-Salih Ayyub, the last ruler of Salah al-Din's Ayyubid Dynasty, was the husband of Shagarat ad-Durr, an indomitable Turkish slave who became ruler of Egypt, single-handedly engineering the succession of the Mamluk Dynasty after the death of her husband in 1249. Look for the custodian with the keys to the adjacent domed mosque.

Diagonally across the street from the gate stand the late 14th-century **Mausoleum, Madrasa,** and **Hospital of Qalawun** in a single complex. Mamluk sultan Qalawun sponsored the construction of these impressive edifices in 1384 before his death en route to attack the Crusader fortress in Akko. The façade is extensive and ornate and the windows Romanesque—no doubt Qalawun's architects were influenced by the Crusader architecture of Syria. Three high *iwans* (vaulted halls) of the original *maristan* (hospital) remain. The ornate stuccowork inside is original, though the undersides of the arches have been restored. To gain access to the mausoleum farther along, hunt down the guard, present your entrance ticket, and ask to have the door unlocked. The exquisite wood screen, separating the tomb from the rectangular fore-court, dates from the original construction. Before the 14th century, Egypt was the world's center for glasswork; many of Cairo's mosques have stained-glass windows, and nowhere is this feature exploited to greater effect than at the mausoleum of Qalawun. This intricately embellished tomb caused quite a controversy because Islamic doctrine bans displaying wealth at the time of burial; ostentatious tombs were frowned upon as vain. By the 11th century, however, the practice of building ornate tombs, especially for rulers, was not unusual; by the 13th century, lavish burial sites had become commonplace. (Complex open daily 9am-6pm. Admission LE3, students LE1.50.)

On the side street just north of Qalawun's mausoleum and tomb stands his son's, the **Mausoleum-Madrasa of an-Nasir Muhammad,** completed in 1304. An-Nasir Muhammad's 40-year reign marked the height of prosperity and stability in Egypt under Mamluk rule. The square minaret exhibits an exceptional, intricately carved stucco surface. (Open 10am-8pm. Admission free.) Next door, to the north along al-Muizz St., is the **Mosque of Sultan Barquq.** Barquq was the first Circassian Mamluk sultan and seized power through a series of heinous assassinations. His mosque was erected in 1386, a century later than Qalawun's complex, and the difference in styles is striking. Barquq's minaret is slender and octagonal, and the high, monumental portal crowned by *muqarnas* (stalactites) gives it away as classic Mamluk architecture. The inner courtyard has four *iwans,* the largest and most elaborate of which doubles as a prayer hall. Its beautiful timber roof has been restored and painted in rich hues of blue and gold. Four porphyry columns, quarried in pharaonic times from the mountains near the Red Sea coast, support the colorful ceiling. The round disks of marble floor are slices of Greek and Roman columns, used because Egypt has no indigenous marble. (Open daily 10am-8pm. Admission LE3, students LE1.50.)

Al-Muizz St. comes to a fork north of the Mosque of Barquq. Walk 25m down Darb Kermez St., the small sidestreet to the right of the fork, and you'll find all that remains of **Qasr Bishtak,** a lavish palace from the 14th century which originally stood five stories high. All floors of the palace had running water, a technological achievement unmatched in Europe for another 300 years and currently unmatched in many of Egypt's budget hotels. (Open daily 8am-5pm. Admission free.) In the center of the fork is the slim 18th-century **Sabil Kuttab of Abd ar-Rahman Kathuda** (Open 8am-5pm. Admission free). Bear left at the fork and continue north along al-Muizz St. to the next right-hand sidestreet. On the corner stands the small but architecturally important Fatamid **Mosque of al-Aqmar.** Built in 1125, this was the first Cairene mosque to have a stone façade and shell motif within the keel-arched niche. *Al-Aqmar* means "moonlit," and refers to the way the stone façade sparkles in the moonlight. The archway of the northern corner is typical of later Cairene architecture; the height of the cut is just about equal to that of a loaded camel, and the chink was intended to make the turn onto the side street easier for hump-laden creatures to negotiate. (Open 7:30am-9pm. Admission free).

Proceeding north from al-Aqmar Mosque, turn right on ad-Daub al-Asfar (the next sidestreet on the right) and follow the winding alley about 50m. The doorway on the left marked with a small, green plaque is the entrance to Cairo's finest old house, the 16th-century **Bayt al-Suhaymi.** The *sheikh* of Al-Azhar Mosque, Suhaymi built this elaborate residence to house himself and his various wives. The house sports carved wooden ceilings, stained glass windows, tile mosaics, marbled floors, and fountained salons. (Open daily 10am-5pm. Admission LE3, students LE1.50.) Walk along the same alley, away from al-Muizz St., and you'll eventually come to al-Gamaliya St. Across the street is the façade of the 14th-century *khanqah* (Sufi establishment) of **Baybars al-Gashankir.** Erected in 1310, this building is the oldest surviving example of a *khanqah* in Cairo. From here, continue walking north on al-Gamaliya St. until you pass through Bab an-Nasr.

Northern Walls

Islamic Cairo is bordered on the north by the extensive remains of the Fatamid walls, once vital to keep out Mongol invaders. Built in 1087 CE, the colossal fortifications are the best surviving example of Islamic military architecture from pre-Crusader times. They did the trick; medieval Cairo was never besieged after their construction. Medieval Europe, which borrowed most of its knowledge of siege warfare and fortification technology from the Arab world, produced nothing comparable to these formidable walls.

Three of the fortified gates originally built into the ramparts still stand. **Bab an-Nasr** (at the top of al-Gamaliya St.) and **Bab al-Futuh** (at the northern end of al-Muizz ad-Din Allah St. just in front of the al-Hakim Mosque) are connected by a stretch of wall so thick it accommodates a tunnel; these walls once wrapped all the way around the Fatamid city to **Bab Zuwayla.** The northern gates with domed roofs were constructed with stones plundered from the temple complex at neighboring ancient Heliopolis, as the hieroglyphics and reliefs on the interior walls indicate. Bab al-Futuh is flanked by two rounded towers, as is Bab Zuwayla. Bab al-Futuh's unusual interior consists of a single large room connected by tunnel to the other gates. Although this arrangement subjected the soldiers to cramped living conditions, it was not without its advantages during popular uprisings; as late as the 19th century, when Napoléon conquered the city, the walls protected soldiers from hostilities occurring both within and outside the city. You can still examine Napoléon's vandalism in the French names he ordered carved into the walls of each tower.

The Fatamid **al-Hakim Mosque,** just inside the walls between the two gates (entrance off al-Muizz St.), was built between 990-1010 and remains the second largest mosque in Cairo. Al-Hakim was known as the "Mad Caliph"; his unpredictable rages meant death to Christians, Jews, his enemies, his friends, and, on one occasion, all the dogs of Cairo. He was murdered soon after he announced that he was an incarnation of the Divinity. His chief theologian, ad-Darazi, fled to Syria where he founded the Druze sect. The structure was recently restored (amid great controversy) by a group of Isma'ili Shi'i Muslims. Rather than restoring the mosque according to its original appearance, they chose to curry it up with an Indian interior, outraging many art historians and Islamic experts. (Open daily 9am-9:30pm. Admission LE3, students LE1.50.)

Al-Azhar and Khan al-Khalili

The oldest university in the world and the foremost Islamic theological center, the **Mosque of al-Azhar** stands just a few steps from the midpoint of al-Muizz St. at the end of al-Azhar St., facing the large square. Al-Azhar University was established in 972 CE and rose to preeminence in the 15th century as a center for the study of Qur'anic law and doctrine, a position it still holds. The mosque has been extensively restored. To reach the central court, enter through the double arched gate and pass under the minaret of Qaytbay (1469). The stucco decoration of the courtyard's façade is a reconstruction, but the *mihrab* in the central aisle is the real thing. The library, just left of the main entrance, holds over 80,000 manuscripts.

The curriculum has remained virtually unchanged since the Mamluk era, although Al-Azhar University has added mathematics, physics, and medicine. You can still see the traditional form of instruction, a process of Socratic questioning with a professor seated in the center of a circle of students. For about 50pt the caretaker will allow you to climb one of the locked minarets for a fantastic view of the complex. Women without headcoverings must don one of the long wraps provided at the entrance. (Open Sat.-Thurs. 9am-7pm, Fri. 9am-noon and 2-7pm. Admission LE3, students LE1.50.)

Across the street, 100m to the north of the main entrance to al-Azhar through al-Hussayn Sq., stands **Sayyidna al-Hussayn,** Cairo's most venerated Muslim shrine, revered throughout the Islamic world as the resting place of the skull of al-Hussayn, grandson of the prophet Muhammad. The head is rumored to have been transported to Cairo in a green silk bag in 1153, almost 500 years after the death of its owner in the battle of Karbala (in Iraq). The present edifice is of recent construction, and the garish interior includes green neon lights that glow with the name of God. Officially, non-Muslims are not allowed to enter.

On *mullids* (feast days), the president of Egypt traditionally comes to pray at Sayyidna al-Hussayn while boisterous festivities take place in the large square. During Ramadan, this square is the best place to witness the breaking of the fast after evening prayers (about 8pm). Restaurants display their fare half an hour before prayers begin, and famished patrons stampede to the tables afterwards. After blood sugar levels return to normal, the square hosts a nightly celebration.

Behind Sayyidna al-Hussayn stands the 18th-century **Musafirkhana Palace** (tel. 92 04 02). To reach the palace, walk north down al-Gamaliya St. (toward Bab an-Nasr), passing four sidestreets on the left. The fifth lefthand sidestreet, on the corner of which sits the small 14th-century **Mosque of Gamal ad-Din al-Ustadar,** is across al-Gamaliya St. from Kasr ash-Shouk St., which almost immediately becomes Darb at-Tablaoui St.—here you will find the palace; go to the end of this street and *voilà* (you are now either there or very, very lost). Built during the Ottoman period in imitation of the Mamluk style, the Musafirkhana Palace served as the residence of the Egyptian royal family and state guests during the 19th and early 20th centuries. The interior is currently being restored, but Mr. Mahmud Badeer, a self-appointed dignitary, can provide a complete history. (Open daily 9am-4pm. Admission LE3, students LE1.50.)

Almost all streets south of the palace will lead you back to al-Azhar St. and Sayyidna al-Hussayn. Turn down any of the passageways leading west from Sayyidna al-Hussayn and you'll immediately encounter the swish alleys of **Khan al-Khalili,** the largest tourist bazaar in Egypt. Stretching between Sayyidna al-Hussayn and al-Muizz St., this may be the world's most stereotypical, expensive, and commercial Middle Eastern bazaar. As you walk through the labyrinth, you'll see the traditional butcher, baker, and candlestick maker, but most of all you'll see hundreds of tourist shops pushing everything from exquisite furniture to fake pharaonic antiquities; even the most humble souvenir stands accept all major credit cards. You'll also be accosted in English at every turn with offers to "get a special guide," and "just come in and look." Striking a good deal in Khan al-Khalili requires ferocious bargaining and patience in saintly proportion; many shopkeepers will quote a starting price 10 times an object's value. Some stores post fixed prices that are nothing of the sort. Leave the bazaar without a camel, but not without admiring the lavish marble inlay on the Mamluk gates of Sultan al-Ghouri.

Far more authentic, vastly less tourist-ridden, and less expensive is **al-Muski,** the long bazaar where Egyptians shop for men's cologne, shoes, cloth, furniture, pillowcases, and food. Al-Muski stretches from al-Muizz St. all the way to Port Said St., running parallel and one block north of al-Azhar St. If you're walking between Islamic and downtown Cairo, al-Muski offers the most picturesque route.

Southern al-Muizz Street

During the Fatamid period, al-Muizz Street was the main avenue of the city, running through the heart of Cairo and connecting the southern and northern entrances, Bab al-Futuh and Bab Zuwayla. Today the street is a minor thoroughfare bisected by the much larger al-Azhar St. At the southern corners of the intersection of al-Azhar St. and al-Muizz St. stand two impressive Mamluk structures. The **Madrasa of Sultan al-Ghouri** (1503) occupies the southwest corner (tel. 90 08 23). A custodian sporadically provides tours, complete with a climb to the roof and minaret (LE1 *baksheesh*). The long chains hanging in front of the *mihrab* were used to suspend glass lamps; today a marginally different effect is achieved with neon.

The **Wakala of al-Ghouri** (tel. 92 04 72 or 90 91 46) is easier to overlook. From the mausoleum, turn left onto al-Azhar St. then right (east) onto Sheikh Muhammad Abduh St. At #3 (on your right) you'll see a magnificently preserved *wakala* (1505), now transformed into a center for handicrafts and folkloric arts. The courtyard is often used as a theater and concert hall. The structure originally served as a commercial hotel.

The *madrasa,* mausoleum, and *wakala* are all open Sat.-Thurs. 8am-2pm and 4-10pm. Admission to any or all of the three is LE3, students LE1.50.

Two blocks from the Madrasa al-Ghouri down al-Muezz St. on the left is a small street on the left of which sits the **House of Gamal ad-Din,** a 16th-century mansion. Unhitch the latch and walk in, but be prepared to encounter the mentally unstable watchdog. The house is one of the most splendid of the surviving Ottoman residences in the city, with beautiful wooden ceilings and outstanding Turkish tiles. (Open 8am-5pm. Admission LE3, students LE1.50.)

Farther south along al-Muizz St. on the left at the corner of Ahmad Maher St. is the entrance to the **Mosque of al-Muayyad,** built between 1415 and 1420. Strategically located at Bab Zuwayla and the market area, it is the last of the great *al fresco* congregational mosques. Look for the two minarets towering atop the Fatamid gate, a stone-carved dome, and an imposing *muqarnas* portal. The interior has a pleasant garden, and the *qibla riwaq* (porch along the southeast wall) is covered by an extensively restored ceiling. At the northern end of the *qibla* wall is the mausoleum of Sultan al-Muayyad. The second mausoleum, at the other end of the wall, is an Ottoman addition. (Open 9am-9:30pm. Admission LE3, students LE1.50.)

Across the street from Bab Zuwayla and to the right stands the **Zawiya of Sultan Faraj** (1408), a small rectangular structure. During the 19th century, execution by strangulation was carried out beside the railings outside. Access is difficult if you are a non-Muslim. Opposite this structure, to the left across the street from Bab Zuwayla, stands the small, elegant **Mosque of Salih Talai,** built in 1160. When the mosque was erected, the street was at the level of the series of shops standing behind the iron railing. The five keel arches form a remarkable projecting portal, unique in Cairo. The courtyard opens into a small *qibla riwaq.* The custodian (who will expect *baksheesh*) will show you to the roof. (Open 3:30am-9pm). Continuing south on al-Muizz St. you enter a covered bazaar known as the **Street of Tentmakers,** followed a few blocks down by a similar covered alley called the **Street of Saddlemakers.** Turning left as you step out of Bab Zuwayla, you'll find yourself on Darb al-Ahmar St. heading toward the Citadel. A right turn leads to Ahmad Maher St., lined with the shops of carpenters, tombstone-carvers, and metalworkers. The street leads out to Ahmed Maher Sq. on Port Said St., across from the Museum of Islamic Art.

The Citadel

Dominating Islamic Cairo, the lofty **Citadel** (tel. 93 17 35) was begun by Salah ad-Din al-Ayoubi in 1176 and has been continually expanded and modified since then. (Citadel in Arabic is *qal'a.*) To reach the Citadel, take bus #82, 83, or 609 from Tahrir or #401 from Ataba Sq. or minibus #50 or 55 from Ataba Sq. To enter the Citadel complex, walk all the way to the far eastern side, following the road along the southern walls. Don't head for the Goliathan western gateway of Bab al-Azab across from the Sultan Hasan Mosque—this entrance is locked. Enter instead through the eastern gate of Bab al-Qal'a. (Open Sat.-Thurs. 8am-6pm, Fri. 8am-noon, 2-6pm; winter Sat.-Thurs. 8am-5pm, Fri. 8-10am, noon-5pm; Ramadan 9am-4:30pm. Admission LE7, LE5 with student ID, including Muhammad Ali's mosque; camera privileges LE20.) The complex contains three mosques and four operating museums (the police museum is closed). To reach the **Mosque of Muhammad Ali,** head for the thin, unadorned Turkish minarets, the ones that look like pencils.

Before you reach the goliath Muhammad Ali Mosque, you will pass the oldest of the Citadel's three mosques (built 1337 CE). Pop into this green-domed construction to get a feel for the basic architectural principles that preceded the creation of the Citadel's magnum opus. All mosques of these periods lacked easy access to microphones, so they were built to amplify and echo the readings of the Qur'an. A sharp eye will notice that one of the mosque's columns is not like the others. This white marble column, of a different shape, bears a Coptic cross at its head. It is not yet known from which Coptic church it was taken.

During his reign in the first half of the 19th century (1805-1848), Muhammad Ali laid the foundations of the modern Egyptian state, sparked the Europeanization of the country, introduced education in the arts and sciences, and paved the way for an independent dynasty. Muhammad Ali leveled the western surface of the Citadel, filling in the famous 13th-century Mamluk Qasr al-Ablaq palace that was there, and built his mosque on top of it to serve as a reminder of Turkish dominion. Modeled after an Ottoman mosque in Istanbul, the edifice is more attractive from a distance; up close, its outline resembles a giant toad. Three years ago, the mosque was refurbished by the Department of Antiquities—its silver domes and marble and alabaster decorations now twinkle on the Cairo skyline. The interior is far more dramatic, especially just after prayers when the large chandelier and tiny lanterns are lit. This mosque, also called the Alabaster Mosque, was built in 1830 CE. It's covered inside and out with the clearest alabaster, hauled over from Beni Suef. (One outer face is not bedecked in alabaster; when Muhammad Ali died, so did the funding.)

The mosque consists of two parts: the **courtyard** and the **House of Prayer.** The attraction of the courtyard is a nameless, 17-meter deep well whose underground cavity is as big as the courtyard itself; call down something polite, because it will be a few minutes before the echoing of the message subsides. The House of Prayer is lighted by a huge chandelier and 365 lanterns for the number of days in a year, and it is bedomed five times and semi-bedomed an additional 15 times. Parisian decor splashes itself across these domes, as Muhammad Ali was a big fan of France. A charming and unexpected French gingerbread clock overlooks the courtyard; King Louis Philippe of France presented the clock in 1845 in appreciation of Muhammad Ali's gift of the pharaonic obelisk that now stands in Place de la Concorde in Paris. Depending on how much you exude *baksheesh*, you may be able to enter the gaudy, gilt **Tomb of Muhammad Ali,** with its five human-sized, silver candlestick holders. The mosque is surrounded by shady, marble gazebos overlooking Cairo against a backdrop of the Sahara and the Pyramids of Giza.

To the south of the Muhammad Ali Mosque stand the remains of the **Qasr al-Goharrah** (the Diamond Palace, named after one of Muhammad Ali's wives), also built by Muhammad Ali (in 1811 CE). A 1974 fire destroyed half of the palace. The other half consists mainly of a large reception room where Muhammad Ali received 500 of his Mamluk allies and cordially slaughtered them. The elaborate wooden benches next to the wall served as accomplices, concealing the murder weapons in a chamber *caché* below the seat. Also on display are a few of the gold- and silver-adorned tapestry coverings of the Ka'ba; every year until 1961 Egypt presented such a work as a gift to Mecca.

The **Military Museum,** just across the square from the Mosque of an-Nasir Muhammad, has a large collection of medieval weaponry and military paraphernalia but will bore all but the most crazed soldier of fortune; the only item of interest is the Chariot of Pharoah Tutankhamen. Another trifle is the **Carriage (Hantoor) Museum,** housing the carriages of the Muhammad Ali family

Near the far eastern end of the northern enclosure is a small, lovely, domed mosque known as the **Mosque of Suleiman Pasha,** built in 1527. Ask the ancient man with the *gallebiah*, a limp, a surprising knowledge of English, and the even more surprising blue eyes to explain the tombs and the intriguing figures planted on them. (LE1 *baksheesh*.)

Central Islamic Cairo

The overwhelming **Mosque of Sultan Hasan,** considered the jewel of Mamluk architecture, is spurned by devotees of pharaonic art because many of its stones were the exterior casing stones pilfered from the Pyramids at Giza. The mosque stands in Salah al-Din Sq., facing the western gate of the Citadel. From downtown, take Muhammad Ali St. from the southern edge of Ataba Sq. and walk east for 2km. Bus #72 and minibus #54 run from Tahrir Sq. Strictly speaking, Sultan Hasan is not a mosque but a combination *madrasa* and mausoleum with an added prayer niche. The commodious interior courtyard belongs to the **Madrasa of Sultan Hasan** and is surrounded by four enormous vaulted *iwans*, each of which would have housed one of the four schools of judicial thought in Sunni Islam. Inside the *iwan*, the *mihrab* is flanked by a pair of

Crusader columns. On either side of the eastern *mihrab,* bronze doors open into the **Mausoleum of Sultan Hasan.** (Open Sat.-Thurs. 9am-5pm, Fri. 9-11am and 2-5pm. Admission LE6, students LE3.)

Directly across the street from the Sultan Hasan Mosque stands the enormous **Rifa'i Mosque** (1912). Though of little architectural or historical importance, its stupendous size and polished interior draw every tour group in Cairo. It is the resting place of many Egyptian monarchs and contains the tomb of the Shah of Iran. Both the Rifa'i and Sultan Hasan Mosques are illuminated at night. (Open Sat.-Fri. 8-11am and 2-6pm. Admission LE6, students LE3).

The first street after the mosques if you proceed around the Salah al-Din rotary in a clockwise fashion is Bab al-Wazir St. This street hugs the northwestern wall of the Citadel. Follow it until it breaks free of the wall and heads north a few blocks. There you'll find the 14th-century **Mosque of Aqsunqur,** commonly referred to as the Blue Mosque, owing to its blue faience-tiled interior. The tiles were imported from Damascus and added in 1652 by a Turkish governor homesick for Istanbul's grand tiled mosques. Turn right as you leave and continue up the same street; its name changes to Darb al-Ahmar (Red Way) in memory of Muhammad Ali's massacre of the Mamluk generals here.

Continue north along Darb al-Ahmar St.; at the corner where the street veers to the left stands the simple and unobtrusive **Mosque of Qijmas al-Ishaqi.** Don't guffaw in derision at the unremarkable exterior; the light from the stained-glass windows emblazons the marble and stucco inside. Under the prayer mats in the east *iwan* lies an ornate marble mosaic floor. As you step out, notice the grillwork of the *sabil* (fountain) on your right and the carved stonework of the columns.

Southern Islamic Cairo

If you see only one mosque in Cairo, let it be the **Mosque of Ibn Tulun,** the largest, oldest (879 CE), and most sublime of the city's Islamic monuments. To reach the mosque, walk west along Saliba St. from Salah al-Din Sq., by the western gate of the Citadel. A number of buses service this area: #72 or #174 from Tahrir Sq., #923 from Giza, #905 from the Pyramids, and minibus #54 from Tahrir. The vast, serene inner courtyard is surrounded by three rows of shaded colonnades. The courtyard covers almost seven acres and contains an inscription of elegant Kufic carved in sycamore wood that runs for over 2km.

Ibn Tulun, son of a Turkish slave, was sent to Egypt as governor of al-Fustat in 868 and became governor of the entire province in 879. He declared independence from Baghdad and built a new royal city north of the original capital of al-Fustat. The grand mosque is all that remains of the Tulinid City. The minaret and its unusual external staircase was probably built in the 13th century to resemble Ibn Tulun's original tower, which in turn was modeled after the minaret at the Great Mosque of Samarra in Iraq. (Open 8am-6pm. Admission LE3, students LE1.50.) Don't mistake the *madrasa* and Mosque of Sarghatmish, which adjoins the northern side of the Mosque of Ibn Tulun, with Ibn Tulun's entrance; Sarghatmish is closed to non-Muslims.

On the right, as you step out of the main courtyard entrance, you will come upon the enchanting **Bayt al-Kritiliya** (House of the Cretan Woman), also called the **Gayer-Anderson House.** Once distinct buildings, these two 16th- and 18th-century Turkish mansions were merged and elaborately refurbished in the 1930s by Major Gayer-Anderson, an English art collector. Today the mansions house a museum containing, among other exhibits, carved wooden *mashrabiyya* screens, which allowed women in the harem to see out without being visible from the streets. (Open daily 8am-3:30pm. Admission LE8, students LE4.)

If the Ibn Tulun Mosque is the boldest and most impressive of Cairo's Islamic monuments, then surely the **Madrasa of Qaytbay** is the most delightful and expressive. A short walk west of the Gayer-Anderson House, the mosque was built by Mamluk Sultan Qaytbay in 1475 as a theological college. The beautifully carved *minbar* and the intricate mosaic floor are two of the finest in Cairo. The caretaker will unlock it for *baksheesh.* (Open daily 9am-4pm. Admission LE3, students 1.50.)

Old Cairo

Some of Cairo's oldest architectural monuments are, appropriately enough, in the southern section of town known as Old Cairo. Nine hundred years before victorious Fatamids founded the city of al-Qahira, the Roman fortress town of Babylon occupied the strategic apex of the Nile Delta just 5km south of the later city site. This outpost became a thriving metropolis during the 4th century CE, and a number of churches were built within the walls of the fortress. One of the rebuilt churches survives as a place of worship for the Coptic community.

Located outside the walls of the Islamic city, Old Cairo also became the center for Cairo's Jewish community. Although most of the Jewish population of the city fled in 1949 and 1956, approximately fifty Jewish families still inhabit this quarter, worshiping at the ancient Ben Ezra synagogue. In addition to a handful of beautiful and well-kept Coptic churches, Old Cairo possesses one of the city's finest collections, the **Coptic Museum.**

The easiest way to reach Old Cairo is to take the Metro from Tahrir Sq. to Mar Girgis (25pt). Buses #92, 134, 140, and 94 also run from Tahrir Sq., stopping directly in front of the Mosque of Amr. If you take a taxi to the outskirts of Old Cairo (LE2-3), tell the driver you want to go to *Masr al-Qadima* or *Gama'a Amr.*

Coptic Cairo

Ancient Egypt invariably inspires images of towering pyramids, hieroglyphics, mummy cases slathered in jewels, and Cleopatra. Many view the pharaonic era as having shifted directly into the Islamic age of mosques, medieval fortifications, and integration into the Arab world. But for a transition period of several hundred years, beginning in the first century CE when the new faith began to take hold in Egypt, Christianity and Hellenistic culture were the dominant forces. Egyptian Christianity was spread by the agency of the Coptic Orthodox Church, which split off from the main body of the Christian Church in 451. Currently, some 7-8 million Egyptians are Copts, and an estimated 4 million Copts reside in Cairo alone. For a brief description of Coptic Christianity, see the General Introduction.

Located in the 19th-century Qasr ash-Shama, the **Coptic Museum** (tel. 84 17 66) houses the world's finest collection of Coptic art. With its tranquil courtyards and shaded, overpriced cafeteria, the museum offers a respite from the hullaballoo of Islamic Cairo. Halls are paved with spotless white marble and a host of elegantly carved wooden *mashrabiyya* screens the windows. An added attraction is the museum's location on the site of the ancient Roman fortress of Babylon. An interesting artistic comparison to make is between an icon of the Virgin Mary suckling the Baby Jesus and a carving of the goddess Isis suckling her son, the sun-god Horus. Though all of the exhibits are excellent, the rarest and most inspiring is perhaps the collection of woodwork and frescoes, parts of which date back to the 4th century. Also not to be missed is the display of Coptic textiles (located on the second floor). Next to these are displayed the Library of Gnostics, a collection of non-standard gospels (e.g., Thomas's gospel) from the 13th and 14th centuries, along with a few more Coptic texts from various periods. Some of these shine with intricate gold foil. The museum also displays a variety of architectural fragments brought from the sanctuary of St. Menas at Maryut and the monastery of St. Jeremiahs at Saqqara, as well as illuminated manuscripts and numerous paintings, icons, and ivories. The labels on each exhibit do not provide excavation dates and are, in general, not exceedingly helpful (for example, "A man presented in a decorative manner, holding a symbol, perhaps a cross"); bring another source of information with you or resign yourself to bumbling through, bereft of clue.

The museum is directly across from the Mar Girgis stop on the Metro. If you arrive by bus or taxi, you'll be let off just outside Old Cairo. Head directly south along the old subway tracks and the museum will be on your left. (Open Sat.-Thurs. 9am-4pm, Fri. 9am-1pm and 2-4pm; winter Sat.-Thurs. 9am-4pm, Fri. 9-11am and 1-4pm. Admission LE8, students LE4, camera privileges LE10).

In front of the museum stands Cairo's only substantial classical ruin. The imposing **Roman battlement** originally flanked the main entrance to the Fortress of Babylon. Built in the first century, the fortress overlooked the Nile before the river shifted west. The *castellum* extended over a full acre, and it took invading Muslims more than seven months to overpower the fortifications in the 7th century. The castle's only surviving tower formed part of a massive harbor quay in ancient times. Today a flight of stairs leads down to the foundation of the bastion, which is currently flooded with water.

Most of Cairo's Coptic churches are tucked away from the street, and the older structures possess simple rather than elaborate entrances. Though none of the churches in Coptic Cairo charges admission, all contain donation boxes (LE1 for posterity, LE2 for penance). The caretaker may not approach you for *baksheesh*, but if you are shown a secluded chapel or crypt, a small tip (25pt) is in order. The churches are open daily, roughly 9am-4pm. Photography is prohibited in all of the churches.

Standing south of the Coptic Museum, the **Church of al-Muallaqa** (The Hanging Church) was built suspended above the gate of Babylon Fortress, 13 meters above the ground. Known also as the Church of St. Mary and St. Dimiana, it is perhaps Coptic Cairo's loveliest church and the earliest known Christian site of worship in Egypt. The original building was erected at the end of the 3rd century CE, but repeated restoration has rendered the early structure virtually undiscernible. Enter al-Muallaqa through the gateway in the walls just south of the museum. Pointed arches and colorful geometric patterns enliven the main nave; in the center, an elegant pulpit rests on 13 slender columns—one for Christ and each of his disciples. The conspicuous black marble symbolizes Judas. The pulpit is used only on Palm Sunday. The 12th-century ebony and ivory *iconostasis* is one of the finest in Coptic Cairo. The Hanging Church is ark-shaped, and its roof held up by eight pillars on each side of the church, one for every member of Noah's family. Because an altar can only administer the Liturgy once a day, this church contains seven altars. Some of these altars are set off, not by an iconostasis, but by a cedar wood altar screen. The screen is inlaid with pentagons and crosses of ebony and ivory—all of which are fit together without nails, like a jigsaw puzzle. Al-Muallaqa houses 110 icons. The icon of St. Mark was written (icons are written, not drawn) with natural pigments of the 10th century, and today, the colors remain impressively strong. The careful observer of the icon of St. Boktor will notice that the tormentor standing above him is striking him with the left hand, traditionally thought of as the weaker hand; thus, putting one and one together, the viewer will realize that Boktor is being tortured, not mercifully killed. The most mesmerizing of the icons is that of the Virgin with her baby Son; the 8th-century eyes seem to follow you around the church. This church holds a special place in the annals of Coptic belief, due to its congregation's involvement in the miracle of Mokattam Mountain. A troublesome caliph, so the story goes, picking on the Biblical claim that those of faith can move mountains, proposed an ultimatum to Pope Ibra'am Ibn az-Zar'a and the Coptic population: prove it or die. The congregation stayed to pray in this church three days and three nights. On the third day, each exalted *Kyrie eleison* (Lord have mercy), accompanied by a bow en masse, shook the earth and moved Mokattam a few inches. Note the ostrich eggs hanging above the alter. Coptic Orthodox Masses are held at al-Muallaqa on Friday 8-11am and Sunday 7-10am. Modest attire is required at all times for both men and women.

North of al-Muallaqa on Mari Girgis St., past the museum, is the 6th-century Greek Orthodox **Church of Mari Girgis** (St. George) a wide, circular building, erected over one of the towers of the Fortress of Babylon. Renovated on several occasions, the present structure preserves the circular plan that was once common in Middle Eastern churches. The icon-clad interior is illuminated by stained glass windows and candles. (Open daily 8am-12:45pm and 2:30-5:15pm.)

To the left of St. George's Church on Mari Girgis St., a staircase descends into Old Cairo proper. After entering the city, the first main doorway on the left is marked with a tin plaque indicating the 14th-century **Convent of St. George.** The nuns here sometimes enact a traditional Coptic ritual of wrapping a person in chains to symbolize the persecution of St. George by the Romans. Venture farther into Old Cairo and continue to the end of the alley with the entrance to the convent. Bear right; and directly ahead will be Coptic Cairo's most renowned structure, the **Church of Abu Serga** (St. Sergius). A dwarfed archway leads off the main street into a narrow passage and the entrance to the church (across from the tourist bazaar). The church, dating from the 10th century, stands several feet below street level. Behind the left side of the *iconostasis,* a set of steps descend to a crypt where the Holy Family is believed to have rested on their journey into Egypt. Rising Nile waters have flooded the crypt in recent years; it is currently closed to the public.

Leaving the Church of Abu Serga, turn right and head eastward to the end of the alley. Immediately to the left lies the cavernous **Church of St. Barbara** (pronounced bar-BAR-a), together with a Church of St. Cyrus and St. John dating from the Fatamid era. Legend holds that when the caliph discovered that both Christian churches were being restored, he ordered the architect to destroy one of them. Unable to choose, the architect paced back and forth between the two buildings until he died of exhaustion. Moved by this tragedy, the caliph allowed both churches to stand. The interior of the Church of St. Barbara closely resembles that of its restored neighbor. The bones of St. Barbara, who was killed by her father when she attempted to convert him, are said to rest in the tiny chapel accessible through a door to the right as you enter the church. The bones of St. Catherine, namesake of the monastery on Mt. Sinai, also reputedly lie here. An inlaid wooden *iconostasis* dating from the 13th century graces the church's ornate interior.

A few meters south of St. Barbara's a shady garden luxuriates in front of the **Ben Ezra Synagogue.** The temple that occupied the site in pre-Christian times was demolished in the first century CE to make room for construction of the Roman fortress. Later, a Christian church was built on the site; the building was transformed into the present synagogue in the 12th century. The distinctive Sephardic ornaments and a valuable collection of ancient manuscripts and 6th-century Torah scrolls have been removed until restoration is complete, which will probably be years. Access to the synagogue's interior remains unhampered by the construction, however, so feel free to walk in and admire the brilliantly detailed ceiling.

Fustat

Adjoining Coptic Cairo to the north are the partially excavated remains of Fustat, one of the oldest Islamic settlements and the capital of Egypt during its first 250 years as a Muslim state. The architectural remains of Fustat are insubstantial, and a stroll through the site reveals little more than traces of cisterns, drains, cesspits, and rubbish. In the northwest corner of the site, the **Mosque of Amr,** Egypt's first Islamic mosque, has been restored to use. In addition to architectural fragments, thousands of pieces of fine Islamic pottery and imported Chinese porcelain have been discovered here; they are currently displayed at the Islamic Museum. In the nearby **pottery district,** you can watch modern-day artisans at work.

To sate your Fustat fetish, take the Metro or a bus from downtown to the Mari Girgis station. Walk north along Mari Girgis St. for about five minutes until you see the Mosque of Amr on your right. Fustat sprawls over the large area behind the mosque. If you venture out to this district in the heat of summer, bring plenty of water. Also beware that the ground near the site is unstable in places.

Fustat was the name of a garrison town that some historians maintain comes from the Latin word for entrenchment, *fossatum.* A more romantic account of the founding of Fustat holds that the conquering general Amr sent word to the caliph in Medina that the magnificent Roman port of Alexandria would be the perfect place for the capital of Egypt. To Amr's dismay, the caliph preferred to establish his outposts in sand, connected by desert trade routes and invulnerable to the naval attacks of seafaring Christians. The disappointed general returned to Babylon to find that a white dove had nested in his tent during his absence. Interpreting this as a divine omen, Amr founded the new capital of Egypt on the site of his tent, and dubbed it *al-Fustat* (City of the Tent).

Credit for the construction of Egypt's first mosque goes to Amr himself, who made many such lasting contributions to the nation. At the time the mosque served as the seat of government, the post office, *caravanserai,* and the city's religious center. The huge, open square could accommodate nearly 12,000 worshipers (the size of Amr's army). Fustat later acquired a large treasury, numerous mansions, and elaborate plumbing and sewage systems, the likes of which were not seen in Europe until the 18th century. Fustat remained the capital of Egypt until the Fatamids established the neighboring city of al-Qahira in 969 CE. By the middle of the 12th century the Fatamid Dynasty was flailing; in 1168 Crusader King Amalric of Jerusalem invaded and fought the Fatamids near Cairo. During the battle, Fustat was burned to the ground to prevent it from falling into the hands of the Crusaders. Except for the great mosque, little survived of the city; by the end of the 14th century Fustat was virtually abandoned.

The present day **Mosque of Amr** occupies the site of the original building of 642, which was barely one-fourth the size of the present edifice. The oldest portion of the mosque is its crumbling southeast minaret, added during the Turkish period. The mosque's 18th-century design includes a single, spacious courtyard lined on four sides by stately white marble columns, pilfered from local Roman and Byzantine buildings during medieval times. The mosque was entirely renovated several years ago. (Admission LE3, students LE1.50. Open 24 hrs.)

Near the Mosque of Amr is **Dayr Abu Saffayn,** a complex of three 8th-century Coptic churches. From the mosque, head north, take the first left, and follow the thoroughfare to the railroad tracks; the wooden entrance to the churches will be slightly behind you and to the north. (Complex open 8am-1pm, but knock loudly to rouse the caretaker if you arrive late.) The main attraction is the **Church of St. Mercurius Felopatir** (or the Church of Abu Saffayn), dating from the 4th century but extensively restored during medieval times. The cathedral contains 14 altars (most of which the modestly-dressed *baksheesh*-forker might be allowed to see), various relics of saints venerated in the Orthodox Church, several early icons, an elaborate gabled roof (fit together like a jigsaw puzzle—no nails), and the original delicate ebony/ivory/cedar wood *hegab* or *iconostasis.* St. Mercurius Felopatir was a Roman Christian who assured his frazzled king that divine assistance would dispose of the annoying Barbars who were invading Rome; after victory, the king promptly beheaded Mercurius. He is called Abu Saffayn (which means "two swords") because an angel gave him a heavenly cleaver to go with his military slicer. Against the wall on the northern side of the main chamber, the eyes of the Virgin Mary on a deerskin icon seem to follow you around the church. Next to her, an icon picturing St. Barsoum marks the entrance to a tiny vaulted crypt where the saint supposedly lived for 25 years with a cobra tamed by the Tamer on High. For 50pt the caretaker will let you descend into the small, dusty burial chamber. Mass is celebrated in the crypt on September 10 to honor St. Barsoum's feast day. If the *bewab* (caretaker or custodian) is in a good mood (LE3-4 slipped into his palm usually lifts his spirits) he'll take you upstairs to see the ancient, tiny Churches of St. George of Rome, St. John the Baptist, and the 144,000 Martyrs—all of which were rediscovered when the plaster was accidentally chipped away to reveal icons and icons-beneath-icons.

Next door is the late 4th-century **Church of St. Shenouda,** one of the most famous Coptic saints. This chapel (undergoing repairs in summer 1992) contains two fine *iconostases*—one of red cedar and the other of ebony—and seven alters. The smallest of the three main structures at Dayr Abu Saffayn is the early 8th-century **Church of the Holy Virgin,** a tiny one-room chapel crammed with icons and small paintings. The *odass* (liturgy) is celebrated in these churches Sun. 6-10am, Wed. 8am-noon, and Fri. 7-11am.

If you leave Old Cairo and head north by bus or taxi you'll pass the impressively preserved 14th-century **aqueduct,** erected by Sultan an-Nasir Muhammad to transport water from the Nile to the Citadel.

Cities of the Dead

The Cities of the Dead teem with life, if you know where to look. The area to the northeast and south of the Citadel contains hundreds of tombs and mausolea from the Mamluk era—hence the name. But, doubling as a residential district or shanty town, the area is home to hundreds of thousands of Cairenes. The modern residents of the medieval necropoli dwell amidst the funerary architecture and many households have even incorporated the grave markers into their houses and yards. Tombs serve as clotheslines, soccer goals, and public benches. On Fridays these quarters swarm with visitors arriving to pay their respects to the deceased. Many of the grave plots are enclosed by walls, encompassing an adjoining chamber and small house where families pray for their dead relatives on holy days. The Egyptian custom of picnicking at the family tomb on feast days may be an ancient holdover from pharaonic times, when the corpse was believed to require nourishment to ensure the spirit good health in the afterlife. Visitors are not permitted to enter the mosques on Fridays or during prayers. There are also many areas of the necropoli which are uninhabited: don't be surprised if you turn a corner and find yourself alone with five apparitions, desperately trying to believe that it's merely your shadow.

Mamluk sultans spared no expense in the construction of their final resting places. Elaborate tomb complexes, fashioned with domed mausolea, mosques, and adjoining *madrasas,* were erected for Cairo's rulers. Gravestones built for the families of Mamluk nobles vary widely; cenotaphs of all shapes and sizes dot the crowded thoroughfares of the royal necropoli.

The **Northern Cemetery,** northeast of the Citadel, is characterized by wide boulevards and courtyards. It contains the finer monuments of the two necropoli, with structures dating from the later Mamluk period (14th-16th centuries) to this century. A visit to the Northern Cemetery is best tacked onto a tour of Islamic Cairo. Head right from al-Azhar Mosque, past the fruit markets and around the north side of the mosque until you reach Bab al-Ghurayyib St. Follow this due east until you hit Salah Salem St. Dirasa lies 0.25km north (look for the blue overpass). Also, buses #77 and #904 from Tahrir Sq. will take you to the vicinity. The **Southern Cemetery** is a far more crowded necropolis, housing Ayyubid mausolea and the oldest Mamluk tombs (12th-14th centuries). The Southern Cemetery is accessible by foot from Ibn Tulun, the Sultan Hasan Mosque, or the Citadel. Bus #82 or #182 from Tahrir Sq. or bus #85 from Ataba Sq. can also take you there (get off at Imani Station). From Ibn Tulun or Sultan Hasan, proceed east to Salah al-Din Sq., just southeast of the Citadel. From here head directly south past the Manshiya Prison to Imam ash-Shafi'i St., the main thoroughfare in the cemetery.

Graveyard groupies visiting either cemetery will successfully avoid the fragrant crowds that waft together at the Pyramids or the Citadel, but the empty streets here can be unsettling, especially for women alone.

Northern Cemetery

Bordered on the west by Salah Salem St., the Northern Cemetery is an outdoor museum of Mamluk art. Its most celebrated article is the 15th-century **Mausoleum of Qaytbay.** Approach it from the north through the open square for the best view of the façade's polychrome striped brickwork, recognizable from the art on the one-pound note. Qaytbay was a Mamluk slave who rose through the ranks of the army to become leader of Egypt during the closing decades of the 15th century. Reigning for 28 years—longer than any other Mamluk except an-Nasir Muhammad—he was a ruthless sultan with a soft spot for beautiful buildings. Enter the complex through the northern doorway, passing through a rectangular sanctuary. The mausoleum proper is a spacious, domed chamber housing the marble cenotaphs of Qaytbay and his two younger sisters. Also in the tomb chamber are two black stones bearing footprints said to be those of the Prophet Muhammad. (Open daily 9am-9:30pm. Admission LE3, students LE1.50.)

South of the Mausoleum of Qaytbay are two 14th-century monuments constructed for members of the royalty. To reach them, follow the main road south of the mausoleum through the **Gate of Qaytbay,** a stone archway that once guarded the entrance to the tomb complex. When this thoroughfare intersects with a paved road, turn right and head west toward Dirasa and Salah Salem St. Just beyond the next main street are the remains of the **Tomb of Umm Anuk** (1348), a ribbed dome adjoining a sweeping pointed archway. Umm Anuk was the favorite wife of Sultan an-Nasir Muhammad, and her devoted husband presented her with an appropriately lavish tomb. He also constructed the **Tomb of Princess Tolbay** across the way for his principal wife. Muslim law required him to treat the two women equally, but the sultan apparently obeyed only the word and not the spirit of Qur'anic law: judging from the inferior work of the second tomb, it's clear who received the sultan's genuine affections.

Follow the cemetery's main north-south boulevard, Sultan Ahmed St., which runs parallel to Salah Salem St., north until you reach the **Tomb of Barsbay al-Bagasi.** Built in 1456, the tomb is decorated with an intricate, geometrical design resembling a tulip, a variation on the Moroccan motif of *dari w ktaf* (cheek and shoulder). The nearby **Tomb of Amir Sulayman** was built about 90 years later; its dome is decorated with a series of zig-zag stripes.

Around the corner to the east is the imposing **Mausoleum of Barquq,** easily identified by its matching pair of ornately sculpted minarets. Built in 1400 for Sultan Barquq by his son, this enormous family plot encompasses an inner courtyard. The *minbar* beneath the western arcade was donated to the mausoleum by the Mamluk ruler Qaytbay. The smaller, central peak covers the thickly decorated *minbar,* while two matching zig-zag domes—the earliest stone domes in Cairo—shelter the family mausolea located in either corner. Sultan Barquq is interred below the northeast corner of the complex, and the remains of his two daughters occupy the chamber beneath the southeast dome. For a little *baksheesh,* the caretaker will show you around the mausolea and let you climb the minaret. In the northeast corner of the complex, the second story holds the remains of a large *kuttab* (Islamic school for orphans) and numerous monastic cells that once housed Sufi mystics. (Open daily 9am-9:30pm. Admission, excluding the tomb chambers and minaret, LE3, students LE1.50.)

The **Mosque and Mausoleum of Sultan Ashraf Barsbay** are 50m south of the mausoleum of Barquq, along the cemetery's main thoroughfare. Originally intended as a *khanqah* (Sufi establishment), the 15th-century mosque has meticulously fashioned marble mosaic floors; lift the protective prayer mats to see the colorful tilework. Adjoining the mosque to the north is the mausoleum, a domed chamber containing a white marble cenotaph, an elaborately decorated *mihrab,* and gleaming mother-of-pearl and marble mosaics. (Open daily 9am-9:30pm. Admission free.)

Southern Cemetery

The Southern Cemetery's most impressive edifice is the celebrated **Mausoleum of Imam ash-Shafi'i.** The largest Islamic mortuary chamber in Egypt, the mausoleum was erected in 1211 by Salah al-Din's brother and successor in honor of the great Imam ash-Shafi'i, founder of one of the four schools of judicial thought of Sunni Islam. In 1178, Salah al-Din had built a large cenotaph over the grave of Imam Shafi'i, which is currently housed within the 13th-century mausoleum and often crowded with Muslims offering prayers. In the center of the mausoleum is the teak cenotaph of Imam Shafi'i, one of the finest surviving pieces of Ayyubid wood carving. In addition to the tomb chamber, the complex contains two mosques, one dating from 1190, the other from 1763. The older mosque is closed to non-Muslims. The more recent, open to all, remains a vital center of worship. (Open daily 6am-7pm. Admission free, but 25pt *baksheesh* appropriate.)

The **Mosque of Sayyida Nafisa,** Egypt's third-holiest Islamic shrine, stands on the western edge of the Southern Cemetery not far from as-Sultaniya. One of Cairo's three congregational mosques, Sayyida Nafisa is a center of Islamic worship and hence closed to non-Muslims. To reach the mosque, go to the main intersection southeast of the Citadel and follow Salah Salem St. alongside the 12th-century **Wall of Salah al-Din** in a southwesterly direction. At the end of the wall, bear sharply right and weave westward through a short maze of side streets to get to the entrance. Sayyida Nafisa, the great grand-daughter of al-Hasan, a grandson of the Prophet, was venerated during her lifetime. After her death in 824, her tomb attracted droves of pilgrims. By the 10th century, the original structure proved too small to contain the multitudes of worshipers, necessitating the construction of successively larger mosques. The present structure dates from the 19th century. So many mausolea were erected in the immediate vicinity of Sayyida Nafisa's tomb that historians suspect the construction of this sacred shrine alone sparked the development of the Southern Cemetery. On Fridays, crowds converge on the mosque.

Adjoining the Mosque of Sayyida Nafisa on the eastern side are the 13th-century **Tombs of Abbasid Caliphs.** At the peak of their authority, the Abbasid caliphs ruled the entire Muslim world (except for Spain) from Baghdad. The last reigning caliph fled from Baghdad in 1258 when invading Mongols toppled the regime. The Mamluk sultan welcomed him upon his arrival in Egypt and went so far as to exalt the deposed caliph in an effort to legitimize his own sinecure. Subsequent Mamluk rulers continued to harbor a succession of caliphs, all the while preventing them from gaining any real power. Finally, the sultan in Istanbul declared himself caliph in 1517, thereby consolidating the authority of the Ottoman Sultanate. With Egypt under Ottoman rule, it was impossible for the regional government to protest the abolition of their local charade of religious authority. Though the Abbasid caliphs have been fully deposed, their succession continues to the present day, and members of the family are still buried within the walls of the 13th-century mausoleum. Inside are wooden cenotaphs marking the graves of the caliphs. (Open daily 24 hrs. Admission free, but *baksheesh* appreciated.)

North of the Tombs of the Abbasid Caliphs, along al-Calipha St., lies the **Shrine of Sayyida Ruqayya** (1160), whose father, Ali, was husband of the Prophet's daughter Fatima and a central figure in Shi'i Islam.

Across the street lies the **Tomb of Shagarat ad-Durr,** the most recent Ayyubid building in Cairo (1250) and the burial place of one of the few women to achieve political prominence in the history of Islam. Shagarat ad-Durr (Arabic for "Tree of Pearls") was a slave who rose to power after marrying as-Salih Ayyub, the final ruling member of Salah al-Din's Ayyubid Dynasty. She concealed the sultan's death in 1249 for three months until her son returned from Mesopotamia to claim the throne; the wily queen, realizing that her frail son would never muster the authority to command a following among Mamluk slave troops, promptly engineered his murder. Proclaiming herself Queen, Shagarat ad-Durr governed for 80 days until she married the leader of the Mamluk forces. The renegade couple managed to consolidate power over the next several years, but their happy rule ended when the queen discovered that her new husband was considering a second marriage: she arranged for his murder. Not to be outdone, the prospective second wife avenged the death of her lover by beating Shagarat ad-Durr to death with a pair of wooden clogs and then hurled her body from the top of the Citadel, where it was left to the jackals and dogs.

Museums

Egyptian Museum

The **Egyptian Museum,** the world's unrivaled warehouse of pharaonic treasures, stands in Tahrir Sq. (Open Sat.-Thurs. 9am-4pm, Fri. 9am-noon and 2-4pm; during Ramadan Sat.-Thurs. 9am-3pm, Fri. 9am-noon and 2-3pm. Admission LE10, LE5 with student ID; camera privileges LE10.) The most conspicuous displays in the museum are not always the most interesting; try not to overlook the smaller rooms tucked away in various niches around the museum. Sadat closed the famed mummy room in 1981 because the display was offensive to some Islamist groups, and the reopening of the room has been delayed because the mummies have since decomposed and are now offensive to just about everyone. Hopefully, the mummies will be treated and the better-equipped New Egyptian Museum will be finished soon.

In the small glass case opposite the entrance, the **Narmer Palette** commemorates the unification of Egypt about 3100 BCE by King Narmer of the First Dynasty. Some believe that King Narmer was actually the incarnation of Menes, the mythical founder of united Egypt. From here, the corridors and rooms leading around the central domed court present a chronological sampling of pharaonic art from the Old Kingdom to the Greco-Roman period.

The unusually well-preserved paint on the statues of Prince Rahotep and his wife Nofret (room #32) expresses the extraordinary realism of these funerary statues sculpted 47 centuries ago. Nearby stands the world's oldest extant magnitudious metal statue, depicting King Pepi I of the 4th Dynasty. The statue was fashioned by beating heated metal sheets around a wooden core.

Proceed to the **Akhenaten room** (#3) at the rear of the first floor, to see statues of the heretical pharaoh who introduced a form of monotheism. He worshiped Aton as the sun god and source of life, representing him as a disk with rays that ended in hands, sometimes holding *ankhs,* the Egyptian symbol for life. Akhenaten also venerated Maat, who was rather indelicately manifested as "truth in artwork."

Of all the collections in the museum, the exuberance of contents from **Tutankhamen's tomb** on the second floor are surely the most outstanding. Originally squeezed into less than 100 cubic meters, the treasures now occupy an entire quarter of the second level. The eastern corridor contains decorated furniture, golden statues, delicate alabaster lamps, weapons, amulets, fossilized undergarments, and other bare necessities for a King of the Underground. Room 4, the most magnificent of all, flaunts the famous coffins and funeral masks, as well as a mind-occluding collection of amulets, scarabs, and jewelry. This impressive room also displays a pair of gilded sandals and a knife with an actual iron blade, a rarity for the times and thus one of the king's prized possessions.

When your eyes become gold-plated, check out the rooms opening off the corridor toward the center of the building. Room 43, off the eastern hall, holds a fascinating collection of toys, tools, weapons, and household items that reveal how people lived and artisans worked thousands of years ago. Animal rights activists would be proud to see Room 53, where mummified cats, dogs, birds, and monkeys repose in honor. (Preserve the whales.) On the northern hall, Room 3 is studded with dazzling jewelry from all periods of dynastic history. Room 12, around the corner on the western hallway, holds funerary items from later royal tombs, including an amusing assortment of bushy wigs worn by priests in the Late Period. During the Old Kingdom, servants were buried alive in order to care for the king in the afterlife, but eventually the Egyptians decided that clay figurines were more willing and jovial companions for the deceased.

Other Museums

The Museum of Islamic Art, off Ahmad Maher Sq. at the corner of Port Said and Muhammad Ali St. About 0.5km west of Bab Zuwayla; easily incorporated into a trip to Islamic monuments. From Tahrir Sq., walk east down Tahrir St. all the way to Ahmed Maher Sq. on Port Said St. at the edge of Islamic Cairo. Houses one of the world's finest collections of Islamic art. There's a little of everything here, from carpets, glassware, and metalwork, to wood carvings, calligraphy, and pottery. (Since the exhibits have recently been rearranged, make sure any guide to the museum is current before you invest.) Usually quiet and uncrowded. One of the most interesting exhibits features a collection of ancient Qur'anic scientific and philosophical manuscripts. Open Sat.-Thurs. 9am-4pm, Fri. 9-11:15am and 1:30-4pm. Admission LE3, students LE1.50.

The Mahmud Khalil Museum, 1 Shaykh Marsafy St., Zamalek. Opposite the north gate of Gezira Sporting Club, across the street from the Marriott Hotel. Contains a fantastic collection of European and Islamic art, including works by Monet, Renoir, Van Gogh, Pisarro, Toulouse-Lautrec, Degas, and Rubens, as well as beautiful Chinese jade carvings and Islamic pottery and tiling. Open Sat.-Thurs. 9am-2pm. Admission LE1, students 50pt. Passport or other ID usually required for admission.

The Museum of Modern Art, Gezira St., Zamelek, near the Cairo Opera House. Features Egyptian paintings 1940s-present. Open Sat.-Thurs. 10am-2pm. Admission LE1, students 50pt.

The Mukhtar Museum, just before al-Galaa Bridge, Zamalek (Gezira). Built by Ramses Wissa Wassef and houses the works of Mahmud Mukhtar (1891-1934), one of Egypt's famous sculptors. Open Sat.-Thurs. 9am-1:30pm, Fri. 9-11:30am. Admission LE2, students LE1.

Museum of Egyptian Civilization (tel. 340 62 59), next to the Gezira Museum. Traces Egypt's development through its Pharaonic, Greek, Roman, Coptic, and Islamic periods. Open daily 10am-2pm. Admission 50pt.

Mogamma al-Fenoun (Center of Arts, tel. 340 82 11), on the corner of Maahad as-Swissry St. and July 26 Bridge. Formerly the residence of Aisha Fahmy, today the center has rotating exhibits by Egyptian and foreign artists. Open mid-Sept. thru mid-July Sat.-Thurs. 10am-1:30pm and 10am-2pm. Free.

The Agricultural Museum, at the western end of the October 6 Bridge, Dokki, behind a large garden. Exhibits on Egyptian agriculture. Also on display is the only remaining mummified Apis bull from the Serapium at Saqqara. Open Sat.-Thurs. 8am-2pm, Fri. 10am-noon. Admission LE1.

The Manial Palace Museum (tel. 84 26 68) at the northern edge of Roda Island; the entrance is next to the Cairo Youth Hostel on Sayala St., which leads to Cairo University Bridge. Built by Muhammad Ali in the last century. Visitors have access to the "reception palace," a private mosque, and a small hunting museum with a collection of stuffed birds and other taxodermic treasures. Also has an enthralling collection of Islamic furnishings. Open daily 9am-4pm. Admission LE1.50. Photo privileges LE5.

Entertainment

If a full day of Cairo hasn't conquered or otherwise flattened you, venture out for Cairene nightlife. The daily English-language newspaper, *The Egyptian Gazette,* lists entertainment and events. *Cairo by Night,* a free weekly periodical available in hotels, occasionally has useful information for the diurnally-challenged, and *Cairo Today,* a monthly magazine sold at newsstands, runs articles on attractions in the metropolitan area. *Cairoscope,* a guide to "culture and entertainment" in Cairo, lists foreign films, musical performances, and art exhibits; it's available at newsstands and major hotels.

The **sound and light show** at the Giza Pyramids is overrated, yet overpriced. At 6:30 and 7:30pm, the three Pyramids are illuminated while the story of the ancient pharaohs is narrated by the Sphinx in English, French, German, or Italian (check *Cairo Today* or call 385 28 80 for language schedule). The chagrined Sphinx's expression, if you look at it in just the right light, suggests it wishes it could get the rest of its head shot off. Tickets go on sale at 6pm for a LE10; arrive early. On Monday, Wednesday, Friday, and Saturday nights the performance is in English. Organized tours (from AmEx or the Hilton) cost LE25, but you can easily take a taxi or bus to Giza and save the expense. Occasionally, the Pyramids' theater hosts concerts. For added surrealism, go on foreign language night ("Ich bin der Sphinx!").

Pubs, Clubs, and Other Diversions

The Four Corners, 4 Hasan Sabri St., Zamalek. Hang out with a bizarre mix of expats, Cairo elite, and AUC students. A Western-style complex including 2 restaurants, a bar, and disco. La Piazza, the "informal" restaurant serves skimpy but delicious Italian dishes for LE9-13; Matchpoint, the video bar, has cosmopolitan prices to match its pretensions: LE6 minimum.

Taverne du Champs de Mars, in the Nile Hilton. The heart of Cairo's gay community. A *fin-de-siècle* bar transported brick-by-brick from Belgium, with piano music Thurs.-Tues. 8pm-midnight. High prices: cover LE9, beer LE6. Open daily 11am-2am.

Audio 9, 33 Kasr al-Nil St., 9th floor. Slightly seedy but convenient for Tala'at Harb budgeters. European and Sudanese clientele. Every Friday night is Sweaty Reggae Night. Cover usually LE4-6. Look for posters in Felfela's.

B's Corner (tel. 341 38 70), 22 Taha Hussayn St., Zamalek. Take Hasan Sabri St. north of July 26 St. until you come to a square 3 blocks down, then take the left prong of the fork; it's 100m down the second street, next to the President Hotel. More of a lounge than a dance club. No cover. Open daily 3pm-1am.

El Patio (tel. 340 26 45), off Shagarat ad-Durr St. to the right, 1 block north of July 26th St., Zamalek. An upscale bar favored by foreigners living in Zamalek. The piano, old movie posters, and swinging wooden doors scream John Wayne. New York cheesecake (LE2.50); imported beers (LE8). Open 6pm-12:30am.

Il Capo (tel. 341 38 70), in the same building as B's. A great place for live music. When popular groups play you have to buy at least LE13 worth of food and drink; on other nights LE4 suffices. Most bands are scheduled to begin at 10pm, but as everywhere in Egypt, schedules exist to be ignored. Open 1am-1pm.

Other night-time options include the swank bars, nightclubs, and discos in most of Cairo's luxury hotels. The **Garden Bar** in the Atlas Hotel (tel. 91 83 11), al-Gomhouria St., offers rock music and draws gay men and the expatriate crowd on Thursday and Friday nights 11pm-1am. Drinks are expensive, but there's no cover charge. **Jackie's** (tel. 76 74 44), at the Nile Hilton, is Cairo's most exclusive night spot. Admission is LE20, and proper dress is required (couples only, really; open 10pm-3:30am). You can gamble at **casinos** in the Nile Hilton, Marriott, and Sheraton hotels, where you must show your passport to enter and can throw away foreign currency only. Enjoy a drink while overlooking the Nile and the Cairo skyline from the terrace on the top floor of the **Shepherd's Hotel** (small bar open daily 1pm-midnight). The hotel is in Garden City on the corniche, just south of the Kasr al-Nil Bridge. During Ramadan, **As-Sokkareya,** near the as-Salam (Hyatt) Hotel at 61 Abdul-Hamid Badawy St., Heliopolis (take bus #50, 128, or 330), features an Egyptian garden setting with superb singers and musicians, a penny arcade, and fortune tellers. The LE10 entrance fee includes all drinks and a *sheesha* (waterpipe). Try *sahlab,* a yummy concoction of buffalo milk, herbs, spices, raisins, coconut, and nutmeg. (Open 8pm-3am during Ramadan. Call the Hyatt at 245 51 55 to confirm.)

Some major hotels host Egyptian dancing and musical performances in their ethnic restaurants. The **Felafel** restaurant at the Ramses Hilton serves an excellent but expensive *prix-fixe* dinner (LE40), which includes a fabulous folk dancing show by the Hasan Troupe. Call the Ramses Hilton for details (tel. 574 44 00).

One of the best dance companies in Cairo is the Egyptian folk dancing **Rida Troupe,** which performs regularly at the **Balloon Theater** on al-Nil St. in Aguza (tel. 247 74 57 or 347 17 18), at the Zamalek Bridge. The Balloon Theater also hosts plays and concerts by famous Arab singers. Admission ranges from LE4-6. Performances every evening (average price LE10, children LE6). There are also performances at the **Gumhurriya Theater** (tel. 91 99 56) by the **Arabic Music Troupe** and the **Cairo Symphony Orchestra**, usually on Friday evenings, and occasional dance and music concerts at the **Sayyid Darwish Theater**, off Pyramids Rd. on Gamal ad-Din al-Afghani St., Giza. The **Cairo Puppet Theater** (tel. 91 09 54), in Azbakiyya Gardens near Opera Sq., offers nightly performances from October-May. The shows are performed in Arabic, but anyone can understand the overnight campesque musicals. Cairo has a handful of **cinemas** that run foreign-language films, most often *Mystic Pizza*. Check *The Egyptian Gazette* for listings. Ticket prices average LE5. Remember that the Egyptian audience reads the subtitles—they don't give a wet slap about the sound. Try to sit in the least popular part of the theater—usually the rear of the orchestra. Evening performances begin about 9pm.

On Wednesday and Saturday nights at 8:30pm the Mausoleum of al-Ghoury on al-Muizz St., just south of the pedestrian overpass in Islamic Cairo, hosts the **whirling dervishes.** The performance is a traditional religious dance performed by members of the mystical Sufi sect of Islam. Free.

AUC runs the **Wallace Theater,** featuring two plays per year performed in English in the New Campus on Muhammad Mahmud St. The university also hosts a variety of concerts from jazz to chamber music. (Open fall-spring.) Check bulletin boards on the buildings of the Old Campus. The **American Cultural Center,** 4 Ahmed Ragheb St., sometimes screens free films on Friday nights. The **British Council,** 192 al-Nil St. (tel. 345 32 81) has a large library and also sponsors performances by visiting British theatrical and musical groups. The **Netherlands Institute,** 1 Mahmud Azmi St. (tel. 340 00 76), Zamalek, offers English-language lectures about Egypt on Thursdays at 5pm September-June.

During Ramadan, nightlife assumes an entirely new dimension in Cairo. Cairenes take to the streets around al-Azhar and Hussayn Sq. and along the corniche and the bridges across the Nile. Starting at 10-11pm, there are street theater performances, magic shows, and general pandemonium. All cinemas have performances starting at midnight.

You may opt, as many Egyptians do, to spend a more relaxing evening having a drink at one of the cafés that line the Nile. Consider lazing on the river itself by hiring a swallow-winged *felucca* (sailboat) to take you out. Most *feluccas* can accommodate up to eight people comfortably. The more passengers, the cheaper, but you still have to bargain for the best rate. *Feluccas* for hire dock just south of the Kasr al-Nil Bridge on the east bank. Across the corniche (on the water) from the Meridien Hotel, boats sail for LE5-6 during the day, LE7 in the evening. The agency across the corniche from the Shepherd's Hotel hires out boats around the clock (LE5-10 during the day, LE12-15 at night).

Near Cairo

The Delta

The loveliest place in the immediate vicinity of Cairo lies 15km north at the **Nile barrages.** Decorated vividly with turrets and arches, the barrages were constructed in the first quarter of the 19th century in an attempt to regulate the flow of water into the Delta. Avoid visiting on a Friday when the crowds burgeon into absurdity. Small bridges connect the islets next to the barrages, where the Nile reaches one of its widest points.

Qanater marks the official beginning of the Delta. Bus #214 sputters to Qanater from the front of the Nile Hilton at Tahrir Sq. A small passenger ferry runs along the Nile between Cairo and Qanater hourly 6am-6pm (LE2, 2 hrs.). Catch the ferry on the west bank of the corniche, north of the Ramses Hilton and in front of the Television Building. It's also possible to hire a *felucca,* but the journey to Qanater from Cairo voraciously consumes much of your time, as the mast of the boat must be lowered for each bridge. Farther north lie the flat agricultural lands of the **Nile Delta,** "the pharaoh's breadbasket," lauded as the most fertile agricultural region in the world.

It was primarily in Lower Egypt that the Old Kingdom thrived, and many looming monuments were erected in the Delta throughout the pharaonic period. Due to the looseness of the soil, the deployment of irrigation canals, and the natural fanning out of the river, almost all of the major pharaonic sites in the Delta have been lost. Southeast of **Zagazig** (80 min. from Cairo via any train bound for Port Said or 1 hr. by service taxi; both LE2.50), between Mustafa Kamal St. and Bulbais Rd., are the ruins of **Bubastis,** one of Egypt's oldest cities and the most accessible of the Delta's pharaonic sites. The name means "house of Bastet" and refers to the goddess of felinity to whom the main temple was dedicated. The festivals here in honor of the cat goddess attracted over 700,000 devotees who would dance and sing, make sacrifices to the goddess, and consume egregious quantities of food and wine. Herodotus marvelled that "more wine is drunk at this feast than in the whole year beside." He described the temple as the most pleasurable to gaze upon in all of the Delta's pharaonic sites. Today it is not, as the sanctuary has become a scattered pile of kitty litter.

Two hundred meters down the road, explore the winding underground passages of the **Cat Cemetery,** where numerous celebrated bronze likenesses of Bastet have been unearthed. In Zagazig, the small **Orabi Museum** displays local archeological fins. (Open Sat.-Thurs. 8am-2pm, Fri. 8am-12pm. Admission LE3, students LE1.50, camera privileges LE5.) Lake Manzalik, the largest in the Delta region, lies 15km from the Ras al-Bahr resort area, not far from Zagazig. The region's most worthwhile pharaonic site is located some distance from Cairo in the northeastern corner of the Delta's fertile triangle (4.5 hrs. by *service* taxi; no buses). Just outside of the village of **San al-Hagar,** at the junction of Bahr as-Sughir and Bahr Facus, the ruins of ancient **Tanis** sprawl over an area of about four square kilometers. The site includes a royal necropolis, the foundations of several temples, a small museum, and a pair of sacred lakes. (Museum open daily 8am-2pm; the ruins are accessible at any time. Admission into the site LE8, students LE4.) The ruins of Tanis are impressive, but not quite impressive as the movie *Raiders of the Lost Ark* would have you believe.

Helwan and Ma'adi

Helwan is an unappealing, polluted factory town that possesses a pair of eccentric sights. Take the Metro from downtown to Ain Helwan station (50pt); 25m from the stop stands the **Wax Museum,** replete with stiff portrayals of Egyptian history and assorted executions, disembowelments, and suicides. Some of the victims are immortalized as tasty lollipops available at the gift shop—impress friends at home with your appreciation of Egyptian culture. (Open daily 9am-4pm. Admission LE1.) From the next Metro station (Helwan, 25pt), take a left, and five blocks ahead you'll find the paltry **Japanese Gardens.** Neither authentic nor well-tended, the grounds are at least shady. (Open daily 8am-12am. Admission LE1.)

The Metro towards Helwan also takes you to the upper-class residential area of **Ma'adi,** home to most Americans in Egypt (35pt). On the Fourth of July, the homesick American budgeteer's dream comes true, as the Cairo American Primary and Secondary School hosts a carnival at which over 5000 American citizens consume all the hot dogs, soft drinks, and pot luck food they can pack into their pot bellies. Just bring your American passport and an appetite—it's all included in your taxes.

Cairo Environs

If you want to break away from the brat pack of lemming-like, camel-obsessed tourists heading for Luxor, linger around Cairo for more than a few days. The Pyramids at Giza and Saqqara, the Coptic monasteries of Wadi al-Natrun, and the sprawling oasis of Fayyum are all worthwhile expeditions.

Giza and the Pyramids الجيزة و الاهرامات

From a distance they look like the world's largest paperweights, but as you approach, you are seized by (in Napoléon's words) "a sort of stupefaction, almost overwhelming in its effect." The last of the seven wonders of the ancient world still extant, the Pyramids at Giza stand as awe-inspiring monuments to human achievement.

Since everyone likes to see awe-inspiring monuments to human achievement, nowhere else is Egypt's ravenous tourist industry so rabid. For a solid mile, souvenir shops, alabaster factories, and papyrus museums conspire to pawn off ancient artifacts made while-u-wait. At the foot of the Pyramids, a sizable army of hustlers will hound you: Bedouin imposters rent camels and Arabian race horses, hawkers peddle tourist dreck at inflated prices, and self-appointed guides ("Pyramid—very big") approach you at every turn. Don't let the racket deter you from spending at least a few hours gaping at the Pyramids.

Practical Information

To get to the Pyramids (*al-Ahramat* or *al-Ahram*), take **bus** #8 (25pt) from the front of the Mugama Building at Tahrir Sq. in Cairo. The last stop on bus #8 leaves you near the entrance to the Pyramids. Get off the more crowded bus #900 as it turns off to the right just before the Mena House Hotel. Don't jump off as soon as you see the Pyramids—they're farther than they look. For more comfortable transport, take **minibus** #83, which leaves from the station just to the right of the Mugama Building (35pt). **Taxis** should cost LE4 from downtown Cairo. The Giza Tourist Office (tel. 85 02 59) is located on Pyramids Rd., next to the police station just before the stables. (Open daily 8am-5pm.)

Go early to beat the crowds. Shoes with traction are neat little life-saving contraptions if you plan to do any internal climbing. The best time to visit is after the Pyramids' official closing time of 5pm, when you'll have free access to the entire site without tourists and hustlers. If you want to attend the sound and light show *gratis*, sit with the hundreds of Egyptians and watch from anywhere on the site. Shining colored lights on the Pyramids to make them look dramatic is like using mirrors to make them look big. The shows are performed twice nightly, at 6:30 and 7:30pm. Call 38 52 880 or check *Cairo Today* to find out when the Sphinx will gab in the language of your preference. Your ticket will admit you to the Pyramids and Sphinx complexes. (Open daily 6:30am-8pm; winter daily 7am-10pm. Pyramids open daily 8am-5pm. Admission to the complex LE10, students LE5. Admission inside the pyramids LE10, students LE5.) You must buy a separate ticket for the Cheops Solar Boat Museum. (Open daily 8am-4:30pm. Admission LE10, students LE5.)

Renting a horse can be fun, although many of the overworked and underfed animals have one hoof in the glue factory. It's best to go in the morning or at dusk, when the weather is cool and the crowd bearable. For longer rides and more reliable beasts, walk down beyond the Sphinx and head to the right after the Sound and Light Auditorium. You'll come to a row of reputable establishments, two of which are **AA Stables** and **S.A. Stables** (tel. 85 02 59). Although the tourist police post prices for an hour ride as LE6 for a horse and LE5 for a camel, the going price is closer to LE10 for a guided trek on either. LE6 is a fair price without a guide, but one should be a confident rider; some mounts only obey hieroglyphics and may gallop off into the desert ignoring riders' hysterical screams. A tourist police station is adjacent to the ticket office. The Pyramids Rest House, a fancy little establishment with a LE4.50 minimum charge, and the Sphinx Rest House have public bathrooms.

Accommodations, Food, and Entertainment

If you enjoy crashing amidst sun and sand, you can stay at Salome Campground, which has fairly clean toilets and showers and a small restaurant for LE3 a night. Go down Pyramids Rd. until you come to the Maroutiya Canal; take a left and follow the signs. For food, the options are bleak, except the **Pyramids Shish Kebab Restaurant** (tel. 385 10 78), 2 blocks from the Sphinx Rest House along the main road (shish kebab LE8, open daily 11am-2am) and **La Rose**, 58 Maroutiya Canal St. (tel. 85 57 12), about 3km from the intersection with Pyramids Rd., towards Kardassa. A Cheops-sized meal here, with free seconds, includes salad, rice, veggies, stuffed grape-leaves, *kufte, taamaya, samoussa*, chicken with kebab and fries, and fried dough balls for dessert. Meet mystically-named proprietor Ala'adin. (Open daily 11am-2am.)

As far as entertainment goes, it's pretty much the pyramids or bust. The **nightclubs** on Pyramids Road are notoriously sleazy, featuring drunk men heckling scantily clad belly dancers. The expensive bars at the **Mena House Hotel** have live music in an elegant setting. If it's solitude you seek, the stables next to the Sphinx can arrange overnight expeditions through the dunes. (See Practical Information.)

Sights

The three main pyramids at Giza were built for three pharaohs: Cheops (or Khufu), Chephren (or Khafre), and Menkaure (or Mycerinus). This father-son-grandson trio reigned during the 26th century BCE. Each of the pyramids was once attached to its own funerary complex, complete with riverside pavilion and mortuary temple, in which the pharaoh's cult was supposed to continue for eternity. A long, narrow causeway linked the mortuary temple with the neighboring waters of the Nile, culminating in the valley temple through which the complex proper was reached. The mummy of the deceased ruler was conveyed by boat across the Nile, carried up the causeway in a solemn procession, and deposited in its sacred resting place at the heart of the giant pyramid.

The **Pyramid of Cheops** is the first pyramid you'll encounter upon entering the site. It initially stood 146m high upon completion, and over the course of four-and-a-half millenia its height has decreased by only 3m. The total weight of Cheops is estimated at 6,000,000 tons. To appreciate its mass, crawl through the narrow passageways inside that lead to the king's chamber in the center of the pyramid. (This arduous climb is not for the faint-hearted or the claustrophobic.) The highlight of the expedition is the tall, narrow gallery with 9m walls formed from 14 massive slabs of granite. The king's tomb chamber is a large, square room containing only the cracked bottom half of the sarcophagus. Its most novel feature is the impressive collection of 19th-century graffiti. The passageway to the queen's chamber, which starts at the bottom of the gallery, is closed off by an iron grille.

Outside, walk around to the southern face of the structure to see the **Solar Boat,** one of the oldest boats in existence, unearthed near the pyramid base in 1954. This vessel most likely transported Cheops across the Nile from the "land of the living" on the east bank to his resting place in the "land of the dead"; the boat was buried close to the pharaoh so he could use it to cross the ocean of death beneath the earth. A plywood and glass structure resembling a Modernist ski lodge houses the boat today (admission LE7. What a bargoon.). On the east side of the pyramid are the meager remains of the **Mortuary Temple of Cheops.** Besides a few sockets for columns, only the foundations remain.

The middle member of the trio, the **Pyramid of Chephren,** is only 3m shorter than the pyramid of Cheops. Portions of the limestone casing that originally covered the monument still sheathe its apex, making it Egypt's most splendid pyramid. The interior of Chephren's tomb is the finest of the three at Giza. The burial chamber contains Chephren's sarcophagus and more 19th century graffiti. The relatively spacious passageways make Chephren the coolest and most comfortable for exploring.

After Mama and Papa comes the Baby **Pyramid of Mycerinus,** comparatively small at only 66m. Its burial chamber once contained a magnificent basalt sarcophagus covered with ornate decorative carving. Unfortunately, this treasure was lost at sea en route to the British Museum during the early 19th century. The smaller pyramids surrounding the Big Three belonged to the pharaoh's wives and children. Outside, at the northeast corner of the temple, lie the quarried remains of the **Mortuary Temple of Mycerinus.** Farther away, the ruins of the unexcavated Valley Temple of Mycerinus are swathed by a blanket of sand.

The **Sphinx** crouches downhill to the northeast of the Pyramid of Cheops. Hewn almost entirely from living rock, the poised figure is 80m long and gazes out over the world from a height of 22m. Known as *Abu'l-Hul* (father of terror), the mysterious feline man wears an inscrutable smile. Opinion is divided over the Sphinx's identity. Some believe the face is a portrait of Chephren, whose pyramid lies behind it to the northeast, while others maintain that the features represent the local deity Horan. Its expression and attitude are clearly discernable, though the soft limestone from which it was sculpted is greatly weathered. Used for target practice during the Turkish occupation, the Sphinx lost not only its nose but also its beard (the latter is now in the British Museum). In addition, in 1988 a large chip fell from its shoulder. A pharaonic nose-job has been prescribed to restore the features and prevent the rest of the face from sliding off; the Sphinx complex is currently open but surrounded by scaffolding.

At the foot of the Sphinx, just around the corner to the south, is the **Valley Temple of Chephren,** discovered in 1853. Sixteen great pillars support the roof of this edifice, soaring to a height of 15m each. Your guide will inevitably hold a candle to the fine grain of the stone; *baksheesh* is expected in return.

The minor **Pyramid of Abu Ruash,** 7km north of the Giza pyramids, is accessible by foot or hired animal. *Service* taxis and minibuses also run to the nearby village of Abu Ruash from Giza Square. The pyramid itself is a 9m-high mound.

Near Giza: Kardassa

On the road from Cairo to Giza, a turn-off to the right at the second canal before the pyramids leads to the village of **Kardassa,** where the Western Desert and camel road to Libya commence. The village has become a popular tourist destination owing to its variety of local crafts. Much of what appears in Cairo's tourist shops is made in Kardassa. The main products of the village are wool and cotton scarves, *galabiyas* (LE20-30), rugs, and Bedouin weavings. The shops are in a sand lot across the canal from the village; the artisans' workshops are usually in the back of the store or the side alleys off the main commercial drag. Unfortunately, the influx of tourists to Kardassa has heavily inflated prices.

Taxis from Giza Sq. to Kardassa cost LE6. Frequent minibuses run to Kardassa from Giza Sq. (35 pt), as well as to the turn-off from Pyramids Rd. (25pt).

Saqqara صقارة

It took clout to end up here—only the pharaohs, aristocrats, and a few dozen mummified Apis bulls are interred at Saqqara. The city boasts the world's oldest pyramid—dating from 2700 BCE—along with the burial ground of the pharaohs who ruled at nearby Memphis. Although not quite as polished as their later cousins at Giza, Saqqara's stepped pyramids have an equally captivating visage. Situated squarely in the Libyan desert, with nothing but sand in every direction, they are less frequented by tourists.

Saqqara consists of five different archeological sites scatted over a large area. The primary destination for most visitors is **North Saqqara,** site of the funerary complex and the great Step Pyramid of Zoser I. The three pyramids of **Abu Sir** lie 6km north of North Saqqara, only a few kilometers from the tiny village of Abu Sir. The two pyramids and the funerary complex of **South Saqqara** are about 4km south of North Saqqara. The historically significant but scanty ruins of the ancient city of **Memphis** are farther from the necropolis of Saqqara, located next to the Nile just south of the village of Mit-Rahine.

Get a very early start—it takes time to travel around the sites at Saqqara. The summer afternoon sun can be immobilizing, so be sure to bring plenty of water. Wear a hat, bring your own food, and make sure you're wearing good shoes. Lighting inside some of the tombs is poor—a flashlight (which you can either bring along or rent for LE1) will enlighten your expedition.

Practical Information

The exuberant and energetic Mr. Salah Muhammad offers a minibus trip to Saqqara, Memphis, Giza, and al-Harania (a delightful rug-weaving museum) under the name "Luxor Tours" (LE15). Bring your own information about the sites, for Salah is a moonlighting accountant, not a tour guide. To arrange a tour, call him between 1 and 5pm at 76 85 37 or look for his posters at budget hotels.

If you choose to say *salaam* to Salah's services, begin your journey at the ruins of **North Saqqara.** Short of hiring a taxi, there's really no simple way to get here. The cheapest way is to take a minibus from Giza Sq. to the village of Abu Sir (35pt). From Abu Sir, the 3km walk to the entrance takes between 30 minutes and an hour, depending on how fast you walk in sand. Walk south (to the left as you arrive) along the canal just before the village and keep following the dirt road by the canal until you reach the paved road. Turn right at the paved road, and it's 200m to the site entrance. Alternatively, you can hire a **pickup truck** at the canal in Abu Sir (about 50pt per person) to take a group to the site. The pyramids of Abu Sir are visible from those of North Saqqara; either hoist yourself onto one of the horses or camels at the stable next door to the ticket office (LE10-20) or put on your shades and start walking (about half an hour).

All the sites are officially open 7am-5pm, but you can always view the monuments from the outside. Make the pyramids of Abu Sir your lowest priority, as they're hollow inside. Admission to North Saqqara is LE10, students LE5, camera privileges LE5. The ticket is good for all Saqqara sites, though unnecessary for Abu Sir. Bring *baksheesh.* A cautionary note for women: ancient stones evidently make cold company, and the caretakers of these monuments can be overly friendly.

Sights

North Saqqara

Saqqara's largest edifice is the mountainous **Step Pyramid** built by Imhotep, chief architect to the Pharaoh Zoser, in about 2650 BCE. This was the first monumental tomb and the inspiration for Egypt's many subsequent architectural wonders. Like most pharaonic structures, the Step Pyramid was built as part of a funerary complex. Most experts believe the tomb began as a *mastaba* (literally "bench," the simple flat brick mortuary structure of the Old Kingdom) and was augmented five separated times until the present six-level building was completed.

Enter the Step Pyramid complex from the eastern side of the limestone enclosure wall. The paneled barrier was designed to resemble the mud-brickwork which graced the fortifications surrounding the cities and palaces of the period. Striding into the complex itself, you pass through a hallway with a stone ceiling that mimics the palm log rafters of earlier wooden structures. Two fixed stone panels, carved to resemble a massive wooden doorway, open off the hallway onto an impressive 40-pillared colonade. The walls and roof have been restored as part of a lifetime project of reconstruction undertaken by the French archeologist Jean-Phillipe Lauer. The Egyptian pillars, ridged to create the stylized effect of a bundle of papyrus stems, are probably the world's first stone columns. This imposing corridor culminates in the **Hypostyle Hall,** a fledgling version of the great hallways found at Karnak and Abydos.

Up the steps to the right of the pit and over the enclosure wall looms the massive **Pyramid of Unis,** the last pharaoh of the 5th dynasty. You can go spelunking in the interior burial chamber of the crumbled monument; find a guard if the door is locked. Although the passage into the tomb is uncomfortably low at points, the central burial chamber is commodious. The ancient carvings on its alabaster walls, known as the **Pyramid Texts,** were discovered in 1881 and constitute the earliest known example of decorative hieroglyphic writing on the walls of a pharaonic tomb chamber. Carefully etched into the shiny alabaster, the well-preserved texts record hymns, prayers, and articles necessary for the afterlife. On the western edge of the main chamber sits the open basalt sarcophagus of Unis, with its lid on the ground beside it.

Opposite the south face of the Pyramid of Unis, an inauspicious shack covers the shaft leading to three of Egypt's deepest burial chambers, the **Persian Tombs** of Psamtik, Zenhebu, and Peleese. A dizzying spiral staircase drills 25m into the ground, terminating in three vaulted burial chambers linked by narrow passageways. According to the ancient inscriptions, Zenhebu was a famous admiral and Psamtik a chief physician of the pharaoh's court. Entrance to these nicely illuminated tombs requires some *baksheesh*, more if you're taking photographs.

To the southwest of the Pyramid of Unis, a 100m path leads into the desert to the unfinished **Pyramid of Sekhemkhet,** a paltry pile of rubble unearthed in 1951. The pyramid was originally intended as a replica of its giant neighbor, the Pyramid of Zoser, but construction was abandoned after its walls reached a height of only 3m. East of the Pyramid of Unis a smooth, narrow causeway runs down the hill. Nearly 1km long, this causeway originally linked the Pyramid of Unis with a lower valley temple at the banks of the river. Strewn by the sides of the causeway are the **Old Kingdom Tombs.** Over 250 *mastabas* have been excavated here, though only a few of the larger and best preserved are open to the public.

The 6th-dynasty **Mastaba of Idut,** adjacent to the southern enclosure wall of Zoser's funerary complex and just east of the Pyramid of Unis, includes 10 chambers. Nearby are the **Mastaba of Mehu** and the **Mastaba of Queen Nebet.** South of the causeway is a pair of enormous **Boat Pits,** side by side 100m east of the Pyramids of Unis. There is some speculation as to whether the pits were intended to house the royal barques (as at Giza) or whether these finely sculpted trenches of stone were meant as simple representations of boats.

At the end of the causeway, head 150m uphill and southward to the **Monastery of St. Jeremiah.** Built in the 5th century CE, the monastery has been repeatedly pillaged, starting in 950 when invading Arabs ransacked the entire edifice. Recently, the Antiquities Service moved all decorative carvings and paintings to the Coptic Museum in Cairo, allowing the despoiled shell to be overrun by advancing sand dunes. What's left of the monastery is best reached by car or horse; it's usually much too hot to walk.

Head back up to the causeway and around the corner to the Great South Court of Zoser's mortuary complex. In the northern end, at the base of the Step Pyramid, lie the remains of the *mastaba* that was the seed of Zoser's tomb. In the center of the pyramid's south face is an entrance to the tomb's interior. This long passageway, the **Saite Gallery,** affords stunning views of the interior frame. (Entrance requires special permission from the Antiquities Service; ask at the Egyptian Museum.) To the east, the **Heb-Sed Court** runs the length of one side of the courtyard. The building is a copy of the pavilion employed at the Heb-Sed Jubilee, a festival during which the king demonstrated his vigor by completing a ritual race around the courtyard. The Heb-Sed Court in the funerary complex and the panels inside the pyramid that depict Zoser running the race were meant to ensure his eternal rejuvenation.

The more substantial **House of the South** stands next door, on the eastern side of Zoser's pyramid. Inside, the walls are inscribed with ancient tourist graffiti left by a starving Egyptian artist in the 12th century BCE. The messages, expressing admiration for King Zoser, were hastily splashed onto the walls with dark paint, scrawled in a late cursive style of hieroglyphics. Heading north, you'll come to the **House of the North.** Nearby, directly in front of the Step Pyramid's northern face, is the most haunting spectacle at Saqqara, the **Statue of King Zoser.** In a slanted stone hut pierced by two tiny apertures, the pharaoh stares fixedly at you. This small structure, known as the **Sardab,** was designed to enable the spirit of the pharaoh to communicate with the outside world. The striking figure is a plaster copy of the original, which has been moved to the Egyptian Museum in Cairo.

If you have a car, you can return to the entrance of Zoser's mortuary complex and drive around to the western portion of North Saqqara. Or you can hike five minutes across the desert to reach the **Tomb of Akhti-Hotep and Ptah-Hotep,** halfway between the Step Pyramid and the canopied Rest House. This remarkable double tomb housed the bodies of a father and son, inspectors of the priests who served the pyramids. The pair designed their own mortuary complex. The structure, which contains some of Saqqara's finest reliefs, is accessible through a long corridor, culminating in the burial chamber of Akhti-Hotep.

West of the Tomb of Akhti-Hotep and Ptah-Hotep is a shady **Rest House** with a bathroom and a small cafeteria. Farther along the highway, where the road jogs sharply to the west, an area has been cleared to reveal badly weathered **Greek statues** said to represent Homer (at the center), Pindar (at the west end), and Plato (at the east end).

The **Serapeum,** a few hundred meters west of the Rest House at the terminus of the main road, was discovered in 1854. An eerie subway system with tiny lanterns, this surrealistic mausoleum houses the **Tombs of the Apis Bulls,** where 25 sacred oxen were embalmed and placed in enormous sarcophagi of solid granite. Only one of the bulls was discovered (the rest had been stolen or roasted) and is now displayed in Cairo's Agricultural Museum.

The Serapeum is the sole legacy of a mysterious bull-worshipping cult that apparently thrived during the New Kingdom. Work on the main portion of the underground complex began in the 7th century BCE with the efforts of Psamtik I and continued through the Ptolemaic era, though much older tombs adjoin this central set of chambers. In the oldest portion of the Serapeum, two large gold-plated sarcophagi and several canopic jars containing human heads were found, as well as the undisturbed footprints of the priests who had laid the sacred animals to rest 3000 years earlier. (This portion of the tomb is no longer accessible.) Recessed tomb chambers flank the main corridor on both sides, each containing a monolithic sarcophagus. It's difficult to imagine these mammoth coffins being transported to the confines of the cave—their average weight is 65 tons. At the final tomb along the passageway stands the largest sarcophagus of all, hewn from a single piece of black granite.

The **Tomb of Ti,** 300m north of the Serapeum, was excavated in 1865 and has since been one of the primary sources of knowledge about both daily and ceremonial life during the 5th dynasty (toward the end of the Old Kingdom, 25th century BCE). Serving under three pharaohs, Ti must have been quite a power-monger—his titles included Overseer of the Pyramids and Sun Temples at Abu Sir, Superintendent of Works, Scribe of the Court, Royal Counselor, Editor, Royal Tea Brewer, and even Lord of Secrets. His rank was considered so lofty that he was allowed to marry a princess, Nefer-Hotep, and his children were considered royalty. In the tomb paintings, the children wear braided hairpieces, which marked them as contenders for the throne.

Although now entirely buried in sand, an **Avenue of Sphinxes** once ran the full width of the site, commencing near the Tomb of Ti, paving a straight course east past the Step Pyramid complex and ending at the river's edge near the **Pyramid of Titi.** This weathered pyramid can now be reached by following the east-west highway past the Rest House to the fork and then heading a short distance north. The interior of Titi's tomb has several interesting sacred inscriptions, but it's usually closed to the public. The 30 rooms comprising the magnificent **Tomb of Mereruka**, just next door to the Pyramid of Titi, are open. The naturalistic portrayal of wildlife found inside the Tomb of Mereruka has enabled scientists to learn a great deal about ancient Egyptian fauna. Various species of fish can be differentiated thanks to the minutely detailed work of the artists.

Farther east is the neighboring **Tomb of Ankhma-Hor.** Though the decorations are relatively sparse, there are several representations of medical operations, including a circumcision and toe surgery. One noted Egyptologist has asserted that the 6th dynasty tendency to depict funerary scenes indicates a growing pessimism among Egyptians about the afterlife as the Old Kingdom went into its final decline.

South Saqqara

The most inter(est)ing funerary monument at South Saqqara is the **Tomb of Shepseskaf** (popularly known as Mastabat Faraun), an enormous stone structure shaped like a sarcophagus and capped with a rounded lid. Though Shepseskaf, son of Mycerinus (whose pyramid stands at Giza), reigned for only three or four years, his brief stint on the throne was long enough to qualify him for a grand tomb. Originally covering 7000 square meters, the Mastabat Faraun is neither a true *mastaba* nor a pyramid. The interior consists of long passageways and a burial chamber containing fragments of a huge sandstone sarcophagus. Ask a guard to admit you.

Abu Sir ابـو صيـر

The pyramids of Abu Sir are isolated in the Eastern Desert just north of Saqqara. You can enjoy them without the camera-clicking clowns, since no tour buses make it here. The pyramids (6km from North Saqqara and 2.5km from the village of Abu Sir) are accessible only by foot or on beast.

The **Pyramid of Neferirkare,** the most imposing of the three main pyramids, stands tall at 68m. This structure originally had a stone facing like its neighbors at Giza, but the casing has completely deteriorated and the exterior now resembles a step pyramid. Nevertheless, the Pyramid of Neferirkare is one of the best preserved monuments in the Saqqara area. The **Pyramid of Niuserre** is the youngest of the trio and yet the most dilapidated. It is possible to enter the **Pyramid of Sahure,** the northernmost member of the group, on its north face. One of the custodians at the site will show you the entrance, which is about 0.5m high and 2m long and requires you to worm your way along the sand floor. The small chamber inside served as the pharaoh's tomb. More pyramids are visible from here than from any other site in the country. If you intend to walk on to the village of Abu Sir, have the guards point out the route.

If you are traveling by animal between Abu Sir and Giza, have your guide stop off on the way at the 5th-dynasty **Sun Temple of Abu Surab,** about 1.5km north of the Pyramid of Sahure. Located on the fringe of cultivated fields, the temple was built by King Niuserre in honor of the sun god Ra; it features an impressive alter constructed from five massive blocks of alabaster. A horse or camel ride from Zoser's pyramid in North Saqqara costs LE10.

Memphis ممفيس

As late as the 13th century, Arab historians wrote with awe about the remnants of the Old Kingdom capital at Memphis. The brick houses of this city of 500,000 inhabitants had melted into mud, but many of the stone monuments were not destroyed until much later, when they were pilfered for use in construction in Cairo. Only the ancient canal responsible for the lush vegetation and a few exhibits housed in the modern **museum** in the village of **Mit-Rahine** remain. Near the museum is the famous alabaster sphinx, which probably stood at the south entrance of the Temple of Ptah. (Museum open 8:30am-4pm. Admission LE10, students LE5. Photo privileges LE10.) The only reasonable way to get to Memphis from either Saqqara of Abu Sir is by rental car; hitchhiking, as always, is potentially dangerous, especially for women.

Wadi al-Natrun وادى النطرون

If the craziness of downtown Cairo made you think that all of Egypt is a circus, come to Wadi al-Natrun—the quiet surroundings and kind-hearted people restore tranquility to even the most shattered of nerves. For the past 1500 years, the 50 monasteries of Wadi al-Natrun have been the backbone of the Coptic community in Egypt. The four that stand today are impressive relics that are also still functional, serving the spiritual needs of Egypt's orthodox Christian population.

The Orthodox Copts introduced the tradition of monasticism; the first Christian monastery was established in Egypt's Eastern Desert by St. Anthony the Great (250-355 CE). In 330, one of Anthony's disciples (St. Maccarius) began monastic life in Wadi al-Natrun. In the 1980s, Coptic monasticism again came into vogue, and new rooms were added to accommodate the novice ascetics living in the Natrun valley. The majority of modern monks are young, college-educated Egyptians.

The monks begin their day in church at 3am. Amid billows of incense, wide-eyed icons, and flickering candlelight, they sing psalms and cantillate the Coptic liturgy for six hours. The service is punctuated by entrancing triangle and cymbal music. (Arrive before 9am to attend the service.) The monks are swathed head to toe in black, indicating that they are symbolically dead—an honored status in this community. When initiated, a new monk "dies" from the former self and the world of corporeal desires. The monks also wear a black hood, said to symbolize the "helmet of salvation" (Ephesians 76), upon which 13 crosses are embroidered; the 12 on the sides represent Christ's apostles and the 13th on the back symbolizes Christ brought to mind. For more information about the monasteries, Evelyn White's *The Monasteries of the Wadi'n Natrun* (1932) tells all.

Practical Information

Just about the only way to reach Wadi al-Natrun from Cairo is by a blue **bus** which leaves from the station behind the Egyptian Museum, north of Tahrir Sq. (LE5, 2 hrs., runs hourly 6:30am-6:30pm, except at 11:30am and 2:30pm). It's unnecessary and usually impossible to purchase tickets in advance; your money will be collected after you board the bus. Buses returning to Cairo or continuing to Alexandria stop at the Wadi al-Natrun Rest House frequently during the day. It may also be possible to rely upon the kindness of pilgrims—Copts flock here by the busload and are often willing to pick up physical or spiritual stragglers. From the Rest House you can hire a **taxi** for the trip to the monasteries (one-way about LE4). Start your journey early if you plan to return to Cairo or Alexandria in the evening. There are no places to stay in Wadi al-Natrun town.

Sights

The General Introduction contains a brief explanation of Coptic Christianity as well as a description of the main features of a Coptic church. When touring the Coptic monasteries, remember that modest attire is the rule—no shorts or sleeveless shirts.

Dayr Anba Bishoi (the Monastery of St. Bishoi), the largest of the four monasteries, is the most accessible to visitors. Fifteen kilometers from the Rest House and 500m from Dayr as-Suryan, this monastery is open daily 8am-5pm (6pm in summer). There are seven churches in the monastery: the Church of St. Bishoi, the Church of St. Iskhiron and the Church of the Holy Virgin (both located within the Church of St. Bishoi), the Church of St. George, the Church of St. Michael, and the recently restored Church of Marcorious and Church of St. Mary. The Church of St. Bishoi has three *haikals* and is part of the most ancient section of the monastery, dating from the 4th century. It was rebuilt in 444 after being sacked by nomads and now contains the remains of St. Bishoi, who is still believed to perform miracles for the faithful. Set in the floor at the western end of the church is the *lakan* (marble basin), which is used in the Holy Thursday Rite of the Foot-Washing. The church has undergone several restorations and was completely redecorated in 1957. The entrance to the keep of the monastery is on the first story through a drawbridge resting on the roof of the gatehouse.

Dayr as-Suryan (the Monastery of the Syrians), named for the Syrian monks who once inhabited it, lies 100m northwest of the Monastery of St. Bishoi and is easy to reach. (Open 9am-3:30pm, 5:30pm in summer.) The monastery was established when a group of monks broke away from the Monastery of St. Bishoi following a 6th-century theological dispute about the nature of the Mother of God. When the dispute ended, this alternative monastery no longer had a purpose. In the beginning of the 8th century it was purchased by a Syrian merchant for use by Syrian monks, the first of whom arrived at the beginning of the 9th century. The monastery was prominent throughout the 10th century and by the 11th housed the largest community in Wadi al-Natrun. The design of Dayr as-Suryan is supposedly based on the model of Noah's Ark.

Be sure to ask to see the **Door of Prophecies** in the Church of the Virgin Mary. The uppermost panels depict disciples, while the panels below depict the seven epochs of the Christian era. The domes of the church are covered with frescoes of the Annunciation, the Nativity, and the Ascension of the Virgin. At the back of the church is a low, dark passageway leading to the private cell of St. Bishoi. The monks will show you an iron staple and chain dangling from the ceiling and explain how St. Bishoi would fasten it to his beard, thereby maintaining himself in a standing position lest he fall asleep during his all-night prayer vigils. The Gaon of Vilna would have been impressed.

Dayr Anba Baramus (The Monastery of the Virgin Mary) is about 4km northwest of the Monastery of St. Bishoi, accessible by taxi from Wadi al-Natrun town. This is the oldest monastery in the al-Natrun valley. Relics of St. Moses and St. Isadore are kept in the first section of the old church. In the old days, the body of St. Moses would shake the hands of passers-by through a small aperture in his casket. For the past 200 years, however, the corpse has not been quite as gregarious and the aperture has been sealed. Tradition holds that a crypt under the altar contains the remains of Maximus and Domidius, sons of the Roman Emperor Valentinus (later St. Valentine) who both dwelt here as monks. The oldest architectural element in the church is the 4th-century column of St. Arsanious.

Dayr Abu Maqar (the Monastery of St. Maccarius) lies roughly 8km southeast of Dayr Anba Bishoi and can be seen to the west of the Cairo-Alexandria desert road (from a point about 129km from Alexandria or 86km from Cairo). The monastery is ordinarily closed. The foundation of Dayr Abu Maqar is associated with the life of St. Maccarius the Great (300-390 CE) and marks the beginning of monastic life in Wadi al-Natrun. It is believed that an angel led St. Maccarius to a rock and ordered him to build a church there. In spite of the monastic community that he founded, St. Maccarius remained a religious hermit throughout his life and lived in a cell connected by a tunnel to a small cave. Virtually no part of the original building remains. In the beginning of the 11th century, the monastery became the refuge of monks fleeing Muslim persecution. During the Middle Ages, the monastery was famous for its library, which remained intact until European marauders discovered the treasures in the 17th century and decided to remove them to European libraries.

Fayyum Oasis واحة فيوم

Fayyum offers a glimpse of a kinder, gentler Egypt that most tourists never see. A little more than 100km from Cairo, Fayyum is a large oasis spreading west and north of the Nile Valley along an offshoot of the river. Although occasionally victim to the same crises of crowding and overnight modernization that plague many parts of Egypt, Fayyum remains primarily agricultural, producing everything from chrysanthemums to straw hats. Those passionate about the pastoral will find an overnight stay blissful; others can easily visit as a daytrip from Cairo or as a stopover on a journey south or north. One warning: the worthwhile spots in Fayyum are scattered outside the main city, so you'll need the better part of a day to enjoy them.

Unlike the other oases of Egypt, Fayyum shares in the life and culture of the Nile and has done so since it was first developed by the rulers of the 12th dynasty (19th and 20th centuries BCE). The Ptolemies, through the construction of canals and irrigation, made the area into a rich province with its capital at Crocodopolis (near the site of modern Fayyum), the center of a cult that worshipped Sebek and other reptilian deities. Roman conquerors used Crocodopolis as a vacation resort as well as one of the primary granaries of the empire. Distanced from the long arm of persecuting authorities, this oasis was an early center of Coptic Christianity; it also sheltered a large population of exiled Jews in the 3rd century CE. The Muslims believed the extensive canals and agriculture to be the work of the biblical Joseph during his stay in Egypt; the main waterway, the Bahr Yusef, is named for the technicolor-bedecked interpreter of dreams. Lake Qaruun to the north is a popular beach resort, and the local government is attempting to develop the rest of the area for tourism.

Orientation and Practical Information

Fayyum is a roughly triangular area, about 90km east to west. The eastern edge is bordered by the Nile. The fresh water **Lake Qaruun,** 40km by 8km, separates the northwest edge from the sandy plateau of the Western Desert. The city of Fayyum is almost in the center and is the transportation hub for the entire oasis. The city runs along the **Bahr Yusef,** which flows west from the Nile; at the center of town the **Bahr Sinnur** leaves the Bahr Yusef at a right angle and flows northward toward the farmlands. The **tourist information office** (tel. 32 25 86, ext. 177), which doubles as the town's **post office,** is a small pre-fab box situated on the Bahr Yusef beside the cafeteria al-Madinat, 50m east of the juncture of the two canals. The four working waterwheels next to the information office are unique to Fayyum and are the oasis's symbol. The **bus station** is located behind the youth hostel about 1km east of the tourist information office. Buses leave for the one-hour trip to Cairo every five minutes until 6:30pm (LE2.50). *Service* taxis also leave here for Giza Sq. in Cairo at all hours of the day and night (LE3-5). Buses and *service* taxis serving Beni Suef, al-Minya, and points south stop at **Hawatem Square;** to reach it, walk to the third bridge over the canal west of the tourist office, turn left, and walk 1km south. The **police emergency number** is 123. The **telephone code** for Fayyum is 084.

Accommodations and Food

You get what you pay for. Clean, non-airconditioned rooms with worry-free bathrooms are found cheapest at the **Palace Hotel** (tel. 32 36 41), centrally located on al-Houreya St. a few blocks west of the tourist information office (singles LE25, doubles with bath LE45, breakfast included). The rooms at the out-of-the-way **Montaza Hotel** (tel. 32 46 33) are substantially cheaper, but can't be accused of being terribly comfortable or clean. Nevertheless, the bathrooms aren't too distressing. Walk north along the left side of Bahr Sinnur from Bahr Yusef. Take a left at the railroad tracks, cross them, continue along the tracks for nine blocks, and take a right onto Ismail al-Midany St. The hotel will be two blocks down on your right. (Singles LE9.65, with shower LE12. Doubles LE10.25, with shower LE19. Breakfast and fans included.) For piaster-pinchers, the **HI youth hostel** (tel. 32 36 82) is 1km east of the tourist office. Turn left at the third bridge past the office or ask for the *Bayt al-Shibab* (LE2 per night, LE4 without HI card; opens at 2pm).

The biblical fourth plague is quaintly reenacted by the swarms of flies infesting the outdoor **Cafeteria al-Madinat** (tel. 32 20 28), beside the four waterwheels in the center of town. Fare is expensive (grilled pigeon, chicken, or kebab LE8-11), but the cafeteria is possibly the only place in town where you can get breakfast (LE3). Open daily 8am-midnight. The **Palace Hotel Restaurant** also offers expensive meals, but with fewer flies and larger variety. If you don't mind the commute, head to **Ain Sileen**, where you'll find several small cafés and many farmer children eager to sell you some of the sweetest mangos you'll ever taste. In town, *kushari*, *fuul*, fresh produce, and juice stands line the street leading south to Hawatem Sq.

Sights

The main attractions within Fayyum city are Egyptians living tourist-free lives. Visitors who weren't ossified by the Islamic architecture in Cairo should visit the Mamluk **Mosque of Khawand Asal-Bay,** about 1km west of the town center along the canal. The restored mosque was named for the favorite concubine of the Sultan Qaytbay. For a quick introduction to the rural life of Fayyum, head north out of town along the Bahr Sinnur. You'll pass farms and boundless green fields, and after about 2km you'll reach the first of seven **waterwheels,** still used in the irrigation system. Unlike Western versions, these great wooden tires are not used to power pumps but are pumps themselves, ingeniously using the flow of the stream to lift the water to a higher level.

The **Ain Sileen** (Sileen Springs) are 9km north of town and the easiest to reach of the area's attractions. Two restaurant-cafés provide a place to sit and imbibe as the streams babble by, but drink from the springs only if you long to battle Dan the Diarrhea Man. The springs feed a small swimming pool crammed with Egyptian children. Foreigners bathing here will create a stir; foreign women will cause widespread apoplexy. (Open 24 hrs. Admission 25pt.)

Fifteen kilometers farther north is **Lake Qaruun,** the south side of which is lined with beaches, casinos, and luxury hotels. Just east of the **Auberge de Fayyum Hotel,** a former royal hunting lodge, **La Promenade** café juts into the water. Waves will slosh on three sides of you as you fork over LE1.50 for a cup of tea. A cheaper option is the **Gabal az-Zina Casino,** 4km west of the Auberge, which is still overpriced but bearable (tea 50pt, coffee 80pt) and next to a beckoning beach. To reach Ain Sileen, Lake Qaruun, or any other place north of Fayyum, walk north from the information stand to the railroad tracks running parallel to Bahr Yusef. Turn left and walk west to the fourth crossing; cross the tracks and you'll be standing in a taxi stand. The pickup trucks shuttle between Fayyum and Ain Sileen (50pt) and Lake Qaruun (LE1). It may be necessary to change taxis at the village of Sanhur to reach the lake; the total price should be the same.

The most prominent historical site in the Fayyum is the **Pyramid of al-Lahun,** near the village of the same name, to the southeast of Fayyum city. To reach the pyramid, take a *service* taxi from Hawatem Sq. to the village and hike 3km to the site. The structure, built by Senusert II of the 12th century, has been robbed of its stone casing but is nonetheless a worthwhile stop for those who just can't get enough.

Nile Valley وادى النيل

> *How doth the little crocodile*
> *Improve his shining tail*
> *And pour the waters of the Nile*
> *On every Golden Scale.*

—Lewis Carroll

Originating in the equatorial high water mark of Lake Victoria, the Nile winds its way through Uganda and the Sudan, pouring into Lake Nasser and Egypt where its banks are home to all but a few of the country's millions. By now the river has surely grown accustomed to the company. Ancient Egyptians likened their country to a lotus of which the Nile was the stem, the Delta the flower, and Fayyum the bud. Teeming cities, lonely necropoli, fertile fields, and desert sands all play significant parts in the drama of the river.

Travelling south from Cairo, it sometimes seems that the longest river in the world is flanked by the planet's longest city. Hardly a meter passes without the appearance of a building and a horde. Also lining the route are relics of ancient glory; pyramids, temples, and roomy burial chambers can be found all along the river's length. From Giza, Memphis, Saqqara, and Cairo, the Nile runs through Middle Egypt, where Minya and Mallawi cope with rapid expansion and where the Pharaohs of the Middle Kingdom left their mark on Beni Hassan and Tel al-Amarna. Further south comes Assyut, Egypt's third largest city, followed by the towering monuments of Luxor and Thebes, and finally, at Egypt's southern border, awesome Abu Simbel. From the first Pharaohs to the modern Egyptians, the country's inhabitants and their conquerors have all tried to leave their mark on the mighty river. The dry desert sun preserves their efforts, bearing witness to their successes and failures.

Remember that despite its spectacular remnants of vanished civilizations, the Nile Valley is far more than an ancient cemetery. Venturing off the tourist trails is a challenge—fewer people speak English and tourist facilities are spotty. But don't make the mistake of spending all your time at the ancient temples—you'll miss out on one of the most exotic and vibrant regions of the world.

Getting Around

In the days of British colonialism, a slow, romantic cruise down the Nile was an aristocratic indulgence. Times haven't changed much. Fares with **Eastmar,** 13 Kasr al-Nil St. in Cairo (tel. 75 72 98/9), start at US$65 per night. Make arrangements with a travel agent before you arrive. *Feluccas* are cheaper and more fun. (See Between Luxor and Aswan section for details.)

The inexpensive **Cairo to Aswan train** stops at several points along the Nile Valley, and is the most comfortable alternative for traveling between Cairo and either Luxor or Aswan. Reserve your seats several days in advance. For shorter trips, trains become more unreliable and less convenient than *service* taxis. (See the Egypt Introduction and Luxor or Aswan sections for more information.) Travel early in the morning, since by mid-afternoon you may have to wait an hour or more before your service taxi fills up with the requisite seven passengers. **Buses** are somewhat safer and cheaper than service taxis but less frequent and slower, except for the zippy Cairo-Luxor express bus. Nile-side navigation is easier than you might think—just follow the river up or down.

In summer, plan to do most of your touring between 6-11am, before temperatures soar above 43 C. From Nov.-May temperatures are much more comfortable, but the madding crowds are not.

Minya and Mallawi المنيا و ملوى

The Upper Egyptian provincial capital of Minya lies along a major canal west of the Nile, halfway between Cairo and Luxor. Already a city of half a million and a university town, the town is striving to add polish to its considerable historical allure. The city of Mallawi, south of Minya, is closer to many of the area's archeological sites.

Exploring the region on your own demands more time and vim than the standard jaunts to the Luxor or Aswan areas, and the sites are not as immediately impressive. But for a chance to see some of the workings of Ancient Egypt from up close without fighting through crowds of cameras and the babble of tour guides, the Minya and Mallawi area can be worth the substantial effort.

Practical Information

Minya lies 250km south of Cairo, on the western side of the Nile; Mallawi is 45km farther south, also on the western bank. The trip from Cairo's Ramses Station by **train** to Minya takes three to four hours. Fare in air-conditioned first-class is LE13.50 (students LE9.50); second-class with air conditioning is LE7.10 for students. *Service* **taxis** leave regularly for Minya from Giza Station (one way LE5.50); the 250km trip takes about four hours, depending on traffic. Service taxis are slightly cheaper (the fare should be a little more than 2pt per kilometer), but less comfortable, especially after a few hours. Unless you're within 150km of Minya (for example, at Beni Suef, Mallawi, or Assyut), your best bet is probably the train. The region can also be reached by **bus** from the Ahmed Hilmi Station, located next to Ramses Station (LE5 to Minya or Mallawi).

Mallawi can be reached by train from Cairo or Luxor—the trip from Cairo takes about five hours—or by local transportation from closer cities such as Minya or Assyut.

You can shuttle between Minya and Mallawi by bus, taxi, or pickup truck, all of which run fairly often and take about an hour. In Minya, go to the station next to the bridge which crosses the canal to the south of the train station; in Mallawi the station is on the western bank just north of the train station. Third-class trains run between the cities, stopping at local villages all day as well. Although they take 15 minutes longer than buses or taxis, trains are cheaper and sometimes less crowded. Fares between the cities run around LE1.

The Minya **train station** lies at the center of town by the canal, about five blocks east of the Nile. **Taxi and bus stations** run along the street parallel to the tracks, crossing over the first bridge about 500m down and lining the western side going south.

The train station in Mallawi is on the eastern bank of the canal across from town. South of the terminal is the taxi station serving points south of Mallawi. Just north of the bank on Essim St., Mallawi's principal road, which runs along the western bank of the canal, is a taxi station serving points north.

The Minya **Tourist Information Office** (tel. 32 01 50) is on the Nile; walk due east from the train station through the town square, then turn left at the corniche and continue for 3 blocks. (Open 8am-2pm and 5-8pm.) There are two **banks** flanking the tourist office (open Sun.-Thurs. 8:30am-2pm, also Sun. 6-9pm, Wed. 5-8pm). The **post office** (open Sat.-Thurs. 8:30am-3pm; no poste restante) and **telephone office** (open 24 hrs.) are located across from the train station. Dial 123 for an **ambulance**; hospitals include **General Hospital** (tel. 32 30 29) and **Mobarah Private Hospital** (tel. 32 30 77). In case of emergency, contact the **Tourist Police** (tel. 32 45 27) or the **Minya police** (tel. 32 31 22 or 32 31 23). The **telephone code** is 086.

Mallawi has no tourist office. The **Bank al-Misr** is across the canal from the train station and about 400m north. (Open Sun.-Thurs. 8:30am-2pm.) To get to the post office, turn down Al-Galah street just south of the bank, walk about 250m until the first wide street, and head left for another half block. (Open Sat.-Thurs. 9am-3pm.)

Accommodations and Food

Hotels in Minya lie along three main thoroughfares: Sa'ad Zaghloul Road, parallel to the railroad tracks; El Gomhoria Street, which begins at the train station exit; and Corniche al-Nil, which is perpendicular to El Gomhoria and runs along the corniche. For comfort and calm it's hard to beat the immaculate **Akhnaton Hotel** (tel. 32 59 18), one block down the corniche from El Gomhoria, where rooms include baths and balconies. Singles LE24, with A/C LE26. Doubles with A/C LE35. Breakfast included. Less elegant but slightly cheaper, the **Beach Hotel** (tel. 32 23 07), on El Gomhoria just before the corniche, offers singles with telephones and A/C for LE20 and similar doubles for LE25. Breakfast included. The **Lotus Hotel** (tel. 32 45 41), a 6-8 minute walk north of the train station on Sa'ad Zaghloul Rd., also offers pleasant rooms and clean bathrooms. Singles LE19.75, LE22.50 with A/C. Doubles LE22.80, LE32.10 with A/C. Or try the friendly **Amoon Hotel** (tel. 32 57 87), across El Gomhoria from the Hammaux Store. Doubles LE10, with bath LE12. For heat and noise, the **Palace Hotel** (tel. 32 40 21) is in the town square on El Gomhoria. A day-glo portrait of Nefertiti greets you in the tiled foyer, and a grand colonial staircase leads up to an airy lobby ringed by dusty rooms. Watch outdoor movies on one side, or stay on the other side and get to sleep early. (Singles LE6.75. Doubles LE11.) The daring or desperate might choose the aptly-named **Hottel Seety** [*sic*] just south of the train station on Sa'ad Zaghloul Rd. Singles LE7. Doubles LE10. Prices negotiable.

Dining options in Minya are less extensive than sleeping options. The **Akhnaten Hotel** and the **Lotus Hotel** both offer safe but unexciting meals for about LE15. The **Savoy Restaurant,** across from the train station, serves full meals in its quiet court-yard for LE4. Along the corniche just north of El Gomhoria is **El Fairouz,** home to aquatic murals and an effigy of St. Nick. Potatoes, rice, shish kebab, and macaroni are the house specialties (meal LE6). Further north, **Aly Baba Restaurant** offers kebab, chicken, and other traditional fare (LE8-10). Also a hot spot for deserts. Those who are strong of stomach might venture to Hussein St., two blocks east of the corniche, where an endless row of eateries offer *shwarma*, shish kebab, and the like. There's a shady tea garden about 1km south of the tourist office that starts serving around 3pm.

Mallawi has only one hotel, the **Samir Amis Hotel and Restaurant** (tel. 65 29 55), on the western bank of the canal just north of the train station (LE5 per person). You may prefer to stay comfortably in Minya and commute to the sites rather than fighting off flies, mosquitos, and noise in Mallawi. If not, and if the hotel is full, have a drink at the restaurant and ask the owner to arrange a room. The restaurant offers filling meals in a convenient location out of the heat (LE4.) For an equally cheap and hearty meal, try the terrific *kufte* at **Restaurant El Huria,** on Bank al-Misr St. just across the bridge from the train station. Top off a local meal with a shot of ice cream or ices served up from machines marked "Expresso" (25pt).

Sights

Getting there may not be half the fun, but it's certainly more than half the trouble. The most easily accessed of the local sights is perhaps the least interesting. The **arche-ological museum** in Mallawi houses artifacts unearthed at the local sites. To get there, follow Al-Galah St. from Bank al-Misr for three and a half blocks. The museum is on the left. (Open Sat.-Tues. and Thurs. 8am-4pm, Fri. 8am-noon. Admission LE3.0, stu-dents LE1.5.) Other local points of interest demand more effort. **Tel al-Amarna** and **Beni Hassan** offer the most striking remains, while **Tuna al-Gabel** and nearby **Her-mopolis** (Ashminein) showcase a touch of the bizarre. Leave at least a half-day for each sight and prepare for energy-sapping desert heat.

You might want to look into hiring a driver from either city. The LE50-90 may well be worth it, especially for groups of three. With a driver, you can fit two or three sights comfortably into a day; otherwise, even one is a stretch. Of the major sights in the re-gion, Beni Hassan is the most easily reached by public transportation.

Beni Hassan بـنـى حـسـن

The rushing waters of an angry mountain stream apparently destroyed the ancient village of Beni Hassan, but the neighboring necropolis, housing 39 pharaonic rock tombs, remains one of the finest Middle Kingdom sites in Upper Egypt. These apart-ments for the afterlife, dating from the 11th and 12th dynasties (2000-1800 BCE), have colorful wall paintings that retain a touch of their original vibrancy, despite the effects of 4 millenia of earthquakes and vandalism.

From either Minya or Mallawi, take a bus or *service* taxi to the sizable village of Abu Qurqas (50pt). Next to the bridge spanning the canal in the center of town, you'll see a sign indicating the road to the antiquities. Cross over the bridge and railroad tracks, then either walk the 3km east to the Nile bank or take a covered pickup truck (25pt). From the government office at the riverside, you can buy a ticket for transpor-tation to the site, including boat fare across the Nile (LE3.75, six or more LE1.25 each) and a minibus from the dock on the far side to the tombs, 500m inland. Admission LE6, students LE3. Permission to take photos costs LE5 per tomb; flashes prohibited. Open 7am-5pm, 7:30am-3:30pm in winter.

Four of the 39 tombs are regularly open to the public; for a little *baksheesh*, several of the other tombs open their doors. The **Tomb of Kheti** (#17; all tombs labelled on the outside) originally contained six lotus columns hewn from solid rock. Two of these graceful supports still adorn the interior. Decorative scenes on the southern wall depict Kheti of the Antelope province (11th dynasty), accompanied by his various servants. These include the essential fan-bearer, sandal-bearer, gnarled dwarf, and others offering sacrifices, such as an entire cow haunch and bread. On the northern wall, women dance in long lines apart from the men. Above them, hunters pursue cattle, though two cows still find the time to copulate. On the rear wall, wrestlers demonstrate nearly 200 different moves; the positions are more than slightly erotic.

Kheti's father, Baket, was responsible for the construction of one of the necropolis's most lavish burial sites. The **Tomb of Baket** (#15) features many themes later repeated in Kheti's tomb. Here, the wrestlers are more colorful and discernible, and gazelles replace cows as the featured animal actors.

The **Tomb of Khumhotep** (#3) was built for one of the province's most prestigious officials, the ruler of the province of Antelope and governor of the Eastern Desert. The base of one 16-sided proto-Doric column remains, and the ceiling is constructed as a triple vault. On the walls, Khumhotep inspects the various activities of his province, including the arrival of the Semitic Amo tribe from Syria. The copious green hieroglyphics outline the history of Khumhotep's family along the bottom of the walls. The tomb features extraordinarily rich colors, especially in an image of Khumhotep with two speared fish on the rear wall.

In the neighboring **Tomb of Amenemhat** (#2), a checkerboard pattern covers the vaulted ceiling, while the upper walls display still more wrestlers and fighting soldiers. But the artwork emoolates the aforementioned no further: the cows are celibate here. Four 16-sided proto-Doric columns remain standing and a badly damaged statue of Amenemhat with his wife and mother rests at the rear of the tomb chamber.

Gabel at-Tair and Tehna al-Gabel جبـل الطيـر و طهنـا الـجبـل

Gabel at-Tair is a monastery above a cave in which Jesus and Mary supposedly hid for three days while fleeing Egypt. Empress Helena, mother of Constantine, had the cloister constructed in 328 CE. The monastery is currently the site of a modern prayer festival; in late May, about 40,000 Copts come to worship at Gabel at-Tair. Tehna al-Gabel is a nearby array of ruins from Old Kingdom and Roman times. The two sites are a workable daytrip from Minya.

To reach **Gabel at-Tair,** take a *service* taxi to the village of Samalut from the first service taxi station south of the train station in Minya (20km, 40pt). Get off at the canal bridge in Samalut and take a pickup truck-taxi east to the Nile; cross the Nile by ferry (LE1). Another pickup can take you from the quarry on the eastern bank up to the monastery. Find someone to open the church (about LE1).

Inside the church are six white columns hewn from the rock. One has been hollowed out and is used for baptisms. (A local legend tells of a mother who hoped to save money by having her first son baptized at the female child rate; she was handed back a daughter to add to her five older ones.) On the walls are 11th-century paintings of Mary, St. George, and a local saint. One fragmented wall from the original monastery has been preserved in a room to the rear of the sanctuary.

You can continue to **Tehna al-Gabel** by walking around the monastery and descending the 100 steps to the dirt road below. Wait there for a pickup going to Tehna (10km, 40pt). At the village, walk about 100m toward the hills, then turn right and walk to the ruins, about 50m. Two columns along the path mark the entrance to the ruined Nero temple, dedicated to the gods Amon and Sobek. Watch out for bats. Continuing counter-clockwise around the ruin, you'll see the remains of a four-faced column consecrated to the god Hatol. Farther along, in a locked room, sacred crocodiles can be seen through a barred window. You can then climb a 4m ledge to view a higher level of the temple. Pass through the ornate doorway guarded by a snake figure into a small cave with reasonably well-preserved carvings of Roman and Egyptian officials from Ptolemaic times. Outside to the right, "This is our home" is chiseled into the rock in Greek, next to the local version of Venus de Milo. Once back on the road, a service taxi can take you to Minya for 50pt.

Hermopolis and Tuna al-Gabel هـرمـوبـوليـس و تـونة الـجـبـل

The appeal of these two sites lies chiefly in the peculiar history and myth that surround them, not in the ruins themselves. In one ancient Egyptian creation story, the sun god sprang from a cosmic egg on the hillock at the ancient capital of Hermopolis, 10km northwest of Mallawi. Twelve kilometers farther west, isolated in an arid plain at the foot of the Western Desert hills, lie the ruins at Tuna al-Gabel. This necropolis features a bizarre collection of funerary remains, including an enormous underground burial area where thousands of sacred baboons and ibises were mummified and interred. Egyptologists suspect that Tuna al-Gabel served as the Hermopolitan cemetery. The two can be visited in a single trip, but unfortunately, public transportation won't take you all the way to either site. You should be able to persuade the driver of a taxi to do the entire route in a half-day excursion from Mallawi for LE20, a good deal for groups. The alternatives—finding a local pickup truck-taxi or walking—will wear you out.

Begin with **Tuna al-Gabel,** and bring an ample supply of water. For 25pt you can take a service taxi or pickup truck from the taxi station on Bank al-Misr St. in Mallawi to the town of Tuna al-Gabel, which is 5km from the necropolis. From here some people try to get a ride with a truck carrying workers to a local quarry (25pt per person). From the turn-off to the quarry, it's a 2km hike to the site—this is where you'll wish you'd hired a private taxi. A truck in the village or your driver from Mallawi may take you out and back for about LE5. The site is isolated; be sure to arrange your return trip in advance. (Open daily 7am-5pm. Admission LE6, students LE3, plus a 25pt toll to enter the desert. Permission to take photos costs LE5 per building.)

Notwithstanding the attendants and a particularly rapacious lot of *baksheesh* seekers, a visit to Tuna al-Gabel can be rewarding. The isolation of the site and the eerie silence of the caves lend drama to the ruins. Most unusual is **as-Sarad-eb** (the Galleries), a series of mysterious underground catacombs where sacred animals were buried during the Ptolemaic and Roman periods. Strewn about the catacombs are broken remnants of the two million sarcophagi used to hold the mummified bodies of baboons, ibises, and other animals. Many were killed as offerings to Thoth, the divine messenger and god of writing.

Farther into the desert on the narrow stone walkway is the **City of the Dead,** filled with royal mausolea laid out like a town, with houses, streets, and walkways half-buried by sand. Most of the tombs here evidence Greece's aesthetic influence. The finest structure is the **Tomb of Petosiris,** high priest of the Temple of Thoth. Just inside, the four proto-Doric columns at the front of the tomb are elaborate stone bas-relief carvings depicting Petosiris's family, Petosiris making offerings and prayers, and Egyptians at work making metal, wine, cloth, and bread. Inside, a vestibule opens up into the central chamber, where a square shaft plummets to the burial chamber. The decorative bas-reliefs on the walls, dating from about 300 BCE, depict pharaonic deities in typical Hellenic poses. The most vivid surviving colors in the tomb are found in the images of nine baboons, twelve women, and twelve cobras, each set representing a temporal cycle. Behind Petosiris's tomb sits the **Tomb of Isadora,** a young woman from Antinopolis who drowned circa 120 BCE. Isadora's mummy is on display inside a glass case: teeth, fingernails, and even traces of hair can still be seen on the corpse, an accomplishment that can be credited to 2000 years of arid desert air, not embalming expertise. The rest of this section of the necropolis is essentially empty, but a hike through the sands to look at additional scattered ruins is worth it.

Slightly south of the Tomb of Isadora, a stone walkway branches north toward **al-Sakiya** (the Well), a huge circular brick shaft that once supplied the necropolis and its sacred aviary with fresh water. The water wheel, built in 300 BCE, pumped water from 70m below the desert floor. For *baksheesh*, the guard will open it and you can descend to the well's bottom after shooing away the bats. The walkway to the ancient well passes through the remains of the great **Temple of Thoth,** which once dominated the entire necropolis. A few of the massive façade columns remain, along with a series of pillars that once enclosed the forecourt.

To visit **Hermopolis,** you need to reach **Ashminein** (a 20-minute drive from Mallawi) or take a pickup from the town of Tuna al-Gabel (at least LE1). All the locals know Ashminein, but none have heard of Hermopolis. Just outside Ashminein stand two huge sandstone baboons, representations of Thoth. They are all that remain of the ancient city of Khnumu. Named Hermopolis by its Ptolemaic Greek citizens, the city dates from at least the 15th dynasty. The two unfortunate apes who once supported the ceiling of the great temple are not what they once were, as their erect phalli were removed by later generations of prudish Egyptians. The temple served as a cult center for Thoth, an enigmatic god who had the body of a man and the head of an ibis; the baboon was one of his sacred animals. The Egyptians revered him as scribe of the divine court, inventor of writing, and patron of wisdom. The Greeks, arriving in the 5th century BCE, associated this learned deity with their own messenger god, Hermes, and named their metropolis in his honor. Forward from the baboons' gaze, in a large grassy field of ruins, lie more remains of Khumu and Ptolemaic Hermopolis, most of which are little more than rubble. One surviving formation retains drawings of the ancient Egyptian deities; these are the remains of a pharaonic pylon. Further on, 24 re-erected rose granite columns demarcate the ruins of the **Agora,** an early Christian basilica. People flag down pickups to get back to Mallawi (at least 15pt).

Tel al-Amarna تــل العمارنة

Less than overwhelming in external appearance, Tel al-Amarna is in fact one of the most intriguing of the Pharaonic ruins, both for its history and for its art. The founder of the city, King Akhenaten, was a maverick who fled Thebes to found a monotheistic cult dedicated to the sun god Aton after the local religious powers resisted his innovations. The new capital of Akhenaten was decorated with countless representations of Aton. The sun god was usually depicted as a brilliant sun disk whose rays terminated in outstretched palms, often holding an *ankh,* a circle-topped cross symbolizing eternal life. The legacy of these decorative efforts is not exclusively religious; Akhenaten's artists created the naturalistic Amarna style of art and made Nefertiti, Akhenaten's wife, a timeless symbol of beauty.

Akhenaten followed his children and Nefertiti to the grave at the age of 35, and conservative political forces quickly stepped in. With Akhenaten's new city razed, the capital was returned to Thebes and Tel al-Amarna was declared unhallowed ground. The taboo helped preserve the remains of Akhenaten's home, since no later civilization would build over the home of this heretic. The necropolis of Tel al-Amarna, 12km south of Mallawi on the eastern bank of the Nile, houses several rock-hewn tombs from Akhenaten's reign.

To reach Tel al-Amarna, take one of the local pickup trucks from the depot south of the Mallawi train station (25pt). The trucks leave from the parking lot at the end of the bridge crossing into town; make it clear that you want the village of Tel al-Amarna. You'll be dropped off at the bank of the Nile. From there, take a ferry, which will drop you off by the site office. At the office you'll pay LE7.25, including round-trip on the ferry, transportation to and from the site on a tractor-pulled bus. At the site there is another charge (LE6, LE3 for students. Site open daily 7am-5pm). Bring a filing cabinet for all the tickets.

There are two groups of tombs. Of the six in the northern group, #1, 3, and 4 are most worthy of a visit. A few of the southern tombs are interesting, but in order to reach them you must return to the village and pay LE15 for the 14km excursion. Visits to tombs #1-6 are included in the northern tour, but if you're not insistent you'll be shown only #3-5 as the others are a bit out of the way. If the lights in the tombs are out of order, the guides have a nifty foil apparatus which illuminates the tomb walls with sunlight. It's not a bad idea, however, to bring a flashlight.

Once inside, you will immediately notice the pervasive vandalism. Later-day pharaohs returned to Tel al-Amarna and defaced much of the local work on account of its heretical nature. The faces of Akhenaten and Nefertiti and the symbol of Aton were favorite targets.

The **Tomb of Huye** (#1) was constructed for the superintendent of the royal harem and steward to the queen mother, Tiy. Its decorative reliefs depict King Akhenaten with his family and closest friends. Look for the small depiction of a sculptor at work in the lower right-hand corner of the far wall, to the right of the doorway.

On the entrance walls of the **Tomb of Ahmose** (#3), the deceased can be seen worshiping the sun. Ahmose was royal fan-bearer to Akhenaten, and is most often depicted praying in his official costume, carrying a fan and an axe. This tomb offers a glimpse of the artistic process. A large sketch of king with chariot graces the left side of this uncompleted tomb. Because of the city's abrupt end, the tomb was left unfinished.

The **Tomb of Meri-Re** (#4), the high priest of Aton, is the largest and best preserved of the group, retaining vibrant colors. Plans of the temples and palaces of Akhenaten adorn the walls of the tomb's hypostyle hall, enabling Egyptologists to deduce the appearance of the ancient city's official buildings. One wall of the tomb features two ornately decorated chariots under the solar symbol of Aton. The famous profile of Nefertiti is identifiable in several places, but has been marred by thieves. Her famous bust-with-crown was discovered here, but kept hidden by its German discoverers for years and then taken to the Berlin Museum.

The **Tomb of Pentu** (#5), chief physician to the royal family, has been badly damaged, as has the **Tomb of Panhesy** (#6), 1km to the south. Panhesy was the Servant of Aton, observer of granaries and herds, and chancellor of Lower Egypt. His tomb was converted into a church by early Christians, but its original decorative carvings survive in reasonable condition, as does a fairly ordinary staircase that leads nowhere.

On the way back to the Nile shore, the tractor-bus will make a detour to the remains of the **Royal Palace** of Akhenaten and Nefertiti. The only things uncovered by the excavations of royal rubble are the locations of streets, but a helpful guide may point out the pool where Nefertiti was known to bathe in the buff.

If you make it to the southern tombs, two are worth touring. The **Tomb of Mahu** (#9), Akhenaten's chief of police, contains several levels of chambers, connected by a winding stairway and adorned with various scenes of the deceased with royal personages. The striking **Tomb of Ay** (#25) was constructed for a man of many trades; Ay was the king's secretary, Queen Nefertiti's nurse, and later, Tutankhamen's successor. Although Ay abandoned his designs here to excavate a more elaborate tomb for himself in the Valley of the Kings at Thebes, the structure was intended to be the finest in the necropolis at Tel al-Amarna. The wall inside the imposing hypostyle hall entrance is covered with scenes depicting the bustling street life of the ancient city, complete with soldiers, visiting officials, and dancing women. On the way south, you'll pass the insubstantial ruins of Akhneton's city, all but leveled by reactionaries after his death (at about the time of Tutankhamen).

Assyut أسيوط

Assyut's most famous native son, the 3rd-century philosopher Plotinus, once remarked that "Every beautiful vision requires an eye that is able to see it." The eye that truly appreciates the beauty of Assyut has been trained in the tourist camps of Luxor and Aswan; when you become afraid your own reflection will try to sell you a souvenir, you are ready to come to Assyut. Located at the geographic center of Egypt, Assyut has always been an important market and commercial center; today, Assyut is the most important city in Upper Egypt and the third-largest in the country, with a large university and an economy that thrives on everything but tourism. Aside from a few scattered tombs, some nearby churches, and the Nile-splitting Banana Island, Assyut has little that fits nicely in a tourist brochure or on a roll of film. But the city's ancient market and its renowned carpet district, the novelty of an Egyptian city with a large and visible Christian presence, the relative care with which its buildings and streets have been maintained, and the natives' indifference to tourists make the town seem almost beautiful, at least to veterans of the Nile Valley.

All transportation connects to and from the main square in front of the **train station.** More than a dozen trains per day travel to Cairo (7hr., 2nd class A/C LE13). Eight southbound trains shuttle to Luxor (A/C, 7hr., LE11.50), four of which continue to Aswan (12hr., LE16). **Buses** are more convenient to the closer cities; the bus station lies just south of the train station. Five buses daily, some originating in Cairo, pass through Assyut en route to Kharga Oasis (4-5hr., LE5), and the 7am bus continues on to Dakhla Oasis (8hr., LE10). Unfortunately, not all buses stop in the city center every day. A surer way to reach Kharga is to grab a *service* **taxi** from the stand 100m south of the train station (LE7). The wait shouldn't be more than an hour or two. *Service* taxis also provide convenient, though perilous, transportation to other Nile cities. Stands for various destinations spread out to the west and south of the train station.

The **post office** is on the street to the right of Hotel Assiout de Tourisme. Adjacent to the train station is the **telephone office** (open 24 hrs.). The **telephone code** is 088. The **Bank of Alexandria,** along with a number of other banks, is on the same street in a square 200m west of the train station and will change traveler's checks. (Open Sun.-Thurs. 8:30am-2pm, additional exchange hours Sun. 6-9pm and Wed. 5-8pm.)

If trouble strikes, the **police station** is located on the Nile, 100m south of al-Helaly St., the main street just south of the train station (tel. 32 25 62 or 122). Assyut University Hospital on University St. is probably the best local medical facility (tel. 32 20 16). Phone 123 in case of **medical emergency.**

Set amidst trees and playgrounds, the **YMCA** (tel. 32 32 18) offers two types of accommodation. Relatively spartan but clean doubles with refrigerators go for LE8 (singles LE6). But the large carpeted rooms with A/C, color TV, and private bath make this place perhaps the best deal in Egypt. (Deluxe doubles LE20. Deluxe singles LE15.) The staff is sometimes elusive, so try to make it as clear as possible what it is that you want to whomever you see. To get to the YMCA, turn right (north) from the train station after 200m; turn right and walk beneath the underpass, past a mosque and a church, and you'll see the entrance on your left (after another 150m). Just before the underpass, the **Windsor Hotel** has bearable large rooms. (Doubles with bath LE4.50.) A bit closer to transportation, the **al-Haramein Hotel** (tel. 32 04 26) is one block east of the train station on the road to the Nile (al-Helaly St.), but it's not always easy to get a room here. (Clean rooms. Singles LE7. Doubles LE14. Fans LE2.) The **Lotus Hotel** (tel. 32 49 29), on the same street at the end close to the Nile, will do in a pinch. (Rooms with private bath LE10 per person.) The **Hotel Assiout de Tourisme** (tel. 32 26 15), across from the train station, has some renovated rooms and aging bathrooms in a grungy building. (Singles LE8. Doubles LE12. No fans.) At the other end, the **Reem Hotel** (tel. 32 62 35), though poorly decorated, is a full service hotel with A/C and private baths in every room. Head south from the train station, make your first left and then your right. (Singles LE36. Doubles LE56.)

A favorite restaurant with locals is the **Mattam al-Azhar,** where a delicious, crispy whole chicken goes for LE7. The restaurant is on the same street as the post office, one block farther on the left. There's no English sign; look for the ornate wooden screen above the door. **Express Restaurant,** in the heart of commercial Assyut, is spotless and lively and serves tiny, tasty hamburgers (75pt) and *shwarma* or kebab sandwiches (50pt). To reach the restaurant, walk 200m north from the station and turn left at Windsor Hotel onto July 26 St. The restaurant is on the right, just after the next intersection. That street is also the best place for *kushari* (50pt) and falafel (15-25pt).

Assyut's *souk* sprawls across the area west of the main square. If you head further west from the Express Restaurant, you will eventually arrive at the *souk*. This maze of covered, tangled alleyways houses some of the country's better carpet shops. Unfortunately, without a local guide it's all too easy to get lost. Ask at your hotel for help, or propose an expedition to one of the local university students eager to practice his English.

As far as other **sights** in the Assyut area, there are several groups of ancient tombs as well as a couple of historic Coptic monasteries, the most interesting and accessible of which being **Dayr al-Muharrak.** Bishop Bakhomous built a monastery here in the 4th century at the legendary refuge of the Holy Family during their whirlwind tour through Egypt. The **Church of Elazraq** is the oldest church in Upper Egypt and was constructed in fulfillment of an Old Testament prophecy about a church in the geographic center of Egypt. The adjacent **Church of St. George** contains more icons of the Holy Family and star-studded Coptic saints. Next to two churches is a four-story tower accessible (when open) only by a drawbridge, built to provide refuge for the monks during the 5th century. Father Athanisos Al-Moharragi will show you around, answer your questions, and practice his best monastic English. To get to Dayr al-Muharrak, take a *service* taxi south to al-Qusiyyah (LE1.50) from outside the Assyut train station, then another service taxi up to the monastery (25pt).

Felucca fanatics might venture out to **Banana Island,** across the river from the city (50pt by *felucca* ferry). If you choose to meander on foot, you'll find the Nile bank of Assyut long and leafy, with a view of the British-built Assyut Barrages to the north.

Sohag سوهاج

Sohag is a center for agriculture, not tourism. It is situated on the west side of the Nile, 467km south of Cairo, 92km south of Assyut, and 204km north of Luxor. Despite its proximity to Abydos and the abundance of old cars which make its streets a living automotive museum, relatively few tourists have heard of Sohag. However, if you find yourself in the neighborhood between July 5 and August 5, be sure to venture out to the nearby monastery, **Dayr Amba Shenouda,** which becomes the focus for Coptic pilgrims during this period.

In Sohag, you'll find the usual Nilonic plentitude of transportation. The **train station** is in the center of town in the middle of al-Mahatta St. Frequent trains head both north and south. The train to Luxor takes four hours and costs LE7.50 in air-conditioned second class. The **bus station** lies 300m south of the train station. Buses leave frequently, especially in the morning, to Assyut (2hr., LE2.25), Qena (3hr., LE3), and al-Balyana, near the ruins of Abydos (1hr., 75pt). **Northbound *service* taxis** can be found in a square 200m north of the train station on al-Mahatta St. (to Assyut 90min., LE3.50). **Southbound *service* taxis** stop by the bus station and depart every 20 minutes in the morning to Qena (LE5) and al-Balyana (1hr., LE2), where you can connect with a service taxi to Abydos for 50pt. **Local taxis** leave from 200m west of the bus station to Dayr Amba Shenouda (50pt), or you can hire a private taxi to the sights for LE10 round-trip.

The three hotels in Sohag stand in a row across from the train station at the heart of the town's boisterous mosque scene. **Andalos Hotel** (tel. 32 43 28), just south of the train station on al-Mahatta, has clean rooms and fans. (Singles LE5.50. Doubles LE8.40, with bath LE11.50. Breakfast included.) **Al-Salaam Hotel** (tel. 32 33 17), south of the station, is a touch cleaner than Andalos and also has fans. (Singles LE6, with bath LE10. Doubles LE8, with bath LE12.) **Ramses Hotel** (tel. 32 23 13), next to al-Salaam, boasts musty odors and a dearth of fans. (Singles LE5. Doubles LE10.) Try to stay on the lower floors; water and electricity don't always make it to the top floors. A cheaper option is the small **HI Youth Hostel** at 5 Port Said St. (tel. 32 43 95). Take a right out of the train station and walk until you reach a square. Cross the train tracks and turn right twice; it's on the right side. Grimy bathrooms but sizable rooms with fans. (Lock out 10am-2pm. 11pm curfew. LE3. Members only, membership LE2.40.) Continue down this street to reach the *service* taxis (25pt) to **Akhmin,** a Coptic community renowned for its cotton weavings, shawls, and batik crafts.

At the end of the street and across the square is a madhouse branch of the **Bank of Alexandria.** (Open Sun.-Thurs. 8:30am-2pm, additional exchange hours Sun. 6-9pm and Wed. 5-8pm.) Other banks lie just north of the post office along the Nile. On the other side of the bridge by the mosque sits the **police station** (tel. 122). The **hospital** lies just across from the bus station. The **post office** is on Nile St.; go left from the station past the mosque and head left to the end of the street. The **telephone office** (open 24 hrs.) is inside the train station. The **telephone code** is 093.

For crusty fresh bread, spicy *taḥina,* and half a roast chicken (LE4.50), stop in at the **El Eman for Roast Grill** a few doors north of Andalos Hotel. Cheaper meals can be found at the nearby *kushari* shops; one is 100m north of the station,another 100m south.

About 10km northwest of Sohag on the edge of the desert are two of the finest Coptic monuments in Upper Egypt. **Dayr Amba Shenouda,** or the Monastery of St. Shenouda, is also known as the White Monastery after the color of its limestone blocks, many of which originally belonged to a pharaonic temple and feature hieroglyphic inscriptions. The monastery was founded in 400 CE by St. Shenoudi. Much of the nave has been destroyed by earthquake, but a small church occupies the apse. Remove your shoes upon entering the carpeted church within the monastery complex. You'll be greeted by a seated Jesus, balancing an eroded globe in his right hand and a Bible in his left. The monastery is especially worth visiting between July 5 and August 5, when hordes of Coptic pilgrims descend upon it. During this period, the monastery becomes a living flea market, especially on Thursdays and Fridays. The pilgrims sprint down the steep slopes of the nearby hills, and childless women wrapped in sacks roll down the hills in hopes of obtaining a divine fertility boost. During the pilgrimage period you can visit Dayr Amba Shenouda sites from Sohag by bus for 25pt.

The smaller **Dayr Amba Bishai (Red Monastery)** is named in Arabic after its founder, St. Bishai, a thief who converted to Christianity and repented through fasting and prayer. Portions of the original red-brick walls from 600 CE still stand within the more modern building. The sanctuary's main fresco depicts the Last Supper, with another view of Jesus and the apostles in the right apse and Mary on the left. Amba Bishai lies in a village of the same name, 4km up the road from Dayr Amba Shenouda. Start walking and try to flag a *service* taxi (25pt).

Abydos أبيدوس

The ancient city of Abydos was the site of a necropolis and temple dedicated to the god Khenti-Amentiu. Pharaohs from the first dynasty onward chose to be buried at the site and eventually corpses from all over Egypt were interred at this necropolis *par excellence*. Never one to rest on his laurels, Osiris, god of the Nile, subtly co-opted Abydos and the worshipers of Khenti-Amentiu during the 6th dynasty. Abydos has all but vanished, save the imposing Temple of Osiris built by the 19th-dynasty Pharaoh Seti I. Though not as imposing as its stupendous first cousins at Luxor and Karnak, the temple is the greatest work of the New Kingdom, noted for its delicately painted murals and magnificent bas-reliefs.

Practical Information

Since there are virtually no accommodations in the area, most people visit Abydos as a long daytrip from Luxor (LE40-75 for a private **taxi** in combination with Dendera Temple). You can also stop en route between Luxor and points farther north. The closest town to the ruins is **Balyana,** 7km away, on the main north-south rail line and relatively accessible. Five of the ten daily Cairo-Luxor **trains** stop at Balyana. From Luxor it's much faster to go by *service* **taxi** to Qena (LE2) and change for Balyana (LE5). Another strategy is to stay in Sohag, the nearest city, and come to Balyana by *service* taxi (LE2). The *service* **taxi station** in Balyana is one block east of the railway station. From here or from the junction of the north-south road and the Abydos-al-Balyana road you can catch a *service* taxi to Abydos (50pt). An infrequent and crowded **bus** runs from town to the village of Balyana (15pt). The correct fare for a **private taxi** to Abydos is LE4 each way, though it can require some hard bargaining. The only beds in Balyana are at the **Hotel Wadi** (tel. 80 16 58), which is crumbling and equipped with Turkish restroom facilities (LE3 per person). There is a small **restaurant** farther down the road from the train station.

Nearby is a grassy campsite called **Osiris Park.** For LE5 per person you can pitch your own tent, and LE10 per person allows access to their big white tents. Prices include breakfast. A number of store offer drinks at inflated prices. The **New Seti Restaurant,** 150m east and to the left, has a chicken meal for LE5. Falafel is for sale at a coffee shop nearer to the temple.

Sights

Abydos became the site for the cult of Osiris because Osiris's head landed there after it was removed by his evil brother Seth. The myth of Osiris was once reenacted annually at Abydos, including a simulation of his death and dismemberment.

With the cult of Osiris gone the way of the "the" in "the Ukraine," about the only thing left at Abydos is the **Temple of Osiris** built by Seti I. Only three of the original seven doors remain to the **Portico of Twelve Pillars,** which guarded the entrance into the temple proper. The central doorway leads to the first hypostyle hall, lined with 24 colossal papyriform columns. This grandiose entrance gives way to the second hypostyle hall, which contains some of the finest bas-reliefs ever carved in Egypt. At the far left corner of the second hypostyle hall a long, narrow corridor known as the **Gallery of the Kings** leads toward the southeast. This simple passage houses one of Egyptology's most treasured finds, the **Kings' List,** which mentions the names of 76 Egyptian rulers from Menes of Memphis to Seti I, although it's missing a few. Correlating this list with prior knowledge, scholars were able to pinpoint the sequence of the Egyptian dynasties.

In the southern wing of the Temple of Abydos, beside the entrance to the Gallery of the Kings, a doorway leads to a chamber with two tiny but not quite picayune chapels adjoining it. The right-hand chapel contains a kinky relief showing the mummy of Osiris impregnating Isis, in the form of a falcon.

Osiris's sanctuary at the temple's rear is more elaborate than others in the complex, opening into the **Inner Sanctuary of Osiris,** a chamber still possessing most of the original painted scenes of Osiris's life. The sanctuary is flanked by three small chapels bedecked with the best preserved reliefs in the temple. (Site open daily 7am-6pm. Admission LE1.50, students 75pt. The ticket covers everything, so there's no need to wound your wallet with *baksheesh.*)

Qena and Dendera ‫قنا و دندرة‬

Qena, the provincial capital of the region that includes Luxor, is a bustling and relatively attractive town. However, unless you are en route to or from the nearby temple at Dendera (8km to the northwest) or on your way to Hurghada, there isn't much reason to come here. The paucity of tourist facilities and the absence of any sights or English signs almost beg foreigners to move on. Qena is an Egyptian city for Egyptians.

Practical Information

Each of Qena's important transit centers is in a different part of town. The best way to get from one train, bus, or taxi terminal to another is to hail a horse carriage (LE1-1.50 for 1-3 people, with bargaining. Don't abuse the horse by cramming more than 3 people in the carriage). The **train station** is located near the center of town at the intersection of al-Mahatta St. and al-Gomhoria St. There are ten trains daily to Cairo (11hr., 2nd-class A/C LE17.70) and ten trains daily to Luxor (2hr., 2nd-class A/C LE3; inconvenient). You can reach the **bus station** by walking forward out of the train station (down al-Gomhoria St.) until you reach a large square (500m). Turn right and continue past the mosques; the station will be on the left. Buses are often slow and crowded. Buses to Hurghada run at least every hour in the morning, more often in the evening (LE5-10; make reservations). Frequent service to Dendera as well (15pt).

Hail **northbound** *service* **taxis** either one block west of the bus station or from a taxi depot just to the east of the Nile bridge, 1km north of the bus station. Service to Dendera is 35-50pt. If you're going to Abydos, say you want to go to Balyana (LE5); if you mention Abydos, which is only 3km farther, you'll have to refuse offers for a special taxi. It's LE5 to Sohag, and taxis go as far as Assyut (LE8). For **southbound** *service* **taxis,** walk to the right from the front of the train station toward the bridge spanning the canal. Cross and walk to the right side of the square. Frequent service to Luxor (LE2) and Aswan (LE9). To reach Esna, change at Luxor. To reach Edfu or Kom Ombo you'll have to pay the full fare to Aswan. Hail taxis to Hurghada at the far corner of the southbound station square, in front of the large mosque (LE8). Hairpin turns near the sea are always taken at top speed.

Local taxis depart from the square beyond the bus station and the Bank of Alexandria, or wherever you happen to find one. Fare to Dendera is LE7-10 round-trip with earnest bargaining.

To reach the banks in Qena, turn right from the main square on al-Gomhoria St. (500m west of the train station). The **Banque du Caire** is 100m down the street on the west side, the Bank of Alexandria 300m farther just past the mosques. (Both open daily 8am-2pm, 6pm-9pm.) To get to the **post office,** go from the train station to the main square, make a left, and walk 100m. (Open Sat.-Thurs. 8am-2:30pm.) The **telephone office** is on your left as you walk west under the aquamarine archway from the main square. (Open 24 hrs.) The **telephone code** is 096. There is a **police** office in the train station (tel. 32 52 84). The main office is just behind the bus station.

Accommodations, Food, and Entertainment

If at all possible, don't spend the night in Qena. Luxor, with its array of cheap, comfortable hotels, is only an hour away. For those who must stay in Qena, there are only two hotels willing to accept tourists. Try the **New Palace Hotel** (tel. 32 25 09), across from the train station behind the Mobil gas station (no English sign—look for the building that looks like a hotel). Screened windows, some rooms with fans, and an efficient elevator ease the sticker shock. (Singles with bath LE10. Doubles LE8, with bath LE17). **Hotel Maka** (tel. 32 29 09), just south of the main square, next door to Studio Express and fronted by a white latticed window, offers dusty rooms and lots of noise. (Singles LE6. Doubles LE9.50.)

The most accessible restaurant in Qena is **al-Prince Restaurant,** on the corner in the main square 0.5km west of the train station. Look for the white sign on the right. Serves the usual Egyptian food (LE4-6) and beer (LE4). **Hamdi Restaurant,** 100m down the street on the right, north of the square, serves complete meals of chicken, rice, and salad for LE4.20. The confectionary shop just south of Hamdi's serves ice cream (LE1) and pastries. The *kushari* stand at the southwest corner of the main square intersection heaps healthy servings of the stuff onto a plate for LE1.25. Qena's produce *souk* begins with tomatoes and melons near Hamdi Restaurant and runs east up a small street for 400m, ending with bunnies and pigeons.

If you're in Qena for more than an hour, head north to the Nile, about 1km from the main square. The view is spectacular, especially at sunset.

An interesting excursion is to **Naqada** (na-GA-da), about 30 minutes south of Qena by taxi, where during the *fin-de-siècle* a monk built the **Pigeon Palace.** This array of brick, mortar pots, and ceramic is home to 10,000 pigeons. The birds are about 200m west of the road through Naqada in the midst of the green fields. (LE2 by service taxi from Qena or West Thebes.) Upon crossing the Western Desert, the weary pigeons park here for food, shelter, and the opportunity to be slaughtered. The caretakers will show you around and then bid you goodbye with outstretched palms.

Sights at Dendera

The cheapest way to reach the antiquities at **Dendera** (8km from Qena) is to take a *service* taxi (25pt) that will drop you off at a fork in the road just 1km from the site. Follow the paved road to the left and you'll come upon the well-preserved remains.

The roof, walls, and inner sanctuary of the **Temple of Hathor** remain largely intact. Hathor, the city's matron deity, was worshiped as early as the Old Kingdom, but this temple dates only from the first century BCE. The late Ptolemies and the Romans found it politically expedient to associate themselves with Hathor; Cleopatra, Augustus, Claudius, and Nero sponsored decoration of the temple. A benevolent goddess, Hathor was usually depicted as cow-headed, or shown wearing a crown of two horns cradling Ra, the sun disk. Because her specialty was love and joy, Hathor, the "Golden One," was identified by the Greeks as Aphrodite. During an annual festival, a statue of Hathor was carried in a sacred procession down the Nile to meet Horus of Edfu.

During the summer, countless bats inhabit the secluded portions of the temple. Glance up at the ceiling and cover your hair before entering the temple's smaller chambers. A flashlight comes in handy.

Eighteen columns are surmounted by cow-goddesses' heads in the **Great Hypostyle Hall.** In the temple's inner sanctum, wall paintings portray the embalmer's art, while the ceiling is decorated with pictures of Nut. In the second hypostyle hall, also known as the **Hall of Appearances,** six columns line the central aisle of the temple, complemented by six small chambers on either side. The function of these chapels is indicated in their frescoes: perfumes used during sacred rituals were kept in the laboratory and across the hall in the temple's treasury. The second hypostyle hall gives way to the **Hall of Offerings** where the daily rites were performed. In the kiosk in the southwest corner of the roof priests performed the ceremony of "touching the disk," in which the soul of the sun god Ra appeared in the form of light. If you look to the right you will notice a gently sloping staircase which leads up to the roof, where you can survey the scene below. Unless you have a fantastic fear of bats, it's worth the climb.

The **Hall of the Ennead** immediately precedes the inner sanctuary. The chamber on the left is the wardrobe, and opposite a doorway leads through a small treasury into the **Court of the New Year** where sacrifices were performed during the festival of the New Year. On the ceiling of the colorful portico the goddess Nut gives birth to the sun, whose rays shine upon the head of Hathor. The **Mysterious Corridor** surrounds the **Sanctuary** on three sides, and 11 chapels, each with a distinct religious function, open off of it. A small chamber known as the **Throne of Ra** sits behind the northernmost of the three doorways which open up behind the sanctuary. A minuscule opening in its floor leads to the crypt, a subterranean hallway embellished with reliefs, some of in-laid alabaster. Wait for a guard to show you around in exchange for *baksheesh.*

The first of the series of small buildings on the right after the front gate is a Roman *mammisis* from the time of Emperor Trajan. The reliefs depict Hathor and Horus raising their god-son. The second building is the scanty remains of a **Coptic Basilica** (5th or 6th century). The third is the *mammisis* of Nakhtanebo featuring more god-raising scenes. Farther around the outside of the temple running counter-clockwise are the remains of a sacred lake, a sanatorium, a small **Temple of Isis** and a well. (Open daily 6am-7pm. Admission to the site LE6, students LE3.)

The **Hotel Dendera** (also known as Happy Land Hotel; tel. 32 23 30) has clean rooms around a shady courtyard, creating a retreat atmosphere. However, it is often filled by tour groups. (LE15 per person, LE20 with private shower.) **Camping** on the adjacent lawn costs LE3.

Luxor الاقصر

Built on the site of Thebes, capital of united Egypt during the New Kingdom (18th-20th dynasties, 1555-1070 BCE), Luxor is now home to several august monuments. Within the town, the Temples of Karnak and Luxor awe even ruins-jaded-travelers with their fusillades of gateways and forests of gigantic columns. Luxor's historic and artistic wealth spills to the other side of the Nile, where fabulous tombs dot the West Theban plain. In the barren Valley of the Kings, pharaohs such as Tutankhamen achieved the immortality they sought: though their preternatural methods may have failed, the international fame of their exquisite tombs lives on millenia later. Luxor is also an excellent base for daytrips to the antiquities at Abydos, Dendera, Edfu, and Esna.

Luxor's relationship with its illustrious past is more parasitic than reverent. Never have so many come so far to see so much that is so dead. Here thousands come looking for that unbeatable photograph, while hundreds of others come to house, feed, and sell alabaster busts to the camera-toting foreigners. There is no shortage of smiling dragoonfolk willing to perform any service for as much as they can get. Fortunately, since the city is completely dependent upon tourism, it's a buyer's market, particularly during the slow summer season. Budget travelers luxuriate in Luxor; a few dollars per day can buy accommodations, food, and access to unforgettable sights.

Orientation and Practical Information

The town of Luxor is located along the eastern bank of the Nile, 670km upstream from Cairo and 220km downstream from Aswan. Surrounded by a heavily cultivated floodplain, Luxor is an agricultural center, with a weekly *souk* (vegetable market) on Tuesdays. The nearby village of al-Habel holds a weekly **camel market**, also on Tuesdays. **Luxor Temple** is on the Nile at the center of town; the **train station** is 0.75km inland on the eastern edge of Luxor; and **Karnak Temple** is 3km northeast of the first two at the northern fringe of town. Although there are only a few street signs in town, finding your way around Luxor is easy as long as you know the three main thoroughfares: **al-Mahatta Street** (Station St.) runs perpendicular to the Nile; **al-Nil Street** runs along it; and **al-Karnak Street** runs parallel to al-Nil.

Tourist Office: At the front of the tourist bazaar next to the New Winter Palace Hotel, just south of Luxor Temple on the Nile (tel. 38 22 15). Staff can tell you official prices for every service. The free *Upper Egypt Night and Day* offers a limited train schedule. Useful map of the west bank sights in *Egypt Tourist Information*. Open daily (including Ramadan) 8am-8pm. Branch at airport (tel. 38 23 06). Open 8am-8pm, 24 hrs. during winter. Another branch at train station, open at indeterminate hours.

Tourist Police: al-Nil St. (tel. 38 66 20), in the tourist bazaar. Also in train station (tel. 38 28 40). Both open 24 hrs.

Passport Office: al-Nil St. (tel. 38 23 18), about 1km south of the Novotel, by the sign for Mandera Restaurant. Passport registration and visa extensions available in the foreigners office. Open daily 8am-2pm and 6-9pm. Visa business Sat.-Thurs. 8am-2pm only. During Ramadan 10am-2pm and 8pm-10pm., visas Sat.-Thurs. 10am-2pm.

Currency Exchange: Bazar Radwan, in the tourist market south of Luxor Temple on the corner of al-Karnak St. and Muhammad Farid St., has the longest hours. Open daily 10am-11pm. Most luxury hotels will change money between 8am and 10pm.

Banks: Banque Misr: Nefertiti St., 1km north of Luxor Temple, off al-Karnak St. Open Sun.-Thurs. 8:30am-9pm, Fri. 8:30-11am, 2-9pm. **Bank of Alexandria:** Al-Karnak St., just north of intersection with Nefertiti St. Open daily 8:30am-2pm, additional currency exchange hours Sun. 6-9pm and Wed. 5-8pm. **National Bank of Egypt,** al-Nil St., 50m south of Old Winter Palace Hotel. Open daily 8:30am-2pm, 5-9pm. **Banque du Caire,** Salah al-Din St., just east of Television St. Open Sat.-Thurs. 8:30am-2pm, Fri. 6-9pm.

American Express: Old Winter Palace Hotel on al-Nil St. (tel. 55 13 01), south of Luxor Temple. Holds mail. Traveler's checks sold to cardholders. Will wire money or send mail through Cairo office. Open daily 8am-7:30pm, sometimes later.

Post Office: Poste Restante on al-Mahatta St., 50m east of al-Karnak St. Another branch in the bazaar near the tourist office. Both open Sun.-Thurs. 8am-2pm.

Telephones: Next to EgyptAir, in front of the Old Winter Palace Hotel on al-Nil St, and in train station (open 8am-10pm). **Central Telephone Office** is off al-Karnak St. directly behind the Savoy Hotel. International and national calls (to Cairo LE1 minimum). Open 24 hrs. Better, more expensive service at luxury hotels along the Nile, including the Savoy and ETAP (to Cairo LE2). **Telegrams** can be sent from the main post office or telephone offices, above. **Telephone code:** 095.

Airport: 5km northeast of town (tel. 38 46 55). Take a taxi (LE4.75). Served by **EgyptAir** (tel. 58 05 81), next to the entrance of the Old Winter Palace Hotel. In summer, to Cairo (3-5 per day, LE282), Aswan (2-5 per day, LE124), and Hurghada (2 per week, LE97). More flights in winter.

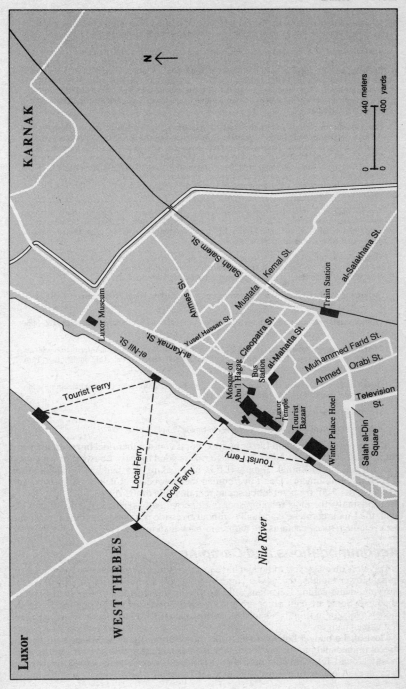

Luxor

KARNAK

WEST THEBES

Nile River

Tourist Ferry

Local Ferry

Local Ferry

Tourist Ferry

Luxor Museum

el-Nil St.

al-Karnak St.

Salah Salem St.

Ahmes St.

Yusef Hassan St.

Mustafa Kemal St.

Cleopatra St.

al-Mahatta St.

al-Salakhana St.

Train Station

Mosque of Abu'l Hagag

Bus Station

Luxor Temple

Tourist Bazaar

Winter Palace Hotel

Muhammed Farid St.

Ahmed Orabi St.

Television St.

Salah al-Din Square

440 meters

400 yards

Egypt's other airline, **ZAS Air** (tel. 38 59 28), on the opposite side of the entrance to the Old Winter Palace Hotel, serves the same airports for the same prices. Both open daily 8am-8pm.

Train Station: At the head of al-Mahatta St. (Station St.), 0.75km inland from Luxor Temple (tel. 38 20 18). Looks like a temple. If you're returning to Cairo on the unreliable train, make reservations the day you arrive in Luxor. With A/C: 10 per day, 12-14hr., 1st class LE32.55, students LE20.90; 2nd class LE20.40, students LE13.90. Sleepers to Cairo (3 per day, LE214.00). To Aswan with A/C: 5 per day, 5hr., 1st class LE13, students LE8.75; 2nd class LE8, students LE6. It's possible to pay a walk-on fee and travel without a guaranteed seat, but the trip to Cairo is too long to risk standing.

Bus Station: intersection of al-Karnak and al-Mahatta St., by the mosque and the Horus Hotel. All buses stop here. Main Luxor terminal is on Television St. off Salah al-Din Sq., 4 blocks southwest of the train station. To Cairo (3 express buses per day, 10hr.; non-A/C 8am and 4pm, LE18.75; A/C 7pm, LE30.50). Seats may be available on the A/C bus from Aswan to Cairo which passes through Luxor at 8:30pm. From 6am-7pm buses run about every hr. to Esna, Edfu, Kom Ombo, and Aswan (LE5); most buses heading south are without A/C. To Qena (LE1.50) and northern Nile towns every hr. 6am-6pm. To Hurghada 7am and noon (LE6.50), 4pm (LE12), and A/C bus at 7pm (LE15).

Service **Taxis:** al-Karnak St., 1 block inland from the Luxor Museum on the Nile. Early morning and late afternoon service taxis leave every 15 min. for Qena (1hr., LE2), Esna (45min., LE2), Edfu (90min., LE5), Kom Ombo (2-3hr., LE7), and Aswan (3-4hr., LE8). There is also a station on the west bank where the local ferry docks.

English Bookstore: Aboudi Bookstore, in the tourist bazaar on al-Nil St. a few doors down from the tourist office. No Beckett. A small newsstand in the middle of the boulevard in front of the New Winter Palace Hotel sells foreign-language newspapers and magazines.

Swimming Pools: The small but pleasant pool at the **Luxor Wena Hotel** charges LE10 for a swim. You can splash about in the dramatically situated soup at the Novotel for the same price.

Laundromat: most accommodations listed below provide free use of washing machines (25-30pt per piece).

24-Hr. Pharmacy: Ahsraf (tel. 38 28 34). Walk 400m on al-Karnak St. from intersection with al-Mahatta St. until you see the Modern Shop on one side and a Suzuki dealership on the other. Turn right and then left on the next block.

Hospital: Luxor General Hospital, al-Nil St. (tel. 38 20 25). north of Luxor Museum near the youth hostel. English spoken. Open 24 hrs.

Medical Emergency: Tel. 123.

Police: Off al-Karnak St., about 200m north of Luxor Temple (tel. 38 20 06).

You can easily get around Luxor by foot, but if you'd rather ride, **horse-drawn carriages** *(kalishes)* line the Nile. A carriage ride is good for easy transport of baggage, a pleasant trip out to Karnak Temple (LE3), and making that budding romance bloom (LE2 plus commitment). Don't overburden the poor beasts. Luckless singles can rent a **bicycle** (LE3-5); try hotel lobbies, and rent this side of the river.

Surprisingly, the most relaxing spot in Luxor is the waterfront. Attractive and elegant, the Luxor corniche is virtually without riverside restaurants and the typical chaos; even the *felucca* captains are more laid-back than in Aswan.

Accommodations and Camping

Travelers on every sort of budget have many resting places to choose from in Luxor. In the slower months, those who come by train will disembark into a crowd of card-carrying, name-calling Egyptians offering you invitations to stay with them, for a fee of course. Some are legit, some are not. Check the place out before you hand over any money. No sign in front is a bad sign, as are extended stories about new management and name changes.

Most of the budget hotels are near the train station, lining al-Mahatta St. and the streets immediately to the north and south. Cheap, comfortable pensions are grouped mostly around Television St., off Salah al-Din Sq. Prices fluctuate by season; summer is cheapest. Competition is usually fierce, and starving student types can lop some piasters or pounds off almost any price any time of year. At many inexpensive hotels you can sleep on a roof or a terrace for LE2. Hot water and fans are the rule in most hotels. Summer rates are listed below, unless noted.

Youth Hostel (HI), 16 al-Karnak St. (tel. 38 21 39), 200m north of the service taxi station. Halfway between Karnak and Luxor Temples, across from the YMCA camp and down a small street toward the Nile. Modern and relatively clean, but inconvenient and relatively expensive. Free lockers. Lockout 10am-2pm. Curfew 11pm. Dorm beds (no fans) LE5. Doubles (with fans) LE12. Nonmembers must join for LE24. Breakfast LE1.50.

Badr Hotel, off al-Mattah St. (tel. 38 22 60), 100m down from train station and to the left. Look for sign across from the Majestic Hotel. Have pleasant dreams at this cozy, relatively well-decorated and laid-back place. Singles LE6, LE12 with shower, LE15 with A/C. Doubles LE10, LE20 with A/C and bath. Pricier in winter.

Moon Valley Hotel, El Shmoos St. (tel. 38 57 10). From Salah al-Din St., make first right off Television St., slanting onto El-Medina-Amanawara St. Hotel is 6 blocks down and to the right. Alpine charm and pleasant if smallish rooms. Singles LE8. Doubles LE15, with A/C and private bath LE20. Includes breakfast.

Titi Hotel (tel. 38 60 94), off Television St., 1 block past the bus station and to the right. Pleasant and comfortable with TV lounge. This, the classiest of the pensions, is run by easy-going, multilingual owners. LE7, less in summer.

The Golden Pension, Muhammad Farid St. (tel. 38 22 34), on the 2nd sidestreet to the right as you head south on am-Manshiya from the train station. You'll feel that you've stumbled across a secret here, but secrecy has its price. 4 rooms which range in size and cost. The smallest is LE10, the largest LE25. Breakfast included.

New Grand Hotel, off Ahmed Oraby St. (tel. 58 10 25). From the mosque by Salah al-Din Square, go left for 150m and follow signs which point you right, left, and left again. Not to be confused with the Grand Hotel or with any kind of grandeur. Manager Muhammad will show you a good time on the roof garden above his cleanish rooms. LE5 per person, including breakfast.

Oasis Hotel, on Muhammad Farid St. (tel. 38 32 79). Take a left out of the train station and another left after 2 blocks. Built in 1989, Oasis has clean, carpeted rooms and commodious lounges which the cleaning staff also finds comfortable. Good for short stays. Singles LE8. Doubles with A/C and shower LE20. Tiny breakfast included.

Happy Home, near the station (tel. 38 58 11), on the first street to the left as you walk down al-Mahatta St. Climb three flights of stairs to reach this teetotalling establishment, which sucks joy from clean, cozy rooms, not from the bottle. LE4 per person. Solo travellers may have to pay LE1 for private quarters.

Mustata Hotel, Television St. (tel. 38 47 21), about 400m south of Salah al-Din Square. Sparkling new digs. Rooms with A/C and private bath, though you may have to go across a hallway to get to the shower. Singles LE20. Doubles LE30, more in winter.

Fontana Hotel, off Television St. Turn left after the bus station and follow the can't-miss signs. Conscientious Mr. Magdy will keep you clean, informed, and reasonably well-read. Singles LE10. Doubles LE20, with shower and A/C LE25.

New Palace Hotel, Muhammad Farid St. (tel. 37 22 97). At the end of the street away from the river. Follow directions to Oasis Hotel and continue for 150m. Clean, quiet, and cheap. LE4 per person, LE5 for one person staying alone. Includes breakfast.

Noubia Home, Kawahbi St. Follow directions to Moon Valley Hotel, go one block further and turn right. Quiet and cozy, though slightly out of the way. Management may treat you to a rooftop party. LE5 per person, including breakfast.

Akhnaton Hotel, Muhammad Farid St. (tel 38 39 79). Next door to Golden Pension. Fancy lobby; not very fancy rooms. Singles LE10. Doubles LE14. Private bath LE2. Breakfast included.

Bob Marley Palace. Head down Muhammad Farid St. and look for sign near Nour Home. Mr. Marley himself will greet you upon arrival to the tidy, tiny, and rather unusual place tucked away amidst the livestock and alleyways of Luxor. LE4 or LE5 per person.

New Karnak Hotel, opposite the train station (tel. 38 24 27). Noisy and a bit tattered. Free book exchange. Singles LE6. Doubles LE8.

Abu al-Haggar Hotel, Muhammad Farid St. (tel. 38 29 58), on the corner of al-Karnak St. Unbeatable views, but beatable prices. Rooms are pleasant and have that look of faded grandeur that budget travelers learn to love. Singles LE20. Doubles LE25, LE40 in winter. Includes breakfast.

Venus Hotel, Youssef Hasan St. (tel. 38 26 25), just east of al-Karnak. Aggressive new management trying to go places. Crowded but reasonably clean. Singles LE8. Doubles LE12. A/C LE7 or LE8. Includes breakfast.

For those wishing to climb a bit upscale, **The Ramoza** on al-Mahatta St., **Horus Hotel** by Luxor Temple, and **Santa Maria** on Television St. offer comfortable accommodations with A/C, baths, bars, and full service at rates that are extremely reasonable, especially in the summer. For LE25-LE35 per person you will find luxurious accommodations indeed.

The **YMCA Day-Camp,** on al-Karnak St. (tel. 38 24 25) 180m north of the service taxi station, offers a flat, grassy area for tents and caravans. During the summer the grounds are noisy with Egyptians partying until midnight or later (about which time the front gates close). You can use the hot shower and toilets, and the enclosed camp is guarded 24 hrs. (LE3 per person, LE1.50 for motorcycles, LE5 for cars, LE25 for caravans.)

Food

While it's no gourmet's paradise, Luxor serves up better fare than most temple-hugging towns. Its menus are a little longer, its dishes are a little stronger, and its restaurants have a little more charm. Many of Luxor's affordable culinarias huddle around the train station and to the north of Luxor Temple on al-Karnak St. Luxor's best deal for food is the *kushari* stand on your left as you walk down al-Mahatta St. from the station (LE1 per plate).

New Karnak Student Restaurant, next to the hotel of the same name. Specializes in tasty omelettes—cheese (LE2.25), chicken, or Spanish—and soups (75pt).

Cafeteria El Hussein, al-Karnak St., behind Luxor Temple. Excellent food, great bread, reasonable service, and music indoors or outside on terrace. Sea bass with rice LE6. Delectable shish kebab (LE5).

Salt and Bread, in front of train station. Good food and great prices. Omelettes for a song (55-90pt). Hamburger and fries LE3.00.

Restaurant Limpy, al-Mahatta St., next to the New Karnak Hotel. Dine outside on terrace or inside listening to almost-rock-and-roll. A little more upscale than its neighbors. Sterilized *shisha* LE1.

El Houda, Television St., about 150m beyond bus station. Hearty, filling pizza with a slight Egyptian twist. If you're disappointed, feed it to the birds. Neapolitan Pizza with olives LE4.

Restaurant Khased Khear, about 100m down from Limpy's on the right side. One of the best places for traditional Egyptian food. Shish kebab LE7.

You might also head for the *souk* which runs parallel to al-Karnak, beyond the tourist shops. And if you want a cold one as bad as a Canadian in Upper Egypt in July, head to al-Mahatta St., where tucked between a leather shop and a cosmetician and across from the Majestic an old man sells beer and wine. The goods are not on display.

Sights

While not as flashy as the West Theban relics and ruins, three of Luxor's sights have more to offer than yet another notch on the traveler's monument meter. Karnak Temple has its immensity, the Luxor Museum its clarity, and Luxor Temple its tranquility. You can visit all three in one day, but it may behoove your sanity to visit them on separate afternoons or evenings, after spending the morning in West Thebes.

Luxor Temple

The grand columns of Luxor Temple, visible from al-Mahatta St., reside in the heart of modern Luxor on the eastern bank of the Nile. New Kingdom Pharaoh Amenhotep

III presided over the first work on the temple, building on the site of a small Middle Kingdom temple to Amon-Ra and rededicating his edifice to the triumvirate of the god Amon, his wife Mut, and their son, the moon god Khonsu. The unfinished work of Amenhotep was completed under Tutankhamen. The most significant later contributions were those of the swell-headed pharaoh Ramses II, among which are the six looming statues of him guarding the entrance. The sanctuary was later restored under Alexander the Great, and when Christianity came to Luxor, part of the complex was used as a church. Only an altar and a few mosaics are left from this period, but the **Mosque of Abu'l-Haggag,** added by the Fatamids, still holds dominion over the temple court and remains in use.

The doorway to the temple's interior is cut through the enormous **Pylon of Ramses II,** nearly 24m tall. Flanking the main doorway are two of the six original **Colossi of Ramses II,** as well as a pink granite obelisk with four praying baboons on one side. The obelisk's twin was removed in 1836 and stands in the Place de la Concorde in Paris. Carved reliefs on the pylon describe Ramses' battles against the Hittites.

Continue through the **Court of Ramses II** to reach the **Colonnade of Amenhotep III.** From here, proceed into the **Court of Amenhotep III.** Beyond this second court rises the hypostyle hall, or antechamber, with its 32 gigantic columns set in four rows. Latin inscriptions to Julius Caesar adorn an altar in one of the rooms to the left of the pillared hall. Alexander appears in pharaonic attire before Amon and other deities in some bas-reliefs in the **Sanctuary of Alexander the Great** at the end of the corridor. The perpetually ithyphallic, overzealous fertility god Min receives disproportionate attention in the sanctuary.

Situated among well-groomed lawns, the temple and its surroundings make for comfortable retreat from the noise and dirt, especially in the late afternoon and at night. (Temple open daily 6am-11pm; in winter 6am-10pm; during Ramadan, 6am-6:30pm and 8-11pm. The lights go on at 7:30pm year-round. Enter on al-Nil St., 400m north of Winter Palace. Admission LE10, students LE5. Half-price after 6pm.)

Karnak Temple

Karnak Temple is overwhelming in its intricacy and proportions. Every major period in the ancient history of Egypt is represented in the additions to this complex of shrines dedicated to Amon and his family. In pharaonic times, Karnak represented the power of the Theban ruler and the importance of the cult of Amon.

An annual festival celebrated the glory of Amon and linked the two great temples of Luxor. The entire 3km distance between the two great temples was connected by the sacred **Avenue of the Sphinxes,** a paved boulevard lined on both sides with hundreds of majestic, human-headed lions, each cradling a statuette of Ramses II, and his monumental ego, between its paws. The final stretch of the avenue remains, complete with two rows of sphinxes, at the northern end of al-Karnak St. by the **Temple of Khonsu,** to the right of the main entry to Karnak Temple.

Enter **Karnak Temple** from the west with the Nile at your back and pass through the **Avenue of the Rams,** another double-rowed boulevard of creatures (lions' bodies with rams' heads) dedicated to Ramses II. The temple is a melange of additions and alterations spanning millennia, but because of the traditionalism of pharaonic architecture, the different pieces comprise a harmonious whole. The Karnak complex expands outward from the center where you will find most of the oldest treasures; the further you proceed from the entrance, the farther back in time you go.

The first pylon is Ptolemaic (2nd century BCE), and the eighth is the contribution of Queen Hatshepsut (15th century BCE). The 10th-century BCE **Great Court,** the area before you as you emerge from the first pylon, is the largest single portion of the Karnak complex. Chambers on the left are dedicated to the Theban Trio of Amon, Mut, and Khonsu. They were built during the 29th dynasty and adorned with bas-reliefs depicting the deities. On the right is a temple built by Ramses III and lined with 20 seven-meter tall statues of guess-who. The three chapels behind the temple's inner court are also dedicated to the Theban Triad.

Return to the Great Court and continue to the right into the **Great Hypostyle Hall,** one of the pinnacles of pharaonic architecture with its sandstone forest of 134 colossal papyrus columns. The sensory overload continues on a smaller scale as every square centimeter of the ceiling, walls, and columns is carved with inscriptions. Note the boastful depictions of the fertility god, Min, doing what he does best.

Walking east toward the fourth pylon, you can find the pink granite **Obelisk of Queen Hatshepsut** at the center of a small colonnade. Passing through the rubble of the fifth pylon and the granite sixth pylon, enter the **Hall of Records,** containing two elegantly proportioned granite pillars, one decorated with carvings of the lotus of Upper Egypt, the other with the papyrus of Lower Egypt. Behind the hall is the **Sanctuary of the Sacred Boats,** a double-breasted chapel famous for its exquisite carvings.

Straight ahead, the **Festival Hall of Thutmose III** dominates the eastern edge of the Karnak complex. The star-studded ceiling survives intact, supported by 52 tapering pillars. Some of the bases were actually whittled down to make room for large processions. In Christian times, the hall was converted into a church; frescos of haloed saints still adorn the interior walls and column shafts. Beyond a low wall to the east, the **Gate of Nectanebo** marks an early entrance to the complex.

Retrace your steps to the central hall, turn right, and walk 50m to see the limpid waters of **Birket al-Mallaha** (Sacred Lake) north of the Festival Hall. Priests purified themselves in the holy waters of this rectangular pool before performing ceremonies within the temple. If your curiosity about Karnak is still unsated, you can visit the **Karnak Open Air Museum,** to the north of the great court; look for a small sign and return toward the entrance. The museum is comprised of three chapels and a motley collection of well-labeled wall fragments. Egyptologists were unable to reassemble the **Red Chapel** of Queen Hatshepsut so it is displayed in long rows of blocks. Unlike most temple decorations displayed this way, each block of the chapel features a self-contained design, which made it more difficult for the archeologists to see the larger picture. The Queen's vertically arranged breasts provided the crucial clue. The **Alabaster Chapel** is a beautiful Middle Kingdom addition to Karnak; the white walls streaked with brown are a welcome relief from the acres of sandstone. The apparent reason for placing the Alabaster Chapel, the Red Chapel, and the **White Chapel** of Sesostris I in the museum is that no one has figured out exactly where the chapels originally stood in the temple; parts of each were pilfered for later additions. (Admission LE1.50, students 75pt.)

It usually takes at least two hours to see the entire temple, so in summer it is advisable to bring plenty of bottled water and come early in the day. Equip yourself with Jill Kamil's excellent paperback guide *Luxor* (LE20), or tag along with a tour group. The temple lies 3km north of Luxor Temple at the end of al-Karnak St., 1 block east of al-Nil St. Walk or bike along the Nile or take a horse-drawn carriage (only if the horse looks like it's well-treated). A local *service* taxi, which you can catch along al-Karnak St., runs between Karnak and the train station. Ask first to make sure the driver is going as far as the temple (25pt). (Temple open daily 6am-6:30pm in summer; 6am-5:30pm in winter. Admission LE10, students LE5.)

Luxor Museum

The Luxor Museum is testament to the fact that less is sometimes more. Facing the Nile midway between Luxor and Karnak Temples, the Luxor Museum has a small but stellar collection displayed with the help of the Brooklyn Museum of New York. Featured are lavish treasures from the neighboring temple complexes and the Valley of the Kings, including a wooden cot, a relief of ancient gymnasts and acrobats, and model funerary boats from the celebrated tomb of Tutankhamen. The New Hall showcases 16 pieces of marble and granite statues, 8 small and 8 large, that are quite magnificent to behold. The giant cobra and the confident Amenhotep III are perhaps the most striking. The museum is within walking distance (1.5km) of both Luxor and Karnak Temples. (Open daily 9am-1pm, additional evening hours 5-10pm in summer, 4-9pm in winter. Admission LE8, with New Hall LE10, students half-price.)

Entertainment

Fritter away late afternoons in Luxor aboard a *felucca* on the Nile. **Banana Island** is a popular destination; two miles upriver, it is a small peninsula studded with palms and fruit trees whence come small green bananas for LE1. Overpriced souvenir stands detract from an otherwise rustic experience. (Round-trip 2-3hrs.; LE10 per person plus tip. *Feluccas* are prohibited from sailing after sunset.)

The Winter Palace, ETAP, Isis, and Sheraton Hotels feature **belly dancers** on most nights. Dancers sign on for six-week contracts; prurient locals usually know which shows are best. There are no set time appearances; just lurk at the bar and wait for these master midriff manipulators to appear. A politically-correct dilemma: Is this a genuine cultural expression and therefore sacrosanct, or is it objectification of women? (Minimum drink charge of LE12-15, which covers anywhere from 1 to 1.5 drinks. 1.5 drinks? How do you order 1.5 drinks?) A low-budget alternative, Luxor's numerous **sidewalk cafés** buzz with flies and nightly gossip about people you'll never meet. Foreign women won't necessarily feel uncomfortable at a café, but a lone woman will probably be hassled.

West Thebes طيبة غربية

> And so sepulchred in such pomp dost lie,
> That kings for such a tomb would wish to die.
> —John Milton

Even while preoccupied with the desire for a great empire, the rulers of Thebes were dedicated to estate planning and life insurance. All ancient kings apparently aspired to a tomb with a view on the western shore of the Nile. Pharaonic obsession with the afterlife made the necropolis of Thebes into possibly the world's best-endowed graveyard. Over the course of centuries, robbers and archeologists have pilfered much of the treasure, but the site still features an unparalleled collection of Egyptian funerary art.

Security was the main concern of the Middle Kingdom rulers who built the Theban tombs. Earlier pharaohs had been, it seems, too trusting and too convinced of the inviolability of their sacred tombs. Thieves soon mastered the delicate process of pyramid pilfering at Memphis, making off with many of the afterlife amenities thought to make the second go-round a little easier for the expired exalted. That simply would not do— a radical change in burial practices was in order to ensure only the most decorous treatment of the deceased.

The western edge of Thebes, capital city of the New Kingdom, was selected as the site for subsequent tombs. In order to conceal the location, contents, and design of the tombs, the work was done in utmost secrecy by a team of laborers who dwelt within the necropolis itself. Perfecting techniques of tomb construction, decoration, and mummification, this community of 300 artisans devoted themselves to the City of the Dead over the course of generations, passing their knowledge down through their families. (Remains of the workers' walled city have been excavated near the Temple of Dayr al-Medina.) Tomb design reflected the new emphasis on secrecy. Instead of a single ostentatious pyramid, there were pairs of funerary monuments: an underground grave, lavishly outfitted with the articles demanded by the hectic afterlife and sequestered in an obscure recess of the desert, and a grandiose mortuary temple where the monarch could be publicly worshiped for eternity. Designers and builders incorporated dead-end passages, fake sarcophagi, hidden doorways, and deep shafts to foil the most cunning robbers. Once a plotzed pharaoh was safely stowed, workers immediately began to construct the tomb destined for his successor.

One region in particular seemed ideal for entombment: a narrow, winding valley captured on three sides by jagged limestone cliffs and approachable by a single rocky footpath. This isolated canyon, known as the **Valley of the Kings,** became the burial place of New Kingdom pharaohs. Although it looked promising on papyrus, it failed to deter the foot-pads; few of the tombs escaped vandalism.

Queens, favored consorts, and select offspring were accorded ceremonial burial with full honors and security precautions in a separate corner of West Thebes, the **Valley of the Queens.** The most esteemed members of the Theban aristocracy also practiced the elaborate burial customs. Several of the **Tombs of the Nobles** in fact rival the royal burial chambers in quality of craft and design. Over 400 tombs are found in West Thebes.

Practical Information

Conduct your exploration of West Thebes in a series of one or more early morning visits. For those who can bear the heat, however, afternoons are less crowded, and some of the more open sights and temples lay abandoned for errant wanderers to examine free of charge and hassle. Especially in the summer, guards at the less visited sights tend to lock up and head home a little early. All sites open at 6am, offering about three hours of peace and pleasant temperatures. The sites officially close at 4pm in winter, 5pm in summer. Drinks are sold at some of the ruins; play it safe by bringing plenty of water.

Take a ferry from Luxor to West Thebes. **Tourist ferries** operate frequently for LE2 round-trip (no bicycles allowed). One tourist ferry docks next to the Savoy Hotel, 300m north of the temple. The other docks in front of the Winter Palace Hotel, 200m south of Luxor Temple. Both tourist ferries shuttle you to the main (non-student) ticketing office on the western bank. (Ferries operate daily 6am-5pm.)

The more logical option for the budget traveler is the two **local ferries,** which terminate their crossings at a site more convenient for donkeys, bicycles, and other vehicles. One docks directly in front of Luxor Temple (25 pt., bicycles 25pt.) and the other leaves from a spot just north of the Novotel (LE1 each way, bicycles free). From the dock, head inland to the student ticket kiosk or walk east to the main ticketing office. (Ferries operate daily 6am-midnight; modest dress should be worn on board.)

Once on the west bank, there are several different ways to explore West Thebes; some require pre-ferry planning, others do not. **Bicycles** are cheap; they also allow you relative freedom and a chance to take in the surrounding scenery of barren mountains and fertile fields. The well-paved and gently sloping roads make for a relatively easy ride, even on one-speeds. Rent your bike in Luxor.

Hiring a **taxi** for the day is surprisingly economical (LE5-12 per person, plus LE1-2 baksheesh at the end of the trip) and allows you to cover the most ground. Approach tourists in Luxor (try the Salt and Bread Restaurant) and ask if they are interested in sharing the cost of a taxi. Then come early and bargain hard with the drivers who wait at both the northern (tourist) and southern (local) ferry docks. Ignore any prattle about government rates and per-person charges. It is also possible to make arrangements in Luxor the day or night before and take the car ferry to the other side.

Mark Twain wrote that riding a **donkey** in Egypt "was a fresh, new, exhilarating sensation...and worth a hundred worn and threadbare pleasures." The novelty of donkey travel (which has a way of wearing off quickly) and the fantastic views afforded by the donkey trail as it climbs its way up and around to the Valley of the Kings has lead to a burgeoning burro-borrow market. Never encourage cruelty to animals. Through your pension, you can arrange an excursion which includes donkey, ferry, and guide (LE10-15). You can also do away with middlemen and hire your own ass. Hiring your own animal allows you more leeway with your itinerary—the tours usually take you to the Valley of the Kings, Dayr al-Bahri, the Ramasseum, and the Colossi of Memnon—but won't necessarily save you money. Or venture along a route on your own. The donkeys usually know the way, they are generally obedient beasts, and besides, guides are usually useless. Try to pay LE8-10 for the donkey, but not until the day is done. Leaving an expired license with the handlers is a good way of hedging your bets—you might even want to hold on to the poor beast.

In the winter, those with time to spare can get around by **foot.** You might want to take a local taxi (about 25pt) to the student ticket kiosk (3km from the ferry dock), from which most of the Theban Necropolis and the Valley of the Queens is within a 3km radius. The Valley of the Kings lies an easy 8km away by road, or a few strenuous kilometers by donkey path.

Guided tours in air-conditioned coaches with English-speaking guides can be arranged through the various corniche travel agents and cost LE65-80 per person, including admission. Most tours visit the Valley of the Kings, the Valley of the Queens, the Collossi of Memnon, and Hatshepsut Temple. The larger your group, the better your bargaining leverage. Often the travel agencies will have prearranged tours and you can pay the full price and tag along. Isis Travel and Misr Travel on the corniche are good places to start. The loss of spontaneity, adventure, and independence is mitigated by convenience and a more thorough description of the sights, which can be enlightening.

Try to bring a flashlight; it'll save you the necessity of paying *baksheesh* to guards. Photography is prohibited at all sites; this regulation is rigorously enforced, as flashes harm the paintings.

The least explored of all options is a **motorbike.** Technically you need a license to operate these machines. Motorbikes for hire are available at countless shops and some pensions. The New Grand and Nefertiti Hotels both offer rental. Renters will often quote you exorbitant sums—LE25-35 is a reasonable day's rate. When you're done with the sights, you might also consider an easy ride through the countryside, but beware of local driving customs.

Although most travelers receive their fill of West Theban sights in two or three days, the wealth of ancient relics could occupy a wannabe Egyptologist for weeks. The best inexpensive specialized guidebook to the area is Jill Kamil's paperback *Luxor* (LE20), available at bookstores in town. The most thorough, though far more expensive, coverage available in English is Nagel's *Encyclopedic Guide to Egypt.*

Accommodations

Though most visitors to the area sleep in Luxor, staying in West Thebes offers a respite from the noise in tranquil, nearly rustic settings and a chance to roll out of bed and to the sights at the opening bell. Unfortunately, you don't get quite as much for your money in West Thebes, as competition is not as fierce. During the high season you should call ahead before lugging your bags across the river. When a three digit number is listed, dial 10 or 25 in Luxor and ask for "west bank number so-and-so." You can also ring up a west bank operator at 38 25 02 or 38 48 35 and ask for your three or four digit extension. A taxi from the ferry docks should cost LE2.

Pharaoh's Hotel, 100m behind the student kiosk along an unpaved road (tel. 207). Reminiscent of a Greek villa. Fronted by an elegant garden; new, stylishly decorated. A/C. Doubles LE40, LE60 with private bath. Breakfast included. Lunch or dinner LE15.

Abul Kasem Hotel, just before the entrance to Seti Temple (tel. 2095 or 438). Large, carpeted rooms in a quaint and tranquil setting. Often hosts large tour groups; student and group discount. LE15 in summer, LE25 in winter. Breakfast and private bath included. Lunch or dinner at the fine adjoining restaurant LE10 (in winter and late summer only).

Queens Hotel, near Medinat Habu Temple (tel. 716). Interestingly contoured but relatively clean rooms and rooftop terrace. LE10 per person. Includes breakfast. Generous meals of beef or chicken upon request (LE7).

Hotel Marsam, the second building away from the front of the student kiosk (tel. 38 24 03). Rustic, exotic setting—Spanish style adobe surrounded by lush fields. No fans. LE15 per person with breakfast, but flexible. Lunch or dinner LE8.

Sights

Plan ahead—you must decide what you would like to see before you head out. Consider content, location, and mode of transport before purchasing tickets. (For example, those planning to ride donkeys should try to reserve the Valley of the Kings for the day of the burro ride.) One suggested donkey route includes the Valley of the Kings, around to Dayr al-Bahri, the Ramasseum, and home. Those with a great deal of energy or with only one day to spare in West Thebes should consider squeezing in the Tombs of Rekhmire and Sennofer and the Tombs of Ramose, Userhet, and Khaemt. A second day by bike or taxi might begin at the Seti Temple, stop off at one or two of the Noble Tombs and the Tombs of Rekhmire and Sennofer if still unvisited, and continue to Dayr al-Medina, the Valley of the Queens, and Medinat Habu. Taxi riders or cyclists with only one day should make sure to include the Valley of the Kings, the Tombs of Rekhmire and Sennofer, the Valley of the Queens, and Medinat Habu in their journey.

Tickets

There are two ticket kiosks. The one for non-students is on the western bank of the Nile next to the tourist ferry dock. The student kiosk is 3km farther inland, just beyond the Colossi of Memnon. Both kiosks are open daily 6am-4pm. Tickets are non-refundable and good for day of purchase only. Non-student prices are as follows (50% student discount with ISIC).

#1	Valley of the Kings (see note below)	LE10
#2	Tomb of Tutankhamen (closed for restorations)	LE6
#3	Dayr al-Bahri (Temple of Hatshepsut)	LE6
#4	Medinat Habu (Temple of Ramses III)	LE6
#5	Ramasseum	LE6
#6	Asasif Tombs	LE6
#7	Tombs of Nakht (Khereef, Nefer-hotep, Kiky and Anch-hor) and Mena	LE6
#8	Tombs of Rekhmire and Sennofer	LE6
#9	Tombs of Ramose, Userhet, and Khaemt	LE6
#10	Dayr al-Medina (Temple and Tombs)	LE6
#11	Valley of the Queens	LE6
#12	Tomb of Nefertari (closed for renovations)	LE6
#13	Seti Temple	LE1.50
#14	Tombs of Khousu, Ushereto Benia	LE6
#15	Tomb of Pabasa	LE6

Note: The Valley of the Kings ticket (#1) grants you admission to three tombs. You may choose among any of the ones that are open (nine in summer 1992). Fortunately, this is the one place you can buy tickets on location. A second admission ticket opens three more tombs.

Valley of the Kings وادى الملوك

The Valley of the Kings lies 5km from the Nile but is accessible only via steep, circuitous routes (or donkey paths). From either ferry dock, head inland toward the ridge and the temples of the Necropolis of Thebes. There are two possible routes to the beginning of the Valley road: students must head 3km straight inland past the Colossi of Memnon to the student kiosk, then northeast past the sites of the necropolis to the beginning of the Valley road. Non-students with tickets from the Nile-side office can turn right (northeast) at the canal (follow the signs) and go 2km along the canal, then turn west by the Abul Kasem Hotel and go 1.5km to the base of the Valley road. The well-paved, gently sloping road winds for 5km into desolate mountain valleys. The Valley of the Kings itself, no more than 400m long and 200m wide, can easily be toured by foot from the clearly marked, well-groomed gravel paths. Over 64 known and numbered tombs honeycomb the valley. Most of them are not open to the public, but the best-known tombs are almost always accessible. Some are kept locked and can be opened only by the mythical site guards. All tombs listed are illuminated with fluorescent lights, but a flashlight can be helpful in revealing dark side chambers.

In the summer of 1992, 9 tombs were open to public view (3 admission tickets' worth). Ramses VI (#9—don't confuse ticket numbers with tomb numbers) and Ramses III (#11) once occupied the best of these; Amenhotep III (#35), Ramses I (#16), and Merneptah (#8) would also be proud of what is left of their burial chambers.

West Thebes's most renowned tourist attraction, the **Tomb of Tutankhamen (#62)**, stands directly in front of the Rest House in the middle of the valley. Visit it first or you'll probably be disappointed after seeing the others; size does make quite an impression. The tomb's celebrated discovery in 1922 by archeologist Howard Carter produced a cache of priceless pharaonic treasures that has toured the world several times and now resides permanently in the Egyptian Museum in Cairo. Egyptologists had expected that the tomb would contain little of interest because the pharaoh reigned only a short time before he died. A determined archeologist, Carter ignored professional censure, toiling for six seasons in the Valley of the Kings. After more than 200,000 tons of rubble had been moved, even Carter's sympathetic patron, the wealthy Lord Carnarvon, reluctantly decided to abort the project. But before admitting failure, Carter made one last attempt: the final unexplored possibility was a site in front of the tomb of Ramses VI, in an area covered with workers' huts. Confounding the critics, he chanced upon an ancient doorway beneath the shanties. The sensational discovery revealed an amazing store of baubles, thoroughly vindicating Carter. The tomb had remained almost intact, barely despoiled by robbers for centuries; it was crammed with decorated furniture, wheat, vegetables, wine, clothing, canopic jars, jewelry, and utensils—including several royal walking sticks—and three mummies, including that of the pharaoh himself. Carter was occupied for 10 years cataloging the contents.

Tutankhamen's mummy was encased in the innermost of three snugly nested, superbly decorated coffins. This dazzling coffin of solid gold is now displayed in the Cairo Museum as is the second mummy-case of inlaid gold foil. Fortunately, the raiding Egyptologists left behind the outermost coffin, a gilded wood extravagance luxuriating in rich jewels, along with Tut's exquisitely carved sarcophagus. Of all the pharaohs buried in the Valley of the Kings, only Tutankhamen has the privilege of resting here in peace. King Tutankhamen's tomb may seem miniature because he reigned as pharaoh for only two years. The interior walls of the burial chamber, perfectly preserved, depict colorful scenes from the *Book of the Dead.*

The 12th-century BCE **Tomb of Ramses IX (#6),** on the left upon entering the valley, features fantastic ceiling murals of gold figures manifesting their *joie de mourir* against a deep blue background. A lengthy corridor slopes down to a large anteroom covered with a proliferation of demons, serpents, and wild beasts. Beyond, through a pillared room and corridor, a pit in the burial chamber once held Ramses IX's sarcophagus.

The **Tomb of Ramses VI (#9),** directly behind and above the Tomb of Tutankhamen, is best known for its unusual ceiling. Bizarre images of men with snakes' heads, little naked figures riding cobras like camels, kneeling headless bodies, and people with elongated limbs and torsos party on the walls and ceilings. Below are scattered the fragmented remains of Ramses VI's sarcophagus, smashed by grave-robbers. This tomb was closed for repairs in 1992.

The steep entrance next to the Tomb of Seti I descends into the **Tomb of Ramses I (#16),** a single burial chamber dominated by Ramses' pink granite sarcophagus. The tomb walls, some of the most vivid in the valley, are painted with scenes of Ramses hobnobbing with the gods. The first corridor is the shortest of any royal tomb in the valley, a consequence of this Ramses's brief rule (1320-1318 BCE).

Named the "Tomb of the Harp Players" after a pair of musicians depicted plucking away in one of its interior chambers, the **Tomb of Ramses III (#11)** boasts an interesting portrayal of ancient races on the left side of the penultimate chamber as you enter the tomb.

West Thebes' most dramatically situated burial site is the cliff-side **Tomb of Thutmose III (#34),** reached by a long, steep staircase that ascends a precipitous ravine squeezed between towering limestone cliffs. To get to the tomb, follow the dirt road that begins next to the Tomb of Ramses III leading southwest up the hill. In no other tomb was greater care taken to camouflage the grave's location. Closed for restorations in 1992.

In 1898, local Egyptian farmers directed France's most eminent archeologist, Victor Loret, to the **Tomb of Amenhotep II (#35).** The tomb lies past the Tomb of Ramses III, west of the Rest House. From the path leading up the western hill to the Tomb of Thutmose III, bear right to the northern cliff face. Although thieves had stolen the best treasures millenia ago, the interior was essentially undisturbed and contained the un-touched mummy of Amenhotep II as well as nine other sacred mummies. The Cairo Museum won custody of these royal remnants, including Thutmose IV, Amenophis III, and Seti II. One red sarcophagus remains. The burial chamber, decorated with a complete set of texts from the *Book of the Dead,* is stunning.

The **Tomb of Seti II (#15)** is southwest of the Rest House. Take the road leading up-hill toward Thutmose III's tomb and then the first right after the path to the Tomb of Amenhotep II. The grave consists of a series of long, descending corridors culminat-ing in a small burial chamber that houses a statue of the pharaoh. Near the tomb en-trance is an anonymous mummy; Seti II's mummy has been transferred to the Egyptian Museum in Cairo. Although the painted decorations and bas-relief on the corridor walls are fairly well preserved, they are less sophisticated than those in neigh-boring tombs. The tomb ends abruptly because the king died before it could be com-pleted.

The **Tomb of Tausert and Sethnakht (#14)** testifies to the thievery of pharaohs themselves. Queen Tausert reigned in 1200 BCE; upon her death, successor Sethnakht usurped her tomb, superimposing his own drawings and inscriptions over the earlier, carefully painted images. The double images represent the dual human-divine role of the pharaoh.

The descent into the **Tomb of Merneptah (#8)** stretches about 80m, and the burial chambers contain a number of huge granite sarcophagus lids. In an effort to preserve the frescos the builders of the tomb covered the walls with a thick layer of plaster, which in fact caused the drawings to crack and fall off. The tomb stands just inside the main gate.

The **Tomb of Ramses IV (#2)** is outside the main entrance to the Valley of the Kings. Walk 100m down the paved road away from the entrance booth; the tomb is on the left. Because it is seldom visited, you may have to ask at the entrance booth for it to be opened. Despite Coptic graffiti, the painted carvings retain most of their original color, but they lack the vitality and expressiveness in many of the other tombs. Don't forget to ogle the biggest sarcophagus in the valley.

The centrally located **Rest House** serves refreshments (complemented by meals in the winter) and charges tourist prices. Public toilets add popular appeal. (Open daily 6am-5pm in summer, 8am-3:45pm in winter.)

Mortuary Temples

As if gripping rock-hewn tombs aren't spectacular enough, West Thebes also boasts some of the finest **mortuary temples** ever built. Treated as gods while living, the pha-raohs continued to be worshiped after death in these edifices. Though overshadowed by Luxor's Karnak Temple in scale and historical importance, the West Theban tem-ples of Hatshepsut, Ramses II, Seti I and Ramses III are still stupefying.

The mortuary temples of the Necropolis of Thebes, all accessible from a road that runs parallel to the Nile, are described from south to north. From the ferry—Seti I—docks, head inland 3km past the Colossi of Memnon until you come to an intersection. A road to the left leads to the temple of Ramses III at Medinat Habu, 0.5km to the southwest. With the exception of Dayr al-Bahri, the mortuary temples afford little shade; they are best visited early in the morning during the summer months.

The largest mortuary temple, that of Amenhotep III, has been destroyed save the **Colossi of Memnon,** a pair of glowering, towering statues seated in magnificent iso-lation on the northern side of the entrance road to the necropolis. Looking out over the plain from a height of 20m, the figures of Amenhotep III were Thebes' greatest tourist attraction during the Roman era. At night, an eerie whistling sound emanated from the stones, which the Romans interpreted as the voice of Memnon, mythical son of the goddess of dawn, Aurora. The sound, according to scientists, was actually produced by grains of sand splitting off from the statues as the rocks contracted in the cool night air. Unfortunately, the Colossi ceased to sing after repairs during the reign of Antoninus Pius.

To the left at the end of the road after the Colossi stand **Medinat Habu,** a series of well-preserved edifices constructed in several stages by various pharaohs. The most impressive structure in the complex is the **Mortuary Temple of Ramses III,** decorated with reliefs of the pharaoh's numerous successful military campaigns.

The Ramasseum

> *My name is Ozymandias, King of Kings,*
> *Look on my works, ye Mighty and despair.*
> > —*Percy Bysshe Shelley*

The first stop as you turn right after the Colossi of Memnon is the Mortuary Temple of Ramses II, better known as the Ramasseum. This is the pharaoh who had Abu Simbel tailor-made to his specifications; the Ramasseum also once housed two of his mammoth exercises in narcissism. Though the chest, shoulder, and one foot remain, the hefty, 1000-ton, 17m **Colossus of Ramses II** had fallen and splintered, thereby avoiding the fate of its twin. The other monolith (the forefingers alone measure over 1m long) was transported in one piece from the pharaoh's granite quarries in Aswan to Thebes. This colossus and its twin originally flanked the passageway leading into the second court, reputedly identified by the Roman historian Diodorus as the Tomb of Ozymandias.

Dayr al-Bahri

Just north of the Ramasseum a paved road leaves the main north-south thoroughfare and heads west, straight for the cliffside **Mortuary Temple of Hatshepsut,** known in Arabic as Dayr al-Bahri. Located in the center of the necropolis, the temple is 500m north of the Tombs of the Nobles. Hatshepsut's masterpiece rises in three broad, columned terraces from the desert floor against a backdrop of sheer limestone cliffs. The Temple's ancient Egyptian name means "most splendid of all."

After the death of her husband Thutmose II, Hatshepsut assumed the role of monarch. Her temple, currently under excavation by a team of Polish archeologists, has been skillfully restored with modern materials. No images of Hatshepsut remain intact; after her death, the soon-to-be-great Thutmose III defaced virtually all of them to avenge his stepmother and aunt, who cleverly displaced him and ruled in his stead.

Walk from the lower court up an absurdly wide ramp to the central court. The colonnaded back wall contains, from left to right, the Shrine of Hathor, Colonnade of the Expedition of Punt, Birth Colonnade, and Shrine to Annubis. Another huge ramp leads to the upper court. Badly ruined, and sadly defaced by Christians who used the temple as a monastery in the 7th century, this court is currently undergoing restoration and is closed to the public; if you happen to be around when a lot of other tourists are not, a dedicated guard may attempt to make your visit complete by inviting you up for a quick peek.

The **Shaft of Dayr al-Bahri,** north of the Temple of Hatshepsut in a gully at the foot of the towering cliffs, was the site of the greatest mummy find in history. In 1876, the local director of antiquities began receiving reports of a steady flow of unknown ancient artifacts appearing on the Luxor market and became convinced that someone was plundering a pharaonic tomb. Later, after a family squabble, the eldest brother of Luxor's most prominent antiquities merchant squealed and led the authorities to a shaft penetrating 12m into the earth. Amenhotep I, Thutmose II, Thutmose III, Seti I, Ramses I, and Ramses III had all been laid to rest in this single shaft along with a host of other royal mummies. Apparently the high priests, realizing that even the most elaborate precautions failed to prevent thieves from disturbing the bodies of deceased pharaohs in their tombs, made a final and successful attempt to hide the mummies by moving their remains to this secret communal grave. The 40 mummies unearthed at Dayr al-Bahri now rest in the Egyptian Museum in Cairo. Strangely, the body of Hat-shepsut was not among them. Though the queen constructed two tombs for herself, one in the Valley of the Kings, and the other south of Dayr al-Bahri, her remains have never been found. The shaft can be opened upon request, though a visit requires *bak-sheesh.*

Temple of Seti I

Ah, yes. You were thinking of coming this way, weren't you? From Dayr al-Bahri return to the main road, turn north, and follow it to the end. Turn right to visit what remains of the **Mortuary Temple of Seti I,** father of Ramses II, a warrior who en-larged the Egyptian empire to include the island of Cyprus and parts of Mesopotamia. The mortuary temple contained some of the booty Seti I obtained on his successful campaigns, as well as some of the finest relief work ever executed in ancient Egypt. The treasure is gone but the carvings remain.

Tombs of the Nobles

A few hundred meters southeast of Dayr al-Bahri is West Thebes's sardinally packed burial site, the more than 400 Tombs of the Nobles. The area is divided into six regions: the Tombs of Rekhmire and Sennofer (ticket #8); the Tombs of Ramose, Userhet the Scribe, and Khaemt (ticket #9); the Tombs of Nakht and Mena (ticket #7); the Asasif Tombs (ticket #6); the Tomb of Pabasa (ticket #15); the Temple and Tombs at Dayr al-Medina (ticket #10). You must buy a separate ticket for each. Tickets #7, 8, and 9 provide the most bang for your tomb-going buck. A guide is unnecessary as the sites are scattered through a village where residents can point the way. If you can get your hands on one, a map of the area is useful.

Throughout the New Kingdom, Theban aristocrats had *de facto* control over much of the pharaoh's empire and served as advisers on matters of state. The pharaoh often remained ignorant of the most crucial political developments while members of the elite fought amongst themselves for control of the kingdom. Some aristocrats affected pharaonic status by amply providing themselves with luxuries for the afterlife and de-vising well-hidden underground tombs. Unlike the divine pharaoh who would live among the gods after his death, Theban aristocrats needed more assurance that a com-fortable existence awaited them in the afterlife. Accordingly, every facet of their earthly lives was carefully recorded on the walls of their tombs; the decoration is thus more naturalistic and mundane than the reliefs found in pharaonic tombs. Because the limestone in this portion of the necropolis was inferior, artisans could not carve in re-lief; instead they painted murals on a whitewashed stone surface.

Tombs of Rekhmire and Sennofer

The tomb at the westernmost portion of the site belongs to Rekhmire, a governor of Thebes who advised Thutmose III and prided himself on his administrative genius. A historian's delight, the **Tomb of Rekhmire (#100)** is comprised of biographical narra-tives depicting the full range of activities Rekhmire oversaw. This tomb is perhaps the most absorbing of all the tombs in West Thebes.

In the first chamber, tax evaders are tried by Rekhmire, who sits with a set of rolled papyrus texts strewn at the foot of his judgment throne; the presence of the papyrus shows that written law existed as early as 1500 BCE. On the inner, left-hand wall, a procession of tribute-paying expeditions arrive from Crete (top), Syria (middle), and the African Kingdoms of Punt and Nubia (bottom). Making a special contribution to the pharaonic menagerie, Nubian representatives offer a giraffe, assorted monkeys, a tiger, and an elephant tusk. The niche at the top of the rear wall was intended to con-tain a statue of Rekhmire himself.

Trek 50m up the hill to the west of Rekhmire's tomb to reach the **Tomb of Sennofer (#96).** This vivid tomb is known as "Tomb of the Vines," after the filigree grapevine crawling all over the ceiling. The delightful lattice of purple and green simulates a shady arbor for Sennofer, overseer of the royal gardens of Amon under Amenhotep II. The plan of the tomb is as unusual as its decor: a curving wall leads into the first room, which in turn leads straight back into the pillared burial chamber. The big, wet eyes of Hathor the cow follow you around the tomb from the tops of the columns. The superb condition of the paintings and their remarkable expressiveness make this small tomb worth the detour.

Tombs of Ramose, Userhet and Nakht

The **Tomb of Ramose (#55),** southeast of the tombs of Rekhmire and Sennofer down a short dirt road, was built during the pharaoh Akhenaten's period of monotheistic religious orientation. Ramose was preeminent during the reigns of Amenhotep III and Akhenaten, and was apparently one of the first converts to the latter's radical devotion to the sun god Aton.

In the columned first chamber, all of Egypt pays obeisance to Aton, a blood-red disk emitting shafts of light which end in small hands holding *ankhs* and other religious symbols. On the wall through which you enter, the images carved in unpainted relief reflect the traditional, stylized tastes of the Old Kingdom, with scenes of Ramose and his family making offerings, and Egyptians cheering Ramose's conversion to the Aton cult. In contrast, the wall to the left as you enter displays expressive and realistic "Amarna-style" scenes of a mourning procession.

Continue up from the depression containing the Tomb of Ramose to the **Tomb of Userhet the Scribe (#56),** a few meters to the south. Although an early Christian monk who made his home within the chamber destroyed most of the female figures adorning the walls, the tomb's decor retains a certain blithe spirit because of the unusual pink tones of the interior frescos. Userhet, Amenhotep II's royal scribe, had his resting place painted with mundane scenes. On the right-hand wall of the first chamber, men wait their turn in line for a chance at an Ed Grimley hairdo from the local barber.

Slightly north of the Tomb of Ramose a trail leads off the main dirt road, winding east a short distance to the recently reopened **Tomb of Nakht.** The first chamber contains a reconstruction of an exquisite statue of Nakht, scribe of the royal granaries under Thutmose IV (the original was lost at sea on its way to the U.S. during World War I), photographs of some of the other removed contents, and a series of well-labeled diagrams explaining the images within the second chamber. The most famous image from the Tombs of the Nobles, three wardrobe minimalist musicians playing the flute, harp, and lute is on the left wall.

Asasif Tombs

Southwest of Dayr al-Bahri lies **Asasif,** a current archeological hotspot, with several research projects in the digging. Asasif became the most popular aristocratic burial area during the 25th and 26th dynasties (about the 7th century BCE). The **Tomb of Kheruef (#192),** constructed during the 14th century BCE, is the finest in this portion of the necropolis. Enter the burial site through an outer courtyard containing other tombs, where a series of well-wrought reliefs stands against a protecting wall. Note the ceremonial dance in which a line of women flop their hair and a jumping bird and monkey are accompanied by flautists and drummers to the left of the doorway. On the right is a striking portrait of Amenhotep III surrounded by 16 swooning princesses.

As you enter the **Tomb of Kiki (#409),** about 10m to the north of Kheruef, the gods Thoth and Anubis discuss the readings of a giant scale. The burial chamber remained unfinished, leaving a series of faceless figures outlined in red. To get to the **Tomb of Nefer-hotep (#48),** walk 100m east along the dirt path from Kiki then turn right (south) and walk 20m to the tomb, immediately in front of a village house. Most of the seated stone figures within the tomb are fairly intact.

Dayr al-Medina

To reach the scanty remains of the **Tomb Workers' Walled City,** start from the student ticket office and follow the small road west to Dayr al-Medina. About 60m west of the guardhouse stands the small **Temple of Dayr al-Medina** (Monastery of the Town), an elegant shrine dating from the Ptolemaic era. Dedicated to Hathor, the goddess of love, and Maat, the deity of justice, the temple was named during Christian times when monks constructed a monastery next door. A single admission ticket includes entrance to the Temple of Dayr al-Medina, Sennutem's tomb, and the Workers' Walled City.

Valley of the Queens وادى ملكات

During the later years of the New Kingdom, a special burial area was chosen for the wives and children of the pharaohs. Traditionally the pharaoh's closest relations were buried beside the monarch, but this arrangement changed during the reign of Ramses I (14th century BCE), when princes, consorts, and wives were buried in the Valley of the Queens. In the southwest corner of West Thebes, directly west of the Colossi of Memnon at the end of the main road, the Valley of the Queens contains fewer than 30 royal tombs. Check at the ticket kiosks to find out which are currently open. Don't be alarmed if you see Egyptians painting the walls: they're preserving the pigments with a special fixative.

The **Tomb of Amon-Hir Khopshef (#55)** is richly bedecked with bas-relief carvings. Ramses III introduces his nine-year-old son to each of the major deities; Amon-Hir Khopshef wears the groomed topknot of a pharaonic prince. The colored scenes of deities and farmers fill entire walls—a rare sight in Theban tombs. The small sarcophagus that held the prince's mummy stands in the rear burial chamber. A mysterious desiccated fetus lies curled in a small glass display next to the sarcophagus. The **Tomb of Queen Nefertari (#66),** the most beautiful tomb in the Valley of the Queens, is, to the chagrin of many, closed indefinitely.

Between Luxor and Aswan

The 220km stretch of the Nile contains the drowsy rural towns of Esna, Edfu, and Kom Ombo. The area is an olio of older Arab *fellaheen* communities and Nubian villages created for those displaced by the High Dam. Each of the major towns is also graced by an outstanding Ptolemaic temple.

Whether you go by taxi, bus, or train, you'll have no difficulty stopping in Esna, Edfu, and Kom Ombo during a day's journey between Luxor and Aswan. These towns and their temples also make excellent day trips: Esna and Edfu from Luxor; Edfu, Kom Ombo, and the camel market at Daraw (near Kom Ombo) from Aswan. If you've got a bit of spare time and cash, glide on a *felucca* for leisurely, low-budget transport. The entire Aswan to Luxor route takes 3-5 days, including ports of call in Esna, Edfu, and Kom Ombo.

By Taxi, Bus, or Train

Traveling by *service* **taxi** is the most efficient, cheap and sensible option for shuttling between the river towns at almost any time of day:

Luxor-Aswan: LE8, 3-4hr.	**Luxor-Edfu:** LE4, 90min.
Luxor-Esna: LE2, 1hr.	**Luxor-Kom Ombo:** LE7, 2-3hr.
Esna-Edfu: LE2, 1hr.	**Aswan-Esna:** LE3.50, 2-3hr.
Edfu-Kom Ombo: LE2, 45min.	**Aswan-Edfu:** LE2.50, 90min.
Aswan-Kom Ombo/Daraw: LE1, 40min.	**Kom Ombo-Daraw:** 50pt, 5min.

The two potential drawbacks to travel by *service* taxi are that you must wait an unpredictable (though usually short) time for a taxi to fill, and that taxi drivers are king-hell crazy speed demons. Mangled Peugeot carcasses in roadside ditches and the Egyptian highway death rate testify to the risks involved. Sure are fast, though. A group of five to seven people may want to hire a **private taxi** (LE65-95 from Luxor to Aswan).

Buses can be convenient because they are frequent (13 per day in both directions) and do not require advance purchase of tickets; simply climb aboard and pay the conductor. The disadvantage is that they stop running about 7pm and most lack A/C. A bus is best for transport out of Luxor or Aswan; you may not find an empty seat when you try to board in one of the towns in between.

Last and least, the seven daily **trains** present more hassle than they are worth for short runs. Air-conditioning is a plus, but probably outweighed by the headache of purchasing a ticket and waiting for a delayed train. Luckily, you can usually get a seat in an air-conditioned car between Luxor and Aswan without advance booking—walk on and pay the LE1.50 surcharge. Second-class air-conditioned travel is slightly more expensive than a *service* taxi (Luxor to Aswan LE8), while second-class non-air-conditioned is a steamy bargain (Luxor to Aswan LE2).

By Felucca

If you're intrigued by the idea of not doing much of anything, not really going anywhere, and getting in touch with the Nile while floating in a boat with a tall mast and a white sail with some friends, newly acquired acquaintances, and a couple of Nubians, then you should make sure to include a *felucca* trip on the Nile in your Egypt travel plans. Hiring a *felucca* and captain is a simple affair. Stroll along the waterfront in Luxor or Aswan and you'll attract them like flies, each willing to give you a "special price." Without wanting to sound like a killjoy, stay alert—hotel comment books from Kom Ombo to Esna are filled with tales of watery woe of mysterious repairs, broken masts, and lost possessions.

First, gather a group of travelers who would like to spend a few days together adrift on the Nile. Next, hunt for a captain. Get referrals—consult fellow travelers, your hotel manager, or the tourist offices in Aswan or Luxor. Be sure to get more than the captain's name; if you go down to the riverside asking for Captain Muhammad, you're likely to learn that he's very busy in the Nubian village, he's vacationing in the Sudan, or he has just met an untimely death. To avoid a wild goose chase to the local Nubian cemetery, find out the name of the captain's boat and a likely place to find him.

More than likely, you'll be embarking from Aswan, where the *felucca* industry thrives. Most trips last two days and end in Edfu. If you'd like to spend more time on the river, you'll have to be very insistent and have a big group to back you; the captains would rather stay close to home. In Aswan, heading from north to south, you might look out for Captain Haman and the large kiwi banner on the good ship *Happy Days*. Captain Fowzy parks his *Sheraton* across from the tourist office. Jimmy and his *Silver Moon* rent behind the Aswan Moon. Further down you'll find Captain Hamdi hanging out in a café behind the police station when he's not in the Valley of the Kings. You might also venture out to Elephantine Island. From the ferry that leaves by El Shati, take a quick right, walk about 10m, and you'll find the Jamaica family home. Brothers Abed and Ahmed (currently in Holland) run a six-boat fleet, and they'll be happy to have you aboard. It's a good idea to try and get to know your captain. Most sleep on their boats and will be happy to conduct introductory meetings. Besides, there isn't all that much to do in Aswan during the day.

The typical large *felucca* sleeps up to eight people, displays a single tall sail, and is piloted by an English-speaking Nubian. Police regulations forbid sailing after 8pm, so passengers either sleep on wooden slats in the docked *felucca* or on the river bank next to the boat.

A conscientious *felucca* captain will help you buy the appropriate ingredients for multi-course Egyptian meals at a cost of LE5 per person per day for a typical trip. The captain may cook on a stove in the *felucca* or arrange to stop at his village for a home-cooked meal. Bring at least three bottles of water per person per day for drinking, cooking, and brewing tea.

Captains generally adhere to the official rates for *felucca* trips as quoted at tourist offices, though you can negotiate down to 50% of this in summer. Officially, members of a 6-8 person group should pay LE25 each to Kom Ombo, LE45 to Edfu, LE50 to Esna, and LE60 for the four days it takes to get to Luxor. This does not include food, water, registration, and any other gear you might bring along. Women may be more comfortable if they bring male companions along.

When you begin the *felucca* trip in Aswan, you will be asked to register your passport and part with LE5 for the registration fee. The government requires travel agencies to register passengers. In Aswan, **Seven Tours** (tel. 32 36 79), on the central corniche next to Maxime's, and **Luxor Tours** (tel. 32 26 15), in front of the tourist office, handle nearly all the *felucca* business. Curiously, the registration requirement is not enforced for trips beginning in Luxor. The Aswan tourist office can explain the latest vagaries of the *felucca* scene.

Esna اسنا

A quiet, provincial town, Esna snoozes on the west bank of the Nile, connected by a bridge to the main highway and rail line on the eastern side. A smaller highway ambles along the western bank to West Thebes. Luxor is 70km downstream; Edfu lies 50km and Aswan 155km upstream. Esna can be reached by taxi, train, bus, or *felucca;* see above for details.

Esna has one main street for tourists. Heading south from the bridge, Nile Street (Bahra St.) crosses the canal, veers left, then continues on by the Nile, running north-south. As you travel down Nile St., you'll first find the **police station** (tel. 40 08 89) just south of the canal. The **tourist police** (tel. 40 06 86) are located near the temple just to the right of Nile St. by the ticket booth (open 6am-5pm). About 1km further down is the **Bank of Alexandria** (open 8:30am-2pm, 6-9pm for exchange). About 150m north of the ticket booth, you'll find the **Post Office** (open Sat.-Thurs. 7am-2pm). The **telephone and telegraph office** is located near the bridge on Nile St. (Open 7am-10pm.) International calls can be made from a small office two blocks south and a quick right.

The **train station** lies to the east of town on the other side of the Nile. A **carriage** will charge about LE1.50-2 for the 4km trip to the temple. The **bus and *service* taxi stations** are at the town's western edge, down the street just south of the telephone office (LE1 to temple).

Despite its pleasant people and atmosphere, there is little to keep you in Esna beyond a temple visit. The only accommodations are at **Al-Haramen** (tel. 40 03 40). Walk 1km south (through the *souk*) from the temple's eastern wall, pass to the right of the white wall enclosing a gray concrete building, and walk another 100m. (Singles LE5. Doubles LE8.) Dirt is pervasive and there are no fans. For **food** in Esna, go to the *souk* or try your luck at **Al-Amana** by the temple, where a chicken meal goes for LE5. The camel market takes place early Saturday morning.

Temple of Khnum

Khnum was a ram-headed creator god who reputedly molded the first human on a potter's wheel. Although begun during the 18th dynasty, the Temple of Khnum is largely a Roman creation and was in many ways a feeble imitation of inherited technical and artistic achievements. Esna was an important regional center for the area south of Luxor, and the pharaohs of the 18th dynasty, seeking stronger popular support, dedicated this temple to the local deity. Archeologists discovered the elaborate hallway in excellent condition. Today the temple forms an incongruous spectacle, lying in an excavated depression next to the *souk.*

The Romans, making an effort to decorate the temple in a traditional pharaonic manner, instead carved a procession of stiff, oddly deformed figures marching solemnly across the walls of the hallway. Look up; the ceiling designs are among the more interesting ones in the temple. Faint blue and red hues on the tops of the 24 columns hint at how brilliant the interior must have been. (Open 6am-6:30pm, in winter 6am-5:30pm. LE4, students LE2.)

Edfu اد فو

Edfu is an unspectacular town with unpaved roads and a modest-sized market. But just beyond the bustle of the central square, silently oblivious to its surroundings and to the passage of 2000 years, stands an astonishingly well preserved ancient site—the mammoth and mesmeric Temple of Horus. This labyrinth of dark chambers and towering pillars ranks with Karnak and Abu Simbel as one of Upper Egypt's most fabulous sites.

Practical Information

Roughly halfway between Luxor (115km) and Aswan (105km), Edfu lies 50km south of Esna along the western bank of the Nile. Travel by taxi, bus, train, or *felucca*. The **bus station** in Edfu is on Tahrir St., 100m north of central **Temple Square.** Tahrir St. runs parallel to the Nile about 1km inland. The wide **al-Maglis Street** links Temple Sq. with the Nile. The Edfu bridge, with the **train station** on its eastern end and the *service* **taxi station** near its western end, is about 300m north of al-Maglis St. along the riverfront road. The last bus out of town in either direction leaves at about 6pm, the last trains at about 9-10pm. To reach the **temple** from Temple Sq., follow the signs and head away from the Nile along al-Maglis St. for 200m. Local **pickup trucks** (25pt) or **private taxis** (LE2) can take you from the train station to the temple.

The **tourist police** (tel. 70 07 24) are located at the entrance to the temple (open 7am-6pm). The main **police station** (tel. 70 08 66) is on the east end of al-Maglis, about 100m from the Nile. The **post office** is on Tahrir St., on the right side 50m south of Temple Sq. Edfu's produce *souk* is on Gomhoria St., parallel to Tahrir St. and 10m further west (open Sat.-Thurs. 8am-2pm). A **Banque Misr** is also on Gomhoria St., about 150m south of al-Maglis St. (open Sun.-Thurs. 8:30am-2pm).

Accommodations and Food

Hotel Dar as-Salaam (tel. 70 17 27), 50m east of the temple on al-Maglis St., is the cleanest of Edfu's three hotels, though by no means immaculate. All rooms have fans. (Singles LE12. Doubles LE20. Negotiable.) Even if you don't decide to stay at the **al-Madina Hotel** (tel. 70 13 26), Taha won't let you go without a cup of tea and a peek at his correspondence. (Quoted prices about LE12; negotiate. Dinner LE5.)

Dining options in Edfu are slim after Mr. Taha's delicious breakfast of fruit, falafel, bread, and eggs for LE3. Across the street from the Sami Ramis Hotel is the clean **Restaurant Zahrat al-Medina** ("City Flower" in Arabic). **Happy Land Restaurant,** on the west bank between the bridge and town, has a wider selection. The **New Egypt Restaurant,** on the left side of Tahrir St. 200m south of Temple Sq., features a rotisserie grill but isn't particularly clean. (Meat meal at any of these restaurants LE5.)

Temple of Horus

This Ptolemaic structure took over 200 years to construct and was not completed until 57 BCE, making it one of the last great Egyptian monuments. The Ptolemaic designers created this temple and the one at Dendera, dedicated to Horus's wife Hathor, as a matched set.

Several important religious festivals centering around the life and death of the falcon-god Horus were celebrated at Edfu. During the annual "Union with the Solar Disk," Horus's earthly form was brought to the roof of the temple to be rejuvenated by the rays of the sun. The rite generally transpired in conjunction with the New Year holiday. Another important ritual was the coronation festival, in which a falcon was crowned in the temple's main court and triumphantly paraded to the interior where it reigned in darkness for one year.

From the site's entrance by the ticket kiosk and tourist police station, walk the full length of the structure and enter the temple at the far end. The main doorway through the pylon is flanked by two battlements rising to a height of 36m and guarded by a noble granite falcon. Only a chunk of his co-sentinel on the right remains. Enter the temple through the 12 gigantic columns of the **Great Hypostyle Hall,** and proceed on to the second Hypostyle Hall, outfitted with a similar arrangement of smaller pillars.

Doorways on either side lead to the **Corridor of Victory,** an exterior passageway running between the temple and its protective wall, so narrow that even an underfed chihuahua might get stuck. The temple is honeycombed with doorways and small passageways that enabled the priests to walk around the entire complex without crossing in front of the sanctuary or having to talk to one another. Recently, holes were made in the ceilings and walls to provide light, damaging many fine stone figures.

Outside the temple, directly in front of the main entrance pylon, is a well-preserved (except for sparrow damage) Roman *mammisis,* where the birth of Horus was annually reenacted with appropriate hoopla. Later generations of prudish Egyptians emasculated the images of the growing god on the columns of the *mammisis.* The site is open daily 6am-6pm in summer, 7am-4pm in winter. (Admission LE10, students LE5.)

Near Edfu: Al-Kab

If you're traveling by bus or private taxi on the main highway north of Edfu and you have a lot of time and energy to spare (or if you're editing a travel book and you have some extra pages to spare), you might consider a stop at **al-Kab,** 15km north of Edfu near the village of al-Mahamid. The excursion fare from Edfu is about 50pt by truck or LE2 by taxi. The religious center of al-Kab was dedicated to the goddess Nekhbet and currently contains comparatively uninteresting ruins from most eras of ancient Egyptian history. From the ticket office on the east side of the road, walk up the stairs on the left to find a series of Middle and New Kingdom tombs up on the hill. Beginning on the right, you'll first see the **Tomb of Daheri,** chief priest, royal tutor, scribe of accounts, and son of pharaoh Thutmosis I. This tomb is the best preserved of the group and features designs of long lines of seated lotus-sniffers and Egyptians cultivating various crops. Next door, the **Tomb of Setau,** high priest of Nekhbet, and the **Tomb of Aahmes,** a military leader, are both devoid of interest unless you want to learn hieroglyphics to communicate with the horses at Giza. To the left is the slightly more intact **Tomb of Renini,** superintendent of priests.

Further along into the desert languish the **Chapel of Thoth** and the **Ptolemaic Temple,** 3.5km up the road from the ticket office. The better-preserved **Temple of Amenophis III** lies 1.5km further. Caravans going to and coming from gold mines deeper into the desert used to stop here for prayer, and there are some nice intact depictions of the goddess Nekhbet ("Lady of the Desert"), especially on the four interior columns. If you're determined to see these lonely remains, bring several bottles of water (there's not a leaf of shade) or try to hire a private taxi—a difficult task on a road where there's as much traffic as rain. Alternatively, you can arrange for private transportation in Edfu for about LE10.

Across the highway from the ticket office lie the remnants of the city of al-Kab, or more precisely the Roman walls that used to surround it. The government has only recently developed al-Kab for tourism, and the site has yet to become popular. (Open daily 8am-6pm. Admission LE5, students LE2.50.) When you've finished looking around, try to catch a ride back to Edfu or on to Esna. On a really bad day you may have to trek the 2.5km to al-Mahamid.

Kom Ombo كوم أمبو

Forty-five kilometers north of Aswan on the east bank of the Nile looms Kom Ombo, the site of an Egyptian temple as renowned for its location as for its rigorously symmetrical construction. Unlike other temples in Egypt, Kom Ombo is still situated along the banks of the Nile, giving virtually the same visual impression today as it did during Ptolemaic times. The sanctuary's more dramatic peculiarity, however, is its meticulous symmetry, which has each element paired with a twin. Double doorways lead into double chambers and sanctuaries after passing through double halls and past double colonnades. The two-fold temple was dedicated to a duo of gods: Sebek, the toothy crocodile god, and Horus, the winged falcon or sky god. The priests were doubly diplomatic and, so as not to offend either deity, ordered everything to be built in tandem. There is double zero shade at Kom Ombo, so wear a boater; and remember:

you can never have two much water. Relax afterwards by strolling in the town; the warm hospitality of the townspeople is a double bonus.

Practical Information

Kom Ombo is easily reached by service taxi, bus, train, or *felucca* from Aswan, Edfu, or Luxor. The **bus station** in Kom Ombo is on July 26 St., which runs parallel to the railroad tracks and the Cairo-Aswan highway, about 400m south of the central square where Gomhoria and the highway intersect. The *service* **taxi station** is also on July 26 St., just south of the intersection with Gomhoria St. The **train station** is on Gomhoria St. across the highway and the tracks. The remains of the temple are 4km west from the central square down Gomhoria.

The **police station** sits 50m north of Gomhoria St. (tel. 50 08 29). The **Bank of Alexandria** is in a small alley next to the mosque, at the corner of the highway and Gomhoria St. (Open daily 8:30am-2pm, during Ramadan 10am-1:30pm, additional currency exchange hours Sun. 6-9pm and Wed. 5-8pm.) To get to Kom Ombo's *souk*, cross over the highway on the footbridge. The **post office** is one block farther in on the right. (Open Sat.-Thurs. 7am-2pm.) A covered pickup truck (25pt.) runs all day between the river (near the ruins) and the center of town. The truck leaves from Gomhoria St. behind the large white mosque with the minaret, one block off the highway. Private taxis cost LE3 each way. If you're coming from Aswan by service taxi or bus, ask to be let off at the well-marked turn-off to the "tembel" 2km south of town. From the turn-off, walk 1.5km through sugar-cane fields to the temple site. (See Between Luxor and Aswan for more transportation arcana.)

Accommodations and Food

The **Cleopatra Hotel** (tel. 50 03 25), just off 26 July St. at the service taxi stand, may have the tidiest rooms between Aswan and Luxor. The bathrooms are somewhat less impressive. (Singles LE5.25. Doubles LE8.70. Fans LE1.50.) The **Roowan Hotel,** 300m south of the white mosque along the highway, has dark, cramped rooms with ceiling fans. (Singles LE5. Doubles LE8.) The recently opened **Restaurant El Noba,** halfway between the mosque and Roowan on the other side of the street, offers a quarter chicken, rice, vegetable, and salad for LE5.

Temple of Kom Ombo

Although a temple has stood at Kom Ombo since the time of the Middle Kingdom, its oldest portions now rest at the Louvre and the Egyptian Museum in Cairo. What remains dates from the Ptolemaic and Roman periods. After its abandonment during the decline of the Roman Empire, the rising waters of the river inundated the site and left the temple almost completely buried in sand. In later years the portions above ground were used as a quarry for neighboring edifices, and as a result the side walls have vanished. Nonetheless, the temple retains much of its original resplendence.

The temple's dualism is apparent in the surviving columns of the hypostyle hall. Designs on the right columns feature Sebek while those on the left depict bird-beaked Horus. The ceiling of the adjoining vestibule managed to escape defacement by unappreciative Christians; bright blue and black images of Horus hover protectively over the chamber. In the interior of the temple are the less substantial remains of the Hall of Offerings and the inner sanctuaries dedicated to Sebek and Horus.

Adjoining the northern edge of the temple are the Roman water supply tanks, comprised of two wells joined to a stepped vat, and, to the west, the remains of a Roman *mammisis*. The guards at the site claim that crocodiles once lived in the well and that Cleopatra's bubble bath is nearby. Climb down the well and check for yourself. The **Chapel of Hathor,** directly south of the main temple, houses a doubly-revolting collection of crocodile mummies unearthed near the road leading away from the site. (Site open daily 6am-6pm. Admission LE4, students LE2.)

Near Kom Ombo: Daraw دراو

Sudanese merchants, Bishari tribespeople, and Egyptian *fellaheen* convene in Daraw (de-RAU) every Tuesday morning for a **camel market.** The Sudanese purchase camels for the equivalent of LE200, march for one month through the desert to Daraw, and resell the be-humped beasts at 500% profit. The Bishari are traditional Saharan nomads with their own language and culture. Some of the men conduct business in full traditional dress: flowing pants, fighting sword and dagger, and a cloak draped over their shoulders. Typically, a Sudanese camel owner will pay a Sudanese or Bishari shepherd to drive his camels north to Egypt. The owner then flies up to oversee the selling. If you think the slobbery creatures are cute, the going rate for a big male camel is LE1200-1500, which will save you close to LE1000 over prices in Cairo.

Tuesday is the only market day in the summer, but camels are sometimes sold on Sundays and Mondays in the winter. On Tuesday, the camel market is adjoined by a **livestock market** where farmers sell cattle, water buffalo, sheep, and goats. The animals are hauled in by truck, or occasionally toted on the merchants' shoulders. On market day, impromptu shaded *fuul* and tea stands refresh merchants, buyers, and gawkers. The camel market runs from 7am-2pm but starts deteriorating after about 11am. A good strategy is to rise very early in Aswan, visit the camel market, and move on to see the temple at Kom Ombo. En route to the camel market, you'll walk through an equally large **fruit and vegetable market** where the Nubians do their weekly shopping.

Service **taxis** careen to Daraw from Kom Ombo, 8km to the north (5min.) and Aswan, 32km to the south (1hr.). All the trains and buses running between Luxor and Aswan stop in Daraw. The **taxi stand, bus station,** and **train station** all lie along the main highway. To reach the market from the taxi, bus, or train station, walk 300m toward the Nile, bearing left when the first street ends, then right. If you're gliding by on a *felucca,* have the captain stop at the Daraw ferry landing and a covered pickup truck will shuttle you to the market. During the winter there may be another location for the market; ask around. The word for camel is *gamel,* and don't be afraid to act like one if you're hard up for directions. It really works.

Aswan أسوان

Within sight of the first cataracts of the Nile, the city of Aswan grew and flourished as Egypt's frontier town: the trading center between Egypt and the rest of Africa and the gateway to the plains of Sudan and Nubia. Modern Lake Nasser adds moisture to the air while its dam powers Aswan's burgeoning industry.

The desert's presence is easily felt in Aswan. Temperatures frequently soar well into the 90s, and unlike other sections of the fertile Nile Valley, the river at Aswan is bounded by inhospitable sand and mountain. The spice added by the large local Nubian community, many of whom relocated to Aswan ahead of the innundation of their homes following the creation of Lake Nasser, contributes to the desert flavor.

Aswan is also a resort town, especially popular in the winter. The city's spotless corniche, perhaps Egypt's most elegant boulevard, graces the Nile for the entire length of the city. One unfortunate result of Aswan's commercialization is that what was once a city where women could feel quite comfortable is now noticeably less so. Still, the pace is relaxed and the heckling confined, making for a pleasant atmosphere, provided one can escape the south Egyptian heat.

Orientation and Practical Information

The southernmost city in Egypt, Aswan is 890km upstream from Cairo and 220km south of Luxor. Frequent taxi, bus, and train service connects Aswan with Luxor. Aswan is the base for exploring the southernmost parts of Egypt. Plan on at least three days: one for Aswan, one for Philae and the High Dam, and one for a round-trip excursion to Abu Simbel. Aswan is also a good starting point for slow *felucca* trips on the Nile.

You are almost never more than two blocks from the river in Aswan. The northern half of the city lies along three long avenues running parallel to the bank of the Nile. By far the most handsome of the trio is the **Corniche al-Nil,** featuring most of the fancy hotels and *Let's Go* stopping points. Two blocks inland, Aswan's busiest lane, **al-Souk St.** (Market St., also known as Sa'ad Zaghloul St.), features everything from merchants peddling mounds of spices to tacky tourist trinket stands with plastic busts of Queen Nefertiti. This street begins at the train station at the northeast corner of town and runs south 2km through the *souk.* In the southern half of town, the corniche continues for another 2km, ending at the **Ferial Gardens.** The northern grid pattern falls apart at the central market. South of the *souk,* inland streets form a labyrinth of alleys and cul-de-sacs. Running between the corniche and the market street, **Abtal al-Tahrir St.** begins at the youth hostel and culminates in a small cluster of overpriced tourist bazaars.

The white local taxis charge about LE2 to travel the length of the city, but walking is easy.

Tourist Office: Corniche al-Nil (tel. 32 32 97), two blocks toward the river from the train station and one block south across from a small park. English-speaking staff and friendly Shukri Sa'ad. Advice on tours to Abu Simbel and travel to Kalabsha and Sudan. A good *felucca* resource, with knowledge of prices and captains. Open daily 8:30am-2pm and 6-8pm; during Ramadan daily 9am-3 or 4pm.

Tourist Police: Main office above the tourist office (tel. 32 43 93); branch on the south side of the train station (tel. 32 31 63). English-speaking cops. Open 24 hrs.

Passport Office: Corniche al-Nil (tel. 32 22 38), 2 blocks south of the Continental Hotel, in the police building at the southern end of the corniche. Enter on the left side of building. Register your passport or extend your visa here. Open Sat.-Thurs. 9am-2pm and 7-9pm.

Banks: On Corniche al-Nil are **Banque Misr** (tel. 32 31 56), **Banque du Caire** (2 branches, tel. 32 24 58), and **Bank of Alexandria** (tel. 32 27 65). Open daily 8:30am-2pm and 5-8pm, during Ramadan 10am-1:30pm. Alex closed Fri. and Sat.; Caire will usually exchange money 2-5pm.

American Express: In lobby of Old Cataract Hotel (tel. 32 29 09), at the southernmost end of the corniche. Offers exchange and banking services and will hold mail. Open daily 8am-7pm.

Post Office: Corniche al-Nil, across from the Rowing Club Restaurant, toward the northern end of town. Open Sat.-Thurs. 8am-2pm. **Poste Restante** is 1 block off the corniche, in the center of town, on a small street behind the Bank of Alex. Open Sat.-Wed. 8am-noon and 6-8pm, Thurs. 8am-noon, Fri. 4-8pm. You can also send mail from major hotels.

Telephones, Telegrams, and Telex: Tel. 32 38 69. Corniche al-Nil, 2 doors south of EgyptAir. Relatively efficient for international calls. Open 24 hrs. Also a telephone and telegraph office in the train station (open daily 8am-10pm). Those wishing to avoid immediate cash charge (LE28 for three minutes to United States) might try international operators at the hotels or at the **Business Center** on corniche, one block south of police building (LE2 per minute). Fax available. Open daily 8am-11pm. **Telephone code:** 097.

Airport: 23km south of town (tel. 48 03 20 or 32 29 87), near High Dam. LE10 one-way by taxi. Served by **EgyptAir,** Corniche al-Nil (tel. 32 24 00; airport 48 03 07), at the southern end, before the Ferial Gardens and Cataract Hotels. Egypt's other airline, **ZAS Air** (tel. 32 64 01), on the corniche just north of Continental Hotel, serves the same airports for slightly less (LE353 to Cairo, compared to EgyptAir's LE387). **Airport Police:** 48 05 09.

Train Station: Northern end of al-Souk St. (tel. 32 20 07), 2 blocks east of the corniche, at the northeast corner of Aswan. To Luxor (4 per day, 5 hrs., 1st class LE13.10, 2nd class LE8). Reservations available in advance. Also trains, originating from Luxor, to the Dam (9 per day 6am-10:30pm, returning 6am-7:30pm, 20pt). Up to 50% discount with student ID.

Bus Station: Abtal al-Tahrir St., 3 blocks south and 1 block west of the train station, 1 block in from the Nile in the northern part of town. North to Daraw, Kom Ombo, Edfu, Esna, and Luxor (18 per day, 5:45am-3pm; to Luxor, 4 hrs., LE5). A/C bus to Hurghada (3 per day, LE26.25). To Cairo: 5:30am, 3:30pm, 4:30pm, LE25-30. South to Hazan/Old Dam (#20 and 59 from Corniche; 14 per day, 6am-9:30pm, 25pt). Also to Abu Simbel (A/C, daily at 8am, 3 hrs., back in Aswan 5-6pm, LE13.50 each way). No bus service to High Dam.

Ferry to Sudan: Nile Navigation Company: To Wadi Halfa on eastern shore of Lake Nasser. Office next to tourist office (tel. 32 33 48; open Sat.-Thurs. 8am-2pm). Boats on Thurs. and Sat., sometimes another day in summer. 1-day trip. Ferry connects with train to Khartoum. Over Mark Templeton's dead body: *Let's Go: Sudan.* Must acquire visa in advance in Cairo or at home. Can handle motor vehicles. 1st class LE135, 2nd class LE75.

Local Ferries: To Elephantine Island from either al-Shati Restaurant on central corniche or across from EgyptAir at the south end of the corniche (6am-9pm, every 15 min., 25pt for foreigners). To west bank tombs and villages from Seti Tours, opposite tourist office (6am-6pm every 30 min.; 6pm-10pm, every hr., LE1).

Service **Taxis:** Taxis leave from the covered station 1km south of the train station on the east side of the railroad tracks, next to a large underpass. To Daraw or Kom Ombo (LE1), to Edfu (LE3.50), to Esna (LE4.50), and to Luxor (LE5.50). For taxis to Aswan environs and south, wait in the square at the corner of Mahmoud Yakoub St. and Abtal al-Tahrir, next to Happi Hotel, 2 blocks south of the bus station. To Hazan/Old Dam (25pt). You can arrange special trips with taxis anywhere in Aswan. See the Aswan Sights, South of Aswan, or Abu Simbel sections, below, for details about taxis to High Dam, Kalabsha, Philae, and Abu Simbel. 7-person taxis cost 40% more than 4-person taxis. You might also look into passenger-bearing **pickup trucks,** which leave from a covered station between Corniche and Abtaak al-Tahrir St. next to the Hotel Abu Simbel. Similar prices. Don't jump off.

Bike Rental: For daily rental, try to stumble upon **Nahas Alley,** near Bata Shoes Store, 1.5 blocks off central corniche from Aswan Moon Restaurant, on southern fringe of the *souk.* Bikes have locks and rear brakes only. Rates negotiable: about LE2 per hour, LE10 per day. Must leave passport, student ID, or first-born. Other bike shops, without signs, are 100m south of Ramses Hotel on Abtal al-Tahrir St. and on Matar St., across from King Aswan Lab (LE1 per hour, LE10 per day). Haggle.

Swimming Pools: New Cataract Hotel (LE10, open daily 9am-sunset) at the southern end of the corniche, and **Isis Hotel** (LE10, open daily 9am-sunset) in the north central segment. Municipal pool does not admit foreigners.

Photo Developing: Photo Sabry, Corniche al-Nil (tel. 32 64 52), will print 36 color exposures in 24 hrs. Open Sat.-Thurs. 8:30am-11pm, Fri. 6:30-11pm.

Pharmacies: El-Nile Pharmacy, Corniche al-Nil (tel. 32 26 74), across from Isis hotel in the central part of the corniche. Open daily 7am-midnight. **Atlas Pharmacy,** next to Mena Hotel on Atlas St. (tel. 32 43 00). Open Mon.-Sat. 9am-2:30pm and 6-11pm. Over-the-counter drugs and contraceptives. If these are closed or out of stock, there are plenty of alternatives in the *souk* and along the Corniche.

Hospital: German Evangelical Mission Hospital, past EgyptAir on the southern end of the corniche (tel. 32 21 76 or call tourist office). Open 24 hrs. There is also a **Government Hospital,** a second choice.

Foreign Press and Books: Corniche al-Nil (tel. 32 43 70), 30m north of Hotel Continental, next to ZAS office. Newsstand on sidewalk has paltry but eclectic selection of used books in English and many other languages.

Laundromat: Many of the accommodations listed below will do laundry for you for 25-50pt per garment.

Medical Emergency: Tel. 123.

Police: Tel. 122.

Accommodations and Camping

During high season (Oct.-April), expect to pay 10% to 50% more than the low-season rates listed below. In summer, hotels sit empty, desperate for business and willing to negotiate; they'll also usually tack on a service charge (often 20% with tax). Rates listed here are for low season, unless otherwise noted. Groups can lower hotel prices to LE6-7 per night. All places listed provide showers, and many have restaurants attached.

Youth Hostel (HI), 96 Abtal al-Tahrir St. (tel. 32 23 13), 1 block west and 1 block south of the train station. Foreigners entrance on the right side of the building. Large, crowded rooms with bunk beds. Musty and dusty, but clean bathrooms. Lockout 10am-2pm. Curfew 11pm. Beds LE3. Nonmembers may purchase membership for LE24, but requirement may be overlooked when hostel is empty.

El-Amin Hotel, Abtal al-Tahrir St. (tel. 32 31 89), 3 blocks south and 1 block west of train station; follow the sign. Clean, pleasant, and inexpensive. Fans. Singles LE9. Doubles LE14, with bath LE16. Rooms with 3-6 beds also available. Breakfast included. Prices negotiable.

Mena Hotel, Atlas St. (tel. 32 43 88). Turn right from the train station, walk to the right of two gas stations, continue straight for two more blocks until the convenience store, and then turn left. Good value, but inconvenient location in northeasternmost corner of Aswan. Amiable service with rooms cleaned daily. Beds are less than sturdy. Comfortable porch, roof garden, and ping-pong table. Sporadic hot water. Singles LE10. Doubles LE16. 5-person suite with salon LE30. Discount for students and 50% discount for seniors, doctors, and nurses. Small breakfast included. Expect to pay LE3 to LE5 more in winter.

Hotel Continental Aswan, Corniche al-Nil (tel. 32 23 11), at the southern end of the corniche, with a long outdoor café in front. Once grand, now so only in name. Cheap and convenient, with some rooms splashed with graffiti. Short on amenities—wear shoes to the bathroom. Rooms for 2 or more. LE5 per bed for Nile view, LE3 without.

Marwa Hotel, Abtal al-Tahrir St., across from the hostel and down a short alley under Eiffel tower lights. Not a bad recreation of prison life: beds, fans, barred windows, and stark yellow walls. Will organize trips. Ceiling fans in all rooms, hot shower on every floor. Singles LE4. Doubles LE7. Triples LE9.

Molla Hotel, Kelanie St. (tel. 32 65 40). Pass through the corridor across from Aswan Moon Restaurant, continue 2 blocks east, veering left past Bata Shoes. Continue for another 50m, go right, then walk another 60m. The proud owners offer organized trips, bazaar, and ceiling fans. Two air-conditioned rooms, which the owners do not give up for less than LE30 until late in the day. Singles LE8, in winter LE10. Doubles LE16, in winter LE20. Private baths LE2. Breakfast included.

Keylany Hotel, from corniche across from Aswan Moon, head down small street, veering left for two blocks, then right. Look up for sign. Spanking new, with spotless rooms in quiet part of town. Singles LE15. Doubles LE25, in winter LE32. All doubles with private shower, singles without. LE9 for extra cot. Breakfast included.

Saber Hotel, al-Souk St. (tel. 32 27 44), 4 blocks south and 1 block west of the train station. Surprisingly clean rooms off dusty hallways. Ceiling fans. Doubles LE10, some with private bath.

Rosewan Hotel (tel. 32 44 97). Turn right as you leave the train station, head past a gas station, and take the next left. The hotel is on the right. Neat and hospitable. Large rooms, all with fans. Convenience store next to lobby. Singles LE10. Doubles LE17. Private bath LE2. Includes breakfast.

Oscal Hotel, Abdas al-Abkad St. (tel. 32 38 51). Turn left from train station and continue for 500m. Turn left on Hememy al-Gabelawy St., then right on Abdas al-Abkad St. and continue for two blocks. Hotel on right. A Las Vegas lobby graces this clean and comfortable hotel. A/C and bath in every room. Singles LE18, in winter LE38. Doubles LE25, in winter LE50.50.

Horus Hotel, 98 Corniche al-Nil (tel. 32 33 23), across from Aswan Moon Restaurant. Tidy, carpeted rooms with A/C, bath, and balconies overlooking the Nile. Singles LE25, in winter LE30. Doubles LE35, in winter LE38. Extra for A/C. Breakfast included.

Hathor Hotel, Corniche al-Nil (tel. 32 25 90), across from Isis Hotel. Clean, bright rooms, some overlooking the Nile. Fans and cramped baths in every room. Features rooftop pool and sundeck. Singles LE20, with A/C LE27. Doubles LE32, with A/C LE38. Breakfast included.

Happi Hotel, Abtal al-Tahrir St. (tel. 32 20 28). One block west of Misr Bank on Corniche. Pleasant, well-decorated rooms with private baths and A/C. Even a hint of luxury. Singles LE30, in winter LE40. Doubles LE40, in winter LE55. Breakfast included.

Abu Simbel Hotel, Corniche al-Nil (tel. 32 28 88), on the corniche, 2 blocks south of the train station. A would-be luxury hotel, with a *patisserie,* outdoor café, and nightclub. Riverfront rooms with bath. Singles LE20, with A/C LE23, in winter LE38. Doubles with A/C LE35. Breakfast included.

El Salam Hotel, Corniche al-Nil (tel. 32 26 51), 25m south of the Isis Hotel on the opposite side of the north-central corniche. Spotless, carpeted rooms, some with balconies overlooking the river and commotion below. All rooms with bath. Singles LE21, with A/C LE23.95. Doubles LE27.50, with A/C LE31. Same prices all year. Breakfast included.

Aswan's **campground,** a magnet for cross-Africa safari groups, also welcomes independent rustics. For LE3 you can pitch a tent on the grass of this spacious enclosure. Facilities include showers, water, and toilets; purchase firewood from local vendors.

The campground, adjacent to the Unfinished Obelisk, lies 2km south of town on Sharq al-Bandar St. From EgyptAir on the corniche, make a left and go about 1km. Look for sign and take a right. After another 1km, look for the campground on left. In the summer heat, the campground is inconvenient without motorized transport—for which you will be charged.

Food, Shopping, and Entertainment

Mood, not menu, sets apart one Aswan eating establishment from the next. You may find yourself on a liquid diet in Aswan—the appetite-suppressing sun, an abundance of tasty drinking options, and menu ennui may combine to put your teeth on vacation.

Fresh fruit, vegetables, bread, and pigeon are available in Aswan's main *souk*. The highest concentration of shops and street vendors is at the southern end of al-Souk St. where it intersects al-Sayyida Nafisa St. (Aswan's older market street); that's three blocks in from the Isis Hotel on the corniche. The vegetable markets lie to the north. A large vegetable *souk* is tucked away near the train station, on the northeast edge of al-Souk St. Shop in the morning for the best produce. At the other extreme, splurge on Italian food at the **Isis Hotel** (meat entrees LE18.50), or at the local deluxe establishments.

Aswan Moon Restaurant, on the river across from the National Bank of Egypt—entrance easy to spot with its wooden castle gate on the corniche. Surprisingly cool dockside restaurant by day becomes an equally cool nighttime café with Nubian musical performances. Classiest of the lot. Prime place for a beer or bottle of wine. Excellent *baba ghanoush* (40pt). Fish, chicken, and meat entrees between LE4 and LE6. Beer LE4. 10% service charge.

Aswan Panorama, on the southernmost part of the corniche. Real ice in drinks. Voluminous menu in floral atmosphere. Try the banana frappe (90pt). 12% service charge. Open noon-10pm.

Maximes Restaurant, across the corniche from Hotel Isis. The name is French; the food isn't. Dinner LE9.20. 10% service charge.

Philac Hotel Restaurant, central Corniche al-Nil. Hearty serving of spaghetti LE1.50. 10% service charge.

Monnalisa, on the corniche next to Aswan Moon. Understated and clean. Entrees LE4-LE6. Delicious Monnalisa cocktail of blended fruit juices for 60pt.

EMY, on the corniche next to Aswan Moon. A little dirtier, a little cheaper. Offers 20% student discount.

El-Shati Restaurant, on the corniche, opposite the Hotel Continental. A refreshing selection of fruit juices: banana, mango, lemon, grape, guava juice or *kirkaday* (all 50-70pt). Shortest menu save a *fuul* stand. Complete meal with choice of beef, chicken, steak or spicy fish (LE5). Ice cream 75pt. 10% service charge.

Trade in nonperishables heats up in the evenings, especially 8-10pm. If you are looking for more than the ubiquitous alphabetical hieroglyphics T-shirt, peruse the market's cloth merchants. **Barakat Nadir Kaldas,** a.k.a. Clark Gable, specializes in making Western-style pants, shorts, shirts, vests, dresses, and belts, all the while weaving fantastic tales of himself and his ancestors. His shop is 50m up al-Sayyida Nafisa St. from the Isis Hotel; look for a big yellow banner emblazoned with his name. Select one of his Egyptian cotton prints, and he'll cut and sew you a garment on the spot (trousers LE10-20, tank tops LE5-10, short-sleeve shirts LE20-25, dresses LE25-50, *galabiyas* LE25-50, and long-sleeve shirts LE25-30). Be sure to heed Barakat's suggestions about added room to preempt shrinkage. (Open Mon.-Sat. 10am-10pm or later.) If you're interested in more traditional Egyptian wear, visit the **Abdel Al-Aleety** family shop, about 60m due south on al-Souk St. from al-Sayyida St. The Aleetys specialize in custom-made, beautifully embroidered *galabiyas* and *kaftans*, a shorter form of the *galabiya* (LE15-500; open daily 9am-2pm and 5-11pm).

The **nightclubs** in the Cataract, Isis, and Oberoi hotels are anything but cheap. No cover, but a minimum charge of LE10-20 per person, which the hefty drinks prices will quickly swallow. In the winter season, the **Aswan Cultural Center,** on Corniche al-Nil between the Abu Simbel and Philae Hotels, features authentic Nubian dancing and handicrafts. (Dancing Sat.-Thurs. 9:30-11pm during winter only. Admission LE3.10.) There is no shortage of clubs and cafés where you can join the locals for a cup of tea, a puff of *shisha*, or a game of dominoes late into the night.

Sights

Aswan's real charm lies in its marvelous location and inviting market streets, not in its excavated antiquities. There are pharaonic, Coptic, Islamic, and modern monuments, but none are outstanding. On the west bank of the river, directly across from the city, the wind-swept sand piles into dunes with pronounced edges and sweeping contours. In the middle of the river float a handful of islets where most of the city's official attractions can be found. The largest of these, **Elephantine Island,** is linked to the mainland by regular ferries. As you disembark, you'll see to your left the **Aswan Archeological Museum,** where you must purchase an admission ticket covering the **museum,** adjacent ruins, and the **Nilometer.** The museum's collection is miniscule, but highlights include a few gilt sarcophagi and a ceremonially mutilated skull. (Open 8:30am-6pm, 8am-5pm in winter. Admission LE5, students LE2.5)

To the left of the museum's entrance, at the water's edge, stands a sycamore tree. Directly beneath the tree and carved into a rock is the **Nilometer,** some parts dating to Roman and pharaonic times, a long stairway-like shaft that measures the height of the Nile. In ancient times nothing was of greater practical significance than the Nilometer's oracle. When it proclaimed that the river was high, heavy annual flooding would ensure a bountiful harvest. When the Nilometer indicated shallow water, it foretold hunger and misery.

Elephantine Island was the original site of the settlement of Aswan. The only remains have been excavated on the southeast corner of the island, directly behind the museum. Some of the ruins, including a large **Temple of Khnum** and a small stone **Temple of Heqa-Ib,** dedicated to one of the island's ancient rulers, are currently closed for display but can be reached by judicious use of *baksheesh.* At the southeastern tip of the island (particularly attractive when viewed from the Nile) is a small Ptolemaic temple dedicated to Alexander II and reconstructed by German archeologists; the rebuilt façade is a disjointed collage of bas-relief fragments.

The central section of Elephantine has three **Nubian villages,** where you'll find congenial residents, brightly painted homes and handicrafts, and gnarled alleyways. The Nubians prefer that you be escorted by one of the villagers and be discreet about photography. Dress modestly—short shorts are frowned upon. The entire northern half of Elephantine Island is dominated by the Oberoi Hotel, surrounded by a tall *cordon sanitaire.* To reach the hotel, take their private ferry from the Aswan corniche.

Behind Elephantine Island and not visible from central Aswan, **Geziret al-Nabatat** ("Island of the Plants," or Kitchener's Island) is a lovely, island-wide botanical garden where African and Asian tropical plant species flourish. The floating arboretum also attracts a variety of exotic and flamboyant birds. To reach the island, you can rent a *felucca* and combine an island visit with stops along the west bank. It is also possible to hire a rowboat, piloted by a Nubian youth, from the west side of Elephantine Island (about LE1 for 1 or 2 passengers only.) If you wait until 7pm when the Egyptians who work on the island head home, you can catch a rowboat back for 50pt. (Island open 7am-sunset. Admission LE5.)

To reach the sights on the west bank of the Nile, it's easiest to hire a *felucca.* The official government rate for *felucca* transport in the vicinity of Aswan is LE18 per hour regardless of the number of passengers, but feel free to negotiate. Specify number of hours. A complete tour of Elephantine Island, Geziret al-Nabatat, the Aga Khan's Mausoleum, St. Simeon's Monastery, and the northern tombs goes for LE30. Insist on at least the official prices, available at the tourist office; in the summer you might be able to swing a deal. To meet other tourists who wish to share a *felucca* try the restaurants along the corniche or the café in front of the Hotel Continental. One or two people can save money by taking the ferry to Elephantine Island (25pt) then hiring a rowboat from the west side to take you to Geziret al-Nabatat, the mausoleum, the monastery, and back to Elephantine Island (LE8 after bargaining). Ferries run to and from the tombs and the east bank for 50pt, so you're better off visiting them separately.

The most accessible attraction on the west bank of the Nile is the **Mausoleum of the Aga Khan,** a short climb from where the *felucca* docks. Aga Khan is the hereditary title of the ruler of the Isma'ili Muslims. The Isma'ili believe that the Aga Khan is the direct descendant of Muhammad and inheritor of his spiritual responsibilities of guidance. The Aga Khans used to rule from Pakistan, but political shifts have since forced them into exile. Aswan became the favorite winter retreat of Muhammad Shah Aga Khan (1899-1957), the flamboyant 48th Imam of the Isma'ili. Upon his death, the Begum (the Aga Khan's wife) oversaw the construction of the mausoleum, where she is also buried. The interior of the shrine, modeled after the traditional Fatamid tombs of Cairo, is more impressive than the exterior. Opposite the entrance stands a marble sarcophagus inscribed with passages from the Qur'an. Each day a red rose is placed on the sarcophagus; contemporary legend tells of the distances across which a red rose was flown when none were available in the area. (Open Tues.-Sun. 9am-4:45pm. Free. *Baksheesh* for the guards is forbidden; caretaker will show you around. Modest dress required.) After leaving the shrine, those tempted by the striking sandswept landscape to take an alternate route back to the dock will be greeted by signs asking them to "Take The Normal Way." If you don't want to be a freak, take the stairs.

Dayr Amba Samaan (Monastery of St. Simeon) stands isolated and majestic in the desert 1km inland from the mausoleum. Built in the 6th and 7th centuries CE and abandoned in the 13th, the monastery sits on a terrace carved into the steep hills visible from the Mausoleum of the Aga Kahn. With its turreted walls rising to a height of 6m, the monastery appears more like a fortress than a religious sanctuary. The original walls of the complex stood 10m high and enclosed a community of 300 resident monks. Upstairs, the monks' cells with their stone beds are currently occupied by bats. The monastery also had a church and accommodations sufficient for several hundred pilgrims and their camels. (Open 9am-6pm. Admission LE5, students LE2.50.) To reach the monastery, follow the paved path which starts in front of the Aga Khan Mausoleum (15-20 min., bring water) or hire a camel near the *felucca* stop. (LE10 per camel; 2 people fit on a camel.)

The **Tombs of the Nobles** lie farther north along the west bank of the Nile, honeycombed into the face of ennobled desert cliffs and impressively illuminated at night. These tombs of governors and dignitaries date primarily from the end of the Old Kingdom and the First Intermediate periods. Years of decay and pilfer have severely damaged most of the tombs. The bright color and detail of the reliefs in the **Tomb of Sarenput II** (labelled as #31) merit the easy trip across the Nile. Farther south on the mountain ridge are the interconnected 6th-dynasty **Tombs of Nikhu and Sabni** (#25 and 26), father and son respectively. The cheapest way to visit the tombs is to take the ferry to the west bank from the corniche (across the small park from the tourist office, 50pt). Once across, walk uphill to the office on the left. (Open daily 5:30am-6pm. Admission LE5, students LE2.5. Permission to take photos LE10.)

Another worthwhile excursion in the Aswan area is a visit to any of the **Nubian villages** in the surrounding region, particularly on the occasion of a wedding. You may be invited to join the celebrations and ululations; the villagers consider it a mark of honor to have guests from far away villages attend their nuptial festivities. Nubian weddings traditionally involve 15 days of partying, but the demands of modern life have trimmed the celebration down to three or four.

Traditional domed roofs characterize Nubian buildings. Their large houses made of Nile mud consist of a half dozen rooms around a courtyard; each cluster of rooms has its own dome or cylindrical roof. While the disruption wrought by the High Dam has threatened to destroy this traditional architecture, Egyptian architect Hasan Fatry has brought it international recognition.

The ferry to the west bank tombs can bring you to **Garb Aswan,** another series of Nubian villages that is less frequented by tourists. From the ferry dock, you can walk or catch a taxi north to the villages. If you are going to Elephantine or the west bank by *felucca,* ask your captain to show you around the village.

For those who dream of being more than a passenger on the Nile, the **Rowing Club** on the corniche (tel. 32 24 46) rents sailboats, windsurfing equipment (LE50 per hr.), and shells, and also has facilities for water-skiing (LE50 per half-hr.). Arrange an outing one day in advance. 10% student discount.

South of Aswan

Aswan itself lacks spectacular antiquities, but the 15km stretch of the Nile south of town more than compensates. This region of the **First Cataract** includes both the **Old Dam** (5km south of Aswan), built in the early 20th century by the British, and the enormous **High Dam** (15km south of Aswan), construction of which created Lake Nasser in the early 1960s. On an island in the lake between the two dams, the exquisite **Philae Temple** proclaims the glory of Isis. Just beyond the west side of the High Dam, the lonely **Temple of Kalabsha** stands guard over Lake Nasser and the surrounding desert. The pharaoh's granite quarries lie on the southern border of Aswan and contain the famous **Unfinished Obelisk.** The area invites daytrips from the comfortable base of Aswan.

Getting Around

Unfortunately, public transportation does not completely extend to many of these sights. An excellent road follows the Nile from Aswan to the village of **Hazan,** site of both the Old Dam and the motorboat launch to Philae. The road crosses the dam and continues south for 10km along the west side of the Nile to reach the High Dam. Getting from Aswan to Hazan is simple, as the route is served by *service* **taxis** (25pt) and by **public bus** (#20 and 59 from corniche; 14 per day, 6am-9:30pm, 25pt). The high dam is served by a frequent train (20pt.) from Aswan. (See Aswan Practical Information.)

Try to travel in a group; up to four can hire a small taxi for 4-5 hrs for LE30. A full itinerary for this fare includes the High Dam, the Old Dam, Philae Temple, and the nearby Unfinished Obelisk and ancient granite quarries; the trip can be a relaxed 7-11am tour. Consider skipping something—maybe the Obelisk or Dam—to make it to Kalabsha. The best place to meet tourists for such a venture is in one of the cafés on the corniche; try those in front of the Hotel Continental.

Another way to see all the sights except the Temple of Kalabsha is to take one of the **taxi tours** occasionally organized by the youth hostel upon request (approximately LE5). Inquire at the hostel at least two nights before you want to go. The tours usually operate in the busier winter months only. Hotel managers at the Marwa, Mena, and Ramses Hotels also organize tours; talk to them or the tourist office. Tours arranged by private operators are less reliable. The outdoor eatery at the Abu Simbel hotel is a favorite hangout of self-proclaimed tour guides.

The Dams and Quarries

The most notorious of the attractions in the area is modern Egypt's great monument, the **High Dam (as-Sadd al-Ali السد العالى)**, completed in 1971. One kilometer thick at its base, 3.6km long, and 110m high, the dam has inundated Nubia with waters as deep as 200m, wiping out 45 villages and requiring the relocation of thousands of people, as well as the removal of numerous ancient monuments to high ground under a UNESCO plan.

The dam may do more for your brain than your eyes; its rather unspectacular construction saps the drama and excitement out of its mammoth size and strategic location. The long-term effects of the massive project are still unfolding: a rise in the Sahara's water table has been noticed as far away as Algeria. Archeologists suspect that the high water table has also damaged the tombs at Luxor.

On the brighter side, the dam's 12 turbines produce over two megawatts of electricity. Thanks to the dam, agricultural productivity has been greatly enhanced, and the acreage of Egypt's arable soil has been increased by 30%. The dam enabled Egypt to enjoy an undiminished water supply during the drought of the past decade, and in August 1988 the dam saved Egypt from the floods suffered by Sudan when the Nile overflowed after heavy rains.

The High Dam at Aswan has had significant international repercussions as well. Plans for the construction were unveiled after World War II when it became apparent that Egypt had achieved maximum agricultural output and could no longer feed its rapidly increasing population. When the United States offered and then refused to provide loans for the High Dam project in 1956, President Nasser ordered the seizure and nationalization of the Suez Canal as a means of generating the necessary hard currency. This triggered the Suez crisis, in which France, Britain, and Israel invaded Egypt. The Soviet Union decided to provide the necessary loans and technology, and work began on the dam in 1960.

The most conspicuous consequence of the High Dam is **Lake Nasser,** the world's largest artificial lake, stretching 500km across the Tropic of Cancer into Sudan. The beauty of the lake, lipped by sands and rocky hills, is tempered by an awareness of its effects: the displacement of an entire people, followed by the slow death of their culture, and the loss of priceless antiquities beneath the waters.

On the eastern bank, just before the dam, the **Visitors Pavilion** features plaques and sculptures blending Soviet socialist-realist motifs with traditional pharaonic figures and symbols. Plans for the construction of the dam—written in Russian and Arabic—include a map with the names of the 45 Nubian villages the engineers doomed. At the center of the pavilion is a 15m model of the High Dam and the surrounding environs, minus the water. The domed pavilion is well off the road from the dam and most taxis will not stop at it unless you insist; ask for the *mekat* (Arabic for model). (Open 7am-5pm. Free, but the Nicholsonian guard will expect some *baksheesh* for opening the place.)

A towering stone monument at the western end of the dam is another remnant of Soviet assistance. A stylized lotus blossom, the monument was intended as a symbol of Soviet-Egyptian friendship. The central image reinterprets Michelangelo with a female worker reaching across the dawn to her male comrade. Shortly after the completion of the dam and Anwar al-Sadat's rise to power, Egypt severed relations with the Soviet Union and turned back to the United States, leaving the lotus to blossom *sans* Soviets. The top of the dam affords excellent views of the islands to the north and Lake Nasser to the south. (Open daily 6am-5pm. Admission to the top LE2.00.)

Eight trains per day travel to the eastern end of the High Dam (see Practical Information), but you'll have to walk the several kilometers across the dam to see the sights. Bring water or fry. The train station usually presents a colorful spectacle, crowded with Sudanese tribespeople (mostly Bishari) camping out while they wait for the next boat home. It's more comfortable (but more decadent) to take a taxi across the dam. The dam closes to traffic at 5pm on most days.

The **Old Dam,** a few kilometers to the north, is less spectacular but more aesthetically pleasing than the High Dam. Built by the British between 1898 and 1902, the dam supplied most of Egypt's power for many years. The Old Dam can be reached by green public bus from the Aswan corniche (see Getting Around). The area known as the First Cataract is extremely fertile and one of the most idyllic spots in the Aswan area. In the picturesque village of **Hazan,** 70-year-old British villas are nestled peacefully within walled gardens.

Situated just below the waters of the First Cataract, **Sehel Island** attracts remarkably few tourists. The island boasts a hospitable Nubian village, scanty ruins, and a variety of inscriptions ranging from the 4th dynasty to the Ptolemaic period. If you're interested in a longer *felucca* ride from Aswan, this island makes a perfect destination (LE25 for a 3-hr. tour).

If you're traveling by taxi back to Aswan after touring the High Dam or Philae, you might ask the driver to stop at the Fatamid Tombs, the adjacent Unfinished Obelisk, and the nearby granite quarries. These sites are all near the camping area, 300m east of the main road at a turn-off 1km south of Aswan. The **Fatamid Tombs** are typical early Islamic shrines: squat, square stone buildings with crescents on their roofs. They are easily spotted on the left side of the road across the street from the Obelisk. The tombs have been more or less abandoned; it can be spooky wandering around the dark cemetery frequented mostly by packs of crazed banshees. The **Unfinished Obelisk** was abandoned at its site because of a flaw in the granite; it was to have soared to a whopping 41.7m on a base 4.2m on each side. In its unadorned state, the obelisk looks—well, it looks unfinished. In fact, it looks like it had never been started. The even less visually arousing **granite quarries** here supplied most of ancient Egypt with the raw material for pyramids and temples. (Obelisk and quarries open daily 6am-6pm. Admission LE5, students LE2.50.)

Philae فيلة

Philae Island's isolation, enhanced by its majestic position above the fertile Nubian frontier, has historically awed visitors. In the Greek and Roman eras, the temples of the cult of Isis drew the pious and curious. The construction of the Old Dam by the British in 1902 partially submerged the temples only a few years after their resurrection as a popular tourist destination. Archeologists feared that the temple would eventually be destroyed by the Nile's strong current after the Dam was enlarged in 1912. The construction of the High Dam alerted the world to the watery plight of Nubia's monuments and provided the impetus needed to save Philae. Between 1972 and 1980, UNESCO and the Egyptian Antiquities Department labored to transfer the complex of temples from Philae Island to higher ground on nearby Agilka Island. In 1980 the new site of the ancient temples opened to a fresh flood of tourism.

You can visit Philae by **taxi** as part of an itinerary including the High Dam, or take a **bus** to the Old Dam from the Aswan corniche; get off when it stops at the checkpoint on the east end of the dam. From the checkpoint, walk south along the shore to the concrete boat dock (about 2km). Whether you come by bus or taxi, you must first purchase an admission ticket and then hire a **motorboat** to reach the island. The proper round-trip fare for a small motorboat is LE16. It is usually easy to find other visitors to share a rental on the motorboat docks. The boat pilot is obliged to wait for you as you tour the site, so don't rush. If you linger for more than an hour, *baksheesh* is in order, but don't shed a pound until you're back on the east bank. (Open daily 7am-5pm; during Ramadan daily 7am-4pm. Admission LE10, students LE5.)

The well-preserved **Temple of Isis** dominates the island's northern edge. Isis was the mother of nature, protector of humans, goddess of purity and sexuality, and sister-wife of the legendary hero Osiris. Her following was so strong that the cult of Isis continued long after the establishment of Christianity, fizzling out only in the 6th century during the reign of Justinian, finally stamped out by patriarchal monotheism. Nearly all the structures on Philae date from the Ptolemaic and Roman eras after the beginning of artistic decline in Egypt—hence the inferior quality of the decorative relief work; Nile waters have hardly enhanced their intrinsic beauty.

From the landing at the southern tip of the island, climb the short slope up to the temple complex past Philae's oldest structure, the **Portico of Nectanebo.** The paved portico once formed the vestibule of an ancient temple. The larger edifice has been washed away, but the eastern side of the colonnade remains unfinished. At the first pylon, towers rise to a height of 18m on either side of the main entrance into the temple. Through this entrance is the central court, on the western edge of which reclines a Roman *mammisis*, its elegant columns emblazoned with the head of the cow-goddess Hathor. To the north is the slightly off-center second pylon, marking the way to the temple's inner sanctum. The *pronaos* (vestibule) was converted into a church by early Christians who inscribed Byzantine crosses on the chamber walls and added a small altar. Farther north is the *naos*, the temple's innermost sanctuary. Just inside the doorway is an amusing piece of ancient graffiti etched into the granite wall in capital letters: "B. Mure Stultus Est" (B. Mure is stupid).

Kalabsha كلبشة

The enormous **Temple of Kalabsha,** dramatically situated above the placid waters of Lake Nasser at the top of the High Dam, is one of the most striking pharaonic ruins in the Aswan area. Dedicated to the Nubian god Mandulis, the temple was begun by Amenhotes II, erected primarily during the reign of Augustus, and used as a church during the Christian era. The West German government paid to have the entire temple dismantled and transported in 13,000 pieces from its Nasser-flooded home to the present site, 50km north of the original. Many Egyptologists consider well-preserved Kalabsha to be second only to the treasures of Abu Simbel.

Slightly out of the way and not well publicized, Kalabsha allows its few visitors a rare chance to explore in the absence of tourists, bazaars, and *baksheesh* seekers. The temple is located on the west bank of the Nile, just south of the High Dam and 2km past the checkpoint. The most convenient way to reach Kalabsha is by **taxi** from Aswan. Try bargaining down to LE15 or LE20 for a large group (more than 5). You can include Kalabsha in an excursion to Philae and the dams (LE30 for a 5-person taxi). You can also reach the road to Kalabsha independently by taking the **train** to the eastern end of the High Dam (20pt; see above), and then walking across the dam (LE2 toll). Don't forget that the dam closes at 5pm. Unless the water level in Lake Nasser has risen dramatically (which would make Kalabsha an island accessible by boat only), you'll walk 2km to the temple, passing the abandoned hulls of a marooned fishing fleet along the way. If you plan to walk in the summer, bring plenty of water—at least enough to make up for the lower lake level. The site is officially open 6am-5pm but the guard may be so surprised to have visitors that you'll be allowed to stay later. (Admission LE6, students LE3.)

An immense causeway of dressed stone leads from the water to the temple's main entrance. The first pylon is off-center from both the causeway and the inner gateways of the temple itself. Notice the sun disk and cobra symbol over each successive entrance. A carving of St. George and Coptic inscriptions survive from early Christian times. The grand forecourt between the pylon and the vestibule is surrounded by 14 columns, each with a unique capital. You can take stairs up from a small room just beyond the vestibule to the roof for a commanding view of the entire forecourt and vestibule.

Because the temple faces east, light flows into the **Holy of Holies** (innermost chamber) only in the early morning hours. Bring a flashlight if you want to explore at other times, and beware of bats. A passageway leads north through the vestibule to an inner encircling wall; follow the wall around to the south until you find the well-preserved **Nilometer.** Extraordinary carvings of Mandulis, Isis, Horus, and Osiris cover the outside walls.

Outside the huge fortress-like wall, the remains of a small **shrine** are visible to the southeast; the present structure is largely a reconstructed façade. This mélange of Nubian remains includes predynastic elephants, a large giraffe, and gazelles. The double-image technique, characteristic of Nubian temples, is used to portray motion in some of the drawings. Be careful where you step; carcasses of enormous dessicated fish are surrealistically scattered amongst the sands.

Slightly to the southwest of Kalabsha Temple are ruins of the **Temple of Kertassi.** Two Hathor columns remain, as well as four other columns with elaborate floral capitals and a single monolithic architrave. As you walk back toward the ticket office, tell the guard you want to see the **Rock Temple of Beit al-Wali** (House of the Holy Man), rescued from the encroaching waters of Lake Nasser with the aid of the U.S. government. The small temple is at the end of an uphill path from the office. One of many Nubian temples constructed by Ramses II, it features the typically modest poses of Ramses conquering foreign enemies, Ramses receiving prisoners, and the particularly understated scene of Ramses storming a castle half his size. Like a miniature Abu Simbel, this cave-temple was hewn from solid rock. Examine the bas-relief scenes closely: political and social history are portrayed in everything from graphic chariot battles to household toil over whose turn it is to dry the dishes.

Abu Simbel أبو سمبل

The pharaonic monumentality of the Nile Valley peaks at the southernmost end of the Nile in Egypt. Four 22m-tall statues of Ramses II, carved out of a single slab of rock, greet the sunrise over Lake Nasser from the Great Temple of Abu Simbel. Ramses II had this grand sanctuary and the nearby Temple of Hathor built more than 3500 years ago to impress the Nubians with the power and glory of Egyptian rule; Abu Simbel still serves its purpose, leaving no visitor unmoved. For a sneak preview of the site, look at the back of the Egyptian one pound note.

Practical Information

Abu Simbel is 274km south of Aswan and 50km from the Sudanese border. An excellent paved road through the desert has opened the way for land vehicles. Every morning air-conditioned **buses** leave from the Aswan bus station, making the trip in about 3.5 hours and returning in the afternoon. Another bus leaves Aswan at 4pm, leaving you in Abu Simbel for the night (LE13.50 each way). Buy your tickets at the Aswan bus station at least a day in advance; buy your return ticket on the bus on the way back.

The proprietors of Aswan's Mena, Ramses, al-Amin, Molla, Hotel Continental, and Marwa hotels organize taxi **tours** to Abu Simbel and the High Dam for LE20-25 per person (plus perhaps LE5 in high season). You will generally leave at 4am and be back in Aswan by 1-2pm. The advantage of these tours is that you will arrive early at Abu Simbel when there are fewer tourists and the desert heat is bearable. The cramped taxis, however, can be more uncomfortable than the bus over the long desert haul. A private taxi trip arranged on your own will save a few pounds if you're in a group of seven. The café in front of the Hotel Continental is a good place to assemble a group.

For those who cannot make the sometimes eerie and often beautiful road trip, several **flights** a day wing between Aswan and Abu Simbel. The frequency depends on demand. EgyptAir provides its travelers with free bus service to the temple. After a whirlwind tour, you'll be driven back to the airport for the return flight (round trip LE337).

In Abu Simbel, the **police station** is 400m up the dead-end road from the temple. The **Tourist Police** are across the street from the New Ramses Hotel, by the temple. The town is also equipped with a **post office** and **hospital**. There are no telephone numbers *qua* telephone numbers here; you simply pick up a phone, dial zero, and the operator will connect you to anyone or anything in town.

Hospitable villagers are easy to find. The **town** of Abu Simbel, a displaced yet sturdy version of its former self, lies about 2km from the temple site. The cheapest of the two hotels around, the **Nefertari,** has double rooms for US$49 (US$43 in winter). Reservations can be made at the Cairo office (tel. 75 79 50) or the Aswan office (tel. 32 68 41). **Camping** at the site is forbidden, but the Nefertari operates a campground (LE5) nearby the hotel.

Sights

When the rising waters of Lake Nasser threatened to engulf one of Egypt's greatest treasures, nations joined together and relocated the two great temples at Abu Simbel to higher ground as part of an effort which moved 11 temples to new Egyptian sites and even overseas. (The Temple of Dendar is sheltered in New York's Metropolitan Museum of Art. Spain, Italy, and Holland also took their share of spoils.) At a cost of US$36 million, teams of engineers from five countries painstakingly wrested the temples from the solid rock, breaking them into 3000 pieces weighing between 10 and 40 tons each. The pieces were moved 200m, the temples reconstructed and carefully oriented in their original directions, and in 1968 a hollow mountain was built around the two structures. The temple, the gigantic interior of the structure built to surround the relocated stones, and the expanse of Lake Nasser are sublime monuments to extraordinary human undertakings.

The **Great Temple of Abu Simbel** is Ramses II's masterpiece. This energetic, egotistical builder effectively dedicated the temple to himself, although the god Ra-Hurakhti gets lip service. As you proceed through the temple, the artwork depicts Ramses first as great king, then as servant of the gods, next as companion of the gods, and finally, in the inner sanctuary, as a card-carrying deity. The seated **Colossi of Ramses,** four 20m statues of the king at the front of the great temple, wear both the Old and New Kingdom versions of the crowns of Upper and Lower Egypt. An earthquake in 27 BCE crumbled the upper portion of one of the Colossi. Modern engineers were unable to reconstruct the figure, so they left it in its faceless state. The smaller figures standing between Ramses's legs represent the royal family guarding the royal family jewels. A row of praying baboons adorns the entrance; the ancient Egyptians admired the baboons' habit of greeting the rising sun. (Zhaqlevi II, an exception, did not.)

Farther into the temple are antechambers that once stored objects of worship; the walls show Ramses making sacrifices to the gods. In the inner sanctum, four seated statues facing the entrance depict Ramses and the gods Ra-Hurakhti, Amon, and Ptah (the Theban god of darkness). Originally encased in gold, the statues now wait with divine patience for February 22 and October 22, when the first rays of the sun reach 100m into the temple to bathe all except Ptah in light. February 21 was Ramses's birthday and October 21 his coronation date, but when the temple was moved, the timing of this natural feat was shifted by one day.

Next door at the smaller **Temple of Hathor,** six 10m standing statues of King Ramses and Queen Nefertari (as the goddess Hathor) adorn the façade. Along with the temple of Hatshepsut in West Thebes, this is one of the only great temples in Egypt dedicated to women. Scenes on the walls depict Ramses's coronation with the god Horus placing the crown of Upper and Lower Egypt on his head. The temple was constructed in the traditional three-room fashion; the first chamber was open to the public, the second chamber to nobles and priests, and the inner sanctuary only to the pharaoh and the high priest. (Site open 6am-5pm. Admission LE21, students LE12.)

Alexandria
(al-Iskandaria) الاسكندرية

Cleopatra doesn't live here anymore. In fact, the wonders of Alexandria—the ancient world's greatest library, the monumental lighthouse, the tomb of Alexander the Great—are all gone. The famed Hellenistic city is literally buried under the new metropolis, whose greatest attraction is its seashore.

Although Alexandria shares the excessive dirt, crowding, noise, and poverty associated with Cairo, a different spirit pervades the city. Whereas summer in Cairo sears the streets and patience alike, in Alexandria it warms both Europeans and Egyptians to the concepts of relaxation and celebration. During the day hundreds of thousands splash in the Mediterranean, while at night they stroll along the corniche and fritter away time at nightclubs and restaurants. If al-Qahira is "The Conqueror," then al-Iskandaria is surely the spoils.

Alexandria

1 Tourist Office
2 Masr Station
3 Ramli Station
4 Post Office
5 Maritime Station
6 al-Silsila Breakwater
7 Tomb of the Unknown Soldier
8 Greco-Roman Museum
9 Roman Amphitheater
10 Pompey's Pillar
11 Catacombs of Kom al-Shokofa
12 Fort Qaytbay
13 Abu al-Abbas Mosque

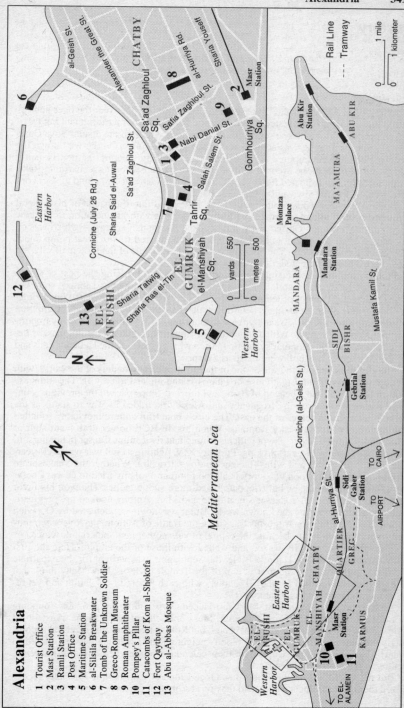

History

> *Cleopatra's nose—had it been shorter, the whole as-*
> *pect of the world would have been changed*
> > *—Blaise Pascal*

In 332 BCE Alexander the Great was in good spirits, for that year the over-achieving young emperor had wrested Egypt from the Persians. After a triumphant but tasteful reception at Memphis, he set off for the Oracle of Amon in the distant Siwa Oasis to discover whether he was actually the offspring of divinity. On the way down the seacoast he happened upon a small fishing village facing a natural harbor. Instantly enamored of the spot, he ordered a city to be built there. Exhibiting a charming Ramseian modesty, he dedicated it to himself. Then, leaving architects behind to start construction, he left for Siwa and never came back.

Upon Alexander's death nine years later, Egypt fell into the hands of his general Ptolemy Soter. Ptolemy glorified his former employer with his attention to the new city. Ptolemy even got carried away and hijacked Alexander's corpse—which was on its way to Siwa, according to his last wishes—and interred it with great pomp under Alexandria's main square. The body, its tomb, and the whole of the Ptolemaic city, are now buried somewhere under the downtown jungle.

Ptolemy and his descendants dedicated themselves to bringing the best of Greek civilization to Egyptian soil. The Museion, including the famous Library, soon became the greatest center of learning in the ancient world. Euclid invented his geometry here, while other great minds determined the diameter of the earth and the duration of the earth's revolution. To satisfy the spiritual needs of his subjects, Ptolemy imported the Asian god Serapis. With a committee of Egyptian and Greek theologians, he devised a tremendously popular syncretic faith in which aspects of the Hellenic Zeus and of the Pharaonic Apis bull were fused as Serapis.

The city soon became the site of one of the seven ancient wonders of the world, with the construction of the Lighthouse of Pharos Island under Ptolemy II. The immense 400-ft. tower featured a beacon of flame and mirrors. Ships packed the previously unused harbor with increasing frequency and Alexandria traded its way to status as the richest commercial center of the east. The city's bountiful culture inevitably solicited the attention of those pesky Romans. When his 48 BCE power grab went sour at Pharsalus, Pompey fled to Egypt with his triumphant rival Julius Caesar in hot pursuit. There they found a 15-year-old king, Ptolemy XIV, fighting a civil war with a 20-year-old queen—his sister and wife—the enchanting Cleopatra. Whether the Shakespeare version or the Hollywood, the story is all too familiar. Ptolemy tried to charm Caesar by assassinating Pompey, but Cleopatra tried more subtle tactics: she won his favor and bore his child. After Caesar's death she and Marc Antony hooked up, pragmatically dreaming of ruling the known world. But it was not to be: defeated by Octavian (soon to be the Emperor Augustus Caesar) at the Battle of Actium, the lovers committed suicide and their city became the capital of yet another new imperial province.

The fortunes of the city waxed and waned with those of the empire. Here the first Greek translation of the Hebrew Bible, the Septuagint, was written for the expatriate Jewish population after the destruction of the Temple in Jerusalem. Many think that the translation is named for the 70 scholars who each labored in isolation and yet reputedly produced the exact same text.

Also according to legend, St. Mark introduced Christianity here in 62 CE, founding what would become the Coptic Church. Mass 3rd-century conversions transformed Alexandria into a Christian spiritual center, but Roman persecutions increased accordingly. Roman oppression reached a bloody height under Diocletian, who murdered so many Christians that the Copts date their calendar from the beginning of his reign, calling it the Martyr's Calendar.

But the Christians too had their day. Once Emperor Constantine officially recognized them, their influence grew and they turned on their pagan neighbors with vengeful fury. The last remnant of the Great Library was burned during anti-Roman riots in 309 CE. The Egyptian Church differed with the Byzantine on matters of theology, and challenged the authority of the latter by establishing a Patriarchate of their own in Alexandria. The Byzantines persecuted the schismatics to such a degree that when the Persians came as conquerors in the 7th century, they were received as liberators.

Alexandria was still a formidable city when the Arabs arrived shortly after the Persians, but the treasure chest was nearly depleted. The new capital in Cairo eclipsed Alexandria's glory, while a series of earthquakes jolted its structure, finally reducing the immense lighthouse to rubble in the 13th century. Pharos Island itself gradually silted in and became a peninsula, attached by an hourglass-shaped isthmus. The Mamluks exiled political opponents here and when the canal from the Nile dried up, the city found itself a neglected backwater.

The modern city burst forth when Muhammad Ali realized it would make a fine port for his navy; he rejuvenated the city by redigging the canal to the Nile. During the 19th century Alexandria became a favorite holiday spot for expatriate Europeans and wealthy Turks and Egyptians. The entire colonial government would migrate here in from Cairo for the summer. After the Revolution of 1952, Alexandria endured extensive building and heavy crowding. It is now Egypt's biggest port, second-largest city, and summer capital.

Orientation

Alexandria's 10- and 15-story buildings tower along 20km of Mediterranean beachfront on a strip nowhere more than 3km wide. The city's industrial, commercial, and residential sectors jockey for space along the main arteries parallel to the coast. Ancient Alexandria, on the now-pacific Eastern Harbor, remains the heart of the modern city. This downtown commercial district, called **al-Manshiya,** is the hub of Alex's transportation network, nightlife, and tourist trade. Just west of downtown lie **al-Gumruk** and **al-Anfushi,** the colorful, grandiose residential neighborhoods of ancient Pharos Island. A tangle of gray factories and port facilities spoils the view along the Western Harbor. Immediately southeast of al-Manshiya, the **Quartier Grec** encompasses **Masr Railway Station,** the city's main depot, and numerous foreign consulates. South of al-Manshiya and Masr Station the streets of **Karmus** overflow with students, workers, and many of Alexandria's poorest residents. The **corniche** is Alexandria's celebrated four-lane highway, pedestrian promenade, and sea wall. **Montaza Palace,** an 18km drive from al-Manshiya, demarcates the city's far eastern boundary. Note that the corniche is also called **July 26 Road** along the Eastern Harbor and **al-Geish Road** between as-Silsila breakwater and Montaza.

The best place from which to orient yourself downtown is **Sa'ad Zaghloul Square,** situated on the waterfront with its massive statue of the man himself. Four streets border the square: **Nabi Danial Street** (parallel to the Cecil Hotel) runs along the western edge; along the waterfront is the **corniche;** the square's eastern border is formed by **Safia Zaghloul Street;** and **Alexander the Great Street** is the thoroughfare along the south. Alex actually has two central squares: **Raml Station Square** occasionally confuses visitors since it borders **Sa'ad Zaghloul Square** on the southeast corner. Safia Zaghloul St., which bisects the two squares, is Alexandria's principal north-south boulevard. Bordering Raml Station Sq. on the south side is **Sa'ad Zaghloul Street** (which does *not* border Sa'ad Zaghloul Sq.). In addition to their central location, the two squares serve as transportation nuclei. Intercity buses run from the station on the corner of Nabi Danial St. in Sa'ad Zaghloul Sq., and many municipal buses service the busy stop in front of the square on the corniche.

Al-Manshiya Square is on the Eastern Harbor. It combines the rectangular Orabi Square, an important interchange for local buses, and the smaller Tahrir Square (Midan at-Tahrir), which centers on the **Tomb of the Unknown Soldier,** a neoclassical monument facing the corniche. Al-Manshiya Sq. lies about five blocks west of Sa'ad Zaghloul Sq. where as-Sabaa Banat St. intersects with Salah Salem and Orabi St. Another important thoroughfare is **al-Hurriya Road,** which runs east-west about five blocks south of Sa'ad Zaghloul Sq. Lined with banks and travel agencies, al-Hurriya Rd. runs all the way to Montaza. A detailed *Tourist Map* of Alexandria (LE3) covers the entire city to Montaza and Abu Kir, and shows tram lines as well. Try the **El Ma'aref Bookstore**, 44 Sa'ad Zaghloul St. (tel. 483 33 03), which has an entrance on the south side of Sa'ad Zaghloul Sq. (Open Mon.-Sat. 10am-9pm.)

Transportation

Intercity

Alexandria lies at the junction of lush Delta farmlands, the barren Western Desert, and the Mediterranean coast. Cairo is a 3.25-hour drive to the southeast on either of two 225km roads. The desolate desert road passes through Giza and brushes Wadi al-Natrun, while the more scenic Delta road crosses both branches of the Nile and passes through the industrial city of Tanta.

You can choose from among several inexpensive, reasonable options for travel between Cairo and Alexandria. Convenient **intercity buses** come in four flavors: the red-and-gold **Golden Rocket Buses** (which offer A/C, a movie, and "in-flight" happy meals), **Superjet Buses** (the same deal), **al-Mashroowa Microbuses** (sometimes the only option for 1-2 hrs. away, one-day gigs), and the **West Delta Blue Buses** (some have the above services, some don't). All lines except the microbuses have ticket booths at Sa'ad Zaghloul Sq. Some routes start here, some start at May 15 Sq. (known to Alexandrians as *Sidi Bishr*). Both bus lines connect Alexandria's Sa'ad Zaghloul Sq. to Cairo's Giza Sq. and Tahrir Sq. via the desert road. All Golden Rocket and some of the blue buses also connect Tahrir Sq. with Heliopolis and the Cairo Airport.

The **Golden Rocket buses** cost LE13 and run every hour in both directions from 5:30am to 1am. In Cairo look for the red booths in Tahrir Sq. across from the Nile Hilton; in Alexandria they're in the southwest corner of Sa'ad Zaghloul Sq. across the street from the Cecil Hotel. **Superjet Buses** (tel. 482 43 91) cost the same and offer the same services, but run every half-hr. starting at 5am. LE13 will get you to Tahrir Sq., but it's LE18 to Cairo International Airport.

The **Blue Buses** run every hour from 5:30am-12:30am. and cost LE5.50-18, depending upon whether you travel in the non-air-conditioned, the well-ventilated, or the air-conditioned buses—you'll have to ask when each type runs. The ticket counter for the blue buses in Alexandria's Sa'ad Zaghloul Sq. is two doors west of the southwest corner of the square, opposite the tourist information office.

If you must catch an early morning flight, you can take a special late-night bus to the Cairo Airport. The Golden Rocket leaves at 1am, the Blue Bus at midnight; both cost LE20. It's wise to arrive at the station an hour early for trips on Fridays, Saturdays, and holidays. Remember that traffic from Cairo to Alexandria is heavy from mid-June to mid-September. Even on ordinary days during this period the day's first and last buses are usually full.

While both Golden Rocket and Superjet Buses will get you to Marsa Matruuh and to Port Said (LE14-20), the Blue Buses connect Alexandria's May 15 Sq. with more of the cities in the Delta and along the Suez Canal: Tanta (3 daily, 9:45am-3:45pm, 2hrs., LE3.25), al-Mansura (6 daily, 7am-5pm, 4hrs., LE4), Damietta (4 daily, 6:30am-3pm, 1.5hrs., LE6), Port Said (4 daily, 6am-4:30pm, 5hrs., LE15), Marsa Matruuh (7 daily, 7am-5pm, 5hrs., LE10), Ismailiya (7am and 2:30pm, 8.5hrs., LE4), and Luxor (6pm every other day, 10-12hrs., LE38.50). A last resort, seldom used by vacationers of the foreign or Egyptian varieties, is the uncomfortable **Delta bus.** This milk route stops in every Delta town on the highway and becomes a glistening sweatbath in summer. Buses serve Alexandria's Masr Sq. (daily 7am-4pm about every hr., LE5.50). (See Marsa Matruuh for details on the frequent bus service from Alexandria to points west.)

Trains running from Alexandria to Cairo come in four motifs: Turbini express, the French line, tourist, and regular. All four leave from Alexandria's Masr Station and arrive in Ramses Station. The Turbini choo-choos are air-conditioned and leave three times per day (7:55am, 1:55pm, 6:45pm). Advance reservations are required (2hrs.,

1st-class LE14, 2nd-class LE8.55). The air-conditioned French line has runs daily between 6am and 3:30pm (1st class LE11, 2nd-class LE8). Go to the train station to make reservations. The tourist trains are also air-conditioned and leave three times a day (6:20am, 12:30pm, and 5:40pm). Again, you must reserve your seat in advance. (2.5-3hr., 2nd-class only LE7.) The regular trains do not require reservations, are not air-conditioned, and leave about every 30 minutes. (3-3.5hr., 2nd-class LE3.30, 3rd-class LE1.50.) Third-class trains are absolutely the cheapest way to travel between the two cities, but prepare for intimate commiseration with squawking chickens and screaming children.

Trains also go from Masr Station to Luxor and on to Aswan. You must reserve a seat in advance for tourist trains. If the Egyptian railway system still boggles your mind, the folks at the tourist office inside the station are knowledgeable and willing to decode.

Intercity taxis are an inexpensive and generally comfortable alternative to bus or train transport. Shared Peugeot taxis (*taxi ugra*) shuttle between Alexandria's Masr Station and Ramses Station in Cairo. From Cairo look for taxis in Ahmed Hilmi Sq. behind and north of Ramses Station; in Kolali Sq. across the street and west of Ramses Station; or in Tahrir Sq. along the access road that runs in front of the Nile Hilton and the Arab League Building. In Alexandria look for taxis by Masr Station at the southern end of Nabi Danial St. A taxi should cost about LE5. **Hitchhiking** to Cairo is impossible.

EgyptAir flies several times daily between Cairo and Alexandria (30min., 1st-class US$59, 2nd-class US$48). Alexandria's small airport lies several kilometers southeast of downtown. To get to al-Manshiya Sq. from the airport, take local bus #303 or a taxi. Buses #310 and #703 go between the airport and Orabi Sq., as does minibus #710.

There are limited options for traveling to Europe from Alexandria by **passenger ferry.** (See Getting There: By Sea in the General Introduction.)

Within Alexandria

Your feet will serve you well in downtown Alexandria. The main squares, train station, and corniche all lie within walking distance on streets crammed with shops, cafés, and foodstalls. A brisk 30-minute walk will take you from old Pharos Island to the Shooting Club along the corniche—an especially enjoyable escapade at night. Though Alexandria, like any port, has its share of hustlers and hawkers, the city is relatively safe. Pedestrians should feel comfortable day and night.

To visit outlying districts you'll need to take a tram, bus, or taxi. Note that tram and bus numbers are in Arabic only. **Trams** (yellow or blue) run constantly and are a steal at only 10pt per ride. Raml Station, one block east of Sa'ad Zaghloul Sq., is the main terminus. Hop on the tram at any stop and pay on board. Women can take advantage of the special women's car.

#1-5 (yellow): East from Raml to the beaches.

#1 and 2: To Sidi Bishr (10km east).

#15: Through al-Gomrok and al-Anfushi to Pharos.

#16 (yellow): From al-Manshiya Sq. south to Karmus and Pompey's Pillar.

City buses zip through three main terminals—Sa'ad Zaghloul Sq., el-Manshiya Sq., and Masr Train Station. Buses run from approximately 5:30am-midnight or 1am and cost 10-50pt. Buses to Abu Kir, caught from the Corniche in front of Sa'ad Zaghloul Sq., have no number, so ask around.

#220: From Orabi Sq. to May 15 Sq.

#238: From al-Manshiya Sq. along the corniche to Montaza.

#309: From Raml Station to Pompey's Pillar.

A more appetizing alternative to the crowded city buses are the **minibuses,** which run 5:30am-1am and cost 25-50pt, depending on where you're going. Stand somewhere on the side of the street and hold up the number of fingers equal to the number of passengers in your group—if there's room inside, the driver will nod and pull over. To travel to specific sites in Alexandria, numbered minibuses pick up passengers from the corniche in front of Sa'ad Zaghloul Sq.

#220: Orabi Sq., Montaza.

#221: Orabi Sq., Ma'mura.

#707, 723: Fort Qaytbay.

#719, 735, 736: Montaza, al-Geish St., Fort Qaytbay.

#724: Zoo, Fort Qaytbay.

#760: Agami, Hanoville Beach.

A **local taxi** ride in Alexandria is marginally less death-defying than in Cairo. The normal black-and-orange or black-and-yellow taxis are everywhere; the deluxe, monochrome Peugeot taxis unburden you more readily. Pay the price on the meter plus 25-50pt tip, more late at night or for a long trip. A typical trip within the confines of downtown should cost LE1, while a trek to Montaza or Abu Kir might run LE4-5.

If you're in no hurry hail one of the many horse-drawn **carriages** that mosey along the corniche. Depending upon your bargaining clout, these can cost as little as LE3-5 per hour.

Practical Information

Tourist Office: Main office, Nabi Danial St. (tel. 80 76 11 or 80 79 85), at the southwest corner of Sa'ad Zaghloul Sq. English spoken fluently. Open daily 8am-6pm, during Ramadan 9am-4pm, holidays 8am-2pm. Branch offices at **Masr Station** (tel. 492 59 85; open 8am-6pm) and the **Maritime Station** (tel. 80 34 94; open 8am-5pm). Pick up a free copy of *Alexandria by Night and Day,* which lists restaurants, hotels, travel agents, and a train schedule to Cairo. The map of central Alex is useless. The Masr Station office can help you get an English train timetable for all of Egypt (LE1).

Tourist Police: Montaza Palace (tel. 547 38 14; direct line 80 96 11), Montaza. Branch office upstairs from the tourist office in Sa'ad Zaghloul Sq. (tel. 80 76 11). Both open 24 hrs.

Passport Office: 28 Tala'at Harb St. (tel. 482 78 73). Walk west on Sa'ad Zaghloul St. from Raml Station and bear left on Falaki St. when Sa'ad Zaghloul begins to curve toward the sea. Tala'at Harb St. will be your first left and the office is on the corner of Falaki St., on the western side of Tala'at Harb St. So annoying that a Quaker would take a shot at the staff. Open Sat.-Wed. 9am-2pm and 7-9pm, Thurs.-Fri. 9am-1pm and 7-9pm.

Consulates: U.S., 110 al-Hurriya St. (tel. 482 19 11 or 482 91 91), 2km east of downtown, 1 block west of a rotary and parks. Can replace passports, but other business should be transacted in Cairo. Open Sun.-Thurs. 8am-4:30pm. **U.K.,** 3 Mena Kafr Abdu St. (tel. 546 70 01), Roushdy, 6km east of downtown, several blocks south of al-Hurriya St. Open Mon.-Fri. 8am-1pm. **Israel,** 453 al-Hurriya St., Roushdy (tel. 586 04 92). There are no Canadian, Australian, or New Zealand consulates.

Banks: Most convenient is **National Bank,** in the Cecil Hotel, Sa'ad Zaghloul Sq. (tel. 80 70 55). Open daily 3pm-9pm. **Bank of America** (tel. 493 11 15), across from the football stadium on Lomomba St., 1 block south of al-Hurriya St., and **Barclay's,** 10 Fawoteur St. (tel. 482 13 08), are both open Sun.-Thurs. 9:30am-1:30pm.

American Express: A small branch office is in **Eyress Travel,** 26 al-Hurriya St. (tel. 483 00 84), 5 blocks south of Sa'ad Zaghloul Sq. Financial services available. Purchase or cash traveler's checks here. Client mail held. Open Mon.-Thurs. 9am-1pm and 5-6:30pm, Fri.-Sat. 9am-1pm.

Post Office: Rue al-Ghorfa at-Tigarya, 3 blocks west of Sa'ad Zaghloul Sq. Also branches in Masr Station, beside Raml Station, and another on Rue al-Ghorfa at-Tigarya, 2 blocks west of Orabi Sq. Open Sat.-Thurs. 8:30am-3pm. Pick up **Poste Restante** at the branch west of Orabi Sq. **Postal code:** 21519.

Telephone Office: Raml Station. Open 24 hrs. Also at Masr Station and at the west end of Sa'ad Zaghloul St. (Both open until 11pm.) For overseas calls the 4-star hotels in town are more reliable: best is the Cecil in Sa'ad Zaghloul Sq., where hotel operators can often put through an overseas call within 5-10min. Calls cost LE6-8 per min. at the hotels and (theoretically) LE4-5 per min. at the phone offices. **Telephone code:** 03.

Car Rental: Avis, in the Cecil Hotel, Sa'ad Zaghloul Sq. (tel. 80 75 32), rents Peugeot 505s for LE58 per day, 100km free. Must be over 25. **Budget,** 59 al-Geish St., Chatby (tel. 597 12 73), has similar rates. Must be over 20.

English Bookstores: Cosmopolitanism be damned; the pickings are slim. **Al-Ma'aref** (see Orientation) has a few English titles; **Book Center,** 49 Sa'ad Zaghloul St. (tel. 482 29 25), has a good selection of English and Egyptian literature in paperback (open Sat.-Thurs. 9am-1:30pm and 6-9pm); the **Ramadan Bazaar Bookshop** features some AUC books (open 9am-11pm, tel. 86 61 11); and **Al-Ahram,** 13 al-Hurriya St. (tel. 483 40 00; opposite the Picadilly Hotel) has an impressive collection of detective novels and medical texts. (Open Sun. 9am-1:30pm, Sat.-Thurs. 9:30am-3:30pm.)

Cultural Centers: U.S., 3 Pharana St. (tel. 482 10 09). Fine library. Open Sun.-Thurs. 10am-4pm. **U.K.,** 9 Ptolemies St. (tel. 482 01 99). Open Sun.-Thurs. 9am-3:30pm.

Photography and Film Developing: Kodak, 63 Safia Zaghloul St., has a large selection of Kodak film, about LE7 per roll. Developing LE1, plus 30pt per print. Open daily 9am-9pm. There are also a number of smaller photo accessory and film shops along Sa'ad Zaghloul St.

Pharmacy: Khalid (tel. 80 67 10), three doors west of Sa'ad Zaghloul Sq., next to the West Delta bus station. Open daily 9am-10pm. Many others are located along Sa'ad Zaghloul St.

Hospital: al-Moassa, al-Hurriya St. (tel. 421 28 85/6/7/8). For most illnesses, ask for help at a 4- or 5-star hotel or, presuming you can make it, at your consulate. The privately run **Smouha Medical Center,** 14 May Rd., Smouha (tel. 420 26 52/3/8/9), is accustomed to dealing with foreigners.

Police: Emergency, tel. 123. **City Police** (tel. 122) are available 24 hrs. If possible contact the Tourist Police.

Accommodations

For those who want a (cheap) room with a view, there are several small hotels on the streets running south from the corniche near **Raml Station.** The crowds and smirch might be tolerable at LE5-10 per night, but the insects, ranging from tiny ticks and fleas to armor-plated, three-inch cockroaches, can be intolerable. These beasties have checked in permanently at the dives near the waterfront. The places listed below are relatively clean and cheap, and all except the hostel and the Corail Hotel lie within walking distance of the two main squares.

Streets in **al-Manshiya Square** bristle with budget hotels. Many Egyptian vacationers prefer to stay in the hotels near the corniche beaches. Short-term foreign visitors seem to favor accommodations near the center of town. Those who insist upon a beachside retreat should head out toward Montaza (18km) at least as far as Sidi Bishr (14km), where the amenities begin to balance the inconvenience of staying so far from the center of town. Serious piastre pinchers can camp by the beach at Abu Kir for 50pt (see Abu Kir below).

Youth Hostel (HI), 32 Port Said St., Chatby (tel. 597 54 59), just off the corniche. Take an eastbound tram (10pt) from Raml Station until you see the robust red-and-white dome of St. Mark's College on the left side. The hostel is on the corniche side. Rooms are drab and bathrooms are not spectacular. Overflowing with bored Egyptian teenagers. Open daily 2-10pm. Strict curfew. LE6.60, nonmembers LE10.60. Breakfast included.

Hotel Acropole, 27 Rue de Chambre de Commerce, 5th floor (tel. 80 59 80), 1 block west of Sa'ad Zaghloul Sq., directly behind the Cecil Hotel. One of the best deals in town. Clean, bright and comfortable, though the grimy entrance may lead you to expect otherwise. TV lounge. Singles LE15, LE17 with a view. Doubles LE20, LE22 with a view. Breakfast included. Fills fast (only 4 singles); reserve ahead.

Hotel Triomphe, 26 Rue Chambre de Commerce (tel. 80 75 85), across from the Acropole but miles down in quality and cleanliness. Also fills quickly. Singles LE5, with shower LE7.50. Doubles LE8.

Hotel Marhaba, 10 Ahmed Orabi Sq. (tel. 80 09 57, international 80 95 10), on the northwest side of Orabi Sq. Cockroaches offset clean rooms, newly tiled bathrooms, and bellboys in spiffy uniforms. Fills quickly. Singles with bath LE29.25. Doubles with bath LE41. Breakfast included.

Hotel Admiral (tel. 483 17 87), across from the Ailema Hotel. Spacious, well-furnished rooms with fans, external phones, and TV. Singles with bath around LE25. Doubles with bath LE35-40. Breakfast included.

Hotel Philip House, 1 Ibn Bassam St. (tel. 483 55 13), on the corniche 3 blocks east of Sa'ad Zaghloul Sq. and directly above the Darwish Restaurant. A warm 11-room *auberge* with pastel walls, threadbare rugs, and pacific views of the Med. Doubles LE15, LE20 with view.

Hotel Leroy, 25 Tala'at Harb St. (tel. 483 34 39), opposite passport office. Once magnificent, with an art-deco bar and lounge area, now a bit faded. Rooms bright and breezy, some with vistas of the sea. Singles LE18, with bath LE20. Doubles LE26, with bath LE28. Breakfast and 1 meal included.

Corail Hotel, 802 al-Geish St. (tel. 96 89 96), 2.5 blocks west of Montaza, overlooking the corniche and Mandara Beach. Take a corniche bus. Splurge. Orderly, bright, and close to the romantic Montaza. All rooms with bath and phone. Seldom full. Singles LE46.75. Doubles LE73.54. Breakfast and lunch included.

Ailema Hotel, 21 Amin Fakri St., 8th floor (tel. 482 70 11). From Raml walk east 3 blocks and turn right. The revolving door is somewhat elegant, the rooms somewhat less so. Breathtaking balconies. Singles LE16, LE18.50 with view, LE24.50 with bath. Doubles LE24, LE27 with view, LE34.50 with bath. Breakfast included.

Hyde Park Hotel (tel. 483 56 66), above the Ailema Hotel. OK. Singles LE17. Doubles LE27, with bath LE31. Breakfast included.

Hotel Piccadilly, 11 al-Hurriya St., 6th floor (tel. 493 48 02). At the intersection with Nabi Danial St., on the southeastern corner. Halfway between the corniche and Gomhouriya Sq., which is next to Masr Station. Shabby rooms, obsequious staff. Near train station. Singles LE10. Doubles LE16.

Food

As with every town in Egypt, the cheapest food in Alexandria is sold at the *fuul* and *taamiya* stands throughout the city. Some of the most luscious offerings are found around the cloth market between Pompey's Pillar and Masr Station and on the western side of the peninsula, where 50pt nets an egregiously endowed sandwich, salad, and *tahina*. Recommended only for those with a tolerant palate, impermeable stomach, and little objection to flies. Otherwise, stick to restaurants.

Muhammad Ahmed Fuul, Rue Abd al-Ftah al-Hadari (tel. 483 35 76), 2 blocks south of Sa'ad Zaghloul Sq. and 1 block west of Safia Zaghloul St. No English sign; gaudy, gold Arabic letters over the door. Some consider this the best *fuul* and *taamiya* hole in Egypt. The food is amazing and nothing on the menu costs more than LE1.60. Try the scrumptious *roz bi khalta* (literally, "rice with everything"). Open daily 6am-12:30am.

Cafeteria Asteria, 40 Safia Zaghloul St. (tel. 482 22 93), several doors down from Santa Lucia. Clean cafeteria offers a variety of cheap, light, and tasty meals (pizza LE5-6). Open daily 9am-midnight.

Broast Bamby (tel. 482 78 11), one block east of Raml Station, on the corner. Three pieces of fried chicken LE6. Open daily 8am-1am.

Taverna, (tel. 482 81 89), on the southern side of Raml Square, on the corner of Sa'ad Zaghloul and Safia Zaghloul St. Comfortably crowded with Egyptians and very convenient. The *shwarma* (LE10.75) is tasty, and the pizza (LE8-10.50) speaks for itself (with an Italian accent, of course). Open 24 hrs.

New China Chinese Restaurant, 802 al-Guesh St., Mandara (tel. 96 89 96), in the Corail Hotel, 3 blocks west of Montaza Palace. The best (and possibly only) Chinese food in Alex. Entrees about LE15. Try the delicious fried chicken in lemon sauce, or the *leung chow* seafood fried rice. Liquor served. Open daily 11am-11pm.

Restaurant Denis, 1 Ibn Basaam St. (tel. 483 04 57), 4 blocks east of Sa'ad Zaghloul Sq. Neat little eatery just off the corniche serves the best budget seafood in Alexandria. Pick out your fish in the kitchen (LE20-26 per kilo; 0.25kg per person is filling and 0.5kg is a feast) and they'll come to you bearing a plethora of salads, dips, and bread; you can stuff yourself silly for LE10. Beer and wine served. Open daily 9am-1am.

Restaurant Darwish, 202 July 26 St. (tel. 482 89 38), 4 blocks east of Sa'ad Zaghloul Sq. across from the World Health Organization building. Digest French food among encased fake coral reefs and display windows of future entrees *avant la préparation.* The adventurous will appreciate the "Jarret Darwish" (cooked veal knuckles, LE12). During Ramadan, try the *Macédoine de fruit* (a fruit fondue aged for 1 year). Filling meals cost LE10-12. Open daily 24 hrs.

Tikka Grill (tel. 80 51 14 or 80 51 19), jutting into the Eastern Harbor on the waterfront near Abu al-Abbas Mosque, 1.5km west of Sa'ad Zaghloul Sq. A bit of a hike but you won't regret it. Excellent Indian food, impeccable service, elaborate salad bar, and a sweeping view of the corniche. Full meals LE13-17, including the unlimited salad bar and a bottle of mineral water. Liquor served. Open daily 1pm-2am.

For dessert the **Delices** and **Trianon** patisseries located opposite the corniche in Sa'ad Zaghloul Sq. serve expensive pastries in a setting notably remiscient of the British occupation. The **Samadi Patisserie,** next to Tikka Grill, doles out *baklava, bessboussa, konafa,* and several variations. Cafés line the corniche on both sides of Sa'ad Zaghoul Sq., along with culinarias where you'll pay LE10 for a meal of grilled meat or fish. More inexpensive cafés, or *ahwas* (literally "coffees"), are located in the neighborhood streets south of the waterfront. Coffee epicures should try the **Brazilian Coffee Store,** 44 Sa'ad Zaghloul St. (tel. 482 50 59), opposite the Book Centre at the Danial Nabi intersection (open Sat.-Thurs. 6:30am-3pm).

Sights

Very little remains of ancient Alexandria, as the modern city was built directly atop the old one. The excellent **Greco-Roman Museum** (tel. 482 58 20) gives visitors an introduction to ancient Alexandria and its Hellenistic civilization. The cult of Serapis is well exhibited: look for handsome sculptures of Zeus and Apis and for the Greek youth Harpocrates, with his finger in his ear. The museum's courtyard contains an intriguing crocodile temple attributed to the cult of Phepheros, as well as a mummified crocodile and other assorted relics from Egypt's Greco-Roman past. To reach the museum walk south from the corniche along Safia Zaghloul St., turn left on al-Hurriya St., and walk until the sign for the museum directs you to the left again. (Open Sat.-Thurs. 9am-4pm, Fri. 9-12pm and 2-4pm, during Ramadan and on holidays 9am-3pm. Admission LE8, students LE4, camera privileges LE10.)

From the museum it's an easy meander to the three major ancient sites, all of which lie within a few kilometers of downtown. Just north of Masr Station is the beautifully preserved white marble **Roman Amphitheater,** the only one of its kind ever discovered in Egypt. Behind the 13-tiered theater struggle the ruins of a Roman bath (to the left) and of a Roman villa and cistern (to the right). Self-styled guides may offer to sneak you in for a fee, but it's not worth it since almost everything of interest is visible from the theater. To get here from Sa'ad Zaghloul Sq. walk down Nabi Danial St. and take the second left after al-Hurriya St.; the entrance will be on your left. (Open daily 9am-4pm, during Ramadan 10am-3pm. Admission LE3, students LE1.50.)

The most famous ancient monument is **Pompey's Pillar,** a single granite erection that thrusts upward to a height of 25m, named by lengthist Crusaders who mistakenly imagined that it had some connection with Pompey and took a liking to its size. The pillar actually dates from the time of Diocletian, several centuries later, and was part of the Serapium, a religious center where the rites of the cult of the bull god were conducted. Not surprisingly, the temple was leveled once the Roman Empire became Christian.

The Roman provincial governor raised the pillar, originally transported from Aswan, in honor of the emperor Diocletian's role in subduing an Alexandrian revolt. Apparently, the feisty emperor, not well-loved by Amnesty International, swore that he would massacre the rebellious people until blood stained the knees of his horse; as he entered the cowering town his mount stumbled into a pool of blood, prematurely fulfilling Diocletian's oath. Thus, the emperor did not sack the city, and the lone pillar remains as a symbol of the people's gratitude to him and his klutzy horse. The ruins of the Serapium around the pillar have been excavated and the best finds moved to the Greco-Roman museum. To reach the site take bus #309 from Raml Station and get off on Karmus St. when you see the pillar. The entrance is on the southern side of the complex. You can also take tram #16. (Site open daily 9am-4pm, during Ramadan 9am-3pm. Admission LE3, students LE1.50.)

Ambling past the entrance to the Serapium (in the direction the bus travels), take your first right and follow it about 0.5km to the eerie **Catacombs of Kom ash-Shokafa.** These Roman tombs descend in three levels to a depth of about 35m and are noteworthy for their bits of sculpture and reliefs depicting Egyptian gods with unmistakably virile Roman bodies. Don't miss the jackal-headed Anubis with the torso of a man; he's near the entrance to the innermost burial chamber. As you enter the central rotunda the creepy capacious room to your left is where the funeral feasts were held. The hall of the goddess Nemesis, farther down and to the left, is menacingly flooded. (Open daily 9am-4pm, during Ramadan 9am-3pm. Admission LE8, students LE4.)

Behind the Governor's residence sits the architecturally-intriguing **Royal Jewelry Museum,** 27 Ahmed Yehia St., Gleem, which contains the gleaming baubles of the Muhammad Ali era. Most memorable are the pieces belonging to the royal family, especially those bestowed on the wives of King Farouk. Take blue tram #2 to get there. (Open Sat.-Thurs. 9am-4pm and Fri. 9-11:30am and 1:30-4pm. Admission LE10, students LE5.) For another quick tourist fix, visit the **Tombs of Chatby,** Port Said St., across from St. Mark's College. Believed to be the most ancient tombs in Alexandria, these tombs date back to the 3rd century BCE. (Open daily 9am-4pm. Admission LE3, students LE1.50.) For the thorough student of Alexandrian history, the **Cavafy Museum** (inside the Greek Consulate, 63 Alexander the Great St., Azarita; tel. 482 58 96) houses an interesting collection of this Greek Alexandrian poet's books and furniture. (Open Mon.-Fri. 10am-1pm. Admission free.)

The neighborhoods of Alexandria lying west and north of the central square reward backstreet investigation. Dilapidated **al-Gomrok** and breezy **Anfushi** are crowded with old mosques, Coptic churches, and finely decorated 19th-century buildings. A few sights here mustn't be missed. The Islamic **Fort Qaytbay** commands the ancient island of Pharos, now the tip of the peninsula separating the eastern and western harbors. The fort symbolizes "the big one that got away"; it was built in the 15th century by the Mamluk Sultan Qaytbay over parts of the old Lighthouse of Pharos. Inside, a naval museum features an exhibition of artifacts salvaged from the sunken French fleet that was destroyed by Nelson at the Battle of the Nile. Notice the small mosque in the center of the tower; the entire fortress is aligned so that its *mihrab* will face Mecca. (Fort open Sat.-Thurs. 9am-4pm, Fri. 9am-noon and 2-4pm, during Ramadan 10am-2:30pm. Admission LE6, students LE3. Camera privileges LE10.)

To reach the fort, take tram #15 west from Raml Station and get off when it makes a sharp left turn. You'll find yourself in the middle of an open-air **fish market,** and lo, it stinketh. At the point where the tram turned left, you should turn right on the road between the Kuwait Airlines sign and the mosque; the fort is at the end of this road. Also accessible by bus #260 to Abu Kir or minibus #707 from Raml Station (these buses take you to the end of the street, not all the way to the Fort).

The **Mosque of Abu al-Abbas,** with its four domes and tall minarets, is located about 1km south of the fort along the corniche and is Alexandria's most prominent and elaborate sample of Islamic architecture. The holy Abu al-Abbas came from Andalucia, Spain, and settled in the Delta. His tomb rests in the back of the mosque. Legend professes that he rose from his tomb to catch bombs falling on Alexandria during World War II raids. Until the arrival of feminism in this part of town, women are permitted to enter the back room of the mosque only. With the coffin surrounded by a glowing green neon-lithic lamp, this might actually be the most intriguing sight. (Open 5am-10pm.)

Another central Alexandrian magnet, the **Fine Arts Museum,** at 18 Menasha St. (tel. 493 66 16), contains a small but interesting collection of modern Egyptian art as well as Alexandria's public library. From Masr Station walk east on Mahmoud Bey Salama St., which runs along the southern side of the railroad tracks. The museum is on the right at the first major intersection (about 1km; Open Sat.-Thurs. 9am-1pm and 5-8pm. Free.)

Those who plan to spend more than a day or two in Alexandria should journey at least once to the eastern beaches. This district's highlight is **Montaza Palace and Gardens** (tel. 86 00 79 or 86 00 56). Formerly King Farouk's decadent summer retreat, the huge complex includes gardens as well as beaches. The palace and its museum have been closed to the public, but the gardens and groves are open and have become a favorite picnic spot for Alexandrians. (Admission to the gardens LE1. Semi-private beach west of the palace LE6).

Entertainment

Alexandria's most popular attractions are its **beaches.** Alarmingly popular, in fact; during the blazing summer months, Cairenes come here by the thousands. The masses will daunt all but the most fanatical sun-worshipers: it's possible to ride up and down the entire 18km coast without seeing a single square meter of free sand. Consider the effects of ever-increasing erosion and exceptionally disagreeable pollution (the net weight of the litter nearly exceeds that of the bathers), and you will doubtless opt to avoid this temptation to court melanoma. The beaches along the corniche are the most crowded and family-oriented. Women bathe fully clothed or, occasionally, in modest maillots. Westernized Egyptians tend to congregate at the slightly less crowded beaches at Mandara, Montaza, and Ma'mura. Ma'mura, just east of Montaza, can be reached by a Montaza bus (minibus #735 or 736, both from the seafront).

Most of Alexandria's nightlife fidgets around the clubs on the corniche. In summer you'll see wedding parties wherever you go along the corniche, and foreigners are often invited to share in the fun. Most clubs require patrons to guzzle (LE5-10 worth) but have no cover charge. **Crazy Horse,** in Raml Station (tel. 482 81 31), is the best known and generally packed with Egyptians (open 8pm-1am). Away from the corniche, **Santa Lucia Restaurant** has a low-key bar that features live music every night except Sundays (open nightly 10pm-2am; cover charge LE13.75; see Food), and a nightclub is also attached to **Au Privé Restaurant,** 14 al-Hurriya St. (tel. 483 80 82; open until 3am). For those hungry for an expatriate atmosphere, **Monty's Bar** in the Cecil Hotel (open 24 hrs.) is where General Montgomery totalled more than tea and planned the British war effort, and where Bogart nursed a cool one.

Also extremely popular are Alexandria's **cinemas.** English-language films usually play at the Amir (tel. 491 79 72) and Metro (tel. 483 04 32) theaters, both on Safia Zaghloul St. (Usually four shows a day, tickets LE2.50-4.50.) Check billboards for details. In late summer an **international film festival** presents foreign films in all of the city's theaters; ask at the tourist information office. Also, the American Culture Center shows films on Tuesdays and Thursdays.

Near Alexandria

The fishing village of **Abu Kir** (commonly pronounced abu-EER) lies on a peninsula 5km past Montaza. The village remains rural, not yet absorbed by Alexandria's relentless eastward expansion. Abu Kir is famous as the site of Nelson's 1798 naval victory over Napoléon, as the former foiled the little Frenchman's vision of Egyptian conquest. More important to the traveler, Abu Kir is a great place to sample Mediterranean seafood and visit an "international" International House of Pancakes. The fare is far superior to what's available in Alexandria, making it well worth the short evening excursion to dine here. You can reach Abu Kir by **local bus** #250, 251, or 260 or by **minibus** #729 from Masr Station (every 30min. from 7am-10pm, 50pt), by **train** from Masr Station (daily 6am-10pm, every 30min., third class 15pt), or by **local taxi** from downtown (LE5-10).

There are two options for eating fish (*samak*) in Abu Kir. If it's daytime and funds are lacking, try eating on the beach; as you step off the train or bus, walk east to the waterfront until you reach a row of tables on the beach. Anglers will come in from the boats anchored offshore and cook the fish you select right at your table.

The second option is a seafood restaurant. Try the well-known **Zephyrion,** 14 Khalid Ibn Walid St. (tel. 560 13 19), an Abu Kir landmark since 1929. The blue and white pavilion has expanded in girth as its popularity has reached new heights. A full dinner of fresh fish with beer and salad typically costs LE15. Cooked fish will cost roughly LE28 per kilo (more for shrimp and other exotica). Appetite dictates financial damage: it's possible to binge for LE22. Try the octopus plate (LE9). (Open daily noon-midnight.) Next door to Zephyrion is another piscatory paradise called **Bella Vista** (tel. 560 06 28), which is not as nice but has slightly lower prices. To reach either restaurant head north to the waterfront from the main mosque; they're right on the beach. (Open daily noon-1am.)

Abu Kir offers little except seafood and is best visited as a daytrip from Alexandria. The town is ideal for campers, though, since Abu Kir Camp, located on Bahr al-Mait St., about 0.5km south of the Zephyrion (tel. 560 14 24), supplies the only consistently available camping possibilities in the Alexandria area. A night's repose will cost you LE1 whether you use one of their tents or bring your own. Alternately, with permission from the local police, you can camp for free on the beach at Abu Kir.

For generations many of the wealthiest Egyptian vacationers in Alexandria have avoided the crowded city beaches by sunning at **Agami,** a resort town 20km west of al-Manshiya. Long famous for its white sand and turquoise waters, Agami lies where Alexandria nudges the Western Desert. In recent years pollution from the city's Western Harbor has sullied some of Agami's beaches, and the crowds have accrued. A bevy of hotels and villas fringe the choppy waters of **Agami Beach** (also called "Bitaash") and the adjacent **Hannoville Beach.** The resort, easily accessible from downtown Alexandria, makes a worthwhile daytrip or overnight excursion.

Buses #750 and #760 leave Masr and Raml Stations and al-Manshiya Sq. for Agami (daily 5:30am-midnight, 50pt). For accommodations, try the **New Admiral** in front of the Gadd Restaurant (tel 34 84 65; singles LE38, doubles LE60) or the slightly cheaper **Costa Planca Hotel** (tel. 430 31 12; singles LE17.50, doubles LE35).

About 75 minutes east of Abu Kir (about 1hr. east of Alexandria) stretches the northern edge of the Nile Delta. Immediately past the barrages the river divides in half, flowing into the Mediterranean at the two ports of **Rosetta** (Rashid) and **Damietta.** The Rosetta Stone was, yes indeed, discovered near Rosetta. The port drips with Islamic architecture. Scattered throughout the town are dozens of provincial Ottoman mosques and houses from the 17th and 18th centuries. The highest concentration of such buildings lies along Port Said St., opposite the bus stop. To get to Rashid, the cheapest option is the **bus** from Misr Station (every hour between 8am and 10pm, LE1.50). There's also a **train** to Rashid (ask at the station), and a **taxi** costs LE2.50. Al-Mashroowa microbuses cost the same per person as a taxi and leave from Muhammad Kareem St. next to Sidi Dimrass Mosque.

The best place from which to orient yourself in Rosetta is the Arab Killy House, also called the Rosetta Museum. Turn left from the bus stop and walk past the scores of noxious fish stands until you reach the corniche, then take another left and continue about 0.5km until you see a large howitzer on your left. This is al-Hurriya Sq., and the Arab Killy House is just behind the howitzer on the right. The museum, built by Mr. Arab Killy (a governor of Rosetta in the 18th century), features nothing of interest except perhaps the ridiculous lifesize diorama of the Rashidan rendition of minutemen inflicting generous amounts of pain on invading British brigades, their plaster visages grimacing in ways that, while anatomically possible, are highly improbable. (Museum open daily 8am-4pm. Admission LE5, students LE2.50, camera privileges LE10.) While the museum is basically a bust, the staff is more helpful and speaks better English than that of the **tourist office** across the street.

Bus #5115 from Alexandria to Rosetta runs every hour, and stops at the station on the north side of Gomhouriya Sq. (90pt). The train (3rd-class only) runs from Masr Station daily at 5:45am and 4:20 pm (75pt). The last bus returning to Alexandria leaves at 5pm. Make it a day trip.

About 5km from Rosetta, the recently restored **Fort of Qaytbay** (not to be confused with the one in Alex) guards the strategic entrance to the Nile. (Open daily 9am-4pm, during Ramadan 9am-3pm. Admission LE6, students LE3.) Built in 1479 by Sultan Ashraf Abu Nasr Qaytbay to serve in the first line of defense against the Ottoman

Turks and the Crusaders coming from the Delta, this structure used to overlook the surrounding land; now, due to soil and clay deposits from the Nile, the ground level is the same as that of the fortress. Fortification of this fortress by the French in 1799 prompted the importation of stone from Upper Egypt, and one of the French soldiers noticed writing on one of the stones. This **Rosetta Stone** enabled Jean-François Champollion to unlock the mystery of the hieroglyphics. The stone (which now resides in London) describes—in Demotic (the common language), ancient Greek (the royal language), and hieroglyphics (the holy language)—the coronation and numerous titles of Pharaoh Ptolemy V. Recent excavations in this and surrounding areas have revealed Rashid (pharaonically named "Bulubatin") to be a site rich with pharaonic history. The cheapest way to get here is by the green-and-white taxis (LE1-2). On the other hand, the romantic way to get here is to find a willing fisherman and go by private boat (20min., LE5-10 depending on your bargaining prowess). You'll see some beautiful scenery on the way.

To visit the peaceful **Mosque of Abu Mandur** perched on the bank of the river, catch one of the southbound taxi boats at the main dock just across from the cannon in al-Hurriya Sq. The boat driver will ask for LE10-15, but don't pay more than LE5-7 round-trip. Ask the royal shoe-taker to take you to the minaret for a film-frying view of the Mediterranean.

Mediterranean Coast

400km of the Egyptian coast are dominated by sea and sand. While opportunities for free, secluded camping are virtually unlimited (simply check in with the nearest police or military office), the most gleaming coastline segments remain tantalizingly inaccessible to budget travelers. The coastal highway between Alexandria and Libya bisects this junction of the Mediterranean and the Western Desert. Buses, trains, and service taxis make regular runs between Alexandria and Marsa Matruuh, the coast's only sizable town. The 290km of coastline in between are *not* served by public transportation. Consequently you must have a private car or risk long treks across the desert to reach resort villages such as **Sidi Abd ar-Rahman,** 44km west of al-Alamein. Marsa Matruuh, a low-key resort town, proffers enough variety of coastal scenery to content the most demanding beach bum.

A detailed, scholarly map of Egypt will tell you that seven or eight towns line the coast between Sidi Abd ar-Rahman and Marsa Matruuh. Experience will tell you otherwise. For the names of these towns cartographers could just as well have printed the names of their residents; the ratio approaches one to one.

You can pass the time on the bus contemplating the grandiose dream of the **Qattara Depression** Project. Desperate to increase the area of arable land in their country, Egyptian planners have long dreamed of channeling water to the nutrient-rich but parched soils of the Western Desert's Qattara Depression. Covering a region the size of the Delta and dipping 134m below sea level, the depression lies 100km inland. The idea is to take water from the Mediterranean Sea, desalinate it, and pipe it past al-Alamein to create vast new tracts of farmland. During Nasser's rule Soviet aid stimulated initial steps, but shifting political alliances and burgeoning costs checked this early optimism. Egypt still seeks enormous amounts of foreign aid for the project, but definite plans for a massive reworking of the desert landscape seem unlikely in the near future.

Marsa Matruuh is the starting point for trips to the saliently memorable **Siwa Oasis.** With its ancient Temple of Amon and memories of a visit by Alexander the Great, this oasis has a venerable history of trade with the coast.

Marsa Mutruuh مـرسة مطـروح

Fanning out from the cobalt blue bay, this resort city looks as if it were built yesterday. Dozens of mold-and-pour concrete villas accommodate the thousands of Egyptians who annually fall victim to the universal human urge to reach the beach. The natural harbor here has served travelers, merchants, and soldiers from Alexander to Rommel; but now the majority of sea vessels in Matruuh are rented by the hour, and the only major military presence in town patronizes the holiday resorts maintained especially for Air Force and Navy officers. As Alexandria's beaches become polluted and crowded, more and more expatriates and members of the Egyptian intelligentsia come to Marsa Matruuh for their summer holidays. Few foreigners make it out here, but those who do are treated to the finest beaches in Egypt and a tepidly hedonistic atmosphere.

Practical Information

The best way to reach Marsa Matruuh is to take a **bus** from Alexandria. The **blue buses** leaving Sa'ad Zaghloul Sq. are convenient and inexpensive (8 per day, 7am-7pm, 5 hrs., LE10, LE15 with A/C). The plush **Golden Rocket** line serves Marsa Matruuh daily at 7:35am (4hrs., LE15). The newer **Superjet** line leaves Alexandria daily at 7:15am (4hrs., LE20). Reserve seats on any of these buses 2 or 3 hours before. All three companies connect from Tahrir Sq. in Cairo (8hrs.; blue buses LE12.75, LE23 with A/C; Golden Rocket LE28.50; Superjet LE30; book 1-2 days in advance at the booths in front of the Nile Hilton). In Marsa Matruuh, blue buses arrive and depart from the **bus station,** about seven blocks inland, three blocks west of Alexandria St. Golden Rocket buses continue to the parking lot next to the tourist office, on the corniche.

Marsa Matruuh's **train station** is at the top of Alexandria St., about 0.5km from the corniche and three blocks east of the bus station. Trains run daily to Cairo's Ramses Station (1st-class LE26.20, 2nd-class with A/C LE15.70, 2nd-class without A/C LE8, *wagon-lits* three times per week, 9hrs., LE32; 50% student discount). To Alexandria's Masr Station (1st-class LE18.20, 2nd-class with A/C LE11.20, 2nd-class without A/C LE5.60; 50% student discount).

Shared *service* **taxis** shuttle between the bus station in Marsa Matruuh, Alexandria's Masr Station, and Cairo's Ahmed Hilmi Sq. or Kolali Sq. (both adjacent to Ramses Station). These taxis leave sporadically and are often effectively camouflaged. In Marsa, the taxis park at the northern side of the bus station (behind the small tea stall). If you travel by shared taxi you won't have to wait in line for a ticket to Alexandria or Cairo, you won't have to come days in advance, and you'll be guaranteed a seat (albeit much like a corset). Moreover, a *service* taxi will cost about the same as the bus. Best of all, you'll travel at break-neck speed. (LE10 to Alexandria, LE15-20 to Cairo).

EgyptAir flies to Marsa from Cairo (2 flights per week during summer only, US$79 one-way). Their office (tel. 93 43 98) is on Galeh St., three blocks west of Alexandria St. and next to the bus station.

You need to know only two streets to find your way around Marsa Matruuh: the lively **corniche,** which stretches the length of the bay, and busy **Alexandria Street,** which runs perpendicular to the corniche from the Marsa Matruuh Governate inland to the hill north of town. Most of the hotels and government offices are clustered along the corniche and the three streets that run parallel to it. Restaurants and cafés glaze lower Alexandria St.

Once you've arrived in Marsa Matruuh, getting around is a breeze. At the bus or train station scores of donkey commanders will besiege you. Don't subsidize those owners who mistreat their poor beasts. For most destinations in town you don't even need a braying companion—you can usually walk to where you're going in under 10 minutes. To travel farther afield rent a **bicycle** from the shop across from the Rady Hotel, four blocks east of Alexandria St. (LE1 per hour, you can negotiate LE10 per day, open 24 hrs.), or from the stand next to the Riviera Palace Hotel, one block from the corniche on Alexandria St. (LE10 for 24 hrs., open 2pm-midnight).

Marsa Matruuh's **tourist office** (tel. 93 31 92), located one block west of Alexandria St. on the corniche, is not as efficient as its well-kept appearance suggests, but they can give you a map of the area which does include major hotels and offices but lacks such pesky details as street names. (Open daily 8am-2pm and 8-10pm.)

The manager of the tourist office also leads the fearless **tourist police.** If you have trouble tracking him down, go to the **Police Station** (tel. 93 30 63), on the first street south of the corniche, two blocks east of Alexandria St. (open 24 hrs.). Next door is Marsa Matruuh's **post office** (open Sat.-Thurs. 8am-3pm), and across the street is the **telephone office** (open 24 hrs.). The City Council, where you must go to receive permission to camp on the beach or to ask passport questions, is across the street from the train station. (Open Sat.-Thurs. 9am-2pm; tel. 93 52 66.) The most convenient **bank** in Marsa Matruuh is the **Bank of Cairo** (tel. 93 53 17), off Alma Rum St., one block east of the Ghazala Hotel (open daily 8:30am-2pm and 6-9pm). The **telephone code** is 03 (even if dialing from Alexandria).

The **hospital** (tel. 93 33 55) is located at the top of Alexandria St. on the right, across from the train station. Facilities here are more limited than those in the large cities, and, for serious problems, it's probably a wise idea, if your condition permits, to catch the next flight to Cairo. **Said Lee Tohami Pharmacy** (tel. 93 47 19) is located on the west side of Alexandria St., about eight blocks from the corniche. In addition to the usual medications, the pharmacy carries Raid electric mosquito-zappers, which restore sanity for a mere LE9. (Open daily 8am-midnight, 8am-9pm in winter.)

Because Marsa Matruuh is so close to Libya, there is a noticeable military presence in the surrounding areas. While unnecessary within the city limits (unless you want to rent a bike), it's wise to carry your passport with you outside of town and on the more obscure beaches to avoid being hassled by officers on power trips. There may also be a passport check on the road into town.

Accommodations

Hotel prices in Marsa Matruuh have skyrocketed in recent years. The tourist season lasts from the beginning of May through the end of October. The month of Ramadan brings crowds of Copts and Muslims to Marsa Matruuh. In the mild and generally sunny off-season many hotels either close entirely or slash their rates, and the luxurious new hotels along the corniche become affordable. For example, the government-run, two-star **Arous al-Baha** (tel. 93 44 19/20) on the corniche drops its full board requirements and prices between October and May (LE38 w/bath and breakfast, doubles LE75 w/bath, breakfast and one more meal. In winter, prices drop close to 50%).

Small, mega-cheap hotels can be found along and nearby Alexandria St., three or four blocks inland. Only Egyptians frequent these places, so many of them have no English signs, and some foreigners, especially women, might find a stay here unpleasant. Talk to the tourist office. Men with small budgets and open minds can rent a bed in a crowded room for LE1-2, but guard your belongings. The hotels listed below are accustomed to foreigners. Unfortunately, women should always be on guard.

HI Youth Hostel, (tel. 93 23 31). Very difficult to find: walk west from Alexandria St. on Galeh St. until you pass the Omar Effendi Store. Follow the street that angles off to your right towards the beach. Otherwise, if you're coming from the Corniche, find the Ministry of Agriculture and peek behind it. The Youth Hostel is a 2-story concrete cube behind similar 3-story buildings, along an unnamed street that juts off to the left about 0.5km north of Omar Effendi. Ask for the *bayt ash-shibab.* If you make it you'll find the best deal in Marsa Matruuh. Mr. Abdallah Kamel, the warden, is fluent in English and is adamant about having the rooms cleaned daily. Fine bathrooms, and purified water taps. In the future, Mr. Kamel dreams of starting a parachuting club which will be open to his patrons. LE5.10, nonmembers LE9.10.

Ghazala Hotel, Alma Rum St. (tel. 93 35 19), a 3-story yellow building just east of Alexandria St., about 6 blocks from the corniche. Speckless rooms. The second best budget bed in town. LE5.

Hotel El Roda Tourist, Zahr Galal St. (tel. 93 41 20), 2 blocks down from Mansour Fish Restaurant heading away from the Corniche. The only remarkable feature of this hotel is the height of one of the managers. Drab but clean rooms, with small but decent bathrooms. Decide between a fan and a sea view. Singles with bath LE5, LE3 in Jan.-Apr. Doubles with bath LE10, LE6 in Jan.-Apr.

Hotel Ageba (tel. 93 23 34), on Alexandria St., a half block closer to the Corniche than the intersection with Mohateh St. Striking lobby; rooms less so. Singles LE15. Doubles LE25. All rooms have bath.

New Lido (tel. 93 45 15), on the corniche 1km west of Alexandria St., 1 block past the mosque. Rents 4-room flats (including kitchen, bath, and balcony) that accommodate 4 comfortably, 5-6 if you don't breathe, for LE100 per night. 4 can fit in the beach bungalows farther down the beach for LE65 per night (no kitchen but private bath). Mixed gender groups should provide marriage certificates. Reservations recommended. Closed in winter.

El Dest Hotel (tel. 93 21 05), on the corner of Alexandria and Alma Rum St., just across from the Ghazala Hotel. Not exceedingly cozy, but centrally located. Clean beds, decent bathrooms. Singles LE7. Doubles LE10.

Cairo Hotel, Tahrir St. (tel. 93 26 48), 3 blocks east of Alexandria St. at the intersection of Port Said St., near the Mosque al-Malaak. In a quiet neighborhood, but concrete rooms with padlocks will give you the disturbing feeling of doing time. Marriage certificate needed for mixed-sex couples to share a room. Singles LE2.50 (in winter LE2), with shower LE5 (in winter LE4). Doubles LE5 (in winter LE4), with shower LE10 (in winter LE8). The **Mena House Hotel** (tel. 93 46 02), across the street, has similar rates and similar compartments, but the bathrooms are even more harrowing.

Rio Hotel, on the corner of Alexandria St. and Galeh St. Due to a bad experience a female Let's Go researcher had with someone who worked here, we cannot recommend this hotel.

Campers have two options. You can receive permission to camp for free on the beach by the bay from the City Council (see Practical Information; the law against camping without a permit is strictly enforced) or you can take an intercity Peugot taxi to **Disney Beach** (also called "Bagoush Village," 48km east of Marsa Matruuh) and set up camp there. Disney Beach is convenient to Libya, home of the dethspicable Qaddaffy Duck. Call (03) 93 66 60/1/2 for information and rates.

Food and Entertainment

The cheapest way for a group to eat in Marsa Matruuh is to shop en masse at the local market. Alexandria St. runneth over with grocery stores, vegetable stands, and fruit markets, and the bread bakery is just one block west on Galeh St. A number of inexpensive restaurants vie for customers on Alexandria St.

Alexandria Tourist Restaurant (tel. 93 23 15), on the east side of Alexandria St., 2 blocks south of the Corniche. One of the best budget meals in town. Try the *bamia* (okra stew) and rice for LE3. Open daily 10am-midnight.

Panayatis Greek Restaurant (tel. 93 42 74), across the street from Alexandria Tourist Restaurant. Nothing particularly Greek about the food here (generous meal LE9). Open daily 8am-midnight.

Hani al-Omda (tel. 93 15 22), two doors east of Alexandria St. on the south side of Tahrir St. next to the Matruuh Tourist Coffee shop. Another fine contender for your stomach. Dimly lit but cool and clean. 0.25kg of mystery meat with bread and salad for about LE5.50. Open 24 hrs.

Mansour Fish Restaurant, Mohatah St. (tel. 93 34 10), 4 blocks east of Alexandria St. and 1 block closer to the corniche than the intersection of Galeh St. and Mohatah St. Lobster (LE10/kilo) and fish (LE22/kilo). Open June-Sept. daily 10am-1am.

Abdu Kofta, Gamal Abd an-Nasser St. (tel. 93 58 38), on the corner of Tahrir St. *Kufte* with salad and bread costs a mere LE6. The *bamia* costs LE1 in this small but clean joint. Open daily 9am-1am.

Restaurant Camona (tel. 93 21 07), on the corner of Galeh St. and Alexandria St. Slurp up a meal of *bamia* and chicken with rice and salad (LE6.50) and then practice your seed-spittin' with some *butteekh* (watermelon, LE1). Open daily 11am-3am.

Most of the fancy hotels along the corniche open their bars or nightclubs to all who wish to surrender their sobriety. Small nightclubs along the bay attract a staid crowd of young Egyptians every summer night. Try **Disco 54,** in the Radi Hotel (tel. 93 48 28), on the corniche four blocks east of Alexandria St. (Open July to mid-Sept. daily 10pm-2am. Admission LE4.)

Sights

Marsa Matruuh's **beaches** will enchant you, but all the beaches are closed after sunset. As part of a government effort to control drug trafficking, soldiers patrol the coast throughout the night.

Five kilometers of soft sand rim Marsa's crescent-shaped bay, from the town's small port on the east to Lido Beach on the west. As in Alexandria, some women here swim fully clothed; as in all of Egypt, bikinis and revealing one-piece suits can incite apoplexy. The Beau Site Hotel has a private beach which is cleaner, less crowded, and more liberal (some belly button sightings reported) than the public beaches. There is no charge for non-guests, but they encourage you to rent an umbrella (LE3 per hour), or a surf kayak (LE6 per hour).

East of the port the shoreline arches into a peninsula that faces the town from across the bay. Hire a donkey cart, rent a bike, or hire a boat from the port to take you over to the peninsula, called **Rommel's Isle.** The **Rommel Museum** contains a mediocre exhibit built into a series of nifty caves that Rommel once used as his headquarters during the North African campaign of World War II. (Open daily 9:30am-4pm. Admission 50pt.) On the ocean side of the peninsula, just past the marine Fouad Hotel, is **Rommel's Beach,** where, according to legend, the Nazi general skinny-dipped every day. Also, on the ocean side of the isle, the rusting wreck of an old U-boat juts out of the water. You can rent a surf kayak to paddle out to the wreck; head straight toward the red buoy on your left. The sub lies parallel to the beach 20m toward the mosque from the red buoy; you'll need a diving mask to discern it.

To the west of the main town beach, the **Beach of Lovers** fondles the western horn of the bay. You can easily reach this beach by foot or kayak. Inconsiderate visitors have recently begun to desecrate the sand while worshiping the sun, and the heaps of litter float out daily. Farther west on the ocean side of the bay you'll encounter more wind, less trash, and **Cleopatra's Beach,** on the far right-hand side of which lies a dwarf cove called **Cleopatra's Bath.** The queen and Marc Antony partook of the legacy of Ramses here. The farthest and most spectacular spot of all is **Agiiba,** about 20km from Marsa Matruuh. Agiiba, which means "wonderful," is an inlet in a series of rocky cliffs interrupted with caves. Bring your own food; there is only a soft-drink stand. Stop along the way at the ruins of the tiny **Temple to Ramses II** which lies neglected in the sand. There is a sandy and crowded beach, but it is also possible to find a private spot below the cliffs and spend the day swimming off the rocks looking for latex.

To reach these western beaches take a shared **taxi** or **microbus** from the bus station (LE2-3 per person to Agiiba), or catch the open-sided *tuf-tuf* bus (LE1.25 to Cleopatra, Ubayyad, or Agiiba). The bus shuttles to and fro from the bus station whenever enough passengers want to go, usually every hour from 9am-4:30pm (summer only). Alternatively you can join one of the Hotel Beau Site's weekly car or boat excursions to the more distant beaches. The LE8 fee includes transportation, a guide, umbrellas, and refreshments. Every now and then the hotel sails a boat to Cleopatra's Beach (LE4).

Al-Alamein العلمين

Al-Alamein means "two worlds," and is best known for its role in World War II. A tiny village set in a broad, barren desert plain, al-Alamein is slightly too distant from the water to attract many tourists. But there was a time when al-Alamein was vastly less quiet, far less out-of-the-way, and infinitely less empty. In November 1942, the Allied forces under the command of the British Field Marshal Sir Bernard Montgomery halted the advance of the Nazi Afrika Corps here. Al-Alamein had been pinpointed by the Nazis the gateway to Alexandria and the key to the control of the continent. The Allied victory here marked the beginning of the end for the Axis Powers in North Africa and simultaneously crushed the mystique surrounding the "Desert Fox," German Field Marshal Erwin Rommel, whose force of Panzer tanks had previously proven invincible. The Battle of al-Alamein was not only one of the war's most important confrontations, but also one of the most violent: nearly 10,000 soldiers lost their lives and 70,000 were wounded.

On the east side of town toward Alexandria lies the **British War Cemetery,** the burial place of 7,367 men, 815 of whose headstones bear only the somber inscription "Known Unto God." Ringed by purple flowers and set against the seemingly interminable desert, the excruciatingly tidy rows are enough to set almost anyone to pondering. The plaque and inscriptions within the shaded alcove explain the battle's significance as well as the diverse backgrounds of the victims interred here. Maintained by the British War Graves Commission, the cemetery is free and almost always open.

The **War Museum** at the west side of the village is near the bus stop and main square. It contains displays of weaponry, military garb, and descriptions of the actions of Rommel, Montgomery, and the other participants in the battle. The room dedicated to Egypt's 1973 war with Israel is somewhat anomalous. Although subsequent tactical mistakes cost Egypt its victory, the smashing of Israel's much-touted Bar-Lev Line along the Suez Canal in the first few hours of the war endures as a point of great pride for many Egyptians. (Open daily 9am-3:30pm, during Ramadan 9am-3pm. Admission LE1.) Eight kilometers west of town, perched on a petite peninsula overlooking the sea, are the less frequently visited German and Italian citadel-like **Cemeteries.**

Without a private car or hired taxi it is difficult to visit the last two monuments. Look for the small marker about 3km west of the town center marking the farthest Axis advance; an arrow pointing east reads: "Il Fortuna, Non Il Valore: Alexandria, 111km."

Getting to al-Alamein is easy; leaving is the hard part. All of the buses that travel between Marsa Matruuh and Alexandria or Cairo make a 30-minute rest stop at al-Alamein. You can disembark, but it may be difficult to board a later bus unless you have already purchased a separate, full ticket at your point of departure. In addition, the buses are usually packed when they arrive here. West Delta buses to Marsa Matruuh cost LE10, LE15 with A/C. It's sometimes possible to board an Alexandria-bound bus and pay half the fare of a full one-way ticket.

The only other patented way to visit al-Alamein without your own car is to hire a *service* **taxi** to make the trip. This means you either have to find six other people who want to take a long pause in al-Alamein on a cross-desert run or have to make a special, round-trip excursion from Alexandria (about LE80 for the taxi with either option).

Another possibility for getting out of al-Alamein, though it's a miserable one, is to catch one of the four daily **trains** that pull very, very slowly through al-Alamein (3 each way, LE2 to Marsa or Alexandria). All trains arrive in the late morning or early afternoon. Inquire at Masr Station in Alexandria or at the station in Marsa for schedule information. The disadvantages of train travel are that coaches are not air-conditioned and the al-Alamein stop is 2km across the desert from the village. Some people arrange a ride with one of the drivers taking a rest stop in al-Alamein by offering to pay a few pounds for the trip.

Accommodations in this tiny village are pretty much nonexistent. For food, check out the **al-Alamein Rest House,** where an omelette costs LE1.35. (Open daily 7am-10pm). The Rest House also doubles as the **bus stop.**

Siwa Oasis واحة سيوة

Almost completely isolated from the rest of Egypt, awash in infinite desert sands, Siwa has developed a unique culture and history. Amidst groves of date palms and cool natural springs, the Siwans have retained most of their ancient customs. But as visitors continue to flood the oasis, the traditional way of life has begun to succumb to the demands of a kitschy tourism. Even so, like Alexander the Great, who made Siwa famous with his pilgrimage to the Oracle of Amon here in 331 BCE, the modern visitor will be richly rewarded.

A bus from Marsa Matruuh takes you through a completely barren landscape on much of the same path followed by Alexander's camel caravan. Today a paved road cuts through the desert, a tendril of modernity, and the 300km trip takes only five hours. Siwa's isolation has made it legendary in the annals of Egypt: ancient historians told odd tales of strange cities and mysterious kingdoms in the desert. Nature, however, defeated most attempts to ascertain the truth; in 500 BCE a desert sandstorm left an entire Persian army into smithereens. This suited the Siwans fine; they have always resented outsider interference in their lives, particularly those invaders who demand taxes.

A romantic perspective on Siwan culture sets the oasis in folktales, with its women donning traditional, vividly colored garb in the fashion of the Berbers of the Saharan plains in Libya, Tunisia, and Algeria. Much has changed. Whereas Siwan women characteristically adorned their necks, heads, and limbs with heavy silver jewelry and braided their hair in elaborate styles, today only the older, married oasis women wear traditional dress: the *troket* (black embroidered veil, sold everywhere and worn on special occasions), the *tarfudit* (blue veil always worn outside the home), and the *agbir* (loose dress, often bright yellow or red, worn every day and for festivities). Unmarried Siwan girls now wear Egyptian fashions. About 90% of the heavy silver jewelry has been sold to tourists and replaced by gold Egyptian jewelry, and hair styles are only a simplified version of the dozens of intricate braids women used to sport.

Assessing women's role in modern Siwan society is more complex than it appears. While visitors are tempted to assume that Siwan customs isolate, exclude, and repress women, an investigation behind the scenes suggests otherwise. Contrary to hearsay, women do leave their homes—to visit friends and relatives, to attend funerals, birth ceremonies, and feasts, and to join other women in craft-making. Siwan women's efforts are in fact responsible for the booming cottage craft industry, a fact not often realized by most tourists. In practice this means that women are the producers of the family income; children and men are generally responsible for selling the handiwork. Siwan girls were traditionally married by the age of 14, but in the last five years that age has risen to 16, which is around the national average. Girls also have more say regarding whom they will wed.

In recent years the national government has been working overtime to make up for long years of neglect. The new road, completed in 1985, has led to an increased number of well-stocked stores and a growing stream of tourists. Universal education, a new quarry, a new desalination plant, and modern agricultural projects are altering Siwan daily life.

The sexual conservatism of Siwa pervades every aspect of life here; for example, only male donkeys are used in order to prevent the corruption of the population who might otherwise witness donkey lust. Foreign visitors should dress modestly. Men should not wear shorts in town; women shouldn't bare their arms or legs. A sign explaining these dress codes is posted in town in English. Women should also avoid wandering into less populated areas alone, especially in the afternoon (when the majority of Siwans take a siesta) and in the evenings.

Those planning to spend more than a day in Siwa should make an effort to glance at a copy of the late Ahmed Fakhry's superb 200-page guide to Siwa. The author, a renowned Egyptologist, conveys his love for Siwa through fastidious descriptions of its history, culture, and geography. Published by the American University in Cairo, Fakhry's *The Oases of Egypt: Volume I, Siwa* is unfortunately out of print. Mr. Mahdi, the local tourist guru, keeps two copies on hand in the tourist office.

Practical Information

Siwa Oasis is enfolded into a desert depression about 300km southwest of Marsa Matruuh, a coastal town 290km west of Alexandria. Siwa's western edge comes within 50km of the closed Libyan border. The most practical way to reach Siwa is by road from Marsa Matruuh, but you *can* hire a camel in the Nile Valley, brave 20 days of sandstorms and endless possibilities for death, and break every Egyptian travel restriction law as you trek across the Western Desert. Those with a group and at least two cars can travel the 420km stretch of the new road from Bahariya. Keep in mind, if you opt for this route, that this road offers no rest house or petrol station—travelling in one vehicle is a bad idea.

The new road from Marsa Matruuh is well-paved but infrequently used. The best way to travel is to catch a **bus** from the main station in Marsa. The buses (*sans* A/C) leave daily at 7am and 3pm and cost LE6, and the air-conditioned but much more crowded version departs Saturday, Monday, and Wednesday at 4pm and costs LE8. (Both buses take 5 hrs. and arrive at the station 30 min. before departure time.)

Non-air-conditioned buses return to Marsa Matruuh daily at 6am and 1pm (LE6), with the morning bus continuing to Alexandria (LE8). Air-conditioned buses also leave Siwa on Sunday, Tuesday, and Thursday at 10am for Marsa Matruuh (LE8) and Alexandria (LE9). The bus station in Siwa is located in the town square, but incoming buses continue through town about 1km and stop in front of the **Badawi Hotel** (see Accommodations). All buses stop at the simple desert **Rest House** halfway between Marsa Matruuh and Siwa, where you can buy soft drinks and snacks but not bottled water. There is an outhouse behind the store. Buses break down on occasion; take bottled water and food with you.

If getting to Siwa wasn't bad enough, getting around Siwa is vicious. The oasis fills a depression that stretches for 82km west to east, and between three and 30km north to south, but most visitors concern themselves only with the **town of Siwa** and the nearby villages and ancient sites. Five days to a week are needed to really get a feel for Siwa and the Siwans. About 12,000 people live in the town; 2000 more Siwans plus a few hundred Bedouin live in villages scattered elsewhere in the oasis. The paved road from Marsa Matruuh ends at the **New Mosque**. The main north-south road in town continues past the mosque into the two squares of the **town market**. The ruined houses of **ancient Siwa** rise in eerie geometric form above the market on a rock acropolis. The narrow streets of Siwa town radiate from the market and the acropolis. The town is graced by a swath of palm trees on its eastern side and fringed by palms on all but the southern side, which rolls gently into the desert.

The **telephone office** (which can handle **international calls** from 9-10am) is located just west of the New Mosque, next to the Arous al-Waha across from the new government hotel. (Open daily 7am-10pm.) Across the street in a modern building is both the **police station** (open 24 hrs.) and the **post office** (open Sat.-Thurs. 9am-2pm). Around the corner and down the street is the brand new **tourist information office** (open Sat.-Thurs. 9am-1pm, Fri. 6-8pm), the domain of the knowledgeable Mr. Mahdi Muhammad Ali Hweiti. A sociology major at the University of Alexandria, fluent speaker of English, and native Siwan, Mr. Hweiti can arrange sight-seeing expeditions and provide maps and information on Siwan events. Mr. Hweiti, one of the country's sharpest businessmen, is largely responsible for the rapid growth of this isolated tourist sight. (Open Sat.-Thurs. 9am-1pm, Fri. 6-8pm.)

New services introduced in Siwa within the past year include a 24-hr. **hospital** beside the Badawi Hotel (tel. 19), a **pharmacy** (open 9am-1pm) next to the Suleiman Mosque, and **Hassan's Handcrafts and English Bookshop,** next to the phone office, which sells English books and traditional Siwan art. Hassan's also rents bikes (LE4/ day).

Siwa has recently introduced covered donkey carts (*carettas*) which can take you outside town for LE1-2 per hour. As always, avoid cruelty to animals. You can rent **bicycles** for LE1 per hour or LE5 per day in the market. The one **local bus** crawls west from Siwa town to al-Maraqi making a 50km loop. Round-trip fare is 75pt; ask Mr.

Hweiti for the schedule. Siwa town has no banking services or travel agencies. Aside from the main telephone office, telephones are unheard of here; the postal service, nevertheless, seems reliable. Streets in Siwa have no names, but most establishments hand out maps like American barracuda lawyers hand out their business cards.

The climate in Siwa is similar to that in Aswan and the other oases. Winter is pleasantly warm, with cool nights. Summer is brutally hot. Round-the-clock electricity was introduced in 1990, but air-conditioning is but a diaphanous mirage. The mild weather and the many local festivals associated with the harvest make fall and winter the best times to visit.

Accommodations and Food

Siwa can't claim to offer a wide variety of accommodations, but you can find decent lodging. Most travelers prefer the new **Cleopatra Hotel,** south of the town square on the main road past the Shali fortress. Cleopatra has the most comfortable rooms within a radius of 290km. Mr. Muhammad Ahmed Khaled, who is fluent in English, awaits the daily bus from Marsa Matruuh, so as to escort disoriented visitors to his hotel. (Doubles with internal private bath LE20, with external private bath LE15.) The government-run, three-story **Hotel Arous al-Waha** (Worth Bride Hotel) stands at the end of the road from Marsa Matruuh. Clean, simple rooms all have baths. If you find the rooms uncomfortably hot (very likely in the summer), you can drag your mattress out onto the gigantic, breezy terrace. (Singles LE15. Doubles LE20. Prices discounted 50% June-Sept.) Binge on a bodacious budget bed at the **Badawi Hotel,** 1km north of the town center, across from the intelligence office. The hotel is managed by the owner's energetic and competent 13-year-old son Badawi, with help from other siblings. Clean rooms, Turkish toilets. Couples without proof of marriage must sleep separately. (LE3 per bed.) Those who hear the call of the date palms and pomegranate trees and feel more comfortable at sea-level should take a *carreta* to the **Amun Hotel** at Dakrur Mountain. (Doubles LE8.) And, for the piastre-pincher, the large, decrepit **Hotel al-Medina** and the cramped **New Siwa Hotel,** across from the military intelligence office, both charge LE2 for a dorm bed. Be ready for a hole-in-one W.C. experience.

Camping is available on Dakrur Mountain, 1km south of the Pool of Cleopatra. Bring your sleeping bag and insect repellent—the shelters on the mountain are free. Camping outside this area is dangerous and forbidden; check with Mr. Hweiti before pitching your tent anywhere.

Several cafés line the two market squares. What you order often bears minimal resemblance to what you receive; you'll usually get whatever is in stock that day. Standard offerings (LE1-3) include macaroni, chicken, *couscous,* omelettes, and *shakshuka* (a mixture of meat, eggs, and sauce). **Abdou's Restaurant,** on the inside northern corner of the square, serves tasty food (meals LE1-4) and has fans to disseminate the flies (open daily 7am-12:30pm or 1pm). Equally devoid of flies and serving fresher, better-prepared food for the same prices is the **East-West Restaurant,** next to the New Mosque. Possibly the only place in Egypt to try Indian Fig Juice (LE5). (Open daily 10am-midnight.) The small **Sohag Restaurant,** a sidekick of Abdou's, extravagantly beflied and inferior to its neighboring eatery, still serves as a good *ahwa.* Enterprising throats can enjoy a menagerie of cheap, exotic drinks (e.g., *louisa,* a sweet mint beverage) and outlandish ice cream flavors (e.g., date, fig, watermelon) for under LE1. (Open daily 9 or 9:30am-1 or 2am). Many of the small, buzzing patrons of Sohag's also hang about **Shalighaly Restaurant,** just west of the town square. Prices similar to those of the other restaurants, but with a more a extensive menu. (Open Sat.-Thurs. 9am-2am.) The cheapest eats in town can be found at **Restaurant Kilani,** where most dishes are less than LE1. The local **stores** are also well stocked with canned goods, cold soda and mineral water, and fresh and dried dates and figs (in season).

Because Siwans tend to be more reserved than residents of most Egyptian towns, the traveler will be lucky to receive an invitation to eat or stay with a local family. Invitations are usually offered by children, but sometimes by men. Sometimes the Siwans will hope to sell you home-made handicrafts (you can get great deals on native silverwork and Siwan designer headcoverings), and sometimes they're just eager to help you use up those last few exposures on your roll of film. Women will be allowed to enter a home much more readily than men. As always, exercise caution before accepting hospitality.

Sights

Siwa is often considered the most beautiful of Egypt's oases. From atop the ruins of **ancient Siwa** you can look out on the quiet streets of Siwa town, which wind from the cluster of mud houses to luxuriant palm gardens. From here you can also see the Sahara: black gashes of rock to the north, waves of sand to the south, and the piercing blue desert sky all around. The weird geometric profiles of crumbling walls looming in the vicinity are the remains of the medieval fortress-town of Shali. Its encircling wall once protected the Siwans from marauding Berbers and Bedouin. As you descend to the paths leading back to the market you understand why the Siwans slowly abandoned their acropolis for the more spacious settlement at its base. The descent began when Muhammad Ali conquered Siwa in 1820 and protected the inhabitants from attacks. The heavy rains, which occur once every five decades and apocalyptically melt Siwan houses, encouraged migration to the new town. By 1930 the ancient city had become a virtual ghost town. Wandering among the haunting skeletons of these ancient abodes, the sojourner will find inhabitants in random dwellings and old men turning unlikely corner on their way to unknown businesses. The most recent rains, in 1985, washed away much of Shali and most of the Siwan mud-dwellings, but, due to the rise of concrete buildings, the devastation was not total. The threat of history and tradition being literally washed away prompted the Canadian ambassador to put forth funds to construct a permanent version of the **Traditional Siwan House.** The house serves as a museum of traditional Siwan garb, silver jewelry, and children's toys. (Open Sat.-Thurs. 9am-12pm. Admission LE1.)

In addition to Shali, a second acropolis rises 1km to the northeast of ancient Siwa. During the bombing of Siwa town by the Italians in World War II, its caves and ancient tombs sheltered the Siwans and the Egyptian, British, Australian, and New Zealand armed forces from the modern marauders. During this period the local people rediscovered several Ptolemaic-era tombs that Romans had robbed and then reused. Called the **Tombs of Jabal al-Mawta** (Hill of the Dead), they merit a visit by every traveler to Siwa. The random human bones and mummy wrappings that litter the sight belonged to the Romans and, sadly, the niches damaging the ancient frescoes are also their doing. A custodian is on hand to unlock the tombs Sunday-Thursday from 9am-1pm, but it is best to confirm the custodian's whereabouts with Mr. Hweiti or your muleteer. Bring a flashlight (or buy one from one of the stores along the road from the town square to the mountain for LE2.50-3), and be sure not to miss the **Tomb of Si-Amon** (literally, Man of Amon, the prominent pharaonic deity). Although damaged by Allied and Egyptian soldiers during the war, it boasts a beautifully painted ceiling depicting the six stages of the sun's journey across the sky. Marred murals on the walls show the bearded, Hellenized portrayal of the bearded nobleman Si-Amon and his sons worshiping Egyptian deities. The **Tomb of Niperpathot** housed the body of a nobleman of the 26th and last pharaonic dynasty. It is the oldest tomb in Siwa, but the real attraction is the once-mummified skull, complete with hair, gaping from a rusty can in one of the niches. The **Tomb of Mesu-Isis** is 20m to the east of Si-Amon, and has ancient frescoes depicting the gods Isis and Osiris in action. The acropolis commands exhilarating views of Siwa town and the oasis; the summit, now a military lookout post, is off-limits. LE1-2 *baksheesh* is appropriate.

In Siwa town hail a *carreta* and rattle off through the palm groves to the village of **Aghurmi.** Like Siwa town, Aghurmi rests peacefully at the foot of a formerly inhabited acropolis. To ascend the acropolis pass through an old gate made of palm logs and then underneath a weatherbeaten but sturdy old mud **mosque.** Up ahead, perched dramatically at the cliff-edge of the acropolis, looms the well-preserved **Oracle of**

Amon. This is where Alexander came to consult the renowned priests of Amon. First, though, he had to pass through the stone temple's simple gateway into the outer, then the inner court, as you must do to see the site. Accounts by ancient Greek and Roman historians paint the scene: priests carried the sacred boat containing the image of Amon as women sang and danced in procession. The oracle of Amon is said to have confirmed suspicion that Alexander was a god-king, proclaiming him the "son of Amon." Alexander never told what he asked the oracle in private, nor what the answer was. The secret died with him, less than 10 years after his visit.

The temple of the Oracle of Amon is thought to date from the 21st dynasty (c. 1000 BCE). It became widely celebrated in later dynasties and was well known to the ancient Greeks, who constructed many shrines to Amon in their own country. Twentieth-century visitors enjoy unrestricted access to the temple and the Aghurmi acropolis— no guards, no fees. You can look around the acropolis, peer down the sacred well where offerings were purified (next to the mosque), and climb the mosque's minaret for a masterful view of the town and fiery sunsets.

If you follow the road heading southeast of Aghurmi, after 1km you'll stumble onto the emaciated remains of the **Temple of Amon,** also known as Umm Ubaydah. Time has been unforgiving to this formerly glorious companion of the oracle temple. In 1897 a government official of Siwa (the Marmur) demolished the temple to acquire materials for the construction of a police station and the modern mosque in Siwa town. All that is left is an inscribed, broken wall amidst the palms.

Beyond the temple, about 2km to the south on the same road, lies the cool and mossy **Pool of Cleopatra.** Like many of the approximately 200 natural springs in Siwa, this one has been encircled with a stone basin, with an irrigation duct running out one end. This pool is popular with local men and boys, but fully clothed women should also feel comfortable swimming here, and are free to enter the enclosure next to the spring. On the other side of town the **Pool of Fatnus** ripples out on an island in the middle of a salt lake (accessible by a small causeway), providing a spectacular setting for an afternoon swim. Although smaller in diameter than the Pool of Cleopatra, this spring is more attractive and less visited. A bathing suit with a shirt on top is acceptable attire for women. The road to **al-Maraqi,** which traverses a low desert pass, is lined with craggy yellow buttes honeycombed with caves and Roman tombs. The village of al-Maraqi lies in its own lush oasis, virtually severed from the rest of Siwa by the clenching fingers of the desert. Several dozen Bedouin families inhabit this western fringe of Siwa. Al-Maraqi makes a good daytrip (by local bus) from Siwa town. After traveling two hours on a twisting road, the bus will stop in al-Maraqi and then turn around for the return trip. The round-trip fare is 75pt. (Contact the tourist office for a bus schedule.) The tourist office can also arrange car trips to al-Maraqi or to Abu Shrouf, noted for its ruined Roman temples and five splendorous springs.

Every October Siwans gather for a huge feast at the rocks of **Dakrur.** A "chief of the feast" oversees the distribution of food to the small groups spread over the plain, and none may begin to eat until the chief climbs to the top of the rock and hollers "Bismillah!" (In the name of God). Tourists are invited to attend; it's an experience not to be missed.

Siwa is also the place to purchase exquisite **handicrafts,** including intricately embroidered clothing and veils, *margunahs* (large decorated baskets that weave elegance into every Siwan household), and heavy silver alloy jewelry. Several stores have sprung up around the town square: **Hassan's Handicrafts,** next to the phone office; **Siwa Crafts,** to the left of Abdou Restaurant; **Fatnas Bazaar,** near the police station; and **Sharif's,** halfway up Jabal al-Mawta. Don't try to bargain in craft shops because the women set the prices and aren't there to haggle. Many crafts are changing to accommodate tourist demands—the baskets and shawls are the most authentic. It's also quite likely that precocious children will drag you into a private home to view their own family's selection of handiwork.

Sinai سيناء

Often (and only semi-justly) dubbed "24,000 square miles of nothing," the Sinai divides naturally into three distinct, individually fascinating regions. The broad sand valleys and wind-carved sandstone formations of the north extend from al-Arish to the Suez Canal. Pharaonic armies crossed this region on their way to conquering Syria and Canaan, as did the Hyksos, Assyrians, Persians, Greeks, Arabs and Turks, off to conquer the Nile Valley. The central region is a wide, limestone plateau called at-Teh, the water-pocketed edges of which, scholars believe, the Israelites traversed during their sojourn in the desert. Last, the mountains of the south (including Mt. Moses) conceal a world of Bedouin gardens and encampments. The desert's imperturbable silence hangs over the entire peninsula.

Four wars between Israel and Egypt have rattled this land, and minefields, trenches, and twisted fuselages still litter parts of the desert. In 1903, Britain drew the borders of the Sinai from Rafiah to Eilat in an attempt to keep Turkey and Germany a safe distance from the Suez Canal. After the 1948 Arab-Israeli war, the Rafiah-Eilat line became the armistice line between Israel and Egypt. In the 1956 Suez War, Israel captured all of the Sinai, but returned it due to intense United States and Soviet pressure as well as a United Nations pledge to keep the Straits of Tiran (formerly under Egyptian blockade) open to Israeli shipping.

In 1967, Israel recaptured the Sinai on the fourth day of the Six-Day War. This time Israel refused to unilaterally return the Sinai and held on to the territory, building a defensive line along the now useless Suez Canal. In the 1973 war, Egyptian forces crossed the Canal in a surprise offensive to recapture the Sinai. The Egyptian army smashed the Israeli Bar-Lev defense line in six hours, but Israeli forces regrouped and recaptured the peninsula. Israel retained the Sinai until the land was returned to Egypt in two stages under the terms of the 1979 peace treaty: the first half in 1979, the second in 1982. U.S. troops stationed in the Sinai monitor the treaty, most visibly at the MFO base in Sharm al-Shaikh. (See the General Introduction for more details of the Sinai's history.)

Today, according to the terms of the Camp David accords, Sinai is apportioned into three somewhat arbitrarily demarcated strips: the easternmost strip, nudging Israel, is a military-free zone. Multi-national forces monitor the borders; when passing their bases, do *not* take photos or your film will be confiscated. The middle strip contains light arms, and the western portion houses the strongest artillery of the Egyptian arsenal. Today, it is primarily nomadic Bedouin who populate the Sinai, most of them descendants of Arabs from the Arabian peninsula. (The Muslim Gebeliya Bedouin who live near and closely interact with the population at St. Catherine's, are an exception. They are descendants of slave families sent by Justinian to service the monastery in the 7th century.) The 12-year Israeli occupation irreversibly mutated the nature of Bedouin culture by slowly introducing Western playthings, and the withdrawal set up borders that interfere with the Bedouin's wandering. Under Israeli rule, the Bedouin began to supplement their income by catering to the tourists.

Sinai Bureaucracy

The bureaucracy in the Sinai is as sensible and orderly as the driving. You'll need a **visa** to visit the Sinai. A regular Egyptian visa is fine as long as you obtain it in advance; if not, Egypt issues a **Sinai-only visa** on the spot at the Israeli border at Taba (valid for 2 weeks). This visa limits travel to the Aqaba Coast and the St. Catherine's area. Unlike ordinary one-month Egyptian visas, the Sinai-only visa has no grace period; overextend your stay and you'll pay a hefty fine. If you're crossing from Israel, you must first pay an NIS28.10 exit tax and receive the appropriate receipt, which you should hold on to if you are returning to Israel. You must then line up at the Israeli passport control (go to the window closer to the Israeli side) to have your passport stamped and to surrender the entry card you filled out upon arrival in Israel. You must then go to the gate and show your receipt and passport to an Israeli border guard. Officially in Egypt now, head for a large shack where you must fill out an entry card (write your middle name as well as your first name in the space marked "forename"). After you hand in the card, an official will stamp your passport with a visa marked "14 Hays," which he will change by hand to "14 Days." The next stop is the metal detector/X-ray machine, basically a formality in this direction. At the Taba Hilton, change money, as the banks further along are frequently closed. At another shack ahead, you'll be asked to "bay" (pay) the entry tax in LE only (the equivalent of US$6). There. That wasn't so bad. A small shop by the checkpoint provides cheap refreshments. Buy water ahead of time.

A number of **regulations** govern travelers to the Sinai. Unguided travel is restricted to main roads and settlements, but you can visit parts of the desert interior with a Bedouin guide. Sleeping on the beach is prohibited in some areas (notably Na'ama Bay), and the police often harass sleeping backpackers. Since these areas are not always marked, ask around before settling down for the night. Nude sunbathing is illegal, as is smoking the oft-hawked hash. You cannot bring a rented car or any four-wheel drive vehicle into the Sinai. If you hold a standard, one-month Egyptian visa, you must register your passport with the police in any town within seven days of your arrival in Egypt. Don't wait until Sharm al-Shaikh to do this, since the passport office there is several kilometers south of the town.

Virtually none of the police in the Sinai speak English; even with a Bedouin translating, confusion looms. If they're uncertain whether you've registered (and they may overlook the rather obvious triangular registration stamp on your passport), they may insist that you register in every town you visit. If you ask a procedural question that stumps them, you may be ordered to go to the main police station at Taba or Sharm al-Shaikh, no matter how inconvenient this may be from your point of view. Don't disregard police orders, but realize that they may not understand your situation. Any Arabic you know goes a long way with the police and other fidgety officials.

Getting There

The Sinai is most easily approached on the way to or from **Israel**. Unfortunately, there are very few buses from Taba into the Sinai, which makes taxi drivers extremely happy. A bus leaves for Nuweiba at 2pm (LE8). Another bus leaves at 3pm with stops at Nuweiba (LE8), Dahab (LE10), and Sharm al-Shaikh (LE12). A bus also leaves for Cairo at 2pm (LE40). Taba to St. Catherine's is a case of you-can't-get-there-from-here; go to Dahab and continue from there with another bus or taxi. Bus #15 leaves from opposite Eilat's central bus station for the border. It is impractical to come through Rafiah and Gaza unless you are going to al-Arish.

Coming from Egypt, your departure point for the Sinai will be either Cairo or Suez. In **Cairo**, buses leave Abbassiya Station, also known as Sinai Station, at the northeast end of Ramses St., in the al-Abbassiya district of Cairo. The daily Sinai buses from Cairo go to Sharm al-Shaikh and St. Catherine's, Nuweiba, and on to Taba. One bus per day travels directly to Nuweiba via the new road across the northern Sinai. A direct bus runs to Dahab, which may stop in St. Catherine's if it's not full.

The city of **Suez** is another transit option, especially for travelers coming from Hurghada. Buses from Suez's Arba'in Bus Station, off Sa'ad Zaghloul St., 1500m from the bay, run the following routes once per day: St. Catherine's, Sharm al-Shaikh and continuing to Dahab; direct to Nuweiba and to Taba. Note that most buses from Cairo to the Sinai bypass Suez, passing through the tunnel north of town. (See Hurghada.)

Getting Around

Well-paved roads connect the Sinai's handful of permanent settlements, but newer roads may not appear on your map of Egypt. Daily **buses** run within the Sinai from Sharm al-Shaikh to Dahab, Nuweiba and Taba; plan ahead. To get to al-Arish, your best bet is to go to Rafiaḥ and find a taxi. Buses in the Sinai are notoriously idiosyncratic; be skeptical.

Taxis have an irritating tendency to follow buses, trying to persuade debarking passengers to go one town farther by cab. Exercise caution when using taxis, and do so preferably in parties of three or more—traveling for hours in the desert with strangers may put you at unnecessary risk. Women should not take taxis alone. Drivers will sometimes agree on a price and then demand additional *baksheesh* when you get out, saying something like "America rich country; give more *baksheesh*." Explaining economic principles such as the fact that national wealth does not equal personal wealth will not help. Saying "no" and hightailing it out of there will.

Laws of traffic do not apply here; sadly, laws of physics do. And the white lines on the road are mere formalities. A sign that says "Very Dangerous Curves" is followed by one that says "Goodbye." For God's sake, use your seat belt.

Infrequent traffic and blistering heat could make **hitchhiking** the last foolish choice you'll ever make. Don't hitch unless someone offers you a ride to your destination or to a place where you can wait in the shade for a bus. Women should *never* hitch alone.

Practical Information

Prices for staples are higher in the Sinai than elsewhere in Egypt, but lower than in Israel. If you're coming from Egypt, change your money before arriving in the Sinai. American cash is accepted by some storekeepers—but don't depend on it.

Budget accommodations are usually only a negligible improvement over sleeping outside, and many travelers prefer the latter option. Bring along a sleep sack, warm clothes, or a sleeping bag (in winter months), and guard your belongings. Inquire at police stations and diving shops about storage. Toilets, showers, and running water are sparse; toilet paper and tampons are as sought after as Levis in Moscow.

Snorkeling fanatics may want to purchase their equipment in Cairo or Israel, and resell the gear before leaving. Stores here are unreliable.

Before kaplunging into the Red Sea, protect all necessary toes. Wear plastic shoes, sneakers, or fins *at all times*. At very least, the coral will make your feet into hamburger. Even better, sea creatures lurking in crevices and on the bottom will sting you, causing pain and sometimes death. Be especially careful if you unwisely walk *on* the coral—if your foot slips into one of the shadowy spaces, a gnarled stonefish may ambush it, causing you to puff up and die within four hours. Sharks are attracted by blood, so never enter the water with an open wound or if menstruating. Panicking and thrashing tends to excite sharks—if you see one, climb calmly out of the water and casually share the joyous news. Most sharks, however, are not aggressive and wouldn't (even if they could) give you the time of day. Not least, remember the sun, and wear a shirt while snorkeling, and use a strong waterproof sunscreen.

You must be certified to rent scuba equipment in the Sinai, but diving shops will take you on a safe, shallow introductory dive with a guide for US$40, or give you a full certification course for about US$250. Dahab and Na'ama are equipped with decompression chambers. If you're certified but you haven't logged a dive in the past three months, most diving shops will require a "proof of competence" dive.

Prepare yourself for the climate in the Sinai. Temperatures can reach 50 C (120 F). On summer nights, the temperature drops to about 30 C (80 F), lower at St. Catherine's; winter nights can be downright cold. Keep chugging bottled mineral water (1.5 liters LE2) even when you're not thirsty—five to six liters per day, more if you're trekking.

Skepticism is a virtue here. Prices, for instance, are almost always negotiable. And never believe anyone who tells you that you're 20 minutes from your destination; this is a stock reply and can mean anything from "two hours to go" to "you're standing there, idiot."

Mount Sinai and St. Catherine's Monastery جبـل مـوسى و ديـرسانت كتـرينة

> *And the Lord came down upon Mt. Sinai, to the top*
> *of the mountain; and the Lord called Moses to the*
> *top of the mountain, and Moses went up.*
> —*Exodus 19:20.*

If you didn't know its history, you'd probably call this remote, bone-dry mountain region God-forsaken. But for Jews, Christians, and Muslims, Mt. Sinai is the site of God's great revelation to Moses.

Gebel Musa is regarded as the mountain where, according to Exodus, Moses ascended, parleyed with God, and returned with the Ten Commandments. This place is a bargain for spiritually needy tourists: you can pump water from the well where Moses met his wife and go barefoot where Moses encountered the burning bush (a shapeless weed overgrowing its stone and chicken-wire shrine) for free. The monastery's private library cloisters the oldest (5th century) translation of the Gospels and, with its collection of over 3000 ancient manuscripts and 5000 books, is a perfect setting for *The Name of the Rose*.

Attracted by the tradition that named the valley below the site of the burning bush (and looking for a place to lay low during times of persecution), Christian hermits began inhabiting caves in the vicinity as early as the 2nd century CE. St. Catherine's monastery began as part of their rudimentary communal life in a small chapel built by Helena, the converted mother of Emperor Constantine. In 342 CE, Justinian ordered the construction of a splendid basilica on the top of Mt. Sinai. When Stephanos, Justinian's trusted architect, found the mountain's peak too narrow, he built the Church of the Transformation next to St. Helen's chapel instead. Justinian, peeved, commanded Stephanos's execution, but the pragmatic builder instead lived out his days in the safety of the monastery and eventually achieved sainthood; his bones are on display in the ossuary. Pilgrims of all persuasions frequent Mt. Sinai throughout the year.

Practical Information and Food

The village of St. Catherine's is hidden away in the mountainous interior of the southern Sinai. Excellent roads run west to the Gulf of Suez and east to the Gulf of Aqaba, both about 100km away. If you come from the west you'll pass through the lush **Oasis of Feiran,** where Islamic tradition holds that Hagar fled in banishment from Abraham and Sarah. One kilometer before the village the spur road leading to St. Catherine's Monastery and the base of Mt. Sinai branches off to the left. The monastery is about 0.5km up this road. Buses make the trip from Cairo and Suez and from other Sinai sites. Leaving St. Catherine's, you can chase the unreliable buses of the East Delta Bus Company to Cairo (LE35); Suez (LE14); Dahab (LE10) and Sharm al-Shaikh (LE12); and Nuweiba (LE10) and Taba (LE15). Don't count on catching any buses to the east after the 1:30pm run.

Service **taxis** occasionally fill up for runs to Dahab (about LE6-7 per person if you have a full taxi, more if there are less people) and elsewhere. *Service* taxis, however, mean long hours in the desert with people you don't know, and hence may unnecessarily threaten life, limb, or pocketbook. Women should generally avoid them unless traveling in groups. If you (male or female) insist on taking one, you should go to the central square (by Supermarket Katreen and the Guest House Restaurant) during daylight hours and look around for a taxi. Ask at the market if you don't see any, and bargain fiercely.

Ask the driver to let you off on the road to the monastery. If you insist on seeing the town, the bus will drop you off in front of the tourist village. Past the overpriced and unimpressive hotel stand a very small **supermarket** and an equally tiny **restaurant,** where a filling meal goes for LE10 (open 24 hrs). The **Cafeteria al-Ekhlas** offers meat, macaroni, vegetable soup, and tomatoes for only LE5-7. Nearby are the village **post office,** and **National Telecommunications Office,** with telegraph and international phone services (open 24 hrs.).

Really, the only reason you would need to go into town is to buy a flashlight for the climb up Mt. Sinai or for a few canned goods to eat while you're up there. These can be purchased at **Supermarket Katreen,** in the square near the bus station, further down the road from the tourist village. Back on the road there's a **hospital** (with round the clock emergency service) and the **tourist police,** and across the street is **Bank Misr.** The bank will exchange money or traveler's checks, but not Eurochecks (open daily 8am-1pm and 6-9pm, Fri. 9-11am). On a hill above the shopping center stands the **police station,** where you can register your passport.

Accommodations

Most travelers come to St. Catherine's to camp on the cool summit of Mt. Sinai (10 C in June nights). If not, the monastery's **youth hostel** (tel. (062) 77 09 45) offers clean but cramped rooms, each with bunkbeds, without A/C and fans, for LE25 (all meals included); attached toilet and shower LE5 extra. Check-in is 8am-2:30pm and 5-7pm (you have to wait for the monks to finish praying). The gates to the monastery close at 9:30pm. A shop at the monastery sells cheap water for your climb up the mountain. Buy lots.

The **Alfairoz Hotel** has rooms that are even more cramped than those at the monastery and cost LE11.50 per bed, LE56 for private doubles with attached toilet and shower. Showers are available. From the bus stop, walk straight toward the tourist village and bear left at the fork. The hotel is at the top of the hill. A third, extremely inexpensive option is **Zeitouna Camping.** The entrance is located at the base of the path to the monastery, but you may want to hire a taxi to drive you the 2km into the campground proper. The stone huts (LE5) offer fresh cushions on raised ledges with thick wool blankets and tented roofs. The bathrooms and low-pressure shower are immaculate. Be sure to arrive before sundown and bring a flashlight or candle since there is no electricity.

Sights

Tradition has it that Justinian ordered St. Stephanos, architect of **St. Catherine's Monastery,** to be executed for not erecting the edifice on the summit of the mountain. The lower location that Stephanos selected, however, is better protected and, while farther from God, closer to an abundant water supply. St. Catherine's is believed to be the oldest unrestored example of Byzantine architecture in the world. The monastery once housed hundreds of orthodox monks, but its population has dwindled to a handful. Members of one of the strictest orders, these monks never eat meat, never drink wine, and awaken sun-shatteringly early each morn when the bell of the **Church of the Transfiguration** is rung 33 times.

Both St. Helen and Justinian dedicated their structures to the Virgin Mary, since according to Christian tradition the burning bush foreshadowed the Annunciation. The main church became known as the "Church of the Transfiguration" owing to its spectacular almond-shaped mosaic of Jesus' transfiguration. The complex was named St. Catherine's Monastery after the body of the martyred Alexandrian evangelist was miraculously found on top of the mountain in the 7th century. About to be tortured on a wheel of knives for converting members of the Roman emperor's family, Catherine was miraculously saved by a malfunction in the wheel. They slit her throat anyway. Also in the 7th century, Muhammad dictated a long document granting protection to the monastery and exempting it from taxes; a copy of this document still hangs in the icon gallery, near Napoléon's 1798 letter of protection to the monastery.

The monastery possesses many treasures, including exquisite icons dating to the 4th century. One of the finest libraries of ancient manuscripts in the world resides here. Unfortunately only the central nave of the Church of the Transfiguration is open to the public (free). On tiptoe you can see mosaics of a barefoot Moses in the **Chapel of the Burning Bush** behind the altar. Should you manage to visit the icons back there, you'll have to remove your footwear—the roots of the sacred shrub extend under the floor. The monks themselves, with the help of the local Gebeliya Bedouin, built the **mosque** within the walls of the fortress to convince advancing Ottoman armies that the complex was partly Muslim, and thus averted destruction. Don't miss the gruesome **Ossuary,** a separate building outside the walls, where the bones of all the monastery's former residents lie in enormous heaps (bishops have special niches in the wall). A **gift shop** sells books on the monastery's history for LE6.50. The ossuary and enclosed part of the monastery are open Mon.-Thurs. and Sat., 9am-noon (free; modest dress required).

The Sinai Peninsula owes its name to the towering 2285m peak of Mt. Sinai. Mt. Moses translates as Gebel Musa in Arabic, but most Egyptians refer to it as Gebel Iti, literally "the Mt. of Losing (Yourself)," because the Israelites "lost themselves" here in the worship of the golden calf as Moses ascended the mountain to speak with God.

Tradition holds that God chose Mt. Sinai as the mountain where he would give the great Ten Commandments because Sinai was the most humble of mountains. Tradition obviously never tried to climb to the summit with luggage. This is not an easy climb, and you should leave all but the bare essentials behind. (The monks will allow you to leave your bags in a room at the monastery for LE2 per piece.) The shorter of the two routes up (about 75 min.), the **Steps of Repentance** is actually the harder route. It is said that the 3000 steps were built by a single monk in order to fulfill his pledge of penitence. Be forewarned: this monk tried to cut corners here and there (who could blame him?) and made many of the steps the height of two or three normal steps. The steps are treacherous by night; if you are ascending on the stairs take them only during the early morning or late afternoon—don't forget a comfy hairshirt—otherwise, take them on the descent. The other route, the **camel path** (2-2.5 hr. by foot), begins directly behind the monastery. You can rent a camel there to trundle you up the path for about US$10 (about 90 min.); it's definitely worth it if you're not a seasoned climber. Unless you know Arabic, conversation with your Bedouin guide will be limited to 90 minutes of "Problem?" and "No problem." If you want to expand the discourse and praise the camel, tell your guide it's *hilwa*. Camels take well to flattery. Unfortunately, the camels are not always available when you need them, and you can't count on having them at your disposal—you may arrive at the dispatch area and find nothing but dung.

About two-thirds of the way up and directly below the camel path's juncture with the steps is a 500-year-old cypress tree which dominates a depressional plain known as **Elijah's Hollow.** Here the prophet Elijah is said to have heard the voice of God. Two small chapels now occupy the site, one dedicated to Elijah and the other to his successor Elisha.

The best time to start the journey is about 5pm—late enough to avoid the most potent heat but early enough to climb by sunlight. The alternative, elected by many travelers, is to hike at night, when the air is chilly but the going tough (even with a flashlight and the glow of the moon). Either way, try to spend the night on the summit. At night, the glowing dusting of infinite numbers of stars on an inky sky will make you a believer, and you will awake to the sunrise and Mt. Sinai's unforgettable view, encompassing the mountains of Africa and Saudi Arabia, the Red Sea, and the Gulf of Aqaba. Sleeping bags form a nocturnal assembly on the mount's peak, so those who seek a less shared spiritual experience should sleep in Elijah's Hollow and be sure to rise before the sun does.

On the summit stands a small chapel, built in 1937 over the remains of a Byzantine church. Moses supposedly hid himself in the cave below when he first came face to face with God: "...while my glory passes by, I will put you in cleft of the rock, and will cover you with my hand until I have passed by" (Exodus 33:22). The chapel is almost always unattended and closed.

Bring enough food for the night and enough water (2-3 bottles) for the ascent. There are refreshment stands on the way up, but as you climb higher so do the prices. There is a refreshment stand at the summit which sells candles (50pt apiece) and rents blankets (LE2.50 per night) for people who haven't followed the Boy Scout motto. There is also a "toilet" at the summit (nothing more than a hole in the ground with little privacy and many flies).

Dress warmly for a night trek and bring a sleeping bag; there's no room to pitch a tent. You don't need a guide. The camel path begins 50m up the valley from the monastery's rear wall. One juncture that usually confuses hikers is the path's intersection with the steps, which awaits soon after you pass through the camel trail's narrow, steep-walled stone corridor. After passing through the corridor, head left and follow the steps up the final third of the ascent. To take the steps all the way, begin at the corner of the monastery's right wall. The steps originate at a sign that says "To Moses Mountain."

Six kilometers to the south of Sinai towers **Gebel Katherina** (Mount Catherine), the highest mountain in Egypt (2642m). The path to the top, more secluded and beautiful than the Sinai highway, begins in the village itself and takes five or six hours to complete. A chapel with water replenishes you at the summit.

Sharm al-Shaikh شرم الشيخ

Like the military commanders of the Egyptian-Israeli wars, travelers will be interested in Sharm al-Shaikh (also spelled Sharm el-Sheikh) for its strategic position only: commanding the southernmost point of the Sinai Peninsula, Sharm is an important transportation interchange. To enjoy the Aqaba Coast's reefs and beaches, head up the spectacular twisting road to Na'ama Bay (6km), to Dahab (100km), to Nuweiba (170km), or to Taba (240km).

Buses leave the bus station in Sharm al-Shaikh for Cairo (no A/C, LE25), and Taba (LE12) with stops at Na'ama, Dahab, and Nuweiba. You can usually find **taxis** outside the Hilton hotel in Na'ama Bay, but expect hassles.

The **HI Youth Hostel** is located on top of Sharm al-Shaikh's hill, near the town's main square. The bus stops in front of the hostel. Usually. Then cross the street and walk up the hill opposite until you see the hostel's basketball court. This hostel is heavy on restrictions (curfew at 11pm, no mixed-sex rooms) and light on toilet paper. HI members pay LE10.60 for dorm beds (includes breakfast). Nonmembers must either become members for LE24 or pay an extra LE4 per night and get a special card stamped each night which, after six nights, turns pumpkin-style into a membership card. Rather crowded but clean. (Lockout 9am-2pm.) Another option is **Safety Land** (tel. (062) 60 03 73), located at the bottom of the hill across the street from the bus station. Budget options include thatched bungalows with locking doors and fans (singles LE27, doubles LE40, extra mattress on floor LE15), three-person tents (LE15 per person), or open tent sites for LE8 per person. Breakfast included. (Reception open 7am-1am).

Walking down the hill from the youth hostel, you'll pass the **tourist police,** a **hospital,** and the **bus station,** where tickets to Cairo can be reserved (open 7am-noon). Continuing south at the bottom of the hill, you'll come to the **police station** (look for the Egyptian flag). To register, follow the road from Na'ama about 1km farther south to the main police station at the port. Walking down the hill, make a right after the bus station and then a left to get to a row of seedy-looking **cafeterias** and **gift shops** and the **South Sinai Supermarket** (open 10am-2pm and 6-10pm).

If you follow the road all the way up the hill and turn right at the top, you'll find the town's main square, which contains three **banks,** all of which exchange traveler's checks. There's also a **post office** (open Sat.-Thurs. 8am-3pm) and **Pharmacy Sharm al-Shaikh** (open 9am-3pm and 6-11pm). A bit further up the road and all the way to the left lies the new **telephone office** (open 24 hrs.), where you can make international calls.

To travel between Na'ama and Sharm al-Shaikh, take the yellow, open-sided *phutphut,* which runs about every hour from the square. Since the bus is erratic and hitching fairly reliable (low volume but of the high-yielding variety), some rash people start out thumbing and flag the bus if it happens to slink by. If you're American and decide to hitch, don't curse your compatriots for not giving you a lift—MFO personnel are forbidden to pick up civilians. Most buses heading north from Sharm al-Shaikh stop at Na'ama. Taxis also run between Na'ama and Sharm; fares (around LE10-15) rise by night. Visible just before you enter Sharm al-Shaikh from Na'ama Bay (back and to the left) is Ras Kennedy, a rock formation that looks so much like the slain president that Mother Nature could not have acted alone in creating it.

Ferries make the 5.5-hr. trip from Sharm al-Shaikh to Hurghada every day except Saturday. The *Mimi Misre* and *Golden Sun* both leave from the port. Tickets (LE60) are usually sold the evening before the date of departure at the Cliff Top Hotel, next to the youth hostel, and at Safety Land and at Spring Tours (tel. (062) 60 01 31/2) in Na'ama Bay.

Na'ama Bay

Don't be confused by Egyptian and Israeli songs; the resort in the southern Sinai is not Sharm al-Shaikh, but Na'ama Bay, located 6km north. Na'ama is not cheap, but features the best underwater territory in the Sinai. Venture to Ras Muhammad and Tiran Island and you may never leave.

The bus stop at Na'ama Bay is in front of the Marina Sharm Hotel. Don't be alarmed if you hear locals and travelers alike referring to the bay as "Marina" or "Marina Sharm." These are the Hebrew names for Na'ama Bay, which is an Israeli-built resort. Buses that leave from Sharm al-Shaikh almost always stop at Na'ama, to the north, a few minutes later.

The only real budget options in Na'ama are the huts at the **Sanafir Hotel** (tel. (062) 06 01 96/7) next to the Camel Diving Club, behind and to the north of the tourist police. The showers and toilets are spotless and fresh water flows 24 hours. (Singles US$15.50. Doubles US$23. Breakfast included.) Sleeping on the beach is illegal.

Public showers are available in the Aquamarine and Hilton hotels. The **tourist police** are located past the Aquamarine. The **National Bank of Egypt** has branches in the Marina Sharm, Gazala, and Hilton Hotels.

Serious divers should head for the **Camel Dive Club** (tel. (062) 60 07 00), a few doors over from the Sanafir Hotel on the southern end of the bay. If you rent their equipment you can camp in back of the shop for free; they also offer 24-hour showers and storage for their clients. Na'ama has quite a few other diving shops; heading north along the beach: **Red Sea Diving Club** (tel. (062) 60 03 42/3), near the Marina Sharm hotel; **Red Sea Diving College** (tel. (062) 60 02 45, fax 60 01 44), across from the Sanafir hotel; **Aquanaute** (tel. (062) 60 06 19) is next, then **Sinai Divers** (tel. (062) 60 01 50/1/2) near the Ghazala Hotel, and finally **Aquamarine** in the Aquamarine Hotel (snorkeling gear US$5-7, scuba gear US$20). Night dives cost US$30, and five-day licensing courses are US$250-275 (Aquamarine and Sinai are the cheapest). Try to pay in pounds. These shops also have showers for customers.

Though Na'ama Bay itself has no quality reefs, two tremendous dive sites are within walking distance. Coral, undersea foliage, and phantasial fish await divers in the magnificent **Near** and **Far Gardens** to the north. To reach the Near Gardens, walk north from Na'ama until you reach the point at the end of the bay (about 30min.); the Far Gardens are about a 30-minute walk farther. Bring water and wear sneakers.

When you've become desmitten with these reefs (i.e., after several months), take one of the diving shops' daily trips to more distant and even better sites. **Tiran Island** and **Ras Muhammad** are the most spectacular. Fish of virtually every imaginable size, shape, and incandescent color frolic in the labyrinthine coral gardens, while manta rays, hammerhead sharks, and other exotica skulk in the depths. Unfortunately, these trips are expensive (US$35-45 per day including equipment and meals). For US$35 per day, visit the reefs at **Ras Masrani, Ras Umm Sidd,** and other nearby sites as a daytrip. Though Jacques Cousteau might rate these a tadpole below Tiran and Ras Muhammad, their slithering splendors should keep you amused for hours.

Dahab دهب

Dahab has three personalities, but most tourists see just one—the tourist trap "Bedouin Village," which resembles a small scale Na'ama Bay. Yet only 3km away, a traditional Bedouin town with palm trees, thatch huts, and meandering goats and chickens is bordered by the small, rapidly growing city under construction nearby. Dahab's residents live off the fish they catch, the few livestock they tend, and the dates they harvest from the palm trees.

Because of its cheap accommodations, cheap food, and plentitude of places to buy schlocky merchandise, Dahab is the best place in the Sinai for travelers to spend a few relaxing sun-and-beach-filled days. The water is unbelievably clear and cool, and the beach is lined with Bedouin blankets and pillow rolls which make for a comfortable—if sweltering—tanning experience.

Buses run twice daily from Dahab to Cairo via Sharm al-Shaikh (LE35, to Sharm LE8); once daily to Suez via Sharm al-Shaikh (LE18, LE5); direct to Sharm al-Shaikh and Na'ama Bay (LE5); to St. Catherine's (LE6); to Nuweiba (LE8); and to Taba (LE8). The bus station is some distance south of the Bedouin Village, and you'll probably want to take a cab there. If you stay in the Bedouin town, keep in mind that at least two of the Bedouin own **shared taxis.**

There are a few budget sleep spots near the bus station: stay on the hotel beach in a thatched hut (LE2, no mattresses, blankets, or sheets) or head for the **Dahab Holiday Village** and stay in a brand new bungalow (LE20 per person) or pitch your tent.

To *really* enjoy Dahab, head north by taxi to the Bedouin town; the LE1 one way fare is a small price to pay to avoid dragging your pack the 3km in the hot Sinai sun. If you can't find a taxi, walk back across the parking lot and head for the two white water towers of the MFO base. Just inside the base the asphalt road ends and a rough dirt track leads to the village—follow this and aim for the far palm grove, barely visible from the base.

Accommodations in the Bedouin village are standard—about 15 so-called "campgrounds" have the same offerings for the same price—a thatched or stone hut. The wolf-proof stone huts all have locks and are much more carefully guarded than the blow-downable thatched huts. Located right on the beach, the **Moon Valley** on the northern end and the **Muhammad Ali Bedouin Camp** are clean and relatively comfortable. Most camps charge LE4 for a bed in a two-person hut with lumpy mattresses on slabs of plaster-covered something; more pristine travelers may appreciate having a sleeping bag with them. Some camps offer rooms with attached shower and toilet for LE15. Clean public showers and toilets are available in most camps.

Like the accommodations, the restaurants in Dahab are clones. The cuisine, luckily, is quite tasty. All of the *gourmandisements* are located on the beach except for the excellent **Scorpions Restaurant,** which is located at the southern end of the dirt road that runs from the beach past Star of Sinai camping. Back on the beach, the **Fighting Kangaroo,** run by a homesick Aussie, specializes in veggie delights. Dinner entitles you to a free breakfast the next morning. Breakfast in Dahab costs LE3-4 for a full meal, and lunch and dinner cost LE5-7.50 per meal. Fish runs LE6-20, and lobster can really pinch you at LE10-30. There are three **supermarkets** in the southern end of the Bedouin camp area (open 7am-midnight). Children run through the Bedouin town area selling fresh pita that contains only a few stones and insects and is otherwise quite tasty. The sweet pita is generally a ticket to diarrheadom.

There is remarkably little to see in Dahab's steamy metropolis, located past the Holiday Village Hotel. Come here to exchange money at the **National Bank of Egypt** (open daily 9am-1pm and 6-9pm; in winter 9am-1pm and 5-8pm). There is also a **post office** (open Sat.-Thurs. 8:30am-3pm), a **supermarket** (open 8am-10pm), the **police**

station, and a **telephone office,** where you can make calls within Egypt only (open 24 hrs.).

The official showers and restrooms are in the holiday village. The hotel charges 50pt per use, but the facilities are never attended.

The only major diving shop in Dahab is **Inmo Diving Center,** located on the beach south of the supermarket/store area at the southern end of the Bedouin camps. Just ask any of the locals for "Inmo" or "Inmo Diving," while making swimming motions. "Inmo, Inmo," they'll shout, and they'll point you in the right direction. Alternatively, they'll look at you like you're crazy, but never mind—there are signs that say "Inmo 500m" everywhere. The center is located in a white building, surrounded by palm trees. You can get a mask, snorkel, and fins here for US$5.50. A full-day dive costs US$35. (Open 8am-8pm. Trips begin at 9am.)

The best of Dahab's reefs begin at the northern and southern ends of the cove on which the town is built; walk either north or south until you see the waves breaking over the coral. To find reefs closer to the modern village, check the map in the diving shop.

Crazy House, halfway up the cove in the Bedouin village, runs the popular Blue Hole lobster tours. Blue Hole, 2km north of the village, features rugged mountain scenery and is an ace dive site. The trip, whose highlight is a lobster feast, leaves in the afternoon and lasts until the next morning. Ask around the Bedouin supermarket about trips to **Wadi Gnay,** a brackish oasis with a Bedouin village. The trip takes one day by camel; agree on the route before you set off, and pay afterwards. The police station at which your guide must obtain permission, and at which you can register, is in the Bedouin town next to the palm huts.

If you stay with the Bedouin, be respectful of your neighbors. When you see the Bedouin men in their long white robes and the women in their austere, black garb, you will be tempted to photograph them, but Bedouin custom prohibits making images of people. Always ask before you take a picture.

Nuweiba نويبع

One of Sinai's natural oases, Nuweiba lies at the mouth of an enormous *wadi* that empties into the Red Sea. For about 10 months of the year the surface of the *wadi* is just drifting sand—but in winter a sudden, rampaging wall of water 3m high charges down its banks to the sea. Nuweiba's tourist heyday ended with Israeli withdrawal; today, there are better places for snorklers and backpackers in Sinai. Its chief attraction is the ferry to Aqaba.

Daily **buses** arrive from Sharm al-Shaikh and Dahab, from Taba, from Cairo or Suez via Sharm al-Shaikh or St. Catherine's, and directly from Cairo. Leaving Nuweiba, you can go to Sharm al-Shaikh (LE8) via Dahab (LE5); to Taba (LE8); to St. Catherine's (LE10); and to Cairo (LE35). Afternoon buses are sometimes more comfortable.

Near the back of the compound you'll find a **police station** where you can usually register during the day. Going through the gate behind the cafeteria and continuing to the north past the Bedouin huts, you will confront the **Nuweiba Holiday Village Hotel** (tel. (02) 76 88 32 or 76 27 01) in the highbrow village. The **tourist police** are at the main entrance to the hotel. To make **international calls** (8am-midnight) or to **change money** (9:30am-2pm and 6-9pm), head for the reception desk of the Holiday Village Hotel.

The hotel also has information about safaris, usually in the mountains near St. Catherine's, from either South Sinai Safari or Emad El Moazen's Wilderness Company. These safaris include land rovers, knowledgeable guides, and Bedouin cuisine. Half-day excursions to the stunning **Colored Canyons,** 4km from Nuweiba, are also available for LE30 per person. Inquire about trips to **Ain Omahmed,** the second largest oasis in South Sinai. These trips, which leave at 8am, cost LE24 per person per day, and the each jeep holds six people; if your jeep is not full, though, you have to pay for the empty seats. For a less blatantly touristic stay in Nuweiba, sleep in the northern campground of the Tarabin Bedouin (1km walk north along the beach, LE5, lunch also LE5).

Nuweiba also makes an excellent base for short **camel trips** into the desert. You can arrange a trip directly with a Bedouin guide (ask around the fish stands or at the cafeteria's picnic tables). A popular excursion from Nuweiba is the one-day trek to the lush oasis of **Ain Furtuga** along the wadi cut in the mountains by a freshwater spring. The trip past Ain Furtaga to **Ain Hudra** takes two days by camel or one by car. Both treks lead through varied and unforgettable scenery, and are well worth the time and the LE35 per day.

Because the desert, St. Catherine's Monastery, and Mt. Sinai are technically off-limits to tourists, your Bedouin guide may have to take your passport to the police the day before you depart and receive permission to make the trip. Some of the best treks are completely illegal.

Ferry from Nuweiba to Aqaba, Jordan

The word you must keep in mind when crossing on the **ferry to Jordan** is "patience." There are two daily ferries. The first departs between 10am-noon, the second 4-6pm; sailing time is about three hours. One-way passage on the deck costs US$25. Show up at or before 9am and 3pm respectively to deal with customs, ticketing, Egyptian bank hassles, and quagmirean queues.

Any Nuweiba bus can leave you at the terminal, or at least at the turn-off, which is 7km south of the tourist center (bus fare 75pt, taxis LE8). The morning bus from Taba comes by at 8am and is convenient for catching the morning ferry. You can also catch a direct bus from Cairo to the ferry, leaving from Abbassiya Station at 11pm and arriving at about 6am. The bus, like the ferry itself, will be crowded with Egyptian workers bound for jobs in Jordan, Saudi Arabia, and the Gulf states. At times when Egyptians are on holiday—especially during Ramadan—all the space may be taken. Ordinarily you can buy a ticket when you arrive at the port.

Non Middle-Easterners will be whisked through the gate and into the customs building on the right, where they can proceed to the head of the line and are obligated to fill out a form for the Egyptian authorities to receive an exit stamp. There is no exit fee. From customs, proceed north across the lot to enter the poorly marked **ticket office** (tel. (062) 77 79 49). Here you must exchange US$25 (in US currency) into LE for the ticket on the spot. (A bank is conveniently located at the port for this purpose.) You must show this receipt for the currency exchange before you will be allowed to purchase a ticket. If you come only with LE and nothing to change, you're not going anywhere.

When you board the ferry, you'll be searched perfunctorily and asked to fork over your passport. During the trip, or immediately after you disembark, a Jordanian visa (valid for either 1 month or 2 weeks) and an entry stamp will be entered into your passport. While it's best to come to Nuweiba with a Jordanian visa already in your passport, you can obtain one en route. Travelers from America, Canada, Australia, New Zealand, and Britain should have no difficulty obtaining this visa. Your passport will be returned at Jordanian customs in Aqaba, or, if you go searching for it, on the boat. In Aqaba you'll have to endure a long wait and pass through a painless customs search before you're freed to catch a taxi or minibus into Aqaba center, 10km north (the drivers will probably accept Egyptian currency).

Travelers with **evidence of a visit to Israel** in their passports might be allowed to board the ferry, **but will not be allowed to disembark.** Passports with an Egyptian Taba entry stamp have been known to pass through, but don't stake your trip on it. Clever sorts who have two passports *must* be sure to get the Nuweiba exit stamp in the passport that has no sign of Israel in it.

Al-Arish العريش

Al-Arish, the most frequently visited settlement in the northern Sinai, has hardly a sight in sight. It is, in fact, a rather uninteresting city of some 30,000 inhabitants. What this city can show you, however, is what Egyptian life is like in the absence of the Western tourist trade. Minus, of course, you.

A number of luxury hotels are under construction near the beach, and every year more and more Egyptians come here to gambol about amidst the sand, palm trees, and charred anti-aircraft guns. It will be several seasons, however, before these facilities are open for business and the foreign tourist troop begins the invasion. The water of al-Arish is patched with a deep teal and a clear aqua. Some of the beaches are stained with a few streaks of tar and you may have an encounter with a jellyfish or two, but the beaches are, on the whole, pleasurable.

Direct **buses** run to al-Arish daily from Cairo's Abbassiya International Station (5hrs., LE10.50) and Ismailiya (3.5hrs.). From Port Said, you must change buses and cross the Suez Canal by the small, free passenger ferry at **Qantara**, about 50km south of Port Said. *Service* **taxis** run directly from all the above locations for LE2-3 extra. There is no transport across the peninsula to the Aqaba coast.

The al-Arish **bus station** is at the southeast corner of Baladiya Sq., the town's main thoroughfare from there. **July 23 St.,** runs north to the ocean, where it meets Fouad Zakry St. The **tourist office** is on Fouad Zakry St., (tel. 34 05 69), about 1km west of its intersection with July 23 St. (Open Sat.-Thurs. 8am-2pm and 7-10pm.) Next door is the **tourist police** (tel. 34 10 16); for some reason police officers are indistinguishable from employees at the tourist office. The **post office** (open Sat.-Thurs. 8am-2pm) and the **telephone office** (open 24 hrs., international calls possible) are across the street from each other, two blocks east of July 23 St. and three blocks north of Baladiya Sq. The easiest way to reach the beach from the middle of town is by **minibus** (50pt) or **taxi** (50-75pt). **Pharmacy Fouad,** on July 23 St. two blocks north of Baladiya Sq., on the west side of the street, is open Sat.-Thurs. 8am-1:30pm and 5pm-midnight, Fri. 8am-midnight; they can put you in touch with a local doctor. The local **hospital** is located on Gish St. (tel. 34 00 10 or 34 10 77), east of Souk Sq.—the first square inland on July 23 St. In case of emergency, call the **ambulance** (tel. 123) or local **police** (tel. 122).

The search for budget accommodations in al-Arish is an ordeal. The beachside **Moonlight Hotel** (tel. 34 13 62; to reserve rooms from Cairo, tel. 24 81 28) on Fouad Zakry St., 50m west of the tourist office, has petite rooms for LE10 and a view of the beach. Singles LE5, with bath LE15. Doubles LE10, with bath LE28. Breakfast included. The more centrally located **as-Salaam Hotel** on July 23 St. (tel. 34 12 19), 1 block north of Baladiya Sq., has shabby but spacious rooms. (Singles LE4. Doubles w/bath LE10.) There are also several **campgrounds** along the beach. The average fee for a two-person tent is LE6; ask at the tourist office for details. It is also possible to camp for free on the beaches near town, but you'll need permission from the tourist police and an HI card.

Groceries are available, and the town has two unsurpassed restaurants. The **Aziz Restaurant,** under the as-Salaam Hotel, serves delicious kebab, *kufte,* and salad for LE5. Groups that call ahead (tel. 34 03 45) can enjoy their meal in the Bedouin tent room, sitting cross-legged at low tables on large, embroidered cushions. (Open daily 10am-midnight.) About 300m down the street, just past the Sultana Café, the **Sammar Restaurant** offers a variety of fried chicken and fish dishes for LE4-9. Filling *hawawshi* (bread filled with meat) can be had for a painless 75pt. (There's no sign in English for this restaurant; look for the Mickey Mouse across the street from Café Bahry.) Another convenient watering hole is the all-wood **Restaurant kadis bil Arish** (Sand of Arish), about 500m east of the Moonlight Hotel, across the street from the Kholafah Mosque (no English sign). Meat and seafood plates LE8-15. (Open daily 8am-midnight; tel. 34 14 24). On your way to the beach, have a look at the town's only tourist attraction—the bizarre, multi-colored brick minaret on your left. July 23 St. is lined with small outdoor bistros where you can get a cup of *shay* or a *fuul* sandwich for a few piastres.

Suez Canal and Red Sea Coast و قناة السويس
شاطئ البحـر الاحمـر

Suez Canal قناة السويس

The strategically-located Suez Canal is a miracle of 19th-century engineering, but strategically-located engineering miracles aren't that much fun for the average tourist. The canal stretches, without locks and at a depth of up to 15m, from Port Said on the Mediterranean, past Ismailiya, to Suez on the Red Sea (112km all told). Construction began in 1859 under the direction of Ferdinand de Lesseps, and the canal opened 10 years later. The waterway allowed rapid travel from Europe to the Indian Ocean, and became a crucial element in the infrastructure of the British Empire. The canal was nationalized by Nasser in 1956; this precipitated a British-French-Israeli invasion. In 1967, with Israeli troops on the Sinai side of the canal, Nasser blocked it with sunken ships. It remained closed through the 1973 war. While the waterway was closed, monstrous ships too big to pass through the canal were built to travel around Africa. Upon its reopening, the canal's clientele never fully returned; canal cities have never fully recovered.

The Suez Canal's business is business, not tourism; Port Said, Ismailiya, and Suez live off ships of commerce. Located near a former international flashpoint, all three cities have suffered heavy war damage. The only evident reconstruction is Ismailiya's newly paved streets and pedicured parks. In a nation as rich with sights as Egypt, this region ranks low on a traveler's itinerary.

Port Said (Bur Sa'id) بـور سعيد

Gateway to the canal and the Mediterranean Sea, Port Said (Bur Sa'id) is the northeasternmost point on the African continent, and the busiest and most interesting of the Suez Canal cities. Rows of tankers, freighters, and cruise ships dock here next to the white colonnade of the port authority, where the canal widens to flow into the Med. Port Said is currently under development as a beach resort, an alternative to the increasingly packed shores of Alexandria. While better beaches exist in Egypt, Port Said's proximity to Cairo and its (current) obscurity make it an appealing destination.

Lying 350km east of Alexandria and 230km from Cairo, Port Said is the northeastern corner of the Delta region. **Buses** run between Cairo's Kolali Sq. in front of Ramses Station and Port Said several times daily. (3 hr., Golden Rocket LE10, Superjet LE10, West Delta LE8 with A/C.) Buses also run daily to Sa'ad Zaghloul Sq. in Alexandria. (Superjet goes via Cairo.) The Golden Rocket bus leaves every day at 10am (4.5hr, LE20), and West Delta departs daily at 6am and 1pm (LE14 with A/C). West Delta also runs half-hourly 6am-6pm to Ismailiya (1.5hr., LE4) and twice daily to Suez at 1pm and 4pm (LE4.25). The West Delta and Golden Rocket **bus depots** are located on the northwest side of Ferial Gardens, two blocks west of Gomhouriya St. The Superjet bus depot is next to the train station at the end of Gomhouriya St. *Service* taxis also run from Cairo's Kolali Sq. (LE6.50). To reach the *service* **taxi stand** in Port Said, take a municipal taxi (LE1-1.50) and ask for a *taxi ugra* to the city you wish to reach.

You can also shuttle between Cairo and Port Said by the **trains** which leave each city daily (1st-class LE10.80, 2nd-class with A/C LE6.50, ordinary 2nd-class LE2.70). These Cairo-bound trains (4.5hrs., 6 times daily) pass through Ismailiya; there are trains which go to Ismailiya but do not continue to Cairo (3 times daily; 1st-class LE3.50, 2nd-class with A/C LE2.50, 3rd-class LE1). There are no trains directly to Alexandria; go from Cairo. To get to the train station go to the southern end of Gomhouriya St. and turn right onto Mustafa Kemal St. The station will be about 1km down, on your left.

Most services are either along the canal or along the beach at right angles to the canal. **Palestine Street** follows the canal; two blocks from its southwestern end is the **tourist office** (tel. 23 52 89), open Sat.-Thurs. 8am-2pm and 3-8pm. The **tourist police** (tel. 22 85 70) are located in the customs building at the southwest end of Palestine St. and has a branch office in the train station. (Both open 24 hrs.) There are a number of small, reputable **currency exchange** offices around town. The most convenient place to change money is **Thomas Cook,** on Gomhouriya St., three blocks from July 23 St. (Open daily 9am-6pm.) A number of countries (including the U.S. and U.K.) have **consulates** in Port Said; the tourist office or tourist police can provide addresses and phone numbers. The emergency phone number for the **police** is 122; for general **medical emergencies,** dial 123.

Port Said's **post office** for Poste Restante is at the southeast corner of Ferial Gardens. (Open Sat.-Thurs. 8:30am-6pm.) The **telephone office** is about halfway up Palestine St. (Open 24 hrs.) Port Said's most modern hospital is **al-Mabarrah Hospital** at the western end of July 23 St. (tel. 22 05 61 or 22 05 60). The **at-Tadaman Hospital** also serves tourists (tel. 22 17 90). **El-Isaaf Pharmacy** (tel. 22 19 47), on Safia Zaghloul St., one block past its intersection with Shohada St., is open 24 hours. The **postal code** is 42511. The **telephone code** is 066.

Most of the better **accommodations** in town are either on or just off Gomhouriya St., which runs parallel to Palestine St. two blocks inland. Two blocks from the southern end of Gomhouriya St. is the **Akri Hotel** (tel. 22 10 13), where cheap, charming rooms have old-fashioned iron bedsteads and views of the canal. (Singles LE9. Doubles LE15. Breakfast included when the cook is in town and in the mood.) About halfway up Gomhouriya St. is the enormous **Hotel de la Poste** (tel. 22 96 55), which has classy rooms with hardwood floors and all the amenities. (Singles LE20, LE26.50 facing the street. Doubles LE23.50, facing the street LE35. No breakfast, no donut.) In the Sea Rangers' building near the Timsah Lake Beach opposite the big station on the corner of New Corniche and al-Amin St. is an **HI youth hostel** (tel. 22 87 02, fax 22 64 33; dorm beds LE3.10, nonmembers LE5.10).

Port Said has a number of cheap, convenient restaurants. **Popeye's Café** (opposite Hotel de la Poste) offers Western amenities such as cappuccino and "classic rock." Spaghetti, salad, and a Coke costs LE6. (Open daily 8am-midnight.) Farther north on Gomhouriya St. is the **Galal Restaurant** (tel. 22 96 68), with standard Egyptian fare at prices similar to Popeye's. Don't miss the "camel-to-the-moon" mural. Try to either ignore or befriend the large plastic crustaceans above your table, or avoid them entirely by dining *al fresco.* (Open daily 7am-1am; closed during Ramadan.) **Restaurant Soufer** (tel. 22 43 95), just past the Akri Hotel on Degla St., off Gomhouriya St. has superb Lebanese food and a tremendous variety of seafood. Try the shrimp platters (LE8-10) or the kebab and *kufte* (LE7.30). (Open daily 8am-midnight; during Ramadan 8am-11pm.) Just outside the Hotel de la Poste is the **Restaurant Lourdat** (tel. 22 99 94) where you can get a *shwarma* sandwich for LE1.25 or a small pizza for LE4. (Open daily 8am-midnight.)

The best way to enjoy the canal is from the Noras floating restaurant (tel. 32 68 04); cruises leave daily at 3 and 9pm. You can pay LE6 (minimum charge LE2) for the cruise and a drink, or pay about LE26 for an elaborate lunch or dinner. The boat departs from Palestine St. at the corner of July 23rd St. across from the Port Said National Museum. Otherwise, take advantage of the free **ferry ride** across the canal to **Port Fouad.** The crossing affords you a good view and the chance to wander around the less mobbed shops of the smaller port. To catch the ferry walk to the southern end of Palestine St., across from the tourist office.

The **Port Said National Museum,** at the north end of Palestine St., houses an impressive olio of Egyptian historical artifacts ranging from ornately painted sarcophagi to Muhammad Ali's horse carriage. It's cool and usually empty, perfect for unharried browsing. (Open Sat.-Thurs. 9am-3pm, Fri. noon-2pm, during Ramadan 8:30am-1pm. Admission LE3, students LE1.50, camera privileges LE10.) Port Said's **Military Museum,** west of the obelisk on July 23 St. (tel. 22 46 57), has dioramas of ancient pharaonic and Islamic battles but concentrates on the early Egyptian victories of the 1973 Arab-Israeli war. (Open daily 9am-3pm. Admission LE2, students LE1, camera privileges LE1.) In front of the museum, the **beach** extends east to the canal. Beach chairs and umbrellas are available for rental, and showers are located every 100m along the beach.

Ismailiya الاسماعيلية

Surprisingly, this tiny, tranquil town of tree-lined boulevards is home to tremendous canal trade and some 50,000 people. Heavily damaged during the Arab-Israeli wars of 1967 and 1973, Ismailiya has been almost completely rebuilt. During the construction of the canal, tremendous care was taken to retain the town's provincial charm. Wander through the quiet, shaded avenues, relax in the sprawling gardens in the middle of town, or hit the beaches at nearby **Lake Timsah** (Crocodile Lake—just a name, not a warning).

Midway along the Suez Canal, Ismailiya is linked by road and the Ismailiya Canal to the Delta, and by highway and railroad to Cairo (160km) and Alexandria (280km). **Buses** leave daily for Cairo every 30 minutes from 6am-8pm (LE5), and depart for al-Arish eight times daily (LE6). You can also get to Cairo by **train;** locomotives leave Ismailiya six times daily (1st-class with A/C LE5, 2nd-class with A/C LE4, 3rd-class with little class LE1.50).

Peugot taxis to Port Said carry seven passengers to other cities from various departure points; from Orabi Sq., taxis sprint to Cairo (LE4.50 per person) and Port Said (LE4 per person), and others join the journey to al-Arish from Souk al-Gohma'a (LE7 per person).

The city's main road runs diagonally southeast from the **train station** at Orabi Sq. to the Ismailiya Canal via Gomhouriya Sq. Many of Ismailiya's restaurants, hotels, and shops are on Sultan Hussein St., which trots north-south about five blocks east of Orabi Sq. The **bus station** is at the northwest corner of town, west of the train station. The **post office** (open Sat.-Thurs. 8am-4pm; closed on holidays) and the **telecommunications office** (open 24 hrs.) are both on Orabi Sq., and the **police station** (tel. 122) is in the Governorate Building along the canal on Saleh Salem St., two blocks south of Gomhouriya Sq. The **tourist office,** also in the Governorate Building, can arrange tours and group discounts on admission.

The easiest place to **change money** is at the **Bank of Alexandria** on the eastern side of Orabi Sq. (Open Sun.-Thurs. 8:30am-2pm, during Ramadan 10am-1:30pm.) The **general hospital** is appropriately located on Hospital St. in the al-Arishayat Masr district (tel. 22 20 46/7; open 24 hrs.). Dial 123 for an **ambulance.** For minor maladies, go to the **Ismailiya Pharmacy** at 24 Sultan Hussein St. (tel. 22 93 19), open daily 24 hours.

As far as accommodations are concerned, the **Nefertari Hotel,** 41 Sultan Hussein St. (tel. 32 28 22), offers budget-bracketed elegance. Located three blocks north of Bank Misr, the Nefertari has a restaurant, agreeable bathrooms, pastel furniture, and some rooms with air-conditioning. (Singles LE10, w/bath LE17. Doubles LE10, with bath LE20. Breakfast LE2 per person.) Another popular bargain (especially for those who detest pink, violet, and mint green) is the **Isis Hotel** (tel. 22 78 21) with checkerboard floors, comfortable rooms, hot water, fans, and spotless bathrooms. (Singles LE7, with bath LE13. Doubles LE12, with bath LE20. Breakfast in the cafeteria LE3 per person.) Purchase your fare from street vendors or try **Nefertiti's** on Sultan Hussein St. (tel. 22 04 94), south of the Nefertari Hotel (full meal LE6). For dessert, **Groppi's** across the street (tel. 382 28) serves tempting pastries for 80pt. (Open Sat.-Thurs. 9am-10pm; closed during the first half of Ramadan.)

The **Museum al-Asar,** near the canal at the northern end of town, has an exhibit on local history from ancient times to the present. (Open Wed.-Mon. 8:30am-1:30pm; during Ramadan 9:30am-1pm. Admission LE5, students LE2.50.) Near the museum, the **Garden of the Stelae** contains sphinxes from the age of Ramses II. (Inquire at the museum entrance for permission to visit.) Otherwise, spend the day soaking up rays on the beaches. Access to some resort clubs requires payment of a ludicrous LE5-10; price includes buffet meals.

Suez (Al-Suweis) السويس

Located at the junction of the Red Sea and the Suez Canal, Suez city's oil refineries and countless ships spew out smoke and fumes in an attempt to equal the air quality of Mexico City if it was on Venus. The only sights in Suez are the canal and the gulf. Most travelers simply hold their noses as they pass through the city en route to the Si-nai by way of the tunnel under the canal 30km north of town, or on their way south along the Red Sea coast.

The only monuments in town are three American-made tanks on the corniche cap-tured the hard way from Israel in 1973. A trip to the beach at **Ain Sukhna,** 60km south along the Red Sea, can be arranged with some ingenuity; getting there is easy, as buses and *service* taxis run down the coast from Suez, but unless you have your own car or a hired taxi, you may never return. If you're lucky, future archeologists will dis-cover your charred body. Decent reefs near the shore make this the only snorkeling spot convenient to Cairo, but do your best not to wander into the minefields under the cliffs. The reefs, as well as a small spring-fed waterfall, are to the north of the small sandy beach. There are no showers but there is one small cafeteria which is open about 6am-midnight. Forget it; just go to Hurghada.

Buses shuttle from Suez to Cairo every 30 minutes between 6am and 8:30pm (LE4.50, LE4.75 with A/C) and to Ismailiya every 15 minutes between 6am and 6pm (LE2.50). *Service* **taxis** travel these routes at similar prices. These cities are also ac-cessible by **train** (50pt) but the coaches are hot and uncomfortable. Buses run from Suez to Alexandria twice per day (LE10). Three buses per day run to Hurghada on the desolate Red Sea Highway (6 hrs., LE10). Tickets to Hurghada should be reserved a couple of days in advance. Since you won't want to stay in Suez that length of time, either take a *service* taxi (6-7 hrs., LE10-12) or travel to Hurghada from Cairo by bus and avoid Suez altogether (are you getting the picture yet?).

Suez is the main launching ground for forays into the Sinai. Buses run daily to Sharm al-Shaikh (LE12-14), St. Catherine's (LE14), Dahab (LE14-17), Nuweiba (LE17-20), and Taba (LE17). Times vary, but buses generally leave twice per day, once in the morning and once in the afternoon.

The few amenities in Suez are on **al-Gaysh Street,** the wide thoroughfare, visible beneath the garbage, that runs east-west from the **bus station** to the seashore. The **tourist police** station is in the bus station just off al-Gaysh St. on the west side of town (open daily 3-6pm). The **train station** is about 4km farther west at the end of al-Gaysh St. The **post office** is on Hoda Sharawi St., parallel to al-Gaysh St. and one block north (open Sat.-Thurs. 8:30am-2:30pm). The **telecommunications office** is about three blocks south of al-Gaysh St. on the side street running next to the Misr Palace Hotel (open 24 hrs.).

The **Misr Palace** (tel. 22 30 31), just off al-Gaysh St., six blocks east of the bus sta-tion and across from the luxury Bel Air Hotel, has dirt-free, furniture-free rooms. Don't get too excited about the building's huge sign for a Korean Restaurant—it's been out of business since stegosaurus rump roast became scarce. (Singles LE10.25. Doubles with bath LE22. Breakfast included. Fans LE2.) Around the corner from the "Palace" hides the more comfortable **Hotel Sina** (tel. 22 03 94); the rooms have more amenities and the bathrooms have less odor. (Singles LE11.20. Doubles LE15.) Conjuring up images of bad bits from Dickens, the **HI youth hostel** on Tarik al-Hurriya St. (tel. 22 19 45), across from the stadium is much too cramped and inconvenient to make the low price worthwhile. (Dorm beds LE3, non-members LE3.50.) Across the street from the hostel is the more comfortable **Hogag Village** (tel. 22 11 60), behind the mosque next to the stadium. (Chalets with 2 beds LE44.20, with 4 beds LE57.60.)

The restaurant of choice in Suez is the **El Tayib Coffee Shop** on Hoda Sharawi St., (tel. 22 59 88), four blocks west of the post office. Fresh orange juice will relieve you of LE1, excellent baked macaroni a mere 75pt. (Open daily 7am-3am.) A more expensive option is the **Magharbel Restaurant** (tel. 22 21 32), several doors east of the White House Hotel on al-Gaysh St., where an ordinary Egyptian dinner costs LE7. (Open daily 11am-12:30am; closed on Islamic feasts.)

Monasteries of St. Paul and St. Anthony

ديــر القديس بــولس و ديــر القديس انطـون

Isolated outposts, the monasteries of St. Paul and St. Anthony lie 30km apart (82km by road) near the edge of the Red Sea. These centers of faith, dating from the beginning of the Christian monastic tradition, are the residences of monks who live in a austere style that differs remarkably little from that of 16 centuries ago.

You had better be serious about it if you want to reach these monasteries. Direct access is limited to private cars and tour buses from Cairo. The Cairo-Hurghada bus makes a stop at **Ras Za'farna** on the Red Sea, about 33km east of the turn-off to St. Anthony's. St. Paul's Monastery is tucked in the mountains 12km inland from the coastal road, about a 90-minute drive from St. Anthony's. You can catch a ride to either monastery with one of the brethren passing by; this should be especially easy in summer. Of course, if not, you're really in deep.

Alternatively, a group of seven can hire a *service* **taxi** from Suez or Hurghada. If you can negotiate with the taxi driver directly, expect to pay LE110 for both monasteries. Travel agencies can arrange the trip starting at LE180.

Still another way to reach the monasteries is to join a church expedition. For further information in Cairo, contact the monasteries' administration office (tel. 90 60 25) or the YMCA at 27 al-Gomhouriya St. (tel. 91 73 60). The former sends a car to the monasteries every week. Note that you *must* have a letter of recommendation from the administration office in Cairo in order to visit St. Paul's monastery. Also contact them in the summer about permission to spend the night at St. Anthony's *gratis*. (In winter you don't need permission to spend the night.) The monks provide food and potable water on the house.

St. Anthony, raised in the Nile Valley, scorned worldly concerns and retreated into the Eastern Desert, where he became the first famous ascetic of the Christian Church. Anthony's dramatic move reflected the restlessness that overtook some Christians in the 4th century CE when Constantine made Christianity the official religion of the Roman Empire. This mainstreaming was a disturbing development for many followers of Christ, who felt that the church had gained worldly security and wealth at the expense of its spiritual focus. In Egypt some of these restless Christians, mostly educated middle-class men, sought to escape the secular world by going to the desert where they could pray in solitude and dedicate their lives to God, not Caesar.

St. Anthony suffered paradoxical popularity; his desert hermitages became popular pilgrimage sites and crowds of the pious and the curious deprived the recluse of precious penitent isolation. Icons of hirsute, barefute Antonius adorn the walls of many Coptic churches in Egypt. Soon after the saint's death, his disciple St. Athanasius told the story of his choice of poverty and hardship, his wild battles with demons, and his wise counsel to monks and layfolk. Athanasius' *Life of Anthony* became the prototype for most later Christian hagiography.

A few years after the death of St. Anthony, his monastic followers settled at the present site and established the first Christian monastery. The **Monastery of St. An-**

thony served as a refuge for some of the monks of Wadi al-Natrun when their own sanctuaries were attacked by Bedouin tribes in the 6th century. During the 7th and 8th centuries the monastery was occupied by Melkite monks, and in the 11th it was pillaged by the army of Nasr ad-Dawla. About 100 years after the sack it was restored and transferred into Coptic hands. The Church of St. Anthony and the southern walls are among the few remains that date from before the construction of the present monastery in the 16th century.

The Church of St. Anthony is divided into five parts: the haikal, the passage in front of the haikal, the nave, the narthex, and the small chapel at the southwest corner of the church. Ancient frescoes embellish each of the sections. East of the Church of St. Anthony, the Church of the Apostles contains three haikals. During Lent, the monks cantellate the liturgy in the 18th-century Church of St. Mark. As in the Wadi al-Natrun monasteries, the Chapel of St. Michael is on the top floor of the keep. The impressive library contains more than 1700 manuscripts.

The major religious attraction in the vicinity of the church is the **Cave of St. Anthony.** The one- to two-hour expedition to the cave, 680m above the Red Sea and 276m above the monastery, is worth the effort. The best time to climb the mountain is when the sun is relatively dormant, before 6am or after 4pm. Try to return before dark, and remember to bring non-saline oceans for libation. St. Anthony's is technically open 9am-5pm, later if you're spending the night. There is a small snack shop there (soda and cookies) and a gift shop. If you spend the night the monks will feed you for free, though it is good etiquette to make a donation.

The **Monastery of St. Paul** has four churches, the most important of which is **Church of St. Paul,** built in the cave where St. Paul is said to have lived for 90 years. Many of the frescos date from the 4th and 7th centuries. Ostrich eggs, symbolizing the Resurrection, hang from the roof. Above the church is the fortress where the monks retreated upon the Bedouin attack. A secret canal from the spring ensured their survival during long sieges.

Hurghada (Ghardaka) الغـردقة

Somewhere between heaven and hell, there is Hurghada. The permanently-under-construction motif of its architecture, the inconvenient layout of its streets, the crowds of holidaying Europeans on package tours, and the unwholesome collection of characters trying to convert Hurghada's popularity into money for nothing might make visitors to Hurghada feel like one of the damned. On the other hand, veterans of the Nile Valley may appreciate the town's relaxed character (where else can you see Egyptians in shorts?) and water you can swim in. Those who venture into the depths of the sea or just gaze at the aquatic splendor from a mask while breathing from a snorkel above may feel like they've caught sight of a bit of paradise. Either way, the town's cheap and comfortable beds together with its relatively varied and tasty menus will please your body if not your soul.

Orientation and Practical Information

Although paved highways link Hurghada with the main population centers, the town is remote. From Qena, 70km north of Luxor in the Nile Valley, it's 160 barren, mountainous kilometers to Port Safaga on the Red Sea coast, and another 50km of empty coastline north to Hurghada. And that's the short way—Suez lies 410km north at the far end of the Gulf of Suez, and Cairo is another 130km.

The main **town** of Hurghada, a cluster of hotels, restaurants, shops, and residences, lies 2km north of the **harbor** (dahar in Arabic) Saqala, which has plenty of diving shops and cafés, but few budget hotels. If you follow the coastal road south from the harbor, you'll pass Moon Valley resort (4km) and the Sheraton Hotel (6km). Jasmine Village (15km) is the last in a long string of tourist resorts along the coast. Convenient minibuses also shuttle back and forth frequently (50pt to the harbor, LE1 to the area around the Sheraton), as do taxis (LE10).

Al-Nasr Way, the main thoroughfare, connects the town and harbor. From south to north along a 2km stretch of this street you'll find all the important points in town. Between Al-Nasr Way and barren, rocky, oft-noticed and seldom-mentioned **Ugly Mountain** to the east are more small streets with hotels, restaurants, and tourist bazaars, all separated from the sea by the distinctly uncomely mount. The town's **beaches** lie along al-Bahr St.; continue straight where Al-Nasr Way turns at a large mosque. Cafés and hotels (in that order) in the harbor line Sheraton St.; coming from town, make a left at the Hurghada police station and then a quick right and take the winding path toward the Sheraton.

Tourist Office: Off Al-Nasr Way (tel. 44 65 13), 750m north of the bus station in a dilapidated, shack-like structure, adjacent to the Ritz Hotel. Look for the sign on Al-Nasr Way facing the other way (north). Branch office inside the bus station. Open Sat.-Thurs. 8am-2pm.

Tourist Police: In the same building as the Tourist Office (tel. 44 67 65). Open 24 hrs.

Banks: National Bank of Egypt (open Sat.-Thurs. 8:30am-2pm, Fri. 9-11:30am, daily 6-9pm) and **Banque Misr** (open Sun.-Thurs. 8:30am-9pm, Fri. 8am-noon and 6-9pm, Sat. 10am-2pm and 6-9pm), both on Al-Nasr Way, 200m north of the bus station.

Passport Office: Al-Nasr Way (tel. 44 07 27), entrance on the left side of the Red Sea Security Department Building at the northernmost edge of town, 1.5km north of the bus station. Open Sat.-Thurs. 8am-2pm and 7-9pm, and Fri. 10am-noon (afternoons and Fridays for visa business only).

Post Office: Al-Nasr Way. Yellowish building on the right, 200m north of the bus station. Open Sat.-Thurs. 8am-2pm.

Telephones: Al-Nasr Way. A large yellow building right after the road turns at the police station (open 24 hrs.). A few shops in the tourist bazaar offer prompt connections abroad for a small surcharge. **Telephone code:** 065.

Airport: 15km south of town (tel. 44 08 83). Take a taxi (LE5). Served by **EgyptAir** (tel. 44 07 88), across from the large mosque at the northern end of Al-Nasr Way in the town, 700m north of the bus station. To and from Cairo (daily, US$90). **ZAS Air** (tel. 44 10 19) is around the corner in the same building.

Buses: Al-Nasr Way, 100m north of the southernmost limits of the town. Book seats at least 1 day in advance. Standing room may be available at the last minute. Direct A/C buses to Cairo (10am,10:30pm, 11pm; 5.5hrs; LE25). Much slower and more crowded service via Suez (6 per day, LE18). To Luxor (5 per day, LE6.50-LE11.50). To Alexandria (7pm, LE32). **Minibuses** run between the town and harbor (60pt) at the station across the street from the post office.

Service **Taxis:** Off Al-Nasr Way, 500m north of bus station, just before the bend in the road. Qena (2 hrs., LE8) is the only realistic destination. From there you can hook up with trains, buses, and trucks to points north and south. Groups may try to arrange "special" *service* to Luxor or even Cairo.

Ferries to Sharm al-Shaikh: Sat.-Thurs at 9am. Must book at least one day in advance. Going to the operators, **Sea Cruisers** (tel. 44 62 82) and **Spring Tours** (tel. 44 70 03), will not save you the LE10 commission taken by the hotels, so you're best off arranging trips through your hotel manager (LE60). The **Love Boat** offers twice weekly service on its luxurious, swimming pool-equipped liner for only LE65.

Bike Rental: Several shops in the area between Al-Nasr Way and Ugly Mountain. Shops in the harbor on Sheraton St. charge LE4 for a half day, LE5-8 for whole day. Rent rickety roadsters for LE5 a day. Rrr.

Laundromat: Most hotels will send your clothes out with the sheets for no charge. **Stop Shop** (tel. 44 66 09) at the southernmost edge of town charges 30pt-LE3 per piece. Open daily 8am-8pm.

Hospital: Hurghada General Hospital (tel. 44 67 40), al-Bahr St., 50m south of Shedwan Golden Beach Hotel.

Police: Al-Nasr Way (tel. 122), at a bend in the road 600m north of the bus station.

Accommodations

If there are any beds left in town, the first thing you'll do in Hurghada is wade through a sea of boisterous hotel-hawkers insisting that you come along with them. As always, ask to see a room and nail down a price before resting your bags and body. If hotels in town are crowded, you may consider taking a taxi south to the harbor, where **New Star, New Ramoza, Coral,** and **Peter** hotels are all viable options. Otherwise, it's probably best to follow one of the enthusiastic card and photo wavers back to a room in town. Before deciding, it's worthwhile to take a close look at the listings, as sequels and mimics are favorites in Hurghada. And since beaches and amenities are relatively far from each other, location may be a serious consideration. The cheapest place to **camp** is on the beach, although you'll have to trek quite a way from town in either direction to find a secluded spot. You must first acquire a permission request form from the small **Security Office** behind the large mosque opposite EgyptAir. Then offer your passport, the form, a prayer, and LE1.30 in stamps at another Security Office on Al-Nasr Way, this time across the street from the large mosque. (Offices open daily 8am-noon and 8-9pm.) LE3 per person buys campers a bureaucracy-free site behind the **Geisum Restaurant.** The owners have made a modestly successful effort to sequester campers from the noisy eatery uphill. In general, the beaches along the Red Sea coast are risky for campers. The military takes a dim view of unofficial crashers and, more importantly, many beaches still harbor land mines.

Youth Hostel (HI) (tel. 44 24 32), 10km south of the bus station across from Sonesta Hotel. Small and very inconvenient, but relatively clean lockers in every room. LE5.10. HI members only.

Beach House: From Abd al-Aziz St., make a right by the Riviera Restaurant and continue for 150m. Mahmoud and Sally will help you relax and take it easy in their crispy, clean little place.

Beach House II: 100m south of Geisum Restaurant. Same owners, different place. Carpeted comfort overlooking the public beach, due to open in late 1992. LE10 per person, includes breakfast.

Alaska Hotel, in the block of hotels between Shakespeare and Hotel California, about 500m from the corner of Abd al-Aziz St. Clean, cozy rooms, and a roof garden from which to watch the sea and the stars. LE7.50 per bed, LE10 with breakfast.

Happy Home, al-Gamea St. From Al-Nasr Way, make a right at Weshahy Restaurant, 100m north of the bus station. Home is on the right, a half block down. The largest of the tourist flats, with no-smirch rooms and fans. LE5. Breakfast LE2.

My Home, Solimon Mazhar St., one block east of fire station on Al-Nasr Way. Coated with Japanese writing and reading materials a propos of a favorable review. Not an overseas takeover. A clean and homey place tucked away behind a walled-in garden. LE5 per person, breakfast LE2.

Shakespeare Hotel, at the corner of Abd al-Aziz St. and the street which leads to the beach. Lounges and fridges on every floor. Clean rooms flanked by a small pleasant garden and topped by a roof restaurant. Singles LE10. Doubles LE20, with private bath LE25.

Pharaoh's Hotel, between Luxor Palace Hotel and Hotel California, 400m from Abd al-Aziz St. (tel. 44 75 77). Huge doubles with views of the water. Traces of luxury in this clean establishment. Relatively small singles LE15. Doubles LE25, with bath LE30.

Happy House II: (tel. 44 68 05), from Al-Nasr Way take a right at Red Sea Restaurant and go east 1 block. Take the first joyous right and then a quick, merry left. It'll be on the right; look for the spray-painted "Happy House tow" on the low, blue building. Nearly clean rooms and the boundless glee of manager Raouf cluster around a small public room. LE5 per bed. Breakfast LE2.

Happy Land Hotel: Al-Sheagh Sebak St. (tel. 44 73 73). From Al-Nasr Way, turn right past the banks and continue, veering right for 300m. Copious shared bathrooms and respectable but fanless rooms. Doubles LE15.

Luxor Palace Hotel (tel. 44 74 58): From the Shakespeare Hotel, continue 500m east. Fading, but not intolerable. Managers still loudly sing its praises. LE7.50 per person, includes breakfast.

Gobal Hotel (tel. 44 66 23), on the corner of Abd al-Aziz and Al-Sheagh Sebak St., near Happy Land Hotel. Spotless if slightly charmless rooms equipped with fans. Singles LE15. Doubles LE25. Breakfast included.

Africa House (tel. 44 66 29), halfway between al-Andalos and Luxor Palace. A little shabby and A/C a function of sea breezes. LE5 per person, includes breakfast.

Africa House II (tel. 44 67 79), 50m down from Happy House. Clean rooms adorned with clichéd pastel works. The focus of a great deal of activity. Singles LE10. Doubles LE20.

Quiet Corner, abutting Beach House. Clean, comfortable rooms. LE10 per person with breakfast.

Hotel California, the last of the string of hotels leading eastward along the road from Shakespeare Hotel. Reasonably clean but cramped rooms near the water. Nice roof garden overlooking water. Doubles LE20, with bath LE25.

Food

Surprise—Hurghada's seaside location makes it a prime spot for seafood. Shrimp, calimari, fish, and even lobster are readily available. In general, Hurghada's menus offer a little more than their counterparts in Upper Egypt. Unfortunately, prices are a little higher here, but for the price of a burger, fries, and a Coke, you can do quite well. And, for a burger and fries, you can still eat the usual Egyptian fare.

The cheapest meals can be had by the bus station, where *kushari* and falafel stands ring the terminal. The stand behind the buses offers a heaping plate for LE1. In the area between Al-Nasr Way and Abd al-Aziz St., traditional meals of *kufte* or roast chicken are served up by a variety of establishments. Meals run from LE4 to LE6. Try **Zekko's,** across from Happy Home.

Along Abel Aziz St., you'll find **Aly Baba's** at the northern end. They'll serve up a heap of calimari for LE8.50. Near the square, 400m south, sits **Tarbouch Restaurant,** which serves up decent and large individual pizzas (LE5-11, depending on the toppings). Two doors down, the **Bella Riviera** offers pasta, steak, and chicken. (Spaghetti with tomato LE1.50.)

For seafood and/or relative elegance you might venture to **Rendezvous,** on Al-Nasr Way by the bus station, for a meeting with red-checked tablecloths, candlelight, and fine food. (Kebab LE10.) The menu includes veal and other such delicacies. **Salsa,** by Happyland Hotel, will actually make you feel that you are out at a restaurant. Reasonable service and relatively tasteful surroundings. (Grilled fish LE8.) Watch out for the flaming tomatoes. **Geisum,** with its pleasant beachfront location, has good food and good prices. Hearty portions of grilled fish for LE7.50. Those attempting to rein in the revolutionary vanguard might opt for lobster thermidor (LE30-40 around town) or try the Chinese restaurant by the Gabal Hotel.

The restaurant situation is comparable in the harbor. The disoriented **Berlin Café,** 300m down Sheraton Street, serves cheap Egyptian fare put together by proprietor Sharif, who will be pleased as punch to meet you.

Sights and Entertainment

Hurghada's main attractions are silent and submerged. Red Sea creatures flabbergast in their dazzling array of colors, shapes, and sizes. Buck-toothed trigger fish, iridescent parrot fish, rays with blue polka dots, sea cucumbers, giant clams, and a million others star in this briny freak show. The shimmering, variegated blues of Hurghada's waters have been spared the terrors of oil exploration (for the moment anyway), and the shifting colors will woo even the sternest terranean.

The tropical sun can give you a crispy burn: wear protective sunscreen or clothing. To walk near the reefs, you'll need shoes—otherwise the coral will make shish kebab out of your feet. If you see something that looks like an aquatic pin cushion, it's probably a sea urchin or blowfish, both of which should be touched only as sushi. Avoid the feathery lionfish as well—its harmless-looking spines can deliver a paralyzing sting. Not least, the rare but well-named fire coral can bloat a leg to mammoth proportions, leaving welts the size of croquet balls. Before plunging in, look at one of the plastic cards that pictorially identifies these nautical nasties—most guides and diving shops carry these cards. You can reach some of the reefs without a boat. An interesting one lies off the beach to the left of the Sheraton; another lies off the string of beaches at the northern end of town on the far side of Ugly Mountain.

To reach Hurghada's most brilliant scenery you must board a barge. The all-day trip to **Geftun Island,** the most popular excursion, usually includes two one-hour snorkeling stops near the island and a fish meal prepared on the boat during the trip. You must make arrangements the night before with the manager of a hotel or tourist flat or directly with one of the "sea trips" agencies. Regardless, the trip will cost LE30. Be sure to take along a hat, suntan lotion, and potable water.

The standard Geftun Island trip takes one full day; the trick for budget travelers is planning for more days of underwater carousing. Try to make arrangements with a hotelier or boat owner so you can take another trip to Geftun and see two different reefs or plan an overnight at Geftun. Prices range from LE60 to LE90 including meals; the exact price depends upon the length of the second day of the trip. Better yet, inquire about excursions to other locales. Adel Shazly of Nefertiti Sea Trips, Muhammad Emad of Sunshine Sea Trips, Muhammad Awad of Red Sea Wonderland (next to Happy House), Sally of Beach House II's Amira Diving Center, and Hosni Bakeet of Hurghada Sea Trips can each provide excellent information. Bakeet's office is the only one unconnected to a tourist flat; to find it, take the street running south across from the telephone office for two blocks and look right.

On any snorkeling trip you can bring your own **equipment** or rent from the guides. Competition among the dive ships in town has brought the rates down to LE5 per day for mask, snorkel, and fins; try any of the above sea trip offices.

Determined underwater explorers who wish to scuba dive will find relatively high prices compared to those elsewhere in Egypt. The quality of the reefs and underwater life is spectacular; you'll encounter clear waters, magnificent colors, and bountiful species. Few places in the world come close. Newly opened, **Amira Diving Center** at Beach House II offers a range of courses (open water US$230, 5 days, 6 dives, all equipment) and general diving packages (US$40 for 1 day/2 dives, US$100 for 3 days). Ask around for prices and names, and take the usual precautions against slime and fraud.

As for the beaches, sand and surf they are not. Beaches in town are unspectacular but convenient, and not far from a decent snorkeling reef; they run north from Geisum Restaurant. The **Geisum** charges LE5 for a spot in the sun, from where it is an easy hop to the pool at the nearby Sand Beach Hotel. Further along, **Shedwan's** pool and beach also cost LE5, the same price demanded by Three Corners Village for the use of their cramped facilities. A free public beach is due to open in late 1992 for tourists just south of Geisum. There is a **free public beach** just south of the Sheraton Hotel, 7km southwest of town, but Western women may feel uncomfortable here if they choose to bare anything more than toes. Better is the semi-private **Shellghada Beach** just before the Sheraton, where LE5 will buy you a day on their soft, clean sand, free soft drinks up to that value, fresh-water showers, and more liberal bathing fashions. The best and most expensive beach in town belongs to the Sheraton (LE10). Minibuses (60pt), local buses (25pt), and taxis (LE5) shuttle between the center of town and the Sheraton throughout the day.

The **Red Sea Aquarium** in the town on al-Bahr St. before Geisum Restaurant has a reasonably impressive display of live fish but is a bit expensive for its size; it may, nevertheless, be a good way to get acquainted with the species you'll encounter in your underwater explorations. (Open daily 9am-10pm. Admission LE4.) Another option for hydrophobic oglers is to take a glass-bottom boat out to the reefs (LE10 for a 2-hr. ride). Check with Shellghada or the hotels by the beaches in town for details.

At night, the **Cha Cha,** in the Shedwan, is the only place in Hurghada which can legitimately call itself a disco. Belly-dancing 11:30pm daily except Tuesday, Hurghada's big night. The Belgian proprietor pipes in the latest music from Europe. Be forewarned: the LE15 minimum charge covers the price of one beer.

Western Desert Oases

Scattered through the expanses of the Western Desert, the oases dot the sea of sand and rock like little green archipelagos. Hot and cold springs, groves of oranges and dates, rice paddies, and fields of watermelons and cucumbers flourish astonishingly amidst the imposing desert. Though the Bedouin and Egyptian *fellaheen* who dwell beside the robust fields greet strangers with comforting hospitality, this is an adventure for the rugged. Getting around is more difficult than along the Nile and tourist facilities are token gestures at best.

The series of oases sprinkled throughout the Sahara—**Kharga, Dakhla, Farafra, and Bahariya**—marks the trail of a prehistoric branch of the Nile. A flow of water from the Sudan supposedly replenished the aquifers annually. This bounty of water has been an impetus for development in crowded and largely water-starved Egypt. In 1958, the government released studies that showed considerable stores of water below the desert floor, accessible with new techniques of drilling deeper wells. The government's New Valley Project was designed to fully exploit this underground water for the irrigation and fertilization of the desert. A mass relocation of landless peasants from the Delta to the New Valley was also planned. Unfortunately, experts are now beginning to question the hypothesis that the underground water is recharged by seepage from the more humid parts of Africa. New estimates indicate that the supply could last only another 100 to 700 years and that it is not replenished yearly; instead, it is simply left over from 6000 to 12,000 years ago.

The fortunes of the people of the oases have ebbed and flowed with the water supply throughout Egyptian history. The Romans, with their waterwheels and aqueducts, were able to tap deeper water and push back the desert. The population burgeoned and prospered for approximately 300 years but overirrigation and abandonment of fallow farming eventually hindered productivity. The oases slipped into a slow decline that lasted into the 1970s, when Anwar al-Sadat targeted the New Valley for development. The plans proved far too ambitious and expensive, even though the new desert wells did open vast regions around the oases for cultivation. Government attention has meant radical change for those living in the oases, as new roads and other recently introduced conveniences funnel in Western culture.

In general, the oases share the climate of Nile Valley cities on the same latitude—Bahariya is like Cairo, Kharga like Luxor. But the air is fresher in the oases, and breezes more common. October through April is unquestionably the best time to visit. It is not unusual for summer temperatures, especially at Kharga, to reach the 50 C mark. Even at night, summer temperatures persist into the upper 20s. And you won't find air conditioning *anywhere*. If you go in summer, finding accommodations will be a cinch.

Check out a copy of Dr. Ahmed Fakhry's *Bahariya and Farafra Oases,* an extremely readable introduction to the life and history of these areas. The volume, along with Fakhry's *Siwa Oasis,* is published by the American University in Cairo Press and is available in the university bookstore on the Old Campus and at several of Cairo's English language bookstores (LE9-10 paperback). The university library on the New Campus also has both volumes for consultation.

Getting Around

Daily **buses** run from the al-Azhar bus station in Cairo to Bahariya, Kharga, Dakhla, and Farafra. A special air-conditioned bus runs from Ataba Sq. in Cairo to Kharga and Dakhla every morning. Inexpensive buses also run from the town of Assyut, halfway down the Nile, to Kharga and Dakhla. Kharga is served by **airplane** from Cairo Aerodrome every Sunday and Wednesday (LE300). *Service* **taxis** travel to Bahariya from Cairo, and to Kharga from Assyut. (See the individual chapters on the oases, Cairo, and Assyut for detailed transportation information.) Some people **hitchhike** from one oasis to the next, but they often have to wait a day or so for a ride, especially between Farafra and Dakhla. The military checkpoints outside each oasis are the most ideal hitching spots. **In the heat and isolation, hitchers run a real risk—*Let's Go* doesn't recommend it.**

Car rental is a convenient and comfortable, though expensive, option for desert travel. Any car must be in top condition in order to survive the long, hot, poorly maintained desert roads—this rules out most of the cars rented to tourists in Cairo. Four-wheel drive is highly recommended. Renting a caravan can solve a lot of problems, including those of transporting food, water, and extra gas, and finding a comfortable place to sleep. If the cost is split among several people, caravans can be economical.

If you have the time and energy, visit all four oases in the Western Desert by making a giant loop along the Great Desert Road and the Lower Nile Valley in either direction. Beginning in Cairo—the best place to rent a car—travel to Kharga via Assyut and proceed north from there. Or drive through the desert to Bahariya and continue to the southern oases; return via Assyut along the Nile, passing by the archeological sites near Minya and Mallawi. The entire trip is about 1700km.

A number of caveats are in order concerning **desert travel.** It is sometimes a long way between gas stations. While every oasis boasts at least one fuel pump, it is probably wise to buy jerry cans in Cairo or Assyut and fill them with enough gas to cover the vast distances between stations. A caravan consumes ludicrous quantities of fuel; buy enough extra to fill an entire tank. Bring along at least one good spare tire; flats are more common than service stations. Several large containers filled with potable water are also essential in case you get stranded.

Foreigners are (probably wisely) prohibited by the military from leaving the main road. Try to drive in the cool of the morning. And finally, never drive at night—the chances of getting lost on the unlit road increase exponentially and potholes veiled in darkness are especially pernicious.

The best alternative to hosteling in the oases is **camping.** Most fertile land here belongs to farmers who'll usually permit you to pitch your tent. The ideal spot is just outside the main town of an oasis, where you can usually find a small pool of water and the sound of silence. The desert itself is also a viable option. Generally the area is free of dangerous fauna. Cool temperatures and breezes carry away the mosquitoes to feast on rest house guests, and sand is a comfortable mattress substitute. Each oasis has at least one bearable and cheap **hotel** or **rest house.** Stockpiling **water** is a wise idea, as only Farafra has a 24-hr. water supply. Local water, since it is groundwater, is reportedly cleaner and healthier than other Egyptian municipal water. **Food** is readily available in the main towns of all the oases.

Women are advised to follow certain guidelines when swimming in oasis springs. In the most isolated springs unfrequented by locals, frolic as you wish. The same goes for pools cordoned off and adjoined to tourist rest houses. Women should not, however, enter pools where men are already bathing. Sometimes there is a separate pool where women may bathe, provided they wear a *galabiya*.

Note that the requirement for foreigners to obtain permission to visit the oases was lifted in 1985-86. Despite what out-of-date sources will tell you, you need only flash a **passport** at the numerous military checkpoints en route—keep it handy. In Dakhla or Kharga you'll be asked to pay a LE4.50 per person **tourism development tax.** The receipt is your admission slip to all the ancient sites in the New Valley. If you pay the tax at a hotel, be sure to keep the receipt as proof; otherwise you'll probably have to pay again at a roadblock.

Bahariya الواحات البحرية

This small oasis is historically significant as a stopover for caravans traveling between the Nile Valley and the rest of North Africa. Since pharaonic times, the arrival of merchants and their heavily laden camels was a major event in Bahariya; for many centuries, pilgrims on their way to Mecca would join traders on the trans-desert trek and enjoy an enthusiastic welcome from the Bahariyan faithful. Nowadays it's caravans of rip-roaring European adventurers gallivanting through the oasis in Land Rovers that cause the intense noise pollution in Bahariya. Because of its relative proximity to Cairo, Bahariya attracts many foreign visitors who crave a couple days of desert but no more.

Bahariya's ancient ruins are scanty and largely inaccessible, and **Bawiti** (pop. 24,000), the main village, is unappealing. Nearby gardens and springs and the desert, however, unequivocally compensate. The town offers conveniences including several food stores, a gas station, a market, and two or three coffee shops. Thus, if you're headed to Farafra, this is a great spot to refuel both body and auto.

All services are on or just off a 0.5km stretch of the main road. Starting from the west end, you'll find the **bus station, hospital, telephone office** (open 7am-11pm), **police station,** and **gas stations.** The **telephone code** is 088; to reach any place in town, dial 1404 and ask the operator to connect you. The **tourist office,** within the Bahariya village government compound, is staffed by convivial city council member Saleh. (Officially open Sat.-Thurs. 8am-2pm.) **Water** in Bahariya is on from 7am-noon and 4pm until the final stroke of seven though hotel storage tanks sometimes provide added relief.

Because local government officials closed down all but the government rest houses to foreigners, accommodations in Bahariya are less than ideal. In Bawati, a rest house which goes by the puzzling and altogether inappropriate name of **Edelweiss** charges LE5 for grungy rooms to be shared with mosquitoes and the desert heat. The bathrooms are slightly less appealing than the multi-bedded rooms, but the small garden in front is quite nice. More appealing are the **bungalows** at Bir al-Matthar, with relatively clean rooms and baths and convenient access to a nearby spring. Unfortunately, Bir al-Matthar is situated 6km from Bawati and 3 long km from the nearest *service* taxi stop; the cost of a bed (LE5) is only half the price of the taxi ride to or from Bawati. Camping here is an attractive option. The outlying springs, particularly Bir al-Ghaba, afford ideal settings for a night's rest.

Abdallah at the **Paradise Motel's** cafeteria serves up solid if unadventurous cuisine (omelettes LE1) and will help orient you in town. The **Oasis Cafeteria,** unconnected to the similarly named hotel, serves a large piece of chicken (LE5) and other typical oasis offerings. For falafel try **Kimo's** by the bus station (one plate with salad 50pt). The **Popular Restaurant** across from the police station, where you may find yourself bargaining for your meal, has more of the same.

Nature—not man—is the area's real attraction. Several local operators organize trips to nearby sights, and they will find you shortly upon arrival. **Bir al-Matthar,** a cold spring, lies 6km southeast of Bawiti. The slightly sulphurous water pours out of a viaduct into a small shaded cement pool. Taxis to this popular place cost LE10 each way. The road to Bir al-Matthar continues southeast through the desert to **Bir al-Ghaba,** 15km from Bawiti, with both a hot and cold spring in another sumptuous oasis landscape. Both men and women can swim in this deserted spot. Daytrips to Bir Ghaba cost at least LE2.50. A steamy spring, 2.5km out of the town center, is within walking distance. On a slightly bizarre and unusual note, a large natural pyramid, surrounded and topped by dunes, lies within the range of local tour operators about 9km away.

Archeological sites of some interest cluster around Bawiti and **al-Qasr,** the older city adjacent to Bawiti in the west. The **Tomb of Bannentiu,** on the eastern outskirts of Bawiti, was discovered by Ahmed "Oasis" Fakhry and dates from the 26th dynasty. Its central and burial chambers are decorated with fairly well-preserved painted reliefs, including murals of the journeys of the sun and moon. The tomb is currently closed for restoration and preservation work; ask locally about when it will be reopened. Bahariya's resident Egyptologist, Muhammad at-Tayib at the Bahariya Department of Antiquities, is the best-informed source; Paradise Motel's Abdallah can contact him and may help you arrange a sneak peek. Fakhry, the bodacious oasis man, has also discovered a many-chambered **ibis burial,** 500m south of Bawiti, where sacred ibises, falcons, and quails were interred in jars. This tomb also dates from late pharaonic times, and was used into the Roman era. The burial chamber cannot be visited, but little was left behind to see anyway. **Al-Qasr** itself, the ancient capital of Bahariya, hides scanty Roman remains among its mud brick dwellings. Ancient walls and the watery geological fault **Bir Bishmo** also make interesting sidetrips.

Getting There

After Kharga, Bahariya ranks as the most accessible of the oases in Egypt's Western Desert. From Cairo, a 400km road leads past the Pyramids of Giza and southwest across the desert to Bawiti. The distance can be covered in four or five hours by private **car.** Two **buses** per day leave from al-Azhar station in Cairo (LE10, with A/C LE12). Book one to two days in advance to secure a seat. From Bahariya, there is a daily bus to Cairo at 7am and at least one additional bus. To purchase tickets and reserve seats, head to the inconspicuous second-story office above the telephone office in Bahariya. From Farafra, there are six weekly buses, running every day except Wednesday (LE7.50). Each day a few *service* **taxis** travel between Cairo and Bahariya (ordinarily in afternoon or evening, LE15), leaving from the front of Kimo restaurant. Taxis from Cairo leave from the inconspicuous Qahwa al-Wahia Café, on a corner of Sharia Qadry, a few blocks south of Port Said St., west of the Citadel in the el-Saiyida district.

The Roads from Cairo and to Farafra

As you leave metropolitan Cairo you'll pass just north of the Pyramids of Giza. Beyond lies the as-yet-uninhabited **October 6th City,** one of Egypt's new planned cities whose name and purpose might have easily been lifted from an anti-utopian novel, designed to accommodate a share of the country's burgeoning population. On the approach to Bahariya, the entire landscape slurches into a deep shade of red. Vast deposits of iron here are quarried by a huge iron mine just off the highway 40km before Bawiti.

Heading southwest toward Farafra you leave the fertility of Bawiti behind. Look for the tiny oasis of **al-Hayz,** 40km to the southwest. The modern settlement (5km east of the main road on a gravel track) is a puny remnant of the sizable, prosperous community that flourished in early Christian times. About 2km down the gravel track from the main road lie sundry and substantial remains of an early **church** and **military camp.** You'll need permission to approach or enter these ruins. (LE45-50 per truckload as a daytrip from Bawiti.)

The paved road from Bawiti to Farafra oasis (180km) features spectacular canyons, wind-blown mesas, and rugged desertscape. The precipitous eastern and western escarpments of the Bahariyan depression meet at a point about 60km south of Bawiti. The road winds through this pass and onto a brief plateau, then plummets into the Farafra depression. Soon you'll enter the fantastic **White Desert,** where the wind has shaped mountains of chalk into giant white mushrooms, sphinxes, and riddling Rorschach-like psychedelia. Several groups arrange camping trips to the White Desert leaving in the afternoon from Bahariya and continuing to Farafra after an evening amid sandy absurdity. (LE250-300 per truckload, including bed and transportation in jeeps. Some quotes are higher, but you shouldn't pay more than LE300.)

Farafra واحة الفرافرة

Even after over a decade of existence, the paved road has enticed few vehicles to Farafra. With a population of 2300, Farafra is the smallest of Egypt's major oases, supporting only two really extended families. The oasis is also one of Egypt's most photogenic: the explosion of lush foliage perches on a sloping hill like a bright green fortress. Tiny dirt paths tip-toe through the gardens behind Farafra's single immaculate settlement; nearby hot springs bubble through the desert floor.

Two government **rest houses** accommodate guests in Farafra. The **Youth House,** adjoining the café which doubles as the **bus station,** has some rooms (more like barracks) and an outhouse facility. You can also move a bed or mattress under a vine-covered canopy—the cooler option in summer. (LE2, mosquito nets 75pt.) 100m down the road, the government rest house boasts more conventional toilet facilities and rooms that are cleaner by a hair (LE3.35). Camping in the nearby desert is always an option. You might also take up some of the locals on their offers of hospitality.

In between the hostelries sit the **police station** and, 30m west, the **post office.** For food, **Saad's Restaurant,** by the government rest house, the café by the bus station and **Husseini's Restaurant** in between offer omelettes (LE1), macaroni (LE1), *kufte, fuul,* and soup (depending on availability) at reasonable prices.

In town, the **Art Museum,** the self-indulgent project of local artist Badr, displays his expressive sculptures and paintings, many of which depict life in Farafra. Mounted local wildlife and an exhibit of Farafran artifacts complete the collection. The museum is near Saad's Restaurant, about 100m to the northwest behind a school; it's a mud-brick building with a decorated façade. (Open capriciously. Contributions welcome.) Many of Badr's murals also adorn the outside walls of local houses. In the middle of the village, 800m west of the café and the main road, a gelid spring gushes into a pool. Men can refresh themselves here, or wash their laundry surrounded by the stupendous scintillations of the nighttime stars. **Well #6 (Bir Sitta),** 4km west of the Farafra town, is an idyllic spot to swim and camp. **Al-Mufid,** a lake 10km from town, is warm enough for swimming in summer. Hamdy, who operates from Saad's Restaurant, will organize a variety of excursions by taxi, jeep, or camel. An overnight excursion into the surreal and eerie White Desert goes for LE150 for a group of 6 or 7, including food.

Getting There

From Dakhla, there is a bus every day except Wednesday (4.5 hrs., LE6.50). Farafra can also be reached from Cairo by way of Bahariya, with daily buses leaving Cairo at either 10am (LE15.20) or 7am (LE19.50). Buses to Cairo leave daily, except Wednesday, at 7am or 10am. Many people find **hitchhiking** to be a viable option; they wait near the military checkpoint outside of Dakhla, Farafra, or Bahariya and they make sure their ride is traveling all the way to their destination.

The Road to Dakhla

The 310km road to Dakhla was constructed in 1982 but is rapidly deteriorating. Much of its foundation is made of chalky rock, heaped up to prevent the road and vehicles on it from slipping into the quicksand on either side: Be careful where you step off the road. Shifting dunes obscured the southern part of this road for years, making travel between Dakhla and Farafra an unpredictable undertaking. The road is now kept partially clear, but still sees markedly little traffic. Don't bank on receiving your American Express refund in these parts.

Ten kilometers south of Farafra you'll come to a tiny, uninhabited oasis officially considered part of the town. The villages take care to cultivate the land here; occasionally a skein of sheeply farmers gambol across the road but otherwise the spot is deserted and quiet—and the best place in the area to pitch a tent. Still farther down the road toward Dakhla, about 50km from Farafra, covers the diminutive, sparsely inhabited **Oasis of Sheikh Merzuq,** where you'll find a sulphur spring with a viaduct carrying water into a concrete pool. The pool is a refreshing spot for men to take a dip; women will have to settle for a sweat bath. The local Bedouin will show you the way to an ancient **Roman well,** where fresh water blurbles from a deep spring.

Dakhla الواحات الداخلة

Dakhla's lush fields, rice paddies, and fruit orchards stubbornly hold out against the harsh, engulfing desert. At two junctures the desert does indeed consume the greenery, segmenting Dakhla into three separate oases, but 65,000 Dakhlans are the clear victors in the struggles of water versus stone and farmer versus dune. Basking in government attention, the people of Dakhla have reclaimed this recalcitrant wasteland, planting peanuts and rice before introducing more fragile crops. The New Valley Project may have rendered the town of Kharga unappealing to visitors, but in Dakhla—dubbed the "pink oasis" for the pink cliffs jabbing the horizon—something of the opposite has occurred. While in oases such as Siwa and Farafra development seems to be enervating local culture, in Dakhla the local oasians beam under broad-brimmed straw hats that look like the offspring of a bowler and a sombrero, and share their infectious enthusiasm with visitors.

Orientation and Practical Information

Farthest from Cairo of all the oases, Dakhla lies 310km from Farafra and 200km from Kharga. The center of the oasis is **Mut** (pronounced MOOT; named for the Egyptian goddess whose husband was Amon), a modern upgrowth and capital. **West Mawhub,** 80km west of Mut, and **Tineida,** 45km east of Mut, are smaller repositories of green at the boundaries of the oases. The cultivated regions dot the main, well-paved highway. These areas are centered at **al-Qasr,** 32km west of Mut; **Balaat** and **Bashendi,** 35-40km east of Mut; and the capital itself.

Life in Mut centers around **Liberation Square** (Midan at-Tahrir) and **New Mosque Square,** 1km south along **New Valley Street.** Liberty Sq. encompasses the intersection of New Valley St. and the east-west Kharga-Farafra Highway.

Tourist Information Office: 2nd floor of Tourist Rest Home (tel. 84 14 07; home tel. 94 17 58 and 94 16 54), in New Mosque Sq., Mut. Ibrahim Muhammad Hassan and Omar Ahmed go the distance to provide assistance. Open Sun.-Thurs 8am-2pm, sometimes 9-11pm, but feel free to call at other times.

Bank: Misr Bank, Liberty Sq. (tel. 94 10 63), opposite the police station. Changes traveler's checks and cash. Open daily 8:30am-2pm.

Post Office: In New Mosque Sq. and branch on al-Ganaim St. (Garden St.), parallel to New Valley St. and about 0.5km east, across from the telephone office. Both open Sat.-Thurs. 8am-2pm.

Telephone Office: al-Ganaim St. From Hamdy Restaurant on New Valley St. walk right (east) to Anwar Restaurant then veer left. International and inter-oasis calls. Open 24 hrs. **Telephone code: 088.**

Intercity Buses: Station located in New Mosque Square. To Kharga (3.5hr.; LE4.50-6) and to Assyut (5 per day; 8hr.; LE9-11). 3 continue to Cairo (3 per day; 14hr.; LE8). Early morning bus to Cairo (16hr.; LE18) with stops in Farafra (4.5hr.; LE6.50) and Bahariya (7.5hr.; LE11). Another bus to Farafra only (4.5hr.; LE6.50). Intercity buses also stop in both the eastern and western villages. Check the schedule at the bus station or the tourist office and book a day in advance. About half the buses from Dakhla are without A/C and are frequently late.

Local buses: travel same route through Mut as intercity buses. To eastern villages (2 per day, 6:30am and 2pm, Balaat and Bashedi 50pt, return to Mut 1hr. later) and western villages (4 per day, 6:30am-2pm, al-Qasr 25pt, return to Mut 2.5hr. later).

Taxis: special sight-seeing tours LE30-35 for 1 day, LE8-10 for a trip to east or west Dakhla. Ask around New Mosque Sq. in Mut and bargain. Special to Kharga LE50-60. Covered pickup trucks shuttle frequently between the intersection of Liberation Sq. and eastern and western villages (50pt for the full trip). Early morning is the best time to catch them.

Bicycle Rental: Hamdy Restaurant and **Abu Muhammad's Restaurant,** both in New Mosque Sq. LE5 per day.

Gas Station: On the outskirts of eastern Mut on the Kharga-Farafra Hwy. Open 24 hrs.

Hospitals: Tel. 94 13 32. Ambulance tel. 333. On the edge of Mut next to the gas station. Smaller ones in each village.

Police: Tel. 94 15 00. Station in Liberation Sq., on the Kharga-Farafra Hwy.

Accommodations and Food

There are three hotels in downtown Mut, all more than a little warm in summer. The **Tourist Rest House** by the bus station is almost clean, but oh-so-steamy and full of flies. (LE3.75 per bed.) The **Gardens Hotel** (tel. 94 15 77) has blue, well-screened rooms and relatively clean bathrooms. From the bus station, turn right at the mosque and continue one block past Hamdy's Restaurant; you'll find the hotel on your right. (Singles LE7.50. Doubles LE10.) Further along past Anwar's Restaurant is the grungy and sweltering **Dar al-Wafden Hotel.** (LE3 for a normal bed, LE4.50 for a bed made special by a slab of carpet on the floor.) A little to the west along the main highway,

Dakhla's finest hotel, **The Mebauez** (tel. 94 15 24), offers fans, well-maintained rooms, and a comfortable lobby. (Singles LE18.70, with bath LE23.40. Doubles with bath LE37.30. Includes breakfast.) 3 km east of town, two rest houses lie near a hot spring and pool, which spills out into a quiet rural setting. **The Roadside "Villa"** features fans and multi-bed rooms, while the **Rest House** further in from the highway just by the pool has quaint rooms, private baths, and only partially effective screens. (LE4.25 per person in either place.) 32km down the road from Mut in the village of al-Qasr, also along the main highway, is a **rest house** with large clean rooms (LE5 per person).

Finally, **camping** is a very viable option. The area behind the hot springs has many dunes and few insects. A number of the nearby springs also provide good spots at which to pitch tents.

While it's not saying much, Dakhla probably has the best food in the oasis. **Hamdy's Restaurant** on New Valley St., halfway between the Mosque and the highway, has a relatively long menu and an engaging proprietor named Nasser (*kufte* LE2.50). One block east of Hamdy's, **Anwar's Restaurant** serves up full meals for LE5. Along the highway, **Shehaab,** just west of New Valley St., is a local favorite (kebab LE3.50). **Abu Muhammad's Restaurant,** another 100m west, is the cleanest place in town, but all that soap and antiseptic has also sterilized the taste and raised prices.

Sights

Don't linger in mangy Mut. The only sight is the **Dakhla Ethnographic Museum,** whose exhibits explain traditional oasis culture through a reconstruction of a typical Dakhlan family dwelling. Expressive clay figurines created by the artist Mabruk recreate scenes of village life, including the preparation of a bride for marriage and the celebration of a pilgrim's return from the *hajj*. The museum is located next to Hotel Dar al-Wafden in eastern Mut. Visits can be arranged through the tourist office or by contacting Ibrahim Kamel Abdallah, the museum's curator. Reach him at the Ministry of Culture office (tel. 94 13 11), the multi-story building on New Valley St. north of Hamdy Restaurant (he's usually there between 8am-2pm and 6-9pm), or at home (tel. 94 17 69). Admission LE1.

Use the capital as a base for travel to the outlying villages. The most edifying daytrip is to the western village of **al-Qasr,** 32km northwest of Mut on the main highway. The charming contemporary town was built in and around the substantial remains of Dakhla's medieval Islamic capital. Its mud buildings remain cool in summer and warm in winter. The **old village** of al-Qasr lies slightly to the north (400m) of the main road through the new village. At the western edge of town on the main road is a large map of al-Qasr, visible from the road. Underneath the map is a small exhibit on traditional Dakhlan culture. Within the old village itself, occasional arrows direct you to the main sights.

The **Minaret of Nasr ad-Din** (21m) is the only extant part of an 11th-century Ayyubid mosque; Sheikh Nasr ad-Din built the present mosque in the 19th century around the old tower. North of the minaret through the gnarled alleys is **Qasr Madrasa,** an intact two-story mud-brick building that is thought to have been either an Ayyubid schoolhouse or an entertainment hall for an Ottoman palace; to bungle matters a little further, villagers later used the building as a courtroom. Many of the doorways of the old village are adorned with ornate wooden lintels that reveal the name of the owner, builder, and carpenter and the date of construction. A pharaonic arch, once used to support the entrance to a house, and a Roman doorway a few doors away hint at al-Qasr's distant pre-Islamic past. On the southern fringes of the old town you can see a water-wheel and functioning **pottery works,** where the villagers churn out everything from ashtrays to chamberpots. A small **restaurant** on the main road at the eastern edge of town serves simple meals of cheese and hard-boiled eggs in summer and a more complete menu in winter.

Three other sights of interest are found near al-Qasr but are beyond walking distance. 2.5km west on the main highway is the turn-off for **al-Mousawaka Tombs.** The local bus to west Mawhub or a pickup truck-taxi can drop you here. Head 1km south on the well-marked track to reach the guarded tombs, hewn into a rock outcropping. The two-chambered **Tomb of Petosiris** features brightly painted funerary scenes with a cast of characters that's half ancient Egyptian, half Greco-Roman. The ceiling is ablaze with Hellenistic angels, portraits of folks passed on, and an overwrought zodiac. The adjacent **Tomb of Sadosiris** features unusual images of a two-faced man, simultaneously looking back at life and toward the afterlife, and of a mummy carrier with wooden wheels, another zodiac, and a plethora of grapes. These are the two most interesting of hundreds of Greco-Roman tombs laid to rest in the immediate vicinity. Unfortunately, they were closed for repairs during the summer of 1992. Check with local tourist officials for an update. (Open 8am-3pm. Admission LE8, students LE4.)

Another 2km west down the main road lies the unmarked white path that leads 3.5km toward **Dayr al-Haggar,** the unguarded ruins of a small Roman temple. Follow the path south until it ends in a small village, turn right, then take the first left to the back of the village. The temple is southeast another 1.5km, out of sight from the back of the village but soon visible in a small depression. One kilometer east of al-Qasr is the turn-off for **Bir al-Gabel,** a hot spring connected by a road to the highway. After a 5km walk (you may be lucky to catch a ride with a truck on its way to a nearby quarry), you'll arrive at a paradisiacal little pool adorned by swarming insects and mysterious objects floating on the water's edge.

Returning to Mut, a 5km eastward detour at the Bedouin village of **ad-Drous,** will bring you to an **Islamic Cemetery.** Three kilometers before Mut, stop for a dip at the so-called **Tourism Wells,** where the rest houses are located. Here hot spring water (42 C) has been tapped to fill two swimming pools, open to both sexes, before it flows into irrigation channels (free if you paid the New Valley tourism development tax).

Two historic villages on the eastern side of Mut may restore your faith in rural living. In the crowded old section of **Balaat** (pop. 5000), elongated dark passageways burst into a courtyard with palm fronds and grape vines.

The unguarded red-brick tombs of **ad-Daba,** still under excavation, inhere to lands 3km northeast of the main road behind the village. First walk 2km east from the official bus stop to a bantam military base, identifiable by its white stone columns; from there walk 2km straight into the desert and never return. At **Bashendi,** 5km farther east (and 40km from Mut), the accomplishments of a "model village" have prompted cities everywhere to ask their village spawn, "Why can't you be more like Bashendi?" The village actually lies on top of a recently discovered ancient temple, but excavation is improbable for the near future. The large stone **Tomb of Ketenus** contains four rooms, including one decorated with scenes of its 2nd-century Roman owner mingling with the gods Min and Seth. (The key is held by a villager whom locals will hunt down upon request. Admission LE8, students LE4.) Next door, the prominent **Tomb of Bash Endi,** the base of which is Roman but whose domed roof is distinctly Islamic, commemorates the village's beloved namesake. You might join locals who decorate the inside of the holy man's tomb with henna in hopes of finding missing objects and links. The village leaders will inevitably direct you to the Bashendi **carpet works,** where local youths are trained to weave. If the guard isn't around to open the tombs, you may be invited in by a hospitable villager while you wait. In between and all around these sights are sprinkled several hot and cold springs to which locals can direct you.

Assorted natural pyramids notwithstanding, the antenna of desert along the **road to Kharga** has unusually little to inspire the muse. The rest house, at the midway point, doesn't even offer food. Crescent-shaped sand dunes creep across the road just outside Kharga, necessitating occasional detours.

Kharga الخارجة

Egypt's most convincing attempt at a desert boomtown is the city of Kharga, the most accessible and developed of all the oases. Since the New Valley Project, Kharga's population has approached six digits. Model villages have sprung up all over the oasis to house the peasants who work the fledgling fields. Aesthetics, however, do not appear to be high on the local priority list. The town looks functional, even by Egyptian standards, and the Old Town, while not quite lifeless, is not overly inspiring or appealing. A handful of nearby monuments add a touch of flavor but can't lift the ugly duckling label from this town.

Orientation and Practical Information

Kharga lies closest to the Nile Valley of all the oases in Egypt's Western Desert—240km from Assyut via a passable road. The greenery begins about 20km north of the town of Kharga, the capital of the New Valley. A newly paved road heads south from Kharga, skirting sand dunes and small oases en route to **Bulaq,** 15km south, **Baris,** (90km), and numerous smaller settlements in between.

In sprawling Kharga town, the main road is **Gamel Abd an-Nasser Street.** It becomes the road to Assyut at its northern end and intersects with the road to Dakhla several blocks south near Cinema Hibis. A few blocks farther south, al-Nasser St. intersects with **An-Nabawy al-Mohandis Street,** which connects New and Old Kharga, 3km to the southeast. **Ash-Showla Square,** the cynosure of Old Kharga, is linked to Al-Nabawy St. by Port Said St. Convenient **covered truck-taxis** scurry to and fro between Showla Sq. and the Hotel al-Kharga at the northern end of an-Nasser St. (10pt).

Tourist Information Office: an-Nasser St. (tel. 90 12 05), in an egg-white building in a square with modern statues at the northern end of an-Nasser St., just south of Hotel al-Kharga. Open Sat.-Thurs. 9am-3pm.

Tourist Police: Tel. 90 15 02. Opposite new tourist office building. Open daily 8am-2pm.

Banks: Misr Bank, opposite Cinema Hibis. Exchanges cash and traveler's checks. Open Sun.-Thurs. 8:30am-2pm.

Post Office: Main office on an-Nasser St., behind the Cinema Hibis. Another in Old Kharga's Showla Sq. Both open Sat.-Thurs. 8am-2pm.

Telephone and Telegram Office: Next to the main post office. Intermittent international service. Open 24 hrs. **Telephone code:** 088.

Planes: On Sun. and Wed. from Cairo (dep. 5:30am) via Luxor to Kharga and back to Cairo (dep. 8am). Cairo-Kharga LE30. Airport turn-off is 3km north of town on Assyut Rd., then another 2km southeast; minibus or shared taxi from Showla Sq. (50pt).

Buses: Station in Showla Sq. To Assyut (6 per day 6am-8pm, 4hr., LE5), Cairo (6am, 9am, 7pm, and 8pm, 10hr., morning buses LE15, evening buses LE18), Dakhla (7am and 5pm, 1pm bus from Assyut and Cairo stops in Kharga en route to Dakhla, 3hr., LE4.50, most buses not A/C), and Baris (noon and 2pm, 2hr., LE1.25).

Service Taxis: Opposite bus station. Fairly frequent service to Assyut (LE8). Possible to Baris (LE1.50) or occasionally to Dakhla (LE7). Special (unshared) to Dakhla, total LE40. For local sight-seeing LE25-30 per day. All the sights including Baris LE60-70.

Hospital: Tel. 90 07 77. Main branch off al-Nasser St. south of an-Nabawy St. intersection. Open 24 hrs.

Police: Tel. 90 07 00. In same building as Tourist Police.

Accommodations and Food

The two low budget alternatives in town are passable, if nothing more. The **Waha Hotel** (tel. 90 03 93) dominates the intersection of an-Nasser and an-Nabawy St. The hotel has fairly clean rooms, some with carpeting, but no fans and feeble water pressure on the top two floors. (Singles LE5. Doubles LE8. LE5 for bath.) **New Valley Tourist Homes,** 23 July St. (tel. 90 07 28), is next to a large church, 200m west of an-Nasser St. The turn-off from an-Nasser St. is midway between the tourist office and a mosque; look for the sign facing north on an-Nasser St. Known only as "Metalco" to locals, this hotel's 14 bungalows, surrounded by giant sunflowers, resemble barracks for migrant workers. Simple rooms with semi-private baths. No water 11pm-5am. (LE3.65 per person.) A pricier option is the spotless and airy **Hamadulla** hotel (tel. 90 06 38), 300m south of an-Nasser St., about 1km east of the tourist office. Fans and shower in every room. (Singles LE16.90. Doubles LE27.30. A/C LE2.)

Kharga town serves mediocre oasis cuisine. The *souk* adjacent to Showla Sq. satisfies fresh produce cravings, and a **falafel** stand at the front of the *souk* in Showla Sq. supplies tasty sandwiches (25-30pt). **Restaurant** (no other English name) in Showla Sq. and **Restaurant El Zhra** on an-Nabawy St., about 100m back toward New Kharga from Port Said St., offer the usual Egyptian favorites of chicken, kebab, and *kufte* (LE2-4). Or try the hotels: Metalco serves iron meals if there's at least a handful of hungry tourists around (breakfast LE2, dinner LE3); a calm café beneath the Waha Hotel offers standard inexpensive Egyptian fare for lunch and dinner (LE3-7).

Sights

Welcome, if only temporary, relief from Kharga's New Town can be found in the narrow alleyways of the Old Town. Locally made ceramics, carpets, and souvenir beef entrails and heads are available in the *souk,* which begins at Showla Sq.

Surrounding the market are Kharga's original mud-and-brick homes. Most have fallen prey to neglect as waves of migrant tenants have afforded owners the opportunity to move to modern quarters. Ambling from Showla Sq. on Salah Salim St. you will come upon a large intersection in the market; turn right and then left after 50m under a short thatched roof to explore the passageways of **Sendediya Alley** (ad-Darb ash-Sendediya). This sunken walkway meanders under homes and the enormous wooden lintels that support them.

Kharga's important ruins cluster at the northern end of town. A shared covered taxi will take you as far as the Hotel al-Kharga (possibly farther), whence you can walk to the sites. The **Temple of Hibis,** 2km north of the Hotel al-Kharga and close to the road on the left, was built by the Persian emperor Darius I (about 500 BCE). The temple is one of only a few surviving monuments from the Persian period. The artistic style is noticeably less refined than in pharaonic temples. The temple was later dedicated to the Egyptian god Amon. (Admission free, except for *baksheesh* to the guardians of the key.) Across the road and to the southeast, the **Temple of Nadura** crowns a knoll. Little of the temple is still standing, but the site exudes an exemplary view of the oasis and desert beyond.

The spooky 263 above-ground tombs (also called chapels) of the Christian **Necropolis of al-Bagawat** stand at the desert's edge, 500m past Hibis Temple on the road to Assyut. From the 3rd-8th centuries CE, a sizable Christian community inhabited Kharga; the domed, mud-brick mausolea here are the only surviving traces. The necropolis is visible from the road, and an asphalt path leads to the ticket booth. If you go up the hill along the marked path, you'll come to the **Chapel of Exodus.** Inside, the ceiling mural depicts Pharaoh's Roman-looking army chasing the Jews as they flee from Egypt. Other scenes show Adam and Eve and *ankh*-like crosses. In front of the Chapel of Exodus are the interconnected chapels **#23-25.** Down the hill and up the path on the right stands the **Chapel of Peace (#80).** The interior frescoes of biblical scenes exemplify Coptic painting of the early Alexandrian style. Greek inscriptions identify Adam and Eve, Noah's Ark, and the Virgin Mary. Atop the cemetery's central hill wallow the remains of a 4th-century mud-brick basilica. (Open 8am-5pm. Admission LE10, students LE5.)

The Roads to Baris and to Assyut

If you've got time to spare, take the road along the old 40-day camel trail south to Baris. This legendary caravan route extended from western Sudan all the way to the Egyptian Nile Valley. The numerous ancient ruins in the small oases south of Kharga substantiate the claim that Egypt's current rulers are not the first to take special interest in this remote district.

Vast sandscapes are all that thrive between Kharga and **Khwita Temple,** 17km to the south. The impressive 10m walls of the temple-*cum*-fortress command a hill 2km east of the road. The temple, dedicated to Amon, Mut, and Khonsu, rises above a complex of adobe and sandstone—remnants of a once-flourishing Ptolemaic settlement. At the 25km mark you'll come across shaded **Nasser Wells,** and, farther on, the better-developed **Bulaq Wells.** Both wells offer modern government-run **rest houses** (beds LE3) and hot springs that encourage participants to let off steam. **Zayan Temple,** a mud and brick structure dedicated to Amon, is 5km east of Nasser Wells near the village of Araf, on a road that loops around from the north of Khwita Temple to a point north of Bulaq.

The secluded village of **Baris** (known locally as Paris-on-the-Pond) is 90km south of Kharga. Merchants make a 40-day camel trek from here to the border of Chad to purchase an ingredient used in local soap. It is estimated that each expedition brings the merchant LE20,000 in profit. Think twice before going into business for yourself, however, since only one family in town is privy to the location of vital water wells en route. There is a government **rest house** north of town, but no sign to mark it; look for the yellow, grey, and red buildings in a row perpendicular to the highway, about 0.5km north of the "Bienvenue à Paris/Au Revoir" sign. You can arrange your stay through the manager whose office is in the town on the road to Dush, across from the police station. Half a dozen small kiosks sell soda, mineral water, and canned goods. The blue structure resembling a doghouse sells kebab, *fuul,* and *taamiya* every day except Friday.

Three hundred meters northwest of the rest house stands a public housing complex designed by Hassan Fathy, a modern Egyptian architect who utilizes the cooling properties of traditional oasis architecture in his work. Sponsored by the government, construction was halted during the 1967 war with Israel and was never resumed; the government decided that villagers would not want to live in buildings that resemble tombs.

A recently paved road leads 23km southeast to the **Dush Temple,** which has an overabundance of heat and isolation to recommend it. The temple, originally built for the worship of Serapis and Isis, dates back to the Roman emperors Justinian, Trajan, and Hadrian, and is in the process of being excavated. The sand is slowly parting, revealing a church and a well with clay pipes leading to an underground city. Pottery shards litter the site. All signs indicate that Dush was once a prosperous area, eventually abandoned as a result of well dessication. The temple is the tallest structure for miles around.

The easiest way to get to these sights is to hire a taxi for a day, but that's an expensive proposition (up to LE80) unless you have several people. Hitchhiking can be difficult and dangerous—the road is sparsely traveled. Each day, two buses go to Baris (2hr., LE1.50) and two return. That's comforting. You must plan ahead if you intend to disembark at Khwita, Nasser Wells, or Bulaq Wells. The 2pm bus to Baris sometimes continues on to Dush (2.5hr. from Kharga, LE1.50), but doesn't return until the next morning (6am). Drivers in Baris will make a special return trip to Dush for LE10 (including waiting), but it's sometimes tough to find an ipsemobile. To get public transportation to Zayan Temple, take the 6am bus to Khartoum (LE1.25) and tell the driver where you want to go.

The 240km **road to Assyut** passes through endless miles of monotonous desert that do little to inspire consciousness. The town of Kharga is surrounded by a moonscape of rock outcroppings. As you leave, it becomes evident that the oasis tangos in the middle of a 200 square kilometer depression. The al-Obbur Rest House, replete with water and refreshments, is halfway to Assyut. *Shantih shantih shantih.*

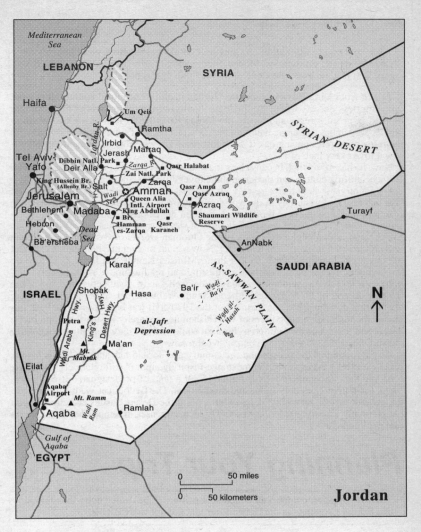

JORDAN (AL-URDUN) الاردن

US $1 = 0.66 Jordanian dinar (JD)
CDN $1 = JD 0.55
UK £1 = JD 1.26
IR £1 = JD 1.19
AUS $1 = JD 0.48
NZ $1 = JD 0.36

JD 1 = US $1.53
JD 1 = CDN $1.81
JD 1 = UK £0.79
JD 1 = IR £0.84
JD 1 = AUS $2.09
JD 1 = NZ $2.81

> For important information on Climate, Useful Organizations and Publications, Documents and Formalities, Money, Safety and Security, Border Crossings, History, and Religion, see the General Introduction to this book.

Take it from King Hussein's mouth: "Jordan itself is a beautiful country. It is wild, with limitless deserts where the Bedouin roam, but the mountains of the north are clothed in green forests, and where the Jordan River flows it is fertile and warm in winter. Jordan has a strange, haunting beauty and a sense of timelessness. Dotted with the ruins of empires once great, it is the last resort of yesterday in the world of tomorrow. I love every inch of it."

Now, he has to say that, because he's the king, of every inch of it. But he has a point. It *is* a beautiful country, and the geographic diversity is fascinating and appealing. Jordan's countryside is indeed strewn with imperial rubble. (And as for that line about "the last resort of yesterday in the world of tomorrow," well, that makes no sense.)

In ancient days, this was the land where John the Baptist baptized Jesus in the famous Jordan River. Once a remote branch of desert trade routes and of the Roman Empire and later a neglected chunk of the Ottoman *vilayet* of Syria, modern Jordan was created by a stroke of a British pen ("Now a giant mixing machine called the West has thrown us together," wrote former Prime Minister Kamel Abu Jaber, "and here we are loving it and hating it, constantly adjusting and readjusting...."). This small kingdom with its commensurate king today finds itself sandwiched between some of the rougher players in a rough neighborhood: Saudi Arabia, Israel, Syria, and Iraq. There are internal divisions, too; the memory of the 1970 civil war between radical Palestinians and conservative supporters of the Hashemite monarchy is still fresh and bitter. The recent trauma of the Gulf crisis brought some of these intra-Jordanian tensions to the surface again, although the country is calm now.

As engrossing as the people and the country are, Jordan has another bonus for the plucky budget traveler: even the most awe-inspiring sight is still relatively undiscovered and thus uncommercialized. Jordan is not a land of predesignated, freshly polished, for-tourist-eyes-only sights and experiences. The Bedouin at Wadi Rum are still the genuine article, unspoiled. Close your eyes at the Desert Castles or Petra and you can be in any century; explore caves and hidden staircases in remote castles as a bona fide explorer.

Planning Your Trip

> If your passport contains an Israeli stamp you will be denied entry into Jordan. See Border Crossings in the General Introduction for more details.

Work, Apprenticeships, and Archeological Digs

It's hard for foreigners to find jobs in Jordan. Formal positions must be arranged before arrival, and you must name your employer to obtain a work visa. **Work permits** can be secured from the Ministry of Labor. **Residence permits** are also required for stays of more than three months.

Some apprenticeships are available for science students through the **International Association for the Exchange of Students with Technical Experience (IAESTE).** (See Alternatives to Tourism in the General Introduction.) This exchange program is open to undergraduate and graduate students. The internship lasts 2-18 months and provides housing, transportation, and stipend.

Volunteers for **archeological digs** are ordinarily in demand. Most archeological journals list digs abroad; *Biblical Archeology* is an excellent source. Also try The Archeological Institute of America (see General Introduction), which publishes the *Archeological Fieldwork Opportunities Bulletin.*

Study

Two Jordanian universities are open to foreign students. The **University of Jordan** (Al-Jubaiha, Amman) has a more liberal atmosphere than the conservative **Yarmouk University** in Irbid. Students interested in Islamic culture, however, may enjoy the more rapid pace of study at Yarmouk. The University of Jordan has a special foreign students program and summer programs which are popular for those seeking colloquial and classical Arabic language instructions. Both schools also guarantee dormitory housing for women. A Jordanian embassy or consulate can provide further information on either school, or you can write to the universities themselves. The Jordanian **Ministry of Education** is P.O. Box 1646, Amman, Jordan (tel. 66 91 81).

Once There

Communication

Postage stamps may be purchased from 7am to 7pm at the downtown post office in Amman and during regular business hours elsewhere. An **air mail letter** to North America costs 320fils, and an aerogramme or postcard is 240fils; the cost to Europe is 240fils and 160fils, respectively. Mail from Jordan to North America and Europe takes one to two weeks. **Packages** may be sent through the parcel office, located behind the downtown post office. **Poste Restante** operates at the downtown post office in Amman and in the larger cities. **American Express offices**, located in Amman and Aqaba, also hold mail.

The **telephone system** is functional and automatic, but often overloaded. The rare pay telephones are particularly erratic and require 50fils regardless of whether or not your call goes through. If you ask shop owners where to find the nearest pay phone, they will probably invite you to use theirs as long as the call is local. Another option is to use a hotel phone, but be sure to inquire about surcharges before doing so. Both push-button phones and rotary dials should be operated slowly for the correct number to register. And prayer never hurts.

International calls can be made in Amman from the telephone center around the corner and up the hill behind the downtown post office on Prince Muhammad St. (See Amman Practical Information.) When calling North America, the first three minutes will cost about JD6.600; you pay at the desk afterwards. In other parts of Jordan, international calls can be made at luxury hotels, where service will be faster, clearer, and more expensive. Late night and early morning are the best times to dial overseas. The easiest option is to use a private phone and reimburse the owner. You can dial directly to the U.S., Europe, and Australia (JD1.540 per minute between 10pm and 8am, JD2.200 otherwise; to the U.S. dial 00 and international code). Although there has been talk of it during the recent Middle East peace talks, neither phone nor mail service extends to Israel. For an international operator, dial 0132. Dial 131 for information on local codes. For other information, dial 121. No **collect calls** can be made from Jordan. AT&T calling cards do work.

The **international phone code** for calling to Jordan is 962.

Telegrams can be sent to North America (180fils per word) from larger post offices, the telephone office, and some hotels.

Currency and Exchange

The **Jordanian dinar (JD)** is a decimal currency, divided into 1000fils. Prices are always labeled in fils, but the usual spoken practice is to call 10fils a piastre (pt). Thus, 500fils will be written as 500fils, but referred to as 50pts. A piastre is also sometimes called a "qirsh" and a 0.5pt is a "t'arifeh." Clear? Bills come in denominations of JD50, 20, 10, 5, 1, and 500fils. Coins are silver for 250fils, 100, 50, and 25, and copper for 10 and 5. Since confusion enriches life, the numerals Westerners call "Arabic" are not used in the Arab world, so it's a good idea to learn the Arab forms (see Arabic Numerals in the Appendix and look at car license plates that are in both scripts). Keep in mind that numbers go from left to right even though Arabic script is written right to left. Denominations on currency are also written in Arabic and modern Arab numerals.

Currency exchange is easy to find in Amman, but harder elsewhere. Bank exchange hours are regularly 9:30am-12:30pm, with some banks opening for an hour or two later in the afternoon. Branches of the national **Housing Bank** are the best bets outside of Amman. Queen Alia Airport has exchange facilities for incoming passengers. A passport is *always* required to change traveler's checks. Credit cards are not accepted except in expensive hotels.

Tipping

Tips are expected in restaurants, unless "service included" appears on the menu. Taxi drivers do not expect tips, but will round off fares to their advantage. If you are with a large sight-seeing group, tip the bus driver about 500fils. A small tip (300-500fils) to the room cleaners and porters in hotels is appropriate.

Business Hours

Jordan's business timetable has been shaped by various natural, religious, and economic forces. The desert sun converts the lunchtime hours into a Mideastern siesta. Most stores and offices open around 8-9:30am, close from 1-3 or 4pm, and open again in the late afternoon. In Amman, retail stores usually close around 8 or 9pm, when the transportation system also dwindles. In some areas, such as Jebel El-Hussein, stores often close as late as 11pm. Banks and government offices retain only a skeleton staff in the afternoon; if you care about getting something done, take advantage of the morning. Government offices are open Sat.-Thurs., 8am-2pm (9:30am-2:30pm during Ramadan).

Friday is a holiday throughout the Muslim world, although it is less scrupulously kept in Amman and Aqaba. Foreign banks and offices generally observe both Friday and Saturday as weekday holidays, though they may keep longer hours during the rest of the week. Museums are closed on Tuesdays. The only reliable schedule for the last few centuries has been the Islamic call to prayer: five times per day, the faithful kneel facing the holy city of Mecca.

Accommodations

Though the Jordanian government has gone to great lengths to establish adequate, regulated accommodations for some tourists, budget travelers have been for the most part left out. Regulated tourist hotels charge prices as high as Jordan's temperatures, though the devaluation of the dinar in recent years has made some regulated prices reasonable. Jordan has no Hostelling International hostels.

Hotels

Jordanian hotels are inspected annually and regulated by the government according to a five-star system. Bargaining is difficult, but hotel owners may be more flexible in the off-season summer months. Fall and spring are the busiest times throughout Jordan, though sunny Aqaba sees the most activity during the winter season. Single women may feel uncomfortable at some of the cheaper hotels, and may on occasion not be admitted. Jordanian law bars unmarried couples from sharing a room. The law is rarely applied to foreign travelers, but if you are asked to split up, console yourself by remembering that in cheap hotels, the price is usually per bed rather than per room.

The Ministry of Tourism provides a comprehensive list of classified hotels and their prices (available at the Ministry's Public Relations Office in Amman). Below is a table of the minimum rates set by the government binding through September 1, 1992.

Class	Singles	Doubles
Five-star deluxe	US$100	US$120
Five-star	$85	$100
Four-star	$70	$90
Three-star	$40	$55
Two-star	$20	$25
One-star	$11	$15

Most hotels add a 10% service charge; ask whether it's included in the quoted price. If business is slow, use this surcharge as a bargaining chip. Some of the cheaper places charge an extra 500fils for a hot shower; many have European-style toilets. The unclassified places usually have clean beds, but toilets and showers can be heinous. Hotel owners may ask to hold your passport for the length of your stay.

Alternate Accommodations

Hotels are rare outside Amman and Aqaba. The primary alternatives elsewhere are the government **Rest Houses** in Petra, Karak, Azraq, Um Qeis, Wadi Rum, and Dibbin National Park. Not all of the Rest Houses have overnight facilities, and rates vary among those Rest Houses that do. If you plan to stay at one, especially in the spring or fall, reserve a room in advance with the **Tourist Investment Department**, P.O. Box 2863, Amman, Jordan (tel. 81 32 43).

Camping

Camping is an option virtually everywhere in the country, although organized facilities are nonexistent. Favorite sites include the beach north of Aqaba, the caves and ledges at Petra (ask for permission first), and Dibbin National Park. In addition, camping is allowed next to most of the government Rest Houses (JD1 per night, plus 10% government tax), and many hostels and hotels will let you camp out on the roof for a small fee. You'll need a sleeping bag for the cool summer nights, and winter evenings can bring sub-freezing temperatures.

And of course, you can always spend a night with the Bedouin. Tea, Arabic coffee, and meals always accompany an invitation, although showers and toilets rarely follow. While the Bedouin won't accept money, a pack of Marlboros will always be appreciated.

Transportation

Most visitors to Jordan stay long enough to see the major sites at Petra and Jerash, yet not long enough to master the transportation system. Organized **bus tours** and private **taxis** can cost JD8 to JD50 per day. The country has a fine **train** system, but only for freight, and the only reliable long-distance **bus company, JETT**, offers a limited number of routes. Fleets of **shared taxis** (called *service* and pronounced "ser-VEES") and collective **minibuses** shuttle between all cities, towns, and villages. Hitchhiking is a common practice among Jordanians, though more so in the north than in the south, where a wagging thumb gesture is often mistaken for a friendly wave.

Travel to the **West Bank** requires a special permit available only at the Ministry of Interior in Amman. (See Border Crossings in the General Introduction as well as Practical Information in Amman for details.) Travel restrictions change with the political winds; check with the Ministry of Tourism or travel agencies for the latest developments.

Taxis and Service

Private taxis, useful mainly in Amman, are yellow and conveniently have "taxi" written in Roman letters on them. Jordanian taxi drivers take their horns seriously, their fares a little less so, and the law not in the least. Insist that the driver use the meter. Most will. A few, however, specialize in ripping off newly arrived tourists; be wary of those driving souped-up, chrome-encrusted Mercedes. The starting fare is 150fils. Drivers may also charge extra (illegally) for large amounts of baggage.

Service taxis are shared taxis, usually white or gray Mercedes with a white sign written in Arabic on their roofs. The front doors have the route and number on them (again in Arabic letters only). *Service* can be hailed en route. Payment takes place whenever the rider feels like it, traditionally just as the cab is on two wheels negotiating an insanely sharp curve. With drivers sneering at speed limits and holding their cars together with such things as tin foil, *service* rides range from entertaining to traumatic. Travel within Amman is generally easier on foot (except when you have to go uphill), but the *service* taxis are invaluable for inter-city travel. There are specific *service* routes in Amman and between the central transport terminals in the larger cities. In Amman, *service* cost 70 to 120fils; a ride may cost up to JD2.910 from Amman to Aqaba. Shared taxis rarely run in the evenings and the long-distance ones may make only two or three trips per day. Schedules are (predictably) unpredictable—they leave when all five seats are occupied. If you get into one alone and want to leave before it's full, you'll have to pay for five.

Service to the northern part of the country depart from the depots in **Abdali Station** (North Station) on King Hussein St. Fares are 470fils to Jerash, 690fils to Ajlun, 850fils to Irbid, 300fils to Salt, and 1150fils to the King Hussein/Allenby Bridge. From Irbid, it's 285fils to Um Qeis and 460fils to al-Hemma. *Service* to the southern part of Jordan leave Amman from **Wahadat Station** (South Station) in Jebel Ashrafieh. The station is several kilometers from downtown Amman between the Abu Darwish Mosque and the Wahadat Refugee Camp. *Service* leave from Wahadat Station to Madaba (330fils), to Karak (JD1.180) down the King's Highway, and to Ma'an (JD1.870) via the newer Desert Highway. At Ma'an you can transfer for service to Wadi Musa (Petra) and Aqaba (475fils and JD1.130, respectively). All of these prices are government regulated.

Buses

Public buses supplement the *service* taxi system in Amman. The inter-city bus network is sparse due to the monopoly granted by the government to the **Jordan Express Tourist Transport (JETT)** company. Private buses, however, cover the most popular routes, and private minibuses travel to more remote areas. Regular service on JETT buses is limited to daily schedules from Amman to Aqaba, Petra, and the King Hussein/Allenby Bridge, from Amman to Damascus, and to Cairo via Aqaba and the Sinai. (See Amman Practical Information for details about schedules and the station.) JETT also sponsors tours to Jerash, Madaba, Petra, Ajlun, and the Desert Castles. For information, call tel. 66 41 46/7. The **Arabella** and **Hijazi** bus companies travel to Jerash and Irbid. Minibuses operate widely as well; destinations are written in Arabic only.

Bus fares are slightly lower than *service* rates, but buses travel more slowly. The JETT luxury coaches cost more than regular buses, but are usually air conditioned, and those running from Amman to Aqaba come with hosts and professional wrestling videos. Do note, however, that you will be charged for each and every "in-flight" bologna and mayo sandwich you eat, regardless of how earnest the attendant seems when handing you one. The buses depart more or less on schedule. Booking ahead is advisable and often necessary. Most towns have one main terminal shared by inter-city buses and *service* taxis; Amman and Irbid have several. In Amman, most buses follow the pattern of *service,* with traffic to the north leaving from Abdali Station and buses to the south leaving from Wahadat Station.

Cars

Some of Jordan's greatest attractions are not served by the public transportation system. For groups of four to six, renting a car can be an affordable and efficient way to reach less accessible sights. With a car, for example, the round-trip to Azraq via four or five desert castles can be done in 8-12 hours. The unsurpassed Kings' Highway route, hardly served by other modes of transportation, can be seen from a private car in another full day. Some rental agencies will even let you return a car from Amman in Aqaba; ask around.

If you can't split the costs, car rental in Jordan will break your budget. Most rental agencies charge from JD22 to JD29 per day, including insurance, plus 45 to 55fils per kilometer. Unlimited mileage deals are cheaper (JD17-20 per day), but you must rent the car for at least a week. (See Amman and Aqaba Practical Information sections for details.) Always ask whether the car has a fire extinguisher. Really. The desert heat warrants it and the police require it. The four-wheel drive cars that companies push are unnecessary except to reach Qasr Touba, south of Azraq. Ordinary cars will do even at Wadi Rum.

Gas costs about 220fils per liter. The law requires seatbelts to be worn (JD5 fine for naughtiness), and speeding tickets can cruise to an exorbitant JD50. Many rental companies require an International Driver's License. **Road accidents** should be reported to the traffic police (tel. 89 63 90), and an **ambulance** can be called at tel. 193.

Hitchhiking

Let's Go does *not* recommend this. *Service* and minibuses are cheap enough to make hitching unnecessary except in remote areas such as along the King's Highway. For those feckless die-hards who ignore this sound advice, rides between small towns (Jordan Valley, Amman environs, Irbid area) are easy to come by. As with anything in the Middle East, be aware that even short waits in the sun can be dangerous; bring lots of water and cover your head with a straw boater.

When hitchhiking within a city (Amman, Irbid, Jerash, Ajlun), empty taxis will pester you with their horns as they careen by. The steady stream of trucks serving the port facilities compensates, with many drivers eager for company on their long trans-Jordan hauls.

We repeat: *Let's Go* does *not* recommend hitchhiking. Women especially should *never* hitchhike alone.

Dress and Etiquette

Jordan is predominantly Muslim and socially conservative, making modest dress a necessity. You will not be arrested, but inappropriate dress will alienate you from the very people you have come to meet. The same modesty is required of both men and women. The code is simple: Do not wear shorts. Your pants should come down to at least mid-shin (women may wear pants). Shirts should cover the shoulders and upper arms. Women should wear head scarves in mosques. Feet can be exposed freely. The exception to these rules is hedonistic Aqaba, where both men and women can wear shorts.

Non-Muslims should not enter mosques during prayers, which occur five times a day.

Life in Jordan

Government and Politics

After about ten minutes in Jordan, you'll notice pictures of a little bald man with a smooth smile everywhere you look. Refrain from jokes; he's the king, and you are in his kingdom. Officially known as the Hashemite Kingdom of Jordan (that's what H.K. stands for), Jordan is very much the fiefdom of little Hussein ibn Talal. Jordan was a 1921 gift from Britain to the Hashemite royal family (for details see History in the General Introduction), who are not shy about trumpeting their status as *sharifs*—that is, they trace their lineage directly to the Prophet. King Hussein has ruled since 1953. He divorced his first two queens, Dina and Muna al-Hussein (a Briton who changed her name from Antoinette Gardiner); his third, Alia (a Palestinian), died in a plane crash. "It was the Amman Go-Kart Club that really brought us together more informally," the king sighed about Muna. The current queen, Noor, was born Lisa Halaby, an American and a graduate of Princeton. Hussein's brother Crown Prince Hassan serves as advisor and heir to the throne. Educated in Britain, King Hussein is generally moderate and pro-Western, but, as Palestinians will tell you remembering their 20,000 dead from the 1970 civil war, he can be brutal if his throne is at stake. Above all, he is a slippery and brilliant politician; these skills have kept him alive through assassination attempts and several wars. (Luck has also been a factor; the same bullets that killed his grandfather, King Abdallah, bounced off a medal on the young Hussein's chest.) After Kim Il Sung of North Korea, Hussein is the longest-ruling head of state in the world.

Undeniably, tension between Israel and Jordan runs deep; Jordan has never recognized Israel, and despite recent peace overtures and a long record of clandestine Hashemite negotiations with Israeli leaders, the two countries technically remain at war. Most of the Jordanian population is of Palestinian descent, and the *intifada* (Palestinian uprising) across the river in the West Bank and Gaza has aggravated internal disputes. In the summer of 1988, King Hussein cut all ties with the West Bank, allowing the Jordanian government to focus its efforts on relieving economic ills and East Bank tensions; recently, Amman has started reextending its influence back into the West Bank. In April 1989, the country witnessed violent street riots protesting government price hikes.

King Hussein's rule is a constant balancing act in the face of such pressures. He has accommodated and integrated his Palestinian subjects over the years, opening his cabinet to them as well as to the Bedouin that are the bedrock of the monarchy's support. Jordan is the only Arab country that will offer Palestinians citizenship. The conservative Hashemites have faced opposition from pan-Arabists, Nasserists, radical Palestinian nationalists, and, most recently, Islamists organized in the Muslim Brotherhood. An attempt at democratic reform didn't turn out as the monarchy had hoped; in Jordan's first general elections in 22 years, held in November 1989, Islamists won almost half the seats in parliament. A rising tide of pan-Arabism and frustration with Western power led many Jordanians to support Saddam Hussein in the Gulf War, and thus pushed the king to do so too. The monarchy, always flexible, has been reingratiating itself with the West ever since.

A flood of refugees into Jordan from Kuwait and Iraq following the 1991 Gulf War has begun to disrupt the usually placid Jordanian lifestyle. Jordan's cities are now overcrowded, and crime rates are on the rise. Travelers are advised not to wander through the country alone and should **consult their embassy** or a reputable international newspaper for up-to-the-minute information on the political situation.

Economy

Unlike its Arab neighbors, Jordan is blessed with neither oil reserves nor abundant natural resources. Because of this, Jordan remains dependent upon Arab and American financial aid. Remittances from Jordanian workers in the Gulf states have traditionally constituted another important supplement to the Jordanian economy. With the outbreak of the Iran-Iraq War in 1980, Iraq became a major importer of Jordanian goods and services and the economy boomed. Recently, though, Jordan's economy has been ailing. With a 2-3% annual growth rate, the country's economy cannot keep pace with its burgeoning population. In the late 1980s, when Iraq began threatening not to pay its war debts, Jordanian exporters held an ugly mountain of worthless Iraqi IOUs.

In April 1989, following steep government-imposed price hikes on gasoline and other goods, Jordanians took to the streets in protest until King Hussein fired Prime Minister Zaid Rifai and the cabinet. Stability soon returned, but the monarchy was sobered and remains jittery.

On top of that, the 1990-91 Persian Gulf crisis dealt a devastating blow to Jordan's economy. In addition to the complex task of absorbing and caring for tens of thousands of refugees fleeing the turmoil, Jordan's decision to side with Iraq cost the country dearly. The United States, along with Saudi Arabia and the other Gulf countries, suspended most aid to Jordan. Furthermore, Palestinian and Jordanian workers in the Gulf were sent home and largely replaced by Egyptians, whose government the Saudis found to be more politically correct. 320,000 of these unhappy Jordanians are now crowded into the cities, often in miserable conditions. Among this group, unemployment is 80%. Unemployment in the general population, once alarming at 15-20%, may have hit 25-30%. But Washington, by now less miffed over Jordan's pro-Iraq tilt, has hinted none too subtly that it may reward Jordanian cooperation in the Arab-Israeli peace process by once again lending a hand.

Festivals and Holidays

The most important festivals of the year are Islamic celebrations, including the holy month of **Ramadan** (approx. Feb. 22-March 24 in 1993) and the three-day **Eid al-Adha** (Feast of Sacrifice, May 31 in 1993). Jordan's other major holidays are **New Year's Day, Mawlid an-Nabi** (Muhammad's Birthday, Sept. 10), the feast of **Isra Mi'raj** (Jan. 19, commemorating Muhammad's Night Journey from Mecca to Jerusalem), **Arab Revolution and Army Day** (June 10, marking the 1916 Arab Revolt against Ottoman rule), **Labor Day** (May 1), **Independence Day** (May 25), and, of course, King Hussein's **Accession Day** (Aug. 11) and **Birthday** (Nov. 14). Muslim holidays are determined according to the lunar calendar and thus differ every year. Expect difficulties in making international flights between Muslim countries during Ramadan and Eid al-Adha. Note also that Muslims traditionally count years beginning with the Hijra, or Muhammad's emigration from Mecca to Medina. Therefore, 1993 is 1413 AH in the Muslim world. The Western calendar is used in daily life. Government offices and banks close on national holidays.

For the Christian community, the **Easter Celebrations** (some following the Gregorian calendar, others the Julian) are the most spectacular of the year. **Christmas** is a smaller feast, especially for the Coptic and Abyssinian Churches, which celebrate the holiday during the second week of January rather than on December 25.

The two-week **Jerash Festival** is held every year during July or August. Amidst brilliantly illuminated Roman ruins and inside ancient amphitheaters, visitors witness performances by international artists. For more information, contact the **Jerash Festival Office** in Amman (tel. 67 51 98).

Literature

The Arabic language is shared by many nations, and Arabic literature from these countries serves the whole of the Arab world. The Jordanian region itself has a long tradition of prose: the oldest example of a Semitic script, the Mesha Stele, was found in Karak. Unfortunately, few Jordanian works are translated into other languages and thus remain inaccessible to most foreigners.

Among English travel accounts, C. M. Doughty's *Arabia Deserta* and Wilfred Thesiger's more recent *Arabian Sands* are powerful adventure stories inspired by a romanticized version of Bedouin lifestyle. T.E. Lawrence's *Seven Pillars of Wisdom* contains vivid descriptions of the battles fought and the territory explored during the Arab Revolt of 1916; even if you don't reach Wadi Rum in the Jordanian desert, see *Lawrence of Arabia* on the big screen. King Abdallah's two-volume *Memoirs*, and King Hussein's *Uneasy Lies the Head*, are self-serving but dispel once and for all the myth that it's good to be the king. The Arab Legion chief of the 1940s and '50s, John Bagot Glubb (Glubb Pasha), wrote *A Soldier With the Arabs* and several books based on his life. A little less adventurous but more erudite is Jonathan Raban's *Arabia: A Journey through the Labyrinth.* Gertrude Bell, one of the first Western female travelers in the region, writes of her travels through Jordan and Syria in *The Desert and the Sown.*

For the archeologically and historically inclined there are G.L. Harding's *Antiquities of Jordan* and Julian Huxley's *From an Antique Land.* Ian Browning's *Petra* is wonderfully comprehensive. Finally, Agatha Christie's *Argument with Death* is a light introduction to the mesmerizing power of Petra.

The Arts

Both the Jordanian government and private groups are currently taking measures to promote and foster the arts. Like that of other countries of the Arab world, Jordanian art is an expression of Arab and often Muslim identity. But Jordanians are not sticklers for the traditional; contemporary artists have many more Western tendencies and use art as an outlet for personal as well as cultural expression. Modernity is eroding the traditional Islamic taboo against the portrayal of animate objects. Jordan's architecture, painting, and sculpture have all developed substantially in this century.

When it comes to their folk art, Jordanians do abide by tradition. Techniques developed over centuries make these people skillful weavers of wool and goat-hair rugs and tapestries. Leather handicrafts, pottery, ceramics, and coral curios also belong to the family of mastered Jordanian folk art. It is wood-carving, though, that is the Jordanian specialty. Artists can do beautiful carvings of your name right on the street, for an appropriate fee, naturally. You will find most of these crafts sold proudly on the streets of Jordan.

Popular Culture

Homesick Yankees who aren't sticklers for highbrow culture can look for Bart Simpson to brighten their day or *Empty Nest* to remind them of those Saturday nights in front of the TV. These and other popular American shows appear on Jordanian television with Arabic subtitles. More authentic Jordanian programming includes music videos and disco dance extravaganzas. Much of the pop music in Jordan is Egyptian; listen for traditional Arabic sounds through the cacophony of not-quite-Western sounds. Jordanian chintz runs to ubiquitous pictures of the king, often forcing a constipated grin. Jordanians do, however, have their own traditional expressions of pop culture, most notably a strong oral tradition of stories, songs, and ballads. Villagers often have their own individualized songs commemorating births, circumcisions, weddings, funerals, and planting. Several Cossack dances, including a sword dance that has to be seen to be believed, are popular in Jordan, as are the *dabkeh*, dances performed to the resonating rhythm of feet pounding on the floor.

Food

Jordanian cuisine has evolved through centuries of Bedouin cooking. The national dish, *mensaf,* ideally consists of 8-10 kilos of rice on a tray at least a meter across, topped with pinenuts and the stew of an entire lamb or goat. The Bedouin still serve the head of the lamb on top, reserving the prize delicacies—eyes and tongue—for speechless and visually jaded guests. The right hand is used to ball the rice, and the flat bread to pull off chunks of meat and dip them into the *jamid* (dried flour and milk).

Most other dishes include the main ingredients of *mensaf.* Traditional dinners, served between 2-3pm, are rarely as spicy as those in other Arab countries. Popular dinners are *musukhan*—boiled chicken with olive oil and onions and a delicious spice called *sumac,* served with *khoubz* (bread)—and *mahshi,* a tray of vine leaves, squash, or eggplant stuffed with mincemeat, rice, and onions. *Mezze,* loosely translated as "hors d'oeuvres," encompasses a wide range of dishes which include hummus with olive oil, *mutabal* (an eggplant dip), *labneh* (thickened yogurt), cucumbers, tomatoes, and pickles. Supper is usually a smaller meal; *fuul* (pulped fava beans in olive oil scooped up with bread, and pronounced "fool") is a standard breakfast.

At restaurants, if the uninitiated can read the menu, you can't afford the food. Omnipresent *fuul* is always a cheap option. Kebabs and *shwarma* are skewered lamb or chicken. Fresh *ka'ik,* a bread ring with sesame seeds, is a street favorite, and you'll see long lines at the market for *knaffeh,* a delicious creamy confection made of soft cheese and wheat.

Water in Amman is piped in from Azraq oasis and the Euphrates River in Iraq. Although certainly potable, it is hardly pure. Toting bottled water (260fils, more if it's cold) or iodine tablets, like extra molars, is a sign of wisdom. As the desert recedes, more vegetables venture into the country's diet, but raw salads and fruits can be problematic if not washed properly—fruits and vegetables that can be peeled are best.

Amman عمان

Like Rome, Amman is built on seven hills, called *jebels.* Unlike Rome, it *was* built in a day—almost. Just before 1948, Amman was a tiny Jordanian village, much diminished from its former status as the Ammonite capital in biblical times and the city of Philadelphia in Roman times. But Amman's population exploded when the Arab-Israeli wars of 1948 and 1967 brought waves of Palestinian refugees. Now most Palestinians in Jordan live in and around Amman, making Amman demographically the world's largest Palestinian city. Egyptian workers, originally attracted by the dinar's strength and employment opportunities in Amman, composed an important segment of the city's population. Though the Jordanian economy isn't what it once was, Amman still bustles with activity. Gulf Arabs in town on business, burly truck drivers, and frustrated Palestinians trying to obtain visas home give Amman a peculiarly gripping character.

Amman is a convenient base from which to explore the rest of Jordan. Many of Jordan's best sights are daytrips from here. In addition to being the country's transportation hub, Amman offers cheap accommodations, government services, and the embassies or consulates of the countries you may plan to visit next. But don't sacrifice time here that could be better spent marveling at Petra, Jerash, and Jordan's rural landscapes.

Orientation

The downtown district of Amman, called **al-Balad** in Arabic, lies in a valley neatly framed by several *jebels.* Streets from the city's large western districts pour off the *jebels* into **King Faisal Street,** the perpetually crowded heart of the downtown commercial communities. Faisal St. runs into the **al-Husseini Mosque,** the center of modern Amman. Several blocks southwest is the market; to the northeast lie the graceful **Roman Amphitheater** and the new piazza.

The steep hills of Amman encircle the downtown area. Though distances between *jebels* appear short on a map, traversing these slopes is a hack hiker's nightmare. **Jebel Amman,** along whose summit you can see the neon signatures of budget-breaking luxury hotels, is the governmental and diplomatic core of the city. Amman's eight **numbered traffic circles** follow a line leading westward out of town; traffic circles beyond Fourth Circle have been replaced by busy intersections that are still called "circles." From Seventh Circle, traffic heads south to Queen Alia International Airport and the Desert Highway (Aqaba 335km), to the Kings' Highway via Madaba (35km; Karak 125km; Petra 260km), and via Na'ur to the Dead Sea and to Jerusalem (90km). From the Eighth Circle, you can continue west to Wadi Seer, or head north to Jerash (50km). From the Ninth Circle, there are no mirrors, there is no exit.

To the northwest of Jebel Amman slopes the suburb of **Shmeisani,** with its numerous luxury hotels. **Jebel al-Weibdeh,** across the wadi to the north of Jebel Amman, is a quiet residential district. Its northern slope descends to **King Hussein Street,** where the JETT and Abdali (north) Bus Stations have attracted a swarm of food stands and busy hotels. Beside Abdali Station, the blue dome and octagonal minaret of the enormous new **King Abdallah Mosque** are visible from the surrounding jebels. Opposite the mosque stands the **National Parliament** building. **Jebel Hussein,** up the slope to the northeast, is residential as far as its northern boundary at the **Ministry of Interior Circle** (officially known as Jamal Abd an-Nasser Square). Permits to visit the West Bank are issued here. From this circle, traffic heads northwest to Jerash (50km).

Across from the Roman Theater towers rocky **Jebel Qala'a** (Citadel Hill), where the Archeological Museum sits amidst unearthed remains of Roman and Umayyad palaces, temples, and hilltop fortifications. To the south, in the direction of the airport, rises **Jebel Ashrafieh;** its ornate Abu Darwish Mosque can be seen above the Wahadat (south) Bus Station and the Wahadat Palestinian refugee camp. Beyond the other residential *jebels,* the city recedes into the surrounding desert sands.

The names of the streets in downtown Amman are generally preserved in the collective memory of its residents rather than in anything so gauche as signs. Most streets elsewhere are clearly marked in English. In general, however, no one refers to street names. You will need to learn some of the landmarks to avoid unnecessarily long cab rides.

Getting Around

Buses and *service* taxis to the north central and northwestern parts of the country, including the Jordan Valley, leave from **Abdali Bus Station** on King Hussein St. on Jebel al-Weibdeh. **Hashemi Street Station,** near the Roman amphitheater, launches traffic to the northeast, including Zarqa, Mafraq, and points east of Irbid. Traffic to and from the south is based at **Wahadat Station** near the Abu Darwish Mosque on Jebel Ashrafieh.

To reach locations within the city or to find the departure point for buses and *service,* ask a downtown shopkeeper—at a minimum, you'll be pointed in the right direction, and quite possibly you'll be escorted there. You can flag buses and *service* anywhere along their routes, but expect to wait quite a while before a vehicle with space for another biped creature stops. Public transportation stops about 8-9pm, and a couple of hours earlier than that on Fridays; after that, walking is the only alternative to the expensive regular taxis. These yellow, metered cabs prowl the streets in search of fares until 11pm, sometimes later. Cabs charge 150fils plus about 100fils per kilometer. The approximate cost to travel from downtown to Third Circle, or from Third to Sixth Circle, is 500fils. The trip from downtown to Abdali costs around 350fils. A taxi between the two bus/*service* stations (Abdali and Wahadat) should cost 800fils. (See Transportation in the Jordan Introduction.)

Although *service* are the best bet when leaving Amman, within Amman **buses** travel from the downtown area and cost about 100fils for city trips, slightly more to areas

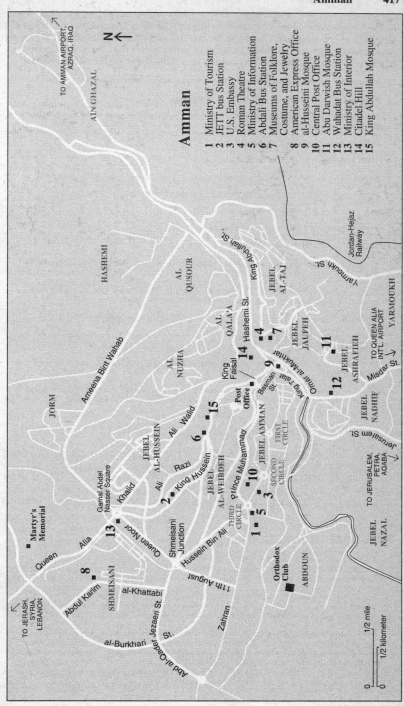

Amman

1 Ministry of Tourism
2 JETT bus Station
3 U.S. Embassy
4 Roman Theatre
5 Ministry of Information
6 Abdali Bus Station
7 Museums of Folklore,
   Costume, and Jewelry
8 American Express Office
9 al-Husseini Mosque
10 Central Post Office
11 Abu Darwish Mosque
12 Wahadat Bus Station
13 Ministry of Interior
14 Citadel Hill
15 King Abdullah Mosque

just outside Amman. Flag any bus traveling in your direction and ask the driver if it stops where you want to go, or ask at the bus station which bus you should get on. Be sure to have exact change. Buses going on different routes may display the same number, so what worked one time may not the next. Still, these are the alleged routes:

#10 and 53: Travel to the university and the American and British Institutes.

#10 and 59: Go to the Sports City (north of Shmeisani).

#21, 23, and 24: Pass the Armenian Quarter and the Abu Darwish Mosque on the way to Wahadat Station.

#31B: Runs to Queen Alia Airport.

#39: Climbs Jebel Amman to the numbered circles.

#41-45: Head directly to Third Circle before passing Fourth, Fifth, Sixth, and Seventh Circles.

#53-61: Pass Abdali Station, the JETT offices, and the Ministry of Interior Circle.

#61: Travels on Jebel Hussein to Duwar Firas.

#61-63A: Pass the Archeological Museum on the Citadel.

The following are the *service* routes in Amman:

#1: Travels on Jebel Amman between Center City and Third Circle, passing First and Second Circles (70fils).

#2: Starts downtown on Basman St. (look for the Basman Theater) and travels on Jebel Amman to Malik Abd Ribiya St. between Second and Third Circles (70fils).

#3: Starts downtown on Kureisha St. and travels on Jebel Amman to Fourth Circle (80fils).

#4: Runs from Basman St. to al-Amaneh Circle and gardens, passing near all points of interest on Jebel Weibdeh (70fils).

#5: From Basman St., travels up Jebel Weibdeh to Queen Alia Institute, just uphill from Abdali Station (70fils).

#6: Starts downtown at terminus on Malik Razi St. (better known as Cinema al-Hussein St.) then travels along Kings Faisal and Hussein St. to Jamal 'Abd an-Nasser Circle, passing Abdali and JETT Stations (80fils).

#7: Starts by Cinema al-Hussein St. and runs past Abdali Station to Shmeisani near the Ambassador Hotel and the Gallery Alia (80fils).

Service and minibuses to Wahadat Station start at Kureisha St. (also called Sakfi Seil) near Petra Bank and pass near Abu Darwish Mosque on Jebel Ashrafieh. *Service* directly to Wahadat Station from Abdali costs 120fils. Another route starts at Shabsough St. near the Gold Market in Center City, passing Abdali Station and Jebel Hussein to Ministry of Interior Circle (80fils). *Service* between here and Third Circle cost 70fils.

Practical Information

Ministry of Tourism: P.O. Box 224 (tel. 64 23 11). From Third Circle on Jebel Amman, walk past the somewhat wary guard in front of the American Cultural Center and take your first right. Distributes free maps, hotel price lists, and other tourist literature. Open Sat.-Thurs. 8am-2pm.

Ministry of Interior, on the southwest side of Ministry of the Interior Circle near the Marriot Hotel, Jebel Hussein (tel. 66 31 11). Issues free permits to visit the West Bank and Jerusalem. Bring two photos and your passport at least three days before your trip. Open Sat.-Thurs. 8am-2pm.

Banks and Currency Exchange: Banking hours are ordinarily Sat.-Thurs. 9:30am-12:30pm, although foreign banks sometimes close later. Authorized money changers are open daily, usually late into the evening, and offer roughly the same exchange rates as banks. You may have to wait 20-30 min. to get cash for your travelers' checks. Bring your passport. The nationwide **Housing Bank** is your best bet in small towns. The **Industrial Development Bank** by the Second Circle on Jebel Amman (tel. 64 22 16) offers all banking services.

American Express: International Traders, King Hussein St , P.O. Box 408 (tel. 66 10 14/5) in Shmeisani, opposite the Ambassador Hotel. Holds mail and can obtain visas at no charge for card-holders. Open Sat.-Thurs. 8am-1pm and 3-6pm.

Downtown Post Office: Prince Muhammad St., at the bottom of the staircase where the *service* to Center City let you off. Stamps and **Poste Restante** open Sat.-Thurs. 7am-7pm, Fri. 7:30am-1pm. Cables can be sent from this office. For **international registered express mail,** go to inter-national office (tel. 68 81 90) next to central post office (between Jebel al-Hussein and Shmei-sani). Call and ask for directions. Open Sat.-Thurs. 7:30am-7pm, Fri. and holidays 8am-4pm.

Telephone Office: Omar al-Khayyam St. Walking uphill from the downtown post office, turn right into the alley past the red phone booths and walk up the stairs at the end of the alley. At the top of the stairs, turn right. Telephone office will be halfway down the hill on your right. Open daily 7:30am-midnight. Rate for 3 minutes to the U.S. JD6.600, to Great Britain JD5.445. 30% cheaper after 10pm. Overseas calls can be made from any post office, from most hotels at any time for a surcharge, or by dialing directly from a friend's private phone and reimbursing the lucky Jor-danian. For telephone and postal information, dial 121. Neither phone calls nor mail to Israel are possible without going through third parties in the U.S. or Europe. **Telephone code: 06.**

Airport: Queen Alia International Airport, 35km south of Amman. Buses leave from the air-port for Abdali Bus Station every 30 min. (5:30am-9pm, 500fils). Bank and tourist office (tel. (08) 53 070; bank open 24 hrs.) in the airport. Jordanian visas available at the airport upon arrival, but good for only a month. There is a JD10 exit fee.

Buses: JETT Bus Station, King Hussein St. (tel. 66 41 46), 600m uphill from Abdali Station. Air-conditioned buses to King Hussein/Allenby Bridge (Sun.-Fri. 6:30am, JD5.500); to Petra (6:30am, JD5.000; round-trip tour including guide, horse, and lunch, JD25.500); to Aqaba (7am, 9am, 10am, 2:30pm, 3:30pm, 4pm, JD3.500). Also to Damascus (7:30am, 3pm, JD4.500); to Cairo (8am, US$46); to Baghdad (10am, 11am, JD12.000 plus JD4.000 departure tax). Reserve at least one day in advance, especially to bridge, Aqaba, and Petra. Office open daily 8am-6pm. **Minibuses** to Jordanian towns from various points. (See Transportation in Jordan Introduction.)

Service **Taxis:** To Jordanian towns and King Hussein/Allenby Bridge from Abdali and Wahadat Bus Stations. (See Transportation in Jordan Introduction.)

Car Rental: Many possibilities, but most very expensive. Local agencies have the best deals. *Your Guide to Amman* lists numerous specials. International drivers license is often required. Try **Bisharat Travel Corporation** next to the Intercontinental Hotel or **Dirani Rent-a-Car** (tel. 66 06 01), across from Jabri in Shmeisani. Another rental agency is attached to the **Marriott Hotel.** Age restrictions vary from birth to 21 years of age.

English Bookstores: University Bookstore (tel. 63 63 39), Jebel Weibdeh, near Khalaf Circle. Books on the archeology of Jordan. Open 8am-7pm. **Amman Bookstore,** on Prince Muhammad St., near Third Circle, and the more expensive bookstores in the **Marriott** and **Intercontinental** hotels carry books on the Middle East as well as maps and guides to Jordan's sights. The Inter-continental also has many works on Palestinians. **InterBooks,** near the Second Circle on Zahran St., sells local and foreign newspapers and magazines in English.

Publications: *The Jordan Times* lists useful telephone numbers, cultural events in Amman, and current government prices for fruits and vegetables (helpful for bargaining in the market). The weekly *Jerusalem Star* lists cultural events. *Your Guide to Amman,* published monthly and avail-able free at larger hotels and travel agencies, has more complete listings.

Department of Antiquities: From Third Circle, walk up Zahran St. Turn left at the traffic light, then immediately right (tel. 64 44 82). Research office and library with information on the latest digs. Distributes books and detailed maps of the country's 3 regions (Amman/Irbid, Karak, and Ma'an), highlighting archeological sites. Open Sat.-Thurs. 8am-2pm.

Friends of Archeology: P.O. Box 2440. A private local organization sponsoring weekly field trips to historical sites. Travelers can hitch a ride with some trips. Call American Center for Ori-ental Research (tel. 84 61 17), or read their newsletter posted at cultural centers. Free field trips usually leave from Department of Antiquities.

American Cultural Center: Jebel Amman just south of the Third Circle (tel. 64 15 20). Free American films every Sun. and Thurs. Occasional lectures on Jordan, Aseel Rabie, or the dialec-tics of both. Library open Sun., Tues., Thurs. 8am-7pm, Mon. and Wed. 8am-5pm.

British Council: Rainbow St. (tel. 63 61 47). From First Circle walk 200m downhill along the right-hand tine of the fork; it's on the right. Sponsors films and lectures in the winter on why Jor-danians speak such proper English. Library (with A/C) open Sat.-Wed. 8am-1:45pm and 3:30-6:30pm, Thurs. 8am-1:45pm.

Laundry: Al-Jamm'a Laundry (tel. 84 78 57), on your first right heading away from the city past the main gate of Jordan University. Wash and dry JD2. Hotels often have reasonably priced services, and in the cheapest places you might be able to do your laundry for free, or at least bargain.

Pharmacies: The *Jordan Times* lists all-night pharmacies. In the downtown area: **As-Salam** (tel. 63 67 30) or **Nayroukh** (tel. 61 47 24). Jebel Hussein: **Firas** (tel. 66 19 12). Near Wihadat: **Ibn Al-Nafees** (tel. 74 51 05) or **Deema** (tel. 78 70 40). Call for directions.

Emergency: Call the American Embassy 24-hr. hotline (tel. 64 43 71) and ask them to call the police or ambulance. **Medical Emergencies:** Tel. 63 03 41, 62 11 11, or 63 77 77. **Ambulance:** Tel. 193. **Traffic Accidents:** Tel. 89 63 90. *Your Guide to Amman* contains list of doctors and hospitals. **Police:** Tel. 192 or 62 11 11.

Diplomatic Missions

United States: Zahran St., (tel. 64 43 71), halfway between the Second and Third Circles on Jebel Amman, across from the Intercontinental Hotel. Not particularly helpful for West Bank permits. Consular division open Sun.-Thurs. 9am-3pm. Observes all Jordanian and most American holidays.

Canada: in Shmeisani near the Petra Bank (tel. 66 61 24). Open Sun.-Thurs. 8am-4pm.

Britain: Abd al-Damascus St., (tel. 82 31 00), near the Orthodox Club in Abdoun. Consular division open Sun.-Thurs. 8:30am-noon.

Australia: Fourth Circle on Jebel Amman (tel. 67 32 46). Helpful with foreign visas. Open Sun.-Thurs. 8am-2:30pm. Open for inquiries Mon., Wed. 9am-noon.

Egypt: Jebel Amman (tel. 62 95 26). Consulate is at the First Circle, across from the Iraqi embassy. Same day visas: bring a photo, JD12, and come before noon. Americans get can visas at the airport upon arrival. Open Sat.-Thurs. 9am-3pm.

Iraq: Between First and Second Circle on Jebel Amman (tel. 62 31 75). Neither British nor American citizens are allowed to visit Iraq.

Lebanon: Second Circle on Jebel Amman (tel. 64 13 81). Visas require a letter from your embassy. Consular hours 8-10am.

Syria: Jebel Amman, up from Third Circle toward the Holiday Inn (tel. 64 19 35). Take a left at the 5-way intersection. For a visa bring one photo and JD9.750 for Americans, JD37.500 for British nationals. You must have a Jordanian entry stamp on your passport and no evidence of visits to the West Bank or Israel. Open for visas Sun.-Thurs. 9-11am.

Accommodations

Many clean and reputable hotels are located near the **Abdali Bus Station** in Jebel Weibdeh. Close to the city center and convenient for transport out of Amman, this is also the safest area for female budget travelers. Just beyond Jebel Weibdeh lies the opulent **Shmeisani** district with a few reasonably priced accommodations.

The **city center,** on the other hand, is overgrown with small, seedy hotels. Since every block has three or four hell-holes and every alley at least one, look carefully so as not to get burned. Most of these are not too clean, rattle with each passing truck, and may still be full of Iraqis in no hurry to return home. But the hotels *are* cheap: singles usually JD3, doubles JD5. (Feel free to bargain.) Women alone should definitely avoid staying in this area. Establishments of similar quality cluster near the **Wahadat Bus Station.**

Official hotel prices are set by the government and posted conspicuously at each hotel. During the summer and other slow times it's often possible to bargain. In the dirt cheapest places—those catering mostly to foreign workers—governmental edicts reflect the pipe dreams of local proprietors rather than reality. And although beds with clean sheets are easy to find, toilet paper and decent washing facilities are definitely not. Most places will keep your passport until your bill is paid.

Near Abdali Station

Remal Hotel, 4 Sa'id Bin al-Harith St. (tel 63 06 70, fax 61 55 85). From Abdali, walk up the hill next to the police station; the hotel's on your right. Newly renovated, the Remal boasts bright, clean, freshly-painted rooms. Singles JD8.500. Doubles JD10.500.

Canary Hotel, Jebel Weibdeh (tel. 63 83 53), on Karmaly St. near Terra Sancta College. From Abdali, walk 1.5 blocks downhill to the fork at the base of Abdali, bear right, and take the first right after the fork. Convivial, family-like atmosphere, complete with backgammon and name-sake canaries on the patio out front. Singles JD14.000. Doubles JD17.500.

Sunrise Hotel, King Hussein St. (tel. 62 18 41), on the left of Abdali as you face downhill. Under renovation, but functional. Mirrors, plants, big windows on every landing. Singles JD8.500. Doubles JD10.500.

Al-Monzer Hotel, King Hussein St. (tel. 63 94 69), not far from the Sunrise. Spacious, bare rooms with ceiling fans. Comfortable lobby. Singles JD8.500. Doubles JD10.500.

City Center/Al-Husseini Mosque Area

Cliff Hotel, King Faisal St. (tel. 62 42 73), at the top of the street across from the "Seiko" fork, at the base of King Hussein St. On the 3rd floor. One of the most popular budget places in Amman. Cheap and clean, with an excellent view of the café scene. Sinks in each room and reliable luggage storage. Manager Abu Suleiman has more information than the Ministry of Tourism and will write out taxi directions in Arabic. Singles JD3. Doubles JD5. Hot shower 500fils, laundry free. Often full.

Bader Hotel, Prince Muhammad St. (tel. 63 76 02), up the alley opposite the Cliff Hotel on King Faisal St., a few blocks down from post office. Quiet, plain, and extremely popular. Small valuables can be locked up for free. Singles JD5.500. Doubles JD7.500.

Palace Hotel, King Faisal St. (tel. 62 43 27), 1.5 blocks from al-Husseini Mosque. Turn left into a small alley with clothing stores; entrance on left. Roman pillar decor and mandatory glittery picture of King Hussein hanging over the desk. Singles JD8.500, some without bathrooms. Doubles JD10.500.

Metro Hotel, King Hussein St. (tel. 63 91 91), in the alley beside the blue and yellow Housing Bank. Peeling brown wallpaper, hefty rooms with sinks, cozy nook on the roof. Both pit toilets and regular ones; rudimentary showers. You get what you pay for. Singles JD3. Doubles JD5. Shower 500fils.

Haifa Hotel, King Faisal St., near the large Arab Bank. Traditionally a good bet, but closed for renovations during summer 1992. Scheduled to open sometime in early 1993.

Outlying Districts

Nefertiti Hotel, 26 al-Jahiz St. (tel. 60 38 65), in Shmeisani off 11th of August St. Bright rooms and soft beds. Checkout at noon. Singles JD8.500. Doubles JD10.500. Service charge 10%.

American Center for Oriental Research (tel. 84 61 17), across from Jordan University and up the hill from the 7-Up billboard. Home base for field workers in Jordan: English and archeology spoken here. Southwestern-style lobby, cozy library. Arabic-American lunch often includes brownies and pecan pie. Private showers (free) and laundry (US$4-5 per load). Students US$20, visitors US$24. Discounts for affiliates. Reservations recommended. Monthly rates available.

Food

Amman's edibles combine the city's Bedouin and Palestinian heritages. The better sit-down restaurants cluster near Third Circle and in Shmeisani; these places usually add a 10% service charge to the bill. Endless varieties of street food are cheap and plentiful, but your stomach's safest on the main thoroughfares.

Shwarma is always available for about 200fils, but the most succulent stuff comes from the stands on Prince Muhammad St. just downhill from Third Circle, and on the Second Circle near the Lebanese Embassy. Falafel and corn on the cob go for 100fils and 250fils respectively. Common sides include hummus plates and salads for 250-350fils.

Bread is, well, a staple. *Khoubz* (flat-bread), is the most convenient; *ka'ik* (sesame rings), the most tasty. Both are available at almost any stand for 100-200fils. Ask for *za'atar* (dried thyme) to sprinkle on top. For more variety, try cheese or meat *sfiehah* (Arabic pizzas) or *manaish* (bread baked with olive oil, *za'atar,* and other spices).

In the **downtown** area, rolled falafel sandwiches are a budgeteer's dream (100fils). Two busy stands opposite al-Husseini Mosque are open until 11pm. Freshly squeezed **juices,** found in stands throughout Amman, are too refreshing to miss (250-300fils). Options range from tomato and orange to banana, carrot, and a mysterious brown concoction that tastes like mangoes.

If you're in the Shmeisani district, ask for directions to the **Ata Ali Café** across from the Housing Bank. This popular spot for Amman teens is no Ben & Jerry's, but it *is* ice cream. Unabashedly homesick Americans should head to the **Pizza Hut** in the Petra Center building in Shmeisani. Though prices are not higher than what you'd pay back in the States, a pizza will still cost more than your Jordanian hotel room. Stop in at **Zalatimo Sweets** for a cavity-catalyst of Arabic candy and pastries. It's in the large gray building at the top of the hill on which Abdali is located.

Al-A'eelat Restaurant, Prince Muhammad St. (tel. 63 72 46), on the left as you walk 10 min. uphill from Faisal St. Sign is in Arabic; look for the Suleiman Tannous Chevrolet dealer opposite. Small, but unbeatable prices. Sandwiches 200fils. Falafel 10 fils each. Open Sat.-Thurs. 8am-3pm.

Cairo Restaurant, between King Talal St. and Omar al-Mukhtar St., the two broad avenues heading southwest from al-Husseini Mosque. Walk about 100m from the mosque toward the market and look left for a side street clucking with roasting chickens. The Cairo is big, bright, and orange, on the mosque side of the street. Hearty, inexpensive meals: one-half roast chicken 900fils, kebabs 800fils, *fasula* (bean soup) 500fils, and breakfast *fuul* plates 250fils. Open daily 5am-11pm, often later.

Indian Chicken Tikka Inn, Prince Muhammad St. (tel. 64 24 37), downhill from the Third Circle. Tiny upstairs room with A/C. Curry dishes JD1.750. One-half chicken tikka 1200fils. Mix *paratha* (Indian bread) and ḥummus for 300fils. Another location at Seventh Circle.

Salaam Restaurant, King Faisal St. (tel. 62 26 26), a half block away from al-Husseini Mosque on the left-hand side of the street. No English sign, but look for spitted chickens in the window. The colorful crowd, tasty food, and A/C compensate for the gloomy interior. JD2.160 buys you bread, bird, and fries. *Sfiehah* and *manaish* 150 fils each. Menu is in Arabic but servers can describe the dishes in English. Open daily 7am-10pm.

Golden Chicken Restaurant, Muhammad Tash St. (tel. 62 11 49). From the park in Jebel Weibdeh, walk down Ahmad Shawqi St. and take the first left onto Muhammad Tash. *Mezze* dishes 220fils each, grilled chicken JD2.150. Open daily 11:30am-11pm.

Abu Ahmad's New Orient Restaurant, 10 Orient St. (tel. 64 18 79). Take the last right before Third Circle as you approach it from Second. The first left is Orient St. Award-winning charcoal-grilled dishes for only JD2.300. Canopied *al fresco* dining with excellent service. An order of *mensaf* (JD2.300) is enough for two. Will take travelers' checks. Open daily noon-midnight.

Sights

Although Amman is usually considered an inhabited way station between Jordan's major attractions, it has several worthwhile sights. The **Roman Theater,** downtown on Jebel al-Qala'a, is the most renowned. Built by Antoninus Pius (138-61 CE), the theater could accommodate 6000 spectators. (Open daily 8am-5pm. Free.) Beyond the Odeon, a smaller theater, is a new **piazza.** The short stroll between **al-Husseini Mosque** and the **Nymphaeum** is crowded with pedestrians and twinkling evening lights.

Two museums are built into the foundations of the theater on either side of the stage area. The **Folklore Museum** (tel. 65 17 42) has two rooms filled with mannequins impersonating an entertaining cast of Jordanian characters, as well as smaller rooms displaying Palestinian embroidery. (Open Wed.-Mon. 8am-5pm. Admission 250fils.) The **Museum of Costumes and Jewelry** (tel. 65 17 60) shows off current attire and Jordanian jewels. Learn about the origins of regional embroidery and why the white shawl is called "the thrilling of the soul." The gallery to the right of the entrance displays 6th-century mosaics from Madaba and Jerash. (Open Wed.-Mon. 8am-5pm. Admission 250fils.)

From the Roman Amphitheater, or any downtown locale, you can climb the steep steps and streets to the flat top of **Citadel Hill.** On the southern slope of Jebel al-Qa-la'a, the citadel is the site of ancient Amman, called Rabbath-Ammon, or the "Great City of the Ammonites." Neighbors of the Israelites, the Ammonites make frequent guest appearances in the Bible. King David besieged Rabbath-Ammon twice, the second time improving his chances of marrying the already pregnant Bathsheba by putting her husband Uriah in the front line of battle. A few Byzantine and Umayyad ruins remain. Taxis go to the summit, and bus #63 passes nearby. The wadi below and to the right of the Roman Theater is Center City; across from it are Jebel Ashrafieh and the black-and-white checkered dome of the **Abu Darwish Mosque,** built in the 1940s by Circassians. To the east, you'll see the **Royal Palace** at Raghadan, although you'll have to get a little closer to see the stylishly virile red and black regalia of the Circassian guards.

Apart from the sweeping view, the main attraction on Citadel Hill is the **Archeological Museum** (tel. 63 87 95), which contains a chronologically organized series of finds from ancient sites throughout Jordan. Displays range from 200,000-year old dinner leftovers to Iron Age anthropomorphic sarcophagi, minimalist Nabatean portraits, and a Roman marble statuary. (Open Wed.-Mon. 9am-5pm. Admission 250fils.) In front of the museum are the foundations of a 2nd-century Roman temple that once housed a 10m statue of Hercules, to whom the temple was probably dedicated. Three giant marble fingers beside the museum steps and ponderous column segments scattered about the site hint at the shrine's former glory.

The best preserved and most intriguing ruins lie behind the museum. Vaulted chambers tower 10m over a spacious courtyard where elaborate floral decorations can still be seen in the stonework. The 7th-century structure once supported a huge stone dome and was used as a mosque, audience hall, and living accommodation. Below the Roman walls directly to the north, an open pit leads into the underground passageway that connected the fortified city to a hidden water supply. With a flashlight and fancy footwork you can enter the cavernous rock-hewn **cistern** by this route. The more conventional approach is from the gate on the street below.

The Citadel was the heart of ancient Amman; today the pulse emanates from downtown, in and around the **al-Husseini Mosque.** The Ottoman-style structure was built in 1924 on the site of an ancient mosque, probably also the site of the Old Cathedral of Philadelphia. The area around the mosque is full of second-hand shoe shops.

For a selection of indigenous products, wander through the **Jordan Craft Center** (tel. 64 45 55), downhill from the Lebanese Embassy (Second Circle) and on the left. This is a non-profit exhibition of rugs, silver, glass, jewelry, embroidery, caftans, and pottery (open Sat.-Thurs. 9am-1pm and 4-7pm; in winter Sun.-Thurs. 9am-1pm and 3-6pm). Amman also features a number of galleries that display national and regional art; these are found in the ministry and luxury hotel districts. The **Jordan National Gallery,** on Jebel Weibdeh (tel. 63 01 28) at Muntazah Park displays contemporary artwork from around the Muslim world as well as 19th-century paintings of the Middle East by European artists. (Open Wed.-Mon. 8am-5pm. Free.)

Amman's finest Byzantine artifact is the 6th-century **Suwaiffiyeh mosaic,** unearthed during construction at the western edge of the city. Ask the caretaker to hose down the floor for a better look at the design of bizarre creatures, including leaf-bearded men, eagles with ears, eelie fishmen, and quayles with brains. To reach the site, follow the signs from the first left west of Sixth Circle. (Open Sat.-Thurs. 8am-4pm, Fri. 9am-2pm. Free.) The **Martyr's Monument** and **Military Museum** (tel. 66 42 40) sit in an odd square building overlooking the Hussein Sports City (open Sun.-Fri. 8am-4pm. Free). They're occasionally closed to visitors, so call ahead.

Entertainment

Amman is not known for its rollicking nightlife, but nocturnal enthusiasts will find fulfillment on dance floors or in restaurants; most of Amman's major hotels have late-night fests. On the far side of Shmeisani (about twice as far as the Ambassador Hotel, on the same road) is the **Middle East Hotel,** which hosts an excellent disco on Friday and Sunday nights. The crowd is mostly foreign, the tunes mostly reggae. Out by Sixth Circle the **Amra Hotel** also has a fairly lively nightclub on Fridays and Saturdays. Cover charge at these places is usually around JD6 and drinks cost JD3.000-JD3.500. The **El Cesar Restaurant** on Jebel Weibdeh offers more traditional Jordanian music and dancing, but few affordable comestibles.

At first glance, the city center seems to lack the traditional Middle Eastern constellation of cafés and tea houses. Look up: they're mostly perched on second floors. One of these is the downtown **Hilton Café,** overlooking the royal intersection of King Hussein and King Faisal St. (above the Seiko watch sign). There's a crowded and noisy *al fresco* hangout on the second floor. You can learn the local card games over a cup of Amman's sludgiest Arabic coffee (100fils and up) and entertain your suddenly acquired best friends by choking on the dense charcoal and tobacco smoke of a *nargileh* (300fils). There is a "boys' club" atmosphere (whatever that means), and though foreign women are welcome they are likely to cause a stir. (Open daily 8am-11pm.) **Babiche Café** in Shmeisani serves coffee and drinks.

During the late afternoon and early evening, Amman's central *souk* (market) becomes the city's most happening spot. The *souk* swallows several blocks southwest of al-Husseini Mosque. Most people rest between 2-4pm (*service* and buses become scarce), but cafés allow homeless budget travelers to linger over coffee in the shade. Try **Maatouk's** on Third Circle (coffee 200fils).

Near Amman

Salt الصلط

During Turkish rule, Salt (pronounced "sult") was the chief administrative center for the surrounding area, and in the 1920s it seemed a likely choice for the capital of the newly independent state of Jordan. But the city was bypassed in favor of the smaller but more centrally located village of Amman. While development obliterated Amman's rural charm, Salt has retained much of its original flavor. The focal point of Salt is the mosque on Jebel Yushah, which, according to Muslim legend, covers the site of the tomb of the prophet Hosea (Yushah).

A survey of the crowded Ottoman houses and buildings clinging to the steep slopes can be the most rewarding part of a visit to this sleepy town. Venture up into the hills via one of the narrow stairways in the downtown area. Many of the yellow stone buildings date from the late 19th century. The Ottoman barracks, still intact, were built over a 13th-century fortress that was destroyed to prevent its capture at Crusader hands. Salt is also known for its large Christian community: church towers pepper the hillsides.

Taking a minibus up Wadi Sh'eib is the most dramatic approach to Salt. Lush, terraced farmlands and eucalyptus groves tumble down the wadi to the southwest of town, descending to Shuneh Nimrin (South Shuneh) on the busy route from Amman to the King Hussein/Allenby Bridge (Jordan Valley Highway). From King Abdullah St. on the east side of Amman, bus #57 crawls 30km northwest to Salt, stopping at Fifth Circle and the town of Suweileh en route (175fils). A *service* from Abdali Station costs 300fils. Salt has no tourist office, hotels, or restaurants to pamper travelers. The **post office** (tel. 55 49 78) is located uphill from the circle on the left (open Sat.-Thurs. 7:30am-7pm, Fri. 8am-1:30pm). Next door is the **police station** (tel. 55 56 32). Change money at the **Bank of Jordan**, the **Jordan Islamic Bank**, or the **Housing Bank,** all of which have branches in Salt.

The **Archeological Museum** (tel. 55 56 53) is located uphill from the bus station near the Jordan Islamic Bank (open Sat.-Thurs. 8am-2pm, free).

If the adventurous spirit moves you, wander downhill from the bus station into Wadi Sh'eib. Unexplored caves and abandoned stone houses dot the area, and numerous dirt paths lead you further down. Here, pink flowers and fruit trees line the banks of the narrow stream that winds through the bottom of the valley. And leave a trail of bread crumbs, or you might not find your way out of the valley.

Wadi Seer وادى السيـر

Burgeoning Amman has poked its urban tentacles westward to Wadi Seer, yet this small town stubbornly maintains a rural personality. Wadi Seer, like much of the fertile hill country to the north and west of Amman, was settled by Circassians. These fair-skinned Muslims came from Russia during the Czarist persecutions of the 1870s and account for most blonde Jordanians. Amman's Folklore Museum displays the traditional Circassian costume—a cylindrical fur cap, and black waistcoat with red trim.

At Wadi Seer, the high desert plateau suddenly gives way to the Jordan Valley. The town's namesake, a muddy little stream, snakes through the countryside on its way to the Dead Sea. The narrow asphalt road that follows this valley out of town seems designed for daytripping motorists and tramping backpackers. It's a 30-minute hitch from Amman; *service* and minibuses also make the trip.

Verdant tobacco plants and olive trees, along with a multitude of young children, line the 12km road which runs from Wadi Seer southwest to the ruins at **Iraq al-Emir** and the nearby grottos. An occasional Bedouin tent or woman herding her goats peek out from the hills as the road approaches the ruins. The villagers of Wadi Seer believe that the identity of the site's mysterious builders is encoded in the carvings on the monolithic blocks of brown stone that stand between the town and the caves. The only clue offered by the caves themselves is the Aramaic inscription "Tobiah" near two of the cave windows.

Local legend holds that **Qasr al-Abd** (Castle of the Slave) was built by a love-smitten slave named Tobiah. While his master was away on a journey, Tobiah built a palace and carved lions, panthers, and eagles into its walls in order to win the hand of the master's daughter. Unfortunately, the master returned before Tobiah could finish the work, and the slave's efforts and attraction went unrequited. Kill-joy historians explain the inscription and the castle remains with reference to Tobiah the Ammonite Servant. Although this Tobiah was a rich priest in Jerusalem, the name of the castle refers to his occupation as a servant of God. Josephus, a historian before the profession became overrun with kill-joys, also records the wealth of a Tobiah family and the exploits of the young son Hyrcanus who built a strong fortress, constructed entirely of white marble and enclosed by a wide, deep moat. The ruins, restored in 1987, resemble a Hellenistic palace more than a defensive fort. Several red stone lions remain intact.

About 2-3km on the way from Wadi Seer to Iraq al-Emir, you pass **al-Bassa springs,** the source of the valley's fertility and the swimming pool for many of the area's kiddies. Above the left bank of the wadi, the monastery **al-Deir** is carved into the face of the cliff. This extraordinary building deserves the 20-minute clamber, even if you don't find any of the Roman gold villagers claim is buried under the floor. The walls inside are covered with thousands of triangular niches, each of which once cradled a gaping skull: the chamber is an ossuary which stored remnants of monks.

Service to the municipality of Wadi Seer leave from Third Circle (165fils). A minibus (95fils) leaves from Wahadat Station and will let you off either in Wadi Seer or at the al-Bassa springs. From Abdali Station, a minibus runs to Suweilah where you can connect with a minibus to Wadi Seer. To get to the village of Iraq el-Emir take a minibus from Wadi Seer (110fils) to the city and ask the driver to point out the path to Qasr al-Abd. The village store sells supplies. Past the castle the road ends, making passage to the Jordan Valley unmanageable for ordinary vehicles. To reach the Dead Sea you'll have to backtrack to Amman.

Northern Jordan
Jordan Valley and Dead Sea

The greatest obstacle in reaching Deir Alla, Pella, and the Dead Sea is getting to the highway that follows the contours of the Jordan River along the length of the valley. Once there, hop on one of the many buses or *service* shuttling up and down the road. Perhaps the simplest method is first to take a bus (285fils) or *service* (460fils) west from Amman to South Shuna (Shuneh Nimrin), a busy village on the Jordan Valley Highway. A bus also runs to South Shuna from the Ras al Ain area in southern Amman, near the intersection of Ali Bin Abi Taleb and Jerusalem St. near Jebel Nadhif. From South Shuna, buses (85fils) and *service* (145fils) travel north to Deir Alla via Karemah or south to Suweilah and the Dead Sea Rest House. Another method would be to take a bus directly from Amman to either Deir Alla (370fils) or the Dead Sea (570fils). The Dead Sea bus stops in ar-Rameh, where you can catch another bus to South Shuna. Don a fedora and bring plenty of water, and don't forget your passport—you'll be asked for it at several military roadblocks along the way.

Dead Sea البحــر المـيت

> *"Tell me, General, how dead is the Dead Sea?"*
> *—George Bush, to the Jordanian army chief of staff*

Icthyologically, very dead; tourism-wise, pretty lively. The only stretch of sand that is open to visitors stretches along the Dead Sea's northern shore, 90 minutes from Amman or Deir Alla. During the middle of the day the sun reflects off the sea's still surface, creating the illusion that the entire body of water is about to spill into the Jordan Valley. The peculiar buoyancy of this briny water, which forces even the densest swimmer into a back float, attracts many Jordanians; there is almost never room for hitchhikers in the cars heading south from the King Hussein/Allenby Bridge or South Shuna. The salt water causes even a paper cut to feel like an amputation without anaesthetic, so pay attention when you shave. The only overnight accommodations available along the Dead Sea are at the very expensive Dead Sea Spa Hotel, a couple of kilometers past the **Dead Sea Rest House** (tel. (05) 57 29 01). The Rest House offers showers (250fils) to relieve you of Lot's wife's encrusted fate. Unless you swim around the barrier on the north, which closes off the nicest section of beach, you'll have to pay 500fils to enter the resort enclave. The complex contains the showers, the air-conditioned Rest House, and an overpriced restaurant (buffet lunch JD4.950 per person). The Rest House beach is rock-hard and echoes with loquacious local dogs, but if you miss the last bus (about 4pm) and can't get a ride, you can sleep here for JD1.925, which includes entrance to the resort enclave and showers. The sunset almost justifies getting stranded. (Rest House open daily 8am-10:30pm, with swimming allowed only until sundown.) About 4 or 5 km past the Rest House, a natural swimming pool is nestled between the colorful cliffs.

Within 30km south on the highway to Aqaba (Rte. 65) is **Zarqa Ma'in,** a cascading hot spring. (See Madaba, Kings' Highway for details.)

Deir Alla and Pella (at Tabaqat Fahl) ديـر عـلـى و طبقـات فـحـل

Deir Alla, 50km north of the Dead Sea, is the spot where Jacob supposedly snoozed after wrestling with the angel. On and around the sandy *tel* overlooking the modern town, archeologists have collected Bronze Age, Iron Age, Roman, and Islamic artifacts documenting over 20 centuries of history. Two temples dating back as far as 1300 BCE have been excavated. To the casual observer, however, the *tel* tells no tales:

baked mud walls of ancient temples and shrines blend into the top of the tanned mound, only vaguely suggesting the former structures. For elucidation, consult the exhibit at the dig headquarters, stationed on the left at the end of the dirt road as you pass by the foot of the *tel*. A map, an explanation of the excavation, and an extensive array of its spoils are on display here.

The best way to reach Deir Alla is to take a minibus from South Shuna (see above). *Service* (590fils) and buses (370fils) also run sporadically from Amman's Abdali Station to Deir Alla village next to the site. Some foolish travelers try to hitch to Deir Alla from Salt; this is a risky trek, as few cars pass. The route from Salt passes through **Zei National Park,** about 5km beyond Salt, where lovely free camping grounds await.

A 30km ride north of Deir Alla brings you to the serene surroundings of **Tabaqat Fahl,** the biblical **Pella.** A thriving city during the first century CE owing to membership in the Decapolis commercial league, Pella is gradually being unearthed by American and Australian archeologists. On the bank of a tortuous wadi, a stark row of Roman pillars frames bald hills and gaping ancient tombs. Far below, a Byzantine amphitheater opens onto green lawns and cool springs at the wadi's mouth. Locals have dammed the spring to create pools that are great for splashing but not for drinking: bring potable water. Across from the Archeological Station lie the ruins of an Umayyad mosque and cemetery. Renovations of the church and civic center behind the theater unearthed the skeletons of camels and their keeper, buried since an earthquake in 747 CE. To reach the site from the main road, hike 2km up the paved turn-off to Tabaqat Fahl (Pella). The trail leads to the Australian compound on the hill to the right.

The trip from Deir Alla to Pella (Tabaqat Fahl) takes about an hour by bus. Pella is also accessible by bus from Irbid's North Station (1 hr., 360fils). Buses to al-Mashareh—a 20-min. walk from Tabaqat Fahl—run from South Shuna via al-Karameh (70fils) or from Irbid's west bus station (300fils). A minibus from Amman's Abdali Station to Suwalheh costs 370fils, plus another 250fils to al-Mashareh from there.

Jerash جرش

Dubbed Gerasa in ancient times, Jerash is one of the most extensive extant provincial Roman cities. Gerasa, along with Pella, was a member of the Decapolis, a commercial league of ten cities in Rome's Asian Province (the Antiquities' answer to the European Economic Community). Because of its isolation in a remote valley among the mountains of Gilead, Jerash survived long after the other nine cities were destroyed.

Unlike the other great cities of the classical period in this area, Jerash is typically Roman in design. The city trampled over earlier settlements, so little evidence of pre-Roman days remains. Inscriptions calling the town Antioch reveal that the Seleucid king of that name had a prominent outpost here, but Jerash entered its golden age only after its conquest by the Roman Emperor Pompey in 63 BCE. For the next three centuries, Jerash prospered: granite was brought from as far away as Aswan and old temples were razed and rebuilt according to the latest architectural fads. The Emperor Trajan annexed the Nabatean lands in 106 CE and built a highway from Damascus to Aqaba that passed through Jerash. Hadrian visited the town in 129; the Triumphal Arch built for the occasion still stands. The town was converted to Christianity and had a bishop by the mid-4th century.

Following the destruction of the Syrian trading center at Palmyra and the decline of the Nabatean kingdom, trade routes shifted from the desert to the sea. Frantic construction continued through the 6th century. Without their former wealth, though, Jerash's citizens could only replace the older monuments with flashy, inferior structures which were then plundered by invading Persians in 635 CE. The great earthquake of 747 CE relegated what little remained to the hands of the Muslim Arabs, who by then controlled the city. The Crusaders described Jerash as uninhabited, and it remained abandoned until its rediscovery in the 19th century. After the invasion of the Ottoman Turks, Circassians built the modern town on the eastern slope of the stream valley in what was once the main residential area of ancient Jerash.

Practical Information and Food

Jerash is minuscule—barely 1km long from the South Gate down the Street of Columns to the North Gate. The tiny Chrysoras River (Golden River) separates the ancient ruins on the western bank from the new town on the east. The **Visitors Information Center** (open daily 7am-7pm) is on the left of the main road entering the city from the south, about 400m north of the Triumphal Arch. Groups of any size can hire guides for JD4. Booklets which include maps and explanations of the sights facilitate more leisurely exploration and range in price from JD1 to JD6. The visitors center also has a small **post office** (open daily 8am-2pm).

Buses and *service* leave from Jerash's **bus station** on the western edge of the new city. Buses to Amman's Abdali Station cost 370fils (slightly more with A/C), to Ajlun 250fils, and to Irbid 290fils; *service* cost about 60% more. Public transportation shuts down at about 7pm. Hitchers to Amman, Dibbin, or Ajlun are known to walk south about 1km from the visitors center to the intersection with Highway 20. Turning right leads to Ajlun and the Dibbin National Forest with its new camping facilities. Going straight takes you to Amman; buses pass frequently and are easy to flag. The main road through Jerash continues north to Irbid. Hitchers go to the northern edge of town, just before the branch of road that splits off to the left.

Because Jerash is such an easy daytrip from Amman, there are no accommodations in the town; some people, however, discreetly camp along the western edge of the enclosed site. You might also consider either camping at Dibbin National Park, about 8km away, or instead taking a room at the Dibbin Rest House. The **Jerash Rest House** (tel. 45 11 46), to the left as you enter the site from the visitors center, overlooks the ruins and serves traditional Jordanian food as well as burgers. (kebabs JD1.800, hummus 300fils, soft drinks 300fils, and excellent banana splits for 650fils. Open daily 8am-9pm.) At the **Al Khayyam Restaurant,** just past the visitors center on the main road, JD2.500 buys bread, salad, and grilled meat (open daily 11am-10 or 11 pm). Street stands surrounding the bus station in town sell cheap falafel and *fuul*.

Sights

Jerash's dusty claim to fame is its extensive ruins, even though the best parts are probably lying beneath your feet (90% of ancient Jerash is still unexcavated). Enter the site by the visitors center or the north gate. The ruins are open daily 7:30am-7:30pm; admission is 500fils, JD1 during the festival. We'll walk you through the ruins from south to north.

The **Triumphal (or Hadrianic) Arch,** 400m south of the ancient walls, honors the arrival of Emperor Hadrian in the winter of 129 CE. Walking from that monument to the main entrance you'll pass the extensive remains of the **Hippodrome,** including stables and spectator seats. From the entrance, the **Forum of Ionic Columns** opens up into a main street intersected by two perpendicular avenues.

A footpath leads from the forum up to the astounding **South Theater**. Greek doodles reveal that 4000 of Jerash's wealthiest citizens could reserve seats here. The two-story backstage, still furnished with curtains and marble statues, once dominated the setting. The ruined **Temple of Zeus** lies behind the theater's seats. The **Street of Columns** runs the distance between the forum and the North Gate. Its 260 pairs of columns are Corinthian replacements for earlier Ionic columns and were once capped by aqueducts carrying water throughout the ancient city. The huge paving stones show grooves worn by the chariots that clattered through the streets. The occasional holes were designed for the drainage of rain water into a sophisticated sewage system. Massive sidewalk coverings protected pedestrians from the sun, but only traces of these cosmopolitan parasols remain. On the right, halfway down the Street of Columns, sits the **Jerash Antiquities Museum.** Tall display cases mounted along the walls have neatly arranged artifacts from the Neolithic to Ottoman periods. Coins, jewelry, theater "tickets" made of stone, and other household items highlight the museum's small collection. (Open Sat.-Thurs. 7:30am-5pm. Free.)

Walking through the first intersection (named **South Tetrapylon** for its four slabs), look for the **Cathedral** and **Nymphaeum** to the left. The "crow-step" designs on these buildings and the Nabatean coins found here bear witness to the strong commercial links with the desert kingdom at Petra. The ornamental fountains of the Nymphaeum were used in an annual reenactment of the Miracle at Cana, where Jesus changed water into wine. Several hundred meters behind the cathedral, three churches possess the finest mosaics to survive Caliph Yazid II's attempt to destroy all "images and likenesses" in 720 CE.

The **East Baths** are across the wadi, just north of the mosque in the new town. Scattered around the western part of the city are the ruins of some 13 churches of more recent vintage. When first built, the stones were pillaged from the larger monuments and ornamentation carelessly flailed about. They're of little interest today. The **Northern Gate** was built in the 2nd century CE to open onto the newly completed road to Pella in the Jordan Valley.

Occasionally, during the summer months, there is a 60-minute **sound and light show** among the ruins, with special JETT buses running to and from the show. Check with the JETT office in Amman (tel. 66 41 46) for details.

Jerash is undergoing eternal restoration, as the government attempts to raise the city's profile. The **Jerash Festival**, which has been running since 1981, takes place every summer in late July and is under royal patronage. Check with the Ministry of Tourism for details (tel. 64 23 11) or see *The Jordan Times* for complete coverage. The South Theater and Artemis Steps provide a dramatic setting for musical, theatrical, and dance groups from all over the world, and recently featured Andrew Lloyd Webber's breathtakingly mediocre composition, *Starlight Express*. Shows range from the Gary Burton Quintet to Radio Jordan Orchestra to the Azerbaijan State Ballet to Crown Prince Hassan in a tutu. Shows begin at 7:30 and 9:30pm each evening except Fridays. Tickets to the different events vary in cost, but admission to the grounds costs JD1. You will be searched upon entry, and may be required to hire a guide if you arrive during the day. An international telephone exchange, set up in the grounds, charges average fees.

Transport to and from Jerash during the festival is chaotic. Do not expect to hitch unless you are leaving town before 4pm. *Service* are also crowded. Coming home at about 10pm is less of a problem, though most cars are still full and thus will not stop for hitchers.

Near Jerash

Ajlun عجلون

Atop the highest peak overlooking Ajlun is Qalat al-Rabadh, a huge Arab castle built between 1184 and 1185 by Azz ad-Din Ausama, a commander under Salah al-Din. Crusader knights spent decades unsuccessfully trying to capture the castle and nearby village. The name Kafranjah, a town in the area famous for its olive trees, suggests that the crusading Franks (*Franjis* in Arabic) did some time here—if only as prisoners. The Crusader threat quelled, Mamluks began using the castle to transmit messages by beacon and pigeon: from Baghdad to Cairo, day or night, the relay could be made in 12 hours. (Castle open daily 6:30am-6 or 7pm. Free.)

Ajlun lies a hilly 24km west of Jerash, an easy hitch or bus ride from that town, from Amman (73km), or from Irbid (88km). *Service* from Amman takes 75 minutes (690fils). From Ajlun's main traffic circle, which revolves around a sickly henna tree gasping from the fumes, it's 4km of gently sloping road to the summit. You can catch a taxi at the traffic circle for JD1 round-trip. Ajlun's **post office** is located on Amman St., on your right as you enter the town (open Sat.-Thurs. 7:30am-7pm, Fri. and holidays 8am-1:30pm). Exchange money at either the **Housing Bank**, next door to the post office, or the **Bank of Jordan**, on Irbid St. uphill from the circle (regular banking hours Sat.-Thurs. 8am-12:30pm).

The only lodgings are the **Rabadh Hotel** (tel. (04) 46 22 02; singles JD14, doubles JD17.500) and the **Ajlun Hotel** (tel. (04) 46 25 24; singles JD7, doubles JD12). Both are between Ajlun and the castle.

The Rabadh Hotel's terrace restaurant charges eye-moistening prices for its view of the fortress and valley: shish kebab or a full breakfast for JD2. If you stick to *mezze* dishes at 250fils per plate you can afford an enjoyable light lunch. Those who prefer to court their bellies rather than their eyes should stop in at the **Green Mountain Restaurant** in Ajlun's center circle. A half-chicken costs 800fils, hummus and *fuul* 220fils, and 650 fils buys a complete meal which includes rice, meat, and a vegetable. (Open daily 6:30am-8:30pm.)

Dibbin National Park

The Aleppo pines and oaks of the fertile woodland are a remarkable sight in this desert country. Located in the hills 10km southwest of Jerash and 65km north of Amman, Dibbin National Park encompasses some 20km of forest stretching south from the town of the same name.

The government subsidizes refreshments, shaded bungalows, and camping facilities (JD1). On the old road to Jerash near Dibbin is a government **Rest House** (tel. (04) 45 24 13) with singles for JD8.500 and doubles for JD13.200; extra beds JD4.500. The access road leaves the Amman-Jerash Highway about 2km south of Jerash; look for the signs. You'll have to take a car as neither buses nor *service* accesses the park. The Rest House fills up during holidays, so it's best to call ahead and make reservations.

Irbid اربد

Much like Amman, Irbid (one hour north of Jerash) is an industrial center which has overwhelmed the site of its ancient Decapolis city (Arbila). But while expansion in Amman has left some areas uninhabited, Irbid's narrow streets remain stuffed with merchants, kung fu theaters, and restless taxis. Besides the tiny **Natural History Museum** (open Wed.-Mon. 8am-5pm) on the sedate campus of **Yarmouk University,** there is little to do here but plan your junket to Um Qais or al-Hemma.

Irbid has several hotels and restaurants to suit the budget traveler. The **al-Amin al-Kabir Hotel** (tel. 24 23 84) on Maydan Malik Abdallah St., one block down from the city center and the Ministry of Antiquities building, has pleasant, breezy rooms and exceptionally courteous management. (Singles JD3. Doubles JD5. Bathroom 500fils.) Around the corner on Jameel St. in the same building as the Bank of Jordan is the more communal **Abu Bakr Hotel** (tel. 24 26 95), where snoozing is the main event. (Singles JD3. Doubles JD5.) The **al-Nasseem Hotel** (tel. 27 43 10) on Idoun St., the south side of the Yarmouk campus, desperately needs new carpeting but the somewhat unkempt rooms are comfortable. With the main entrance to Yarmouk University on your left, walk uphill and take the first left. The al-Nasseem will be on your right before you reach al-Nasseem Circle. (Singles JD5. Doubles JD7.700.) The three-star **al-Razi Hotel** (tel. 27 55 15), across the street from University Mosque, is a bit expensive but its restaurant serves delicious Arabic-style pizzas for less than JD1. The newly-renovated **Cafe Amon Italian Restaurant**, downhill from the al-Razi Hotel and right on the circle, serves a variety of entrees, mostly under JD2. (Open daily 8am-11pm.) Downtown, **al-Katkoot** serves supreme Jordanian dishes, or try the **Hungry Bunny** to get that wabbit.

Many have an easy time hitching to Irbid via Jerash, but the quickest way to the city is by the Arabella or Hijazi Bus Companies. **Minibuses** from Amman, Jerash, and Ajlun take somewhat longer and drop you off at Irbid's South Station, at which point you can take **service** to downtown (55fils) and then from downtown to North Station (55fils). You can also catch a taxi to Yarmouk (700fils, JD1 at night). The last buses depart for Amman at about 8pm, sometimes as early as 5pm in the winter. Irbid's **post**

office (open Sat.-Thurs. 7:30am-7pm; Fri. and holidays 8am-1:30pm) and **telephone office** with international phone and telex services (open Sat.-Thurs. 7:30am-10pm; hours vary Fri. and holidays) are located just off the central square. **ANZ Grindlay's Bank** in Central Square, across from the post office, exchanges cash and traveler's checks (open Sat.-Thurs. 8am-12:30pm). The **telephone code** is 02.

Near Irbid: Um Qais and al-Hemma ام قيس و الـحـمـى

Um Qais was the biblical Gadara, where Jesus exorcised a sinner's demons into a herd of pigs which stampeded down the hill to drown in the Sea of Galilee. This thriving Decapolis city, once a resort for Romans vacationing at al-Hemma's therapeutic hot springs, was renowned for its theaters, writers, philosophers, and, among lowbrows, for its orgiastic extravagances. The city was probably founded sometime in the 4th century BCE and was later ceded by Caesar Augustus to Herod the Great, but it perished in the Jewish Rebellion of 66-70 CE.

Today, much of the **Roman amphitheater** survives; covered passageways stand in the back, and the six-foot, headless marble goddess that once sat at the front of the stage has moved inside. Nearby, squat, square pillars litter the ruins of the bathhouse; at one time they bolstered the bath floors to allow steam to circulate underneath. In front of the theater stand the columns of a Byzantine Church. A gatekeeper will show you around and explain the sights—a tip will be expected. (Open daily. Knock.)

The **Um Qais Rest House** (tel. 21 72 10, ext. 59), a joint project of the Department of Antiquities and the American Center for Oriental Research (ACOR), serves over-priced refreshments to desperate travelers. No overnight lodging is available—hit the hills for a serene, scenic campsite. There is a **post office** along the main road through modern Um Qais (open Sat.-Thurs. 7:30am-7pm, Fri. 8am-1:30pm.)

From Um Qais, wait for the next minibus from Irbid headed to **al-Hemma,** 10km away. (Foolish hitchers have to watch out for the skull-and-bones signs that identify mine fields.) Shortly beyond Um Qais, at the first of several checkpoints, a soldier will ask to see your **passport.** Just after the military roadblock, the valley of the Yarmouk River gapes below. The high plateau across the vale is the Golan Heights.

After that exquisite descent, the arrival in al-Hemma itself (entrance fee 200fils per car) may be a letdown. Swimming in the mineral springs complex costs 500 fils; JD3.500 if you reserve a private bath with slightly cooler water. (Open daily 6am-8pm). After 8pm, you can reserve the mineral springs complex for JD5 per hour—if you don't mind the egg-gregious stench of sulphur. The **Hotel al-Hemma al-Urdun** (tel. (02) 21 72 03), built like a staircase around the springs, has clean, no-frills rooms. (Doubles JD5 or JD6. Chalet triples complete with mineral water JD15.) For food, the **Jordanian Hammi Restaurant** (tel. (02) 21 72 03) on the east side of the complex serves kebabs for an outlandish JD1.600. You're better off heading for the old tropical village—complete with mud huts, thick pomegranate groves, and banana palms—and bargaining with the villagers for local specialties. **Buses** (300fils) travel to Um Qais and al-Hemma from Irbid's North Station. The last minibus leaves at around 5:30 or 6pm.

Azraq and Desert Castles الـزرق

Adjacent to sultry desert lava fields, Azraq's dusty green foliage comes as a welcome respite. As T.E. Lawrence (of Arabia) rather obscurely noted, *"Numen in est"* ("Where's the latrine?"). The springs at Azraq are the only permanent bodies of water in an expanse of over 2500 square kilometers of barren sand-and-scorpion desert. Thus, the oasis serves as a resting stop for truck drivers from three continents and hundreds of species of exotic birds molting their way through Jordan's desert.

The discovery of an enormous cache of flint hand-axes indicates that either pale-olithic settlers or extremely sophisticated camels hunted in the area 500,000 years ago. The most remarkable records of human habitation are the scattered Umayyad castles, a group of structures that originally formed a chain from the north of Damascus to

Khirbet al-Mafjar near Jericho. Built in the 7th and 8th centuries by the Umayyads, the castles were mysteriously abandoned a century later. The imposing stonework of **Qasr Harraneh** and strategic location of **Qasr Azraq** and **Qasr Mushatta** support speculation that the castles sheltered caravans along the trade route between Syria, Arabia, and the Far East. The baths near **Qasr al-Hallabat** and the magnificent frescos at **Qasr Amra** brought creature comforts to the desert.

Practical Information

A trip to Azraq oasis and the Desert Castles is a journey fraught with uncertainty, to say nothing of a pain in the ass. A taxi will take you from Zarqa to Qasr Azraq (500fils), but it's up to you to find transportation to the other castles. Excluding Qasr al-Touba, which lies far to the south and is accessible only by four-wheel drive vehicles, the castles lie on a paved highway loop, with the western end at Amman and the eastern end at Azraq. It is possible to reach some of the castles by hitchhiking, but **renting a car** in Amman with a group is infinitely wiser. Jordan's modern highway system enables you to visit all of the castles in one day. JETT buses provide full day tours of the desert castles, but only for groups.

Hitchhikers, before undertaking this risky and potentially dangerous fool's errand, will need an immense supply of food and water, a taste for adventure, and careful planning. There is some traffic on the Damascus highway from Amman to **Zarqa** (30km), but there are also other hitchhikers, mostly soldiers and Arab workers. Alternatively, *service* from Abdali Station near the Roman theater can take you there quickly and cheaply (300fils). Be careful about accepting rides from military vehicles since most will take you only as far as some desolate desert depot. The highway to Azraq passes right by Qasr al-Hallabat (30km from Zarqa) before reaching Azraq (87km from Zarqa). From Azraq junction you'll have to hitch 13km north to reach Qasr Azraq and then return to Azraq. If you take the southern highway back to Amman you will pass near Qasr Amra (25km from Azraq), then Qasr Kharaneh (40km from Azraq) and Qasr Mushatta (about 90km from Azraq and 40km from Amman).

A Clockwise Tour

The following description of the castles and Azraq details a road trip that takes the northern route from Amman to Azraq and the southern highway on the return trip. This direction serves hitchhikers better because there is more traffic; if you have a car, you could as easily make a counterclockwise tour. The road from Amman to Zarqa passes through Jordan's most notorious speed trap, where gimlet-eyed cops dispense fines at a honking JD50.

Approximately 30km east into the desert from Zarqa, **Qasr al-Hallabat** enters into view. Angle off at the right turn onto the paved road and turn left up the track to the gate. The Bedouin gatekeeper's tent sits to the left of the crumbling castle; you're free to roam around whatever is left of the castle. Keep in mind that any gatekeeper who provides you with information will expect a dinar tip in return.

Back on the main highway, note the difference between the sand and limestone desert to the south and the grey volcanic desert to the north. Just off the road to the south is the **Hammam Sarah,** the ruined bathhouse modeled after Amra. The thousands of stones thrown into the well over the last 1000 years haven't noticeably affected its depth.

On the long and grinding road east of Hallabat you'll hear nothing but the phlegmatic entreaties of your overheating engine. After kilometers of drab desert, you'll suddenly come upon the 12 square kilometers of lush parklands, pools, and gardens of the **Azraq oasis.** These wetlands are Jordan's only permanent body of fresh water. Relax and reassemble your bearings (both mental and mechanical) at Azraq Junction, where the highway to the northeast heads off for Iraq and the southeastern road leads to the southern castles and on into Saudi Arabia.

A two-minute walk away from Qasr Azraq is the palatial **Al-Sayyed Hotel and Restaurant.** Though the dozens of apparently Cézanne-inspired still-lifes by some no-talent named "Lydia" might make a bad impression, doubles are only JD17.500, singles JD14.000 (prices negotiable). For JD3, you can also take a plunge in their pool, with bathing suits provided if you forgot yours. Restaurant open 8am-11pm. Although inconveniently located at the southern edge of town, the **Zoubi Hotel** (tel. 64 76 22) is an even better deal. Surprisingly modern, the place is so clean that you might have to step through puddles of soapy water to see your room. (Singles JD5, doubles JD7.) The Zoubi Hotel serves many customers from nearby Saudi Arabia and operates only during June, July, and August. The requisite picture of the manager with King Hussein is hanging above the TV and VCR.

About 13km north of Azraq junction on the highway to Iraq squats **Qasr Azraq.** Most of the castle is in excellent condition thanks to extensive restoration. The Druze gatekeeper will muscle open the three-ton portal of the castle and show you his Lawrence of Arabia photograph collection if you inquire with sugar on top. (Many of the photographs look suspiciously like the gate-keeper himself.) The most interesting attractions lie within a few meters of the entrance. Carved into the pavement behind the main gate is a Roman board game. Just above the entrance you'll find the room used by the aforementioned British charmer during his short stay on the premises—it is no longer the fetid dungeon where he sought to punish himself for the failure of one of his missions. The castle, which was first built by the Romans as a fort in 300 CE and later rebuilt by the Ayyubids in 1237, used to rise up in three levels. Only parts of the second level survived the 1926 earthquake, including a ceiling that exposes a web of huge basalt beams.

Throughout the trip, keep an eye out for desert wildlife. The Jordanian government tries to protect varied desert habitats since many indigenous species are disappearing. In the **Shaumari Wildlife Preserve,** southwest of Azraq near Qasr Amra, the government is reintroducing gazelle, armadillo, Himalayan dwarf hamsters (no relation to the Hashemite dwarf king), ostriches, and Arabian oryxes. In remote desert regions to the northeast and southwest of Azraq, cheetah and even desert wolves roam around doing the rare animal thing. (Admission 300fils, students 100fils.)

Despite the ill-fitting glass windows, the hunting lodge and bath complex of **Qasr Amra** impresses onlookers with the elegant simplicity of its design. The interior is also the best preserved of the desert palaces; its vaulted ceilings are splashed with colorful frescoes, and mosaics grace some of the floors. Restoration of these ancient works is underway, so don't be surprised by scaffolding. As centuries of Bedouin campfire soot are removed, a fascinating portrait of Umayyad refinement is slowly reappearing. An early portrayal of the zodiac covers the domed ceiling of the *caldarium* (hot room). The frescoes are all the more riveting since they date from the earliest days of Muslim culture, when human and animal depictions were permissible. You can reach Qasr Amra on the road heading southwest of Azraq Junction, about 28km from Qasr Azraq.

Qasr **Harraneh,** named for the small black stones that blanket the area, remains an enigma. Some experts believe that it was a defensive fort, while others argue that it was a *caravanserai*. Others believe it was a *khan*, or inn—one of the first in the Islamic world. The latest interpretation holds that it served as a retreat where Umayyad leaders discussed matters of state. A painted dedication in a second-story room of the well-preserved castle dates its construction to 92 years after the Prophet's flight from Mecca to Medina (711 CE). The "defensive" theory of Harraneh is supported by the four corner towers and the solid, square plan of a Roman fortress, but the lack of narrowly slit windows from which guards could fire arrows upon attackers casts doubt. The Greek inscription in the doorjambs implies that the Umayyads built upon an earlier structure.

Continuing west you'll move through more expanses of desert, dotted with Bedouin tents. To reach **Qasr Mushatta,** take the highway or any turn-off to Queen Alia International Airport. You may want to hire a *service* from the village of Muwaqaar in the north to reach the castle. The castle is on the left as you approach the airport from the north, but the public access road turns off to the right and loops about 4km around the airport. If you're walking from the airport, don't take this marked turn-off. Instead, continue to the left of the airport, past the Alia cargo terminal, until Mushatta appears on the left (a 30 min. walk). Soldiers and guards at checkpoints will ask to see your **passport.** The façade of the 8th-century castle beckons at the entrance with wonderfully carved floral designs. Most of the carved stones, however, were delivered to Kaiser Wilhelm as a gift from Ottoman Sultan Abdul Hamid II, and only fragments remain at this site. From Qasr Mushatta and the airport it's easy to hitchhike back to Amman or catch a taxi or bus into the city.

Kings' Highway (Al-Mujib)

Three roads link Amman and Aqaba: the **Wadi Araba Highway,** the **Desert Highway,** and the **Kings' Highway.** The **Wadi Araba Highway** hugs the Dead Sea Coast. Owing to its proximity to Israel, the highway serves as a military road; a permit from the police is required for civilian use. By contrast, enormous trucks rumble impassively along the **Desert Highway,** the artery that ties the cities of the north to Aqaba's port. Since the Iran-Iraq War, the Desert Highway has become the chief link from Europe and Turkey to the Persian (Arabian) Gulf. Major new road construction is supposedly in the planning to make the highway smooth and swift, but the government can do little about the scenery—three hours of unchanging desert to Petra and five hours of the same to Aqaba. Only the antics of deranged drivers playfully bumping the narrow shoulders or squeezing between oncoming cars break the monotony. Gas and telephones along the way are scarce. Many travelers find hitching easy on the Desert Highway.

Unless you are rushing from Amman to Aqaba or want to spend every one of your three days in Jordan at Petra, the **Kings' Highway** (Wadi Mujib Road in Arabic) is the ideal way to travel the length of Jordan. This ancient route journeys through spectacular canyons, crisscrossing numerous historical sites along the way. Known by the same name in biblical times, this road was traveled by the Israelites during their exodus from Egypt. Caravans filled with cinnamon and myrrh crept from Arabia to Palestine and Syria along the Kings' Highway en route to Europe. Biblical sites, Byzantine churches and mosaics, Crusader castles, and soul-stirring scenery await you along this route.

Service run most of the way from Amman to Petra, as do minibuses, but generally in the mornings only. Karak is a convenient overnight stop. Nothing leaves Tafilah after 4pm except *service*, so get an early start. Because many drivers shun the Kings' Highway, hitchhiking is reportedly poor. Drivers tend to head for the first entrance to the Desert Highway—check that they intend to stay on the Kings' before climbing in. Since, for some inscrutable reason, roadside bystanders often wave at passing cars in salutation, hitchers generally point at the curb beside their feet—that's the gesture used to hail buses. Hitchers find a light pack and lots of water crucial.

The distances are manageable: 33km from Amman to Madaba, 98km from Madaba to Karak, and 150km from Karak to Petra. The total distance from Amman to Petra is 282km along the Kings' Highway or 262km along the Desert Highway. Many people find camping sites in the wadis north of Karak or in the desert regions between Karak and Petra. A Rest House and a couple of hotels in Karak provide the only indoor accommodations.

To take the Desert Highway from downtown Amman, hitchhikers head south on Jerusalem St. (in Jebel Nadhif across Wadi Abdoun), which metamorphoses into the Desert Highway (Rte. 15). To get to the Kings' Highway they then take a *service* from Amman's Wahadat Station all the way to Madaba (330fils) and then try their luck on the road to Karak, which passes out of Madaba by the Apostles' Church; alternatively, some head south toward Queen Alia International Airport. Eighteen kilometers south of Amman, at the intersection of the Kings' Highway and the Desert Highway, small groups of hitchhikers stand by the mini-obelisk marking this fork. People reach the intersection by taking the Madaba-bound *service* from Wahadat Station, or by hitching south from Seventh Circle.

Madaba مادبا

Madaba is located on a plateau of orange groves overlooking the Jordan Valley. The scanty Roman columns next to the government Rest House hardly evoke visions of a flourishing trade center that once was the size of Jerash. Yet the elaborate mosaics scattered throughout the town are testament to Madaba's importance as a Byzantine ecclesiastical center. Leveled by an earthquake in the 8th century CE, Madaba lay untouched for nearly 1100 years until Christian clans from Karak reinhabited the city in the late 1800s.

The prominent, yellow-brick Greek Orthodox **Church of St. George** stands in the center of town, right off the town square. Inside, parts of the 6th-century Map of Palestine, originally composed of 2.3 million tiles, remain intact. The map includes the Palestinian cities of Byzantium, most notably Nablus, Hebron, and Jericho. At one time the map depicted the entire Middle East, as shown by the few remaining tiles of Turkey, Lebanon, and Egypt. A map of Jerusalem, with representations of the buildings existing in the 6th century, including the Church of the Holy Sepulchre, is the most interesting and renowned section. The church is best known by some devout and imaginative local Christians and Muslims for hosting the Virgin Mary in 1980. A small shrine in the crypt pictures Mary as she purportedly appeared, with a green "healing hand." (Open daily 7am-1pm and 3-6 or 7pm; ask around for the caretaker. Free, but a donation box in the church requests money for the poor.)

Madaba's ramshackle **museum** features an extensive resident collection of mosaics, including a well-preserved depiction of the Garden of Eden, traditional dresses representative of the different regions in Jordan, and jewelry and pottery dating back to various ages. Divided into three sections—the Old House of Madaba, a Folklore Museum, and an Archeological Museum—the museum sits in the southern part of town. Ask for directions at the tourist office. (Open Wed.-Mon. 9am-5pm, Fri. and holidays 10am-4pm. Admission 250fils.) The **Apostles' Church** on the left, at the second right uphill from the museum, houses the town's largest intact mosaic. Use Freud or Monty Python to figure out the mosaic's symbolism, a woman surrounded by mythical sea creatures in the center of a field of parrots. Ex-parrots, that is. The church, built in 578 CE, is gone, an ex-church, but the mosaics are perfectly preserved under a modern hangar. Ask the guardian to spray water on the stones to make them glimmer. The Apostles' Church was closed to visitors during the summer of 1992.

The **tourist office** (tel. 54 33 76) across from St. George's church deals with Madaba as well as Mt. Nebo and nearby sights. (Open Sat.-Thurs. 8am-2pm.) The **Rest House** (tel. 54 40 69) next door serves a full meal complete with seven *mezze* dishes (hummus, *mutabal*, etc.) and traditional Jordanian dishes such as *mensaf* or *maqlouba* for only JD3.000. (Open daily 7:30am-9pm.)

The central **post office** (open Sat.-Thurs. 8am-7pm, Fri. 8am-1:30pm) is located on King Abdallah St. around the corner from the tourist office. The **Housing Bank** (open Sat.-Thurs. 8am-12:30pm) is on the other side of King Abdallah St. but not directly opposite the post office. Madaba also has a police station. The nearest hospital, 1km from Madaba, is **Nadim Hospital** (tel. 54 40 08). Madaba's **telephone code** is 08.

Service (330fils) and **buses** (175fils) run back and forth between Madaba and Wahadat Station in southern Amman regularly until 6 or 7pm.

Near Madaba: Mount Nebo and Zarqa Ma'in

No wonder Moses's last request to God was for a view from **Mount Nebo**. On a clear day you can see across the Jordan Valley to the glistening Dead Sea and beyond to Jericho. The Bible says "no man knows the place of his burial to this day" (Deuteronomy 34:6), but Moses's grave is rumored to be in a secret cave somewhere along the **Ain Musa**. There are only a few tombs on Nebo itself, but on the higher Mount Pisgah stands an enigmatic serpentine cross next to the **Memorial of Moses.** The memorial houses the baptismal fonts and well-preserved "Mosaic" mosaics of a Byzantine church dedicated to Moses. It also contains restored mosaic panels unearthed by an Italian archeological team and Franciscan monks, whose mountaintop excavations have uncovered monasteries dating back to the 3rd century CE. The buildings close at 6pm, but walk beyond them for an evening view of the Dead Sea.

Traffic is too light for convenient hitching from Madaba to the mountaintop, but you can take a taxi round-trip, including about 30 minutes to look around (price negotiable). Just beyond Faysalieh, a small town near Mount Nebo, a marked turn-off leads to **Khirbet al-Mukhaiyat**. If you've yet to deem mosaics prosaic, you may want to make the one-hour detour (round-trip) to see secular scenes of fishing, hunting, and wine-making that decorate another finely-preserved Byzantine church floor. Cigarettes are the preferred *baksheesh* for the Bedouin gatekeeper who lives next to the mosaic on the hill at the end of the paved road. (Open as late as the gatekeeper is willing, usually dusk.)

Herod the Great, Governor of Judea in 40 BCE, frequented the hot mineral springs at **Zarqa Ma'in** to relieve his great rheumatism. As he lay dying, he was carried here from his fortress at nearby Mukawer—where Salome danced and John the Baptist lost his head (Matthew 14:1-12). The road from Madaba tumbles southeast from a high escarpment to the Zarqa Ma'in River, into which spring water cascades from the low cliffs. From the road you can see the hills of the West Bank rising across the Dead Sea. JD3.300 (JD5.500 with lunch) allows you to enter the new **Ma'in Spa Village**, located at the end of the road in the center of a ring of mountains and hills. Get your swaddlings and Fungo therapy here. In addition, both men and women can swim in **Hamman az-Zarqa,** the hot indoor pool sunk in the cliff face, or bathe under the voluptuous torrents of hot waterfalls. Reach Zarqa Ma'in by **bus** from Madaba (95fils). The JETT Bus Company in Amman offers 8am-6pm daytrips to the springs for JD8 round-trip—including a lunch that's nothing to write home, or in a travel guide, about.

The Kings' Highway from Madaba to Karak chugs over plateaus and wadis. Forty kilometers south of Madaba the road descends into the vast **Wadi Mujeeb**, 4km wide and 1100m deep. On one escarpment lies the Biblical **Dibon** where the Mesha Stele was found in 1868. (The original tablet, engraved by King Mesha with the earliest Hebrew script found up to that time, now resides in the Louvre. Copies may be seen in both the Karak and Madaba Museums.) An ancient Roman mile marker is on the road approaching the modern town of Dhiban and the wondrous Wadi Mujeeb unfurls after the town disappears from view.

Few buses run directly from Madaba to Karak along the highway. The easiest way to go is to hitch or catch a minibus to **al-Qasr,** which features a ruined Roman temple (c. 350 CE) and a bus to Karak (200fils).

Karak الكرك

The ancient capital of Moab, Karak now humbles itself in the shadow of **Karak Castle,** the largest of the mountaintop Crusader castles, which stretch from Turkey to southern Jordan. In 1132 CE, Baldwin I built the castle midway between Shobak and Jerusalem. Although the fortress wall has mostly collapsed, its building blocks remain large enough to inspire awe. Inside, the vaulted stone ceilings span only a few meters, resulting in a network of long narrow audience halls and barracks. You can still see the bolt holes for mammoth stone doors that have since turned to dust or, worse, souvenirs. The castle is riddled with secret passageways and hidden rooms. To the west across the moat you can see battlements from which the charming Renauld de Chatillon cast prisoners to their deaths (with wooden boxes attached to their heads to preserve their consciousness). The tower in the northwest corner is a 13th-century addition. Below, a 50m tunnel leads out of the town through an arched gateway. (Open daily 8am-7pm. Free.)

To the right of the castle entrance, a stone staircase descends to the **Archeological Museum.** It holds Nabatean and Roman coins, Mamluk pottery, insipid descriptions of the incredible archaeological site at Bab adh-Dhira and of the biblical cities of

Buseirah and Rabbah, and a plaster copy of Dhiban's Mesha Stele, too. (Open Wed.-Mon. 8am-5pm. Admission 250fils.)

Walking downhill from the Karak Castle, take your first right. Above the Castle Hotel is a genially useless **tourist office** (open Sat.-Thurs. 8am-2pm). The **police station** is located down the street and on the right, next to the huge radio tower. The **post office** (open Sat.-Thurs. 7:30am-7pm, Fri. 8am-1:30pm) is across the street from the Castle Hotel. Karak also has a hospital, the **Italian Hospital** (tel. 35 10 45 or 35 11 45), downhill from the turn-off up to the Castle, next to the public park. The **Housing Bank,** where you can exchange traveler's checks and cash, is located uphill from the Italian Hospital (open Sat.-Thurs. 8am-12:30pm). The **telephone code** for Karak is 03.

Occasional minibuses make the trip to Karak from Wadi Musa (near Petra) for a few hundred fils. *Service* (JD1.070) and buses (600fils) from Wadahat Station in Amman are more reliable but less scenic—they run directly to Karak via the Desert Highway, skirting the gorgeous wadis north of Karak.

There are several ways to get from Karak to Petra: Continue down the Kings' Highway to Tafilah by bus and see more evocative scenery (76km, 480fils), or catch a faster bus to Ma'an via the Desert Highway and a *service* from there to Petra. If you're going as far as Aqaba, you can take the Wadi Araba (Jordan Valley) Highway (bus from Karak leaves at 2:30pm, 3.5hr., JD2.360). You must receive permission to use the highway from the police in Karak by presenting your passport (if you're driving it's done while you wait). No hitching is allowed.

Accommodations in Karak are limited but adequate. The rooms at the government **Rest House** (tel. 35 11 48) are acceptable and have private baths and fans. (Singles JD13.500. Doubles JD17. 10% service charge.) The best cheap and seemingly safe lodging is the **Castle Hotel** (tel. 35 24 89). (Singles JD5.500. Doubles JD6.) A couple of tiny hotels near the center of town offer less comfortable rooms for less.

The prosperous modern town of Karak extends away from the castle on its northern and eastern slopes and serves as an ideal resting place for travelers on the Kings' Highway. A snack or meal at the government **Rest House** (tel. 35 11 48) near the entrance to the castle affords you a view of the Jordan Valley's descent to the Dead Sea. (Beer JD2, hummus 350fils, full lunch or dinner JD3.850.) To avoid these inflated prices, try the **Fida Restaurant** (tel. 60 73 52 or 60 76 77), across the street from the police station and the radio tower. (Open daily 8am-10pm.) True budgeteers picnic atop the sublime ruins.

Near Karak

Highway 80 west from Karak drops from the Kings' Highway for 20km until it reaches the Dead Sea "port" of Mazra'ah and the al-Lisan (tongue) Peninsula. About 5km before reaching Mazra'ah and the Wadi Araba Highway to Aqaba, Highway 80 passes **Bab adh-Dhira.** The cemeteries at this ancient site contain some 20,000 shaft tombs enshrining 500,000 bodies (an unfortunate body-per-tomb ratio) and over 3 million pottery vessels. The length of the bones indicates that the average height in Bab el-Dhira was a sturdy 2m.

Hitchers report that there is very little traffic between here and Karak, and on the Wadi Araba Highway along the Dead Sea to Aqaba. Stop in at the **Mazra'ah Police Post,** 5km north of the junction, if you need assistance. The Wadi Araba highway, running right beside Israel, is sometimes closed to civilian travel.

Traveling east on Highway 80 toward Qatrana on the Desert Highway you'll pass the turn-off for **al-Lejjun,** where archeologists have excavated the Roman Empire's southeasternmost frontier post. Streets, barracks, a tower, a church, and a *principium,* dating from 30 CE and destroyed by an earthquake in 551, have all been unearthed. The main ruin site is 2km north of the turn-off, on the hill below the Turkish barracks. The barracks were constructed from stone pillaged from the site in order to defend the nearby railway against T.E. Lawrence and his posse (now used as stables). Take a *ser-*

vice (450fils) or bus (310fils) toward Qatrana and ask the driver to let you off at the "Lejjun" turn-off (the sign is in Arabic only).

The tremendous hospitality of locals is virtually guaranteed and your only hope in towns just north of Karak on the Kings' Highway (Rabba, Qasr) and immediately to the south (Mazar, Tafilah). The mosques at Mu'tah and at the nearby village of Mazar commemorate the Islamic generals who died in the first great battles between the forces of Islam and Byzantium in 632 CE. The green-domed mosque in Mazar houses a small Islamic museum on the first floor.

Shobak شـوبك

As the desert becomes more desolate and Petra's small brook more resonant from only a half-hour drive south, the village of Shobak (Nijil-Shobak) emerges. From the marked turn-off at the northern edge of town, travel 4km to **Shobak Castle,** the first of seven castles built by the Crusader King Baldwin I in 1115 to control the triangular trade route between Syria, Egypt, and Saudi Arabia. It didn't work; the castle fell to Salah al-Din in 1189. Although most of the castle is gone, the view from the approach road across the natural moat is inspiring, with colossal white stones silhouetted against desert brush and a cobalt sky. Villagers who lived inside the castle walls and depended upon the water from the rock-hewn well, 375 steps deep, have recently abandoned the area, leaving a secluded spot for free camping.

Shobak town can possibly be reached in a shared minibus from Karak and Wadi Musa (near Petra), although much of the traffic between those towns takes the Desert Highway. If you hire a taxi, make sure the driver will not gouge you for waiting while you investigate.

Petra متـرى

> *"Rose-red Petra, half as old as time."*
> —*John William Burgon*

The once-lost city of Petra is now easy to find; ease of access hardly lessens its magnificence. Nothing could. After hiking about 2.5m through a natural 3m-wide fissure, one approaches a towering sculpture, raw mountains fashioned by human hands into impossibly delicate structures. This is Khazneh, the so-called "treasury," Petra's finest monument to the vigilant gods of the dead. Petra, meaning "stone" in ancient Greek, is perhaps the most astounding ancient city left to the modern world—and certainly the biggest must-see in Jordan. It's worth changing your travel plans just to explore this insane Nabatean city built to rival the imposing proportions of the surrounding mountains.

For 700 years, Petra was lost to all but the few hundred members of the Bedouin tribe who guarded their treasure from outsiders. In the 19th century, the Swiss explorer Johann Burkhardt heard Bedouin speaking of the "lost city" and vowed to find it. Initially he was unable to find a guide, but he knew that if this were the Petra of legend, the biblical Sela, then it must be close to Mount Hor, the site of Aaron's tomb. Impersonating a pilgrim, Burkhardt found a guide and, on August 22, 1812, walked between the cliffs of Petra's *siq* (entrance). Awed and driven to sketch the monuments and record his thoughts, this pragmatic pilgrim aroused the suspicion of his Bedouin guide. The guide warned him of the spiritual significance of the ancient rocks, and a chastened Burkhardt left—but announced his discovery to the world. In the nearly two centuries since, Petra has been molested by visitors ranging from the film crew of *Indiana Jones and the Last Crusade* to hordes of tourists from Bethesda, Maryland, asking, "Where's the ladies' room?"

The area's principal water source, Ein Musa (Spring of Moses), is one of the many places where Moses supposedly struck a rock with his staff and extracted water (Exodus 17). Human history in the area dates back to the 8th millennium BCE, when farmers settled in this area and put to use the newly developed techniques of agricultural cultivation. By the 6th century BCE, the Nabateans, a nomadic Arab tribe, had quietly moved onto land controlled by the Edomites and had begun to profit from the trade between lower Arabia and the Fertile Crescent. Over the next three centuries the Nabatean Kingdom flourished, secure in its easily defended capital. During this era the Nabateans carved their monumental temples out of the mountains, looking to Egyptian, Greek, and Roman styles for inspiration. Unique to the Nabateans are the crow-step (staircase) patterns that grace the crowns of many of the memorials. A legend explains these decorations: the crow-steps so decidedly resemble inverted stairways that the people of Meda'in Salih (a miniature Petra in Saudi Arabia) claim that to punish Petra's wickedness, God threw Petra upside down and turned it to stone.

More historically verifiable evidence suggests that in 63 BCE the Nabatean King Aretas defeated Pompey's Roman Legions. The Romans controlled the entire area around Nabatea, however, prompting the later King Rabel III to strike a deal: as long as the Romans did not attack during his lifetime, they would be permitted to move in after he died. In 106 CE the Romans claimed the Nabatean Kingdom and began to develop the city of rosy Nubian sandstone.

In its heyday, Petra may have housed 20,000-30,000 people. But after an earthquake in 363 CE, a shift in the trade routes to Palmyra (Tadmor) in Syria, the expansion of the sea trade around Arabia, and another earthquake in 747 CE, all but Petra's rock-hewn tombs deteriorated to rubble. The city fell under Byzantine and then Arab control for the few centuries before the Crusaders tried to resurrect it by constructing a new fortress. By this time, though, its importance had so declined that even its location was forgotten. A few explorers futilely searched for Petra, but not until Burkhardt schemed his way in was the city visited by anyone other than the Bedouin.

For decades, the resident Bedouin adapted to the influx of tourists by providing food and accommodations inside Petra for them. In 1984-85, however, the government removed them, out of concern for the fragility of the monuments. Virtually all of Petra's Bedouin have been relocated to a housing project near Wadi Musa and spend their days hawking souvenirs at the site. Burkhardt had a big mouth.

Practical Information

Petra is located in the rocky wilderness near the southern extreme of the Kings' Highway about 280km from Amman, or 260km via the Desert Highway. Air-conditioned **JETT coaches** leave Amman daily at 6:30am and arrive about three and a half hours later; they return at 4pm from Petra (one way JD5; round-trip JD9.500; complete tour including lunch, guide, and horse JD25.500). Reservations should be made at JETT stations well ahead of time, especially during the busy fall and spring seasons. You'll be dropped off at the visitors center in Petra.

Service to Petra from Wahadat Station takes about five hours, plus a wait in Ma'an (JD2.345, JD1.650 if you take the bus directly from Amman to Wadi Musa). Drivers will drop you off at either the al-Anbat or the Wadi Musa Hotels. From Aqaba, the two-hour trip costs 930fils by minibus. There are also special JETT trips from Aqaba. Start early in the morning to make any of these connections. Leaving Petra, you can catch minibuses or s*ervice* to Aqaba, Ma'an, or Amman at the center of Wadi Musa, near the post office, between 5:30 and 6am. A local bus to Ma'an leaves at 6am, returns at 2pm, and costs 475fils one way.

To reach Petra from the Kings' Highway, take the well-marked turn-off and head west into the colorful, steep-sided town of Wadi Musa. You'll pass the main traffic circle and travel through the main market area of Wadi Musa. After a tortuous 5km, the spur road leaves town and ends at the entrance to Petra. The cluster of buildings here includes the visitors center, the government Rest House, the lavish Forum Hotel, and the gatehouse to the valley that leads to the *siq* and Petra proper.

The tourist police munch on cigar ends at the **Petra Visitors Center** (tel. (03) 830 60), where you can hire an official guide for JD5 per trip. (Open daily 7am-6pm in summer, 7am-5pm in winter.) It's easy to tag along behind a group with a guide or to form a group of your own. The various guidebooks available at the visitors center are helpful, but there's no substitute for the expertise of an official guide for trips to the more remote sites of al-Barid or al-Madras. On the other side of the visitors center are the **Rest House** and the swinging gate marking the beginning of the trail down to the *siq*. You can rent a horse for the short ride (JD4.500), but it's more interesting to walk, admiring the tower cliffs of Jebel Khubtha to the right, Jebel Madras to the left, and the monuments you come upon every few meters.

Admission to the ancient city is JD1 for adults, 100fils for children. Petra is open daily from 6am-6pm, but these hours are loosely enforced. The generous guard at the entrance to the *siq* often admits people as late as 8pm.

Accommodations, Camping, and Food

Budget accommodations are not exactly plentiful in Wadi Musa and near Petra, but competition is fierce (especially off-season) and the quality generally as rosy as the sandstone. Shop around before you decide. Closest to Petra is the government **Rest House** (tel. (03) 830 11) which charges a hefty JD20 for singles, JD30 for doubles, and JD10 per extra bed. About 200m up the hill to your left, before the Visitors Center, is the **Sunset Hotel** (tel. (03) 835 79), which has doubles for JD12, JD9 without a bathroom. You can also camp on the roof for JD3. Although located further up the hill in Wadi Musa, the **Musa Spring Hotel** (tel. (03) 833 10) and **al-Anbat Hotel, Restaurant, and Student House** (tel. (03) 832 65) are probably the best bet for budget travelers. Both provide free transportation to and from Petra at regular intervals, and have helpful staff. The Musa Spring is slightly farther out of town and marginally cheaper. (Roof beds JD1. Doubles JD5. Breakfast JD1, lunch or dinner JD2. Free hot showers.) **Al-Anbat** is a smidgen larger and affords an incredible view of the valley. (Camping on the roof JD1.500. Singles JD5. Doubles JD8. Prices negotiable.)

For **camping** inside Petra proper, write to the minister of antiquities in Amman (Dept. of Antiquities, P.O. Box 88, Amman, Jordan) at least three weeks ahead of time for a permit. Although you'll probably never be found if you illegally hole yourself up in one of Petra's vacant caves, security has been tighter in recent years. Explaining your story to Jordanian police could turn you pinker than the monuments.

The **Rest House Restaurant** is worth a visit only because it was built into one of Petra's Nabatean tombs; have a drink in the tomb's lively inner-chamber-*cum*-bar. In the separate eatery, a filling meal costs JD3.850 (both open until 11pm daily). The Rest House's new restaurant should be open by January 1993. About JD2.500 gets you a tasty meal at the **Sunset Hotel**, and at the **New Petra Restaurant**, adjoining the al-Anbat Hotel, you can get grilled meat and salad for JD2.500 or a breakfast of eggs, hummus, and tea for JD1. The only place to grab a bite in Petra itself is a small and expensive sandwich shop below the museum. The town has a post office next to the Musa Spring Hotel (open Sat.-Thurs. 7:30am-7pm, Fri. 7:30am-1:30pm), numerous stores, and a **health center**. There is also a **post office** right behind the Petra Visitors Center (same hours as above).

Sights

Aside from a number of revered monarchs, the Nabateans worshipped only two deities: Dushara, the god of strength, symbolized by hard, sculptured rock, and al-Uzza (or Atargatis), the goddess of water and fertility. Still, the number of temples and tombs in Petra seems infinite. Despite cars now occasionally squeezing through the *siq*, a little climbing allows you to escape the tour groups that crowd the Khazneh and inner valley. A few of the spectacular monuments are close enough to be viewed in a one-day junket, but the majority require sweaty exploration. Be sure to bring plenty of water—Bedouin selling bottled water will take advantage of your desperation.

Even before the *siq*, caves stare from distant mountain faces and large *djinn* monuments (ghost tombs) woo. (An unsettling thought: some archeologists theorize they might be sacrificial altars.) On the left, built high into the cliff, stands the Obelisk

Tomb. Closer to the entrance of the *siq*, rock-cut channels once cradled ceramic pipes which brought Ein Musa's waters to the inner city as well as to the surrounding farm country. A nearby dam burst in 1963 and the resulting flash flood killed 28 tourists in the *siq*. While designing a new dam, excavators uncovered the ancient Nabatean dam and used it as a model for the new one.

As you enter the *siq*, walls towering 200m on either side begin to block out the light, casting enormous shadows on the niches that once held icons of the gods to protect the entrance and hex unwelcome visitors. The *siq* winds around for 1.5km, then slowly admits a faint pink glow as it widens at the **Khazneh** (Treasury), standing guard over the exit. At 90m wide and 130m tall, it is the best preserved of Petra's monuments, although bullet holes are clearly visible on the upper urn. Believing the urn to be hollow and filled with ancient pharaonic treasures, Bedouin periodically fired at it, hoping to burst this impervious piñata. Actually, the treasury was a royal tomb and, like almost everything else at Petra, is quite solid. The colors are incredible; in the morning the sun's rays give the monument a rich peach color, while in late afternoon it glistens rose and then turns blood-red with the sunset.

Down to the road to the right as you face the Khazneh, Wadi Musa opens up to the large **Roman Theater** (straight ahead) and the long row of Royal Tombs on the face of Jebel Khubtha (on your right as the road curves to the right in front of the Roman Theater). The Romans built their theater under and into the red stone Nabatean necropolis, whose caves still yawn above it. The theater seats some 3000 people and is being restored to its 2nd-century appearance; appreciative audiences are returning for the first time in over 1500 years. A marble Hercules (now in the museum) was discovered just a few years ago in the curtained chambers beneath the stage.

Across the wadi are the **Royal Tombs.** The **Urn Tomb,** with its unmistakable recessed façade, commands a soul-scorching view of the still-widening valley. Nearby is the **Corinthian Tomb,** allegedly a replica of Nero's Golden Palace in Rome. The **Palace Tomb** (or the Tomb in Two Stories) literally juts out from the mountainside. The tomb had to be completed by attaching preassembled stones to its upper left-hand corner. Around the corner to the right is the **Tomb of Sextus Florentinus,** who was so enamored of these hewn heights that he asked his son to bury him in this ultimate outpost of the Roman Empire.

Around the bend to the left, several restored columns dot either side of the paved Roman **main street.** Two thousand years ago, columns lined the full length of the street, with markets and residences branching off. Nearby the raised **Nymphaeum** ruins outline the ancient public fountain near its base. Farther along is the triple-arched **Temenos Gate,** formerly thought to have been constructed to herald a visiting emperor who never arrived. Recent excavations reveal that it was actually the front gate of the **Qasr Bint Faroan** (Palace of the Pharaoh's Daughter), a Nabatean temple built to honor the god Dushara. Across the road to the right, before the triple-arched gate, recent excavations have uncovered the **Temple of al-Uzza (Atargatis)**, also called the **Temple of the Winged Lions.** In the spring you can watch the progress of the American-sponsored excavations, which have already uncovered several workshops and some cracked Nabatean crocks. On your left as you pass through the triple-arched gate is the **Nabatean Temple.** On the trail leading off behind the temple to the left, a single standing column gloats beside its two fallen comrades—the **Zib Faroan** (Pharaoh's Phallus, perhaps Ramses') marks the entrance to the ancient Roman city. (The priggish Arabic sign actually reads "Amoud Faroan," Pharaoh's Pillar.) To the right of the Nabatean temple, a rock-hewn staircase leads to a small archeological **museum,** which holds the spoils of the Winged Lions dig and carved stone figures from elsewhere in Petra. (Open daily 6am-6pm. Free.)

Hikes

Up to this point, particularly if you're visiting Petra during the peak spring and fall seasons, you'll have shared this splendor with a drove of peregrinating shutterbugs. Many people, content with daytrip dosage, will go home raving about Petra's first ten percent. But it's only the tip of an inverted iceberg: the magnificent rest of Petra is nestled in dozens of high places scattered over a vast area. At least two days are necessary for the following four treks and another two or three days if you venture beyond Petra proper—assuming you don't get indulgently lost at least a few times. The Bedouin say to appreciate Petra you must stay long enough to watch your nails grow long.

The shortest and easiest of the hikes leads down the wadi to the left of and behind the Temple of the Winged Lions. Fifteen minutes of strolling down the road that runs through the rich green gardens of **Wadi Turkimaniya** guide you to the only tomb at Petra with a Nabatean inscription. The lengthy invocation above the entrance beseeches the god Dushara to safeguard the tomb and to protect its contents from violation. Unfortunately, Dushara took an interminable sabbatical and the chamber has been stripped bare.

A second, more interesting climb begins at the end of the road that descends from the Pharaoh's Phallus to the cliff face, a few hundred meters left of the museum. The trail dribbles up to the **Qasr Habis** (Crusader Castle), outclassed by many of Petra's other splendors. The steps have been recently restored and the climb to the top and back takes well under an hour.

Jebel Harun and Jebel Umm al-Biyara جبـل هـارون و جيـل ام بـيارة

The third climb begins just to the right of Jebel Habis below the museum. A sign points to **ad-Deir** (the Monastery) and leads northwest across Wadi Siyah, past the Forum Restaurant to Wadi Deir and its fragrant oleander. As you squeeze through the narrowing canyon you will confront a human-shaped hole in the façade of the **Lion's Tomb.** A hidden tomb awaits daredevils who try to climb the cleft to the right; less intrepid wanderers can backtrack to the right and find it a few minutes later. Again on the path, veer left, and eventually stone steps lead past a providential Pepsi stand to Petra's largest monument.

Ad-Deir, 50m wide and 45m tall, was undertaken in the first century CE but never completed, and is less ornate than the Khazneh. On the left a lone tree popping through a crack in the rock marks more ancient steps, which continue all the way up to the rim of the urn atop the monastery. Straight across the wadi looms the highest peak in the area, **Jebel Harun** (Aaron's Mountain or Mount Hor). On top of the mountain a white church reportedly houses the **Tomb of Aaron.** The whole trip takes a couple of hours, a few more if you detour into **Wadi Siyah** and visit its seasonal waterfall on the way back.

The fourth hike climbs **Jebel Umm al-Biyara** (Mother of Cisterns), which towers over the Crusader castle on Jebel Habis. Follow the trail from the left of the Nabatean temple past the Pharoah's Phallus and down into the wadi to the right. If you scramble 50m up the rock chute to the left of the blue sign you'll reach the beginning of a stone ramp and stairway that leads to the top. It was here, at the site of Petra's original acropolis and the biblical city of Sela, that a Judean king supposedly hurled thousands of Edomites over the cliff's edge. The gigantic piles of shards, over 8000 years old, are the only remnants of the mountains' first inhabitants. This grueling excursion takes three hours.

If instead of climbing Umm al-Biyara you continue south along Wadi Tughra, which runs by its foot, you'll eventually reach the **Snake Monument**, one of the earliest Nabatean religious shrines. From here it's about two hours to Aaron's Tomb on Jebel Harun. The path meanders around Mount Hor before ascending it from the south. When it disappears on the rocks, follow the donkey dumpings. As you start to climb Jebel Harun you'll see a lone tent. A Bedouin inside, the official holder of the keys, will escort you the rest of the way and open the building for you to explore. The entire trek takes five or six hours.

The High Place

One of the most popular hikes is the circular route to the **High Place** on Jebel al-Madbah, a place of sacrifice with a full view of Petra. A staircase sliced in the rock leads to the left just as the Roman Theater comes into view. Follow the right prong when the trail levels and forks at the top of the stairs. On the left, **Obelisk Ridge** presents one obelisk to Dushara and another to al-Uzza. On the peak to the right, the Great High Place supports a string of grisly sights: two neatly cut altars, an ablution cistern, gutters for draining away sacrificial blood, and cliff-hewn bleachers for a delightfully unobstructed view of the slaughter. To mollify sangrophobic nerves, head downhill past the Pepsi stand, leaving the obelisks behind you, and backtrack neologistically under the western face of the Great High Place. If you hunt around you'll find a staircase leading down to a sculptured **Lion Fountain.** The first grotto complex beyond it is the **Garden Tomb.** Below it is the **Tomb of the Roman Soldier** and across from it a rock *triclinium* (feast hall), which has the only decorated interior in Petra. The trail then leads into Wadi Farasa by the Katute site, the dwelling of a merchant apparently driven away by the Romans' nearby waste disposal site. You'll leave the trail near the Phallus. The circle, followed either way, takes about 90 minutes.

Al-Madras and al-Barid المدرس و الـبـارد

The region around Petra harbors a wealth of minor archeological pleasures, but only those within walking or donkey-riding distance are accessible. All roads in this isolated area lead back to the Kings' Highway, not to outlying sites. The peripheral location of the sites is a blessing; outside Petra, imported commercialism has neither altered the Bedouin lifestyle nor chased away wildlife.

A trail branches to your left just past the Obelisk Tumb and just before the entrance to the *siq*. The route leads to **al-Madras,** an ancient Petran suburb with almost as many monuments as Petra itself. On the way, watch for the short-eared desert hare and a full spectrum of long lanky lizards—purple, fuchsia, and iridescent blue. Come with plenty of water, a snack, and a Bedouin guide. The round-trip takes four to eight hours.

Past the Tomb of Sextus Florentinus and the **Mughar al-Nasara** (Caves of the Christians), a trail chisels into the rock leading to the northern suburb of **al-Barid.** A road passing the new hotel in Wadi Musa also approaches this archeological site. Al-Barid is a curious miniature of Petra, complete with a short *siq,* several carved tombs and caves, and inscriptions on high and mighty places. Also off the new road past the hotel is **al-Beidha.** Excitement runs high among the members of the excavating expedition here because they have uncovered traces of a pre-pottery Neolithic village, a sedentary society dating to the 8th century BCE. This finding would make it, along with Jericho, one of the earliest known farming communities in the world. A Bedouin guide can lead you here via a painless trail (about 3 hrs. each way). Again, bring munchies, hydrogen and oxygen in a 2:1 ratio, and an extra JD2-3 or some of your own native trinkets to trade—a ukelele, fuzzy dice, or a mood ring.

Southern Jordan

Aqaba العقبة

Set in a natural amphitheater beneath a curtain of rugged hills, Aqaba is land-locked Jordan's sole toe-hold on the Red Sea. A more spectacular scene than the reddish mountains, however, lurks under the sea: legions of brilliantly colored creatures flit through a surreal universe of coral. Aqaba is an important trade and military center, and as a swinging resort, it has become the darling of the Arab elite in need of a periodic escape from dry cityscapes. Backpackers may hyperventilate at the expensive accommodations and restaurants. Highfalutin' travelers from Germany might very well demand you leave "their" beach chairs; although you may have paid for it here, they paid for it back in Munich and still have first dibs.

With its strategic and commercial potential, Aqaba has never suffered neglect. In biblical times, Solomon's copper-laden ships sailed for Ophir from the port of Etzion-Geber. The Romans stationed their famous Tenth Legion here, the Crusaders fortified the port and the little Isle of Greye 7km off the coast, and the successors of Salah al-Din built the fort, whose remains grace a waterfront park today. During the 1917 Arab Revolt, Faisal ibn Hussein (played by Sir Alec Guinness in *Lawrence of Arabia*) and T.E. Lawrence (Peter O'Toole) staged a desert raid on the Ottomans' fortifications and valiantly captured the port. In 1965 King Hussein shrewdly traded the Saudis 600km square of southeastern desert for 13km of coastline, and started developing the city into a tourist's paradise. After the reopening of the Suez Canal in 1957 and the increased traffic caused by the Iran-Iraq War, the harbor became packed with huge juggernauts bulging with cargo. During the 1991 Gulf War, the blockade of the port, which became Iraq's chief illicit outlet to shipping lanes, slowed traffic considerably. Trade had resumed under international supervision, by the summer of 1992.

Practical Information

Visitors Center: (tel. 31 33 63 or 31 37 31), on the grounds of the new Islamic Museum between Salah al-Din's fort and the southern waterfront. Staff helpful to campers. Currently open 8am-2pm daily; hours to be extended to 5pm eventually.

Visas: Egyptian visas can be obtained in 1 day at the Aqaba consulate (tel. 31 61 71). Bring JD12, your passport, and 1 photo to the consulate on al-Istiqlal St.; turn right along the curve about 800m northwest of the Aquamarina II Hotel. Look for an empty guard booth in front. Consulate open daily 9am-1:30pm.

American Express: International Traders Travel Agency Office (tel. 31 37 57), 1 block west of Ailah Sq., a few doors from the Ali Baba Restaurant. P.O. Box 136. Open Sat.-Thurs. 8am-1pm and 4-7pm, a couple of hours Fri. mornings if business is good.

Central Post Office: 2 blocks uphill from Ailah Sq. (tel. 31 39 39), next to the large radio tower. **Poste Restante, international calls,** and **telegrams** here. Open Sat.-Thurs. 7:30am-7pm, Friday 7:30am-1:30pm. **Telephone code:** 03.

Air Travel: Alia has regular flights to and from Amman (about 45 min., JD15.600 one way, JD18 round-trip if you stay less than 10 days). Buses from Aqaba Airport to the center of the city are run by various hotels. The trip by taxi costs JD2 per person.

JETT Buses: Station 1km west of Ailah Sq. (tel. 31 52 22), on the corner of a dumpy shopping complex by the Miramar Hotel. Regular bus service to Amman only (7 buses daily: 7, 8, and 9am, and 1:30, 2, 3:30, and 4pm; 4hr.; JD3.500). Bus to Petra Mon., Wed., and Fri. (JD3.500 one way, JD18.500 for a complete tour including lunch, guide, horse, and round-trip transportation) leaves at 8:30am, returns at 4pm. Best to reserve in advance. JETT buses are luxury class, with hostess service, A/C, and videos.

Buses and *Service*: Station 2 blocks uphill of Ailah Sq. Serves points north of Aqaba. Several minibuses per day to Petra, depending on demand (JD1.750). Regular taxis offer groups quick transport to Petra (JD25). You can sometimes find taxis to Wadi Rum (1 hr., JD25 round-trip). Taxis to Aqaba ferry terminal (10km, JD1.500).

Ferries to Egypt: Jordanian National Lines to Nuweiba in the Sinai (daily, around 11am, 2pm, and 4pm; 3.5hrs; US$18 plus JD6 departure tax). Several hour waits are not uncommon. Overnight facilities at Nuweiba (hotels and camping) if you arrive late. Buses from Nuweiba to Cairo meet the boats (6-10 hrs., JD6). In Aqaba purchase tickets from any agency; in Amman at the JETT Station or Za'artarah Shipping on Prince Muhammad St., off Third Circle (open Sat.-Thurs. 8:30am-7pm, Fri. 8:30am-noon). Jordan National Lines headquarters are in Amman (tel. (06) 78 27 82).

Car Rental: Prices are controlled by the government and range from JD16 to JD27 per day, plus 50-70fils per km. Call around for specials. Rental agencies include **Rum** (tel. 31 35 81), **Manama** (tel. 31 81 22), and **al-Cazar** (tel. 31 41 31).

English Bookstore: Yamani Bookshop (tel. 31 22 21) opposite the post office. Decent selection of magazines and tourist guides. Also sells film, snorkeling equipment, suntan lotion, tobacco, and sundries. Open 10am-2:30pm, 6-10pm daily.

Pharmacies: Bayla Pharmacy (tel. 31 50 50) and the **Jerusalem Pharmacy** (tel. 31 47 47) are open 24 hrs.

Medical Emergency: Princess Haya el-Hussein Hospital (tel. 31 41 11/2), near the JETT Station on the way into town. One of Jordan's best hospitals, with decompression chambers and a staff capable of dealing with diving accidents.

Police: Station down the steps and 100m to the right of the Palm Beach Hotel (tel. 31 24 11/2). Issues camping permits for JD1.

Extending from King Hussein's villa on the Israeli border to the huge, fenced-in port facilities 4km down the arching corniche to the southeast, Aqaba is one elongated beach. Luxury hotels and military complexes have gobbled up a good part of the beach near town. Four countries come together in the small northern tip of the Gulf of Aqaba: Egypt meets Israel near the conspicuous resort hotels at Taba, Israel's Eilat faces Jordan's Aqaba across a quiet buffer zone, and Saudi Arabia looms on the southeast horizon.

Assorted shops line the streets of central Aqaba that branch from **Ailah Sq.** South of the port and 10km from central Aqaba, the **ferry dock** handles the thousands of Egyptian workers and occasional foreign travelers who cross the Gulf of Aqaba to Nuweiba or Suez in Egypt (see Ferries to Egypt above). If you'll be taking the ferry, be sure to arrive with an **Egyptian visa** already in hand. (See the Nuweiba Ferry section in the Sinai chapter for information on traveling to Aqaba from Egypt.) One kilometer past the ferry port you'll come to the Marine Research Center building, just past which you'll find Aqaba's finest coral reefs and a sandy beach that stretches south to a factory and the Saudi border.

Those who hitch in and around Aqaba find it easy because an army of trucks serves the port. Herds of six-wheeled beasts cover vast stretches along the highway 2km north of town. These truck stops make strategic starting points for hitching trips to the north. Taxi fare out to the truck stops is about 500fils; the road to the port, which bumps the eastern side of town, has closer hitching points.

Aqaba's overheated atmosphere has a discernible effect on human behavior. People drive like idiots here, even more so than in the rest of the country; there are (ignored) road signs telling drivers to lay off their horns. Aqaba is also far more lax about morality than the rest of Jordan. In the evenings it is not uncommon for hotel guests to drink, and both men and women can wear shorts in and around Aqaba. Finally, women should be especially careful about unwanted advances.

Accommodations and Camping

A question has long circulated among budget travelers (or at least among budget travelers trying to impress other budget travelers): which is higher in Aqaba—temperatures, tan lines, or prices? Sleeping near the beach or in an air-conditioned room will set you back several dinars. Several cheap hotels occupy the streets near Ailah Sq.—shop around before you decide. The only laundry facilities outside of hotels are at **Friends Laundry** (tel. 31 50 51), in the open area near the bus and service station.

Al-Shula Hotel, Raghadan St. (tel. 31 51 55), behind the Hussein ibn Ali Mosque. Color TV, refrigerators, bidets, balconies, and a charming view of Eilat. Red curtains cast a gory pall over the rooms on sunny afternoons. Singles JD14. Doubles JD17.500. Breakfast included.

Nairoukh Hotel 2 (tel. 31 29 80/1), down the street from the mosque. New and clean. Comparable to al-Shula in terms of amenities and prices. Knowledgeable staff. Singles JD13. Doubles JD17.

Nairoukh Hotel (tel. 31 29 84/5), adjoining the Red Sea Hotel. Quiet and clean. Singles with A/C, TV, bath, and refrigerator JD6. Doubles JD8.

Aqaba Hotel (tel. 31 40 91), along the waterfront 1.5km west of Ailah Sq. For the self-indulgent who must be close by the beach. Very friendly staff. Puff on pungent *nargileh* out on the beach. Regular rooms will break your budget, but you can sometimes put 3 people in a bungalow for JD40.

Red Sea Hotel (tel. 31 21 56), in a tall, prominently labeled building just off the northwest corner of Ailah Sq. Fans *and* a crosswind. Congenial management. Singles with bath JD6. Doubles JD7, with A/C, TV, and fridge JD12.

Jordan Flowers Hotel (tel. 31 43 77), a half block north of the Jerusalem Hotel. Welcoming and weedless. Two-star hotel with A/C, TVs, baths, and balconies in every room. Singles JD8.500. Doubles JD10.500.

Jerusalem Hotel (tel. 31 48 15), on the 2nd floor of the street running south from Ailah Sq. Plenty of fans, showers, and low prices. Best to sleep on the roof (with its own mattresses and showers) for 600fils. Singles JD2. Doubles JD3.500.

Nile Palace Hotel (tel. 31 51 77/8), at the northeast corner of Ailah Sq. Park, across a vacant lot full of bottles and bricks from the Arab Bank. Not quite palatial—psychedelic wall murals and grimy bathrooms. Plenty of fans. Singles JD1.500. Doubles JD3.

The only legal **camping** north of the port is in the lots beside some of the larger hotels. The **Aqaba Hotel** has hard ground (it's basically a parking lot) and the JD4.400 fee also admits you to the private beach and showers. Six kilometers south of the port are the new and wonderfully scenic government camping facilities with showers and bathrooms for only 750fils.

Food

Aqaba's fare is only fair. Fresh fish, the obvious staple of a sea-side town, is actually a rarity here. Because of the low plankton content in the clear northern waters of the Gulf of Aqaba, there are few edible sea creatures afloat. Jordanians are not permitted to fish richer Saudi waters and the Egyptian export tax is outlandish. There is a **market** just up from Ailah Sq. where you can fill up on fresh fruit, bread, and cheese, though your snout may be overwhelmed on windless summer days. Shops on the streets surrounding the square sell delicacies from fried sloth to ice cream, all at high prices.

Ali Baba Restaurant (tel. 31 39 01), on the corner north of the mosque, downhill from Ata Ali. Aqaba's hip hangout, specializing in fresh fish (entrees JD5 and up) and Lebanese *hors d'oeuvres* (220-770fils). Service gives lots of time to admire campy fish fountain dedicated to King Hussein and the 40 thieves. Open daily 8am-11pm.

Chicken Tikka, An-Nahda St. (tel. 31 36 33), 100m west of the Aquamarina II Hotel on your right. Red-and-white modern decor. Slim menu but best fries in Jordan. Try the Tikka Special— 2 pieces of spicy chicken, fries, and *burri*— JD1.600. Open daily 11am-11pm.

Captain's Restaurant, An-Nahda St. (tel. 31 69 05), west of the Aquamarina II Hotel, or look for the blue-and-white veranda. Cheery staff, pleasant manager, plastic seaweed. Delectable spaghetti dishes (JD1.100-1.300) and fresh fish (JD4). Omelette 300fils. Open daily 8am-midnight or 1am.

Chili House Restaurant (tel. 31 24 35), behind the Captain's Restaurant and to the left of Mickey Mouse. Extraordinary double cheeseburger (JD1.100), fish sandwiches (JD1.150), and slushpuppies (250fils). Look for the photo of a sheepishly grinning King Hussein on waterskis above the counter. Open daily 11am-midnight.

Ata Ali Café (tel. 31 52 00), to the north of the Hussein ibn Ali Mosque. Pink-and-white chairs. Filling meals for JD3-JD3.500; hard or soft *knaffeh* 400fils. Mouthwatering 3-scoop sundaes and sugar cones, 500fils. Open daily 11:30am-midnight.

Sights

With all due respect, we tell you: go soak your besnorkeled head. **Yemenieh Reef,** just south of the Marine Research Station beyond the port, ranks among the world's best for scoping fish, if that's what you go for. The new **Royal Diving Center** (tel. 31 75 30) in the Yemenieh Area rents out snorkeling and diving equipment. Most luxury hotels also rent out equipment and organize outings. With a mask, snorkel, and pair of fins you can wander off on your own to some of the more isolated spots near the Saudi border, where the fish run on super-octane. Always cover your feet; the coral can slice them at the lightest touch. Also be careful about what you poke: urchins, fire coral, chicken fish, and stone fish might poke back. All are painful and the last three sometimes deadly. (For emergency medical help call 31 41 11.)

The **Seastar Watersports Center** (tel. 31 41 31/2), located in the al-Cazar Hotel, conducts dives daily at 9am and 2pm (arrive 30 min. early). Equipment rental for divers is US$19, JD5 for snorkelers, including transportation. Try-out dives are also possible for beginners. If you have five days and are serious about submerging, you might want to take the official (American) PCEI training course (US$250 plus approximately US$42 for supplies). If you plan to spend more than a few days snorkeling, you could invest in your own equipment and go solo. The **Yamani Bookstore** across from the post office has the biggest selection of masks (JD8-12) and fins (JD12-20).

Meet fish on your own terms at the **aquarium** in the Marine Research Center (tel. 31 51 45), just beyond the port. (Admission 300fils. Open Sat.-Wed. 7am-2:30pm, Thurs. and Fri. 9am-3:30pm; daily 7:30am-3:30pm in the winter.) Another option is a costly **glass-bottom boat ride** (about JD10) traveling up and down the coast, worthwhile if you've never been to a tropical fish store.

In early mornings and late afternoons the winds are strong enough to make **windsurfing** possible; the Aquamarina Club charges JD3 per half-hour for a board. The Aquamarina also offers waterskiing and, for the less adventurous, paddle-boating. Windsurfers risk being blown across the border illegally into Eilat as you swerve between tankers—makes a hell of a story to tell your grandkids.

The Aqaba Hotel will gouge you JD2.200 for the privilege of burning your plebeian feet on its patrician white sands—shade and lounge chairs are reserved for guests. Near the excavations of **Aila** (medieval Aqaba) in front of the Miramar Hotel is a free and relatively clean **public beach.** (In the 7th to 10th centuries, Aila—"god" in ancient Aramaic—was an early Islamic port trading as far away as China.) The majority of Aqaba's most scenic, clean, and empty free beaches are quite a distance away. Indigent sun and coral worshippers often walk southeast to the free pebble beach behind a "Restricted Area—No Camping" sign. It's mostly an all-male scene, and women may become the focus of more attention than they want. The trek past the port on the 10km strip leading to Saudi Arabia is long and the hitch difficult, but if you've got a whole day to conquer and a grand picnic, this is the place to go. A poke-bonnet and sunscreen are necessities, no matter how tan you think you are.

Aqaba should thank its lucky starfish for its aquatic splendors because the sights above sea level don't hold much water. The recently discovered ruins of Aila are the only exception, and they're not all that exceptional. In a seemingly plain beachside lot across from the Miramar Hotel, archeologists have uncovered the original 120 by 160m 10th-century port. The sight is always open and visitors are free to wander amidst the signs explaining the paltry ruins. Items recovered in the excavations, including Greek and Arabic inscriptions, pottery shards, and other small items are displayed in the recently completed **Aqaba Museum,** in the same building as the visitors center between the Fort of Salah al-Din and the southern waterfront (open daily 8am-2pm. 250fils donation requested). The **Medieval Fort** itself, behind a dilapidated mosque and a palm grove, is gradually being restored by the Department of Antiquities.

An accord between the Jordanian and Egyptian governments has recently opened up the Egyptian **Isle of Greye** (7km off shore) to tourists with Jordanian visas. Day-passes can be obtained in Aqaba and the boat ride takes about 45 minutes (JD20). There is boffo swimming and snorkeling (bring your own equipment) around the island (known in Arabic as Djezirat Faraum, Pharaoh's Isle), and on it stand the ruins of a castle that originally guarded this extreme end of the Crusader Kingdom of Jerusalem. Salah al-Din took it in 1171 but abandoned it in 1183 after counterattacks by the Europeans. The site has recently undergone extensive restoration.

Wadi Rum وادى رام

Those who most appreciate the majestic grandeur of Wadi Rum revel in its inaccessibility. No buses or *service* come here, and most Jordanians have never been to this area located nearly 300km south of Amman. Buses and *service* along the Desert Highway can drop you off 25km north of Aqaba at the turn-off marked "Rum-30km."

From there many people hitch a ride east and south to the **Desert Police Headquarters** within Wadi Rum. Hitching, always dangerous, is not a feasible option in the summer due to the lack of traffic in the area. *Do not attempt it.* A far wiser option is to form a group and either hire a taxi in Aqaba to transport you to and from Wadi Rum (JD25 per taxi) or rent a car on your own. Some of the more expensive Aqaba hotels organize their own trips; ask in advance. The journey is 90 minutes from Aqaba; the entrance fee, which includes tea or coffee in a Bedouin tent, is JD1. The Jordanian government has decided to push Wadi Rum as a tourist attraction—Douglas Scott climbed it in 1975 and they feel it's in your best interest to do the same.

Not without reason. Two tectonic plates have split to create the wide desert valley of Rum, and a sunset here is a wonder of darkness and light. At the southern end of the valley is the fort of the Desert Camel Corps, the descendants of the British-trained Arab Legion. In *Seven Pillars of Wisdom*, T.E. Lawrence wrote that when he passed between these rusty crags his "little caravan fell quiet, ashamed to flaunt itself in the presence of such stupendous hills." The unabashed members of the Desert Patrol, however, are proud to be photographed in their best bib and tucker. When not posing for visitors, they chase smugglers and renegade Bedouin.

Beyond the ruins of the Nabatean temple and behind the Bedouin tents, the great massif of Jebel Rum shoots up to 1754m. A jeep, or better yet, a camel, can take you farther through the sheer rust-colored cliffs towering above the mudflats. These whopping slabs of granite and sandstone erupted through the desert floor millions of years ago, and their striations in the bays and grottoes point toward prodigious vistas down the 30km-long wadi. The other-worldly lavender mountains cast against the empty sky have inspired the name **Valley of the Moon.** For JD4 a Bedouin will lead you on a camel to a crack in the rocks, the origin of the springs that support all the wadi's life. Dark stains point out the conduits carved by the ancient Nabateans to conserve that precious water. You may also be shown **Lawrence's Well,** where T.E. used to doze. The Bedouin can point to many places where mammoth boulders are inscribed with Thamudic graffiti thousands of years old. Such script, which evolved into modern Ethiopic, can be seen from Mada'in Salih in Saudi Arabia to Ma'an.

Only jeeps or camels can continue through Wadi al-Umran to Khirbet Kithara back on the Desert Highway near Aqaba. Riding a camel ranges in price from JD1.500 to JD24, depending on the destination. Jeep trips can cost anywhere from JD5 per car to Lawrence's Well, to JD22 to the Rock Bridge.

The clean and comfortable government **Rest House** maintains a monopoly on food and refreshments. (Bottled water 550fils, Pepsi 770fils, buffet lunch JD4.) Visitors who decide to stay overnight must sleep in one of the tents next to the Rest House (JD2 per person per night). A larger tent beside the small campground is often the site of traditional Bedouin music and singing in the evenings.

The night sky is ablaze with meteorites over the desert. Make a wish.

Language Glossary

Arabic (al-'Arabi) العـربى

In addition to a rather complex grammar, Arabic uses several sounds that are unfamiliar to speakers in English. *Kh* is like the German or Scottish *ch*. Another letter, the *'ayn* (usually indicated by an apostrophe) is simply a glottal stop, as in "co-operate," indicating a sound made by tightly constricting the back of the throat. In addition, vowels and consonants can be either long or short. You linger an instant more on the vowel in *salaam* (peace) than you do in *ahram* (pyramids). Furthermore, a doubled consonant can mean the difference between *ham-mam* (toilets) and *hamam* (pigeons). There are two kinds of *k* in Arabic: one that is pronounced as the *k* in English and the other which comes from deep inside the back of the throat. The latter can be dropped, so if you are looking for the Mausoleum of Barquq, someone will give you directions to the Mausoleum of Bar'u'. *R* is pronounced as a rolling growl, as in French. The aspirated ḥ is hissed from the back of the throat. In Egypt, *g* is pronounced hard (as in "gobble") whereas in Jordan and other Arab countries a *g* is pronounced like a *j*. The definite article is the prefix *al*, which is often written *el*. It is pronounced somewhere in between the two; when before the consonants t, n, d, s, sh, or z, the *l* is not pronounced. Also remember that adjectives describing females (grammatical or real) add an "-eh" at the end. *Yaa* is the Arabic equivalent of "Yo!" and is considered polite when addressing someone directly.

Numerals

0	1	2	3	4	5	6	7	8	9	10	20
sifr	wahid	itneen	talatta	arba'a	hamsa	sitta	sab'a	tamanya	tis'a	'ashara	'ishrin

Useful Words and Phrases

Greetings and Courtesies

ahlan or *ahlan wa-sahlan*	hello (informal)
salaam aleikuum	hello (formal)
aleikuum as-salaam	(response)
sabaḥ al-khair	good morning
sabaḥ en-nuur	(response)
masaḥ al-khair	good evening
masaḥ an-nuur	(response)
ma'a salaama	goodbye
aiwa or *nam*	yes
la'eh or *la*	no
afwaan	please
shukran	thank you
insha'allah	God willing
al-hamda li-lah	Praise God
mah ismaak?	what is your name?
ismi...	my name is...
kifak? (to men) or *kifik?* (to women)	how are you?
izzayik	how are you? (more common)
Ana kwais	I'm fine (male)

449

Ana kwais-eh	I'm fine (female)
Ana mish kwais	I'm not well
Ana mabsut	I'm excellent
Ana ta'baan	I'm tired
Ana mish khoaga	I'm not a dumb tourist
taalib	student (male)
taliba	student (female)

Getting Around

feen or *a'ina*	where?
imta	when?
li matha	why?
Ana raihah illa...	I'm going to...
Ana dawar bi...	I'm looking for...
Ana harbar min...	I'm running from...
Fe...	There is...
Mafeesh...	There is no...
Ta'rif feen...	Do you know where...is?
mataam	restaurant
bosta or *maktab al-berid*	post office
sharia or *shaaraa*	street
souk	market
met-haef	museum
mazged (in Egypt) or *masjid* (in Jordan, West Bank)	mosque
kineesa	church
gam'eh	mosque or university
fonduuq or *hotel*	hotel
ghurfa	room
mataar	airport
sa'a	hour, time
youm	day
usbu'ah	week
shahar	month
sanah	year
al-yoam	today
imbareh or *ams*	yesterday
bukhra	tomorrow
youm il-ḥadd	Sunday
youm al-itneen	Monday
youm it-talat	Tuesday
youm il-arba'	Wednesday
youm il-khams	Thursday
youm gum'a	Friday
youm is-sabt	Saturday
addeish as-sa'a?	what time is it?
yameen	right (direction)
shimal	left
utubeese	bus
taxi or *serveese*	taxi
utumobeel	automobile
siyyahi	tourist

Shopping and Dining

fee 'andik ...?	do you have...?
bikaam?	how much?

mish mumkin	impossible (i.e., no way I'm paying that much money)
imshi	go away!
fuluus	money
saraf	change
Ana biddeh-aqul...	I would like to eat...
Gib lee...	Give me...
ra'ees	waiter (lit. "president")
maiya	water
ah'weh or *qah'weh*	coffee
shay	tea

Emergency

B'itkallim englizi?	Do you speak English?
Ana mish batkellam arabi	I don't speak Arabic.
polees askari	policeman
musteshfa	hospital
doktuur	doctor
gawaz safar	passport
safireh	embassy
Ana mela'un, mela'un, mela'un	I am damned, damned, damned
maalish	never mind, no big deal

Hebrew (Ivrit) עיברית

(אם אתה יכול לקרוא את זה, אין לך צורך במילון שלנו.)

The transliterations *ḥ* (ח) and *kh* (כ) are guttural, as in the German word *ach*. Hebrew vowels are also shorter than English ones, which leads to discrepancies in transliteration. Extended vowels are the hallmark of an American accent and make Israelis giggle. Arabic, Russian, German or French can also be helpful.

In Hebrew, vowels are found below or, less commonly, above the consonant; but in day-to-day writing (and *Let's Go*), the vowels are omitted altogether. Thus, as a rough rule of thumb, a consonant, with its invisible vowel, makes a syllable. Two consonants, א and ע, make no sound of their own, only that of their vowel.

Although Hebrew is read right to left, numbers are read left to right.

Alphabet

alef	א	varia ble vowel
bet	ב	B as in Bush being badly beaten by Bill (Clinton)
vet	ב	V as in Van-Damme, whose movies some people actually watch
gimel	ג	G as in *gevalt* ('ג is a J as in Josh)
dalet	ד	D as in Dan
hay	ה	H as in hellfire, sometimes silent at the end of a word
vav	ו	V as in Veritas, can represent vowels
zayin	ז	Z as in Zaphod Beeblebrox or Zonker Harris
ḥet	ח	guttural H sound as heard in Bach
tet	ט	T as in Terminator
yad	י	Y as in Yousef, can represent vowels
kaf	כ	K as in kvetch
khaf	כ	guttural H sound as heard in Bach
khaf-sofit	ך	same as כ, appears only at end of words
lamed	ל	L as in landshark
mem	M מ	as in Mike, the assistant editor's not-so-little brother
mem-sofit	ם	same as מ, appears only at end of words
nun	נ	N as in narcolepsy
nun-sofit	ן	same as נ, appears only at end of words

samekh	ס	S as in <u>s</u>ignature <u>s</u>carcity
ayin	ע	variable vowel, as in <u>A</u>dina (sometimes)
pay	פ	P as in <u>p</u>oorly-<u>p</u>aid <u>p</u>artisan <u>p</u>olemicizing <u>p</u>olitical <u>p</u>undit
fay	פ	F as in <u>F</u>rada, who reads *Let's Go* religiously
fay-sofit	ף	same as פ, appears only at end of words
tzadi	צ	Tz as in g<u>ri</u>ts (gritz?)
tzadi-sofit	ץ	same as צ, appears only at end of words
kuf	ק	K as in <u>K</u>nesset <u>k</u>raziness
reish	ר	R as in <u>R</u>abie the <u>r</u>eckless <u>r</u>esearcher-<u>r</u>iter
shin	ש	Sh as in <u>sh</u>muck
sin	ש	S as in <u>s</u>ubliminal messages
tav	ת	T as in <u>T</u>erminator 2

Useful Words and Phrases

Greetings and Courtesies

shalom	hello or goodbye or peace
ahlan	hello (informal)
boker tov	good morning
erev tov	good evening
l'hitra'ot	goodbye
ma nishma?	how are things?
ken	yes
lo	no
toda	thank you
sliha	excuse me
bevakasha	please/you're welcome
eikh korim likhah/lakh?	what is your name? (to male/to female)
shmi...	my name is...
ma shlomkha/shlomekh?	how are you? (to male/to female)
b'seder	fine, OK
lo tov	not good
mitzuyan	excellent
ayef/ayefa	tired (male/female)
talmid/talmida	student (male/female)

Getting Around

aifo...?	where is....?
matai	when
lama	why
ani nosaya l'...	I'm going to...
yesh...	there is...
ain...	there is no...
ata yodea (aht yoda'at) aifo nimtza...	do you (you, a female) know where...is?
rega	wait (backhanded gesture with four fingers touching thumb)
nahon or b'emet?	really, honestly?
mis'adah	restaurant
beit do'ar	post office
rehov	street
sderot	boulevard
midrehov	pedestrian mall
shuk	market
muzaion	museum
beit knesset	synagogue
knaissia	church
tahana merkazit	central bus station

malon	hotel
akhsaniya	hostel
ḥeder	room
universita	university
ḥof	beach
makolet	grocery store
mirpeset	balcony
kama zeh?	how much is it?
ma zeh?	what is this?
okhel	food
sha'a	hour, time
yom	day
shavua	week
ḥodesh	month
shana	year
ha'yom	today
etmol	yesterday
maḥar	tomorrow
yom rishon	Sunday
yom shaini	Monday
yom shlishi	Tuesday
yom rivi'i	Wednesday
yom ḥamishi	Thursday
yom shishi	Friday
shabbat	sabbath, Saturday
ma hasha'a?	what time is it?
yamin	right (direction)
smol	left
monit	taxi
miḥonit	automobile
rakevet	train
otoboos	bus

Shopping and Dining

yesh likha...?	do you have...?
kama zeh oleh?	how much?
ani rotzeh/rotza...	I want... (male/female)
lo rotzeh/rotza...	I don't want... (male/female)
ani lo fryer	I'm not a pushover
histalek	go away
balagan	utter chaos
lekh l'azazel	go to hell
kesef	money
odef	change (lit. "leftovers")
meltzar	waiter
mayim	water
kafeh	coffee
teh	tea

Emergencies

ata (aht) midaber (midaberet) Anglit?	do you speak English? (to female)
ani lo midaber (m'daberet) Ivrit	I don't speak Hebrew (female)
mishtara	police
beit ḥolim	hospital
rofay	doctor
darkon	passport
s'deh t'ufa	airport

INDEX